Mr. Joseph Provost

HISTORY OF
AMERICAN
PRESIDENTIAL
ELECTIONS

1789–2008

FOURTH EDITION

VOLUME III
1944–2008

HISTORY OF AMERICAN PRESIDENTIAL ELECTIONS

1789–2008

FOURTH EDITION

VOLUME III
1944–2008

GIL TROY
ARTHUR M. SCHLESINGER JR.
FRED L. ISRAEL

Editors

Facts On File
An Infobase Learning Company

HISTORY OF AMERICAN PRESIDENTIAL ELECTIONS, 1789–2008, FOURTH EDITION

Facts On File, Inc.
An imprint of Infobase Learning
132 West 31st Street
New York NY 10001

Library of Congress Cataloging-in-Publication Data
History of American presidential elections, 1789-2008 / Gil Troy, editor ; Arthur M. Schlesinger, Jr.
[and] Fred L. Israel. — 4th ed.
     p. cm.
  Rev. ed. of: History of American presidential elections, 1789–2001. Philadelphia : Chelsea House
Publishers, c2002.
  Includes bibliographical references and index.
  ISBN 978-0-8160-8220-9 (acid-free paper) 1. Presidents—United States—Election—History.
2. Presidents—United States—Election—History—Sources. 3. United States—Politics and government.
4. United States—Politics and government—Sources. I. Troy, Gil. II. Schlesinger, Arthur M. (Arthur Meier),
1917–2007. III. Israel, Fred L. IV. History of American presidential elections, 1789–2001.
  E183.H58 2010
  324.973—dc22   2010025576

Facts On File books are available at special discounts when purchased in bulk quantities for businesses, associations, institutions, or sales promotions. Please call our Special Sales Department in New York at (212) 967-8800 or (800) 322-8755.

You can find Facts On File on the World Wide Web at http://www.InfobaseLearning.com

Text design by Erika K. Arroyo and Annie O'Donnell
Composition by Annie O'Donnell
Cover printed by Yurchak Printing, Landisville, Pa.
Book printed and bound by Yurchak Printing, Landisville, Pa.
Date printed: October 2011
Printed in the United States of America

10 9 8 7 6 5 4 3 2 1

This book is printed on acid-free paper.

Contents

Election of 1944

Election Overview

Election Year 1944

Election Day November 7, 1944

Winning Candidates

- ⭐ **President:** Franklin D. Roosevelt
- ⭐ **Vice President:** Harry S. Truman

Election Results [ticket, party: popular votes (percentage of popular vote); electoral votes (percentage of electoral vote)]

- Franklin D. Roosevelt and Harry S. Truman, Democratic: 25,612,916 (53.39%); 432 (81.4%)
- Thomas E. Dewey and John W. Bricker, Republican: 22,017,929 (45.89%); 99 (18.6%)
- No candidate, Texas Regulars: 135,439 (0.28%); 0 (0.0%)
- Other: 210,806 (0.44%); 0 (0.0%)

Voter Turnout 55.9%

Central Forums/Campaign Methods for Addressing Voters

- Stumping
- Whistle-stop tour
- Radio addresses
- Personal appearances, speeches
- Pamphlets, ads, newspaper endorsements, editorials, newsreels

Incumbent President and Vice President on Election Day Franklin D. Roosevelt and Henry A. Wallace

Population (1944) 138,397,000

Gross Domestic Product

- $219.8 billion (in current dollars: $2,035.2 billion)
- Per capita: $1,588 (in current dollars: $14,706)

Number of Daily Newspapers (1940) 1,878

Average Daily Circulation (1940) 41,132,000

Households with

- Radio (1940) 28,048,000

Method of Choosing Electors Popular vote (mostly general ticket system/winner take all)

Method of Choosing Nominees

- National party convention
- Presidential preference primaries

Key Issues and Events

- First wartime presidential campaign since 1864
- Rumors Roosevelt would suspend elections "for the duration" of the war
- Growing anxiety about postwar economy and postwar relations with the Soviets

Leading Candidates

DEMOCRATS

- Franklin D. Roosevelt, president of the United States (New York)

REPUBLICANS

- Thomas E. Dewey, governor (New York)
- Robert A. Taft, senator (Ohio)
- Wendell Willkie, businessman and 1940 presidential nominee (New York)
- John W. Bricker, governor (Ohio)
- Everett Dirksen, representative (Illinois)
- Douglas MacArthur, general of the U.S. Army (Wisconsin)
- Harold Stassen, former governor (Minnesota)
- Riley A. Bender, businessman (Illinois)

Trajectory

- Roosevelt is renominated easily despite growing opposition to his economic and social policies among conservative Democrats, especially in the South.
- Thomas Dewey wants to run despite promising to serve his entire four-year term when elected governor of New York in 1942. He does not actively campaign or announce his intentions for the Republican nomination. His name is on write-in ballots in state primaries, and Republican state conventions pledge delegates to vote for him at the Republican convention, where, on June 28, he captures the nomination with near unanimous delegate support.
- At the Democratic National Convention, July 19–21, Roosevelt's declining health and suspicions of concealed health problems prompt the party's conservatives to oppose the renomination of Vice President Henry Wallace, whom they consider too left wing, too indiscreet, and too "mystical." (Wallace wrote coded letters discussing Roosevelt and Winston Churchill to his controversial Russian spiritual guru, Nicholas Roerich.) In the "new Missouri Compromise," party leaders propose Missouri senator Harry Truman, a moderate, and chairman of a Senate wartime investigating committee. Roosevelt refuses to support any vice-presidential candidate publicly.
- After the convention, Arthur Krock of the *New York Times* reports that Roosevelt told the Democratic National Committee chair, Robert Hannegan: "Go down and nominate Truman before there's any more trouble. And clear everything with Sidney." This statement feeds fears that union leader Sidney Hillman wields too much power in Washington.
- Roosevelt takes to the stump September 23, 1944. His first radio address, known as the "Fala Speech," may be his best campaign speech ever. Dismissing Republican claims that his administration wasted taxpayers' money, he particularly ridicules a GOP charge that he sent a U.S. Navy warship to pick up his Scottish terrier, Fala, in Alaska, noting that "Fala was furious" at such rumors.
- In response, Dewey gives a blistering partisan speech in Oklahoma City a few days later on national radio, accusing Roosevelt of being "indispensable" to corrupt big-city Democratic organizations and American Communists; he also calls FDR's cabinet a "motley crew" and accuses the president of incompetence, arrogance, inefficiency, fatigue, and senility.
- American battlefield successes in Europe and the Pacific boost Roosevelt, including D-Day (June 1944), the liberation of Paris (August 1944), and the Battle of Leyte Gulf, Philippines (October 1944).
- Roosevelt wins an unprecedented fourth term, but he is physically ailing.

Conventions

- Republican National Convention: June 26–28, 1944, Chicago Stadium, Chicago
- Democratic National Convention: July 19–21, 1944, Chicago Stadium, Chicago

Ballots/Nominees

REPUBLICANS
Presidential first ballot
- Thomas E. Dewey 1,056
- Douglas MacArthur 1

Vice-presidential first ballot
- John W. Bricker 1,057

DEMOCRATS
Vice-presidential second ballot after shifts
- Harry S. Truman 319.5; 477.5; 1,031
- Henry A. Wallace 429.5; 473; 105
- John H. Bankhead 98; 23.5; 0
- Scott W. Lucas 61; 58; 0
- Alben W. Barkley 49.5; 40; 6
- J. Melville Broughton 43; 30; 0
- Paul V. McNutt 31; 28; 1
- Prentice Cooper 26; 26; 26
- Scattering 118.5; 20; 7

Primaries

- Democrats: 14; 36.7% delegates
- Republicans: 13; 38.7% delegates

Primaries Results

DEMOCRATS
- Franklin D. Roosevelt 1,566,218; 79.24%
- Joseph T. Ferguson 164,915; 8.34%
- Harry F. Byrd Sr. 109,000; 5.51%
- Claude R. Linger 59,282; 3.00%
- Unpledged 57,299; 2.90%

REPUBLICANS
- Douglas MacArthur 662,127; 28.94%
- Earl Warren 594,439; 25.99%
- John W. Bricker 366,444; 16.02%

- Thomas E. Dewey 278,727; 12.18%
- W. Chapman Revercomb 91,602; 4.00%
- Unpledged 87,834; 3.84%
- Harold Stassen 67,508; 2.95%
- Riley A. Bender 37,575; 1.64%
- Charles A. Christopherson 33,497; 1.46%
- Wendell Willkie 27,097; 1.18%

Party Platform

DEMOCRATS

- Continue the New Deal
- Roosevelt should carry on as commander in chief until the end of the war.

REPUBLICANS

- Anti–New Deal
- Smaller government, greater fiscal restraint
- Accusations of abuse of power

Campaign Tactics

DEMOCRATS

- Roosevelt would not stump at first, too busy being commander in chief.
- Tired of Dewey's attacks, Roosevelt starts stumping in mid-September. He plans to give five speeches.
- To refute rumors of declining health, Roosevelt makes a vigorous campaign swing on October 21, rides in an open car through New York City streets, seen by an estimated 3 million New Yorkers in a downpour.

REPUBLICANS

- Dewey is the only candidate on the stump at the start of the general campaign.
- Dignified stance: efficiency, finely honed (unexciting) speeches, impeccable dress, cool demeanor, perfect timing for speeches and press conferences.
- Does not attack Roosevelt's foreign policy, endorses much of the New Deal, emphasizes the need for fresh leadership.

Popular Campaign Slogans

DEMOCRATS

- "Vote Democratic for Victory *and* Peace"
- "The Fighting President"

REPUBLICANS

- "For Victory *and* Lasting Peace"
- "We're Marching to Victory with Dewey"

Campaign Songs

- Democrats: "We're Going to Win the War"
- Republicans: "Keeping Score in 44" to the tune of "Oh, Susanna"

Influential Campaign Appeals or Ads

DEMOCRATS

- Fala Speech shows Roosevelt's wit, vigor, but also a condescending arrogance.
- "Hell-Bent for Election," a 13-minute cartoon sponsored by the United Auto Workers, depicts Roosevelt as a slick diesel train competing against a broken-down Dewey steam engine dragging along the "Business as Usual" sleeper car and the ugly Jim Crow caboose.

REPUBLICANS

- "Clear Everything with Sidney."
- "It's your country and why let Sidney Hillman run it?"
- "Everything in your government will be cleared with the radical Sidney Hillman and his Communist friend Earl Browder."
- "Sidney Hillman and Earl Browder's Communists have registered. Have you?"
- "Clear it with Sidney, you Yanks. / Then offer Joe Stalin your thanks, / You'll bow to Sid's rule / No matter how cruel, / For that's a directive of Frank's."

Campaign Finance

- Roosevelt: $2,169,077 (in current dollars: $25,079,800)
- Dewey: $2,828,652 (in current dollars: $32,706,100)

  Overall:
  - Democratic Party: $7.4 million (in current dollars: $85,563,000)
  - Republican Party: $13.5 million (in current dollars: $156,092,900)

Defining Quotations

- "I don't know whether you are going to support me or not, and I don't give a damn. You're a bunch of political liabilities, anyway." *Wendell Willkie speaking bluntly to Missouri businessmen in St. Louis, October 15, 1943*
- "Well, you see, you have come to the wrong place, because—gosh, all these people haven't read the Constitution. Unfortunately, I have." *Franklin D. Roosevelt at a February 8, 1944, press conference,*

reassuring a reporter there will be elections despite the war

- "Does anyone suggest that the present national administration is giving either efficient or competent government? We have not heard that claim made, even by its most fanatical supporters. No, all they tell us is that in its young days it did some good things. That we freely grant. But now it has grown old in office. It has become tired and quarrelsome. It seems that the great men who founded this nation really did know what they were talking about when they said that three terms were too many." *Thomas E. Dewey, address accepting the presidential nomination at the Republican National Convention in Chicago, June 28, 1944*

- "I like him [Vice President Henry A. Wallace] and I respect him and he is my personal friend. For these reasons I personally would vote for his re-nomination if I were a delegate to the convention. At the same time, I do not wish to appear in any way as dictating to the convention, obviously the convention must do the deciding" *Franklin D. Roosevelt to Indiana senator Samuel D. Jackson, permanent national chairman of the Democratic Convention, regarding Vice President Henry A. Wallace, July 11, 1944*

- "They will decide on the record—the record written on the seas, on the land, and in the skies. They will decide on the record of our domestic accomplishments in recovery and reform since March 4, 1933. And they will decide on the record of our war production and food production—unparalleled in all history, in spite of the doubts and sneers of those in high places who said it cannot be done. They will decide on the record of the International Food Conference, of U.N.R.R.A., of the International Labor Conference, of the International Education Conference, of the International Monetary Conference. And they will decide on the record written in the Atlantic Charter, at Casablanca, at Cairo, at Moscow, and at Teheran. We have made mistakes. Who has not? Things will not always be perfect. Are they ever perfect, in human affairs?" *Franklin D. Roosevelt, address to the Democratic National Convention in Chicago, July 20, 1944*

- "Well, here we are—here we are again—after four years—and what years they have been! You know, I am actually four years older, which is a fact that seems to annoy some people. In fact . . . there are millions of Americans who are more than eleven years older than when we started to clear up the mess that was dumped into our laps in 1933." *Franklin D. Roosevelt, campaign dinner address, September 23,*

1944, Washington, D.C., International Brotherhood of Teamsters, Chauffeurs, Warehousemen and Helpers of America

- "These Republican leaders have not been content with attacks on me, or my wife, or on my sons. No, not content with that, they now include my little dog, Fala. Well, of course, I don't resent attacks, and my family doesn't resent attacks, but Fala does resent them. You know, Fala is Scotch, and being a Scottie, as soon as he learned that the Republican fiction writers in Congress and out had concocted a story that I had left him behind on the Aleutian Islands and had sent a destroyer back to find him—at a cost to the taxpayers of two or three, or eight or twenty million dollars—his Scotch soul was furious. He has not been the same dog since. I am accustomed to hearing malicious falsehoods about myself—such as that old, worm-eaten chestnut that I have represented myself as indispensable. But I think I have a right to resent, to object to libelous statements about my dog." *Franklin D. Roosevelt, campaign dinner address, September 23, 1944, Washington, D.C., International Brotherhood of Teamsters, Chauffeurs, Warehousemen and Helpers of America*

- "He was like a veteran virtuoso playing a piece he has loved for years, who fingers his way through it with a delicate fire, a perfection of tuning and tone, and an assurance that no young player, no matter how gifted, can equal. The President was playing what he loves to play—politics." Time, *October 2, 1944, describing the Fala speech*

- "Roosevelt's dog and Dewey's goat." *One jibe about the Fala speech*

- "Let's not be squeamish. . . . It is convention, not the Constitution . . . which forbids open comment on the possibility that a President may be succeeded by his Vice President. . . . Six Presidents . . . have died in office." New York Sun *front-page editorial, mid-October, 1944*

- "Nothing wrong organically with him at all. He's perfectly O.K. . . . He does a terrific day's work. But he stands up under it amazingly. The stories that he is in bad health are understandable enough around election time, but they are not true." *Admiral Ross McIntire, the president's personal physician, statement on Roosevelt's health, quoted in* Time, *October 23, 1944*

- "Now, Mr. Roosevelt in his recent speech from the White House very softly disavowed communism. But the very next day, at a meeting right here in Boston, Earl Browder made a speech for Mr. Roosevelt and a collection was taken up for the fourth term. And not a voice in the New Deal was raised in protest. . . . Now, by the self-same tried and familiar tactics and with the aid of Sidney Hillman, the Communists are seizing control of the New Deal, through which they aim to control the Government of the United States." *Thomas E. Dewey, Boston, Boston Garden, November 1, 1944*

Lasting Legacy of Campaign

- Only time a president was elected to a fourth term (ratification of the Twenty-second Amendment to the Constitution in 1951 will limit the number of presidential terms to two).

- Historic fight over the Democratic vice-presidential nomination ultimately determines the next president. Roosevelt dies of a cerebral hemorrhage on April 12, 1945, less than three months after beginning his fourth term. Truman, not Wallace, becomes the nation's 33rd president.
- Last election in which a Democratic presidential candidate carries every state in the South.
- First election since Grover Cleveland's reelection in 1892 in which Ohio goes to the losing candidate
- Last election in which any candidate receives over 90% of the vote in any state.

Election of 1944

The midterm elections of 1942 marked the low point of the Roosevelt Era. The war was still going badly. In the European theater, the Germans controlled almost all the land between the Atlantic and the Volga; Nazi panzer divisions roamed at will in the Caucasus, approached the Baku oil fields, attacked Stalingrad in force, and threatened Moscow again. Rommel's forces had advanced into Egypt, and only a few British divisions stood between the Germans and the Suez Canal. German submarines had become so effective that they could pick and choose their targets at will even in American waters, and oil tankers going from the Gulf of Mexico to the East Coast were regularly torpedoed. There was little to cheer about in the Pacific. The defeat of the Japanese Fleet at Midway in June 1942 was the only significant naval victory in a year. The Marines had landed in Guadalcanal in August, but the Japanese resisted fiercely, sinking four American cruisers and inflicting heavy casualties on the ground troops. In New Guinea, General Douglas MacArthur had, at long last, begun an offensive, but advances were tortuously slow. The arrows in the maps of the daily newspapers still showed Axis advances almost everywhere.

On the home front, Roosevelt demonstrated sporadic leadership in mobilizing the economy for the war. A series of new "alphabet agencies" had been established: WPB (War Production Board), WMC (War Manpower Commission), OES (Office of Economic Stabilization), OPA (Office of Price Administration), WLB (War Labor Board), and many others to deal with production preferences, resource allocation, wage and price controls, and rationing. But their jurisdictions overlapped, there was constant bickering between the administrators, and no overall policy was established to guide the agencies. A typical problem arose over the rubber shortage. Donald Nelson, the WPB chief, told Roosevelt that the nation had only a 15-month supply of that vital product. He urged Roosevelt to impose strict gasoline rationing so as to curtail automobile use and thus conserve rubber. Roosevelt resisted, fearing hostile public reaction. Instead, he went on the radio and asked Americans to turn in all the scrap rubber they could find. Although nearly a half-million tons were collected, that solution proved at best temporary, and eventually all the drastic measures suggested by Nelson had to be imposed.

Inflation was also a problem. The price of food increased significantly during the summer of 1942. As a result, the pressure from labor for wage increases became stronger. A dispute over wages in the steel industry was settled by a 15 percent increase, and this became a model for other areas of the economy. Roosevelt realized that until food prices could be stabilized, the unions would insist on higher wages, but getting Congress to impose necessary controls in an election year was proving extremely difficult. FDR finally sent a strong message to Congress on September 7 requesting farm price stabilization and increased taxes, and he followed it up with a "fireside chat" radio broadcast. "We are not doing enough" in support of our valiant young men dying throughout the world, the president asserted, as he pledged to fight "economic chaos" through presidential decree if Congress failed to act.

Reluctantly, Congress returned to work on the tax and food price laws, and by October 2 a compromise farm bill was on the president's desk. Three weeks later, Congress passed a disappointing tax measure raising only $7 billion in new revenues. Nevertheless, Roosevelt signed the bill while planning another financial attack for early 1943.

With farmers unhappy about farm price controls, workers disappointed about wage restrictions,

(continues on page 1134)

☆ ☆ ☆

1944 ELECTION CHRONOLOGY

1941

January 6, 1941: In his State of the Union address, President Roosevelt outlines four freedoms he hopes will form the basis of the postwar world order.

March 11, 1941: Roosevelt signs the Lend Lease Bill, providing armaments to the Allied powers.

June 22, 1941: Operation Barbarossa, the Axis invasion of the Soviet Union, begins.

December 7, 1941: Japan bombs Pearl Harbor.

December 8, 1941: Declaring the date of the Japanese attack "a day that shall live in infamy," Roosevelt summons Congress to declare war.

December 11, 1941: Germany and Italy declare war on the United States.

1942

January 16, 1942: Roosevelt establishes the War Production Board to coordinate munitions production.

January 30, 1942: Roosevelt signs the Prices Control Act, which gives the government the power to control the prices for most consumer goods.

February 20, 1942: Roosevelt signs Executive Order 9066, which sends Japanese Americans on the Pacific Coast to detention camps in the interior.

June 3–6, 1942: The U.S. Navy inflicts a major defeat on the Japanese Fleet at the Battle of Midway. It is the turning point in the war in the Pacific.

November 3, 1942: The Republicans make large gains in the midterm elections, taking 45 seats from the Democrats in the House of Representatives and 10 seats in the Senate. The Democrats retain narrow majorities in both houses. Thomas Dewey is elected as Republican governor of New York, having promised not to be a candidate in the 1944 presidential election.

November 8, 1942: In Operation Torch, American troops land in North Africa.

1943

January 14, 1943: Roosevelt travels to meet with Winston Churchill and other Allies at Casablanca, where they agree to demand the unconditional surrender of the Axis powers.

September 3, 1943: Allied forces invade Italy.

November 28, 1943: Roosevelt attends a summit at Tehran with British prime minister Winston Churchill and Soviet premier Joseph Stalin. The allies agree upon an invasion of France in 1944, with General Dwight D. Eisenhower to be in command of the operation.

1944

January 30, 1944: A Gallup poll finds that Governor Thomas Dewey enjoys a commanding lead as presidential nominee among Republican voters, with 42 percent support against 28 percent support for Wendell Willkie and 19 percent support for General Douglas MacArthur.

February 1, 1944: Minnesota senator Joseph H. Ball begins a campaign to draft former Minnesota governor Harold Stassen, currently serving as a lieutenant commander in the Pacific theater, as a candidate for the Republican nomination. Like General MacArthur, whose name is also placed on the ballot in several states, Stassen does not campaign for the nomination.

April 4, 1944: Thomas Dewey sweeps the Wisconsin Republican primary, electing 18 out of 24 delegates. Former presidential candidate Wendell Willkie, who had staked his candidacy on a victory in Wisconsin and campaigned there for several weeks, fails to elect a single delegate and withdraws from the race. The victory cements Dewey's status as the frontrunner for the nomination.

June 6, 1944: D-Day: Allied forces land in Normandy, beginning the liberation of France.

June 22, 1944: Roosevelt signs the GI Bill, guaranteeing a wide range of benefits to U.S. veterans.

June 26–28, 1944: The Republicans hold their convention in Chicago. Governor Thomas Dewey of New York is easily chosen as the presidential nominee on the first ballot. Governor John W. Bricker of Ohio, who had unsuccessfully sought the nomination in the primaries, is selected as the vice-presidential nominee. Despite not having campaigned in the primaries or entered his name in many states, Dewey benefits from the support of the party establishment. He is the first Repub-

lican presidential nominee to attend his party's convention.

July 12, 1944: Due in part to the president's failing health, there is a heated contest for the vice-presidential nomination. After a critical meeting with aides the day before, Roosevelt signs a letter supporting either Missouri senator Harry Truman or Supreme Court justice William O. Douglas for the vice presidency, which boxes out Roosevelt's close aide James Byrnes and incumbent vice president Henry A. Wallace, whom party leaders fear as too liberal.

July 16, 1944: As intrigue grows because Roosevelt has reassured both Byrnes and Wallace of his support, party leaders are now told that Roosevelt wants Byrnes. The Democratic National Committee chairman, Robert Hannegan of Missouri, then supposedly tells Mayor Ed Kelly of Chicago, "The president said, 'Clear it with Sidney,'" meaning labor leader Sidney Hillman.

July 19–21, 1944: The Democrats hold their convention in Chicago. President Roosevelt does not attend the convention, but is renominated by acclamation. After a bitter struggle, Harry S. Truman, a moderate senator from Missouri, is nominated for vice president on the third ballot.

July 20, 1944: Roosevelt delivers his acceptance speech via radio from San Diego, where he is inspecting naval and marine bases.

August 12, 1944: In an address from Puget Sound Navy Yard, Bremerton, Washington, Roosevelt rambles and looks uncomfortable as he struggles with his leg braces. The performance encourages speculation about the president's ailing health.

August 25, 1944: The Allies liberate Paris.

September 7, 1944: Dewey starts his formal campaign, which will mix traditional stumping with 30-minute radio speeches and advertisements.

September 15, 1944: Before a crowd of 93,000, including dozens of movie stars, Dewey gives a dry exposition on Social Security. Reporters are critical that Dewey lacks passion.

September 23, 1944: Roosevelt begins his campaign for the presidency, delivering his famous "Fala Speech" in a radio address to the Teamsters Union. He ridicules Republican criticisms of his administration's extravagance, particularly the claim that he sent a U.S. warship to pick up his dog Fala in Alaska.

September 25, 1944: Dewey, starting to get riled up, responds in a blistering radio address delivered in Oklahoma City. The Republicans run an increasingly aggressive campaign, attacking the president's domestic record and accusing the administration of corruption and Communist sympathies. The objective of the Republican campaign is to draw the president into the fray as a political candidate, while saying little about foreign affairs and his conduct as a wartime leader.

October 21, 1944: Roosevelt demonstrates his vigor by traveling in an open motorcade over four boroughs in New York City, passing an estimated 2 million cheering fans, despite a driving rain. In truth, the trip exhausts the president.

October 26–23, 1944: American forces win the battle of Leyte Gulf, the largest naval battle of World War II, against the Japanese. The battle paves the way for the liberation of the Philippines in the months that follow.

November 1, 1944: Increasingly vituperative, Dewey warns of the "Red menace," saying, "The Communists are seizing control of the New Deal."

November 4, 1944: In his final campaign address at Boston's Fenway Park, Roosevelt says bitterly: "Never before in my lifetime has a campaign been filled with such misrepresentation, distortion, and falsehood. Never since 1928 have there been so many attempts to stimulate in America racial or religious intolerance."

November 7, 1944: Roosevelt is reelected to an unprecedented fourth term as president, winning 53.39 percent of the popular vote and 432 electoral votes. The Republican ticket receives 45.89 percent of the popular vote and 99 electoral votes. The election is seen as ratification of President Roosevelt's wartime leadership, though the Republicans win more votes than in any previous election fought against Roosevelt.

December 18, 1944: Presidential electors cast their ballots in their respective state capitals.

1945

January 6, 1945: A joint session of Congress assembles to count the electoral votes.

(continued from page 1131)

consumers grumbling about rationing, and little good news from the war fronts, it was no surprise that the Republicans gained heavily in the November congressional elections. They won 47 new seats in the House (leaving the Democrats with a working majority of only 9) and 9 seats in the Senate. (The Democrats still controlled the Senate, 58 to 37.) The only candidate that FDR personally supported, Senator George Norris, the great independent from Nebraska, lost to Republican Kenneth S. Wherry. But the election returns did not mean any wholesale disillusionment with Roosevelt. Because of the large number of voters in the armed forces or in widely scattered war industries, total voter turnout was far lower than in 1940. Especially hard hit were the northeastern industrial states—New York, for

example, had the lowest number of votes cast in eight years.

Roosevelt had hoped to report some encouraging news immediately before the midterm election. Initial plans for Operation Torch, the landings in North Africa under General Dwight D. Eisenhower, called for a late-October invasion. But the difficulty of gathering enough landing craft (a recurring problem throughout the war) and marshaling all the men and material in time led Eisenhower and the British generals to postpone the date to November 8, five days after the election. In fact, the two-week period immediately after November 3 also saw important turning points in other war theaters. British troops under General Bernard Montgomery broke Rommel's advance into Egypt at El Alamein and by November 12 had taken Tobruk in Libya. Marshal Georgy Zhukov

Because World War II continued to go badly for the Allied forces, the midterm elections of 1942 marked the low point of the Roosevelt Era. This photograph shows an aerial view of a U.S. tanker torpedoed by an Axis submarine. *(Library of Congress)*

had commenced his great counterattack at Stalingrad and in a giant pincer movement encircled the 22 German divisions under General von Paulus. A strong Japanese counterattack on Guadalcanal was beaten back on November 12 with heavy losses to both sides. While Roosevelt cautiously told the American people that "it would seem that the turning point in this war has at last been reached," Churchill described the situation in his famous phrases: "Now, this is not the end. It is not even the beginning of the end. But it is, perhaps, the end of the beginning."

Roosevelt devoted a substantial part of the following year to his duties as commander in chief, attending many high-level conferences in Washington and elsewhere. In January 1943, Roosevelt made the first presidential trip to a war theater since Abraham Lincoln. At Casablanca, Morocco, he met Churchill for a grand strategy meeting. The conference produced continued wrangling about the date for the cross-channel invasion of France, which Stalin and the American generals wanted as soon as possible. Although it was scheduled for August 1943, the British persuaded Roosevelt to postpone the invasion in favor of Churchill's "soft-underbelly" approach through Sicily and Italy.

On his return to Washington in February 1943, the president played host to numerous Allied dignitaries, including Madame Chiang Kai-shek, who spoke about the Asian war to a cheering session of Congress. (The fight against the Japanese was far more popular among the conservatives in Congress and the Hearst–McCormick press than the European war, in which the hated Russians were our allies.) In private, she complained bitterly about General Joseph W. Stilwell, the American military leader in China who was insisting on better performance from the Chinese army before additional American aid would be forthcoming. Anthony Eden, the British foreign minister, arrived in Washington during March to talk about anticipated diplomatic problems of the postwar period, including the establishment of the United Nations, new boundaries for Poland and Germany, and Russian domination of the Baltic states. Churchill also came to Washington for two weeks in May 1943, and final plans were then made for the Normandy invasion, rescheduled for May 1, 1944. Practically every important diplomat and general from the two countries attended the meetings, and every phase of the war was thoroughly discussed.

Roosevelt kept in close touch with his military advisors on the final Tunisian campaign (which ended in June 1943) and the invasion of Sicily (July 10, 1943). In mid-August, Churchill returned for a new series of conferences at Hyde Park, and then Roosevelt and his staff went to Quebec in late August for still further discussions with the British on the structure of the United Nations,

the treatment of the new Badoglio government in Italy, which had replaced Mussolini, and the Chinese theater of operations. Further military discussions with Churchill were held in Washington in September in preparation for the climactic Cairo and Teheran conferences in November and December.

At Cairo, Roosevelt and Churchill met with Chiang Kai-shek and urged him to greater efforts against the Japanese on the Asian mainland. The president and the prime minister then flew on to Teheran, where on November 28, 1943, FDR met Stalin for the first time. The meetings continued for a week, the three "Titans," in Robert Sherwood's words, "determining the future course of an entire planet." Sherwood described the scene as follows:

> This was indeed the Big Three. Churchill employed all the debater's arts, the brilliant locutions and circumlocutions, of which he was a master, and Stalin wielded his bludgeon with relentless indifference to all the dodges and feints of his practiced adversary; while Roosevelt sat in the middle, by common consent the moderator, arbitrator and final authority. His contributions to the conversations were infrequent and sometimes annoyingly irrelevant, but it appears time and again—at Teheran and at Yalta—that it was he who spoke the last word.

Military operations were the first order of business—final plans for Overlord (the Normandy landings), Anvil (the secondary invasion of southern France), and the Italian campaign, as well as the Pacific theater. The three leaders spoke of the future of Germany (Stalin was for dismembering the country) and the United Nations. On the afternoon of December 2, Roosevelt spoke privately with Stalin, telling him that he would probably run for president in 1944. He wanted Stalin to understand that he had to consider the 6–7 million Americans of Polish extraction whose votes were needed for his election, and therefore he could not publicly discuss Polish boundaries or a postwar Polish government. When Roosevelt made the same point about voters from the Baltic republics, Stalin demurred, stating that the president should engage in "some propaganda work" among those peoples.

From Teheran, Roosevelt flew back to Cairo for more military discussions (Eisenhower was chosen for command of Overlord), and then to Tunis, Sicily, and Malta. He did not return to Washington until December 17. Thus, Roosevelt was outside the United States for more than two months during 1943; 20 days in January at the Casablanca conference; almost a week in Quebec in August;

and 38 days for the Big Three meetings in November and December.

Roosevelt's presence at these global meetings, and his superb playing of his role as commander in chief, his favorite title during the war, gave him a stature in the eyes of the nation superior to the one he had earned during the happiest days of the New Deal. Even William Allen White, the midwestern Republican journalist, acknowledged the "vast impudent courage" of the president. "We are compelled to admit," White wrote after Casablanca, "that Franklin Roosevelt is the most unaccountable and on the whole the most enemy baffling President that this United States has ever seen. . . . Well, damn your smiling old picture, here it is. . . . We, who hate your gaudy guts, salute you."

But Roosevelt could not always remain on the Olympian heights as the global commander in chief. Many thorny domestic affairs demanded his attention. One recurring difficulty was labor. Hardly a week passed in 1943 without a major union threatening a walkout in a critical industry. John L. Lewis and his coal miners presented the severest problem. In early January, 15,000 miners went out on a wildcat strike, and although they obeyed a presidential order to return to work, Lewis demanded a $2-a-day boost in wages when the UMW contract with the mine owners expired. Then in April, when Lewis threatened another strike, Secretary of the Interior Harold Ickes, at the president's command, seized the mines. The union allowed the War Labor Board to assume jurisdiction but then refused to obey its orders. Congress, furious with Lewis's defiance, reacted by passing the Smith–Connally "No-Strike Law," which severely restricted labor's right to strike and its political activities. Roosevelt vetoed the bill, but Congress overrode the veto by large majorities.

The Railroad Brotherhoods were another headache for the president. Although many of the nonoperating unions accepted some form of arbitration, the more important operating unions did not. Roosevelt spent many hours in December (immediately after his return from Teheran) trying to mediate the dispute but finally had to resort to seizing the railroads.

Following the sizable Republican victories in the 1942 elections, Roosevelt's relations with Congress sank to a new low. Early in 1943, the president asked for continued authority to limit all salaries in the nation to $25,000 per year. (Using emergency executive powers, Roosevelt had actually imposed such a limit in 1942.) But a congressional majority ignored Roosevelt's patriotic blandishments and defiantly terminated the president's power to restrict salaries. Later in the year, Roosevelt suffered another setback when Congress overrode a presidential veto of a bill increasing farm parity prices.

Roosevelt's most serious domestic problem remained taxes. While he called for higher taxes to absorb consumer purchasing power and to meet a large percentage of the war costs out of current revenue, Congress cut his requests. Beardsley Ruml, a presidential advisor, proposed a "pay-as-you-go" tax plan that would start by forgiving all 1942 taxes. The Ruml plan actually passed the Senate, but was stopped in the House. Secretary of the Treasury Henry Morgenthau proposed $10.5 billion in new revenue. The House agreed to only $2 billion, and the Senate was even more stingy, although it was generous in granting special tax concessions to commercial airlines, lumber interests, and oil companies. While the Democratic leaders told Roosevelt that the new bill was the best they could obtain, Roosevelt vetoed the measure on February 22, 1944, with a blistering attack on Congress: "It is not a tax bill but a tax relief bill providing relief not for the needy but for the greedy." Alben Barkley, the Senate majority leader who had been a loyal New Dealer and had pushed hard for the president's programs, was affronted by the sarcasm of the veto message. The next day, Barkley rose before a packed Senate gallery to defend the tax measure, attack the president's veto, and resign his position as majority leader. The Democratic senators immediately reelected him while Roosevelt dispatched a soothing message from Hyde Park. Naturally, Congress overrode the veto, and the bill was the first revenue act to become law in that manner.

Congress and the President also strongly disagreed over the Soldiers' Vote bill. While Congress was usually quite generous toward the men in uniform—the GI Bill of Rights had been enacted in late 1943, granting educational and other benefits to returning veterans—it was unwilling to move on a law facilitating servicemen's suffrage rights. The issue was a significant one. There were more than 11 million men in service who faced restrictive absentee-ballot laws in their home states. (In 1864, the votes of the Union soldiers unquestionably accounted for Lincoln's victory in several states.) The anti–New Dealers, who assumed that most of the soldiers would back their commander in chief, were not about to provide the president any new advantages. The best that Congress was willing to do initially was to recommend to the various states that they pass better absentee-ballot provisions. This, Roosevelt said, was a "fraud upon the soldiers and sailors and a fraud upon the American people." Our fighting men, the president declared, "do not have any lobby or pressure group on Capitol Hill to see that justice is done for them." The Republicans quickly counterattacked. Senator Robert A. Taft charged that the soldiers would be ordered to vote for Roosevelt. Another Republican speculated that the law would pass only if Roosevelt took himself out of the running. In the House, Southern

This Clifford Kennedy Berryman World War II cartoon titled "The Pedestrian Has the Right of Way" shows President Roosevelt as a policeman stopping a large truck labeled "New Tax Program," driven by House Ways and Means Committee chairman Robert Doughton, to allow a little boy (shown as John Q. Public and labeled "Taxpayer") to pull a small wagon of papers labeled "3rd War Loan" across the street. A frightened woman (labeled "Morgenthau") covers her eyes. In September 1943, Secretary Henry Morgenthau and the Treasury Department launched the Third War Bond Drive and the president spoke out strongly endorsing the effort. At the same time it was reported that the House Ways and Means Committee was meeting to draft a new tax bill. Berryman suggests that Roosevelt is promoting the war loan to keep the public from being frightened from purchasing bonds by the threat of new taxes. In actuality it was Morgenthau who was proposing new taxes ($10.5 billion), while Doughton eventually only agreed to a little more than $2 billion. *(Library of Congress)*

congressmen worried aloud that black soldiers would be allowed to vote, and John Rankin of Mississippi accused Communists and Jews of promoting the law. In final form, the bill extended a special federal ballot to only 85,000 overseas servicemen.

During the debate, Democratic Senator Abe Murdock of Utah brought to the surface what had been common knowledge in Washington for months, namely that Roosevelt would be a candidate for a fourth term. Murdock said: "I know it is the prayer . . . in the heart of every . . . good, old, stand-pat Republican in the United States today . . . that Franklin D. Roosevelt would eliminate himself from politics and give them at least a shadow of a chance to bring in the Grand Old Party again. But I say to them . . . the American people still want Roosevelt."

Any doubts that may have existed as to the president's candidacy were erased on January 11, 1944, when Roosevelt gave his 11th State of the Union address, which James MacGregor Burns has described as "the most

radical speech of his life." In it Roosevelt discussed the legislation he considered necessary to expedite the war effort: a realistic tax law, a new cost-of-food law, and a new national service law, "which, for the duration of the war will prevent strikes, and, with certain appropriate exceptions, will make available for war production or for any other essential services every able-bodied adult in the Nation." (Roosevelt had not consulted any of his economic advisors on the last recommendation, and Byrnes was so furious when informed of it that he threatened to resign.) The president then proceeded to outline measures that he thought vital to establishing postwar prosperity and "an American standard of living higher than ever before known." "We cannot be content," he stated, "no matter how high that standard of living may be, if some fraction of our people—whether it be one-third or one-fifth or one-tenth—is ill-fed, ill-clothed, ill-housed, and insecure." The political rights protected by the Constitution have proven "inadequate to assure us equality in the pursuit of happiness." He continued: "We have come to a clear realization of the fact that true individual freedom cannot exist" without economic security and independence. "Necessitous men are not free men. People who are hungry—people who are out of a job—are the stuff of which dictatorships are made." A second Bill of Rights was necessary for the nation, an economic Bill of Rights, and one that included:

> The right to a useful and remunerative job in the industries or shops or mines of the Nation;
> The right to earn enough to provide adequate food, clothing, and recreation;
> The right of farmers to raise and sell their products at a return which will give them and their family a decent living;
> The right of every businessman, large and small, to trade in an atmosphere of freedom from unfair competition and domination by monopolies at home and abroad;
> The right of every family to a decent home;
> The right to adequate medical care and the opportunity to achieve and enjoy good health;
> The right to adequate protection from the economic fears of old age and sickness and accident and unemployment;
> And finally, the right to a good education.
> All of these rights spell security. And after this war is won we must be prepared to move forward, in the implementation of these rights to new goals of human happiness and well-being.

In Roosevelt's mind, the establishment of a postwar, open society, providing economic security for all its citizens, required his victory in November. But in early 1944, this did not seem an especially easy task. Despite the president's wartime popularity, the 1942 congressional elections showed that the Republican Party had a bedrock support of about 20 million votes. If the approximately 10 million independent voters became disillusioned with Roosevelt's conduct of the war or skeptical of his capacity to cope with peacetime problems, a Republican victory was certainly possible. (The fact that Churchill was unceremoniously voted out of office in July 1945 showed how fickle an electorate can be with its wartime leaders.)

Faced with this arithmetic, Republican strategists attacked the weakest point of the Democratic administration—bureaucratic inefficiency and wrangling—while stressing that governmental wartime controls would lead to a future administrative dictatorship—one that would include strong Communist influence. The Democrats' inability to spark the economy was also an important argument. And then there was the dark rumor: Roosevelt was a dying man who would never complete another term.

The charge that Roosevelt was a terrible organizer and administrator came not only from his political enemies. Secretary of War Henry Stimson, for example, recorded in his diary that the president was "the poorest administrator I have ever worked under." It also piqued him that "inexperienced men appointed largely for personal grounds have constant and easy access to him." When the able Byrnes took over as head of the Office of War Mobilization, there was discernible improvement, but the charges against Roosevelt on this point were largely true. Instead of coordinating the agencies, making responsibilities clear, and giving extensive authority to a chief of staff, Roosevelt too often contributed to administrative conflicts by creating still another agency. Furthermore, his penchant for secrecy and for encouraging rivalries among his aides (to keep them honest and running hard, he once explained to Secretary of Labor Frances Perkins), which may have worked well in the 1930s, created confusing problems during the war when quick decisions, strict lines of authority, and comprehensive planning were absolutely necessary. Dean Acheson, then an assistant secretary of state, disclaimed as "nonsense" the charge that Roosevelt deliberately catered to confusion, and he attributed the disorganization in the administration to the fact that Roosevelt "was tone deaf to the subtler nuances of civil government organization. This was messed up in his administration for the simplest of reasons: he did not know any better."

The confusion in the State Department was a case in point. Although Cordell Hull was the nominal chief, Roosevelt had severely limited his authority by dealing directly with Hull's subordinates and making major decisions without consulting the secretary. George Kennan, then chargé d'affaires in Lisbon, describes in his *Memoirs* a meeting with the president, arranged by Harry Hopkins, during which Roosevelt enunciated a new policy toward Portugal without a prior word to the State or War Department. When Kennan mentioned his superiors, Roosevelt assured him, "Oh, don't worry about all those people over there." Undersecretary of State Sumner Welles, for another example, had easier access to the president and had a more important decision-making role than did Secretary Hull. From Hull's viewpoint, it was bad enough to have Harry Hopkins as the most important voice in foreign affairs, but worse still to have Welles as a presidential spy within the department. But the secretary swallowed his pride, helped force Welles's resignation in 1943, and did not resign himself until forced to by illness in November 1944.

But the Republicans were not content merely to echo legitimate complaints about the administration's inefficiency. Outrageous stories were spread about members of the presidential team on the theory that if you cannot strike at the king, you can at least throw mud at his ministers. Harry Hopkins was always a special target, along with Justice Felix Frankfurter, presidential speechwriter Samuel I. Rosenman, and administrative assistant David Niles—three of the highest-ranking Jews in the national government. Hopkins remarried in June 1943, and immediately the anti-Roosevelt press concocted a series of slanders about the new couple. Lord Beaverbrook, it was said, had given the bride $500,000 in emeralds in recognition of Hopkins's help in securing Lend Lease for England. Then a published story claimed that Hopkins had ordered the Coast Guard to requisition a yacht for his honeymoon cruise and that a Michigan businessman had been forcibly taken off his boat so that Hopkins could use it. After Bernard Baruch had arranged for a wedding dinner for Hopkins in a Washington hotel, columnists reported that a bacchanalian feast had taken place just when the president was calling for greater sacrifices.

And then there were the Communists. The House Un-American Activities Committee was at its zenith in 1943. Throughout that year, Communist-front organizations continued to be investigated. Even members of the Executive Department were not immune from the committee's scrutiny. Many were compelled to explain their support of the Spanish Loyalists during the 1930s or to justify their signatures on a Socialist Party petition in the 1920s. The Republicans went all out to capitalize on the leftist issue, especially since Roosevelt in May 1942 had pardoned Earl Browder, who was serving a federal prison sentence for perjury.

But the Republicans' most compelling argument (which they could only hint at) was the president's health.

From late in 1943 to March 1944, Roosevelt was plagued with colds and bronchial miseries that ultimately led to hospitalization. At Bethesda Naval Hospital late in March 1944, doctors discovered that Roosevelt's heart was enlarged, that his blood pressure had increased, and that he suffered from arteriosclerosis and hypertensive heart disease. They recommended that he rest, lose weight, and take digitalis. The president readily agreed to the new regimen, which began with a month's vacation in Hobcaw, Bernard Baruch's estate in South Carolina.

While he was recuperating in the South, rumors of his frail condition circulated through Washington, but on his return to the capital in May, the president seemed rested and in better spirits. His doctor claimed that he was in "good condition for a man of his age [62]." White House reporters and visitors, however, continued to be worried about his haggard appearance. Admiral Ross T. McIntire, Roosevelt's physician, later wrote, "The baggy coat and ill-fitting shirts, much too large for his shrunken neck, did as much as anything else to give an effect of illness and physical deterioration." Even his closest advisors commented on the dark circles under his eyes, the slump in his shoulders, his emaciated neck, and the shakiness of his hands when he lit a cigarette. Thus, despite optimistic reports put out by his doctors, whisperings continued as to the perilousness of the president's physical condition.

By the time Roosevelt returned from Hobcaw in early May, it was clear that Governor Thomas E. Dewey of New York would be his election opponent. The frontrunner at the start of the campaign, however, had been Wendell Willkie, the 1940 GOP candidate. Willkie had commanded nationwide attention as the chief Republican spokesman throughout the war. His worldwide travels in 1942 kept him in the limelight, and his book *One World,* with its plea for a strong international organization after the war, was highly popular. All members of the United Nations should be represented in the war councils, Willkie claimed, or else postwar suspicion and distrust would grow. In many speeches, he harshly condemned Roosevelt's cooperation with the Vichy government and vehemently attacked the president's one-man rule and inept administration. But Willkie had no elective position to use as a base of operations. Furthermore, he was out of tune with the isolationist, violently anti-Roosevelt sentiment of the Republican Old Guard, which had regained control of the party machinery after the 1942 elections. His supporters were barely represented in the party councils, and Willkie had built no organization of his own at the grassroots level. Nevertheless, he bounded out with enormous energy to enter the party primaries in the spring of 1944. He completed a 12-state speaking tour through the Far West in January and February and made a deal with Governor Earl Warren whereby he (Willkie) agreed not to challenge Warren's favorite-son candidacy in the California primary in exchange for vague intimations of later support. Willkie also campaigned vigorously in New Hampshire, Wisconsin, and Nebraska.

In the New Hampshire primary, Willkie won a small victory (6 of 11 delegates). The Wisconsin primary was next, and Willkie barnstormed the state for two weeks, speaking to crowds in six or seven towns a day. Although no other candidate stepped foot inside the state, the regular Republican machine supported a slate of delegates pledged to Dewey. On April 4, the voters elected not a single Willkie delegate. Although he disavowed all the efforts on his behalf, Dewey had won 17 delegates. There were also 4 pledged to Douglas MacArthur and 3 to Harold Stassen. Willkie recognized the inevitable and withdrew from the race the very next day. *Newsweek* immediately commented on the importance of the Wisconsin primary: "By Wednesday noon, April 5, the day after the primary, it was apparent that Wisconsin voters had not merely administered an unprecedented defeat to Willkie, they had virtually chosen the next Republican presidential nominee in the person of Dewey, three months in advance of the GOP national convention."

General Douglas MacArthur (*Library of Congress*)

The prediction was accurate. The only drama left in the campaign for the Republican nomination revolved around Douglas MacArthur. He was certainly a favorite of the *Chicago Tribune* and the Hearst press, who were both pressing for a Pacific-first strategy. His reputation as a brave and skillful wartime commander may have been dimmed somewhat by the quick Japanese takeover of the Philippines—MacArthur had been the military commander in Manila for five years before the war and had given optimistic reports about the islands' defenses—but as the senior military man in the Pacific, he benefited from the growing number of victories over the Japanese. In his prewar career, he had spoken out against communism, pacifism, and foreign entanglements, and his routing of the Bonus Marchers in 1932 endeared him with those favoring strong action against radicals. There was no doubt about his antipathy toward Roosevelt and the New Deal, his isolationist ideas, or his desire for a strong military rather than an international organization as the best means to guarantee peace. The most reactionary elements in the party, including General Robert E. Wood, the former head of America First, pressed for his nomination. More skillful managers would have kept his name out of contention until an opportune time presented itself at the convention. But an overeager supporter, Representative A. L. Miller of Nebraska, became anxious about Dewey's growing lead and made public an exchange of correspondence between himself and MacArthur, in which the general endorsed the congressman's vitriolic attack on the New Deal. Miller had written to MacArthur in September 1943, "I am certain that unless this New Deal can be stopped this time, our American way of life is forever doomed. You owe it to civilization and the children yet unborn to accept the nomination." MacArthur answered a month later, "I did not anticipate in any way your flattering predictions, but I do unreservedly agree with the complete wisdom and statesmanship of your comments." He added, "I knew your state well in the days of used to be. I have enjoyed many a delightful hunting excursion there. . . . Those days seem singularly carefree and happy compared to the sinister drama of our present chaos and confusion." Encouraged, Miller wrote back to MacArthur in January 1944, "If this system of left-wingers and New Dealism is continued another four years, I am certain that this monarchy which is being established in America will destroy the rights of the common people." To which MacArthur responded in February, "I appreciate very much your scholarly letter. Your description of conditions in the United States is a sobering one indeed and is calculated to arouse the thoughtful consideration of every true patriot. . . . Out here we are doing what we can with what we have. I will be glad, however, when more substantial forces are placed at my disposal."

Miller released the letters, evidently hoping to start a MacArthur drive and to show that the leading general in the Pacific was not getting enough troops or supplies. Instead, the press and the political professionals reacted with astonishment that the general could be so naive as to endorse such a reactionary position. When he saw the furor his letters had raised, MacArthur issued an explanatory statement claiming that the letters "were neither politically inspired nor intended to convey blanket approval of the Congressman's views. . . . I entirely repudiate the sinister interpretation that they were intended as criticism of any political philosophy or any personage in high office." Early in May, MacArthur, faced with the almost universal negative reaction to his letters, ended any speculation that he was a candidate: "I was not a candidate for the position. . . . I do not covet it, nor would I accept it."

MacArthur's withdrawal left no doubt that the Republican candidate would be Dewey. The New York governor was one of the few challenging candidates in modern history who won a nomination without having to declare his candidacy or leave his home state. His political rise had been spectacular. Born in the small Michigan town of Owosso in 1902, he attended the University of Michigan and Columbia University Law School. He joined a New York law firm and impressed his colleagues and other members of the bar with his ability and hard work. When George Z. Medalie was appointed U.S. attorney for the Southern District of New York in 1931, he picked Dewey as his chief assistant. He succeeded Medalie as top federal attorney within a year and quickly won a national reputation as a vigorous prosecutor when he indicted Waxie Gordon and other racketeers for income tax evasion. He resigned in 1933 and resumed private practice. Two years later, when a runaway grand jury complained that the district attorney was blocking its efforts to investigate organized crime, Governor Herbert Lehman chose Dewey to be a special prosecutor, and he soon won popular acclaim by successfully prosecuting such well-known figures as Legs Diamond and Lucky Luciano. In 1937, he was overwhelmingly elected district attorney of New York County. In 1938, at the age of 36, he ran for governor against the popular Lehman and lost by only 64,000 votes. A man in a hurry, he announced his candidacy for the presidency in December 1939, and remained the leading Republican contender throughout the spring of 1940. Dewey won most of the Republican primaries and had the largest bloc of delegates until the Willkie hurricane swept the Philadelphia convention. In 1942, he was elected governor of New York by a heavy margin (650,000 votes) over John J. Bennett.

In the 1944 campaign for the Republican nomination, Dewey was in a much better position than he had been four years earlier. He had gained valuable experience, had a smashing political victory under his belt, and commanded a strong political base in the nation's largest state; he was respected (if not liked) by party regulars and had access to the biggest money-raisers in the party; and there were no new attractive figures in any real position to deny him the prize.

On November 1, 1943, the Gallup Poll reported that Willkie was the choice of 32.5 percent of registered Republicans, while Dewey was preferred by 17.9 percent. By January 1, Dewey had taken the lead, 29.6 percent to 22.6 percent, and by February 15 the margin was even greater, 36.9 percent to 19.6 percent. On April 15, it was 50.3 percent to 9.3. No doubt the early figures reflect the fact that Willkie was still the titular head of the party. The Dewey surge began in November 1943, when his personal choice for lieutenant governor of New York, Joe R. Hanley, was elected to the office. The victory seemed a clear indication of Dewey's strength and influence in New York, and there was never any doubt that the Empire State was crucial for a Republican victory. In January, Dewey received a further boost when a number of complimentary articles appeared in national magazines.

Dewey was also the chief beneficiary of the anti-Willkie movement initiated by party regulars. In the process of stopping Willkie, however, they built up Dewey's

This Clifford Kennedy Berryman cartoon shows former Republican presidential candidate Wendell Willkie as a farmer, sitting on a fence, talking to Governor John Bricker of Ohio and Governor Thomas E. Dewey of New York. Willkie tries to reassure them, saying, "Buck up, boys, we can win in 1944." Bricker responds, "WHO does he mean by 'WE'?" Willkie was a Wall Street public utilities lawyer, but he was portrayed by the media as a homespun Indiana boy. Although he captured the Republican nomination in 1940, he was widely distrusted by the party regulars because of his internationalist views. When Willkie began to take steps to capture the nomination again, he was opposed by the conservative wing of the party led by Bricker and Dewey. *(Library of Congress)*

strength to a point where his lead was insurmountable. In short, the party regulars had lost control of the situation.

There were some minor obstacles that Dewey had to overcome. When running for governor in 1942, he had pledged that he would complete a full four-year term. If he actively sought the presidential nomination, he would certainly be violating that promise. His strategy was thus to make the drive for the presidency seem as much like a draft as possible. Dewey therefore refused to announce his candidacy, never undertook a political tour outside the state, and never spoke out on any important political issues then dividing the party. The one notable exception was a foreign policy speech in April 1944 in which he vaguely supported an international organization and attacked Roosevelt for not supporting Secretary of State Hull. His silence had its advantages. The *New York Times* commented in April that Dewey's reluctance to discuss the issues "permits different groups in different sections of the country to interpret his silence on controversial issues as they wish to interpret it for the sake of the most practical political results and to portray Mr. Dewey in different lights to different groups of people . . . this is a highly effective way of achieving a superficial political unity."

There were also some doubts about Dewey's voter appeal. He certainly lacked the common touch. As Irving Stone wrote later, "His legislature found him cold, hard, dictatorial, unsympathetic, and unfriendly; they didn't like him as a person. . . . Newspapermen disliked him cordially, found him overbearing, opportunistic in making them work for his purposes, but always leaving them out on a limb for the material they published." During a governors' conference at Mackinac Island in 1943, Dewey had offended many of the Midwestern party leaders by calling on farmers to help reduce grain prices by slaughtering their hogs and sending the grain that would otherwise be used as feed to the Eastern states. He also urged importing grain from Canada if prices did not go down. *Newsweek* commented that some party leaders were skeptical as to whether "Dewey will play the game, that he will make the deals and trades and compromises" necessary for a successful political campaign.

But Dewey's lieutenants worked efficiently at lining up delegates for the convention. His campaign team consisted of J. Russel Sprague, the county executive for Nassau and the New York Republican national committeeman; Edwin F. Jaeckle, a Buffalo lawyer and the state Republican chairman who had been temporarily dropped from the Dewey councils in 1942, after it was discovered that Jaeckle's law firm had represented the German Bund before the war; and Herbert Brownell, then forty years old and later attorney general under Eisenhower, who had served in the New York Assembly from 1932 to 1938 and who had been named Republican national chairman after Dewey's nomination. Other advisers were Roger W. Straus, president of American Smelting and Refining; John Foster Dulles, Dewey's chief foreign policy adviser (later Dewey appointed him to the Senate and Eisenhower chose him as secretary of state); and George Z. Medalie, Dewey's old boss in the U.S. Attorney's Office. Elliott Bell, a former Willkie aide, became Dewey's chief speechwriter, and James C. Hagerty, son of the *New York Times* political reporter James A. Hagerty and later Eisenhower's press secretary, handled press relations.

Dewey's team set up national headquarters in the Roosevelt Hotel in New York City, from which invariably came the message that only Dewey could carry New York, and New York was essential for a Republican victory. The Dewey staff relied heavily on polls, which continually showed increasing Dewey popularity and delegate strength. As early as April 17, James A. Hagerty reported in the *New York Times* that Dewey had pledges from an absolute majority of delegates. Dewey's strong showing in the primaries also helped his bandwagon. He garnered over 20,000 write-in votes in Nebraska, where his name was not on the ballot. Stassen, who was on the ballot, received only 45,000 votes. In Pennsylvania, close to 150,000 Republican voters wrote in his name, while the next leading Republican, MacArthur, received a mere 8,000. In May, he beat both Harold Stassen and John W. Bricker in Oregon by a large margin. In the states that selected delegates by convention rather than in a primary, the party leaders chose slates either committed to Dewey or strongly leaning toward his candidacy.

The Republican convention in late June was a dull anticlimax. In fact, Willkie was not even allowed to speak to the delegates, as Dewey's managers feared a repetition of 1940. A vaguely internationalist platform was adopted endorsing a United Nations plan. New Deal centralization was condemned: "The measures we propose . . . shall avoid . . . detailed regulation of farmers, workers, businessmen, and consumers, to the end that the individual shall be free." The platform promised to protect small business, the farmer, and foreign trade. It called for a revision of the tax laws and a balanced budget. In a bid for the labor vote, the platform supported extension of the old-age insurance and unemployment insurance systems to all employees. Another plank stated the party's acceptance of "the purposes of the National Labor Relations Act, the Wage and Hour Act, the Social Security Act, and all other Federal statutes designed to promote and protect the welfare of American men and women, and we promise a fair and just administration of these laws."

Before the final vote, on June 28, Governor John W. Bricker withdrew his name from consideration. "I come here this morning conscious of the fact that it is the desire of the great majority of the delegates of this convention to

Earl Warren *(Library of Congress)*

nominate the gallant, fighting Governor of New York for President. I believe in party organization." With no other candidate available, the convention, on the first ballot, gave 1,056 votes to Dewey, with one lone maverick from Wisconsin spoiling unanimity with a vote for MacArthur. It was the most one-sided victory for any candidate not then an incumbent president in the history of the party.

The political professionals had hoped to make Governor Earl Warren of California the vice-presidential candidate. He had won an impressive victory over Democrat Culbert Olson in 1942, and California's electoral vote was important in November. But before the balloting, Warren declined the probable nomination because of "certain commitments in my home state as governor which I have not yet been able to complete." During his 1942 campaign for governor, Warren, like Dewey, had promised that he would remain in office for a full term. Most probably, Warren saw no point in jeopardizing his own political career by taking second place on what still looked like a losing ticket. Warren's withdrawal left the way open for Bricker, who was unanimously chosen as the vice-presidential candidate.

In his acceptance speech, Dewey hit hard at the quarreling Democratic administration: "It is at war with Congress and at war with itself. Squabbles between cabinet members, feuds between rival bureaucrats and bitterness between the President and his own party members, in and out of Congress, have become the order of the day. . . . It has grown old in office. It has become tired and quarrelsome." Dewey also focused on unemployment: "In 1940 . . . there were still 10,000,000 unemployed. After seven years of unequalled power and unparalleled spending, the New Deal had failed utterly to solve that problem. . . . It was left to be solved by war." It was a sober, statesmanlike speech, in keeping with the high-level campaign that both parties thought, at first, was appropriate to wartime.

Roosevelt did not make his availability official until the last minute, although there was little doubt that he would be the candidate. The polls consistently showed that he was the only Democrat who could win. Some polls even indicated that as many as 50 percent of those planning to vote for Roosevelt would vote Republican if he did not run. Furthermore, many of those surveyed responded that they would vote for Roosevelt only if the war was still going on in November. In short, the president's chief asset was the fact that he was the wartime commander, and the people wanted him to continue in that role until hostilities closed.

Roosevelt's refusal to announce gave the Democrats the chance to organize a ground-swell campaign demanding that he stay on. Labor leaders, Democratic politicians, and veterans groups issued public statements that Roosevelt had to be the candidate or else the work of the New Deal and the victorious conclusion of the war would be put in jeopardy. Although a small anti-Roosevelt boomlet led by former secretary of war Harry Woodring formed within the party, the newspapers gave it more coverage than it warranted. Finally, on July 11, 1944, just a week before the Democratic convention began in Chicago, Roosevelt released a letter stating that as a "good soldier" he would accept renomination.

But who would be Roosevelt's running mate? Whenever a vice president succeeds to the highest office, the machinations by which he was picked for the second place provoke the greatest interest of later observers. And no selection of a vice-presidential candidate ever contained more intrigue, suspense, confusion, and political maneuvering than the nomination of Harry S. Truman.

It was clear that incumbent vice president Wallace had done nothing as vice president to endear himself to the Democratic political bosses. In their eyes, according to the *St. Louis Post Dispatch,* he was "impractical, theoretical, enigmatic, and 'too damned independent.' He is too pro-labor, too outspoken for racial equality. And besides, he speaks Russian." The party leaders, Ed Flynn of the Bronx, Edwin Pauley, the party treasurer, Postmaster General Frank Walker, Robert E. Hannegan, chairman of the Democratic National Committee, and Mayor Ed Kelly of Chicago were adamant against Wallace. He had been

trouble enough in the past four years, and they certainly could not visualize him as president should the rumors of Roosevelt's disintegrating health prove true. Two key White House aides, Edwin "Pa" Watson and Steve Early, also opposed Wallace's renomination.

In their struggle against Wallace, party professionals directed and maintained a stream of anti-Wallace reports to the White House; his presence on the ticket would cost 3 million votes and at least ten states; there would be a nasty floor fight at the convention if Wallace was pushed for the vice presidency; a number of state delegations had specific instructions not to vote for Wallace; Congress would not go along with the president's postwar program if Wallace remained. Ed Flynn even told the president that it was doubtful he could win New York State with Wallace on the ticket.

Whether Roosevelt believed all this conjecture is unclear. Certainly the labor leaders and other liberal elements within the party, including his own wife Eleanor, expressed their support of Wallace, and the polls continued to show his popularity with the rank and file. But the depth of feeling against Wallace among the professionals and in his own cabinet made Roosevelt wary. Ickes had been Wallace's bitter enemy for years, and Hopkins was something less than a Wallace admirer. Hull told the president in June that he thought Wallace was "intellectually dishonest" and that his election would place the secretary in "an impossible position."

Roosevelt expressed his feelings about the subject to Rosenman at the end of June:

> I am just not going to go through a convention like 1940 again. It will split the party wide open, and it is already split enough. . . . It may kill our chances for election this fall, and if it does, it will prolong the war and knock into a cocked hat all the plans we've been making for the future.

He instructed Rosenman to inform Wallace "that I'd like to have him as my running mate, but I simply cannot risk creating a permanent split in the party by making the same kind of fight for him that I did at the convention four years ago. I am sure he will understand and be glad to step down." Rosenman immediately got in touch with Wallace's office (he was then on a mission to China), telling his secretary that he had to see Wallace as soon as he returned to the United States. Wallace's staff was extremely elusive about telling Rosenman the vice president's travel plans, and Wallace, well aware of what was up, tried to avoid meeting Rosenman until he at least had a chance to talk to the president. But Rosenman was insistent and arranged a breakfast meeting for July 10, at which time he and Harold Ickes told Wallace of the president's decision. Wallace listened to the message but then informed the two men he did not wish to discuss politics until he had spoken to the president about his China mission.

That very afternoon he did speak with Roosevelt. Instead of remaining adamant, the president weakened. As Rosenman explained his behavior, "his unwillingness to be unpleasantly frank was notorious among those who knew him well . . . his performance in 1944 on the Vice-Presidential nomination was the most extreme expression of it I ever experienced." Although Wallace offered to step down, the president said he was his own personal choice for second place, and he urged Wallace to remain in the race. Wallace asked for a written statement that Roosevelt preferred him, and the president promised to provide it.

Wallace was not the only recipient of a presidential promise of support. James F. Byrnes had been approached by both Harry Hopkins and Frank Walker about running for the second position. Then on June 14 Byrnes met with the president about plans for the convention. Roosevelt wanted him to be permanent chairman. When Byrnes demurred, Roosevelt reminded him that Senator Joe Robinson had been permanent chairman in 1928 and had handled matters so well that the convention chose him for the

In this Clifford Kennedy Berryman cartoon, labor leader Sidney Hillman, with CIO president Philip Murray, asks grinning city bosses Edward Kelly, Edward J. Flynn, and Frank Hague, "What did I do wrong?" Despite the fact that he was strongly supported by the labor unions and the liberal wing of the Democratic Party, Vice President Henry Wallace was denied renomination at the Democratic National Convention in 1944, losing to Senator Harry Truman, who was more acceptable to the South and the city bosses. Democratic leaders, fearing that Roosevelt's health was uncertain, were determined to prevent Wallace, viewed as an unpredictable, wild-eyed visionary, from being next in line for the presidency. *(Library of Congress)*

second spot on the ticket. "History will repeat itself," said the president. Byrnes was greatly encouraged and genuinely believed that he was the president's personal choice.

The key meeting on the ultimate selection took place on July 11. Bob Hannegan, Frank Walker, Ed Pauley, Ed Kelly, George Allen, and Ed Flynn were dining at the White House. During coffee, the subject of the vice presidency came up, and the participants examined each candidate's qualifications. Byrnes, they decided, would not go over with the black or labor vote. Besides, he was an ex-Catholic and as such might alienate the big city vote. Barkley was too old. Roosevelt then suggested Supreme Court Justice William O. Douglas, but the others felt he added no visible strength to the ticket. Then Truman's name came up. He had been a protégé of Tom Pendergast in Kansas City and understood the ways of the big city machines. He had done a commendable job in the Senate as the head of a committee to investigate the defense program and had courageously uncovered both graft and inefficiency. He had fought in World War I and was sympathetic to veterans' problems. Ed Flynn summed up the sentiment for Truman:

> Truman was the only one who fitted. His record as head of the Senate Committee to Investigate the National Defense Program was excellent, his labor votes in the Senate were good; on the other hand, he seemed to represent to some degree the conservatives in the party, he came from a border state, and he had never made any "racial remarks." He just dropped into the slot. It was agreed that Truman was the man who would hurt him least.

When the conference ended, Roosevelt said to Hannegan, "Bob, I think you and everyone else here want Truman." Hannegan also asked the president for a written statement confirming the acceptance of Truman. Roosevelt dashed off a short note, stating, "Dear Bob: You have written me about Harry Truman and Bill Douglas. I should, of course, be very glad to run with either of them and believe that either one of them would bring real strength to the ticket." Presumably, the president added Douglas's name so that he would not seem to be dictating to the convention as he did in 1940, although there was no strong feeling for Douglas among the party leaders. The next day, Hannegan returned to the White House and had the letter typed on White House stationery and signed by the president. It was dated July 19, although it was signed July 12. Hannegan then kept both copies for use at the convention.

Walker was given the task of telling Byrnes that he was dropped. He did so on Wednesday July 12. But Byrnes did not give up any more easily than Wallace. He immediately called the president to find out why he had changed his mind. Roosevelt again refused to verify the unpleasant news. He told Byrnes, "You are the best qualified man in the whole outfit and you must not get out of the race. If you stay in, you are sure to win."

The next day, Roosevelt spoke to Byrnes again. He told him that he could not ask the vice president to step aside since he considered him a close friend. In fact, he was going to publicly announce that he personally preferred Wallace. But he knew he could not be renominated, and he wanted Byrnes to stay in the running. Not a word was said about Truman. Later in the day the president saw Wallace and told him he would write a personal letter to Senator Sam D. Jackson, the permanent chairman of the convention, indicating his personal preference for Wallace. "While I can't say this publicly," the president said, "I hope it's the same old team again." The letter was sent out the next day.

On Friday, July 14, Walker and Hannegan again spoke to Byrnes. For the first time, the president's preference for Truman was mentioned. Byrnes got the president on the phone again and asked him about the letter of endorsement of Truman and Douglas. "We have to be damned careful about language," the president said. "They asked me if I would object to Truman and Douglas and I said no. That is different from using the word 'prefer.' This is not expressing a preference because you know I told you I would have no preference." Hannegan was not in a position to translate Roosevelt's remarks to Byrnes as Rosenman might have done, and Byrnes continued to think he was the president's favorite. Byrnes then called Truman, asking him to place his name in nomination for vice president. The Senator readily agreed, thinking Byrnes was the president's choice.

The action then shifted to Chicago. Roosevelt was on a train heading for San Diego and the Pacific, but he made a brief stop in Chicago to consult for a few minutes with Hannegan and Kelly about the nomination. What happened on the train is unclear. Kelly came away with the idea that Byrnes was the president's choice. On the other hand, Grace Tully, the president's secretary, claimed that Hannegan asked her to type a new letter for the president to sign endorsing Truman and Douglas. (She later wrote that the original letter of July 11, typed up on the 12th, mentioned Douglas's name first, a position that Rosenman disputed and Hannegan denied. Since everyone agreed that Truman was the choice of the July 11 meeting, it would not have made any sense for Roosevelt to have put Douglas's name ahead of the senator's.)

At a July 16 dinner for various Democratic leaders, Hannegan and Kelly indicated that the president's choice was Byrnes. But before any public announcement could be made, one last matter had to be cleared. Hannegan then reportedly said to Kelly, "Ed, there is one thing we forgot.

This Clifford Kennedy Berryman cartoon shows President Roosevelt jovially greeting Vice President Henry Wallace, who carries a briefcase covered with Asian characters. As the 1944 Democratic convention approached, Roosevelt played a devious hand, letting a number of people think that he supported their candidacies for vice president. Wallace had just returned from a trip to the Far East, a trip that some observers thought was designed by the president to keep him out of the way. In the end, Wallace was dumped, and Senator Harry Truman of Missouri was nominated instead. *(Library of Congress)*

The president said, 'Clear it with Sidney.'" (After Arthur Krock published an account of the meeting that he got from Byrnes, Hannegan denied making the statement.)

The "Sidney" referred to was, of course, Sidney Hillman, the head of the CIO (Congress of Industrial Organizations) Political Action Committee. Labor had organized for the election as it never had in the past, and the PAC campaign fund was bulging. Twenty percent of the $7 million contributed to the Democratic campaign fund during 1944 came from Hillman's group. With that much muscle, labor could not be ignored in making the decision for vice president. Hillman let it be known immediately that Byrnes was totally unacceptable.

In the meantime, Truman had been busily denying that he was a vice-presidential hopeful. He told his Missouri delegation that he did not want the honor, and told reporters that he wanted to remain a senator. When Hannegan told him confidentially he was Roosevelt's choice, he still rejected the position. Hannegan panicked and told Walker, "It's all over; our candidate won't take it—we have no candidate!" Truman repeated his denial to certain labor leaders, notably Philip Murray of the CIO.

The crucial break came when Ed Flynn arrived from New York on Monday afternoon, July 17. When he heard of the swing to Byrnes, he could not believe it. The last he knew, Truman had been picked on July 11. He immediately called a meeting with Hannegan, Walker, and Kelly for Monday night and insisted that they call the president, then en route to San Diego. Away from the personal influences of Byrnes and Wallace, Roosevelt reaffirmed his choice of Truman.

Now it became necessary to put all the pieces together. Byrnes was notified of the president's final decision. Later, during the evening of July 17, Hannegan and Walker met with Hillman, Philip Murray, president of the CIO, and A. F. Whitney, president of the Brotherhood of Railroad Trainmen. Hannegan let Hillman think that Byrnes was still the first choice while Hillman insisted that Wallace be renominated. The stage was set for an obvious compromise on Truman later in the week, and Hannegan thought he would have no problem in securing the vital labor votes for his candidate.

Byrnes later wrote that Truman was then told that he was the president's candidate, and he came to see Byrnes that Monday night, asking to be released from his pledge of support. But Truman in his *Memoirs* tells a different story. He claims that he was a Byrnes man until Thursday, July 20, and that he did not accept the nomination until the following telephone conversation took place on July 20:

> FDR to Hannegan: "Have you got that fellow lined up yet?"
> Hannegan to FDR: "No. He is the contrariest Missouri Mule I've ever dealt with."
> FDR: "Well, you tell him, if he wants to break up the Democratic Party in the middle of a war, that's his responsibility."
> Truman: "Well, if that's the situation, I'll have to say yes, but why the hell didn't he tell me in the first place."

It seems likely that the conversation took place earlier than Thursday, probably on that Monday night. Byrnes told his supporters on Tuesday that he was not the president's candidate and announced it publicly on Wednesday. Truman would hardly have continued as a Byrnes backer for two days after Byrnes's withdrawal.

But if the bosses had agreed, the delegates were totally confused. Most had no idea that Wallace had been eliminated, especially after the president's letter of personal preference for Wallace had been released on Monday. Speculation about the contents of the letter had been front page news for days, with the political analysts claiming that only a demand for Wallace's renomination by the president could save him. In their view, the president's endorsement of Wallace was strong, but not strong enough. Hillman was pledged to support Wallace, and he had to go through the motions until the time came to

switch to Truman. On Tuesday and Wednesday, delegate enthusiasm for Wallace began growing uncontrollable. When he entered the convention hall on Wednesday night, he received a 15-minute standing ovation.

Hannegan decided that he had to take drastic steps to stop the Wallace drive. He called an early morning press conference on Thursday and released Roosevelt's letter endorsing Truman or Douglas. But the letter did not produce the desired effect.

When Wallace seconded Roosevelt's nomination on Thursday night, the galleries exploded again. Shouts of "We Want Wallace" continued long after his speech had ended. The chanting continued until the chairman adjourned the meeting to a chorus of "noes." On Friday the police screened the galleries to keep out Wallace supporters. The leaders spoke to the delegates, insisting that Truman was Roosevelt's choice. Nevertheless, after the first ballot Wallace led 429.5 to Truman's 319.5. The rest went to favorite sons. On the second ballot, the state delegations began to fall in line, and Truman's nomination was secured, by a vote of 1,031 to 105.

John Gunther later called the switch to Truman as "the worst double-cross in Roosevelt's history." But surely the facts show otherwise. Roosevelt's concern about a split in the party was a legitimate one, and the difficulties at the convention resulted more from his vacillation than from his initial decision. Hannegan was no Harry Hopkins, who was able to understand his chief's wishes even when he contradicted himself. Kelly, Flynn, and Hannegan could not handle Byrnes and did not want to offend him, particularly when Roosevelt refused to do so. The "Clear it with Sidney" story may have been Hannegan's way of shifting the burden of vetoing Byrnes to labor rather than keeping it himself or putting it upon the president's shoulders.

While all these maneuverings were going on in Chicago, Roosevelt was in San Diego inspecting the naval and marine base and preparing for a trip to Hawaii. He gave his acceptance speech from San Diego, stating that he would "not campaign in the usual sense. . . . In these days of tragic sorrow, I do not consider it fitting. And besides, in these days of global warfare, I shall not be able to find the time." He outlined the job ahead: to win the war, to form an international organization to make war impossible, and "to build an economy for our returning veterans and for all Americans—which will provide employment and provide decent standards of living."

One of the pictures taken of Roosevelt while he was speaking showed him with his mouth open, stooping forward, looking especially thin and gaunt. Ordinarily, Steve Early would check all news pictures before they were released, but he was not with the president on the Pacific trip and the photograph was sent out. It later appeared in Republican campaign literature.

Roosevelt sailed on to Pearl Harbor, where he was greeted by the chief Pacific-area admirals and generals. MacArthur arrived at the last minute, driven in what Rosenman called the "longest open car I have ever seen." The car contained only one chauffeur in khaki and "one lone figure" in the back seat, MacArthur. He climbed the gangplank, acknowledging applause from the dock. Roosevelt remarked about his uniform, "Hello, Doug. What are you doing with that leather jacket—it's darn hot today." MacArthur answered, "Well, I've just landed from Australia. It's pretty cold up there."

The president went over the final war plans for the Pacific area and paid several visits to army and navy hospitals in Hawaii. At one point, MacArthur asked him about Dewey. He replied that he thought he was a "nice little man." (Ickes reportedly once said that Dewey looked "like the groom on the wedding cake.") MacArthur later told Charles Lindbergh that Roosevelt looked terrible but that his voice was still strong and his mind as quick as ever.

From Hawaii, Roosevelt sailed to the Aleutians to visit naval installations and finally returned to the United States on August 12. He then delivered a report on his Pacific trip

at the Bremerton Naval Base near Seattle. None of his regular speechwriters were with him, and the speech was rambling and pedestrian. Furthermore, Roosevelt decided to stand up while speaking and used his braces for the first time since Teheran, eight months before. The braces did not fit because of his loss of weight, and the steel stays bit into his legs. The destroyer deck on which he spoke sloped sharply, putting an even greater strain on the president. He had to grip the lectern so hard that he was unable to concentrate on the speech, which, as a result, was faltering and unsure. During the first half of the speech, Roosevelt suffered sharp pains in his chest that radiated to both shoulders. With a strong wind blowing, the audience could barely hear the president and did not react to his remarks. All in all, it may have been Roosevelt's worst public performance during his entire political career, and his advisers, listening on the radio, were thrown into a panic.

The polls reported a dramatic increase of support for Dewey after the Bremerton speech, and Democratic leaders advised Roosevelt to start a series of campaign speeches to offset the trend. But Roosevelt decided he still had ample time—and besides, there was a war to win. He

Vice President Henry A. Wallace at the Democratic convention in Chicago turns to greet delegates while seeking the vice-presidential nomination for another term. *(Library of Congress)*

would continue to stay above the political arena as commander in chief until the appropriate moment.

Early in September, Churchill arrived in Quebec for a war conference that Roosevelt attended. At the meeting, Henry Morgenthau introduced his plan for dismantling all the German industries after the war and making the country strictly an agricultural, "pastoral" nation. The plan ran counter to all the wisdom of the Versailles settlement in 1919, and Churchill himself had previously opposed any such war settlement, though he appeared to acquiesce in this one. Roosevelt's other advisors also spoke against it, and the introduction of the proposal made for some uneasy moments. But the parties soon turned their attention to the more immediate problem of winning the war, and good spirits returned.

While Roosevelt was in Quebec, Dewey started his formal campaign in Philadelphia on September 7. He contrasted the "exhausted quarreling and bickering administration" with the "fresh and vigorous" government that the Republicans would put in. He accused the Democrats of failing for eight "straight years to restore our domestic economy." He turned his attention to a statement made by General Lewis Hershey, the director of Selective Service and a man inclined even then to making foolish remarks. Hershey had said in an August press conference held in Denver, "We can keep people in the Army about as cheaply as we could create an agency for them when they get out." Dewey seized on this statement to prove that the administration had no plan to keep the peacetime economy moving. The Democrats "kept this country in a continuous state of depression for seven straight years," and they were afraid to let soldiers return lest they bring on further unemployment.

After a long train trip to the West Coast, Dewey spoke in Seattle on September 18 about his labor policy. He accused Roosevelt of ignoring the established legal processes to settle strikes and relying instead on "personal government instead of government by law, politics instead of justice." Labor relations "have been smothered under a welter of agencies, boards, commissions, and bureaus." In Portland, Oregon, he claimed that Roosevelt had tried for 12 years to "bring the Congress of the United States into disrepute," and that he was claiming "to be indispensable to peace and prosperity." In San Francisco, Dewey declared that "we are not going down the New Deal road to total control of our daily lives." The next day, in Los Angeles, Dewey delivered his most radical speech, calling for extended Social Security as well as old-age and unemployment coverage to 20 million workers not then covered. "We must [also] help to develop a means for assurance of medical service to those of our citizens who need it and cannot otherwise obtain it."

Thomas E. Dewey address a crowd midway between Chicago and Milwaukee. *(Library of Congress)*

In commenting on this tour, the *New York Times* editorialized, "Mr. Dewey just about completed the process of running for the Presidency on the domestic platform of the New Deal." Party regulars, according to Arthur Krock, complained that his position "was too close to Roosevelt's." Rather than stick to his original plan of appealing to the independent vote with a sober and careful criticism of the New Deal while accepting many of its positive features, Dewey heeded the warnings of the regulars and soon found himself pushed far to the right, swinging wildly at the Democrats. *Time* magazine, which supported Dewey, observed other shortcomings after the Los Angeles speech. "However well the speech was aimed at the 'Ham 'n Eggers' in Southern California, at the Coliseum, it was a total flop. The newsmen wrote it down as another demerit for Dewey. In more than two weeks of junketing, they had noted other demerits: the Dewey lack of humor, his tinge of Scoutmasterishness (when excited he used phrases like 'Oh, Lord' and 'good gracious'), his lack of warmth (he rarely visited journalists in the lounge car), and his superefficiency (which sometimes led him, in normal conversation, to say 'period' at the end of a sentence, as if he were dictating)."

In September, the president finally turned his attention to the campaign. He had agreed to talk before the International Brotherhood of Teamsters on September 23, 1944, and worked for some weeks on the speech. He was enjoying the preparation. When Robert Sherwood returned from Europe to help on the campaign, Roosevelt invited him to his office and laughingly read a few of the tidbits he had prepared. In Roosevelt's view, it was going to be a major event.

The speech, carried to the nation via radio, probably exceeded even Roosevelt's expectations. Rosenman later called it the greatest campaign speech of Roosevelt's career. Sherwood added, "It can well be studied as a masterpiece of political strategy and tactics." The audience, which had arrived apprehensive and uncertain about Roosevelt's stamina or capacity to lead the country, came away buoyant, excited, and confident about the campaign. More important, they came away laughing.

Roosevelt delivered the speech in a conversational chatty style, as if he were talking to a roomful of friends instead of a nationwide radio audience: "Well, here we are together again—after four years—and what years they have been! I am actually four years older—which seems to annoy some people. In fact millions of us are more than eleven years older than when we started in to clear up the mess that was dumped in our laps in 1933." He accused the Republicans of showing concern for labor and the poor only before an election. Roosevelt said he "got quite a laugh" from one plank in the Republican platform in which the party accepted the aims of the National Labor Relations Act and other New Deal laws. The Republican leaders who approved the plank "would not even recognize these progressive laws if they met them in broad daylight. Indeed they have personally spent years of effort and energy—and much money—in fighting every one of these laws in the Congress, in the press, and in the courts." Roosevelt acknowledged that there were many progressive elements in the Republican Party who had fought to bring it up to date (this was Roosevelt's bid for support from the Willkie branch of the party), but the Old Guard Republicans were still in command.

The same Republican leaders who in 1939 and 1940 had fought against Lend-Lease and insisted there was no chance of war were now asking the American people to entrust to them the conduct of military and foreign affairs. The same Republican leaders who accused the Democrats of having failed to prepare for the war had "tried to thwart and block nearly every attempt that this administration made to warn our people and arm our nation."

The president then acknowledged the great contributions of labor toward supplying weapons and munitions. As for the strikes that made all the headlines, only one-tenth of 1 percent of man-hours had been lost by strikes since Pearl Harbor. All the responsible labor leaders had condemned war industry strikes, save one (John L. Lewis) who was "not conspicuous among my supporters."

Roosevelt hit the Republicans hard for refusing to pass a strong soldiers' vote bill, for trying to keep the vote down in November, for attacking labor's right to contribute to "any wicked political party" while rich businessmen gave thousands to the GOP. He accused the Republicans of deliberate falsification in claiming that there was still a depression in 1940. "Now there is an old and somewhat lugubrious adage which says, 'Never speak of a rope in the house of a man who's been hanged.' In the same way, if I were a Republican leader speaking to a mixed audience, the last word in the whole dictionary that I would think of using is that word 'depression.'"

As for the charge that the administration was planning to keep men in the Army when the war was over because there might not be any jobs for them in civilian life, Roosevelt pointed out that a method of speedy discharge had already been announced by the War Department. "This callous and brazen falsehood about demobilization was . . . an effort to stimulate fear among American mothers and wives and sweethearts. And, incidentally, it was hardly calculated to bolster the morale of our soldiers and sailors and airmen who are fighting our battles all over the world."

Then came what James MacGregor Burns calls the "dagger thrust . . . the blade lovingly fashioned and honed, now delivered with a mock serious face and in a quiet, sad tone of voice, rising briefly to indignation." It was the defense of his dog, Fala:

> These Republican leaders have not been content with attacks on me, or on my wife, or on my sons. No, not content with that, they now include my little dog Fala. Well, of course, I don't resent attacks, and my family doesn't resent attacks, but Fala does resent them. You know, you know, Fala's Scotch, and being a Scottie, as soon as he learned that the Republican fiction writers in Congress and out had concocted a story that I had left him behind on an Aleutian island and had sent a destroyer back to find him—at a cost to the taxpayers of two or three or eight or twenty million dollars—his Scotch soul was furious. He has not been the same dog since. I am accustomed to hearing malicious falsehoods about myself—such as that old, worm-eaten chestnut that I have represented myself to be indispensable. But I think I have a right to resent, to object to libelous statements about my dog.

The reaction of the audience to these remarks was uproarious laughter. All the doubts that Roosevelt had lost his touch, that he did not have the stomach for another campaign fight, were instantly dissipated. Rosenman described the scene at the end of the speech:

> The applause and cheers when he finished were startling even to those of us who had seen him out campaigning in 1932, 1936, and 1940. Never

had there been a demonstration equal to this in sincerity, admiration and affection. In the mind of every friend and supporter who stood and cheered and applauded in that large dining room was the same thought: "The old maestro is back again—the champ is now out on the road. The old boy has the same old fighting stuff and he just can't be licked."

The Fala speech accomplished three objectives for the Democrats: it gave the campaign much needed excitement; it stimulated Roosevelt supporters to register and vote; and it angered Dewey and the Republicans to such an extent that they began a series of wild accusations, which in turn stimulated voter interest even further. The excitement of the last six weeks of the campaign initiated by the Fala speech, coupled with the registration drive of the CIO-PAC, brought the total vote to over 47 million—7 million more than had been predicted. And Roosevelt was unquestionably the beneficiary of the larger turnout.

Dewey heard the speech on his campaign train in California and immediately prepared an angry response, which he gave in Oklahoma City on September 25. "Last Saturday night," Dewey charged, "the man who wants to be President for sixteen years made his first speech of this campaign. Gone was the high-sounding pledge [not to campaign in the usual sense]. Forgotten were these days of tragic sorrow. It was a speech of mud-slinging, ridicule, and wise-cracks." Dewey claimed he would never divide America by inciting one group of people to hatred and distrust of another group. He repeated his charge that the government had no plans for swift demobilization and that the New Deal had kept the depression going for 11 years "by waging relentless warfare against our job-making machinery." He stated that Roosevelt was indispensable to many individuals: "He is indispensable to Harry Hopkins, Madame Perkins, Harold Ickes . . . to America's leading enemy of civil liberties—the Mayor of New Jersey [Frank Hague]. He's indispensable to those infamous machines in Chicago and the Bronx. He is indispensable to Sidney Hillman and the Political Action Committee, he's indispensable to Earl Browder, the ex-convict and pardoned Communist leader."

On October 5, Roosevelt repudiated all Communist support and at the same time launched an attack on those "labor baiters, bigots, and . . . politicians who use the term 'communism' loosely and apply it to every progressive social measure and to the views of every foreign born citizen with whom they disagree." Dewey responded by again lumping Browder and Roosevelt together and insisting that the president's repudiation was a "soft disclaimer" of Communism. In Charleston, West Virginia, on October 7 Dewey claimed that Browder had urged the victory of Roosevelt since it was "essential to his aims.

This is the same Earl Browder, now such a patriot, who was convicted as a draft dodger in the last war, convicted again as a perjurer and pardoned by Franklin Roosevelt in time to organize the campaign for a fourth term." Dewey also quoted a 1939 statement by A. A. Berle, then assistant secretary of state, to the effect that "over a period of years the Government will gradually come to own most of the productive plants in the United States." The quote was completely wrenched from context. In an angry response, Berle pointed out that in the statement from which the quote was excerpted he had maintained that if capital did not flow into necessary enterprise, the government would have to invest itself and become the owner of certain industries, which, said Berle, was "just what we wanted to avoid." (This type of distortion became more frequent as the campaign continued.) The GOP candidate further charged that the New Deal was leading to a corporate state where government "would tell each of us where we could work, at what, and for how much." He further insisted that the "great Democratic Party was taken over by Earl Browder and Sidney Hillman."

Throughout the campaign, the Republicans linked Hillman's PAC with the Communists and tried to taint Roosevelt with both. The PAC had been formed in July 1943 as labor's political action arm to support its candidates in politics and punish its enemies. When the Smith–Connally Act forbade labor unions to contribute to federal elections, the PAC raised money by having individual union members contribute one dollar to a special fund that it could use as it wished. A National Citizens Political Action Committee (NC-PAC) was also formed, composed of individuals outside the labor movement who wished to work for PAC candidates.

Hillman had been the head of the Amalgamated Clothing Workers for 30 years and was an astute labor leader and a careful student of politics. He knew that the PAC could not take on all its enemies in Congress, and he carefully chose those who were vulnerable on other grounds and worked for their defeat. The PAC was successful in five primary elections in 1944, and their large campaign fund and eager workers alarmed conservatives throughout the country. The House Un-American Activities Committee and the Justice Department peered over the PAC's shoulder throughout the year, looking for some legal violation. In fact, Hillman seemed to spend more time in Washington defending his group before Congress than he did in running its affairs. The Republicans became concerned—quite rightly, as it turned out—that the PAC would bring out the labor vote for Roosevelt and contribute heavily to his campaign. The PAC organized right down to the precinct level and promoted a mammoth get-out-the-vote drive that proved extremely successful in industrial states such as Michigan—one of the few states that had more voters in 1944 than in 1940. It brought union members out for Democratic rallies, distributed campaign literature in the millions of copies, and gave far more money to the Democrats than any other organization or individual. The PAC collected $1,024,814 and the NC-PAC $380,306. The next largest contributor, the One Thousand Club (consisting of businessmen who gave at least a thousand dollars to the Democratic Party) collected $252,055. (All in all, the Democrats raised $7.4 million and the Republicans $13.5 million.)

Convincing themselves that there was a strong anti-Hillman sentiment in the country, the GOP adopted and widely used the slogan "Clear it with Sidney" to attack Roosevelt, although as noted, it is doubtful that Roosevelt ever made any such statement. Hannegan purportedly quoted the president in the context of the Byrnes candidacy for vice president. If Hannegan did say it (he later denied making the remark himself), he probably was trying to avoid responsibility for denying Byrnes the nomination. But it was passed on to Byrnes, who told Arthur Krock of the *New York Times,* who published the account. The Republicans seized on the statement, changed the phrase to "Clear everything with Sidney," and used it

WHAT IS THAT, HENRY?

LOOKS LIKE A BOOMERANG. WE BETTER DUCK.

This Clifford Kennedy Berryman cartoon shows President Roosevelt staring in the distance at Sidney Hillman, shaped like a boomerang, and asking Vice President Henry Wallace what it is. Wallace answers, "Looks like a boomerang. We better duck." Hillman was head of the CIO Political Action Committee, the most powerful political group supporting Roosevelt in his campaign for a fourth term as president. It was rumored that Roosevelt had consulted with Hillman before picking Senator Harry Truman as his new running mate. The Republicans seized on this story and gleefully used "Clear it with Sidney" as one of their campaign slogans. *(Library of Congress)*

as their chief campaign slogan to charge Roosevelt with selling out to radical labor and the Communists. There were variations of the theme in other slogans: "Destroy the Browder–Hillman Axis," and "Sidney Hillman and Earl Browder's Communists have registered. Have you?" Bricker claimed that the name of the PAC should be the Political Auction Committee since it was "trying to put labor up for sale and put a great political party up for sale." In a speech in Boston, Bricker lamented the "insidious and ominous forces of Communism linked with irreligion that are working their way into our national life. These forces are attempting to take a stranglehold upon our nation through the control of the New Deal party. These subversive forces are class hatred and pressure politics under the leadership of Sidney Hillman and Earl Browder and must be driven from high places in our American political life."

The accusations about Communist influence and the violently anti–New Deal remarks that Dewey and Bricker threw around in October drew hoots and loud applause from partisan audiences, but made many responsible Republicans and independents more sympathetic to Roosevelt. (Four years later, Dewey maintained a highly nonpartisan pitch to the very end in his losing battle against Truman.)

As the campaign drew to a close, world affairs played into Roosevelt's hands. American troops drove into Germany, and on October 20 MacArthur made his famous return to the Philippines, landing at Leyte. The Philippine invasion undercut the Republican charge that MacArthur was not being given sufficient manpower and supplies. Despite these advances, however, it was clear that the war was far from over, and victory in the Pacific seemed years away. If the polls, which indicated that most people wanted Roosevelt to continue as commander in chief and end the war, were right, then a Democratic victory seemed certain. Although 60 percent of newspapers and magazines, including the powerful Luce publications, supported Dewey, many papers in the nation switched their 1940 editorial position and backed Roosevelt. The *New York Times* editorialized, "Mr. Roosevelt has a large first hand knowledge of the problems that will arise in the making of the peace. Moreover, the great prestige and personal following among the plain peoples of the world which he has won with his war leadership might easily prove in itself to be one of the most important cohesive forces binding together a new world organization."

Roosevelt launched his final drive in late October. He had scheduled a foreign policy address in New York for October 21 and used the occasion to present himself to the city's voters. After speaking briefly in Brooklyn at Ebbetts Field for Senator Robert Wagner, the president, in a driving, cold rain, rode in a long cavalcade through Queens to the Bronx and then down through Harlem to mid-Manhattan, waving, laughing, responding to the cheers of the people. More than 2 million people turned out despite the wretched weather to see the president on his four-borough tour. His stamina gave the lie to Republican rumors that he was close to death, and the many pictures of the tour convinced many voters that the president could still take it. At the Waldorf Astoria, Roosevelt strongly supported the United Nations and insisted that it have authority to act by force in any international emergency. "A policeman would not be a very effective policeman if, when he saw a felon break into a house, he had to go to the Town Hall and call a town meeting to issue a warrant before the felon could be arrested. . . . [I]f the world organization is to have any reality at all, our representative must be endowed in advance, by the people themselves . . . with authority to act." (Dewey had not squarely faced this issue, although he supported the general idea of the United Nations, and as a result of the speech, Senator Joseph Ball of Minnesota, a leading Republican internationalist, came out for Roosevelt.)

On a highly successful visit to Philadelphia on October 27 (it was Navy Day), Roosevelt gloated over the great naval victory in Leyte Gulf, where the Third and Seventh Fleets under Admirals Thomas C. Kincaid and William F. Halsey had sunk virtually half the remaining Japanese capital ships. Roosevelt, hoping to show the farsightedness of his administration's defense planning, pointed out that the battleships, cruisers, and aircraft carriers in the victorious fleets had all been authorized by the Democratic administration before Pearl Harbor.

The next night, Roosevelt spoke to a hundred thousand wildly cheering voters in Soldier Field in Chicago. He asked them how a government of "quarrelsome, tired old men" (a Dewey phrase) could have built the greatest military machine in the history of the world, which was winning victory after victory in Europe and Asia. He promised further to implement the Economic Bill of Rights that he had enumerated in his annual message in January and to build a postwar economy of "close to" 60 million jobs. (That figure was actually reached in 1947.)

By the last week of the campaign, Roosevelt had grown visibly angry over the bitter and irresponsible charges made by the Republicans. Merriman Smith of the United Press reported that Roosevelt felt nothing but "unvarnished contempt" toward Dewey. Not only did the public charges and distortions disturb Roosevelt, but he thought that an organized rumor campaign about himself, his children, and his aides had been initiated by the opposition. Hopkins wrote in a later memo, "The President told me he meant it when he said that this was the meanest campaign of his life. He said he thought they hit him below the belt several times and that it was done quite deliberately and very viciously." In his last speech in Boston, Roosevelt answered the charges linking him with Communism and attacked the Republicans' whispering campaign:

> Just the other day, you people here in Boston witnessed an amazing demonstration of talking out of both sides of the mouth. . . . A Republican candidate said . . . "the Communists are seizing control of the New Deal, through which they aim to control the government of the United States." However, on that very same day that very same candidate had spoken in Worcester and he said that with Republican victory in November, "we can end one man government and we can forever remove the threat of monarchy in the United States." Now, really—which is it—communism or monarchy?

He then described his own feelings about the campaign:

> I must confess that often in this campaign I have been tempted to speak my mind with sharper vigor and greater indignation. Everybody knows that I was reluctant to run for the Presidency again this year. But since this campaign developed, I tell you frankly that I have become most anxious to win—and I say that for the reason that never before in my lifetime has a campaign been filled with such misrepresentation, distortion and falsehood. Never since 1928 have there been so many attempts to stimulate in America racial or religious intolerance.

Most observers predicted a close race. *Newsweek* reported in its last pre-election issue: "President Roosevelt and Gov. Thomas E. Dewey are so closely matched on election eve that the outcome in the composite opinion of *Newsweek*'s Election Trends panel hinges on which candidate captures Pennsylvania's all important 35 electoral votes." The *New York Times* predicted that Dewey would win at least 150 electoral votes, with several states too close to call. The president himself in an election pool with his aides gave Dewey close to 200 electoral votes.

But the 1944 results were almost exactly the same as in 1940, primarily because the political structure of the country remained fixed during the war. Roosevelt carried the industrial areas of the Northeast, the South remained solid, and the West, which gained in population because of new war industries, also supported him. The war had not undermined the basic Democratic alliance of labor, big-city machines, intellectuals, and the Southern states.

Dewey won 10 of the same states that Willkie had won four years previously—Maine and Vermont in New England, the midwestern tier of North and South Dakota,

This cartoon shows Republican candidates Thomas E. Dewey and John W. Bricker and Democratic candidates Franklin D. Roosevelt and Harry S. Truman sitting on the floor trying to put together a jigsaw puzzle of the states. Uncle Sam admonishes them that they must complete the puzzle before Wednesday morning. A portrait of J.Q. Public, looking distressed, hangs on the wall. The cartoon was drawn shortly before Election Day, November 7, 1944. The Democrats won by a large majority. *(Library of Congress)*

and Nebraska, Kansas, Indiana, Iowa, and Wyoming. The only Dewey gains were Ohio and Wisconsin, but he lost Michigan, a state Willkie had carried. The final electoral count was 432 to 99.

The popular vote was closer, Roosevelt's margin being 3.6 million, the closest of all his elections. But the main reason for this was the predicted drop in the total number of voters. Whereas 49,891,051 people had voted in 1940, the total was 47,977,090 in 1944. A significant drop had again taken place in the industrial states. Pennsylvania, Ohio, and Illinois each had 200,000 fewer voters. The Republican vote in Ohio had been the same in the two elections, but because the Democratic vote dropped from 1,733,000 to 1,570,000, Roosevelt lost the state. On the other hand, he won Michigan because the vote had increased by 170,000—largely due to the efforts of the PAC. The total vote in New York had also increased, although Roosevelt needed the votes on the American Labor Party and Liberal Party lines to carry the state.

Dewey did better than any of his predecessors in the county vote. The Republicans won 1,344 counties to 1,750 for the Democrats. (In 1940, the totals had been Democrats 1,947, and Republicans 1,147.) Roosevelt did poorly in the rural areas of the Midwest and some Western states—Idaho, Oregon, Washington, and California.

Nevertheless, the Roosevelt victory was significant enough to increase his strength in Congress. The Senate stayed Democratic by almost 20 seats (56 to 38), and in the House the number of Democratic congressmen increased from 222 to 242 (the margin over the Republicans from 16 to 52). Some of the new faces coming to Congress were to play crucial roles in the years to come—Wayne Morse, Helen Gahagan Douglas, and Adam Clayton Powell. Gone were some of the most reactionary names, including Gerald Nye of North Dakota and Roosevelt's own congressman from Dutchess County, Hamilton Fish.

For the second time in the nation's history, the electorate had chosen a president in the midst of a major war. In both cases, they decided to let the incumbent bring hostilities to a successful conclusion and to lead the nation in the peace that followed. In both cases, no one could foresee how short a time both President Lincoln and President Roosevelt would have at that task.

—*Leon Friedman*

Selected Bibliography

The personal reminiscences of members of the Roosevelt administration are still the best source of information on the 1944 election. These include Samuel Rosenman, *Working with Roosevelt* (1952); Robert E. Sherwood, *Roosevelt and Hopkins* (1948); James F. Byrnes, *All in One Lifetime* (1958); Grace Tully, *F.D.R., My Boss* (1949); and William D. Hassett, *Off the Record with F.D.R.* (1958). See also George E. Allen, *Presidents Who Have Known Me* (1950). On Roosevelt's relations with Cordell Hull and the State Department, the best books are Fred L. Israel, ed., *The War Diary of Breckinridge Long* (1966), and Dean Acheson, *Present at the Creation* (1969). On the CIO Political Action Committee, see Joseph Gaer, *The First Round* (1945). On voting patterns and campaign contributions, see Louise Overacker, "Presidential Campaign Funds, 1944," *American Political Science Review* 39 (1945). James MacGregor Burns, *Roosevelt, The Soldier of Freedom, 1940–1945* (1970), also has a short account of the election campaign. See also Herman Bateman, "Foreign Policy in the Election of 1944" (unpublished PhD dissertation, Stanford University, 1953); John Morton Blum, *V Was for Victory: Politics and American Culture During World War II* (1976); Hugh E. Evans. *The Hidden Campaign: FDR's Health and the 1944 Election* (2002); Steven Fraser, *Labor Will Rule: Sidney Hillman and the Rise of American Labor* (1990); Frank Freidel, *Franklin D. Roosevelt: A Rendezvous with Destiny* (1990); Robert R. Garson, *The Democratic Party and the Politics of Sectionalism, 1941–1948* (1974); Doris Kearns Goodwin, *No Ordinary Time: Franklin and Eleanor Roosevelt: The Home Front in World War II* (1994); Norman D. Markowitz, *The Rise and Fall of the People's Century: Henry A. Wallace and American Liberalism, 1941–1948* (1973); Richard Polenberg, *War and Society: The United States, 1941–1945* (1972); and Richard Norton Smith, *Thomas E. Dewey and His Times* (1982).

1944 ELECTION STATISTICS

State	Number of Electors	Total Popular Vote	Elec Vote D	Elec Vote R	Pop Vote D	Pop Vote R	Margin of Victory Votes	Margin of Victory % Total Vote
Alabama	11	244,743	11		1	2	154,378	63.08%
Arizona	4	137,634	4		1	2	24,639	17.90%
Arkansas	9	212,954	9		1	2	85,414	40.11%
California	25	3,520,875	25		1	2	475,599	13.51%
Colorado	6	505,039		6	2	1	34,400	6.81%
Connecticut	8	831,990	8		1	2	44,619	5.36%
Delaware	3	125,361	3		1	2	11,419	9.11%
Florida	8	482,592	8		1	2	196,162	40.65%
Georgia	12	328,109	12		1	2	208,307	63.49%
Idaho	4	208,321	4		1	2	7,262	3.49%
Illinois	28	4,036,061	28		1	2	140,165	3.47%
Indiana	13	1,672,091		13	2	1	94,488	5.65%
Iowa	10	1,052,599		10	2	1	47,391	4.50%
Kansas	8	733,776		8	2	1	154,638	21.07%
Kentucky	11	867,921	11		1	2	80,141	9.23%
Louisiana	10	349,383	10		1	2	213,814	61.20%
Maine	5	296,400		5	2	1	14,803	4.99%
Maryland	8	608,439	8		1	2	22,541	3.70%
Massachusetts	16	1,960,665	16		1	2	113,946	5.81%
Michigan	19	2,205,223	19		1	2	22,476	1.02%
Minnesota	11	1,125,529	11		1	2	62,448	5.55%
Mississippi	9	180,080	9		1	2	156,878	87.12%
Missouri	15	1,572,474	15		1	2	46,280	2.94%
Montana	4	207,355	4		1	2	19,393	9.35%
Nebraska	6	563,126		6	2	1	96,634	17.16%
Nevada	3	54,234	3		1	2	5,012	9.24%
New Hampshire	4	229,625	4		1	2	9,747	4.24%
New Jersey	16	1,963,761	16		1	2	26,539	1.35%
New Mexico	4	152,225	4		1	2	10,701	7.03%
New York	47	6,316,817	47		1	2	316,591	5.01%
North Carolina	14	790,554	14		1	2	264,244	33.43%
North Dakota	4	220,171		4	2	1	18,391	8.35%
Ohio	25	3,153,056		25	2	1	11,530	0.37%
Oklahoma	10	722,636	10		1	2	82,125	11.36%
Oregon	6	480,147	6		1	2	23,270	4.85%
Pennsylvania	35	3,794,793	35		1	2	105,425	2.78%
Rhode Island	4	299,276	4		1	2	51,869	17.33%
South Carolina	8	103,375	8		1	3	85,991	83.18%
South Dakota	4	232,076		4	2	1	38,654	16.66%
Tennessee	12	510,692	12		1	2	108,396	21.23%
Texas	23	1,150,331	23		1	2	630,180	54.78%
Utah	4	248,319	4		1	2	52,197	21.02%
Vermont	3	125,361		3	2	1	17,707	14.12%
Virginia	11	388,485	11		1	2	97,033	24.98%
Washington	8	856,328	8		1	2	125,085	14.61%
West Virginia	8	715,596	8		1	2	69,958	9.78%
Wisconsin	12	1,339,152		12	2	1	24,119	1.80%
Wyoming	3	101,340		3	2	1	2,502	2.47%
Total	531	47,977,090	432	99	1	2	3,594,987	7.49%

Roosevelt Democratic		Dewey Republican		Others	
198,918	81.28%	44,540	18.20%	1,285	0.53%
80,926	58.80%	56,287	40.90%	421	0.31%
148,965	69.95%	63,551	29.84%	438	0.21%
1,988,564	56.48%	1,512,965	42.97%	19,346	0.55%
234,331	46.40%	268,731	53.21%	1,977	0.39%
435,146	52.30%	390,527	46.94%	6,317	0.76%
68,166	54.38%	56,747	45.27%	448	0.36%
339,377	70.32%	143,215	29.68%	0	0.00%
268,187	81.74%	59,880	18.25%	42	0.01%
107,399	51.55%	100,137	48.07%	785	0.38%
2,079,479	51.52%	1,939,314	48.05%	17,268	0.43%
781,403	46.73%	875,891	52.38%	14,797	0.88%
499,876	47.49%	547,267	51.99%	5,456	0.52%
287,458	39.18%	442,096	60.25%	4,222	0.58%
472,589	54.45%	392,448	45.22%	2,884	0.33%
281,564	80.59%	67,750	19.39%	69	0.02%
140,631	47.45%	155,434	52.44%	335	0.11%
315,490	51.85%	292,949	48.15%	0	0.00%
1,035,296	52.80%	921,350	46.99%	4,019	0.20%
1,106,899	50.19%	1,084,423	49.18%	13,901	0.63%
589,864	52.41%	527,416	46.86%	8,249	0.73%
168,479	93.56%	11,601	6.44%	0	0.00%
807,804	51.37%	761,524	48.43%	3,146	0.20%
112,556	54.28%	93,163	44.93%	1,636	0.79%
233,246	41.42%	329,880	58.58%	0	0.00%
29,623	54.62%	24,611	45.38%	0	0.00%
119,663	52.11%	109,916	47.87%	46	0.02%
987,874	50.31%	961,335	48.95%	14,552	0.74%
81,389	53.47%	70,688	46.44%	148	0.10%
3,304,238	52.31%	2,987,647	47.30%	24,932	0.39%
527,399	66.71%	263,155	33.29%	0	0.00%
100,144	45.48%	118,535	53.84%	1,492	0.68%
1,570,763	49.82%	1,582,293	50.18%	0	0.00%
401,549	55.57%	319,424	44.20%	1,663	0.23%
248,635	51.78%	225,365	46.94%	6,147	1.28%
1,940,479	51.14%	1,835,054	48.36%	19,260	0.51%
175,356	58.59%	123,487	41.26%	433	0.14%
90,601	87.64%	4,610	4.46%	8,164	7.90%
96,711	41.67%	135,365	58.33%	0	0.00%
308,707	60.45%	200,311	39.22%	1,674	0.33%
821,605	71.42%	191,425	16.64%	137,301	11.94%
150,088	60.44%	97,891	39.42%	340	0.14%
53,820	42.93%	71,527	57.06%	14	0.01%
242,276	62.36%	145,243	37.39%	966	0.25%
486,774	56.84%	361,689	42.24%	7,865	0.92%
392,777	54.89%	322,819	45.11%	0	0.00%
650,413	48.57%	674,532	50.37%	14,207	1.06%
49,419	48.77%	51,921	51.23%	0	0.00%
25,612,916	53.39%	22,017,929	45.89%	346,245	0.72%

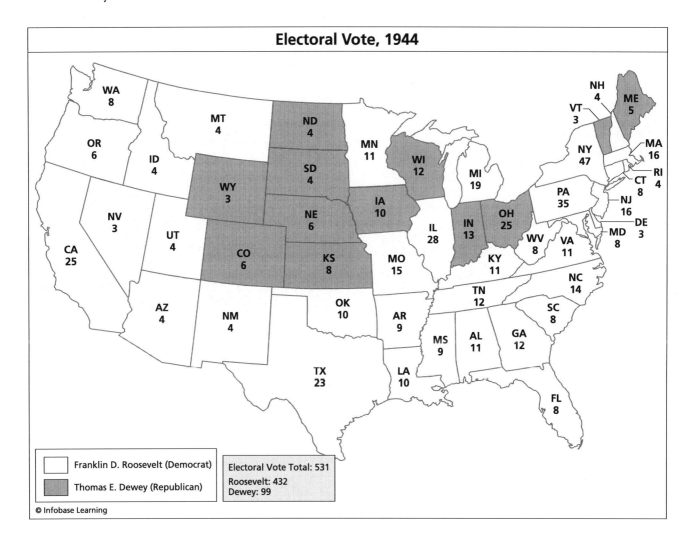

Electoral Vote, 1944

WA 8
OR 6
ID 4
MT 4
ND 4
MN 11
WI 12
MI 19
NH 4
VT 3
ME 5
NY 47
MA 16
RI 4
CT 8
NJ 16
DE 3
MD 8
PA 35
SD 4
WY 3
IA 10
NV 3
UT 4
NE 6
IL 28
IN 13
OH 25
WV 8
VA 11
CA 25
CO 6
KS 8
MO 15
KY 11
NC 14
AZ 4
NM 4
OK 10
AR 9
TN 12
SC 8
GA 12
MS 9
AL 11
TX 23
LA 10
FL 8

Franklin D. Roosevelt (Democrat)
Thomas E. Dewey (Republican)

Electoral Vote Total: 531
Roosevelt: 432
Dewey: 99

© Infobase Learning

Election of 1948

Election Overview

Election Year 1948

Election Day November 2, 1948

Winning Candidates

* **President:** Harry S. Truman
* **Vice President:** Alben W. Barkley

Election Results [ticket, party: popular votes (percentage of popular vote); electoral votes (percentage of electoral vote)]

* Harry S. Truman and Alben W. Barkley, Democratic: 24,179,347 (49.55%); 303 (57.1%)
* Thomas E. Dewey and Earl Warren, Republican: 21,991,292 (45.07%); 189 (35.6%)
* J. Strom Thurmond and Fielding Wright, States' Rights: 1,175,946 (2.41%); 39 (7.3%)
* Henry A. Wallace and Glen Taylor, Progressive: 1,157,328 (2.37%); 0 (0.0%)
* Norman Thomas and Tucker Smith, Socialist: 139,569 (0.29%); 0 (0.0%)
* Other: 150,069 (0.31%); 0 (0.0%)

Voter Turnout 53.0%

Central Forums/Campaign Methods for Addressing Voters

* Stumping
* Whistle-stop tours
* Speeches
* Radio, television
* Ads, newspapers, editorials

Incumbent President on Election Day Harry S. Truman

Population (1948) 146,631,000

Gross Domestic Product

* $269.1 billion (in current dollars: $1,854.2 billion)
* Per capita: $1,835 (in current dollars: $12,645)

Number of Daily Newspapers (1950) 1,426

Average Daily Circulation (1950) 53,829,000

Households with

* Radio (1950): 40,700,000
* Television (1948): 975,000

Method of Choosing Electors Popular vote

Method of Choosing Nominees

* National party convention
* Presidential preference primaries

Key Issues and Events

* After President Franklin D. Roosevelt's death on April 12, 1945, as World War II is ending, Vice President Harry S. Truman becomes president.
* In the 1946 midterm elections, the Republican Party wins control of both houses of Congress and a majority of state governorships (Senate 51–45; House 246–188).
* The Republicans campaign with the slogan "Had Enough?" promising to remove the four Cs: controls, confusion, corruption, and Communism.
* Domestic challenges include high taxes, rising cost of living, labor strife, corruption in Washington.
* The Truman Doctrine seeks to contain Communism, especially Joseph Stalin's Soviet Union and Mao Zedong's China.
* In May 1948 Truman, accused of being soft on Communism, has a 36 percent approval rating, according to Gallup. Republicans seem primed to recapture the White House.

Leading Candidates

DEMOCRATS

- Harry S. Truman, president (Missouri)
- Richard Russell, Jr., senator (Georgia)
- Harley M. Kilgore, senator (West Virginia)
- Alben W. Barkley, senator (Kentucky)

REPUBLICANS

- Thomas E. Dewey, governor (New York)
- Robert A. Taft, senator (Ohio)
- Harold E. Stassen, former governor (Minnesota)
- Arthur H. Vandenberg, president pro tempore of the Senate (Michigan)
- Earl Warren, governor (California)
- Douglas MacArthur, general of the Army (Arkansas)

Trajectory

- "Dump" Truman movement builds momentum along with moves in both parties to draft General Dwight D. Eisenhower, who declines.
- In his "nonpolitical" stumping tour out west, June 3–18, 1948, Truman starts speaking off the cuff. His informal, peppery approach generates enthusiasm, as does his campaign theme attacking the Republican Congress as "the worst in my memory" committed to "the welfare of the better classes."
- Republicans are confident of victory at their national convention June 21–25 and nominate Thomas E. Dewey for president and California governor Earl Warren for vice president.
- Truman starts a dramatic airlift to Berlin on June 26 to break the Soviet blockade and feed 2,400,000 West Berliners. Americans cheer Truman's decisiveness.
- At the Democratic convention in Philadelphia, July 12–15, fights over civil rights splinter the party, as the young mayor of Minneapolis, Hubert Humphrey, pushes through a strong civil rights plank.
- Truman's rousing acceptance speech on July 15 accuses the Republican-dominated Congress of doing "nothing." He calls a special session on July 26, "Turnip Day" in Missouri, asking Congress "to pass laws to halt rising prices, to meet the housing crisis," and to act on "aid to education," "a national health program," "civil rights legislation," and "an increase in the minimum wage." Congress will debate for two weeks, then adjourn with nothing, proving Truman's point.
- The Democratic Party splinters. Southern delegates who walked out to protest the civil rights plank form the States' Rights or Dixiecrat Party, nominating Strom Thurmond of South Carolina for president on July 17. More radical Democrats and New Deal ideologues form a "Progressive Party" and nominate former vice president Henry A. Wallace.
- On September 9, the pollster Elmo Roper says that with Dewey leading Truman 41 to 31 percent, "no amount of electioneering" would change the result by the election. Pollsters George Gallup and Archibald Crossley along with 50 political writers predict a substantial Dewey victory.
- "Give 'em Hell, Harry" Truman spends much of the two months between Labor Day and Election Day speaking from a train, delivering 26 addresses and 244 "whistle stop" talks.
- Dewey plays it safe—and loses the election by about 3 million popular votes.

Conventions

- Republican National Convention: June 21–25, 1948, Convention Hall, Philadelphia
- Democratic National Convention: July 12–15, 1948, Convention Hall, Philadelphia

Ballots/Nominees

DEMOCRATS

Presidential first ballot

- Harry S. Truman 947.5
- Richard B. Russell 266
- James A. Roe 15
- Paul V. McNutt 2
- Alben W. Barkley 1

Vice-presidential first ballot

- Alben W. Barkley 1,234

REPUBLICANS

Third ballot

- Thomas E. Dewey 434; 515; 1,094
- Robert A. Taft 224; 274; 0
- Harold E. Stassen 157; 149; 0
- Arthur H. Vandenberg 62; 62; 0
- Earl Warren 59; 57; 0
- Dwight Green 56; 0; 0
- Alfred Driscoll 35; 0; 0
- Raymond Baldwin 19; 19; 0
- Joseph W. Martin 18; 10; 0
- Carroll Reece 15; 0; 0
- Douglas MacArthur 11; 8; 0
- Everett Dirksen 1; 0; 0
- Abstaining 1; 0; 0

STATES' RIGHTS DEMOCRATS (DIXIECRATS)

- Convenes three days after walking out of the Democratic convention in Montgomery, Alabama, with delegates from 13 states
- Nominates Governor J. Strom Thurmond of South Carolina for president and Governor Fielding Wright of Mississippi for vice president
- Hopes to be a spoiler and throw the election into the House of Representatives, where the Southern states could impose an opponent of civil-rights legislation

PROGRESSIVES

- Henry A. Wallace forms the Progressive Citizens of America in 1947 and the Progressive Party in 1948 to promote world peace.
- Blames the Truman administration for the cold war
- Party convention, July 22, 1948, in Philadelphia
- Nominates Henry A. Wallace for president, Democratic Senator Glen Taylor (Idaho) for vice president
- Delegates include pacifists, reformers, disaffected New Dealers, some American Stalinists and Communists.

Primaries

- Democrats: 14; 36.3% delegates
- Republicans: 12; 36.0% delegates

Primaries Results

DEMOCRATS

- Harry S. Truman 1,419,875; 64.65%
- William Alexander "W. A." Julian 271,146; 12.35%
- Unpledged 161,629; 7.36%
- Harley M. Kilgore 157,102; 7.15%
- W. B. Bixler 136,401; 6.21%
- Others 17,160; 0.78%
- Lynn Fellows 11,193; 0.51%

REPUBLICANS

- Earl Warren 771,295; 26.99%
- Harold E. Stassen 627,321; 21.96%
- Robert A. Taft 464,741; 16.27%
- Thomas E. Dewey 330,799; 11.58%
- Riley A. Bender 324,029; 11.34%
- Douglas MacArthur 87,839; 3.07%
- Leverett Saltonstall 72,191; 2.53%
- Herbert E. Hitchcock 45,463; 1.59%
- Edward Martin 45,072; 1.58%
- Unpledged 28,854; 1.01%
- Arthur H. Vandenberg 18,924; 0.66%
- Others 5,939; 0.21%
- Dwight D. Eisenhower 5,014; 0.18%

Party Platform

DEMOCRATS

- Mild civil rights platform
- Attacks "do-nothing" Republican Congress
- Equal rights for women
- Maintain a strong military force to protect national security
- Expand social welfare legislation of the New Deal.

REPUBLICANS

- Maintain military strong enough to ensure national security
- Encourage small business
- Anti-Communist
- Equal rights for women
- Endorse United Nations, containment strategy

PROGRESSIVES

- Reject the Marshall Plan and the Truman Doctrine
- End the cold war
- Negotiate with Russia

Campaign Innovations

- Twenty-second Amendment of the United States Constitution (1947) limits the number of terms a president can run to two four-year terms
- Republican and Democratic national conventions are the first party conventions ever televised.

Campaign Tactics

DEMOCRATS

- Active campaign, mudslinging; extensive nationwide whistle-stop tour 21,928 miles by rail; and more than 270 speeches beginning on Labor Day and ending Election Day. Speeches to large crowds at "whistle-stops" and big cities.
- Rear platform campaign: appearances on train platforms. Truman introduces his family after short speeches: "Howja like to meet my family?" His wife Bess as "the boss" and daughter Margaret as "the boss's boss."
- Truman runs against the "Do-Nothing Republican Congress," the 80th Congress, rather than his opponent Dewey.
- Carefully mobilize the constituent groups that benefited from the New Deal, including labor unions, blacks, Jews, women.

REPUBLICANS

- Dewey promises a safe, dignified campaign for a president to-be, ignores Truman and avoids specifics in his speeches. Dewey seeks "a unity which is above recrimination, above partisanship, above self-interest," pitching himself as an effective administrator who could unify the country and create an effective foreign policy. Strategy backfires—the public and press find him stuffy.

- By October, Dewey, upset by the mudslinging, wants to engage in a more active campaign. Advisers urge him not to, and Dewey mostly complies, especially regarding foreign policy issues, with American politicians trying to approach such matters with "bipartisanship."

Popular Campaign Slogans

DEMOCRATS
- "With Truman for Civil Rights"
- "Beat High Prices"
- "Phooey on Dewey"

REPUBLICANS
- "All 48 in '48 Dewey-Warren"
- "Dewey Gets Things Done"
- "Truman for Ex-President"

Campaign Songs

- Democrats: "I'm Just Wild About Harry"; "Give 'em Hell, Harry!"
- Republicans: "(What Do We Do on a) Dew-Dew-Dewey Day"
- Progressives: "We Can Win with Wallace"

Influential Campaign Appeals or Ads

DEMOCRATS
- The 80th Congress "the worst in history"
- "Gluttons of privilege"
- "A bunch of old mossbacks"
- "Bloodsuckers with offices in Wall Street"
- "The party of . . . Hoover boom and Hoover depression"
- "The notorious 'do-nothing' Republican Eightieth Congress . . . stuck a pitchfork in the farmer's back."

REPUBLICANS
- "Dew-IT with Dewey" (on oldest printed tee-shirt on record)
- Vow to start "unraveling and unsnarling" the mess the Democrats made
- Letter praising "Dewey the Pawling Farmer"
- Newsreels celebrate Dewey's character
- Dewey-Warren Clubs
- "I have no trick answers and no easy solutions. I will not offer one solution to one group and another solution to another group."

Campaign Finance

- Truman: $2,736,334 (in current dollars: $23,105,400)
- Dewey: $2,127,296 (in current dollars: $17,962,800)

Defining Quotations

- "To err is Truman"
- "I wonder what Truman would do if he were alive."
- "[O]ur people will have greater confidence . . . when life-long professional soldiers, in the absence of some obvious and over-riding reasons, abstain from seeking high political office." *Dwight D. Eisenhower to Leonard Finder, publisher of the* Manchester *(New Hampshire)* Evening Leader, *January 22, 1948*
- "If the Democratic Party departs from the ideals of Franklin Roosevelt, I shall desert altogether from that party." *Former vice president Henry A. Wallace, May 19, 1948*
- "The issue now is squarely drawn. I drew that issue at Chicago, and Omaha, and Butte, and Spokane, and Seattle, and Tacoma, and Portland, and San Francisco, and Los Angeles, and here. They know now what I stand for, and what I have been trying to do. I have been pouring it on them, and they have got the jitters back there. . . . But I haven't been pouring anything on, only what ought to be poured on. The issue in this country is between special privilege and the people. I'm going to, I'm going to, I'm pouring it on and I'm gonna keep pouring it on." *Truman attacking the Republican Congress, during his "nonpolitical" whistle-stop tour, Albuquerque, New Mexico, June 15, 1948*
- "The time has arrived for the Democratic party to get out of the shadow of states' rights and walk forthrightly into the bright sunshine of human rights." *Minneapolis mayor Hubert Humphrey, Democratic Convention Address, Philadelphia, July 14, 1948*
- "Senator Barkley and I will win this election, and make these Republicans like it, don't you forget that. We'll do that because they're wrong and we're right. The reason is that the people know the Democratic party is the people's party, and the Republican party is the party of special interests and it always has been and always will be." *Harry S. Truman, address accepting the nomination at the Democratic National Convention in Philadelphia, July 15, 1948*
- "On the twenty-sixth day of July, which out in Missouri they call Turnip Day, I'm going to call that Congress back and I'm going to ask them to pass laws halting rising prices and to meet the housing crisis which they say they're for in their platform. At the same time I shall ask them to act on other vitally needed measures such as aid to education,

which they say they're for; a national health program, civil rights legislation, which they say they're for; [and] funds for projects needed . . . to provide public power and cheap electricity. . . . What that worst Eightieth Congress does in its special session will be the test. The American people will decide on the record." *Harry S. Truman, address accepting the nomination at the Democratic National Convention in Philadelphia, July 15, 1948*

- "Ours is a magnificent land, don't let anybody frighten you or try to stampede you into believing that America is finished. America's future . . . is still ahead of us." *Thomas E. Dewey, speech in Phoenix, Arizona, September 23, 1948*
- "I will not get down into the gutter with that fellow." *Thomas E. Dewey referring to Truman*
- "Traveling with [Truman], you get the feeling that the American people . . . would . . . give him just about anything he wants except the presidency." *Richard H. Rovere, in The New Yorker, October 9, 1948*
- "The smart boys say we can't win. They tried to bluff us with a propaganda blitz, but we called their bluff, we told the people the truth. And the people are with us. The tide is rolling. All over the country. I have seen it in the people's faces. The people are

going to win this election." *Harry S. Truman, final campaign speech in St. Louis, October 30, 1948*
- "Dewey will be in [the White House] for eight years—until '57 . . 32-page special report on 'What Dewey Will Do' has been prepared and will be mailed to you within a week, embodied in Kiplinger Magazine." Kiplinger Washington Letter, *October 30, 1948*
- "The next president travels by ferry boat over the broad waters of San Francisco Bay." *Caption on a full-page picture of Dewey in* Life, *November 1, 1948*
- "Dewey Defeats Truman." Chicago Tribune *early election-night returns headline*

Lasting Legacy of Campaign

- Considered the greatest election upset in American history. Challenges pollsters to improve.
- Truman's surprise victory is the fifth consecutive win for the Democratic Party in a presidential election. Truman's election confirms the Democratic Party's status as the nation's majority party, a status retained until 1968.
- Truman's pugnacious, populist style and Dewey's aloof, aristocratic approach compel candidates to be more active and aggressive.

Election of 1948

The 1948 election is the delight of romantics. They see a brave man, fighting almost alone against great odds, defying the experts who unanimously predicted his defeat, and emerging as the winner in the greatest upset in American political history. While in touch with some of the realities, the interpretation obscures at least as much as it reveals. It exaggerates the significance of Truman's own efforts, although they must not be neglected, and understates his debts to others. (He did not wage a lonely campaign.) Most important, the romantic view of 1948 pays inadequate attention to some of the most important elements of the situation in which Truman functioned, especially the strengths of the Democratic Party and its New Deal and the weaknesses of the Republican Party and its presidential candidate. The interpretation also neglects Truman's weaknesses. The outcome reflected them as well as his strengths.

Perhaps the most important statement that has been made about 1948 is the classification of it as a "maintaining election." As defined by Angus Campbell, in such an election "the pattern of partisan attachments prevailing in the preceding period persists, and the majority party wins the Presidency." In addition, 1948 was a "low turn-

out" and a "narrow margin" election. Any valid interpretation must explain these features of Truman's victory.

It must be emphasized that Truman had the strength of the nation's majority party behind him. Roosevelt, or the Great Depression and the New Deal, had provided Truman with the base needed for victory. The Democrats had taken control of Congress in 1931 and had maintained control until 1947, and they had moved into the White House in 1933 and were still there in 1948. *Fortune* reported on the eve of that election year that 39 percent of the people thought of themselves as Democrats while only 33 percent regarded themselves as Republicans. And the American Institute of Public Opinion found at the same time that 56 percent of the partisans and 57 percent of the independents preferred the Democrats to the Republicans and that white- and blue-collar workers and farmers had much more confidence in the Democrats than in their opponents.

Basic Democratic strength did not guarantee a Truman victory, however, for weaknesses in the party were obvious by 1948. One of the clearest signs was new Republican strength in Congress. The GOP revival, which had begun in 1938, had reached a new high in the congressional elections of 1946 and produced Republican control

This Edwin Marcus cartoon captioned "House Hunter: 'Hope I'm Not Disturbing You'" shows President Truman looking out of the White House in dismay as New York governor Thomas Dewey nails a new nameplate on the front door. Marcus expresses the popular view that Dewey, the Republican candidate, would defeat Truman in the presidential election of 1948. To almost everyone's surprise, Truman won. *(By Permission of the Marcus Family)*

of Congress for the first time since 1930. The Eightieth Congress (1947–48) contained fifty-one Republicans and forty-five Democrats in the Senate and 246 Republicans and only 188 Democrats in the House of Representatives. This configuration reflected widespread dissatisfaction with the Truman administration and suggested that the Republicans would gain control of the White House as well in 1948. One feature of the troubled Democratic picture was evidence that Northern blacks were returning to the Republican Party. They had been enthusiastic supporters of Roosevelt, but Truman seemed an unworthy successor. They also resented the attitudes and behavior of Southern Democrats and the failure of the federal government to establish a permanent Fair Employment Practices Commission and to outlaw lynching.

The once-powerful Democratic coalition seemed to be falling apart. Liberal dissatisfaction with Truman had developed during 1945 and 1946 as New Dealers moved out of the administration and were replaced by more conservative Democrats, as the administration developed its "get tough" policy toward the Soviet Union, and as Truman clashed with organized labor. He had, it seemed to some, betrayed Franklin Roosevelt. In September 1946, Henry A. Wallace, once Roosevelt's secretary of agriculture and vice president and the most prominent liberal

in the administration, publicly criticized the emerging foreign policy, an act that was quickly followed by his dismissal as Truman's secretary of commerce. Out of office, he campaigned strenuously and stepped up his criticism, going beyond Truman's foreign policy to include basic features of the American political and economic system.

In 1947, Wallace became a candidate for the presidency. The new Progressive Citizens of America (PCA), a group that believed liberals and Communists could work together, provided support and encouragement for Wallace's crusade against the administration, including its Truman Doctrine and Marshall Plan. Members of the Communist Party, sharing the hostility to the new policy of Soviet containment, also rallied behind Wallace. Since the end of the war, they had been making plans for the formation of a new political party, and late in 1947 Communist leaders decided the time was right for such a step and that Wallace should be the new party's presidential candidate. Most members of the PCA agreed; so did the American Labor Party, a few old New Dealers, and a few members of the Congress of Industrial Organizations, the National Association for the Advancement of Colored People, and the National Farmers Union. On December 29, 1947, Wallace, convinced that he had widespread support but would be denied the Democratic nomination, announced that he would run on a third-party ticket.

The Wallace movement owed much to discontent with the administration's foreign policy, and foreign policy became the focal point of the campaign that Wallace waged. His followers, both Communists and non-Communists, agreed essentially on this issue. They regarded the containment policy as the creature of Wall Street and the military, imperialistic and destined to lead the world into atomic war. They could not agree on some other large questions, most notably the future of capitalism. Unlike the Communists, Wallace and his liberal followers believed in the possibility of a dynamic, progressive capitalism, a reformed capitalism, that would supply the material needs of all people. They believed that Roosevelt had moved in the right directions and that his efforts must be resumed.

For Wallace, there was no clash between his domestic and his foreign policy preferences. Reform at home depended on peace in the world. Or, put another way, return to the reliance upon Roosevelt's United Nations would permit a revival of Roosevelt's New Deal. In his view, the groups opposed to reform—big business and big brass—also promoted international conflict.

By early 1948, Wallace seemed a threat to Truman's chances for victory. The polls indicated that at least 6 percent of the voters favored Wallace, that most of these people had voted for Roosevelt in 1944, and that he had substantial strength in the Far West, especially California, and in the big cities, including Chicago and New

York, which had been so important in Roosevelt's victories. In February, voters in a New York City congressional district elected a Wallaceite, Leo Isacson of the American Labor Party, and shortly thereafter Democratic leaders in New York regarded Truman's chances in the Empire State as very slim. Wallace, in short, seemed capable of depriving Truman of badly needed votes.

At the same time, Truman encountered trouble in the right wing of his party. Discontent with the policies of the national party and the national administration had been growing in the South for more than a decade. Many Southerners resented the decline in their influence in the Democratic Party and the expansion of the role of the federal government in their lives. Some of the discontent reflected economic interests and a belief among Southern planters and businessmen that their interests were being subordinated to those of the urban working classes and the rural poor. Of ever-increasing importance was the fear of change in race relations and the resentment of efforts by Washington to promote those changes. Among other developments, the black vote in the South was growing, largely as a result of recent U.S. Supreme Court decisions outlawing the Democratic white primaries. The increasing black vote seemed to threaten the whole pattern of race relations in the South.

Southern discontent began to focus on Truman in late 1947 and early 1948 as he stepped up his own efforts to alter race relations. In October 1947, his Committee on Civil Rights issued a list of bold recommendations, and on February 2, 1948, he incorporated some of them into a special message on civil rights that advocated government action in several areas. Leading Southerners, including Governor Fielding Wright of Mississippi, protested loudly against these developments and began to organize in hopes of forcing party leaders to behave more conservatively. They felt that Truman had betrayed the very Southerners who had battled for him against Henry Wallace for the vice presidency in 1944, and they saw this betrayal as a consequence of Truman's new interest in the black vote in the Northern cities.

J. Strom Thurmond's leading role in this Southern movement demonstrated the basic importance of the race issue and Truman's civil rights proposals. As recently as October 2, 1947, the South Carolina governor had praised the president in a radio address and advocated his renomination. While emphasizing Truman's accomplishments in foreign affairs, Thurmond also indicated that he approved of the labor and farm policies of the Roosevelt–Truman administrations. Those who believed "in a liberal political philosophy, in the importance of human rights as well as property rights, in the preservation and strengthening of the economic and social gains brought about by the efforts of the Democratic Party in

the past several decades" and who believed "this Nation should continue its militant crusade for world peace, the Soviet Union notwithstanding," would, he predicted, "vote for the election of Harry Truman and the restoration of Congress to the control of the Democratic Party." The governor expressed confidence in a Democratic victory, and the president thanked him for the "kind things" he had said.

Four months later, on February 23, 1948, however, Thurmond led a special committee of Southern governors to a meeting with Rhode Island Senator J. Howard McGrath, the chairman of the Democratic National Committee. The governor charged that Truman's proposed civil rights laws "would be unconstitutional invasions of the field of government belonging to the states." He urged the chairman to use his "influence for the adoption in the 1948 party convention of a plank in the party platform upholding the traditional principle of the sovereignty of the several states and opposing such invasions of that principle" as Truman's proposals "and all Federal legislation dealing with the separation of races." And he advised him "at a time when national unity is so vital to the solution of the problem of peace in the world" to use his influence "to have the highly controversial Civil Rights legislation, which tends to divide our people, withdrawn from consideration by Congress."

The Southern revolt moved forward and gained strength. Following the meeting with McGrath, the governors warned that the South was "aroused" and that Democratic leaders would soon realize that the section was "no longer 'in the bag.'" Polling evidence, which indicated a sharp drop in Southern support for Truman and in Southern approval of his handling of his office, supported the threat. Hostility toward the civil rights proposals and toward the nomination of Truman or any advocate of civil rights legislation was widespread. Southerners seemed divided only on the question of the steps to be taken. While some insisted that the South must continue to work within the Democratic Party, others proposed a bolt from it. A conference in Jackson, Mississippi, on May 10 stressed opposition to civil rights legislation and advocates of it, called upon the Democrats to repudiate Truman's proposals, and made plans for a meeting in Birmingham, Alabama, after the Democratic convention, to decide on other measures. The rebels hoped their threats would restrain the Democrats and encourage them to adopt a weak plank on civil rights and nominate an opponent of new civil rights legislation.

The Democratic coalition seemed to be disintegrating, and, as the revolts developed, Truman's popularity declined. Polls at the beginning of the year had hinted that he could defeat any of the serious Republican contenders,

(continues on page 1166)

★ ★ ☆

1948 ELECTION CHRONOLOGY

1945

April 12, 1945: President Roosevelt dies at Warm Springs, Georgia, of a massive cerebral hemorrhage. Harry S. Truman is sworn in as president.

May 7, 1945: VE Day: Germany surrenders to the Allies, bringing an end to the war in Europe.

June 26, 1945: President Truman signs the United Nations Charter at San Francisco.

July 16, 1945: The first atomic bomb is tested at Trinity, New Mexico.

July 18, 1945: Truman attends the Potsdam Conference to discuss the postwar division of Germany.

August 6, 1945: The U.S. Air Force drops an atomic bomb on the Japanese city of Hiroshima.

August 9, 1945: The U.S. Air Force drops a second atomic bomb on the Japanese city of Nagasaki.

August 14, 1945: VJ Day: Japan surrenders to the Allies, bringing an end to the war in the Pacific.

August 18, 1945: Truman announces a return to peacetime production of consumer goods.

1946

May 24, 1946: Truman attempts to bring an end to a crippling railway strike by threatening to nationalize the railroads and use the army as strikebreakers. The workers settle just as the president is addressing Congress on the issue. He receives a standing ovation, but loses support among traditional Democratic supporters in the labor movement.

October 14, 1946: In a televised address, President Truman announces that the wartime controls on the price of meat will be lifted. The price controls are now creating shortages and a growing black market. The decision leads to a steep rise in prices and contributes to the president's unpopularity in the run-up to the congressional elections.

November 5, 1946: The Republicans take control of both houses of Congress in the midterm elections, gaining 55 seats in the House of Representatives and 13 seats in the Senate. The result is a severe rebuke of President Truman's policies.

1947

March 12, 1947: Truman sets out the "Truman doctrine" of U.S. foreign and military aid for states facing the possibility of Communist takeover.

June 5, 1947: Secretary of State George C. Marshall announces the Marshall Plan to provide funds for postwar reconstruction to the European states.

June 20, 1947: Truman vetoes the Taft-Hartley Bill, which he considers to be unfair toward labor. Congress overrides the veto three days later.

July 26, 1947: Truman signs the National Security Act, which unifies the armed forces in a single defense department and creates the Central Intelligence Agency and the National Security Council.

August 11, 1947: Senator Robert Taft of Ohio announces his candidacy for the Republican presidential nomination, in a speech condemning New Deal policies and foreign interventionism. His campaign peters out in the primaries.

November 19, 1947: In a confidential memorandum called "The Politics of 1948," presidential adviser Clark Clifford maps out a blueprint for Truman winning election in 1948.

December 29, 1947: Former vice president Henry A. Wallace announces his intention to run for president on a third-party ticket.

1948

January 3, 1948: Dwight Eisenhower refuses to be a candidate for the nomination of the Republican or Democratic party. A Gallup poll had indicated that he would win by seven points against the president as the Republican candidate.

February 2, 1948: Truman introduces a civil rights package to Congress, risking Southern Democratic support.

March 9, 1948: New York governor Thomas Dewey wins 6 of 8 delegates in the New Hampshire primary, after minimal campaigning.

☆   ☆   ☆

April 6, 1948: A surprise in the Wisconsin primary as former governor Harold Stassen of Minnesota wins 19 of 27 delegates, despite expectations that General Douglas MacArthur would triumph. With a victory the next week in Nebraska, Stassen becomes the front-runner.

May 4, 1948: Stassen stumbles, trying to take on Ohio senator Robert Taft in the Ohio primary, and loses.

May 14, 1948: The United States recognizes the State of Israel.

May 17, 1948: Desperate to revive his campaign with a victory in the Oregon primary, Dewey agrees to a live radio debate with Stassen.

May 21, 1948: Dewey wins Oregon with 53 percent of the vote, cementing his hold on the nomination.

May 30, 1948: A Roper poll finds that four of the leading candidates for the Republican nomination—Thomas Dewey, Harold Stassen, Arthur Vandenberg, and Douglas MacArthur—could each defeat President Truman by a margin of at least 10 percentage points.

June 2, 1948: In response to a letter from a Missouri constituent urging him not to run, Truman responds that he was "not born to run away from a fight." By this time he has won decisively in the Democratic primaries.

June 3–18, 1948: Truman embarks on a "nonpolitical" tour of the Midwest delivering stump speeches condemning the Republican Congress for its inaction and "commitment to the welfare of the better classes." His more peppery, informal style receives a favorable response from audiences.

June 21–25, 1948: The Republicans hold their convention in Philadelphia. New York Governor Thomas Dewey defeats Robert Taft and Harold Stassen to win the presidential nomination on the third ballot. Governor Earl Warren of California is selected as the vice presidential candidate. The convention displays a confident Republican Party, anticipating victory in November.

July 12–15, 1948: The Democrats hold their convention in Philadelphia. President Truman is renominated, winning on the first ballot. Senator Alben Barkley of Kentucky is nominated as the vice-presidential candidate. The convention is marked by division over the party platform, which calls for national health insurance, public housing, and civil rights for African Americans. A group of conservative Southern Democrats breaks away from the party.

July 15, 1948: Truman accepts the nomination with a passionate speech and a surprise call for the Congress to convene for a special "Turnip Day" session.

July 17, 1948: The "States' Rights" or Dixiecrat Party holds its first convention in Birmingham Alabama, nominating South Carolina Governor Strom Thurmond for president and Mississippi Governor Fielding W. Wright for vice president.

June 26, 1948: Truman orders the Berlin airlift, in response to a Soviet blockade.

July 23, 1948: The Progressive Party holds its founding convention in Philadelphia to nominate Henry A. Wallace for president and Idaho's Democratic Senator Glen Taylor for vice president.

July 26, 1948: Truman signs Executive Order 9981, ending racial segregation in the armed forces.

July 26, 1948: Congress convenes for its special session and fails to enact the legislation proposed in the Republican platform, which seemed to endorse much of Truman's ambitious agenda. This allows him to blast the "do-nothing" Republican Congress.

September 1, 1948: Dewey delivers a speech in Albany, promising to purge the federal government of Communist sympathizers.

September 6, 1948: Truman begins his famous "whistle-stop" tour of the nation at Cadillac Square in Detroit, which will become a Democratic tradition until 1972. In his "Give 'em hell Harry" campaign he travels over 22,000 miles, delivering 26 major speeches and 244 "whistle-stop" talks from the rear of his train carriage.

September 9, 1948: Pollster Elmo Roper predicts that Republican candidate Thomas Dewey will beat Truman by 40 to 31 percent, and that no amount of electioneering will be able to salvage the situation. Most leading pollsters agree.

(continues)

1948 ELECTION CHRONOLOGY *(continued)*

September 13, 1948: The Republicans sweep the early Maine elections, winning by their biggest margin in 21 years. Dewey warns Republicans of the danger of overconfidence, but continues to run a cautious campaign and appears sufficiently confident in his chances to campaign for Republican congressional candidates in the Midwest.

November 2, 1948: Truman wins a surprise victory, taking 49.55 percent of the popular vote and 303 electoral votes. The Republicans win 45.07 percent of the vote and 189 electoral votes. The States' Rights Party wins 2.41 percent of the popular vote and 39 electoral votes, while the Progressives win 2.37 percent of the vote and no electoral votes. Norman Thomas, the perennial Socialist Party candidate, wins 0.41 percent.

December 13, 1948: Presidential electors cast their ballots in their respective state capitals.

1949

January 6, 1949: A joint session of Congress assembles to count the electoral votes.

(continued from page 1163)

including Thomas Dewey of New York, Harold Stassen of Minnesota, and Earl Warren of California, and that he would enjoy a landslide victory over the Republican leader in the Senate, Robert Taft of Ohio; but by spring the president had fallen far behind Dewey and Stassen, among others, and Warren and Taft had narrowed the gap. As a consequence of the troubles of the Democratic Party, almost any Republican candidate seemed capable of winning. And as Democratic hopes dimmed, the party ran into trouble obtaining funds for the campaign.

The polls reflected the drop in popular confidence in the president. While 55 percent of the people had approved of his performance as president in October 1947, only 36 percent did so in April 1948. "People are restless, dissatisfied, fearful. They want someone who can 'take over' and solve everything," one member of the administration explained. "Truman is just a man, a likable, courageous, stubborn man. So away with him."

The quest for a strong man caused many to turn to General Dwight D. Eisenhower. Even in late 1947 and early 1948, when Truman's popularity had been high relative to the Republicans, the general seemed a much more popular candidate than the president. And Eisenhower's support remained strong despite his announcement on January 23 that he would not run. A spring poll indicated that 24 percent of the people thought that of all the candidates, Eisenhower would make the best president, while only 11 percent thought Truman would. And in this poll, Eisenhower ranked ahead of Truman with Democrats as well as Republicans and independents.

Taking the lead in an attempt to dump the president was the Americans for Democratic Action (ADA), an anti-Communist liberal organization that had been formed in January 1947. These liberal Democrats liked Truman's major policies. They applauded the Marshall Plan, the domestic policies that he outlined in his messages on the State of the Union and civil rights, his increasingly vigorous liberal rhetoric, and his criticism of the Eightieth Congress. They were displeased, however, with his treatment of old New Dealers in his administration. Most important, the ADA was unhappy with the president as a political leader and looked on him as a certain loser who would lead the ticket to defeat. "We honor President Truman for his unswerving support of the European Recovery Program, for his courageous advocacy of civil rights, and for his wise recommendations for domestic economic policy," the ADA board stated on April 11. "But we cannot overlook the fact that poor appointments and faltering support of his aides have resulted in a failure to rally the people behind policies which in large measure we wholeheartedly support."

Thus, the ADA spearheaded a campaign to substitute General Dwight D. Eisenhower for Truman, hoping desperately to find a charismatic leader of the sort they had lost with Roosevelt's death. And they were not stopped by critics who suggested that Eisenhower's views remained unknown. The general seemed to have the qualities that the nation needed, and the president lacked and seemed capable of spectacular accomplishments at home and abroad, accomplishments that appeared to be beyond Truman's reach. According to the ADA, Eisenhower would "stir the popular enthusiasm which will sweep progressive candidates across the country into Congress" and produce the type of leadership that would "defeat both the forces of vested reaction and the Communist-dominated third party." He would also give the free people of the world "a new infusion of faith and hope" and force Russia to "hesitate in its policy of headlong expansion and aggrandizement."

The Eisenhower boom picked up a strange assortment of participants. In addition to liberals such as California representative James Roosevelt, the list included several city bosses—Jacob Arvey of Chicago and Frank Hague of Jersey City, among others—and several prominent southerners. Each group had its own reasons for being unhappy with Truman and for having different expectations of Eisenhower. The unknown quality of the general's ideas helped the cause along, as did the belief that he was a winner who could carry others to victory with him. Cabell Phillips suggests that "the willingness of southern conservatives and northern liberals to rally together behind a man whose views on the most divisive issue of the day—civil rights—were totally unknown, betrayed a panic born of desperation."

By the spring of 1948, the weaknesses of the Democratic Party were its most conspicuous features. But below the surface lay basic strengths. Could Truman tap them? Could he persuade the voters with Democratic ties and Democratic leanings that they should stick with him rather than follow the rebels or switch to the Republicans?

Although prospects looked dim and Truman frequently appeared and felt weary, he was determined to push on. "The President's stock is very low indeed," David Lilienthal recorded in April. "He doesn't seem to give a hang; he is going to be President as long as his term lasts, come what may." Actually, he was determined to be president beyond 1948. He felt obligated to seek a second term. When a Missourian suggested that he should withdraw, Truman replied that he "was not brought up to run from a fight" and recalled his refusal to surrender when many members of his party tried to defeat him in the senatorial primary of 1940. As Cabell Phillips has observed, "His instinctive response to a challenge was to fight back." Furthermore, he saw the policies and programs in which he believed, both domestic and foreign, as seriously threatened and concluded that he must defend them. Thus, on March 8, he authorized McGrath to announce his candidacy.

Preparations for the campaign had begun long before. And Truman had help in his quest for victory. While some people consciously worked on his behalf, others assisted him indirectly by battling against some of his enemies.

Two groups were especially important in the early preparations: several administration officials, headed by Clark Clifford, and the staff of the Democratic National Committee, chaired first by Robert Hannegan and then Senator McGrath. Clifford, the president's special counsel, and his associates, including Charles S. Murphy, an administrative assistant to the president, had begun to make plans for 1948 shortly after the disastrous elections of 1946. Struggling for

Two sisters, Esther and Louisa Page, look intently at a Truman poster outside the Democratic National Convention in Philadelphia, 1948. *(Library of Congress)*

influence against conservatives such as John Snyder, an old friend of Truman serving as secretary of the treasury, they encouraged the president to become militantly liberal, and they achieved their first major victory with the veto of the Taft–Hartley Act in June 1947.

Throughout 1947, the staff of the National Committee conducted organization and publicity campaigns. The top assistants to Hannegan and McGrath in these efforts were Gael Sullivan, the executive director, and Jack Redding, the publicity director. They attempted to strengthen party organization in the cities of the North and West. One of the methods employed was a series of conferences in Washington that gave the national officials a chance to educate state Democratic leaders on organizational plans and gave the latter an opportunity to visit with the president. Another tool was a highly partisan newsletter that devoted much of its attention to the record of the 80th Congress and sought to spur party workers and furnish them with political ammunition. Industrious registration drives were one product of these efforts.

These committee officials recognized the basic strength of their party and sought ways to exploit it. They realized that their policies were more popular than those of the congressional Republicans and were convinced that the Democrats had lost the 1946 election by default. The great need was to bring the Democratic majority to the polls in November 1948. Truman's "infectious personality," his "smiling, man-in-the-street attitude toward the public" that had impressed the party leaders and that seemed much more attractive than the personalities of the leading Republican contenders, appeared to be a major asset. To take advantage of his charm, the officials suggested that before the party's national convention he "show himself to the Nation via the back platform of a cross-country train," for his "easy manner of speaking when speaking informally has been lost in translation to the People via radio and speaking tours." In addition, he should change his speaking style, gaining "more natural delivery, even if some rhetorical effects are lost." And to dramatize and publicize another major asset, the party's domestic program, Democrats should fight "continuously and vigorously" in 1948 for action on domestic issues, for this was the best way for the party to demonstrate that the Republicans were "failing to meet the real issues." An aggressive campaign would either "get . . . adequate measures . . . under Democratic leadership or put the Republican Party squarely on the spot for failure to come through."

The thinking of a year was drawn together in a confidential memorandum from Clifford to the president on November 19, 1947, dealing with "The Politics of 1948." It was a tough-minded document, with its toughness moderated by the assumptions that the policy that was "politically wise" was also "the best policy for the country," and that "the future of this country and the future of the world" were "linked inextricably" with Truman's reelection. It contained suggestions for more "exposure" for the president, including a "nonpolitical" tour, and advice on ways of dealing with the Wallace threat—liberal appointments, liberal programs, charges of Communist control. The "basic premise" was that the Democratic Party was "an unhappy alliance of Southern conservatives, Western progressives and Big City labor," and the test of Democratic leadership was "its ability to lead enough members of these three misfit groups to the polls." Heavy emphasis was placed on the Western vote and ways of getting it, for it seemed crucial. Warning that Truman and the Democrats could not win "without the *active* support of organized labor" and that labor might "*stay home,*" Clifford insisted that the administration renew its "working relationship with progressive and labor leaders."

Two other passages were especially significant: the advice on how to deal with the second session of the 80th Congress and the suggestions regarding the South and civil rights. Assuming that the congressional Republicans would move "left," the adviser urged Truman to remain left of them. He must exploit conflict rather than legislation and thus must not bargain and compromise. He must tailor his recommendations for the voter, not the congressman. "The strategy on the Taft–Hartley Bill—refusal to bargain with the Republicans and to accept any compromises—paid big political dividends," Clifford reminded the president. "That strategy should be expanded in the next session to include all the *domestic* issues." (High prices, housing, tax revision, conservation, and civil rights seemed especially important.) In his message on the State of the Union, he should present his program to the American people, and he should present it in a simple and clear fashion that would enable them to know what he was asking Congress to do. Thus, he would be in a position "to receive credit for whatever they do accomplish while also being in a position to criticize the Congress for being obstructionists in failing to comply with other recommendations." In this approach, Clifford saw "a fertile field for the development of campaign issues."

On civil rights, Clifford assumed not only that Truman must act but also that he could act without risk. The situation demanded action, for black voters held the balance of power in Illinois and perhaps in New York and Ohio, and the Republicans appeared to be making progress in their efforts to regain black support. And he was free to act since it was thought that no policies "initiated by the Truman Administration no matter how 'liberal' could so alienate the South in the next year that it would revolt." In Clifford's view, the South could be considered "safely Democratic" and could be "safely ignored" in formulating national policy. Anticipating that "Republican strategy at the next session will be to offer an FEPC [Federal Employment Practices Commission], an anti-poll tax bill, and an anti-lynching bill," Clifford advised that "the President go as far as he feels he possibly could go in recommending measures to protect the rights of minority groups." The resulting difficulties with the South would be "the lesser of two evils."

Truman accepted many, but not all, of the suggestions, and with the new year the strategy began to unfold. On January 7, he delivered his State of the Union message, with its long list of proposals for action in both domestic and foreign affairs and its appeals to many groups of voters. And since this broad message dealt with specific issues in general ways, he supplemented it with a series of special messages. One of these called for the extension and improvement of legislation authorizing rent control and emergency financial aids for housing and for new housing legislation that would establish "an integrated program to assist in obtaining more housing at lower cost, both in the immediate future and for the long run." Still another major message called for a ten-point civil rights program that would, among other things, provide federal protection against lynching, protect the right to vote, prohibit discrimination in interstate transportation facilities, and establish a Fair Employment Practices Commission to prevent unfair discrimination in employment.

Clearly, the administration expected that the civil rights message would create difficulties for both Wallace and the Republicans in the black wards. It also became clear, however, that Southern reaction was stronger than expected. The administration and the National Committee now recognized that the South would not be solid and began to work to limit the scope of the Southern revolt. McGrath, in his meeting with the Southern governors and on other occasions, defended the president's message but called attention to the limits on the proposals. "There . . . never has been any intention to upset or invade the rights of the States under the Constitution," he insisted. The president "is for the Federal Government acting only within the limits of the Constitution and according to the regulations which affect interstate commerce." McGrath indicated that he valued Southern contributions to the party, advised Southerners to remain within it, and pointed out that he favored a civil rights plank in the party platform similar to the one adopted in 1944. While refusing to modify the civil rights proposals or withdraw them from Congress, the Administration did not introduce a draft of a civil rights bill and delayed action against discrimination in federal employment and against segregation in the armed forces. Advisers most concerned about the loss of black votes to Wallace urged action, but those who were worried about the Southern revolt counseled delay and, for the moment, dominated the administration's handling of civil rights.

Truman's speech in Los Angeles on June 14 illustrated the new caution on the civil rights issue. Before he headed west, the Research Division of the National Committee called attention to the rising importance of blacks in the West and to the great strides that the Wallace movement was making with those black voters and advised that civil rights should be dealt with in speeches in Chicago, Omaha, and Los Angeles. The president should, for example, comment on the "lack of enthusiasm" that Republicans had shown for the Civil Rights Report. The president did refer to civil rights in Chicago, and his advisers studied Southern reaction to this, found little, and were advised that he could make short statements about civil rights without arousing a bad reaction as long as the major emphasis of the speech was on something else. Some advisers now maintained that he should mention civil rights in Los Angeles and argued that it was one of the three critical areas where Wallace was hurt-

ing Democratic chances and that, next to New York and Chicago, Los Angeles was the city where the president could make the most capital out of his strong civil rights position. By blaming Congress for the lack of action, he could help offset the Wallace claim that inaction on civil rights was Truman's fault. But McGrath advised against this, suggesting that he would rather accept the criticism that would be leveled against the president for the omission than take the chance of arousing a bad reaction in the South. When delivered, the speech contained no reference to the subject.

Truman and his associates in Washington were not forced to work alone on efforts to contain the Southern revolt. They received advice from others on how best to conciliate the South, including restoration of the two-thirds rule in the Democratic National Convention. And in the South, loyal Democrats worked to keep their states within the party.

Truman also received aid from outsiders in his battle against the revolt on the left. Here two groups—labor leaders and anti-Communist liberals—were especially helpful despite their limited enthusiasm for Truman. Only a few labor leaders joined the third party. Most of them, including William Green, Walter Reuther, Michael Quill, most members of the executive boards of the Congress of Industrial Organizations (CIO) and American Federation of Labor (AFL), and the leaders of the Amalgamated Clothing Workers, deprived Wallace of labor support that he hoped for and needed, and subjected him to open attacks that hurt him with others. Philip Murray, the president of the CIO, for instance, had concluded that American labor leaders could not work with Communists. In fact, he began to purge them from his organization and denounced the new party as Communist-controlled.

Most leaders of the labor movement recognized the great importance of the Democratic Party, the party of FDR, and feared any damage that Wallace might do. The years of Democratic rule had been years of progress for the movement and for the working man. As one labor leader explained to an official of the new party:

> Some time ago I publicly stated that I could not support a third political party, for the reason that in my opinion it will divide the progressives of the nation, which would be detrimental to the Democratic Party and helpful to the reactionary Republican Party.
>
> I do not wish to imply that the Democratic Party has not made mistakes; however, I am of the opinion that the liberals of the nation should not have permitted themselves to become divided and should have defended their cause within the framework of the Democratic Party.

To men such as this, the Taft–Hartley Law constituted evidence of what they could expect from the Republicans, while Truman's veto demonstrated the value of the Democratic connection. Passage of the law encouraged them to increase their political activity in hopes of defeating congressmen who had voted for it and bringing about the repeal of the law. Some, including A. F. Whitney, the president of the Brotherhood of Railroad Trainmen, also endorsed Truman. Gael Sullivan worked especially hard to obtain such endorsements.

An interesting footnote to labor's role in the campaign can be found in Truman's refusal to approach John L. Lewis of the United Mine Workers for support. The president felt, rightly or wrongly, that the dour, bushy-browed mine chief had betrayed the Democrats two years before.

Support for the administration's new foreign policy also played a part in labor's refusal to support Wallace. The CIO, for example, endorsed the Marshall Plan at the same time that it condemned Wallace's candidacy, and the AFL charged that the Communists hoped to elect an arch-reactionary with isolationist leanings and that this "would play into the hands of Soviet Russia's expansionist policies."

Liberals in the Americans for Democratic Action (ADA) and the New York Liberal Party evaluated the Wallace movement in a similar way and joined in efforts to weaken it. After failing to persuade Wallace himself that a decision to run would harm the liberal cause, they advised others that a vote for him would help conservative Republicans gain power. Denying that liberals and Communists should work together, they joined in the attack on Wallace's connections and made some of the most sensational and influential presentations of the thesis that the Wallace movement was essentially a Communist movement designed chiefly to destroy Truman's foreign policy.

Clifford had hoped that the liberals would help in this fashion. In his memorandum of November, he had predicted that Wallace would be a candidate and that he would hurt the Democrats in important states, including New York and California. He realized that most Wallace supporters were not Communists but believed that those in control of the movement were. Thus, he called for efforts to identify and isolate Wallace "in the public mind with the Communists." He contended that "the Administration must persuade prominent liberals and progressives—and no one else—to move publicly into the fray. They must point out that the core of the Wallace backing is made up of Communists and fellow-travelers." Now the liberals were performing as Clifford had hoped they would. Truman and the leaders of the National Committee merely supplemented those efforts, employing the theme of Communist control in their own statements and working in other ways to undermine Wallace.

Truman had defenders in the ADA, most notably Paul Porter, a former administration official and now a Washington lawyer, and the National Committee worked with Porter in hopes of promoting cooperation between the organization and the Truman forces. As "dump Truman" sentiment mounted, Sullivan worked with Porter on tactics for the ADA convention in April and agreed that Porter should seek the best solution he could get. While most delegations favored either Eisenhower or William O. Douglas, Truman fans were present, led by Boris Shishkin of the AFL, Lester Granger of the National Urban League, and Ben McLaurin of the Brotherhood of Sleeping Car Porters, in addition to Porter. Walter Reuther of the United Auto Workers and Emil Rieve of the Textile Workers, although favoring an open Democratic convention, opposed any statement critical of the president or any endorsement of Eisenhower or Douglas. One participant who opposed taking a position at the time suggested that "we don't want to abandon the allegedly sinking Truman ship for the sheer joy of getting into the water," while Reinhold Niebuhr called the Eisenhower boom infantile, and Porter described it in similar terms. One staff member of the National Committee believed that Porter had

Henry A. Wallace, Progressive Party presidential candidate, speaking to a crowd during the campaign for the 1948 presidential election. *(Library of Congress)*

done a "fine job," given the very difficult situation, and hoped that Clifford was not too disappointed with the ADA statement that expressed greater enthusiasm for Eisenhower and Douglas than for Truman and advocated an open convention.

The Russians also helped to weaken Wallace. While he preached the possibility of peaceful coexistence between Communists and non-Communists, including Russia and the United States, the Communists staged a coup in Czechoslovakia in February, overturning a liberal regime. Wallace bungled badly in his efforts to explain this development, while Truman responded with a strong speech condemning Russian aggression, advocating enactment of the European Recovery Program, universal military training, and selective service, and denouncing Wallace. "I don't want and I will not accept the political support of Henry Wallace and his Communists," Truman assured a nationwide radio audience. Other Russian and Communist actions also challenged Wallace's thesis. Most important of these was the blockade of West Berlin, beginning in June. Truman responded with the dramatic airlift of supplies to the city. "If foreign Communists had deliberately tried," David A. Shannon stated, "they could not have done much more than they did to hurt the Wallace campaign." Clifford had expected that American relations with Russia would worsen and that Truman would derive benefits from this. "In times of crisis the American citizen tends to back up his President," the adviser had written in November.

Foreign policy questions entered the campaign in other ways at this stage, and Truman again both received help and helped himself. Early in the year, a nationalities division in the National Committee began to work strenuously to capture and hold the ethnic vote, and Truman joined in the efforts, sending messages to the various organizations. This campaign emphasized his anti-Communist foreign policy.

The Jewish vote presented a major problem. Clifford's memorandum had called attention to the importance of this vote in New York and the importance of New York in presidential elections, and had advised that "the Jewish bloc is interested primarily in Palestine and will continue to be an uncertain quantity right up to the time of election." But, recognizing conflicts within the bloc, he suggested that it would be "extremely difficult to decide some of the vexing questions which will arise in the months to come on the basis of political expediency" and that there was "likely to be greater gain if the Palestine problem is approached on the basis of reaching decisions founded upon intrinsic merit." In the early months of 1948, Wallace made gains with Jewish voters; criticism of administration policy mounted as the United States backed away from its earlier support of immediate partition of Palestine; Jewish leaders urged the president to lift the embargo on the sale of arms to the Jews in the Middle East and to recognize the new Jewish state on its establishment, scheduled for May 14; and Democratic leaders in New York and several other states insisted that Truman take dramatic and effective steps on behalf of the Jews in Palestine in order to undercut Wallace and the Republicans. Truman clearly resented the pressures that were being imposed on him, and Drew Pearson caused a storm in New York by publicizing a version of Truman's feelings. Inside the administration, the leading opponent of recognition was the Secretary of State, General George C. Marshall; the leading proponent, Clifford. Finally, Truman agreed with the advocates of recognition, although only, as Ian Bickerton has demonstrated, after persuading himself that this was in America's national interest. So, on May 14, the United States granted *de facto* recognition to the new State of Israel. While Jewish leaders remained critical of the State Department, charging that it was sabotaging the president's policy, and pressed for *de jure* recognition and removal of the embargo on arms sales to Israel, they applauded his prompt action. Once again, any Wallace advantage was undermined.

As these various measures were taken, plans were moving forward for the pre-convention tour that had been suggested by Sullivan, Redding, and Clifford. Before it began, Truman took another step that his advisers had urged: he changed his speaking style. He actually returned to an old style that he had used frequently in his pre-presidential years, but only on informal occasions after he moved into the White House. Then he had attempted to develop a formal manner deemed appropriate for the presidency. It involved efforts to sound like Roosevelt, something that Truman proved incapable of doing. He was, as a consequence, widely regarded as a very poor speaker. Facing this problem squarely, his advisers persuaded him to adopt an informal manner, aided only by notes or an outline, that would permit his own personality to be expressed. He accepted the advice, acknowledging that he read speeches poorly. The "new" method was tested publicly at a meeting of the American Society of Newspaper Editors in April; and, as the response was enthusiastic, the method was employed on three other occasions in May and endorsed for the "nonpolitical" tour by train in June. "You may rest assured that the country will hear a good deal from the President speaking off-the-cuff," his press secretary assured a friend.

To assist in the preparation of speech materials, the National Committee had accepted a suggestion from Clifford and established a research division, headed by William L. Batt Jr., an ADA official. Composed of a small group of people who knew the major issues and were good at research and writing, the division gathered information on the issues and candidates and on the towns Truman would visit, devised campaign plans, prepared drafts and outlines of speeches, and analyzed political situations and reactions to the speeches, all the while working closely with the White House staff. The division pressed for a hard-hitting campaign that would praise the Democratic record, criticize the Republicans as obstructionists, and portray the Democrats as the party that worked in the interests of all Americans and Republicans as working in the interests of the wealthy few. One speech draft referred to Republican foes of the housing bill as "a little group of blind, stubborn men—men who had comfortable homes of their own, men who were sensitive to the whispers of the real estate lobbies but could not hear the desperate voices of millions of homeless Americans." And another draft suggested that the president should respond as follows to Senator Taft's charge that the president would veto everything Congress accomplished:

> The Congress can rest assured that I will NOT veto any proposal aimed at advancing the welfare of ALL the people of the United States. I WILL veto special interest legislation aimed at profiting the few at the expense of the many. I WILL veto any further attempts to repeal the great social and economic gains of the past sixteen years.

Taking advantage of an offer of an honorary degree from the University of California, Truman left Washington on June 3, not to return for two weeks. Traveling several days ahead of the train, Oscar Chapman, the undersecretary of the interior, provided important assistance, talking to local political leaders, mending fences, getting advice on speech topics that should be emphasized in each location, and making other preparations for Truman's visit. The president pushed toward the Pacific Coast, making many speeches in communities from Indiana to Washington. He then journeyed down to Los Angeles and returned through the Southwest and the Middle West, talking from the back platform at every stop. While he emphasized domestic matters, he did not limit his attention to them. He talked also about peace and pictured his foreign and military policies and proposals as ways of avoiding war. Hitting matters of major and special interest to the communities he visited, he covered most of the major issues of the day, stressed Democratic accomplishments and Republican failures, and paid some attention to the threats from Wallace and Eisenhower. Although he made several formal speeches, most of them employed the new style, and as he progressed, his mistakes diminished, his effectiveness increased, and the crowds grew larger. To

many, he seemed much more attractive than ever before. He and his advisers derived a large sense of accomplishment from the venture. It had enabled them to present their views of the issues of the day and to present them effectively. Truman's confidence soared.

Thus, Truman's preparations for the fall campaign were well advanced by the beginning of the summer. He had not made great gains in the public opinion polls, but even they contained several encouraging signs. Approval of his handling of his office was on the rise again, and Wallace was slipping. Clearly, the many forays against the latter were succeeding. As many as 51 percent of the people believed that his party was run by Communists, and only 21 percent rejected this interpretation. Furthermore, Truman was ready for the task that lay ahead and had many people working for him in various ways. The Republicans, on the other hand, had not yet selected his opponent.

At the beginning of the year, the Republicans appeared to have several rather strong choices. According to the polls, Thomas E. Dewey was in the lead. But Harold Stassen, Senator Robert A. Taft of Ohio, Senator Arthur Vandenberg of Michigan, General Douglas MacArthur, and Governor Earl Warren also had substantial followings.

An experienced public official and politician, Dewey represented a middle-ground position in the party. Relatively young, he had been born in Michigan in 1902, the son of a newspaperman, and educated at the University of Michigan and the Columbia Law School. He had become famous as a racket buster in the 1930s and was elected district attorney in New York City in 1937. Failing in bids for the governorship in 1938 and the Republican nomination for the presidency two years later, he won the gubernatorial election in 1942 and the Republican nomination for the presidency in 1944. His defeat in Roosevelt's last campaign did not harm his career seriously, and his reelection as governor of New York by a large margin in 1946 gave him a big boost. His record as governor was one of efficiency, economy, and tempered liberalism, and his moderate stand on national issues involved endorsement of much that had been done by the Democratic administrations, a stand that did not make him attractive to the more conservative Republicans. A man of average height with a neatly trimmed moustache, Dewey was hampered by a rather stiff public manner.

Stassen was the reform candidate and the most militant internationalist. He had been elected governor of Minnesota at the tender age of 31 and had been reelected twice. Resigning to enter the Navy, he saw much action during the war and then served as a delegate to the conference in San Francisco that established the United Nations in 1945. Lacking a base in office and popularity with the party professionals, and trailing Dewey in the polls, he

Candidate's welcome: Thomas E. Dewey with Thomas J. Curran, Manhattan Republican leader, on return from campaign tour. *(Library of Congress)*

campaigned strenuously, beginning in 1946. As Vandenberg was not an active candidate, preferring to concentrate on his work on foreign policy in the Senate and on a platform plank that would commit his party to internationalism, Stassen was the leading internationalist in the field. Unlike Vandenberg, Stassen hoped to transform the party on domestic as well as international affairs. He hoped to commit it to a liberal position. In appearance and manner, he differed significantly from Dewey. The Minnesotan was ruggedly handsome, had a warm and easy smile, and appeared to be very friendly and seriously concerned about the voters' problems.

Of the leading candidates, Taft was the most critical of the Democratic record. The son of a president, he had been elected to the Senate in 1938 and had quickly established himself as a leader of the Republican bloc there and the most distinguished representative of Republican conservatism, although as time passed he became less conservative than many of his followers. Lacking color and the common touch and candid to the point of bluntness, he seemed, according to the polls, likely to lose in a race

with Truman, and the belief that he was a loser hurt him seriously.

But the Ohio senator had great strength with congressional and party leaders, and he placed his emphasis upon recruiting the delegations in states that did not have presidential primaries.

Warren pursued the presidency in much less strenuous fashion than Dewey, Stassen, and Taft did. He had been elected California's governor in 1942 by a large margin and reelected four years later without opposition after winning the Democratic as well as the Republican primary. The fiscal soundness of his administration gave him some appeal to conservatives, while his innovating tendencies made him attractive to liberals. Beyond these assets, this husky, hearty, vigorous man had great personal warmth and charm and a large and very attractive and photogenic family. Despite his limited campaigning, he could not be ignored.

From March to May, the Republican contenders competed in a series of presidential primaries. The first was held in New Hampshire on March 9, and there, after only a small amount of campaigning by Dewey and Stassen, Dewey won 6 of the 8 delegates. The next test came in Wisconsin on April 6, and there MacArthur, serving in far-off Japan, was the predicted winner. With Dewey and Stassen campaigning strenuously, Stassen picked up 19 of the 27 delegates, while MacArthur won only 8, thereby killing the MacArthur boom. The Nebraska primary the next week had a long list of names on the ballot, including Taft, Warren, and Vandenberg, as well as Stassen and Dewey, and Taft joined them in the campaign. Again Stassen won, finishing far ahead of Dewey and even farther ahead of Taft and Vandenberg. Clearly, he had replaced Dewey as the front-runner. But now Stassen overreached himself and not only entered the Ohio primary against Taft but campaigned vigorously against him. Stassen failed to achieve a dramatic victory and thus moved into the Oregon primary of May 21 in a weakened position but still the favorite. Both Stassen and Dewey needed victories, and they campaigned hard. Stassen stirred controversy with his proposal to outlaw the Communist Party, and in a radio debate Dewey challenged this persuasively on civil libertarian grounds and moved on to win 53 percent of the vote and all 12 delegates, a victory that strengthened him substantially.

Dewey had revealed some of his weaknesses as well as his strengths in the primaries, although he had maintained his position as the leading Republican candidate. The Gallup Poll reported that while Stassen had moved ahead among Republican voters in April, and had remained ahead in May, he dropped behind in June. He had narrowed the gap, however. Before the primaries, only 15 percent of Republicans had favored him, while

38 percent favored Dewey. Now, however, the latter had dropped to 33 percent, and Stassen had moved up to 26. MacArthur, Taft, and Warren also lost ground with Republicans during the period. Only Vandenberg, in addition to Stassen, made progress. The senator, it seems likely, benefited from the leading role that he played in producing the March victory in Congress for the popular Marshall Plan, just as Stassen was helped by his own campaigning. Dewey, on the other hand, seemed a somewhat uninspiring performer.

Nevertheless, as the Republican convention drew near, Dewey seemed capable of defeating Truman. For that matter, so did Vandenberg, Stassen, and MacArthur. Dewey, however, led Truman by a slightly larger margin, 44 to 32 percent, or 12 percent, as compared with the 10 percent margins separating the others from the president. Relative to Truman, Dewey, as well as Stassen, had moved since the beginning of the year from a projected loser to a seeming winner. And they had done so despite the preparations the president had been making and the help he had been receiving.

Late in June, the campaign moved beyond the preparatory stage and into the conventions, with some uncertainty concerning platforms and candidates. And decisions in these areas had to be made before another element of uncertainty could be removed. How many parties would nominate serious presidential candidates? It was already certain that Truman's opposition would not be limited to the Republican candidate. Wallace was clearly in the race, although his campaign was not making the gains that had been expected. But would the Democratic right also organize a party and send a candidate into combat? Despite many efforts to produce a negative answer to this question, a States' Rights Party was formed in July and nominated Governors Thurmond of South Carolina and Wright of Mississippi.

The Republicans met first and revealed that the predominant wing of their party was quite liberal and international in point of view. They assembled in Philadelphia on June 21 and, with a significant number of television viewers able for the first time to look in on a national political convention, clashed more than mildly over issues of both domestic and foreign policy. The platform indicated that the faction that dominated the congressional party was not in control of the convention. The platform, which endorsed both the United Nations and the containment policy, was in harmony with the congressional party's record on foreign policy and with its efforts to cut expenditures and taxes, but the platform endorsed many domestic schemes that the 80th Congress had refused to pass, including civil rights legislation, inflation control, public housing, an increase in the minimum wage, and aid to displaced persons. The Platform Committee,

In this Lute Pease cartoon Thomas Dewey rolls up his sleeves, while the Republican elephant, holding Dewey's hat and suit jacket, cheers. *(Library of Congress)*

however, appeased conservatives by omitting reference to federal aid to education by a meaningless compromise on reciprocal trade and by dropping a plan favoring an FEPC. Now Republicans were making their own efforts to court the South.

The contrast between the efficiency of the Dewey organization and the ineptitude of the Taft forces helped Dewey win the nomination. He came to the convention leading in delegate count but with Taft regarded as a serious opponent due to his strength with party leaders. And the New Yorker fell at least 200 votes short of the 548 needed for the nomination. Stassen was regarded as the long shot; Warren and Vandenberg were seen as contenders, and a number of favorite sons were also in the race. Dewey needed the support of the favorite sons in the large states. His top lieutenants, Herbert Brownell, J. Russel Sprague, and Edwin F. Jaeckle, had liaison men assigned to every delegation and a file card on almost every delegate, and, assisted by loyal supporters of the governor, they worked on the unconverted and brought him together with key people and key delegations. The first breakthrough came when Senator Edward Martin of Pennsylvania announced his decision to withdraw and nominate Dewey. Then Representative Charles A. Halleck of Indiana withdrew and announced that he would second the nomination, apparently confident that he had been promised the vice presidency. Next, Governor Alfred E. Driscoll of New Jersey, Senator James P. Kem of Missouri, and Governor Robert F. Bradford of Massachusetts swung most of their delegates behind Dewey.

In the meantime, Stassen and Taft failed in their efforts to check the swing toward Dewey. They worked together and received help from people in the Warren and Vandenberg camps. Former Republican hopeful Alfred M. Landon of Kansas had been trying for weeks to form a Stassen–Taft coalition, with Taft at the head of the ticket and Stassen as the second man. Taft had balked at this, accepted Landon's alternative suggestion that Stassen should become secretary of defense or attorney general, but offended the Minnesotan by delaying discussion of the proposal. At the convention, none of the anti-Dewey candidates would withdraw. They could agree only to stand firm.

Thus, Dewey moved on to victory. He fell short by more than 100 votes on the first ballot, as Taft, Stassen, Vandenberg, and Warren demonstrated substantial strength. Taft gained on the second ballot, but Dewey gained even more, and Stassen slipped back. Stassen then ignored Taft's suggestion that he withdraw. Not until Taft and then Warren conceded defeat did Stassen do so. With the opposition out of the way, the convention nominated Dewey unanimously on the third ballot.

Warren, not Halleck, received the second spot on the ticket. Following Dewey's nomination, he met with a small group of party leaders and personal advisers to discuss the candidates. Halleck's isolationism led to his rejection. Warren, on the other hand, had many qualifications that recommended him. He disagreed with Halleck on foreign policy and was more liberal on domestic questions. He had administrative experience, came from a large state, and was apparently a more attractive person. And he balanced Dewey geographically. Assured that he would play an important role in the Dewey administration and that all elements of the party wanted him, Warren agreed to run. He was nominated quickly and without opposition.

Despite the obvious divisions within the party, great optimism now gripped the GOP, and the polls endorsed the Republican predictions of victory. The *Boston Globe* poll suggested that even in Massachusetts, which had supported the Democratic presidential candidate in the five preceding elections, Dewey would win by a large margin, and the New York *Herald Tribune* poll made a similar prediction. Gallup indicated that the big cities, which had provided strong support for Democrats since the late 1920s, favored Dewey.

A pessimistic band of Democrats followed the Republicans into Philadelphia on July 12. Some of the most prominent men in the party expected to lose with Truman at the head of the ticket and wished that he would step aside, and some labor leaders shared this wish.

The efforts to substitute Eisenhower for Truman continued up to the eve of the convention, when the general made it unmistakably clear that he would not run. Then Leon Henderson, the chairman of the ADA, tried to switch the Eisenhower support to Supreme Court Justice Douglas, but his liberalism made him unacceptable to many who had favored Eisenhower. Senator Claude Pepper announced his candidacy, saying he was the only man available who would carry on the tradition of FDR, but when the ADA and the CIO withheld support, Pepper took himself out of the race. Jacob Arvey of Chicago and William O'Dwyer of New York City issued a joint statement endorsing Truman. Any chances of dumping him had been lost, and those chances had been slim, for, as president, he had a strong hold on the party machinery. It contained many party workers who were now present as delegates and were either loyal to him or unwilling to inflict the damage on the party that would be involved in his repudiation.

Truman's hold on the convention was not total, however. He failed to get the civil rights plank that he advocated, failed to prevent a Southern bolt, failed to receive a unanimous nomination, and failed to obtain his first choice for the vice presidency.

For the most part, the party platform conformed to White House desires. The White House staff, aided by the Research Division, made major contributions to the platform and battled within the Truman camp for a platform that would appeal to liberals and internationalists. On such issues as repeal of Taft–Hartley, support for the international control of atomic energy, Marshall Plan appropriations, reciprocal trade, and aid for Israel, the final product differed significantly from the Republican platform. "The very fact that the Truman forces have fought through to adoption by a divided Resolution Committee a platform which is basically, and in most details explicitly, a rededication to the New Deal, present and future, is evidence," Roscoe Drummond stated, "that Mr. Truman himself is ready to venture losing some traditional Democratic support in order to build for the future."

On civil rights, however, Truman chose the McGrath strategy. The administration's proposal essentially repeated the party's 1944 plank, one that the Southerners had found at least tolerable. It ignored the specific proposals that Truman had made in February and contained the same ambiguous emphasis on limits that had been present in McGrath's statements since the civil rights message. ("We again call upon the Congress to exert its full authority to the limit of its constitutional power to assure and protect these rights.") The proposal involved, in other words, an effort to conciliate the South and contain the Southern revolt as well as a promise to try to obtain for minority groups "the right to live, the right to work, the right to vote, the full and equal protection of the laws, on a basis of equality with all citizens as guaranteed by the Constitution."

The ADA contingent, led by Andrew J. Biemiller of Wisconsin and Hubert H. Humphrey of Minnesota, disliked the proposal and battled successfully to strengthen the plank. Failing with the platform committee, which was dominated by Truman supporters, the liberals decided to take the issue to the convention floor. Biemiller and Joseph L. Rauh proposed the deletion of the ambiguous sentence about what Congress should do and the substitution of one calling on the lawmakers "to support our President" in guaranteeing a set of clearly defined civil rights. A candidate for the Senate, Humphrey hesitated to employ his oratorical powers in a fight that might hurt him and the party but agreed to do so after the insertion of a sentence commending Truman "for his courageous stand on the issue of Civil Rights," a sentence that might help Humphrey retain links with the administration and party leaders. Southerners countered with a states' rights substitute that not only rejected recent developments on civil rights but repudiated the party's 1944 stand as well. This substitute, however, was defeated decisively. With Humphrey supplying a stirring speech and a number of big city bosses rallying behind the liberals, the convention endorsed the ADA proposal, an impressive accomplishment for a group that had suffered a disastrous defeat in its efforts to dump the president. The organization's representatives had made the president's stand of February 2 the official position of the party and had done so despite his desires, for his representatives at the convention had opposed the liberal substitute.

While the change encouraged liberals, it also produced the Southern bolt the administration had feared. Following the acceptance of the civil rights plank, 35 delegates from Mississippi and Alabama withdrew from the convention. Earlier, as part of the effort to keep the South in the party, administration supporters in the convention had worked successfully against an effort to unseat these Mississippians. George L. Vaughn, a black delegate from Missouri, backed by a sizable minority of delegates, all from the North, had argued that the delegation should not be seated because it had come instructed to bolt under certain circumstances.

Most Southerners remained in the convention, but almost all of them now voted against Truman's nomination. They could not veto it. In fact, the Truman forces had worked, again successfully, against Southern efforts to restore the old Democratic rule requiring a two-thirds vote for nomination. But when the role was called, only 13 Southern votes, all of them from North Carolina, were cast for Truman. All of the other Southerners voted for Senator Richard Russell of Georgia, an advocate of settling the civil rights issue within the party. Russell got 263 votes while Truman received 947, but the Southern mood checked any move to make the nomination unanimous.

Although Truman now had the nomination, he could not be fully satisfied with the proceedings. He had not wanted to go as far as the platform went on civil rights, and he would certainly have welcomed a unanimous endorsement. But as a politician with a quarter century of experience, he understood and sympathized with the behavior of Southerners who voted against both his civil rights proposal and his nomination. "I would have done the same thing myself if I were in their place and came from their states," he explained to two members of his administration. And on the convention floor, he praised the members of his party who disagreed "violently" with him on civil rights. Contrasting them with the Republicans, he said the Southern Democrats opposed him "openly" and the people could "tell where they stand."

Truman also failed to get the man he wanted for the vice presidency. His choice was Justice Douglas, a former member of the Roosevelt administration and a member of the liberal bloc on the U.S. Supreme Court who might strengthen the ticket with liberals. But Douglas refused, forcing the president to seek an alternative.

The convention actually supplied the alternative, Senate Minority Leader Alben W. Barkley of Kentucky. Perhaps it would be more accurate to say that Barkley himself, with substantial help from Leslie Biffle, the Democratic secretary in the Senate and the convention's sergeant-at-arms, created the vice-presidential candidate. Barkley did so with a rousing keynote speech that praised the Democratic record and generated a tremendous amount of convention support for him. Thus denied the chance to run with Douglas, Truman turned to the popular senator, and the convention nominated him by acclamation.

In some respects, Barkley was a good choice. He and Truman were close to one another, perhaps too close. Both represented the older generation in the party, the party's ideological center, and the border states. Barkley had provided consistent support for the president in the Senate and could in the future help him work with Congress. An experienced and effective campaigner, the senator could strengthen the campaign in the border states and the South and could help Democratic congressional candidates. Nevertheless, Truman was not enthusiastic about Barkley as the second man on the ticket. Apparently, Truman's dominant consideration in the quest for a running mate was cultivation of the Democratic left. Perhaps, also, he was troubled by the fact that Barkley symbolized the failures at the convention.

Despite his difficulties, Truman now had the nomination and fully intended to make something of it. The first step was to come to the convention and deliver an inspiring acceptance speech. He gave the kind of fighting, optimistic speech that his advisers recommended and drafted, the type he had delivered on his Western

President Harry S. Truman delivers his acceptance speech following his nomination for a full term at the Democratic National Convention in Philadelphia, July 15, 1948. *(Library of Congress)*

trip a month before. "Victory has become a habit of our party . . . it will be elected a fifth time next November," he predicted. "The reason is that the people know that the Democratic Party is the people's party and the Republican Party is the party of special interest."

The most dramatic feature of the speech was its call for a special session of Congress. This matter had been considered for more than a month, and the performance of the Republican convention seems to have decided the issue for the administration. Prior to that convention, William Batt of the Research Division had advised against such a session even though he recognized certain advantages in the suggestion, including the possibility of embarrassing the Republicans, who would "probably have written a fairly liberal platform by then." One of his fears, however, was that the call would commit Truman to a fight with Congress as his principal issue, while the Republicans might nominate someone unconnected with Congress, such as Dewey, who would repudiate it and leave the president "beating a dead horse." But when the Republicans drafted a rather liberal platform and nominated Dewey, and when he failed to repudiate Congress, the Research Division began to battle for the special ses-

sion, seeing it now as a way to dramatize the conflict between the record of Congress and the performance of the convention. They encountered opposition, but several people close to the president, including Clifford and Murphy, concluded that the idea was a good one.

The advocates made their case in a memorandum written a few days after the Republican convention. The memo suggested that the election could "only be won by bold and daring steps, calculated to reverse the powerful trend now running against us," and that calling a special session would be the "boldest and most popular step the President could possibly take." It would focus attention on the "rotten record" of the 80th Congress, force Dewey and Warren to defend that record, "keep a steady glare of publicity on the Neanderthal men of the Republican Party," split that party on domestic issues, and "give President Truman a chance to follow through on the fighting start he made on his Western tour." The advisers discounted objections that Congress would pass legislation that would help the Republicans, arguing that the power in the GOP of the "reactionaries" and the "rich interests" would prevent this from happening. And the memorandum dealt at length with the danger that the Republicans might invite a Southern filibuster by introducing strong civil rights legislation. "The election will be won or lost in the Northern, Midwestern and Western states. The South cannot win or lose the election for the Democratic Party," these advisers argued as they had for months: "If the President supports the introduction of moderate legislation, beating the Republicans to the punch, the credit would go to Mr. Truman and the Democratic Party even if a few diehard Southern senators try to start a filibuster."

Although opposed at first, Truman accepted the counsel of boldness, convinced that the party needed a dramatic move. Contrasting the record of the 80th Congress with the Republican platform, he offered that the special session would be a test. Predicting that the Republicans would fail the test, he concluded his speech with an appeal for help in the election. "The country can't afford another Republican Congress," he warned.

The speech produced the enthusiastic reaction from Democrats outside the South that Truman and his advisers had sought. Surveying the immediate reaction, Batt concluded that Truman had "hit the comeback trail" and that the Dewey–Truman standings in the polls would be reversed "within six weeks."

Southerners lacked enthusiasm, however, and some of them assembled in Birmingham on July 17 for a convention or "conference" of their own. The most important men present were the leading Democrats of Mississippi, the conservative faction of the Alabama Democracy, and Governor Thurmond. Men of less importance came from a number of other states. While most of the southern political leaders stayed away, those who came decided without any dissenting voices that Thurmond should run for the presidency with Wright as his running mate.

The convention expressed in extreme form Southern resentment of recent developments in American life and Southern fears, including fear that the system of segregation would be destroyed. Their platform or "declaration of principles" stated that the way to protect the American people "against the onward march of totalitarian government" was to guarantee the rights reserved to the states in the Constitution. The declaration deplored a "long train of abuses and usurpations of power by unfaithful leaders who are alien to the Democratic parties of the states here represented," denounced the civil rights plank of the Democratic platform, affirmed belief in "the segregation of the races," and called for the defeat of Truman and Dewey "and every other candidate for public office who would establish a police state in the United States of America."

Although they had failed to prevent the Democrats from adopting a strong civil rights plank and nominating an advocate of civil rights legislation, the Dixiecrats, as they were called, still hoped to transform the Democratic Party. They hoped to persuade Southern Democratic parties to accept their candidates as the official party nominees or at least to permit Thurmond and Wright to appear on the ballot under the States' Rights designation. Then they would obtain the South's 127 electoral votes, deny either Dewey or Truman a majority, and throw the election into the House. There, with each state having one vote, the South would be in a very strong position, perhaps capable of electing their candidates. The least that could be expected would be much more attention to Southern wishes in the future by the Democrats, eager to avoid a repetition of the projected defeat of 1948. Southern influence in the Democratic Party would be restored, and that influence would be used to reduce the authority of the central government and to maintain the "Southern way of life."

On July 23, politics returned to Philadelphia for the fourth significant convention of the year. It was the first convention of the new party that now formally adopted the name "Progressive." The meeting was large and colorful. More than 3,000 delegates participated; most of them were young people, many of them women, many black; very few were professional politicians. The delegates did very little drinking for a political gathering and an unusually large amount of singing. Banjoes and guitars rather than a band provided the music; folk songs set the tone, and Pete Seeger sang many of them. An open-air rally at Shibe Park highlighted the gathering. The rally was, according to one sympathetic student of the party,

"a well-staged spectacle—designed to entertain as well as convert or further indoctrinate."

The delegates discussed issues as well as sang songs. They did not, however, need to debate candidates. Long before the meeting, they had agreed that Wallace would be nominated for the presidency and that his running mate would be Glen Taylor, a singing cowboy who had been elected to the Senate by the Idaho Democrats in 1944. Wallace and Taylor were nominated by acclamation. The platform, on the other hand, was discussed at great length, although the basic work on it had also been done earlier. The main ideas had been expressed in Wallace's declaration of candidacy and his subsequent campaign speeches. They emphasized "Peace, Freedom, and Abundance" and included understanding between Russia and the United States, the removal from power of the war-producing elite, opposition to the Marshall Plan and to American intervention in Greece, Turkey, and China, the repudiation of universal military training, the repeal of the draft law, the end of the military buildup, the destruction of the stockpile of atomic bombs, the breaking up of monopolies, better housing, lower food prices, and the abolition of segregation. Although Communists played a large role in drafting the platform, the ideas it contained were not exclusively or essentially Communist ideas. Communist enthusiasm was limited to the planks on foreign and military policies, but that was enough to secure endorsement of Wallace by the Communist Party.

Perhaps the most damaging episode at the convention concerned the "Vermont Resolution." It represented an effort by non-Communists to answer the charge of

Henry Wallace (right), Progressive Party presidential candidate, and his running mate, Senator Glen Taylor, wave to the audience at Madison Square Garden in New York City. (*Library of Congress*)

subservience to Russia and was an attempt to get the delegates to avow that, though they were critical of the present foreign policy of the United States, they did not intend "to give blanket endorsement to the foreign policy of any nation." More than Communist influence was involved in the defeat of this resolution. It also reflected the fear on the part of many non-Communists of being guilty of "red-baiting" and of contributing to the worsening of relations between Russia and the United States.

These attitudes influenced Wallace. One of his longtime associates, Rexford Guy Tugwell, once a member of Roosevelt's Brain Trust and now a leader of the non-Communist faction in the Progressive Party, became disturbed about the large and growing influence of the Communists in the party and urged Wallace to repudiate them. The candidate, however, refused to do so even though he recognized that such a step could produce more votes than it would lose.

The convention produced more converts to the belief that the new party was dominated by the Communists. The press insisted that domination and control, not mere influence, were the terms that should be employed to describe what was taking place. The ADA gained a new opportunity to publicize its interpretation of the Wallace movement when James Loeb attended the hearings of the Platform Committee as a spokesman for the group and gained front-page, national coverage for the ADA view. Wallace's inept handling of the issue of the role the Communists were playing convinced many that he was remote and naive in his political outlook.

Already in decline before the convention met, the Wallace movement became even weaker as a consequence of the convention and its impact on the public. While Gallup had reported early in the year that 7 percent of the people were ready to vote for Wallace in a contest with Dewey and Truman, only 6 percent were listed as Wallaceites in June. By the end of the convention, the percentage of Wallace supporters had reached 5 percent and was still dropping.

Apparently, no candidate benefited from the conventions. At least the immediate consequence was loss of support for Dewey and Truman as well as Wallace. While Gallup had found before the conventions that 49 percent were willing to vote for Dewey and 38 percent favored Truman, the percentages dropped to 48 and 37 before August. Uncertainty alone had increased. Seven percent of the people were undecided about their choice for the presidency in June, but the percentage moved to 10 while the parties held their meetings.

Truman faced a difficult task as time for the fall campaigns approached. If the polls were accurate, Dewey needed only to hold the support that he had already acquired and hope that most of the Wallace people

This Progressive Party campaign poster, titled "The Duet, or A Good Man Is Hard to Find," shows Thomas E. Dewey sitting on an upright piano played by Harry Truman. *(Library of Congress)*

resisted the temptation to vote for the "lesser evil." The president had a tougher assignment. In addition to maintaining the loyalty of those who favored him, he had to convert both the uncertain and some of those who at present seemed devoted to his opponents. He was, however, ready for battle. After all, he was the president and had tremendous power at his disposal to promote his campaign. Furthermore, many of those who wavered toward Dewey or Wallace had strong Democratic inclinations and had voted for Roosevelt in the past. They only needed to be persuaded that the Democratic Party remained very important to them and that Truman really deserved the votes of people who had voted for FDR.

On July 26, the day the members of Congress assembled for the special session, Truman employed one of his powers in a very significant way. He issued two executive orders on civil rights, one dealing with the armed forces, the other with civilian employment in the federal government. The administration had decided early in the year to move on these problems by administrative action rather than by legislation. The southern revolt, however, and also opposition from the army, encouraged delay. On the other hand, black leaders demanded action. A. Philip Randolph, for one, threatened to advise young blacks not to register for the draft if the army remained a segregated institution. For its part, the Republican platform expressed opposition to "the idea of racial segregation in the armed services of the United States." Finally, the Democratic civil rights plank, which included promises of "equal opportunity of employment" and "equal treatment in the service and defense of our Nation," increased the pressure. One of Truman's liberal advisers, Oscar Ewing, the director of the Federal Security Agency, advised the president to do everything he could now to carry out that plank, warning that otherwise he would lose the black vote. Other liberals offered similar advice. "In the world battle of ideas, the weaknesses in our own way of life can no longer be afforded," the chairman of the ADA advised. "We urge you to lead the way so that the armed forces of the world's greatest democracy may become in truth the world's most democratic armed forces." Truman accepted the advice; Clifford, Ewing, and Philleo Nash, a member of the White House staff, drafted the orders; and when confusion arose as to the purpose of the one on the armed forces, Truman stated in a press conference on July 29 that it was intended to end segregation. After McGrath met with Randolph to provide further assurances, the latter brought his civil disobedience campaign to a close. As strategy, the president's action offered a significant contrast with congressional inaction during the special session of late July and early August. He and his advisers recognized that they had placed Dewey in a very difficult situation. The spotlight had been shifted from him to a battle between the president and the Congress.

If Dewey attempted to intervene, the congressional Republicans would resent it; the public, however, would be unhappy if he did not call upon Congress to act. Truman, on the other hand, was now in a position to take credit for any accomplishments and place the blame on the Republicans in Congress for any failures, just as his advisers had anticipated. To accomplish his purposes, the president made a long list of recommendations with the chief emphasis on anti-inflation and housing proposals and with aid to education, increases in the minimum wage and in social security benefits, and civil rights legislation also included. Foreign policy items embraced a loan to the United Nations to build its permanent home in New York City. Special efforts were made to develop close cooperation among the White House, Democrats in Congress, the Democratic National Committee, and interested pressure groups; press and public opinion were studied with care. Republican members of Congress pro-

tested against the call for a special session, participated reluctantly, and, following Taft's lead, rejected advice from the Dewey camp to pass two or three measures that Truman wanted and the Republican platform favored. (Dewey remained aloof on most issues, preferring to wait until he had the powers of the presidency in his hands.) Many Democrats, most of them from the South, shared the unhappiness, and Congress devoted little or no attention to the president's recommendations. Consumer and bank credit controls were enacted; an "emasculated housing bill" was passed instead of the administration proposal; and the loan was made to the United Nations. That was all.

Congress had provided Truman inadvertently with the help that he sought for the campaign that lay ahead. He had suffered but one blow. Republican investigators made substantial progress with the "Communist-in-government" issue during the special session. The chairman of the Democratic state committee in New York was "certain that the President had helped himself tremendously with the special session of Congress" but feared that the "Communist smear" was hurting the party, since the public was being "influenced to think that this administration is covering them up." In the fall campaign, the administration would be forced to deal with this even as it attempted to take advantage of the opportunities that Congress had supplied.

The big decisions about the campaign had already been made. All that remained was to reconfirm and implement them. Truman discussed politics during August with many people, including three former chairmen of the Democratic National Committee—Edward J. Flynn, Frank Walker, and Robert Hannegan—and with Senator Barkley. He also continued to draw heavily upon McGrath and his aides. But the liberals on the White House staff, headed by Clifford and aided by Batt's Research Division, played the leading advisory role.

These top advisers continued to press for a militantly liberal campaign. They placed heavy emphasis on the millions of "independent" voters who had supported the Democrats in the days of Roosevelt, arguing that they could again be persuaded "by driving home to them the failures of the 80th Congress, by linking Thomas E. Dewey closely to the leadership of that Congress, and by presenting the President as a crusader rallying the people to save the tremendous social gains made under the New Deal and carried forward by his administration in a difficult postwar period over the opposition of a reactionary Congress." They also advised Truman to devote most of his time and closely identify himself with "three key groups," the workers, the veterans, and the blacks, contending that they could "swing the election" and were "already predominantly Democratic in their inclinations." This is not to say that the liberals advised neglect of foreign policy. They suggested instead that efforts should be made to emphasize that the president's policy led to peace and that any changes might lead to war. They urged him to speak at meetings sponsored by labor organizations and liberal groups, appear on platforms with their leaders, spend most of his time in "the 17 states which went to one major party or the other by very narrow margins in 1944," and "make his major speeches in the 23 largest city-county areas." These metropolitan areas, the liberals reminded the president, "gave Roosevelt his overwhelming majorities and in most instances were decisive in swinging the electoral votes of their states." To hit these crucial states and cities, the president should make three long tours—one through the Middle West, one through the Far West, and one through the East.

Although the liberals still paid little attention to the Southern vote, they did not advise complete neglect of it. "The Negro votes in the crucial states will more than cancel out any votes he may lose in the South," these advisers suggested. But they also advised "a short side trip into the South" with a speech in Birmingham or Atlanta "on the need for the economic assistance for the South in the TVA pattern," a reminder of the South's "great gains, under the New Deal," and assurance that the welfare of the region was one of Truman's "primary concerns." In other words, Clifford and his associates hoped that the South's interest in economic liberalism, in addition to its attachment to the Democratic Party, would offset its hostility to racial liberalism. The liberal strategy dominated Truman's campaign even though the earlier tests of it had produced the Southern revolt and had not destroyed the Wallace threat. Obviously, no other group had been able to suggest a strategy that made greater sense to Truman. Actually, of course, the civil rights plank prevented him from switching to an emphasis on the cultivation of the South, even if he had desired to do so. And the idea of a strenuous swing around the country had obvious appeal to him, especially now that he had new confidence in his effectiveness as a campaigner.

From Labor Day to Election Day, Truman stumped the country. He began in Michigan, crossed the continent from Pennsylvania to California, and returned to Washington via Texas and Oklahoma, all of this in September. During October, he concentrated on the populous Middle West and East, although he also made a quick trip into the South, stopping only at Miami and Raleigh. He covered more than 20,000 miles and gave more than 250 speeches, most of them informal and many of them delivered from the rear platform of his train. It was the longest and hardest campaign of his career, but, despite his 64 years, he displayed the strength and energy the ordeal demanded.

Truman's liberal advisers dominated his speech-writing team. The Research Division functioned to the end of the campaign and was enlarged to seven members with the addition of another representative of the ADA, David D. Lloyd, a liberal who had not participated in the efforts to dump Truman. They worked in Washington and supplied material to the White House staff, including drafts of both "whistle-stop" and major speeches. The men in the White House who had the major responsibility for the speeches placed a high value on the division's work and drew heavily on it. Clifford was the chief in this operation; Murphy was his top lieutenant; and several men were added to the staff to enable it to carry the heavy burden. Among the additions was Jonathan Daniels, a Southern liberal and North Carolina newspaperman and politician who had voted for Truman at the convention, regarding him as "the only rallying ground for a really national Democratic Party," and who was convinced that Truman had much support in the South and needed to demonstrate that by speaking there. These staff men divided their time between Washington and the campaign train and received help from others, including departments in the executive branch, two White House press secretaries—Charles Ross and Matt Connelly—and the president himself, when his busy schedule permitted.

The speeches had a significant conservative dimension: they sought to preserve the New Deal as well as maintain Democratic control of the national government. Employing hard-hitting and frequently folksy and entertaining language, referring to particular features of a community and to the political leaders of the area, and emphasizing issues of especially strong local interest, the president focused attention on the 80th Congress rather than Dewey and on domestic issues, such as housing, high prices, resource development, social security, health insurance, and Taft–Hartley. His speeches pictured politics as a struggle between the "people," represented by the Democrats, and the "special interests," represented by the Republicans, while at the same time viewing the people as composed of groups with special orientation. The president identified himself and his party with Roosevelt's New Deal, depicted the Republicans as a threat to it, and interpreted the New Deal as beneficial to the interests of his listeners.

One of the authors of the Taft–Hartley Act strengthened Truman's argument that the Republicans represented a threat to the New Deal. In a book that appeared during the campaign, Representative Fred Hartley of New Jersey referred to the "political difficulties of eliminating the New Deal social legislation" and acknowledged that it could not "be repealed at a single stroke." McGrath regarded this as an especially clear "admission" that the "real intention of the Republican Party" was to "do away with all New Deal social legislation." Truman referred to the book several times, warning that the Republicans were "really going to do something to you if they get a chance." "The Taft–Hartley Act is not enough," he warned the Amalgamated Clothing Workers. "The NAM [National Association of Manufacturers] is getting ready to fire both barrels at you this year." Although Truman underscored Congress, he did not ignore Dewey. He attacked and ridiculed the challenger's emphasis on unity, interpreting Republican unity as, for example, "unity in giving tax relief to the rich at the expense of the poor," insisting that "some things are worth fighting for," and listing several worthy foes—"isolationists and reactionaries, the profiteers and the privileged class." He also attacked Dewey's neglect of issues, maintaining that the American people wanted "to hear more than platitudes," and that as long as Dewey was afraid to tell where he stood, he would "lose more votes than he gains."

The campaign paid somewhat greater attention to farmers than had been planned. The liberal advisers, while not overlooking this group, had focused on the cities. But after the campaign got under way, an issue that could be exploited was discovered. It was the failure of Congress to provide grain storage bins. Linking this with

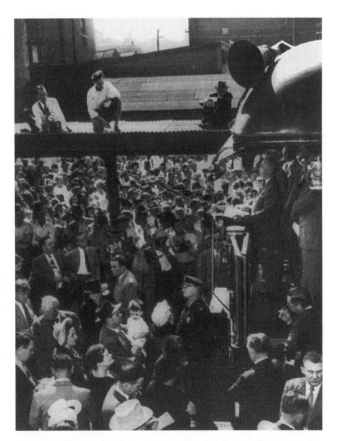

President Truman addresses a crowd from the back of a train on his whistle-stop campaign, September 19, 1948. *(Library of Congress)*

Stassen's contention that the Republicans favored lower farm prices, Truman charged that his opponents wanted to sabotage the price support program, and, with farm prices dropping and farmers suffering from a shortage of bins, he presented the Republicans as a threat to the farm prosperity that the Democrats had produced.

Truman followed the liberals' advice on the South, visiting there only briefly and stressing sectional economics. Offering suggestions for the major speech in Texas, Batt called attention to the importance for the South of regional development programs, reciprocal trade, and agricultural programs, such as rural electrification. Representative Sam Rayburn, who had invited Truman to Bonham, Texas, also felt that Truman should stress these issues. Thurmond wired the president to suggest that he should discuss civil rights in the Lone Star State. But speaking in Bonham on September 27, Truman instead emphasized rural electrification, reciprocal trade, and other efforts to create markets for southern agriculture. And throughout Texas, Truman ignored civil rights and talked chiefly about economic questions such as reclamation, public power, high prices, agricultural prosperity, and flood control. In his other Southern speeches, those in Miami and Raleigh, he emphasized foreign policy and the economic benefits the South had received from the Democrats and warned against helping the Republicans by voting for the third party. In the South, he maintained, Republicanism meant "rule by the carpetbaggers" and "rule by the moneybaggers" or "a rule that treats the South and the West as colonies to be exploited commercially and held down politically."

In Raleigh, Truman also associated himself with three great Southerners—Andrew Jackson, James K. Polk, and Andrew Johnson. Speaking of Jackson and the Nullification Controversy to draw an obvious parallel with his own divided feelings as one who had Southern roots but an obligation to the civil rights of blacks as well, Truman referred to "the pain it cost him [Jackson] to stand against the people so closely allied to him," but insisted "it was his duty, and he did it." The president again called on Jackson's example in his attempt to restore the southern bolters to a better historic perspective. In an obvious reference to the Dixiecrats, Truman stated that Jackson "knew that the way to correct injustice in a democracy is by reason and debate, never by walking out in a huff." The Southerner Daniels was the top adviser on these Southern speeches.

Truman did not pay as much attention to civil rights as his liberal advisers advocated. In fact, he devoted only one speech to it, but that was a major one in Harlem. His aides had recommended a speech there, assuring him that it "would have a powerful effect on Negro voters throughout the United States." He was especially pleased with this part of his campaign. The crowds were large and enthusiastic; the rally was sponsored by the "Truman Crusaders," a black group in Greater New York working for his election, and by the Interdenominational Ministers Alliance, and he received the Roosevelt Memorial Brotherhood Medal of the Colored Presbyterian Churches. In a speech that had been drafted with great care by Philleo Nash, the president discussed the Civil Rights Committee and his efforts to implement its recommendations and promised to keep moving toward the goal of equal rights and equal opportunities "with every ounce of strength and determination that I have."

Declining fears of Wallace may have explained the limited attention devoted to civil rights. As late as August, the liberals had urged Truman to "discuss Civil Rights in California to cut into the Wallace strength," but once again Truman did not discuss the subject in that state.

Fears of Wallace had not altogether evaporated, however, and Truman faced up to them in California. His advisers urged him to make two arguments against a vote for the Progressive Party. He should stress the role of the Communists and point out that a vote for Wallace would hurt the party of effective liberalism—the Democratic Party—and "play into the hands of the Republican forces of reaction." In a major speech in Los Angeles on September 23, Truman hit both themes and concluded, "This is the hour for the liberal forces of America to unite. We have hopes to fulfill and goals to attain. Together we can rout the forces of reaction once again."

Concern about Wallace also affected Truman's handling of the foreign policy issue during the campaign. Although it did not receive as much attention as domestic policy, it was not ignored, and efforts were made to portray the Republican Party as the party of high tariffs and isolationism and the Democrats as the party of international cooperation and peace. While Truman campaigned, he worried about the possibility that the Berlin crisis would lead to war and about the charge, made most frequently by Wallace, that he was not seriously working for peace. Thus, he accepted a suggestion from his advisers that he should send Chief Justice Fred Vinson to Russia in October for talks with Stalin. Secretary of State Marshall, however, talked Truman out of this. In such a difficult campaign, foreign policy questions could prove highly volatile. With this in mind, the State Department, even as it offered some help, urged right along that such questions be handled with utmost caution. The wisdom of this advice was borne out when the press learned of the aborted Vinson plan and threw the glare of publicity upon it. The Republicans were quick to exploit the opening. Their criticism became so vociferous that it behooved Truman to issue a public explanation. But this was not enough. His advisers, deeply troubled about the

affair, pressed him to discuss it in a campaign speech and worked out a response to the criticism. Addressing the American Legion convention in Miami on October 18, Truman maintained that his purpose had been "to ask Premier Stalin's cooperation in dispelling the present poisonous atmosphere of distrust which now surrounds the negotiations between the Western Powers and the Soviet Union." He further insisted that he was determined "to utilize every opportunity to work for peace." And behind the scenes, he and his staff continued to seek some dramatic and effective way of making progress on the Berlin crisis before the end of the campaign.

Israel was another foreign policy question that figured in the campaign. At first, Truman resisted pressure to discuss the issue, but Dewey upset him and his advisers by charging that the president had retreated from the Democratic platform with its promises of additional steps on Israel's behalf. As a consequence, Truman issued a statement on October 24 declaring that he stood "squarely on the provisions covering Israel in the Democratic platform," and then, addressing a Madison Square Garden rally on October 28, sponsored by the Liberal Party, he spoke of his "desire to help build in Palestine a strong, prosperous, free, and independent democratic state" and insisted that he had "never changed" his position. Despite these statements, some Democrats continued to worry that not enough had been said and done to maintain Jewish support. Although he might have strengthened himself with Jewish voters by doing so, he refused to extend *de jure* recognition and to lift the arms embargo before Election Day.

Also in the foreign policy area, Truman dealt with Republican charges that Communists had dangerously infiltrated the Roosevelt–Truman administrations. His advisers believed that the "Communist issue" was a major one and suggested a speech that would have "the widest possible radio audience." They urged him to discuss it in the Middle West, for there the voters were generally concerned over the issue, having been especially upset by the congressional investigations. Oklahoma City was chosen as the site, and the speech was prepared with great care by Stephen Spingarn of the White House staff, who checked it with the attorney general, among others.

Speaking in Oklahoma City to a nationwide radio audience on September 28, Truman presented his party as the effective foe of Communism and charged that the Republicans were "unwittingly the ally of the Communists in this country." In support of his claim about the Democrats, he pointed to the "strong foreign policy" that he had developed and that "checked" the "Communist tide," to the domestic programs of the Roosevelt–Truman administrations that prevented the Communists from making "any progress whatever in this country," and to his loyalty program that made sure "that Communists and other disloyal persons are not employed by the Federal Government." On the other side of the ledger, he listed "considerable opposition from the Republican rank and file . . . in Congress" to his foreign aid program and successful Republican opposition to his efforts "to strengthen democracy at home," and he charged that the Republican investigations were both ineffective and harmful. They lacked, for example, "the democratic safeguards of the loyalty program."

Wallace's presence in the campaign helped Truman tackle this issue. He charged that the Communists were backing Wallace because they wanted a Republican victory, and he explained that they wanted a Republican administration for they thought that its "reactionary policies" would "lead to the confusion and strife on which communism thrives."

This hard-hitting campaign was not a lonely venture. Truman traveled on a crowded train, filled with advisers and aides, members of the Secret Service, and newsmen. His wife and daughter made the trips and were frequently introduced to the crowds. Politicians climbed aboard the presidential special, many of them remaining for short trips, and representatives of the Democratic National Committee and organized labor also frequently rode the train. Politicians now seemed eager rather than reluctant to be associated with the president and to have him refer to them in his speeches. This was not difficult to explain, for large and enthusiastic crowds greeted the train at the stops, lined the streets when Truman traveled by car, and filled the halls and ballparks in which he made his major speeches.

Once again, Truman did not battle alone; he had much help. The assistance provided by the White House staff and the Research Division was especially important, but aid also came from others. Although most cabinet officers remained at their desks, three—Attorney General Tom C. Clark, Secretary of Agriculture Charles F. Brannan, and Secretary of Labor Maurice J. Tobin—campaigned with vigor. Clark hit the Communist issue. He pointed to the loyalty program and to the Justice Department's prosecution of the leaders of the Communist Party for violation of the Smith Act and argued that the administration had a very effective internal security program. He also charged that the 80th Congress had frustrated his efforts to secure additional and needed internal security laws. Brannan, who had been promoted to the secretaryship in the spring, in part because of his ties with the liberal National Farmers Union, dealt with agriculture. He interpreted Stassen's charge that the administration had deliberately attempted to keep food prices high as an attack on the price support program and moved on to charge that the Republicans had deliberately crippled that program

by passing a provision restricting the grain storage activities. The president admired his officials' "vigorous and effective" campaigning. Tobin, who was also new to his job, delivered close to 150 speeches in more than 20 states and focused his attack on the Taft–Hartley Law.

Another member of the administration, Undersecretary of the Interior Oscar Chapman, also made major contributions. Devoting full time to the campaign, he traveled several days ahead of the train, contacting politicians and civic and labor leaders, making detailed arrangements for the President's visits, and otherwise helping to make them successful. Some who worked with him believed he deserved promotion to the top spot in the Department of the Interior for his efforts.

The Democratic National Committee and state and local Democratic organizations also worked for Truman's victory. The National Committee made many of the arrangements for Truman's trips and enlarged its publicity and registration drives, making special efforts with particular groups, such as blacks and the foreign-born, seeking to combat criticism as well as to take advantage of the opportunities provided by administration—and also Republican—policies and trying to offset Republican advantages in the press. Louis Johnson, a wealthy lawyer and active Democrat, accepted the chairmanship of the committee's Finance Division and worked strenuously and quite successfully on the party's serious financial problems. Out in the cities and states, many Democratic leaders and organizations performed a variety of chores—recruiting enthusiastic crowds for the president's visits, providing transportation and entertainment for the rallies, distributing buttons and literature, making speeches, offering advice on the president's speeches, introducing Truman, arranging visits for him with various groups, etc.

Many Democrats supplemented Truman's meager efforts in the South. The National Committee, convinced that Truman must carry the South to win, worked at this; Representative Rayburn and Senator Barkley campaigned strenuously there, and Brannan and other administration officials also spoke in the South. Prominent Southerners—such as Senators George of Georgia and Pepper of Florida, Governor Folsom of Alabama, and Estes Kefauver of Tennessee—openly supported Truman, while others worked more quietly behind the scenes. Loyal Democrats, especially representatives of the liberal wing of the party, worked to prevent further bolts, to obtain a place for Truman on the ballot, as the Democratic candidate if possible or as an independent if necessary, and to keep their states in the Democratic column at a time when some Southern conservatives, while remaining in the party, refused to work for Truman or to punish those who endorsed his foes. The loyal Democrats appealed to party loyalty. "My fellow Southerners, for a century and a half the Democratic Party has sheltered you," Senator Pepper reminded a Montgomery audience. In some states, most notably North Carolina, Virginia, and Tennessee, fear of a rather serious Republican threat helped to hold Democrats in their party. In Mississippi, where leaders had already bolted, Truman Democrats formed a new organization that received recognition and help from the National Committee.

Like Truman, these campaigners in the South stressed economics. They emphasized the economic benefits the South had received from Democratic administrations and the threat to the Southern economy that the Republicans represented. They also urged Southerners to think in broad national terms, such as the dangers of a depression, and not to be governed by narrow concerns, such as the desire of a state to control oil in the tidelands. While Southerners as close to the President as Rayburn opposed him on civil rights, they urged other Southerners to wage their battles on this issue within their party. Southern defenders of the president's civil rights proposals, such as Pepper, were in short supply. For most Southern liberals, liberalism meant government action only in the economic realm.

Others helped Truman get and hold labor and liberal votes. Almost all labor leaders formally or informally endorsed him, although John L. Lewis was a major exception. Many had reservations about Truman as president and strong doubts that he could win, but they liked his record, beginning with the Taft–Hartley veto, and his platform. The unions gave greater attention to congressional elections, hoping that either Dewey or Truman would face a strong prolabor bloc in Congress that would repeal the new labor law. But labor's efforts on behalf of other Democratic candidates, which the White House encouraged, as well as more direct efforts to build support for Truman, such as Whitney's, helped him, for they publicized the Democratic stand on issues, including Truman's record on civil rights, and encouraged normally Democratic workers to register and vote. In many places, unions performed functions that had been performed by Democratic organizations in their stronger days, and at times labor organizations and party organizations combined their efforts. Dewey, on the other hand, obtained almost no help and received much criticism from organized labor.

The ADA joined in to rally liberals behind the president. Many of them remained critical of him, had mixed feelings about his campaign, expected that he would lose, and even made preparations for new liberal efforts after Dewey's election. But ADA formally endorsed Truman and worked actively for him as well as other Democratic candidates, focusing on the Wallace challenge, stressing the Communist role in the new party

Published on the cover of a collection of *Washington Star* cartoons, this illustration shows a teddy bear taking a photograph of Harry Truman, Thomas Dewey, Harold Stassen, and Henry Wallace. *(Library of Congress)*

and the contribution that a vote for it would make to the hopes of reactionaries, blunting Republican charges of Democratic radicalism, and cultivating liberals who regarded Truman as an unworthy heir. The National Independent Committee for Truman and Barkley, patterned after earlier efforts to recruit liberal support for Roosevelt, supplemented the ADA's efforts, and one of the most prominent recruits was Roosevelt's secretary of the interior, Harold Ickes. Troubled by Wallace's efforts to "wrap" himself "in the glory of Franklin Roosevelt," Ickes circulated an ADA statement that he hoped would be signed by "all of the prominent men and women associated with the Roosevelt Administration" and that would "disabuse many who may still regard Wallace as a spokesman for the Roosevelt tradition." The statement argued that the Progressive Party represented a "repudiation of the methods and purposes of Franklin D. Roosevelt" and "the most serious attempt in the history of our nation by a totalitarian group to capture and destroy American liberalism." It pictured Roosevelt and Wallace as far apart in their attitudes toward the Soviet Union and collaboration with Communists, presented Truman and the Democratic platform as "a liberal alternative to the fake progressivism of the Progressive Party," and urged all followers of Roosevelt to oppose Wallace and vote for Truman.

While Truman and his allies exerted these massive efforts, Dewey waged a relatively dull campaign that differed greatly from Truman's. After the Republican convention, he and his advisers decided to discard the aggressive methods he had employed in 1944 and in this year's battle for the nomination to pitch the campaign on a high level. Several considerations influenced this decision. One was the belief that he had made a mistake in 1944. Another was the divided character of his party. He hoped that lofty generalizations would alienate neither the right nor the left wing. The high-level approach would conceal the divisions within the party and his differences with many members of it, uniting all behind him. Also involved was a rather low estimate of the impact of campaigns, a tendency to believe that voters had reached decisions by summer. Along this line, perhaps nothing was more important than Dewey's confidence that he would win. With victory assured, he felt that he did not need to wage a militant campaign in the Truman manner. Furthermore, if he radiated confidence, voters would have confidence in him; and if he spoke like a statesman, preached the need for national unity, reminded the people of the blessings that were theirs as Americans, he could easily make the transition from the campaign to the presidency and would not worsen the international situation he would face in January. So his reasoning went. When, late in the campaign, he became troubled by Truman's slashing attacks and feared they might be effective, his advisers talked him out of changing his approach, arguing that his campaign was going well, that no one believed the president anyway.

So, Dewey did not feel compelled to work as hard as Truman. He did not start in as early; instead he called on Stassen to campaign on Labor Day, an assignment he handled rather ineffectively; and after Dewey finally hit the campaign trail, he began his days later than Truman did and brought them to a close earlier. He failed to cover nearly as many miles, and, to an even greater degree than Truman, he confined his attention to the East, the Middle West, and the Far West. He made fewer speeches; and a higher percentage of those he made were the formal kind that imposed fewer demands on his memory, his sense of humor, and his ability to identify with the public.

Although he was fearful that the Democrats would gain control of the Senate (he devoted an unusually large amount of time to the congressional races), Dewey did not tackle Truman's criticism of the 80th Congress. Perhaps he agreed with some of Truman's charges, for Dewey's point of view was rather close to the president's on many issues, both domestic and foreign. He did, in fact, endorse much of Truman's program. In retrospect, per-

haps he should have made a greater effort to persuade the farmers that his party would not destroy the New Deal farm program. He surely recognized that the Republican record created some difficulties for him in the big cities and that a militant defense of it would not guarantee victory. On the other hand, however, he could not join in the criticism, for that could only help the Democrats and weaken his chances of getting a Congress that would work with him. So he tended to remain silent, or to praise Congress mildly and infrequently. And this meant that he ignored weaknesses in the Democratic record, such as Democratic failure to pass Truman's domestic proposals when the Democrats controlled Congress, or did not attack them vigorously. It also meant that he seldom praised Republican accomplishments, such as crucial Republican support for the European Recovery Program. The question was, would praise for Republican support for Truman's foreign policy help Dewey more than Truman? Dewey, in short, suffered from certain Republican weaknesses and Democratic strengths that, despite his confidence, he at least dimly perceived.

Dewey seldom subjected Truman to the type of heated attack that the latter made upon the Republicans. The GOP candidate did suggest that more should be done to help the Nationalist Chinese but did not hit the point very hard. On this issue, Republicans were torn between a belief that China deserved more help, including military aid, and doubts concerning the Chinese situation and fears of deep involvement in China's problems. Dewey also tapped the issue of Communists in government but only infrequently and with restraint. And he did not fully exploit the Vinson episode. Nor did he remind the voters that the man who was calling the Taft–Hartley Act a "slave-labor law" had urged as recently as 1946 that striking railroad workers should be drafted, and that the man who spoke of Wall Street domination of the Republican Party employed many men from Wall Street in his own administration.

Dewey did not depend, of course, on only his own efforts to combat Truman's campaign. He had the help of most of the nation's press: 65 percent of the dailies favored him, while only 15 percent favored Truman.

The Republican chairman of the House Un-American Activities Committee, J. Parnell Thomas of New Jersey, attacked Truman during the campaign. Thomas charged that the administration had failed to keep the people informed about the "dangerous" Communist "infiltration into the Government service," had attempted "to obstruct and thwart" and "to dismiss and discredit" the committee's work, and had ignored the evidence of Communist espionage. Thomas also charged that in Oklahoma City the president "made some ridiculous accusations" against the committee, and the congressman credited it with the actions that had been taken against subversives and proclaimed that he would not be "deterred or intimidated" by Truman's attacks.

Others denounced Truman's foreign policy and his handling of it in the campaign. His administration was blamed for Communist control of Poland, Czechoslovakia, and other countries, and Senator Vandenberg attacked Truman's criticism of the 80th Congress as a "do-nothing" Congress, maintaining instead that it deserved much of the credit for the accomplishments in foreign affairs in 1947–48. In a nationwide address on October 4, Vandenberg discussed his party's record on foreign policy and suggested "that this makes the 80th Congress, in all that related to our foreign affairs, not 'the second worst in history' as we sometimes hear in general attack, but the best."

Vandenberg came to doubt that he had helped the party. The president called him to the White House for a private chat and praised him for his speech and reaffirmed his belief in the importance of the bipartisan foreign policy. "If that isn't a strange reaction to a campaign speech, I never heard one," Vandenberg wrote to his wife. "It almost makes me wonder whether it did the GOP any good." The senator's complaint suggests that Dewey's situation was not as favorable as it seemed.

Governor J. Strom Thurmond of South Carolina, States' Rights presidential candidate, delivers a campaign speech in Austin, Texas, on October 29, 1948. *(Library of Congress)*

Dewey did not receive as much help from the Dixiecrats and the Progressives as had been expected. Thurmond limited his campaign almost exclusively to the South, and there he had to contend with the opposition of most of the press and most of the politicians and to campaign with but little financial support. He and his allies battled fiercely with the Truman Democrats over control of the Democratic Party name and machinery but succeeded in capturing them in only four states: Alabama, Louisiana, Mississippi, and South Carolina. Elsewhere, the movement was clearly a third-party movement that had to contend against the Southerner's allegiance to the party label.

Thurmond waged a strenuous "crusade against centralization." He did not limit his attention to civil rights. In his telegram to the president in Texas, for example, he asked him to discuss his "veto of the act of Congress confirming the title of the states, including Texas, to their submerged coastal lands, including the oil lands of the Texas coast, which belong to the schoolchildren of Texas." But most of the telegram dealt with civil rights and did not support a claim that Thurmond "discussed issues on a rational plane" and made "a dignified and intelligent appeal." The governor professed to see an "amazing parallel between the ideology and administrative provisions of the proposed FEPC bill . . . and Communistic Russia's all races law promulgated by Stalin." He criticized the civil rights plank of the Democratic platform, and Truman's executive orders of July 26 "ending segregation in government jobs and breaking down the segregation pattern in the Armed Forces against the advice and judgement of military leaders who have the responsibility for the morale of the Armed Forces and the safety of the nation," and he condemned the president's "whole so-called 'civil rights' program calling for the end of segregation in the schools and the forced mingling of the races in public facilities." The race question had become the central feature of Thurmond's political life.

While other Dixiecrats ranged beyond civil rights to express hostility to other policies of the Roosevelt–Truman administrations, their heaviest emphasis, too, was upon race relations. Many of the speeches appealed to racial prejudices and racial fears. They stressed fears of racial violence and racial intermingling and distorted Truman's proposals.

Wallace campaigned much more extensively than Thurmond did but could not check the decline in the Progressive Party. His campaign surpassed Truman's in miles covered as he visited every part of the country and spent much more time in the South than Truman did. Unlike orthodox campaigners, the Progressives charged admission to their rallies and took up collections. They continued to provide a Broadway touch and to sing, with Paul Robeson and Pete Seeger lending their voices to the cause.

Wallace devoted a substantial amount of attention to civil rights. Unlike Truman, he did not talk of this only to Northerners but stressed the issue in the South as well. There, he and his partisans refused to obey Jim Crow laws, held numerous unsegregated meetings in a large number of Southern cities, and tested segregation ordinances and practices in other ways. His Southern foray challenged the Dixiecrats, but Wallace's criticism extended to Truman also, for he charged that the president was an insincere champion of civil rights.

Foreign policy remained the focal point of Wallace's campaign. All else seemed to depend on the solution to the problems in this realm. The nation had to free itself from its war-breeding policy before it could solve its domestic problems. And change in that policy depended on destruction of the power of big business and the military.

Although Wallace did stimulate some discussion of foreign policy by other campaigners, he could not make it the dominant issue as he had hoped to do. This failure was typical of his experiences in the fall. The party could point to two successes: it had candidates on the ballot in almost every state and enough money to support their campaigns. But beyond was a long list of problems, including the behavior of the Communists in Berlin. Liberals continued to desert the party, alienated by the Communists, and, as the liberals left, the Communists became more important and the party became more vulnerable to the attack being made by the president, the ADA, and others. The leader of the Socialist Party, Norman Thomas, a militant anti-Stalinist, as well as many liberals and labor leaders, hampered Wallace's efforts to hold his followers and gain new recruits, and Truman's liberal campaign, combined with the liberal aspects of his record and his troubles with the Dixiecrats, produced further major difficulties. Attempting to combat the charge that they were helping reactionaries by splitting the liberal vote, the Progressives withdrew congressional candidates who were running against liberal Democrats, thereby providing fresh evidence of weakness as a party and of the strength of liberalism in the Democratic Party. Organizational problems and the opposition of the nation's press added shades of darkness to the new party's prospects. Furthermore, as Wallace, Taylor, and other campaigners moved about the country, they had to contend with roughnecks eager to use violent means of expressing their hostility.

And almost everywhere that Wallace went, the crowds were smaller and less enthusiastic than they had been earlier.

The polls revealed that Wallace lost ground during the campaign. They also suggested that Truman had been the most effective campaigner. He alone, of the four presidential candidates, gained support during the fall. He narrowed the gap separating him from Dewey as the latter, as well as Wallace, fell back. Nevertheless, the pollsters remained confident that the Republican would win, although in a rather close election. And the pollsters continued to predict a Dewey victory despite the evidence they presented that the Democratic Party remained much more popular than its leading opponent. In other words, according to the polls, the Democrats seemed to have the strongest party and the most effective campaigner, yet the Republicans seemed certain to elect a president.

Placing a higher value on campaigns than the pollsters did, Truman did not accept their prediction, and his advisers were encouraged by their analyses of the political situation and by their evaluation of his campaign to believe that he could win, although few of them were as confident as Truman himself. Outside of the president's camp, few informed observers expected a Truman victory. They were not swayed by the large crowds that Truman drew or the many other signs that brought some cheer to the Democrats.

To the great surprise of almost everyone, Truman won. He received more than 24 million votes or 49.6 percent of the total, while Dewey received fewer than 22 million or 45.1 percent. Wallace and Thurmond trailed far behind, dividing slightly more than 2.3 million votes almost equally. In the Electoral College, Truman's performance was more impressive; Wallace's, more dismal. The Democratic candidate gained 303 electoral votes or

A smiling Harry S. Truman holds up the mistaken edition of the *Chicago Daily Tribune. (Library of Congress)*

57 percent of them, while Dewey's total was 189 and Thurmond obtained all of the 39 others.

How had Truman accomplished his surprising victory? Basically, the answer is that he had taken advantage of the strength of his party, much of which had been developed by Franklin Roosevelt. Two major factors were involved: party strength and rather effective campaigning. Truman had battled so strenuously that many observers gave him all of the credit. While they provided a distorted view, so do those who treat the campaign as insignificant.

The question that has been raised, however, produces distortions if one does not go beyond it. Much of the impact of the question actually rests on the failures of the pollsters to understand the political situation. Had they been more perceptive, then the victory would not have been so surprising, and more attention would have been paid to the size of the victory and less to the simple fact of it. To focus on the victory by itself distorts the picture in favor of Democratic strong points. Equally significant were the weaknesses shown by the president's coalition. These can best be appreciated by assessing the narrow margin of his election, the kind of victory he won.

Those who give Truman exclusive credit ignore the contributions of many people in 1948, including Clark Clifford and other Truman advisers. They also ignore the importance of the strength that the party had developed. Truman's advisers understood that element of the situation, devised a strategy to exploit it, and helped Truman implement the strategy. The election results confirmed the wisdom of their analysis. Of the twenty-eight states that voted for Truman, all but five had supported Roosevelt each time he ran; and of the five, three had voted for Roosevelt three times, and two had supported him twice.

Truman maintained most but not all the strength that the Democratic Party had developed by the 1940s. He returned five states to the Democratic column after they had deserted it in 1940 or 1944, but this accomplishment was more than matched by the loss of eight states that had supported Roosevelt in every election year and of four that had supported him in each of his last three elections. Truman also failed to carry Michigan, although it had supported Roosevelt in every year but 1940. The strategy had worked well enough but not perfectly.

A swing to Truman had taken place during the fall. In September, Dewey had been in the lead, but Truman had caught up by mid-October and moved into the lead in the final weeks. The pollsters missed this swing. They made errors in sampling and interviewing, stopped collecting data too early, and did not know how to predict the voting behavior of the large number who remained undecided in early October and even of those who stated a preference. In the final weeks, Truman lost the support of some, but most of them decided not to vote; but he gained the support of many who either moved away from Dewey and Wallace or reached a decision they had been unable to make earlier. The net result of a large number of shifts favored Truman.

Most of those who moved behind Truman during the campaign were rallied rather than converted to the Democratic cause. They had voted Democratic in the past but had become dissatisfied with Truman, regarding him as an inadequate replacement for FDR, and had lost interest in the kind of issues that characterized the New Deal. Some of them did develop a more favorable view of Truman during the fall, but a belated revival of interest in socioeconomic issues was even more important. The same kind of issues that had helped the Democratic Party become the majority party in the 1930s once again became most important to the people who returned to the Democratic Party. These were, of course, the issues that Truman emphasized.

In the campaign, Truman had successfully identified himself with the New Deal and persuaded a sufficient number of people that he was a sincere fighter for policies and programs that had benefited them. His stand on foreign policy was less important to the people who voted for him. They saw him as a New Dealer, as a friend of the worker, the farmer, the African American, and the "common man," and as the champion of programs that were in their interest and would protect the prosperity that many of them had come to enjoy in recent years. His stand on domestic issues was the most important factor; his personal qualities as they related to those issues were not insignificant.

Much of Truman's strength was in the cities, although they were not so strong for him as they had been for Roosevelt. Truman's plurality in the 12 largest cities fell nearly 750,000 below Roosevelt's 1944 plurality. Also, he failed to carry several highly urban states—Maryland, Delaware, New Jersey, Pennsylvania, New York, Connecticut, and Michigan—that had supported Roosevelt all or most of the time. But Truman did win in the biggest cities. Two highly urban states—Ohio and Wisconsin—returned to the Democratic fold after deserting it in 1944, and 4 other states with cities among the top 12—Massachusetts, Missouri, Illinois, and California—and also densely populated Rhode Island remained Democratic, as they had been in the Roosevelt period. Almost everywhere, Truman defeated Dewey in the densely populated areas; and in them, the late swing to Truman by those who had planned to vote for Dewey or Wallace or who had been undecided was very substantial. In New York City, for example, Dewey drew close to Truman during the summer but then lost by a wide margin (better than 15 percent). Truman gained very late in the campaign chiefly by getting the support of Democrats and independents who had planned to vote for Dewey or Wallace or had been undecided and who were influenced by the president's position on civil rights, Israel, and labor, and by recognition that Wallace finally had no chance. Truman's campaign obviously helped to produce the swing in the nation's largest city.

Most of the urban support for Truman was support from the working classes. Concern about the high cost of living, hostility toward the Taft–Hartley Act, and a belief that the Democrats best served their interests influenced these groups significantly. Many of these people had recently joined a new, blue-collar middle class, and they were grateful to the Democrats for their prosperity and looked to them for the preservation of it. The unskilled among them endorsed Truman by a wide margin; a much higher percentage of the skilled and semiskilled voted, and they supported Truman by an even wider margin. And of these workers, union members were both much more inclined to vote and much stronger supporters of Truman than were nonmembers. Obviously, political action by labor unions had helped him. Furthermore, workers shifted heavily toward Truman late in the campaign, a shift that reflected their traditional political bias as well as the effectiveness of the campaigns. Although support from labor was not enough to produce Truman victories in the industrial states of Michigan, Indiana, Pennsylvania, New York, New Jersey, and Connecticut, it was a major factor in his victories in Rhode Island, Illinois, Ohio, and West Virginia.

Also important in the cities were the votes of Catholics, Jews, and blacks. Although most of them were members of the working classes and influenced by class interests, religious and ethnic considerations also affected their voting patterns. No matter what their class status, they voted more heavily for Truman than for Dewey.

While Catholics had voted for Roosevelt, even more of them supported Truman. Among the factors at work here were his clashes with Communists in Europe and America, his troubles with Henry Wallace, and the work of the Nationalities Division of the Democratic National Committee.

Most Jewish voters also supported Truman. They did not provide so much support for him as they had for Roosevelt in 1944, since their enthusiasm for Hitler's enemy had been unusually strong. Also, some of them believed that Truman's support for the Jews in Palestine had not been sufficiently strong or consistent. But most found his overall record satisfactory. In addition to his recognition of Israel, they liked his support for the United Nations, his program of economic aid for Europe, his social welfare and labor policies, and his proposals and policies on civil rights.

Black voters in the northern and western cities also provided significant support for Truman. His civil rights record, his campaign, and the Dixiecrat revolt contrib-

uted to this. When the revolt took place, blacks, according to a Harlem editor, "felt if they didn't support Truman no other politician would ever defy the Southerners again." Furthermore, the revolt persuaded many of the skeptical that Truman was sincere in his civil rights proposals, and the executive orders provided additional evidence. The Harlem speech also helped, for it was the first speech there by an American president. In every black voting district, Truman ran far ahead of his opponents, and in Illinois, Ohio, and California, where his victory margins were very small, the contributions of black voters were crucial. It is interesting to note that he succeeded with these voters despite the opposition of almost all of the large black newspapers.

Truman's success in the cities reflected the high degree of success of the anti-Wallace efforts. Almost all of the support that Wallace did receive came from urban blacks and Jews who regarded Truman's stand on civil rights and Israel as unsatisfactory. What's more, he did hurt Truman in three urban industrial states—New York, Maryland, and Michigan. But Wallace needed about 10 million votes in order to create the foundations for a permanent party and to demonstrate strong opposition to administration policies, and he received even less than the 4 percent of the total the pollsters had predicted in October.

The efforts to check the Southern revolt were also quite successful. The Dixiecrats did obtain 38 electoral votes in the Deep South—in Louisiana, Mississippi, Alabama, and South Carolina—and one in Tennessee. Those Deep South states had voted for Roosevelt every time. In fact, they had supported Democratic presidential candidates in every election since Reconstruction. But, though the losses were significant, they were not enough to throw the election into the House of Representatives. Furthermore, Thurmond placed third in six Southern states and third in the entire South, getting less than 25 percent of the vote and running behind Dewey as well as Truman. Despite the revolt, the president obtained 50 percent of the Southern popular vote, better than 55 percent in four states— North Carolina, Georgia, Arkansas, and Texas—and all but 39 of the South's 127 electoral votes.

The revolt had been largely confined to a section of a section. Nearly 99 percent of Thurmond's vote came from the South, and his best performance outside of the states that he carried was in Georgia, where he received less than 21 percent of the vote. In Texas and North Carolina, he fell short of 10 percent. The four states that he carried provided better than 55 percent of his votes and were the states—the only ones—in which the Dixiecrats had obtained control of the Democratic machinery and appeared on the ballot as the Democratic Party. In Alabama, Truman was denied any place on the ballot and received no votes. In the other three, his vote ranged from 10 percent in Mississippi, where Thurmond received nearly 90 percent, to 33 percent in Louisiana, where Thurmond fell short of 50 percent.

The area of Dixiecrat control was the part of the South in which the black population was especially large and also incapable of voting in significant numbers. The black population of the states Thurmond carried ranged from better than 45 percent in Mississippi to about 32 percent in Alabama, while in the other Southern states the range extended from below 31 percent in Georgia to approximately 11 percent in Texas. Below the state level, Thurmond usually polled his heaviest vote in the counties with the highest proportion of blacks. Clearly, racial fear was the strongest force working for revolt.

To the people who voted for Thurmond, the national leadership of the Democratic Party now seemed to threaten change in race relations. In 1861, their counties had provided strong support for secession, while in 1928 they had firmly resisted the Republican challenge. Since then, the South's relations with the Democratic Party had changed significantly. But to these people, the Republican Party as yet did not provide an attractive alternative.

Several forces had worked against the Southern revolt. The most obvious was the strength of the Democratic tradition in the South. Where Truman was able to run as the Democratic candidate, he was able to win. Another factor was the relative weakness of racial concerns in areas where the black population was relatively small. There, those concerns were not strong enough to overwhelm forces working to hold voters in the Democratic Party. And there were advantages for the South and for Southerners in their connections with the national administration. They meant economic programs that served Southern interests and helped the South develop, influence in the national government, and federal jobs. Many political leaders were eager to maintain those connections, and the list included even prominent champions of white supremacy like Herman Talmadge of Georgia. Furthermore, many Southerners, even those who disliked some or all of the president's civil rights proposals and believed in segregation, disliked even more the extreme foes of those proposals; and many Southerners distrusted the Dixiecrats, regarding them as dominated by crass motives, such as a desire to gain control of tidelands oil. "Today the Dixiecrats have only succeeded in making themselves look contemptible," Jonathan Daniels wrote shortly after the election. "Their furies in retrospect look comic by the disclosure of their lack of power even in the South. Fortunately, the South of good sense and good will was not captured by them. And it does not wish to be represented by any men of their spirit."

While weaker in the South and East than Roosevelt had been, even in his poorest race in 1944, the president partially compensated for these losses by gains in the Far West and the Middle West. He failed to carry one Western state (Oregon) in which Roosevelt had been strong but regained the support of two others (Colorado and Wyoming) that had deserted Roosevelt after the 1930s. The net gain was 3 electoral votes, and the total was 65 of the West's 71 votes. Most Westerners liked his stand on the development of their region, while particular groups—labor, farmers, and blacks—preferred his positions on issues of special importance to them. Truman's liberalism appealed to the West. Wallace, on the other hand, proved to be much weaker on the West Coast than had been expected.

In the Middle West, Truman lost Michigan, where Roosevelt had been strong, but pulled Iowa, Wisconsin, and Ohio back to the Democratic Party and held onto the support of Illinois, Minnesota, and Missouri. He picked up 101 electoral votes in the region, 26 more than Roosevelt's total in 1944. The outcome was a surprise.

Especially surprising was the large farm vote for Truman throughout the region. Farmers alone did not produce his victory there—city and small-town voters also contributed significantly—but the Democratic pluralities in many of the cities dropped below 1944, and the farm vote was crucial in Wisconsin, Iowa, and Ohio. Had the farmers in those states provided no more support for him than they had given Roosevelt in 1944, Truman would have failed to win his victories there.

Farmers throughout the nation provided substantial support for Truman. For many, 1948 meant a return to their way of behaving in the 1930s. Then they had resented Republican handling of farm policy and looked on Roosevelt's New Deal for agriculture as their salvation. But in 1940, they turned away from FDR for a variety of reasons, including objections to his foreign policy. But now Truman, aided by Brannan, the 80th Congress, a drop in farm prices, and a shortage of storage facilities, had revived old loyalties. Once again, farmers had concluded that the Democratic Party served their economic interests and that those interests should guide their behavior in the polling booths. The Republican Party seemed to threaten the economic gains they had made since 1932.

Dewey had received more electoral votes than he had in his first bid for the presidency. Running against Roosevelt, he had gained only 93. Running against Truman, his total jumped to 189. While falling back in the West and the Middle West, he made substantial gains in the East. He added the 121 votes of New York, Pennsylvania, New Jersey, Maryland, Delaware, Connecticut, and New Hampshire to the 8 of Maine and Vermont. Dewey's popular vote, however, fell short of his 1944 total by more than 36,000. With the voters, he suffered from both personal weaknesses and weaknesses in his party. The upper-income groups, the better educated, the professional and managerial classes, and the older people tended to prefer him to Truman, while white-collar workers, middle-income people, and Protestants divided their votes about equally between the two leading candidates. Dewey had a substantial bloc of loyal Republicans on whom he could depend, and they had a strong tendency to go to the polls. But not even the desire for a change that some voters felt was enough to compensate for the minority status of the Republican Party and its identification with big business in the eyes of many. And Dewey's personality and his campaign certainly failed to close the gap. Although he was regarded as experienced, capable, and intelligent by many, many more found him unappealing. To them, he seemed patronizing, cold, complacent, and smug. And his campaign was regarded as filled with weaknesses, including neglect of the issues. Even many Republicans found him inadequate as an individual and a campaigner. Most important, he had been unable to maintain the support of many of the Democrats and independents who had thought seriously of voting for him, and, by the same token, he had been unable to capture many of the votes of those who were undecided and of those who became disenchanted with Truman or Wallace as time passed. These groups tended to switch to Truman or stay at home.

In the popular vote, however, Dewey had not fallen far behind Truman. It was a narrow-margin election. Roosevelt's margin had reached as high as 24.5 percent, had dropped no lower than 7.5, and had averaged 14.75. Truman's, on the other hand, was about 4.5, the lowest since 1916 when Wilson's was 3 percent.

Truman was less popular than many other Democratic candidates in 1948. In Illinois, to take one example, the party's candidate for the governorship, Adlai E. Stevenson, won by a wide margin, while Truman's was slim indeed. Winning presidential candidates before him had led their congressional tickets, with the margin since 1896 averaging 7.5 percent. Truman, however, ran behind his congressional ticket. This can be explained in part by the appeal of Wallace and Thurmond to some Democrats; but in some places, other candidates in Truman's party, or the active supporters of those candidates—above all, organized labor—carried him to victory. Interest in congressional elections was relatively high, partly because of organized labor's efforts. Truman probably contributed to this by focusing his campaign on Congress. And the popularity of congressional Republicans was low as Dewey ran ahead of his ticket. His party was less helpful than Truman's.

The basic strength of the Democratic resurgence can best be seen in the new alignments in Congress and in the capitals of the various states. Seventy-five Democrats replaced Republicans in the House, and nine Democrats replaced Republicans in the Senate. Thus the 81st Congress would be composed of 263 Democrats and 171 Republicans in the House and 54 Democrats and 42 Republicans in the Senate. In the state houses, the parties moved from an even split to a 29–19 division in favor of the Democrats. It has also been pointed out that 700,000 people who voted for local offices did not bother to vote for the presidency.

The election also revealed that Truman as well as Dewey had weaknesses as a party leader. In addition to being a narrow-margin election, 1948 was also a low-turnout election. Fewer than 49 million people voted. This total was less than 750,000 above 1944, a war year; and it was more than a million below 1940 despite the growth in population from slightly above 130 million in 1940 to more than 150 million in 1950. (In 1952, more than 61 million voters would go to the polls.) Clearly, many people found Truman as well as Dewey uninspiring. He was less successful in drawing Democratically inclined voters to the polls than Dewey was in attracting voters with Republican attachments or leanings. Truman had, of course, a more difficult task, because Republican groups were more inclined to vote than most groups with Democratic ties. Many former Roosevelt supporters in the big cities, including wage-earners, stayed at home and thereby helped Dewey carry Maryland, Pennsylvania, Connecticut, and New Jersey with only slightly larger votes than he had received when he lost them in 1944, and to carry New York and Michigan even though larger totals in those states had failed to carry them for him in 1944. While a critic of Dewey's campaign suggests that he would have won if he had made a better effort, a leading student of American voting behavior points out that most nonvoters preferred the Democrats and concludes that an increase in the total turnout would have favored them "unless some selective stimulus were present that would have induced only Republican non-voters to go to the polls while the far more numerous nonvoting Democrats remained at home." Perhaps a slashing, anti–New Deal campaign would have rallied these Republicans, but it may have helped Truman attract even more Democrats.

Angus Campbell regards the "extraordinarily low turnout" as the "most striking feature" of the election and refers to 1948 as "the prototype of the low-stimulus presidential election." Nothing had "aroused strong public interest in the choice of alternatives" and thus "the turnout was low."

Dewey and Truman had been unable to draw large numbers to the polls, and they had also failed to change the political faith of many voters. Campbell points out that "partisanship of the vote was determined largely by the established party loyalties of the voters." According to the work of his Survey Research Center, 74 percent of the Democratic vote for president came from Democratic Party "identifiers," and 71 percent of Dewey's vote came from Republican identifiers, while only 6 percent of the vote for each candidate came from those who identified with the opposing party.

The election was not a "realigning election." Popular feelings associated with politics were not so strong that the basic partisan commitments of a portion of the electorate changed. The 1930s had been such a period, and Truman benefited and Dewey suffered from the party realignment that had taken place then.

In sum, the election of 1948 was a maintaining election. Truman and his aides had maintained Democratic control of the White House. He had accomplished this despite his weaknesses, and he had not worked alone. Many people had helped him, including some perceptive political analysts on the White House staff. Beyond Truman and his closest advisers, many other people made contributions to his victory: the leaders of the Democratic National Committee, strong campaigners like Brannan and Barkley, loyal party members working openly or behind the scenes against party rebels, the ADA, organized labor, and strong candidates for other offices, among others. The participation of many people in the campaign demonstrated that the party still possessed much of the strength and vitality it had developed in the age of Roosevelt. And one of its greatest strengths was the approach to domestic issues with which the party had become identified then, an approach that emphasized the use of the powers of the national government to deal with the nation's social and economic problems. This point of view had been endorsed by the voters. "Conservatives had better get a firm grip on their chairs, for a rebirth of the New Deal is in prospect," *Newsweek* warned. "Mr. Truman campaigned on the issue and he won." It should also be noted that liberals interpreted Truman's victory as a victory for Roosevelt and the New Deal. It demonstrated that Truman deserved their support and provided a mandate to move forward. It also erased the need for party realignment. Dewey lacked the personal qualities needed to compensate for the weaknesses of his party, and he helped Truman by waging a dull, uninspiring campaign that failed to swing the independent voters and the discontented Democrats behind him.

While Truman received much help, he was also his own best advocate. Although his personal campaign was not a one-man affair, Truman himself was perhaps its greatest asset. He played rather skillfully—and very strenuously—the role that his advisers had suggested. He demonstrated that he was a political man of strength as well as weaknesses. Recognizing that his situation contained advantages as well as disadvantages, he exploited those advantages and helped his party maintain control

of the presidency for four more years. Although he failed to rally a spectacular number of voters behind him or to convert a substantial bloc to his political faith, he and his aides attracted enough support to accomplish their immediate objective.

—*Richard S. Kirkendall*

Selected Bibliography

This essay rests heavily upon the rich manuscript collections of the Harry S. Truman Library in Independence, Missouri. The best book on the election is Irwin Ross, *The Loneliest Campaign: The Truman Victory of 1948* (1968). He recognizes the "maintaining" character of the election, corrects errors in Truman's account (Harry S. Truman, *Memoirs*, 2 vols., 1955–56), and carries the discussion of the work of Truman's campaign advisers beyond the significant handling of that story in Cabell Phillips, *The Truman Presidency: The History of a Triumphant Succession* (1966). Ross's leading competitors are Gary A. Donaldson, *Truman Defeats Dewey* (2000), which is solid if workmanlike, and Jules Abels, *Out of the Jaws of Victory* (1959). This book, however, is seriously flawed by its exaggeration of the importance of Dewey's campaign. Zachary Karabell, *The Last Campaign: How Harry Truman Won the 1948 Election* (2000), is a well-written analysis of this critical campaign. The best Truman biography is Alonzo L. Hamby, *Man of the People: A Life of Harry S. Truman* (1995). In the rich social science literature on 1948, Angus Campbell and Robert L. Kahn, *The People Elect a President* (1952), is a pioneering work, while Bernard Berelson, Paul Lazarsfeld, and William N. McPhee, *Voting: A Study of Opinion Formation in a Presidential Campaign* (1954), makes use of repeated interviews with a sample of the population of Elmira, New York. Both of these voting studies document the late swing to Truman. Also important is Samuel Lubell, *The Future of American Politics* (1951), which relates 1948 to the "Roosevelt Revolution." The orthodox view of the Wallace campaign, emphasizing Communist influence and control, is advanced in David A. Shannon, *The Decline of American Communism: A History of the Communist Party in the United States Since 1945* (1959), and in David J. Saposs, *Communism in American Politics* (1960). The challenge to this interpretation has been supplied by Karl M. Schmidt, *Henry A. Wallace: Quixotic Crusade 1948* (1960), and by Curtis MacDougall, *Gideon's Army* (1965). See also Robert J. Donovan, *The Presidency of Harry S. Truman* (2 vols., 1977, 1982); Alonzo L. Hamby, *Beyond the New Deal: Harry S. Truman and American Liberalism* (1973); Richard S. Kirkendall, ed., *The Harry S. Truman Encyclopedia* (1989); Norman D. Markowitz, *The Rise and Fall of the People's Century: Henry A. Wallace and American Liberalism, 1941–1948* (1973); David McCullough, *Truman* (1992); and Richard Norton Smith, *Thomas E. Dewey and His Times* (1982).

1948 ELECTION STATISTICS

State	Number of Electors	Total Popular Vote	Elec Vote D	Elec Vote R	Elec Vote SR	Pop Vote D	Pop Vote R	Pop Vote SR	Margin of Victory Votes	Margin of Victory % Total Vote
Alabama	11	214,980			11	9	2	1	130,513	60.71%
Arizona	4	177,065	4			1	2	-	17,654	9.97%
Arkansas	9	242,475	9			1	2	3	98,700	40.71%
California	25	4,021,538	25			1	2	6	17,865	0.44%
Colorado	6	515,237	6			1	2	-	27,574	5.35%
Connecticut	8	883,518		8		2	1	-	14,457	1.64%
Delaware	3	139,073		3		2	1	-	1,775	1.28%
Florida	8	577,643	8			1	2	3	87,708	15.18%
Georgia	12	418,764	12			1	3	2	169,591	40.50%
Idaho	4	214,816	4			1	2	-	5,856	2.73%
Illinois	28	3,984,046	28			1	2	-	33,612	0.84%
Indiana	13	1,656,214		13		2	1	-	13,246	0.80%
Iowa	10	1,038,272	10			1	2	-	28,362	2.73%
Kansas	8	788,819		8		2	1	-	71,137	9.02%
Kentucky	11	822,658	11			1	2	3	125,546	15.26%
Louisiana	10	416,336			10	2	3	1	67,946	16.32%
Maine	5	264,789		5		2	1	-	38,318	14.47%
Maryland	8	596,735		8		2	1	5	8,293	1.39%
Massachusetts	16	2,107,146	16			1	2	-	242,418	11.50%
Michigan	19	2,109,609		19		2	1	-	35,147	1.67%
Minnesota	11	1,212,226	11			1	2	-	209,349	17.27%
Mississippi	9	192,190			9	2	3	1	148,154	77.09%
Missouri	15	1,578,628	15			1	2	5	262,276	16.61%
Montana	4	224,278	4			1	2	-	22,301	9.94%
Nebraska	6	488,940		6		2	1	-	40,609	8.31%
Nevada	3	62,117	3			1	2	-	1,934	3.11%
New Hampshire	4	231,440		4		2	1	6	13,304	5.75%
New Jersey	16	1,949,555		16		2	1	-	85,669	4.39%
New Mexico	4	187,063	4			1	2	-	25,161	13.45%
New York	47	6,178,502		47		2	1	8	60,959	0.99%
North Carolina	14	791,209	14			1	2	3	200,498	25.34%
North Dakota	4	220,716		4		2	1	5	19,327	8.76%
Ohio	25	2,936,071	25	0		1	2	-	7,107	0.24%
Oklahoma	10	721,599	10			1	2	-	183,965	25.49%
Oregon	6	524,080		6		2	1	-	17,757	3.39%
Pennsylvania	35	3,735,148		35		2	1	-	149,771	4.01%
Rhode Island	4	327,702	4			1	2	-	52,949	16.16%
South Carolina	8	142,571			8	2	3	1	68,184	47.82%
South Dakota	4	250,105		4		2	1	-	11,998	4.80%
Tennessee	12	550,283	11		1	1	2	3	67,488	12.26%
Texas	23	1,249,577	23			1	2	3	520,768	41.68%
Utah	4	276,305	4			1	2	-	24,749	8.96%
Vermont	3	123,382		3		2	1	-	30,369	24.61%
Virginia	11	419,256	11			1	2	3	28,716	6.85%
Washington	8	905,059	8			1	2	-	89,850	9.93%
West Virginia	8	748,750	8			1	2	-	112,937	15.08%
Wisconsin	12	1,276,800	12			1	2	-	56,351	4.41%
Wyoming	3	101,425	3			1	2	-	4,407	4.35%
Total	531	48,794,710	303	189	39	1	2	3	2,188,055	4.48%

Truman Democratic		Dewey Republican		Thurmond States' Rights		Wallace Progressive		Others	
0	0.00%	40,930	19.04%	171,443	79.75%	1,522	0.71%	1,085	0.50%
95,251	53.79%	77,597	43.82%	0	0.00%	3,310	1.87%	907	0.51%
149,659	61.72%	50,959	21.02%	40,068	16.52%	751	0.31%	1,038	0.43%
1,913,134	47.57%	1,895,269	47.13%	1,228	0.03%	190,381	4.73%	21,526	0.54%
267,288	51.88%	239,714	46.52%	0	0.00%	6,115	1.19%	2,120	0.41%
423,297	47.91%	437,754	49.55%	0	0.00%	13,713	1.55%	8,754	0.99%
67,813	48.76%	69,588	50.04%	0	0.00%	1,050	0.75%	622	0.45%
281,988	48.82%	194,280	33.63%	89,755	15.54%	11,620	2.01%	0	0.00%
254,646	60.81%	76,691	18.31%	85,055	20.31%	1,636	0.39%	736	0.18%
107,370	49.98%	101,514	47.26%	0	0.00%	4,972	2.31%	960	0.45%
1,994,715	50.07%	1,961,103	49.22%	0	0.00%	0	0.00%	28,228	0.71%
807,833	48.78%	821,079	49.58%	0	0.00%	9,649	0.58%	17,653	1.07%
522,380	50.31%	494,018	47.58%	0	0.00%	12,125	1.17%	9,749	0.94%
351,902	44.61%	423,039	53.63%	0	0.00%	4,603	0.58%	9,275	1.18%
466,756	56.74%	341,210	41.48%	10,411	1.27%	1,567	0.19%	2,714	0.33%
136,344	32.75%	72,657	17.45%	204,290	49.07%	3,035	0.73%	10	0.00%
111,916	42.27%	150,234	56.74%	0	0.00%	1,884	0.71%	755	0.29%
286,521	48.01%	294,814	49.40%	2,476	0.41%	9,983	1.67%	2,941	0.49%
1,151,788	54.66%	909,370	43.16%	0	0.00%	38,157	1.81%	7,831	0.37%
1,003,448	47.57%	1,038,595	49.23%	0	0.00%	46,515	2.20%	21,051	1.00%
692,966	57.16%	483,617	39.89%	0	0.00%	27,866	2.30%	7,777	0.64%
19,384	10.09%	5,043	2.62%	167,538	87.17%	225	0.12%	0	0.00%
917,315	58.11%	655,039	41.49%	42	0.00%	3,998	0.25%	2,234	0.14%
119,071	53.09%	96,770	43.15%	0	0.00%	7,313	3.26%	1,124	0.50%
224,165	45.85%	264,774	54.15%	0	0.00%	0	0.00%	1	0.00%
31,291	50.37%	29,357	47.26%	0	0.00%	1,469	2.36%	0	0.00%
107,995	46.66%	121,299	52.41%	7	0.00%	1,970	0.85%	169	0.07%
895,455	45.93%	981,124	50.33%	0	0.00%	42,683	2.19%	30,293	1.55%
105,464	56.38%	80,303	42.93%	0	0.00%	1,037	0.55%	259	0.14%
2,780,204	45.00%	2,841,163	45.98%	16	0.00%	509,559	8.25%	47,560	0.77%
459,070	58.02%	258,572	32.68%	69,652	8.80%	3,915	0.49%	0	0.00%
95,812	43.41%	115,139	52.17%	374	0.17%	8,391	3.80%	1,000	0.45%
1,452,791	49.48%	1,445,684	49.24%	0	0.00%	37,596	1.28%	0	0.00%
452,782	62.75%	268,817	37.25%	0	0.00%	0	0.00%	0	0.00%
243,147	46.40%	260,904	49.78%	0	0.00%	14,978	2.86%	5,051	0.96%
1,752,426	46.92%	1,902,197	50.93%	0	0.00%	55,161	1.48%	25,364	0.68%
188,736	57.59%	135,787	41.44%	0	0.00%	2,619	0.80%	560	0.17%
34,423	24.14%	5,386	3.78%	102,607	71.97%	154	0.11%	1	0.00%
117,653	47.04%	129,651	51.84%	0	0.00%	2,801	1.12%	0	0.00%
270,402	49.14%	202,914	36.87%	73,815	13.41%	1,864	0.34%	1,288	0.23%
824,235	65.96%	303,467	24.29%	113,776	9.11%	3,920	0.31%	4,179	0.33%
149,151	53.98%	124,402	45.02%	0	0.00%	2,679	0.97%	73	0.03%
45,557	36.92%	75,926	61.54%	0	0.00%	1,279	1.04%	620	0.50%
200,786	47.89%	172,070	41.04%	43,393	10.35%	2,047	0.49%	960	0.23%
476,165	52.61%	386,315	42.68%	0	0.00%	31,692	3.50%	10,887	1.20%
429,188	57.32%	316,251	42.24%	0	0.00%	3,311	0.44%	0	0.00%
647,310	50.70%	590,959	46.28%	0	0.00%	25,282	1.98%	13,249	1.04%
52,354	51.62%	47,947	47.27%	0	0.00%	931	0.92%	193	0.19%
24,179,347	49.55%	21,991,292	45.07%	1,175,946	2.41%	1,157,328	2.37%	290,797	0.60%

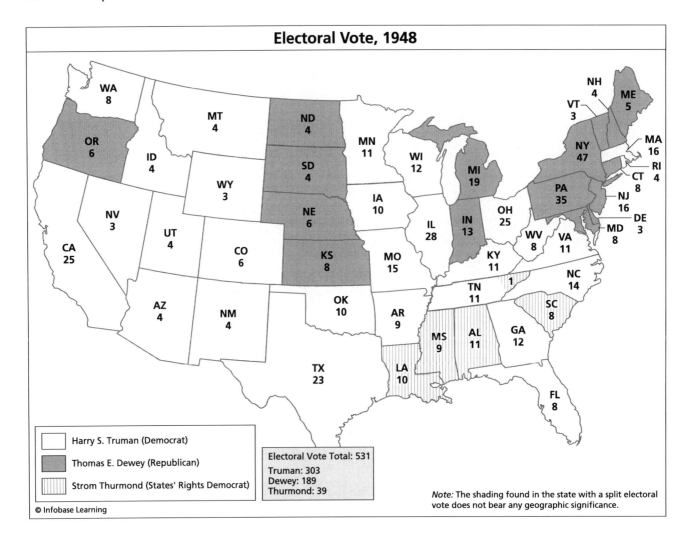

Electoral Vote, 1948

WA 8 · OR 6 · ID 4 · MT 4 · WY 3 · NV 3 · UT 4 · CA 25 · AZ 4 · NM 4 · CO 6 · ND 4 · SD 4 · NE 6 · KS 8 · OK 10 · TX 23 · MN 11 · IA 10 · MO 15 · AR 9 · LA 10 · MS 9 · AL 11 · WI 12 · IL 28 · IN 13 · OH 25 · KY 11 · TN 11 · GA 12 · MI 19 · WV 8 · VA 11 · NC 14 · SC 8 · FL 8 · NY 47 · PA 35 · VT 3 · NH 4 · ME 5 · MA 16 · RI 4 · CT 8 · NJ 16 · DE 3 · MD 8

Harry S. Truman (Democrat)
Thomas E. Dewey (Republican)
Strom Thurmond (States' Rights Democrat)

Electoral Vote Total: 531
Truman: 303
Dewey: 189
Thurmond: 39

Note: The shading found in the state with a split electoral vote does not bear any geographic significance.

© Infobase Learning

Election of 1952

Election Overview

Election Year 1952

Election Day November 4, 1952

Winning Candidates

* ★ **President:** Dwight D. Eisenhower
* ★ **Vice President:** Richard M. Nixon

Election Results [ticket, party: popular votes (percentage of popular vote); electoral votes (percentage of electoral vote)]

* Dwight D. Eisenhower and Richard M. Nixon, Republican: 34,075,529 (55.18%); 442 (83.2%)
* Adlai Stevenson and John Sparkman, Democratic: 27,375,090 (44.33%); 89 (16.8%)
* Other: 301,323 (0.49%); 0 (0.0%)

Voter Turnout 63.3%

Central Forums/Campaign Methods for Addressing Voters

* Whistle-stop tour
* Speeches
* Radio
* Introduction of television (ads, speeches)

Incumbent President and Vice President on Election Day Harry S. Truman and Alben W. Barkley

Population (1952) 156,954,000

Gross Domestic Product

* $358.3 billion (in current dollars: $2,243.9 billion)
* Per capita: $2,283 (in current dollars: $14,297)

Number of Daily Newspapers (1950) 1,426

Average Daily Circulation (1950) 53,829,000

Households with

* Radio (1950): 40,700,000
* Television (1950): 3,875,000

Method of Choosing Electors Popular vote (mostly general-ticket system/winner take all)

Method of Choosing Nominees

* National party convention
* Presidential preference primaries

Key Issues and Events

* Fears of Communism grow as faith in President Truman wanes.
* Senator Joseph McCarthy and others charge that Communists are infiltrating the State Department.
* America's "Winter of Discontent" from 1951 to 1952, with a stalemated Korean War and an unpopular President Truman not committing to seek another term.

Leading Candidates

REPUBLICANS

* Dwight D. Eisenhower, general of the Army (New York)
* Robert A. Taft, senator (Ohio)
* Harold E. Stassen, former governor (Minnesota)
* Earl Warren, governor (California)

DEMOCRATS

* Adlai Stevenson, governor (Illinois)
* Estes Kefauver, senator (Tennessee)
* Richard Russell Jr., senator (Georgia)
* W. Averell Harriman, former secretary of commerce (New York)
* Alben W. Barkley, vice president (Kentucky)
* Robert S. Kerr, senator (Oklahoma)

Trajectory

- On January 7, 1952, General Dwight Eisenhower makes it clear that he is open to a Draft Eisenhower movement. On March 11, 1952, Eisenhower wins the New Hampshire primary by 50% to 38% over Robert Taft. The general then returns to the United States.
- After losing the New Hampshire primary to Estes Kefauver, Truman announces on March 29, 1952, "I shall *not* be a candidate for reelection."
- Vicious battle pitting Eisenhower, a popular, moderate, heroic newcomer, against "Mr. Republican," Senator Robert Taft, a well-known, veteran conservative. Eisenhower wins the nomination. To placate conservatives, Eisenhower chooses Senator Richard M. Nixon of California as his vice-presidential candidate.
- Kefauver wins 12 of 16 primaries, but party leaders oppose him. Truman prefers Governor Stevenson of Illinois, who declines to run, or Vice President Alben Barkley. Southerners rally around conservative senator Richard Russell.
- Democratic convention begins July 21. Adlai Stevenson's rousing speech welcoming the delegates prompts the delegates to choose Stevenson as the compromise candidate, despite Stevenson's reluctance. Stevenson is the first candidate legitimately drafted to the nomination since Garfield in 1880.
- In September, Eisenhower meets with Senator Taft in New York for two hours. They agree that the campaign will be for "liberty against creeping socialism" and affirm the K_1C_2 Republican formula for victory: Korea, Communism, and corruption. Democrats mock the "surrender of Morningside Heights."
- On September 18, the *New York Post* reveals a "secret Nixon fund" with over $18,000 for Nixon's expenses as senator. Eisenhower wonders how to run against corruption, if his running mate is enmeshed in scandal.
- On September 23, Nixon delivers his "Checkers" speech on television. To defend the fund as legitimate, Nixon accounts for his personal finances and recounts his humble upbringing before the largest television audience to date. The Republican national headquarters receives thousands of letters, cards, and telegrams supporting Nixon.
- On October 3, in Milwaukee, Eisenhower wants to defend his friend General George C. Marshall against McCarthyite accusations of disloyalty. The passage is in the press release, but Eisenhower succumbs to pressure from party leaders and omits the defense from the speech.
- On October 24, 1952, Eisenhower proclaims, "I shall go to Korea," stirring Americans and securing his electoral victory.

Conventions

- Republican National Convention: July 7–11, 1952, International Amphitheatre, Chicago
- Democratic National Convention: July 21–26, 1952, International Amphitheatre, Chicago

Ballots/Nominees

REPUBLICANS

Presidential first ballot after shifts

- Dwight D. Eisenhower 595; 845
- Robert A. Taft 500; 280
- Earl Warren 81; 77
- Harold E. Stassen 20; 0
- Douglas MacArthur 10; 4
- Thomas E. Dewey 1; 0

DEMOCRATS

Presidential third ballot

- Adlai Stevenson 273; 324.5; 617.5
- Estes Kefauver 340; 362.5; 275.5
- Richard B. Russell 268; 294; 261
- W. Averell Harriman 123.5; 121; 0
- Alben W. Barkley 48.5; 78.5; 67.5
- Robert S. Kerr 65; 5.5; 0
- Paul A. Dever 37.5; 30.5; 0.5
- Hubert Humphrey 26; 0; 0
- J. William Fulbright 22; 0; 0
- Scattering 26.5; 13.5; 8

Party Platform

REPUBLICANS

- Condemn the Roosevelt and Truman administrations
- End the war in Korea
- End "Communist subversion"
- Support for the Taft-Hartley Act
- Restrict activities of labor unions

DEMOCRATS

- Continue agricultural price supports
- Repeal the Taft-Hartley Act
- Eradicate discrimination
- Defend the Korean War

Campaign Innovations

- Use of television to address the nation amid controversy: Richard Nixon's "Checkers" speech
- Eisenhower sound bites/ads: "Ike for President," "You like Ike, I like Ike, everybody likes Ike"

- Stevenson buys 30-minute blocks on TV for long speeches, but few watch because the speeches are too long.

Campaign Tactics

REPUBLICANS
- Republican strategy: "Attack! Attack! Attack!"
- Focus on partisan stay-at-homes rather than independent voters
- Advertising: "packaging" Eisenhower as a product, emphasizing his character
- Great faith in television commercials, especially toward the end of the campaign
- Traveling by train and plane, Eisenhower covers 33,000 miles and gives 228 speeches, 40 televised.
- Eisenhower never takes the low road in attacks against the Democrats, but Senators William Jenner and Joseph McCarthy, along with Eisenhower's running mate, Richard Nixon, launch the harsh attacks on Adlai as "Alger" and "Adelaide," and, in Nixon's famous words, as having a "Ph.D. from Dean Acheson's College of Cowardly Communist Containment."

DEMOCRATS
- Stevenson stumps. He is a witty, substantive campaigner.
- Pitches the appeal on the success of Roosevelt and Truman in spreading middle-class prosperity
- Wants to "talk sense to the American people"
- Resents peddling the presidency like a bar of soap

Popular Campaign Slogans

REPUBLICANS
- "I Like Ike"
- K_1C_2: Korea, Communism, and Corruption
- "Ike: For Prosperity Without War"

DEMOCRATS
- "All the Way with Adlai"
- "We Need Stevenson Badly"
- "Go Forward with Stevenson-Sparkman"

Campaign Songs

- Republicans: "I Like Ike"
- Democrats: "Don't Let 'em Take It Away"

Influential Campaign Appeals or Ads

REPUBLICANS
- "Time for a change"
- "Ike for President"
- Run short commercials: "Eisenhower Answers America" and introducing "The Man from Abilene,"

denouncing "High Prices," highlighting "Nixon on Corruption"
- Labeling Stevenson and his aides as "eggheads"
- Stevenson mocked for having a hole in the bottom of his shoe

DEMOCRATS
- Stevenson: A New Man in American Politics
- "You Never Had It So Good" emphasizes Roosevelt's New Deal and Truman's Fair Deal.
- "Ike is running like a dry creek"

Campaign Finance

- Eisenhower: $6,608,623 (in current dollars: $50,749,000)
- Stevenson: $5,032,926 (in current dollars: $38,648,900)

Defining Quotations

- "[O]ne of the greatest soldiers in history, a fine educator, a man who really understands the problems of the world." *Thomas E. Dewey on television endorsing Dwight D. Eisenhower, October 15, 1950*
- "If you decide to finish the European job (and I don't know who else can) I must keep the isolationists out of the White House. I wish you would let me know what you intend to do." *President Truman inquiring about General Eisenhower's plans, December 18, 1951*
- "I do not feel that I have any duty to seek a political nomination, in spite of the fact that many have urged to the contrary. Because of this belief I shall not do so." *Eisenhower's reply to Truman, January 1, 1952*
- "Any American who would have that many other Americans pay him that compliment would be proud or he would not be an American." *Dwight D. Eisenhower's reaction to winning the New Hampshire primary, March 11, 1952*
- "Behind Tom Dewey is the same old gang of Eastern internationalists and Republican New Dealers who ganged up to sell the Republican party down the river in 1940 and in 1944, and in 1948. They are trying it again this year." *"SINK DEWEY," a pamphlet distributed at the Republican Convention and issued by Taft Committee's David S. Ingalls*
- "The boys in the smoke-filled rooms have never taken very well to me." *Estes Kefauver quoted in* Life, *April 14, 1952*
- "I would shoot myself if nominated. For the last time, I'm not going to run for the Democratic nomination." *Adlai Stevenson, July 13, 1952*

- "The ordeal of the twentieth century, the bloodiest, most turbulent era of the whole Christian age, is far from over. Sacrifice, patience, understanding, and implacable purpose may be our lot for years to come. Let's face it. Let's talk sense to the American people. Let's tell them the truth, that there are no gains without pains, that there—that we are now on the eve of great decisions, not easy decisions, like resistance when you're attacked, but a long, patient, costly struggle which alone can assure triumph over the great enemies of man—war, poverty, and tyranny—and the assaults upon human dignity which are the most grievous consequences of each." *Adlai Stevenson, address accepting the presidential nomination at the Democratic National Convention in Chicago, July 26, 1952*

- "We talk a great deal about patriotism. What do we mean by patriotism in the context of our times? I venture to suggest that what we mean is a sense of national responsibility which will enable America to remain master of her power—to walk with it in serenity and wisdom, with self-respect and the respect of all mankind; a patriotism that puts country ahead of self; a patriotism which is not short, frenzied outbursts of emotion, but the tranquil and steady dedication of a lifetime. The dedication of a lifetime—these are words that are easy to utter, but this is a mighty assignment. For it is often easier to fight for principles than to live up to them." *Adlai Stevenson, speech to the American Legion Convention, August 27, 1952*

- "One other thing I probably should tell you, because if I don't they'll probably be saying this about me too, we did get something—a gift—after the election. A man down in Texas heard Pat on the radio mention the fact that our two youngsters would like to have a dog. And, believe it or not, the day before we left on this campaign trip we got a message from Union Station in Baltimore saying they had a package for us. We went down to get it. You know what it was. It was a little cocker spaniel dog in a crate that he sent all the way from Texas. Black and white spotted. And our little girl—Trisha, the 6-year-old—named it Checkers. And you know the kids love the dog and

I just want to say this right now, that regardless of what they say about it, we're gonna keep it." *Richard M. Nixon's "Checkers" speech, September 23, 1952*

- "I know that charges of disloyalty have . . . been leveled against . . . Marshall. I have been privileged for thirty-five years to know General Marshall personally. I know him, as a man and as a soldier, to be dedicated with singular selflessness and the profoundest patriotism to the service of America. And this episode is a sobering lesson in the way freedom must not defend itself." *Dwight D. Eisenhower, text of October 3, 1952, passage not delivered*

- "The biggest fact about the Korean war is this—it was never inevitable, it was never inescapable. . . . It will begin with its President taking a simple, firm resolution. The resolution will be: To forgo the diversions of politics and to concentrate on the job of ending the Korean war—until that job is honorably done. That job requires a personal trip to Korea. I shall make that trip. Only in that way could I learn how best to serve the American people in the cause of peace. I shall go to Korea. That is my second pledge to the American people." *Dwight D. Eisenhower's "I Shall Go to Korea" speech, October 24, 1952*

- "They tell me I laugh too much. I don't see how in hell you could do this job without laughing about it occasionally. . . . I'm glad the General wasn't hurt. But I wasn't surprised that it happened—I've been telling him for two months that nobody could stand on that platform. . . . GOP: Grouchy Old Pessimists. . . . My opponent has been worrying about my funnybone; I'm worrying about his backbone." *Samples of Adlai Stevenson's campaign wit*

Lasting Legacy of Campaign

- Farmers return to support the Republican Party.
- The South continues to move toward supporting the Republicans.
- Consensus develops that a military man is the best candidate to end the war in Korea and deal with the cold war and Communist subversion.
- Television dominates as the medium for communicating with the people.

Election of 1952

On March 29, 1952, President Harry S. Truman greatly improved the political fortunes of his party by declaring that he would not be a candidate for reelection. His own popularity was near its nadir, and his administration had become a major liability to the Democrats. Many voters

blamed the president for our Korean involvement, corruption, Chinese aggression, and Communism, as well as high taxes and inflation. A large number of voters had grave doubts about the party that had occupied the White House for almost a generation.

In the normal course of events, the Truman administration would have been voted out of the office in 1948, but somehow Thomas E. Dewey, the Republican standard-bearer, managed to extract "defeat from the jaws of victory." While Dewey waited for the voters to ratify the judgments of the experts, who predicted a Republican landslide, Truman, fighting vigorously for his political life, pulled together a dispirited party in his "give 'em hell" campaign. He also benefited from the Progressive Party, which absorbed much of the taint of Communism from the administration, and from the Dixiecrats, whose bolt placed many white liberals and Northern blacks behind Truman. For his part, the president was successful in patching together the tattered New Deal coalition of urban workers, Western farmers, Northern blacks, and Southern whites. Furthermore, by concentrating his attack on the GOP right wing (Robert A. Taft, in particular), Truman was able to exploit the fears of a depression and to blame the Republican 80th Congress for its antilabor legislation, its failure to restrain prices, and its "soak the poor" tax cut.

Soon after its victory, however, the unstable Democratic coalition crumbled. Within a year of the election, China fell to the Communists and the Truman administration was blamed for the defeat of Chiang Kai-shek. Conveniently forgetting that few in the Republican Party had shown much interest in China until late in 1947, the Republicans attacked the administration. How, asked the GOP, could the administration commit itself to stopping communism in Europe and yet propose that Chiang ally with Communists in China? Although few Republicans had been willing to commit American troops to Chiang's aid before the collapse of China, they still saw no contradiction in condemning Truman for not acting to "save" China. Unfortunately for Truman, he had not extended the bipartisan foreign policy to the Far East, and the GOP was not about to share responsibility for the loss of China.

Because the administration left the American people unprepared for victorious revolutions, and particularly for the fall of China, many troubled citizens defined the problem in unrealistic terms: Why had America "allowed" a Communist triumph? Unwilling to acknowledge the limitation of American power, and promised success in the long run by the administration, they concluded that only bumbling or betrayal could explain the seemingly unexpected Communist victory, and such interpretations were not the monopoly of the Republicans and the right wing of the Democratic Party. In the House, for example, a young Democrat, John F. Kennedy, in discussing China, declared, "What our young men had saved [in World War II] our diplomats and our President have frittered away."

Unfortunately for the administration, its failure in China coincided with apparent evidence of espionage and subversion—by Alger Hiss, Judith Coplon, and Julius

This Art Bimrose cartoon titled "Good Luck, Pal!" shows the 1948 pollster on crutches wishing good luck to the 1952 pollster who is about to walk out on a limb. On the eve of the 1952 presidential election, Bimrose recalls the fiasco in 1948 when the public opinion polls unanimously predicted the election of Thomas E. Dewey. *(Library of Congress)*

and Ethel Rosenberg. The result was an indictment of the New Deal–Fair Deal government's handling of Communism at home. In the view of some, the Democrats had willingly harbored Communists, even placed them in positions of power, and thereby betrayed the nation. In 1948, and even earlier, the GOP had tried unsuccessfully to exploit these themes for significant partisan advantage, but the evidence had seemed less impressive, and the Progressive Party had drawn off the charges of red taint. The apparent failures of the loyalty program, as well as the fall of China, made the administration even more vulnerable.

The GOP's assaults on the loyalty and judgment of the administration were also encouraged by the administration's fluctuating, and seemingly contradictory, policies in Korea: first, the effort to push North Korean armies back to the 38th Parallel and restore the *status quo ante bellum*; then, the attempt to conquer North Korea and unify the nation; and finally, after the intervention by the Chinese Communists in the autumn of 1950, the acceptance of stalemate, proclamation of limited war, and a shift to more limited objectives. (It was not a "pointless and inconclusive struggle," declared Dean Acheson in 1951,

(continues on page 1204)

☆ ☆ ☆

1952 ELECTION CHRONOLOGY

1949

October 1, 1949: Mao Zedong proclaims the People's Republic of China as Chinese Nationalist forces evacuate to Taiwan.

1950

February 9, 1950: During a speech in West Virginia, Senator Joseph McCarthy of Wisconsin claims to have a list of 205 known Communists in the federal government.

May 3, 1950: The Senate votes to establish a special subcommittee to investigate interstate crime. The committee holds a series of televised public hearings across the country, questioning leading organized crime figures. With the hearings the most closely followed program on television, its chairman, Tennessee Democrat Estes Kefauver, becomes an instant celebrity.

June 25, 1950: North Korean launches a surprise invasion of South Korea, occupying much of the country within a short period of time. The U.N. demands the North Koreans' withdrawal.

June 30, 1950: President Truman commits American forces to enforce the U.N. demand.

September 15, 1950: American forces land at Inchon, launching a successful counteroffensive that drives across the North Korean border.

October 14, 1950: Chinese forces cross the Yalu river, beginning an offensive that eventually drives the U.N. force south of the 38th parallel and captures Seoul.

November 7, 1950: The Republicans gain 28 seats in the House of Representatives and 5 seats in the Senate in the midterm elections, though the Democrats remain in control of both houses. Among the victorious senators is Richard M. Nixon of California.

1951

February 26, 1951: The Twenty-second Amendment, which limits presidents to two terms, is ratified, although it is not binding on the current White House occupant.

March 18, 1951: U.N. forces recapture Seoul, and the war becomes a stalemate.

April 11, 1951: Truman relieves General Douglas MacArthur from command of the U.S. and U.N. forces in the Far East.

July 10, 1951: Peace negotiations begin between the U.N. and North and South Korea.

1952

January 4, 1952: President Truman announces he will decide whether to run for the Democratic presidential nomination when he is ready, contradicting Ohio Congressman Wayne L. Hays, who had claimed on January 1 that the president had told him he planned to announce his decision by February 1.

January 5, 1952: Tennessee senator Estes Kefauver indicates he is interested in running for the Democratic nomination, and will announce his decision after President Truman decides.

January 7, 1952: General Dwight Eisenhower makes it clear that he is open to a Draft Eisenhower movement.

January 15, 1952: Truman meets with Kefauver at the White House. He indicates he has not yet decided whether he will run, but states that he would not object to a presidential campaign by the senator.

January 16–18, 1952: Republican leaders meet in San Francisco to prepare for the July convention. Senator Robert Taft of Ohio, former Minnesota governor Harold Stassen, and California governor Earl Warren address the party bosses, as does Senator Henry Cabot Lodge of Massachusetts, representing the movement to elect Dwight Eisenhower.

January 23, 1952: Estes Kefauver announces he will seek the Democratic nomination, stressing his anticommunism, support for a balanced federal budget, and ideas for fighting crime. He embarks on a vigorous stumping campaign, often wearing a coonskin cap to emphasize his populism and Tennessee roots.

February 6, 1952: In a surprise announcement, President Truman indicates he will enter the New Hampshire primary, a week after saying he would withdraw.

☆   ☆   ☆

March 11, 1952: Eisenhower defeats Senator Robert Taft in the New Hampshire Republican primary by 50 to 38 percent. Eisenhower then returns to the United States.

March 11, 1952: President Truman loses the New Hampshire Democratic primary to Estes Kefauver. Truman soon withdraws from the race and announces his plan to retire.

April 8, 1952: Truman orders the seizure of several steel mills to prevent strikes by steelworkers. The Supreme Court later judges the order to be unconstitutional.

April 29, 1952: Eisenhower wins the Massachusetts primary, his third major state victory in a row, having won New Jersey two weeks earlier and Pennsylvania a week earlier. Taft runs an aggressive primary campaign stressing his conservative, isolationist credentials in contrast to the more moderate, internationalist Eisenhower, but the general proves more popular than "Mr. Republican."

July 7–11, 1952: The Republicans hold their convention in Chicago. General Dwight Eisenhower receives the presidential nomination on the first ballot, defeating Senator Robert Taft. To placate conservatives, Eisenhower chooses California Senator Richard M. Nixon for the vice presidency.

July 16, 1952: President Truman signs a bill extending the provisions of the GI Bill to Korean War veterans.

July 21–26, 1952: The Democratic National Convention meets in Chicago. Estes Kefauver enters the convention with a lead, having won 12 out of 16 state primaries, while Southern conservatives have rallied around Georgia senator Richard B. Russell. But Illinois governor Adlai Stevenson's rousing welcoming speech, combined with the support of the party bosses, helps him win the presidential nomination on the third ballot. Congressman John J. Sparkman of Alabama is chosen as the vice-presidential nominee.

July 26, 1952: Adlai Stevenson delivers one of the great acceptance speeches, exclaiming: "Let's Talk Sense to the American People."

August 7, 1952: Adman Rosser Reeves pitches an elaborate advertising plan to Eisenhower and Nixon, focusing on short "spot ads" in key electoral college battlegrounds, focusing on three issues: fighting corruption, lowering taxes, and the problems with the Korean War.

August 17, 1952: Stevenson indicates in a letter to the *Oregon Journal* that he received the Democratic nomination without owing anything to anyone, including the unpopular incumbent president. He pledges to launch an intensive whistle-stop campaign, which ultimately is a prop-stop campaign—by airplane, too—covering 32,000 miles. Although Stevenson is an effective speaker, Eisenhower's rallies continue to draw more voters.

September 1, 1952: In a Labor Day speech in Milwaukee, President Truman heartily endorses Stevenson, claiming he is the most qualified presidential candidate ever nominated by the Democratic Party.

September 11, 1952: Eisenhower spends a day filming what becomes "Eisenhower Answers America": a campaign of 28 20-second spots and 3 1-minute spots, with "average Americans"—taken from the queue at Radio City Music Hall—pitching him issue-oriented questions.

September 12, 1952: Eisenhower hosts Robert Taft at home in Morningside Heights, New York, and agrees to adopt a series of domestic policy positions more in line with conservative Republicans. Democrats ridicule "the surrender of Morningside Heights," using it as an excuse to attack Taft as a surrogate for the more popular Eisenhower.

September 18, 1952: The *New York Post* reveals the existence of a secret $18,000 fund to cover Nixon's expenses as a senator. The charges of corruption are harmful to the Republican Party, and Eisenhower considers dropping Nixon from the ticket.

September 23, 1952: Nixon defends his financial integrity on national television, eliciting sympathy from the viewing audience by mentioning Checkers, the cocker spaniel a supporter gave his children. The "Checkers" speech saves Nixon's career and demonstrates TV's power.

(continues)

1952 ELECTION CHRONOLOGY *(continued)*

September 27, 1952: While campaigning in Kentucky, Stevenson hears that a platform collapsed under Eisenhower at Richmond, Va. Stevenson cracks: "I've been telling him for two months that nobody could stand on that platform." These quips feed the legend of Stevenson's wise and witty but ultimately quixotic 1952 campaign.

October 1, 1952: At a press conference, George Ball of the Stevenson campaign, describing leaked plans of the Republican spot-ad campaign, says Republicans are trying to "sell an inadequate ticket to the American people in precisely the way they sell soap, ammoniated toothpaste, hair tonic, and bubble gum." In fact, Democrats will also run some spot ads, although they favor longer 30-minute televised speeches, and Stevenson will not appear in the short ads.

October 2, 1952: Ball files a complaint with the Federal Communications Commission (FCC) that the Republicans' ad campaign violates the Equal Time Provision of the Communications Act of 1934 and/or parts of the Corrupt Practices Act. On October 9, the FCC dismisses the charges.

October 3, 1952: Eisenhower plans to defend his friend and comrade General George C. Marshall against charges of Communist sympathy leveled by the McCarthyites, but deletes the defense at the last minute.

October 3, 1952: Stevenson takes up the charge against Republican advertising, complaining:

"This isn't a soap opera, this isn't Ivory Soap vs. Palmolive. . . . This is a choice for the most important office on earth."

October 16, 1952: Nixon, playing the role of partisan hatchet man, says Stevenson has a Ph.D. from Secretary of State "Dean Acheson's College of Cowardly Communist Containment."

October 24, 1952: In a major address, Eisenhower proclaims, "I shall go to Korea," arguing that a personal visit by the president will be necessary to resolve the ongoing conflict.

October 24, 1952: The Republicans begin airing their "spot ads" in 62 counties in 12 states.

October 28, 1952: Senator Joseph McCarthy delivers a nationwide address attacking Adlai Stevenson for supposedly aiding the Communists. Twice McCarthy calls Adlai "Alger," linking the Democratic nominee to Alger Hiss.

November 4, 1952: Eisenhower wins by a decisive margin, taking 55.18 percent of the popular vote and 442 electoral votes. Adlai Stevenson wins 44.33 percent of the vote and 89 electoral votes. The Republicans narrowly gain control of both houses of Congress.

December 15, 1952: Presidential electors cast their ballots in their respective state capitals.

1953
January 6, 1953: A joint session of Congress assembles to count the electoral votes.

(continued from page 1201)
for the United States had achieved "a powerful victory" by defeating "Communist imperialist aims in Asia" and stopping the Communist conquest of Korea.) This final redefinition of aims baffled and angered many citizens, who found stalemate an unwise and cowardly policy. "It all fits into a pattern," declared Senator George Malone, Republican of Nevada. "We deliberately lose Manchuria, China, Korea, and Berlin. We follow the pattern of sometimes apparently unrelated events—but it all adds up to losing strategic areas throughout the world."

Some were also suspicious of the administration's contention that bombing China, particularly the area near

Manchuria, would lead to war with Russia. Certainly the administration's contention was neither self-evident nor necessarily realistic, and it did seem incompatible with earlier assurances that encircling Russia with bases would not lead to war. How, many asked, could bombing China mean war with the Soviet Union when the administration promised that arming Western Europe and planting U.S. bases around the Soviet Union would not provoke Soviet antagonism? Truman's critics were not denying the Sino–Soviet defense pact; they were simply questioning whether the Soviets would honor it if, as it seemed, the pact meant the sacrifice of Soviet interests and welfare. "The whole Atlantic Pact, certainly the arming of Germany," asserted Taft, "is an incentive for Russia to enter the war before the army is built up. I cannot see that any bombing of China without invasion can be regarded in any way by Russia as an aggressive move against Russia itself, or a reason for war, unless they have made up their minds to start a third world war anyway."

The administration was also victimized by its own tactical mistakes. In June 1950, when Truman had committed U.S. forces to Korea, he had not asked for a declaration of war and thereby left the GOP free later to criticize his decision. In June, most congressmen endorsed his decision and only a few, like Senator Robert A. Taft, criticized him for acting without congressional authorization. But by the winter of 1950–51, as the Chinese forces overran United Nations positions and American casualties multiplied, many Republicans blamed Truman for entering the war, for refusing to extend the war to China, and for continuing in a war he would not seek to win. For Truman, the price of seeking victory was too high; he feared all-out war, antagonizing suspicious European allies with a "go-it-alone policy," and the possibility that the United States might lose Europe by becoming bogged down in Asia. For many Republicans, a policy of stalemate was less attractive than withdrawal or expansion.

Republicans had long been agitating for the employment of Chiang's troops to open what Minority Leader Joseph Martin, Republican from Massachusetts, ambitiously entitled "a second front in Asia." Looking forward to nearly 800,000 Nationalist soldiers (150,000 was more realistic), he contrasted that number with the 200,000 soldiers in the United States and emphasized that the addition would be "the cheapest operation" possible in Asia. But "if we are not in Korea to win, then this administration should be indicted for the murder of thousands of American boys." Persuaded that the Nationalists had been sold out earlier by the administration, he warned, "If we want a strategy that will save Europe and Asia at the same time . . . , we must clear out the State Department from top to bottom, starting with Dean Acheson." Though most Democrats opposed the use of Chiang's troops as foolhardy and dangerous, few Democratic congressmen would defend Truman's embattled secretary of state, who, despite his avowed anticommunism and his strategy for building American strength, had become the symbol of appeasement, sometimes even of betrayal.

Many in the GOP were obviously seeking to exploit the issue of the war for partisan advantage, but their analyses were also often sincere and flowed from deep convictions about the use of American power and the nature of American policy. When in April 1951 Truman fired General Douglas MacArthur, the supreme allied commander in the Pacific, Truman provided an outlet for the nation's pent-up emotions. Expressing the senti-

ments of many Americans, Senator Joseph McCarthy of Wisconsin declared, "The son of a bitch ought to be impeached." All parts of the GOP, stretching from the so-called "internationalist" wing, represented by Dewey and Harold Stassen, to the so-called "isolationist" wing, represented by Taft and Senator Kenneth Wherry, criticized Truman. But it was primarily the latter group who accused Truman of dismissing MacArthur because the United Nations commander wanted to win the war.

MacArthur, justifiably removed after numerous acts of insolence and insubordination, had wanted to take the war to China—by blockading the coast and bombing her industrial capacity—and to use Chiang's troops in Korea, while also allowing Chiang to engage in "diversionary action (possibly leading to counter-invasion) against vulnerable areas of the China mainland." It was MacArthur himself who called those who wished to limit the military the "new isolationists"—a term later applied by liberals to MacArthur and his supporters. Challenging the wisdom of the administration policy, the general concluded that the "only way to prevent World War III is to end the Korean conflict rapidly and decisively." MacArthur, usually more concerned about Asia than Europe, had expanded the administration's argument that aggression in Asia must be blocked in order to save Europe, thus reaching the dubious conclusion that Europe would remain safe only if Communist aggression was defeated in Asia.

Though liberals called such demands irrational, many others found them no less rational than what the administration was offering—limited war, limited aims, continued bloodshed. If the administration was right in saying late in 1950 and afterward that Russia might enter the war if China was bombed, then the administration was probably wrong earlier in the year when Secretary Acheson emphasized that China and Russia were not reasonable allies and that China had good reason to fear Russia. (At the same time, he called the Soviet attempt to control Outer and Inner Mongolia, Manchuria, and Sinkiang "the single most . . . important fact" in Asian developments. He had concluded that the United States, not Russia, could prove to be the friend of China and was obliquely suggesting an ultimate Sino–American rapprochement and the abandonment of Formosa—which angered many Republicans.) Neither estimate was self-evidently valid, but they did seem incompatible. Those Republicans who concluded that the Soviet Union was exploiting China—that nation was a victim of "Russian imperialism," according to Acheson—and was therefore unwilling to go to war to protect her, were actually following some of the lines of the administration's own analysis. These Republicans, however, were unsympathetic to the administration's argument that an expanded war would destroy the American alliance with Western

Europe. Angry that Europe contributed so little to the war, and persuaded that European nations depended on the American alliance for protection, they were antagonized by Truman's declaration that "We cannot go it alone in Asia and go it with company in Europe."

The GOP blamed the Truman administration for the war. In fact, members of both parties charged that Secretary of State Dean Acheson had invited red aggression when in January 1950 he had defined Korea outside the American defense perimeter in the Far East. The GOP conveniently overlooked General MacArthur's similar statements a few months earlier. Republicans also charged that the administration had not given South Korea adequate equipment to resist aggression. The GOP conveniently neglected to point out substantial earlier Republican opposition to financial aid for Korea, and the administration was unwilling to explain publicly that it had not provided heavy armored tanks and other material because the Korean dictator, Syngman Rhee, could not be trusted. ("Some appeaser in the State Department," sneered Taft in 1951, "was afraid that with real arms they might have attacked . . . North Korea.") In the years before the Korean War, American advisers had warned periodically that Rhee might invade the North in an attempt to unify the divided nation, and he had made the most recent of his public threats on this theme only a few weeks before the war started.

Some in the GOP raised another vexing question about foreign policy: If Acheson was wise in January 1950 when he declared Korea outside the American defense perimeter, why was Korea so vital in June 1950 or in 1952 and worth defending? The administration replied obliquely that Acheson had indicated the possibility of the United States, under United Nations auspices, assisting South Korea if she was attacked. The administration also responded that Korea was the test case of Communist aggression, that a Communist victory there would unleash the forces of revolution and expansion elsewhere, and that the United Nation's resistance would halt the Communist surge. "This is the Greece of the Far East," declared Truman. For many Americans, as the war dragged on and sapped the nation's patience and resources, the administration's self-defense seemed highly questionable.

Savoring victory in 1952, the Republicans were sure that the voters would repudiate the party of Truman and rectify the "mistake" of 1948. For many in the GOP, the first—ultimately the most—significant battle was the struggle within the party between the liberal and conservative wings. The liberal Eastern wing, financed by some of the nation's major financial and industrial firms, had captured the presidential nomination in the past three elections. Led by Dewey, this wing included

such prominent men as Senators Henry Cabot Lodge and Leverett Saltonstall of Massachusetts, Ralph Flanders and George Aiken of Vermont, Irving Ives of New York, and James Duff of Pennsylvania, ex-governor Harold Stassen of Minnesota, and Governor Sherman Adams of New Hampshire. It included bankers like Winthrop Aldrich of the Chase National Bank and John H. Whitney of J. H. Whitney Co., and industrialists such as Paul Hoffmann of Studebaker and Thomas Watson of IBM. In foreign policy, this wing, led by Senator Arthur Vandenberg until his death, had endorsed the basic approach of the Roosevelt–Truman foreign policy.

The conservative wing, rooted primarily in the Midwest and financed largely by Midwestern interests, was led by Senator Robert Taft of Ohio. It included Senators John Bricker of Ohio, Everett Dirksen of Illinois, Karl Mundt of South Dakota, Homer Capehart and William Jenner of Indiana, Kenneth Wherry of Nebraska, and Joseph McCarthy of Wisconsin. It drew heavy financial support from men like General Robert E. Wood of Sears Roebuck Co. and Henry Timken Jr. of Timken Roller Bearings, and press support from Robert R. McCormick's *Chicago Tribune*. It received advice on foreign policy from men like Arthur Bliss Lane, Truman's former ambassador to Poland, William C. Bullitt, Roosevelt's former ambassador to the Soviet Union, and Generals MacArthur and Albert C. Wedemeyer. Both had served in the Pacific during World War II and were long embittered by the Truman–Roosevelt emphasis on Europe first.

Senator Robert Taft of Ohio, leader of the conservative wing of the Republican Party *(Library of Congress)*

The leading candidate of the conservative forces was Taft, the brilliant "Mr. Republican," who had announced his candidacy in October 1951. The slightly paunchy figure, with his thinning hair, round face, and glasses, was a familiar figure in American politics. The son of William Howard Taft and a graduate of Yale University and Harvard Law School, he was a Midwestern patrician. He was also a self-proclaimed foe of the New Deal and Fair Deal at home and abroad. Denied the GOP presidential nomination in 1948, Taft, unlike Wendell Willkie and Dewey, wanted a clear-cut departure from Democratic foreign and domestic policies. He was the candidate of the rock-ribbed Republicans who resented the quadrennial dominance of the internationalist, more liberal, Eastern wing of the party.

Taft's strictures and attacks were often extreme; for example, he warned that the New Deal, excessive federal spending, and economic planning meant socialism—for him, the end of American liberties. Yet he had actually supported aid to agriculture, public housing, higher minimum wages, expanded Social Security, and federal grants to education and hospitals. And although he vigorously emphasized economy in government and opposed the welfare state, he was legitimately concerned about unfortunate Americans—estimated by Taft as no less than a fifth of the nation—whom he was prepared to offer what he openly called federal "charity." He opposed price and wage controls immediately after World War II, but he was not a doctrinaire advocate of laissez-faire; he usually put his faith in the free market and distrusted government red tape and bureaucracy. Despite his concern for a balanced budget, he did not believe that the budget had to be balanced annually and, as a result, endorsed the major tax cut in 1945, even though it clearly meant a deficit in 1946.

Fearing bureaucracy and viewing the state as a threat to liberty, he preferred local government, which he assumed was close to the people, to centralized government. He was also generally unconcerned about business power and private restraints on competition, except for labor unions. He also emphasized in the case of labor unions the dangers of leaders, misusing funds or of coercing their members. His solution—the Taft–Hartley law—was poorly constructed, though it was not a "slave labor" bill, as labor leaders and the administration had charged.

So great was his concern with liberty and his fear of the federal government that he had opposed the draft in 1940. Along with many congressmen in the early cold war years, he again was a proponent of voluntarism until reluctantly retreating from this position in 1948 so that America could meet its increased foreign commitments. In combating Communism at home, he had shown similar concerns about protecting individual liberty. He was unwilling to outlaw the party, and he opposed government interference in colleges to root out reds. Taft could on occa-

sion appear foolish, as when he opposed the nomination of David Lilienthal to the chairmanship of the Atomic Energy Commission because the former New Dealer was "soft on Communism." As the election approached, Taft's concern for political liberties seemed to wane, and he even supported Joseph McCarthy. First regarding him as reckless, Taft, repudiating his own values, was later quoted as saying that the senator from Wisconsin "should keep talking and if one case doesn't work out, he should proceed with another." "It was the pro-communist policies of the State Department which fully justified . . . McCarthy in his demand for an investigation," Taft declared. He also played loosely with the truth when he declared that McCarthy's investigation had been "fully justified by repeated dismissals of employees of doubtful loyalty."

It was in foreign policy, more than in domestic policy, that Taft's position differed from that of the administration and the Eastern wing of the GOP. Taft was more critical of national objectives and more wary of the ways in which American influence was being expanded. Unlike the Eastern leaders, he denied that America had a mission to extend democracy abroad, and he warned against trying to impose American democratic institutions in foreign lands. It was not, as was so often charged, that Taft was an isolationist and they were internationalists, but rather that he was usually more conscious of the limitations of American power and less willing to extend American commitments abroad. A supporter of America First before Pearl Harbor, he had denied that Germany constituted an imminent threat to the United States, and therefore he had been considered an isolationist. During the war years, when Soviet–American friendship was a popular theme and American policy makers publicly praised the Soviet Union and its democracy, he warned that the alliance was grounded in common need and common enemies, not common values. In the late war years, Taft, like many Republicans, was a supporter of the U.N., though, unlike Vandenberg, then a celebrated internationalist, Taft foresaw more of the world organization's shortcomings and problems, concluding that it would not solve many of the basic problems in international relations. Each wanted the world organization to be an instrument of American foreign policy, but Taft, always more interested in law, despaired that the U.N. could not develop or enforce international law.

Differing with the early Truman foreign policy, as well as the similar policies of the Eastern wing of his own party, Taft repeatedly questioned efforts to extend American influence abroad and to establish international peace and prosperity. He challenged their firm belief that the American economy depended significantly on foreign trade, and he doubted whether expanding foreign trade and investment were necessary in order to increase domestic employment or produce prosperity. He did not believe that America was in danger of economic stagnation. Like other critics of earlier American economic expansion abroad, he believed that the domestic market, not the foreign market, was the key to American prosperity, and he supported tariffs to reduce foreign competition in the home market. He also feared that greatly increased investments abroad would "build up hostility," not friendship. As a critic of economic multilateralism, Taft, unlike the administration or the Eastern wing, did not have the same faith that the reduction of trade barriers and the expansion of world trade would necessarily reduce world tension and promote peace.

In 1947, Taft objected to Truman's request for military and economic aid to Greece and Turkey and emphasized that America's action was dangerous and provocative. "I do not want war with Russia," he said. Moreover, the Truman Doctrine could mean "domination over the affairs of those countries [which is] similar to Russia's demands for domination in her sphere of influence." Unlike many Americans, he pointed to the dangers of a double standard: "If we assume a special position in Greece and Turkey, we can hardly . . . reasonably object to the Russians asserting their domination in Poland, Yugoslavia, Rumania, and Bulgaria." Reluctantly he acceded to the president's request, lamely explaining that the Senate should not rebuff the chief executive on such an important matter and thereby damage his prestige. Taft also supported the Marshall Plan, though he tried often to reduce appropriations, and he emphasized the dangers to the domestic economy, contending that exports would contribute to inflationary conditions. Taft drew strong support from the limited number who shared his sophisticated analysis, but much of his support on foreign policy came from the larger number who simply mistrusted aspects of America's new role in the world. And it was the latter position that prominent GOP House leaders like John Taber, Joseph Martin, and Harold Knutson seemed to represent.

In 1949, when the administration presented the North Atlantic Treaty to the Senate, Taft led the opposition and tried to break the bipartisan consensus on foreign policy. He denied that Russia was committed to military expansion or that it constituted a military threat to Western Europe or the United States. A military alliance with nations on the border of Russia, he stressed, was dangerous and might well provoke Russia into war. In addition, he posed some major legal objections: that the treaty violated the U.N. charter; and that it obligated the United States to send troops and arms to Europe. He was not opposed, however, to the concept of American involvement in Europe and recommended, in lieu of the pact, that Congress pledge that the United States would retaliate militarily if the Russians attacked Western Europe. In

effect, he was contending that the United States should make explicit its reliance on the nuclear deterrent and extend that protection to western Europe. Because he feared weakening the domestic economy through excessive expenditures for defense and he was reluctant to commit more troops abroad, he emphasized an American defense based on air and sea power. It was not "isolationism" or a "Fortress America" that he was proposing but rather a different strategy for defending America and the areas he regarded as useful, though not essential, to her security. Unlike the administration and the Dewey wing, he did not regard Western Europe (outside Britain) as essential to American security. To defend this area, he was not proposing massive retaliation, but he was offering policies "to deter Russia from military aggression [without being] so provocative as to give Russia a sound reason for such aggression."

Taft was defeated by the bipartisan coalition on foreign policy. They swept away his arguments and stressed that the alliance was essential to stop Russian military expansion into Western Europe. (Administration spokesmen, under probing questioning, admitted a different case: the treaty was essential, not to block Soviet expansion, but to bind the European nations together, to restrain impulses for "appeasement," and to strengthen American influence in Europe.)

In 1951, facing the same bipartisan coalition in the so-called Great Debate on foreign policy, Taft, Herbert Hoover, and other conservative Republicans were blocked in their efforts to trim the defense budget, redesign American strategy, and cut American commitments abroad. Like many Americans, Taft and his cohorts were angry that America's European allies had not created large armies for their own defense, and for this reason, having little sympathy for Europe's economic problems, the Republicans favored avoiding what they judged an unnecessary, costly, and dangerous troop commitment to Europe. Europe's paltry armies, even when supplemented by American ground troops, could neither deter nor defeat a Soviet attack, these men concluded.

Hoover, warning of the danger of land war in Europe and fearful of weakening the American economy, recommended that the United States concentrate on the defense of the Western Hemisphere (a "Fortress Gibraltar") and rely on building up the navy and air force, not the army. Taft, advancing the same concern about the economy, also raised fundamental strategic objections to building up American forces in Europe: a great increase by the United States might at first provoke an arms race, but if the Soviets feared that they would ultimately lose ground, they might be provoked into attacking first. Put bluntly, if the American buildup was designed to offset the Soviets, and if it would not be completed for about three years, why should the Soviets delay? "If they have no intention to attack," as Taft concluded, "then we don't need the armed forces."

The administration relied on General Dwight Eisenhower, who returned from Europe to testify on behalf of the program. His testimony, however, supported portions of the Taft–Hoover analysis. He did not argue that the addition of American troops would deter or defeat the Russians; he claimed only that American troops would improve the morale of Europeans and make them more likely to expand their own armies and improve their own defense. In substance, he was agreeing with Taft and Hoover that Europe was primarily responsible for its own ground defense, but he was disagreeing on the means of inspiring Europeans to construct that defense. Eisenhower, unlike Hoover and Taft, however, did assert that Europe was essential—not just useful, as Taft purported, or unnecessary, as seen by Hoover—to American security.

When Secretary of Defense George Marshall indicated that the United States intended to send no more than four more divisions to Europe, the debate dwindled to narrow, but important, disputes over presidential power and secrecy. The latter, probably the more important in the long run, received the least attention. Taft and a few others complained that the administration concealed so much strategic information on the grounds of military security that the Senate could not properly exercise its authority. The administration and its supporters avoided a direct confrontation on this issue. Instead, they focused on defending their contention that the president, without explicit authority from the Senate, had the power to commit troops to the NATO defense. The fundamental question was partially resolved by passage of a Senate resolution that "it is the sense of the Senate that no troops in addition to such four divisions should be sent to Western Europe in implementation of the North Atlantic Treaty without further Senatorial approval." On this vote, 38 Republicans and 11 Democrats triumphed over a coalition of 35 Democrats and 8 Republicans. It was this minority of Republicans, all members of the Eastern liberal wing of the party, who sought to protect the GOP and the nation from Taft and his followers by blocking his presidential candidacy.

To stop Taft, the liberal, "internationalist" wing of the Republican Party sought a candidate who could win and maintain the European orientation of the bipartisan coalition on foreign policy. As early as the autumn of 1950, Governor Thomas Dewey had removed himself from the campaign and proposed Dwight D. Eisenhower, "a very great world figure, the president of Columbia University, one of the greatest soldiers of history, a fine educator, a man who really understands the problems of the world."

The popular commander of the allied forces in Europe during World War II, Eisenhower had been coveted by the politicians of both parties since the defeat of Germany. So enamored of him was President Truman in 1945 that he had told him (but later denied), "There is nothing that you may want that I won't try to help you get. That definitely and specifically includes the Presidency in 1948." Though the general's political affiliation was unknown, liberal Republicans had tried to enter him in presidential primaries in 1948, and that year the Americans for Democratic Action had sought to dump Truman in favor of Eisenhower. Although he rebuffed both parties, Eisenhower still remained the favorite hope of many in both parties.

"Nothing in the international or domestic situation especially fits for the most important office in the world a man whose adult years have been spent in the country's military forces," he explained in 1948. "My decision to remove myself completely from the political scene is definite and positive." When he completed his term as chief of staff in 1948, he told reporters that he had no presidential ambitions: "I don't believe a man should even try to pass his historical peak. I think I pretty well hit my peak in history when I accepted the German surrender in 1945. Now why should I want to get into a completely foreign field and try to top that? Why should I go out and deliberately risk that historical peak by trying to push a bit higher?"

His refusals deterred few. His claims of inadequacy were interpreted as modesty, thereby contributing to his greatness. To politicians and pundits, the amiable general seemed an embodiment of virtue and a potentially powerful political leader. Unlike the arrogant, austere MacArthur, who could command respect but seldom affection, Eisenhower was the GI's general—understanding, knowledgeable, sympathetic; in short, a wise father. Born into a Texas family in modest circumstances, reared in Kansas, he became in his own lifetime a legend. With his magnetic grin and personality, he was a candidate worthy of a PR man's invention. Even his failure as president of Columbia was little known beyond the university, and few politicians or other citizens would begrudge him his interest in football and his lack of interest in education.

Fortunately for Eisenhower, he was quickly lifted out of Columbia when President Truman asked him in late 1950 to become the supreme allied commander in Europe, where he would struggle to create a strong North Atlantic Treaty Organization (NATO) force. Symbolizing collective security and a Europe-first orientation, the general rendered himself an even more attractive candidate. By the spring of 1951, a Gallup Poll indicated that 40 percent of the Democrats favored him for the presidency, while only 20 percent wanted Truman. Among GOP voters, Eisenhower was also the front-runner: Eisenhower 30 percent, Taft 22 percent, Dewey 16 percent, and Earl Warren, governor of California, 13 percent.

By late summer of 1951, a Draft Eisenhower organization was taking form. Its sponsors were Dewey, Herbert Brownell (Dewey's former campaign manager), Senators James Duff of Pennsylvania, Henry Cabot Lodge and Leverett Saltonstall of Massachusetts, Frank Carlson of Kansas, and Irving Ives of New York; and Governors Sherman Adams of New Hampshire, Val Peterson of Nebraska, Edward Arn of Kansas, Arthur Langlie of Washington, Walter Kohler of Wisconsin, and Dan Thornton of Colorado. At the same time, a group of Eisenhower's friends, including Philip Reed, chairman of the board of General Electric, and General Lucius Clay, then a Wall Street financier-industrialist, were independently organizing to promote Eisenhower. In October, the prestigious *New York Herald-Tribune*, a major Republican paper, endorsed the general, and Lodge, selected by the Draft Eisenhower group, became the campaign manager of the uncommitted candidate.

In 1951, politicians of both parties scurried to Supreme Headquarters Allied Powers, Europe (SHAPE) in Paris to enlist Eisenhower in the presidential race. While the general refused to commit himself and still seemed unwilling to seek the nomination, there is evidence that men on his staff, presumably with his knowledge, were working for his nomination. In November, when he returned to Washington for military talks with Truman, Eisenhower, according to Washington reporter Marquis Childs, seemed to be leaning toward becoming a candidate. The general "held a press conference at which the 'no' was so faint as to become the equivalent of 'yes.'" When reporters asked whether he had authorized Senator Duff to work on his behalf, he replied evasively, "If I have friends that have been my friends so long they know how I would act and react under given circumstances, that's their own business and I have never attempted to interfere with any man exercising his own privileges as an American citizen." This ambivalence persuaded many that the General was indeed in the running.

Looking back on this period in later years, Eisenhower stressed the importance of the September visit by Lodge, who implored the general to become a candidate. More than a year before, in June 1950, Lodge also had discussed the subject with Eisenhower and told him that he might have to run in order to preserve the two-party system and avoid permanent Democratic hegemony, the death of the GOP, and what Lodge's biographer, William Miller, calls "the inevitable drift into a third-rate socialism." Eisenhower admitted that, if those were the threatening possibilities that his election could forestall, he would run, though "it would be the bitterest moment of my life." In

their 1951 meeting, Lodge, emphasizing the need of the GOP and the dangers of deficit spending, inflation, and centralization of power, found Eisenhower (as the senator later reported) "in substantial agreement." The party, they concurred, needed someone who would reverse the trend at home but avoid the Old Guard's "fatal errors of isolation." (Eisenhower told a publisher privately, "Taft is no more an isolationist than I am. In fact, he goes farther in some things than I do, not as far as I do in other things, but he certainly is not an isolationist.") "For the first time," Eisenhower later wrote, "I had allowed the smallest break in a regular practice of returning a flat refusal to any kind of proposal that I become an active participant. . . . I began to look anew—perhaps subconsciously—at myself and politics." When Truman queried him in December about his political intentions, Eisenhower responded that there had been no change in his "personal desires and aspirations," but he also noted that "fervent desire may sometimes have to give way to a conviction of duty."

What the liberal internationalists had was a prospective candidate willing to be drafted but unwilling to plan a draft or struggle for the nomination. On January 4, 1952, Lodge, acting without Eisenhower's express approval, declared that the general was a Republican and entered his name in the New Hampshire primary. "I will not be repudiated," he told reporters. "Go and ask the General." A day later, Eisenhower confirmed Lodge's statement that he was a Republican but still emphasized that he would not "seek nomination to political office." Stressing the importance of his duties at NATO, he said, "In the absence of a clear-cut call to political duty, I shall continue . . . [at this] vital task." Alongside the statement of obligation and duty was an assumption of some arrogance, for Eisenhower was suggesting that the politicians and the party might bestow the nomination on him without even knowing his position on many issues. His supporters put together reprints of his earlier remarks, and from these often vague statements the staff tried to piece together his policies.

It was difficult for Eisenhower's opponents to run against the "phantom candidate," as some of Taft's supporters unwisely described the general. But it was equally difficult for the professional politicians backing him, for they feared that his chief rival would secure delegates while the general presided over NATO. To demonstrate Eisenhower's popularity to politicians and to Eisenhower himself, his backers arranged a late-night rally (after a prize fight) at Madison Square Garden in February. Fifteen thousand enthusiastic supporters attended, and the jamboree was put on film, which was immediately flown to Paris for Eisenhower's viewing. To emphasize the growing support, 19 Republican members of Con-

This Daniel Robert Fitzpatrick cartoon, titled "Well, There It Is," shows a cook outside a building labeled "Eisenhower Headquarters" shouting, "Come an' git it" to a startled GOP elephant. It comments on the first real indication that General Eisenhower would accept a Republican nomination for the presidency in the election of 1952. Senator Henry Cabot Lodge reported on January 6 that Eisenhower would consider running, and the general did not repudiate the statement. *(Library of Congress)*

gress urged him to return and campaign actively for the nomination.

On March 11, in the New Hampshire primary, the first in the nation, the Taft and Eisenhower candidacies met. Actually, it was a three-cornered race, with the irrepressibly ambitious Harold Stassen, the youthful ex-governor of Minnesota, then on leave from the presidency of the University of Pennsylvania, also an announced candidate and staking out roughly the same terrain on foreign policy that Eisenhower would occupy. Stassen toured the state, and Taft, who had been campaigning in Colorado, moved into New Hampshire. The senator attacked the general for his absence and warned the voters not to support a man without knowing his position. Taft expected defeat but hoped for a close race, feeling he could not afford to let Eisenhower win by default. Against Taft, the Eisenhower forces massed a powerful array of supporters: Governor Sherman Adams, several former New Hampshire governors, and Lodge, who helped win for the general an even greater victory than Taft had feared. The Dewey group had even advertised in New York that New Hampshire voters living in the city could get a

free ride home for the primary. Not even MacArthur's telegram to a backer, "Suggest you support Taft," could reverse the tide. Eisenhower received 46,661 votes, Taft 35,838, and Stassen 6,574. "The way is clear and victory stands at the end for all to see," declared the powerful *Washington Post* in support of the general. From Paris Eisenhower announced his gratitude in characteristically wooden prose. "Any American who would have that many Americans pay him that compliment would be proud or he would not be an American."

Eight days later, his candidacy received an unexpected boost in Minnesota, the home state of favorite son Harold Stassen. A local attempt to put Eisenhower on the ballot, despite the protests of the national organization, which wanted to avoid a clash with Stassen, had been rejected because of defective petitions, but the general's supporters in the state decided just five days before the election to launch a write-in campaign. When the votes were counted, Eisenhower had been edged by Stassen by only about 20,000 votes (129,076 to 108,692), with Taft, without an organized write-in campaign, a distant third, receiving 24,093 votes. In response to the so-called "Minnesota Miracle," Eisenhower told reporters that he was "astonished." "The mounting number of my fellow citizens who are voting . . . [for] me . . . are forcing me to reexamine my present position and past decision."

During these victories, the Taft organization was working effectively to secure delegates and stressing the Ohio senator's popularity with the people and with GOP rank-and-filers. Repeatedly cast on the defensive by charges that Taft could not win the presidency and that labor would oppose him, his backers stressed his landslide victory, by the greatest margin in Ohio history, over his Democratic opponent for the Senate in 1950. They neglected to mention that the opponent was a nonentity and that Ohio's popular Democratic governor had backed Taft. The Taft organization also worked feverishly to circulate the results of favorable polls and to conduct their own. In a poll of Republicans shortly before the primaries, Taft received 34 percent, Eisenhower 33 percent, and MacArthur, Stassen, and Earl Warren each 14 percent. In a poll of House Republicans in February, 81 of 144 responding favored the senator and only 37 preferred the general. By late March, after the selection of delegates was completed in four states (Florida, New Hampshire, Oklahoma, and North Carolina) and almost completed in five others (Minnesota, Tennessee, Pennsylvania, Kansas, and Arkansas), the Associated Press gave Taft 50 delegates, Eisenhower 32, Stassen 22, and MacArthur 2, with 18 uncommitted.

During the spring, the Taft forces continued to lead in lining up delegations, though the results in the primaries and state conventions suggested a near standoff.

Eisenhower clearly was more popular on the East and West coasts, and Taft was stronger in the Midwest. In the Wisconsin primary, which the Eisenhower forces did not enter, Taft won a plurality over Warren and Stassen but lost in three congressional districts in and around Milwaukee and Madison, thereby prompting renewed fears that labor and city voters would oppose him. In Nebraska, where both Eisenhower and Taft were write-in candidates, the senator won 36 percent (79,357) of the votes, while Eisenhower received 30 percent (66,078), and Stassen, who was on the ballot, got 24 percent (53,238). It was a bitter campaign in which the Taft organization charged that "Eisenhower . . . is the candidate of those who would have American boys die as conscript cannon fodder thousands of miles across the ocean."

On April 11, Eisenhower asked to be relieved of his duties by June 1, and his campaign organization, then receiving able guidance from Herbert Brownell of the Dewey machine, became more optimistic with the prospect that their man would return in time to meet and court the convention delegates.

Four days after Ike's announcement, the general won the New Jersey primary by almost 160,000 votes over Taft, who had tried unsuccessfully to withdraw after Governor Alfred Driscoll broke his pledge of impartiality and backed Eisenhower. In Massachusetts, all but one member of the Taft slate was defeated by the "unpledged" delegation that represented Eisenhower. Taft, as expected, won in the uncontested primary in his home state, as well as all but one delegate in West Virginia. In the Oregon primary, however, the Eisenhower forces triumphed, as they did at the state conventions in Washington and Connecticut. Both major candidates stayed out of the California primary on June 3, won by Governor Earl Warren—a favorite son, liberal, Republican, and dark horse candidate, who was hoping for a convention deadlock. The same day, in South Dakota, Taft won a narrow victory over Eisenhower, 64,695 to 63,879.

On June 2, Eisenhower retired from the army and returned to Abilene, Kansas, his boyhood home, where he enjoyed his second homecoming in seven years. At the celebration, he offered the townspeople his counsel: "In spite of the difficulties of the problems we have, I ask you this one question: If each of us in his own mind would dwell more upon those simple virtues—integrity, courage, self-confidence, an unshakable belief in the Bible—would not some of these problems tend to simplify themselves? . . . I think it is possible that a contemplation, a study, a belief in those simple virtues would help us mightily." That evening the general offered a nationwide audience the same simple thoughts. He was calling for the regeneration of American life. He looked for responsible citizenship and promised that neither "international dif-ficulties nor internal problems . . . [could] defeat the real America." He warned of four threats to American life—disunity at home, inflation and swollen federal spending, the federal bureaucracy, and Communism abroad. He proclaimed his faith in "peace with honor" and "reasonable security with national solvency," and concluded that he believed "in the future of the United States."

In the next few weeks Eisenhower actively campaigned for the nomination. Glad-handing delegates as far east as New York, he also made speeches throughout the Midwest and Texas. He opposed socialized medicine, called for the end of price and wage controls "as rapidly as possible," endorsed state ownership of off-shore oil, promised not to send an ambassador to the Vatican, favored reducing the voting age to 18, warned of the worldwide Communist threat, and urged "sound fiscal practices and integrity in government." In an attack on the Taft–Hoover wing, he warned against those "who preach that we need do nothing except maintain a destructive retaliatory force for use in the event the Russian army should march." He urged support for the UN and, in a clear challenge to Taft, called for support of NATO. He also broke publicly with the Taft–MacArthur Far Eastern strategy by opposing a military victory in Korea because it could lead to a general war. Chiang's troops were needed in Formosa, he further maintained, and could not be deployed in Korea or encouraged in assaults on the mainland.

By July 6, when the Republican convention opened in Chicago, Taft, according to the *New York Times,* led in the number of delegates with 530 (including 72 contested), needing only 74 for the nomination. Eisenhower had 427 (including 21 contested), with Warren having 76, Stassen 25, 20 were scattered, and the other 118 uncommitted. A Gallup poll predicted that in a race against Adlai Stevenson, the general would receive 59 percent of the vote against Kefauver's 55 percent. In contrast, both Democrats received more support than Taft: Stevenson 45 to the senator's 44 percent; and Kefauver 55 to 41 percent.

Despite the polls, however, the Taft forces had reason for confidence that the Ohio senator would win the nomination. After all, they controlled the National Committee and therefore were able to dominate the convention machinery, an important asset to a strong candidate. They named General MacArthur, who himself still hoped for a popular draft, as the keynoter, made a Taft supporter the temporary chairman, and loaded the list of speakers with such right-wing senators as McCarthy, James Kem of Missouri, and Harry Cain of Washington. In control of the convention, the Taft forces expected to be able to settle in their own favor the disputes over the 68 delegate seats of Texas, Georgia, and Louisiana. Of the three, the one involving the Texas delegation became a cause célè-

Enthusiastic Seconds

In this Reg Manning cartoon, President Truman and Senator Robert Taft duel with an axe and broadsword in contrast to the more delicate fencing of presidential candidates Eisenhower and Stevenson. Manning reflects the vigorous campaign tactics of some of the Republican and Democratic supporters during the presidential election of 1952. *(Library of Congress)*

bre and its resolution shaped the decision on the other two and forecast the outcome of the convention.

The National Committee met in Chicago the week before the convention to settle the disputed delegate issue. The committee promptly refused the request of the Eisenhower camp for telecasts and broadcasts of its deliberations. "Let the people see and hear the evidence," declared Dewey. Guy Gabrielson, chairman of the GOP and a Taft supporter, presented Taft's compromise on the Texas delegation: 22 delegates for the senator and 16 for the general, probably the fairest resolution of the complex problem. Lodge, rejecting the proposal, declared, "General Eisenhower is a no deal man." Undoubtedly, Lodge realized that the National Committee, after Taft's offer, had to endorse the compromise, and he saw no advantage in burying an emotional issue that could still be exploited. Planning to appeal to the convention, Lodge believed that the Eisenhower forces might also gain some of the 17 Georgia and 11 Louisiana delegates that the National Committee had awarded to Taft.

At the convention, the delegates, despite the objections of many Taft supporters, passed the so-called fair play amendment named and proposed by the Eisenhower forces—that contested delegates who had failed to receive at least a two-thirds vote by the National Committee could not vote on the credentials of others. Actually, just a few minutes before the opening session, Taft's managers had agreed to the substance of this proposal, but Lodge, who wanted a public victory, rejected the offer and urged support of the "fair play" amendment, which, to his delight, the Taft group refused to endorse on the floor. The wisdom of this strategy was confirmed when Eisenhower won, 658 to 548, on this first test. Truman, recognizing the significance of the vote, remarked with a smile, "I am afraid that my favorite candidate is going to be beaten."

On the convention floor, the court of last appeal, the Taft forces lost on the Georgia delegation, as had been expected, and then they decided to yield on the Texas delegation. Apparently, they were unwilling to risk another loss on a roll-call count. Not only had Taft lost some delegates to whom he was probably entitled, but he had also lost moral prestige, and his movement had lost momentum. The embittered Taft group tried to regain the initiative by concentrating their attack on Dewey, who, they charged, was the mastermind of the Eisenhower crusade. They attacked him as "the most cold-blooded, ruthless, selfish political boss in the United States today." During the debate on seating the contested delegation, Senator Everett Dirksen, the Taft representative, contributed to one of the ugly incidents at the conventions, as television viewers watched him point accusingly at Dewey and remark that the GOP "had a habit of winning conventions and losing elections." When Dirksen charged Dewey with taking "us down the path to defeat," and warned, "don't take us down that road again," the Taft delegates began booing the New York governor, and then Dewey's supporters assailed Dirksen with boos. Dewey, contributing to the division in the party earlier, had given orders that the New York delegation should absent itself from MacArthur's keynote address.

Taft, not Eisenhower, probably better represented the politics and hopes of the delegates. But many were convinced that he could not win. Echoing this judgment, Clare Booth Luce, delegate from Connecticut and wife of the powerful *Time-Life* publisher, a political enemy of the senator, also argued that Eisenhower's defeat "would be taken by European communists as the signal that America was going home. It would give Stalin the only real political victory he has had in Europe since the formation of SHAPE." Committed to the same theme, the prestigious *New York Times* ran three editorials entitled "Mr. Taft Can't Win." Reporting from the convention, James

Reston wrote, "It is difficult to overestimate the bitterness of the men, now in their fifties and sixties, who have devoted all their mature lives to this political struggle."

According to the estimates of the *New York Times* on the eve of the convention, Taft needed about 75 votes beyond those pledged to secure the nomination. When he lost the three disputed delegations, he needed 120, and his chances waned. Of the delegates either uncommitted or committed to dark horses and favorite sons, Taft could not make sufficient inroads. The 24 Maryland votes, initially pledged on the first ballot to favorite son Governor Theodore McKeldin, were released, with Eisenhower getting 16 when the governor was selected to nominate the general. The Minnesota delegation, pledged to Stassen, a longtime adversary of Taft, could not have been lured into the Taft camp. Nor could Taft have secured Warren's support and the votes of his delegation, for Warren's hopes rested on a deadlock, and his Republican politics were antithetical to Taft's. During the second and third days of the convention, when the Eisenhower forces secured majorities in the previously uncommitted delegations from Michigan and Pennsylvania, it was becoming clear that Eisenhower would triumph. In Michigan, politically powerful Arthur Summerfield entered his camp, and in Pennsylvania, Governor John Fine, after a patronage deal, also joined the Eisenhower camp. Taft also lost 13 delegates from New York, when Dewey, reminding them that he had "a long memory," intimated a loss of patronage should they stay with the Ohioan.

On July 10, the first roll call confirmed the predictions of observers and the fears of the Taft forces. Before states began switching, Eisenhower secured 595 votes, Taft 500, Warren 81, Stassen 20, and MacArthur 10. In the South and Far West, the candidates were about even, but Eisenhower had run 230 votes ahead (301 to 71) in the Northeast, easily offsetting the senator's lead of 120 votes (232–112) in the Middle West. When Minnesota shifted and cast 19 votes for Eisenhower, he officially became the party's nominee. Even then, 280 delegates, 212 from the Middle West, refused to turn their backs on Taft until there was a move by his campaign manager, John Bricker, to make the nomination unanimous.

In looking back on the race, Taft attributed his defeat to several powerful forces: (1) the New York financial community and interests subject to New York influence, which, despite exceptions like banker Lewis Strauss, strongly backed Eisenhower; (2) many of the influential GOP newspapers, which outside the McCormick, Hearst, and Knight chains, "continuously and vociferously" objected to Taft, with many "turning themselves into propaganda sheets for my opponent"; and (3) the opposition of most GOP governors. Taft regretted not having put on a "real primary campaign" in Pennsylvania, New York, Michigan, and Oregon, states whose delegates voted 198–28 for Eisenhower. "The difficulty," the senator noted, "was the tremendous expense involved and the lack of time to make an adequate campaign against newspaper influences."

For Warren and Stassen, the convention was the expected disappointment, for MacArthur a source of bitterness. Hoping to be drafted, the vain general, recently second in public esteem behind Eisenhower, was now only a grand old man to the Grand Old Party, to be revered but not fully trusted. Hoover, privately explaining part of MacArthur's weakness, said the general "has an approach to all great questions in the spirit of the St. James version of the Bible. . . . He had a Napoleonic bent to put through the ideas which he holds very strongly." Rejected by the GOP, this general ultimately became an unwilling candidate, along with eager Jack Tenney, California's local version of Joe McCarthy, on Gerald L. K. Smith's Christian Nationalist Party. The party, gaining a place on the ballot in nine states, affirmed the importance of Christianity, decried traitors in government, and called for MacArthur's "victory" strategy in Asia. It drew support from the extreme right wing of the GOP and underlined the alienation of some of the disgruntled general's loyal supporters, but at no time did the split seriously trouble GOP leaders.

In selecting a vice-presidential candidate, the Eisenhower camp had an opportunity to heal party divisions by offering the position either to Robert Taft or to Taft's own candidate, Everett Dirksen. They were unwilling to make that concession. Instead, Eisenhower's advisers chose Richard Nixon. Nixon, a 39-year-old junior senator from California, had long flirted with the nomination. He offered the party fine geographical balance, an appeal to youth, a record of opposition to corruption, and impressive credentials as a crusading anticommunist. He was also the bête noire of many liberal Democrats because of his red-baiting campaigns in California. "A vote for Nixon is a vote against the communist-dominated PAC," he had declared in 1946. In 1950, Nixon assailed liberal Representative Helen Gahagan Douglas, who had first been unfairly red-baited by her opponent in the Democratic primary as "a member of a small clique which joins the notorious party-liner, Vito Marcantonio of New York, in voting time after time against measures that are for the security of his country." Nixon had already received recognition and acclaim for his tenacious pursuit of Alger Hiss, a probe that ended with a jury finding that the former New Dealer had committed perjury and with the widely held conclusion that he committed espionage.

Regarded by many Republicans as a responsible investigator of Communism, Nixon also evoked strong sympathy from such anticommunist crusaders in the Taft

Dwight Eisenhower arrives at Washington's National Airport on September 10, 1952, and is met by GOP vice-presidential candidate Richard Nixon of California, who holds his four-year-old daughter. With them is chairman of the Republican National Committee, Arthur Summerfield, center. *(Associated Press)*

wing as Senators Jenner, Cain, and Kem. His record was eminently acceptable to the Dewey wing. He had supported the Truman Doctrine, the Marshall Plan, NATO, and troops for Europe, though he had voted for some cuts in foreign aid. Like many Republicans, he was fond of blaming Truman for the Korean War and castigating him for the removal of MacArthur. On domestic economic issues he was more willing to use government power than were such staunch conservatives as Joseph Martin of Massachusetts and Charles Halleck of Indiana but less willing than, say, Jacob Javits of New York. In the 82nd Congress, for example, Nixon had generally supported price and wage controls and favored federal support for school construction, but opposed tax reform, expanded public housing, aid to medical schools, and liberalization of the immigration laws.

Described by one journalist as a "Republican meld of Paul Revere and Billy Sunday," Nixon in the preceding two years had become one of his party's more sought-after speakers. The year before in an address entitled "The Challenge of 1952," he had urged the party to conduct a "fighting, rocking, socking campaign." He attacked the administration for "the whining, whimpering, groveling attitude of our diplomatic representatives who talk of America's fear rather than of America's strength and of America's courage." Sharply critical of Truman's government, he charged that "top administration officials have refused time and time again to recognize the existence of this fifth column . . . and to take effective action to clear subversives out . . . of our government."

The GOP platform represented an uneasy compromise between the Taft and Eisenhower factions and managed by its ambiguities and vagueness to avoid antagonizing either faction. Beginning with a catalog of sins, the Republicans charged the Democrats with depriving citizens of rights, fostering class strife for political purposes, debauching the money system, striving to establish socialism, allowing corruption in high places, shielding traitors, appeasing Communism at home and abroad, and plunging the nation into war without the approval of Congress or the "will to victory." They assailed the administration for past mistakes, affirmed the danger of excessive spending for defense, promised greater preparedness at a lower price, and endorsed the value of collective security. Following Taft and his cohorts, they repudiated "secret understandings such as those at Yalta which aid communist enslavements," condemned the administration for losing the peace in Europe and allowing Mao to win in China, and they proclaimed the end of containment.

The foreign policy section, drafted by Senator Eugene Millikin of Colorado and Clarence Buddington Kelland, two Taft men, and by John Foster Dulles, a former member of the bipartisan coalition of foreign affairs and a representative of Eisenhower, was prepared without bitter disputes. As early as May, Taft had told Dulles confidentially that his speeches indicated "a large area of possible agreement," suggesting that the two camps could write a mutually acceptable plank. Early in the convention, Dulles confided that he had been instructed by the general's political advisers not to reveal that there would be agreement "for they thought it useful to keep the issues alive." The foreign policy plank followed, reflecting much of Dulles's recent article ("A Policy of Boldness") in *Life*. There he had called for "liberation" of the captive peoples of Eastern Europe and implied that American opposition to their enslavement and the inspiration of the Voice of America would lead them to revolt against their oppressors. In the platform this theme was more muted: "The policies . . . will inevitably set up strains and stresses within the captive world which will make the rulers impotent to continue . . . and [will] mark the beginning of their end." In short, the GOP was promising "liberation" without much American expense or the use of American troops.

The platform, while pledging the United States to some undefined "aid" to Europe, also contained a subtle rebuke to the European allies, who had failed so far to provide the military forces they had promised. Such criticism was certainly compatible with Eisenhower's position as well as with Taft's analysis. Seeking to chart a course between the "China-first" and the Europe-first wings of the party, the platform tried to solve the problem by condemning the administration for an "Asia-last" policy and implied that both Asia and Europe could be first. Conveniently, the party neglected to mention that Eisenhower's own efforts

had contributed to the emphasis on Europe and, therefore, to the comparative neglect of Asia.

The party assailed the administration for past mistakes in Korea: the withdrawal of occupation troops "in the face of the aggressive, primed-for-action communist military strength"; the announcement that "Korea was no concern of ours"; the commitment of the U.S. to fight "under the most unfortunate conditions." The platform also complained that the administration did not seek victory: "by their hampering orders they produced stalemates and ignominious bartering with our enemies, and no hope of victory." The GOP, however, was not prepared to endorse MacArthur's strategy of bombing Red China and left unclear what strategy would achieve victory or what victory would mean.

The section on civil rights, particularly when contrasted with the anticommunist crusade, was pitifully weak. The party, aside from condemning bigotry, affirmed the federal government's responsibility to "take action toward the elimination of lynching . . . , the poll tax . . . [and] segregation in the District of Columbia." Retreating from the 1948 platform, which implied compulsory adherence to the Fair Employment Practices Commission (FEPC), the 1952 platform emphasized the obligation of states "to order and control [their] . . . domestic institutions" and lamely suggested that the "Federal Government should take supplemental action to further just . . . employment practices." The party, torn between hopes of bringing blacks back into the GOP fold, on the one hand, and fears of federal power and expectations of making inroads into the South on the other, wrote off blacks.

Appraising the platform, the *New York Times* concluded that it was "broad enough to cover the diverse elements of the party, vague enough not to offend minority or special interests, and denunciatory enough to provide phrases for the campaign ahead." Its meaning, of course, would be defined in the campaign and later by the man in the White House.

No Democratic candidate could fully escape from the liability of the administration, but men distant from Truman at least had a chance of asserting their independence. Such a man was Estes Kefauver, the 48-year-old junior senator from Tennessee. Catapulted to fame by the daily national television coverage of his special Senate Crime Investigating Committee, Kefauver had become a familiar household figure as a result of his crusade against crime. An outsider, a foe of conservative Senator Kenneth McKellar, and conqueror of the corrupt Crump machine in Memphis, Kefauver entered the Senate in 1948 after 10 years in the House. In Congress he had followed the New Deal–Fair Deal domestic and foreign policies. Troubled by the stalemate in Korea, however, he did differ with the administration on strategy. He wanted the U.N. to set terms for a truce, give the Communists a deadline for agreement, and then carry the war to Manchuria if the Communists did not agree.

Emphasizing his independence, he rebuked the administration for failing to root out corruption. Unfortunately for him, his expertise seemed unduly restricted, and his war against crime lacked heroic proportions. Also, as a result of his bold investigations, he had uncovered links between organized crime and big city Democratic bosses, which rendered him unacceptable to powerful men in the party. Indeed, Scott Lucas, former Senate majority leader from Illinois who lost his seat in 1950, blamed his defeat on the exposés of the Kefauver committee. In addition, Kefauver's opposition to the filibuster and his support for home rule in the District of Columbia, which Southerners saw as an assault upon segregation, made him unacceptable to the South.

A few weeks after Kefauver's declaration and before Truman's withdrawal from the race, two other senators entered the contest—Robert Kerr of Oklahoma and Richard Russell of Georgia. Kerr, however, promised to withdraw if Truman decided to become a candidate, while Russell, who had polled 263 votes in the 1948 convention, asserted that he would remain a candidate regardless. Kerr, the respected junior senator from Oklahoma, with only two years experience in the upper house, was near the inner circle of the Senate and had already exercised power in the upper house. Previously a governor of his state and keynote speaker at the 1944 presidential convention, he was a millionaire partner of the powerful oil firm of Kerr–McGee. Because he wore a company button in his lapel, and had used the Congress to advance the interests of his company and the industry, he was sometimes called the "Senator from Kerr–McGee." He generally supported Truman's foreign and domestic policies.

In contrast, Richard Russell was an archenemy of the Fair Deal. As head of the Southern caucus and chairman of the Armed Services Committee, he was one of the most powerful men in the Senate. He had blocked much of Truman's reform legislation and had maintained an effective alliance with the GOP in opposing the administration's domestic program. Loyal to the Democrats in 1948, when the Dixiecrats bolted, Russell was clearly a sectional candidate in 1952. His chances were slim, and probably his candidacy was designed primarily to gain leverage within the party for the Southern interests. Probably to strengthen his position, he hinted that he might accept a third-party nomination if he failed within his own party.

In the first scheduled primary, in New Hampshire in early March, Kerr and Russell stayed on the sidelines, while Kefauver confronted Truman. To the surprise of the nation, Kefauver defeated the president, 19,800 to 15,927, thereby possibly pushing Truman to announce his withdrawal from the race. In Key West, in 1951, the president had confided to close associates that he would not seek another term, and there is no evidence that he wavered in that decision, but there is also none that he had planned before this defeat to make such an early announcement of his plans. Probably the primary did not shape his decision to withdraw, for he knew that he could have the nomination if he wanted it. But the primary did confirm evidence of mass disaffection for the man and his administration, and thereby emphasized that he probably could not be reelected.

With Truman's announced withdrawal, the party bosses needed a man who could stop Kefauver. Neither Kerr nor Russell could rally national support, and in the absence of popular rivals, the senator from Tennessee was winning primaries. Securing twenty-eight delegates in the Wisconsin primary, in which he was unopposed by Kerr and Russell, Kefauver also won in Nebraska, receiving 64,531 votes to Kerr's 42,467. He continued to win the preferential vote primaries—in Illinois, New Jersey, Massachusetts, and Maryland—but in the first three states the delegates by law remained unpledged. Not until May in Florida, against Russell, did Kefauver suffer defeat in a preferential poll, 368,000 to 285,000, thereby losing 19 of the 24 delegates. That defeat seemed to confirm predictions that Kefauver would not receive any Southern votes

This Edmund Duffy cartoon shows Uncle Sam staring in amazement at Truman, who is wearing one of his famous sport shirts decorated with "1952? No! Maybe. Yes." Duffy chides the president for his failure to decide whether to run again in the 1952 election. *(Library of Congress)*

aside from Tennessee's at the convention and that Russell would carry the South.

The candidate many party leaders wanted was Adlai Stevenson, the scholarly and reflective governor of Illinois. Urged by Truman in January to become a candidate and promised support by the president, Stevenson claimed to prefer to run again for the governorship. Admired for his ability and eloquence, the 52-year-old Stevenson, a Midwestern patrician, had established an enviable record: he had cleared up the Republican corruption in Illinois, established a reputation as a reformer, and yet demonstrated that he could work effectively with Jacob Arvey, the Democratic boss of Cook County. Moreover, as a former member of the Roosevelt administration, Stevenson could claim a portion of the New Deal mantle; and his service as assistant secretary of the navy and assistant secretary of state offered the promise of expertise in foreign and military affairs. His chief liability, aside from his comparative obscurity, was that he was a divorced man.

Reluctant to become a candidate despite Truman's offer of support, Stevenson seemed to be favoring W. Averell Harriman, Mutual Security administrator and former secretary of commerce. "If Presidents are chosen for their vision, their courage, and conviction, for their depth of understanding of the meaning of this revolutionary era and the mission of America, you will find them all in [Harriman]," Stevenson declared in late May at a testimonial dinner. As a former ambassador to the Soviet Union for Roosevelt and Truman, Harriman, of all the candidates, was most closely allied with the Roosevelt–Truman administrations. Even though his experience was largely in foreign affairs, and despite the fact that he was a multimillionaire, he was acceptable to labor. Within the party, he appealed to the liberal wing and sought to reconstruct the New Deal coalition, but he lacked the organization and support to extend his candidacy much beyond his native state of New York.

On the eve of the Chicago convention, which opened on July 20, the delegates were widely split: Kefauver 257, Russell 161, Harriman 112, Kerr 45, and Stevenson 41. Stevenson seemed the favorite among party leaders, Kefauver the leader among Democratic voters, and Russell the Southern choice.

Truman, opposed to Russell, Kerr, and Kefauver, had given up on Stevenson and recognized that Harriman could not win. In the days before the convention, the president leaned toward Alben Barkley, the popular vice president, who could, Truman believed, unify his party. A Kentuckian, remembered fondly as the majority leader during the New Deal years, Barkley was likely to be acceptable to both the Northern and Southern wings of the troubled party. But labor bosses blocked him, osten-

Presidential candidate Adlai Stevenson at the Democratic National Convention, Chicago, July 1952 *(Library of Congress)*

sibly because he was too old, but also because they feared that the Kerr–Russell forces might unite behind his candidacy and exercise disproportionate control in the party.

With Barkley rebuffed by labor and forced to withdraw from the race, the convention became a battleground for sectional forces. There were disputes over civil rights and party loyalty, the latter issue emerging in a fight over credentials. It started as a seating contest over the 70 delegates from Texas and Mississippi. The loyalists, representing groups who had backed the national ticket in 1948 and who had promised to do so in 1952, challenged the elected delegates of the states' rights group, who some feared would bolt or refuse to support the convention's nominee if a strong civil rights plank was included. The Kefauver and Harriman forces, looking for support (and opposed to the states' rights groups), backed the loyalists. This liberal coalition sponsored a loyalty pledge, approved by the convention over the bitter opposition of the South, that no delegate could be seated unless he assured the Credentials Committee "that he would exert every honorable means . . . in [his] official capacity . . . to provide that the nominees of this Convention . . . or . . . electors pledged to them, appear on the election ballot under the . . . Democratic Party." On the urging of the president and party officials, the Southern coalition finally agreed to a weak pledge: "That for the convention only, such assurance shall not be in contravention of the existing law of the state, nor of the instruction of the state

Democratic governing bodies." This compromise allowed the seating of the Texas and Mississippi delegations.

Even under the relaxed rule, however, Louisiana, South Carolina, and Virginia refused to file the required statements. Senator Harry Byrd, the dominant power in Virginia politics, explained, "We're just going to sit here and maybe they'll have to throw us out." When the votes of Virginia were challenged publicly, the convention, on the first reading of the roll, opposed seating the delegates. At first it appeared that the efforts at compromise by Frank McKinney, chairman of the party, and Speaker Sam Rayburn, permanent chairman of the convention, had failed; but the Illinois delegation, presumably under the guidance of Arvey, shifted its votes and led a turnabout. In explaining the shift a year later, Arvey said that he realized suddenly that "the strategy of the Kefauver supporters and the northern liberal bloc was to make impossible demands on the Southern delegates so that they would walk out of the convention" and thereby reduce the opposition to the senator from Tennessee. Completing the defeat of this liberal coalition, the convention also voted to seat the other two states.

On the disruptive civil rights issue, the early position of the liberals was weakened through defection and compromise. From the beginning, it was clear that not even moderate Southerners, like Senator John Sparkman of Alabama and Representative Brooks Hays of Arkansas, would accept a platform that included the formation of a compulsory fair employment practices commission. Nor would they accept repeal of the Senate rule on cloture. When some liberals on the 24-member Platform Committee agreed to retreat on these issues, a compromise solution engineered by Sparkman and Dawson was hit upon. There was no specific mention of changing the rules of cloture or of establishing a compulsory fair employment practices commission. The final civil rights plank, retreating from the position of 1948, remained wonderfully vague and was, in substance, a surrender to the southern wing of the party.

The nature and politics of this compromise, as well as the hostility of the convention management and the bosses to Kefauver, made it clear that Stevenson was the likely candidate. Long the choice of party officials and considered the man most likely to consolidate sectional factions, Stevenson disclaimed interest in the nomination without, however, asserting unequivocally that he would not run.

Prior to the nomination, Stevenson emerged as a man of self-doubt, uneasy modesty, indecision, ambivalence: he would not seek the office nor would he refuse it. He sought power, prestige, and responsibility, but he also felt unworthy, inadequate, unsure. By late June, he acknowledged that he would accept a genuine draft, yet he pleaded not to be drafted. Appearing at the caucus of the Pennsylvania delegation, he denied "indecision . . . coyness and . . . uncertainty." "I couldn't, wouldn't, did not wish to be a candidate for President," he told the group. "I ask you therefore in the spirit of our cause . . . to abide by my views and do not nominate me." Wrote columnist Doris Fleeson, who was close to high-ranking Democrats, "It looks as though . . . Stevenson will be dragged to the Presidential altar, his shrieks are growing fainter, his suitors more importunate."

For many party leaders, Stevenson was an alternative to Barkley, who was too old and rejected by labor; to Russell, who was too clearly identified with the South and segregation; to Kerr, a marginal candidate who represented the oil and gas industries; to Kefauver, who had antagonized party leaders; and to Harriman, who was too liberal and without luster.

By the fourth day of the convention, July 24, Stevenson, having slowly resolved his ambivalence, decided to become a candidate. The rest of the drama unfolded in roughly predictable form. Although the Kefauver camp tried to launch a "stop-Stevenson" movement, other liberals, viewing Stevenson's nomination as inevitable, chose

This Don Hesse cartoon shows the Democratic donkey apprehensively clinging to a large rock (labeled "South") that is precariously balanced on another rock. Hesse questions whether all of the Southern states will continue to support the Democratic ticket during the presidential election of 1952. *(Library of Congress)*

to jump on the bandwagon and hoped thereby to move Stevenson away from the Southern camp and toward their own political orbit. Truman, without an alternative candidate and once more wanting Stevenson, backed the governor.

The first ballot was highly inconclusive: Kefauver 340, Stevenson 273, Russell 268, Harriman 123, Kerr 65, and Barkley 48. On the second ballot, Kerr released his votes, Stevenson's vote increased by 50, Russell's and Kefauver's each by 20, and Barkley's by 30. The vice president, who had allowed his name to be placed in nomination, had a brief flurry of hope that his candidacy might emerge from a deadlocked convention. His hopes were dashed even before the third-ballot voting had begun. Harriman, as he had earlier promised Stevenson, announced his withdrawal in favor of the Illinois governor. Governor Paul Dever of Massachusetts, a favorite son, followed suit. Shortly thereafter, Kefauver tried to announce his withdrawal, but Rayburn, the presiding chairman, apparently eager to rebuke him publicly, denied him this privilege and unwisely refused to let him interrupt the roll call. At the end of the roll call but before the results were announced, Stevenson was 2 votes short of the necessary majority. Kefauver was then recognized and withdrew, followed immediately by Russell. The delegates then made the nomination unanimous. A man largely unknown to the nation or even to party members—except for the eloquent welcoming address he had given the convention as governor of Illinois—had been chosen by the Democrats in a convention that had so far avoided the schism of 1948.

The next day, in what is usually an anticlimactic decision, the party moved formally to consider a vice-presidential candidate. The leaders were unwilling to risk antagonizing the South with Kefauver, and they could not risk estranging the North with Russell. The ideal candidate would have been one who would placate many in one section and delight those in the other; a suitable candidate, however, need only please one section and not antagonize the other. In order to soften the blow to the defeated candidates, a meeting of leaders, including Stevenson, Rayburn, Truman, and McKinney, decided to exclude from candidacy all who had been contenders for the presidential nomination. Apparently concerned with conciliating the South, they decided to endorse Senator John Sparkman of Alabama, Russell's floor manager at the convention.

Regarded as a liberal on economic matters, he had voted against granting tidelands oil to the states, for price controls and increased public housing, and against the McCarran Act. On foreign policy, he had backed the administration on the important issues: the Marshall Plan, NATO, arms and troops to Europe, and Point IV.

His record on civil rights, however, was unsatisfactory to liberal Democrats. While not succumbing to open racism, he had demonstrated that he would struggle within the party to defend segregation and racial inequality. "If the nomination of Sparkman was a slap in the face of the Negro voters," declared the Nation, "it was given a special sting by the dishonest attempt to induce Negroes to accept him as something he is not and to justify his record on the grounds that, after all, a Southern liberal must hedge on civil rights measures."

Sparkman was one of the architects of the compromise on civil rights engineered to bring the South into the fold. So disgruntled were 50 of the black delegates, including Congressman Adam Clayton Powell of New York, that they bolted the convention. "They [can] cram a candidate down our throat," declared Powell, "but they cannot make us vote for him."

On most domestic matters, the platform adhered to the New Deal–Fair Deal liberalism: extension of Social Security and unemployment assistance, implementation of the public housing program, maintenance of maximum production, repeal of Taft–Hartley and the McCarran–Walter Immigration Act, and continuation of a strong farm program. The party congratulated itself for its loyalty program, which "has served effectively to prevent infiltration

Adam Clayton Powell (Library of Congress)

by subversive elements and to protect honest and loyal public servants against unfounded malicious attacks." In addition, the platform promised to continue the fight against inflation and, in a clear attempt to run once more against Herbert Hoover, to maintain prosperity.

Undoubtedly, the most important section of the platform was the portion devoted to foreign policy. Under the theme of "peace with honor," the party endorsed intervention in Korea, asserted that such action established that the U.N. would resist aggression, declared that Communist aggression had been halted, and promised that the United States would welcome "a fair and effective" peace. In a direct rebuke to the GOP, the Democrats affirmed their commitment to balanced military forces (and not reliance on the air force) and declared that the economy could support the expenditures that security required. Endorsing collective security, including the Truman Doctrine, the Marshall Plan, NATO, and the Japanese–U.S. military alliance of 1951, the party pledged that it would "not abandon the once-free peoples of Central and Eastern Europe who now suffer under Kremlin tyranny in violation of the Soviet Union's most solemn pledges at Teheran, Yalta, and Potsdam."

The party, proclaiming the accomplishments of the past 20 years, had written a platform defending its past and promising a continuation on most issues of the Fair Deal policies at home and abroad.

For the Eisenhower campaign, the initial strategy for victory was well defined. A "Campaign Plan," prepared by a former advertising man and revised by Eisenhower's advisers, called for the general to court the normal GOP support that was often still attached to Taft and to seek significant inroads among the approximately 45 million "stay at homes." They, not the 4 million independent voters courted by Dewey, were deemed the pivotal voters. Recognizing that the GOP was a minority party and assuming that the "stay at homes" would vote if sufficiently agitated, the recommended strategy was to launch a wholesale offensive. The GOP candidate, by attacking, could define the issues. "The whole spirit of a campaign conducted on this level," explained the plan, "would be one which could inspire a crusading zeal that is impossible to engender by the 'me too' approach, or anything which promises only to better what the administration is doing." Eisenhower, conceiving of himself as a candidate who could unify the country left badly divided by Truman's bungling at home and abroad, had been offered a strategy that corresponded with his hopes for a "Great Crusade." He did not then clearly foresee what others would come to lament: the candidate and the program were being merchandised.

In line with the general strategy, Eisenhower consulted with party leaders, consolidated his control of the party,

and journeyed to the Midwest to meet with Taft supporters who feared his position on international affairs and who resented his victory over the Ohio senator. In August, he also developed the outlines of his tactics; his early speeches criticized the administration for corruption, stressed its failures in foreign policy, and warned against Communism in government and in the nation.

On August 25, appearing before the American Legion in Madison Square Garden, Eisenhower presented his first statement on foreign policy since his acceptance speech. He echoed the themes of "liberation," declaring that the American "conscience" could never rest until the people behind the Iron Curtain were free, but he carefully avoided specifying the means of freeing them. Like the GOP platform, his declaration offered promises without responsibility, a pledge without tactics. Yet, in words that did frighten some Europeans, he did assert that peace with the Soviet Union was impossible as long as there were captive peoples. He offered an analysis of Soviet goals and strategy—"economic containment and gradual strangulation of America." He explained that the Soviets were aiming to destroy America's productive power and economic strength by slowly gaining control of the many areas (through "infiltration" or "seizure") on which the American economy depended for critical materials. Stalin, Eisenhower declared, would never attack until the Soviet Union had gathered the materials and men that would guarantee victory. He concluded that America had time, that war was not near, and that a strong military with "great retaliatory power" (the phrase he had earlier deleted from the platform) would deter attack.

He had avoided the slam-bang assault on the administration that his supporters were counseling. The closest he came to harshness was the complaint that the administration had allowed the "disintegration" of America's military strength and prestige, and lost China "through . . . false starts, fractional measures, loud politics, and faint deeds." He also congratulated the Legion for its efforts in ferreting out Communists at home without "recklessly injuring the reputations of innocent people." His critics rightly concluded that he was insensitive to the need to protect civil liberties, while most supporters applauded his acknowledgment of the internal Communist menace and the need of private groups to take action. It remained for admirers, following *Time,* to interpret this statement as a subtle rebuke to Senator Joe McCarthy.

So disappointed were Eisenhower's admirers in the lackluster performance of their candidate, so dismayed were they that he refused to slug the administration, that sour jokes at his expense soon circulated. One reporter, after a speech by the general, remarked, "He just crossed the thirty-eighth platitude." "Ike is running like a dry creek," declared the front-page editorial of the Scripps-

Howard papers. On the public rostrum, he continued to be a disappointment; he was vague and lifeless, often poorly informed, frequently indefinite and floundering. Aside from Eisenhower's personal weaknesses, the problem as *Newsweek* explained was "how to make such a moderate position dramatic and exciting enough to the millions of independent and Democratic voters the Republicans must enlist if they are to win."

For the next few weeks, the campaign pepped up somewhat as Eisenhower continued to dwell on the themes of bungling in Korea and Communism and corruption in government—what Karl Mundt, in outlining GOP strategy, called "K_1C_2." On September 4, for example, he lashed out at the administration: "This Washington mess is not a one-agency mess or a one-bureau mess . . . it is a top-to-bottom mess. . . . Washington waste and extravagance and inefficiency; of incompetence in high places and low places; of corruption . . .; of bungling in our affairs at home; of fumbling in the life and death matter of war and peace."

Throughout September, however, the chief concern in the Eisenhower camp was not the general's speeches but two other developments: the rapprochement with Taft and the Nixon Fund. On September 12, Taft, accepting Eisenhower's invitation, journeyed to the presidential candidate's home at Morningside Heights to confer on the campaign. What resulted, labeled by Democrats as "the surrender of Morningside Heights," was a retreat by Eisenhower on domestic policy and the endorsement of many of Taft's positions.

Taft, knowing well the value of his support, had an advance guarantee that the general would meet his demands. The senator brought to the meeting a prepared statement that Eisenhower slightly revised before Taft issued it. Taft declared that they agreed "100 percent" on domestic policy and "to a large extent" on foreign policy. They agreed also that the issue between the Republicans and Democrats was "liberty against creeping socialism," that the nation needed a "drastic reduction in federal spending" (to $70 billion, not the $78.5 billion later proposed by Truman for fiscal 1954, and to $60 billion in fiscal 1955), and that Taft–Hartley was basically right. The statement on domestic policy was a retreat from the position that Lodge and Dewey had earlier staked out for the general, but it was a necessary concession by the victorious forces in the party. On foreign policy, however, despite Democratic charges of "surrender," there was nothing more than a vague phrasing that might be taken as retreat: their differences were simply of "degree." It was a matter largely of symbols, not of substance. Eisenhower's greatest concession was not on matters of policy but on party spoils: he promised, if and when elected, not to discriminate against the Taft wing in making appoint-

ments. In return, Taft promised to urge his supporters to work for Eisenhower, and the senator agreed to campaign vigorously in 13 states for the GOP ticket. The "great crusade," quipped Stevenson, had become the "great surrender." He said that the general had sat in the love seat with Taft, "matching pennies against principles." In short, Eisenhower, who had claimed originally to be seeking the GOP nomination to save the nation from Taft, was now embracing him and minimizing differences in order to win the presidency.

On September 18, Eisenhower's "Great Crusade" stumbled on an unexpected embarrassment: the charges that Richard Nixon had received a private "slush fund" of about $16,000 from California businessmen. Declaring the "existence of a 'millionaire's club' devoted exclusively to the financial comfort of Senator Nixon," the New Deal–Fair Deal *New York Post* broke the story that afternoon under the headline "Secret Rich Men's Trust Fund Keeps Nixon in Style Far Beyond his Salary," and it was promptly picked up by the nation's press and splashed on front pages. For the Eisenhower campaign, which condemned corruption in Truman's government, the charges meant scandal, the besmirching

This Adlai Stevenson Democratic Party poster warns against a return to the Republican policies of Herbert Hoover. (*Labor's Committee for Stevenson & Sparkman Campaign*)

of Eisenhower's case, maybe even the dumping of his running mate. How could Eisenhower promise a clean sweep when his handpicked vice-presidential candidate, charging the Democrats with a "scandal a day," was taking money under the table?

At first, few in the party realized the explosive nature of the charges. Nixon issued a prompt statement: the money, collected by some supporters in the 1950 campaign, had been used to defray the political expenses—for travel, postage, and secretaries—which he felt could not be charged to the federal government. Soon the Eisenhower group recognized the danger. The short-run strategy was to delay until the issues could be assessed, until there was more time for public reactions, until advisers could confer. Keeping Nixon could be a liability. But his dismissal might be even more costly. Sherman Adams later reported that Eisenhower had told him privately, "If Nixon has to go, we cannot win." The evening after the *Post*'s story, Eisenhower announced that Nixon would provide a full accounting of the fund. Departing from his prepared text on corruption in government, Eisenhower told a Kansas City audience, "Knowing Nixon as I do, I believe that when the facts are known to all of us, they will show that Dick Nixon would not compromise with what is right. Both he and I believe in a single standard of morality in public life."

The *Washington Post* and the *New York Herald-Tribune,* which were supporting the GOP ticket, called for Nixon's resignation. Volunteers for Eisenhower across the country joined the chorus. In the New York office of the Eisenhower headquarters, most of the nonprofessionals, like speechwriter Emmet Hughes, favored dumping Nixon. His support came chiefly from the professional politicians. Robert Taft, for example, declared that there was no impropriety in accepting financial assistance as long as there were no favors in return. Adlai Stevenson avoided condemnation and offered a similar standard. (Years later, when Nixon looked back on what he had first considered Stevenson's charity, he saw it as an effort to avoid disclosure of the governor's own political fund, which was used to assist underpaid officials.)

Two days after the *Post* story, the chief trustee of the fund made public the details of the fund (actually $18,235) and confirmed Nixon's statement that the money was for political expenses. There were 76 contributors (the average was $250 and the largest was $1,000) whom *Time* called a "Who's Who of Southern California business"—oilmen, department store owners, bankers, and industrialists. Denying any wrongdoing or any attempt to win influence, he explained that the fund was established "because Dick Nixon is the best salesman against socialism and government control of everything in this country." Allen Haywood, CIO executive vice

president, charged that the businessmen had "earned handsome dividends," and he cited Nixon's support for the oil depletion allowance, his vote against raising the capital gains tax, and his opposition to public housing and rent control.

Nixon, cast on the defensive, lashed out at his attackers. He blamed the "smear" on the "communists and the crooks in the Government," who were trying to stop his attacks on them. Senator Karl Mundt of South Dakota, co-chairman of the Republican Speakers Bureau, called the assault on Nixon a "filthy" tactic devised by "left-wingers, fellow-travelers," and a "self-admitted three-year member of the Young Communist League," James Wechsler, the anticommunist editor of the *New York Post.*

To regain support, Nixon had to take his case to the people; to remain pure but to avoid condemning Nixon, Eisenhower had to let the people decide whether the senator should remain on the ticket. Nixon, partly on the advice of Dewey, presented his case on national television. Appearing on September 23, just five days after the story first broke, Nixon addressed the largest television audience ever assembled to that date. His speech, described variously as a "masterpiece" and a "soap opera," detailed the argument he had made earlier, disclosed information about his debts and the disbursement of funds, jibed at Democrats ("Pat doesn't have a mink coat"), scolded Democratic Senator John Sparkman for having his wife on the payroll, and included a tearjerker. He was putting his future in the hands of the people, but there was one present he would not return: "Checkers," the young cocker spaniel given to his daughters. They loved him too much, and he would not hurt his children. Declaring that his record was unblemished, that he was no "quitter," that he was dedicated to Eisenhower and to driving "the communists and those that defend them out of Washington," he asked the American people to determine his future by wiring or writing to the GOP National Committee.

In the Cleveland auditorium where Eisenhower was scheduled to speak, nearly 15,000 had watched Nixon's performance. "Many women were weeping," reported the *New York Times.* Eisenhower tossed away his prepared speech and discussed the Nixon case: "Tonight I saw an example of courage." Before making a final decision, however, he concluded that he should speak privately with Nixon. The vice-presidential candidate, feeling rebuffed and believing that the general should have immediately offered his public blessing, briefly considered resigning. The deluge of telegrams—nearly 200,000—to the National Committee, as well as the unanimous support of all national committeemen who could be reached, made Eisenhower's decision inevitable and politically safe. At the airport, he met Nixon, announced, "You're my boy," and in fatherly fashion put his arm around the shoulder of the man whom some still regarded as the wayward son.

In his speech, Nixon had jabbed at Stevenson, who, it had been revealed, also had a private, secret political fund. The Illinois governor had explained a few days before that he used his fund ($18,700 from his 1948 gubernatorial campaign, and later supplemented by $2,900) "to make gifts, usually around Christmas time, to a small number of key executives who were making sacrifices to stay in State Government." The real question, in both cases, was not whether the monies swelled the wealth of the candidate but whether the donors received special benefits, though unkind rumors continued to linger around Nixon.

Eisenhower, having made peace with Taft and having weathered the storm over Nixon, still had to maintain unity in the party, particularly in the right wing. After the convention, when asked whether he would back red-hunters like Senators Jenner and McCarthy, the general had declared that he would endorse all GOP candidates but would not support "anything that looks . . . like unjust damaging of reputation." The first major test of this policy occurred in mid-September in Indiana, where the general appeared on the same platform with Jenner, who had called General George Marshall, Eisenhower's former superior, a "front man for traitors," and received from the senator two or three public embraces. "I felt dirty from the touch of the man," Eisenhower later told an associate. When the "Great Crusade" rolled toward Wisconsin, McCarthy joined the campaign train, met with Eisenhower for an hour's conference, which the senator told reporters had been "very, very pleasant," and then introduced Eisenhower at one of the stops in Wisconsin. Earlier, among Eisenhower's staff, there had been considerable confusion about whether McCarthy would introduce the presidential candidate. Eisenhower himself, in one address when McCarthy was on the campaign train, said, "The differences between me and Senator McCarthy . . . have nothing to do with the end result we are seeking . . . of ridding this government of the incompetents, the dishonest, and above all the subversives and the disloyal. The differences apply to method."

On October 3, in Milwaukee, the general was scheduled to deliver a major address, which included a strong rebuke of McCarthy and a staunch defense of Marshall, whom the senator had called a "traitor." "I know that charges of disloyalty have . . . been leveled against . . . Marshall. I have been privileged for thirty-five years to know . . . [him] personally. I know him, as a man and as a soldier, to be dedicated with singular selflessness and the profoundest patriotism to the service of America." That statement, originally drafted at Eisenhower's request, was also deleted at his request. Apparently when the

paragraph was shown to Governor Walter Kohler of Wisconsin, he pleaded, Sherman Adams later recalled, that "it should be omitted since it was out of context and a too obvious and clumsy way to take a slap at a Senator." Under pressure from other state GOP leaders and his advisers, particularly "Jerry" Persons, Eisenhower concluded that the offending section should be stricken. (Commenting later on the event, Emmet Hughes, author of the offending passage, remarked, this incident "gave warning that certain qualities of the man, even virtues in himself, could be wrenched in the play of politics. . . . Clearly, there was in him a profound humility—a refusal to use the full force of his personal authority or political position against a critical consensus.") Pained by the deletion, Arthur Hays Sulzberger, publisher of the powerful pro-Eisenhower *New York Times,* cabled the general, "Do I need to tell you that I am sick at heart?" Stevenson, who was chided by Eisenhower for his humor, remarked that "My opponent has been worrying about my funnybone. I'm worrying about his backbone." There was little comment from Democratic critics when Eisenhower, two weeks later in Cleveland, called Marshall one of the "great American patriots."

As the Eisenhower campaign seemed in its practices and politics to be moving toward the right, the general received further assistance from his running mate and from McCarthy. Nixon, a master of tasteless invective, called Stevenson "Adlai the appeaser" and a "Ph.D. graduate of Dean Acheson's College of Cowardly Communist Containment." He assailed Stevenson for his "satisfaction with the appeasing, disaster-bent policy of 'containing' global communism" and for his "soft attitude toward the communist conspiracy at home." By the middle of October, as the campaign heated up, Nixon charged that Stevenson had been "duped by Communist Alger Hiss," and he condemned the Democratic nominee for having testified on behalf of Hiss. "Can such a man as Stevenson," Nixon asked on a nationwide broadcast, "be trusted to lead our crusade against communism?"

Stevenson had been asked in 1949 to testify on the basis of "the speech of . . . persons [who have known Hiss], what was his reputation" for integrity, loyalty and veracity. To which the Illinois governor had responded, "Good." Manipulating that evidence, Nixon challenged Stevenson's judgment and cast doubts on his loyalty. In response, Stevenson explained that he had had a responsibility to answer the deposition and that he could not lie: "Hiss's reputation—so far as I had heard from others—was good. [That was] the simple, exact, whole truth." Stevenson also pointed out that Dulles, in 1946, before Hiss was installed as president of the Carnegie Endowment, of which the Republican foreign policy expert was president of the Board of Trustees, had been told that

Hiss had a "communist record" and was offered evidence to support the charge. Dulles rebuffed the informer and affirmed his confidence in Hiss's "complete loyalty." Moreover, the Board, including Dulles and Eisenhower, later rejected Hiss's resignation after he was indicted, and instead granted him a leave of absence. Despite Stevenson's efforts in his own defense, and even his charges against Dulles and Eisenhower, Nixon's attacks helped to blame the Democrats for subversion at home and Communist victories abroad. Eisenhower, while not dwelling on the theme, was willing to exploit the same charges. The administration, he declared, had "allowed the godless Red tide to . . . engulf millions [and had] failed to see the Red stain seeping into the most vital offices of our Government."

McCarthy, in his campaigning, hit on the same themes. On October 28, just eight days before the election, McCarthy delivered a nationwide address devoted to establishing that Stevenson aided the Communist cause. Twice during the speech McCarthy called Adlai "Alger." Inventing falsehoods, fabricating quotes, and misusing evidence, he charged Stevenson with "conniving" with Communists in 1943 and surrounding himself with such allegedly pro-Communist advisers as Arthur Schlesinger Jr., Wilson Wyatt, James Wechsler, and Archibald MacLeish. He conveniently overlooked the anticommunism of these notable liberals and of the Americans for Democratic Action (ADA), which he found red-tainted, and he stated falsely that the Communist Party was supporting Stevenson in 1952. Governor Sherman Adams, offended by McCarthy's vicious onslaught, dissociated himself from the senator and hoped that the speech would not cost Eisenhower votes. The general remained silent. The Democratic Party promptly rebutted McCarthy's charges, stressed Stevenson's anticommunism and that of his advisers, and emphasized that the *Daily Worker* was not supporting the Democratic nominee.

Earlier, when Arthur Summerfield, Eisenhower's appointee as GOP chairman, had charged that Stevenson's selection of Wilson Wyatt as campaign manager "clearly demonstrates that the ultra-left wingers—not the Democratic Party—will have complete charge of the campaign," the ADA responded that Wyatt had always been in the "conservative faction of the body." Adding to the innuendoes from the right, Everett Dirksen, already known for his mellifluous, purple prose, asked, "Just how well does [Stevenson] think his associates look—Alger Hiss, Dean Acheson, Wilson Wyatt, ADA, and the 'lavender lads' of the State Department?"

Eisenhower, having made concessions to the right wing of the GOP, which cost him the support of Senator Wayne Morse, was also pursuing his Southern strategy. He spent more time in the South than had any other Republican

presidential candidate. His caution on civil rights, as well as his endorsement of state ownership of the valuable tidelands oil, was winning defectors from the Stevenson ticket. Introduced in New Orleans by the mayor of the city and the governor of the state before a huge crowd, he called the Democratic platform "un-American" and spoke, in reference to tidelands oil, of "the policy of the Washington power mongers as a policy of grab." In Dixie, he did affirm the need for equal rights for black men, but he would not support any mechanism to accomplish this reform, and even his muted calls for a revision of spiritual values did not threaten racial prejudice or estrange the Southerners he sought to woo. Earlier, he had warned that a compulsory FEPC, then much hated in the South, would only increase racial antagonisms. Even in the North, where his voice on civil rights was stronger, he was usually vague. He claimed credit for the GOP for the gradual advancement of civil rights under Republican governors, and he affirmed the value of a voluntary FEPC over the compulsory agency that Truman had requested. He also attacked Truman's civil rights record as senator, and charged (with

This Edmund Duffy cartoon, titled "There Seems to Be a Tide in the Affairs of Elephants, Too!," shows the GOP elephant in a barrel floating on a stormy sea riding a wave labeled "1952" and carrying a flag labeled "Ike." A bell on a buoy rings out in the foreground. Referring to Shakespeare's prediction in *Julius Caesar* ("There is a tide in the affairs of men which, taken at the flood leads on to fortune"), Duffy comments on the election of 1952 when Eisenhower was elected president and the Republicans took control of Congress. *(Library of Congress)*

some accuracy) that the president had exaggerated his friendship for blacks. "Would a true friend advocate on an all-or-nothing basis measures to improve race relations that were so extreme as to be certain of uncompromising opposition?" Eisenhower asked. In Harlem, he avoided civil rights, aside from claiming falsely that he had worked in the army to eliminate military segregation and promising as president to complete the task (which actually was not even started in Europe until 1952). In this election, unlike 1948, civil rights was not a popular issue, and the GOP would not invest much capital in a cause that did not enlist its sympathy or concern.

Eisenhower, by accepting the New Deal, removed from the campaign the dispute over welfare so dear to the hearts of many right-wing Republicans. "Social security, housing, workman's compensation, unemployment insurance, and the preservation of the value of savings—these are the things that must be kept above and beyond politics and campaigns," he concluded. "They are rights, not issues." When explaining the GOP farm plank at the United Plowing Contest in Kasoon, Iowa, he ended by backing away from it and endorsing the Democratic program of federal restrictions and subsidy payments at a high level of parity.

To many observers within and outside the campaign, Eisenhower seemed to be losing control of his own "crusade." At an early briefing when advisers and advertising men were talking about how best to merchandise his candidacy, he felt neglected, disgusted. "All they talked about was how to win on my popularity," he complained to an associate. "Nobody said I had a brain in my head." The "great crusade" was carefully planned: advance men, crowd builders, telephone campaigns to get out the masses, cheerleaders recruited to toss confetti. So detailed was the planning that there was a 39-page blueprint for his appearance at Philadelphia's Convention Hall. It called for "fresh cut roses (25,000) . . . noisemakers (3,000) . . . flags (5,000) . . . programs (25,000)." The final touch was that Eisenhower should stand so as to be photographed with his right hand on the Liberty Bell.

The merchandising reached its climax with the plan for a $1.5-million campaign of radio and television "spots" in 62 key counties in 12 states in an "all-out saturation blitz" during the last three weeks. In New York City alone, there were 130 "spots" in one day. The emphasis, selected by Gallup, was on the Korean War, corruption, taxes, and the cost of living. The dialogue of "Eisenhower Answers the Nation" went like this: Man-in-the-Street—"Mr. Eisenhower, what about the high cost of living?" Eisenhower—"My wife, Mamie, worries about the same thing. I tell her it's our job to change that on November 4." To a similar question another time, he replied—"Why, there is only one answer. Get that high price crowd out of Wash-

ington." Man-in-the-Street—"General, the Democrats are telling me I never had it so good." Eisenhower—"Can that be true when America is billions in debt, when prices have doubled, when taxes break our backs and we are still fighting in Korea? It is tragic. It is time for a change."

As the campaign unfolded, it became clear how often the major domestic issues were related to the war and to the fight against Communism. High prices, high taxes, and the high budget, the products of rearmament and war, were important issues to consumers. Eisenhower, by promising to cut expenditures for defense, was able to offer military security at a lower price. In substance, his message was prosperity without war, high incomes without high taxes and high prices. Challenging the Democrats' claims that they had established prosperity, Eisenhower charged that war and the threat of war had created good times. Moreover, he pointed out that the average real family income had failed to rise appreciably since World War II, and that the sense of greater prosperity was largely illusory. Not only had the New Deal failed to lift the nation out of the Depression, but the Fair Deal, he charged, was plunging the nation into a recession, averted only by the Korean War and the rearmament program. The slogan "You've never had it so good," he warned, "is a slick Fair Deal paraphrase for, 'You'll never have it any better under us—unless military expenditures keep the economy steamed up.' The Democrats could purchase full employment only at the price of dead and mangled bodies of young Americans."

As the campaign progressed, Eisenhower was slowly making the main issue foreign policy, particularly the war. The general, unwilling to remove this issue from politics as Truman had requested, charged the administration with squandering American prestige and power. Midway through the campaign, on October 2, he spoke for the first time on the peace negotiations that had been dragging on for nearly 15 months. Like many others, particularly those in the right wing of his party, he concluded that the negotiations were a "swindle," a "Soviet trap" designed to allow the North Koreans to repair their weaknesses. Turning from direct criticism of the Truman administration, he offered his own "plan" for conducting the war: prepare the South Koreans to defend their own front lines. "If there must be a war [in Korea], let it be Asians against Asians, with our support on the side of freedom." He was counseling what the administration was seeking to accomplish: train the South Koreans to bear a greater burden. But his thought was so loose, so ambiguous, that he could also be interpreted as proposing total withdrawal of American troops and letting the South Koreans alone continue the battle. In bitter responses, Truman and Stevenson, backed up by General James Van Fleet, U.S. commander in Korea, pointed out

This Don Hesse cartoon shows the Democratic donkey sitting on top of an enormous bag of money singing, "You've never had it so good." Hesse derides the Democratic claims during the presidential election of 1952 of the benefits they have provided in the face of the large public debt. *(Library of Congress)*

that the South Korean troops could not take over more of the fighting. This "proposal of a quick and easy way out of Korea . . . is false," Stevenson declared.

In early October, Eisenhower reversing his position of June, announced that "I have always stood behind General MacArthur in bombing those bases on the Yalu from which fighter planes are coming." He also found it a "useless war," though in July and August he had defended Truman's decision. He still continued to stress that all-out war in Korea had to be avoided, and he admitted that he had no solution to the war. "I am not going to be put in a position that I am personally a messiah," he explained. While the general was unwilling to claim the mantle of "messiah," others in the GOP were willing to make bold claims for Eisenhower. Stalin is most afraid of Eisenhower, certainly not Stevenson, declared Dewey. The road to peace, both major parties agreed, was to force the Soviets to yield, and Dewey and Dulles, along with their cohorts, were promising peace through the election of Eisenhower.

On October 24 in Detroit, Eisenhower moved beyond his earlier caution. He promised that, if elected, his administration would "concentrate on the job of end-ing the Korean War—until that job is honorably done." "That job," he continued, "requires a personal trip to Korea . . . I shall go to Korea." That promise, apparently introduced at the recommendation of Emmet Hughes, galvanized many voters who sought relief from the war. (The speech greatly angered Truman, who sharply asked the general, "Are you sure that you are much better than your old colleagues—Generals Bradley, Ridgeway, and Van Fleet?") The great impact of the speech rested on the military prestige of the general, a man whom many believed could end the war. Stevenson, also contemplating a similar gesture, had rejected it as an unworthy gimmick, and undoubtedly it would have been unsuccessful for him. The Illinois governor, despite his experience in the State Department, did not command the same respect for his prowess as a guardian of American freedom and a resolver of problems in foreign policy. "We can trust the man who won the peace," House Minority Leader Joseph Martin and Senate Minority Leader Styles Bridges announced. In the last 11 days before the election, Eisenhower's speeches were dotted with promises to end the war. How? What did he mean by "honorable terms"? The terms on which he would end the war remained unstated. History would define them.

Stevenson's style and strategy, unlike much of his program, contrasted sharply with Eisenhower's. While the general attacked Truman, the Illinois governor, saddled with the poor record of the administration, was seeking desperately to establish his independence of the president. Stevenson, quickly capturing the fancy of intellectuals, promised in his campaign to "talk sense to the American people," which evoked cheers from many who disregarded his dubious assertion that the Democratic platform "neither equivocates, contradicts, nor evades." The intellectuals were also pleased by his eloquence, realism, and nationalism. He warned of the need for "sacrifice, patience, understanding and implacable purpose"—words that were to bridge the rhetoric of the Roosevelt and Kennedy years.

The nominee, hoping to reweave the tattered New Deal coalition, sought to regain the South, keep the black and labor vote, and make substantial inroads in the Far West and Midwest. In short, he aimed to win the support that had returned Truman to the White House, but he hoped at the same time to escape from the liabilities of that administration. It was a campaign that Stevenson, until recently unknown to many Americans, did not seem to believe he could win. The Democratic nominee, by necessity a defender of the recent past, was by conviction a celebrator of American life and an enthusiastic protector of the administration on the important issues—not Truman, but the New Deal–Fair Deal state and the bipartisan Cold War policy.

Assisting him in his venture were talented speechwriters who also offered style and wit. Unlike Eisenhower, Stevenson drew upon a distinguished group of liberal intellectuals: Arthur Schlesinger Jr., the young, brilliant, Pulitzer Prize-winning Harvard historian; David Bell, a Truman assistant, former Budget Bureau official, and later John F. Kennedy's budget chief; John Kenneth Galbraith, the Harvard economist and former *Fortune* editor; Bernard De Voto, Pulitzer Prize winner, literary critic, and essayist; John Fischer, an editor of *Harper's;* Carl McGowan and W. Willard Wirtz, able Illinois attorneys; Herbert Agar, a popular author; and John Bartlow Martin, a skilled journalist. The campaign manager was Wilson Wyatt, ADA'er and briefly Truman's housing expert, who was assisted by George Ball, law partner and close friend of the candidate. Only Bell and Clayton Fritchey, Pulitzer Prize–winning Southern editor, were closely identified with Truman. The team had a clear ADA flavor, and Stevenson counted heavily on them to assist him in explaining the issues to the people. The candidate, unlike Eisenhower, remained throughout in control of the content and the style of his speeches. He decided what he wanted to say, and they helped him say it. No advertising men, perhaps unfortunately for Stevenson, shaped the campaign or merchandised the man.

To Truman's displeasure, in mid-August Stevenson had announced that he could clean up the "mess in Washington." Wounded by this admission that corruption was an acute problem, the president warned that such attacks on him would only injure the party and its presidential ticket. "I am the key of the campaign," he asserted. Stevenson, after Truman's successful Labor Day tour, invited the enthusiastic president to join the campaign. In early September and again in October, Truman sought to assist the ticket, but, as he complained later, there was little coordination between his Washington headquarters and Stevenson's office in Springfield. "How Stevenson hoped he could persuade the American voters to maintain the Democrats in power while seeming to disown powerful elements of it, I do not know," Truman later wrote.

Whether the president's efforts proved a liability or asset is difficult to determine. He did draw crowds and arouse enthusiasm. In the early stages of the campaign, he patronized Eisenhower: a good man duped by the GOP "right wing." Truman's message was that Eisenhower and the nation had to beware of the isolationists: they would cut foreign aid, slash the defense budget, and embark on a reckless policy of "liberation." But as Eisenhower's attacks on the administration sharpened, and when he failed to repudiate McCarthy, the general became the butt of Truman's scorn. The president, loving the combat of the campaign, even charged that Eisenhower was "willing to accept the very practices . . . [of] the master race."

Stevenson, though trying to distance himself from the administration, did not depart from Truman on such matters as federal responsibility for the economy or the farm issue. He continued the New Deal–Fair Deal line in appealing to farmers and workers, and in warning against a GOP-created depression. He periodically conducted the campaign against Hoover, not Eisenhower. It was not "time for a change," he declared, countering the GOP propaganda. On labor, he deviated slightly from Truman's policy and denied that Taft–Hartley was a "slave-labor act," but he did assert that it was "biased and politically inspired," concluding that it should be revised. He wished to restore the closed shop, which Taft–Hartley outlawed; to remove the antistrike injunction, which Taft–Hartley authorized; and to establish flexible, but ill-defined, measures to deal with critical strikes. While these proposals won the support of labor's leaders, who still regarded Taft–Hartley as a vital political issue, he also offered two revisions that won less favor: the need to maintain prohibitions similar to those in Taft–Hartley against unfair labor practices (such as jurisdictional strikes), and a rule barring unions from restricting blacks and other minorities from union membership because of race.

Of all the domestic issues, it was on civil rights that Stevenson departed most from Truman. The president, initially a wary advocate of rights for blacks, had moved during his years in the White House to assaults on Jim Crow in American life and to efforts to advance the welfare of the black man. Though Truman's rhetoric was usually bolder than his actions, he had become by 1952 a conscience for his party on civil rights. He had wanted a stronger plank in the platform and had reluctantly acceded to political necessity and accepted the retreat from a commitment to a compulsory FEPC. Stevenson, moving slowly and under pressure from blacks, finally went beyond the platform: he supported restrictions on filibusters and endorsed establishment of a modified compulsory FEPC (with judicial, not executive, enforcement) in cases where states did not have commissions. By these decisions, Stevenson, despite Sparkman's record on civil rights, was able to woo Adam Clayton Powell and other black Democratic defectors back into the fold.

Stevenson's success in courting the black vote, assisted by the Democratic record and Truman's efforts on behalf of the ticket, contrasted sharply with his failure in the South. His statements on civil rights, according to the *New York Times,* "did not make much of a stir in the South," where party officials knew that the filibuster could block any legislative effort to change race relations. Many Southerners, long estranged by the New Deal–Fair Deal reforms, regarded Stevenson's shift on civil rights as additional evidence that the "presidential party" would

This Fred Little Packer cartoon, titled "As of Someone Gently Rapping—!," shows a raven croaking "Nevermore" sitting on a bust of President Truman. The cartoon is based on Edgar Allan Poe's poem, "The Raven," in which a raven, sitting on a bust of Pallas, invoked dire predictions for the future. Packer reflects Democratic candidate Adlai Stevenson's charges that the Republicans would pursue a dangerous foreign policy by cutting the defense budget and foreign aid, promoting restrictive trade policies, and endorsing isolationism if they won the election in 1952. *(Library of Congress)*

sell out the South to northern liberals, big city bosses, and blacks. Some Southerners were also angered by his position on tidelands oil.

Stevenson, approving Truman's veto of a bill bestowing the multibillion resource on the states, declared that the federal government should retain title to the land. As a result, the Texas Democratic Party, after fulfilling its pledge to place Stevenson and Sparkman on the official ticket, endorsed the Eisenhower–Nixon slate. "Every Democrat in Texas," they declared, should "vote and work for the election of Dwight D. Eisenhower." They were not bolting the party, only the ticket. In Louisiana, Governor Robert Kennon and his machine also moved

to Eisenhower. In South Carolina, James F. Byrnes, Truman's former secretary of state, declared that Stevenson had succumbed to "Trumanism" in domestic policy, and he announced his support for Eisenhower. Virginia's Senator Harry Byrd, long an opponent of the New Deal and Fair Deal, also backed the general. Elsewhere, conservative Democrats, attracted by Eisenhower and his program, and estranged from the Northern wing of the party, were moving toward the GOP, thereby promising it the first success in Dixie since Hoover cracked the South in 1928. The South's powerful Richard Russell, despite promises that he would campaign for the ticket, offered one perfunctory testimonial and then retreated into silence. Speaker Sam Rayburn, Senator Lyndon Johnson, and Sparkman struggled to halt the defections.

Throughout the campaign the voters received many examples of the Stevenson wit. After a platform on which Eisenhower had been standing collapsed, Stevenson quipped, "I'm glad the General wasn't hurt. But I wasn't surprised that it happened—I've been telling him for two months that nobody could stand on that platform."

On another occasion, the Democrat nominee remarked, "If the Republicans will stop telling lies about us, we will stop telling the truth about them." In Phoenix, he complained that the GOP was a "two-headed elephant." "One head agrees with everything I say and the other head fumes and curses at everything I say." When Eisenhower sharply scolded Stevenson for taking the issues lightly, for regarding it as "amusing that we stumbled into a war [and] . . . that there are Communists in government," Stevenson responded that GOP stood for "Grouchy Old Pessimists."

Stevenson's humor delighted the intellectuals but may have offended other Americans who regarded him sometimes as undignified. His strong support for civil liberties, his firm anticommunism, and his clear dedication to patriotism won support from liberals. He called for patriotism, which he defined—in what then seemed platitudinous terms—as "putting country before self." Fingering McCarthy amid the senator's supporters at the American Legion convention, Stevenson bravely condemned those self-styled patriots who "for political or personal reasons" attacked the loyalty of men like General Marshall. Stevenson was not soft on Communism, he was quick to add, in what had become a reflex action for McCarthy's opponents; he just did not want to "burn down the barn to kill the rats." Communism, he knew, meant "the strangulation of the individual . . . , death for the soul. Americans who have surrendered to this malignant ideal have surrendered their right to our trust." By opposing vigilantism before the American Legion, Stevenson was faithful to his ideals and won the praise and respect of liberals.

This Daniel Robert Fitzpatrick cartoon shows the GOP elephant pushing an oil truck labeled "Tidelands Oil" while carrying the banner, "I like oil" (a play on the Republican campaign slogan, "I like Ike"). Fitzpatrick is satirizing the decision of the Republicans to add state ownership of offshore oil to their platform during the presidential election of 1952. *(Library of Congress)*

In foreign policy, where Stevenson was willing to run on the substance of the Truman record, his views were straightforward. He accepted the cold war, attributed it to Soviet malevolence and expansion, and viewed the United States as the protector of freedom in the world. Looking at Europe, he defended NATO as the necessary bulwark against Soviet aggression, but never adequately explained how the understaffed armies could stop Russia, how the Europeans could realistically rely on anything but the nuclear deterrent, or why the deterrent would be credible. Affirming collective security in Europe and warning the nation that Eisenhower was a captive of Taft and his fellow isolationists, Stevenson counseled that American policy must acknowledge limited means and therefore restrict itself to limited goals: victory was not always possible. By increasing American military strength, he hoped to achieve an eventual settlement in the cold war. "I think the Soviet Union," he explained, "will be influenced only by the steady, serious, undeviating determination to build up the strength of the free world—not with a view toward war but with a view toward preventing war and negotiating the conditions of peace."

Along with Truman, he warned against MacArthur's strategy for victory—an attack on China across the Yalu—as well as against proposals for American withdrawal from Europe and Asia. "I am . . . proud," he asserted, "that we have had the fortitude to refuse to risk extension of the war despite extreme Communist provocations and reckless Republican criticisms." The military budget, he concluded, could not be cut significantly without impairing America's international obligations and endangering her security. His message was the "lesson of Munich": strength and will would restrain aggression. In turn, he deplored the Republican policy that "proposes to reduce our contribution to free world strength . . . while it steps up its verbal threats against the enemy."

Confronted by Eisenhower's charges that the administration had made "a mess of foreign affairs," "lost" China, abandoned millions to Soviet tyranny in Europe, and "bungled" the nation into Korea, Stevenson admitted that the administration had made minor "mistakes," but stressed that China could not have been saved, nor the Iron Curtain rolled back without war. He decried "liberation" as either reckless or meaningless. The Korean War, he implied, could have been averted if America had not allowed rapid postwar demobilization, underestimated Soviet strength, and withdrawn troops from Korea. Stevenson declared that the GOP had to share responsibility for these mistakes: Dewey had criticized the government for delaying demobilization; Eisenhower had supported demobilization; and the general had badly estimated Soviet intentions when, for example, he had told a congressional committee in November 1945, "Nothing guides Russian policy so much as a desire for friendship with the United States." Moreover, the general, as chief of staff of the army, had joined in the recommendation of the Joint Chiefs of Staff that South Korea was of little strategic value to the United States and that American troops should be withdrawn from the peninsula.

In defending American participation in the war, Stevenson declared that Korea "was the testing point for freedom throughout the world. . . . Everyone of us knows in his heart why we had to stand up and fight in Korea." Had the United States not intervened, the price would have been great: the Communists "could have picked away at the free world and engulfed more millions, piece by piece . . . [until] we would have had to fight"; the free world would also have lost Japan and East Asia, with her valuable manpower, rubber, tin and oil. He lashed out at those GOP congressmen who had originally greeted the war with enthusiasm and now "attempt to make you believe that it was almost an act of treason." "We are not," he declared, "a race of whimpering adolescents who can't face the truth, but a race of men and women, proud, courageous and unafraid." To the question "How long can we keep up the fight against this monster tyranny?" he answered, "As long as we have to." The high budget, high taxes, inflation, even deaths in Korea, in his view, were the price America must pay to maintain freedom—for itself and the world. The battle was against "the Antichrist."

Opposing any extension of the war into China, agreeing with General Omar Bradley that war with China would be "the wrong war, at the wrong place, at the wrong time, and with the wrong enemy," Stevenson promised "by perseverance [to] win the military decision in Korea": an honorable peace that would halt the Communists at the 38th Parallel. When Eisenhower electrified the nation with his promise "I will go to Korea," Stevenson sharply criticized the general for not having a program. The truce negotiations, the Democratic nominee rightly explained, were stalled because the United States refused to accede to Communist demands for forced repatriation of all prisoners. What would Eisenhower do with these 50,000 prisoners, many of whom had reputedly declared that they preferred death to repatriation? Would Eisenhower, like Senator Homer Capehart, the Indiana Republican, force the prisoners to return? Not only was this position "identical with that of the Communists," emphasized Stevenson, but "if we give up on this point . . . we will no longer lead the coalitions of the free world." America, he explained, symbolized freedom. That was her greatest asset in the cold war, and it would be lost if the United States acceded to forced repatriation.

In 1952, the cold war consensus was challenged only by the fringe parties of the left. The most interesting was the Progressive Party, which in 1948 had briefly threatened to ruin Truman's chances by snaring enough disaffected Democrats to throw the election to Dewey. By 1952, however, Henry Wallace, its standard-bearer, and many other noncommunist stalwarts had departed, leaving only a fragmented shell. Some left because they felt that Communists were dominating the party, while others, like Wallace, perhaps tired of being embattled, seceded when the party's executive council opposed American intervention in the Korean War. "The Russians could have prevented the attack by the North Koreans and undoubtedly they could now stop the attack if they wish," Wallace declared three weeks after the war erupted. "When my country is at war and the United Nations sanctions that war, I am on the side of my country and the United Nations."

Behind Wallace's bolt was a longstanding dispute on whether the Soviets shared some responsibility for the cold war or whether America was solely to blame. In 1948, Wallace had acknowledged that the Soviets were sometimes culpable, and the platform had hinted that the Soviets shared responsibility for the cold war. After 1950, despite many defections, the disagreement on Soviet

responsibility continued, and the 1952 platform suggested that the Soviet Union had contributed in some minor, unstated way to the cold war.

Unlike the major parties, the Progressives had steadfastly opposed the Truman Doctrine, the Marshall Plan, NATO, the arms and troops programs for Europe, rearmament of Germany and Japan, the alliances with Franco and Chiang, and the support of colonialism. As the Truman administration had forged military alliances abroad and begun establishing what Acheson called "situations of strength," the Progressives castigated the government for "warmongering." However, because they believed they were preserving the heritage of Roosevelt, the Progressives were unable ideologically to challenge the New Deal tradition in foreign policy. As a result, like many postwar liberal critics, they argued simply that Truman and the bipartisan coalition had reversed Roosevelt's foreign policy of accommodation with the Soviet Union.

The Progressives called for the halt of stockpiling nuclear weapons, an international agreement outlawing these weapons, and repeal of the draft. How America would be protected they did not need to explain, for, in their view, there was no Soviet threat, no aggressive

This Don Hesse cartoon shows a sword labeled "Korean War" stuck into the surface of a desk labeled "President of the United States." Hesse suggests that the person who wins the 1952 presidential election will be faced with the problem of ending the Korean War. *(Library of Congress)*

impulse to be thwarted. For evidence, they emphasized that administration officials had admitted that they did not expect the Soviet Union "to start a war now or at any time." To suspicious Americans, who had come to believe that their nation's safety depended upon a nuclear arsenal and a large military establishment, the Progressives simply offered negotiations and "peaceful understanding and peaceful relations" with the Soviet Union; that is, peaceful coexistence. To settle the German "problem," they proposed a neutral, disarmed, united Germany. To assist the underdeveloped nations, the party recommended a fund of $50 billion, to be distributed by the U.N. In addition, the Progressives wanted the elimination of trade barriers between the United States and Communist nations, and endorsed the recognition of Red China and withdrawal of recognition from Chiang's government.

In 1952, the party's nominees were Vincent Hallinan, a prominent California attorney who was serving a sentence for contempt of court, and Charlotta Bass, a black former editor of the California *Eagle*. During the campaign, Bass proudly declared, "Win or lose, we win by raising the issues." Whether or not the Progressives found consolation in such analysis is difficult to say, but certainly it contained an element of truth. In many respects, the Progressives saw more deeply the defects, and also the possibilities, of American life. In condemning the "tweedle-dum, tweedle-dee" approach of the major parties, they were heirs to a part of the nation's radical tradition. "Both old parties," asserted Hallinan, "are sold to a program of war against labor, against the Negro. . . . They are both captive parties and both parties are captive to the same interests." Although his analysis may have been overwrought, distorted, and too simple, he did focus on three major problems in American political life: the cold war, poverty, and race relations.

For the Socialist Party, already torn by doubts about its own relevance and possessing less support than the Progressives, the campaign of 1952 was again ritualistic. Norman Thomas, the party's perennial presidential candidate, had announced in 1950 that he would not run again, arguing that the party should no longer support a national ticket but channel its energies into educational efforts and the election of liberals. Others in the party, particularly outside New York, the stronghold for Thomas's position, were reluctant to withdraw for the electoral success of liberals and wanted a national campaign in order to maintain the party and promote socialism. In 1952, the party nominated Darlington Hoopes, a Reading attorney, for the presidency, and Samuel Friedman, a New York labor leader, as his running mate. Correctly anticipating an even smaller vote than in 1948, they spoke before small enclaves and appeared

on the ballot in only 16 states. The ticket received the formal support of Thomas and his cohorts, though he asserted that he hoped that Stevenson would win and thereby hinted that Socialists should not "waste" their ballots on Hoopes.

The Socialist platform, technically to the left of the Progressives on domestic issues, once more proclaimed the value of democratic socialism and called for nationalization of major industries. Like the Progressives, the Socialists urged abolition of segregation in all public and public-supported institutions, including housing and the armed forces. They called for antilynching legislation and protection of the right to vote. They also demanded enforcement of the Fourteenth Amendment and the reduction of congressional representation in cases where citizens were deprived of the right to vote. Unlike the Progressives, the Socialists, who were having doubts about centralization of power, openly and perceptively recognized the need for action on the community level to abolish segregation that could not be eliminated by legislation. Like the Progressives, however, they were unable to devise effective tactics for challenging America's racism.

On foreign policy, the parties on the left differed significantly. The Socialists, despite serious divisions on other matters, were stridently anti-Stalinist. Whereas the Progressives agreed that America was primarily responsible for the cold war and argued about the amount of Soviet guilt, the Socialists stressed Soviet guilt and argued about American responsibility. Norman Thomas, for example, zealously attacked Soviet foreign policy while remaining a sympathetic critic of recent American policy. Pledging himself "to do everything possible" to defend socialism, he labored to block efforts within the party to condemn American imperialism and to treat the United States and the Soviet Union as equally culpable in the cold war. Privately he explained his fears of a platform "couched in one or another of the numerous doctrinaire Marxist sets of formulas or which would backtrack [on our support for Truman's intervention in Korea] in favor of a curious blend of pacifism and near-Trotskyism." In order to prevent problems at the convention, he prepared an advance draft of the platform that he hoped would establish "approximate agreement" among party leaders. It did not.

Hoopes, Thomas's running mate in 1944 and the representative of the party's left wing on foreign policy, rejected Thomas's analysis. The party, he declared, should not go along with "distasteful features" of American policy—for example, NATO, and support of dictators and European colonialism. He denied that these policies were simple "mistakes." They were "inherent in the nature of our capitalistic government, and until we make a clean break with these policies we cannot fight communism."

At the party convention in Cleveland, the delegates hammered out a compromise. Peace, they explained, was blocked by "four tremendous obstacles": first and most important, "the aggressive imperialism of the [totalitarian] Soviet Union"; second, the militarization in the West that developed in response; third, unfair dealings with underdeveloped nations; and fourth, capitalism.

On election eve, both major parties made their final appeal on national radio and television. Truman, Barkley, Stevenson, and Sparkman spoke for the Democrats. Truman, attacking the GOP's "campaign of fear and deception," declared that the choice was between prosperity or depression, between extending civil rights and liberties or succumbing to "smear and fear," between stopping Communism and retreating before the red menace or plunging the world into atomic warfare. Stevenson summed up the themes of his campaign: prosperity could not be entrusted to the GOP; "we are winning the worldwide struggle with communism"; and the times were difficult and demanded Democratic leadership.

Following this performance, the GOP had an hour-long telecast emphasizing the people's dedication to the "Great Crusade." Opening with Eisenhower and his family and friends, the camera moved to sequences of Alger Hiss, of "five-percenters," of men in battle in Korea, of Eisenhower with Churchill and the GIs, and of the general at home in Abilene with his grandson. The camera then flashed to supporters. A veteran, asked why he was backing Eisenhower, said, "Well, all the guys I know out in Korea figure there's only one man for the job," the general. There was also a San Francisco typist "crusading" for Eisenhower, a Nisei physician in Seattle, a youngster who had organized "Tykes for Ike," a Gary steelmaker, a suburban housewife and mother, and a Los Angeles "Coffee-with-Eisenhower" meeting that ended with a prayer. Throughout, the theme was the same: the nation needed Eisenhower to end the "mess" at home and abroad. At the end of the program, the general and Mrs. Eisenhower cut a victory cake.

The campaign had been long, expensive, and fatiguing. Eisenhower had traveled 33,000 miles, two-thirds by air, visited the South twice, gone to 44 states, skipping only Nevada, Maine, Vermont, and Mississippi, and delivered 228 speeches, of which 40 were major and nationally televised. Nixon, making 375 speeches, had journeyed 42,000 miles. Stevenson had traveled 32,500 miles, appearing in 32 states and delivering 203 speeches, of which 21 were on national television. Sparkman, going to 38 states, had delivered more than 450 speeches. The two major parties, it was estimated, had spent nearly $80 million on the campaign, the first that relied heavily on television to reach American voters.

So close did the forthcoming election seem that most pollsters, still wary after their mistakes in 1948, would not predict a victor. They painfully recalled the late shift of the "undecided" vote in 1948. The *New York Times,* in its final election survey, concluded that the outcome was "highly uncertain." Louis Bean, who had been correct in 1948, begged off, asserting this time that there were "too many factors involved for which there were no statistical analyses." Samuel Lubell foresaw substantial defections from the Democratic ranks but also warned of other likely developments that could offset this shift. George Gallup of the American Institute of Public Opinion, while finding substantial Eisenhower strength, warned that a continuation of the late-developing trend to Stevenson would give him a majority: he needed the same 3-to-1 ratio that Truman had received from the undecided or uncommitted voters, who were about 13 percent (about 7 million voters) of the expected total vote of 55 million.

"Ike in a landslide," declared election day headlines. In retrospect, to many it all seemed inevitable. The general, in gathering 34,075,529 votes, 55.18 percent of the two-party vote, had won by the largest popular vote of any presidential candidate to that date. Stevenson, with the second largest Democratic vote in history, had received 27,375,090 votes, 44.33 percent of the vote, from the greatest turnout of voters in American history. Eisenhower carried 39 states for 442 electoral votes, while Stevenson had triumphed in only 9 states—in West Virginia and 8 in the South—with 89 electoral votes.

By the end of his 1952 presidential campaign, Dwight D. Eisenhower had traveled 33,000 miles, visiting all but four states. He is shown here campaigning in Baltimore, Maryland, in September 1952. *(Dwight D. Eisenhower Library)*

So great was the support for the GOP ticket that 670 counties outside the South that had supported Democratic presidential candidates since 1932 broke and backed the general. Eighteen states that had always cast their electoral votes for Roosevelt and Truman went Republican. There was no denying the landslide victory, though it should be remembered that Harding in 1920, Coolidge in 1924, and Roosevelt in 1932 and 1936 exceeded Eisenhower's plurality.

Eisenhower easily captured the key states of New York, California, Illinois, Ohio, Michigan, and Pennsylvania by pluralities ranging between 269,000 and 848,000. In 1948, in contrast, Truman had narrowly lost the last four but won Michigan and New York by small pluralities. In the West, Eisenhower won all 11 states by a margin of 57.3 percent. In New England, he was the first Republican since Coolidge to sweep all 6 states. In the Midwest, a comparative stronghold of GOP sentiment, the general easily moved to victory, with Minnesota recording his lowest percentage (55.6). Even in the South, the traditional Democratic stronghold, the general polled the largest vote ever received by a Republican, as he won 4 states: Florida (55.0 percent), Virginia (56.3 percent), Tennessee (50.0 percent), and Texas (53.1 percent).

Across the country there had been substantial defections from the Democratic coalition—among white urban and some black-belt Southerners, among Irish, Poles, and Germans, among Catholics, among low-income families, among skilled and semiskilled workers, and among the members of labor union families. All income classes, reversing the normal patterns, had given Eisenhower a majority of the votes cast. In addition, sources of traditional GOP strength, particularly the suburbs, turned out unusually high votes for Eisenhower, and new voters, both young and old, had also favored the general. The farmers, an unexpected source of support in Truman's surprising victory, also returned in large numbers to the GOP column.

Nearly 25 percent of the final vote for Eisenhower, concluded Angus Campbell and his associates at the Michigan Survey Center, came from those who had voted for Truman in 1948. In 1952, unlike 1948, the issues and the candidates broke down party affiliations in many cases. This shift alone was almost sufficient to create an Eisenhower victory. Added to that was the fact that almost 13 million "new" voters—one-third were too young in 1948 and the rest had not voted then—provided significant support for the general. The young supported him 57–43 percent, and the almost 9 million older citizens, the GOP's "stay-at-homes," endorsed him by a 53–47 percent margin. (In contrast, Louis Harris, depending on Roper polls, contended that these young voters, troubled by Eisenhower's concessions to Senators Jenner, McCarthy, and Taft, backed Stevenson 56–44 percent.) Not only

had the turnout of voters (63.3 percent) been the highest since 1908, but the GOP strategy of seeking votes among this group had been successful. These "new" voters did not make a decisive difference, however, because they supported both candidates at about the same rate as did the rest of the electorate. Had they split the way the uncommitted had gone in 1948, and had they been evenly distributed throughout the nation, however, the result in 1952 would have been a Stevenson victory. The difference, primarily, was that those who switched each increased the Eisenhower plurality by two.

Unlike 1948, when domestic issues dominated the campaign and shaped the votes, the dominant issue in 1952, according to most surveys, was the Korean War. "It was probably our most emotional election" since Bryan and McKinley in 1896, concluded Lubell, who found widespread frustration and anger about the war, the stalemate, and the growing battlefield death toll. Apparently, the campaign helped convert the war into a major issue. In January, according to a Roper survey, 25 percent of those asked to indicate the most important problem facing the nation mentioned the war; in June the figure had reached 30 percent, in September 33 percent, in mid-October 39 percent, and in late October 52 percent. The Roper poll also found in June that there was no agreement on what should be done to end the stalemate. Thirty percent had faith in negotiations; slightly more than 30 percent wanted to step up the war and try to drive the Communists out of Korea; less than 20 percent favored a "pull-out." About 75 percent of the voters most concerned about the war believed that Eisenhower could bring it to an end more quickly. The war issue, concluded Louis Harris, "was easily the Achilles heel of the Democratic campaign."

The Survey Research Center, in contrast to Harris's and Lubell's analysis, found foreign policy to be slightly less important than domestic issues for the voters in 1952. Thirty-two percent cited foreign policy as their reason—some gave more than one—for voting for the GOP, while 36 percent mentioned domestic policies. Only 13 percent of those who endorsed the GOP thought the party would solve the war. It is clear on the basis of this study, as well as those by Lubell, Gallup, and Harris, that many who selected the GOP because of their concern about the war did so because of their favorable view of Eisenhower. Indeed, 47 percent of the sample that voted for Eisenhower mentioned his personal qualities, his experience, or his being "the best man" as an important reason for their vote. Very few cited party allegiance.

The issue of Communists in government, according to Harris, was less significant than many feared. Never in 1952 did more than 11 percent of the people volunteer it as a major issue. Only when they were offered it as a pos-

Vice president–elect Richard M. Nixon and his wife, Pat Nixon, examine election results. *(Library of Congress)*

sible issue did substantial numbers select it as important. As additional, but indirect, evidence of its small influence is the fact that McCarthy and Jenner, who had closely identified themselves with the issue, ran well behind the national ticket and their party's gubernatorial candidate, and three GOP senators who exploited the Communism-in-government issue were defeated.

Corruption was another major issue, with nearly one-third of the electorate citing it. But it did not significantly aid the general and the GOP, despite their efforts at "marketing" the issue. About half thought it would continue if Stevenson was elected, and about half thought he would end it. By the end of the campaign, after Truman's vigorous activity, about five out of every eight concerned about corruption believed it would continue under Stevenson. Harris concluded that, in the last stages of the campaign, most citizens "who were disturbed and upset about Korea and communism in government also tended to be more upset about corruption." In turn, those least distressed by the war were less concerned about corruption.

Consequently, the importance of corruption as an influence on the vote declined as Election Day approached, but the issue was "another significant nail Eisenhower was able to drive in the Democratic coffin."

Economic issues in 1952 were a mixed bag. Concern with high taxes and government spending, despite the widespread complaints, apparently did not have much effect on the election. Two-thirds of those who cited these as major problems revealed, when questioned, that they did not believe that the Republicans would improve the situation. The problem of high prices, however, was a more significant issue; like Communism, it was a "trailer" issue, Harris found. "It's bad enough to have so many fine young men slaughtered in Korea," explained one housewife in a typical comment, "but to make it worse we have to have the terribly high cost of everything you buy these days. And it's all because of that war over there." Some charged the administration and the Democratic-controlled Congress with failing to restrain prices, an issue that Eisenhower ably exploited and on which Stevenson did not adequately defend himself. Of the many who cited high prices as a major problem, 60 percent concluded that the GOP would do a better job in restraining inflation.

Both Harris and Lubell concluded that the fears of depression were responsible for a "great deal" (Harris's words) of Stevenson's 44 percent. For many, particularly those in the working class, economic security was still associated with the Democrats. Hoover's depression, Hoovervilles, and breadlines had not been forgotten by a generation of Americans, many of whom incorrectly lauded the New Deal, rather than World War II, for restoring prosperity. "No working man can vote Republican," many workers told the pollsters. "The Democrats are the friend of the working man." "The pocketbook argument," Harris concluded, "was a formidable one. It turned out to be nearly the only appeal the Democrats had on a mass basis." Economic security and the war, with its associated problems, were the two opposite poles tugging at Democratic voters in 1952. Many who broke with the Truman–Stevenson party let the war overpower them. In some cases they even saw prosperity as war-inspired ("Stop trading blood for money," one said) and chose to vote *against* the war, not *for* security.

Of professional men and managers, nearly 60 percent (up from 57 percent in 1948) voted Republican, while 27 percent (up from 15 percent) voted Democratic. While Stevenson ran behind among all white-collar groups, only among the managers and professionals did he improve on Truman's percentage. Among most other groups, Eisenhower gained substantially over Dewey, while Stevenson generally fell behind Truman: other white collar—Eisenhower 52 percent (Dewey 39), Stevenson 28 (Truman 38); skilled and semiskilled workers—Eisenhower 34 (Dewey 15), Stevenson 40 (Truman 52); unskilled workers—Eisenhower 19 (Dewey 12), Stevenson 40 (Truman 33). Only among manual workers did Eisenhower run behind the Democratic nominee. But when the voting is analyzed in terms of income classes, the general triumphed in all three. Among the low-income (to $1,999), he won 34 percent to Stevenson's 22 percent, though Truman had topped Dewey 28 to 16. In the middle-income group ($2,000–4,999), Eisenhower gained 40 percent and Stevenson 36 percent, while Truman had topped Dewey 36–24. Among the high-income group, Eisenhower received 57 percent and Stevenson less than half of that with 28 percent, though Dewey had beaten Truman only 46 to 28.

Among farmers, of all major occupational groups, there was the greatest defection from Truman to Eisenhower. In 1948, when only 42 percent had voted, nearly two-thirds had supported Truman. In 1952, however, when two-thirds of all farmers voted, 63 percent of them supported the General. The figures for rural areas, including farm families and farm-related enterprises, are almost identical. Outside the South, farmers had returned to their normal GOP anchorage. In 1948, Truman, aided by a late downturn in prices, had carried Minnesota, Iowa, and Wisconsin, but in 1952 the last two states reverted to their GOP pattern of 1944, and Minnesota also went Republican. In Kansas, Nebraska, South Dakota, and North Dakota, states where Truman had received between 45 and 48 percent of the two-party vote, Stevenson fell to between 28 and 31 percent. Eisenhower, by promising a continuation of farm prosperity, had removed the major reason for rural support for Stevenson and Sparkman outside the South.

In the cities in 1952, the GOP candidate weakened the New Deal coalition, cutting into the normal Democratic margins. Chicago, which had given Truman about 55 percent, gave Stevenson only 50.3 percent; in Cleveland, which Truman had taken with 54.6, Stevenson received 46.3; Boston, which gave Truman 69 percent, gave Stevenson 60 percent; and in New York City, Stevenson won only 55 percent, not Truman's 59 percent. In Pittsburgh, where Truman had a plurality of 73,000 votes, Stevenson slipped to 13,800. In Los Angeles and San Francisco, the general swept to victory. In the suburbs, Eisenhower rolled up great margins, wiping away the Democratic plurality in five of the eight largest cities that had gone Democratic. As Jacob Arvey, Cook County boss, put it, "The suburbs are murder."

German-Americans, Irish-Americans, and Polish-Americans, but not Italian-Americans, contributed significantly to the defection from the Democratic Party. German-Americans, constituting about 14 percent of the electorate, heavily backed Eisenhower. Harris concluded that nearly 79 percent of the German Protestants, and 73 percent of the German Catholics, endorsed the general. Between September and October, many shifted to the GOP candidate as they concluded that a Democratic vic-

tory was not essential to their well-being. Unhappiness with the war, linked to concern about Communism in government, was of particular concern to this group, especially the Catholics. In the case of the Irish (nearly all Catholics), there was an even split on McCarthy, but there was wider concern among the group about Communism in government. Again issues of the war, joined with the secondary issue of Communism, cut into the normally strong Democratic ranks and significantly reduced their support for the Democratic Party, and thereby helped to produce the general's victory. Like the Germans, the Irish had been torn between economic security (identified with the Democratic Party) and the war and Communism, but by October they resolved this dilemma, and a substantial number bolted to Eisenhower.

Poles, too, worried about Communism in America, as well as in their homeland, which many thought Roosevelt had sold out. They defected in great numbers to the GOP ticket. Their usual 70 percent Democratic vote dropped all the way to 50 percent. Italians (nearly all Catholics), however, were more impressed by the administration's foreign policy, especially its aid to Italy, and believed also that their economic security depended on the continuation of the Democratic Party in power. As a result, they stayed with the New Deal–Fair Deal party, with between 55 and 60 percent of their votes going to Stevenson.

In terms of religion, the sharpest break occurred among Catholics, long the backbone of the big-city machines. In 1948, two-thirds of all Catholic voters had supported Truman, but in 1952 that percentage had been sliced to 51.2. Labor union membership seemed, however, to place a brake on defections. Less than one out of every ten voting Catholic union members bolted to the GOP. Among Catholics without union members in the family, nearly 62 percent backed Eisenhower, a dramatic reversal of the pattern of 1948. In general, the evidence shows that the union member vote held for the Democratic Party. Yet, it is dubious that the political efforts of the unions had much effect. Most likely, union members, like their leaders, preferred the Democrats for the same reasons: the preservation of economic security and the rights of labor. Ironically, while the union man was voting for Stevenson (60 to 40 percent), his family was defecting to Eisenhower by a 55 to 45 percent margin.

The role of women in the voting is less clear. Gallup and Harris both estimated that about 17.6 million women voted for Eisenhower and about 12.7 million for Stevenson. The Michigan Survey, however, found there was little difference—a conclusion that Samuel Lubell also supported. Whatever the precise answer, all agreed that a majority of the voters of each sex cast ballots for Eisenhower.

For many the most interesting question about 1952 was: what happened in Dixie? Ike, securing 48.9 percent of the two-party vote in the South, had been more successful than any GOP candidate since Hoover (49.7), whose strength was sometimes in similar sectors, particularly in Tennessee, Virginia, Arkansas, Georgia, and North Carolina. There was also a loose relationship between the Democratic defections to the Dixiecrats in 1948 and those to Eisenhower in 1952. Eisenhower lost in the four states that went Dixiecrat in 1948—Alabama 35.2, Louisiana 47.3, Mississippi 40.1, and South Carolina 48.3. In three, however, Eisenhower made deep inroads into the black-belt area, the source of Dixiecrat strength; but in other states, like North Carolina, Tennessee, Texas, and Virginia, his major support lay elsewhere. Most significantly, middle- and upper-income white areas in cities and suburbs went for Eisenhower, while the low-income areas, sometimes the residences of minorities, went for Stevenson.

In the South as well as in the North, Stevenson was most successful, and Eisenhower least successful, with black voters, whose ballots carried South Carolina and Louisiana for Stevenson. Overall, they were the only ethnic group to give the Illinois governor substantially greater support than Truman had received. The Survey Research Center concluded that Stevenson received 81 percent of the black vote, while Truman had won about 64 percent. Civil rights, the Roper pollsters found, dominated the voting decisions of Northern blacks. They were also concerned about the cost of living (which they thought Democrats were most likely to restrain) and a depression (which they felt the Democrats would be most likely to avert). They bought the Democratic slogan, "You've never had it so good." On foreign policy, however, they differed with the Democrats and wanted to withdraw from Korea and cut aid to Europe. For them, civil rights and foreign policy coalesced: dollars sent abroad could be used instead to assist the underprivileged at home. Another minority, the Jews, Harris found, backed Stevenson by 74 to 26 percent, or roughly a margin of a million votes. They were also the strongest supporters of Truman's foreign policy in Korea and Europe, and they admired the administration's record on civil rights.

Looking at the landslide victory, students of politics might wonder whether there had been a fundamental shift in the party loyalties of voters. Was there a Republican majority? Despite the hopeful estimates of some GOP analysts at the time, the answer was no. True, in the South, the defections suggested the possibility of building a Republican Party—among the new rich, the urban middle-classes, and some black-belt whites—but most were still loyal to the Democrats on the local level. Their protest, despite the GOP victory in four contests for the House, was primarily against Washington, against the national or presidential party. Often the contest within

the state was a struggle for power within the party. Symptomatic of their concern for the state Democratic Party was the demand by Governor Kennon of Louisiana, who was supporting the Eisenhower ticket, that the GOP withdraw two candidates from congressional races. Throughout most of the country it was clear that the general's popularity had helped to carry other GOP candidates to victory. Local and congressional candidates, who usually run slightly behind the national ticket, had on average run far behind Eisenhower (nearly 19 percentage points). In the face of the greatest GOP landslide since Coolidge and Hoover, the party had barely captured the Congress. In the House, they gained only 21 seats for a majority of 9. In the Senate, they captured 23 of 35 races, gaining 3 over their previous number and thereby securing just 48 seats. In ten states—six outside the south—the voters had endorsed Eisenhower but split enough ballots to return Democrats to the Senate. Among the governors, the Republicans won 20 of the 30 races, for a gain of 5. Alfred DeGrazia concludes that Eisenhower's strength among Democrats and independents (including the GOP's "stay at homes") was so great that his presence on the ballot increased the GOP congressional and local vote by nearly 5 percent of his own total. If that percentage was spread evenly throughout the country, it would have accounted for Republican victories in 39 congressional, 13 Senate, and 7 gubernatorial contests. Thus, he finds the 83rd Congress owed "its Republican majorities to Dwight D. Eisenhower's candidacy."

The Democrats, it appeared, had lost an election, but they had lost it to Eisenhower, not to the GOP. Many candidates had run on the general's coattails. "If the voters liked the Republicans the way they liked Ike," cracked one Democrat, "the two-party system would be in bad shape." The Michigan Survey Study found that 47 percent of the voters considered themselves Democrats, while only 27 percent thought of themselves as Republicans. In 1952, the GOP remained a minority party, though its members' hopes for the future were strong. Perhaps with Eisenhower's assistance, they could be transformed into the majority party. The new moderate Republicans like Senators Jacob Javits and Irving Ives of New York, John Sherman Cooper of Kentucky, and Ralph Flanders of Vermont, if aided by Eisenhower, might offer an attractive alternative to the Old Guard and the Democrats. Perhaps Eisenhower could transfer much of his popularity, and the administration's successes would aid the GOP. Only later would the break in 1952 and 1956 clearly become what V. O. Key has called a brief "Republican interlude."

In 1952, other aspects of the voting pattern attracted less attention. The Progressives, as expected, ran poorly, receiving 140,023 votes, far behind 1948, when they received slightly more than a million votes. Lacking a well-known candidate and subjected to red-baiting, they tallied more than half of their votes in two states: California 24,106 and New York 64,211. If the pattern of 1948 obtained, they probably did disproportionately well among blacks and Jews, two minorities with elements most likely to be disaffected from the two-party system. The Socialist Party, placing its national ticket on the ballot for the last time, received only 19,685 votes, with two-thirds from three eastern states: Pennsylvania, the home of Hoopes, 8,771; New Jersey 8,593 (almost the same vote as in 1948); and New York 2,664. In 1952, they even fell, for the first time, behind the DeLeon Socialist-Labor Party and climbed only slightly ahead of various MacArthur tickets. The results dramatically confirmed what most citizens knew: the American "left" was dead. In New York, the American Labor Party, the strength of the Progressives, soon collapsed. Elsewhere, many on the "left" went into political retreat: many who had devoted years of their lives to reforming America gave up politics and devoted themselves to participating in other parts of American culture. Their children in a later generation would often rediscover politics beyond the two-party, even the electoral, system, and demand of their parents and the nation what the "left" was groping toward in 1952. In that year, perhaps the death knell of the "left" was best symbolized by the *Partisan Review* symposium among intellectuals on "Our Country and Our Culture." Rejecting their own past, many asserted new values in rediscovering the value of American culture, in announcing the uniqueness of America, and in affirming the success of American democracy in extending benefits to its citizens.

The results of the 1952 election also contributed to a growing faith that class was of marginal importance in American society. The two-party system, in the Eisenhower landslide, had contributed to the blunting of the class orientation of American politics, a process underway since the election of 1940 had revealed that the sharp class cleavage of 1936 had been softened. Put bluntly, the poor, the middle- and upper-income groups in 1952—all favored the GOP ticket. In turn, among the wealthy, Stevenson had done slightly better (28–22) than among the poor who had voted. What many neglected, however, was that, of all the economic groups, the poor were also the most likely not to vote. Their rate of nonparticipation is striking: 47 percent of the poor did not vote, as compared to 24 percent of middle-income adults and 14 percent of high income. Amid the great celebration that characterized the 1950s, this fact should have suggested disaffection or alienation of an important, sizable, neglected portion of the citizenry—to be known later as "the other America."

—*Barton J. Bernstein*

Selected Bibliography

The *New York Times, Washington Post,* and *New York Herald-Tribune* provide careful coverage of the major parties and events. Use of these sources is supplemented profitably by examination of *Time, Newsweek, U.S. News and World Report, Nation,* and *New Republic,* all of which provide sharply opinionated views on the major issues and events. *U.S. News* has also published valuable interviews with the vice-presidential candidates and useful features on some of the leading issues, including the training of the South Korean army. Most of the major political speeches in 1952 are available in the *New York Times, Vital Speeches,* or the *Congressional Record.* A good selection of Stevenson's campaign speeches is also available in Adlai Stevenson, *Major Campaign Speeches of Adlai E. Stevenson* (1953). Truman's public statements are reprinted in *Public Papers of the Presidents: Harry S. Truman, 1952–53* (1966). For information on the parties and conventions, see Paul David et al., eds., *Presidential Nominating Politics in 1952* (5 vols., 1954).

The analysis of Taft's thought and policies relies primarily upon material in the *Congressional Record,* as well as in his papers at the Library of Congress and his *A Foreign Policy for Americans* (1952). Other useful sources are: Russell Kirk and James McClellan, *The Political Principles of Robert A. Taft* (1967), William S. White, *The Taft Story* (1954), and Henry Berger, "A Conservative Critique of Containment; Senator Taft on the Early Cold War Program" in David Horowitz, ed., *Containment and Revolution* (1967). The now "standard" interpretation of the Taft wing, from which Barton Bernstein's essay dissents, is presented by Norman Graebner, *The New Isolationism* (1956); Ronald Caridi, *The Korean War and American Politics: The Republican Party as a Case Study* (1969), which also discusses the Dewey–Eisenhower wing; and Arthur M. Schlesinger Jr., "The New Isolationism," *Atlantic* 189 (May 1952).

Eisenhower's movement toward candidacy and his campaign are discussed in his memoirs, *The White House Years: Mandate for Peace* (1963); Emmet John Hughes, *The Ordeal of Power* (1962); Sherman Adams, *Firsthand Report* (1961); Marquis Childs, *Eisenhower: Captive Hero* (1958); and William J. Miller, *Henry Cabot Lodge* (1967). The Eisenhower collections at the Eisenhower Library, as well as the John Foster Dulles and H. Alexander Smith Papers at Princeton, provide additional information, and the Eisenhower Library also has a complete file of the general's campaign speeches. Earl Mazo, *Richard Nixon: A Political and Personal Portrait* (1959), a sympathetic view; William Costello, *The Facts About Nixon: An Unauthorized Biography* (1960), a critical view from the liberal perspective; and Richard Nixon, *Six Crises* (1962), treat the GOP vice-presidential candidate.

Adlai Stevenson's campaign and background are discussed in Stuart G. Brown, *Conscience in Politics: Adlai E. Stevenson in the 1950's* (1961); Bert Cochran, *Adlai Stevenson: Patrician Among the Politicians* (1969); Kenneth Davis, *The*

Politics of Honor: A Biography of Adlai E. Stevenson (1957); and Herbert Muller, *Adlai Stevenson: A Study in Values* (1967).

The most important sources on the Socialist Party are the Norman Thomas Papers at the New York Public Library. On the Progressive Party, the American Labor Party Papers at Rutgers University are useful and informative.

See also Stephen E. Ambrose, *Eisenhower*, Vol. 1: *Soldier, General of the Army, President-Elect, 1890–1952* (1983); Robert

J. Donovan, *Tumultuous Years: The Presidency of Harry S. Truman, 1949–1953* (1982); John Robert Greene, *The Crusade: The Presidential Election of 1952* (1985); John Bartlow Martin, *Adlai Stevenson of Illinois* (1976); Donald R. McCoy, *The Presidency of Harry S. Truman* (1981); Porter McKeever, *Adlai Stevenson: His Life and Legacy* (1989); Chester J. Pach Jr. and Elmo Richardson, *The Presidency of Dwight D. Eisenhower* (rev. ed., 1991); and James T. Patterson, *Mr. Republican: A Biography of Robert A. Taft* (1972).

1952 Electoral Map and Statistics

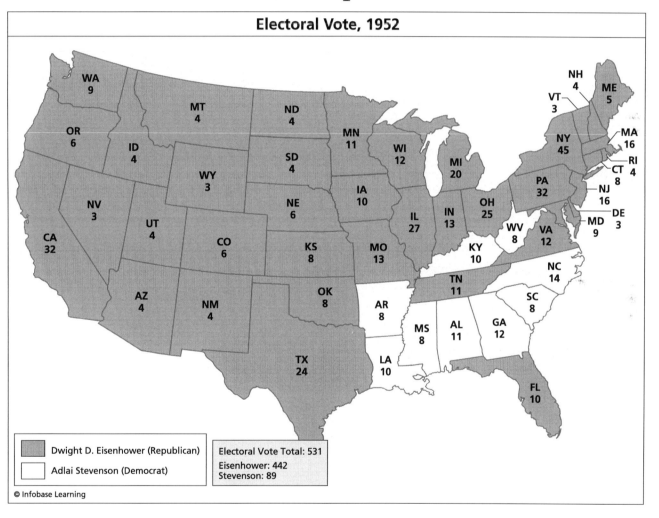

1952 ELECTION STATISTICS

State	Number of Electors	Total Popular Vote	Elec Vote R	Elec Vote D	Pop Vote R	Pop Vote D	Margin of Victory Votes	Margin of Victory % Total Vote
Alabama	11	426,120		11	2	1	125,844	29.53%
Arizona	4	260,570	4		1	2	43,514	16.70%
Arkansas	8	404,800		8	2	1	49,145	12.14%
California	32	5,341,603	32		1	2	777,941	14.56%
Colorado	6	630,103	6		1	2	134,278	21.31%
Connecticut	8	1,096,911	8		1	2	129,363	11.79%
Delaware	3	174,025	3		1	2	6,744	3.88%
Florida	10	989,337	10		1	2	99,086	10.02%
Georgia	12	655,803		12	2	1	257,844	39.32%
Idaho	4	276,231	4		1	2	85,626	31.00%
Illinois	27	4,481,058	27		1	2	443,407	9.90%
Indiana	13	1,955,325	13		1	2	334,729	17.12%
Iowa	10	1,268,773	10		1	2	357,393	28.17%
Kansas	8	896,166	8		1	2	343,006	38.27%
Kentucky	10	993,148		10	2	1	700	0.07%
Louisiana	10	651,952		10	2	1	38,102	5.84%
Maine	5	351,786	5		1	2	113,547	32.28%
Maryland	9	902,074	9		1	2	104,087	11.54%
Massachusetts	16	2,383,398	16		1	2	208,800	8.76%
Michigan	20	2,798,592	20		1	2	320,872	11.47%
Minnesota	11	1,379,483	11		1	2	154,753	11.22%
Mississippi	8	285,532		8	2	1	59,600	20.87%
Missouri	13	1,892,062	13		1	2	29,599	1.56%
Montana	4	265,037	4		1	2	51,181	19.31%
Nebraska	6	609,660	6		1	2	233,546	38.31%
Nevada	3	82,190	3		1	2	18,814	22.89%
New Hampshire	4	272,950	4		1	2	59,624	21.84%
New Jersey	16	2,419,554	16		1	2	358,711	14.83%
New Mexico	4	238,608	4		1	2	26,509	11.11%
New York	45	7,128,241	45		1	2	848,214	11.90%
North Carolina	14	1,210,910		14	2	1	94,696	7.82%
North Dakota	4	270,127	4		1	2	115,018	42.58%
Ohio	25	3,700,758	25		1	2	500,024	13.51%
Oklahoma	8	948,984	8		1	2	87,106	9.18%
Oregon	6	695,059	6		1	2	150,236	21.61%
Pennsylvania	32	4,580,969	32		1	2	269,520	5.88%
Rhode Island	4	414,498	4		1	2	7,642	1.84%
South Carolina	8	341,086		8	2	1	4,922	1.44%
South Dakota	4	294,283	4		1	2	113,431	38.54%
Tennessee	11	892,553	11		1	2	2,437	0.27%
Texas	24	2,075,946	24		1	2	133,650	6.44%
Utah	4	329,554	4		1	2	58,826	17.85%
Vermont	3	153,557	3		1	2	66,362	43.22%
Virginia	12	619,689	12		1	2	80,360	12.97%
Washington	9	1,102,708	9		1	2	106,262	9.64%
West Virginia	8	873,548		8	2	1	33,608	3.85%
Wisconsin	12	1,607,370	12		1	2	357,569	22.25%
Wyoming	3	129,251	3		1	2	33,113	25.62%
Total	531	61,751,942	442	89	1	2	6,700,439	10.85%

Eisenhower Republican		Stevenson Democratic		Others	
149,231	35.02%	275,075	64.55%	1,814	0.43%
152,042	58.35%	108,528	41.65%	0	0.00%
177,155	43.76%	226,300	55.90%	1,345	0.33%
3,035,587	56.83%	2,257,646	42.27%	48,370	0.91%
379,782	60.27%	245,504	38.96%	4,817	0.76%
611,012	55.70%	481,649	43.91%	4,250	0.39%
90,059	51.75%	83,315	47.88%	651	0.37%
544,036	54.99%	444,950	44.97%	351	0.04%
198,979	30.34%	456,823	69.66%	1	0.00%
180,707	65.42%	95,081	34.42%	443	0.16%
2,457,327	54.84%	2,013,920	44.94%	9,811	0.22%
1,136,259	58.11%	801,530	40.99%	17,536	0.90%
808,906	63.75%	451,513	35.59%	8,354	0.66%
616,302	68.77%	273,296	30.50%	6,568	0.73%
495,029	49.84%	495,729	49.91%	2,390	0.24%
306,925	47.08%	345,027	52.92%	0	0.00%
232,353	66.05%	118,806	33.77%	627	0.18%
499,424	55.36%	395,337	43.83%	7,313	0.81%
1,292,325	54.22%	1,083,525	45.46%	7,548	0.32%
1,551,529	55.44%	1,230,657	43.97%	16,406	0.59%
763,211	55.33%	608,458	44.11%	7,814	0.57%
112,966	39.56%	172,566	60.44%	0	0.00%
959,429	50.71%	929,830	49.14%	2,803	0.15%
157,394	59.39%	106,213	40.07%	1,430	0.54%
421,603	69.15%	188,057	30.85%	0	0.00%
50,502	61.45%	31,688	38.55%	0	0.00%
166,287	60.92%	106,663	39.08%	0	0.00%
1,374,613	56.81%	1,015,902	41.99%	29,039	1.20%
132,170	55.39%	105,661	44.28%	777	0.33%
3,952,815	55.45%	3,104,601	43.55%	70,825	0.99%
558,107	46.09%	652,803	53.91%	0	0.00%
191,712	70.97%	76,694	28.39%	1,721	0.64%
2,100,391	56.76%	1,600,367	43.24%	0	0.00%
518,045	54.59%	430,939	45.41%	0	0.00%
420,815	60.54%	270,579	38.93%	3,665	0.53%
2,415,789	52.74%	2,146,269	46.85%	18,911	0.41%
210,935	50.89%	203,293	49.05%	270	0.07%
168,082	49.28%	173,004	50.72%	0	0.00%
203,857	69.27%	90,426	30.73%	0	0.00%
446,147	49.99%	443,710	49.71%	2,696	0.30%
1,102,878	53.13%	969,228	46.69%	3,840	0.18%
194,190	58.93%	135,364	41.07%	0	0.00%
109,717	71.45%	43,355	28.23%	485	0.32%
349,037	56.32%	268,677	43.36%	1,975	0.32%
599,107	54.33%	492,845	44.69%	10,756	0.98%
419,970	48.08%	453,578	51.92%	0	0.00%
979,744	60.95%	622,175	38.71%	5,451	0.34%
81,047	62.71%	47,934	37.09%	270	0.21%
34,075,529	55.18%	27,375,090	44.33%	301,323	0.49%

Election of 1956

Election Overview

Election Year 1956

Election Day November 6, 1956

Winning Candidates

- ★ **President:** Dwight D. Eisenhower
- ★ **Vice President:** Richard M. Nixon

Election Results [ticket, party: popular votes (percentage of popular vote); electoral votes (percentage of electoral vote)]

- Dwight D. Eisenhower and Richard M. Nixon, Republican: 35,579,180, (57.37%); 457 (86.1%)
- Adlai Stevenson and Estes Kefauver, Democratic: 26,028,028 (41.97%); 73 (13.7%)
- Unpledged Elector-Independent: 196,145 (0.32%); 0 (0.0%)
- Other: 217,975 (0.35%); 0 (0.0%)

Voter Turnout 60.6%

Central Forums/Campaign Methods for Addressing Voters

- Whistle-stop tour
- Speeches
- Radio
- Television ads

Incumbent President and Vice President on Election Day Dwight D. Eisenhower and Richard M. Nixon

Population (1956) 168,221,000

Gross Domestic Product

- $437.4 billion (in current dollars: $2,549.7 billion)
- Per capita: $2,600 (in current dollars: $15,157)

Number of Daily Newspapers (1960) 1,763

Average Daily Circulation (1960) 58,882,000

Households with

- Radio (1960): 48,504,000
- Television (1960): 46,312,000

Method of Choosing Electors Popular vote (mostly general-ticket system/winner take all)

Method of Choosing Nominees

- National party convention
- Presidential preference primaries

Key Issues and Events

- Republicans lose control of Congress in the 1954 midterm elections
- Korean War ends
- "McCarthyism" declines with Joseph McCarthy's censure in the Senate in 1954
- President Dwight D. Eisenhower remains popular
- Eisenhower's heart attack in September 24, 1955, injects uncertainty into his reelection bid, but he recovers quickly.

Leading Candidates

REPUBLICANS

- Dwight D. Eisenhower, president of the United States (New York)

DEMOCRATS

Presidential candidates

- Adlai Stevenson, former governor (Illinois)
- Estes Kefauver, senator (Tennessee)
- W. Averell Harriman, governor (New York)
- Lyndon B. Johnson, Senate majority leader (Texas)

Vice-presidential candidates
- Estes Kefauver, senator (Tennessee)
- John F. Kennedy, senator (Massachusetts)
- Albert Gore Sr., senator (Tennessee)
- Robert F. Wagner Jr., mayor (New York)
- Hubert Humphrey, senator (Minnesota)

Trajectory

- Adlai Stevenson struggles at first in seeking the presidency again, as Tennessee senator Estes Kefauver wins the New Hampshire primary on March 13 and the Minnesota primary March 20. Stevenson becomes more populist and wins Oregon, Florida, and California by a 2–1 margin.
- On February 29, with his doctors' approval, Eisenhower announces his candidacy for reelection. On June 8 Eisenhower suffers an ileitis attack but returns to work quickly and reaffirms his intention to run again
- Harold E. Stassen, President Eisenhower's special cabinet assistant on disarmament, leads a movement to Dump Nixon, and, at least twice, Eisenhower encourages Nixon to choose a cabinet post. Nixon refuses, and on April 25 Eisenhower affirms that his running mate will be Nixon.
- At the Democratic convention, August 13–17, Stevenson is nominated on the first ballot. Stevenson invites the delegates to choose his running mate. After a strong surge by the young Massachusetts senator, John F. Kennedy, Kefauver wins the vice presidential nomination on the third ballot.
- One Stevenson elector defects to an Alabama judge, Walter Jones, as a protest against federal, court-ordered desegregation.
- Eisenhower accepts the nomination in person at the Republican convention on August 23.
- On the eve of the election, October 29, Israel, cooperating with Great Britain and France, overruns the Sinai Peninsula in response to Egypt's decision on July 26 to nationalize the Suez Canal. Two days later, Eisenhower, feeling betrayed by his allies, condemns the use of force, and a ceasefire goes into effect at midnight November 6. On November 4, in Budapest, Soviet tanks crush the Hungarian uprising that began October 23. Fearing war with the Soviets, Eisenhower does not help the Hungarian government but does condemn the invasion and offer to help Hungarian refugees. Both the Suez Crisis and the Hungarian Revolution reinforce Americans' faith in Eisenhower's experience and steadiness, and he wins by more than 9 million popular votes.

Conventions

- Democratic National Convention: August 13–17, 1956, International Amphitheatre, Chicago
- Republican National Convention: August 20–23, 1956, Cow Palace, San Francisco

Ballots/Nominees

REPUBLICANS
Presidential first ballot
- Dwight D. Eisenhower by acclamation

DEMOCRATS
Presidential first ballot
- Adlai Stevenson 905.5
- Averell Harriman 210
- Lyndon B. Johnson 80
- Stuart Symington 45.5
- Albert Chandler 36.5
- James C. Davis 33
- John S. Battle 32.5
- George B. Timmerman 23.5
- Frank J. Lausche 5.5

Vice-presidential second ballot after shifts
- Estes Kefauver 466.5; 551.5; 755.5
- John F. Kennedy 294.5; 618; 589
- Albert Gore Sr. 178; 110.5; 13.5
- Robert F. Wagner Jr. 162.5; 9.5; 6
- Hubert Humphrey 134; 74.5; 2
- Luther Hodges 40; 0.5; 0
- P. T. Maner 33; 0; 0
- LeRoy Collins 29; 0; 0
- Clinton Anderson 16; 0; 0
- Frank G. Clement 14; 0; 0
- Pat Brown 1; 0; 0
- Lyndon B. Johnson 1; 0; 0
- Stuart Symington 1; 0; 0

Primaries

- Republican Party: 19; 44.8% delegates
- Democratic Party: 19; 42.7% delegates

Primaries Results

REPUBLICANS
- Dwight D. Eisenhower 5,008,132; 85.93%
- John W. Bricker 478,453; 8.21%
- Unpledged 115,014; 1.97%
- William F. Knowland 84,446; 1.45%
- Joseph J. "Joe" Foss 59,374; 1.02%
- S. C. Arnold 32,732; 0.56%
- Lawrence "Lar" Daly 27,131; 0.47%

- John B. Chapple 18,743; 0.32%
- Others 1,963; 0.03%

Democrats

- Adlai Stevenson 3,069,504; 50.70%
- Estes Kefauver 2,283,172; 37.71%
- Unpledged 380,300; 6.28%
- Frank J. Lausche 278,074; 4.59%
- John W. McCormack 26,128; 0.43%

Party Platform

DEMOCRATS
- End the peacetime draft
- H-bomb test-ban treaty
- Reduce military spending

REPUBLICANS
- Oppose Stevenson proposals; Eisenhower considered expert on military issues
- Strong military
- Fiscal responsibility

Campaign Tactics

- Television appearances take precedence over stumping. Greater reliance on five-minute TV spots, actually four minutes and twenty seconds. These advertisements are cheaper for parties, less disruptive for networks, and more effective in reaching viewers as a captive audience between programming.

REPUBLICANS
- Eisenhower wants a more dignified campaign befitting a sitting president.
- Minimizing speeches also preserves his health
- Deliver carefully planned, formal speeches running on his record
- Restrain Nixon's red baiting. The New Nixon travels 42,000 miles in his speaking tour.

DEMOCRATS
- Energetic campaign to demonstrate vigor unlike Eisenhower
- Series of speeches for Stevenson to envision a "New America" with five policy papers addressing senior citizens, health, education, natural resources, economic policy
- Sweeping peace agenda to end the draft; develop a trained professional volunteer defense corps, and push a nuclear bomb test-ban treaty

- Democrats denounce Republican advertising as commercialized, superficial, undignified, like peddling breakfast cereal
- Criticize Eisenhower's decisions during the Suez crisis and Hungarian Revolution—"the total bankruptcy of the administration's foreign policy"

Popular Campaign Slogans

REPUBLICANS
- "Draft Ike in 1956"
- "Peace and Prosperity"
- "I Still Like Ike"
- "Don't Change the Team in the Middle of the Stream"

DEMOCRATS
- "Adlai and Estes—The Bestest, the Winning Team"
- "Vote Democratic, the Party for You and Not Just a Few"
- "How's That Again, General?"

Campaign Songs

- Republicans: "I go for I-K-E (yes sir, yes sir, yessiree)"
- Democrats: "Believe in Stevenson"

Influential Campaign Appeals or Ads

REPUBLICANS
- Pushing "Peace, Prosperity, and Progress"
- Targeted ads such as "Taxi Driver and Dog" and "Women Voters"

DEMOCRATS
- Titled "The Man from Libertyville" series of ads debunk attacks that Stevenson is an aloof egghead and sell the Democratic Party as the "true voice of the American people"

Campaign Finance

- Eisenhower: $7,778,702 (in current dollars: $58,197,000)
- Stevenson: $5,106,651 (in current dollars: $38,205,800)

Defining Quotations

- "I shall be a candidate for the Democratic nomination for President next year, which, I suspect, is hardly a surprise." *Adlai Stevenson, announcing his candidacy, November 15, 1955*
- "One of the great dangers of the present campaign in California is that the Old Guard politicians are

using the campaign of Mr. Stevenson to climb back into power." *Estes Kefauver during the primary campaign, May 31, 1956*

- "The choice will be yours. The profit will be the nation's." *Adlai Stevenson handing over the vice-presidential choice to the convention delegates, August 16, 1956*
- "As President it would be my purpose to press on in accordance with our platform toward the fuller freedom for all our citizens, which is at once our party's pledge and the American promise." *Adlai Stevenson, Democratic acceptance speech, Chicago, August 17, 1956*
- "This idea that you can merchandise candidates for high office like breakfast cereal—that you can gather votes like box tops—is, I think, the ultimate indignity to the democratic process." *Adlai Stevenson, Democratic acceptance speech, Chicago, August 17, 1956*
- "And finally: they tell us that peace can be guarded—and our nation secured—by a strange new formula. It is this: simultaneously to stop our military draft and to abandon testing of our most advanced military weapons. Here perhaps, I may be permitted to speak in the first person singular. I do not believe that any political campaign justifies the declaration of a moratorium on ordinary common sense. I, both as your President and the Commander-in-Chief of the Armed Forces of the United States of America, cannot and will not tell you that our quest of peace will be cheap and easy. It may be costly—in time, in effort, in expense, and in sacrifice. And any nation unwilling to meet such demands cannot—and will not—lead the free world down the path of peace." *Dwight D. Eisenhower, address at the Hollywood Bowl, Beverly Hills, California, October 19, 1956*
- "And distasteful as this matter is, I must say bluntly that every piece of scientific evidence we have, every lesson of history and experience, indicates that a Republican victory tomorrow would mean that Richard Nixon would probably be President of this country within the next four years." *Adlai Stevenson implying Eisenhower would not live through the term, November 5, 1956*

Lasting Legacy of Campaign

- Last campaign with a candidate born in the nineteenth century
- Last campaign prior to Alaska and Hawaii gaining statehood

Election of 1956

The dim shadows behind the general election of 1956 began to take a discernible pattern soon after Dwight D. Eisenhower took office in 1953. In the interim before the midterm congressional elections, it soon became apparent that, on several significant legislative measures, the president was receiving stronger support from the Democrats in Congress than from his own party. This was particularly true in the domain of foreign affairs, as several polls of the *Congressional Quarterly* documented in 1953 and 1954.

The Democratic leadership strategy was exercised with a sure sense of command and skill. Senator Lyndon Baines Johnson, the minority leader from Texas, quickly made it known that he was not addicted to the parliamentary dictum that the duty of the opposition was to oppose. Far from it. He announced that the Democratic purpose would be selective; Democrats would give vigorous support to the president's proposals deemed in the transcendent public interest, criticize and oppose those it considered unsound or ill-advised. It was a strategy that paid off handsomely. As both the midterm and presidential elections rolled around, the Democrats were able to say to the electorate, "The president really needs us. Look how we have given this popular president more support than his own party on some of the really critical votes."

Also at work in dismantling Republican election strategy during Eisenhower's first term was the unusual political matrix formed by the two leaders of the opposition, Speaker of the House Sam Rayburn and Senate Minority Leader Lyndon Johnson, and President Eisenhower. A warm affection existed among the three principals—one that continued after the Democrats became the majority in Congress right down to January 20, 1961, when Eisenhower left office. Eisenhower himself had been born in Texas and had known both men over many years, and it is improbable that a more supportive relationship ever existed between a president and the opposition congressional leadership.

One more ingredient in the faltering and shaky pointing up of the Republicans toward future congressional contests was the switch of the Republican command in the Senate soon after Eisenhower took office. After one of the most dramatic pre-convention tangles in history, Senate Majority Leader Robert Taft and Eisenhower compacted a political treaty, and Taft thereafter gave strong, muscular support in the Senate. Seven months after Eisenhower became president, Taft died of cancer.

In a context where many feared that too many Republicans had been out of power and in the opposition so long that they only knew how to oppose rather than propose, the loss of a man of the creative stature of Taft was a serious blow to the president. One may only conjecture what Taft might have done in the explosive tribal warfare that developed subsequently within the Republican Party over Senator Joseph McCarthy. There is reason to believe that, because of his responsibilities as Senate majority leader, he would have put a collar on the Wisconsin senator before the embittered struggle got out of hand.

Following the 1954 midterm elections, the wafer-thin Republican margin of 3 in the House disappeared, and the Democrats took control by 232 seats to 203. In the Senate, Democrats also took over the reins but by a smaller margin—49 to 47. Credited with part of the responsibility for the remarkable number of Democratic victories was Adlai Stevenson, who carried a spirited campaign into many critical states. Facing the dilemma of all presidential candidates who have the hollow husk title of "titular leader" thrust on them following defeat, Stevenson initially took on the responsibility of reducing the party deficit from the 1952 campaign and of trying to rebuild the organization stone by stone. This he sought to accomplish with his personal choice for national chairman, Stephen A. Mitchell. In 1953, Stevenson took a personal world tour that received wide coverage in the nation's press. It is perhaps significant that in the course of this tour he discovered that abroad he was acclaimed as a statesman with public responsibilities, much after the fashion of the leader of the "loyal opposition" in British politics. Operating without any beachhead in public affairs, such as a governorship or Senate seat, Stevenson

Adlai E. Stevenson addresses a crowd in Madison Square Garden, New York City. *(Library of Congress)*

was able to win what no other man without such a beach-head had in modern political life—a presidential nomination, and a renomination at that. Wendell Willkie tried it between 1940 and 1944, and Harold Stassen attempted it in two serious bids for the presidency between 1946 and 1952 (and several times since), but without success.

Stevenson did not court renomination between his defeat in 1952 and the 1956 Democratic convention, but he was clearly the front-runner in all the polls during this period, and he was widely acclaimed as leader of his party. His first overt act suggesting more than a passing interest in a second presidential nomination was a major speech in 1955 attacking the foreign policies of the Eisenhower administration.

The dark months of uncertainty that befogged the 1956 presidential race for such a protracted period began shortly after 2:30 in the morning on September 24, 1955, at Denver, Colorado, when Mrs. Eisenhower, worried about the president's restlessness, woke him up. The president complained of a severe pain in his chest, soon to be diagnosed as a serious heart attack.

It was Saturday afternoon, almost 12 hours after the heart attack, that the news was broken to the world. Monday the stock market took its worst plunge since the Great Depression, but made a quick recovery. Later, as Vice President Nixon began presiding at cabinet meetings and as the nation anxiously watched the steady stream of medical bulletins from Fitzsimons Hospital at Lowry Air Force Base gradually turn from caution to guarded optimism, the endless speculation that is the very breath of life of politics turned all eyes on a single event: leadership succession in 1956 if the president's health didn't permit a second term.

Napoleon III's minister of justice, Eugene Rouher, once said that "in politics one must never say never," and if ever there was a period in the nation's lifeline when no one, including the principal (Eisenhower), knew what the shape of things to come would be, it was the next five months. Initially, restraint was the watchword of both major parties. But even as brave, bold words were spoken about full recovery, it is no overstatement to conclude that neither Eisenhower nor most of the world thought he would seriously consider running for the presidency again in 1956. A turbid stream of possible candidates appeared as the months wore on. In the Republican camp, these included Senator William Knowland, then Senate minority leader; the former governor of New York, Thomas Dewey; Vice President Nixon; United Nations Ambassador Henry Cabot Lodge; Governor Christian Herter of Massachusetts; Sherman Adams, assistant to the president; former governor of Minnesota Harold Stassen; and the president's favorite brother, Milton Eisenhower, president of Johns Hopkins University.

Titled "Not What He Wanted for Christmas," this Edwin Marcus cartoon shows the GOP elephant in his pajamas, sitting in front of a Christmas tree, gazing in some dismay at a package labeled "The '56 Dilemma." Marcus refers to the question of whether President Eisenhower would be able to run for another term as president in 1956 after his September 1955 heart attack. Eisenhower did run and was reelected. *(By Permission of the Marcus Family)*

So remarkable was the president's recovery, however, that by the time he reached Gettysburg, Pennsylvania, on November 14 to begin his convalescence, the question of his own candidacy was very much front stage center. These were difficult days for the President. Any inactivity always dampened his morale, and his irritability showed up quickly. He had not suffered the depression in the hospital so customary after a coronary thrombosis; but at Gettysburg everything seemed to conspire to make his convalescence a stressful experience. At least two of the capitol's most sensitive, thoughtful reporters—Robert Donovan, then with the *New York Herald Tribune,* and Edward Folliard of the *Washington Post*—felt that Ike's chafing, restless retirement for many weeks at Gettysburg was a powerful factor in his eventual decision to run for a second term. Yet no one knew. In a press conference at Key West, Florida, on January 8, 1956, the president spoke of what "a critical matter it is to change governments in this country at a time that is unexpected." Following the press conference a poll of White House correspondents indicated that, by a 5-to-1 margin, this group was convinced Ike would not run. But within days (on January 13, at a highly secretive meeting at the White House of Ike's closest friends and advisers), the first field goal was kicked in persuading Ike to declare. Opinion was unanimous among this group that he should run, though his brother Milton, who summed up the reasons for and against, pointed out that Eisenhower, now 65 years old, had already been in public service for 40 years and was

entitled to do some of the things he so enjoyed but which had been crowded out of a busy life. Dr. Eisenhower also advanced one affirmative argument, however, that was most persuasive. His brother's overriding concern for

1956 ELECTION CHRONOLOGY

1953
July 27, 1953: An armistice stops the Korean War.

August 12, 1953: The Soviet Union tests its first hydrogen bomb.

December 8, 1953: Eisenhower delivers his "Atoms for Peace" speech to the United Nations, calling for the peaceful development of nuclear energy and an international Atomic Energy Agency.

1954
May 17, 1954: The Supreme Court declares racial segregation of schools unconstitutional.

November 2, 1954: In midterm elections the Democrats gain 19 seats in the House of Representatives and 2 seats in the Senate, becoming the majority in both houses of Congress. They will control the House of Representatives for the next 40 years.

December 2, 1954: The Senate censures Republican senator Joseph McCarthy of Wisconsin, ending his anticommunist witch-hunt.

1955
January 19, 1955: Eisenhower holds the first televised presidential news conference.

August 12, 1955: Eisenhower signs a bill increasing the minimum wage to a dollar an hour.

September 24, 1955: Eisenhower suffers a heart attack, which raises speculation as to whether he will run again. He recovers quickly.

November 15, 1955: Former Illinois governor and presidential candidate Adlai Stevenson announces his candidacy for the Democratic presidential nomination.

December 16, 1955: Tennessee senator Estes Kefauver announces he will seek the Democratic presidential nomination.

1956
February 29, 1956: With his doctors' approval, President Eisenhower announces he will seek a second term as president.

March 13, 1956: Kefauver wins a decisive victory over Stevenson in the New Hampshire primary.

March 20, 1956: Kefauver defeats Stevenson in the Minnesota primary with 57 percent of the popular vote.

April 25, 1956: President Eisenhower confirms that his running mate in 1956 will be Vice President Richard M. Nixon, after failing to convince Nixon to accept a cabinet post.

May 18, 1956: After beginning a more intensive, populist stumping campaign, Adlai Stevenson defeats Kefauver in the Oregon primary and goes on to win the remaining primaries by a margin of 2 to 1.

June 5, 1956: Stevenson wins the California primary by a decisive 2-to-1 margin.

June 8, 1956: Eisenhower suffers from an attack of ileitis and is operated on, but quickly returns to work. Eisenhower will run a more hands-off campaign, focusing on major speeches while Vice President Nixon conducts a more energetic stumping campaign.

June 29, 1956: Eisenhower signs the National Defense Interstate Highway Act, the largest public works program in American history.

July 26, 1956: Egypt nationalizes the Suez Canal.

August 1, 1956: Kefauver withdraws from the campaign and endorses Stevenson.

August 13–17, 1956: The Democratic National Convention meets in Chicago. Adlai Stevenson of Illinois wins the presidential nomination on the first ballot. He leaves the choice of the vice-presidential nominee up to the convention, which chooses Senator Estes Kefauver of Tennes-

peace, he said, could not be channeled effectively from retirement. If he were to exercise leadership effectively, it would have to be from the White House, not from his farm at Gettysburg. Moreover, a Democratic president would not want a retired president intruding into the domain of foreign affairs.

This argument drove straight to the target. Since the Geneva Conference in 1955, Eisenhower felt that he was

---

☆   ☆   ☆

see, despite a strong showing by Senator John F. Kennedy of Massachusetts.

August 20–23, 1956: The Republican National Convention meets at the Cow Palace in San Francisco. President Eisenhower is elected overwhelmingly on the first ballot. Former Minnesota governor Harold Stassen opposes Richard M. Nixon's renomination, but Eisenhower pressures him to propose Nixon's nomination. The vice president wins easily, on the first ballot. Eisenhower accepts his nomination in person on August 23.

September 5, 1956: Stevenson returns to an issue he first broached in an April 21 speech, and proposes banning all H-bomb tests. He also advocates ending the military draft in favor of an all-volunteer army. This attempt to prove he is not the "issueless candidate" backfires, as Americans have more faith in Eisenhower regarding national security.

September 12, 1956: Eisenhower launches his fall campaign with a picnic at his Gettysburg, Pennsylvania, country house.

September 13, 1956: Adlai Stevenson launches his official campaign for the presidency at the Farm Show Arena in Harrisburg, Pennsylvania. The normally cerebral Stevenson presents himself as the populist "New Stevenson," attacking the president as "a part-time leader."

October 3, 1956: The influential African American congressman Adam Clayton Powell of New York endorses Eisenhower due to the president's international standing and civil rights stand. With AFL-CIO president George Meany wavering in his support for Stevenson, the Democratic coalition Franklin Roosevelt forged is teetering.

October 15, 1956: In a nationwide TV broadcast, Stevenson vows to make a nuclear test ban his "first order of business" as president.

October 23, 1956: The Stevenson campaign holds a major rally at Madison Square Garden in New York, culminating in a half-hour speech by the candidate televised on CBS. The crowd is enthusiastic, though smaller than the one that greeted him at a similar rally in 1952. Stevenson focuses mainly on foreign policy and calls on Democrats to ignore the pollsters, who have consistently predicted his defeat.

October 25, 1956: The Eisenhower campaign holds a major rally at Madison Square Garden in New York City. The president is greeted by "Ike Girls" and serenaded by a marching band before delivering a half-hour speech dealing mainly with foreign affairs. The "Citizens for Eisenhower and Nixon" committee spends $250,000 to have the speech televised on NBC.

October 29, 1956: In response to Egypt's nationalization of the Suez Canal, Israeli forces invade the Sinai, while British and French forces take control of the canal. Eisenhower condemns the action and effectively forces a ceasefire.

November 4, 1956: Soviet forces crush a popular uprising in Budapest, which began on October 23 and nearly toppled the Communist regime. Eisenhower condemns the intervention and offers help to Hungarian refugees, but avoids confronting the Soviets directly. Eisenhower's handling of these two world crises reinforces Americans' faith in him.

November 6, 1956: Dwight Eisenhower is reelected by a landslide, winning 57.37 percent of the popular vote and 457 electoral votes. The Democrats win 41.97 percent of the vote and 73 electoral votes. The election affirms the public faith in Eisenhower's era of peace and prosperity.

December 17, 1956: Presidential electors cast their ballots in their respective state capitals.

1957

January 7, 1957: A joint session of Congress assembles to count the electoral votes.

breaking new ground with the Russians. He believed that he had gotten along with Khrushchev, and he had great hopes of at least starting to initiate some positive actions that would begin at last to defrost the East–West conflict. No decision was reached that night, but Attorney General Herbert Brownell, in an aside as the group broke up, observed that he thought Ike would decide to run. Yet, in the days that followed, Eisenhower continued to reaffirm to confidants something he had said repeatedly both before and after he took office in January 1953: he wanted to be a one-term president.

Meanwhile, the uncertainties were becoming more than a little bothersome for the unity of the Republican Party. Senator Knowland—chief spokesman for the conservative wing—said he would enter the race if the president did not announce by February 15, while Harold Stassen said he would wait until July if necessary. On January 30, in a strongly worded front-page editorial the *New York Herald-Tribune* urged Eisenhower to run. The *Tribune* foresaw a Republican defeat without Eisenhower at the head of the ticket, citing a Gallup Poll showing a 3-to-2 lead for him against any Democratic candidate, and a poll of the *Des Moines Register and Tribune* indicating that the Republicans would lose Iowa without him.

In the welter of contradictions that circulated with ever-growing intensity, Eisenhower did declare that he would make a decision by March 1. Soon after, the president's personal physician, Major General Howard Snyder, insisted that the president needed a little more time, and Eisenhower went to Walter Reed Hospital for a checkup that was to be critical for his final decision. The damaged heart showed no enlargement since the president had returned to more or less normal activity. This was a crucial indicator of his physical condition. At a press conference three days later, the celebrated heart specialist, Dr. Paul Dudley White, put it this way: "Medically I think we would agree that his present condition and the favorable chances in the future should enable him to carry on his present active life satisfactorily for this period, as I have said, for five to ten years, knowing full well, as we have just emphasized, the hazards and uncertainties of the future." Asked if he would vote for the president if he ran again, White said he would.

From this day forward, Eisenhower seemed to have made up his mind. The following day he went to Georgia for some golf and quail hunting and was elated that strenuous walking "didn't bother me." By the end of the month the president was making plans to announce his intentions, and, at a suspense-filled press conference on March 1, he told reporters that he "would go on television that night to tell the American people that I don't know, certainly for certain, that the Republican convention after hearing the entire story wants me . . . but my answer will be positive; that is, affirmative." That night, with his fam-

ily watching, he addressed the American people from the handsome Oval Office in the West Wing of the White House, concluding, "The work I set out to do four years ago has not yet reached the state of development and fruition that I then hoped could be accomplished within the period of a single term of office."

In the riptide of Republican uncertainty, the Democratic pre-convention contest began to jell as the year 1955 ground to a close. With Senator Estes Kefauver of Tennessee already in the race, Stevenson announced his candidacy in November. Whether Stevenson would have taken the big leap had he known what Eisenhower's subsequent decision would be on March 1 is an enigma never solved. In any case, any backing down after Eisenhower's entry into the race was unthinkable. By this time, Governor Stevenson was not only committed, but regretfully, to his own taste, he was also committed to an expensive and exhaustive string of presidential primary hoedowns against Senator Kefauver. Kefauver, unopposed, took the nation's first primary in New Hampshire on March 13. On March 20, the first serious derailment of the Stevenson candidacy took place in Minnesota. Four years earlier, veteran observers had called it the "Minnesota Thunderclap" when Eisenhower, not even a candidate and not even in the country, had almost defeated favorite son Harold Stassen in a last minute write-in campaign. In 1956, all of the heavy gunboats were on Stevenson's side in the Minnesota presidential primary—Senator Hubert Humphrey, Senator Eugene McCarthy, and Governor Orville Freeman. Although the *Minneapolis Tribune* poll forecast a Kefauver victory, citing the effectiveness of his folksy, hand-pumping campaigning and his attacks against Democratic bossism, not many really believed it. When the returns were footed up, however, Kefauver had indeed won, and thumpingly so, capturing 57 percent of the popular vote and all but four delegates. Since there was no major Republican contest, there is good reason to believe that, under Minnesota's open primary, thousands of Republicans crossed over just to be perverse and embarrass the state's Democratic leaders.

Many Democratic professionals watching the weathercock swing in the wind speculated that the Minnesota primary might be a fatal blow to Stevenson. Some began to talk about new candidates like Lyndon Johnson or Senator Stuart Symington of Missouri. The South started a drive for Johnson that was spearheaded by the early backing of Senator Richard Russell of Georgia. As expected, Stevenson carried the Illinois primary, but by the end of April a state-by-state survey of Democratic prospects indicated no Democratic candidate was likely to win nomination on the first ballot. Averell Harriman, midway in his first and only term as governor of New York, was now in the race with the backing of former President Truman (who initially said he would be strictly

Unidentified members of the Republican Club view President Eisenhower on television at the club's New York City headquarters at 54 West 40th Street as he told the nation of his availability for a second term during a broadcast from the White House, February 29, 1956. *(John Lent/Associated Press)*

neutral), Judge Samuel Rosenman, Franklin Roosevelt's gifted ghost writer, former secretary of state Dean Acheson, and some of the big urban Democratic chieftains like Carmine DeSapio of New York and Thomas Pendergast of Kansas City.

An impressive win in the Oregon primary buoyed Stevenson forces the third week in May, but the Florida primary a week later, preceded by a debate between Stevenson and Kefauver where both seemed in agreement on all issues, was inconclusively close. The California primary, a jumpy internal factional battle, would be the decisive contest.

While the Democratic contest whipsawed through the sullen snows of Minnesota to the sun-veiling smog of California, all eyes in the Republican camp after March 1 were trained on a single question. Would Eisenhower's running mate be Nixon again, or would the vice president be replaced by another candidate? For several weeks, Eisenhower would neither affirm nor deny that he wanted Nixon, and a supermarket of rumors went out that Nixon

would be dumped. Nixon's own account of this story, which he identified as one of the crises in his book *My Six Crises,* leaves no doubt that this was a possibility. Indeed, the president, under the pulling and hauling of many persons who tried to persuade him to pick another running mate, did summon Nixon and suggest to him that he appoint him to the cabinet, where he might advance his political career even more advantageously than in the prison of the vice presidency. It was an immensely emotional experience for Nixon, but he stood his ground and turned down the president's suggestion.

Eisenhower was irritated at the suggestions that he was trying to jettison Nixon, but it was not until the end of April that he made a pale pass at the subject. Emerging from a meeting with the president, Nixon told reporters, "I informed the President that, in the event the President and the delegates to the convention reached the decision that it was their desire for me to serve as the nominee of the Republican Party for their Vice President, I would be honored to accept that nomination again . . . as I did in 1952."

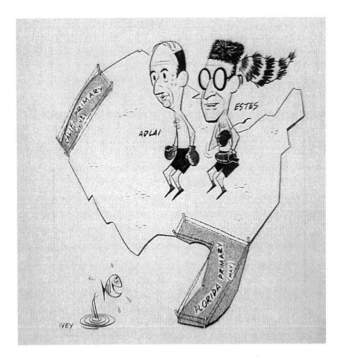

This Jim Ivey cartoon, titled "Coast to Coast Bouts," shows Democratic presidential candidates Adlai Stevenson and Estes Kefauver as boxers, standing on a map of the United States, poised between two boxing rings, one labeled "Florida Primary (May)" and one "Calif. Primary (June)." Ivey comments on the tight schedule for the candidates in the 1956 presidential election. Stevenson won both primaries. *(Library of Congress)*

At this point Press Secretary James Hagerty interrupted to say, "The President has asked me to tell you gentlemen that he was delighted to hear of the Vice President's decision." Some observers are inclined to cite the president's tightrope walking on Nixon's renomination together with his lateness in jumping into Nixon's 1960 campaign against John F. Kennedy for the presidency as a lack of complete confidence in Nixon or a lack of real affection for the man. While Eisenhower was certainly under pressure from some staffers and associates who wanted Nixon off the ticket, he was also well aware of the compelling need for a president to keep his options open. He was, in short, carefully feeling out the situation to determine how well Nixon stood in a test of wills within his own party. Also, in 1960 Eisenhower was determined to support Nixon in any way the vice president desired, but he also was extremely anxious not to intrude in any way that would detract from the Nixon candidacy or deter the vice president from striking out on his own in the production of new policies and new programs. Above all else, he wanted to avoid a presidential election like 1916, where Charles Evans Hughes and Woodrow Wilson were the candidates, but, as Theodore Roosevelt jumped into the campaign to help Hughes, everybody talked about Roosevelt or Wilson and Hughes lost.

As the clamorous campaign within the Democratic camp closed with a 2-to-1 win for Stevenson in Califor-

nia on June 5, it began to look as though the Republican ticket would definitely be Eisenhower and Nixon again.

But, on June 8, the president was operated on for an intestinal obstruction. Once more the names of William Knowland, Tom Dewey, Richard Nixon, Christian Herter, and Milton Eisenhower jumped into contention as presidential possibilities; Governor Goodwin Knight of California was also mentioned. Interestingly, although none of these possibilities generated strong support among the party professionals, a Gallup Poll indicated that Milton Eisenhower would be the strongest Republican candidate if his brother declined to run.

The ileitis attack of the president generated an immense conjectural crisis for two reasons. First, of course, it was major surgery—a serious operation following closely on the heels of a severe heart attack. Second, Eisenhower had said specifically at a March 7 press conference that he would withdraw from the race if his physical condition was seriously impaired. The *London Daily Mirror* renewed an earlier demand that the president retire, and stories soon sprouted up that the health issue would favor the Democrats.

Eisenhower's remarkable regenerative capabilities, however, soon dispelled all doubts about who would head the GOP ticket. On June 25, 20 Republican governors, without mentioning Nixon, urged him to run. On July 7, Eisenhower announced from his farm at Gettysburg that he was requesting Ambassador John Sherman Cooper to return from India to run for a United States Senate seat in Kentucky. He also began to inform Republican leaders that he would run for the presidency. Knowland himself broke the news publicly on July 10 that Eisenhower would run, adding that Nixon was not discussed. Then on July 12, Republican chairman Leonard Hall, who had steadfastly insisted from the outset that Nixon would be Eisenhower's running mate, emerged from a conference at Gettysburg to say that the president had made it absolutely clear that he wanted Nixon.

The inner mystery of this announcement is one of the most difficult matters to assess of that entire election year. At least some of the president's closest associates insist that Eisenhower had not made up his mind yet about the vice-presidential nominee. One high staffer was so stunned by the statement that he called a reporter of the *New York Times* to verify the Hall quote. The Republican chairman was not repudiated, however, and everything now appeared set for a routine ratification of an Eisenhower–Nixon slate by the impending national convention—almost, that is, except for one last abortive attempt by former governor Harold Stassen to keep Nixon off the Republican ticket.

On July 24, Stassen urged that Christian Herter replace Nixon as the GOP vice-presidential candidate. In support of his proposal, Stassen produced a poll showing that such a ticket would run at least six percentage points stronger than one with Nixon. This particular maneuver was reported by the *New York Times*'s James Reston as having Eisenhower's tacit consent. Stassen was granted a month's leave from the White House to pursue his campaign to nominate the Massachusetts governor, as the question of Herter's eligibility was raised because of his birth in Paris. Meanwhile, Chairman Hall shot down Stassen's proposal by announcing that Herter himself would nominate Nixon at the convention. Finally, when Senator Jacob Javits of New York announced he was supporting Nixon and 180 Republican congressmen came out with a declaration for the vice president, the issue seemed closed.

But still the hummocks and troughs in the long story of Nixon's political career persisted. On August 8, a small group met to organize the "eggheads for Ike." Called CASE, the Committee of Arts and Sciences for Eisenhower, it was cochaired by Dean Harry Carman of Columbia, and Helen Hayes, the actress. Others included physicist Isadore Rabi, Arthur Flemming, president of Macalester College in Minnesota, J. P. Baxter, president of Williams College, law professor Arthur Larson, Gabriel Hauge, economics adviser to the president, and Malcolm Moos. No mention was made of Nixon.

Along the Democratic pre-convention campaign trail, Stevenson's fortunes tilted sharply upward on August 1, when Kefauver gave up the chase and came out for him. Harriman claimed half of Kefauver's delegates, but a truly deliverable vote, as every political pro knows, just isn't packageable. In a televised comment on who has it and who hasn't, Judge Rosenman complained that Stevenson "lacked the New Deal spirit," while Harry Truman (now for Harriman) called Stevenson a "hesitant man" aligned with the conservatives and reactionaries who would abandon the New Deal–Fair Deal. Eleanor Roosevelt's reply to these charges was, "It was time to let the young folks run the country." The only question now was whether Stevenson would make it on the first ballot. A strong stand that he took on the civil rights section of the platform was thought by some to jeopardize his chance for a first ballot nomination, but such was not the case. At Stevenson's request, he was placed in nomination by John F. Kennedy, and, after defeating Harriman 905.5 to 210 on the first ballot, the convention made the vote unanimous.

In a surprise move, Stevenson stressed to the delegates that 7 of our 34 presidents had been vice presidents, and that the same high qualities guiding the search for a presidential nominee should likewise be required for the vice-presidential candidate. Departing from the time-honored tradition that the presidential nominee selects his running mate, Stevenson threw the decision to the convention. Taken unawares, the convention turned into a mad scramble of alignments and realignments.

The forces behind John Kennedy mobilized quickly, and for a time it looked as though he would make it. Kennedy supporters had pressed a drive for the vice-presi-

dential nomination at the June Governors' Conference, and his friends were actively working for his candidacy all during the convention. One particular effort of JFK backers, however, turned out to be quite controversial. An elaborate statistical study was distributed to the delegates purporting to document the importance of the Catholic vote in major urban areas in revitalizing the highly successful Democratic ethnic–labor minority group coalition that had dissolved in 1952 under the impact of Eisenhower's popularity. The document was criticized on the ground that Senator Kennedy was immovably correct in urging that candidacy on a national ticket should not be discouraged because a man was Catholic, but that, by the same token, one should not argue that his Catholicism would bring a definite advantage to the ticket. In short, you couldn't have it both ways.

After an inconclusive result on the first ballot, Kennedy jumped to a commanding lead on the second ballot following an open floor fight. With 648 votes, he led Kefauver by a wide margin. But before the results were announced, delegates began switching. Senator Albert Gore of Tennessee, running third, withdrew in favor of Kefauver, and Kennedy lost by a vote of 755.5 to 589.

By Republican convention time in late August, the last tattered shards of Stassen's drive to unhorse Nixon had disappeared. On August 22, Eisenhower, after conferring with the former Minnesota governor, called a press con-

Harold E. Stassen *(Library of Congress)*

ference to announce the collapse of Stassen's campaign. The next day Stassen seconded Nixon's nomination.

Only one event enlivened what otherwise would have been what H. L. Mencken liked to call a "gratification convention." When the secretary was proceeding with the call of the roll of states for nominations for vice president, a delegate from Nebraska named Terry Carpenter asked for recognition. He said he wanted to nominate Fred Seaton, a former governor and United States senator from the Cornhusker State, but convention chairman Joe Martin ruled this was impossible because it was against Seaton's wishes. At this point, Delegate Carpenter nominated Joe Smith, while the convention rocked around uncertainly for a few moments as newsmen tried unsuccessfully to gain access to the floor to find out who Joe Smith really was. Later, Carpenter said he produced Joe Smith as a symbol of an open convention, but he joined with other Nebraska delegates in voting for Nixon. Persistent newsmen never were able to find the real Joe Smith, if indeed he ever existed other than symbolically. Gleeful Democrats, however, made frequent reference to the Joe Smith incident as indicating a lurking disenchantment with Nixon within the ranks of the GOP.

On August 27, some of the pale prefigurations of difficulty for the Democratic campaign were not altogether papered over by the action of the AFL-CIO executive council vote backing the Stevenson-Kefauver ticket 17 to 5. As Stevenson opened his campaign at Harrisburg on September 13, and Eisenhower opened his own with a picnic at Gettysburg the day before, it quickly became evident that the roles of the two candidates would be sharply reversed from what they had been in 1952. While Ike talked in lofty terms—"leave the yelling to the opposition"—Stevenson concentrated on sharp attacks. He accused the Republican administration of "guile in international dealings," and scored Ike as "a part-time leader," as an indirect way of raising questions about the president's health. Stevenson also stressed the need for party organization more than he did in his earlier campaign; it was a strategy born of the hope that if the old Democratic coalition could be reincarnated, he could still overcome Ike's personal popularity. The switch in posture from his 1952 campaign produced many misgivings among Stevenson's followers.

Stevenson's highly talented writers included Willard Wirtz, John Bartlow Martin, John Hersey, Arthur Schlesinger Jr., and John Kenneth Galbraith. He also had, as in 1952, a brilliant constellation of egghead support—the Arts Committee for Stevenson, which included such luminaries as Alan Jay Lerner, Dory Schary, and Cass Canfield. But overtones of a drop-off from the 1952 campaign persisted right from the outset when George Meany, president of the AFL-CIO, indicated his great reluctance to endorse the Democratic ticket.

The Republican campaign rested on a tripod of three central themes—peace, prosperity, and unity at home. Stevenson might charge that it was Stalin's death, not Eisenhower's election, that stopped the Korean War, but the fact that Eisenhower was credited with negotiating the truce was a powerful arrow in the Republican campaign quiver right down to Election Day.

Early in the contest, Eisenhower insisted that the conduct of domestic, not foreign, affairs was the issue. By taking foreign affairs out of the debate and following a disarmingly simple strategy—make Eisenhower the central issue—the Republicans sought not only a presidential triumph, but a congressional one as well. Complementing this strategy was the additional advantage for the incumbents that the entire campaign was executed in a period of economic prosperity.

Early in October, another unanticipated dividend dropped into the Republican camp. On October 3, Adam Clayton Powell returned from a three-month trip in Europe to announce that he was backing Eisenhower. His stated reasons were: Eisenhower's prestige abroad and his stand on civil rights; unelaborated, but apparently much on his mind, were a series of snubs from the Stevenson headquarters. Critics were swift to link the switch with an alleged administration intercession for a Powell aide on a tax case. But the accusation failed to blunt the impact of the Powell endorsement. Elsewhere, other elements helped the president improve his vote among blacks over his 1952 track record. An African American who had always voted Democratic, when asked why he planned to switch, replied that for the first time he could now go to Washington, D.C., and register in a first-class hotel. A presidential executive order had made this possible in the District of Columbia and was taken as a hopeful sign of the shape of things to come.

As the campaign wore on, no brainstorming session of the Stevenson strategists could seem to dismantle the towering, commanding figure of Eisenhower. Certainly, events between 1952 and 1956 had not swept away the earthy appeal of the Democratic Party as the preferred instrument of economic and social reform. But the country still appeared to welcome a breathing spell; unity and stability loomed larger than the desire for change, even though profound change was already on the way—and soon—in the storm-swept years about to follow. And with serenity a Republican was on the bridge in the White House without serious economic trouble. The recession of 1957 was not yet visible, and the harrowing memories of the Great Depression and President Hoover had finally begun to dissolve. Adding also to the invincibility of the Eisenhower shield was his acceptance and embracement of many New Deal reforms. On the issue of war and peace, the pollsters all agreed that in the majority view, people believed that Eisenhower, rather than the Democrats, could keep the peace.

Against these heavy odds, the Democratic strategy appeared uncertain and vacillating. It aspired to reunite the factions within the party that had been feuding since the New Deal–Fair Deal coalition began to break up, to create an "issue" campaign, and to go all out in running against Nixon instead of Eisenhower. The original design to concentrate on Nixon, however, was revised in midcampaign when a decision was taken to mount a more direct attack against the president and have Stevenson devote himself to issues while Kefauver raced about urging the Democratic faithful to vote a straight ticket. Eisenhower's "invincibility is a myth," declared Hubert Humphrey, the vigorous campaigner from Minnesota.

The attempt to generate issues and draw them into sharp focus was sputtering and sporadic. Some years before, Mencken had written, "When I was a boy, presidential campaigns were characterized by a high serious purpose. But now all that is happily past." He was referring to the me-tooism and unity theme of the Dewey campaign in 1948. In 1956, the prevailing mood of the nation did not stir up a buzz of hearty partisan excitement. Unfairly or not, Stevenson was tagged as the "issueless candidate" by his critics both within and outside his own party. His chief issue, which he flogged hard throughout the campaign, was a pledge to end all H-bomb tests. He also urged that the military draft be replaced by a professional, highly paid volunteer defense corps. Clearly, these were not gelatinous campaign choices, although Stevenson spoke up for them with great conviction. But in tangling with a military hero in the White House on the H-bomb, draft, and national defense issues, he was challenging the one area in which people believed Eisenhower to have the greatest judgment and competence. Again, the challenge of events was against Stevenson.

On July 26, Egypt seized the Suez Canal under a nationalization decree after President Nasser had denounced the Western withdrawal of a proposal to finance the Aswan Dam. In the public mind, this takeover highlighted Eisenhower's competence as a crisis manager in stressful situations—a feeling well documented by the polls. But the real wallop to affect the campaign was to come later.

On October 23, the Hungarian revolt, broke out in Budapest against the Soviet-dominated regime. The Soviet response was immediate and bristling with militancy. Soviet tanks and troops crushed the revolt, and the last resistance collapsed November 4—two days before the election.

Coinciding with the Hungarian uprising was yet another crisis that was to hit the campaign with the greatest muzzle-velocity of all—the Israeli penetration of Egypt's Sinai Peninsula on October 29. When Egypt rejected a cease-fire demand made by France and Great Britain, the two nations bombed Egypt in an air attack on October 31 and landed ground forces on November 5 and

This Edwin Marcus cartoon, titled "No Question About This Plank," shows the Democratic donkey and the GOP elephant carrying a long board labeled "Unity on Suez Issue." In the distance, a Russian man looks on unhappily. In the fall of 1956 as the presidential election neared, both parties supported the U.S. government's position in regard to the Suez Crisis. Marcus suggests that the Soviet Union had hoped that this would become a divisive issue. *(By Permission of the Marcus Family)*

6. The United States denounced this attack and supported the cease-fire demand of the United Nations that Israel and Egypt accepted. The fighting halted on November 7.

By November 1, a survey of 12 major cities produced strong evidence that the Middle East crisis between Israel and Egypt was strengthening Eisenhower. National estimates varied but generally agreed that the boiling tensions in the Middle East were worth from 3 to 5 percent to Eisenhower in the final election outcome. The only erosion of the president's strength over the Middle East crisis occurred in some areas of strong pro-Israel sentiment.

Stevenson's equivocation on civil rights undoubtedly disenchanted some elements of the Democratic black vote and cost him important newspaper support among this minority group. Many major black newspapers eventually backed Eisenhower, including the *Amsterdam News* in New York, the *Pittsburgh Courier,* the *Louisville Defender,* and the *Afro-American* in Baltimore.

The chief mischief-makers in the Republican campaign were discontent in rural areas because of cuts in farm price supports, the high-cost-of-living issue, and conservation—the latter particularly in the West. Many Democratic strategists felt that the distress among small businessmen as they reviewed their economic status in relation to big business would have become an important issue if more aggressively exploited. Others thought the Eisenhower health issue might have been damaging to the Republican ticket if it had been handled with the same explosive force that the Republicans had hurled the "crime, corruption, communism, and Korea" charge at the Democrats in 1952. But the health issue was a most delicate, sensitive matter, and any tasteless reference here could be a colossal blunder and probably backfire. Stevenson did raise the question of Eisenhower's health late in the campaign in speaking of Nixon as a successor, and on November 4 he said an Eisenhower victory would make Nixon president within four years. This suggestion hastily produced an indignant reaction, but any discernible impact it may have had on the outcome was difficult to assess.

The windup of the campaign brought in the usual newspaper endorsements, with the *New York Times* lauding Stevenson as the best possible man the Democrats could have picked but backing Eisenhower, while the *Baltimore Sun* came out for Eisenhower with reservations about Nixon. Just before the election, *Editor and Publisher* reported that, of 1,760 dailies polled, 740, or 62 percent, backed Eisenhower, and 189, or 15 percent, were supporting Stevenson, with the former accounting for 60 percent of the total circulation and the latter 10 percent.

As the campaign cranked into its final phase, Eisenhower was quoted on November 2 as being so confident of victory that he would do no more campaigning, and the following day he told Press Secretary James Hagerty that he would win by over 400 electoral votes. Interestingly, the CBS ratings by Trendex found that throughout the campaign Stevenson enjoyed slightly larger television audiences than Eisenhower—an average of 30 million. Once again, as in 1952, however, Stevenson fussed over his speeches so that he sometimes ran over the allotted television time, and had the climax of his talk cut off.

Election Day, November 6, turned into a sunburst for Eisenhower as the returns flashed in. With more than a 9 million–vote plurality, Eisenhower won the presidential steeplechase even more impressively than he had four years earlier. In 1956, Eisenhower's plurality was 3 million greater than his 1952 margin; in the electoral vote he captured 457 to his opponent's 73. Looked at strictly in terms of the Presidency, the sweep was a thumping Republican victory. Eisenhower carried all the mid-Atlantic, Midwest, and Rocky Mountain states, and everything beyond the Rockies. He also carried the border states of Oklahoma, Tennessee, and Kentucky, and invaded the South to win Virginia, Florida, Texas, and Louisiana—the latter slipping into the Republican column for the first time since 1876.

Elsewhere, evidence of the scope of the landslide abounded. Ike carried the Empire State by a plurality of 1.5 million; he not only carried several major cities, but he also ran unusually strong in the black precincts—a feat in both instances unachieved by a Republican candidate since 1928. The 1956 contest was the most spectacular presidential victory since Franklin Delano Roosevelt's electoral romp in 1936, when he won by a 10 million–vote plurality and carried every state but Maine and Vermont. Stevenson, courtly, gracious, and eloquent in defeat, said he was "disappointed but not bruised."

And yet, beneath this shiny, showcase, presidential triumph lurked stark ballot statistics that tarnished the sense of victory. Incredibly, Eisenhower led the Republican congressional ticket by over 6.5 million votes. The Rayburn–Johnson strategy of cooperation rather than opposition evidently paid off. Eisenhower became the first president since Zachary Taylor in 1848 to begin a term with both houses of Congress in the hands of the opposition party—an event that had occurred only four times in history. Only four years before, in the superheated preconvention contest between Ohio senator Robert Taft and General Eisenhower for the Republican presidential nomination, a highly persuasive document had been circulated underscoring Eisenhower's coattail power. Only with a superstar like Eisenhower, his supporters argued, could the Republican Party carry a sufficient number of the hundred-odd critical marginal districts to win control of Congress. But now, while the psephologists sought explanations for the reversal of the coattail theories, that argument seemed shattered as a president began his second term with both houses of Congress securely in the hands of the Democrats, and with the additional handicap of serving as the first chief executive to function under the Twenty-second Amendment limiting a president to two terms.

Sectionally, the Democratic Party made more substantial gains in the West than in the nation as a whole. In California, the Democratic Party fared so well except for the presidency (however, Ike's margin over Stevenson was 92,229 less than in 1952) that it captured the legislature for the first time in this century.

"Life is a mysterious fabric, woven of chance, fate, and character," wrote the philosopher Dilthey near the end of his long life, to which both victor and loser of the 1956 presidential contest might lustily agree.

In overview, the personalities of both men were dramatized at the expense of issues. Stevenson characterized the Republican platform as "propaganda, sprinkled with piety," while Eisenhower accused the Democrats of "willful, wicked nonsense." Stevenson, in taking measure of his losing fight and comparing 1956 with his 1952 campaign, observed that a major miscalculation of his campaign was his failure to realize how much effort, as well as funds, the presidential primaries would consume. But once he had

With upraised arms, President Dwight D. Eisenhower and Vice President Richard Nixon salute cheering Republicans at election headquarters in Washington, November 7, 1956, after Adlai Stevenson conceded, with the Republicans winning in a landslide. *(Associated Press)*

started, he felt he could not pull out. Nonetheless, he said, he had no regrets that he had entered and stayed the course.

To the end, Stevenson felt his main hope was in the Democratic machine and its broad appeal as the party of social and economic reform. But the configuration never materialized, and the farm revolt that tipped the scales for many winning Democratic congressional candidates was not strong enough to help Stevenson.

Stevenson also blamed the administration, the press, and the Democratic Party itself for their failure to discuss basic issues. "In a word," he said, "the Democrats failed to get through to the people." And yet they did. The over-simplified, coattail notion that somehow a good actor can carry a bad play, that a fabulously popular president could coast a majority of congressional candidates to victory, simply did not work in 1956.

—*Malcolm Moos*

Selected Bibliography

In addition to works cited in the 1952 bibliography, see Eisenhower's memoir, *The White House Years: Waging Peace* (1965), which is important for his personal account of his administration. See Arthur Larson, *A Republican Looks at His Party* (1956); Samuel Lubell, *Revolt of the Moderates* (1956); and Heinz Eulan, *Class and Party in the Eisenhower Years* (1962). A study of the campaign is Charles Thomson and Frances Shattuck, *The 1956 Presidential Campaign* (1960). The Eisenhower movement in Texas is covered by Edward McMillan, "Texas and the Eisenhower Campaigns" (unpublished PhD dissertation, Texas Tech, 1960). See also Stephen E. Ambrose, *Eisenhower: The President* (1984); Stephen E. Ambrose, *Nixon: The Education of a Politician, 1913–1962* (1987); Jeff Broadwater, *Adlai Stevenson and American Politics: The Odyssey of a Cold War Liberal* (1994); Fred I. Greenstein, *The Hidden-Hand Presidency: Eisenhower as Leader* (1982); and Herbert S. Parmet, *Eisenhower and the American Crusades* (1972).

1956 ELECTION STATISTICS

State	Number of Electors	Total Popular Vote	Elec Vote R	Elec Vote D	Elec Vote O*	Pop Vote R	Pop Vote D	Margin of Victory Votes	Margin of Victory % Total Vote
Alabama	11	496,871		10	1	2	1	85,150	17.14%
Arizona	4	290,173	4			1	2	64,110	22.09%
Arkansas	8	406,572		8		2	1	26,990	6.64%
California	32	5,466,355	32			1	2	607,533	11.11%
Colorado	6	663,074	6			1	2	130,482	19.68%
Connecticut	8	1,117,121	8			1	2	306,758	27.46%
Delaware	3	177,988	3			1	2	18,636	10.47%
Florida	10	1,124,220	10			1	2	163,478	14.54%
Georgia	12	663,480		12		2	1	224,442	33.83%
Idaho	4	272,989	4			1	2	61,111	22.39%
Illinois	27	4,407,407	27			1	2	847,645	19.23%
Indiana	13	1,974,607	13			1	2	398,903	20.20%
Iowa	10	1,234,564	10			1	2	227,329	18.41%
Kansas	8	866,243	8			1	2	270,561	31.23%
Kentucky	10	1,053,805	10			1	2	95,739	9.09%
Louisiana	10	617,544	10			1	2	85,070	13.78%
Maine	5	351,706	5			1	2	146,770	41.73%
Maryland	9	932,351	9			1	2	187,125	20.07%
Massachusetts	16	2,348,506	16			1	2	445,007	18.95%
Michigan	20	3,080,468	20			1	2	353,749	11.48%
Minnesota	11	1,340,005	11			1	2	101,777	7.60%
Mississippi	8	248,149		8		2	1	83,813	33.78%
Missouri	13	1,832,562		13		2	1	3,984	0.22%
Montana	4	271,171	4			1	2	38,695	14.27%
Nebraska	6	577,137	6			1	2	179,079	31.03%
Nevada	3	96,689	3			1	2	15,409	15.94%
New Hampshire	4	266,994	4			1	2	86,155	32.27%
New Jersey	16	2,484,312	16			1	2	756,605	30.46%
New Mexico	4	253,926	4			1	2	40,690	16.02%
New York	45	7,093,336	45			1	2	1,589,571	22.41%
North Carolina	14	1,165,592		14		2	1	15,468	1.33%
North Dakota	4	253,991	4			1	2	60,024	23.63%
Ohio	25	3,702,265	25			1	2	822,955	22.23%
Oklahoma	8	859,350	8			1	2	88,188	10.26%
Oregon	6	735,597	6			1	2	77,189	10.49%
Pennsylvania	32	4,576,503	32			1	2	603,483	13.19%
Rhode Island	4	387,611	4			1	2	64,029	16.52%
South Carolina	8	300,583		8		3	1	47,861	15.92%
South Dakota	4	293,857	4			1	2	49,281	16.77%
Tennessee	11	939,404	11			1	2	5,781	0.62%
Texas	24	1,955,545	24			1	2	220,661	11.28%
Utah	4	333,995	4			1	2	97,267	29.12%
Vermont	3	152,978	3			1	2	67,841	44.35%
Virginia	12	697,978	12			1	2	118,699	17.01%
Washington	9	1,150,889	9			1	2	97,428	8.47%
West Virginia	8	830,831	8			1	2	67,763	8.16%
Wisconsin	12	1,550,558	12			1	2	368,076	23.74%
Wyoming	3	124,127	3			1	2	25,019	20.16%
Total	531	62,021,979	457	73	1	1	2	9,551,152	15.40%

* One elector voted for Walter B. Jones for president.

Eisenhower Republican		Stevenson Democratic		Others	
195,694	39.39%	280,844	56.52%	20,333	4.09%
176,990	60.99%	112,880	38.90%	303	0.10%
186,287	45.82%	213,277	52.46%	7,008	1.72%
3,027,668	55.39%	2,420,135	44.27%	18,552	0.34%
394,479	59.49%	263,997	39.81%	4,598	0.69%
711,837	63.72%	405,079	36.26%	205	0.02%
98,057	55.09%	79,421	44.62%	510	0.29%
643,849	57.27%	480,371	42.73%	0	0.00%
216,652	32.65%	441,094	66.48%	5,734	0.86%
166,979	61.17%	105,868	38.78%	142	0.05%
2,623,327	59.52%	1,775,682	40.29%	8,398	0.19%
1,182,811	59.90%	783,908	39.70%	7,888	0.40%
729,187	59.06%	501,858	40.65%	3,519	0.29%
566,878	65.44%	296,317	34.21%	3,048	0.35%
572,192	54.30%	476,453	45.21%	5,160	0.49%
329,047	53.28%	243,977	39.51%	44,520	7.21%
249,238	70.87%	102,468	29.13%	0	0.00%
559,738	60.04%	372,613	39.96%	0	0.00%
1,393,197	59.32%	948,190	40.37%	7,119	0.30%
1,713,647	55.63%	1,359,898	44.15%	6,923	0.22%
719,302	53.68%	617,525	46.08%	3,178	0.24%
60,685	24.46%	144,498	58.23%	42,966	17.31%
914,289	49.89%	918,273	50.11%	0	0.00%
154,933	57.13%	116,238	42.87%	0	0.00%
378,108	65.51%	199,029	34.49%	0	0.00%
56,049	57.97%	40,640	42.03%	0	0.00%
176,519	66.11%	90,364	33.84%	111	0.04%
1,606,942	64.68%	850,337	34.23%	27,033	1.09%
146,788	57.81%	106,098	41.78%	1,040	0.41%
4,340,340	61.19%	2,750,769	38.78%	2,227	0.03%
575,062	49.34%	590,530	50.66%	0	0.00%
156,766	61.72%	96,742	38.09%	483	0.19%
2,262,610	61.11%	1,439,655	38.89%	0	0.00%
473,769	55.13%	385,581	44.87%	0	0.00%
406,393	55.25%	329,204	44.75%	0	0.00%
2,585,252	56.49%	1,981,769	43.30%	9,482	0.21%
225,819	58.26%	161,790	41.74%	2	0.00%
75,700	25.18%	136,372	45.37%	88,511	29.45%
171,569	58.39%	122,288	41.61%	0	0.00%
462,288	49.21%	456,507	48.60%	20,609	2.19%
1,080,619	55.26%	859,958	43.98%	14,968	0.77%
215,631	64.56%	118,364	35.44%	0	0.00%
110,390	72.16%	42,549	27.81%	39	0.03%
386,459	55.37%	267,760	38.36%	43,759	6.27%
620,430	53.91%	523,002	45.44%	7,457	0.65%
449,297	54.08%	381,534	45.92%	0	0.00%
954,844	61.58%	586,768	37.84%	8,946	0.58%
74,573	60.08%	49,554	39.92%	0	0.00%
35,579,180	57.37%	26,028,028	41.97%	414,771	0.67%

Electoral Vote, 1956

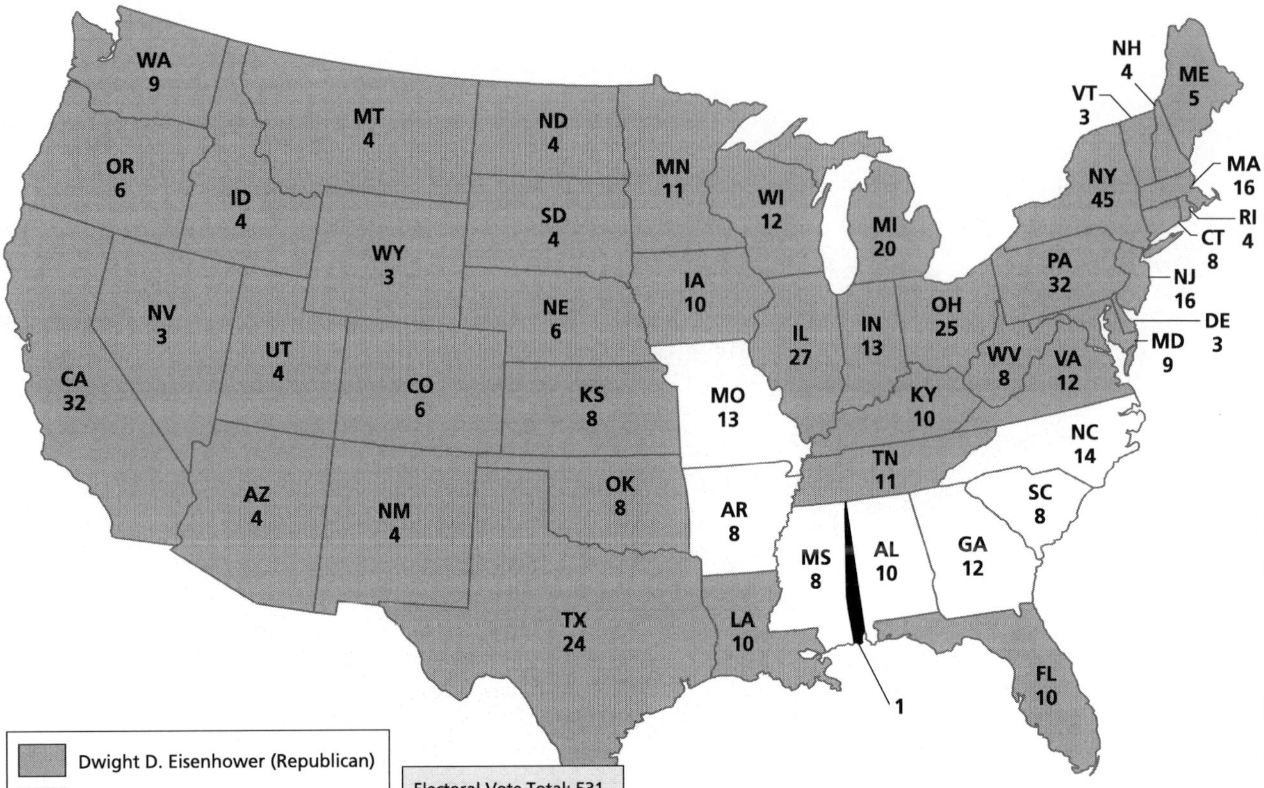

WA
9

OR
6

ID
4

MT
4

ND
4

MN
11

WI
12

MI
20

NH
4

VT
3

ME
5

NY
45

MA
16

RI
4

CT
8

NV
3

WY
3

SD
4

IA
10

NJ
16

PA
32

UT
4

NE
6

IL
27

IN
13

OH
25

WV
8

VA
12

MD
9

DE
3

CA
32

CO
6

KS
8

MO
13

KY
10

NC
14

AZ
4

NM
4

OK
8

AR
8

TN
11

SC
8

GA
12

MS
8

AL
10

1

LA
10

TX
24

FL
10

Dwight D. Eisenhower (Republican)

Adlai Stevenson (Democrat)

Walter B. Jones

Electoral Vote Total: 531
Eisenhower: 457
Stevenson: 73
Jones: 1

Note: The shading found in the state with a split electoral
vote does not bear any geographic significance.

© Infobase Learning

Election of 1960

Election Overview

Election Year 1960

Election Day November 8, 1960

Winning Candidates

- **President:** John F. Kennedy
- **Vice President:** Lyndon B. Johnson

Election Results [ticket, party: popular votes (percentage of popular vote); electoral votes (percentage of electoral vote)]

- John F. Kennedy and Lyndon B. Johnson, Democratic: 34,220,984 (49.72%); 303 (56.4%)
- Richard M. Nixon and Henry Cabot Lodge Jr., Republican: 34,108,157 (49.55%); 219 (40.8%)
- Unpledged Electors, Democratic: 286,359 (0.42%); 15 (2.8%)
- Other: 216,982 (0.32%); 0 (0.0%)

Voter Turnout 63.06%

Central Forums/Campaign Methods for Addressing Voters

- Speaking tour
- Radio
- Television
- Televised presidential debates

Incumbent President and Vice President on Election Day Dwight D. Eisenhower and Richard M. Nixon

Population (1960) 180,760,000

Gross Domestic Product

- $526.4 billion (in current dollars: $2,830.9 billion)
- Per capita: $2,912 (in current dollars: $15,661)

Number of Daily Newspapers (1960) 1,763

Average Daily Circulation (1960) 58,882,000

Households with

- Radio (1960): 48,504,000
- Television (1960): 46,312,000

Method of Choosing Electors Popular vote (mostly general-ticket system/winner take all)

Method of Choosing Nominees

- National party convention
- Presidential preference primaries

Key Issues and Events

- The Twenty-second Amendment prevents the popular president Dwight Eisenhower from seeking a third term, although his declining health and Americans' yearning for more vigorous leadership are also concerns.
- The cold war is at its height.
- The postwar boom continues.
- The civil rights revolution heralds even more dramatic changes.

Leading Candidates

DEMOCRATS
- John F. Kennedy, senator (Massachusetts)
- Lyndon B. Johnson, Senate majority leader (Texas)
- Stuart Symington, senator (Missouri)
- Adlai Stevenson, former governor (Illinois)
- Hubert Humphrey, senator (Minnesota)

REPUBLICANS
- Richard M. Nixon, vice president (California)
- Nelson Rockefeller, governor (New York)
- Barry Goldwater, senator (Arizona)

Trajectory

- Democratic senator John F. Kennedy of Massachusetts, deemed by many too young, inexperienced, and Catholic to win, proves himself by running in nine primaries, beating Senator Hubert Humphrey in heavily Protestant West Virginia on May 10, 1960. Senator Lyndon B. Johnson challenges Kennedy to a televised debate before a joint meeting of the Texas and Massachusetts delegations, which Kennedy wins, demonstrating Johnson's limited appeal beyond the South. And liberals who would have supported Adlai Stevenson are pledged to Kennedy by the time Stevenson enters the race.
- At the Democratic convention, July 11–15, Kennedy asks Johnson to be his running mate and help woo the South. John Kennedy's brother, Robert Kennedy, objects. Liberals believe Kennedy betrayed them by choosing Johnson.
- On July 22, Vice President Richard M. Nixon secretly meets his leading rival, New York governor Nelson Rockefeller, at Rockefeller's Manhattan apartment to determine the Republican platform. Many conservatives denounce Nixon for accommodating Rockefeller's more liberal demands at this "compact of Fifth Avenue," but it sews up Nixon's nomination.
- Nixon campaigns as the more experienced candidate in domestic and foreign policies in comparison to Kennedy's "youth and immaturity." President Eisenhower undercuts Nixon's experience claim when reporter Charles Mohr of *Time* asks the president during his August 24 press conference which major decision Nixon has been involved in and Eisenhower responds, "If you give me a week, I might think of one." Eisenhower supposedly made the comment as a joke, but it is so damaging the Democrats use it in a campaign commercial.
- With anti-Catholic tracts and ugly rumors circulating, Kennedy attempts to defuse the religion issue in a speech to the Greater Houston Ministerial Association on September 12. The televised address assures many Protestant voters—and articulates a vision of mutual acceptance—but does not settle the issue.
- During the first televised presidential debate ever, September 26, 1960, Kennedy comes across as smoother and friendlier than Nixon. Both campaigns experience major upturns in crowd size and excitement after the televised appearance.
- On October 19, two days before the final Kennedy-Nixon debate, civil rights leader Martin Luther King Jr. is jailed while trying to desegregate a Georgia restaurant. King is sentenced to four months of hard labor due to a probation violation. Fearing for her husband's life, King's wife, Coretta, calls Harris Wofford, a Kennedy campaign aide. John Kennedy telephones King's wife, while Robert Kennedy negotiates with the judge, arranging for King to get released on bail. In contrast, Nixon consults with Eisenhower's attorney general, who advises him not to intervene in the matter. The Kennedys' intervention gains Democratic support from blacks.
- After sitting out most of the campaign, President Eisenhower makes a vigorous push for Nixon during the final 10 days. Eisenhower boosts Nixon, and by Election Day the polls indicate a virtual tie.
- Just before midnight on election night, the *New York Times* headlines its morning edition, "Kennedy Elected President." Managing editor Turner Catledge hopes "a certain midwestern mayor would steal enough votes to pull Kennedy through." The *Times* wants to avoid the embarrassment the *Chicago Tribune* endured in 1948 when announcing Dewey beat Truman.
- Nixon makes a speech at 3 A.M. but does not formally concede. Only on the afternoon of Wednesday, November 9, will Nixon give a formal concession speech and Kennedy claim victory.
- Republicans, including Nixon and Eisenhower, believe voter fraud is involved in the slim margin of victory, especially in Texas, Lyndon Johnson's home state, and Illinois, with Mayor Richard Daley's powerful Chicago political machine. The electoral votes from those two states sway the election.
- Nixon's campaign staff wants him to contest the election, especially in Illinois, Missouri, and New Jersey. Three days later, Nixon announces he will not contest the election.
- Republican national chairman, Senator Thruston Morton of Kentucky, challenges the results in 11 states. The case remains in the courts until summer of 1961, and the results in a recount switch Hawaii into Kennedy's column.

Conventions

- Democratic National Convention: July 11–15, 1960, Los Angeles Memorial Sports Arena, Los Angeles
- Republican National Convention: July 25–28, 1960, International Amphitheatre, Chicago

Ballots/Nominees

DEMOCRATS

First presidential ballot

- John F. Kennedy 806
- Lyndon B. Johnson 409

- Stuart Symington 86
- Adlai Stevenson 79.5
- Robert B. Meyner 43
- Hubert Humphrey 41
- George A. Smathers 30
- Ross Barnett 23
- Herschel Loveless 2
- Edmund G. "Pat" Brown 1
- Orval Faubus 1
- Albert Rosellini 1

Vice-presidential ballot
- Lyndon B. Johnson 1,521 votes

Primaries

- Democratic Party: 16; 38.3% delegates
- Republican Party: 15; 38.6% delegates

Primaries Results

DEMOCRATS
- John F. Kennedy 1,847,259; 31.43%
- Edmund G. "Pat" Brown 1,354,031; 23.04%
- George H. McLain 646,387; 11.00%
- Hubert Humphrey 590,410; 10.05%
- George A. Smathers 322,235; 5.48%
- Michael V. DiSalle 315,312; 5.36%
- Unpledged 241,958; 4.12%

REPUBLICANS
- Richard M. Nixon 4,975,938; 86.63%
- Unpledged 314,234; 5.47%
- George H. Bender 211,090; 3.68%
- Cecil Underwood 123,756; 2.15%
- James M. Lloyd 48,461; 0.84%
- Nelson Rockefeller 30,639; 0.53%
- Frank R. Beckwith 19,677; 0.34%

Party Platform

DEMOCRATS
- National defense
- Disarmament
- Civil rights
- Immigration
- Foreign aid
- Labor and tax reform

REPUBLICANS
- Strong national defense
- Enforcement of civil rights laws
- Nuclear test ban agreement
- Tough opposition to Soviet Union

Campaign Innovations

- Televised primary debate between Johnson and Kennedy
- Four televised presidential debates between Kennedy and Nixon
- Norman Mailer attends the Democratic convention and writes his famous profile of Kennedy, "Superman Comes to the Supermart," published in *Esquire,* helping to pioneer a more personal, more psychological "New Journalism."
- Creation of ad hoc groups to manage advertisements but give the candidate full control of the ads

Campaign Tactics

REPUBLICANS
- To attract independents and Democrats, Nixon pledges to campaign in all 50 states and undertakes a grueling campaign schedule. In August, a knee infection gets him hospitalized for two weeks. His advisors fail to convince him to abandon his pledge.
- Nixon campaigns as a more experienced and known candidate, minimizes party labels in speeches, and emphasizes that voters should pick the better man.
- Forms ad hoc groups to manage advertisement, which he names Campaign Associates.

DEMOCRATS
- Main theme of the campaign is America's "decline" under the Republican administration and the need for young, vigorous leadership.
- Attempts to undercut Nixon's accusations that he is inexperienced.
- Stumping along with more than 200 television commercials.

Presidential Debates

- September 26, 1960: Chicago
- October 7, 1960: Washington, D.C.
- October 13, 1960: broadcast from New York and Los Angeles
- October 21, 1960: New York
- Nixon campaigns up to a few hours prior to the first debate telecast. Still recovering from his knee infection, he appears pale, wan, and with a five o'clock shadow, because he refuses makeup. Kennedy appears tanned and rested, because he is. Kennedy speaks to the audience while Nixon addresses his opponent. Nixon is far more effective in the remaining debates.
- Alas, for Nixon, only a fraction of the viewers watch the remaining debates. The first debate attracts 70

million viewers, but a combined total of approximately 50 million watch the remaining three debates.

Popular Campaign Slogans

DEMOCRATS
- "Kennedy: Leadership for the '60s"
- "For America's Greatness"
- "A Time for Greatness"
- Campaign theme: "We Can Do Better"

REPUBLICANS
- "Nixon-Lodge: They Understand What Peace Demands"
- "Peace, Experience, Prosperity"
- "American Needs Nixon-Lodge: Side by Side Our Strongest Team"
- "Experience Counts"

Campaign Songs

DEMOCRATS
- "High Hopes"
- "Marching Down to Washington"

REPUBLICANS
- "Click with Dick"

Influential Campaign Appeals or Ads

- Democratic Party: 200 commercials vary. In one, Jacqueline Kennedy speaks in Spanish to the voters; in another, the singer Harry Belafonte appeals for African American vote support.
- Republican Party: Ad series shows Nixon sitting in an office fielding questions on policy, demonstrating superior policy and leadership experience.

Campaign Finance

- Kennedy: $9,797,000 (in current dollars: $67,354,000)
- Nixon: $10,128,000 (in current dollars: $69,629,700)

Defining Quotations

- "I think it well, that we recall what happened to a great governor when he became a Presidential nominee. Despite his successful record as governor, despite his plain-spoken voice, the campaign was a debacle. His views were distorted. He carried fewer states than any candidate in his party's history. To top it off, he lost his own state that he had served so well as a governor. You all know his name and his religion—Alfred M. Landon, Protestant." *John F. Kennedy, Alfred E. Smith memorial dinner in New York, October 22, 1959*
- "Do not leave this prophet without honor in his own party. Do not reject this man." *Nominating speech by Minnesota senator Eugene McCarthy for Adlai Stevenson, Democratic National Convention, July 13, 1960*
- "The problems are not all solved and the battles are not all won. We stand today on the edge of a New Frontier, the frontier of the 1960s, a frontier of unknown opportunities and perils, a frontier of unfulfilled hopes and threats." *John F. Kennedy, Democratic presidential nomination acceptance speech, July 15, 1960*
- "This is the kind of political expedient Franklin Roosevelt would never have used—except in the case of John Nance Garner." *Kennedy adviser John Kenneth Galbraith at the Democratic convention, complimenting Kennedy's designation of Lyndon Johnson as a running mate.*
- "I am not the Catholic candidate for President. I am the Democratic Party's candidate for President who also happens to be a Catholic. I do not speak for my Church on public matters—and the Church does not speak for me." *John F. Kennedy to the Greater Houston Ministerial Association on September 12, 1960*
- "The Vice-President and I came to Congress in 1946, I've been there for fourteen years, the same period of time that he has, so that our experience in government is comparable. . . . Mr. Nixon is experienced, experienced in policies of retreat, defeat, and weakness." *John F. Kennedy in response to Nixon's charges that he was inexperienced, first presidential debate, September 26, 1960*
- "I had expected to vote against Senator Kennedy because of his religion. But now he can be my President, Catholic or whatever he is. It took courage to call my daughter-in-law at a time like this. He has the moral courage to stand up for what he knows is right. I've got all my votes and I've got a suitcase and I'm going to take them up there and dump them in his lap." *Martin Luther King Sr. after John Kennedy called Coretta Scott King and helped release Martin Luther King Jr. from jail, October 27, 1960*
- "Did you see what Martin's father said? He was going to vote against me because I was a Catholic, but since I called his daughter-in-law, he will vote for me. That was a hell of a bigoted statement, wasn't it? Imagine Martin Luther King having a bigot for a father! . . . Well, we all have fathers, don't we?" *John*

Kennedy to Harris Wofford, a few days before the election

- "I'm getting sick and tired of hearing this constant whimpering and yammering and wringing of the towel with regard to the poor United States." *Richard M. Nixon in response to Kennedy's "Get this country moving again" slogan, November 2, 1960*
- "A race between the comfortable and the concerned, a race between those who want to be at anchor and those who want to go forward." *John F. Kennedy, November 7, 1960*
- "To all Americans I say that the next four years are going to be difficult and challenging years for us all, that a supreme national effort will be needed to move this country safely through the 1960s. I ask your help and I can assure you that every degree of my spirit that I possess will be devoted to the long range interest of the United States and to the cause of freedom around the world." *John F. Kennedy, November 8, 1960*

Lasting Legacy of Campaign

- John F. Kennedy first Roman Catholic elected president
- Excruciatingly close electoral vote margin and popular vote; debate remains whether there was vote theft in certain states, which clinched Kennedy's victory.
- First presidential election in which Alaska and Hawaii participate (they were granted statehood on January 3 and August 21, 1959, respectively)
- First election with both major party candidates for president born in the twentieth century: Nixon in 1913, Kennedy in 1917
- Theodore White, author of *The Making of the President, 1960* (1961), creates a vision of a noble campaign in a narrative, character-driven journalistic style that continues to shape—some say distort—campaign coverage.

Election of 1960

The 1960 presidential election was a watershed in American political history. The oldest man ever to serve in the presidency was succeeded by the youngest man ever elected to it. It was the first time that the nation had elected a Catholic president, the first time that a major party had nominated two incumbent senators for president and vice president, and the first time that the Democrats had sent a sitting senator to the White House. He was in addition the first Democratic presidential nominee from New England in over a hundred years.

Other entrenched assumptions were cast aside—including those that proclaimed the necessity of a winning candidate's possessing a large state electoral base, executive experience as governor or general, and the backing of his party's elder statesmen and best-known political leaders in the pre-convention struggle. The medium of television and the mechanics of public opinion polling played far greater roles in 1960 than ever before. The suburbs surrounding the nation's great cities became a hotly contested key to the outcome for the first time. The professional politicians and party organizations played a lesser role than they ever had. For both parties it was at that time the most expensive campaign in history. Not surprisingly, it produced the largest vote in history and the closest popular vote in 76 years.

Eight years under President Eisenhower had produced no war, no depression, not even a single clear-cut issue to seize the electorate or rouse the Democratic opposition. Eisenhower had been an enormously popular president, presiding over a relatively united Republican Party that had far more support from the nation's newspaper editors and political donors than any Democratic contender in 1960 could hope to muster. He had been reelected in 1956 with an overwhelming margin from a comfortable, contented, complacent electorate. Had the Constitution not been amended after Franklin Roosevelt's death to prohibit a third presidential term, he could have easily been reelected again. For the divided opposition party to switch enough votes in such states as New York, New Jersey, Michigan, and Pennsylvania—not one of which had been won by a Democratic presidential nominee since 1944—to turn the Republicans out of the executive branch seemed contrary to all historical precedent. For a youthful, controversial Roman Catholic senator with no executive experience to do it seemed impossible.

To some, the presidential campaign of 1960 seems in retrospect a romantic chapter in the often sordid history of American politics. A young idealist surrounded by amateurs and intellectuals emerged from his battles with death and racketeering to overcome the forces of bigotry and bossism and narrowly win the nation's greatest prize after a grueling contest with a widely distrusted opponent, only to be killed a thousand breathtaking days later.

(continues on page 1268)

☆ ☆ ☆

1960 ELECTION CHRONOLOGY

1957
October 4, 1957: The Soviet Union launches *Sputnik*, the first man-made satellite into orbit. The Soviet breakthrough prompts a nationwide debate over the adequacy of education, space, and missile programs in the United States.

1958
November 4, 1958: Blaming Republicans for the previous year's recession, Democrats gain 16 seats in the Senate during the midterm election, and 49 seats in the House.

1959
July 24, 1959: Vice President Richard Nixon confronts Soviet Premier Nikita Khrushchev at an American exhibition in Moscow. When this "Kitchen Debate" is broadcast in the United States, Nixon enjoys national acclaim as the nation gears up for the presidential election.

December 26, 1959: Staffers convince New York governor Nelson A. Rockefeller he cannot win enough Republican primaries to secure the nomination. He announces he "shall not be a candidate for the nomination of the Presidency. This decision is definite and final."

1960
March 24, 1960: Missouri senator Stuart Symington announces his campaign for the Democratic nomination for president. Like fellow candidate Lyndon Johnson, the Senate majority leader, Symington plans on working the state caucuses and other informal networks for selecting delegates, rather than the party primaries, which are essential to the strategies of Massachusetts senator John F. Kennedy and Minnesota senator Hubert Humphrey.

April 5, 1960: Kennedy beats Humphrey in the Democratic primary race in Wisconsin. The state boasts a large Catholic population, which helps Kennedy.

May 1, 1960: Francis Gary Powers is shot down in a U2 spy plane over Russia, casting a shadow over the Eisenhower administration's handling of foreign policy. His "definite and final" comments notwithstanding, Nelson Rockefeller calls for a national debate on the subject and announces his candidacy for the presidency.

May 4, 1960: With the primary approaching in West Virginia, Kennedy and Humphrey meet in a debate in Charleston, West Virginia.

May 10, 1960: In the overwhelmingly Protestant state of West Virginia. Kennedy beats Humphrey in the primary. Humphrey withdraws from the presidential race.

May 20, 1960: Kennedy wins his last major primary in Oregon with 51 percent of the vote, on his way to attracting nearly one out of every three Democratic primary votes in a crowded field. Nixon wins 93.1 percent in Oregon and nearly nine of every ten Republican votes.

June 9, 1960: Eleanor Roosevelt, fearing that John Kennedy is too young, too callow, too much his father's son, and not sufficiently liberal, endorses Adlai Stevenson. Roosevelt will head a Draft Stevenson Committee. Stevenson feigns disinterest but is quite interested.

July 3, 1960: Former president Harry S. Truman questions whether Kennedy is "quite ready" for the presidency, urging the 43-year-old senator to step aside in favor of "someone with the greatest possible maturity and experience."

July 11, 1960: The Democratic National Convention meets at the Los Angeles Memorial Sports Arena.

July 12, 1960: Senate Majority Leader Lyndon Johnson challenges Kennedy to a debate, which takes place before the Massachusetts and Texas delegations to the Democratic National Convention but is nationally televised.

July 13, 1960: The Democratic convention nominates John F. Kennedy for president on the first ballot. After some jockeying among delegates, and

☆ ☆ ☆

a bitter fight among Kennedy supporters, Democrats will nominate Lyndon B. Johnson for vice president.

July 22, 1960: Vice President Richard Nixon secretly meets with New York governor Nelson Rockefeller at Rockefeller's Manhattan apartment to determine the Republican platform. Conservatives denounce this "compact of Fifth Avenue," but it secures Nixon's nomination.

July 25–28, 1960: The Republican National Convention meets at the International Amphitheatre in Chicago. Richard M. Nixon wins the nomination on the first ballot, with Senator Henry Cabot Lodge Jr. of Massachusetts selected as his running mate.

August 22, 1960: Members of the House of Representatives shout their approval for the Senate's suspension of the "Equal Time Rule," allowing the TV networks to mount presidential debates only involving the nominees of the two major parties.

August 24, 1960: A reporter asks President Eisenhower about Nixon's role in major decisions. "If you give me a week, I might think of one," the president responds. The remark plays repeatedly in Democratic campaign commercials.

September 12, 1960: Kennedy attempts to defuse the religion issue in the campaign with a televised speech at the Greater Houston Ministerial Association. The address reassures many Protestant voters, but anti-Catholic bigotry lingers.

September 26, 1960: Kennedy and Nixon meet in Chicago for the first-ever televised debate between presidential nominees during the general campaign. Facing a nationwide TV audience of 70 million, Kennedy comes across as smooth and friendly, while Nixon, recently released from the hospital due to a knee injury, looks shifty, sweaty, and weary.

September 27, 1960: More than 600,000 people mob Kennedy's motorcade in Ohio, reflecting the surge in enthusiasm after the televised debate. Nixon's crowds grow in size and intensity, too, reflecting television's magnifying effect.

October 7, 1960: The second presidential debate is held in Washington, D.C. The candidates clash over the fate of two small islands off the coast of China, Quemoy and Matsu.

October 13, 1960: For the third presidential debate, Kennedy broadcasts from New York, while Nixon broadcasts from Los Angeles.

October 19, 1960: Civil rights leader Martin Luther King Jr. is jailed while trying to desegregate a Georgia restaurant. John F. Kennedy and his brother Robert quietly intervene, gaining them important support from African Americans.

October 21, 1960: During the final debate the candidates clash about American relations with Cuba.

November 6, 1960: Nixon flies to Alaska, fulfilling his pledge to campaign in all 50 states, which many Republicans feared had him ignoring the necessary Electoral College strategy.

November 7, 1960: President Eisenhower, after sitting out most of the campaign, makes a vigorous push for Nixon during the final 10 days of the race. Eisenhower's assistance boosts Nixon. By the eve of the race, polls indicate a virtual tie.

November 8, 1960: Election Day. In one of the closest elections of the 20th century, John F. Kennedy wins 49.72 percent of the popular vote to Nixon's 49.55 percent. Kennedy wins the electoral vote, 303–219.

November 11, 1960: Despite possible vote fraud in Illinois, Missouri, and New Jersey, Nixon announces he will not contest the election.

December 19, 1960: Presidential electors cast their ballots in their respective state capitals. Fourteen unpledged Democratic electors and one faithless Oklahoma elector vote for Senator Harry F. Byrd, a segregationist.

1961

January 6, 1961: A joint session of Congress assembles to count the electoral votes.

(continued from page 1265)

Other more cynical observers regarded the 1960 election essentially as a contest between two ruthlessly ambitious young men, both smoothly skilled in politics and public relations, and both possessing more cool reserve than deep emotional convictions. Neither of these two pictures conveys the whole truth, but only time will shake the tenacity of those still convinced that either one is correct.

Others at the time emphasized the extent to which the election of 1960 passed the torch to a new generation of leaders. Richard Nixon and Hubert Humphrey were defeated. Lyndon Johnson, losing his bid for the presidential nomination, settled for the vice presidency. Nelson Rockefeller found he could not even enter the arena. All of these men, it was widely said, were permanently out of the presidential picture, which the Kennedy brothers might well dominate for many years to come. These prophecies turned out to be badly mistaken.

All presidential campaigns in modern times necessarily begin well before election year. Few begin a full four years earlier as completely as did the 1960 contest. In 1956, both Richard M. Nixon, vice president of the United States, and John F. Kennedy, United States senator from Massachusetts, fixed their courses on respective routes from which they would not swerve for four years.

Despite the distinguished precedent set by Adams and Jefferson, no American vice president since Van Buren had been elevated into the presidency by election. Frequently placed in the second spot on a campaign ticket for reasons other than their ability to lead the nation, the occupants of this somewhat peculiar and amorphous office were destined to reach the White House only on the death of the president they served. Vice President Nixon conducted himself with widely admired discretion and delicacy in late 1955 when President Eisenhower suffered a serious heart attack, and much of the world wondered

On August 16, 1956, in Chicago, Massachusetts senator John F. Kennedy placed before the Democratic National Convention the name of Adlai Stevenson for the presidential nomination. Four years later, Kennedy would become the Democratic nominee for president. *(Associated Press)*

whether Nixon was about to succeed him or act for him. That episode helped persuade Eisenhower and the Republican Party to disregard an attempt more publicized than powerful by White House advisor Harold Stassen and others to prevent Nixon's renomination as vice president at the 1956 convention. Solidifying himself with party leaders as he crisscrossed the country supporting their local candidates and raising money for them, and standing out as the only political star on the Eisenhower team so long as Chief Justice Earl Warren remained on the bench, Nixon from 1956 on was the heir apparent.

The Democratic National Convention of 1956 also produced a new star for that party, though it could hardly be said to have guaranteed the 1960 presidential nomination for anyone. Troubled by the conflicting claims on his friendship and presidential prospects that were made on behalf of various vice-presidential aspirants, and seeking a public contrast with the Republican convention's pre-ordained selection of Nixon, Democratic presidential nominee Adlai Stevenson took the unprecedented step of asking an open convention to select his vice-presidential running mate. In the scramble that followed, the name of Senator John F. Kennedy rose surprisingly rapidly to the top. He was backed by urban delegations who hoped his Irish Catholic credentials would help the ticket in their areas, by Southern delegations who found him more acceptable than his chief rival, Senator Estes Kefauver of Tennessee (whose brand of liberalism was largely indistinguishable from Kennedy's but struck his fellow Southerners as traitorous), and by others impressed with his World War II heroism as a PT boat skipper as well as his personality, writings, and speeches. A cliffhanging, seesaw roll-call contest between Kennedy and Kefauver captured the imagination of the delegates and television audience, and, despite the Tennessean's emergence as the nominee, the young Massachusetts senator's graceful concession speech made him an instant nationwide attraction. Speaking invitations poured into his Senate office, and the presidency became his unspoken goal.

But Kennedy was not alone on that trail. As the American economy faltered in 1957–58 and the Russian launch of *Sputnik* shocked the nation into a debate over the adequacy of our education, space, and missile programs, the creaking Democratic coalition slowly began to recover from its 1952 and 1956 trouncings at the hands of General Eisenhower. To the dismay of Nixon and others, Eisenhower had made little effort to translate his enormous personal popularity into a solid top-to-bottom Republican political organization. As a result, the Democrats had, with one brief exception in 1952, maintained their position as the majority party in the Congress and country, and in the congressional elections of 1958 won a tremendous victory. Thus, it was natural that several Democrats began to

edge toward a presidential race, convinced that a Democrat had a better chance to win than in 1956, that Nixon was beatable in an election on his own, and that Kennedy's youth and religion made him an unlikely nominee despite his high standing in the Gallup poll.

To an extent unprecedented since the days of Webster, Clay, and Calhoun, the presidential spotlight between 1956 and 1960 turned on the United States Senate. Both parties in the past had more often looked for presidential candidates among the governors of large states with their executive experience. But national and international problems, with which governors had little contact—on which senators, however, spoke every day—increasingly dominated public affairs after the Great Depression and World War II. Governors, beset by rising state government costs and taxes, had little opportunity to become known in the nationwide media that focused on Washington and New York. As the Republican governor of New York itself, Nelson Rockefeller—elected to that post in 1958—was an obvious exception. But Democratic governors Edmund Brown of California, Robert Meyner of New Jersey, J. Leroy Collins of Florida, and G. Mennen Williams of Michigan found their own ambitions for the presidency overshadowed by the struggle on the Democratic side of the Senate. At least eight Democratic senators were prominently mentioned as 1960 presidential possibilities, and four of them—Lyndon Johnson, Hubert Humphrey, Stuart Symington, and John Kennedy—became active candidates.

Lyndon Johnson, a tall, complex Texan, not only was the leader of the Democratic majority in the Senate but dominated that body as had no one else—not even Robert Taft or Alben Barkley—in many years. Working closely with his fellow Texas Democrat, Speaker of the House Sam Rayburn, Johnson's influence in Washington was second only to that of the Republican president in the White House. Some Democratic partisans complained that the Johnson–Rayburn team too often compromised with the administration on issues that might otherwise have been valuable campaign ammunition. But Johnson was a shrewd head-counter as well as a remarkably persuasive arm-twister. Valuing the respect he had earned from the nation's press as well as from the president for refusing to take his party down a straight obstructionist path, he carefully employed his slender Senate majority to build a record of congressional legislation passed rather than presidential vetoes provoked, challenging the president only on those few economic and social issues on which all wings of the Democratic Party could unite.

By judicious use of his influence on committee assignments, bill advancements, and other legislative favors, Johnson won the gratitude and loyalty of virtually every Democratic senator, including all of the other leading presidential contenders. Not surprisingly, a poll of Senate Democrats showed him to be their favorite for the presidency. But senators rarely control, and in most cases barely influence, their home state national convention delegations, and reliance on their support may have temporarily misled Johnson, who was comparatively inexperienced and untraveled in national politics outside of Texas and Washington.

Close to Johnson personally but far more outspoken on liberal issues, Minnesota senator Hubert H. Humphrey was one of that body's most tireless and agile debaters. He had campaigned more openly than the others for the vice-presidential nomination under Stevenson in 1956 and had been painfully rebuffed by the convention; but he remained a hero to the Stevenson forces, who saw him as their logical champion if the 1952 and 1956 nominee stepped aside in 1960. Humphrey's ability to speak forcibly and interestingly, if lengthily, on every issue had earned him scorn in less liberal quarters but endeared him to the farm, labor, civil rights, disarmament, education, social welfare, housing, and countless other groups whose causes he had so eloquently and energetically championed.

Minnesota and other businessmen were in this category, for Humphrey worked hard on behalf of all his constituents and had earned the respect of many moderates by gradually toning down his rhetoric in the decade following his 1948 election to the Senate. A boundless campaigner for other liberals around the country, he possessed, more than most, a keen knowledge of those individuals outside of Washington—particularly in the Midwest and West—who were key to the presidential nomination. Late in 1958, an extraordinary eight-hour interview with Soviet leader Nikita Khrushchev gave him the kind of enormous publicity splash of which all candidates dream.

The following year, Khrushchev again played a major role in America's presidential picture—not only by a tour of this country as President Eisenhower's guest but also by engaging in a highly publicized, widely photographed "debate" with Vice-President Nixon at an American exhibition in Moscow. Khrushchev—who in 1960 would again have an impact on American politics when he denounced Eisenhower at an abortive Paris summit conference in the spring, and still again when he attended the United Nations General Assembly in the fall—was increasingly important in American politics as well as American foreign policy because he symbolized the issue to which would-be candidates were more and more addressing themselves: namely, the growing Soviet military, economic, and political strength that offered a challenge if not a threat to the United States. Foreign policy questions, such as the alleged "missile gap" between American and Russian total war capacities, were rapidly coming to the forefront of political debate in the latter years of the Eisenhower presidency.

Missouri Senator Stuart Symington's prospects for the Democratic presidential nomination rested largely on that single issue of military preparedness. A handsome, wealthy, former Air Force secretary under Truman with a business background, he had pursued that subject with single-minded determination since even before his election to the Senate in 1952. Hoping to emulate his hero Winston Churchill by sounding the alarm before others recognized the need, he followed a soft-spoken moderate approach on other issues that befitted a border-state senator. He lacked the nationally renowned stature, intellectual depth, and platform zest of the other major contenders; but he had the right location both ideologically and geographically to become the compromise choice that could hold the party together. As the handicaps of the other candidates were weighed in practical political circles, Symington's name emerged as either the favorite choice or the most predictable winner in various polls of congressmen and political leaders.

It was indeed a strange political season as 1960 neared, and the talk in Democratic ranks centered more on the candidates' liabilities than on their assets, as though the nomination would be made by a process of elimination rather than elevation. Lyndon Johnson was a Southerner, and not since the Civil War had one so identified been nominated or elected president. Johnson insisted that he was a Westerner and a national Democrat in the Franklin Roosevelt tradition. He skillfully guided two civil rights bills through the Senate over Deep South opposition. But the more Southern Democrats of all stripes united on his candidacy, the more doubts Northern Democrats expressed as to whether he was acceptable in their cities among black and labor union voters.

Hubert Humphrey in turn was regarded as unacceptable to the South and to other old-line or small-state Democrats who feared his controversial reputation as an outspoken liberal. Adlai Stevenson, who had not yet decided on his 1960 role, was dismissed by many of the professionals as a two-time loser whose reluctance to plunge into the ordeal of a presidential campaign once again was matched by their reluctance to campaign with him once again. Jack Kennedy was not only too young and inexperienced, said the professionals, but his membership in the Catholic Church made him in the eyes of all who remembered the party's debacle in 1928 non-electable as president and a popular choice for vice president. Symington, according to his supporters, was everyone's second choice, but his detractors made exactly the same point.

All of these candidates had considerable assets as well. Kennedy's included a Pulitzer Prize for his *Profiles in*

Soviet leader Nikita Khrushchev and Vice President Richard Nixon meet for a televised appearance at the American exhibit in Moscow in 1959. *(Library of Congress)*

Courage, a study of senators risking their careers for what they regarded to be right; a campaign team and technique well honed in Massachusetts, which reelected him to the Senate in 1958 by a record margin; a beautiful wife; and both the physical and intellectual attributes necessary to communicate clearly and appealingly on the television screen as well as the public platform. He also possessed some mixed blessings: a famous father who had good judgment and connections but a mean reputation as a conservative isolationist; an impassioned investigator brother Robert, along with whom he had incurred the wrath of politically powerful labor leaders as well as the praise of millions of TV viewers for doing battle against corruption in the union movement; and a family fortune that stirred resentment and presumably set the young senator apart from the average American but also enabled him to organize in advance a fully staffed campaign with all the necessary trimmings.

The Kennedys were wealthy, very wealthy. But their riches paled in comparison with those of the only serious Republican threat to Nixon's nomination, New York's Governor Nelson A. Rockefeller. Charming, hard-driving, and well-connected by family fame and fortune as well as his government experience, the handsome governor appeared at first to be a formidable contender. His popularity among Republicans had been at a peak immediately after the 1958 elections. His sweeping victory over Averell Harriman contrasted sharply with the resounding setbacks suffered by Republican candidates across the nation, despite Vice President Nixon's backbreaking campaign on their behalf. Speaking out strongly on such national issues as defense, medical care, and economic growth, his stands did not differ sharply from those of the Democratic contenders. Nor did his office require him to defend the Eisenhower administration. Recruiting a vast and talented team of aides, advisors, researchers, political scouts, and publicity men, he sought to position himself to moderate and liberal Republican president-makers as a fresh, exciting alternative to Nixon (whom he disliked), an alternative who would be less vulnerable to Democratic attack and more appealing to that majority of voters outside the regular Republican tent.

But the vice president, with far more political experience and know-how, could not be dislodged from the inside track. He alone was identified among Republican leaders with their popular president. He alone had gained the necessary contacts and political IOUs in his trips across the country. The New York governor's advocacy of state tax increases caused adverse reactions far beyond the boundaries of Rockefeller's own state. His increasing preoccupation with state issues largely confined him to Albany. His only real chance of defeating Nixon for the nomination lay in a sweep or near-sweep of the presidential primaries; and his scouting reports and poorly received personal trips into other states persuaded him that his prospects of winning over the regular Republican vote in those primary states was clearly too slim to justify the time away from his Albany duties that such a campaign would entail.

Thus, in late December 1959 the Republican contest for the presidential nomination virtually ended before it had formally begun. A public statement issued by Governor Rockefeller concluded, "I am not, and shall not be, a candidate for the nomination for the Presidency. This deci-

sion is definite and final." While this guaranteed Nixon's nomination, the vice president had already felt assured of that prize and was genuinely disappointed at being denied the opportunity to gain more exposure for himself and experience for his organization in a series of contested primaries that he was confident he could win. He had reason to believe, moreover, that Rockefeller would remain waiting in the wings for a Nixon slip.

His judgment was correct. While the vice president entered all Republican primaries in order to rally his followers, these were largely uneventful non-contests that could not compete with the Democratic primaries in the same states for headlines and voter interest. Rockefeller, meanwhile, publicly rejected suggestions that he serve as Nixon's running mate or as convention chairman, stating that he would not even attend the national convention in Chicago. After an American U-2 "spy plane" had been downed over Russia at a time destined to wreck the Paris

In hotel headquarters on July 27, 1960, in downtown Chicago, Vice President Richard Nixon and his wife, Pat Nixon, watch the Republican convention on television. On screen, Oregon governor Mark Hatfield places Nixon's name before the convention for the presidential nomination. *(Associated Press)*

summit conference and cast a shadow over the Eisenhower administration's handling of foreign policy, Rockefeller called for an open national debate on that subject. Immediately thereafter, he indicated his availability to be drafted for president. In June he issued a challenge to the Republican Party and its platform drafters to, in effect, repudiate the Eisenhower administration policies on a whole host of national security, civil rights, and other issues.

A successful and spontaneous draft of an unwilling presidential candidate is a rarity, if not an impossibility, in modern American politics. Nelson Rockefeller in 1960 was not unwilling, the large Draft Rockefeller movement with all its bands and banners was not spontaneous, and it had no chance of being successful.

Nixon, nevertheless, in order to avoid a bitter platform fight and to build a united party for the November elections, flew to New York for a long, secret meeting with the governor that produced a compromise statement on the disputed issues. Conservative Republicans were furious at what appeared to be Nixon's surrender, and for a brief moment they threatened to put forward their champion, the articulate and personable Senator Barry Goldwater from Arizona, as a serious presidential candidate. Eisenhower also was reported unhappy with the wording that implied his administration's inadequacies.

But a smooth Nixon operation eventually quieted all storms. His swift nomination by the convention, his selection of the popular United Nations ambassador Henry Cabot Lodge as his running mate, his excellent acceptance speech that rang all the right notes for Republicans everywhere, all left the Grand Old Party united and prepared for the November election. "I believe in the American dream," Nixon told an enthusiastic convention, "because I have seen it come true in my own life. . . . When Mr. Khrushchev says our grandchildren will live under Communism, let us say his grandchildren will live in freedom."

This show of Republican harmony was in sharp contrast with the Democratic picture. The number and diversity of Democratic candidates contending for the presidential nomination in 1960 had enlivened the political year but increased the scars in the party. Not all of these contenders entered the primaries. Adlai Stevenson remained undecided about a third try for the nomination, though rejecting the pleas of other candidates for his endorsement and acquiescing without commitment in the efforts of many of his longtime supporters and financial backers to organize a Draft Stevenson movement. Stuart Symington, continuing on the course of caution he hoped would result in his emergence as a compromise candidate after the other candidates damaged each other, decided to stay out of all primaries. Lyndon Johnson, with no desire

to tackle Kennedy and Humphrey in primary contests that appeared to be unfertile territory for a Texan, felt his route to the nomination lay through his Senate majority leader's office. These may well have been crucial decisions. Johnson would later encounter skepticism on his claim that he could carry Northern states, because he had no primary victories to prove it. Had Symington entered and won in Indiana, or Stevenson in Oregon, or Johnson in West Virginia, the convention decision in July would probably have been different.

For Kennedy and Humphrey, the primaries were not a matter of free choice. Neither had a chance of being nominated without entering and winning these pre-convention contests to disprove their critics, and both knew it. Neither one had the support of the party's power brokers, who would select a safer candidate if the decision were left to them in a "managed" convention. Both had to prove their acceptability to a cross section of rank-and-file voters beyond the borders of their home states, Kennedy because of his age and religion, Humphrey because of his reputation for extreme liberalism. Nor did either one have any hope of obtaining the necessary convention majority so long as the other was in the race. Thus, while neither could wrap up the nomination in the primaries, either or both could lose it on those battlefields, and each hoped to knock the other out of the contest.

Thus, early in 1960 the battle was joined in a series of primary contests from the coast of New Hampshire to the coast of Oregon. Senator Wayne Morse made a dark-horse entry into a handful of those fights, but Symington, Johnson, and Stevenson stayed away. Their supporters hoped for a double knockout or, failing that, at least the elimination from the contest of Kennedy, who was the front-runner in the public opinion polls. Kennedy at one point charged that the others were "ganging up" on him, but it would have been a difficult charge to document, other than the existence of some fund-raising for Humphrey by Stevensonians.

This was natural. Although both Kennedy and Humphrey had been warm Stevenson supporters in 1952 and 1956, the Minnesotan had a closer relationship with the former standard-bearer and his principal adherents, as well as a better-known record of support for the various liberal causes dearest to their hearts. Many of them were suspicious of Kennedy's religion, wealth, father, or brother, and regarded the Massachusetts senator as a young opportunist who had equivocated on civil liberties and civil rights. His record in the Senate was not as noteworthy as that of Humphrey, who had been elected to that body in 1948, four years before young representative Kennedy had upset the incumbent Massachusetts senator Henry Cabot Lodge.

But Kennedy was not lacking in assets in this battle between two inexhaustible campaigners. In the three and a half years following his sudden arrival on the national scene at the 1956 Democratic National Convention, he had fulfilled speaking invitations in every one of the 50 states and appeared on dozens of national television shows. The delivery of hundreds of speeches—consistently crammed with statistics and literary or historical allusions, and inevitably beginning with humor and ending with a dramatic quotation—had considerably improved his style and increased his inventory of subjects. Despite warnings from the experts that he was starting too early and attracting too much attention too soon, he had been either author or subject of several dozen prominent magazine articles and had collected his best speeches and writings in another book. He had maintained through mailings, telephone calls, Christmas cards, and visits frequent and friendly communication with important Democrats—not merely the nationally known names who were largely hostile or skeptical regarding his candidacy but also those lesser known leaders at the state, county, and city levels who were more likely to be, to choose, or to influence delegates to the 1960 national convention. He had built a small, efficient, devoted staff that had almost no national political experience but matched the candidate's determined and confident zeal.

Finally, and of considerable importance, the Kennedy family had ample funds and Humphrey did not. Both men had to raise money to finance a nationwide campaign; but the inherent advantage of a wealthy candidate—symbolized by the Kennedy family plane and his retention of a private pollster—was understandably resented by the Humphrey team. Despite round after round of criticism on this subject, it appeared to influence few voters.

The two key primaries were in Wisconsin and West Virginia. Humphrey had not contested Kennedy in the latter's neighboring state of New Hampshire, and Kennedy for the same reason had been fearful of accepting Humphrey's challenge to contest with him in Wisconsin. But knowing that his own political handicaps required him to risk all in order to gain all, and encouraged by his private polls, Kennedy literally moved himself, his family, and his campaign team into Wisconsin for the month of March 1960. He shook hands outside meat factories at 5:30 in the morning with the temperature at 10° and visited dairy farms deep in mud. He talked about Wisconsin issues—milk, timber, waterways—as did Humphrey, whose record on agriculture was far more appealing in a farm state than that of the Bostonian.

The press, however, emphasized another issue, the religious issue, despite Humphrey's prompt repudiation of all bigoted attacks on Kennedy in the state. When Kennedy won the primary on April 5, his victory was tarnished by the prominence given in most news analyses to the religious identity of those voters and districts supporting and opposing him. While geography appeared to some to be a more decisive factor than religion—Humphrey having run best particularly among farm voters in the areas bordering Minnesota—undoubtedly the Massachusetts senator's religion was at least one reason many voters preferred him and others opposed him. The press (which had predicted he would sweep all ten Wisconsin districts, not merely the six that he carried) refused to grant him the verdict he sought: namely, that defeating Hubert Humphrey next door to Minnesota demonstrated Kennedy's electability and Humphrey's nonviability as a candidate.

One result was to encourage Humphrey to abandon his plans for withdrawal and to carry the battle into the next contested primary state, West Virginia. Another result was to make the entire country, including 95 percent Protestant West Virginia, acutely aware of the religious issue; and the same private pollster, whose earlier survey showing a 70–30 margin for Kennedy over Humphrey had helped to induce the Bay State senator to enter West Virginia's primary, now predicted a 60–40 victory for Humphrey in that state on the basis of a new poll. The Kennedy family and team moved in, aided by Franklin D. Roosevelt Jr., but vigorously opposed by a coalition of unions and other candidates' supporters. The open manifestations of anti-Catholic sentiment were overwhelming. In a Washington speech before the American Society of Newspaper Editors and thereafter throughout the hills and hollows of West Virginia, Senator Kennedy met the religious issue head-on, emphasizing his record on separation of church and state, on independence from ecclesiastical authority, and against public aid to parochial schools:

> I am not the Catholic candidate for President. I do not speak for the Catholic Church on issues of public policy, and no one in that Church speaks for me. . . . Are we going to admit to the world that a Jew can be elected Mayor of Dublin, a Protestant can be chosen Foreign Minister of France, a Moslem can sit in the Israeli Parliament but a Catholic cannot be President of the United States?

Despite a tide of anti-Catholic sermons and pamphlets in West Virginia, responsible Protestant clergymen there and across the nation began to deplore the issue. Humphrey again made it clear he wanted no votes on that basis. Both candidates—despite some acrimonious personal exchanges inspired by Humphrey's bitterness at Kennedy's far greater spending and Kennedy's bitterness at Humphrey staying in the race when he no longer had a chance to be nominated—stressed the importance of other issues in that hungry and impoverished state. The wealthy young Bostonian, visibly moved by the human misery he saw as never before among the unemployed coal miners and their families, came away from West Virginia in May with a far deeper feeling about poverty in America.

He came away also with an upset victory by a 61–39 percent margin. Humphrey made a tearfully stirring statement of withdrawal from the presidential race and returned to Minnesota to seek reelection to the Senate. Kennedy continued on to the Maryland and Oregon primaries, having also won unopposed in Indiana and Nebraska. The results were no longer in doubt or even very close. But he knew that the votes of the primary states were not enough. Even during the primaries, he had continued his quest of delegates in other states, flying to various state Democratic dinners, conventions, and committee meetings, soliciting endorsements, recruiting delegates, neutralizing opponents. His remarkable knowledge of the delegate selection process, and his inexhaustible energy in pursuing it, outmaneuvered the other candidates in much the same way as Senator Goldwater would in his party four years later.

Humphrey's withdrawal did not leave Kennedy alone in the 1960 field. Stuart Symington, backed by former President Harry Truman, had formally announced in March; but his search for delegates as a compromise second-choice candidate had lost much of its force among Northern leaders unable to deny the impact in their states of Kennedy's primary victories. Symington had to hope for a deadlocked convention. Lyndon Johnson also hoped for a stalemated convention—one in which the votes cast for favorite sons and other candidates would make a Kennedy majority impossible, causing the convention to turn eventually to the party leader in the Senate, with his genius for accommodation and his ties to nearly every state. That prospect strongly depended on a sizable vote among Northern delegations for Adlai Stevenson; and the former nominee's resistance to seeking renomination openly had not deterred his supporters from stepping up their efforts for him and increasing his schedule of speeches.

The growing prominence of foreign policy issues (on which Stevenson was a recognized leader) following the collapse of the Paris summit conference, combined with Stevenson's repeated refusal to take his name out of the race or back any other candidate, spurred on the Draft Stevenson volunteers. They, too, counted on a convention deadlock, on Kennedy being unable to obtain a majority on an early ballot. Much as Symington and Johnson and their respective supporters were doing, the Stevenson leaders crisscrossed the country seeking delegate votes or

Titled "I See a Democratic President in 1960," this Gib Crockett cartoon shows Missouri senator Stuart Symington as a psychic looking into the future and seeing himself as the winner of the 1960 presidential race. *(Library of Congress)*

alternatively urging them to stay uncommitted or stick with favorite sons. The movement toward Kennedy after the West Virginia primary made their task difficult. But all estimated head counts made clear that every delegate vote was crucial. If Johnson could add to his Southern bloc enough votes in the West and Midwest—where he now openly campaigned against Kennedy as a boyish appeaser of the Soviets—and if Stevenson could pick up enough votes in the big states, then the convention deadlock of which three presidential camps dreamed was a certainty.

But there was no deadlock. Kennedy's 65,000 miles of air travel in two dozen states during 1960 prevented the "Stop Kennedy" coalition from obtaining impressive support outside the South. Nor was it ever a real coalition. Had Johnson and Symington united their forces behind Stevenson, or had the Stevenson liberals and Johnson Southerners compromised on Symington, the Kennedy surge might have been stopped. Instead, a nationally televised attack on Kennedy's age (and, some felt, implicitly on his religion) by former president Truman virtually on the eve of the convention served only as an excuse for a masterful Kennedy reply that helped demolish the whole youth and inexperience argument. A shabby attempt by Johnson's managers in a press conference to cast doubt on Kennedy's physical fitness enabled the young senator to refute the rumors that had long circulated because of an old adrenal condition. Stevenson supporters in large numbers picketed the outside of Convention Hall in Los Angeles and cheered wildly on the inside for both their leader, who made a brief address, and for Senator Eugene McCarthy's brilliant nominating speech; but Stevenson's home state of Illinois stood firm for Kennedy. Johnson challenged Kennedy to debate before their two delegations, but Kennedy's graceful and gently humorous response to the majority leader's charges solidified the front-runner's standing.

Many of the experts still predicted a Stevenson–Kennedy ticket. Former first lady Eleanor Roosevelt, a longtime Stevenson admirer, was among those urging Kennedy to take second spot, where he would have an "opportunity to grow and learn." Humphrey endorsed Stevenson; but his longtime ally, Minnesota governor Orville Freeman, made the nominating speech for Kennedy. Privately, Kennedy was nervous. If he did not win a majority on the first roll call, he felt, defections could lead to a deadlock and a compromise choice.

Aided in the last hours by the withdrawal of a favorite-son candidate in Iowa, and by narrow majorities in two other states deciding to give him all their delegates, Kennedy received his majority as the first alphabetical roll call reached Wyoming, the last state to be called. Unanimous support from New England, victory in every primary entered, the backing of all the big Northern states and half the votes from the Western states comprised his majority. He received only 13 votes in the entire South compared to the 307 cast for Johnson, who finished second with 409 votes behind Kennedy's 806.

It was logical, therefore, for Kennedy in his immediate quest for a running mate to turn first to Johnson—the runner-up in the convention, the candidate of the one area most opposed to Kennedy, the leader of the Democratic Party in the Senate, and a man who had not only the suitably Protestant, rural, and big-state background, but also the kind of genuine ability that Kennedy respected. The new presidential nominee could not have known, however, that Johnson would accept the second spot, for the majority leader had been publicly scornful of this possibility for months. But, in a decision that would help shape American presidential politics not only in 1960 but in 1964 and 1968, Johnson did accept. Outraged protests from labor and liberal delegates were quieted. An exhausted Kennedy delivered his acceptance address on "The New Frontier"—"not what I intend to offer the American people but what I intend to ask of them." And the race was on.

Both candidates expressed confidence, yet both recognized that a close, difficult contest lay ahead. The Democratic primaries and convention battles had given Senator Kennedy more recent nationwide publicity than Vice President Nixon had been able to garner from his

relatively smooth track to the nomination. But Nixon had been nominated by a more united party and a less tumultuous convention. He was better known nationally as the result of eight years of almost constant campaigning in the vice presidency. Nixon's running mate, although he would prove to be a far less industrious and effective campaigner, was also better known nationally than Kennedy's as a result of television coverage of U.N. debates. The Democratic Party was still regarded as the majority party in the country, but this was largely due to Democratic strongholds in the South, which Nixon expected to crack. A Gallup Poll taken immediately after both conventions gave Nixon a 50–44 lead with only 6 percent undecided.

In truth, there were many more undecided, and many of those voters saw only the superficial similarities between the two major party nominees. Both were comparatively young and earnest men first elected to Congress in 1946 but still shy and nervous in many circumstances that political veterans instinctively enjoyed. Both were widely traveled abroad and preferred foreign policy as a specialty over domestic policy. Both were proud to be professional politicians and were more expert in their knowledge of that profession than any of their advisers. Both possessed an understanding of the unique importance of the office of the presidency, a genuine dedication to advancing the national interest, and a sense of dignity and self-confidence as presidential candidates. Both had an uneasy time trying to please the disparate regional and other factions of their respective political parties, although in the end it was the Republican nominee who pursued this balancing act longest and suffered the most for it. Both had, on at least one notable occasion, won the scorn of the nation's intellectual liberals, Nixon for his zealous role on the House Un-American Activities Committee and his famous "Checkers" speech of 1952 defending his use of private funds in Washington, and Kennedy for going unrecorded even by "pairing" in 1954 when illness caused him to be absent on the Senate roll-call vote censuring Senator Joseph R. McCarthy.

But the grueling campaign would in time reveal to these undecided voters substantial differences based on party, personality, and philosophy. In his speeches, the Democratic challenger looked to the future—to the fate of new generations and new nations, the conquest of space and disease, the realization of the American dream for all. President Eisenhower's deputy was required to look more often than his opponent to the past—to the preceding eight years, in which the American people had on the whole been more prosperous and contented than ever before. The younger candidate spoke in idealistic terms about what the nation could do; the incumbent vice president spoke in proud terms about what his administration had done. To many, Nixon had shown a tendency toward flexibility and expediency over the years that raised doubts in their minds whether he had any deep convictions to which he was committed, other than a narrow anticommunist militancy.

The first phase of the campaign saw setbacks for both candidates. A serious infection from a knee bump suffered on a successful tour of the South confined Nixon to a hospital for nearly two weeks, thereby diminishing both his visibility and his vitality at a crucial time. Kennedy had felt equally frustrated by his earlier confinement to a late August session of Congress to which Johnson and Rayburn had committed their respective houses before the convention recess. At the time, it had been regarded by many as a ploy in Johnson's campaign, designed to give him increased stature and leverage with reluctant liberal and labor delegates who desired specific bills passed and to give him as well post-convention exposure in a setting he could turn to his own advantage as presidential nominee. Whatever the original motive, the session was a disaster for the Democrats. It revealed the deep split in their party over civil rights, gave them an appearance of impotence in their inability to enact any of the items in their new liberal platform, and kept Kennedy on the Senate floor, where he was least effective politically, and away from the campaign circuit, where he was most effective.

But once they were released from their frustrating confinements, both candidates spent nearly every waking hour of every remaining day and night in action. Kennedy concentrated on the large industrial states and hoped, with Johnson's help, to pick up enough Southern and other states to achieve the necessary electoral college majority. Nixon, aware of Kennedy's big-state strategy but unable to write off those states, pledged to campaign in every one of the 50 states, a pledge that he maintained despite pleas from his advisers—particularly after his loss of time in the hospital—that he focus his efforts on the most crucial states. Both men relied on enormous national organizations, with advance men to drum up crowds, organizers to register and solicit the faithful, fund-raisers and speechwriters, press agents, pollsters, transportation and communications aides, researchers, advisers and all the rest.

Both men on the stump deviated constantly from the mimeographed texts given to the press, to the latter's dismay. But Kennedy was more accessible to the press than Nixon, gave them more variety in his extemporaneous remarks, and was generally regarded by many of the veteran reporters covering both campaigns as being more considerate and relaxed in his relations with them. Such differences in reaction were bound to be reflected in the dispatches filed by these correspondents to their newspapers back home. The atmosphere of rapport and genial-

ity on the Kennedy campaign caravan also added to the sense of confidence that continued to emanate from the candidate and his staff, and this affected press predictions as well.

But by 1960, television had replaced the newspaper as the most influential medium affecting voter opinion, and Nixon had planned from the outset to make the most of his shrewd and intimate knowledge of this means of communication. A devout believer in timing the pace of a campaign so that it "peaked" exactly on Election Day, he planned a saturation television effort for the weeks leading up to that day topped off by a four-hour telethon on the final day. The Kennedy campaign—which began cutting back expenditures as his party went deeply into debt—could not match the Nixon investment in television or his expertise on its use. Nevertheless, the senator's ability to communicate effectively on this medium was rated higher than the vice president's. He was natural, relaxed, extremely handsome, and spoke in cool tones and language more suited to the living room audience than was the political hall oratory of most candidates. He, too, made extensive use of television, preferring five-minute televised segments of his campaign in action to 30-minute nationwide addresses, and seeking all the free time possible on panel interview and other public events programs.

For both candidates, the crucial use of television came in their series of four nationally televised debates over all major TV and radio networks at prime viewing time in late September and October. These were made possible by a generous network offer and a congressional suspension

This Edmund S. Valtman cartoon shows the Democratic donkey and the GOP elephant as competing organ grinders, each with a monkey begging for votes. The organs are actually television sets, one showing the head of Democratic candidate John F. Kennedy, the other showing Republican candidate Richard Nixon. *(Library of Congress)*

of the equal-time rule that would have required inclusion of numerous fringe party candidates. To the surprise of both his advisers and his adversaries, a confident Nixon accepted Kennedy's challenge. Thus, the largest campaign audience in American history—estimated at 70 million adults—watched the candidates confront each other face-to-face on September 26.

All agree that the first debate was a turning point in the campaign. Kennedy, well rested and well briefed, appeared forceful yet at ease in answering questions posed by a panel of newsmen to the two candidates. Nixon appeared to be tired, uneasy, and defensive, and holding in check his customary aggressive debater's style for fear of undermining his new image as statesman. It is doubtful that either of them scored any decisive points in formal debate terms. Both men were well informed and articulate, both appeared nervous in their opening statements, both used lines previously tried out on campaign audiences. But if Kennedy did not win the first debate, Nixon lost it. He was still underweight from his hospital stay; and his makeup and gray suit under the studio floodlights made him look pale beside the always tan Kennedy. Nixon's sometimes hesitant and weary manner contrasted sharply with Kennedy's more confident and vigorous style.

Kennedy, moreover, had gained merely by showing up. If the first debate resulted in a draw, as the pundits of the press all declared, Kennedy had still become better and favorably known to millions who had previously heard only that he was a rich, young Catholic. Nixon's basic argument that as vice president he was more experienced and had "stood up" to Khrushchev in their debate now had less appeal to those who had watched him debate with the more decisive and determined Kennedy.

If—as some said—only a tiny fraction of the voters moved from Nixon to Kennedy as a result of the debate, that was enough in a close election. The widespread assumption that the experienced Nixon would trample Kennedy made even a draw helpful to the Democrat. Most importantly, the debate solidified Kennedy's strength in his own party, where Nixon had counted on major defections. Stevenson Democrats, suspicious of their party nominee's running mate and his refusal to commit himself on their hero as secretary of state, now rallied to the party banner. Previously cool Protestant Democrats and conservative Democrats were also among those moving from the ranks of undecided into the Kennedy column.

The remaining three debates were less important but preserved the gains Kennedy made through the first one. Nixon returned to a more aggressive style and appearance, and was at his best in the third round when he was not required to be present in the same studio as Kennedy. These three debates were judged to have aided both can-

didates about equally; but the private pollsters for both Kennedy and Nixon as well as subsequent in-depth surveys concluded that the four debates as a whole had on balance aided the Democratic nominee.

The issues raised in these four confrontations, like most of the issues raised in the campaign generally, had less effect than the general impressions left by the candidates. The Peace Corps was the only important new proposal to come out of the campaign, and even that had been suggested in various forms for several years. Kennedy's basic theme was the necessity "to get this country moving again," to confront the challenges of the 1960s instead of complacently drifting as in the 1950s, and thereby to increase America's prestige abroad, economic progress at home, and national security standing. Nixon's basic theme was the continuation of the peace and prosperity achieved under Eisenhower. He accused Kennedy of unpatriotically running down the nation, of lacking the necessary experience, and of advocating radical programs that would bankrupt the Treasury and inflate the cost of living. Kennedy urged his audiences to cast off inertia and indifference and meet their responsibilities as Americans to maintain freedom. Nixon warned his audiences not to tamper with the strength of America's leadership and economy with a naive young president who did not know what it was like either to be poor or to deal with the Communists. Kennedy stressed the historical

Senator John F. Kennedy (left) and Vice President Richard Nixon shake hands in a TV studio after meeting in the first of their four nationally televised debates on September 26, 1960. Center is the moderator of the program, Howard K. Smith. (© Bettmann/ CORBIS)

negativism of the Republican Party and, never criticizing Eisenhower by name, deplored the greater Russian progress in space, the decline in U.S. prestige abroad, and the lag in America's appeal to the developing world. Nixon, always mentioning Eisenhower by name but rarely the Republican Party, proposed a variety of peace missions and conferences as well as domestic programs that went well beyond those of the Eisenhower administration. He gibed at Kennedy's wealth, youth, and allegedly left-wing advisers and supporters. Kennedy accused Nixon of lacking credibility and consistency.

The unusual place occupied by President Eisenhower in the American political scene posed a delicate problem for both candidates. Kennedy privately held Eisenhower responsible for the national drift and disarray that constituted the premise of his campaign attack, and he also regarded the president as more conservative on most domestic issues than his vice president. But Eisenhower's continuing popularity made it impossible to campaign against him by name. Nixon recognized the value of his identification with Eisenhower and the need for the president's direct intervention in the campaign. But he disliked being forced to defend another man's record and decisions and was sensitive about his having merely served Eisenhower in a secondary role—a sensitivity increased by Eisenhower's presumably but not clearly facetious remark at a press conference that he would need a week to think of some Nixon contribution to administration policy. The vice president did not feel he could pressure the older man, who not only was his chief but also had a recent history of ailments and a well-known disdain for political combat, into an earlier and more intensive role in the campaign. Nor did he want his own independence in the campaign overshadowed by presidential speeches that stressed their minority party and some of their administration's less popular policies. As a result, the all-out participation of President Eisenhower in Nixon's effort that fall was delayed. When it began, the president drew tremendous crowds and responses. But the shape of the campaign was by that time fairly well set, and Kennedy continued to press the same issues he had raised all along.

The three most solidly identifiable foreign policy issues in the campaign turned out to have very little real substantive content. Kennedy, along with Symington, Johnson, and others in both parties, voiced alarm about the possible dangers of a future U.S.–Soviet Union "missile gap." This helped illustrate his generalized complaint about America making a second-best effort during the contented 1950s. In fact, aerial photographic intelligence collected early in 1960 by the Central Intelligence Agency indicated that the Russians had not converted their head start in rocketry and engine thrust into a massive military superiority based on intercontinental ballistic missiles.

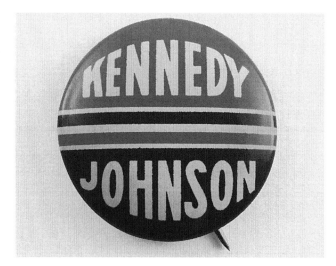

A Kennedy-Johnson campaign pin from the 1960 presidential election (Steve Wood/Shutterstock)

The Democrats, however, were given no hard information on this intelligence and were suspicious of Republican efforts to dampen the issue in a campaign year. Many of the administration's own experts in previous years had warned that the Soviets possessed the industrial and technological capacity to seek a dangerous first-strike advantage. Nixon was not at liberty to reveal the contents of these secret intelligence reports and was forced to reply to his opponent's charges with general reassurances.

Nixon was similarly unable to reveal the administration's plan to assist an army of Cuban exiles seeking the overthrow of Fidel Castro. Thus, he could not respond directly to a loosely worded call for action along these lines released by Kennedy, a call from which Kennedy later retreated. He continued, however, to cite the Castro-Communist takeover of Cuba only 90 miles from American shores as an example of the drift and decline under the Republicans that he had been stressing. A sharp divergence on a minor issue arose when Kennedy told a questioner that two little islands off the coast of Communist China, Quemoy and Matsu, should be evacuated by the Nationalist Chinese as indefensible. Nixon responded that not one inch of "free soil" should be yielded to the Communists. Eventually both candidates buried the issue by agreeing on America's commitment to defend Formosa, Kennedy insisting that Quemoy and Matsu should not be defended unless that was essential to protect Formosa, and Nixon insisting that they should be defended as essential to the protection of Formosa.

Even the more generalized foreign policy issues, though central to Kennedy's theme of "getting the country moving" and to Nixon's theme of "experience," were not decisive. Domestic problems played a far more important role in the final outcome. Here fate conspired against Nixon, as an economic slowdown of sizable proportions began to affect American industry across the country. It was the third recession in Eisenhower's eight years, undoubtedly related to his tight budget and interest-rate policies; and while it was not visible at the start of the campaign to those untrained in economics, its impact was felt by hundreds of thousands who lost their jobs or their overtime pay at the very time that Kennedy was calling for greater economic growth and job development. Nixon had been warned of this prospect early in the year; but administration actions to correct it were too little and too late to curb voter dissatisfaction in the major industrial centers. The vice president had little choice but to deny the existence of the recession and to defend the Eisenhower administration record, while Kennedy was presented with grim evidence of his basic theme.

African Americans as always were particularly and unfairly hard hit by the worsening of the economic climate. At first cool to Kennedy, as the campaign mounted they responded with increasing fervor to his calls for better social and economic legislation and his illustrations of the need for action that often cited their mistreatment. Nixon, realizing that the black vote was largely Democratic by tradition anyway, concentrated more on wooing Southern whites displeased with Kennedy's civil rights stand. Nixon's running mate, who had been assigned the pursuit of minority votes, endangered this strategy by baldly promising that Nixon would appoint a black to his Cabinet and then embarrassed the whole ticket by vacillating on this question after horrified Nixon aides reached him.

When civil rights leader Martin Luther King Jr. was jailed in Georgia on a traffic violation, an indignant Kennedy put in a sympathetic phone call to King's wife, while, unbeknown to him, his brother Robert (who was his campaign manager) called the local judge. Nixon and the administration remained silent on grounds of legal propriety, and Kennedy himself made no speech or press announcement about his action. Most of his advisers had opposed it as a useless gesture that would lose more votes than it would win. But word of his action spread rapidly among black voters, aided by a Kennedy pamphlet distributed outside black churches on the Sunday before election, and his symbolic action was enthusiastically received.

Race, however, was a far less divisive factor in the campaign than religion. Kennedy's Catholicism posed a difficult dilemma for both presidential nominees. Far from being "buried in the hills of West Virginia" as the senator had hoped, this issue dominated private and to a lesser extent public discussions of the campaign in a manner that 50 years later seems hard to comprehend. Kennedy felt he had answered in the spring all legitimate questions on the subject—namely, his views on such issues as education, birth control, censorship, an ambassador to the Vatican, and his own freedom of conscience and action on all public policy questions. If he remained silent in the fall, however, the continuing charges that came from an array of Catholic-fearing spokesmen ranging from thoughtful libertarians to right-wing bigots would lose him the debate by default. If he spoke out again in defense of his views, on the other hand, the Republicans would accuse him of deliberately raising the issue in order to gain sympathy and Catholic votes, while many Catholics would resent his appearing defensive and apologetic. If Vice President Nixon repudiated the support of those attacking his opponent on these grounds, he would be accused of injecting the subject in order to keep it alive in the minds of the voters. If he remained silent, on the other hand, he was accused of accepting or even encouraging the tactics of those who stirred this controversy.

Undoubtedly, some Nixon backers were genuinely troubled by what they regarded as legitimate questions concerning the Catholic Church's influence on an adherent in the White House, and undoubtedly some Kennedy supporters did play on the bigotry theme for political purposes. But there is no evidence that either candidate ever encouraged, much less personally engaged in, such tactics. Both, to their credit, remained silent on the issue when urged by their advisers to speak out in the closing weeks of the campaign. Both no doubt devoutly wished the whole subject would disappear.

The most important and dramatic blow against the religious issue—which caused it virtually to disappear from most serious (as distinguished from scurrilous) campaign discussions—was struck by Kennedy early in the campaign in a September appearance before the Houston Ministers Association. The previous week the issue had been brought to a boil by a highly publicized Washington convocation of prominent conservative Protestant clergymen, many of them well-known Republicans, who accused the Catholic Church of openly intervening in political affairs and of assorted other evils, all of which they ascribed to candidate Kennedy without regard to his publicly stated positions. Their selection of Vice President Nixon's prominent friend, the Reverend Norman Vincent Peale of New York, as chairman and press spokesman, increased the group's prestige and media coverage. When this challenge was emblazoned across the country, Kennedy accepted the Houston group's request that he address the Protestant clergymen of that city on the church–state issue.

His speech did not silence the bigots automatically opposed to any Catholic. It did not end the distribution of more than 20 million pieces of hate literature against him. But it offered reassuring answers to all reasonable questions on this subject and was commended by

Protestant and Jewish organizations as an unequivocal endorsement of constitutional church–state separation. Television coverage of the speech, and taped replays of segments purchased by the Kennedy campaign organization for wide distribution thereafter, made clear to all his belief in "an America that is officially neither Catholic, Protestant nor Jewish . . . where there is no Catholic vote, no anti-Catholic vote, no bloc voting of any kind . . . and where religious liberty is so indivisible that an act against one church is treated as an act against all."

Thereafter he rejected all advice to devote another campaign speech to attacks on his religion, even when his position was undermined by the Catholic hierarchy in Puerto Rico instructing all church members on that island to vote against the incumbent governor with whom the church had quarreled. This event, to the dismay of Kennedy supporters, coincided with Nixon's final two-week drive, which was masterfully designed to peak his campaign on Election Day. Aided by President Eisen-

hower's hard-hitting speeches attacking Kennedy's inexperience, and aided as well by a stepped-up and skillful use of television, the vice president crammed into those two weeks an extraordinarily full traveling and speaking schedule that reached millions of people across the country. "When a President makes a decision," he cried, "it is for keeps." "He can't call a bullet back after he shoots from the hip. . . . [I]n these critical times we cannot afford to have as President of the United States a man who does not think first before he speaks or acts." Because television in general and the debates in particular had generated unusual public interest in the campaign, both candidates drew enormous, excited crowds. Both utilized every available minute to speak to every possible cluster of voters; and both were in a state of physical and mental exhaustion when Election Day dawned.

The turnout of voters set a record—an increase of more than 10 percent over 1956. The Gallup Poll's final report to its readers termed the election too close for any safe predic-

Senator John F. Kennedy, seated on the back of a convertible, campaigning in Yonkers, New York, 1960 *(Library of Congress)*

tion. The results could hardly have been closer. Kennedy's popular vote margin was less than 120,000 out of nearly 69 million votes cast. He won 12 states, including Illinois, with less than 2 percent of the two-party vote, and lost 6 states, including California, by an equally close margin. His electoral vote total of 303 was the same as Truman's 1948 figure; but the winner-take-all electoral system frequently magnifies tiny popular vote margins into more comfortable electoral vote results. Had fewer than 12,000 more people in five states—Illinois, Missouri, Nevada, New Mexico, and Hawaii—voted for Nixon instead of Kennedy, an electoral vote majority would have elected the Republican ticket.

The very narrowness of the margin made possible a variety of interpretations. The number of blacks voting for Kennedy exceeded his edge in enough states to account for his Electoral College margin. The same can be said of the number of white Southerners voting for Kennedy. The same can be said of the votes of newly unemployed workers in six industrial states. A similar conclusion could be reached regarding the millions who made up their minds on the basis of the debates, or the millions of Democrats newly registered in a major drive that fall, or those voting in the 12 (out of 19) most important suburban areas, which Kennedy to the surprise of most Democrats carried after an intensive campaign. Winning 26 of the 40 largest cities, including all of those in the East, was another key reflection of his original electoral strategy.

The single factor influencing more swing voters than any other, however, according to in-depth post-election analyses, was not unemployment or foreign policy or civil rights, but Kennedy's religion. While it undoubtedly helped woo back to the Democratic column large numbers of Catholic Democrats who had voted for Eisenhower over Stevenson, these were more than offset by a loss of some 4.5 million Protestant Democrats switching from Stevenson in 1956 to Nixon in 1960. Only because large numbers of Protestants who voted for Eisenhower also switched to Kennedy (very few longtime Republican Catholics deserted Nixon, and their votes helped him carry several states)—indeed only because large numbers of citizens in every category or in no particular category switched to Kennedy—was he able to compensate for the number of votes lost on this single issue. In the South, only an extraordinarily vigorous campaign by Johnson invoking party traditions and economic issues had stemmed an earlier tide to Nixon in that region, in which religion had been even more important than civil rights. Sympathies aroused when a right-wing crowd in Dallas, Texas, jostled the Johnsons may also have been decisive in that state.

The narrowness of the result was aggravated by the decision of 14 "free electors" elected in Mississippi and Alabama to cast their votes for a conservative Virginia Democrat,

Senator Harry F. Byrd. Had the other Alabama electors, and those from Louisiana, Georgia, and South Carolina, joined in this movement, Kennedy would have been denied an Electoral College majority, and the election by virtue of an archaic rule of the Constitution would have been decided by the House of Representatives under a system in which each state, regardless of population, casts one vote. When such a move failed in the Louisiana state Democratic committee by a margin of 1 vote out of 100, this threat faded. Republican charges of voting irregularities in Chicago also faded when it was realized that even a total switch of the outcome in Illinois would not affect the final result.

Because of the votes cast for these Southern "free electors" and for minor party candidates, Kennedy—like every Democratic president except Roosevelt during the preceding hundred years—received less than a majority of the total popular vote. His party's proportion of the two-party vote had shown, however, an increase over its 1956 level in every state except for six in the South and border regions. Kennedy, whose uphill fight had from the start succeeded only by his surviving a series of near-defeats (and before that near-death in wartime), commented that it was a "miracle" that he had won at all. His campaign over, he turned to the tasks before him. "The margin is narrow," he said, "but the responsibility is clear."

—*Theodore C. Sorensen*

Selected Bibliography

Theodore H. White's *The Making of the President 1960* (1961) is an excellent and extremely well-written account of the campaign. See also Herbert E. Alexander, *Financing the 1960 Election* (1962); Edmund F. Kallina, *Courthouse Over White House: Chicago and the Presidential Election of 1960* (1988); Christopher Matthews, *Kennedy and Nixon: The Rivalry That Shaped Postwar America* (1996); David Pietrusza, *1960: LBJ vs. JFK vs. Nixon: The Epic Campaign That Forged Three Presidencies* (2008); and W. J. Rorabaugh, *The Real Making of the President: Kennedy, Nixon, and the 1960 Election* (2009).

A number of good biographies of Kennedy have been written by his associates. See, for example, Arthur M. Schlesinger Jr., *A Thousand Days* (1967); Theodore Sorensen, *Kennedy* (1965); and Pierre Salinger, *With Kennedy* (1966). For Nixon, see Stephen Hess, *Nixon: A Political Portrait* (1968), and Nixon's memoir *Six Crises* (1962). On the famous television debates, see Sidney Kraus, ed., *The Great Debates: Background, Perspective, Effects* (1962). The religious issue is covered in Lawrence H. Fuchs, *John F. Kennedy and American Catholicism* (1967). See also Stephen E. Ambrose, *Nixon: The Education of a Politician, 1913–1962* (1987); Lucy Dawidowicz and Leon J. Goldstein, *Politics in a Pluralist Democracy: Studies of Voting in the 1960 Election* (1963); Irving Foladare, *Determinants of Voting Decisions in the 1960 Presidential Election* (1966); and Herbert S. Parmet, *JFK: The Presidency of John F. Kennedy* (1983).

1960 Electoral Map and Statistics

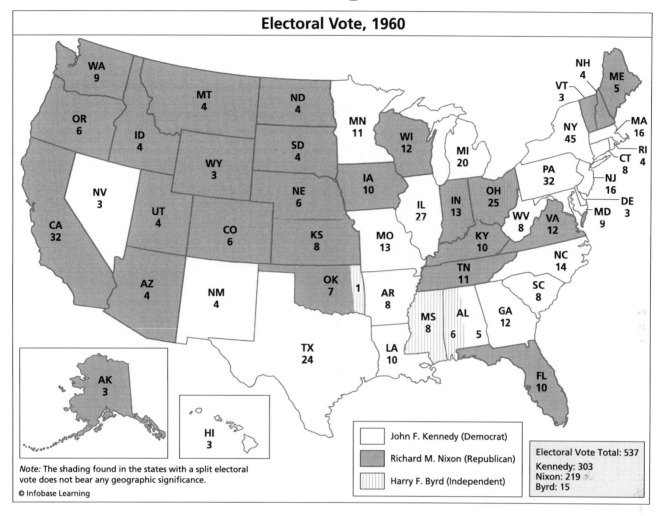

Electoral Vote, 1960

WA 9 | OR 6 | ID 4 | MT 4 | ND 4 | SD 4 | WY 3 | NE 6 | KS 8 | OK 7 | 1 | MN 11 | IA 10 | MO 13 | AR 8 | WI 12 | MI 20 | IL 27 | IN 13 | OH 25 | WV 8 | KY 10 | TN 11 | NY 45 | PA 32 | NJ 16 | CT 8 | RI 4 | MA 16 | ME 5 | NH 4 | VT 3 | DE 3 | MD 9 | VA 12 | NC 14 | SC 8 | GA 12 | FL 10 | NV 3 | CA 32 | UT 4 | CO 6 | AZ 4 | NM 4 | TX 24 | LA 10 | MS 8 | AL 6 | 5 | AK 3 | HI 3

Note: The shading found in the states with a split electoral vote does not bear any geographic significance.

© Infobase Learning

John F. Kennedy (Democrat)

Richard M. Nixon (Republican)

Harry F. Byrd (Independent)

Electoral Vote Total: 537
Kennedy: 303
Nixon: 219
Byrd: 15

1960 ELECTION STATISTICS

State	Number of Electors	Total Popular Vote	Elec Vote			Pop Vote			Margin of Victory	
			D	R	I	D	R	I	Votes	% Total Vote
Alabama	11	564,473	5		6	1	2	-	80,322	14.23%
Alaska	3	60,762		3		2	1	-	1,144	1.88%
Arizona	4	398,491		4		2	1	-	44,460	11.16%
Arkansas	8	428,509	8			1	2	-	30,541	7.13%
California	32	6,506,578		32		2	1	-	35,623	0.55%
Colorado	6	736,246		6		2	1	-	71,613	9.73%
Connecticut	8	1,222,883	8			1	2	-	91,242	7.46%
Delaware	3	196,683	3			1	2	-	3,217	1.64%
Florida	10	1,544,176		10		2	1	-	46,776	3.03%
Georgia	12	733,349	12			1	2	-	184,166	25.11%
Hawaii	3	184,705	3			1	2	-	115	0.06%
Idaho	4	300,450		4		2	1	-	22,744	7.57%
Illinois	27	4,757,409	27			1	2	-	8,858	0.19%
Indiana	13	2,135,360		13		2	1	-	222,762	10.43%
Iowa	10	1,273,810		10		2	1	-	171,816	13.49%
Kansas	8	928,825		8		2	1	-	198,261	21.35%
Kentucky	10	1,124,462		10		2	1	-	80,752	7.18%
Louisiana	10	807,891	10			1	2	3	176,359	21.83%
Maine	5	421,773		5		2	1	-	59,449	14.10%
Maryland	9	1,055,349	9			1	2	-	76,270	7.23%
Massachusetts	16	2,469,480	16			1	2	-	510,424	20.67%
Michigan	20	3,318,097	20			1	2	7	66,841	2.01%
Minnesota	11	1,541,887	11			1	2	-	22,018	1.43%
Mississippi	8	298,171			8	2	3	1	7,886	2.64%
Missouri	13	1,934,422	13			1	2	-	9,980	0.52%
Montana	4	277,579		4		2	1	-	6,950	2.50%
Nebraska	6	613,095		6		2	1	-	148,011	24.14%
Nevada	3	107,267	3			1	2	-	2,493	2.32%
New Hampshire	4	295,761		4		2	1	-	20,217	6.84%
New Jersey	16	2,773,111	16			1	2	-	22,091	0.80%
New Mexico	4	311,107	4			1	2	-	2,294	0.74%
New York	45	7,291,079	45			1	2	-	383,666	5.26%
North Carolina	14	1,368,556	14			1	2	-	57,716	4.22%
North Dakota	4	278,431		4		2	1	-	30,347	10.90%
Ohio	25	4,161,859		25		2	1	-	273,363	6.57%
Oklahoma	8	903,150		7	1	2	1	-	162,928	18.04%
Oregon	6	776,421		6		2	1	-	40,658	5.24%
Pennsylvania	32	5,006,541	32			1	2	-	116,326	2.32%
Rhode Island	4	405,535	4			1	2	-	110,530	27.26%
South Carolina	8	386,688	8			1	2	-	9,571	2.48%
South Dakota	4	306,487		4		2	1	-	50,347	16.43%
Tennessee	11	1,051,792		11		2	1	-	75,124	7.14%
Texas	24	2,311,084	24			1	2	-	46,257	2.00%
Utah	4	374,709		4		2	1	-	36,113	9.64%
Vermont	3	167,324		3		2	1	-	28,945	17.30%
Virginia	12	771,449		12		2	1	-	42,194	5.47%
Washington	9	1,241,572		9		2	1	-	29,975	2.41%
West Virginia	8	837,781	8			1	2	-	45,791	5.47%
Wisconsin	12	1,729,082		12		2	1	-	64,370	3.72%
Wyoming	3	140,782		3		2	1	-	14,120	10.03%
Total	537	68,832,483	303	219	15	1	2	-	112,827	0.16%

* Note: Unpledged electors won in Mississippi with 116,248 votes. These eight electors along with six unpledged electors in Alabama and one rogue Nixon elector in Oklahoma voted for Harry Byrd.

Kennedy Democratic		Nixon Republican		Others	
318,303	56.39%	237,981	42.16%	8,189	1.45%
29,809	49.06%	30,953	50.94%	0	0.00%
176,781	44.36%	221,241	55.52%	469	0.12%
215,049	50.19%	184,508	43.06%	28,952	6.76%
3,224,099	49.55%	3,259,722	50.10%	22,757	0.35%
330,629	44.91%	402,242	54.63%	3,375	0.46%
657,055	53.73%	565,813	46.27%	15	0.00%
99,590	50.63%	96,373	49.00%	720	0.37%
748,700	48.49%	795,476	51.51%	0	0.00%
458,638	62.54%	274,472	37.43%	239	0.03%
92,410	50.03%	92,295	49.97%	0	0.00%
138,853	46.22%	161,597	53.78%	0	0.00%
2,377,846	49.98%	2,368,988	49.80%	10,575	0.22%
952,358	44.60%	1,175,120	55.03%	7,882	0.37%
550,565	43.22%	722,381	56.71%	864	0.07%
363,213	39.10%	561,474	60.45%	4,138	0.45%
521,855	46.41%	602,607	53.59%	0	0.00%
407,339	50.42%	230,980	28.59%	169,572	20.99%
181,159	42.95%	240,608	57.05%	6	0.00%
565,808	53.61%	489,538	46.39%	3	0.00%
1,487,174	60.22%	976,750	39.55%	5,556	0.22%
1,687,269	50.85%	1,620,428	48.84%	10,400	0.31%
779,933	50.58%	757,915	49.16%	4,039	0.26%
108,362	36.34%	73,561	24.67%	116,248	38.99%
972,201	50.26%	962,221	49.74%	0	0.00%
134,891	48.60%	141,841	51.10%	847	0.31%
232,542	37.93%	380,553	62.07%	0	0.00%
54,880	51.16%	52,387	48.84%	0	0.00%
137,772	46.58%	157,989	53.42%	0	0.00%
1,385,415	49.96%	1,363,324	49.16%	24,372	0.88%
156,027	50.15%	153,733	49.41%	1,347	0.43%
3,830,085	52.53%	3,446,419	47.27%	14,575	0.20%
713,136	52.11%	655,420	47.89%	0	0.00%
123,963	44.52%	154,310	55.42%	158	0.06%
1,944,248	46.72%	2,217,611	53.28%	0	0.00%
370,111	40.98%	533,039	59.02%	0	0.00%
367,402	47.32%	408,060	52.56%	959	0.12%
2,556,282	51.06%	2,439,956	48.74%	10,303	0.21%
258,032	63.63%	147,502	36.37%	1	0.00%
198,129	51.24%	188,558	48.76%	1	0.00%
128,070	41.79%	178,417	58.21%	0	0.00%
481,453	45.77%	556,577	52.92%	13,762	1.31%
1,167,567	50.52%	1,121,310	48.52%	22,207	0.96%
169,248	45.17%	205,361	54.81%	100	0.03%
69,186	41.35%	98,131	58.65%	7	0.00%
362,327	46.97%	404,521	52.44%	4,601	0.60%
599,298	48.27%	629,273	50.68%	13,001	1.05%
441,786	52.73%	395,995	47.27%	0	0.00%
830,805	48.05%	895,175	51.77%	3,102	0.18%
63,331	44.99%	77,451	55.01%	0	0.00%
34,220,984	49.72%	34,108,157	49.55%	503,342	0.73%

Election of 1964

Election Overview

Election Year 1964

Election Day November 3, 1964

Winning Candidates

- ★ **President:** Lyndon B. Johnson
- ★ **Vice President:** Hubert Humphrey

Election Results [ticket, party: popular votes (percentage of popular vote); electoral vote (percentage of electoral vote)]

- Lyndon B. Johnson and Hubert Humphrey, Democratic: 43,129,040 (61.05%); 486 (90.3%)
- Barry Goldwater and William Miller, Republican: 27,175,754 (38.47%); 52 (9.7%)
- Unpledged Electors: 210,732 (0.30%); 0 (0.0%)
- Other: 125,757 (0.18%); 0 (0.0%)

Voter Turnout 61.9%

Central Forums/Campaign Methods for Addressing Voters

- Whistle-stop tour
- Speaking tour
- Radio
- Television
- Ads

Incumbent President on Election Day Lyndon B. Johnson

Population (1964) 191,927,000

Gross Domestic Product

- $663.6 billion (in current dollars: $3,392.3 billion)
- Per capita: $3,458 (in current dollars: $17,675)

Number of Daily Newspapers (1960) 1,763

Average Daily Circulation (1960) 58,882,000

Households with

- Radio (1960): 48,504,000
- Television (1960): 46,312,000

Method of Choosing Electors Popular vote

Method of Choosing Nominees

- National party convention
- Presidential preference primaries

Key Issues and Events

- After America's popular young president, John F. Kennedy, is assassinated in November 1963, Vice-President Lyndon B. Johnson becomes president.
- The Civil Rights Act of 1964 advances the civil rights agenda dramatically. The evening of July 2, after signing the law, President Johnson says to his aide, Bill Moyers, "I think we just delivered the South to the Republican Party for a long time to come."
- More broadly, Lyndon Johnson wants to launch a war on poverty, so America can become a "Great Society."
- The war in Vietnam is not yet a major issue but is becoming a serious military and political mess.
- The Harlem Riot, which is sparked on July 18, 1964, shows that for all the goodwill emanating from Johnson's White House, broad discontent remains.

Leading Candidates

DEMOCRATS
- Lyndon B. Johnson, president of the United States (Texas)
- George Wallace, governor (Alabama)

"Favorite-sons"

- Daniel B. Brewster, senator (Maryland)
- Edmund G. "Pat" Brown, governor (California)
- Albert S. Porter (Ohio)
- Jennings Randolph, senator (West Virginia)
- John W. Reynolds, governor (Wisconsin)
- Matthew E. Welsh, governor (Indiana)
- Sam Yorty, mayor (Los Angeles, California)

REPUBLICANS

- John W. Byrnes, representative (Wisconsin)
- Hiram Fong, senator (Hawaii)
- Barry Goldwater, senator (Arizona)
- Walter H. Judd, former representative (Minnesota)
- Henry Cabot Lodge Jr., former senator and 1960 vice-presidential nominee (Massachusetts)
- James A. Rhodes, governor (Ohio)
- Nelson Rockefeller, governor (New York)
- William W. Scranton, governor (Pennsylvania)
- Margaret Chase Smith, senator (Maine)
- John W. Steffey, senator (Maryland)
- Harold E. Stassen, former governor and candidate for the 1944, 1948, and 1952 nominations (Minnesota)

Trajectory

- Preaching "Let us continue," while burning his own brand on his new administration, Lyndon Johnson coasts to nomination by acclamation at the Democratic convention.
- The Republican Party is torn between conservatives seeking a candidate willing to reject the New Deal's welfare state and liberal Republicans led by New York governor Nelson Rockefeller.
- After leading all Republicans by 17 percentage points in an April 1963 Gallup Poll, Rockefeller remarries a divorcee in May 1963, alienating public opinion. Rockefeller's stumble boosts the prospects of Arizona's conservative senator Barry Goldwater. When Republicans meet on July 13–16, 1964, at the Cow Palace in San Francisco, moderates are increasingly frustrated, having seen Pennsylvania governor William Scranton fail to stop Goldwater. Conservatives dominate the convention. Goldwater wins the nomination, selecting the conservative New York congressman William Miller as a running mate, the first Catholic nominated on a Republican ticket.
- At the Democratic Convention on August 24–27 in Atlantic City, N.J., a fight breaks out over the integrated Mississippi Freedom Democratic Party (MFDP) claiming delegate seats for Mississippi to protest the delegates elected in a segregated primary. In a careful compromise, the party grants MFDP two seats and a promise to ban segregation in future primaries, prompting white delegates from Mississippi and Alabama to walk out.
- Johnson dominates the convention, resisting Robert Kennedy's efforts to secure the vice-presidential nomination and instead selecting a key ally in civil rights, Senator Hubert Humphrey.
- Goldwater starts the campaign sounding shrill, proclaiming in his acceptance speech on July 16, "Extremism in the defense of liberty is no vice." Goldwater's attacks on corruption in Washington and chaos on the streets resonate, but his accusations of "socialism" and appeasement backfire with Johnson caricaturing him as a radical who will threaten to dismantle Social Security and bring America to the brink of nuclear destruction.
- Democrats brutalize Goldwater, most famously in the "Daisy" commercial counting down to nuclear war, only shown once on September 7. Meanwhile, Johnson tries to take the high road, acting presidential, but cannot resist a vigorous, 42-day stumping finale.
- On October 7, Johnson's close White House aide Walter Jenkins is arrested for "disorderly conduct" in a Washington YMCA men's room with another man. The news is only reported a week later. As Jenkins resigns and goes to the George Washington University Hospital suffering from "exhaustion," this sex scandal threatens to confirm all of Goldwater's allegations regarding corruption and moral turpitude.
- Back-to-back-to-back foreign shocks push Jenkins off the front-page. On October 14 the Politburo deposes Soviet premier Nikita Khrushchev, sending him into internal exile. On October 15, Harold Wilson and the Labour Party unseat the Tories in England. On October 16, the People's Republic of China successfully tests its first nuclear device. As in 1956, foreign crises work to the incumbent's advantage. Johnson's landslide is even greater than many pollsters predict.

Conventions

- Republican National Convention: July 13–16, 1964, Cow Palace, San Francisco
- Democratic National Convention: August 24–27, 1964, Convention Center, Atlantic City, New Jersey

Ballots/Nominees

DEMOCRATS
Presidential first ballot

- Lyndon Johnson (acclamation)

REPUBLICANS

Presidential first ballot

- Barry Goldwater 883
- William Scranton 214
- Nelson Rockefeller 114
- George Romney 41
- Margaret Chase Smith 27
- Walter Judd 22
- Hiram Fong 5
- Henry Cabot Lodge Jr. 2

Primaries

- Democratic Party: 17; 45.7% delegates
- Republican Party: 17; 45.6% delegates

Primaries Results

DEMOCRATS

- Edmund G. "Pat" Brown 1,693,813; 27.26%
- Lyndon B. Johnson 1,106,999; 17.81%
- Sam Yorty 798,431; 12.85%
- George C. Wallace 672,984; 10.83%
- John W. Reynolds 522,405; 8.41%
- Albert S. Porter 493,619; 7.94%
- Matthew E. Welsh 376,023; 6.05%
- Daniel B. Brewster 267,106; 4.30%
- Jennings Randolph 131,432; 2.12%
- Unpledged 81,614; 1.31%
- Robert Kennedy 36,258; 0.58%

REPUBLICANS

- Barry Goldwater 2,267,079; 38.33%
- Nelson Rockefeller 1,304,204; 22.05%
- James A. Rhodes 615,754; 10.41%
- Henry Cabot Lodge Jr. 386,661; 6.54%
- John W. Byrnes 299,612; 5.07%
- William W. Scranton 245,401; 4.15%
- Margaret Chase Smith 227,007; 3.84%
- Richard M. Nixon 197,212; 3.33%
- Unpledged 173,652; 2.94%
- Harold E. Stassen 114,083; 1.93%

Party Platform

DEMOCRATS

- Expand government programs
- Continuing the Great Society
- Oppose war with Soviet Union

REPUBLICANS

- Oppose big government
- Strong on defense
- Strong anticommunist stance

Campaign Innovations

- "Lady Bird Special": First time the wife of a candidate, first lady, goes on a solo whistle-stop or stumping tour for her husband's presidential campaign

Campaign Tactics

- *Time* calls the campaign a "You're another" campaign, basically a name-calling contest with Goldwater attacked as a "kook" and Johnson as a "crook."
- Heavy reliance on advertising makes many believe that this is the campaign when television became the dominant political medium.

DEMOCRATS

- Johnson focuses on being president, getting his accomplishments covered.
- Emphasizes "consensus," continuing John F. Kennedy's programs and policies.
- Party attacks on Goldwater as warmonger and as a wild westerner who will destroy the post–New Deal prosperity put Goldwater on the defensive.
- At the end of September Johnson embarks on a 42-day stumping tour covering 60,000 miles, delivering 200 speeches. Johnson loves campaigning by motorcade, making impromptu speeches through a handheld bullhorn, shaking countless hands as he is mobbed.
- "Lady Bird Special": Unprecedented whistle-stop tour by the first lady attempting damage control among the once solidly Democratic South following the Civil Rights tumult. From October 6 through 9, Lady Bird Johnson covers 1,628 miles, giving 47 speeches in 47 towns throughout the South to over half a million Southerners.

REPUBLICANS

- Emphasize conservative principles, especially the danger of big government and creeping "socialism."
- Play to "white backlash," North and South. Goldwater targets the Southern states, because he supports states' rights, and refuses to endorse civil rights legislation. Also tries exploiting the Northern "white backlash" vote, as resentment of riots, crime, and ghetto life grows, especially in the large cities in the East.
- To emphasize his authenticity, Goldwater frequently speaks off-the-cuff and rarely tailors speeches to match the constituency he is addressing—as a result he frequently contradicts himself.
- Goldwater focuses on corruption in Washington. He accuses Johnson of amassing a fortune through devious means and questions the president's associ-

ation with Robert G. "Bobby" Baker, Billie Sol Estes, and Matt McCloskey, all accused of shady business dealings. Feeling pressured, Johnson discloses an audit of his financial holdings.

Popular Campaign Slogans

DEMOCRATS

- "Vote for President Johnson on November 3. The Stakes Are Too High for You to Stay at Home"
- "Goldwater in '64, Hot-Water in '65"
- "LBJ for the USA"
- "Vote LBJ the Liberal Way"
- "In Your Heart You Know He Might, In Your Head You Know He's Wrong, and In Your Guts You Know He's Nuts."

REPUBLICANS

- "In Your Heart You Know He's Right" (Democrats respond: "Yes—Extreme Right.")
- "We Need a Space Age Candidate—Go Goldwater in '64!"
- "A Choice, Not an Echo"
- "Yearn for a Return to Conservative Principles"

Campaign Songs

- Democratic Party: "Hello, Lyndon"
- Republican Party: "Go with Goldwater"

Influential Campaign Appeals or Ads

DEMOCRATS

- "Peace Little Girl (Daisy)" aired once, during the NBC Movie of the Week on September 7, 1964. A young girl picks the petals of a flower counting up from 1 to 10. When she reaches 10—after one charming mistake—a narrator enters into a countdown, and the bucolic image of the girl dissolves into an image of a nuclear mushroom. Demonstrates the danger of putting Goldwater in charge of the nuclear arsenal. Republican Party objects, and the ad is never aired again.
- Withdrawn commercial: a little girl with an ice cream cone poisoned with strontium-90, because "there's a man who wants to be president of the United States" who voted in 1962 against the nuclear test-ban treaty with Russia.
- "Goldwater for Halloween—Vote for Goldwater and Go to War."

REPUBLICANS

- Defensive ads; harking back to Eisenhower's Answers America, talking head commercials.

- Use half-hour broadcast speeches for fund-raising appeals, most notably Ronald Reagan's "A Time for Choosing," October 27, 1964, thereafter known as "the speech" that helped launch his national political career.

Campaign Finance

- Johnson: $8,757,000 (in current dollars: $57,485,200)
- Goldwater: $16,026,000 (in current dollars: $105,202,400)

Defining Quotations

- "Thus, for the American conservative, there is no difficulty in identifying the day's overriding political challenge: it is *to preserve and extend freedom . . .* the Conservative's first concern will always be: *'Are we maximizing freedom?' . . .* Throughout history, government has proved to be the chief instrument for thwarting man's liberty." *Barry Goldwater,* The Conscience of a Conservative, *1960*
- "Have we come to the point in our life as a nation where the governor of a great state—one who perhaps aspires to the nomination for president of the United States—can desert a good wife, mother of his grown children, divorce her, then persuade a young mother of four youngsters to abandon her husband and their four children and marry the governor?" *Republican senator Prescott Bush of Connecticut on New York governor Nelson Rockefeller, quoted in* Time, *June 14, 1963*
- "For a century we labored to settle and to subdue a continent. For half a century we called upon unbounded invention and untiring industry to create an order of plenty for all of our people. The challenge of the next half-century is whether we have the wisdom to use that wealth to enrich and elevate our national life, and to advance the quality of our American civilization. Your imagination and your initiative and your indignation will determine whether we build a society where progress is the servant of our needs, or a society where old values and new visions are buried under unbridled growth. For in your time we have the opportunity to move not only toward the rich society and the powerful society, but upward to the Great Society." *President Lyndon B. Johnson at the University of Michigan, Ann Arbor, May 22, 1964*
- "This is still a free country, ladies and gentlemen. These things have no place in America. But I can personally testify to their existence. And so can countless others who have also experienced anonymous midnight and early morning telephone calls, unsigned threatening letters, smear and hate literature, strong-arm and goon tactics, bomb threats and bombings,

infiltration and take-over of established political organizations by Communist and Nazi methods. Some of you don't like to hear it, ladies and gentlemen, but it's the truth." *Nelson Rockefeller speaking at the Republican National Convention, July 14, 1964*

- "I would remind you that extremism in the defense of liberty is no vice. And let me remind you also that moderation in the pursuit of justice is no virtue." *Barry Goldwater, address accepting the presidential nomination at the Republican National Convention, San Francisco, July 16, 1964*

- "We don't want our American boys to do the fighting for Asian boys. We don't want to . . . get tied down in a land war in Asia." *Lyndon B. Johnson treating Barry Goldwater as the militant regarding Vietnam, September 25, 1964*

- "I wanted to educate the American people to lose some of their fear of the word 'nuclear.' When you say 'nuclear,' all the American people see is a mushroom cloud. But for military purposes, it's just enough firepower to get the job done." *Barry Goldwater, quoted in* Time, *September 25, 1964*

- "My heart is aching today for someone who has reached the point of exhaustion in dedicated service to his country. Walter Jenkins has been carrying incredible hours and burdens since President Kennedy's assassination. He is now receiving the medical attention that he needs." *Lady Bird Johnson statement about Walter Jenkins, October 15, 1964*

- "This is the issue of this election: Whether we believe in our capacity for self-government or whether we abandon the American revolution and confess that a little intellectual elite in a far-distant capital can plan our lives for us better than we can plan them ourselves. You and I are told increasingly we have to choose between a left or right. Well I'd like to suggest there is no such thing as a left or right. There's only an up or down—[up to] man's old—old-aged dream, the ultimate in individual freedom consistent with law and order, or down to the ant heap of totalitarianism. And regardless of their sincerity, their humanitarian motives, those who would trade our freedom for security have embarked on this downward course." *Ronald Reagan, "A Time for Choosing," televised campaign address for Goldwater presidential campaign, October 27, 1964*

Lasting Legacy of Campaign

- Johnson achieves the fifth-largest margin of victory with 22.6 percentage points (after the margins of the 1920, 1924, 1936, and 1972 elections).
- Johnson wins 61.1% of the popular vote, highest popular vote percentage since 1820.
- No post-1964 Democratic candidate has managed to better Johnson's 1964 electoral result.
- Goldwater as a pioneer in the modern conservative movement

Election of 1964

The 1964 election was supposed to raise the most fundamental issues of American policy—war and peace in the nuclear age and the proper role of government in a free society—but it turned out to be one of the silliest, most empty, and most boring campaigns in the nation's history.

The great debates it promised originated in the Republican Party, and to understand this it is necessary to glance backward briefly. From the Civil War to the turn of the century, the Republican Party had been the dominant party in the United States. Between 1900 and 1912, however, it began to split into two wings, and the split was along ideological lines: progressive versus conservative. In 1912, the split produced Republican disaster. The conservatives clung to power within the party during the Wilson years and, in the euphoria of the 1920s, were able to win back the presidency. The Roosevelt revolution defeated them in the nation—but not in the party. Throughout the 1930s, the conservative wing continued to dominate the Republican Party—and to lose elections. By 1940, it was clear to the party managers, even the conservative ones, that something new must be tried lest the Republican Party go the way of the Whigs, and so, reluctantly, they nominated Wendell Willkie. And during the rest of the 1940s they nominated a relatively liberal candidate, Thomas E. Dewey of New York. But Dewey, like Willkie, was the choice of the Eastern establishment, the men from the power centers of Wall Street, advertising agencies, public relations firms, newspaper, magazine, and book publishing houses, big business, Ivy League universities, and big law offices—men who shuttle between New York and Washington, between New York and Paris, between government and private power; men deeply concerned about America's role in world affairs; men who had long since recognized that the larger role assigned to government at home by FDR was here to stay and that the best thing for them, and for the country, was to go along with it.

These men were anathema to Republican Party rank-and-file workers beyond the Alleghenies, and the farther west (and south) one went, the deeper ran the resentment of Eastern power. Wendell Willkie and Tom Dewey were the choices of the Eastern establishment; they were most emphatically not the choices of the county chairmen and the convention delegates from the Midwest, the Rocky Mountain states, and the South. When Dewey lost the "sure-thing" election to Harry Truman in 1948, the conservatives discerned in the loss proof that the Easterners had led them astray, had forced them to nominate what the *Chicago Tribune* called "me-too" candidates, candidates indistinguishable from their liberal Democratic opponents, and that as a consequence an enormous "silent" vote of disgusted conservatives had stayed home and refused to vote. They turned to their hero, Senator Robert A. Taft of Ohio, determined to nominate him in 1952. Once again, however, they were foiled: General Dwight D. Eisenhower, urged on by the Eastern establishment, made himself available, and although the die-hard conservatives fought his nomination in 1952, the more realistic party managers, including many whose hearts lay with Taft, saw in Eisenhower the key to certain and overwhelming victory. They were right.

President Eisenhower, had he been a politician, might have been able to heal the ancient split in his party. But his eight years in the White House only postponed the resumption of the conservative–liberal feud. In 1960, obliged to choose a new candidate, the party turned to Vice President Richard M. Nixon. He was opposed at the convention by Governor Nelson Rockefeller of New York on a more liberal platform than, in all probability, the majority of delegates wanted. Nixon, anxious to heal wounds, sought to compromise with Rockefeller, thereby alienating some of his more extreme right-wing supporters. These turned to Senator Barry Goldwater of Arizona, but they were only few, and Nixon was nominated. In the course of the ensuing campaign, Nixon tried to appease both wings of his party, and pleased neither. As the campaign progressed, ending with the narrowest of margins for John F. Kennedy, many of Nixon's own party leaders accused him of throwing the election away.

During the wrenching four years that followed, encompassing President Kennedy's assassination and the accession of Lyndon B. Johnson, the ancient feud inside the Republican Party resumed. Nixon's defeat for the governorship of California in 1962 seemed to eliminate him as a candidate, and the feud polarized around Rockefeller and Goldwater, with two new Republican governors, George Romney of Michigan and William Scranton of Pennsylvania, in the wings. Apparently, neither Rockefeller nor Goldwater wanted to feud; they liked each other. Rockefeller wanted the presidency and was

eager to please the conservatives. Goldwater, an amiable man, seemed not at all sure he wanted it. He occasionally persuaded his more extreme followers not to harass the New York governor, and he met Rockefeller privately several times seeking party unity. By 1963, Goldwater was becoming convinced that a Rockefeller nomination might not damage the conservative cause.

Beyond them, however, in the hinterland, something more important was going on. It was a vague unease, a malaise, a dislike of the way things were going, an inchoate "whither are we drifting" feeling. It had many wellsprings. The Supreme Court's school desegregation decision, and its firm implementation by John Kennedy and his brother Robert, the attorney general, along with civil rights legislation, had created resentment in the white South and "white backlash" in the Northern cities, where many white workingmen, particularly those of Eastern European extraction, felt themselves threatened by black men. Vestiges of the corrosive McCarthyism of the 1950s remained—a hatred of communism, a suspicion of the government, all further inflamed by the frustrations of Southeast Asia and other seemingly unmanageable events. Stretching back even farther, the isolationism of the late 1930s stirred again as America's power and foreign commitments increased. Sheer population growth pressed people closer together and required them to have numbers so the federal government and its computers could keep track of them. Bearded youths on college campuses, along with showgirls in topless dresses, offended the small-town morality. New right-wing extremist groups kept popping up: the John Birch Society, the Minutemen, and more, some armed or eager to arm. At the fringe were lunatics who hated communists, Jews, Catholics, blacks, waste, or big government (or any government, it sometimes seemed) indiscriminately. The Wyoming legislature in 1963 called for replacing the Supreme Court with a "court of the union" composed of 50 state chief justices, getting the United States out of the U.N. and the U.N. out of the United States, and abolishing foreign aid. (Earlier it had favored repealing the federal income tax.)

And at the same time the conservative rank-and-file Republican Party workers contended that what they needed was, as the slogan soon put it, "a choice, not an echo"—that is, a candidate who would clearly oppose the Democratic drift toward big government and internationalism and thus bring the "silent conservative vote" to the polls to overwhelm the forces of error and evil.

Moreover, authentic voices of intellectual American conservatism were heard in the land: the young rightist intellectuals and older ex-Communist intellectuals associated with William F. Buckley Jr.'s *National Review*, including L. Brent Bozell, Buckley's brother-in-law, frequent contributor to the *National Review,* and a Goldwater ghostwriter.

What all these troubled ordinary people, disgruntled Republican politicians, and conservative intellectuals needed was a candidate. They found him in Barry Goldwater.

Goldwater, who for a few months in 1964 was cast in the role of fanatic, had been anything but a fanatic throughout his life. Born January 1, 1909, in Phoenix, Arizona, the grandson of a Polish immigrant merchant, son of an Orthodox Jewish father and a Protestant Episcopal mother, he himself belonged to Trinity Cathedral in Phoenix but was an infrequent churchgoer. An indifferent student but a good cadet at Staunton Military Academy in Virginia, he spent only part of one year in college at the University of Arizona. He became president of the family department stores, married the daughter of an Indiana manufacturer, and took up hobbies—aviation, golf, photography, Indian lore, sports cars, and shortwave radio. As a conservative and well-to-do businessman, he disliked Roosevelt's New Deal. Ineligible for combat in World War II, he ferried bombers to India and was discharged a lieutenant colonel in the U.S. Army Air Corps. Later, he became chief of staff of the Arizona Air National

☆ ☆ ☆

1964 ELECTION CHRONOLOGY

1961

April 17, 1961: CIA-trained Cuban exiles mount an invasion at the Bay of Pigs in Cuba in an attempt to depose Fidel Castro's Communist government. The failed attempt embarrasses the Kennedy administration.

1962

November 6, 1962: Democrats lose four seats in Congress and gain two seats in the Senate from the midterm elections, keeping their comfortable majorities in both houses.

November 7, 1962: Following his defeat in the California gubernatorial race to Edmund G. "Pat" Brown, Richard M. Nixon makes what he promises to be his "last press conference," saying to reporters: "You won't have Nixon to kick around anymore."

1963

April 9, 1963: Peter O'Donnell, the Texas Republican state chairman, holds a press conference announcing the formation of the National Draft Goldwater Committee to draft Barry Goldwater, the Arizona senator and author of the 1960 blockbuster *The Conscience of a Conservative.*

May 4, 1963: Republican front-runner Nelson Rockefeller marries a divorcee, alienating public opinion. The stumble erases his commanding lead and boosts Goldwater's prospects.

October 24, 1963: Senator Barry Goldwater of Arizona announces his intention to run for the Republican nomination.

November 7, 1963: Nelson Rockefeller announces he will seek the nomination.

November 22, 1963: President John F. Kennedy is assassinated in Dallas, Texas, while riding with his wife in a motorcade. Vice President Lyndon B. Johnson is immediately sworn in as president.

1964

March 10, 1964: Goldwater and Rockefeller battle in the New Hampshire primary, considered by analysts to be one of the most important in the 1964 Republican race. Both are defeated by a write-in candidate, Henry Cabot Lodge, then the U.S. ambassador to South Vietnam.

May 15, 1964: Even though Oregon is another key Republican battleground state, Goldwater chooses not to campaign there. Rockefeller wins with 33 percent of the vote.

May 19, 1964: After winning the Wisconsin primary on April 8 and the Indiana primary on May 9, segregationist governor George C. Wallace of Alabama wins Maryland's Democratic presidential primary. President Lyndon Johnson's nomination is ensured, but the three Wallace victories are a protest against Johnson's civil rights stance.

June 2, 1964: Goldwater wins the California primary with 51 percent of the votes.

Guard and, as a major general in the USAF Reserve, commanding officer of the 999th Combined Air Force Reserve Squadron, made up of members of Congress and congressional employees. He remained forever a friend of the military.

In 1949, Goldwater ran on a nonpartisan reform ticket for the Phoenix City Council and won. In 1950, he managed the successful campaign of Howard Pyle, a popular radio announcer, for governor of Arizona. Goldwater was widely known to Rotarians, Kiwanians, and other such groups throughout Arizona, and had spoken to them as a businessman. He used this acquaintanceship to help the

Republican cause in Arizona and was rewarded in 1952 with the party's nomination for the U.S. Senate. He rode in on Eisenhower's coattails—Eisenhower carried Arizona by 42,000 votes, Goldwater by 7,000.

Goldwater entered the Senate as an Eisenhower Republican, having backed Eisenhower against Taft at the bitter nominating convention. To be sure, he favored "fiscal responsibility," but he also favored peace, workers' compensation, and racial reconciliation. In a campaign speech, he said he wanted to retain the social gains made in the past 20 years, including the Social Security system, unemployment insurance, old-age assistance, aid

---

☆ ☆ ☆

July 1, 1964: As the primary season ends, Goldwater leads the Republicans with 38 percent of pledged delegates, followed by Rockefeller and Ohio governor James A. Rhodes.

July 2, 1964: President Johnson signs the Civil Rights Act into law. The bill overturns the Jim Crow laws in the South, prohibits public discrimination in government and public facilities, and makes it illegal to compel segregation between the races.

July 13–16, 1964: Meeting at the Cow Palace in San Francisco, the Republican National Convention nominates Barry Goldwater of Arizona for president on the first ballot and New York representative William E. Miller for vice president.

July 16, 1964: Accepting the Republican nomination, Goldwater proclaims: "Extremism in the defense of liberty is no vice . . . and moderation in the defense of justice is no virtue."

July 18, 1964: After a New York City police officer shoots and kills a 15-year-old boy, a protest at Harlem's 28th Police Precinct turns violent. A riot ensues, lasting nearly five days.

August 7, 1964: After U.S. destroyers are allegedly fired upon by Vietnamese torpedo boats in the Gulf of Tonkin, President Johnson asks and receives a joint resolution from Congress to use military force in Southeast Asia without the declaration of war.

August 24–27, 1964: Meeting in Atlantic City, New Jersey, the Democratic National Convention nominates President Lyndon Johnson for president and Minnesota senator Hubert Humphrey for vice president. White delegates from

Mississippi and Alabama bolt, protesting the two seats awarded the integrated Mississippi Freedom Democratic Party (MFDP).

September 7, 1964: Democrats air the "Daisy" commercial, contrasting imagery of a young child with footage of detonating nuclear bombs. The ad never runs again.

October 7, 1964: Johnson's close White House aide Walter Jenkins is arrested for disorderly conduct in a Washington YMCA men's room with another man. The news is only reported a week later. Jenkins resigns immediately.

October 14, 1964: The Politburo deposes Soviet Premier Nikita Khrushchev.

October 15, 1964: Harold Wilson and the Labour Party unseat the Tories in England.

October 16, 1964: The People's Republic of China successfully tests its first nuclear device. All this foreign instability reinforces President Johnson's message that Goldwater is too unreliable a leader in an unstable world.

November 3, 1964: Election Day. Democrats Lyndon B. Johnson and Hubert Humphrey defeat Republicans Barry Goldwater and William Miller with 61 percent of the popular vote and 486 Electoral College votes. Voter turnout is 61 percent.

December 14, 1964: Presidential electors cast their ballots in their respective state capitals.

1965

January 6, 1965: A joint session of Congress assembles to count the electoral votes.

to dependent children and the blind, the FHA, and stock market regulation. In the Senate he voted to outlaw the filibuster, and at a time when Eisenhower and Nixon were considering coming to the aid of the French in the war in Indochina, Goldwater proposed to end foreign aid to France unless she freed Vietnam, Laos, and Cambodia.

During this period, and later, Goldwater employed a breezy Western manner that captivated campaign audiences. In private conversation and in public appearances he displayed a disarming candor. He once told the Platform Committee of his party's national convention that it ought not to have a platform; instead, it ought to have a "declaration of principles," and he later explained that "principles" were easier to live with than specific platform proposals—a declaration such as "we believe in the freedom of the individual" could be interpreted with equal ease by himself and Senator Jacob Javits, the New York liberal. Such candor—or cynicism—is rarely displayed openly by politicians, and is therefore attractive. When he

Lyndon B. Johnson *(Library of Congress)*

ran for president in 1964, Goldwater decided not to run for reelection to the Senate at the same time, though it would have been legal in Arizona, because in 1960 he had criticized Lyndon Johnson for seeking the vice presidency and a Senate seat at the same time. When a reporter asked about it, he said he couldn't run for both offices: "After what I said about Lyndon in 1960—they'd run me out of the country. But if I hadn't opened my big mouth so loud, I might do it." He told the same reporter, "You know, I haven't really got a first-class brain," and added that once he had read his wife a speech he planned to deliver, and when she seemed unimpressed, asked, "What the hell is the matter?" Mrs. Goldwater replied, "Look, this is a sophisticated audience, they're not a lot of lamebrains like you; they don't spend their time looking at TV Westerns. You can't give them that corn." In 1963, a reporter asked how he felt about the possibility that he might become president, Goldwater replied, "Frankly, it scares the hell out of me." Weighing the possibility of his candidacy, he once told *Newsweek,* "If I thought I'd get my tail whipped badly, I'd say the hell with it." He was a handsome man, cheerful, amiable, agreeable, friendly. In November 1963, heading toward the nomination, he once said, "God knows, I'm still wishing something would happen to get me out of all this. It's all a little frightening." That same year, a reporter asked why he had voted for a $6 billion agricultural appropriations bill after having ceaselessly called for a "prompt and final termination of the farm-subsidy program." Goldwater denied the action, and when shown that he had indeed supported the bill, he promptly called the clerk of the Senate and had his vote changed to no. He once said, "I know nothing about farming."

All this is wholly inconsistent with the candidate who, in 1964 and for some years before, appeared before the people of the United States as the apocalyptic Savonarola of the Republican Party, scourging sin, smiting big government and all its acts, including the Social Security system and the Tennessee Valley Authority (TVA), threatening nuclear war to wipe out Communism everywhere. That Goldwater said in 1963, "I'd drop a low-yield nuclear bomb on Chinese supply lines in North Viet Nam." He said in 1960, "I do not propose to promote welfare. . . . Let welfare be a private concern." In 1963, in response to the question, "Would you, as President, favor getting out of the United Nations?" he said, "I would." He suggested, in 1961, "I think TVA should be turned over to free enterprise, even if they could only get one dollar for it." But in a later book, *Where I Stand,* he wrote, "I believe the United States should make the fullest possible use of its membership in the U.N." And, he added, "I favor a sound Social Security system, and I want to see it strengthened," and "The Tennessee Valley Authority is an enterprise unique in our nation. Some of its elements have been successful and should be continued." However, during his whistlestop campaign in 1964 he demanded of the pretty girls who cheered him, "What good is prosperity if you are a slave," and on television, more often than not, he glowered at his audience.

It was Richard Rovere's theory that there were two Goldwaters. "There is," he wrote, "on the one hand, the Senator on the hustings, the agreeable man with the easy, breezy Aw Shucks Western manner who speaks in rightist platitudes but has only a loose grip on ideology and not, apparently, much interest in it. And there is, on the other hand, the dour authoritarian polemicist whose name is signed to *The Conscience of a Conservative, Why Not Victory?* and to many hundreds of articles, columns, and press releases so heavily freighted with smarmy theology and invocations of Natural Law ('Right-to-work laws derive from Natural Law') that they have won for the Senator the warm approval of Archduke Otto of Austria, and the admiration of the ranking ideologues of the Franco regime in Spain. There is the Goldwater who can dispose of a large national problem by saying, 'If we get back to readin', writin', and 'rithmetic and an occasional little whack where it will help, then I think our educational system will take care of itself.' And there is the portentous Goldwater, abounding in theory: 'We have forgotten that the proper function of the school is to transmit the cultural heritage of one generation to another. . . . The fundamental explanation of this distortion of values is that we have forgotten that purpose of education. [It] is not to educate, or elevate, society, but rather to educate the *individual*. . . . [We must] recapture the lost arts of learning.'" Rovere believed that Goldwater was captured by the intellectuals associated with the *National Review,* among others, and that they churned out under his name unnumbered words totally out of keeping with his natural style and stance. Rovere added that the invented Goldwater was far less attractive and salable than the original, or natural, Goldwater, a case unique in recent history. Goldwater once told Stewart Alsop of the *Saturday Evening Post,* "Oh, hell, I have ghosts all over the place." Rovere reported, "Things got so bad late in 1963 that the staff had to take on some microfilm and punch-card people to sort out what Goldwater had been saying, or had been having said for him, over the years and to determine exactly what commitments had been made for him and by him."

Precisely when the intellectual conservatives took him over is uncertain, but by 1957 Goldwater had broken with President Eisenhower, claiming that Eisenhower's appropriations requests were "abominably high" and calling the Republicans' fiscal policies "a betrayal of the people's trust." Asked to comment on the president's brother Milton as a party leader, he said, "One Eisenhower in a gen-

eration is enough." In the last Eisenhower Congress, he supported the president only 52 percent of the time. He alone in the Senate voted against the Kennedy–Erwin labor reform bill of 1959 and called it "the most important [vote] of my Senate career." *Congressional Quarterly* reported, "A large portion of Goldwater's national reputation is based on his articulate and consistent opposition to 'big labor.'" Goldwater favored "right-to-work" laws, a ban on union spending in politics, mandatory secret union votes before strikes could be called, and limitations on industry-wide bargaining by any one union. "As early as his first term in Congress," *CQ* noted, "Goldwater was accused by national labor publications of 'tyranny,' 'neo-fascism,' and an attempt to 'smash' organized labor." As a member of Senator McClellan's "Rackets" committee, Goldwater engaged in bitter exchanges with Walter Reuther, head of the United Auto Workers (UAW) and said that Reuther and the UAW were "a more dangerous menace than the Sputniks or anything else Russia might do."

Goldwater was also a relentless enemy of high government spending and taxation. He said he considered the 16th Amendment to the Constitution, which legalized the graduated income tax, "a very poor amendment," and, though pessimistic about the prospects of eliminating the income tax altogether, vigorously condemned its progressive nature. While favoring income tax reform, he consistently defended the oil and gas depletion allowance. In a speech to the Economic Club of New York early in 1964, Goldwater said, "We are told . . . that many people lack skills and cannot find jobs because they did not have an education. That's like saying that people have big feet because they wear big shoes. The fact is that most people who have no skill, have no education for the same reason—low intelligence or low ambition." In 1962, he said he did not think Social Security should be repealed. "I do not think it can be. I would like to see us correct it. I think it should be voluntary, for one thing." In 1963, he stuck to his guns: "I think Social Security should be voluntary. This is the only definite position I have on it. If a man wants it, fine. If he does not want it, he can provide his own." He said in a Senate speech in 1961 that he considered TVA "an unfortunate socialist adventure," and in 1963, "I am quite serious in my opinion that TVA should be sold." With admirable consistency, he favored returning offshore oil to the states and exempting independent natural gas producers from federal control, opposed the national wilderness preservation system, and favored a private communications satellite system over one run by the government. As for education, in *The Conscience of a Conservative* he claimed, "Federal intervention in education is unconstitutional" and consistently voted against programs of federal aid to education.

Similarly, Goldwater stood firm for "states' rights": "I fear Washington and centralized government more than I do Moscow," he told a political rally in Spartanburg, South Carolina, in 1960, and he took the position in *The Conscience of a Conservative* that the 10th Amendment "recognizes the states' jurisdiction" in all matters not specifically designated as federal elsewhere in the Constitution. Therefore, he wrote, the whole idea of "civil rights" was constitutionally invalid and the conflict between states' rights and civil rights was only an "imagined" one. While "it may be just or wise or expedient for Negro children to attend the same schools as white children . . . they do not have a civil right to do so." Goldwater felt that education was reserved to the states by the Tenth Amendment. This was patently absurd. A great many of today's problems were not dealt with—and did not exist—when the Tenth Amendment was written. Goldwater went on to say, "It so happens that I am in agreement with the objectives of the Supreme Court as stated in the Brown [school desegregation] decision. I believe it is both wise and just for Negro children to attend the same schools as whites, and that to deny them this opportunity carries with it strong implications of inferiority. I am not prepared, however, to impose that judgment of mine on the people of Mississippi or South Carolina." Goldwater himself seems to have been personally opposed to racial discrimination and introduced numerous bills intended to improve the lot of the American Indian. But when the chips were down, he sided with the segregationists. In 1964 he voted against the bipartisan Civil Rights Act.

Goldwater's views on foreign policy were summed up in the title of his 1962 book, *Why Not Victory?* He believed that America's foreign policy objective should be "total victory" over "the all-embracing determination of Communism to capture the world and destroy the United States." He believed that negotiations with Communists were fruitless and dangerous; he favored breaking relations with the Soviet Union, keeping mainland China out of the U.N., and considering pulling the United States out. Goldwater advocated a policy aimed at overthrowing Castro and liberating Russia's east European satellites. In a debate with Senator J. William Fulbright, who challenged his position in 1962 as impractical and risky, he said, "The President of the United States [should] declare officially that it is our purpose to win the cold war, not merely wage it in the hope of attaining a standoff. . . . It is really astonishing that our government has never stated its purpose to be that of complete victory over the tyrannical forces of international communism." Asked what kind of total victory he envisaged, he replied, "Well, the victory would not be a military victory necessarily."

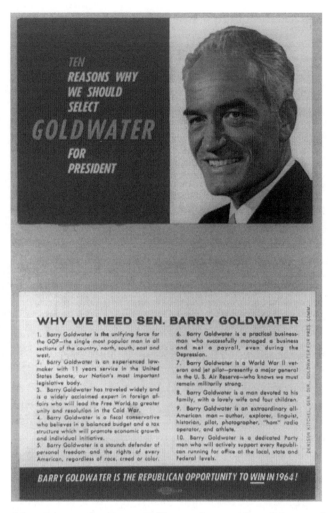

Advertisement for Barry Goldwater for president *(Library of Congress)*

Goldwater disliked most foreign aid programs as well as disarmament negotiations and agreements. Suspecting the Soviet Union's intentions, he rejected the creation of a U.S. Arms Control and Disarmament agency in 1961, and he strongly opposed ratification of the limited nuclear test ban treaty in 1963. He said in 1961, "I hope the Administration will call for an immediate resumption of the [nuclear] tests. Frankly, I do not care what the rest of the world thinks about us." Goldwater frequently advocated the use of low-yield atomic weapons in certain tactical situations. At a press conference in Hartford, Connecticut, on October 24, 1963, he was quoted as saying that North Atlantic Treaty Organization (NATO) field commanders should have the authority to use tactical atomic weapons at their discretion. He later claimed misquotation—claiming he had said only that the NATO commander should have "that authority, to some extent." His aides, seeking to "clarify" the matter further, said that when Goldwater said "commanders," he had not meant local field commanders but rather the string of supreme NATO commanders who succeeded each other over the years.

Goldwater seemed to have a loose grip on policy. Asked in 1964 if he stood by his 1960 suggestion that nuclear weapons should be used to help uprisings in eastern Europe, he answered, "If that became necessary, if that were the only way, yes." In 1961, during the Berlin crisis he said, "I have been very much concerned about the emphasis on conventional weapons [at Berlin]. I am the first to recognize that we should have a greater mix; that we should have conventional weapons; but that we should not exclude nuclear tactical weapons in our rush toward the conventional type." In 1963 he told *Newsweek,* "I'd drop a low-yield atomic bomb on Chinese supply lines in North Viet Nam." Interviewed by the *New York Times* that year, he explained, "I think we could probably return a third—maybe half—of our forces if we gave the NATO command the right to use nuclear weapons—tactical weapons—when they were attacked." Again in 1964 he added, "All NATO forces stationed in Europe, regardless of nationality, should be equipped with and trained in the use of nuclear weapons, particularly of the so-called battlefield or tactical variety."

Goldwater's Vietnam views followed a similar line: "I would strongly advise that we interdict supply routes, wherever they may be, either by sea, or most importantly, through North Vietnam, Laos or Cambodia." He felt Chinese leaders should be told that, unless they stopped delivering supplies to the Viet Cong, the United States would bomb bridges and roads leading into South Vietnam. "There have been several suggestions made. I don't think we would use any of them. But defoliation of the forest by low-yield atomic weapons could well be done. When you remove the foliage, you remove the cover." Goldwater soon claimed that this last statement had been misinterpreted—then went on to say, "I would go to the Red River Valley approaches in South China. I would first take out the bridges. If that wouldn't do the job, I would take out the railroads. I would use conventional weapons. I would not use atomic weapons when conventional weapons will do the job. But I would leave it up to the commanders." Asked by *Der Spiegel* in June 1964 what he thought of the theory that he was an impulsive man who occasionally shot from the hip, he said, "Well, that may be so. But, every time I've shot from the hip, it has later come to be the accepted position of this country." He cited his advice to tear down the Berlin Wall and give NATO forces "our modern weapons," and then added, "Now I'll have to admit that I possibly do shoot from the hip. I'll have to admit also that, while I'm not the most intelligent man in the world, and a lot of people think I'm quite ignorant, that I've traveled more in this world, I've done more things probably than most men in this Congress. So I've been exposed to problems and I don't have to stop and think in details about them."

Goldwater stood loyally and consistently with the military. Although he opposed Democratic efforts to increase defense appropriations during the Eisenhower administration, in general he supported a strong U.S. defense establishment and, during the Kennedy–Johnson administration, favored increases in defense budgets, especially for continuation of the manned bomber program. It troubled him that civilians sometimes vetoed military recommendations. He once said, "I am more concerned over civilian meddlers who decide an invasion of Cuba doesn't need air support than I am over military men who recommended use of enough strength to assure the success of our venture in the Bay of Pigs."

Thus, many of Goldwater's views put him outside the national consensus, but the movement that claimed him stood even farther outside the consensus. It came to be called the Goldwater movement. In the beginning, however, it was not his, but rather, a movement of rightist extremists, rightist intellectuals, super-patriots, fringe-group kooks, and conservative rank-and-file Republicans.

Among those in the movement was Robert Welch, leader of the rightist John Birch Society. Welch wrote in 1958, "I know Barry fairly well. He is a great American—I raised around $2,000 in my state and sent it to him early in 1958. . . . He is absolutely superb in his Americanism. I'd love to see him President of the United States, and maybe someday we shall." He said later that, although he personally favored Goldwater for president, the society had taken no official position. Goldwater himself, while consistently denying he was a member of the Birch Society, refused repeatedly to repudiate the support of its members and at the 1964 national convention blocked any platform amendments repudiating extremist groups. Goldwater always saw far more danger to the country from the "radical left," mainly the Americans for Democratic Action, than from such "radical right" groups as the John Birch Society. In his 1958 Senate campaign, Goldwater accepted contributions from H. L. Hunt, an extremely conservative Dallas oilman, and from Americans for America, another right-wing group. He appeared several times on the Manion Forum, run by Clarence E. Manion, a former Notre Dame Law School dean, which fought the "confiscatory, Marxist income tax" and other wickedness. Several right-wing groups tried to promote Goldwater for the presidential nomination in 1960.

It was natural that such people would turn to Goldwater. He had been one of the staunchest supporters of Senator Joseph McCarthy, and although he privately advised McCarthy to apologize to several senators to avoid censure by the Senate, when the vote on censure came Goldwater voted against it. During the censure debate he said:

> Like him or not, McCarthy is the strongest voice now speaking in America against communism. . . . To remove such a man from honor and influence in America at this juncture would be a strong victory for Moscow in the field of American public opinion . . . [and] a propaganda triumph for the Attlees, the Mendes-Frances, and the double-talking co-existence-with-Russia crowd here at home, which could be incalculable in its consequences. . . . All the discredited and embittered figures of the Hiss–Yalta period of American dishonor have crawled out from under their logs to join the efforts to get even. The news columns and the airwaves have been filled with their pious talk about "civil liberties," "ethical codes," and "protection of the innocent," while at the same time these people have dipped into the smut pot to discredit Senator McCarthy and his work against communism.

After Senator McCarthy's death, Goldwater spoke emotionally to the Wisconsin Republican state convention: "Joe and I became friends long before either of us entered the Senate. . . . He was a faithful, tireless and conscientious American. Joe McCarthy gave himself—his life—to the service of his God and his country. . . . Because Joe McCarthy lived, we are a safer, freer, more vigilant nation today. This fact, even though he no longer dwells among us, will never perish." Goldwater's affection for McCarthy was grounded in his own strong anticommunism. He wrote in *Why Not Victory,* "Our objective must be the destruction of the enemy as an ideological force and the removal of Communists from power wherever they hold it." Opponents might point out that this would entail perpetual foreign wars and crusades for ideological ends; it was music to the ears of the John Birchers and others.

However, it was not the extremist groups that converted the movement into the effective political organization that captured control of the Republican Party in 1964. It was, rather, a handful of little-known, rank-and-file Republican backroom organization men. One was F. Clifton White, a public relations consultant from Rye, New York, who after World War II had become an important figure in New York Young Republican politics and a supporter of Governor Dewey. He developed into an expert political technician and became national chairman of the Young Republicans, an important post that he firmly held from 1950 to 1960. After the Dewey defeat in 1948, White began to drift toward conservatism; he broke with Rockefeller in a New York state contest in 1948, and Nixon's 1960 loss convinced him that the Republican Party needed a new kind of candidate—a conservative one. Others felt the same way—such men as John Grenier, an urbane, bright young Birmingham lawyer who became Alabama Republican state chairman, and Peter O'Donnell, a young, rich Texan, who soon became chairman of the Texas State Republican Party. They had the active support of various business executives.

On October 8, 1961, Clifton White and a score of his friends around the country met secretly in Chicago at the Avenue Motel to see whether it might be possible to seize control of the national Republican Party as White had seized the Young Republicans and then to nominate a conservative candidate who could bring out the full Republican vote in 1964. They decided to try, and White told Goldwater about the decision. Goldwater seemed indifferent but at the same time unwilling to repudiate the effort. They met again on December 10—this time a few more attended, including the governor of Montana—and divided the nation into nine regions, authorized White to open an office, and set out to raise sixty thousand dollars, all aimed at mobilizing conservatives. From his office in New York, White began traveling through the nation, talking with regional volunteer directors who also were being drawn to Goldwater. On August 24, 1962, White sent an unsigned and "confidential" memorandum to his select mailing list of conservatives around the country. The memorandum did not mention Goldwater's name, but it sounded notes of urgency and conspiracy: "There are four months left in 1962"; "We must be prepared to move into high gear in January of 1963"; "There are some of you from whom I have not heard since April. I am anxiously awaiting word as to your state of health." White had been in 28 states at least once. He reported "many encouraging signs": Hayes Robertson (an almost fanatic Goldwater man) had become Cook County (Chicago) chairman and had met congenially with White; White had attended a "highly successful" regional meeting in Phoenix; and a conservative county chairman had been elected in Allegheny County (Pittsburgh) in Pennsylvania and would meet shortly with White "to discuss his work and association with us." (The new Pittsburgh County chairman was an enthusiastic Goldwater man.)

This was the start of the underground movement to capture the Republican Party and hand it over to Goldwater. Across the nation, few state and county Republican chairmen were aware of what was going on. They—and Goldwater, Rockefeller, Romney, Scranton, and nearly everyone else—were preoccupied with the 1962 midterm elections; White and his cabal wanted the presidency.

It was hard going, however. In October, again at Chicago and in the same motel, at a meeting so secret that

White did not mention it in his confidential memos, he and his associates discussed how to proceed in view of Goldwater's own unresponsiveness. Approached repeatedly, Goldwater had remained indifferent. Moreover, he was now praising Rockefeller. Conservative funds were drying up—White had been unable to attend the September convention in Phoenix of the National Federation of Republican Women for lack of money. They decided to go ahead anyway and hold a meeting of the entire underground organization in Chicago on December 1 and 2, 1962. White announced the plans in a confidential memorandum dated October 18: "This meeting will determine where we go—whether we are serious or dilettantes." It was held in downtown Chicago at the Essex Motor Inn, nearly 100 attended, and word of a "sinister" Draft-Goldwater movement finally leaked to the press. In fact, it leaked in such detail that White felt sure a tape recorder had been smuggled into the motel room. The cabal saw their prospects this way, according to one published account: solid Goldwater states—435 votes, mostly from Southern and Mountain states plus Indiana, Maine, Missouri, Nebraska, Oklahoma, Virginia, and Washington; "almost-as-solid" states—81 votes from Georgia, Kentucky, South Dakota, and Tennessee; states that could be won with extra effort—142 votes from Illinois, Iowa, Ohio; a total of 658 votes, plus 43 additional votes from split delegations in California, Connecticut, and Michigan, for a grand total of 701, more than enough to nominate. This seemed wildly optimistic at the time. White hoped that it would persuade Goldwater to run.

Instead, it dismayed him. Annoyed at the publicity, Goldwater told reporters he hoped the group would do nothing during 1963 and give him until January 1964 to make up his mind. He claimed, "I don't know who the group was, where they met or what it's all about. . . . I still plan to run for the Senate two years from now. . . . Things change, and it's too early to be absolutely certain." But a little later, Goldwater had already declared he would not run for the vice presidency, and said that as for the presidency:

> I'd rather stay in a fluid position for the rest of this year and then see how the situation looks. . . . Assume I am interested in the Presidency. It still makes more sense for me to delay. I've done my backroom work already. Nobody's been around the country more in the last ten years than I have. I know the county chairmen. I know the potential convention delegates. Rockefeller and Romney still have to meet those people, but they're already friends of mine. Another thing. I am the only conservative in the presidential picture. The others—Rockefeller, Rom-

ney, and Scranton—are liberals. You might say, "let them fight it out for awhile."

White called a highly secret meeting of the inner circle at the O'Hare Inn in Chicago for early 1963. They decided to surface and compete openly with Rockefeller, who at this time was ahead in all the polls. Peter O'Donnell, the Texas Republican state chairman, would head the effort in order to convince people that bona fide party leaders, not backroom conspirators, were in charge. And so on April 9, 1963, at a press conference in the Mayflower Hotel in Washington, D.C., O'Donnell publicly announced the formation of the National Draft Goldwater Committee. Then he and White uneasily awaited Goldwater's reaction. It came: "It's their time and their money. But they are going to have to get along without any help from me." This was all White and O'Donnell and the others needed. Soon they got more. On April 27, Goldwater, asked about the draft movement, said, "I've given up trying to stop it. It's like trying to stamp out a forest fire with your feet. It's coming up too many places, too often." He also commented when asked whether he was really running for president, "I'm doing all right just pooping around."

White, O'Donnell, and others planned a strategy to close the gap between Rockefeller and Goldwater. First, since they probably lacked time to round up enough solid Goldwater delegates to nominate him before the convention, they would try to encourage the candidacies of numerous favorite sons in order to deny delegates to Rockefeller. Second, they would propagandize to the press—and the Republican Party—to prove that Goldwater could win. This was the famous "southern strategy" set forth in Draft Goldwater Committee pamphlet. It conceded to President Kennedy, then considered the certain nominee of the Democrats, 14 states: New York, Massachusetts, Connecticut, Rhode Island, New Jersey, Delaware, West Virginia, Michigan, Minnesota, Missouri, Nevada, Oregon, Alaska, and Hawaii. It called California doubtful and claimed everything else. This would give Goldwater 301 electoral votes (270 were needed to win) and Kennedy 197. The pamphlet said, "Barry Goldwater will take all 128 electoral votes of the eleven Southern States! In 1964 Goldwater will give 'the solid South' dramatic new meaning! *This is the key to Republican success!*" To the South, Goldwater would add, "the dependable Republican states of the Midwest, Rocky Mountains, and Northern New England." Thus would he win. It was, as Robert D. Novak later observed, "revolutionary doctrine." Goldwater would concede several previously vital battlegrounds—New York, Pennsylvania, Michigan, California—on the assumption that Goldwater could do what no other Republican ever had done: sweep the South. He alone, the pamphlet said, could do it. Finally, White and

O'Donnell would promote the idea that Rockefeller could not win. They would show that Rockefeller's popularity in New York had declined because of his quarrels with the legislature and scandals in his administration. They even hired a polling firm to find out how Rockefeller would run against Kennedy in New York State, and the result showed Kennedy's victory by a landslide.

The attempt to cut down Rockefeller's commanding lead proved unnecessary because Rockefeller himself destroyed it that spring. On March 16, 1962, he had been divorced and on May 4, 1963, he remarried. His bride was Margaretta "Happy" Fitler Murphy. In April, before Rockefeller's remarriage, the Gallup Poll had shown that 43 percent of rank-and-file Republicans across the nation favored Rockefeller for the nomination and 26 percent favored Goldwater. A month later, after the wedding, Gallup found that Goldwater had pulled ahead of Rockefeller, 35 percent to 30 percent. Reporters soon were writing about "hysteria" over the marriage. Congressional mail was running violently against Rockefeller, they said. Clergymen took up the moral outcry, much of which concerned the new Mrs. Rockefeller's four young children by her previous marriage. The question of their custody had not been settled before her divorce from her former husband. Republican politicians heretofore friendly to Rockefeller began to desert him. Rovere has suggested that they never really supported him wholeheartedly and only wanted an excuse to desert. Saying that Rockefeller's remarriage doomed him politically helped make it so.

About this same time, the civil rights revolution had begun in Birmingham and soon was spreading across the South and into the Northern cities. White backlash in the North and the "southern strategy" in the South were Goldwater's meat and potatoes. By the summer of 1963, Goldwater was unquestionably the leading contender for the Republican nomination. Goldwater, who had been chairman of the Republican Senatorial Campaign Committee from 1955 to 1963, had crisscrossed the United States innumerable times, speaking to the state chairmen, the county chairmen, the precinct captains, and the party money men. He knew them all, as he often pointed out. Now on September 1, he announced a two-month schedule of speaking engagements in 10 states. He had already said he would decide by January whether to be a candidate. "I'm playing this thing by ear day by day. I wouldn't want to say 'yes' or 'no' now, because I think it's much too early." He added that any candidate interested in the nomination should enter next spring's primaries.

It seemed almost certain that Goldwater intended to run. He hardly needed the 23-man "advisory committee" headed by the reactionary former Senate majority leader, William F. Knowland of California, to help him decide whether to enter the California primary of 1964.

Denison Kitchel, Goldwater's old Arizona campaign strategist, moved to Washington and set up coordinating headquarters in October. By then, Goldwater supporters were claiming 500 solid delegates and 82 more leaning to him. White had already undertaken a purge of extremists from the volunteer organization, for Kitchel decided that Goldwater, now about to become a serious candidate, would have a problem with extremists. The regional volunteers had formal organizations in 32 states. Indeed, in South Carolina the official state Republican committee passed a resolution declaring that it was now reconstituted as the state's Draft Goldwater Committee; and in several other states matters were moving in that direction. On October 24, Goldwater said he would accept the nomination if it were offered. On November 7, Rockefeller announced he would seek the nomination and would enter the March 10 New Hampshire primary. At a Republican leadership conference in Charleston, South Carolina, most delegates expressed a strong preference for Goldwater, and the Republican national chairman, William E. Miller, said Goldwater could sweep the South in 1964. Then, on November 22, President Kennedy was assassinated.

Goldwater announced, on December 5, that he was reassessing his position. The accession of a Southerner, Lyndon Johnson, undermined Goldwater's whole "southern strategy." Beyond politics, however, Goldwater, though opposed to President Kennedy, had liked him. He fondly recalled that once in 1961, waiting for the president in his inner Oval Office, he sat down in the president's rocking chair, as though to test it. Kennedy, finding him there, had asked, "Do you want this job?" and Goldwater had replied, "No, not in my right mind," and Kennedy had said, "I thought I had a good thing going up to this point." After the assassination, Goldwater was hurt by abusive letters from people who blamed the president's death on right-wing elements.

Goldwater's backers asked him on December 5 to make up his mind—if he was to enter the New Hampshire primary, they had to get started. He asked for a few more days. They met again, but still he gave no definite answer, though they talked more of tactics than of whether he would run. By mid-December his managers were sure he would enter the New Hampshire primary against Rockefeller. Goldwater himself made it official, announcing that he would seek the nomination.

Unlike the primary elections of other years, those of 1964 were not decisive. The most important ones were, in order, New Hampshire, Oregon, and California, and even these were inconclusive.

In New Hampshire, Rockefeller seemed to encounter mistrust because he was a New York liberal, a governor of a big state with a reputation for big spending, and a

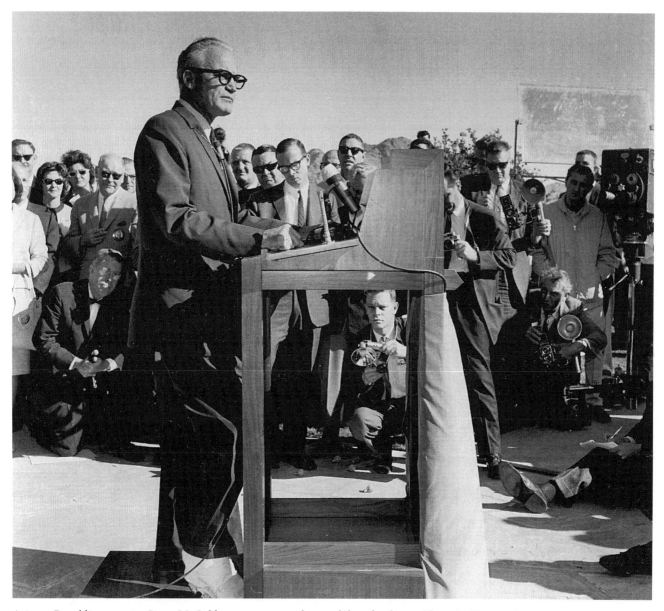

Arizona Republican senator Barry M. Goldwater announces his candidacy for the presidency in Phoenix, Arizona, January 3, 1964. The senator is wearing a cast on his right foot. *(Associated Press)*

divorced and remarried man. But Goldwater did worse. He frightened the voters half to death by calling American missiles "undependable," urging that Social Security be made voluntary (in a state that had a higher percentage of the elderly than all but three others), denounced the U.N. (New Hampshire is extremely proud of its attachment to the U.N.), declared that government couldn't stop depressions and shouldn't aid education (to an audience of students), advocated "carrying the war to North Viet Nam," and declared that the United States should send the Marines to Guantanamo to turn on the water that Castro had cut off. It was pure Goldwater, off the cuff, and Rockefeller, battling uphill for his political life, used it all mercilessly against him. Theodore H. White wrote

later, "It was Rockefeller, of course, who destroyed Goldwater—not out of malice but, at this stage, out of the need of his own campaign to score through on New Hampshire conservatives."

In the end, neither Rockefeller nor Goldwater won in New Hampshire—a write-in candidate, Henry Cabot Lodge, who spent the primary in the U.S. Embassy in Saigon, swept New Hampshire on March 10 with 35.3 percent of the vote to 23 percent for Goldwater and a little less for Rockefeller. Clearly, neither Rockefeller nor Goldwater had pleased New Hampshire's Republicans, who had turned to someone they thought they knew and could trust. This search by the Republicans for a *Republican* solution to their problem—not an outside movement's solution—was to continue through the summer and even into the fall.

Oregon was next. Goldwater, hurt in New Hampshire, decided not to campaign there but, rather, to concentrate on crucial California, the last big primary. Oregon citizens voted on May 15. Rockefeller won with 33 percent of the vote, Lodge was second with 27.7 percent. Goldwater was third with 17.6 percent.

In California, the primary was only two weeks away. Lodge threw his support to Rockefeller, hoping to stop Goldwater. Eisenhower released a statement describing the candidate he hoped would be nominated; it was interpreted as excluding Goldwater, which Eisenhower quickly denied. The polls indicated Rockefeller was ahead in California, but California is a peculiar state, perhaps the most difficult in the union for a politician, and even more difficult in a primary than in a general election. California, an empire in itself, is almost too big to get hold of. It contains everything: endless acres of suburbs sheltering rootless people, the "little old ladies in tennis shoes," the bearded students on campuses, blacks and Mexican-Americans, transplanted Arkansas, Oklahoma, and Texas farmers, fractured labor unions, innumerable power centers, an industrial-military complex around San Diego, and a political system whose legal structure makes organization, or machine, politics all but impossible. California politics is unstable, its electorate volatile, and nobody can count on much of anything in California.

Both Rockefeller and Goldwater threw their best men into California. Both organized excellent campaigns. In addition, Goldwater had his fanatic volunteers ringing doorbells. Rockefeller's managers went after Goldwater hard, mailing out a pamphlet entitled "Who Do You Want in the Room with the H-Bomb?" and widely distributing Goldwater quotes intended to picture him as an irresponsible bomber and enemy of Social Security. Nevertheless, Goldwater won. When California Republicans voted on June 2, they gave Goldwater 51.4 percent of their votes—and 86 delegate votes.

Still and all, the primaries had hardly been conclusive. Lodge had won one, Rockefeller had won one, and now Goldwater had won one. The rank-and-file Republican voters had given their convention no clear mandate. All spring, while public attention had been focused on these primaries, something else had been going on. The capture of the Republican Party by Goldwater's men proved decisive. It had begun, as we have seen, in 1961 with the meetings of Clifton White's men. Their loyalty was not primarily to the Republican Party; some of their financial backers were Southwest speculators, former Democrats, with no tradition of Republicanism. The loyalty of the men of this underground was to themselves and to the

conservative ideas they believed in. They transferred this loyalty to Goldwater and Goldwaterism.

They accomplished their objective quietly during the spring. They did it in precinct meetings, in county and state committee meetings, and in state conventions across the country. While others were watching New Hampshire, Oregon, and California, Clifton White and his men were watching—and operating in—other places on other dates. They got 25 of 26 delegates from North Carolina in district conventions early in February before the state convention met on February 28 and 29. They got all 22 delegates from Oklahoma at the state convention on February 29. They got 16 supporters for Goldwater from South Carolina on March 21. They got 2 new delegates on February 23 from the Fifth Congressional District of Georgia, which included Atlanta, previously a liberal stronghold. In the state of Washington, only 2,500 precincts out of 5,500 formerly had had Republican precinct organizations. Clifton White's men went to work, filled the rest of the precincts, and by the end of 1963, 65 percent of the state's precincts were controlled by Clifton White. Early in 1964, when the precinct caucuses were held in homes and apartments all over the state to choose delegates to the county conventions, which in turn would choose delegates to the state convention, which in turn would choose delegates to the national convention, the Goldwater people were in command. When in June the state convention met to select 24 national delegates, the Goldwater people elected at least 70 percent of them.

Such things were happening all over the country, especially in the South, the Midwest, and the West. On April 19, 1964, an Associated Press poll of GOP county chairmen and other Republican leaders reported that 526 thought Nixon the most likely nominee but said their personal preference was Goldwater. Goldwater won the Texas presidential primary with 75.3 percent of the vote, the Indiana primary with 67 percent, the Illinois presidential preference poll with 62 percent. He did not win them all: Scranton won the all-write-in Pennsylvania preference primary (Goldwater ran a poor fourth); Lodge won the all-write-in Massachusetts primary with 79.5 percent (Goldwater was second with 10.5 percent); and Rockefeller won the West Virginia primary (Goldwater was not entered). But by the time California voted, nearly everybody agreed that Goldwater had more than 500 delegate votes. With the exception of Champ Clark in 1912, no candidate in modern times has entered a national convention with so many votes and left it without the nomination. And by June 16, when the Texas convention gave Goldwater its 56 votes, the Associated Press estimated that he had 647 pledged

"BARRY'S THE CAPTAIN AND IF HE SAYS THIS IS
THE MAINSTREAM, THAT'S GOOD ENOUGH FOR ME"

This cartoon by John R. Fischetti shows Republican presidential candidate Barry Goldwater of Arizona steering a large group of supporters in a boat sailing down a narrow trickle of water surrounded on both sides by desert. Senator Goldwater and his backers insisted that there was a hidden majority of Republicans who supported his conservative views. *(Library of Congress)*

or favorable votes. The convention in San Francisco was less than a month away.

Almost immediately after the California primary, what looked like a stop-Goldwater movement began. Except for Lodge's managers, not one of the Easterners who opposed Goldwater had seen fit to give Rockefeller any help in his desperate fight in California. Now, faced with an imminent Goldwater coup engineered by his underground cabal, they suddenly stirred themselves, invoking "Republican principles." Seldom have men in high office, or men seeking it, or men recently freed from it, behaved more foolishly.

On Saturday, June 6, Governor Scranton saw former President Eisenhower at Gettysburg and emerged from a long talk with the impression that Eisenhower had urged him to challenge Goldwater for the nomination at the Conference of Governors, due to open on Monday in Cleveland. Scranton felt that if he did, Eisenhower would openly support him for the nomination. The governors gathered in Cleveland over the weekend, Republican governors frantic at the prospect of the Goldwater coup, Democratic governors watching from the sidelines,

vastly pleased. On Sunday, Governor Romney proposed to his fellow Republican governors a strong statement denouncing Goldwater; they discussed it at length. Governor Scranton arrived, prepared to announce his candidacy on a television interview show that same day, and was told that General Eisenhower was trying to reach him. He called Eisenhower, who cautioned that he hoped Scranton hadn't misunderstood him at Gettysburg. The newspapers were saying Eisenhower was supporting Scranton but, Eisenhower said, he could not lend his name to an anti-Goldwater move. Scranton must let his conscience be his guide. Scranton hastily assessed the situation among the governors, hoping to find them prepared to fall in line behind him. Instead, they were still debating Romney's proposed statement. Scranton departed for the TV studio but, in a miserable performance, failed to declare his candidacy or even to speak out against Goldwater. Romney, a determined if ineffective crusader, let loose his denunciation of Goldwater at a press conference. Rockefeller, in a sardonic mood, held a press conference, too. Asked if he felt that Scranton was displaying responsibility of leadership, he answered,

"Did you see him on television?" Scranton, returning to the conference, organized meeting after meeting, frantically seeking a candidate, and late that night the governors decided that Romney must be the man. Romney, however, had gone home. They telephoned him, and for two days they all squirmed, telephoned, held meetings, plotted strategies. Romney was informed he would be politically dead in Michigan if he broke his pledge to run for reelection. Herbert Brownell, Eisenhower's former attorney general and an old Dewey and Eisenhower campaign strategist, declined to manage a Romney campaign. So did Len Hall, another Eastern professional. Richard Nixon showed up in Cleveland long enough to get in trouble with everybody. The whole stop-Goldwater movement collapsed in utter confusion.

There was one more try. On June 12, two days after the governors' conference broke up, Governor Scranton suddenly announced his candidacy; then he set forth across the nation in a final flailing struggle to overcome Goldwater and his underground apparatus. To call the struggle uphill would be bad geography. It was up-cliffside, straight up, with nothing to latch onto. He had less than five weeks in which to campaign. Without campaign machinery, his personal staff lacked experience in national politics. And as Scranton began, Goldwater had, by the Associated Press's count, 540 first ballot votes, Rockefeller 128, Scranton 84, Lodge 45, Nixon 14, and others 109, with 204 uncommitted. Even as Rockefeller endorsed Scranton, the Texas convention gave Goldwater its 56 votes, bringing his strength to 647, by AP calculation, with 655 needed to nominate.

Yet Scranton persisted, traveling everywhere, appearing incessantly on television, visiting Republican leaders across the nation. He began to attract what looked like popular support, and Lodge hurried home from Saigon to help him. What was really happening became clear when Scranton appeared before the caucus of the Illinois delegation at O'Hare Inn in Chicago. He saw it cast 48 votes for Goldwater, 8 abstentions, 2 passes, and none for himself. Senate Majority Leader Everett McKinley Dirksen of Illinois announced he would put Goldwater's name in nomination at the convention.

The convention was to open in San Francisco at the Cow Palace on July 13. During the preceding days, Governor Rhodes of Ohio, who had promised Scranton that he would hold the Ohio delegation firmly for himself as a favorite son in order to help the stop-Goldwater cause, suddenly released his delegation, and most of it went to Goldwater. Scranton knew then it was hopeless, but in San Francisco he continued his quixotic fight and, over the weekend before the convention opened, met with the Eastern party leaders. The Platform Committee was clearly in Goldwater's control. Scranton's support-

ers decided to make a floor fight to get a stronger civil rights plank and two additional planks—one condemning extremist groups and the other pledging continued presidential control of the use of nuclear weapons. They hoped to get Eisenhower's support on the nuclear issue, and for a few hours after the old general arrived in San Francisco, they thought they had it. Then Eisenhower reaffirmed his neutrality. He claimed a former president should not discuss secret nuclear policy in public politics. Goldwater called on him, and subsequently Eisenhower said he would campaign for Goldwater if he were nominated and expressed general approval of the platform draft. Scranton appeared before delegate caucuses and on television, trying to go over the Goldwater apparatus to the people and the rank-and-file delegates. A desperate member of his staff sent a letter to Goldwater, forging Scranton's name to it, which challenged Goldwater to debate and denounced him in furious language:

> Your organization . . . feel they have bought, beaten and compromised enough delegate support to make the result a foregone conclusion. With open contempt for the dignity, integrity and common sense of the convention, your managers say in effect that the delegates are little more than a flock of chickens whose necks will be wrung at will. . . .
>
> You have too often casually prescribed nuclear war as a solution to a troubled world.
>
> You have too often allowed the radical extremists to use you.
>
> You have too often stood for irresponsibility in the serious question of racial holocaust.
>
> You have too often read Taft and Eisenhower and Lincoln out of the Republican Party.
>
> In short, Goldwaterism has come to stand for a whole crazy-quilt of absurd and dangerous positions that will be soundly repudiated by the American people in November.

Goldwater, of course, refused to debate and said, accurately, that Scranton himself probably had not written the letter. In a TV interview, Scranton concurred but said he would stand by its contents. As Theodore White wrote later, "[The letter] made the Republican Convention the stage for the destruction of the leading Republican candidate. What Rockefeller had begun in spring, Scranton finished in June and at the Convention: the painting for the American people of a half-crazed leader indifferent to the needs of American society at home and eager to plunge the nation into war abroad."

Goldwater's managers, and Goldwater himself, confirmed the image at the convention. Many of his delegates were attending their first convention. They were not kooks, but the galleries were full of kooks. They were well dressed, but they were not run-of-the-mill professional politicians; the spirit of compromise was alien to them. At every turning point in the convention, the delegates made it plain that they were not out for mere political victory; they wanted total ideological victory and total annihilation of those who opposed them. Governor Romney proposed a civil rights amendment that could not have embarrassed Goldwater and might indeed have come from his platform committee; since it came from Romney, and was supported by Rockefeller and Lodge and Scranton, the Goldwater legions hooted it down. They were told that other platform amendments renouncing extremist groups would make it easier to carry Northern industrial states. The delegates could not have cared less, for they were determined to do nothing to offend the John Birch Society. (Its lobbyist claimed that 100 delegates belonged to the society.) When Rockefeller tried to speak, they booed him. He taunted them; the galleries raged at him, and the delegates squashed his proposals. With the hall in explosive tumult, Rockefeller said, "These things have no place in America. But I can personally testify to their existence. And so can countless others who have also experienced anonymous midnight and early morning telephone calls, unsigned threatening letters, smear and hate literature, strong-arm and goon tactics, bomb threats and bombings, infiltration and take-over of established political organizations by Communist and Nazi methods." The galleries roared at him and he said, "Some of you don't like to hear it, ladies and gentlemen, but it's the truth." As they booed and yelled, all America saw a spectacle on television that could only be described as one of savage fury. The delegates got their platform, and they got their candidate, too. Goldwater was nominated on the first ballot when the roll call reached South Carolina, giving him 663 votes, 8 more than needed. He picked as his vice-presidential candidate William E. Miller, an upstate New York congressman and Republican national chairman, unknown except to Republican Party workers, and a man whose views, far from balancing the ticket, were considered to parallel Goldwater's own.

All day after Goldwater's nomination, Eisenhower waited in his hotel suite; Goldwater did not call him. Instead, he held his first press conference as his party's nominee. He called President Johnson "the greatest faker in the United States . . . the phoniest individual that ever came around." He also struck a new note, and seemed to find a handle on the explosive race issue. General Eisenhower, in a speech to the convention, had already suggested it when he said, "Let us not be guilty of maudlin sympathy for the criminal who, roaming the streets with switchblade knife and illegal firearms seeking a help-

less prey, suddenly becomes upon apprehension a poor, underprivileged person who counts upon the compassion of our society and the laxness or weaknesses of too many courts to forgive his offense." Now at his press conference Goldwater put crime in the cities second only to foreign policy as an issue. He told the press, "I think the responsibility for this has to start some place, and it should start at the federal level with the federal courts enforcing the law. . . . As President, I'm going to do all I can to see that women can go out in the streets of this country without being scared stiff." He sounded the theme again that night in his acceptance speech, listing "violence in our streets" as the number-two issue.

He also did something more in his acceptance speech. Two sentences, both underlined, defiantly drove the final nail into the heart of the liberal wing of the Republican Party and into the heart of Republican political pragmatism, ending any possibility of unity: *"I would remind you that extremism in the defense of liberty is no vice. And let me remind you that moderation in the pursuit of justice is no virtue."* "I like that," Goldwater is reported to have said when he came upon it in the ghostwritten speech. Governor Rockefeller thought the passage "frightening." So did many other people. Goldwater heard that general Eisenhower was upset and made the single conciliatory gesture of the convention. He visited Eisenhower and explained that when the general had led the invasion of Normandy, he had been behaving like an extremist.

The convention was over. Goldwater and his men set forth to do battle. They had gotten everything they wanted, everything they had worked for since 1960. They had also taken a stand on the race issue. Goldwater, himself no racist, had said he had opposed the civil rights bill only because he thought two sections of it usurped states' rights. He had said repeatedly that he hoped the question of race could be kept out of the campaign. Nonetheless, he had accepted the support of racists and segregationists of the most extreme sort. He wanted to hold those people; they were crucial to his "southern strategy." Goldwater wanted votes in the industrial North, too, and the best place to look for them was in the white backlash against blacks in Northern cities. Earlier he had said he would not seek those votes either, because that would be racism. Now Goldwater—or Eisenhower, or someone who wrote speeches for one or the other of them—had suddenly found a way to seek backlash votes without ever mentioning "blacks" or "Negroes." Even Northern whites who favored school desegregation feared the newly militant blacks on the streets of the great cities. Crime was rising—though it was always rising—and blacks were blamed by fearful whites. Goldwater would now play on those fears. He would seek Northern backlash votes by talking about "morality," "law and order," and "violence in the streets." What he could do about it if elected president was not clear. How he squared federal intervention in local law enforcement with his states' rights doctrine was not clear either. This did not matter—he had found a stand on the race issue that would not drive away his Southern segregationist supporters and might attract fearful voters in the Northern industrial cities. It was a position he would use throughout the campaign, and one that Richard Nixon would use, with more success, four years later. The campaign that had begun as an underground cabal had found at last a code word for racism.

The situation of the Democratic Party in 1964 was far simpler than that of the Republican Party and needs only a brief description. In the days following the shattering events of Dallas on November 22, 1963, a dazed nation felt that Lyndon Johnson had somehow saved it, saved it by a single phrase in his speech to the Congress, "Let us continue." President Kennedy, in his inaugural address had said, "Let us begin." Johnson's sentence, pledging allegiance to the martyred president's program and ideals, summoning American unity, somehow seemed to help

heal the wounds. In the weeks that followed, the nation looked to him for help as he looked to the nation for *consensus,* his favorite word. Lyndon Johnson really did want to be, as he often said, the president of all the people, and for a time, he really was.

President Kennedy had been assassinated less than a year before the next election. President Johnson had to hold his consensus together for less than a year to be elected in his own right, and he succeeded. True, during the eight months between the assassination and the Democratic convention, small clouds appeared on his horizon. A number of President Kennedy's key aides resigned. To avoid being forced to take Attorney General Robert F. Kennedy as his vice-presidential candidate, President Johnson was obliged to announce that no member of his cabinet, nor anyone who sat regularly with it, would be considered. A new coup occurred in Vietnam. Black rioting began in the cities. George Wallace, the segregationist governor of Alabama, polled a surprisingly big vote in the Indiana Democratic primary, principally white backlash votes. Aware that his every

Barry Goldwater waves to delegates at the Republican National Convention in San Francisco, July 16, 1964. *(Associated Press)*

move was compared with "what Kennedy would have done," President Johnson seemed at times uncertain. It seemed that he felt he was, somehow, a usurper in his own White House. Comparisons of his "style" with Kennedy's hurt him. People talked about his vulgar idiom, his habit of swimming nude, his dislike of intellectuals and of long position papers and analyses. And the more President Johnson attempted to hold the grip on the American imagination that John F. Kennedy had held, the more he repelled those whose imaginations Kennedy had held most firmly.

Lyndon Johnson was a vain, proud, insecure man. He required loyalty, even servility. Sensitive almost to the point of paranoia, he could charm and he could bully. He had lusted for power and had gotten it. Johnson was a master at senatorial politics and palace politics, and in his first months as president, he seemed a master, too, of national politics, an entirely different skill. He seemed a man able to weld a true national purpose, but as later events proved, he had only the loosest grasp on national politics, especially of the national mood, purpose, and will. In the end, this defeated him.

Much of this was muted in the spring of 1964. The Congress gave him just about everything he asked for, including the sweeping Civil Rights Act that Kennedy had been unable to get passed and that Goldwater opposed. The nation was prosperous as never before. He asked the Congress to join him in declaring war on poverty, and the Congress assented. He asked the Congress to authorize him, in the Tonkin Gulf Resolution, to "take all necessary measures" to defend American forces and to "prevent further aggression" in Southeast Asia, and the Congress did. This last statement resulted from attacks on U.S. destroyers in the Gulf of Tonkin off Vietnam on August 2 and 4, just after the Republican convention and just before the Democrats met. President Johnson responded with a bold, precise, and carefully limited counterattack on North Vietnam torpedo boat bases. His restraint was used throughout the campaign to contrast with what Democrats called Goldwater's rashness. Richard Rovere has suggested that the Tonkin Gulf incident was linked to Goldwater's nomination and that the administration, wishing to demonstrate its own restraint and firmness, had "declared the existence of a major crisis before it knew that one existed." By and large, by the time the Democrats convened at Atlantic City on August 24, their prospects, and Lyndon Johnson's, never looked better.

It was Johnson's convention all the way. The platform emphasized Johnson's new theme of the "Great Society." It proclaimed "war on poverty," and declared, "America is *One Nation, One People*. . . . Accordingly, we offer this platform as a covenant of unity. . . . We offer as the goal of this covenant PEACE for all nations and FREEDOM

In 1964 Congress passed the Civil Rights Act proposed by the late President Kennedy. President Johnson signed it into law during a ceremony in the East Room of the White House on July 2, 1964. *(Library of Congress)*

for all peoples." The platform was far more moderate, far less militantly liberal, than that of 1960, for this was a Johnson, not a Kennedy, platform, and Johnson wanted a tent big enough for all Americans to gather under. The platform stated that "the world is closer to peace today than it was in 1960" and that the nation had enjoyed "forty-two months of uninterrupted [economic] expansion under Presidents Kennedy and Johnson . . . the longest and strongest peacetime prosperity in modern history." It pledged "enforcement" of the Civil Rights Act (as opposed to the "full implementation and faithful execution" promised in the Republican platform). It insisted that control of nuclear weapons remain in the hands of the president alone, and condemned "extremism, whether from the right or left, including the extreme tactics of such organizations as the Communist Party, the Ku Klux Klan and the John Birch Society."

The convention was one of the dullest in recent memory. The only moments of true drama came in a conflict over the seating of the Mississippi delegation. The regular all-white delegation was challenged by an insurgent, largely black "Mississippi Freedom Democratic Party." A compromise gave the rebels two convention seats at-large and, more importantly, established an antidiscrimination requirement for party groups naming delegates to future conventions. Both insurgents and regulars, however, rejected the compromise. In an effort to generate more drama, President Johnson toyed with various aspirants to the vice-presidential nomination, toyed with them—and with the press—publicly and for days. Then, at the last moment, he went before the convention himself shortly after his own nomination and "recommended" that the convention nominate Senator Hubert H. Humphrey of Minnesota for vice president. It did. In their acceptance speeches, Johnson and Humphrey worked hard to pre-empt the middle ground of American politics. Johnson called the Democrats "a party for all Americans," and Humphrey urged Republicans to join them because their own party had been captured by men who had made it a party "of stridency, of unrestrained passion, of extreme and radical language."

It was Lyndon Johnson's convention, except for one brief moment on the last day, when Robert F. Kennedy, after standing more than 20 minutes before the convention unable to speak because of the applause and cheers of the multitude, evoked his brother's memory with a speech that ended with a quotation from *Romeo and Juliet*:

> when he shall die
> Take him and cut him out in little stars,
> And he will make the face of heav'n so fine
> That all the world will be in love with Night
> And pay no worship to the garish Sun.

After that, a film in memoriam to John Kennedy was shown; the delegates and galleries wept. Johnson's managers, however, had made sure the speech would be made and the film shown only after the nominations were over.

After the extraordinary coup at San Francisco, and after the performance of President Johnson in his first months in office, the campaign itself was an anticlimax. From the moment it began to the end, with a single brief interruption in mid-October, just about everybody knew who would win.

Barry Goldwater and his managers had hoped to raise and seriously debate the most fundamental issues of American policy, and, in doing so, to give the voters, as his people put it, "a choice, not an echo." They wanted the voter to make a clear-cut decision between two sets of policies, even between two theories of government. In foreign affairs, they tried to make a case for "victory" over, not accommodation with, international communism. At home, they wanted to argue against federal intervention in civil rights, linking it with violence in the streets, and morality; to question the quality of American life; to decry the increase in crime and alcoholic consumption,

and (as they saw it) sexual immorality, including homosexuality. They had hoped to crusade successfully against all aspects of big centralized government, including its tendency, in a computerized world, to reduce individuals to numbers.

Somehow it all came out wrong. And the man responsible was, by and large, Barry Goldwater himself, with assistance from Johnson and his strategists.

Concerning the crusade against Communism, Goldwater had said in Hartford in 1963 that American ground forces in Europe could probably be cut by at least a third if NATO commanders in Europe had the power to use tactical nuclear weapons on their own initiative. The Johnson people handled this extremely complicated question simply. They "hung the bomb around Goldwater's neck," as one put it, and put a one-minute spot on national television, showing a little girl picking petals from a daisy, counting them. The film then faded to a countdown at an atomic testing site, and the entire scene dissolved in a mushroom cloud. Republicans, immediately aware their candidate had been badly, perhaps mortally, wounded, protested violently, and the spot was withdrawn—to be replaced by another, which showed another little girl licking an ice cream cone. In the background a voice explained strontium-90 and said that Goldwater was against the test ban treaty. Lyndon Johnson stood for peace, nuclear control, and military restraint, while other nationally known Democrats launched attacks on Goldwater that pictured him as the mad bomber prepared to permit "any second lieutenant" in NATO to loose holocaust upon the world. Thus, from the start, and during the cruel months of September and October, Goldwater was forever on the defensive on the issue he himself had given highest priority: victory over Communism.

Goldwater's second issue was, really, a complex of issues—morality and "crime in the streets." The Democrats feared this more than the rest, since nobody really knew how many backlash voters there were in the Northern cities, nor how many Goldwater could mobilize. If he succeeded here, he might hurt the Democrats badly.

But again, somehow he never made full use of the issue. Over and over he demanded, "What kind of country do we want to have?" and President Johnson replied, "The kind we've made it," and went on to talk about prosperity, progress in education, health, and welfare, and then prophesied the Great Society beyond the New Frontier. Goldwater's moral strictures soon began to sound preachy; he almost castigated Americans for their wickedness. Johnson simply said he thought America was a mighty fine place and Americans were mighty fine folks: "We're in favor of a lot of things, and we're against mighty few." Goldwater looked not only like the mad bomber, but like the half-crazed moral zealot.

This is the view President Lyndon Johnson and his guests had of the closing session of the Democratic convention in Atlantic City, August 27, 1964. Left to right: Ethel Kennedy and her husband, Robert F. Kennedy; Lady Bird Johnson, the president looking at the camera, Muriel Humphrey, Luci Baines Johnson, and Lynda Bird Johnson. *(John Rous/Associated Press)*

Goldwater's third issue, big government, was also extremely complicated, for indeed much of the bureaucratic apparatus appropriate to the Roosevelt days was obsolete. The Democrats stripped the question down to a single understandable statement: Barry Goldwater would do away with Social Security. He had never said exactly that, but he had come close enough to permit the attack. The Democrats put a spot on television showing a pair of hands tearing up a Social Security card; they showed it throughout the campaign, over and over. Johnson and other speakers hammered at the issue with the result that here, too, Goldwater was on the defensive, obliged to explain and re-explain what he had really said. The big-government issue never really went anywhere at all, and the great confrontation on policies never came off.

Both campaigns were technically well organized (or at least as well organized as so huge and confused an enterprise as a presidential campaign can be). Johnson had the edge—he was an incumbent, an enormous advantage, and, like any Democrat, he could command the aid of several state and big-city organizations plus that of aca-

demics and intellectuals experienced in politics. Moreover, he had with him a party that was, for the most part, united. In 1964, the year after President Kennedy's assassination, it was more united than at any time in its recent history. Goldwater, on the other hand, was badly hurt by the profound division in his own party, a division that had been deepened by himself and his fanatic followers and by their means of winning the nomination. In state after state, leader after leader of the Republican Party refused to appear with him, or appeared with him only perfunctorily. Senator Kenneth Keating of New York, whose reelection was strongly contested by Robert F. Kennedy, openly disassociated himself from the national ticket. So did Governor Romney, who even refused to appear on a platform with Goldwater. Senator Milton Young of North Dakota did the same. Charles Percy, running for governor of Illinois, boarded Goldwater's train for three joint whistlestop appearances, but by the end of September the Republican professionals knew it was all over—Ray Bliss, Ohio state chairman, said, "As things stand right now, we face another 1936, and any goddamn fool that doesn't believe it had better." Republican candidates everywhere scattered for cover and campaigned on their own. Democratic candidates, by contrast, went to inordinate lengths to clutch Lyndon Johnson's coattails.

At the outset, Goldwater's support had been deep but very narrow; he had to broaden it. Johnson's support, on the other hand, had been broad but quite shallow; he needed to deepen it. Neither man ever really succeeded. Goldwater scarcely tried; Johnson, however, did. Lyndon Johnson tried to keep his broad support because he wanted all the votes. He wished to win not only bigger than John Kennedy had won in 1960, but bigger than anybody had won ever. Moreover, he wanted people to vote for him, not against Goldwater; he wanted all the American people to vote for him because they loved him.

In these circumstances, it might be expected that it would be difficult to restrain Johnson from racing to his airplane to start campaigning the minute the convention ended. However, from the outset, Johnson's strategy for his own personal campaign—as distinguished from the campaigns of the National Committee, local organizations, labor unions, other speakers, the advertising agency's television operatives, and other battalions and divisions—and that of his senior advisers had been to "stay presidential," that is, remain in the White House running the country, above the battle, at least through September, and see whether Goldwater would beat himself. Johnson would then reassess his position and decide his October strategy. By and large, this is what he did. It was sensible; why raise issues when you're ahead?

Far more important, however, than a hoary political truism is the power of the incumbency. A president running for reelection need not race around the country shaking hands and making speeches in order to get his name in the paper. Everything a president does is news. The White House is constantly under TV lights and reporters' eyes. Thus, Johnson, on signing the Housing Act on September 2, permitted himself a few "remarks": "I believe that we have a commitment to assure every American an opportunity to live in a decent home, in a safe and a decent neighborhood." The same day, at the swearing in of a member of the Council of Economic Advisers, he again allowed himself a few words: "This summer, 72,400,000 Americans have been at work, more than have ever been at work in our history." The day his Medicare Bill passed the Senate, the president issued a statement: "The vote in the Senate was a victory not only for older Americans but for all Americans. . . . In a free and prosperous society there is no need for any person, especially the elderly, to suffer personal economic disaster and become a tragic burden upon loved ones or the State through major illness when, by prudently setting aside the employers and employees contributions this can be avoided." And so

on, almost daily throughout September, President Johnson uttered brief remarks on appropriate occasions. He signed the Wilderness Bill and the Land and Water Conservation Fund Bill. He signed the Nurse Training Act of 1964. He issued a statement on Labor Day and one about the North Pacific Fisheries Negotiations. He held press conferences, exchanged messages with the president of Brazil, expressed his sorrow at the death of a Finnish ambassador serving as a U.N. mediator in Cyprus, and received a report of his Committee for Traffic Safety. He flew to Florida and Georgia to inspect damage done by a hurricane, was photographed, and issued a statement. He presented the Medal of Freedom Awards and the Harmon International Aviation Trophies. There was almost no end to what he could do—and did. He made a few campaign speeches—greeted the National Independent Committee for Johnson and Humphrey in the Cabinet room at the White House, spoke to labor unions in Detroit, at a Democratic dinner in Harrisburg, at the convention of the

Campaign poster for Johnson and Humphrey *(Library of Congress)*

International Association of Machinists in Miami Beach, and inspected space facilities at Cape Kennedy. Johnson traveled to the far Southwest, to El Paso, to meet President López Mateos of Mexico and mark the settlement of the Chamizal dispute. He went to the Pacific Northwest to meet with Prime Minister Pearson of Canada to proclaim the Columbia River Treaty, and took occasion on the trip to stop over in Seattle and speak at a dinner honoring the "United States and Canadian Partnership in Progress." His subject that evening was the control of nuclear weapons, and he commented, "The release of nuclear weapons would come by Presidential decision alone." He also praised President Kennedy's efforts for nuclear control, declared he would work to avoid war by accident or miscalculation, and said he had worked to limit the spread of nuclear weapons. He added that the improvement of conventional weapons made unnecessary as well as unwise the use of "nuclear power to solve every problem," and pledged ceaseless work toward arms control. It was all aimed straight at Barry Goldwater's throat, but reading the text without knowledge of when it was delivered it seemed only a nonpolitical statement of American nuclear policy. Similar comments could be made of other speeches Johnson made that month: lofty, low-keyed, noncombative, above all presidential. Lyndon Johnson simply smothered Barry Goldwater.

The people were bored. One of the president's staff aides made a trip through the Midwest—which, Johnson strategists agreed, would be "the battleground"—and found that almost nobody was paying much attention to the campaign. Johnson's aide found a newspaper publisher who supported Goldwater who noted, "It's a cream puff campaign so far. There's no enthusiasm." A Democratic governor commented, "There's no fire in the campaign. They've made up their minds to vote against Goldwater. They admire Johnson, think he's safe, but they don't have the enthusiasm they had for Kennedy." A labor leader said, "There's no enthusiasm for either candidate." A cabdriver: "People don't like either candidate." A housewife: "People are afraid Goldwater will take Social Security away." The president's aide found that a few Democratic backlash votes seemed to be shifting to Goldwater, but he found the backlash far less important, even in Indiana, than anticipated. He believed that many Republican votes—and independent votes—would go to Johnson because, as one put it, "Goldwater scares people. The bomb." The old FDR coalition seemed broken by prosperity, Goldwater's warlike talk, and, to some extent, the backlash. Goldwater's best issue in the Midwest was racism. Johnson's was prosperity, plus the "don't-rock-the-boat" attitude. People did not trust Johnson personally, but they feared Goldwater. In conclusion, the president was informed

that people were saying, "It's a choice between a crook and a kook"; and he was advised to go to the streets and sidewalks of the nation, particularly the Midwest, and let the people see him as he really was.

Johnson did. Bullhorn in hand, he ploughed his way through enormous crowds in state after state, in city after city, stopping his motorcade to shake hands with frantic citizens, yelling at them, "Y'all come on down to the speakin.'" In Peoria and other Midwest towns, he talked pocketbook politics, telling the people how prosperous they were. Once in New Orleans he burst out with a quotation from an aging Southern senator who had said, "I would like to go back down there and make them one more Democratic speech. I just feel like I have one in me. The poor old State, they haven't heard a Democratic speech in thirty years. All they hear at election time is Negro, Negro, Negro!" In Providence and in Hartford, Johnson's crowds were enormous, bigger, Theodore H. White thought, than John Kennedy's had been in 1960. The people clutched at him; he stopped his motorcade and climbed up on the back seat of his limousine or stood on top of a closed car and grabbed a microphone or bullhorn and said, "I'm grateful to each one of you. About ten months ago there came this terrible tragedy and we lost our beloved President John F. Kennedy. Give me your help, your hand, your prayers, and I'll do the best job I can as your President." Sometimes he invited them down to the inauguration. Sometimes he demanded, repeatedly, whether they intended to vote Democratic. And sometimes he gave them a speech straight out of his Texas Populist past. He loved it. And in those warm October days they loved him; Johnson seemed certain to get every vote there was.

Then a news story broke that threatened Lyndon Johnson's entire campaign and future. One of his closest White House aides, and one who had been with him longest, Walter Jenkins, had been arrested a week earlier with a homosexual in the basement of the Washington YMCA and charged with disorderly conduct. The Republican National Committee, at least two newspapers supporting Goldwater (the *Chicago Tribune* and the Cincinnati *Enquirer*), and Goldwater himself had heard about it, but said nothing. On Wednesday, October 14, the Washington *Star* called Jenkins to ask if the story was true. Jenkins went to Abe Fortas, a close friend and senior advisor to President Johnson, and Fortas consulted Clark Clifford, another close friend and senior adviser. Together they tried to persuade Washington editors not to print the story on grounds of humanitarianism. Jenkins, a husband and father, was hospitalized, but the United Press International sent the story over its wires. That night the West Wing of the White House was alternately pandemonium and a wake, as staff aides and advisers talked about, as one put it, "how to save the election." What had looked like a landslide suddenly promised to be a debacle. This issue played straight into the hands of Goldwater. He had been focusing on the morality issue all along, sometimes coming close to attacking the president's morals, something his more extreme supporters had done with relish. Throughout the campaign, hate literature aimed at Johnson, some of it produced in Texas, circulated widely throughout the country. The underground campaign was one of the dirtiest of the century. Moreover, years ago, Senator Joseph McCarthy had warned against permitting homosexuals to have access to classified documents, since they were vulnerable to blackmail. Had Jenkins had such access? One would assume so. The issue was fearful because its effects were so hard to gauge.

Jenkins, of course, resigned, but this solved nothing. What mattered was the national security—had it been compromised? Johnson, in Washington at the Al Smith dinner, consulted with Abe Fortas by telephone and ordered an FBI investigation. Then he ordered a pollster to find out quickly and quietly how many votes this would shift. Johnson's aides debated what he should do.

Nobody will ever know what effect the Jenkins affair might have had on the election's outcome, because three other events followed immediately. Within 48 hours, Nikita Khrushchev fell from power, the mainland Chinese exploded their first nuclear bomb, and the 13-year-old Tory government of England was voted out of office. The Jenkins case, as an important factor in this campaign, was over.

All election campaigns, or nearly all, are influenced by unexpected dramatic events outside the framework of the campaign itself. It is hard to recall so extraordinary a collision of events as those of mid-October in 1964. In all probability, Johnson would have been elected anyway, even with the Jenkins problem on his hands and without the help of the Soviets, the Red Chinese, and the British electorate. He might well have been elected by a lesser margin, however.

As it was, after having issued a brief statement on Jenkins, he could now devote days to CIA and Pentagon briefings on the significance of the Chinese bomb, and to discussions with State Department and other advisers on the Soviet Union and Great Britain. Once again he could become, not a candidate with a "deviant" aide but, simply, the president. And then, after that, once more the candidate, campaigning.

Johnson had already begun to make a few serious political speeches. At Johns Hopkins University he had reiterated America's determination "to defend freedom wherever it is attacked," warned against the unrestrained use of American nuclear power, and predicted the down-

Captioned "Maybe They Could Use an Experienced Politician," this Gib Crockett cartoon shows Soviet leader Nikita Khrushchev reading that the U.S. election scene is in turmoil and wondering if he might have a shot. Khrushchev fell from power on October 14, 1964. *(Library of Congress)*

fall of "the ancient enemies of mankind—disease, intolerance, illiteracy, and ignorance." On national television he had attacked head-on the Goldwater thesis (without naming Goldwater) that the government should withdraw from domestic affairs because it was "radical" and dangerous to prosperity and progress. He also denounced Goldwater's suggestions that we should consider using atomic weapons in Vietnam, breaking relations with Russia, and so on. All this was outside the mainstream of American foreign policy as established by both parties during the last 20 years and would gravely endanger the peace of the world.

Campaigning in New York, he heartily embraced Robert Kennedy and, as in earlier speeches, John F. Kennedy. To the Liberal Party, he attacked Goldwater doctrine briefly, but spent most of his time projecting the Great Society. He went on national television to report to the people on "recent events in Russia, China, and Great Britain," reassuring the people that the Soviet ambassador had informed him that Khrushchev's fall meant no change in basic foreign policy. Johnson said, "I told him that we intend to bury no one, and we do not intend to be buried." Goldwater, on the other hand, predicted that Khrushchev's fall portended a Soviet–China rapprochement. As to the Chinese nuclear device, the president claimed the United States would continue to support the limited test ban treaty, that China should sign it, and that he would work to end all nuclear tests and to stop nuclear proliferation. As for Great Britain, "We congratulate the winners. We send warm regards to the losers. The friendship of our two nations goes on. . . . This has been an eventful week in the affairs of the world." For the rest of the campaign Johnson concentrated on the great issue of war or peace, pledging, among other things, "no wider war" in Southeast Asia.

Goldwater was swinging wildly—pulling out a copy of the Communist *Worker* to belabor the Democrats for accepting Communist support, hardly a great issue in this election. He held a big rally in Madison Square Garden, whistle-stopped through the Midwest, then headed west to Cheyenne, Las Vegas, Tucson, and Los Angeles. He went home to sleep in Phoenix, then off to Texas and South Carolina. On the final day before the election, he went to San Francisco, but he was weary, and so were his listeners. At San Francisco he made—and said he was making—the same speech with which he had opened his campaign. "The issues have not changed. I have not changed. The challenge and the choice has not changed." However, all of them had, really. The issues—victory, big government, morality—which had sounded so good a year or so ago in the locker room of the Camelback Inn in Arizona had not sounded nearly so good on national television. Goldwater himself may not have changed, but the kind of campaign he had been obliged to make—and which had been made for him—had certainly changed. As for the challenge and the choice, the challenge had hardly been made, the choice hardly presented. It was all rather sad.

The result was a Johnson landslide. Johnson carried 44 states and the District of Columbia, with 486 electoral votes; Goldwater won only 6 states with 52 electoral votes. Johnson received 43,129,040 votes, or 61.0 percent of the total vote cast (compared to 60.7 percent for Roosevelt in 1936); Goldwater got 27,175,754 (Johnson's percentage of the total two-party vote was slightly less than FDR's and, for that matter, less than Harding's in 1920), and won only his own Arizona and five Deep South states: Alabama, Georgia, Louisiana, Mississippi, and South Carolina. Johnson carried New York by more than 2 million, Michigan, Ohio, and California by more than a million each, and Illinois by almost a million.

What had happened? The country, still in shock after President Kennedy's assassination, had drawn together. Many voted for Johnson because they could not vote for Kennedy. Many voted less for Johnson than against Goldwater. Goldwater had frightened them. Goldwater—and the extremism of the right-wing movement—had beaten himself. The great conservative crusade of 1964 had begun with a proud slogan: "In Your Heart You Know He's Right." Democrats had responded with a jeer: "In Your Guts You Know He's Nuts." Together they composed a fitting epitaph on the 1964 campaign.

—*John Bartlow Martin*

Selected Bibliography

Theodore H. White, *The Making of the President 1964* (1965), is an excellent summary. Two fine accounts are Herbert E. Alexander, *Financing the 1964 Election* (1966); and Gary Donaldson, *Liberalism's Last Hurrah: The Presidential Campaign of 1964* (2003). The best biography of Lyndon Johnson is Robert Dallek, *Flawed Giant: Lyndon Johnson and His Times, 1961–1973* (1998). Robert David Johnson, *All the Way with LBJ: The 1964 Presidential Election* (2009), is a particularly good and resonant campaign monograph, as is J. William Middendorf II, *A Glorious Disaster: Barry Goldwater's Presidential Campaign and the Origins of the Conservative Movement* (2006). Rick Perlstein, *Before the Storm: Barry Goldwater and the Unmaking of the American Consensus* (2001), puts 1964 in broad historical context.

The views of Senator Goldwater are set forth in his books: *The Conscience of a Conservative* (1960), *Why Not Victory?* (1962), and *Where I Stand* (1964). President Johnson's views were set forth in various tracts, though the definitive texts are in the *Public Papers of the Presidents of the United States: Lyndon B. Johnson, 1963–1964* (2 vols.). Phyllis Schlafly, *A Choice Not an Echo* (1964), presented the Goldwater view of Republicanism. Her book was widely circulated during the campaign. The *New York Times* published a useful *Election Handbook* (1964). See Eric Goldman, *The Tragedy of Lyndon Johnson* (1969); Sam Houston Johnson, *My Brother, Lyndon* (1970); Richard Rovere, *The Goldwater Caper* (1965); Clifton White, *Suite 3505: The Story of the Draft Goldwater Movement* (1967); and Richard Hofstadter, "Goldwater and Pseudo-Conservative Politics," in *The Paranoid Style in American Politics and Other Essays* (1967). Herbert Alexander discusses campaign costs in *Financing the 1964 Election* (1966). See also Vaughn Davis Bornet, *The Presidency of Lyndon B. Johnson* (1983); Milton C. Cummings Jr., *The Presidential Election of 1964* (1966); Karl A. Lamb and Paul A. Smith, *Campaign Decision-Making: The Presidential Election of 1964* (1968); and Lionel Lokos, *Hysteria 1964: The Fear Campaign against Barry Goldwater* (1967).

1964 ELECTION STATISTICS

State	Number of Electors	Total Popular Vote	Elec Vote D	Elec Vote R	Pop Vote D	Pop Vote R	Margin of Victory Votes	Margin of Victory % Total Vote
Alabama	10	689,817		10	-	1	268,353	38.90%
Alaska	3	67,259	3		1	2	21,399	31.82%
Arizona	5	480,770		5	2	1	4,782	0.99%
Arkansas	6	560,426	6		1	2	70,933	12.66%
California	40	7,057,586	40		1	2	1,292,769	18.32%
Colorado	6	776,986	6		1	2	179,257	23.07%
Connecticut	8	1,218,578	8		1	2	435,273	35.72%
Delaware	3	201,320	3		1	2	44,626	22.17%
District of Columbia	3	198,597	3		1	2	140,995	71.00%
Florida	14	1,854,481	14		1	2	42,599	2.30%
Georgia	12	1,139,336		12	2	1	94,027	8.25%
Hawaii	4	207,271	4		1	2	119,227	57.52%
Idaho	4	292,477	4		1	2	5,363	1.83%
Illinois	26	4,702,841	26		1	2	890,887	18.94%
Indiana	13	2,091,606	13		1	2	259,730	12.42%
Iowa	9	1,184,539	9		1	2	283,882	23.97%
Kansas	7	857,901	7		1	2	77,449	9.03%
Kentucky	9	1,046,105	9		1	2	296,682	28.36%
Louisiana	10	896,293		10	2	1	122,157	13.63%
Maine	4	381,221	4		1	2	143,563	37.66%
Maryland	10	1,116,457	10		1	2	345,417	30.94%
Massachusetts	14	2,344,798	14		1	2	1,236,695	52.74%
Michigan	21	3,203,102	21		1	2	1,076,463	33.61%
Minnesota	10	1,554,462	10		1	2	431,493	27.76%
Mississippi	7	409,146		7	2	1	303,910	74.28%
Missouri	12	1,817,879	12		1	2	510,809	28.10%
Montana	4	278,628	4		1	2	51,214	18.38%
Nebraska	5	584,154	5		1	2	30,460	5.21%
Nevada	3	135,433	3		1	2	23,245	17.16%
New Hampshire	4	288,093	4		1	2	80,035	27.78%
New Jersey	17	2,846,770	17		1	2	903,828	31.75%
New Mexico	4	327,615	4		1	2	62,179	18.98%
New York	43	7,166,015	43		1	2	2,669,597	37.25%
North Carolina	13	1,424,983	13		1	2	175,295	12.30%
North Dakota	4	258,389	4		1	2	41,577	16.09%
Ohio	26	3,969,196	26		1	2	1,027,466	25.89%
Oklahoma	8	932,499	8		1	2	107,169	11.49%
Oregon	6	786,305	6		1	2	218,238	27.75%
Pennsylvania	29	4,822,690	29		1	2	1,457,297	30.22%
Rhode Island	4	390,091	4		1	2	240,848	61.74%
South Carolina	8	524,756		8	2	1	93,348	17.79%
South Dakota	4	293,118	4		1	2	32,902	11.22%
Tennessee	11	1,143,946	11		1	2	125,982	11.01%
Texas	25	2,626,811	25		1	2	704,619	26.82%
Utah	4	400,310	4		1	2	38,946	9.73%
Vermont	3	163,089	3		1	2	53,185	32.61%
Virginia	12	1,042,267	12		1	2	76,704	7.36%
Washington	9	1,258,556	9		1	2	309,515	24.59%
West Virginia	7	792,040	7		1	2	284,134	35.87%
Wisconsin	12	1,691,815	12		1	2	411,929	24.35%
Wyoming	3	142,716	3		1	2	18,720	13.12%
Total	538	70,641,539	486	52	1	2	15,953,286	22.58%

* Note: Other vote in Alabama includes 210,732 votes for unpledged Democratic electors.

Johnson Democratic		Goldwater Republican		Others	
0	0.00%	479,085	69.45%	210,732*	30.55%
44,329	65.91%	22,930	34.09%	0	0.00%
237,753	49.45%	242,535	50.45%	482	0.10%
314,197	56.06%	243,264	43.41%	2,965	0.53%
4,171,877	59.11%	2,879,108	40.79%	6,601	0.09%
476,024	61.27%	296,767	38.19%	4,195	0.54%
826,269	67.81%	390,996	32.09%	1,313	0.11%
122,704	60.95%	78,078	38.78%	538	0.27%
169,796	85.50%	28,801	14.50%	0	0.00%
948,540	51.15%	905,941	48.85%	0	0.00%
522,557	45.87%	616,584	54.12%	195	0.02%
163,249	78.76%	44,022	21.24%	0	0.00%
148,920	50.92%	143,557	49.08%	0	0.00%
2,796,833	59.47%	1,905,946	40.53%	62	0.00%
1,170,848	55.98%	911,118	43.56%	9,640	0.46%
733,030	61.88%	449,148	37.92%	2,361	0.20%
464,028	54.09%	386,579	45.06%	7,294	0.85%
669,659	64.01%	372,977	35.65%	3,469	0.33%
387,068	43.19%	509,225	56.81%	0	0.00%
262,264	68.80%	118,701	31.14%	256	0.07%
730,912	65.47%	385,495	34.53%	50	0.00%
1,786,422	76.19%	549,727	23.44%	8,649	0.37%
2,136,615	66.70%	1,060,152	33.10%	6,335	0.20%
991,117	63.76%	559,624	36.00%	3,721	0.24%
52,618	12.86%	356,528	87.14%	0	0.00%
1,164,344	64.05%	653,535	35.95%	0	0.00%
164,246	58.95%	113,032	40.57%	1,350	0.48%
307,307	52.61%	276,847	47.39%	0	0.00%
79,339	58.58%	56,094	41.42%	0	0.00%
184,064	63.89%	104,029	36.11%	0	0.00%
1,867,671	65.61%	963,843	33.86%	15,256	0.54%
194,017	59.22%	131,838	40.24%	1,760	0.54%
4,913,156	68.56%	2,243,559	31.31%	9,300	0.13%
800,139	56.15%	624,844	43.85%	0	0.00%
149,784	57.97%	108,207	41.88%	398	0.15%
2,498,331	62.94%	1,470,865	37.06%	0	0.00%
519,834	55.75%	412,665	44.25%	0	0.00%
501,017	63.72%	282,779	35.96%	2,509	0.32%
3,130,954	64.92%	1,673,657	34.70%	18,079	0.37%
315,463	80.87%	74,615	19.13%	13	0.00%
215,700	41.10%	309,048	58.89%	8	0.00%
163,010	55.61%	130,108	44.39%	0	0.00%
634,947	55.50%	508,965	44.49%	34	0.00%
1,663,185	63.32%	958,566	36.49%	5,060	0.19%
219,628	54.86%	180,682	45.14%	0	0.00%
108,127	66.30%	54,942	33.69%	20	0.01%
558,038	53.54%	481,334	46.18%	2,895	0.28%
779,881	61.97%	470,366	37.37%	8,309	0.66%
538,087	67.94%	253,953	32.06%	0	0.00%
1,050,424	62.09%	638,495	37.74%	2,896	0.17%
80,718	56.56%	61,998	43.44%	0	0.00%
43,129,040	61.05%	27,175,754	38.47%	336,745	0.48%

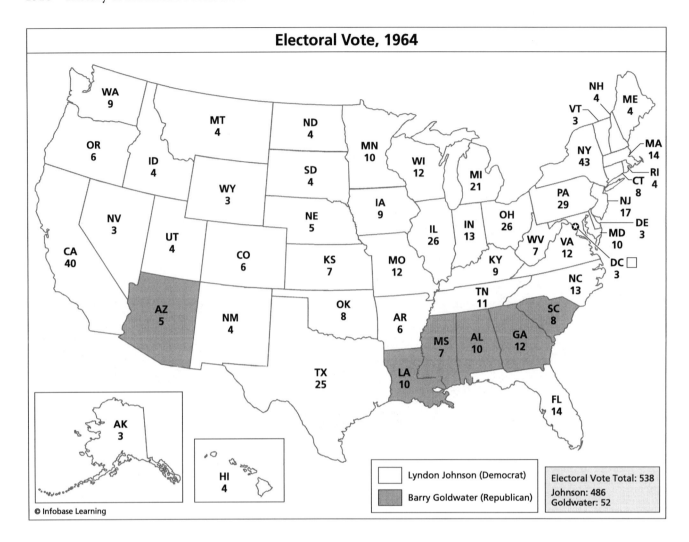

Electoral Vote, 1964

WA 9
OR 6
ID 4
MT 4
ND 4
MN 10
WI 12
MI 21
NH 4
VT 3
ME 4
NY 43
MA 14
RI 4
CT 8
NV 3
UT 4
WY 3
SD 4
IA 9
IL 26
IN 13
OH 26
PA 29
NJ 17
DE 3
MD 10
DC 3
CA 40
CO 6
NE 5
KS 7
MO 12
KY 9
WV 7
VA 12
NC 13
AZ 5
NM 4
OK 8
AR 6
TN 11
SC 8
MS 7
AL 10
GA 12
LA 10
TX 25
FL 14
AK 3
HI 4

Lyndon Johnson (Democrat)
Barry Goldwater (Republican)

Electoral Vote Total: 538
Johnson: 486
Goldwater: 52

© Infobase Learning

Election of 1968

Election Overview

Election Year 1968

Election Day November 5, 1968

Winning Candidates

- ★ **President:** Richard M. Nixon
- ★ **Vice President:** Spiro Agnew

Election Results [ticket, party: popular votes (percentage of popular vote); electoral votes (percentage of electoral vote)]

- Richard M. Nixon, Spiro Agnew, Republican: 31,783,783 (43.42%); 301 (55.9%)
- Hubert Humphrey, Edmund Muskie, Democratic: 31,271,839 (42.72%); 191 (35.5%)
- George Wallace, Curtis LeMay, American Independent: 9,901,118 (13.53%); 46 (8.6%)
- Other: 243,259 (0.33%); 0 (0.0%)

Voter Turnout 60.8%

Central Forums/Campaign Methods for Addressing Voters

- Speaking tours
- Rallies
- Radio
- Print ads
- Television ads, forums, coverage

Incumbent President and Vice President on Election Day Lyndon B. Johnson and Hubert Humphrey

Population (1968) 200,745,000

Gross Domestic Product

- $909.8 billion (in current dollars: $4,133.4 billion)
- Per capita: $4,532 (in current dollars: $20,590)

Number of Daily Newspapers (1970) 1,748

Average Daily Circulation (1970) 62,108,000

Households with

- Radio (1970): 46,108,000
- Television (1970): 60,594,000

Method of Choosing Electors Popular vote (mostly general-ticket system/winner take all)

Method of Choosing Nominees

- National party convention
- Presidential preference primaries

Key Issues and Events

- The Tet Offensive raises fears of losing the Vietnam War
- Assassinations of Martin Luther King Jr. and Robert Kennedy
- Urban riots, especially following King's murder
- College demonstrations
- Crime wave starting

Leading Candidates

REPUBLICANS
Presidential

- Richard M. Nixon, former vice president and 1960 presidential nominee (California)
- Nelson Rockefeller, governor and candidate for the 1960 and 1964 nominations (New York)
- Ronald Reagan, governor (California)
- George W. Romney, governor and candidate for the 1964 nomination (Michigan)

- Harold E. Stassen, former governor and candidate for the 1948, 1952, and 1964 nominations (Minnesota)

Vice-presidential candidates
- Spiro Agnew, governor (Maryland)
- Edward W. Brooke, senator (Massachusetts)
- George H.W. Bush, representative (Texas)
- David F. Cargo, governor (New Mexico)
- John Chafee, governor (Rhode Island)
- Daniel J. Evans, governor (Washington)
- Robert H. Finch, lieutenant governor (California)
- Mark O. Hatfield, senator (Oregon)
- Jacob Javits, senator (New York)
- Warren P. Knowles, governor (Wisconsin)
- John V. Lindsay, mayor (New York)
- John A. Love, governor (Colorado)
- Rogers C.B. Morton, representative (Maryland)
- Charles H. Percy, senator (Illinois)
- Ronald Reagan, governor (California)
- James A. Rhodes, governor (Ohio)
- Nelson Rockefeller, governor (New York)
- George W. Romney, governor (Michigan)
- John G. Tower, senator (Texas)
- John A. Volpe, governor (Massachusetts)

DEMOCRATS
- Hubert Humphrey, vice president (Minnesota)
- Robert Kennedy, senator and former attorney general (New York)
- Eugene J. McCarthy, senator (Minnesota)
- George S. McGovern, senator (South Dakota)
- Lyndon B. Johnson, president of the United States (Texas)

Trajectory

- In 1966, showcasing the "New Nixon," Richard Nixon preaches harmony and helps fellow Republicans rack up gains in the 1966 midterm elections. Skeptics, remembering that as early as 1953 there was talk of a "New Nixon," detest him as the same old "Tricky Dick."
- George Romney, the early Republican front-runner, withdraws in February 1968 after claiming he "originally" supported Johnson's Vietnam policy because he had been "brainwashed" by government briefing officers.
- In New Hampshire primary on March 12, Democratic antiwar candidate Eugene McCarthy finishes a strong second against President Johnson, thanks to his "children's crusade" of student activists.

- Four days later, on March 16, New York senator Robert Kennedy enters the Democratic race, after months of entreaties.
- On March 31, a shaken President Johnson declines to run for reelection and announces a bombing halt north of the 21st parallel in Vietnam.
- Assassinations of Martin Luther King Jr. on April 4 and of Robert Kennedy on June 5 shock Americans, while paving the way for Vice President Hubert Humphrey as the Democratic nominee.
- Richard Nixon, appealing to what he will call "the silent majority," promising to heal America by restoring "law and order," is nominated on August 8. He designates Maryland governor Spiro Agnew as his running mate.
- The Democratic National Convention, convening in Chicago on August 26, erupts in chaos inside and outside the convention hall, as delegates fight over an antiwar plank, and student radicals clash with police.
- By September, Alabama governor George Wallace succeeds in getting his third party on the ballot in all 50 states. Wallace's candidacy will pull Southern conservatives from their traditional but increasingly uncomfortable base in the Democratic Party, unintentionally helping Nixon's campaign.
- On September 30, in a nationwide telecast, Humphrey breaks with Johnson by vowing to order a bombing halt in Vietnam. This announcement allows liberals to rally around him. Then Johnson's "October surprise," actually stopping the bombing on October 31, boosts Humphrey further. But it is too little too late. Nixon wins, barely.

Conventions

- Republican National Convention: August 5–8, 1968, Convention Center, Miami Beach
- Democratic National Convention: August 26–29, 1968, International Amphitheatre, Chicago

Ballots/Nominees

REPUBLICANS
Presidential first ballot after shifts
- Richard M. Nixon 692; 1,238
- Nelson Rockefeller 277; 93
- Ronald Reagan 182; 2
- James A. Rhodes 55
- George W. Romney 50
- Clifford Case 22
- Frank Carlson 20
- Winthrop Rockefeller 18

- Hiram Fong 14
- Harold E. Stassen 2
- John V. Lindsay 1

Vice-presidential first ballot
- Spiro Agnew 1,119
- George W. Romney 186
- John V. Lindsay 10
- Edward Brooke 1
- James A. Rhodes 1
- Not voting 16

DEMOCRATS
Presidential first ballot
- Hubert Humphrey 1,760
- Eugene McCarthy 601
- George S. McGovern 146
- Channing Phillips 67
- Daniel K. Moore 17.5
- Edward M. Kennedy 13
- Paul W. "Bear" Bryant 1.5
- James H. Gray 0.5
- George Wallace 0.5

Vice-presidential first ballot
- Edmund Muskie 1,942.5
- Not voting 604.25
- Julian Bond 48.5
- David Hoeh 4
- Edward M. Kennedy 3.5
- Eugene McCarthy 3.0
- Others 16.25

Third-Party Candidates & Nominations

AMERICAN INDEPENDENT PARTY
- Former Alabama governor George Wallace for president; General Curtis LeMay for vice president
- Wallace known for defying federal college desegregation orders in Alabama; forms the party, and appeals to Middle America
- His supporters place his name on the ballot in all 50 states.
- His strategy is to block a majority in the Electoral College, play the kingmaker in the House of Representatives.
- Accused of promoting racism and segregation in his campaign

Primaries

- Democratic Party: 15; 40.2% delegates
- Republican Party: 15; 38% delegates

Primaries Results

REPUBLICANS
- Ronald Reagan 1,696,632; 37.93%
- Richard M. Nixon 1,679,443; 37.54%
- James A. Rhodes 614,492; 13.74%
- Nelson A. Rockefeller 164,340; 3.67%
- Unpledged 140,639; 3.14%

DEMOCRATS
- Eugene J. McCarthy 2,914,933; 38.73%
- Robert Kennedy 2,305,148; 30.63%
- Stephen M. Young 549,140; 7.30%
- Lyndon B. Johnson 383,590; 5.10%
- Thomas C. Lynch 380,286; 5.05%
- Roger D. Branigin 238,700; 3.17%
- George A. Smathers 236,242; 3.14%
- Hubert Humphrey 166,463; 2.21%
- Unpledged 161,143; 2.14%

Delegate count (prior to Robert Kennedy's assassination)
- Hubert Humphrey 561
- Robert Kennedy 393
- Eugene McCarthy 258

Total popular vote
- Eugene McCarthy 2,914,933; 38.73%
- Robert Kennedy 2,305,148; 30.63%
- Stephen M. Young 549,140; 7.30%
- Lyndon B. Johnson 383,590; 5.10%
- Thomas C. Lynch 380,286; 5.05%
- Roger D. Branigin 238,700; 3.17%
- George Smathers 236,242; 3.14%
- Hubert Humphrey 166,463; 2.21%
- Unpledged 161,143; 2.14%
- Scott Kelly 128,899; 1.71%
- George Wallace 34,489; 0.46%
- Richard M. Nixon (write-in) 13,610; 0.18%
- Ronald Reagan (write-in) 5,309; 0.07%
- Edward M. Kennedy 4,052; 0.05%
- Paul C. Fisher 506; 0.01%
- John G. Crommelin 186; 0.00%

Party Platform

DEMOCRATS
- Continuing the Great Society
- Ending the Vietnam War
- Civil rights/civil liberties

REPUBLICANS
- Ending the Vietnam War
- Ending the draft
- Call for increased law and order
- Slow/limit Great Society reforms

Campaign Innovations

- Heavy reliance on television advertising
- Nixon airs question and answer sessions on television.
- Pat Nixon campaigns for her husband at press conferences and on TV interviews.

Campaign Tactics

REPUBLICANS

- United party, efficient campaign staff, crisp scheduling, well-financed, much newspaper support
- Very targeted, well-organized campaign, following the theories of Marshall McLuhan that the "medium is the message" and that Nixon must be a "cool," not "hot," performer on TV
- Nixon, coddled to stay "cool," only campaigns in crucial states, gives major addresses, makes use of television to address voters in carefully staged question-and-answer sessions. Appears statesmanlike and calm, refuses to debate Humphrey.
- Speaks in general terms about the issues and Vietnam, not to jeopardize the Paris negotiations. Claims he has a secret plan to end the war.
- Calls for calm—and more explicitly—links Humphrey to the national unrest.
- Spiro Agnew, originally dismissed as "Spiro Who?" is more pugnacious but also more gaffe-prone, using words like "Polacks," skipping a visit to a ghetto by saying, "If you've seen one slum, you've seen them all," accusing Humphrey of being "soft on Communism," and calling a reporter a "fat Jap"—although the last expression was indeed the reporter's nickname and other journalists unfairly made Agnew appear more insensitive than he was.

DEMOCRATS

- Little money or organization and no campaign schedule until Lawrence O'Brien is appointed chairman of the Democratic National Committee.
- Humphrey at first is 8 to 10 percentage points behind Nixon in the polls and heckled everywhere he goes to speak.
- Democrats attack Nixon as "Tricky Dick" while mocking Spiro Agnew.
- Humphrey's "politics of joy" seems out of place. He spends more time trying to reunite the party while distancing himself from President Johnson and Vietnam.

Popular Campaign Slogans

REPUBLICANS

- "Vote Like Your Whole World Depended on It"

- "Nixon's the One"
- "He's Good Enough for Me in '68"

DEMOCRATS

- "Humphrey-Muskie, Two You Can Trust"
- "Unite with Humphrey"
- "Two Hearts Beat as One: Elect This Team!"

Campaign Songs

REPUBLICANS

- "Nixon's the One"
- "Vote for Nixon"

DEMOCRATS

- "Hubie Humphrey—We Love You!"

Influential Campaign Appeals or Ads

REPUBLICANS

- "Hubert Humphrey defends the policies under which we have seen crime rising ten times as fast as the population. If you want your President to continue with the do-nothing policy toward crime, vote for Humphrey. If you want to fight crime, vote for Nixon."
- "Convention" ad by the documentary filmmaker Eugene Jones intersperses images of Vietnam, race riots, and poverty with Humphrey smiling at the Democratic convention, as "Hot Time in the Old Town Tonight" plays again and again.

DEMOCRATS

- Wallace and LeMay: "Bombsy Twins"

Nixon

- "Richard the Silent" and "Richard the Chicken-hearted"
- "Apologize now, Spiro, it will save time later."

George Wallace

- "Send THEM a message."
- "There's not a dime's worth of difference between the Democrat and Republican parties."

Anti-Democrat

- "Stop the war! Stop the war! Dump the Hump, dump the Hump!"

Pro-Democrat

- "Hecklers for Humphrey—We Came Back."

Campaign Finance

- Nixon: $25,402,000 (in current dollars: $148,542,600)
- Humphrey: $11,594,000 (in current dollars: $67,798,000)

  - The cost of television ads fuels a huge rise in the cost of campaigning. Since 1956, overall campaign spending has doubled from $155 million to over $300 million, while the amount spent on broadcast media—production and, especially, airtime—has increased from $10 million to $60 million.

- 8 percent of the voting population contributes to candidates at some level—federal, state, or local.

Defining Quotations

- "Television is no gimmick, and nobody will ever be elected to major office again without presenting themselves well on it." *Television producer and Nixon campaign consultant Roger Ailes, c. 1967*
- "My candidacy would not be in opposition to his [Eugene McCarthy's], but in harmony." *Robert F. Kennedy announcing his candidacy to run for the Democratic nomination, March 16, 1968*
- "I shall not seek and I will not accept the nomination of my party for another term." *President Lyndon B. Johnson, March 31, 1968*
- Considering the new circumstances that confront the nation . . . I frankly find that to comment from the sidelines is not an effective way to present the alternatives." *Nelson Rockefeller returning to the race for the Republican nomination after the assassination of Martin Luther King Jr., April 1968*
- ". . . thanks to all of you and now on to Chicago and let's win there." *Robert Kennedy's last words, in his victory speech after winning California, only to be shot moments later, at 12:15 a.m. June 5, 1968*
- "It is another voice, it is a quiet voice in the tumult of the shouting. It is the voice of the great majority of Americans, the forgotten Americans, the non-shouters, the non-demonstrators. . . . They're good people. They're decent people; they work and they save and they pay their taxes and they care. . . . And this I say, this I say to you tonight, is the real voice of America. In this year 1968, this is the message it will broadcast to America and to the world." *Richard M. Nixon accepting the Republican Party nomination for president, August 8, 1968*
- "Like my three brothers before me, I pick up a fallen standard." *Edward Kennedy, August 21, 1968*
- "Gestapo tactics on the streets of Chicago." *Connecticut senator Abraham Ribicoff in his nomination speech for George McGovern, August 28, 1968*
- "Mr. Chairman, most delegates to this convention do not know that thousands of young people are being beaten in the streets of Chicago! I move this convention be adjourned for two weeks and moved to another city." *Donald Peterson, head of the Wisconsin Democratic delegation, August 28, 1968*

- "The President has not made me his slave and I am not his humble servant." *Hubert Humphrey, September 25, 1968*
- "As President, I would stop the bombing of the North as an acceptable risk for peace because I believe it could lead to success in the negotiations and thereby shorten the war." *Hubert Humphrey, Salt Lake City nationwide telecast, September 30, 1968*
- "I tell you when November comes, the first time they lie down in front of my limousine it'll be the last one they ever lay down in front of; their day is over!" *George Wallace at a Madison Square Garden rally, referring to a protestor who blocked President Johnson's limousine, October 24, 1968*
- "In the last thirty-six hours, I have been advised of a flurry of meetings in the White House and elsewhere on Vietnam. I am told that top officials in the Administration have been driving very hard for an agreement on a bombing halt, accompanied possibly by a cease-fire in the immediate future. I since learned that these reports are true. I am also told that this spurt of activity is a cynical, last-minute attempt by President Johnson to salvage the candidacy of Mr. Humphrey. This I do not believe." *Richard Nixon, October 25, 1968*
- "I have reached this decision on the basis of developments in the Paris talks, and I have reached the belief that this action will lead to progress for a peaceful settlement of the Vietnam War." *President Lyndon B. Johnson announcing the cessation of bombing in Vietnam, October 31, 1968*
- "I have been hoping for months that it would happen, for months." *Hubert Humphrey after Johnson's "October surprise" announcement on October 31, 1968, that he was halting bombing in Vietnam*
- "Hubert Humphrey defends the policies under which we have seen crime rising ten times as fast as the population. If you want your President to continue with the do-nothing policy toward crime, vote for Humphrey. If you want to fight crime, vote for Nixon." *Richard Nixon quoted in* Time, *November 1, 1968*
- "I saw many signs in this campaign, some of them were not friendly and some were very friendly. But the one that touched me the most was one that I saw in Deshler, Ohio, at the end of a long day of whistle-stopping—a little town, I suppose five times the population was there in the dusk—but a teen-ager held up a sign, 'Bring Us Together.' And that will be the great objective of this administration at the outset, to bring the American people together. This will be an open administration, open to new ideas, open to men and women of both parties, open to the

critics as well as those who support us. We want to bridge the generation gap. We want to bridge the gap between races. We want to bring America together."
Richard Nixon, victory speech, November 8, 1968

- "The old Democratic coalition was disintegrating, with untold numbers of blue-collar workers responding to Wallace's blandishments, Negroes threatening to sit out the election, liberals disaffected over the Vietnam War, the South lost. The war chest was almost empty, and the party's machinery,

neglected by Lyndon Johnson, creaked in disrepair." Time, *November 15, 1968*

Lasting Legacy of Campaign

- Realigning election as the Republican victory signals the rise of conservatism; end of the Roosevelt/New Deal alignment that commenced in the 1932 election
- Effective third-party candidate; no other third party since George Wallace has won the electoral votes of a state

Election of 1968

The central paradox of the 1968 election was that a year of almost unprecedented violence and turmoil, a year of wild political oscillations and extremes, produced a terribly conventional result. A year that saw repeated challenges from the nation's political left and right wings ended with the country dividing with almost mathematical equality between two candidates of the center. A year that saw more than the usual amount of internal warfare within the major parties and the birth of the most ambitious third party in 44 years ended in an election that vindicated the two-party system. A year that posed a constant threat of constitutional crisis ended with an electoral verdict, rendered in the customary way, without recourse to Electoral College bargaining or a contingent election in the House.

Some will see 1968 as a year when the party system and the election process failed to give the voters a real choice on the issues that were dividing the country. Others will see in it evidence that the cohesive forces of our political system proved themselves strong enough to survive terrible stresses.

All that we can agree on at the outset, perhaps, is that it was a year of resounding paradox.

There is a tendency, in writing the history of modern elections to perform the historian's function of searching out links with earlier events or longstanding political trends. As we shall see, when we come to analyze the voting patterns, most voters in 1968 (the Wallaceites being the notable exception) voted very much along customary lines—or at least, as people of similar occupational, educational, and economic status have traditionally voted.

But neither the continuity of voting patterns nor the conventionality of the post-convention campaigns should blind us to the fact that 1968 was, in important respects, an extraordinary political year.

Not since the Democrats in 1932 has a party come back so far, so fast from the previous election's defeat as

did the Republicans in 1968. Richard Milhous Nixon, the former two-term vice president (1953–61), who carried the Republican banner in 1968, was himself defying tradition in his election bid. Nixon had been defeated for president by John F. Kennedy in 1960, lost a race for governor of California in 1962, and decided not to seek the 1964 Republican nomination. Not since William Jennings Bryan in 1908 had a major party renominated a defeated former candidate after an interval of more than four years. Early in the year, Governor George Romney of Michigan set a precedent of another sort. The earliest of the Republican candidates to declare, Romney was also the first major candidate to withdraw—and he did so on the basis of his private surveys of the New Hampshire primary, thus adding important new testimony to the power of the opinion polls. After Romney's withdrawal, Governor Nelson A. Rockefeller of New York attempted to use that other modern political tool—mass media advertising—for the first time as the main weapon in a campaign for the presidential nomination. The effort failed, but it is likely to be remembered as a significant development in nomination politics.

At least two events in the Democratic Party in 1968 represented sharp breaks with precedent. Senator Eugene J. McCarthy of Minnesota, in his challenge for the Democratic nomination, for the first time mobilized large numbers of college-age youths as the largest component of a serious presidential campaign. Particularly in the New Hampshire primary, where the McCarthy campaign was almost entirely student-staffed, did this "student power" exert itself as a political force. McCarthy's New Hampshire success and his anticipated victory over President Lyndon B. Johnson in the primary in Wisconsin caused the president to do what few had thought possible and virtually none had thought likely—withdraw from contention for renomination and reelection. Johnson's action weakened, if it did not destroy, the political axiom that a healthy incumbent who is constitutionally eligible and

Senator Robert F. Kennedy is held onto by an aide as he stands on a seat while campaigning in a motorcade in Sacramento, California, May 16, 1968. *(Associated Press)*

politically available for a second term can compel his own renomination.

In addition to these landmark developments in the Democratic campaign, we should note that the truncated campaign and assassination of Senator Robert F. Kennedy of New York marked, sadly, another stage in the routinization of frenzy and violence as political techniques. Those same forces were unleashed in unprecedented fashion by the demonstrators and police at the Democratic convention in Chicago, raising serious doubts as to the viability of the convention as a major decision-making institution in the nomination process and triggering a major effort by the Democratic Party, designed to reform and improve its structure and operations.

The feat of former governor George C. Wallace of Alabama in gaining a place for himself and his American Independent Party electors on the ballots of all 50 states showed that the obstacles to third-party operations in our election system were not nearly so intimidating as had been supposed. Remarkable as Wallace's organization was, it was matched by the propaganda campaign undertaken in the fall of 1968 by the leaders of organized labor, which sufficiently reduced Wallace's support from blue-collar families outside the Deep South to deny him his goal of

deadlocking the election. That union-financed campaign was a classic in the power of mass political propaganda.

Finally, one should mention that the election outcome—the choice of a president of one party and a Congress controlled, in both houses, by the opposition—marked the first time since 1848 that a newly elected president found himself at the head of a divided government, with all the implications for presidential leadership and party responsibility that flow from that fact.

More than most years, the 1968 election year was thus a precedent-breaking and a precedent-making year for American politics.

The conditions that produced the 1968 campaign stemmed directly from the circumstances of President Johnson's accession to office in 1963, his election in 1964, and his administration of foreign and domestic matters thereafter. The 1968 election was, in essence, the fallout from the explosive breakdown of the artificial consensus of the Johnsonian years.

Unlike most 20th-century presidents, Lyndon B. Johnson was the product of a one-party state. His adult life had been spent in the House and Senate, where for a period of more than 25 years he polished and perfected his natu-

(continues on page 1326)

☆ ☆ ☆

1968 ELECTION CHRONOLOGY

1965

January 31, 1965: President Lyndon Johnson orders the first American bombing raids on North Vietnam.

July 30, 1965: President Johnson signs the Social Security Act of 1965 into law, creating the Medicare and Medicaid programs, which provide federal health insurance to the elderly and the poor.

August 6, 1965: President Johnson signs the Voting Rights Act into law, outlawing many of the discriminatory practices that had been used to disenfranchise African Americans.

August 11–15, 1965: Widespread rioting in the Watts neighborhood of Los Angeles leaves 34 dead and 1,032 injured.

1966

January 12, 1966: Johnson delivers the State of the Union address, promising that American engagement in the Vietnam War could continue without domestic cutbacks.

November 1, 1966: In House and Senate midterm elections, Republicans pick up 47 seats in the House, three seats in the Senate, and eight governorships.

1967

October 21, 1967: Some 100,000 protestors demonstrate at the Lincoln Memorial and the Pentagon against the Vietnam War.

November 18, 1967: Governor George W. Romney of Michigan announces his candidacy for the Republican nomination.

November 30, 1967: Senator Eugene McCarthy of Minnesota announces that he will enter several Democratic primaries as the antiwar and anti-Johnson candidate.

1968

January 29, 1968: The Viet Cong and North Vietnamese Army launch a surprise offensive during the Tet holiday in an attempt to spark a general uprising against U.S. forces. The Tet Offensive prompts many Americans to question their early support of the war and the Johnson administration's claims of progress.

February 1, 1968: Richard Nixon declares his candidacy for the Republican nomination.

February 8, 1968: George Wallace, the former governor of Alabama and an outspoken advocate for segregation, announces his intention to run for president as a third-party candidate for the American Independent Party.

February 28, 1968: Governor Romney, the early Republican front-runner, withdraws from the race after being ridiculed for claiming he "originally" supported Johnson's Vietnam policy because he had been "brainwashed" by government briefing officers.

March 5, 1968: Speaking in Hampton, New Hampshire, trying to show that he is the "New Nixon," Nixon promises that his "new leadership" will "end the war and win the peace in the Pacific."

March 12, 1968: In the New Hampshire primary, the Democratic antiwar candidate Eugene McCarthy finishes a strong second against President Johnson, thanks to his "children's crusade" of student activists.

March 16, 1968: After months of entreaties, New York senator Robert Kennedy enters the Democratic race.

March 31, 1968: President Johnson announces that he will not run for reelection and that he has ordered a bombing halt north of the 21st parallel in Vietnam.

April 2, 1968: McCarthy defeats President Johnson in the Wisconsin primary, taking almost 57 percent of the vote.

April 4, 1968: Martin Luther King Jr. is assassinated in Memphis, Tennessee, prompting a wave of riots in nearly 60 cities.

April 27, 1968: Vice President Hubert Humphrey formally enters the race, praising Johnson's "dramatic leadership" and dedicating himself to practicing the "politics of happiness."

April 30, 1968: Governor Nelson Rockefeller of New York announces that he is back in the race,

despite having publicly declined to enter it on March 21.

May 7, 1968: Robert Kennedy wins the Indiana primary with a plurality of 42 percent of the vote, edging out McCarthy.

May 14, 1968: Kennedy repeats his victory over McCarthy in the Nebraska primary.

May 28, 1968: McCarthy beats Kennedy in the Oregon primary. In the same race, Nixon beats California governor Ronald Reagan by a 3-to-1 margin.

June 4, 1968: In a win that his supporters hope will clinch the nomination, Kennedy defeats McCarthy by 46 to 42 percent in the California primary.

June 5, 1968: At 12:15 a.m., just after midnight, Robert F. Kennedy is assassinated at the Ambassador Hotel in Los Angeles. He dies the next day.

June 11, 1968: As the primary season ends, Reagan leads the Republican nominees in delegates, followed closely by Nixon, while McCarthy leads the Democrats. Still, Nixon's support is broader than Reagan's.

August 5–8, 1968: The Republican Party holds its national convention in Miami Beach. Richard M. Nixon of California wins the nomination on the first ballot and selects Governor Spiro T. Agnew of Maryland as his running mate.

August 10, 1968: Senator George McGovern of South Dakota, an early critic of the Vietnam War and a close Kennedy ally, announces his candidacy for the Democratic nomination.

August 26–29, 1968: The Democratic Party holds its national convention at the International Amphitheater in Chicago. The convention erupts in chaos inside and outside the convention hall as delegates fight over an antiwar plank and student radicals clash with police. Vice President Hubert Humphrey wins the nomination and chooses Senator Edmund S. Muskie of Maine as his running mate.

September 4, 1968: Nixon formally opens the Republican campaign in Chicago in front of a crowd of half a million.

September 9, 1968: Humphrey kicks off the Democratic campaign in Philadelphia, where hecklers drown out his speech.

September 30, 1968: In a nationwide telecast, Humphrey breaks with Johnson by vowing to order a bombing halt in Vietnam.

October 3, 1968: George Wallace of the American Independent Party selects retired Air Force general Curtis L. LeMay, former chief of the Strategic Air Command, as his running mate. LeMay immediately causes problems for the campaign by advocating the use of nuclear weapons.

October 9, 1968: Wallace publicly charges that opinion polls have been rigged to show his fortunes declining.

October 11, 1968: The Paris Peace Talks begin, the first significant private discussions between American and North Vietnamese representatives regarding a possible agreement that would stop the U.S. bombings.

October 25, 1968: Nixon accuses the White House of arranging an "October surprise" that would stop the bombing to boost Humphrey's campaign in the final days of the race.

October 29, 1968: McCarthy formally endorses Humphrey.

October 31, 1968: Johnson announces that the Paris talks have been successful, and that he will order the bombing of North Vietnam to cease and formal peace talks to begin on the day after the election.

November 1, 1968: The head of the Saigon government announces that the American decision is "unilateral" and that he is not prepared to enter the talks. Rumors swirl that Nixon officials have urged Saigon leaders to hold out for a "better deal" under a Nixon administration.

November 5, 1968: Republicans Richard Nixon and Spiro Agnew win with 43 percent of the popular vote and 301 Electoral College votes.

December 16, 1968: Presidential electors cast their ballots in their respective state capitals.

1969
January 6, 1969: A joint session of Congress assembles to count the electoral votes.

(continued from page 1323)
ral gift as a political mediator. The special genius of Lyndon Johnson's politics was to discern areas of agreement between men who considered themselves enemies (on a particular issue at least) and to frame liberal programs in a way that did not (or did not appear to) jeopardize the vital interests of the business groups in Texas and the country that were very much part of Johnson's personal and political constituency.

Coming to office in the shock of President Kennedy's assassination, Johnson's talents were quickly put to the service of restoring calm and confidence to a badly shaken American and international public. He obtained from Congress most of the major bills—notably tax and civil rights legislation—Kennedy had proposed.

In the 1964 election (as detailed in the previous chapter), Johnson was favored with a Republican opponent, Senator Barry M. Goldwater of Arizona, who represented a minority faction of the minority party and conducted a campaign that specialized in raising settled questions of American policy in a manner so self-destructive as to seem almost deliberately perverse.

Johnson won in 1964 with nearly all the Democratic vote, a large majority of Independents, and a significant slice of Republicans. And he carried with him the most heavily Democratic Congress since 1936.

The immediate by-product of his landslide was the "Great Society" domestic program, rushed through the 1965 and 1966 sessions of the 89th Congress in order to take advantage of what he suspected to be temporarily inflated Democratic majorities.

There was an element of risk in the legislative strategy: to achieve his social reform goals, Johnson pushed Congress hard, stirring resentment in Democratic ranks and enabling the minority Republicans to lodge a plausible claim of one-man government. On one memorable night, he kept the House in session for almost 14 hours—until 12:51 a.m.—in order to pass a highway beautification bill that had become a personal project of Mrs. Johnson's.

There were more serious problems than the bruised feelings of the congressmen. Some of the legislation that was pushed through in the early days—the antipoverty program, for example—was little understood by the lawmakers. No time was spent building public support for the long-term effort that was needed. In the later years of his administration, the president found it difficult or impossible to rally public opinion behind the effort to execute and finance laws that were passed in haste.

Finally, the commitments undertaken at such a hectic pace put a heavy strain on the budget—a strain that Johnson denied long after it was evident to others.

In his 1966 State of the Union message, for example, Johnson refused to accept the notion that the Vietnam War required domestic cutbacks. "I believe," he told Congress, "we can continue the Great Society while we fight in Vietnam," and he recommended a $113 billion budget with no tax increase.

This refusal to set priorities—so understandable in a "consensus politician" who depends on satisfying, simultaneously, the conflicting aspirations of all the diverse elements in his constituency—led directly to the problem of inflation that plagued Johnson's last years in the presidency.

And then there was Vietnam—the issue that finally became his downfall. Retracing the course of his policy on the war is beyond the scope of this essay.

It is essential, however, to note that in the 1964 campaign Johnson created the impression that he was opposed "to supply[ing] American boys to do the job that Asian boys should do." Then in February 1965, less than a month after his inauguration, Johnson ordered American bombing raids on North Vietnam. In August of that year, the massive troop movements began that were to send more than a half-million Americans to Vietnam.

The seeming reversal of the campaign policy aggravated a reputation for deceitfulness, bred by Johnson's penchant for secrecy and surprise. Political opposition spread from the college campuses to the hearing room of the Senate Foreign Relations Committee. Three weeks of nationally televised hearings by that committee in early 1966 provided a forum for critics to challenge the logic of the large-scale U.S. intervention in Vietnam.

While the war preoccupied the country, a series of riots occurred in black areas of many large cities. Violent confrontations between looters and arsonists and armed police and national guardsmen in Los Angeles, Detroit, Newark, and hundreds of other cities inflamed race relations and mocked the ambitions of the president's domestic program and the pretensions of the Great Society.

From late 1965 on, in a steady curve, the Johnsonian consensus declined—its fragile structure shattered by the war, inflation, racial strife, and the public disillusionment with the leadership and personality of the president.

Meantime, the Republicans were taking the steps necessary to restore their party to a competitive position for the 1968 election. The first move was to liquidate the Goldwater experiment by removing from their posts of command the men the Arizona senator had installed in control of the party machinery.

For two months after the 1964 election, a furious intraparty battle raged over the head of Dean Burch, the young Arizona lawyer who was picked by Goldwater as chairman of the Republican National Committee. Republican governors, predominantly liberal in their leanings, joined forces with some traditional Midwestern Republican Party leaders who were shocked by the losses of 1964.

Together, they persuaded Goldwater to accept a face-saving compromise that replaced Burch with Ray C. Bliss, the veteran Ohio Republican chairman who had earned a reputation as the party's top political technician. Determinedly nonideological, Bliss set the party to work on the pedestrian task of rebuilding its shattered local organizations. He also created a Republican Coordinating Committee, whose membership represented the diverse tendencies of the congressional leadership, the governors, and past presidential candidates, and whose task was to bridge the intra-party ideological gaps of 1964. With two-time nominee Thomas E. Dewey taking a leading role, the committee had notable success in its assigned task, and its reports over the four-year period furnished most of the framework for the 1968 GOP platform.

In November 1965, six months after Bliss took office, Republican morale received a major boost—and the argument for political pragmatism a solid endorsement—when John V. Lindsay was elected mayor of New York City. The liberal congressman, who had refused to support Goldwater in 1964, won the mayorship with Liberal Party support over a divided, dispirited Democratic opposition—thus giving dramatic demonstration of the viability of Republicanism even in a traditional Democratic stronghold.

The midterm elections of 1966 confirmed the Republican comeback. The GOP gained 47 seats in the House, 3 seats in the Senate, and 8 governorships. The victories were spread from the industrial East through much of the South and California, and the winners included both liberals and conservatives.

These reverses triggered the first major Democratic rebellion against President Johnson's leadership. Meeting at White Sulphur Springs, West Virginia, a month after the election, Democratic governors publicly blamed the party's losses on "an anti-Administration trend," and upbraided the president for what they called his neglect of party affairs and the weakening of the Democratic National Committee. Governor Harold E. Hughes of Iowa, later to be a leader in the dump-Johnson movement, told reporters after the extraordinary caucus that he and his colleagues were convinced Johnson "would have a very tough race" if he sought reelection. The 1966 election not only served as a warning to Johnson but defined the field of likely Republican challengers: George Romney, Nelson Rockefeller, and Ronald Reagan.

Governor George Wilcken Romney of Michigan, a 59-year-old sometime Mormon missionary who had become a national figure in the 1950s as president of the American Motors Company, which successfully challenged the Big Three auto manufacturers by introducing the Rambler, the first American compact car. A dynamic personality with maverick political views, combining an essentially conservative economic philosophy with a strong commitment to civil rights, Romney ended 14 years of Democratic control when he was elected governor of Michigan in 1962. He was reelected by a wider margin in 1964, after publicly breaking with Goldwater over the latter's civil rights views and declining to support the national nominee. In 1966, Romney won a third term (this time for four years) and paced a Republican sweep that also gave the party a Senate seat and five additional Republican congressmen. With this win, though he was still unproven in national politics, Romney became the front-runner of the liberal wing for the 1968 nomination.

Governor Nelson A. Rockefeller of New York, the 58-year-old heir to one of America's great fortunes, was (depending on one's viewpoint) the hero or villain of the 1964 GOP nomination struggle. In 1965, Rockefeller foreswore any future presidential ambitions and concentrated on a difficult campaign for a third four-year term as governor. By a massive outpouring of energy, funds, and advertising talent, Rockefeller in 1966 reversed the odds and won a plurality victory with less than 45 percent of the total vote against separate Democratic, Liberal, and Conservative Party opponents. Though Rockefeller adhered to his declaration that he was not a presidential contender and gave an early endorsement to Romney, his talent and his resources made him a constant fallback possibility for liberal Republicans and a constant threat to other aspirants.

HOPING FOR THE JACKPOT

This Gib Crockett cartoon shows the GOP elephant hoping to win the jackpot in the 1968 presidential election by using the "crime issue." *(Library of Congress)*

Governor Ronald Reagan of California, a 57-year-old actor, who made a spectacular leap from the entertainment world into politics with his victory over incumbent Democratic governor Edmund G. "Pat" Brown in 1966. Reagan, a veteran motion picture and television performer, came to national prominence with a televised fund-raising appeal for Goldwater in the closing stages of the 1964 presidential campaign. The speech stamped him as perhaps the finest television personality in the GOP ranks. Despite his almost complete lack of governmental experience, a group of conservative California businessmen, most of them Goldwater supporters, staked Reagan to a run for the governorship of the largest state. Under careful management from the political public relations firm of Spencer, Roberts, and Associates, Reagan defeated former San Francisco mayor George Christopher in the primary and then went on to defeat Brown by over 1 million votes. His program for California, premised on the need for a reduction in the role and power of government, was called "The Creative Society." It was, by design, a conservative alternative to Johnson's Great Society, and Reagan was, from the moment of his election, the conservative hope for the 1968 Republican nomination.

In a real sense, however, the big Republican winner of 1966 was none of these successful candidates but the campaigner whose name appeared on no ballot anywhere—55-year-old Richard M. Nixon. Nixon had been in political eclipse since losing his bids for the presidency and for governor of California. After that second defeat, he quit his native state and joined a prestigious Wall Street law firm, taking up an apartment in the same building where his old rival, Nelson Rockefeller, lived.

After Kennedy's death, Nixon toyed with the idea of seeking the 1964 Republican nomination, but abandoned that hope after Goldwater's victory over Rockefeller in the California primary made certain the Arizonian's nomination.

In a conference at his favorite Montauk Point, Long Island, retreat, with a pair of close political associates just before the 1964 convention, Nixon worked out the strategy that he was to follow for the next four years. Recognizing that Goldwater's defeat by Lyndon Johnson was as inevitable as his nomination, Nixon set out to position himself to take command of the Republican ruins. He played the role of party unifier at the disastrous 1964 Republican convention, introducing Goldwater in a speech that was designed to blur the differences that had divided the convention. Though his tactic failed, Nixon stumped the country for Goldwater and other Republican office seekers—covering 36 states in a six-week tour—an investment of energy (at a time when many others were shunning the national ticket)

that earned him dividends of political gratitude from Goldwater and other conservative Republicans. As the symbol of party unity, Nixon presided at the 1965 Republican National Committee meeting where Bliss replaced Burch as party chairman. He took a leading role in the Republican Coordinating Committee, and in 1966 took to the road again—stumping 35 states for 86 candidates. This time, Nixon found himself with the aura of a winner; two-thirds of those for whom he campaigned won their races, and Nixon himself predicted the outcome with notable accuracy. So established was he as the preeminent Republican spokesman by the end of the 1966 campaign that, when the television networks made time available to the GOP to answer a partisan speech by President Johnson, it seemed perfectly natural to everyone that Nixon should make the reply.

The four men mentioned—Romney, Rockefeller, Reagan, and Nixon—dominated the GOP presidential field as 1967 began, along with the usual crop of dark horses, of whom the most prominent were Governor James A. Rhodes of Ohio and Senator Charles H. Percy of Illinois. Nixon made the first major tactical move in the nomination battle by announcing a "sabbatical" from politics that was to keep him offstage, traveling throughout the world and writing, for most of 1967. It was a calculated risk on his part, for Nixon was in a position to "cash in his due bills" and assert a claim to the nomination that any other Republican might have found hard to break. He did not do so—for he had already determined in his own mind that he could erase his "loser's image" only by taking the presidential primary route. Any effort to tie up the delegates with early commitments, as Goldwater had done four years before, would have been doomed to failure; after the 1964 debacle, the GOP was oriented to "looking for a winner."

As Nixon calculated, his leading rival for the nomination, George Romney, did not have the self-discipline (or the professional advice) to play a similar waiting game. Immediately after his third-term victory, Romney plunged headlong into pursuit of the nomination. He took the spotlight as a guest on the *Meet the Press* interview show the Sunday after the November 1966 election; by February 1967, he was off on a speaking trip that took him as far as Alaska, with a retinue of 40 newsmen in a mock-up presidential caravan.

Unfortunately for Romney, these early excursions served chiefly to demonstrate his shakiness on national issues—particularly the war in Vietnam. A series of contradictory statements, some supporting and others opposing administration policy, provoked such a crisis in his campaign that by April 1967 he was forced to make a major address on Vietnam in an effort to combat the impression that his views on that issue were hopelessly muddled. His address, in Hartford, Connecticut, was a balanced but critical appraisal of American policy in the war, but its contents were blurred and distorted by a White House comment characterizing it as an endorsement of the Johnson policy. Throughout the summer, Romney continued to issue "clarifying" statements about Vietnam, but the impression of confusion persisted. On Labor Day weekend of 1967, he told a television interviewer that his initial support of the American intervention in Vietnam resulted from his having been "brainwashed" by American briefing officers during a visit to that country in 1965. Romney's unfortunate phrase—implying that responsible American officials had deliberately lied to him and/or that he had been a dupe—brought to the surface all the accumulated doubts about his capacity in international affairs and caused the *Detroit News*, hitherto a staunch supporter of his, to urge him to abandon the race.

Romney attempted to ride out the storm, formally declaring his candidacy on November 18, 1967, and then embarking on a world tour. But, as events were to prove, he never really recovered from the damage to his reputation. In January 1968, he plunged into an active campaign in New Hampshire, but after two months of intermittent stumping, private polls indicated he was trailing Nixon by a 7-to-1 margin and making no significant gain. On February 28—13 days before the New Hampshire voters were scheduled to cast their ballots—Romney dramatically withdrew from the race, probably the first major presidential candidate to end his bid before the first vote was cast and solely on the basis of public opinion polls.

Ironically, many of the positions that Romney took on Vietnam appear to have been vindicated by history. The main theme of his Hartford speech was a warning against "Americanizing" the war in pursuit of total victory. He declared that the Vietnamese must themselves work out the terms of a "peace with amnesty" that would produce a popular government, not tainted by outside dictation from either North Vietnam or the United States. In May 1967, Romney specified his support of direct negotiations between Saigon and the Viet Cong—a position that was later adopted by the American government. In July 1967— nine months before President Johnson so acted—he called for limitation of U.S. bombing of North Vietnam and a sharp step-up in the training of South Vietnamese troops to replace American soldiers in combat duty—a step that became the keystone of the Nixon policy two years later.

But Romney's early vagueness and lack of precision in discussing Vietnam obscured the essential wisdom of his final analysis of the issue and caused the liberal Republicans to lose the candidate who was, on his record in Michigan, perhaps their strongest campaigner—and all this before the race truly began.

Romney's surprise withdrawal on the eve of the New Hampshire primary left Nixon without an avowed opponent for the nomination. Nixon had declared his candidacy on February 1, 1968, and announced plans to enter at least six primaries: New Hampshire, Wisconsin, Indiana, Nebraska, Oregon, and South Dakota. On his initial swing through those states, Nixon displayed the new campaign style he was to follow throughout the year. He kept to a deliberately slow pace, usually making not more than one or two speeches a day, with each rally carefully designed by his experienced campaign crew for maximum impact on the live audience and the television networks as well. During those early days of 1968—when the enemy's Tet offensive was causing many Americans to question their earlier support of the war—Nixon, while campaigning in the primary states, caught the shift of public opinion and moved adroitly off his well-defined position as an advocate of military victory in Vietnam. By March 5, just five weeks after he announced, he told the voters in Hampton, New Hampshire, in a speech that was to be one of the best remembered of his whole campaign, that his "new leadership" would "end the war and win the peace in the Pacific."

Nixon, though confident of beating Romney, had wanted the governor to remain in the race—both as a convenient opponent for himself and as a block to a Rockefeller candidacy. When Romney withdrew and left Nixon without an active opponent, he upset Nixon's whole strategy of restoring his credentials as a winner through the primaries.

But if Romney's withdrawal caused problems for the front-runner, they were small compared to the dilemmas Reagan and Rockefeller now faced.

Reagan, under the tutelage of F. Clifton White, strategist of the 1964 Goldwater nomination victory, had announced early in 1967 that he would confine himself to the role of a California favorite son. He made frequent out-of-state speaking trips, exploiting his proven capacity to arouse Republican audiences, but vehemently denied that he planned to seek the 1968 nomination. White's strategy was based on the expectation that the Romney–Nixon primaries would produce no clear-cut winner and that Reagan and the other favorite sons would control enough votes to make Miami Beach "a brokered convention." When the brokering was done, White figured that Reagan, the fresh face unscarred by past battles or the warfare of the primaries, would be the convention choice. But now Nixon was left without an active opponent— unless Rockefeller ran, and Rockefeller was wavering.

Even before Romney's withdrawal, the New York governor had begun softening his flat declarations of non-availability, saying he would run if drafted but really didn't want to be president. Rockefeller was in Washing-

FEBRUARY MORN

Titled "February Morn," this Gib Crockett cartoon shows Romney sticking his toe into a body of water labeled "the issues," but finding the water too cold to go in any further. *(Library of Congress)*

ton on February 28 when Romney withdrew, during the midwinter meeting of the National Governors' Conference. He immediately plunged into meetings with other liberal-leaning governors and on March 1 told a press conference he was "ready and willing" to run if the party wanted him. He left open the question of challenging Nixon in the late primaries, but the public activities of the following three weeks appeared to be the orchestration for a formal announcement that he would step into Romney's shoes as the liberal challenger. When he scheduled a news conference in New York on March 21, everyone assumed he was ready to announce, but in fact he had concluded not to run. He told a startled nation he was there to reiterate that "I am not a candidate campaigning directly or indirectly for the presidency of the United States." He said he would accept a draft, but added, "I expect no call and will do nothing to encourage such a call." When a reporter asked him if his decision did not virtually guarantee Nixon's nomination, the governor replied, "I think that's a fair conclusion."

The main ingredient in Rockefeller's surprise decision was his conclusion that Nixon was probably unbeatable. As he put it himself, "I find it clear at this time that a considerable majority of the party's leaders want the candidacy of former Vice President Richard Nixon. And it appears equally clear that they are keenly concerned and

anxious to avoid any such divisive challenge within the party as marked the 1964 campaign."

Rockefeller's decision was a shattering blow to liberal Republicans. For two years, they had allowed themselves to think that if their front-runner Romney stumbled, they had a stronger horse in the stable. Now their fallback candidate had decided not to run. The whole scene was an ironic replay of Rockefeller's 1959 Christmas Eve performance. Then, too, he had allowed himself to be persuaded that challenging Nixon was futile. The shock of this second capitulation was heightened by the fact that Rockefeller, though attended by the largest and best-paid entourage of political advisers in the country, neglected the elementary political courtesy of informing his main backers of his decision. The governor's closest allies and staunchest supporters—governors, senators, and finance men who had staked their own political reputations on his expected candidacy—learned of his decision not to run in the same way the rest of the country did—by watching his televised press conference. The reason for this oversight on Rockefeller's part is not known, but the result was to add rage to the frustration felt by his supporters. Ironically, one of the men trapped by Rockefeller's insensitivity was the novice governor of Maryland, Spiro T. Agnew, who, in an unsophisticated display of simple enthusiasm for Rockefeller's qualities of leadership, had undertaken to organize a national Draft Rockefeller headquarters in Annapolis. Agnew had put his backing behind Rockefeller in early 1967, when the New Yorker was resolutely disavowing any intention of running, and now that his champion seemed ready to enter the lists, Agnew was prepared to collect the rewards for virtue and prescience. He invited Maryland reporters to watch the Rockefeller press conference with him, and with cameras trained on him, underwent the public humiliation of seeing his candidate disappear. "I must confess," he said, "I am tremendously surprised. I also frankly add that I am greatly disappointed."

There and then began the journey that was to make Spiro Agnew vice president. As it turned out, though Rockefeller asked to be "spared any measure of the distrust" commonly felt toward politicians because "I mean—and I shall abide by—precisely what I say," his March 21 "no" was not to be a final "no." Less than six weeks later, he was to reverse himself—but in those six weeks the shape of the political world had been totally altered by developments in the Democratic Party and the country.

The Democratic Party appeared, quite simply, to be coming apart. The first and least surprising revolt had come from the Deep South, led by a skillful demagogue and ardent opponent of integration, ex-governor George Wallace of Alabama.

Wallace, a short, pugnacious man of 48, with a quick wit, a folksy speaking style, and an almost insatiable drive for publicity, had been elected governor in 1962, vowing at his inaugural to maintain "segregation now—segregation tomorrow—and segregation forever." In his first year in office, however, the first black students were admitted under federal court order to the University of Alabama—but not before Wallace, in a typically theatrical gesture, had "stood in the schoolhouse door" to bar their admission until President Kennedy federalized the Alabama National Guard and a deputy attorney general ordered Wallace to stand aside. Through a series of such carefully staged confrontations, Wallace won himself a national reputation as the leading Southern opponent of "forced integration." In 1964, he decided to test his appeal outside the South by entering Democratic presidential primaries in Wisconsin, Indiana, and Maryland. To the chagrin of Democratic regulars, Wallace—campaigning with colorful language against the courts, civil rights legislation, big government, and "coddling" of criminals—won between 30 and 40 percent of the vote against the organization candidates (two governors and a senator) heading the pro-Johnson slates in those states. It was the first demonstration that racial "backlash" in the North had reached dimensions where it could fuel a real challenge to the local organizations.

Wallace toyed for a time with running as a third-party candidate for president in 1964, but withdrew from the race after the Republicans nominated Goldwater. His national ambitions, however, remained.

Unsuccessful in an effort to remove the Alabama constitution's prohibition on a governor seeking reelection, Wallace managed to keep his political base intact by the simple expedient of running his wife, Lurleen, for governor in the 1966 election. Mrs. Wallace, a slight, shy woman, already ill with cancer that was to claim her life in early 1968, was up against a strong field of Democratic rivals. But with her husband making her campaign speeches for her and promising to serve as her "No. 1 adviser," she won the primary, without the expense of a runoff, and easily defeated the Republican who had the temerity to oppose her in the general election.

Once his wife was inaugurated, Wallace launched his preparations for a serious third-party presidential bid in 1968. He toured the country, announcing there was not "a dime's worth of difference" between the Republicans and Democrats on the major issues. If Northern audiences had been receptive in 1964, they were enthusiastic now. After the civil rights movement had reached its high point with the passage of the landmark legislation of 1964 and 1965, the riots in Watts, in Newark, in Detroit, and dozens of other cities hardened the lines of racial conflict. Wallace broadened his rhetoric to play on all the fears and resentments of the lower-income whites, not only their dislike of blacks but also their frustration with rising taxes, with bureaucracy, and with the machinations of all those "pointy-heads" Wallace told them were running the country into the ground.

His grassroots organizations, using a few patronage employees from Alabama to lead the squads of volunteer workers he found available in almost every state, astonished the professionals by the ease with which they secured the signatures needed to place Wallace's name on the state ballots. Skeptics had said he would fail in his first big test in California, where 66,000 names were required, but the Wallace organization secured far more than the requisite number by January 1, 1968. By the time Wallace announced on February 8, opinion polls showed him with 10 to 12 percent of the national vote and threatening to lead the major party candidates in the South. This year, it was clear, the Alabamian was not going to "stand aside" for anyone.

On the far opposite flank of the Democratic Party, the liberal, intellectual Left that since New Deal days had exerted an influence disproportionate to its numbers, another rebellion was brewing. In direct contrast to Wallace, the liberal Left applauded Johnson's ambitious domestic program—especially the civil rights laws—but decried the expansion of the war in Vietnam.

As their disaffection on the war increased—fed by the ever-mounting protest from the college campuses

Nelson A. Rockefeller campaign poster *(Library of Congress)*

that climaxed in the march on the Pentagon of October 1967—the liberal Democrats were searching desperately for a candidate. Among them was Allard K. Lowenstein, a young New York lawyer (he was elected to the House of Representatives in 1968) with wide contacts in the student and liberal movements.

In the summer of 1967, during the convention of the National Student Association (the largest organization of college students), Lowenstein, a former NSA president, and younger colleagues publicly launched the effort to unseat the incumbent president. Help came from some, but not all, the leaders of the 20-year-old liberal organization Americans for Democratic Action, from the California Democratic Council, and similar groups. Many who shared Lowenstein's opposition to the Vietnam War nonetheless hesitated to join his call for an anti-Johnson coalition. Their reason was simple—the dump-Johnson movement had no candidate.

Lowenstein's search for a champion took him through the ranks of the Senate Democratic "doves." He started with Robert Kennedy—who two years earlier had made his public break with the Vietnam War policy he had supported in his brother's cabinet. Kennedy declined to run, citing both the political hazards of the project and the danger that the great debate on Vietnam would be lost in the public preoccupation with his well-publicized personal feud with Johnson. In turn, Senator George McGovern of South Dakota and Senator Frank Church of Idaho (both up for reelection in 1968) turned Lowenstein down. And then, when Lowenstein had about exhausted his list, quite unexpectedly he found the man he had been looking for.

He was Eugene Joseph McCarthy, the handsome, gray-haired, 51-year-old senator from Minnesota. McCarthy, a soft-voiced, intellectual Catholic, endowed with a caustic wit, had been a member of Congress since 1948. He was a leader of the younger liberal Democrats in his decade in the House but, since coming to the Senate as Hubert Humphrey's junior colleague in 1958, had made little mark in that body. He first came to public prominence with his eloquent nominating speech for Adlai Stevenson at the 1960 convention—probably one of the great speeches in convention history—and he retained a small personal following within the liberal Stevensonian wing of the party.

In 1964, he had sought the vice-presidential nomination that went to Humphrey but thereafter returned by choice to his back-bench Senate seat and let other, more vociferous critics take the lead in the criticism of the Vietnam War.

On November 30, 1967, McCarthy announced he would enter several Democratic presidential primaries in order to challenge what he called the administration's policy of "continued escalation and intensification of

Captioned "We'll let the overcoat out all the way, and the robe will hardly show at all," this Herblock cartoon shows presidential candidate George Wallace tailoring a coat, "3rd Party" and "'Law-and-Order' Talk," to fit over a Ku Klux Klan robe. (*A Herblock Cartoon, copyright by the Herb Block Foundation*)

the War in Vietnam." Unless the policy were reversed, he said, he would carry his challenge all the way to the Democratic convention—but would not run as an independent candidate if defeated there.

From the very beginning, the McCarthy campaign was a curious enterprise. His announcement left it unclear whether he was seriously seeking the nomination or merely applying pressure for a change in policy. Though McCarthy had been at odds with the Kennedy family since the 1960 convention, he told reporters he would have been happy to stand aside for Robert Kennedy and would consider it "wholly proper" for Kennedy to enter the race if McCarthy defeated the president in the early primaries. In his announcement, McCarthy said he hoped his candidacy "may alleviate the sense of political helplessness and restore to many people a belief in the processes of American politics and of American government. On college campuses especially . . . it may counter the growing sense of alienation from politics." The students heard him and came flocking to his cause in numbers that had no parallel in earlier elections. It was well for McCarthy that they did so, for his candidacy at first drew negligible support from professional politicians, not even from congressional colleagues who had shared his criticism of the war. Kennedy, McGovern, Church, Fulbright—the whole roster of Senate "doves"—stayed studiously neutral, awed by McCarthy's audacity but skeptical that his energy, skill, or resources were sufficient to bring down the president.

Johnson, in the beginning of 1968, was maintaining the normal posture—for an incumbent—of disdaining to take time from his duties to indulge in partisan politics. But while the president withheld announcement of his plans, several of his close political associates opened an office, next door to the Democratic National Committee headquarters in Washington, to coordinate pre-convention activities on his behalf. Of this group, only Postmaster General Lawrence F. O'Brien appeared to have taken McCarthy's candidacy seriously from the start.

The tactical decision was made early in the year to keep the president's name off primary ballots where it was not required that it be entered. The theory—again wholly in accord with traditional political thinking—was that Johnson could win enough delegates in the non-primary states, through organization support, to ensure renomination, and there was no need to risk possible embarrassment by putting his name before the voters in the primaries.

In New Hampshire, site of the earliest primary, the pro-Johnson Democratic organization was told it could run a write-in campaign for Johnson, in order to keep McCarthy from capturing delegates and prestige, but could not put his name on the ballot or expect any direct campaign aid from Washington. Initially, those conditions seemed unimportant; most observers were guessing in January that McCarthy would do well to win 15 percent of the New Hampshire vote. He was not well known in the state; the entire Democratic hierarchy was against him; and the small, Catholic, working-class vote expected in the primary was thought to be "hawkish" on Vietnam.

This forecast, like so many others in 1968, could scarcely have been more wrong. The Viet Cong's Tet Offensive, which began on January 29 and raged through the cities and countryside for two weeks, bringing the war right to the doorstep of the American Embassy in Saigon before it was finally repulsed, shook public confidence in administration claims of progress in the war. For the first time, the tide of opinion shifted toward serious contemplation of political compromise or withdrawal from Vietnam.

Reinforcing this shift, so far as the voters of New Hampshire were concerned, was the massive, youthful army of college students who came to stand on the doorsteps of their homes, talking of their doubts about the wisdom and morality of the American effort in Vietnam and asking votes for McCarthy.

There were other things, too—including the tactical mistakes of the pro-Johnson regulars, who were heavy-handed and inept and finally panicky in their reaction to McCarthy and his youthful brigade. (The Democratic governor said a McCarthy victory would be "greeted with great cheers in Hanoi.") On March 12, the New Hampshire voters made political history by repudiating the President. McCarthy trailed Johnson's write-ins very narrowly (23,280 to 27,243), and in separate polling the senator's supporters actually won 20 of the 24 delegate contests. That night, for the first time, McCarthy predicted nomination for himself.

While not many others were ready to make that judgment, the New Hampshire returns changed the entire political prospect. The first man to react was Robert Kennedy, who had been having serious second thoughts about his own earlier refusal to get into the race. Some members of his family, many members of his staff, and virtually all the young Democratic Party activists with whom Kennedy identified himself were telling him that Vietnam was a moral issue and that he could not avoid challenging the president without losing his claim to his constituency. Others still argued, however, that an anti-Johnson campaign on his part would be politically imprudent and self-defeating, that it could end only in the wreckage of the Democratic Party and the election of Nixon.

In accounts published after his death, many Kennedy associates said Kennedy had decided a week or ten days before the New Hampshire primary to enter the race. Their testimony is persuasive, but Kennedy gave no public indication of his decision until after the returns were in. Then, he did so with a speed and bluntness that offended McCarthy and most McCarthy supporters. Only a day after the primary, Kennedy announced he was "actively reconsidering" the decision not to run, and, three days later, made the formal announcement that he was entering the race, "not in opposition to McCarthy's candidacy but in harmony." "I run," he told a press conference in the same Senate caucus room where his brother John had declared for the Presidency eight years earlier, "to seek new policies, policies to end the bloodshed in Viet Nam and in our cities, policies to close the gap that now exists between black and white, between rich and poor, between young and old in this country and around the rest of the world. . . . I run because it is now unmistakably clear that we can change these disastrous, divisive policies only by changing the men who are now making them."

Kennedy said he would support McCarthy in the Wisconsin, Massachusetts, and Pennsylvania primaries,

Robert F. Kennedy campaigns in Los Angeles during the 1968 primary election. (*Evan Freed*)

whose filing deadlines had already passed, and would run in primaries in California, Oregon, and Nebraska (he later added Indiana and South Dakota), which were still open to him. Kennedy expressed the vague hope that somehow "Senator McCarthy's forces and mine will be able to work together in one form or another," but practically, Kennedy's announcement meant that he and McCarthy would contest for the leadership of the antiwar wing of the party in the late spring primaries. McCarthy quickly refused Kennedy's offer of help against Johnson in the early primaries. "I can win in Wisconsin alone as I won in New Hampshire without any outside help," he said, adding, in a bitter aside, that when he began his challenge "a lot of other politicians were afraid to come down on the playing field. They were willing to stay up on the mountain and light signal fires, bonfires and dance in the light of the moon, but none of them came down." The split that began in the first few hours of Kennedy's candidacy—and that was perhaps foreordained by the personalities and histories of the two men—never healed, and the antiwar, anti-Johnson ranks never closed.

Kennedy plunged into an immediate speaking tour, starting at Kansas State University and swinging across the country. Both on campuses and in the cities, he drew very large and enthusiastic audiences. His rhetoric ranged from the iniquities of the war to the failings of Johnson. The stringency of his attack mounted with the size of his crowds. In speeches that first week of his campaign, he said "those who make present policy" had, among other things, "removed themselves from the American tradi-

tion . . . and called upon the darker impulses of the American spirit."

Meantime, in Wisconsin, where Johnson's name was entered automatically on the primary ballot under state law, administration loyalists mounted a last-ditch effort to save the president from a second setback at McCarthy's hands. Humphrey and several cabinet members stumped the state on behalf of the still undeclared president, but McCarthy drew larger crowds and every preelection survey pointed to the likelihood of his outpolling the president in the April 2 vote.

And then, on Sunday evening, March 31, less than 36 hours before the Wisconsin polls were to open, President Johnson went on national television for what had been billed in advance as a major address. The moment was made for drama. The fires of controversy over Vietnam—which Mr. Johnson had tried time and again to quench—were burning higher than ever, since the Tet Offensive, the New Hampshire results, and the combined campaigning of Kennedy and McCarthy.

Sequestered in the White House, surrounded by his still-loyal staff, Johnson was like an aging medieval baron besieged by his enemies, still proud and still defiant. He had said little publicly since the storm broke on him with renewed fury at the beginning of the month. On March 19, he asserted the Tet Offensive was a failure and that the Communists would never "crack America's will. We have set our course. We will pursue it as long as aggression threatens us, and we will prevail." Three days later, he told his press conference he hoped there would not be "brutal" partisanship in the coming campaign. As for his own candidacy, he said, "When I get to that bridge, I will cross it. I am not there yet."

On the morning of the March 31 speech, the Gallup Poll showed only 36 percent of the American voters approved of Johnson's handling of his job, while 52 percent disapproved.

Unless the surveys were wrong, outright defeat at the hands of McCarthy awaited Johnson in Wisconsin two days later. It was a bitter comedown for the man who had won such a sweeping victory in 1964.

The speech—from the White House—began with the announcement of a major policy reversal in Vietnam. That reversal had its beginnings early in March, when Clark Clifford, a Washington lawyer who had been in the inner circles of the Democratic Party for 20 years, replaced Robert McNamara as secretary of defense. Clifford came to office as a supporter of the Vietnam policy, but, as he examined the strategy for the war in the Pentagon, he became skeptical of its underlying assumptions. Clifford communicated his skepticism and—for the first time—the air of official optimism maintained by the inner circle around the president was broken. With Clifford questioning the military logic, the other "doves" in the Pentagon and on the White House staff began speaking up, and Secretary of State Dean Rusk and National Security Adviser Walt W. Rostow were challenged. The debate—one of the most momentous of recent times—cannot be detailed here, but in the end the president came down with the "doves," rejected the field commanders' call for an additional 206,000 troops for Vietnam, and ordered a severe cutback in the bombing of North Vietnam. It was this decision—and the invitation to Hanoi to open peace talks—that consumed the early portion of the Johnson speech. Then—with a little gesture to his wife, watching off-camera—the president took on a more personal tone.

"There is a divisiveness among us all tonight," he said. "And holding the trust that is mine, as President of all the people, I cannot disregard the peril to the progress of the American people and the hope and prospect of peace for all peoples."

Johnson recalled his accession to the office "in a moment of tragedy and trauma" and the rallying of the American people that followed. Then he said:

> What we won when all of our people united, just must not now be lost in suspicion and distrust and selfishness and politics among any of our people. And believing this as I do, I have concluded that I should not permit the Presidency to become involved in the partisan divisions that are developing in this political year.
>
> With American sons in the fields far away, with America's future under challenge right here at home, with our hopes and the world's hopes for peace in the balance every day, I do not believe that I should devote an hour or a day of my time to any personal partisan causes or to any duties other than the awesome duties of this office—the Presidency of your country.
>
> (He paused a moment—as if savoring that awesome power for the last second.)
>
> Accordingly, I shall not seek and I will not accept the nomination of my party for another term as your President.

The shockwaves rolled out across the country and the world. Only a handful of men and Mrs. Johnson knew of the president's decision even a few hours in advance; most administration and Democratic Party leaders had no advance warning.

Later, the president was to say he had resolved on this course of action as early as 1964 and had reaffirmed the decision in the fall of 1967, had been ready to announce it in January, when he made his State of the Union speech,

but had decided it would be inappropriate then. There is no reason to reject Johnson's word, but it is hard to reconcile the reported decision with his permitting his old friends and political associates to begin organizing a renomination and reelection campaign, as they did in the winter and early spring of the year. Indeed, some of them held a campaign strategy meeting in the White House on the afternoon of March 31.

If the Democratic battle had been intense before Mr. Johnson's withdrawal, it now exploded in the sudden vacuum created by his announcement.

McCarthy, the instrument of his downfall, confirmed his popular strength by defeating the president in the April 2 Wisconsin primary, taking almost 57 percent of the vote. "We have demonstrated in Wisconsin," said the no-longer-diffident candidate, "the ability to win the election in November."

Kennedy, who had been campaigning almost as if he were as eager to destroy Johnson's prospects as to enhance his own, attempted a quick change of direction, now that he was in a position to court the pro-Johnson regulars. He said the president's decision reflects "both courage and generosity of spirit," and asked for a meeting—which Johnson granted—"to discuss how we might work together in the interest of national unity during the coming months."

But the greatest change was in the status of Hubert Humphrey. Humphrey had been told of Johnson's decision a few hours before the speech, but had flown off to Mexico City for a previously scheduled diplomatic visit, uncertain (or so he later said) whether he had managed to dissuade Johnson from that course.

Humphrey returned to Washington two days later, but even before that time his aides were on the phones, working to stem the expected Kennedy blitz and pleading with pro-administration Democrats to hold fast. On Thursday afternoon, April 4, Humphrey went to Pittsburgh for a previously scheduled speech to the Pennsylvania AFL-CIO convention. The leaders of organized labor, still "hawkish" on Vietnam, suspicious of Kennedy, and totally uncomfortable with McCarthy and his "kiddie campaign," were desperate for a candidate and pressured Humphrey to announce, on the spot. I. W. Abel, president of the Steelworkers Union, endorsed Humphrey in his introduction, and the union delegates shouted at the vice president, "Tell us now." Humphrey declined the formal declaration but said, "I will not run away from the record of this Administration. I will do everything in my power—if the Lord gives me strength—to carry the record of the Johnson–Humphrey administration to the people in the months ahead."

Then Humphrey flew back to Washington, where a fund-raising dinner for Democratic senatorial and congressional candidates was scheduled that night. When he returned, he received word of an event that altered his timetable and shook America as severely as the Tet Offensive.

The Reverend Dr. Martin Luther King Jr., the single strongest leader and the international symbol of the civil rights movement of the 1960s, had been shot by an assassin while in Memphis, Tennessee, to lend his prestige and presence to a strike of municipal garbage collectors. It was Humphrey who announced the news of King's death to a stunned audience of Democrats that night.

The next afternoon, flying back to Washington from a speech on Long Island, which he turned into a eulogy of the slain civil rights leader, Humphrey gazed out on perhaps the most awful sight to greet the eyes of a 20th-century American. A thick pall of smoke hung over the capital city and, from the air, fires appeared to ring the White House and the downtown government buildings.

Rioting and looting and arson that began in the early hours of April 5 had grown steadily worse through the day. Before the week was out, similar riots had taken place in more than a hundred cities, taking 37 lives and destroying millions of dollars in property and an immeasurable degree of America's poise, prestige, and self-confidence.

Politics stopped, as all the 1968 contenders, declared and undeclared, attended funeral services for King at Atlanta's Ebenezer Baptist Church, then halted their campaigning out of respect.

During the pause, Humphrey had time to plan his strategy. Private checks confirmed that Kennedy had scored no "blitz" in the immediate aftermath of Johnson's withdrawal. The leaders of labor were ready to offer Humphrey their endorsement, and most of the Southern Democratic governors and party officials were also in his corner—if only because they found Kennedy's civil rights record as attorney general and McCarthy's antiwar stand even less palatable to their constituents than Humphrey's liberalism. The Northern city Democratic bosses—Richard J. Daley of Chicago, James H. J. Tate of Philadelphia, and Joseph M. Barr of Pittsburgh, and the rest—were either pro-Humphrey or staying uncommitted.

By April 27, the vice president had the promise of adequate organizational and financial support to enter the race. At a kickoff rally in Washington, he praised President Johnson's "dramatic leadership" of the nation and dedicated himself (in a phrase that later came back to haunt him) to practicing "the politics of happiness."

All this occurred before Nelson Rockefeller, on April 30, announced he was back in the presidential race he had declined to enter on March 21. The reason he gave was that in "the gravity of the crises that we face as a people" and "the new circumstances that confront the nation, I frankly find that to comment from the sidelines is not an effective way to present the alternatives." Rockefeller had discovered that the nomination would not come to him without a fight; he had also admitted what many others had long since guessed—that whatever the unlikelihood of his winning, he could not be satisfied unless he tried.

The next six weeks were an odd, disjointed time in American politics. Humphrey and Rockefeller had, by design, timed their announcements too late to qualify themselves for the ballot in even the late presidential primaries. Humphrey preferred to rely on his support among the party regulars in the South and the big cities and labor; Rockefeller still believed that after the bitterness of 1964 he could afford no direct clash with Nixon, the favorite of the organization men.

As a result, the major spring primaries lost most of their significance. Nixon, for all practical purposes, was unopposed on the Republican side; Kennedy and McCarthy were battling each other for the same antiwar, anti-administration votes, while their real opponent, Humphrey, was elsewhere rounding up the delegates.

As a result, the primaries probably had less bearing on the outcome of the nomination struggle in 1968 than in any recent election year. In late April, McCarthy won the Pennsylvania and Massachusetts preference polls with no organized opposition; but only in the latter did his victory give him the delegate votes.

The Indiana primary, on May 7, brought the first McCarthy–Kennedy test, with Governor Roger Branigin (originally a stand-in for President Johnson) also in the race. After an expensive, hard-fought campaign, Kennedy emerged a plurality winner (with 42 percent of the vote), with Branigin narrowly edging McCarthy for second place. Nixon, running unopposed on the Republican side, easily outdrew Kennedy. On the same day, a pro-Kennedy slate beat a pro-Humphrey slate in the District of Columbia primary.

A week later, in Nebraska, Kennedy repeated his victory over McCarthy, this time polling a narrow majority, even when write-ins for Humphrey and Johnson were counted. Once again, Nixon was a landslide winner on the Republican side, taking 70 percent of the GOP vote against Reagan, whose name was automatically listed on the ballot (because he was a declared favorite-son candidate in California) but whose campaigning was limited to a few television commercials.

On May 28, in Oregon, McCarthy turned the tables on Kennedy, beating him by 20,000 votes. The Minnesotan had the advantage of a strong local organization, and in Oregon Kennedy found few of the black or ethnic voters from whom he drew his strongest support.

In addition to the McCarthy upset, Oregon also provided the most important primary win for Nixon. He rolled up a 3-to-1 margin over Reagan, whose support-

Minnesota senator Eugene McCarthy is followed by college student supporters after making a speech in Racine, Wisconsin, March 20, 1968. *(Associated Press)*

ers mounted a full-fledged television blitz for the absentee governor, who, as in Nebraska, was on the ballot but did not campaign in person. Rockefeller's local supporters staged a last-minute write-in campaign for him, but it netted so few votes (barely 4 percent of the Republican total) as to be an embarrassment.

The final showdown between Kennedy and McCarthy came a week later—June 4—in California, with the prize being not merely the 174 votes (one-eighth of those needed for nomination) but the clear leadership in the fight to deny Humphrey the nomination. (Nixon did not enter the Republican primary in his native state out of deference to Reagan's favorite-son candidacy.) After McCarthy's surprise showing in Oregon, Kennedy switched strategy and agreed to debate the Minnesotan—an encounter he had been avoiding all spring. Neither their hour-long confrontation on the Saturday before the voting nor their frantic personal campaigning appeared to have much influence on the California outcome. Kennedy had an advantage in the race, because of the solidity of his support in the sizable black and Mexican-American voting blocs and his alliance with State Assembly Speaker Jesse M. Unruh, proprietor of the most effective organization in populous Los Angeles County. McCarthy ran well in northern California

and in the middle- and upper-class white areas, where the volunteer political strength of the California Democratic Council was greatest. But Kennedy won, 46 to 42 percent, with the slate headed by Attorney General Thomas C. Lynch (another of the stranded pro-administration favorite-sons) a distant third, with 12 percent. (On the same day, a Kennedy slate beat slates favorable to McCarthy and Humphrey in the South Dakota primary.)

McCarthy took his setback with the same equanimity he displayed throughout the primary campaigns, saying he would continue his bid for the nomination and insisting there was no evidence that in a general election "Kennedy can get any votes that I can't get."

But his backers were more prepared than McCarthy himself to recognize the realities of the situation. Several of McCarthy's student organizers had accepted invitations to meet with Kennedy for breakfast on June 5. As the New York senator left his Ambassador Hotel suite to make his victory statement, he asked that a call be placed to Al Lowenstein, the young lawyer who had recruited McCarthy for the antiwar, anti-Johnson cause so many months before. Prodded by his aides, Kennedy left before the call could be completed; his over-the-shoulder instructions were to tell Lowenstein he would call him as soon as he got back to the suite.

He was, of course, never to return. Leaving the platform after rallying his supporters with the cry, "on to Chicago," he turned back into the hotel kitchen, where an assailant, firing from point-blank range, shot Kennedy three times with a .22 caliber pistol and then sprayed the room, wounding five other persons. The assassin, a 20-year-old Jordanian immigrant named Sirhan Bashira Sirhan, was overpowered and captured. (He was brought to trial in 1969, convicted of first-degree murder, and sentenced to death.) Kennedy underwent emergency surgery for the most serious of his wounds—a bullet that entered the right side of his head and lodged in midbrain—but died at 1:44 a.m. on June 6, at Good Samaritan Hospital in Los Angeles, 25 hours after the assault. Like his brother, President John Kennedy, Robert Kennedy found in a demented marksman the nemesis for which none of the stratagems of conventional politics provided an answer.

Once again, as with the murder of King two months earlier, the whole machinery of political life ground to a halt. The surviving actors in the 1968 drama—the president, the vice president, Nixon and Rockefeller, McCarthy and the rest—assembled again as mourners, this time in St. Patrick's Cathedral in New York City, on June 8. Kennedy's last journey was by train from New York to Washington—with saddened crowds lining the tracks and filling the stations where it passed—and then by motorcade to Arlington Cemetery, where he was buried after dark, by candlelight, just down the slope from his slain brother. In a very real sense, neither Humphrey nor McCarthy nor the Democratic Party ever recovered in 1968 from the shock of the Kennedy murder.

All overt campaigning stopped for several weeks. In mid-June, during the lull, McCarthy's fortunes received a brief boost when his supporters defeated backers of Humphrey in the majority of the district delegate contests in New York and a McCarthy supporter won an upset victory in a three-way primary for the Senate nomination. However, in New York and other industrial states, party regulars quickly closed ranks against McCarthy, and the passing weeks saw a diminution both in McCarthy's drive for the nomination and in his chances of winning it.

As July turned into August, attention swung back to the Republicans, preparing for their convention in Miami Beach. Nixon was far in front of Rockefeller and Reagan in the delegate counts, but there was some uncertainty whether the two governors and the favorite sons could withhold enough votes to deny him the first-ballot nomination his strategy required.

Rockefeller's effort was deliberately soft-sell, for the governor and his advisors still believed that he could make no overt attack on Nixon without incurring the regulars' wrath as a habitual party wrecker. Their hope was to persuade the delegates that *only* Rockefeller could win in the fall. Crucial evidence would be the preconvention public opinion polls, and to influence those polls, Rockefeller invested at least $4 million in an unprecedented pre-nomination advertising campaign. Concentrated in newspapers and television stations in the big states, these ads spelled out his position on the issues. Rockefeller was more liberal than Nixon on domestic problems; after Kennedy's death, he shifted still further left, hoping to graft some of Kennedy's support onto his own. The advertising blitz began in early June and ran seven weeks, timed to reach its climax just 10 days before the convention, when the final pre-convention polls would be taken. If they showed Rockefeller beating Humphrey and McCarthy, while Nixon was losing, the delegates might switch.

That, at least, was the theory. But by himself, Rockefeller knew, he could not stop Nixon. The very stands and tactics that might swing delegates to him in the urban, industrial states would solidify the rural states and the South against him. To stop Nixon on the first ballot, Rockefeller would need a major assist from Reagan. Early on, the two men came to an unspoken understanding; the difference in their ideologies and the clash of their egos made alliance impossible; but each understood that his only chance on winning would come if, together, they could stop Nixon on the first ballot.

Reagan, as we have seen, was anything but uninterested in the prize, despite his public cloak of noncandidacy. But the script Clif White, the Goldwater strategist, had devised for him was not playing as he had hoped. White had expected the television campaigns for Reagan in the Wisconsin, Nebraska, and Oregon primaries—each more expensive than the one before—to produce a crescendo of votes for the absentee candidate that might fuel talk of a Reagan groundswell. The votes (as we have seen) were embarrassingly small.

Nonetheless, Reagan plunged into active pursuit of the nomination in late June and July, still undeclared, but crisscrossing the country and concentrating on the South, exerting his powerful charm and showing his oratorical powers to the delegates.

The South was vital to Nixon's calculus for winning nomination and election. In the convention, the 13 Southern states had 356 votes, more than half the 667 needed for nomination. On May 31 and June 1—immediately after the Oregon primary—Nixon had gone to Atlanta for two days of private talks with the Republican leaders of the Southern states; they were old friends, for he had campaigned to build a Republican Party in all their states. The talk was frank; what they most wanted was assurance that he and his running mate would campaign in a way designed to block the thrust of Wallace's third-party appeal, which menaced the growth of Republicanism in their region. They also wanted assurance that if Nixon was successful they would have access to the front door of the White House and not be treated as disreputable poor relations. These assurances Nixon gave, and he left Atlanta with the pledge of support of the leaders of virtually every Southern state—most notably, Senators Strom Thurmond of South Carolina, John Tower of Texas, and Howard Baker of Tennessee, and the Republican chairmen of Florida, Georgia, Virginia, and Mississippi.

But sewing up the Southern delegations was not quite that easy. For it was Reagan, far more than Nixon, who made Southern pulses race: far harsher in his denunciation of "forced" integration, far more strident in declaiming his allegiance to "law and order," and far more hawkish in his pronouncements on the Vietnam War. If Reagan could take the Southerners out from under Nixon, if Rockefeller could best Nixon in the polls, if enough of the favorite sons held firm on the first ballot, then maybe, just maybe, the Miami Beach drama would not run on Nixon's carefully drawn script.

The delegates had barely unpacked when the challengers' hopes began to go awry. Rockefeller's reliance on the polls left him peculiarly vulnerable when on July 29, the morning that pre-convention platform hearings began in Miami Beach, the Gallup Poll announced that Nixon had moved ahead of both Humphrey and McCarthy, while Rockefeller was still deadlocked with the two Democratic contenders. In fact, Nixon's advantage was so small—2 percentage points in one case and 4 points in the other—as to fall within the range of statistical error for the sample size Gallup was using. Moreover, the Gallup results were to be contradicted by another poll released by the Harris organization later in the same pre-convention week. It showed Rockefeller ahead of both Democrats and Nixon trailing them. In a futile effort to resolve the confusion, Gallup and Harris issued a joint statement on August 1, asserting that, when the differences in the timing of the two polls and a third study made privately for Rockefeller by the Crossley organization, were taken into account, the results were not contradictory. Rather, they said, they showed a sequence of readings indicating that Rockefeller "has now moved to an open lead over both possible Democratic candidates, while a Nixon–Humphrey–Wallace contest is a virtual toss-up." Though this final conclusion was favorable to Rockefeller, so much confusion had been engendered by the "battle of the polls" that all the findings tended to be viewed with suspicion, and the political effect of any poll blunted. (In an effort to avoid a repetition of the Miami Beach fiasco, the major pollsters later in 1968 formed an association authorized to set standards for accredited polling organizations and to increase public understanding of the uses and limits of survey data.) Thus, for at least the third time in the Republican presidential race, the polls undercut the efforts of the liberal Republican hopeful.

Meanwhile, on the other flank of the party, Reagan was finding the resistance of the pro-Nixon Southern GOP leaders hard to overcome. The Californian made a dramatic appearance before the platform committee on July 31, drawing repeated bursts of applause from the audience with his hard-line stance against criminals, dissident students, and the Viet Cong. But White found the going tough in picking away at Nixon supporters in the Southern delegations. On Monday, August 5, the opening day of the convention, Reagan was forced to drop his disguise and become an avowed candidate. For the next 48 hours, the battle waged hot and heavy in the Southern delegations. Reagan cracked North Carolina and several times seemed close to turning the majority in Florida, Alabama, Mississippi, and Louisiana to his side. But the lure of being with a winner proved too strong, and with Thurmond, Goldwater, and Tower working for Nixon among the Southern delegates, Reagan was blocked.

At the same time, Northern favorite-son delegations were crumbling under the pressure of Nixon's apparent bandwagon. After a major struggle, Nixon adherents in New Jersey broke the efforts of pro-Rockefeller senator

This cartoon by Herblock shows the Democratic donkey, holding a newspaper with a picture of former vice president Richard Nixon with a five o'clock shadow, perkily asking a dour GOP elephant, "So what's new?" Herblock comments on the fact that the Republican National Convention, held in Miami in 1968, was a boring affair in which the nomination of Nixon, who had been the party's nominee in 1960, was a foregone conclusion. (*A Herblock Cartoon, copyright by the Herb Block Foundation*)

Clifford P. Case to hold the delegation on the first ballot for himself and took 18 of the 40 votes to Nixon. Agnew, the Maryland governor so disillusioned by Rockefeller's unexpected March decision not to run an active campaign, not only released his delegation (with 18 of the 26 votes going to Nixon) but also agreed to make Nixon's nominating speech. In the end, only three major governors—Reagan, Rhodes of Ohio, and Romney—were able to hold their delegations substantially intact as first-ballot favorite sons.

Nixon won on the first roll call, but his total vote—692, or 25 more than the 667 needed for nomination—showed how close the implausible Rockefeller–Reagan combination had come to stopping him. The backbone of his support was in the South, the border states, and the smaller states of the Midwest and the West. He received a majority of the votes in none of the major Northern industrial states except Illinois. Nonetheless, Nixon had achieved a remarkable comeback victory, and he had done it as he wished—without indulging in the kind of strong-arm tactics that might damage his chances in the general election.

Two other aspects of the Republican convention—the platform and the vice-presidential nomination—are worth noting. The platform was adopted, without floor debate, and met with general approbation from all wings of the party. This healing of the ideological wounds of the 1964 struggle was attributable to several factors. For one thing, the platform committee was able to draw heavily on the policy papers issued during the previous four years by the Republican Coordinating Committee, the all-embracing leadership group Bliss had set up soon after becoming chairman in 1965 (its members included leading governors, senators, representatives, party officials, and past presidential nominees). Second, its chairman, Senator Everett McKinley Dirksen of Illinois, was a man of tested parliamentary skill who took on his duties determined to write a document "any of our candidates can run on." Third, none of the candidates—and particularly not Rockefeller—wanted to lead a repetition of the 1964 struggle, for fear of being castigated as a party-wrecker.

The document that emerged from long hours of debate by the committee members was notably strong in its condemnation of crime, deliberately vague in its treatment of civil rights and domestic welfare programs, and rather more "dovish" on Vietnam than had been expected, pledging "de-Americanization" of the war effort and a negotiating position aimed at something more than "a camouflaged surrender," but less than total victory. In all these respects, the platform reflected Nixon's own positions at convention time, and it was in no way an impediment to the kind of campaign he planned to conduct.

The other matter, the choice of the vice-presidential nominee, proved more vexatious to Nixon. In the pre-convention maneuvering, he had followed the time-honored custom of hinting to every susceptible politician with a bloc of delegates at his disposal that he was under consideration for the number two job. But behind all the artfulness, there appeared to be genuine uncertainty as to in which direction to move. In 1960, Nixon had picked a man of high prestige, Henry Cabot Lodge, a former senator from Massachusetts, then serving as ambassador to the United Nations, over several men preferred by the politicians in his party. Lodge's performance as the number two man on the ticket had drawn much unfavorable comment in postmortems on the campaign. Nixon was anxious to avoid a similar mistake. He knew, too, that the vice-presidential choice would be regarded as the first important indication of the electoral strategy he would follow in 1968.

Rockefeller and Reagan eliminated themselves from consideration by their vehement statements of disinterest in the number two job. But there remained in contention, with varying degrees of support, a wide spectrum of Republicans, ranging from Tower, Baker, and Representative George Bush of Texas, on the right, to Senator Mark Hatfield of Oregon, Senator Charles H. Percy of Illinois, and Mayor John V. Lindsay of New York on the left. Lindsay, the most liberal of the group by far, also had the most interesting support, for his backers included not only the Eastern liberals who had just gone down to defeat with Rockefeller, but also such practical politicians as Ohio's Jim Rhodes and such avowed conservatives as Representative Bob Wilson of San Diego, the chairman of the Republican Congressional Campaign Committee. Rhodes argued that Lindsay alone could bring in support from blacks and other urban groups; Wilson asserted, on the basis of a poll of congressional candidates, that the mayor would add most to the ticket in the marginal congressional districts in the Northern states, where Republican hopes of capturing a House majority rested.

But Lindsay—the 1964 party bolter, the man whose 1965 city platform was somewhat to the left of Lyndon Johnson's Great Society—was more than Strom Thurmond or Barry Goldwater could stomach. Others of easy ideological identification were vetoed by the men who met in Nixon's suite in the early morning hours of August 8. At 4 a.m., the session broke up with no choice made. At 9 a.m., Nixon convened a second, smaller meeting and finally retired an hour or two later with his closest associates to make his choice. From all subsequent reports of the participants, it was clear the selection had come down to "political neuters," men of no marked ideology and also no significant personal constituency. At this point, author Theodore H. White later reported and the White House confirmed, Nixon renewed an earlier invitation to his close friend from California, Lieutenant Governor

Robert H. Finch, to become his running mate. Finch, who had won election in his own right for the first time in 1966, demurred at accepting, telling Nixon he would be more valuable to him as a counselor and saying that his selection for the number two place would smack of cronyism. (Nixon later persuaded him to enter his cabinet as secretary of health, education and welfare.)

The choice then came down to two relatively unknown governors, John A. Volpe of Massachusetts and Spiro Agnew of Maryland. Volpe, a short, aggressive man who had made a fortune as a contractor and served as highway administrator in the Eisenhower administration, was in his third term as governor of Massachusetts, with a record as an effective administrator and successful campaigner in a Democratic state. He had worked almost openly for the number two job, laying heavy stress on the appeal he would have as an Italian Catholic in urban, industrial areas.

Agnew was, comparatively, a newcomer to politics, having served one term as executive of Baltimore County, and a bit less than two years as governor of Maryland. After his break with his original candidate, Rockefeller, Agnew and Nixon had several meetings, and the Marylander apparently impressed Nixon as much as Nixon impressed him. The presidential nominee spoke admiringly of Agnew's grasp of urban problems, his poise, and the competence of his performance in delivering the nominating speech.

Moreover, Agnew's image—to those who knew him at all—was sufficiently ambivalent to meet the needs of the ticket. In his first year as governor, he had pushed through the Democratic legislature a substantial program of tax reform and social legislation and gave vigorous support to an effort to overhaul the antiquated state constitution. But in the spring of 1968, after the new constitution was defeated in referendum and serious riots broke out in Baltimore's black ghetto, Agnew appeared to shift to the right. He denounced moderate black leaders in the state for failing to curb the riots and used strong rhetoric in criticizing demonstrators. While he was not the first choice of Thurmond and the Southerners (they would have preferred Reagan, Tower, or Baker), he was probably more acceptable to them than Volpe, whose civil rights record included support of a law for busing pupils to integrated schools in Massachusetts.

Outside the small world of Republican professional politicians, however, Agnew was a virtual unknown; when Nixon went on television at midday on August 8 to announce Agnew as his choice, the reaction among most delegates and guests in Miami Beach was, "Spiro who?" As Agnew himself told reporters at a press conference that day, "I agree with you that Spiro Agnew is not a household name."

Spiro T. Agnew *(Library of Congress)*

Among liberal Republicans, the reaction quickly became one of anger. Rockefeller noted a bit testily that Nixon had not consulted him at any point about the choice. An effort was made to persuade Lindsay to challenge Agnew on the convention floor, but Nixon nipped that in the bud by the simple expedient of asking Lindsay to second Agnew's nomination. That night, in considerable confusion, a few of the liberals indicated their unhappiness with the Agnew choice by nominating Romney for vice president. But the efficient Nixon floor managers easily beat that move, 1,119 to 186, and when Nixon came to the rostrum to deliver his acceptance speech, he was surrounded by his defeated challengers and leaders of every wing of Republicanism, in a show of harmony that Barry Goldwater, four years earlier, had never been able to achieve.

Nixon's 40-minute speech, regarded by many as the oratorical highlight of his campaign, was aimed at the "forgotten Americans," the workers and taxpayers he said were angered and frustrated by the war in Vietnam, the violence at home, and the squeeze of inflation. To them and to the country he promised "new leadership" that would bring "an honorable end to the War in Vietnam," and "reestablish freedom from fear in America and freedom from fear in the world."

As Richard Nixon was being nominated in Miami Beach, there began three nights of rioting in the black ghetto of Miami, some 10 miles distant. Three people were killed, and some 600 soldiers were moved in to help seal off a large section of the city. But careful security arrangements kept the violence from intruding on the pageant of Republican unity Nixon had carefully staged, and the impression the viewing public had was of a party and a candidate serenely confident of the future. The lift that Nixon's campaign received from his skillful management of the Republican convention was clearly evidenced in the polls. Whereas three polls by the Gallup and Harris organizations in July showed Humphrey in a virtual deadlock with Nixon, the first post–Miami Beach surveys of the two organizations gave Nixon a lead of 6 to 16 points over Humphrey. Even before he was nominated, Humphrey was well behind in the race.

His problems in regaining the lead were enormously complicated by the events of the Democratic convention in Chicago during the last week in August. That convention requires serious attention, for the forces that converged there and the response to them, by the delegates and by the country, made it not only a critical factor in the 1968 campaign but a turning point in the long-term process of party reform.

This is true even though there was minimal conflict and virtually no suspense over the main business of the convention—the choice of the national ticket. At no time after Robert Kennedy's death was Humphrey's nomination really in doubt. McCarthy's erratic campaign continued to run downhill from the night of his defeat in California. When it became apparent that McCarthy was not going to be able to unite the anti-administration forces, Senator George McGovern of South Dakota, another early critic of the war and a close ally of the Kennedys, announced a desperation candidacy of his own on August 10, barely two weeks before the convention opened.

There were several flurries of interest in Senator Edward M. Kennedy of Massachusetts, surviving brother of the star-crossed family. In late July, after Humphrey had indicated he would like him as his running mate and several leading Democrats had urged him to accept that post, the 36-year-old senator issued a statement declining the vice presidency because of the "change in my personal

Delegates hold up signs urging "Stop the War," referring to the Vietnam War, during the 1968 Democratic National Convention in Chicago, in August. *(Associated Press)*

situation and responsibilities" resulting from his brother's murder the previous month.

A move to draft Kennedy for the presidential nomination was begun when the delegates assembled in Chicago on August 26. It was led by the California delegation of Robert Kennedy supporters and apparently had the covert support of Chicago mayor Richard J. Daley, who withheld his expected endorsement of Humphrey on the eve of the convention. Stephen Smith, Kennedy's brother-in-law, met privately with McCarthy on the second day of the convention, and McCarthy told him he was willing to release his delegates to Kennedy after his own name went into nomination. But the shakiness of the prospects and his own personal disinclination to make the race prompted Kennedy to ask his supporters to "cease all activity in my behalf" on the morning of August 28, and the boomlet collapsed at that point.

On the other flank of the party, Georgia's segregationist governor, Lester Maddox, announced his candidacy on August 17, but failed to draw support from other Southern states. The major Southern governors maintained their favorite-son status until well into convention week, using their bargaining power to limit Humphrey's concessions to the anti-administration elements on the issues of Vietnam and convention reform. But the Southerners had no place to go but Humphrey, and the threat of a Kennedy draft brought virtually all of them into line for the vice president.

When the roll was called near midnight on August 28, Humphrey was an easy first-ballot winner. He received 1,760 votes—well over the 1,312 needed for nomination—while McCarthy had 601 and McGovern 146, with the remainder scattered. (As a historical footnote, it should be noted that the Reverend Channing E. Phillips, a black activist and Kennedy supporter, was nominated as the District of Columbia's favorite son and received 67 votes from 26 delegations. He is believed to be the first black man nominated for a major party presidential nomination.)

As his running mate, Humphrey chose, and the convention readily accepted, Senator Edmund S. Muskie of Maine. Muskie, an unflamboyant but highly skilled legislator, had specialized in such unglamorous fields as air and water pollution and intergovernmental relations since coming to the Senate after two terms as the Democratic governor of normally Republican Maine. Although as little known to the general public at the time of his nomination as Agnew, he was to prove himself far more adept as a national campaigner and became a major asset to the ticket.

If conventions were—as many suppose—exclusively concerned with nominating presidential candidates and ratifying their choice of running mates, Humphrey would have had a triumph in Chicago. But conventions are also forums for resolving (or at least debating) party policy, caucuses for composing (or exacerbating) factional differences, and, most of all in this television era, pageants where the party shows its best (or worst) face to the public that will soon be deciding its future.

In each of these respects, the Chicago convention was a disaster for the Democrats in general and for Humphrey in particular. From the beginning, every circumstance seemed to conspire against its success. President Johnson had awarded the convention to Chicago back in 1967, over several competing cities, as a reward to Mayor Daley, the most loyal (so Johnson thought) of the big-city bosses. The date had been set unusually late, on the assumption that Johnson would be the unopposed nominee for reelection and that the convention would serve as the springboard for his general election campaign. Since the convention was planned as a giant celebration of the president's accomplishments (and of his birthday, which conveniently fell on the second day of the scheduled meeting), there was no reason to limit the number of celebrants. The Democrats authorized a total of 5,611 delegates and alternates—a number that far overtaxed the capacity of the floor of the old International Amphitheatre in Chicago's stockyards district and that guaranteed maximum discomfort for the delegates and minimum access for the press and public interested in attending the event.

Control of the arrangements of the convention had been given initially to a national committee functionary named John Criswell, who reported to the White House through the president's former appointments secretary, Postmaster-General Marvin Watson. Even after Johnson's withdrawal, the lines of control ran straight to the White House. Humphrey, the presumptive nominee and administration candidate, at no point attempted to take over control of convention arrangements.

A variety of developments made the selection of Chicago as the convention site seem questionable. Militant antiwar groups announced in the spring that they would organize mass demonstrations against the war and the Democratic candidate who supported it. Daley, who had publicly reprimanded his own police force for its alleged laxity in putting down violence and looting by blacks after Dr. King's assassination, grimly declared that he was prepared to cope with anything the antiwar groups attempted. Thus the stage was set for a confrontation on the streets—in a city where the location of the hotels and the convention hall made the problems of security much greater than they were in Miami Beach.

Later, a strike of communications workers that severely restricted the installation of equipment needed by newspapers and television networks covering the convention produced demands that it be shifted to Miami—another reason for doing so, which the White House and Daley rejected. Finally, on the eve of the convention, most Chicago cabs went on strike, adding a paralysis of transportation to the impaired communications already roiling tempers in the sweltering city. And all this Hubert Humphrey watched, apparently impotent to act.

Accounts published subsequent to the campaign make it clear that Humphrey was caught between two conflicting sets of pressures.

On one side, he recognized as a practical politician that he had to divorce himself from Johnson in the public mind to have any hope of winning the election. The evidence of the polls and of the Democratic primaries made it clear that a majority of voters in both parties had rejected Johnson's policies and leadership. Unless he could present himself as something other than an echo of the president, Humphrey knew he was doomed.

But on the other side, he was under a variety of heavy obligations to Johnson. As a matter of principle and personal loyalty, Humphrey did not feel he could denounce the policies in Vietnam he had supported for four years as vice president or break completely with the man who had elevated him to that position; as a matter of practicality, he did not believe he would look anything but opportunistic in doing so. Moreover, there was doubt in his mind that he was free to do so, even had he wished. Many of the Southern delegations whose votes he counted on were

Hubert Humphrey *(Library of Congress)*

loyal to the president. Governor John Connally of Texas and others were hinting publicly that they would withhold votes from Humphrey, and even enter Johnson's name against him, if he "sold out," as they put it, to the dissidents on Vietnam. Apparently, Humphrey himself entertained suspicions that Johnson might be having second thoughts about his decision to step down. The president became more secretive than usual with Humphrey just before the convention.

So Humphrey, on the eve of his almost certain nomination, was a man beset by uncertainties, recognizing that the convention that nominated him might well seal his defeat, and yet seemingly incapable of acting boldly to take control of the situation.

His advisers worked out a strategy that they hoped would establish Humphrey's independence of Johnson without jeopardizing his nomination. The tactic was most successful in the areas of credentials and rules, and it is in these areas that the seeds were planted for the changes that may in time substantially reform the makeup and proceedings of the nominating conventions—if those conventions survive.

An unprecedented number of credentials challenges, involving some or all of the delegates from 17 states, came before the convention committee. Most were initiated by McCarthy supporters, protesting procedures in their states that they claimed deprived them of their just share of representation. These were, for the most part, rejected by the pro-Humphrey Credentials Committee, and the committee decisions that were challenged on the floor were sustained.

However, significant concessions to black insurgents were made in the cases of Mississippi and Georgia. The Mississippi case, which had its origins in a 1964 convention compromise, resulted in 1968 in a clear-cut victory for the interracial delegation over the regular Democratic organization loyal to segregationist Governor John Bell Williams. In the Georgia case, the Credentials Committee decided to split the seats between a predominantly white delegation of regulars headed by, and picked by, Governor Maddox and a challenging interracial group headed by state Representative Julian Bond. The convention failed narrowly to oust the Georgia regulars entirely, and Maddox and most of his regulars walked out rather than accept the compromise. In these cases, the Humphrey leaders (outside the South) voted with the insurgent groups and set the important precedents for an interracial or even black-led Democratic Party in the South.

However, Humphrey and his men balked at the insurgents' floor challenge to the key Texas delegation and to those of two other Southern states.

Along with the credentials of many delegates, the McCarthy insurgents and their allies also attacked some of the rules governing the selection of delegates and the operation of the convention. Their major target was the unit rule, under which some states instructed that the entire vote of their delegation be cast as the majority of the delegation determined. This rule, which had been enforced in national Democratic conventions (but not Republican) for over a century, was attacked by the McCarthyites as a device for denying representation of minority viewpoints.

Humphrey, recognizing that he could easily afford the minor loss of votes that would result from abolition of the unit rule and eagerly seeking areas of accommodation with the insurgents, announced a month before the convention that he was releasing any delegates pledged to him under the unit rules of their states. Later, he recommended "suspension" of the unit rule at the 1968 convention and abolition of it in future years. This concession on his part brought a vigorous protest from the Texas regulars—one of the largest delegations with the unit rule—but on the opening night of the convention, Texas failed on a voice vote to upset the recommendation of the Humphrey-controlled Rules Committee that the unit rule not be enforced on any question that an individual delegate felt would "violate his individual conscience."

The next day, when permanent rules were adopted, the insurgents sought to broaden the attack on the unit rule and, somewhat to their own surprise, won their only major victory of the convention.

By a roll-call vote of 1,350 to 1,206, the convention approved the minority report abolishing the unit rule at the 1968 convention and forbidding its use at any stage of the delegate-selection process, down to the precinct level, in future years.

Abolition of the unit rule was probably the most significant change in the internal workings of the Democratic convention since the abolition of the two-thirds rule for presidential nominations in 1936. But the minority report on rules, approved by the convention, set the stage for even more sweeping changes in the delegate-selection process by requiring that in the future each state select its delegates "through a process in which all Democratic voters have had full and timely opportunity to participate." In addition to forbidding the use of the unit rule at any level, it required each state to certify that "all feasible efforts have been made to assure that delegates are selected through party primary, convention or committee procedures open to public participation within the calendar year of the national convention." This recommendation—which was paralleled in language of the conventional Credentials Committee—was directed at problems identified in a report compiled just before the convention by an ad hoc committee on party reform headed by Iowa governor (later senator) Harold E. Hughes. It found that in some

states most delegates were, in effect, appointed by public or party officials. It said that more than one-fifth of the delegates were chosen by a process that began more than two years before the convention itself met. In few states did the apportionment of delegates conform to the principle of one person, one vote. These and other problems were referred to a party commission on delegate selection headed by Senator McGovern and a companion commission on party rules headed by Representative James G. O'Hara of Michigan, which began work in 1969. Their recommendations appear likely to alter significantly the makeup and procedures of future conventions.

In all these areas, Humphrey succeeded in walking the narrow line between the reformers and insurgents on one side, and the regulars on the other. But these issues, whatever their long-term significance, carried none of the immediate emotional impact of Vietnam, and in the Platform Committee debate over Vietnam, compromise proved to be unattainable.

There were two crucial issues in the Vietnam debate—the composition of the Saigon government and a halt in American bombing of North Vietnam. McCarthy had insisted throughout his campaign that no settlement was possible until the Viet Cong or National Liberation Front was admitted to a share of power in the interim government that would conduct elections to determine South Vietnam's future. Humphrey had just as consistently opposed what he called "imposition of a coalition government" on Saigon. Robert and Edward Kennedy had also indicated some misgivings about McCarthy's adamant stand on this point. In order to compose differences among the antiwar factions, the wording of the minority plank was softened to the following language: "We will encourage our South Vietnamese allies to negotiate a political reconciliation with the National Liberation Front looking toward a government which is broadly representative of these and all elements in South Vietnamese society. The specific shape of this reconciliation will be a matter for decision by the South Vietnamese, spurred to action by the certain knowledge that the prop of American military support will soon be gone." The Humphrey-supported majority plank said nothing directly on whether or how an interim government was to be created, but rather called for "an effective international presence to facilitate the transition from war to peace" and to ensure "fair and safeguarded elections" to determine the composition of the postwar government.

There was, thus, a genuine difference between the prospective nominee and his opponents on this issue. But it is questionable whether, by itself, it would have split the convention. The crucial difference was on the bombing question. Here, McCarthy, McGovern, and Edward Kennedy were unanimous and explicit in their view that an unconditional halt to all bombing of North Vietnam was the first step toward a negotiated settlement. There is strong evidence that Humphrey wanted to meet their demand on this point. (After the campaign, he confirmed reports that he had opposed the initial decision to bomb North Vietnam.) On August 11, two weeks before the convention, he said, in response to a question about a platform plank calling for a bombing halt, "There isn't any problem as far as we are concerned about halting the bombing if we have some kind of restraint or reasonable response from North Vietnam." He reiterated that view in a formal statement the next day, and on August 19, Muskie, appearing before the platform committee on behalf of the Humphrey forces, said the convention could state a "willingness to support our government in taking such calculated risks as halting the bombing if such a risk will improve the chances of an early peace." But Johnson, for personal or diplomatic reasons, was not yet ready to see his party make such a concession. On the same day, August 19, Johnson told the Veterans of Foreign

Poster drawn by Ben Shahn for Senator Eugene McCarthy's campaign *(Library of Congress)*

Wars, "This administration does not intend to move further until it has good reason to believe that the other side intends seriously to join us in de-escalating the war and moving seriously toward peace. We are willing to take chances for peace but we cannot make foolhardy gestures for which our fighting men will pay the price by giving their lives." An immediate, unconditional bombing halt, he said, would allow Hanoi to move "men by the thousands and supplies by the tons . . . against our American sons and our allies without obstruction."

Four days later, he reinforced the message at a White House briefing for congressional leaders, including Representative Hale Boggs of Louisiana, the House Democratic whip who had been picked by Johnson without consultation with Humphrey as chairman of the Platform Committee. Boggs flew back to Chicago for the final drafting session with a warning from the president and the field commander in Vietnam that a bombing halt would (as he later told the convention) permit the enemy to increase his strength near the demilitarized zone "on the order of five times what he now has."

With the line thus drawn, Humphrey had no room for maneuver or compromise. The majority plank said only that the United States should "stop all bombing of North Vietnam when this action would not endanger the lives of our troops in the field; this action should take into account the response from Hanoi."

Debate on the minority and majority planks on Vietnam came to the convention floor on the afternoon of August 28. For almost three hours, many of the party's most distinguished leaders went to the microphone—alternating between advocates of the minority and majority plank, in a debate of rare cogency and emotional power. At the end, the majority plank was sustained by a roll-call vote of 1,567 to 1,041. As the afternoon session was adjourned, supporters of the minority plank on the convention floor and in the gallery donned black armbands and remained in their seats, singing the civil rights anthem, "We Shall Overcome."

The mood of the dissident delegates had been growing increasingly bitter with each passing day. To the inevitable aggravations caused by the overcrowded conditions on the convention floor—movement down the aisles was almost impossible without being bumped, shoved, and pummeled—were added the tightest security regulations ever imposed on a national convention. Delegates had to present special passes for electronic surveillance on entering the amphitheater and again when going onto the floor. Packages and purses were opened and searched. Newspapers, in many instances, were confiscated—ostensibly because of the fear of fire. Private police employed to keep interlopers off the floor and in the vain effort to unsnarl the aisles often used more force in their work than some delegates thought justified, and there were frequent scuffles. Finally, there were persistent complaints that the dissident-controlled delegations like California and Wisconsin were not being recognized by the pro-Humphrey, pro-administration convention chairman, House Majority Leader Carl Albert of Oklahoma.

The first session, on Monday, August 26, began at 7:30 p.m. and adjourned—after three roll calls on credentials fights—at 2:43 the next morning, when weary delegates went back to a city without cabs.

The next day, August 27, was full of conflicting rumors about draft-Kennedy stratagems and the possibility of the president's arrival for a birthday celebration. The session began at 6 p.m. Early in the evening, members of the regular delegation from Georgia walked out to protest the division of their seats with the insurgents. In the turmoil, a television reporter was knocked down, in plain view of the cameras, by security guards. Various delegates began burning credentials and making other protests of security arrangements. At 12:40 a.m., after six and a half hours of speeches and three roll calls on credentials and rules, Albert brought Boggs to the podium to begin presentation of the platform. Dissident delegates—claiming it was an effort to put the Vietnam plank through at a time when the television audience was smallest—began shouting for adjournment. Albert first ruled them out of order and then recognized Daley, who stirred the dissidents further by accusing "people in the balcony" of "trying to take over this meeting." Finally, at 1:17 a.m., with the floor in a state of incoherent pandemonium, Albert agreed to adjourn the session.

By Wednesday night, August 28, with their Vietnam plank defeated and the inevitable Humphrey nomination ahead of them, the despair and anger of the dissident delegates was at its height.

Meantime, outside the amphitheater, in downtown Chicago, a drama of far greater violence was being enacted. As promised, the militant antiwar youth groups had assembled some 10,000 demonstrators in the city by the beginning of convention week. (The number would probably have been much larger except that McCarthy's organization, fearing trouble, actively discouraged its young workers from coming to the city.) Negotiations for rally sites and march permits were sabotaged by city officials, and the request that the demonstrators be allowed to camp overnight in city parks was also refused. On Sunday and Monday nights, as the convention opened, there were clashes between police and demonstrators who refused an order to vacate Lincoln Park, some distance from the convention site. On Tuesday, the main body of demonstrators moved into Grant Park, across from the main convention hotel, the Conrad Hilton. Late that night and throughout the predawn hours on Wednesday,

they shouted slogans at the delegates—watched by armed police and National Guardsmen.

Already, there had been so much violence that convention rioting was competing for space in the newspapers and time on television with the proceedings inside the amphitheater. But Wednesday, August 28, nomination day, was to see much worse. In the afternoon, as the Vietnam plank was being voted, there was a major battle when police waded into demonstrators near the bandstand at Grant Park, after one of the youths hauled down an American flag. Four hours later, as the night session of nominations was beginning, there was another and more serious clash on the street in front of the Conrad Hilton. According to the most careful study of the incident, a report to the National Commission on the Causes and Prevention of Violence by a study group headed by Daniel Walker, chairman of the Chicago Crime Commission, "what followed was a club-swinging melee. Police ranged the streets striking anyone they could catch. To be sure, demonstrators threw things at policemen and at police cars; but the weight of violence was overwhelmingly on the side of the police."

Television crews—themselves the target of police clubs—filmed the battle as it occurred, and scenes of the violence were shown time and again during the nominating speeches. Delegates, watching on sets in the convention hall, were appalled and angered. Senator Abraham Ribicoff of Connecticut, making the nominating speech for McGovern, departed from his text to say, "With George McGovern, we wouldn't have Gestapo tactics on the streets of Chicago." That brought Daley to his feet in the front row of the Illinois delegation, shouting curses at Ribicoff, while a nation watched and the hall exploded again in pandemonium. Efforts by pro-McCarthy delegates to adjourn the convention until the violence ended were overruled. Their boos filled the amphitheater.

Humphrey, watching the scene from his 25th floor suite in the Hilton, had gotten a whiff of the CS gas used to disperse the demonstrators. But the real damage he suffered was far more severe than that. All pretense of party unity was shattered by the events in Chicago. McCarthy, who had spent the night of the nominations comforting the wounded demonstrators brought into the hotel for medical treatment, flatly refused to appear with Humphrey at the traditional reconciliation scene of losers and winners. (His bitterness was increased when police broke into the McCarthy floor of the Conrad Hilton at 3 a.m. the next morning, arresting and attacking students whom they accused of throwing objects on them from the hotel.) Anti-Humphrey delegations went home angry and unappeased—complaining not only of the outcome of the convention but of its conduct. In the later election, Humphrey was to lose to Nixon every one of the states where

McCarthy and Kennedy had waged their primary campaigns—New Hampshire, Wisconsin, Indiana, Nebraska, Oregon, South Dakota, and California. And the turmoil and hostility were such that President Johnson decided it was imprudent for him even to appear before the delegates of the party whose banner he had carried to victory four years before.

Thus, Humphrey came before the public on the night of his acceptance speech as the standard-bearer of a party racked by internal controversy, beset by violence, and seemingly incapable even of ordering its own affairs. Humphrey urged the Democrats to "take heart" and "make this moment of crisis . . . a moment of creation," but he knew and they knew that he emerged from the convention a beaten man. The polls after the convention showed Humphrey had failed to get the normal lift from his party's heavy television exposure. In early September, as the campaign began, he was running 8 to 12 percentage points behind Nixon, and no more than 8 to 10 points ahead of Wallace.

For Nixon, the position of front-runner provided several concrete advantages. Campaign funds were available early and remained more than adequate throughout the race. In the vital area of television, a compilation by the Federal Communications Commission showed Nixon outspent Humphrey by a margin of $12.6 million to $6.7 million, and that only in the last week was Humphrey able to match Nixon in time purchases.

Television played a major part in the campaign, and this time, unlike 1960, Nixon used it to advantage. He was able to avoid a television debate with his principal opponent (which many blamed for his defeat in 1960) by insisting that he would not appear in a three-way confrontation with both Humphrey and Wallace. When Wallace, late in the campaign, relinquished his demand that he be included, Nixon said it was too late to alter his schedule to meet Humphrey alone. The most successful of Nixon's television techniques was a series of regionally broadcast, live, hour-long interrogations by a panel of questioners. Although the members of the

Third party candidate George Wallace waves from his car through noon-hour crowds along State Street in Chicago, September 30, 1968. (*Associated Press*)

panel (usually including only one professional reporter) were selected by the Nixon campaign, the impression viewers received was of Nixon bravely facing a rugged, prolonged interrogation. His skill in formulating answers was evident; the regional pattern of the broadcasts ensured that issues of prime concern to that region would be emphasized; and the audiences for these programs were far larger than was typical for a political program of that length. Only in the last two weeks of the campaign, after some criticism developed of these Nixon-run quiz programs, did he appear on the network interview programs with professional reporters, *Face the Nation* and *Meet the Press*.

Nixon also employed network radio for a series of substantive speeches, where he outlined his views on major issues and his concept of the presidency. These broadcasts, low in cost, had small audiences, but the speech texts provided material for newspaper stories and grist for editorial writers convinced that campaigns ought to be devoted to elucidating the issues.

Nixon's stump talks were quite different from the radio speeches. Most of them were simply repetitions, with minimal variation, of the major themes of his acceptance speech, plus optimistic reports on the progress of the campaign, designed to encourage local organization workers. Unlike in 1960, Nixon made no effort to visit every state, nor did he squander his energies on multiple appearances in a single day. Typically, he would hold one rally in the forenoon (early enough for film to be available for the major network evening newscasts) and one in the evening.

Nixon's electoral strategy at the outset of the campaign focused on two sets of states. His solid base of support lay in the smaller states of the Midwest and West, which he had carried in 1960. From Indiana to the Pacific, these states (exclusive of giant California), won by Nixon in 1960 and leaning to him this time, promised 109 electoral votes. Missouri, Nevada, and New Mexico, which he had narrowly lost in 1960, would (and ultimately did) add 19 more votes. Thus, Nixon had an ensured base of about half the 270 votes needed for victory.

One major battleground, he determined, would be the "Big Eight" states of New York, Pennsylvania, New Jersey, Ohio, Michigan, Illinois, Texas, and California—with 227 votes. In 1960, Nixon had carried only two of the eight—California and Ohio—and thereby had lost the election. In 1968, he figured, he needed at least three and perhaps four of the eight to win. Except in Texas, where polls showed Wallace with considerable strength, the fight in those states would be essentially against Humphrey. Early September polls, incredibly, showed Nixon leading in all eight, but only in California, Illinois, and Ohio did the lead appear comfortable. At about this time, Nixon

advised some friends to "watch California and Pennsylvania; whoever wins both of them will be President."

The second key group of states, in the Nixon strategy, was what he called "the new South," the upper tier of Dixie plus Florida and perhaps Georgia, with a total of 81 votes. Of these, Nixon had carried only Tennessee, Kentucky, Virginia, and Florida in 1960. It was vital that he hold these and if possible expand his base—both to provide some insurance against losses to Humphrey in the "Big Eight" and to prevent Wallace from garnering enough electoral votes to create an Electoral College deadlock and force the election into the House. The battle in this set of states was complex. Nixon could count on only minimal help from Humphrey in combating Wallace; except for the newly registered black voters, more numerous than in the past but still a minority, Humphrey had little support in these states. Nixon could hope that Humphrey would erode Wallace's strength among "loyalist" white Democrats, but he could not count on it. Public and private polls indicated that a heavy majority of the Wallace voters in those states, though nominally Democrats, would prefer Nixon over Humphrey in a two-man race. Nixon stood to gain ground, then, if Wallace's strength declined—but only so long as his campaign did not directly antagonize the Wallace voters. Therefore, the key to his strategy in this bloc of states was the argument, which he made and that Thurmond made for him, that a vote for Wallace was a wasted vote and, worse, a vote that might elect Humphrey by denying Nixon an electoral majority.

Nixon opened his campaign, symbolically, in Chicago, the scene of Humphrey's downfall. On September 4, he received an enthusiastic welcome from a crowd of half a million in the Loop and that night conducted the first of his television interview shows. The pattern of the Chicago visit—enthusiastic crowds and skillful exploitation of television—held throughout the month of September. In that first month, Nixon touched down in 24 of the 30 states he had selected for personal campaigning, disposing of virtually all the small Midwestern and Western states he was confident of carrying and making his first forays into each of the "Big Eight" and into the contested South. He largely skipped central city and black neighborhoods and concentrated on the suburbs. In a typical talk to a suburban audience, Nixon told a crowd in White Plains, New York, on September 10, "The people in the suburbs don't need federal projects suddenly imposed upon them. . . . [They] need men in Washington who will ask them how Washington can cooperate in what they're doing already."

Even more important than this appeal to the "forgotten Americans" of the suburbs was Nixon's bid, early in the campaign, for what had been called, four years earlier, the "backlash" vote. In a television interview on September 12 for the Carolinas, Nixon indicated his disagreement with the Johnson administration policy of withholding federal aid funds from school districts that balked at desegregation. "I believe that the Supreme Court decision was a correct decision," he said, "but on the other hand, while that decision . . . said that we should not have segregation, when you go beyond that and say that it is the responsibility of the federal government and the federal courts to, in effect, act as local school districts in determining how we carry that out, and then to use the power of the federal treasury to withhold funds or to give funds in order to carry it out, then I think we are going too far." The syntax may have been sloppy, but the sentiment was clear. When reporters questioned Nixon two days later, he conceded that Congress had authorized the fund cutoffs in the 1964 Civil Rights Act but said he would use that power "only as a last resort. Our schools are for education, not integration." An important signal had been given to Southern whites, and to their sympathizers in other sections.

If there was any cloud at all on Nixon's horizon in those September days, it was the performance of his vice-presidential running mate. Agnew had set out to make himself "a household name," but not exactly in the way campaign strategists might have wished. He began on September 10 by telling a group of reporters that Humphrey over the years had been "soft on inflation, soft on communism, and soft on law and order." He and Nixon, Agnew said, "are not going to be as squishy soft as this Administration has been." Republican congressional leaders Dirksen and Ford quickly repudiated Agnew's attack, and the governor publicly withdrew the charge, adding, incredibly, that he never would have used the term "soft on communism" if he had known the "political history" of the phrase. Soon thereafter, there was another imbroglio when Agnew said the Republican ticket was withholding its recommendations for a settlement in Vietnam, because "if we shot all our ammunition now the whole campaign would collapse in boredom by the end of October." When that stand was challenged as opportunistic, Agnew quickly retreated and said, "I didn't mean to imply that we have plans to solve the war." In the next few weeks, he stirred further controversy by referring to Polish-American voters as "Polacks," calling a Nisei reporter "the fat Jap," and otherwise raising questions about Nixon's comment that "you can look him [Agnew] in the eye and know he's got it. . . . When it comes to poise under pressure and carrying the attack and resisting the attack, he's got it."

Aside from the Agnew problem, as it came to be called in the Nixon camp, the Republican contender was riding high in September. Scarcely less ebullient was Wallace, the third-party nominee. Disdaining the formality of a national convention, Wallace had spent the summer raising some $6 million in funds for his campaign. The process of getting his name on the ballot was astonishingly successful. By September, Wallace was on the ballot in all 50 states, though it took an order by his old enemy, the Supreme Court, to secure a place for him in Ohio. Only the voters of the District of Columbia were deprived of the right to cast ballots for Wallace; in that predominantly black constituency, Wallace failed to achieve the requisite signatures for his petition.

Nixon was not an ideal Republican candidate from Wallace's viewpoint; he would rather have had Rockefeller at the head of the GOP ticket; but Nixon was not as clear a threat to his electoral base as Reagan would have been. And Humphrey's nomination in the violence-marred Chicago convention suited Wallace fine. Commending the Chicago police for their "restraint" in handling the demonstrators, Wallace added, "I think the people watching can tell the trends in this country. The mess in Chicago and the mess both national parties have gotten us into have put us in an excellent position to win the election."

Making frequent forays into Northern industrial cities, Wallace muted the racism that lay at the base of his political career and portrayed himself as the little man's candidate, arrayed against the bureaucrats, the intellectuals, the downtown preachers and publishers, and all the other "pointy-heads" (to use his favorite word) whose meddling schemes for social improvement he said had brought America to its present impasse.

It was not clear at this time whether Wallace himself believed he had a chance to win. He might well have thought so, for in many medium-sized cities, he drew crowds that would have done credit to a major-party candidate. And the flow of small contributions—sometimes more than ten thousand letters in a single day—testified to the ardor of his supporters.

In mid-September Wallace told reporters traveling with him he had hopes of winning—on a plurality basis—17 Southern and border states and 8 outside that region, with a total of 357 electoral votes. His real base, of course, was much smaller—consisting of the Deep South states of Alabama, Mississippi, Louisiana, and Arkansas, which he was virtually conceded, and such others as Georgia, South Carolina, Tennessee, Florida, and North Carolina, where he was clearly in contention. These could provide Wallace with almost 100 electoral votes—perhaps enough to stalemate the election. Early in September, Wallace made it plain what he would do in such a situation. "I don't believe it is going to go to the House of Representatives," he told the Miami Herald. "I'd say the electoral college would settle the presidency before it gets to the House."

Wallace said he preferred the word "covenanting" for the bargaining he had in mind, but it came down to the same thing. Wallace had secured written pledges from his electors, binding them to his instructions. If the returns gave him the balance of power, he would "covenant" with Nixon or Humphrey—in return for unspecified concessions—to see that his policies "have some representation in the attitude of the new administration."

This was the threat, then, of Wallace's presence. But it would be a reality only if Wallace could maintain or increase his strength in the closing weeks of the campaign, and only if Humphrey and Nixon divided the vote outside the South on a relatively equal basis. And as September began, Nixon was running so far ahead of Humphrey that the possibility of a stalemate seemed remote.

The Humphrey campaign in its opening phases was, quite simply, a disaster. For reasons that have never been clear, Humphrey and his staff had devoted little time or thought to the general election campaign—not even after Kennedy's murder made it virtually certain that Humphrey would be the nominee. Larry O'Brien, having started the year with Johnson and campaigned for three months for Kennedy, joined Humphrey just before the Chicago convention. To the displeasure of some of those already on Humphrey's staff, O'Brien was named convention coordinator, but no decision was made beyond that. Only on the day following the convention did Humphrey arrange to have O'Brien named as chairman of the Democratic National Committee, replacing John M. Bailey of Connecticut, and as manager of the presidential campaign. O'Brien's first move was to bring in Joseph Napolitan, an old friend, to handle the television phase of the campaign; Robert Short, a Minneapolis businessman friend of Humphrey's, took on the fund-raising chore. What confronted them, eight weeks before election day, was chaos. The Democratic organization in the major states, victimized by years of neglect under Johnson, was now further weakened by the brutal infighting of the nomination campaign and the convention. Dozens of top-level Democrats had left Chicago cursing their own party and its nominee. Nothing had been done to arrange itineraries for the candidates or to prepare television ads. Hundreds of thousands of dollars had been squandered on a needless pre-convention TV blitz for Humphrey, leaving his campaign in debt and the treasury empty. And the first post-convention polls, showing Nixon a virtual shoo-in, made Short's fund-raising task formidable.

In this setting, and with these odds, Humphrey set out on September 9 on his first swing of the campaign—and promptly compounded his own problems.

He began in Philadelphia. The turnout in that Democratic bastion was dismal, and much of his formal speech was drowned out by hecklers. In an informal meeting with campaign workers, he dropped the remark that "negotiations or no negotiations, I think I can safely predict we can start to remove some of the American forces [in Vietnam] in early 1969 or late 1968."

While Humphrey flew west late that afternoon, Secretary of State Rusk denied the validity of his prediction. But there was worse to come. In Denver, his second stop, there were more hecklers. And there, Humphrey astounded everyone by saying the minority and majority planks on Vietnam were "so mildly different" that "I would have no difficulty at all" accepting the minority plank, had it won.

Aboard the flight to Los Angeles (where he was snubbed by many of the party leaders, who skipped his airport arrival), Humphrey told reporters he had not meant to imply acceptance of an immediate, unconditional bombing halt. The next day, President Johnson, speaking to the American Legion, appeared to repudiate Humphrey directly when he said, "no one can predict" when Americans could begin to leave South Vietnam. That night, in Houston, Humphrey waved a newspaper headline about the return to the United States of a particular Marine regiment, and told an audience of Democrats in the president's home state that he, not Johnson, was right about troop withdrawals. The next morning, after Humphrey had received a corrective phone call from Secretary of Defense Clark Clifford, his press secretary conceded that the Marine unit was on rotation and its return "in no way indicates any general American withdrawal of troops."

By the end of the first week, when Humphrey got back to Washington, he had raised serious doubts about his relations with his own administration and about his capacity to campaign.

The pattern of trouble continued for most of the next three weeks. Antiwar hecklers dogged his trail, forcing Humphrey to shout himself hoarse and giving television coverage of his rallies the same destructive atmosphere of violence and turmoil that was present at Chicago. On September 19, when he went into Democratic Boston at the side of Edward Kennedy, who had already endorsed the ticket, even the presence of a Kennedy did not spare him from a jeering demonstration.

Only if one looked carefully in September could one see some signs of developments that were, in time, to prove important to Humphrey's October comeback.

For one thing, his running mate, Muskie, was proving to be as adept a campaigner as Agnew was inept. Muskie's style was deliberately low-key—an appeal, as he said, to reason and to trust in a time when the nation seemed almost literally to be splintering. He campaigned among his fellow Poles in Chicago and asked them to realize that blacks were seeking the same freedom that their own ancestors sought in coming to America. More than his words, it was Muskie's calm but forceful style, presence, and personality that impressed his audiences and the reporters traveling with him. In Washington, Pennsylvania, he dealt with a group of youthful hecklers by inviting their leader to take the microphone for a few minutes. It was an old politicians' gambit: but Muskie's performance was so adept—and appeared to reflect so sincere a desire to exchange views rather than insults—that it was featured on that night's television news programs and gave the Democrats perhaps their first favorable publicity of the whole campaign.

There were other, less conspicuous developments helpful to Humphrey. On September 16, President Johnson formally endorsed the ticket in a message to the Texas Democratic convention, and the next day Governor John Connally followed suit. Their action put the prestige of the conservative Democratic "establishment" of the state behind Humphrey's cause. In Texas, thereafter, a com-

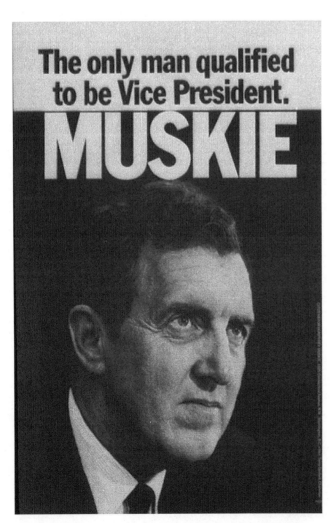

Campaign poster for Edmund S. Muskie *(Library of Congress)*

plex but effective two-headed campaign emerged—with the Connally–Johnson conservatives manning one set of headquarters and the labor–liberal–black faction of Senator Ralph Yarborough (a pre-convention McCarthy supporter) running the other. Their antagonism and suspicion never abated, but together they were to carry the stage against Nixon and Wallace—a feat that seemed impossible in September.

Nationally, labor began gearing up a massive effort for the Democratic ticket. The AFL-CIO endorsed Humphrey in mid-September, as did the major independent unions like the United Auto Workers. Wallace sentiment was strong in many of the industrial unions (a Harris poll in mid-September found one of every six Wallace voters in the North and two of every five in the South were union members). To counter it, the unions pledged—and raised—their largest political education fund in history. By the time it reached its peak in late October, the labor campaign was to dwarf in size anything either of the parties mustered: an estimated 125 million pamphlets, 100,000 door-to-door canvassers, 4 million phone calls. Of the two messages—anti-Wallace and pro-Humphrey—the emphasis was on the first. And the most effective tactic was not to meet Wallace head-on on the race issue but to create countervailing forces (and fears) by portraying him as an enemy of labor. "Wallace's Alabama is a low-wage, right-to-work state," the pamphlets said. "Wallace's election will cut your pay $1,000 a year."

The technique was crude and in some respects—the comparison of Alabama wages with national norms, for example—as demagogic as anything Wallace himself attempted. But it was, as we shall see, to prove itself highly effective.

But all these moves to rescue the Humphrey campaign were coming from the elements of the Democratic Party that had supported his nomination. His crucial problem, as he began to recognize, was to regain the support of the dissident Democrats who had opposed him in Chicago. And the key to this was—as it always had been—his stance on Vietnam.

So long as Humphrey seemed tied to the Johnson policies on Vietnam, he could not bring the dissident Democrats into his corner. So long as he seemed tied to the Johnson policies on Vietnam, Nixon could retain his patent on the promise of "new leadership" and "new policies" to end the war.

In early September, Nixon had borrowed Wallace's catchphrase and told an audience in Houston, "There's not a dime's worth of difference between the policies Hubert Humphrey offers America and the policies America has had for the last four years." On September 24, he returned to the same theme, saying Humphrey "has not disagreed with one policy" of the Johnson administration. "He is the most articulate and the most uncompromising defender of the Johnson Administration," Nixon said.

The next day, Humphrey finally began the process of disengagement. He told a Los Angeles press conference that "if I had any reason to believe that stopping the bombing this afternoon could lend itself to . . . de-escalating the war, I would recommend it tomorrow morning." He said he would not be embarrassed to suggest it to the president, because "the President has not made me his slave and I am not his humble servant. I am his partner and I am Vice President of the United States." Three days later, on September 28, campaigning in Seattle, Humphrey encountered the heaviest heckling of his entire campaign, and correspondents described him as being near the breaking point. That weekend, with the Gallup Poll showing Humphrey 15 points behind Nixon and only 7 ahead of Wallace, there was an emergency conference, with O'Brien and other campaign advisers and George Ball, who had just resigned as ambassador to the United Nations to join the Humphrey campaign, bringing with him the news that the Paris peace talks had reached the point where there was genuine hope of a favorable response from Hanoi to a bombing halt proposal.

The decision was made to commit the little money left in the Democratic treasury to a half-hour television speech on Vietnam, which Humphrey delivered from Salt Lake City on Monday, September 30. In the key passage of the speech, he said that "as President, I would stop the bombing of the North as an acceptable risk for peace." There were conditions attached to the offer, along with proposals for "de-Americanizing" the war and moving forward the negotiations. But the specifics of the speech were less important than the evidence that Humphrey had moved ahead of the Johnson policy and had liberated himself from White House strictures.

The most immediate effect was to restart the flow of contributions to the Democratic treasury. Within a matter of days, it was evident that the heckling from antiwar demonstrators had been cut in volume and vituperation. Four days after the speech, the national board of the Americans for Democratic Action, which had endorsed McCarthy for the nomination, threw its support to Humphrey. And, most important, the candidate himself seemed liberated by the Salt Lake City speech, and for the first time began campaigning as if his heart was in his work.

The day after the Salt Lake City speech, Humphrey went south to Nashville, lit into Wallace as a "charlatan" and "demagogue," and ridiculed Nixon's "perfumed, deodorized, detergentized campaign."

For the first time in the year, Nixon found himself forced to react to an opponent's initiative. He said Humphrey's bombing halt speech might undercut the negotia-

tors in Paris. "I would hope," he said, "that Vice President Humphrey would . . . make it clear that he is not pulling the rug out from under our negotiators, is not destroying the only trump card they really have." It was a good rhetorical reflex, but Humphrey had taken the precaution of checking in advance with the head of the American delegation at the peace talks, Averell Harriman, and he knew his suggestion would not be repudiated. Nixon's negative response, as we will see, was to prove embarrassing a month later when Johnson ordered the bombing stopped.

Two days later, Nixon again appeared to be reacting to a Humphrey tactic, when he made his first direct attack on Wallace in the campaign. Referring to Wallace's standard remark that "any demonstrator who lies down in front of my presidential limousine, it will be the last one he lies down in front of," Nixon said, "Anybody who says that shouldn't be President of the United States."

As October began, Wallace found himself under attack from many quarters. After flirting with several possibilities, he finally picked retired Air Force General Curtis E. LeMay, former chief of the Strategic Air Command, as his vice-presidential running mate. To Wallace's acute embarrassment, LeMay allowed himself to be led into a discussion of nuclear weapons in Vietnam at his first press conference on October 3. "I don't think nuclear weapons are needed in Vietnam," he said, "but I'm not going to stand up here and tell our enemies that we will never use nuclear weapons . . . We seem to have a phobia about nuclear weapons. . . . The world won't come to an end if we use a nuclear weapon."

Wallace immediately recognized the seriousness of LeMay's blunder, and sent him off on an inspection trip to Vietnam. But the damage had been done. Every other candidate immediately leaped to the attack on LeMay. Cartoonists began caricaturing the American Independent Party ticket as the men who would run you down or blow you up. The focus of the heckling shifted from Humphrey to Wallace, and brawling between his supporters and the hecklers took over the television news shots of his rallies. By October 9, only six days after LeMay joined the ticket, Wallace was publicly charging that the opinion polls had been rigged to show his fortunes declining, and demanding a congressional investigation of their manipulation by the "Eastern money interests." The mid-October polls did show that Wallace had apparently peaked off at about 20 percent of the vote and was beginning to slide. They also showed the first slight gain for Humphrey, with Nixon holding steady at the same 43 or 44 percent of the vote he had held since September.

At this point, a crucial assumption of the Nixon campaign came into question. The Nixon strategists, as we have seen, had counted on a Wallace slump as election day approached, and voters felt pressure to be sure their vote counted in picking a winner. They had also calculated that Nixon would inherit the vast majority of those Wallace votes—on the plausible assumption that they were being cast by "aginners," by people who wanted to protest the policies of the incumbent Democratic administration.

What happened was something quite different. Wallace's strength did not ebb evenly around the country, but chiefly in those northern industrial areas where labor had concentrated its anti-Wallace propaganda barrage. And in those areas, the movement of blue collar workers was not predominantly from Wallace to Nixon but directly from Wallace back to Humphrey. In state after state, and in the national polls outside the South, the surveys in October showed Nixon stuck in the low 40s, while Humphrey gained rapidly by recapturing dissident Democrats from Wallace.

This development caught Nixon unprepared. As the campaign moved with distressing slowness toward Election Day, he continued to deliver the same speech to the same rallies and answer the same questions at his controlled television interviews.

It was, to all appearances, a race between Nixon's diminishing lead and Humphrey's diminishing supply of campaign days. As the polls shifted, late money—"nervous money," the politicians call it—came into the Democratic treasury, and Napolitan's effective campaign film on Humphrey was shown more and more often. One after another, the northeastern industrial states fell into Humphrey's column—Massachusetts and Connecticut first; then Michigan; then the enormous prize of New York; Pennsylvania and Texas were teetering to Humphrey; and even Illinois, California, and Ohio, which had seemed locked up and safe for Nixon, looked less than secure. And then, with two weeks to go, began a drama of international dimensions—whose details are still unclear—that was to have perhaps a decisive effect on the election.

On October 11, in Paris, there was the first significant private discussion between American and North Vietnamese representatives at the preliminary peace talks of a possible package agreement. The Americans would halt the bombing of North Vietnam in return for the North Vietnamese guaranteeing the integrity of the demilitarized zone and stopping their shelling of South Vietnamese cities. Then representatives of the National Liberation Front and the Saigon government would be invited to join the talks. It was a tentative proposal, but promising enough that it sent tremors of excitement through the diplomatic–political community. Though there is no reason to think the agreement was timed to the American election, no one could be oblivious of its possible effect on the campaign. On October 16, Johnson saw enough

hope in the situation to call the three candidates and brief them on the possibility of a breakthrough in the talks. The next day, Nixon publicly declared his readiness to support the president if he determined a bombing halt was in the interests of peace. "We do not," he said, "want to play politics with peace."

What happened next in the negotiations is still partially concealed by official secrecy, but apparently both Hanoi and Saigon began laying down additional terms for their agreement to the package. The Saigon regime was particularly upset about the bombing halt; at least twice its officials appeared to agree and then rejected the plan. On October 20, Humphrey said publicly that the United States had a right to expect Saigon to be "cooperative" in negotiations and could not allow it to impose a veto on a bombing halt. On October 23, Nixon accused Humphrey of being "unable to mind his tongue when negotiations are going on." Plainly, the tension of the tightening race and the uncertain political impact of a bombing halt were getting to both men. But still the diplomatic talks went on, with no official word from the president.

At this particular juncture, for reasons that are unclear, Nixon chose to make a speech that was by far the most hard-line military utterance of his whole campaign. On October 24, he accused the Johnson administration of allowing "a gravely serious security gap" to develop between the United States and the Soviet Union, and pledged as president to restore "clear-cut military superiority" in weapons. The next day, Defense Secretary Clifford declassified secret data on the missile strength of the two countries to refute Nixon's charge. Humphrey unloaded his heaviest oratory of the campaign, saying Nixon had committed himself to a "needless and mortally dangerous escalation of the arms race." Throughout the campaign, Humphrey had hammered at Nixon's advocacy of delay in ratification of the nuclear nonproliferation treaty. Now, with Nixon's own words, he was able to dramatize their differences on arms control. As the first candidate to propose a bombing halt and now as the enemy of the arms race, Humphrey was emerging suddenly as the "peace" candidate in the election. Now, if peace talks and a bombing halt became a reality, it might turn the tide.

On October 25—ten days before the election—Nixon issued a remarkable statement. He said, "In the last 36 hours I have been advised of a flurry of meetings in the White House and elsewhere on Vietnam. I am told that top officials in the Administration have been driving very hard for an agreement on a bombing halt, accompanied possibly by a cease-fire, in the immediate future. I since learned these reports are true. I am also told that this spurt of activity is a cynical, last-minute attempt by President Johnson to salvage the candidacy of Mr. Humphrey. This I do not believe."

It was a remarkable example of setting up and knocking down a straw man, and the president promptly accused Nixon of making "ugly and unfair" statements, to which Nixon replied that he was being "quite responsible in . . . making it clear that I did not share the views of those that thought the President would use these negotiations politically."

Meantime, the efforts to bring the Saigon government into line on the bombing-halt agreement were still proceeding. On Monday, October 28, prospects seemed good enough for the president to schedule a speech for October 30. On Tuesday, October 29, a week before the election, McCarthy ended his long silence and endorsed Humphrey for president. On October 30, there was another, unexplained, last-minute snag in the negotiations, but finally on October 31 Johnson went on television to announce that he had ordered bombing of North Vietnam to cease and that formal peace talks would begin in Paris on the day after the election.

In the euphoria of the first reaction, few persons noted the peculiar phrasing the president had used, when he said Saigon would be "free to participate" in the talks.

Less than 24 hours later, the blow fell. The head of the Saigon government announced the American decision was "unilateral" and said his government was not prepared to enter the talks. The South Vietnamese National Assembly publicly condemned Johnson for "betrayal of an ally."

The hopes for peace were quickly drowned in a wave of doubt. Was it just an election trick? No one knew. Only later was it revealed that the Saigon leaders had been encouraged in their objections to the bombing halt by one Anna Chennault, the Chinese-born widow of an American flying hero of World War II, who maintained a lavish Washington apartment, enjoyed many close friendships with Asian diplomats in the capital, and was, with former first lady Mamie Eisenhower, the co-chair of the Women for Nixon–Agnew Committee. Johnson reportedly learned immediately of Chennault's intervention and satisfied himself in a phone call to Nixon two days before the election that the Republican candidate had not encouraged or authorized her to promise the Saigon leaders a "better deal" from his administration if they balked at Johnson's terms. If Humphrey knew of the Chennault caper—and the evidence is that he was informed—he made no use of it against Nixon in the final 48 hours of the campaign, when the effect of the charge of Republican sabotage of the peace talks might have been devastating.

The polls on the weekend before the election showed the rapid swing in public opinion. Harris and Gallup on Sunday, November 3, both gave Nixon a 42–40 lead over

Under a huge banner reading "Nixon's the One," the Republican candidate campaigns in Philadelphia in September 1968. Seated beside him and waving is his wife, Pat Nixon. *(Associated Press)*

Humphrey, with Wallace down to 12 percent (Harris) or 14 percent (Gallup) of the vote. Harris re-polled the next day and announced that Humphrey had moved ahead, 43 to 40, presumably on the strength of the bombing halt.

On November 5, 1968, 73,359,762 persons voted. The turnout, estimated at 60.8 percent of the voting-age population, was slightly lower than in the previous two elections and slightly below expectations.

Nixon led Humphrey 31,783,783 votes to 31,271,839, with Wallace receiving 9,901,118 votes. Nixon's 43.3 percent share of the vote was the lowest for a winning candidate since Woodrow Wilson in the three-way contest of 1912. Not until almost noon on Wednesday, when Illinois went Republican, did Humphrey concede defeat. But in the final electoral count, Nixon won a clear majority. He carried 32 states with 302 electoral votes—though he later lost one of them in the official count, when a North Carolina Nixon elector cast his ballot for Wallace. Humphrey carried 14 states with 191 electoral votes and Wallace 5 states with 45 electoral votes, plus the maverick elector from North Carolina.

The returns validated Nixon's original strategy. He carried all the Western states except Washington and

Hawaii, held four of the Big Eight—California, Illinois, Ohio, and New Jersey—against Humphrey's closing surge, and took Kentucky, Tennessee, Virginia, North and South Carolina, and Florida away from Wallace. In what was perhaps a measure of the pulling power of the rival vice-presidential candidates, Muskie swung Maine into the Democratic column but Agnew failed to sway Maryland into the GOP column. Of the 26 states he had carried against Kennedy in 1960, Nixon lost only Maine and Washington in 1968. He added the electoral votes of Delaware, Illinois, Missouri, Nevada, New Jersey, New Mexico, North Carolina, and South Carolina.

Measured by its comeback from the 1964 Republican rout, Nixon's victory was almost miraculous. But in other dimensions it was not that impressive. Republicans gained five more governorships, bringing their total to 31. (The Maryland governorship reverted to the Democrats when Agnew was sworn in as vice president.) They gained five seats in the Senate, bringing the total to 42. But in the House, the Republicans gained only 4 seats, leaving the Democrats with a 243–192 majority, and making Nixon the first president in 120 years to enter the White House with both branches of Congress controlled by the opposition.

The most striking shift from past voting patterns occurred in the South. Of the 13 states in that once-solid Democratic bastion, Humphrey carried only Texas, losing 5 states to Wallace and 7 to Nixon. Wallace's showing was not particularly impressive. He was able to hold only about one-third of the total vote in the South, trailing Nixon slightly in that region. Outside the South, he received only 8 percent of the vote.

Yet Wallace was clearly a major factor in the election. In only 20 of the 45 states they carried were Nixon or Humphrey able to win a clear majority of the votes; in the other 25, Wallace represented the balance of power. A shift of only 43,000 votes would have denied Nixon an electoral majority and given Wallace the bargaining position he sought.

The sharpest line of demarcation in the major voting groups was on racial lines. The post-election Gallup survey indicated Humphrey was supported by 85 percent of blacks, while winning only 38 percent of the white votes.

In other respects, the voting patterns resembled those of earlier years. Nixon, like most Republican candidates since 1932, found his strongest support among professional and business classes, farmers and white collar workers with high school or college education, Protestants, and those over 50. Humphrey led Nixon, as a Democrat usually has led a Republican, among those under 50, among manual laborers, union members, those with grade school educations, Catholics, and Jews.

Outside of the South, the old Democratic coalition came through the rigors of 1968 in surprisingly healthy condition. Yet there were many observers who—combining the Nixon and Wallace vote as a "conservative" bloc—proclaimed the 1968 returns as the death knell of New Deal–Fair Deal–New Frontier–Great Society liberalism.

Neither the preservation nor the destruction of the Roosevelt coalition could be demonstrated conclusively from the 1968 returns, nor could it be said with certainty at the time whether the Wallace campaign was more than a brief episode in electoral politics.

What was clear was that in 1968—a year of trauma and tragedy in America—the electoral system once again produced a president; that the major parties survived to fight again another day; and that the last chapter of the story had not yet been written.

—David S. Broder

Selected Bibliography

Among the many good works on this election, see Herbert E. Alexander, *Financing the 1968 Election* (1971); Stephen E. Ambrose, *Nixon: The Triumph of a Politician* (1987); Lewis Chester, Godfrey Hodgson, and Bruce Page, *An American Melodrama: The Presidential Campaign of 1968* (1969). Rick Perlstein, *Nixonland: The Rise of a President and the Fracturing of America* (2008), examines Nixon as a unique and powerful phenomenon; Lewis L. Gould, *1968: The Election That Changed America* (1993), helps people appreciate the importance of the election.

For Senator McCarthy and his campaign, see Ben Stavis, *We Were the Campaign: New Hampshire to Chicago for McCarthy* (1969); Eugene McCarthy, *The Year of the People* (1969); and Arthur Herzog, *McCarthy for President* (1969). On Robert Kennedy, see Jack Newfield, *Robert Kennedy: A Memoir* (1969), and Jules Witcover, *Eighty-Five Days: The Last Campaign of Robert Kennedy* (1969). Richard Nixon is covered in Ralph de Toledano's friendly *One Man Alone: Richard Nixon* (1969), and in Garry Wills, *Nixon Agonistes* (1970). An amusing insider's account of Nixon's use of the media is Joe McGinniss, *The Selling of the President, 1968* (1969). Hubert Humphrey is covered in several biographies. See Allan Ryskin, *Hubert* (1968), and Robert Sherrill and Harry Ernst, *The Drugstore Liberal* (1968). On Wallace, see Marshall Frady, *Wallace: The Classic Portrait of Alabama Governor George Wallace* (1996). Theodore H. White has covered the campaign in *The Making of the President, 1968* (1969). See also Stephen E. Ambrose, *Nixon: The Triumph of a Politician, 1962–1972* (1989); Vaughn Davis Bornet, *The Presidency of Lyndon B. Johnson* (1983); Edward W. Knappman, *Presidential Election, 1968* (1970); Karl A. Lamb and Paul A. Smith, *Campaign Decision-Making: The Presidential Election of 1968* (1968); and Richard Nixon, *The Memoirs of Richard Nixon* (1978).

1968 Electoral Map and Statistics

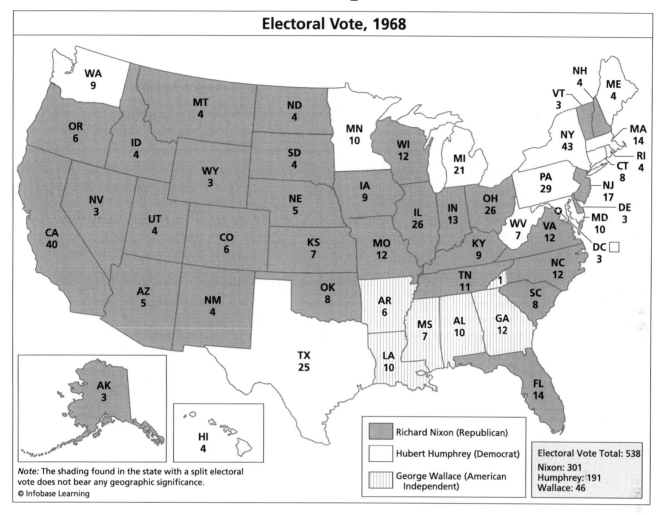

Electoral Vote, 1968

Legend:
- Richard Nixon (Republican)
- Hubert Humphrey (Democrat)
- George Wallace (American Independent)

Electoral Vote Total: 538
Nixon: 301
Humphrey: 191
Wallace: 46

Note: The shading found in the state with a split electoral vote does not bear any geographic significance.

© Infobase Learning

1968 ELECTION STATISTICS

State	Number of Electors	Total Popular Vote	Elec Vote R	Elec Vote D	Elec Vote AI	Pop Vote R	Pop Vote D	Pop Vote AI	Margin of Victory Votes	Margin of Victory % Total Vote
Alabama	10	1,049,917			10	3	2	1	49,656	4.73%
Alaska	3	83,035	3			1	2	3	2,189	2.64%
Arizona	5	486,936	5			1	2	3	96,207	19.76%
Arkansas	6	609,590			6	2	3	1	4,161	0.68%
California	40	7,251,587	40			1	2	3	223,346	3.08%
Colorado	6	811,199	6			1	2	3	74,171	9.14%
Connecticut	8	1,256,232		8		2	1	3	64,840	5.16%
Delaware	3	214,367	3			1	2	3	7,520	3.51%
District of Columbia	3	170,578		3		2	1	-	108,554	63.64%
Florida	14	2,187,805	14			1	2	3	210,010	9.60%
Georgia	12	1,250,266			12	2	3	1	45,671	3.65%
Hawaii	4	236,218		4		2	1	3	49,899	21.12%
Idaho	4	291,183	4			1	2	3	76,096	26.13%
Illinois	26	4,619,749	26			1	2	3	134,960	2.92%
Indiana	13	2,123,597	13			1	2	3	261,226	12.30%
Iowa	9	1,167,931	9			1	2	3	142,407	12.19%
Kansas	7	872,783	7			1	2	3	175,678	20.13%
Kentucky	9	1,055,893	9			1	2	3	64,870	6.14%
Louisiana	10	1,097,450			10	3	2	1	52,080	4.75%
Maine	4	392,936		4		2	1	3	48,058	12.23%
Maryland	10	1,235,039		10		2	1	3	20,315	1.64%
Massachusetts	14	2,331,752		14		2	1	3	702,374	30.12%
Michigan	21	3,306,250		21		2	1	3	222,417	6.73%
Minnesota	10	1,588,510		10		2	1	3	199,095	12.53%
Mississippi	7	654,509			7	3	2	1	62,128	9.49%
Missouri	12	1,809,502	12			1	2	3	20,488	1.13%
Montana	4	274,404	4			1	2	3	24,718	9.01%
Nebraska	5	536,851	5			1	2	3	150,379	28.01%
Nevada	3	154,218	3			1	2	3	12,590	8.16%
New Hampshire	4	297,299	4			1	2	3	24,314	8.18%
New Jersey	17	2,875,395	17			1	2	3	61,261	2.13%
New Mexico	4	327,281	4			1	2	3	39,611	12.10%
New York	43	6,790,066		43		2	1	3	370,538	5.46%
North Carolina	13	1,587,493	12		1	1	3	2	163,079	10.27%
North Dakota	4	247,882	4			1	2	3	43,900	17.71%
Ohio	26	3,959,698	26			1	2	3	90,428	2.28%
Oklahoma	8	943,086	8			1	2	3	148,039	15.70%
Oregon	6	819,622	6			1	2	3	49,567	6.05%
Pennsylvania	29	4,747,928		29		2	1	3	169,388	3.57%
Rhode Island	4	385,000		4		2	1	3	124,159	32.25%
South Carolina	8	666,982	8			1	3	2	56,576	8.48%
South Dakota	4	281,264	4			1	2	3	31,818	11.31%
Tennessee	11	1,248,617	11			1	3	2	121,359	9.72%
Texas	25	3,079,406		25		2	1	3	38,960	1.27%
Utah	4	422,568	4			1	2	3	82,063	19.42%
Vermont	3	161,404	3			1	2	3	14,887	9.22%
Virginia	12	1,361,491	12			1	2	3	147,932	10.87%
Washington	9	1,304,281		9		2	1	3	27,527	2.11%
West Virginia	7	754,206		7		2	1	3	66,536	8.82%
Wisconsin	12	1,691,538	12			1	2	3	61,193	3.62%
Wyoming	3	127,205	3			1	2	3	25,754	20.25%
Total	538	73,199,999	301	191	46	1	2	3	511,944	0.70%

Nixon Republican		Humphrey Democratic		Wallace American Independent		Others	
146,923	13.99%	196,579	18.72%	691,425	65.86%	14,990	1.43%
37,600	45.28%	35,411	42.65%	10,024	12.07%	0	0.00%
266,721	54.78%	170,514	35.02%	46,573	9.56%	3,128	0.64%
189,062	31.01%	184,901	30.33%	235,627	38.65%	0	0.00%
3,467,664	47.82%	3,244,318	44.74%	487,270	6.72%	52,335	0.72%
409,345	50.46%	335,174	41.32%	60,813	7.50%	5,867	0.72%
556,721	44.32%	621,561	49.48%	76,650	6.10%	1,300	0.10%
96,714	45.12%	89,194	41.61%	28,459	13.28%	0	0.00%
31,012	18.18%	139,566	81.82%	0	0.00%	0	0.00%
886,804	40.53%	676,794	30.93%	624,207	28.53%	0	0.00%
380,111	30.40%	334,440	26.75%	535,550	42.83%	165	0.01%
91,425	38.70%	141,324	59.83%	3,469	1.47%	0	0.00%
165,369	56.79%	89,273	30.66%	36,541	12.55%	0	0.00%
2,174,774	47.08%	2,039,814	44.15%	390,958	8.46%	14,203	0.31%
1,067,885	50.29%	806,659	37.99%	243,108	11.45%	5,945	0.28%
619,106	53.01%	476,699	40.82%	66,422	5.69%	5,704	0.49%
478,674	54.84%	302,996	34.72%	88,921	10.19%	2,192	0.25%
462,411	43.79%	397,541	37.65%	193,098	18.29%	2,843	0.27%
257,535	23.47%	309,615	28.21%	530,300	48.32%	0	0.00%
169,254	43.07%	217,312	55.30%	6,370	1.62%	0	0.00%
517,995	41.94%	538,310	43.59%	178,734	14.47%	0	0.00%
766,844	32.89%	1,469,218	63.01%	87,088	3.73%	8,602	0.37%
1,370,665	41.46%	1,593,082	48.18%	331,968	10.04%	10,535	0.32%
658,643	41.46%	857,738	54.00%	68,931	4.34%	3,198	0.20%
88,516	13.52%	150,644	23.02%	415,349	63.46%	0	0.00%
811,932	44.87%	791,444	43.74%	206,126	11.39%	0	0.00%
138,835	50.60%	114,117	41.59%	20,015	7.29%	1,437	0.52%
321,163	59.82%	170,784	31.81%	44,904	8.36%	0	0.00%
73,188	47.46%	60,598	39.29%	20,432	13.25%	0	0.00%
154,903	52.10%	130,589	43.93%	11,173	3.76%	634	0.21%
1,325,467	46.10%	1,264,206	43.97%	262,187	9.12%	23,535	0.82%
169,692	51.85%	130,081	39.75%	25,737	7.86%	1,771	0.54%
3,007,932	44.30%	3,378,470	49.76%	358,864	5.29%	44,800	0.66%
627,192	39.51%	464,113	29.24%	496,188	31.26%	0	0.00%
138,669	55.94%	94,769	38.23%	14,244	5.75%	200	0.08%
1,791,014	45.23%	1,700,586	42.95%	467,495	11.81%	603	0.02%
449,697	47.68%	301,658	31.99%	191,731	20.33%	0	0.00%
408,433	49.83%	358,866	43.78%	49,683	6.06%	2,640	0.32%
2,090,017	44.02%	2,259,405	47.59%	378,582	7.97%	19,924	0.42%
122,359	31.78%	246,518	64.03%	15,678	4.07%	445	0.12%
254,062	38.09%	197,486	29.61%	215,430	32.30%	4	0.00%
149,841	53.27%	118,023	41.96%	13,400	4.76%	0	0.00%
472,592	37.85%	351,233	28.13%	424,792	34.02%	0	0.00%
1,227,844	39.87%	1,266,804	41.14%	584,269	18.97%	489	0.02%
238,728	56.49%	156,665	37.07%	26,906	6.37%	269	0.06%
85,142	52.75%	70,255	43.53%	5,104	3.16%	903	0.56%
590,319	43.36%	442,387	32.49%	321,833	23.64%	6,952	0.51%
588,510	45.12%	616,037	47.23%	96,990	7.44%	2,744	0.21%
307,555	40.78%	374,091	49.60%	72,560	9.62%	0	0.00%
809,997	47.89%	748,804	44.27%	127,835	7.56%	4,902	0.29%
70,927	55.76%	45,173	35.51%	11,105	8.73%	0	0.00%
31,783,783	43.42%	31,271,839	42.72%	9,901,118	13.53%	243,259	0.33%

Election of 1972

Election Overview

Election Year 1972

Election Day November 7, 1972

Winning Candidates

* ★ **President:** Richard M. Nixon
* ★ **Vice President:** Spiro Agnew

Election Results [ticket, party: popular votes (percentage of popular vote); electoral votes (percentage of electoral vote)]

* Richard Nixon and Spiro Agnew, Republican: 47,168,710 (60.67%); 520 (96.7%)
* George McGovern and R. Sargent Shriver, Democratic: 29,173,222 (37.52%); 17 (3.2%)
* John Schmitz and Thomas Anderson, American Independent: 1,100,868 (1.42%); 0 (0.0%)
* John Hospers and Theodora Nathan, Libertarian: 3,674 (0.00%); 1 (0.2%)
* Other: 297,553 (0.38%); 0 (0.0%)

Voter Turnout 55.2%

Central Forums/Campaign Methods for Addressing Voters

* Speaking tours
* Rallies
* Television print/ads

Incumbent President and Vice President on Election Day Richard M. Nixon and Spiro Agnew

Population (1972) 209,924,000

Gross Domestic Product

* $1,237.90 billion (in current dollars: $4,647.7 billion)
* Per capita: $5,897 (in current dollars: $22,140)

Number of Daily Newspapers (1970) 1,748

Average Daily Circulation (1970) 62,108,000

Households with

* Radio (1970): 46,108,000
* Television (1970): 60,594,000

Method of Choosing Electors Popular vote (mostly general-ticket system/winner take all)

Method of Choosing Nominees

* Presidential preference primaries
* Caucuses

Key Issues and Events

* "Body count" of the Vietnam War mounts despite Vietnamization
* Antiwar demonstrations persist
* Inflation grows
* Nixon emerges as a polarizing president
* Republicans lose nine House seats and eleven governorships but pick up two Senate seats in the 1970 midterm elections
* Nixon arrives in China on February 21 and in Russia on May 22, launching détente
* Nixon's poll numbers slipping

Leading Candidates

REPUBLICANS

* Richard M. Nixon, president of the United States
* Pete McCloskey, representative (California)
* John M. Ashbrook, representative (Ohio)
* Harold E. Stassen, former governor (Minnesota)

DEMOCRATS

* George McGovern, senator (South Dakota)
* Hubert Humphrey, former vice president (Minnesota)

- George Wallace, governor (Alabama)
- Edmund Muskie, senator (Maine)
- Eugene J. McCarthy, former senator (Minnesota)
- Henry M. "Scoop" Jackson, senator (Washington)
- Shirley Chisholm, representative (New York)
- Terry Sanford, former governor (North Carolina)
- John V. Lindsay, mayor (New York)
- Wilbur Mills, representative (Arkansas)
- Vance Hartke, senator (Indiana)
- Fred Harris, senator (Oklahoma)
- Sam Yorty, mayor (Los Angeles)

THIRD PARTY CANDIDATES & NOMINATIONS
AMERICAN PARTY
- John G. Schmitz (Republican representative) on the ballot in 32 states

LIBERTARIAN PARTY
- John Hospers and Theodora Nathalia Nathan on the ballot in Colorado only. Hospers and Nathan receive one electoral vote from a disaffected Republican elector in Virginia (first woman to receive an electoral vote)

SOCIALIST WORKERS PARTY
- President: Linda Jenness
- Vice President: Andrew Pulley

PEOPLE'S PARTY
- President: Benjamin Spock
- Vice President: Julius Hobson

Trajectory

- Richard Nixon runs for reelection as "The President," boosted by his groundbreaking trips to China in February 1972 and to the Soviet Union that May.
- Democrats feel cursed after Edward Kennedy's lethal 1969 Chappaquiddick car accident, Edmund Muskie's possibly teary moment during the New Hampshire primary, and the attempted assassination of George Wallace on May 15, 1972.
- George McGovern's "Come Home, America" campaign builds unexpected momentum fueled by his antiwar stance and his mastery of the new primary system he helped design. A June 17 break-in to Democratic National Headquarters at the Watergate complex in Washington, D.C., seems to be more than just a burglary but will have little impact during the campaign.
- Young, sloppily dressed, long-haired "hippie" delegates seem to dominate the Democratic National Convention in Miami in July, feeding perceptions that McGovern is the candidate of "Acid, Amnesty, and Abortion."
- "Stop McGovern" effort fails, but AFL-CIO union head George Meany says McGovern is not "good material" and charges that a "small elite of suburban types and students took over the apparatus of the Democratic Party." Instead of the decades-long tradition of an AFL-CIO endorsement, a "Labor for McGovern Committee" is established, representing the unions that do endorse him.
- The revelation in July that the newly announced Democratic vice-presidential nominee, Senator Thomas Eagleton, underwent electroshock therapy makes McGovern look sloppy and amateurish. When McGovern backs Eagleton "1,000 percent," then backtracks within days, accepting Eagleton's resignation and ultimately choosing Sargent Shriver as a running mate, McGovern further loses his reformist luster, appearing to be just another politician.
- On October 26, just days before Election Day, Secretary of State Henry Kissinger announces "peace with honor" in Southeast Asia is imminent. Americans' belief that "peace is at hand" undercuts McGovern's appeal.

Conventions

- Democratic National Convention: July 10–13, 1972, Convention Center, Miami Beach
- Republican National Convention: August 21–23, 1972, Convention Center, Miami Beach

Ballots/Nominees

REPUBLICANS
- Richard Nixon 1,347
- Pete McCloskey 1

DEMOCRATS
- George McGovern 1,864.95
- Henry M. Jackson 525
- George Wallace 381.7
- Shirley Chisholm 151.95
- Terry Sanford 77.5
- Hubert Humphrey 66.7
- Wilbur Mills 33.8
- Edmund Muskie 24.3
- Edward M. Kennedy 12.7
- Sam Yorty 10
- Wayne Hays 5
- John V. Lindsay 5

- Fred Harris 2
- Eugene McCarthy 2
- Walter Mondale 2
- Ramsey Clark 1
- Walter Fauntroy 1
- Vance Hartke 1
- Harold Hughes 1
- Patsy T. Mink 1

Primaries

- Republican Party: 21; 56.8% delegates
- Democratic Party: 21; 65.3% delegates

Primaries Results

REPUBLICANS
- Richard M. Nixon 5,378,704; 86.79%
- Unpledged 317,048; 5.12%
- John M. Ashbrook 311,543; 5.03%
- Paul N. "Pete" McCloskey Jr. 132.731; 2.14%
- George Wallace 20,907; 0.34%
- Others 8,916; 0.14%
- None of the Names Shown 5,350; 0.09%

DEMOCRATS
- Hubert Humphrey 4,121,372; 25.77%
- George McGovern 4,053,451; 25.34%
- George Wallace 3,755,424; 23.48%
- Edmund Muskie 1,840,217; 11.51%
- Eugene J. McCarthy 553,990; 3.46%
- Henry M. "Scoop" Jackson 505,198; 3.16%
- Shirley A. Chisholm 430,703; 2.69%
- Jason Terry Sanford 331,415; 2.07%
- John V. Lindsay 196,406; 1.23%
- Sam Yorty 79,446; 0.50%
- Wilbur D. Mills 37,401; 0.23%
- Walter E. Fauntroy 21,217; 0.13%
- Unpledged 19,533; 0.12%
- Edward M. Kennedy 16,693; 0.10%
- Vance Hartke 11,798; 0.07%
- Patsy T. Mink 8,286; 0.05%
- Others 9,276; 0.06%

Party Platform

REPUBLICANS
- Celebrate a "new era of diplomacy"
- Support the "Nixon doctrine," having other countries shoulder the burden of defending themselves
- Support Vietnamization
- A "modern, well-equipped force"
- An all-volunteer army
- Welfare reform
- Oppose granting amnesty to draft dodgers
- Health care reform

DEMOCRATS
- Peace platform
- Ending the Vietnam War
- Unconditional withdrawal of U.S. forces
- Welfare system overhaul including guaranteed incomes for the poor
- Gun control, banning small pistols ("Saturday night specials")
- Equal Rights Amendment
- Elimination of Electoral College

Campaign Innovations

- "26ers," U.S. citizens aged 18 to 21, vote for the first time thanks to the 26th Amendment lowering the voting age to 18.
- McGovern-Fraser Commission democratizes the nominating process by increasing the number of states holding primaries to decrease the influence of party bosses, union leaders, and officeholders. Seeking transparency, consistency, and integrity, the new rules outlaw old practices such as proxy voting, mandatory assessments on delegates for easy party fund-raising, and the unit rule favoring front-runners and the majority. State parties to designate uniform times with adequate public notice for delegate selection, require quorums of at least 40 percent of all party committee members, and in general create a process more grassroots and less boss-driven.
- Changes in delegate selection rules requiring "reasonable representation" of minority groups boost the numbers of women, African Americans, and young people at conventions but raise prospects of quotas and a backlash by Democratic regulars.
- The Federal Election Campaign Act (FECA) of 1971 limits individual contributions to $1,000 per candidate per election, $5,000 per year to a political action committee (PAC), and $20,000 per year to a political party. In total, an individual cannot donate more than $25,000 to a campaign.
- FECA also allows unions and corporations to form Political Action Committees, which will—unexpectedly—flood the system with corporate money.
- The Revenue Act of 1971 offers public funding of major party presidential campaigns, with qualifying thresholds for candidates. The funding comes from a voluntary $1.00 checkoff on income tax forms.

Campaign Tactics

- The 1970 census shows that for the first time, more Americans live in the suburbs than in the cities, and both campaigns build strategies trying to mobilize suburban voters.

REPUBLICANS

- Nixon runs a restrained, dignified campaign.
- Runs as a bold world leader, with staffers, members of Congress, cabinet members functioning as "presidential surrogates" on the campaign trail.
- Well organized, identifying voters by consumer identities as well as traditional groups with: the Hairdressers Committee, the Veterinarians Committee, the Motorcyclists Committee, the Indians-Aleut-Eskimos Committee.
- Huge reliance on television, on media markets, on ads. As the journalist Theodore White remarked: "It was easier to cover the President on campaign in 1972 by staying home and watching television—which was the way the President wanted it."
- Establishes the Committee to Re-Elect the President (CREEP), independent of the party, housed across from the White House, filled with Nixon—rather than party—loyalists.
- CREEP builds a formidable fund-raising apparatus. Known at the time for being extremely aggressive, during the Watergate investigation it emerges that dirty tricks, money laundering, and other shady or illegal acts characterized CREEP's operation.
- Nixon as the peace candidate, continually withdrawing troops from Vietnam, under his "Vietnamization" of the war; establishing détente with Communists thanks to historic trips to Beijing in February and Moscow in May; starting strategic arms-limitations talks (SALT)
- Southern strategy: winning traditionally Democratic Southern states by opposing desegregation (busing), civil rights, the New Left, Vietnam protests, the counterculture.
- Paints McGovern as a radical.
- Nixon did not necessarily need to campaign but stumps toward the end, attacking busing and permissiveness, calling McGovern's foreign policy proposals dangerous to the country.

DEMOCRATS

- Heavy emphasis on television, but also grass roots, with activists noting that New York mayor John V. Lindsay's primary campaign was almost solely reliant on television, and failed.
- Improvises campaign organization, difficulty making the transition from a primary insurgency to a general campaign.
- The Eagleton mess and the democratization of the Democratic Party alienate many Democrats, voters, and influential party leaders, some of whom defect to become "Democrats for Nixon."
- Attracts young activists who would lead the party in the future, the pollster Patrick Caddell, his campaign manager Gary Hart, and volunteers Bill Clinton and Hillary Rodham.

Popular Campaign Slogans

REPUBLICANS

- "Now More than Ever"
- "Re-Elect the President"
- "Four More Years"

DEMOCRATS

- "Make America Happen Again"
- "Come Home, America"

Campaign Songs

- Republican Party: "Nixon Now"
- Democratic Party: "Bridge over Troubled Water"

Influential Campaign Appeals or Ads

- Republicans: Democrats as the party of "Acid, Amnesty, and Abortion"
- Democrats: "Don't Switch Dicks in the Middle of a Screw, Vote Nixon in '72."

Campaign Finance

- Nixon: $61,400,000 (in current dollars: $298,919,600)
- McGovern: $30,000,000 (in current dollars: $146,052,000)

Defining Quotations

- "The most painful new phrase in the American political vocabulary is the 'credibility gap'—the gap between rhetoric and reality. Put bluntly it means people no longer believe what their leaders tell them." *Senator George McGovern of South Dakota launching his presidential campaign, January 18, 1971*
- "I was just goddamned mad and choked up over my anger." *Edmund Muskie, explaining his press conference in the snow March 4, 1972, which resulted in his being mocked for supposedly crying while defending his wife against slurs*

"The people don't know McGovern is for amnesty, abortion and legalization of pot. Once middle America—Catholic middle America, in particular—finds this out, he's dead." *Senator Thomas F. Eagleton, speaking off the record to Robert Novak for a column published April 27, 1972—Eagleton's identity was revealed 35 years later*

"They say that George McGovern is for the legalization of marijuana, but I say—I tell you that George McGovern does not advocate the legalization of marijuana. They say George McGovern is for abortion on demand, but I tell you—But I say to you that George McGovern is against tampering with our state laws on abortion." *Nebraska governor Frank Morrison introducing McGovern at a meeting in a large Catholic high school in Omaha, building up to the Nebraska primary, May 9, 1972*

"The McGovern-O'Hara-Fraser commission reform is reforming the party out of the Presidency, and maybe right out of existence." *Ohio congressman Wayne Hays shouting at a closed-door caucus of Democratic House members, June 1972*

"And within 90 days of my inauguration, every American soldier and every American prisoner will be out of the jungle and out of their cells and then home in America where they belong. And then let us resolve that never again will we send the precious young blood of this country to die trying to prop up a corrupt military dictatorship abroad. This is also the time to turn away from excessive preoccupation overseas to the rebuilding of our own nation. America must be restored to a proper role in the world. But we can do that only through the recovery of confidence in ourselves." *George McGovern, address accepting the presidential nomination at the Democratic National Convention in Miami Beach, Florida, July 14, 1972*

"I think we lost the election at Miami. . . . The American people made an association between McGovern and gay liberation, and welfare rights and pot-smoking and black militants, and women's lib, and wise college kids." *Congressman James O'Hara after the Democratic National Convention, July 1972*

"This campaign has a soul of its own. The volunteers don't want it to become just another political campaign. There is a mystique about it." *McGovern's 34-year-old campaign manager, Gary Hart, quoted in* Time, *July 17, 1972*

"I am 1,000 percent for Tom Eagleton and I have no intention of dropping him from the ticket." *Statement issued by George McGovern on July 26, 1972, five days before dropping Eagleton from the ticket*

"I am not embarrassed to be George McGovern's seventh choice for Vice President. We Democrats may be short of money but we're not short of talent. Pity Mr. Nixon—his first and only choice was Spiro Agnew." *Sargent Shriver after receiving the vice-presidential nomination, August 8, 1972*

"And I ask you, my fellow Americans, tonight to join us not in a coalition held together only by a desire to gain power. I ask you to join us as members of a new American majority bound together by our common ideals. I ask everyone listening to me tonight—Democrats, Republicans, independents—to join our new majority—not on the basis of the party label you wear in your lapel, but on the basis of what you believe in your hearts." *Richard M. Nixon, remarks on accepting the presidential nomination at the Republican National Convention, August 23, 1972*

"We did agree that we would make a major effort to conclude the negotiations by October 31. As far as Saigon is concerned, it is of course entitled to participate in the settlement of a war fought on its territory. Its people have suffered much and they will remain there after we leave. We believe that peace is at hand. We believe that an agreement is within sight. It is inevitable that in a war of such complexity that there should be occasional difficulties in reaching a final solution." *Henry Kissinger, press conference, October 26, 1972*

"I am not going to insult your intelligence tonight or impose upon your time by rehashing all the issues of the campaign or making any last-minute charges against our opponents. You know what the issues are. You know that this is a choice, which is probably the clearest choice between the candidates for President ever presented to the American people in this century. I would, however, urge you to have in mind tomorrow one overriding issue, and that is the issue of peace—peace in Vietnam and peace in the world at large for a generation to come. As you know, we have made a breakthrough in the negotiations which will lead to peace in Vietnam." *Richard Nixon, remarks on election eve, November 6, 1972*

"Last year we opened the doors of the Democratic party, as we promised we would, and twenty million Democrats stalked out. For years, I wanted to run for President in the worst possible way—and I'm sure I did!" *George McGovern in 1973, looking back at the campaign in a speech at Washington's Gridiron Club*

Lasting Legacy of Campaign

- Nixon's landslide victory results in the fourth largest margin of victory at 23.2% for percentage of the popular vote.

- Nixon receives the largest margin of victory by winning 18 million more popular votes than his opponent.
- Break-in at the Watergate complex in Washington, D.C., embroils President Nixon in the cover-up and ultimately leads to his resignation in 1974.

Election of 1972

In retrospect, historians can always find significance in any presidential election. If the results of a given election are close, that in itself creates importance; if the margin is great, the landslide is given great meaning. And, regardless of the outcome of an election, the twists and turns of the campaign trail inevitably ensure that no contest is devoid of historical importance or without interpretive possibilities.

The election of 1972 has its own unique dimensions. For example, it was the first election under newly instituted guidelines for delegate selection in the Democratic Party, a change that drastically altered the selection process and ultimately affected Republican politics as well. The election illustrated the continuing decline of party dominance as independents became more important factors in national politics. For the first time, people between the ages of 18 and 21 could vote (following the passage of the Twenty-sixth Amendment), and the election, as a result, measured the more lasting effects of the upheavals of the 1960s that had been produced by the Vietnam war and racial unrest at home. It was also the first presidential election after the Census Bureau noted in 1970 that more people lived in suburbs than in cities, a finding that strongly influenced campaign strategies. But, most significantly, political corruption was epitomized that year by a gross breach of trust, perhaps the most deceitful act in American political history, which for the first time forced a President to resign in disgrace. In itself, Nixon's landslide victory would have sufficed to give the 1972 election historical noteworthiness, but underneath the surface churned powerful and baffling forces that not only would present historians with dramatically new perspectives, but also would dominate American society for decades to come.

The beginning of wisdom about the election of 1972 is an understanding of the 1960s, for the contest actually began on August 16, 1968, when Senator George McGovern stood at his fourth-floor window of the Blackstone Sheraton Hotel in Chicago. Outside, thousands of demonstrators in and around Logan Park taunted a stiff, glaring blue line of helmeted police. Suddenly, the tense scene erupted and a wild melee followed. Policemen wielded nightsticks while the demonstrators threw rocks and bottles. Cries and screams were heard above the sound of shattering glass. A few hours later, the National Guard replaced the police and installed barbed wire to protect the string of hotels on Michigan Avenue. As the sour smell of CS gas seeped into the South Dakotan's room, the internal peace of the country had seldom seemed so fragile. It looked as though the country's social fabric might break apart and the ugly emotions produced by the present national conflicts would spill out over the nation. The flashing police clubs, the obscenities of the crowd, the sting of the gas, the rumors of riots and racial war in other parts of the city, the sight of young National Guardsmen pitted against agitated young students, showed that unless something could be done, America might not reach its 200th year in recognizable form. In the future loomed worsening race relations, the greater despair of the poor, the growing cynicism of the young, and the people's deepening disappointment with the quality of their lives. At the center of the nation's sickness was the perceived bankruptcy of its values and its leadership. The assassination of three of the country's most popular leaders, John and Robert Kennedy and Martin Luther King, shocked the American consciousness and symbolized the violent forces that were unleashed in this decade.

Five miles southwest of the Blackstone Hotel, the Democrats debated the Vietnam War—the issue that had drawn the angry crowds to Logan Park. America's involvement in the Southeast Asian conflict seriously divided the nation. The issue had shattered the incumbent president's hopes for reelection; now the party that had coasted to victory in the 1964 contest was feeling similar strains. The mood on the convention floor was volatile. At one point, Senator Abe Ribicoff accused host Mayor Richard J. Daley of using "gestapo tactics" to control the demonstrators, to which Daley responded with an obscene gesture. The war issue did, in fact, receive

This anti-Nixon poster featured a gruesome image from the My Lai Massacre during the Vietnam War. *(Library of Congress)*

rational and orderly debate over national television before the delegates upheld the Johnson administration's conduct of the war by 163 votes. There were even touching moments, as when many delegates tearfully sang the "Battle Hymn of the Republic" after viewing a film biography of John F. Kennedy.

In McGovern's view, the election of Richard M. Nixon, the Republican nominee, would mean continued violence at home and abroad. Nor did other public figures seem to offer the prospect of the kind of leadership that could harness the social forces swirling across the country. Certainly there were devoted statesmen who in ordinary times could occupy the Oval Office with intelligence and dignity. But the times were not ordinary, and there was scarcely any expectation that they soon would be.

George McGovern came to believe that he could provide the needed leadership. In fact, the convention had been a personal triumph for him. He had begun his candidacy only 18 days before its opening. His decision to run stemmed from the dilemma of Robert Kennedy's delegates, now without a candidate following the assassination. Though many drifted to Humphrey or McCarthy, others found the primary wounds too deep and sought a

more legitimate heir to the legacy they had just fought to secure. McGovern had supported JFK and later became head of his Food for Peace program. Moreover, the senator from South Dakota had been close to Robert Kennedy and shared his belief that the great priorities of the nation were ending the war in Vietnam and reconciling competing social groups at home. Indeed, RFK had given McGovern his finest testimonial when he called him "the most decent man in the Senate."

During the four turbulent days of the Chicago convention McGovern provided new leadership to his 200 delegates, most of whom had never met him before. (Some, in fact, were not even sure where he came from. One supporter, when told the candidate was from South Dakota, cried in anguish, "Christ, I've been telling everyone he's from Iowa.") At every caucus, McGovern pledged to support the nominee of the convention. He was always careful to tell some of his angriest followers that under no circumstances would he lead a walkout or entertain a third-party candidacy. The night of Humphrey's victory, much against the wishes of his key advisers, he joined the Democratic candidate on the rostrum in a demonstration of support. George McGovern, alone among national figures, walked out of the convention a larger man than he went in.

As he left Chicago, McGovern had turned to an aide and remarked, "If that's the competition, I can handle it." He was not thinking of 1968 at that moment, but of four years ahead. No doubt he had thought of the presidency before. After all, he came from Middle America, where mothers still dreamed of such miracles. More importantly, as a senator he came to know well the kind of individuals "mentioned" for the nomination; as a historian, he was unawed by the gauge of men who had dominated the public scene in the past.

Yet 1972 was four years away and the obstacles were formidable. The first was reelection to the Senate from South Dakota. As he began his senatorial campaign, McGovern was greeted by a poll showing his margin over his challenger at only four points, a sharp decline from the previous spring. The decline seemed foreboding since South Dakota was a Republican state and his own margin of victory in 1962 had been less than 500 votes. Hence it was essential to arrest the decline. The senator went back to the kind of campaigning he liked best—face-to-face conversations with South Dakotans, small meetings and endless traveling across the plains. An inept opponent certainly helped the cause. Though Nixon handily carried the state in the 1968 presidential election, McGovern was reelected that year with 55 percent of the vote, a performance unequaled by any Democrat in the history of South Dakota.

Richard Nixon's presidential victory, however, dampened the euphoria, for it meant that the man George McGovern most distrusted would occupy the White House for four years and would undoubtedly be the Republican nominee in 1972. This was particularly bitter since McGovern's early hero in American politics had been Adlai Stevenson, the man whom Nixon savaged in both 1952 and 1956. "That man is outside the breastworks," he once said, unconsciously repeating an earlier judgment made of Nixon by Sam Rayburn. Nixon had pledged to end the war if elected, but McGovern never believed him, reminding the voters that as early as 1954 Nixon had advocated the committing of American troops in Vietnam. Furthermore, the new president was a dedicated cold warrior who might well widen the war in the guise of ending it. What had been a personal desire to run in 1972 now took on a new urgency.

The experience of 1968, however, produced another imperative: there might not be a viable Democratic Party, much less a McGovern nomination, if the system of delegate selection to the next convention was not changed. The system had grown up over a long period of time. In essence, the states determined delegate selection procedures under their own party rules or general statutes.

Some had primaries, others called conventions, still others used complicated caucuses. In addition, there were wide variations from state to state, and every system was laced with unfairness, secrecy, and even chicanery. Part of the problem in Chicago had been the unrepresentativeness of a convention that largely reflected the party establishment without an adequate leavening of the new forces—blacks, Hispanics, women, and the young. "The lesson I would like to see our party learn," McGovern said in Chicago, "is that we have to open up the party once again to the voice of all our people and break these repressive procedures" so that "the average citizen in this land can have a voice in the selection of our presidential nominees and in the writing of the platform." In fact, the convention had adopted this view by mandating a commission to reform party procedures for the 1972 convention.

A few months after the 1968 election, Senator Fred Harris, the Democratic national chairman, appointed George McGovern to head a 15-member commission to do the job of party reform. At the time the position looked like no gift. Some of the senator's closest associates advised him against accepting, arguing that it would

A 1972 campaign poster for George McGovern *(Library of Congress)*

only put him in the middle of factional infighting and that no document, however skillfully contrived, could satisfy everyone. Yet McGovern felt a duty to try. He had always been an organization man and believed that

the Democratic Party was the best available instrument for responsible and liberal government. It now faced internal divisions that might destroy it. As a historian he could look back to Baltimore in 1856 and Chicago in

☆ ☆ ☆

1972 ELECTION CHRONOLOGY

1971

January 18, 1971: Senator George McGovern announces his candidacy for the Democratic nomination in his home state of South Dakota. "The most painful new phrase in the American political vocabulary," he says, "is the 'credibility gap.'"

June 30, 1971: The Supreme Court allows publication of the *Pentagon Papers,* the government's secret history of its involvement in Vietnam. Furious, President Richard Nixon looks for creative ways to plug the constant "leaks" to reporters. This leads to the establishment of the secret White House "plumbers" unit, which will cause his downfall.

July 1, 1971: The Twenty-sixth Amendment to the Constitution is ratified, lowering the voting age from 21 to 18. Young voters in this election will be called "26ers."

August 11, 1971: New York mayor John Lindsay leaves the Republican Party and announces his intention to run in the Democratic primaries.

1972

January 24, 1972: Democratic senator Edmund Muskie of Maine wins the Iowa caucus.

January 25, 1972: Representative Shirley Chisholm from New York announces her candidacy for the Democratic presidential nomination. She does not win but, as a serious African-American woman candidate, helps blaze a trail toward more gender and racial equality.

February 4, 1972: The *Manchester Union Leader* publishes a letter to the editor implying that Democratic frontrunner Senator Edward Muskie of Maine is prejudiced against French Canadians.

February 21–28, 1972: After months of behind-the-scenes diplomacy, President Nixon pays a

state visit to China, marking the first step in normalization between the two countries.

March 4, 1972: Muskie seems to be crying as he defends his wife against campaign smears while delivering a speech in New Hampshire. Muskie later claims the "tears" were actually snow melting on his face.

March 7, 1972: Muskie wins the New Hampshire primary with 46.4 percent of the vote to 37.1 percent for McGovern, but in light of Muskie's crying, the media considers McGovern the victor.

March 22, 1972: Congress passes the Equal Rights Amendment to the Constitution and sends it to the states for ratification. It will languish for a decade before failing to win the necessary approval.

April 4, 1972: McGovern wins the Wisconsin primary with 30 percent of the vote, well ahead of Minnesota Senator Hubert Humphrey's 22 percent and Alabama Governor George Wallace's 21 percent. John Lindsay withdraws.

May 15, 1972: Governor Wallace is shot while campaigning in a Maryland shopping center. He survives, but is permanently disabled and drops out of the race.

June 6, 1972: Primary season ends. Nixon leads the Republicans with 86 percent of pledged delegates. McGovern takes the California primary, but Humphrey's strong showing in the state narrows McGovern's lead. They both command 25 percent of pledged delegates going into the convention.

June 17, 1972: The first national convention of the Libertarian Party nominates John Hospers for president and Theodora Nathan for vice president. Nathan will end up receiving the first electoral vote ever cast for a woman when a "faithless" Republican elector votes for her.

June 17, 1972: Five men break into the Democratic National Committee headquarters in the Water

1912 to know that the two-party structure proved fragile under prolonged stress. His risk was undoubtedly high; but what would the nomination of a divided party be worth?

In addition, the offer was important in itself. The fact that the National Committee had turned to him indicated that McGovern had come out of Chicago with the respect of people from both the "old" and "new" political camps.

☆ ☆ ☆

gate hotel and office complex in Washington, D.C. They bungle the job and are arrested, beginning what becomes known as the Watergate scandal.

June 19, 1972: White House spokesman Ron Ziegler dismisses the Watergate case as a "third-rate burglary."

June 23, 1972: President Nixon and White House chief of staff H. R. Haldeman plot to use the CIA to obstruct the FBI's investigation of the Watergate burglary. This conversation is taped and becomes the "smoking gun"—evidence that the president obstructed justice—that ultimately forces Nixon's resignation in August 1974.

July 10–13, 1972: The Democratic Party holds its national convention in Miami Beach, nominating Senator George McGovern of South Dakota for president. He selects Senator Thomas F. Eagleton of Missouri as his running mate.

July 14, 1972: At 2:48 a.m., McGovern delivers his acceptance speech, after a drawn out vice presidential nomination process. By that time, most television viewers are sleeping, depriving McGovern of a crucial opportunity to make his case to the American people.

July 25, 1972: Reporters break the story that Thomas Eagleton, George McGovern's running mate, has a history of "nervous exhaustion" and has undergone electroshock treatment. McGovern and Eagleton try to minimize the damage with a joint press conference at Custer, South Dakota.

August 1, 1972: Eagleton formally withdraws from the Democratic ticket.

August 8, 1972: A special meeting of the Democratic National Committee selects R. Sargent Shriver, the first director of the Peace Corps, first director of the Office of Economic Opportunity, and John F. Kennedy's brother-in-law, to be the new vice-presidential nominee.

August 21–23, 1972: The Republican Party holds its national convention in Miami Beach, and re-nominates President Richard Nixon for president and Vice President Spiro Agnew as his running mate.

August 23, 1972: Nixon delivers his acceptance speech, on time, to a prime-time television audience. Appealing to moderate Democrats, he says: "To those millions who have been driven out of their home in the Democratic Party, we say come home. We say come home . . . to the great principles we Americans believe in together. And I ask you, my fellow Americans, tonight to join us. . . . as members of a new American majority bound together by our common ideals."

October 26, 1972: National Security Adviser Henry Kissinger declares that "peace is at hand" in Vietnam. The announcement boosts Nixon's reelection prospects, even though an agreement with North Vietnam is not reached until January 9, 1973.

November 2, 1972: In a speech broadcast from the library of the White House, President Nixon calls for "peace with honor" in Vietnam.

November 6, 1972: McGovern ends his campaign with a mad cross-country dash flying from New York to South Dakota, but touching down in Pennsylvania, Kansas, and California along the way.

November 7, 1972: Election Day. Republicans Richard Nixon and Spiro Agnew defeat Democrats George McGovern and R. Sargent Shriver with 520 electoral votes and 60.7 percent of the popular vote.

December 18, 1972: Presidential electors cast their ballots in their respective state capitals. One "faithless elector" from Virginia, Roger MacBride, votes for the Libertarian ticket.

1973

January 6, 1973: A joint session of Congress assembles to count the electoral votes.

He was also convinced that the demand for reform was so widespread that sensible recommendations would be accepted by nearly all segments of the party. Nor was he oblivious to the openings into all factions that the chairmanship involved, since hearings would take him to every part of the country and bring him into contact with local leaders and reporters. In short, McGovern thought the assignment necessary, feasible, and opportune.

Two central matters needed resolution: first, the procedures of delegate selection should be made fair and clear; second, there had to be a guarantee of adequate representation of the aggrieved groups within the Democratic Party. The first problem required a great deal of work, but involved little controversy; the latter, the representation issue, contained dangers of the highest magnitude.

"Adequate representation" was hard to define. Did it mean that the convention itself was to mirror the party's constituents? Or did it merely require that all groups have equal access to the machinery that produced delegates? The commission trod warily through this minefield, and finally adopted the phrase "reasonable representation" to each group's share of the population. The members insisted unanimously that quotas were not intended. Yet they had unwittingly placed a thorn in the party's side that has since irritated and festered. McGovern himself patiently, if not persuasively, asserted that the object was to open up the process, not to exclude anyone. Somebody, however, would ultimately have to decide what "reasonable representation" was.

A few months after the commission had unanimously approved the "equal representation" guidelines, the National Committee ratified the new regulations without dissent. A quiet revolution had been accomplished with little notice and scarcely a tremor. Nearly every state had to change its rules to qualify for convention seats; now ordinary party members had a sporting chance to occupy them. In December 1970, Senator McGovern stepped down as chairman of the commission amidst the thanks of the party leaders and a firm commitment to support the guidelines by the new national chairman, Lawrence O'Brien, who observed wryly, "They are my survival kit."

By this time, too, the general argument for a McGovern candidacy had been fashioned. More than any other possible nominee, with the exception of Senator Edward Kennedy, he could hold together the antiwar movement within the Democratic Party. In the gloomy and angry aftermath of 1968, some disappointed McCarthy supporters broached the idea of a new party, and they kept this threat alive during the intervening years. If 1972 turned into another Chicago, they warned, there would be a fourth party in the field (George Wallace was expected to lead a third-party challenge). The continuing ambiguity of Eugene McCarthy's own statements and the on-and-

off flirtation of Senator Harold Hughes of Iowa with the prospect strengthened this strategy. Only McGovern's nomination promised to keep this sizable, if loosely organized, element within the party, because his peace and reform credentials were unassailable.

In addition, his loyalty to the party reassured the regulars. He might be a liberal on the issues, but he was no organizational maverick. His performance in 1968 had demonstrated that. Moreover, his career in South Dakota marked him as a party professional. In 1956 he took a state that had two Republican senators, a Republican governor, and 100 Republican legislators out of 102, and within a decade made it broadly Democratic. Regular politicians could relate to that, especially because South Dakota was such a conservative state. McGovern had good personal relations with many party leaders who respected his candor as well as his success. Mayor Richard Daley, for example, encouraging him after 1968, observed, "The good Lord sometimes opens another door when He closes the first one."

Beyond the nomination, of course, lay the broader electorate, and here the case seemed even more persuasive. The country was drifting to the right as it recoiled from the upheavals of the 1960s. Yet the Democratic Party's tradition was clearly liberal. McGovern's entire career had been based on selling progressive ideas to essentially conservative voters in South Dakota. He had never fudged on the issues at home, but his low-key, prudent manner had made new trends acceptable in his own state. Would not 1972 require a Democratic candidate who could sustain his party's historic liberalism while making needed changes palatable to a cautious public?

At this time, there was virtually no discussion of the general election. It was assumed that Richard Nixon would be renominated and would be more vulnerable than in 1968. A further supposition was that Wallace would also be in the race and take roughly the same 13.5 percent of the votes. The Democratic goal was 45 percent, or a few points higher than Humphrey's performance. McGovern, it was argued, would hit the president in his Achilles heel—character. The contrast between the candid, open, and honest senator and a dissembling, secretive, "Tricky Dick" Nixon would be compelling, notwithstanding the traditional advantages of incumbency.

The route to the nomination seemed at least possible, even if formidable. Ever since Estes Kefauver had forced Adlai Stevenson into a few contests in 1956, primaries assumed increasing importance in the selection of the Democratic nominee. JFK disposed of the Catholic issue through a string of primary victories, and in 1968 President Johnson's experience in New Hampshire and Wisconsin prompted his withdrawal from the race. Each year more states dispensed with old and usually unrepresentative convention and caucus systems, until by 1972 nearly half had primaries, choosing well over half the delegates who would attend the convention.

For McGovern, the primaries were the key to victory. Their number, however, posed real problems. Where would the money come from? How could he recruit a staff large enough to organize 20 states? The solution was clear: enter wherever there was enough support to warrant a dignified showing, but concentrate on key states. Previous experience had created what one strategist called the "historic corridor"—that set of primaries that had been crucial in previous elections. The corridor contained the first and the last primaries, New Hampshire and New York; between lay Wisconsin, Nebraska, Oregon, California, and perhaps West Virginia. Anyone who carried these seven could not be denied the nomination without the risk of an irreparably divided party.

Even this limited activity, however, required money. Staff projections ran into the millions, though they varied widely. In the long run, McGovern's innocence of large election costs proved a great asset. His presidential bid in 1968 had cost only $80,000 and his successful reelection campaign for the Senate only slightly more. He came to the conclusion that if there was a candidacy there would be money; if not, none. To start down a two-year road without foreseeable financing seemed lunacy to some. It was, to be sure, arrogant; it also led to a remarkable innovation in American politics.

McGovern explained his decision to run to the people of his home state in a television address on January 18, 1971, and with a national press conference in Washington, D.C., the next day. His message was that all of the issues that had racked the nation in 1968 remained. The war in Vietnam continued; race relations had worsened;

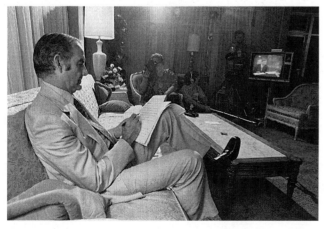

While Democratic National Convention delegates were preparing to pick him as their presidential candidate, Senator George S. McGovern sat quietly in his hotel suite in Miami Beach, July 12, 1972, studying and correcting the draft of the speech he would deliver as he accepted the nomination. *(Associated Press)*

the number of poor had increased; the young remained alienated. Indeed, the Nixon administration had irritated the exposed nerves of American society in a most calculated manner for four years. But McGovern's central concern from the beginning was the decreasing confidence of the American people in their leaders. "The most painful new phrase in the American political vocabulary," he told his fellow South Dakotans, "is the 'credibility gap'—the gap between rhetoric and reality. Put bluntly it means people no longer believe what their leaders tell them." He promised a campaign that would "rest on candor and reason."

The second part of the announcement scenario was a long letter to antiwar activists detailing the reasons for the early candidacy. It frankly asserted that he had no substantial financial support and would have to rely on modest contributions to run. Signed by McGovern himself, it launched a new technique of campaigning, later widely adopted by both parties (and, ironically, exploited especially by the New Right), where the candidate reached over party organizations to their membership by direct mail. Observers later emphasized its success in fund-raising, yet more significant was the way it tied a McGovern constituency to the senator in a personal sense. As the mailing lists multiplied, they contained the names of the troops for the primaries.

Other potential candidates came largely from the liberal wing of the party—a long list that included Senators Edmund Muskie of Maine, Birch Bayh and Vance Hartke of Indiana, former senator Fred Harris of Oklahoma, 1968 presidential candidate Eugene McCarthy of Minnesota, and former attorney general Ramsey Clark. An unexpected factor arose in New York when Mayor John Lindsay changed party affiliation as a prelude to a bid for the presidential nomination on the Democratic ticket. Of all, the Kennedy possibility was always the most complex problem for McGovern. He had "stood in," so to speak, for the RFK delegates in 1968; he was personally close to Edward Kennedy, and a large portion of his active supporters came from earlier Kennedy campaigns. In retrospect, the Kennedy shadow was helpful because it emphasized McGovern's connection to the party's central figure, and so long as it remained, other candidates were seriously handicapped. Kennedy's neutrality was always benevolent, permitting old JFK and RFK veterans to move to the South Dakotan or sit it out.

The conventional wisdom calculated that the most likely candidate was Edmund Muskie. The January 1972 Gallup Poll showed him leading even Senator Kennedy, 32 to 27, with McGovern barely visible at 3 percent. The Democratic "establishment," or what was left of it, assumed the inevitability of his nomination. Muskie had the proper liberal voting record; he had favorable public exposure as Hubert Humphrey's running mate in 1968; though clearly cautious, he quietly exuded a solid composure and thoughtfulness; and, in a fractured party, he made few enemies during the charter years of the preceding decade. Throughout 1971 he put together a veteran organization and lined up an impressive string of endorsements that read like a "Who's Who" of elected officials. Labor maintained its historic formal neutrality. Indeed, its leadership may have preferred Senator Henry "Scoop" Jackson, but some international unions and many AFL-CIO locals were quite active for Muskie. And no one worried about money. Only some unforeseen event or blunder of his own separated Muskie from the 1972 nomination.

Actually, Muskie's formidable backing concealed two land mines. The first was the continuing war in Vietnam. As the year began, its intensity continued unabated. The nightly news put the fighting into every living room. The "body count" designed to show the United States winning the conflict inevitably included an increasing number of Americans. President Johnson had once observed that support for the war would wane when "the caskets start coming home." The prolonged conflict, with no "light at the end of the tunnel," embittered both its advocates and its opponents. Muskie had been deeply troubled by American policy, but his ambivalence created an opening for the more resolute antiwar forces.

The second event affecting Muskie's chances was the adoption of the Twenty-sixth Amendment to the Constitution. This extended the vote to those between 18 and 21 years old. Women had been enfranchised in 1920, and the Voting Rights Act of 1965 secured for blacks what the post–Civil War amendments had originally intended. Now those "old enough to die" would be able to vote. Many of those who could now vote were not anxious to enlist in an unpopular war. Large numbers of college students finessed the draft and transformed their antiwar sentiments into a larger attack on American institutions, beginning with university governance. Campuses across the nation mixed the mutiny against college regulations with protest against American involvement in the Vietnam War. Student activity was highlighted on the nightly news and provided excitement and a good environment for Democratic presidential aspirants. In a flush of enthusiasm, young people registered in significant numbers. It was no small matter; the "26ers," as the regulars called them, provided McGovern with his margin of victory in key primary states.

The Muskie campaign, despite its logical grounding and its traditional support, never quite caught on with Democratic voters. It was suddenly aborted in New Hampshire, the first primary state. The *Manchester Union Leader* published a bogus letter claiming the Senator's wife once referred to Canadian-Americans as "Canucks." Muskie responded with a tearful defense of his wife. In itself the episode was inconsequential, in fact, movingly human. But since he had been projected as cool and restrained, the event contradicted expectations. The cadence of the Muskie parade was broken and could not be restored. Although the senator from Maine won the New Hampshire primary with 46 percent of the vote, the media converted McGovern's 37 percent into a virtual victory. The Muskie effort unraveled, and it finally ended with the Wisconsin primary three weeks later.

In the days between New Hampshire and Wisconsin, a political Halley's Comet streaked across the sky, lighting up the landscape for a brief moment and then disappearing almost as rapidly. John Lindsay, the mayor of New York, a Republican, handsome and articulate, elected without the support of either party, the spokesman for cities beleaguered by violence and decay, announced in the spring that he was changing his party affiliation and would seek the presidency through the Democratic primaries. His strategy was transparent: skip the early primaries and enter Florida, with its large concentration of retired New Yorkers, and then Wisconsin, with its sizable antiwar student population and the antiparty tradition of the La Follettes.

The Lindsay campaign, however, had a more important dimension than the candidate himself. It was the first campaign for the presidency conducted entirely through the media. It sought to invent a serious candidacy through television exposure. The youthful mayor of the nation's largest city was above all things telegenic. New York had survived the worst disorders of the 1960s; as a Republican turned Democrat, he could attract independents; and he was the preeminent representative of the party's urban base. Moreover, David Garth, a pioneer in media politics who had engineered the mayor's reelection, took total control of the campaign. An astute mix of the evening news and paid commercials, it was argued, could make John Lindsay a household name in the primary states. It was a "state-of-the-art" candidacy, yet it proved no more substantial than the evanescent images on the television screen. After a humiliating defeat in Wisconsin, Lindsay withdrew.

The other candidates floundered from the outset. Typically they began with bold announcements, firm assurances of financial support, and many staff appointments. Soon, however, the entrance fee to the presidential sweepstakes became too high, and most had to find a graceful way out. Of the marginal liberal aspirants, only Hartke made it into New Hampshire. One by one, as the ill-starred ships went down, the life rafts drifted toward McGovern. The serious field narrowed to McGovern and Muskie as the Wisconsin primary approached.

The Badger State was important in other ways. Everyone was in the contest—Muskie, Humphrey, Wallace,

Senator Edmund S. Muskie gives a victory sign at a "victory party" in his New Hampshire headquarters in Manchester, March 7, 1972. *(Associated Press)*

Lindsay, and McGovern. The state comprised a cross-section of the country, though not in precise proportions. It had a tradition of heavy voting in the primaries; indeed, the law encouraged voters of both parties to participate in the contest. It was also perfect for McGovern. His best organizers had been there for 15 months; like Humphrey, he was a neighbor, enjoying a close psychological connection with the voters, particularly in the farm districts. The state university with its scattered branches provided a ripe recruiting ground for campaign volunteers. And Wisconsin's historical tradition, including as it did both Robert La Follette and Joe McCarthy, was profoundly independent. Only Milwaukee with its ethnic enclaves presented a problem, though the burgeoning suburbs promised to balance off any substantial losses in the city.

As Muskie hobbled into Wisconsin, Wallace charged in. Fresh from a victory in Florida and drawing on the nagging discontent of ordinary Americans, he suddenly became McGovern's most serious opponent. He had little organization, and his campaign had gotten a late start, but he had done well four years earlier and had come to Wisconsin several times in 1968. In addition, he could draw from Republicans as well as from disenchanted Democrats in the primary. As the other contenders faded away, the Alabama governor grew more prominent. On primary day he ran a strong second to McGovern.

It had been expected that Wallace's impact in the general election in 1972 would be the same as it had been four years before when he won over 13 percent of the vote as an independent candidate. But Florida and Wisconsin thrust him into the race inside the Democratic Party. In addition, the Alabama governor's candidacy had firmer roots than the other, more conventional candidates. No

less than McGovern, Wallace represented those alienated by traditional party politics. He appealed to what the press liked to refer to as "middle Americans"—Southern whites, blue-collar and skilled workers, low-level clerks and small businessmen, portions of the emerging immigrant groups, and all who resented the upward surge of the blacks and the young. His broader constituency was among those who felt, often vaguely, that too much power had moved to Washington. The first of a long line of "outsiders" to seek the office, Wallace attacked the bureaucracy, the elites, the intellectuals, and the leaders of both parties. His outrageous language and caustic wit actually softened his indictment, but his slogan, "Send them a message," became part of the nation's political vocabulary.

Suddenly, on May 15, an assassin's bullet ended George Wallace's candidacy. Campaigning in a Maryland shopping center, he was gunned down by a young man wearing a Wallace hat and sporting other campaign paraphernalia. Though not killed, Wallace was hospitalized and permanently paralyzed from the waist down. A stunned nation remembered again the grim days of 1963 and 1968. Violence clearly knew no ideological bounds, nor did the sympathy of the American public. In Michigan, the voters gave Wallace a sweeping victory in the primary, and for weeks the country's most prominent leaders were photographed at his bedside.

The removal of Wallace did not alter the race for the nomination, but it governed the outcome in the general election. Liberal Democrats, especially McGovern, had assumed that an independent Wallace candidacy in November would attract from 10 to 14 percent of the vote, mostly from those who would otherwise have voted for Nixon. With Wallace removed, Nixon had a plush cushion, permitting him to sit out the campaign and forcing McGovern into a clumsy and unsuccessful attempt to win Wallace votes. The South Dakotan was so firmly rooted in his party's liberal tradition that the reach to the right had an awkward and artificial air. Worse still, it dampened the enthusiasm of his earlier supporters, most of whom viewed Wallace as racist and reactionary. The bullet that wounded George Wallace in May killed the McGovern candidacy in November.

With Wallace out of the picture, Humphrey moved in to take up the slack in a narrowing field. Though Nebraska and Oregon came next in the historical corridor, he fixed on California, the second-largest delegation and a winner-take-all primary. If McGovern could be ambushed there, he would be denied a first-ballot victory, and a deadlocked convention would conceivably turn to Humphrey. Intra-party bitterness had been increasing from primary to primary, though it never reached the savage level of 1968. Suddenly, the latent divisions erupted in California. Humphrey, McGovern's old friend and neighbor, headed

"I hope the Nixon people
do to George McGovern what the
Democrats did . . . underestimate him.
If they do that
. . . WE'LL KILL THEM."

Gary Hart
McGovern Campaign Director
Washington Post May 14, 1972

This quote from Gary Hart, George S. McGovern's campaign director, was published in the *Washington Post* on May 14, 1972. *(Library of Congress)*

for the jugular with uncharacteristic ferocity. He particularly attacked McGovern's proposals for a deep cut in the defense budget and cash payments to all taxpayers, calling them reckless and irresponsible. McGovern's wide lead in the California primary plummeted; his eventual margin of victory was a thin 5 percent. Worse still, the closeness of the results prompted a raucous credentials fight on the convention floor a month later in Miami.

McGovern's larger problems were obscured by a resounding sweep in New York two weeks later. He not only picked up 241 delegates (25 more would be added later from the at-large bonus), but his delegates had defeated 60 out of 62 county chairmen, including the state chairman. Only the Albany machine prevailed—and that by the thinnest margin in half a century.

Just before the New York primary, early on the morning of June 17, five men broke into the Democratic National Committee headquarters in the Watergate Hotel in Washington to replace already installed surveillance devices. Though equipped with all the latest gadgets, they bungled the job badly and were caught. American politics had never known this kind of activity before, and no one really knew how to judge it. Surely it seemed farfetched to think that the Republican Party, much less the president, had anything to do with it. The most probable explanation was that overzealous Nixon supporters had decided to help out their candidate in their own way. The fact that some were anti-Castro Cubans encouraged the "uncontrolled fanaticism" theory. Only a handful of observers connected the episode with the GOP, and fewer still with the Oval Office.

One of these was George McGovern. From the outset he was convinced that what came to be called Watergate was a part of a broader pattern of official corruption fully in keeping with his low opinion of Richard Nixon. While most Democrats running for office or addressing party affairs delighted in making fun of the bizarre event, McGovern held a dark and grim view of the break-in, which he articulated again and again during the cam-

paign. The president, however, separated himself from the break-in with such surgical dispatch that he remained untouched by the consequences until the next year. By June, the historical corridor had been secured, with New Hampshire, Wisconsin, Nebraska, Oregon, California, and New York witnessing an impressive string of McGovern victories. Results elsewhere had been mixed or worse, but the public assumed that the senator from South Dakota had earned the nomination. Yet these states in themselves did not comprise enough delegates, and the candidates hoping to stop McGovern now turned to other areas for assistance. When the tabulations began, however, it was clear that McGovern had done surprisingly well in the convention and caucus states, and their delegates, added to the primary harvest, brought him within hailing distance of a first-ballot decision.

McGovern's victories in the non-primary states stemmed directly from the new regulations surrounding delegate selection, which ensured a fair process and representative results. His Washington staff always understood this and quietly and efficiently picked up delegates all over the country. They found support in such unlikely places as Louisiana and South Carolina, and did well in Georgia and Texas. By midyear, McGovern had become a national candidate, drawing delegates from all parts of the country and nearly every state.

A last minute "stop-McGovern" coalition inevitably arose at the convention, which opened in Miami on July 10. The crucial moments came in the seating of the California and Illinois delegations, where the contest involved the rules of delegate selection. With California it was, ironically, the issue of proportional representation; Humphrey had taken over 40 percent of the vote without winning a single delegate. The issue with Illinois was whether the Cook County delegation had been properly elected. In both cases, McGovern turned back the challenges. Indeed, they were futile as well as desperate. If the candidate who had won most of the primaries had been denied the nomination, there would have been a massive walkout and the Democratic Party would have been hopelessly, and perhaps permanently, divided.

The convention itself stood in marked contrast to previous ones. The number of women delegates had risen to nearly 40 percent; young people amounted to another quarter; blacks and Hispanics were represented above their share of the population but below their portion of enrolled Democrats. In the New York delegation, 250 of the 278 representatives had never attended a convention before. Who was not at Miami was significant, too. Governors, mayors, senators, and congressmen accustomed to participation were onlookers, if they came at all. Labor leaders who used to be automatic delegates from the big industrial states watched the proceedings on television in their hotel

'BUT DON'T YOU SEE? IF THE DEMOCRATIC PARTY IS TO STAY YOUNG AND VIGOROUS WE JUST HAD TO DROP THE ABORTION PLANK'

This Edmund S. Valtman cartoon shows a diverse group of young people listening to an earnest young man explain why the McGovern campaign will not support an abortion plank. The Democratic Party refused to include a pro-choice plank in the platform, fearing that it would make the candidate look too extremist. *(Library of Congress)*

suites. Those prominent in the old ethnic politics—Irish, Italians, Eastern Europeans—complained of their "exclusion." In fact, it was not categories of voters, but their established leaders who were absent. Ethnic proportions were not greatly altered, but it was housewives, teachers, and students who represented them rather than prominent spokesmen. Of course, the participation of youth was new, a direct result of the 26th Amendment. Moreover, under the reformed Democratic National Committee rules, the convention conducted its business in serious fashion, not closing up shop each day until the early hours of the morning. A national poll later showed that 67 percent of the voters held a positive opinion of the whole affair.

To some extent, McGovern's nomination was anticlimactic. He had established his control over the convention during the credentials contests the first night and was never seriously challenged again. The party platform contained few surprises. Basically it extended the positions the party had held since 1960. The Vietnam plank, to be

sure, was sharper and crisper; crime received the attention it demanded; revenue sharing became more explicit; and tax reform was elevated to a critical level. Floor fights highlighted the growing concern over the social issues of abortion, drugs, and amnesty for Vietnam War resisters that had previously lain outside political discussion. These debates contributed to the general notion that the convention was dominated by radical elements, even though moderates won all of the roll call votes.

With the nomination secured, McGovern turned to the task of choosing a running mate. His first choice was Edward Kennedy, who would have brought strong connections with organized labor, Catholics, and party regulars, as well as the formidable family name and resources. When the Massachusetts senator refused, the selection became something of a lottery. The criteria were clear: the vice-presidential candidate ought to be from a large state, acceptable to labor and traditional party leaders, and preferably a Catholic. A long list was whittled down to a half dozen, and at the last moment McGovern announced that Senator Thomas Eagleton of Missouri was the man. Though unknown to most of the delegates, Eagleton had all the required credentials and more—he came from a border state, as a former attorney general he could handle the "law and order" issue, and he had demonstrated appeal to suburban voters.

The delegates had scarcely gone home when the bombshell exploded. Newspaper reporters discovered that Senator Eagleton had a history of "nervous exhaustion" and had been hospitalized three times. Once, at the Mayo Clinic in Minnesota, doctors had used shock treatment as part of their therapy. Unfortunately, Eagleton had not revealed these facts to McGovern at the time of the nomination. The two called a joint press conference (appropriately, it turned out, at Custer, South Dakota) to disclose the facts in an orderly and sober fashion and avoid a sensational exposé by the press. But nothing could minimize the impact of the revelations, and McGovern was forced to seek out a new running mate.

The damage had been done—those seven days shook the campaign, and it was never the same again. Though McGovern had acted deliberately and decently, it seemed to many that he lacked decisiveness. Worse still, debate over the issue only lessened; it did not disappear. Even staff members, eager to escape blame, kept the question alive by contradictory statements about the conversation with Eagleton in the hectic hours before the fatal decision to choose him as a running mate. The intense round of campaign planning never took place, and throughout the next few months the effort had an air of improvisation rather than clear direction.

Finding another running mate was not a simple matter. McGovern offered the spot to six others, including Senators Humphrey and Muskie, before deciding on R. Sargent Shriver. The irreverent charged he was a "second-string Kennedy," but Shriver had impressive credentials of his own. As former chairman of the Chicago School Board, he had gained firsthand knowledge of the crisis in education; his tenure as the first director of the Peace Corps had given him invaluable experience in foreign affairs; and as head of President Johnson's War on Poverty he had been a pioneer in the difficult world of urban revival. In addition, he was known to be an articulate and energetic campaigner.

The whole delay, however, had cost the Democrats the advantage they had gained with an early convention. McGovern's next step was to reach out to those elements in the party that he had defeated in order to get the nomination. Well-publicized meetings with Lyndon Johnson, George Wallace, Richard Daley, and Southern governors demonstrated that to win he had to put together what the primaries had pulled apart. Overtures to George Meany and the AFL-CIO high command were less successful,

and he finally had to rely on a Labor for McGovern Committee comprised of many of the larger and more effective unions, but without the formal labor endorsement usually accorded a Democratic presidential candidate.

This strategy distracted McGovern from the media campaign that increasingly dominated the entire effort. Since the media had replaced the party as the means of communication with the voters, it was believed that McGovern's central concern should not be with traditional campaigning, but rather with television, particularly the news spots at 6 and 11. These required "visuals" showing the candidate at a shopping mall, a hospital, or a factory, talking with ordinary people about their problems and concerns. Schedules were built around this strategy, requiring the candidate to fly from one time zone to another to accommodate the demands of television. Thus, it was argued, millions of people could be exposed to the candidate instead of the thousands who attended even the best organized rallies. On the last day of the campaign, McGovern flew from New York and ended up in South Dakota, but not before touching down in Pennsylvania, Kansas, and California in between—a fitting summary of the new "media politics."

The logistics of the media strategy did, however, isolate the candidate from the voters. Every day the routine was a morning "visual" and perhaps a press conference, then "wheels up" for a flight to another city, where the sequence would be repeated for the local cameras. Each stop required clumsy disembarking while the candidate waited for 200 reporters to get off their plane and be bused to the next "event." It was not unusual to be airborne for three or four hours, with another four hours eaten up coming and going to airports. This left little time for more intimate conventional campaigning—street rallies, luncheons with the party faithful, or private meetings where McGovern could get a sense of the voters' thinking. At the

Campaign poster for George McGovern (right) and Sargent Shriver. *(Library of Congress)*

end, the "people's candidate" was a picture on a screen, almost as isolated as the president. And the press, with nothing much else to do, took to writing damaging stories about internal staff differences. The authors of this strategy had intended to manipulate the media, but instead the needs of the camera governed the campaign.

While McGovern's campaign from the start featured surprise and uncertainty, the incumbent president had little turmoil on his path to renomination. The Watergate break-in occurred in June; the Republican convention was in August. The full dimension of the affair was not known until after the election, and during the campaign the incumbent was wreathed in the authority of the office. There was no overt party opposition, nor any "historical corridor" to the nomination. He was free to choose the themes for the general election.

To be sure, the press continued to nag at Nixon's heels (though newspapers editorially supported him, with 753 for him as against only 56 for McGovern), and he was never able to shake off the image of "Tricky Dick." Moreover, the war continued and indeed widened, and a Democratic Congress thwarted his domestic programs. Yet even his constraints enlarged his area of maneuverability by turning his attention to foreign affairs. In February 1972, he visited China; later he blockaded Haiphong and bombed Hanoi; next he was in Moscow. All these initiatives overshadowed the Democratic Party's complicated primaries and caucuses. And public opinion polls indicated that each move was popular. Moreover, he and his aides masterfully exploited the communications system—television, radio, and the press. He avoided questions about his policies by simply not having press conferences. (His predecessors, from Roosevelt to Johnson, had averaged between 24 and 36 press conferences a year while Nixon had a total of 7 in the election year, about the same number as in each of his first three years in the White House.) Daily communications were left to official surrogates, who deflected or absorbed criticism and obscured the president's intentions. This aloofness contrasted sharply with the persistent and bitter conflict within the Democratic Party, and especially George McGovern, who was anxious, often indiscreetly so, to court the media.

Neither did Nixon have to worry about a formally divided party. The GOP was clearly the minority party in 1972 whether measured in voter enrollment or officeholders. Yet it had the brass ring, the White House. The party's historic moderate wing was crippled; the right was not so disaffected as to launch a campaign against an incumbent president. Hence, he decided to run his campaign outside the party altogether. Very early on, he established the Committee to Re-Elect the President (CREEP). He located its headquarters across the street from the White House and staffed it with people loyal to himself, not the party. The committee would organize and direct the campaign, raise the money, and alone would have direct access to

the Oval Office. Though two years later this arrangement proved troublesome, it indicated that even after a quarter of a century within the GOP, Nixon was as much an outsider as George McGovern. Both won their party's nomination, but neither had any important relationship to his party's national committee or establishment. Nixon had trouble finding someone to take the position of national chairman of the Republican Party. McGovern's choice was a woman who would reflect the rising influence of feminism. But leadership in both campaigns came from outside the national committees.

Mercifully protected from any primary challenge, Nixon had only to bask in the enthusiasm of his own convention. The location was the same as the Democrats had chosen, Miami, but the conventions could not have been more different. The mechanics of the Republican operation were a model of efficiency and precision directed to television's prime time. Nixon's acceptance speech was only two minutes late; McGovern's was five hours behind schedule. A brief scuffle over rules early in the gathering was easily defeated; the Democrats had engaged in endless roll calls. The seats in the Republican convention were filled by middle America, successful and middle aged, mostly white and male. The genial chaos of the Democrats gave way to an orchestrated celebration of Nixon's first term; the slogan that rang through the hall was "Four More Years."

Nixon's acceptance speech, like the GOP platform, was hardly arresting, but did include the broad themes of the campaign. He attacked the Democrats for supporting quotas, asserted that McGovern was the spokesman for a party that had lost its legitimate past and embraced a radical future, waged an assault on "paternalism" and planners, and made a strong statement on the Vietnam War that would become his centerpiece. "There are three things" that we will never do, he said, "abandon our prisoners of war . . . join our enemies in imposing a communist government on our allies . . . or stain the honor of the United States." He also said he was happy to run again with his vice president, Spiro T. Agnew, adding in a reference to the Eagleton affair, "I am not going to change my mind tomorrow."

By Labor Day it was clear that the Nixon strategy was working wonderfully. The president remained aloof and inaccessible. He refused to debate, kept away from the press, and used short radio speeches to explain his record, with no chance for interruption or rebuttal. His extraordinary fund-raising permitted extensive and repetitive commercials in the big media markets of the large industrial states. Direct mail was targeted to crucial political districts, while phone banks brought the message to special groups of voters. Nixon might complain that the Democrats cynically exploited "interest groups," but Theodore H. White identified some new ones working for Nixon, including the Hairdressers Committee, the Veterinarians Committee, the Motorcyclists Committee, and the Indians–Aleuts–Eskimos Committee. This was the first fully electronic campaign in history, complete with television and radio commercials, phone banks, labeled direct mail, and, as Watergate would reveal, electronic surveillance of the opposition. In despair, Teddy White, the chronicler of many campaigns, observed wryly, "It was easier to cover the President on campaign in 1972 by staying home and watching television—which was the way the President wanted it."

Yet all this organization, efficiency, and money did not ease the public's increasing impatience and frustration with the war in Southeast Asia. This had always been McGovern's special issue. As early as 1963, in his maiden speech on the floor of the Senate, he had warned about the consequences of American involvement. It was the antiwar issue that galvanized the students; it was the same issue that financially floated his campaign. Then on October 26, 12 days before the election, Henry Kissinger announced that "peace is at hand" as a result of some negotiations in Paris. It turned out, of course, not to be true, but the last remaining thin thread of hope snapped. Big crowds in the closing days for both candidates kept some interest alive, but not even George McGovern, son of a Methodist minister, thought any miracle was on the way.

By November it was clear that McGovern was hopelessly behind and that the surge that brought Humphrey almost abreast of Nixon in 1968 would not develop in 1972. Though McGovern's crowds were large and enthusiastic, the polls persistently showed a spread of 20 or more points. The results confirmed their prediction. Nixon won over 60.7 percent of the popular vote and nearly swept the Electoral College. McGovern carried only Massachusetts and the District of Columbia. The Wallace vote had obviously moved to the president *en masse,* and the defection of the traditional white Democrats, a trend that had been visible for over a decade, intensified. Only the blacks by a large margin and the young by a narrow one remained firm. But unlike the Goldwater rout in 1964, state and local slates usually escaped the presidential landslide.

The overwhelming Nixon victory led to a search for an explanation within the Democratic Party. Regular leaders, still smarting from their primary defeats, quickly blamed the "McGovern people," who had presumably excluded them from the convention in Miami and then from the campaign. Columnists tended to emphasize the broken momentum that began perhaps as early as the California primary and certainly became critical with the Eagleton episode in July. Others dwelt on the staff problems that persistently plagued the senator's entourage. Still other voices asserted that Nixon's tactics of isolation and aloofness prevented any contest, much less a rational choice for the electorate.

Yet none of these analyses explained the more than 20-point difference between the candidates. No doubt the Eagleton affair cost votes; the disaffection of the regulars accounted for more; a better-disciplined staff would at least have saved some embarrassment; and Nixon's strategy did indeed make a genuine choice difficult. Any one of these factors might explain a close election, but not even all of them together account for the extraordinary gap in the popular vote.

Rather, what lay beneath the surface was a massive national backlash against the tumultuous events of the 1960s. The Nixon years may have been uninspiring and tinged with irregularity and fraud, but they had not seen cities in flames or campuses in turmoil. Television screens no longer featured the violent rhetoric or ugly confrontations that dominated President Johnson's second term. Moreover, the war, which agonized even those who supported it, had seemingly "wound down." Somehow, voters in 1972 believed, or at least hoped, that the country had returned to "normalcy." Underneath, all the vexing questions remained—race, injustice, war, and a new, impatient generation—but the daily upheavals of the previous decade had all but disappeared. The tide that had swelled in 1968 had receded, and though most of the wreckage lay in full view across the beach, most Americans preferred to look beyond to a more tranquil sea.

Richard Nixon, of course, had little to do with the fact that the tide was going out, but he was the president, and

THE OLD MAN AND THE SEA

This Edmund Valtman cartoon shows Senator George McGovern as a fisherman in a small boat with the remains of a large fish, labeled "War Issue," lashed to its side, battling against high seas. Valtman alludes to Ernest Hemingway's *The Old Man and the Sea,* which recounts the story of an old fisherman who catches a giant marlin. Despite his efforts, the fish is largely eaten by sharks before he returns to port with little more than the skeleton. In the 1972 presidential election, Democratic candidate McGovern hoped to make opposition to the Vietnam War his central issue, but his campaign was undermined by a series of tribulations that included attacks on his inconsistent stands on many issues and the revelation that his vice-presidential running mate, Thomas Eagleton, had been hospitalized on two occasions for psychiatric problems. *(Library of Congress)*

the public associated four years of relative social calm with the man who presided over it. Similar comfort could be found in foreign affairs, where Nixon's new détente with China and the Soviet Union relieved international tensions and quieted anxieties about future wars. Furthermore, the end of the draft in the spring of 1972 took the immediacy of foreign policy away from the campuses and the family dinner tables. To be sure, there was no peace, but there was less war.

The Nixon campaign shrewdly capitalized on the national uneasiness that underlay the calm. By refusing to campaign conventionally, by attacking busing without disclaiming civil rights, by replacing the debate about poverty with a restatement of the "work ethic," and by blaming much of the unrest on "permissiveness," he at once reassured people about the things that bothered them, while appearing himself to be a moderate rather than an arch-conservative. At the same time, voters equated the McGovern campaign with the disturbing events of the 1960s. His peace theme, for example, conjured up ugly memories of student unrest and the Chicago convention. Among his followers were the blacks, Hispanics, and young people who had been the rough cutting edge of the decade of demonstrations. Added to this was the emergence of militant feminism, with its unsettling tactics and unpredictable consequences. It was to preserve a fragile social tranquility that so many voted for a man whose own political career, ironically, had been built around the most divisive events of the previous 20 years and who would later be forced from office in disgrace.

Even so, McGovern ran only 3 percentage points behind Hubert Humphrey's total in 1968. The nearly 10 million Wallace votes of the previous election went over almost completely to Nixon. No liberal Democrat could have won or done measurably better. Wallace had offered a convenient halfway house for disgruntled Democrats leaving the party, an exodus that began in the 1950s and continued unabated except for the brief Kennedy years. This movement was difficult to gauge in national elections, but it surfaced continuously in state and local contests and party primaries.

Working-class whites composed the largest contingent of the refugees. Enjoying better jobs and higher pay, they had just enough money to move to more pleasant neighborhoods and to see their children have a chance for a college education. Yet, they had little financial security. Economic forces—recession or inflation—affected them first and most damagingly, and prolonged illness could wipe out everything. Behind these anxieties lay the ultimate fear of unemployment and the knowledge that there was a thin line separating what the economists called "full employment" and the handout.

Recently a new breed of political analyst has tried to tie this phenomenon to an ethnic base. Second- and third-generation Americans made up much of the emergent

Nixon campaign poster (*Library of Congress*)

working class in the Northern cities and, at least since the Depression, they had voted heavily Democratic. Overwhelmingly Catholic, the Irish, Italians, and Poles began to drift away from the party mooring even as they moved to the suburbs. One reason was clearly economic, for as a group they had benefited from the almost continuous prosperity since World War II. In addition, the G.I. Bill of 1944 gave them an opportunity for college that their parents had never dreamed of. Though they hesitated to join the GOP, which they equated with hard times and Herbert Hoover, they no longer felt they needed the party of Franklin Roosevelt.

But another, deeper cause for their disaffection lay in the problem of race. The better neighborhoods on the edge of the city or nearby suburbs pulled them, and the enormous growth of the urban black population gave them a push. Swarming into the Northern cities from the South, blacks increasingly occupied the residential center of the metropolis. Desperate for housing and jobs, they crowded into old working-class areas. Here they competed for the neighborhood; at the factory gate they competed for employment. Both groups had been voting Democratic for generations, but now this elemental collision fractured the party. Blue-collar whites, feeling that the national leadership was too committed to the blacks, drifted away. In the late 1960s the ghettos erupted, accelerating the flight. The elections of 1960 and 1964 concealed the attrition on the national level. The rioting and confrontations brought the schism into the open and into the Democratic Party. George Wallace's surprising surge in the 1968 primaries and his early victories in 1972 came from a shrewd exploitation of this widening fissure.

Analyses of this new trend in voting preferences of the white ethnic groups emphasized the immigrant background of many of these working-class voters and tied their recent "independence" to a heightened consciousness of Old World traditions and values now adapted to the American experience. The argument is sometimes merely a thin cover for bigotry. But in its more serious form this view asserted the primacy of ethnicity over both race and class. It is supposedly the "Irishness" or "Italianness" or "Polishness" that best explains their political behavior, with Catholicism providing another link among immigrant groups that had previously been bitter rivals. This theory arose largely from election statistics drawn from the urban North. As convenient and compelling as this analysis may seem for New York, Chicago, or Boston, it does not explain why blue-collar voters of older, Protestant stock reacted the same way. The blue-collar exodus from the party occurred everywhere. The west end of Louisville and the south side of Atlanta, each with only a trace of immigrant background, witnessed the same development as Cleveland and Chicago, with their endless layers of ethnicity.

The volatility of the blue-collar workers showed just one dimension of the growing independence of the American electorate. Every poll indicated that voters in general were drifting away from the old parties, and a disturbing number were dropping out of electoral politics altogether. The sources of the disaffection varied, but they touched every age, race, and income group. The result was that neither party could gain a majority. Or, to put it differently, the United States contained an increasingly antiparty electorate operating within the framework of a traditional two-party system. In the past, the unattached, called "independents," had been thought to be liberal; they probably were until the 1930s and still were in 1972 in a few places. By the 1970s, however, that large indeterminate group had clearly become conservative, particularly fearful of the changes portended by the radical mutiny of the 1960s. The Wallace candidacy of 1968 ought to have sent that message; in fact, it concealed its importance because party leaders and political commentators considered the 13.5-percent Wallace vote as indicative of a lack of enthusiasm for either party's nominee. The 1972 election, with its clear choice, defined the independents as cautious voters who had deep forebodings about the future; hence neither party could depend on their support.

The election of 1972 also presaged the suburban captivity of American politics. The 1970 census revealed that, for the first time in history, more people lived in suburbs than cities, and also showed that the suburbanites voted in greater percentages than their urban neighbors. The result was an inevitable shift of power to the outer parts of metropolitan areas. This tidal change in voting strength had been concealed in the presidential elections of the previous decade, but was abundantly clear on the local level. Indeed, in 1972 Nixon's largest majorities came from the crabgrass country. The Democrats retained their urban base, but it had shrinking significance. Moreover, the suburbs were no longer the exclusive preserve of the well-to-do, but rather the habitat of the white postwar generation. Suburbs were now as representative of the nation as the cities had been in the days of the New Deal. Surely their power would stretch well beyond 1972.

The election of 1972 gained more importance in retrospect than it seemed to have on the morning after Nixon's victory. In the next months the *Washington Post* revealed the broader dimensions of the Watergate scandal. The break-in at the Democratic headquarters was not just an act of excessive enthusiasm by Nixon supporters; instead, it was only a small part of a larger web of corruption that extended beyond the Committee to Re-Elect the President and reached into the Oval Office. The president, of course, left Washington in shame, and indictments were also handed down against three former cabinet members, including two attorney generals; two of the president's assistants quit when faced with court charges; officers of CREEP were indicted for perjury; and corporate officials awaited judicial action: ultimately, testimony before congressional committees and grand juries disclosed manipulations that made the Grant and Harding administrations seem virtuous. Congress itself moved to impeach the president, who escaped that fate by resigning. The "mandate of 1972" had quickly evaporated, and Nixon's triumphant reelection was followed by the most serious constitutional crisis since the Civil War.

—*Richard C. Wade*

Selected Bibliography

See Herbert E. Alexander. *Financing the 1972 Election* (1976); Stephen E. Ambrose, *Nixon: The Triumph of a Politician, 1962–1972* (1989); John R. Ehrlichman, *Witness to Power: The Nixon Years* (1982); H. R. Haldeman, with Joseph DiMona, *The Ends of Power* (1978); C. Richard Hofstetter. *Bias in the News: Network Television Coverage of the 1972 Election Campaign* (1976); George McGovern, *An American Journey* (1974); Stanley I. Kutler, *The Wars of Watergate: The Last Crisis of Richard Nixon* (1990); Richard Nixon, *The Memoirs of Richard Nixon* (1978); Maurice Stans, *The Terrors of Justice* (1978); Theodore H. White, *The Making of the President, 1972* (1973); and Kristi Witker, *How to Lose Everything in Politics Except Massachusetts* (1974). Hunter S. Thompson, *Fear and Loathing: On the Campaign Trail '72* (1973) is psychedelic, eccentric, but interesting, a real period piece; Timothy Crouse, *The Boys on the Bus* (1973), is still extremely informative about the pack mentality of modern reporters.

1972 Electoral Map and Statistics

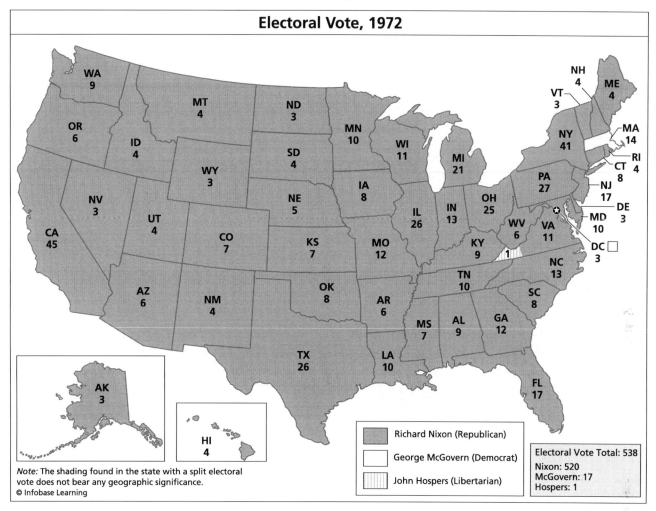

Electoral Vote, 1972

WA 9

OR 6

ID 4

MT 4

ND 3

MN 10

WI 11

MI 21

NH 4

VT 3

ME 4

NY 41

MA 14

RI 4

CT 8

NV 3

UT 4

WY 3

SD 4

IA 8

IL 26

IN 13

OH 25

PA 27

NJ 17

DE 3

MD 10

CA 45

CO 7

NE 5

MO 12

KY 9

WV 6

VA 11

DC 3

AZ 6

NM 4

KS 7

OK 8

AR 6

TN 10

NC 13

SC 8

MS 7

AL 9

GA 12

TX 26

LA 10

FL 17

AK 3

HI 4

Note: The shading found in the state with a split electoral vote does not bear any geographic significance.
© Infobase Learning

Richard Nixon (Republican)

George McGovern (Democrat)

John Hospers (Libertarian)

Electoral Vote Total: 538
Nixon: 520
McGovern: 17
Hospers: 1

1972 ELECTION STATISTICS

State	Number of Electors	Total Popular Vote	Elec Vote R	D	L*	Pop Vote R	D	Margin of Victory Votes	% Total Vote
Alabama	9	1,006,093	9			1	2	471,778	46.89%
Alaska	3	95,219	3			1	2	22,382	23.51%
Arizona	6	653,505	6			1	2	204,272	31.26%
Arkansas	6	647,666	6			1	2	246,852	38.11%
California	45	8,367,862	45			1	2	1,126,249	13.46%
Colorado	7	953,884	7			1	2	267,209	28.01%
Connecticut	8	1,384,277	8			1	2	255,265	18.44%
Delaware	3	235,516	3			1	2	48,074	20.41%
District of Columbia	3	163,421		3		2	1	92,401	56.54%
Florida	17	2,583,283	17			1	2	1,139,642	44.12%
Georgia	12	1,174,772	12			1	2	591,967	50.39%
Hawaii	4	270,274	4			1	2	67,456	24.96%
Idaho	4	310,379	4			1	2	118,558	38.20%
Illinois	26	4,723,236	26			1	2	874,707	18.52%
Indiana	13	2,125,529	13			1	2	696,586	32.77%
Iowa	8	1,225,944	8			1	2	210,001	17.13%
Kansas	7	916,095	7			1	2	349,525	38.15%
Kentucky	9	1,067,499	9			1	2	305,287	28.60%
Louisiana	10	1,051,491	10			1	2	388,710	36.97%
Maine	4	417,271	4			1	2	95,874	22.98%
Maryland	10	1,353,812	10			1	2	323,524	23.90%
Massachusetts	14	2,458,756		14		2	1	220,462	8.97%
Michigan	21	3,490,325	21			1	2	502,286	14.39%
Minnesota	10	1,741,652	10			1	2	95,923	5.51%
Mississippi	7	645,963	7			1	2	378,343	58.57%
Missouri	12	1,852,589	12			1	2	455,527	24.59%
Montana	4	317,603	4			1	2	63,779	20.08%
Nebraska	5	576,289	5			1	2	236,307	41.00%
Nevada	3	181,766	3			1	2	49,734	27.36%
New Hampshire	4	334,059	4			1	2	97,289	29.12%
New Jersey	17	2,997,229	17			1	2	743,291	24.80%
New Mexico	4	385,931	4			1	2	94,522	24.49%
New York	41	7,161,830	41			1	2	1,241,694	17.34%
North Carolina	13	1,518,612	13			1	2	616,184	40.58%
North Dakota	3	280,514	3			1	2	73,725	26.28%
Ohio	25	4,094,787	25			1	2	882,938	21.56%
Oklahoma	8	1,029,900	8			1	2	511,878	49.70%
Oregon	6	927,946	6			1	2	93,926	10.12%
Pennsylvania	27	4,592,105	27			1	2	917,570	19.98%
Rhode Island	4	415,808	4			1	2	25,738	6.19%
South Carolina	8	677,880	8			1	2	289,157	42.66%
South Dakota	4	307,415	4			1	2	26,531	8.63%
Tennessee	10	1,201,182	10			1	2	455,854	37.95%
Texas	26	3,472,714	26			1	2	1,144,605	32.96%
Utah	4	478,476	4			1	2	197,359	41.25%
Vermont	3	186,946	3			1	2	48,975	26.20%
Virginia	12	1,457,019	11		1	1	2	549,606	37.72%
Washington	9	1,470,847	9			1	2	268,801	18.28%
West Virginia	6	762,399	6			1	2	207,529	27.22%
Wisconsin	11	1,852,890	11			1	2	179,256	9.67%
Wyoming	3	145,570	3			1	2	56,106	38.54%
Total	538	77,744,030	520	17	1	1	2	17,995,488	23.15%

* One elector voted for Libertarian candidate John Hospers for president.

Nixon Republican		McGovern Democratic		Others	
728,701	72.43%	256,923	25.54%	20,469	2.03%
55,349	58.13%	32,967	34.62%	6,903	7.25%
402,812	61.64%	198,540	30.38%	52,153	7.98%
445,751	68.82%	198,899	30.71%	3,016	0.47%
4,602,096	55.00%	3,475,847	41.54%	289,919	3.46%
597,189	62.61%	329,980	34.59%	26,715	2.80%
810,763	58.57%	555,498	40.13%	18,016	1.30%
140,357	59.60%	92,283	39.18%	2,876	1.22%
35,226	21.56%	127,627	78.10%	568	0.35%
1,857,759	71.91%	718,117	27.80%	7,407	0.29%
881,496	75.04%	289,529	24.65%	3,747	0.32%
168,865	62.48%	101,409	37.52%	0	0.00%
199,384	64.24%	80,826	26.04%	30,169	9.72%
2,788,179	59.03%	1,913,472	40.51%	21,585	0.46%
1,405,154	66.11%	708,568	33.34%	11,807	0.56%
706,207	57.61%	496,206	40.48%	23,531	1.92%
619,812	67.66%	270,287	29.50%	25,996	2.84%
676,446	63.37%	371,159	34.77%	19,894	1.86%
686,852	65.32%	298,142	28.35%	66,497	6.32%
256,458	61.46%	160,584	38.48%	229	0.05%
829,305	61.26%	505,781	37.36%	18,726	1.38%
1,112,078	45.23%	1,332,540	54.20%	14,138	0.58%
1,961,721	56.20%	1,459,435	41.81%	69,169	1.98%
898,269	51.58%	802,346	46.07%	41,037	2.36%
505,125	78.20%	126,782	19.63%	14,056	2.18%
1,154,058	62.29%	698,531	37.71%	0	0.00%
183,976	57.93%	120,197	37.85%	13,430	4.23%
406,298	70.50%	169,991	29.50%	0	0.00%
115,750	63.68%	66,016	36.32%	0	0.00%
213,724	63.98%	116,435	34.85%	3,900	1.17%
1,845,502	61.57%	1,102,211	36.77%	49,516	1.65%
235,606	61.05%	141,084	36.56%	9,241	2.39%
4,192,778	58.54%	2,951,084	41.21%	17,968	0.25%
1,054,889	69.46%	438,705	28.89%	25,018	1.65%
174,109	62.07%	100,384	35.79%	6,021	2.15%
2,441,827	59.63%	1,558,889	38.07%	94,071	2.30%
759,025	73.70%	247,147	24.00%	23,728	2.30%
486,686	52.45%	392,760	42.33%	48,500	5.23%
2,714,521	59.11%	1,796,951	39.13%	80,633	1.76%
220,383	53.00%	194,645	46.81%	780	0.19%
478,427	70.58%	189,270	27.92%	10,183	1.50%
166,476	54.15%	139,945	45.52%	994	0.32%
813,147	67.70%	357,293	29.75%	30,742	2.56%
2,298,896	66.20%	1,154,291	33.24%	19,527	0.56%
323,643	67.64%	126,284	26.39%	28,549	5.97%
117,149	62.66%	68,174	36.47%	1,623	0.87%
988,493	67.84%	438,887	30.12%	29,639	2.03%
837,135	56.92%	568,334	38.64%	65,378	4.44%
484,964	63.61%	277,435	36.39%	0	0.00%
989,430	53.40%	810,174	43.72%	53,286	2.88%
100,464	69.01%	44,358	30.47%	748	0.51%
47,168,710	60.67%	29,173,222	37.52%	1,402,098	1.80%

Election of 1976

Election Overview

Election Year 1976

Election Day November 2, 1976

Winning Candidates

* **President** Jimmy Carter
* **Vice President** Walter Mondale

Election Results [ticket, party: popular votes (percentage of popular vote); electoral votes (percentage of electoral vote)]

* Jimmy Carter and Walter Mondale, Democratic: 40,831,881 (50.08%); 297 (55.2%)
* Gerald Ford and Robert Dole, Republican: 39,148,634 (48.01%); 240 (44.6%)
* Eugene McCarthy, Independent: 740,460 (0.91%); 0 (0.0%)
* Other: 810,609 (0.99%); 0 (0.0%)

Voter Turnout 53.5%

Central Forums/Campaign Methods for Addressing Voters

* Stumping
* Speaking tours
* Rallies
* Speeches
* Print and television ads
* Interviews
* Television, resumption of televised presidential debates

Incumbent President and Vice President on Election Day Gerald Ford and Nelson Rockefeller

Population (1976) 218,086,000

Gross Domestic Product

* $1,824.60 billion (in current dollars: $5,141.3 billion)
* Per capita: $8,366 (in current dollars: $23,575)

Number of Daily Newspapers (1980) 1,745

Average Daily Circulation (1980) 62,201,840

Households with

* Radio (1980): 79,968,240
* Television (1980): 76,300,000

Method of Choosing Electors Popular vote (mostly general-ticket system/winner take all)

Method of Choosing Nominees

* Presidential preference primàries
* Caucuses

Key Issues and Events

* America reeling from Vietnam War loss and Watergate scandal
* President Ford's pardoning of Richard Nixon
* Honesty in government, faith in Washington, fears about America's future amid the bicentennial celebrations
* Busing and affirmative action
* Rampant inflation
* Energy crisis
* Détente with Soviet Union

Leading Candidates

DEMOCRATS

* Jimmy Carter, former governor (Georgia)
* Jerry Brown, governor (California)

- George Wallace, governor (Alabama)
- Morris Udall, representative (Arizona)
- Henry M. Jackson, senator (Washington)
- Frank Church, senator (Idaho)
- Robert Byrd, senator (West Virginia)
- Sargent Shriver, former U.S. ambassador to France (Maryland)
- Fred Harris, former senator (Oklahoma)
- Birch Bayh, senator (Indiana)
- Lloyd Bentsen, senator (Texas)
- Terry Sanford, former governor (North Carolina)
- Milton Shapp, governor (Pennsylvania)

REPUBLICANS
- Gerald Ford, president of the United States (Michigan)
- Ronald Reagan, former governor (California)
- Harold E. Stassen, former governor and candidate for the 1948, 1952, 1964, 1968, and 1972 nominations (Minnesota)

Trajectory

- President Ford's pardon of his disgraced predecessor, Richard M. Nixon, on September 8, 1974, triggers a nationwide backlash.
- Former California governor Ronald Reagan launches his candidacy on November 20, 1975, saying, "Our nation's capital has become the seat of a buddy system that functions for its own benefit—increasingly insensitive to the needs of the American who supports it with his taxes."
- On January 19, 1976, an obscure former one-term governor of Georgia, Jimmy Carter, wins the Iowa caucus, and on February 24 he wins the New Hampshire primary. These two victories make him the Democratic front-runner.
- After winning 16 primaries to Reagan's 10, President Ford wins the nomination at the Republican convention, August 16 to 19, but barely, with 1,187 delegates to Reagan's 1,070.
- Carter's campaign is almost derailed in late September and his "born again" image tarnished when his interview with *Playboy* is published in which he admits, "I've committed adultery in my heart many times."
- For the first time since 1960, presidential candidates debate each other in the first of three televised encounters, with one vice-presidential debate. In the second debate on October 6, Ford slips, saying, "There is no Soviet domination of Eastern Europe and there never will be under a Ford administration."

- Anticipating Ronald Reagan's upbeat, nostalgia-drenched, "aw shucks," patriotic campaign in 1980, Ford's advisers mount a celebration of America's "return," with the campaign ditty "I'm feeling good about America, I'm feeling good about me," a ride on a campaign train, "The Honest Abe," and a series of softball television appearances with NBC baseball announcer Joe Garagiola Sr.
- Ford's upbeat campaign considerably narrows the 33-point gap in popularity Jimmy Carter enjoyed in the summer, making Carter's ultimate victory margin surprisingly slim.

Conventions

- Democratic National Convention: July 12–15, 1976, Madison Square Garden, New York
- Republican National Convention: August 16–19, 1976, Kemper Arena, Kansas City

Ballots/Nominees

DEMOCRATS
Presidential first ballot
- Jimmy Carter 2,239 (74.48%)
- Morris Udall 330 (10.98%)
- Jerry Brown 301 (10.01%)
- George Wallace 57 (1.90%)
- Ellen McCormack 22 (0.73%)
- Frank Church 19 (0.63%)
- Hubert Humphrey 10 (0.33%)

REPUBLICANS
Presidential first ballot
- Gerald Ford 1,187 (52.57%)
- Ronald Reagan 1,070 (47.39%)
- Elliot L. Richardson 1 (0.04%)

THIRD PARTY CANDIDATES & NOMINATIONS
- Eugene McCarthy runs as an Independent

Primaries

- Democratic: 27; 76.0% delegates
- Republican: 30; 71.0% delegates

Primaries Results

DEMOCRATS
- Jimmy Carter 6,235,609; 39.19%
- Jerry Brown 2,449,374; 15.39%
- George Wallace 1,955,388; 12.29%
- Morris Udall 1,611,754; 10.13%
- Henry M. "Scoop" Jackson 1,134,375; 7.13%

- Frank Church 830,818; 5.22%
- Robert Byrd 340,309; 2.14%
- Sargent Shriver 304,399; 1.91%
- Unpledged 283,437; 1.78%
- Ellen McCormack 238,027; 1.50%
- Fred Harris 234,568; 1.47%

REPUBLICANS
- Gerald Ford 5,529,899; 53.29%
- Ronald Reagan 4,760,222; 45.88%
- Others 37,044; 0.36%
- Unpledged 34,717; 0.33%
- Lawrence Daly 7,582; 0.07%

Party Platform

DEMOCRATS
- Noncontroversial platform
- Wide-raging Democratic goals
- Comprehensive national health insurance system with universal and mandatory coverage, welfare reform, protection of the environment, energy conservation, new energy sources
- Ratification of the Equal Rights Amendment

REPUBLICANS
- Ratification of the Equal Rights Amendment
- Foreign policy, secret agreements banned
- Against big government
- Against "massive, federally funded public employment programs"
- Overhaul the welfare system
- "In pursuing détente we must not grant unilateral favors."

Campaign Innovations

- Following Watergate, Congress establishes a full-time bipartisan Federal Election Commission in 1974 (with amendments in 1976) to enforce campaign finance law. There are now limits of $1,000 on contributions to individual candidates and $5,000 to PACs.
- In *Buckley v. Valeo* (1976), the Supreme Court finds spending money on a campaign equivalent to free speech, meaning that spending limits cannot be imposed on candidates. Candidates can voluntarily accept limits in exchange for federal campaign funding.
- Increase in number of states participating in the primaries
- Jimmy Carter's new model: a strategy of intensive, relentless grassroots campaigning in every primary and caucus state, determining how much time to spend in each one based on a calculation of how many delegates were at stake, what opposition existed, and what was the potential media impact of each victory.
- Carter's intense "retail" door-to-door strategy and his focus on the early Iowa caucus set a template for insurgencies.
- Carter uses his autobiography, *Why Not the Best?*, to resurrect the genre of campaign biographies and autobiographies while emphasizing the selling of the individual's personal story on a mass scale.
- The presidential debate reintroduced, first time since 1960
- First vice-presidential debate
- Georgia "cornpone": Carter deploys his entire, quite colorful family, especially his acerbic, independent mother "Miz Lillian," his buffoonish, outspoken brother Billy, his evangelist sister Ruth Carter Stapleton, his Harley-Davidson riding sister Gloria Carter Spann, his cute daughter Amy, and his "Steel Magnolia" wife Rosalynn. While not quite the Plains Kennedys, the Carters show how a candidate in the age of media can use his family as surrogates and to help spin an attention-getting narrative.

Campaign Tactics

DEMOCRATS
- Carter runs as an "untainted" Washington outsider, honest reformer, "born again" Christian
- Populist "retail" campaign, door-to-door style, mixed with a media-savvy strategy appealing to Americans fed up with dishonesty ("I'll never lie to you") and incompetence ("Why not the best?")
- In 1974, Carter—with surrogates including his family—starts crisscrossing the country. By June 1975, he has already traveled more than 50,000 miles, visited 37 states, delivered over 200 speeches, and appeared on 93 radio and TV shows.
- Focusing on the Iowa caucus works. Right after that victory, the new "front-runner" Carter receives three to four times the media coverage of his competitors.
- Active campaign, nasty attacks against Ford: "an appointed President"; "Can you think of a single program that he's put forth that's been accepted?"

REPUBLICANS
- "Rose Garden" strategy of Ford "acting presidential," through ceremonial, patriotic, and high-profile presidential events, rarely leaving the White House.
- Actively campaigns only in October

- Television commercials sponsored by the President Ford Committee show Ford as a family man.
- Big emphasis in the bicentennial year on America as being "back," turning the corner after the 1960s.

Debates

- September 23, 1976: Presidential debate in Philadelphia
- October 6, 1976: Presidential debate in San Francisco
- October 15, 1976: Vice-presidential debate in Houston
- October 22, 1976: Presidential debate in Williamsburg, Virginia
- The League of Women Voters sponsors the series of debates between Ford/Carter.
- Ford accuses Carter of inexperience. Carter is vague on many of the issues but promises to end busing. Ford wins the first debate and narrows Carter's lead by half.
- In the first debate, an engineering malfunction keeps both candidates onstage, silent, seemingly frozen for 27 minutes until the technicians solve the problem.
- Ford stumbles in the second debate by suggesting Eastern Europe is free of Soviet domination. With the media playing the story intensely, within 24 hours 61 percent believe Carter won the debate.
- Vice-presidential debate between Walter Mondale and Robert Dole. Dole appears harsh and partisan, calling World War II and other noble wars "Democrat wars."

Popular Campaign Slogans

DEMOCRATS
- "Why Not the Best?"
- "I'll Never Lie to You"
- "Not Just Peanuts,"
- "A Leader, For a Change"

REPUBLICANS
- "He's making us proud again"
- "Let's Make America Great Again"
- "The Time Is Now"

Campaign Songs

DEMOCRATS
- "Ode to the Georgia Farmer"

REPUBLICANS
- "I'm Feeling Good About America"

Influential Campaign Appeals or Ads

DEMOCRATS (QUOTING CARTER)
- "My view of détente is that it has been a one-way street. The Soviet Union knows what they want in détente, and they have been getting it. And we have been out-traded in almost every instance."
- "Why Not the Best?"
- "I'll Never Lie to You"

REPUBLICANS (QUOTING FORD)
- Jimmy Carter is a man who "will say anything, anywhere to be president."

Campaign Finance

- Carter: $21,800,000 (in current dollars: $77,966,200)
- Ford: $21,786,641 (in current dollars: $77,918,400)

Defining Quotations

- "I'll never tell a lie, I'll never knowingly make a misstatement of fact. I'll never betray your trust. If I do any of these things, I don't want you to support me." *Jimmy Carter on the primary campaign trail, spring 1976*
- "I never characterized myself as a conservative, liberal, or moderate and this is what distinguishes me from them." *Jimmy Carter on the primary campaign trail, spring 1976*
- "Despite Mr. Ford's evident decency, honesty, and patriotism, he has neither the vision nor the leadership necessary to halt and reverse the diplomatic and military decline of the United States." *California governor Ronald Reagan at a press conference in Orlando, Florida, March 4, 1976*
- "Governor Reagan couldn't start a war. President Reagan could." *Tagline coined by Stuart Spencer of pro-Ford ads building up to the California primary, June 1976*
- "I'm ready to lay down the burden of race, and Jimmy Carter comes from a part of the country that, whether you know it or not, has done just that." *Andrew Young, black congressman from Georgia, seconding Carter's nomination July 14, 1976*
- "My name is Jimmy Carter, and I'm running for President. . . . As I've said many times before, we can have an American President who does not govern with negativism and fear of the future, but with vigor and vision and aggressive leadership—a President who's not isolated from the people, but who feels your pain and shares your dreams and takes his strength and his wisdom and his courage from you." *Jimmy Carter, "Our Nation's Past and Future," address accepting the presidential nomination at the*

Democratic National Convention in New York City, July 15, 1976

- "When Jimmy Carter says he'll beat you, he'll beat you, and he beat us fair and square. As I leave the convention hall tonight, I'm going to have one of those green buttons that dogged me all over America." *Arizona representative Morris Udall, July 15, 1976*

- "To you, an American citizen: You are about to read the 1976 Republican Platform. We hope you will also find time to read the Democrats' Platform. Compare. You will see basic differences in how the two parties propose to represent you. 'The Platform is the Party's contract with the people.' This is what it says on the cover of the official printing of the Democrat Platform. So it should be. The Democrats' Platform repeats the same thing on every page: more government, more spending, more inflation. Compare. This Republican Platform says exactly the opposite—less government, less spending, less inflation. In other words, we want you to retain more of your own money, money that represents the worth of your labors, to use as you see fit for the necessities and conveniences of life. No matter how many statements to the contrary that Mr. Carter makes, he is firmly attached to a contract with you to increase vastly the powers of government. Is bigger government in Washington really what you want? Make no mistake: you cannot have bigger programs in Washington and less government by Washington. You must choose." *Preamble to the 1976 Republican Platform, adopted August 18, 1976*

- "Tonight I can tell you straightaway this Nation is sound, this Nation is secure, this Nation is on the march to full economic recovery and a better quality of life for all Americans. And I will tell you one more thing: This year the issues are on our side. I am ready, I am eager to go before the American people and debate the real issues face to face with Jimmy Carter. The American people have a right to know firsthand exactly where both of us stand." *Gerald Ford, remarks in Kansas City upon accepting the Republican presidential nomination, August 19, 1976*

- "There is no Soviet domination of Eastern Europe and there never will be under a Ford administration." *Gerald Ford, second presidential debate, October 6, 1976*

- "I don't believe . . . that—the Yugoslavians consider themselves dominated by the Soviet Union. I don't believe that the Rumanians consider themselves dominated by the Soviet Union. I don't believe that the Poles consider themselves dominated by the Soviet Union. Each of those countries is independent, autonomous: it has its own territorial integrity and the United States does not concede that those countries are under the domination of the Soviet Union." *Gerald Ford in the second presidential debate, October 6, 1976*

- "If I should ever decide in the future to discuss my deep Christian beliefs . . . I'll use another forum besides *Playboy*." *Jimmy Carter, October 22, 1976, third presidential debate*

- "So I say to you, on November 2—it has been tough the last 2 years, but I have been proud to be your President in a period when adversity almost overcame us, when difficulties were awesome. But because you supported me, because our form of government worked, because America is great, it was a privilege to be your President. But now, as skies get brighter, I ask you to give me an opportunity. I would be highly honored to serve as your President for the next 4 years. We had a magnificent Bicentennial. There was a rejuvenation of the American spirit. There was a rebirth of our faith. So, I would look forward to representing you, to doing the best I could, and I pledge that to you. Therefore, on this occasion I ask you not only to confirm me with your prayers but to support me with your ballots. I won't let you down." *Gerald Ford in Syracuse, New York, October 30, 1976*

- "I've looked on a lot of women with lust. I've committed adultery in my heart many times. This is something that God recognizes I will do—and I have done it—and God forgives me for it. But that doesn't mean that I condemn someone who not only looks on a woman with lust but who leaves his wife and shacks up with somebody out of wedlock. Christ says, Don't consider yourself better than someone else because one guy screws a whole bunch of women while the other guy is loyal to his wife. The guy who's loyal to his wife ought not to be condescending or proud because of the relative degree of sinfulness." *Jimmy Carter,* Playboy *interview, November 1976 issue*

- "There's no really big issue moving people to vote one way or another. It's which man the voters feel more comfortable with." *Ron Nessen, Ford's press secretary, toward the end of the campaign*

- "There was a tremendous yearning in the country this year for something of substance that you could put some faith in. . . . People all over the land were looking for something they thought they had known once and somehow had lost touch with. I think that pine trees and home towns said something even to people who have never seen a small town, because they suggested something that they wanted." *Carter's press secretary, Jody Powell, after the election*

Lasting Legacy of Campaign

- Jimmy Carter is the first president elected from the Deep South after the Civil War; Zachary Taylor was the last in 1848.

- First Democrat to carry the Deep South's electoral votes since Kennedy in 1960; first since Johnson in 1964 to win a majority of the South
- Carter one of five Democrats (along with Samuel Tilden, Franklin Roosevelt, Lyndon Johnson, and Barack Obama) to receive popular vote majority since the Civil War.

Election of 1976

The race for the Democratic nomination in 1976 was one of the more extraordinary in American history. Jimmy Carter, a former one-term governor of Georgia barely known to the country at the beginning of the campaign, raced to the front after the first caucus and never seriously lost momentum during the following three and one-half months of primaries. By summer, it seemed he had acquired almost magical powers. Opposition faded after the last primaries, and the Democratic convention seemed more like a coronation than a contest. Theodore H. White, a journalist who has spent his professional life covering political leaders, told the *American Time Recorder* on August 15, "I think Jimmy Carter has a chance to become the first candidate ever to win all fifty states in an election."

The remarkable aspect of Carter's rise was that he had not come in on the wave of a clearly articulated protest movement, as had Democrats William Jennings Bryan in 1896 and George McGovern in 1972. Nor was he the choice of the leaders of his own party. Even on his home turf in Georgia, most Democratic officeholders failed to endorse him until it became apparent that he could not be stopped.

Carter won because his campaign was best geared to the new primary system, because the media provided the

Campaign poster for Jimmy Carter *(Library of Congress)*

fuel to sustain him, and because he understood the mood of the country, now disillusioned by the loss of the Vietnam War and by Watergate. He met the people's need for a president who could restore their confidence in themselves and in the political process. Ironically, the very fact that the public had little perception of what Carter was really like enabled him to shape his image to meet the demands of new circumstances.

There were nine candidates at the opening of the presidential campaign in January 1976. The most prominent was Senator Henry Jackson of Washington. Throughout his 30 years in the Congress, Jackson had shown himself to be an old-style New Deal liberal on domestic issues; on foreign affairs, however, he was perceived as a conservative, having backed the war in Vietnam, a strong defense buildup, and a tough line against the Soviet Union. Also, he opposed busing as a means to racial integration. Lloyd M. Bentsen Jr. of Texas, with only two years in the Senate, was the other middle-of-the-road contender. To their right stood Alabama's governor George Wallace, who had based his political career on opposing Washington and the federal attempt to integrate schools in the South. He had received 10 million votes as the American Independent Party candidate in 1968 and was ahead in the popular vote in the 1972 Democratic primaries until he was shot in a Maryland shopping center. Although confined to a wheelchair, by 1976 he had recovered to the point where he was ready once again to try for the presidency. The liberal field was crowded with Senator Birch Bayh of Indiana; seven-term congressman Morris Udall of Arizona; R. Sargent Shriver Jr., former director of the Peace Corps and the Anti-Poverty program and George McGovern's running mate in 1972; Governor Milton J. Shapp of Pennsylvania; Fred Harris of Oklahoma, a Southern populist without racist accoutrements; and Terry Sanford, the president of Duke University and a former governor of North Carolina.

Standing in the wings was Senator Hubert H. Humphrey of Minnesota. In the late fall of 1975, Humphrey had told Congressman Paul Simon of Illinois that he was available, although he would not lift a finger to obtain the nomination. Throughout the campaign, Humphrey hinted he would come in at the end if there was no other clear choice, but he still declined actively to seek the nomination. His strategy was to be everyone's second choice in case of a deadlock at the convention.

Carter defied categorization. It was clear from his rhetoric and earlier career that he rejected Wallace's racism. But it was also clear to those who looked at his record that he was not a traditional, big-spending, old-line Democrat. His support of Jackson in the 1972 Democratic primaries and of a strong national defense, along with his stand against busing, suggested that he would be no flaming liberal in the White House. But Carter refused to apply political labels to himself and obscured his stands on controversial issues.

According to R. W. Apple of the *New York Times,* the front-runners at the campaign's outset were Jackson, Bayh, Humphrey, and Carter. The inclusion of Carter was certainly not based on his standing in the polls. He had not even been mentioned in the Gallup polls as a presidential possibility until the spring of 1975, when he secured approximately 1 percent of the Democratic and independent vote. In December, Carter ranked only in the 8 percent of "all others" category among Democratic voters. Nor was he popular with political leaders. Early polls of regional Democratic meetings in the Northeast and Midwest showed Carter as having practically no party support. The December Gallup Poll found that only 17 percent of a national elite sample (drawn from leaders in business, government, and education) thought Carter would make a good president. A majority (52 percent) of the respondents felt they knew too little to judge whether or not Carter would make a good president.

Three days before his formal announcement, Carter said on *Meet the Press* that he would run in every state primary. Seventy percent of the delegates, Carter later told Tom Ottenad of the *St. Louis Post Dispatch,* would be chosen in these primaries, and weights were assigned to each state based on the delegates to be chosen, the potential media impact of a victory, and the relative strength of the opposition. Carter's plan was to apportion the 250 days available for campaigning the next year in accordance with these weights. The highest priority was given to New Hampshire, though Hamilton Jordan, Carter's campaign manager, thought it best to play down their effort. A strong showing would have more impact if it came as a surprise. "The press," Jordan pointed out, "shows an exaggerated interest in the early primaries as they represent the first confrontation between candidates, their contrasting strategies and styles." Florida and Illinois ranked second and third. Iowa, which turned out to be the first caucus state, initially ranked behind the others.

In organizing the early primary states, Carter did not rely on local party leaders. Much like John F. Kennedy in 1960, Carter built up his own personal organization in a few key states. What was unique about the Carter effort was that he accomplished it with little money, a small personal following, and only a handful of aides.

Because he had no official responsibilities, Carter could campaign early and full time. By June 1975, according to his staff's figures, he had traveled more than 50,000 miles, visited 37 states, given over 200 speeches, and appeared on 93 radio and TV shows. He accepted invitations that better-known politicians would have ignored. His first trip to Iowa, for example, was in response to an invitation to attend a retirement party in Le Mars for Marie Jahn, an official of Plymouth County. Flattered that a candidate for the presidency would bother to attend such a small event, she and several of her friends immediately committed themselves to his campaign. Though he did recruit a few public officials and political activists, Carter mainly relied on family, friends, and Georgia volunteers to bear the brunt of the canvassing. In January 1976, for example, the Peanut Brigade, a planeload of Georgians, paid $150 each for a chartered jet flight to New Hampshire to canvass for Carter.

In addition to his strategic and organizational skills, Carter showed finesse in managing the media. By the fall of 1975, the national press was looking for any straw in the wind to mark the leaders in the presidential race, and Carter aides knew exactly how to promote Carter into that category. Early qualification for federal matching funds under the new campaign finance law—$5,000 in each of 20 states—was the first hurdle. After some unexpected difficulties (due to the requirement that candidates report their contributions minus fund-raising costs), Carter was able to pass the qualifying test by September. Secret Service protection, which was offered after he qualified for federal matching funds, was accepted with alacrity.

Polls showing where party leaders were leaning were used to Carter's advantage. When Tim Kraft, who was handling the Iowa effort, learned that the *Des Moines Register and Tribune* planned a poll at a party dinner on October 25, he mobilized Carter supporters. Although only about a quarter of the 4,000 diners bothered to vote, Carter came in first. On November 16, in the presidential preference poll at the Florida Democratic state convention, Carter won a "whopping" 697 of the 1,035 votes cast. Milton Shapp, the only other candidate to attend the convention, came in second with 60 votes. Carter said, "This vote in Florida was the first major test of strength in the South . . . a good indication of what's going to happen in 1976."

Knowing that first impressions are apt to be lasting, the Carter people took other steps to influence the media's initial perception of their candidate. Carter's autobiography, *Why Not the Best?,* came out in 1975. With its idyllic portrait of his roots and his religious and political life, the book suggested that he was a new kind of political leader who could heal the country's wounds. When reporters interviewed him, Carter would invariably ask, "Have you read my book?" Moreover, his chief aides—Hamilton Jordan, Jody Powell, Peter Bourne, and Patrick Caddell— influenced the interpretation of the campaign by taking reporters into their confidence, sometimes giving them peeks at strategy memos. The impact of information thus leaked was heightened by its confidentiality. By the time journalist Kandy Stroud was allowed to see the Jordan memorandum of November 1974, it was treated like the Magna Carta. As she wrote in her book, *How Jimmy Won,* "The original was kept under lock and key. . . . And any-one wishing to read the memo was required to make a special appointment in Jordan's office and any excerpts were to be approved by Jordan himself. . . . No exact quotes were to be used."

To obtain steady, often complimentary, copy, Carter presented a drama with a continuing story-line and a col-orful cast of supporting family characters. Lillian, Billy, Ruth, Gloria, Uncle Alton, and Cousin Hugh were all interesting in their own right, as well as tangible proof of how close Jimmy was to many American types. The decision to base the campaign in Carter's hometown of Plains, Georgia, despite the problems of accessibility, was a masterstroke. Big-city reporters could see for themselves the virtues of a friendly small town, unspoiled by urban blight, smog, and impersonality. Even the peanut became a symbol; after some hesitation, the staff decided that it would introduce a note of humility in the campaign. As one aide noted, "Humility was not our long suit."

Carter's handling of the media paid off. After that "silly poll on Iowa" (as Morris Udall called it), R. W. Apple noted that Carter "appears to have taken a surprising but solid lead" in Iowa's delegate race. Major newspapers and syndicated columnists began to take him seriously. Mar-quis Childs wrote on December 16, 1975, "Visionary as it seems, I believe Carter at the present moment has a better chance than any of the others to win the nomination."

On January 19, Carter "won" the caucuses in Iowa. Of those designating a favorite, 27.6 percent chose him— more than double the 13.1 percent of the votes Birch Bayh received. Afterward, UPI and *Time* marked him as the potential front-runner, and he acquired the press retinue that ensured him widespread coverage for his New Hamp-shire campaign. George Wallace's smashing victory over Carter in the Mississippi caucuses the next week and Har-ris's tie with him in the Oklahoma caucuses two weeks after that were not perceived as genuinely competitive contests and did not change these perceptions of Carter.

In the New Hampshire primary on February 24, 23,000 people voted for Carter, giving him 28.4 percent of the vote to Udall's 22.7 percent, Bayh's 15.2 percent, Har-

The peanut became a symbol associated with presidential candi-date Jimmy Carter, who was a peanut farmer from Plains, Geor-gia. *(Library of Congress)*

ris's 10.8 percent, Shriver's 8.2 percent, and Humphrey's 5.6 percent. The liberal field took more than 60 percent of the total vote, and Carter had no competition from conservatives, with Jackson and Wallace bypassing the state. But Carter led each of the men in the race, and so he reaped the publicity bonanza Jordan had anticipated would go to the winner of the first primary. His face was on the covers of *Time* and *Newsweek,* the stories totaling 2,630 lines, compared to 300 for all the others, of which 96 went to Udall, the second-place finisher. In the week following the New Hampshire primary, as the politi-cal scientist Thomas Patterson pointed out in *The Mass Media Election,* Carter received three times the television news coverage and four times the newspaper coverage of his competitors.

Once the press declared Carter the front-runner, there was a subtle shift in the way it treated other candidates. They were now only the challengers. The Massachusetts

(continues on page 1394)

☆ ☆ ☆

1976 ELECTION CHRONOLOGY

1974

August 9, 1974: President Richard Nixon resigns. Vice President Gerald Ford becomes president, vowing to "heal" the nation.

September 8, 1974: President Ford pardons Nixon.

September 23, 1974: Senator Edward Kennedy announces he will not run for president in 1976.

October 8, 1974: Ford addresses Congress, promising to "Whip Inflation Now," reflecting the serious economic crisis afflicting the United States.

October 15, 1974: Reacting to the Watergate scandal, President Ford signs a campaign finance law, building on a 1971 law, providing federal funding for federal campaigns in return for spending limits, as well as contribution limits. The law also establishes an eight-member, full-time, bipartisan Federal Election Commission.

November 5, 1974: Damaged by Watergate, 38 Republican members of Congress are voted out of office in the midterm elections. Democrats end up with 291 seats in the House of Representatives and with 61 Senate seats.

December 12, 1974: Georgia Governor Jimmy Carter announces his long-shot candidacy for president, saying, "With the shame of Watergate still with us and our 200th birthday just ahead, it is time for us to reaffirm and to strengthen our ethical and spiritual and political beliefs."

1975

August 26, 1975: The Libertarian Party National Convention meets in New York City and nominates Roger MacBride for president and David Bergland for vice president.

October 11, 1975: A new show called *NBC's Saturday Night* debuts (only becoming *Saturday Night Live* in 1977). Comedian Chevy Chase's impersonation of President Ford as bumbling helps make the show a popular phenomenon.

November 20, 1975: California governor Ronald Reagan announces his candidacy for the Republican nomination for president, opposing détente with the Soviets, big government, high taxes, and excessive regulation.

1976

January 19, 1976: Jimmy Carter's victory in the Iowa caucus with 29.1 percent of the vote kicks off a media frenzy as he does "better than expected."

February 24, 1976: Carter wins the New Hampshire primary with 29.4 percent of the vote, making him the front-runner in a large field of Democratic candidates, which includes Arizona representative Morris Udall, who received 23.9 percent, Indiana senator Birch Bayh with 16.2 percent, former Oklahoma senator Fred Harris with 11.4 percent, and former vice presidential nominee Sargent Shriver with 8.7 percent. Among Republicans, President Ford beats Reagan 50.6 to 49.4 percent, despite Reagan's strong standing in state polls for months before the primary.

March 9, 1976: Carter's victory in the Florida primary derails former Alabama Governor George Wallace's campaign. Ford's victory over Reagan continues an impressive winning streak for the president.

March 16, 1976: After Carter's big win in the Illinois primary, two latecomers enter the Democratic race, California governor Jerry Brown and Idaho senator Frank Church.

March 31, 1976: Carter's losses to Washington senator Henry Jackson in Massachusetts, and in New York a week later, reflect growing Democratic discomfort as Carter builds momentum.

April 2, 1976: A New York *Daily News* reporter quotes Carter supporting people maintaining the "ethnic purity" of their neighborhoods, which critics see as a code word for segregation. The firestorm rages for a few days until Carter apologizes.

May 1, 1976: Reagan resurrects his campaign and starts his own winning streak, when he wins the Texas primary 66 to 33 percent. Carter upsets a favorite-son candidate, Senator Lloyd Bentsen.

May 18, 1976: Ford wins in Maryland and his home state of Michigan, stopping Reagan's momentum. In Maryland, California governor Jerry Brown beats Carter, as Democrats worry about the Georgian's electability, even as Carter beats Udall in Michigan.

July 4, 1976: America celebrates its bicentennial in a sober mood, but the festivities boost President Ford, as he follows a "Rose Garden Strategy" of appearing presidential.

July 7, 1976: The White House hosts a state dinner for Queen Elizabeth II and Prince Philip as one of many bicentennial events that play well for Ford, who will not assume a full campaign schedule until October.

July 12, 1976: The Democratic National Convention meets in New York City, at Madison Square Garden. By the start of the convention, Carter has enough delegates to win the nomination and will soon enjoy a 33-point lead in the polls over President Ford.

July 15, 1976: After selecting Minnesota senator Walter Mondale as his vice presidential nominee, Jimmy Carter delivers his acceptance speech, stating, "As I've said many times before, we can have an American President who does not govern with negativism and fear of the future, but with vigor and vision and aggressive leadership—a President who's not isolated from the people, but who feels your pain and shares your dreams and takes his strength and his wisdom and his courage from you."

August 16, 1976: The Republican National Convention is held in Kansas City, Missouri. Going into the convention, Ford has won 16 primaries, Reagan 10. Ford enjoys a narrow delegate majority of 1,102 to 1,063 delegates, but Reagan believes he can still wrest the nomination because Ford remains 28 delegates short.

August 19, 1976: Emerging victorious after a rollicking convention, Gerald Ford delivers his acceptance speech, following Kansas senator Bob Dole's nomination as vice president. Ford strikes an optimistic chord, stating: "Tonight I can tell you straightaway this Nation is sound, this Nation is secure, this Nation is on the march to full economic recovery and a better quality of life for all Americans." Still, his words are upstaged by Reagan's eloquent concession speech challenging Americans to make a better future for themselves and the world.

September 6, 1976: Carter launches his general election campaign at Warm Springs, Georgia.

September 23, 1976: The *New York Times* runs an article entitled "Carter's Comments on Sex Cause Concern," discussing reactions to the Democratic candidate's interview with *Playboy*. During the interview, which appears in the November 1976 issue, Carter admits, "I've committed adultery in my heart many times."

September 23, 1976: The first televised presidential campaign debate since 1960 is held in Philadelphia. Ford performs well and is deemed the winner by some opinion polls. Both candidates stand uncomfortably on stage for 27 minutes when the power fails on their microphones during the debate.

October 6, 1976: The second presidential campaign debate takes place in San Francisco. Ford mistakenly states that "There is no Soviet domination of Eastern Europe and there never will be under a Ford administration." As reporters pounce on Ford's "gaffe," 61 percent of people polled believe Carter won the debate.

October 15, 1976: The first vice presidential debate in American history is held in Houston. Dole sounds partisan and needlessly harsh, especially when he calls World War II a "Democrat War."

October 22, 1976: The third presidential campaign debate is held in Williamsburg, Virginia. Referring to the *Playboy* interview, Carter sighs, "If I should ever decide in the future to discuss my deep Christian beliefs . . . I'll use another forum besides *Playboy*."

October 25, 1976: Leaving the "Rose Garden" behind, President Ford gives a series of seven substantive speeches in the final 10 days of the campaign. His campaign also broadcasts what critics call the "Joe and Jerry Show," half-hour television shows in Illinois, Pennsylvania, California, New York, Ohio, and Texas with former baseball star and TV personality Joe Garagiola asking the president "softball" questions.

October 30, 1976: Speaking in Syracuse, New York, Ford states, "We had a magnificent Bicentennial. There was a rejuvenation of the American spirit. There was a rebirth of our faith. So, I would look forward to representing you, to doing the best I could, and I pledge that to you. Therefore, on this occasion I ask you not only to confirm me with your prayers but to support me with your ballots. I won't let you down."

(continues)

1976 ELECTION CHRONOLOGY *(continued)*

November 1, 1976: A final Republican campaign broadcast features Joe Garagiola and singer Pearl Bailey. This last phase of Ford's campaign draws heavily on patriotic imagery, as well as a feel-good brand of patriotism with Americans singing, "I'm feeling good about America, I'm feeling good about me." This appeal narrows the gap between Ford and Carter considerably and foreshadows Ronald Reagan's successful campaigns in the 1980s.

November 2, 1976: Jimmy Carter and Walter Mondale win the election, but barely, with 297 electoral votes to 240, the narrowest margin since 1916, and only 1.7 million more popular votes out of 80 million cast.

December 13, 1976: Presidential electors cast their ballots in their respective state capitals. One Washington elector casts his presidential vote for Ronald Reagan instead of Gerald Ford.

1977

January 6, 1977: A joint session of Congress assembles to count the electoral votes.

(continued from page 1391)

primary on March 2, the first in which all candidates were running, could have been disastrous for Carter. He ran a poor fourth (13.9 percent) behind Jackson (22.3 percent), Udall (17.7 percent), and Wallace (16.7 percent). Only Harris (7.6 percent), Shriver (7.2 percent), and Bayh (4.8 percent) ran behind Carter. But even that did not cause Carter to lose front-runner status. Most media saw it as *Time* did: Massachusetts had "slowed the momentum" for Carter, and to "recapture that forward thrust" he had to "run strongly (not win) against Wallace" in Florida, Illinois, and North Carolina.

The Carter people had proposed Florida—with its 81 delegates—as Carter's first crucial test. Riding the anti-busing wave, Wallace in 1972 had captured 42 percent of the vote and won every congressional district. Carter presented himself in 1976 as the man who could beat Wallace on his own turf and remove him as a factor in national politics. As a Southerner who had campaigned against Washington and the "big shots," Carter would appeal to potential Wallace voters. As a moderate on racial matters, he was the candidate for anti-Wallace liberals. When the liberal contenders were persuaded to stay out of Florida, labor and liberal activists fell in behind Carter—some only for the Florida race. The United Auto Workers, for example, campaigned for Carter in Florida in order to weaken Wallace before the Michigan primaries. What Carter understood—and many liberals did not—was that, if he beat Wallace in Florida, it might be too late for liberal voters to go to more congenial candidates later. With Wallace weakened, Carter would have a free run in the South, racking up delegates and gaining momentum.

On March 9, Carter edged out Wallace by a small margin of 34.3 to 30.6 percent, with Jackson taking 23.9 percent. He was aided by a silent issue that neither he nor Jackson (the only major Northern candidate to enter the race) discussed. Wallace had to campaign in a wheelchair. "All they see is the spoke of my wheelchair, all humped over, saying the same thing," Wallace told one journalist. "It's hard to beat." According to an NBC exit poll, over 50 percent of the voters said they agreed with George Wallace, but 19.5 percent of them had voted for someone else because they were concerned about Wallace's health. After Carter's Florida win, the press provided the publicity that would keep his campaign going. Scarce on resources and personnel, the Carter people had not been able to organize past Florida. As Joel McCleary, Carter's national financial director, said, "After Florida it was NBC, CBS, and *The New York Times*." Patrick Caddell noted, "After Florida, there was one serious candidacy—Carter's . . . because the media had made it that way." The run-everywhere strategy enabled Carter to enter the Illinois primary without appearing to challenge Chicago mayor Richard J. Daley. Aside from the uncommitted slate led by the mayor in Cook County (where Carter ran no delegates), the only real opposition was from a weakened George Wallace. The two liberal candidates on the ballot—Fred Harris and Sargent Shriver—never got their campaigns off the ground. In the vote on March 16, Carter led the popularity poll with 48.1 percent of the vote (to Wallace's 27.6 percent, Shriver's 16.3 percent, and Harris's 5 percent) and won 55 delegates.

Carter's impressive win in North Carolina on March 23 (53.6 to 34.7 percent for Wallace) was aided by the fact that former governor Terry Sanford had withdrawn from the race the day after the Mississippi caucuses. The other conservative Southern alternative, Lloyd Bentsen of Texas, pulled out of the race after his poor showing in Oklahoma.

In New York on April 6, Jackson took 38 percent of the vote, Udall 25.5 percent, and Carter only 12.8 percent, while 23.7 percent of the vote remained uncommitted. The press could have raised questions about the viability of Carter's candidacy. This was the second major industrial state in the North where Carter had had real competition, and he was overwhelmed. Ben Wattenberg, then with the Jackson campaign, recalls how he woke up the morning after in a hotel room and saw the following on what he thought was the *Today Show:* "'Well, it's now a showdown between Carter and Humphrey.' I literally fell off the bed. Instead of it finally being a head-to-head clash between Jackson and Carter, it was still Carter versus the pack, and the pack then was Udall and Jackson, symbolized by Humphrey."

Actually, most newspapers and television stations that morning featured a photograph of a triumphant Carter, in a Harry Truman–like pose, reading the headlines of a Wisconsin paper that earlier in the evening had proclaimed Udall the winner in that state. Because the New

York race had seemed a foregone conclusion, NBC and CBS had shifted their attention to Wisconsin, where Carter was in a tight race with Morris Udall. When Carter's win became apparent later on election night, by 271,220 to 263,771 (a margin of 7,449 votes), he had a major press bonanza.

The ethnic-purity flap was the only serious crisis Carter faced during the entire primary campaign. On April 2, in an interview with Sam Roberts of the New York *Daily News,* Carter responded to a question about scattered-site public housing by saying, "I see nothing wrong with ethnic purity being maintained. I would not force a racial integration of a neighborhood by government action. But I would not permit discrimination against a family moving into the neighborhood." Four days later, when Ed Rabel, the CBS correspondent traveling with Carter, asked Carter to explain this statement, Carter noted his opposition to governmental programs designed to "inject black families into a white neighborhood," and talked of not being opposed to ethnics and blacks who try to maintain the "ethnic purity of their neighborhood," and said he considered it a natural inclination to do so.

Astonished, the reporters with Carter gathered in the back of the press bus and played their tapes again, to see if they had heard Carter correctly. For all his black sup-

President Gerald Ford (at podium) on stage with George Wallace (left) at a campaign stop in the South *(Library of Congress)*

port, could Carter be a closet racist? When they pushed at Carter at later press conferences, he dug himself in even deeper, speaking of a "diametrically opposite kind of family," and "the intrusion of alien groups into a neighborhood." The whole issue was put to rest, however, on April 13 when Martin Luther King Sr., at a rally in downtown Atlanta, assured a cheering audience that Carter's slip of the tongue did not represent his thinking, that all men make mistakes, and that he personally forgave Carter.

By the time of the primary campaign in Pennsylvania, which Jordan had identified as the "make-or-break" state, Carter was receiving much better press coverage than either Jackson or Udall. One day when all three were in Philadelphia, the Philadelphia *Bulletin* featured two front-page stories on Carter and ran his picture twice in the first four pages. The other candidates were covered in brief paragraphs.

Jackson and Udall, moreover, were mortally wounded by the freeze on federal funding from March 22 to May 21 due to problems in the makeup of the Federal Election Commission. Both had counted on federal matching funds for Pennsylvania and had to curtail severely their advertising and travel. Carter, however, was able to take advantage of a loophole in the federal campaign finance law. The Supreme Court had ruled that a candidate could spend as much of his own money as he wanted. With his own personal wealth, friends in the banks of Georgia, and front-runner status in the presidential lottery, Carter was able to secure large personal loans to fund the Pennsylvania and later campaigns. From March through May, Jimmy Carter and the Committee for Jimmy Carter borrowed a total of $775,000 from various Georgia banks.

On election day in Pennsylvania, April 27, Carter took 37 percent of the preferential vote to Jackson's 24.6 percent, Udall's 18.7 percent, and Wallace's 11.3 percent. Carter took 64 of the delegates to Udall's 22, Jackson's 19, Shapp's 17, and Wallace's 3—with the rest to be appointed later on the basis of strength in the preferential context. A *Washington Post* exit poll showed that 46 percent of the voters would have preferred Humphrey, had he been a declared candidate. Organized labor and the political professionals who had rallied around Jackson, in an "Anyone but Carter" effort, had not been able to deliver this vote to the senator from Washington. Many people voted for Carter because he was the best known. According to Thomas Patterson, 25 percent of the voters by the time of the Pennsylvania primary knew only Carter, and most of these voted for him. Of those voters who knew all three candidates, Carter received half the votes cast.

After the Pennsylvania primary, Carter acted as if his nomination were a foregone conclusion. He would cut back his campaigning pace, he said, in order to concentrate on unifying the party, identifying the issues, and preparing for the general election. Carter's aides began suggesting to tardy politicians that they should get on board the bandwagon before it was too late. At a breakfast fund-raiser in New York, Carter supporter William van den Heuvel offended New York governor Hugh Carey, who had not committed to any candidate, with the statement, "The train is leaving the station."

Certainly Carter seemed to have a clear field ahead. Birch Bayh had "suspended" his campaign on March 4 after his seventh-place finish in the Massachusetts primary. Shriver quit on March 22, and Harris followed on April 8. (Both needed the federal matching funds, so they technically remained in the race, leaving their names on the ballots in several states.) Before the Pennsylvania primary, Humphrey had said he would enter the race only if Carter seemed likely to enter the first ballot with fewer than 1,100 delegates. After the Pennsylvania primary, Carter appeared too strong, and Humphrey disappointed his followers by announcing on April 29 that he had insufficient time and organization to campaign actively for the nomination. "The one thing I don't need at this stage of life is to be ridiculous," he said with tears in his eyes. Shortly after this press conference, Jackson, out of money, flew home to Seattle, where he announced that he would no longer actively pursue the nomination.

These withdrawals left Udall as the only one among the original starters who could possibly stop Jimmy Carter. A charming, intelligent man, Udall had run a good, issue-oriented campaign. Unlike the other starters, he held his personal following even as Jimmy Carter had built up momentum. Had he taken Wisconsin, he would have become a serious contender. But he never received the press attention that might have won him a state and brought him the money to win other states.

There were two late entries in the presidential sweepstakes. After the Illinois primary, Idaho's Senator Frank Church and California's Governor Edmund "Jerry" Brown Jr. announced that they would seek the nomination. Brown, the youngest of the candidates at 38 and a proponent of the neoliberal doctrine that Americans would have to lower their expectations of government, decided to enter the race after the Massachusetts primary. Frank Church, an old-style liberal who had opposed the Vietnam War, had planned to enter the race earlier, but his work as the head of the Senate committee investigating the CIA kept him out of the race longer than he intended. At the time he plunged in, he assumed that, as the only late entry in the race, he could clean up in the Western states, including California, and then pick up other votes at the convention.

Neither Brown nor Church, however, had much chance of stopping Carter. They were starting with zero delegates at a time when it was too late even to acquire field delegates and to build organizations in many of the remaining states. Moreover, Carter had momentum. Network exit polls suggested that Carter had broadly based support—the black vote, the Wallace vote, the labor vote, the business vote, and the liberal and conservative votes. A *Time* poll showed that he was the candidate who could best beat Ford in the fall campaign. Voters came to regard Carter more favorably as he began to look like the winner. Money was pouring in. After the Florida primary, Carter began to surpass all his competitors in money received. With his Pennsylvania victory, Carter soared way above all the others. He reached a peak of $2.25 million by May 31, fully $1.5 million ahead of his closest competitor. Federal matching funds followed private money.

The first primary after Pennsylvania reinforced the impression that Carter was unstoppable. On May 1 in Texas, he beat Lloyd Bentsen, now running as a favorite son, winning 92 out of 98 delegates. On May 4, he won Indiana with 68 percent of the vote and his home state of Georgia with 83.4 percent. (The Georgia primary had been postponed from its original March 9 date, giving Carter time to get his bandwagon going.) On May 6, Carter took

Tennessee by 77.6 percent, although he lost Alabama to Wallace, taking only 8.6 percent of the delegates.

Yet, beneath the surface Carter remained vulnerable. By May 4 he had 553 delegates, according to the *New York Times*—slightly over one-third of the 1,505 needed to nominate. And not all Democrats were happy with this rush to Carter. As a *Time* poll showed, Carter was the choice of 39 percent of Democratic voters, with 59 percent favoring other candidates. More Democrats would prefer Humphrey if they were voting solely on the basis of issues.

From mid-May, Carter began to suffer reversals that, had they occurred earlier, might have knocked him out of the race. On May 11, Frank Church beat Carter in Nebraska (38.5 to 37.6 percent). Brown, who had been drawing enthusiastic crowds of the sort that Carter never attracted, won Maryland on May 18 (48.4 to 37.1 percent). On the same day, Udall ran only 1 percentage point behind Carter in Michigan (43.4 to 43.1 percent). Had it not been for the 5,738 votes that went to Shriver and 4,081 to Harris, Udall, who was only 2,425 votes behind Carter, might have won. Carter's victory was even less impressive considering he had the support of Henry Ford, UAW

Democratic presidential candidate Jimmy Carter speaks to a crowd at a campaign stop in Pittsburgh. *(Library of Congress)*

president Leonard Woodcock, and Detroit mayor Coleman Young. On May 25, Carter lost Oregon and Idaho to Church, and Nevada to Brown. On June 1, he suffered a dismal defeat at the hands of Church in Montana, and Rhode Island went to a slate of ostensibly "uncommitted" delegates (really pledged to Brown or Humphrey) in an extremely close contest.

Carter's decision to run everywhere minimized the impact of these losses, for each was usually offset by a countervailing win. When Carter lost Nebraska on May 11 he achieved a narrow win over Udall in Connecticut. The night of his defeats in Idaho, Nevada, and Oregon, he had compensatory wins in Arkansas and Kentucky. The night he lost Rhode Island and Montana, Carter won in George McGovern's home state of South Dakota. Even when Brown and Church won, Carter picked up delegates. In late May, Carter told reporters in New York City that his wins in the three southern primaries and some caucus states had put him over the 1,000 mark. In Los Angeles in early June, Carter advised Jerry Brown to count delegates: "I would say that someone who has 1,000 delegates is ahead of someone who has 25."

To avoid a possible tailspin after the last primaries—California, New Jersey, and Ohio on June 8—Carter enlisted the support of Mayor Daley. Brown would almost certainly be victorious in California. The slate of uncommitted Brown/Humphrey delegates in New Jersey had held together and now emerged as a fairly solid stumbling block for Carter. Only Ohio, where Udall and Church were both entered, looked promising for Carter. Governor John J. Gilligan was supporting him, and there was a sizable conservative vote in the southern part of the state. To focus attention on Ohio, Daley explained in a press conference on primary day that a Carter win there would be decisive. No one, Daley added in obvious allusion to Humphrey, should have the nomination handed to him after refusing to take part in the primaries.

That evening Carter lost big in California—Brown taking 59 percent of the vote to Carter's 20.4 percent. In New Jersey, the uncommitted slate received 42 percent to Carter's 28 percent. But in Ohio, Carter captured 52.3 percent of the vote against Udall's 21.2 percent and Church's 13.9 percent. Overall, he won 218 delegates that day, bringing his total count up to 1,117—short of the 1,505 required for nomination.

Within the next few days, everyone agreed with Daley about Ohio, and the opposition to Carter collapsed. Wallace, Humphrey, Jackson, Shapp, Church, and Harris all released their delegates and offered full support. Though Udall technically remained a candidate, he released his delegates to vote as they pleased. On June 25 Brown also conceded, saying, "Governor Carter appears certain to be nominated, and if he is, I will enthusiastically support his candidacy in the fall."

Humphrey's vacillation had contributed to the political vacuum through which Carter had driven to secure the Democratic nomination. Gallup Polls showed Humphrey the first choice of Democratic voters from January through late May. According to the various exit polls, he could have won the Iowa caucuses and the Florida, Illinois, and Pennsylvania primaries had he entered. As it was, his shadow candidacy cast a pall over the other liberal candidates. Organized labor frittered away its influence, giving desultory support to a variety of candidates. Party leaders such as Joseph Crangle and Paul Simon dissipated their energies on draft Humphrey movements that went nowhere. Most important, Humphrey's apparent availability for a draft encouraged the media and the party not to take other liberal candidates too seriously. According to the *New York Times,* just before the Pennsylvania primary, Speaker of the House Thomas P. O'Neill Jr. told friends that he preferred Humphrey to any of the candidates then in the race. Jackson was seriously weakened in Pennsylvania because he was widely perceived as a stalking horse for Humphrey. Brown's later victories, as the *New York Times* suggested on May 11, were generally viewed as a boost for Humphrey.

Ironically, Humphrey, the old-line professional, was less aware than Jimmy Carter, the supposed amateur, that the 1976 primaries were a new ball game. Since 1968, the percentage of delegates chosen in primaries had risen from 30 to 70 percent. This and the abolition of the winner-take-all primaries made it very unlikely that late entrants could win the race. Moreover, a decision at the convention to nominate someone who had avoided most of the primaries would have raised serious questions of legitimacy. "A whole lot worse things could happen to the country," the *Washington Post* said on April 29, "than for Hubert Humphrey to be his party's nominee. But it matters how he gets there."

Still, there was an outside chance of stopping Carter after Pennsylvania if his three remaining opponents had worked together. But ideological differences, divergent ambitions, and fears of being labeled as spoilers prevented this. Representatives from the three campaigns did meet to discuss the possibility of strategically dividing up the territory so that Carter would have to face each opponent one on one. Thus, attempting a political power block, Udall stayed out of Nebraska, where Church had been campaigning, and Maryland, where Brown was ahead. The plan foundered, however, when self-interest took over and Brown ran a write-in campaign in Oregon where Church was competing with Carter, and Church competed with Udall in Ohio. To make matters worse, none of the previously withdrawn candidates would endorse Udall, Brown, or Church.

With the collapse of the opposition after June 8, Carter worked to solidify the party. As early as mid-April, he had solicited information on vice-presidential possibilities. In early June, he made public a large list of candidates, drawing from all segments of the party. His designation of Walter Mondale was not announced until the convention, but in choosing the liberal Minnesota senator he threw out a line to the party professionals and liberals he had beaten in the primaries.

To avoid party divisiveness at the convention, Carter's aides began working on the platform in early June. A draft plank pledged to breaking up vertically integrated oil interests was reduced to a vague commitment to free competition in the crude oil industry. Red-flag issues such as decriminalization of marijuana and protection of homosexual rights were avoided altogether. Southerners agreed to sidestep the busing issue. Blacks agreed to a restricted welfare reform plank. Former anti–Vietnam War protesters agreed to a provision to permit the president to grant pardons to deserters on a case-by-case basis, dropping a previous plank pledging blanket pardons. Even organized labor accepted general statements on full employment and national health insurance, foregoing specific references to the Humphrey–Hawkins full-employment bill or the Kennedy–Corman national health insurance bill.

At the convention, the presentation of the platform was less an occasion for debate than a chance for a parade of leading Democrats to signify by their presence that the party was now a family. Four names were placed in nomination: Carter, Udall, Brown, and Ellen McCormack (the anti-abortion candidate committed to one side of an issue that had been brushed over in this extraordinary campaign). Carter won by 2,238 votes to Udall's 329, Brown's 300, Wallace's 57, and McCormack's 22, with a scattering of votes for others.

In his acceptance speech, Carter invoked the names of Roosevelt, Truman, Kennedy, and Johnson, saying he had always been a Democrat. But in his rhetoric he was still the outsider and the populist. "I have never met a Democratic President," he said. And he proclaimed his opposition to "special influence and privilege." Carter saw "no reason why big shot crooks should go free and the poor ones go to jail." He called for a fairer tax system and denounced exclusive private schools, as well as the self-perpetuating alliance between money and politics. "Too many have had to suffer at the hands of a political and economic elite," he said.

It was unusual rhetoric coming from a man whose forces had successfully blunted any radical edge in the platform. But the Democrats were in no mood to note contradictions. After Carter's acceptance speech, party chairman Robert Strauss invited the most important

Jimmy Carter and Senator Hubert Humphrey at the Democratic National Convention, July 15, 1976 *(Library of Congress)*

Democrats to the podium—Jackson, Udall, Church, Brown, Wallace, Daley, Humphrey, Representative Barbara Jordan, Senators Edmund Muskie and John Glenn, Mayor Abraham Beame of New York, and Governor Reubin Askew of Florida. Linking arms and joining hands, they sang "We Shall Overcome."

Carter won over the traditional party leaders because of his apparent appeal to so many different voting groups. As Leonard Woodcock noted when he endorsed Carter, "If a political genius had offered to produce a candidate who could carry the working class as well as the crucial black, moderate, and liberal vote in the North, and at the same time beat the strident segregationist of the South, he would have been called a dreamer. And yet, that is what Jimmy Carter has done."

He had done this, in part, by downplaying the role of issues in his campaign. As Carter told a group of network executives, the only "Presidents he knew of who [had] emphasized the issues were Dewey, Goldwater, and McGovern." Instead, Carter affirmed principles to which few could object: Government should be honest and open, rational, and efficient; laws should be administered evenhandedly; and government officials should be chosen on the basis of merit rather than of politics. His television commercials showed him pulling weeds in a field or walking along the corn rows on his farm as he spoke of the work ethic and recalled his experience in balancing budgets on the farm.

On controversial matters that could not be avoided, Carter would make general statements designed to please one section of his audience, and then at the end slip in conditions that would appeal to another. Thus he supported the principle of the right-to-work provision in the Taft–Hartley Act but would not oppose legislative measures to do away with it. He was against abortion, but he accepted the right of every woman to choose for herself what she would do.

Carter's other major rhetorical technique consisted of the use of code phrases to imply attitudes that he did not have to spell out and that would create common ground between himself and his audience. In announcing his candidacy in 1974, he identified himself as "a farmer, an engineer, a businessman, a planner, a scientist, a governor, and a Christian." In *Why Not The Best?* he wrote, "I am a Southerner and an American . . . a father and a husband . . . a naval officer, a canoeist, and among other things, a lover of Bob Dylan's songs and Dylan Thomas's poetry." Citing his born-again Christian faith and his work as a lay missionary, he appealed to evangelical Christians. At the same time, he quoted Reinhold Niebuhr, Søren Kierkegaard, Paul Tillich, and Karl Barth for the intelligentsia. The emphasis on his small-town, agrarian, religious, and family roots convinced social conservatives that he was at one with them. But his close relationship with the Allman Brothers country rock band sent the message that he was no uptight Bible thumper and would not condemn partying, drinking, or even drug use. In proclaiming "Maggie's Farm" (which describes the burning resentment of a white farmhand toward his middle-class farm owners) his favorite Dylan song, Carter suggested that he might even be a closet radical.

Equally important was Carter's refusal to position himself within the conventional political spectrum. "I never characterized myself as a conservative, liberal, or moderate, and this is what distinguishes me," he said in January 1976. Or, as he stated on *Face the Nation* in March 1976, the voters "just feel that I'm the sort of person they can trust, and if they are liberal, I think I'm compatible with their views. If they are moderate, the same; and if the voter is conservative, I think they still feel that I'm a good President." In an interview after his speech accepting the Democratic nomination, Carter called the speech "uniformly populist in tone." But when pressed to explain what the term "populist" meant, Carter demurred. "I will let you define it." Indeed, one of Carter's political advisers, Charles Kirbo, remarked in July 1976 that Carter had "a wide area of populism" in him, but "I'm not sure what, politically, he cares about. Right now, I imagine he's caring about being President more than anything else."

Actually, the deeper issue in 1976, as Carter suggested, was "simply the desire of the American people to have faith in government, to want a fresh start." By his evocative use of what journalist Thomas Ottenad called the "three Rs" (region, race, religion), Carter met this need. The South, as his own political career suggested, was leading the country in a movement to give outsiders an increasing role in government. Southerners, moreover, could draw on their traditional intimacy with blacks to show the rest of the country how the races really could relate. "I sometimes think," Carter said, "that a Southerner of my generation can most fully understand the meaning and impact of Martin Luther King's life. He and I grew up in the same South." In his unabashed discussions of his born-again religious experiences—in *Why Not the Best?*, at a fund-raiser in North Carolina, and at his Sunday school classes at the Plains Baptist church each Sunday—Carter suggested that religion could be a healing force in American life. Plains itself evoked idyllic images of pre-industrial America, where the sky was always blue, the water clear, the land unspoiled, and the people cared, really cared for each other.

As Jody Powell observed shortly after the election, "There was a tremendous yearning in the country this year for something of substance that you could put some faith in. . . . People all over the land were looking for something they thought they had known once and somehow had lost touch with. I think that pine trees and hometowns said something even to people who have never seen a small town, because they suggested something that they wanted."

Carter's self-presentation, moreover, suggested that he had the power to accomplish important things. When asked to explain his audacity in running for president, Carter had said that he "always had self-assurance" and that he was at "complete peace" with himself and the world around him. His toughness was evident in the extraordinary self-discipline and sangfroid he showed on the campaign trail. He set a brutal pace for himself and reporters traveling with him. While other candidates might start as late as 9 a.m., Carter began each day around 5 a.m. His campaign plane flew on time, leaving lagging reporters behind. Even the softball games in Plains gave evidence of his drive, his competitive streak.

Stories about his past—how he had read *War and Peace* three times when a boy, how he had been a candidate for a Rhodes scholarship, his work as a nuclear engineer—all hinted at scientific and intellectual depths. Carter's charm was evident in his ability to weave his magic before blacks, county sheriffs, children, college students, the aged. As Tom Wicker observed, anyone who doesn't understand "the mystical appeal of Jimmy Carter to the American people in 1976" should have attended the senior citizens' center gathering where he discussed America's problems with Vietnam and Watergate.

Any fears that he might misuse his power were allayed by the compassion he professed for those less fortunate than himself. Carter himself proclaimed his capacity to love anonymous people he met on factory lines. His rectitude, he suggested, would keep him from abusing power. "I don't want anything selfish out of government," he often said. "I think I want the same thing you do. And that is to have our nation once again with a government as good and honest and decent and truthful and fair and competent and idealistic and compassionate, and as filled with love as are the American people." In contrast to Nixon, Carter suggested he would have no all-powerful palace guard or shadow cabinet. Even his aides would be selected on the basis of merit rather than politics. Most important, he looked you in the eye and said, "I'll never lie to you . . . never make a misleading statement . . . never betray your trust." Whatever uneasiness Carter observers might have felt at those times when he seemed rough or tough or manipulative, it could be put to rest by the conviction that here was a deeply religious man.

His perfection was always tempered with assurances that he was one of the people. "I think my greatest strength," he said, "is that I am an ordinary man, just like all of you, one who has worked and learned and loved his family and made mistakes and tried to correct them without always succeeding." And this ordinariness was shown in the many little things he did on the campaign trail. He carried his own luggage, washed his own clothes in hotel rooms, and made his own bed when he stayed in private houses. He even gave his phone number and address to campaign audiences, urging them to keep in touch.

Carter thus presented himself as self-confident but humble; tough but compassionate; intellectual but in no way snobbish; ambitious for justice but not for himself. He was, in essence, an extraordinary ordinary man.

His self-presentation was aided by eager and hopeful journalism. For Garry Wills, Carter was a "real Southerner," unlike more liberal Southerners like Terry Sanford or Reubin Askew, whom Northern liberals preferred. His background gave him a "a southern respect for the military without the awe that naval amateurs like the two Roosevelts displayed." He might even respect his promise never to be compromised. "The scary thing is that he might have some way of keeping it." Other journalists affirmed Carter's passion for social justice, though the record suggested he was really fairly conservative. Anthony Lewis concluded in the *New York Times* that "he cares about the powerless in society—genuinely I am convinced." When Carter talked conservatively, Stanley Cloud of *Time* implied, he was simply doing what Roosevelt had done in 1932, that is, hiding liberal views under a conservative cover in order to win an election.

At times these bigger-than-life projections of Carter were a function of the interests of the journalists involved. Generally, reporters working and traveling and joking with a candidate come to have a shared interest in obtaining good publicity for him—to help the candidate win the election, and to help themselves advance their own careers. As David Jones, national news editor of the *New York Times*, explained in 1976, "When our political reporters get on that campaign they get trapped; they're in a cocoon and it distorts their perception of everything that is happening in the campaign because they don't see the broader dimensions." This symbiotic relationship was intensified in Carter's case by another factor. Because he was not well known at the beginning, established reporters were not assigned to him. As he gained prominence, he gave younger reporters the opportunity to get ahead and to challenge their own establishment. As Richard Reeves later wrote:

> Jimmy Carter, it turned out, was my candidate. . . .
> He was, as I thought about it, the candidate of a frustrated generation of American political reporters. . . . For years, we had seen our business defined by a generation that came along with John F. Kennedy—the Hugh Sideys and Joe Krafts—who had been able to report politics as the institutionalized ambition of their candidates, the Kennedys, Nixon, Humphrey, and Rockefeller.
>
> Then we found someone they didn't know—an outsider. We began touting Jimmy Carter in early 1976; they began mocking him. To me, he was a transitional figure who understood symbolic communication in media-world; to James Reston, he was the slightly laughable "Wee Jimmy."

Basically, Carter and the press held out to Americans the hope that after Vietnam and Watergate they could find once again a president they could admire and trust. By 1973, polls showed that 75 percent of the people thought the government had lied to them to some extent. Carter's genius lay in sensing that underneath the prevailing cynicism a deep longing remained for the good authority in which Americans had once believed. Carter was smart, tough, and disciplined, and voters expected that he could exercise power as strong presidents have traditionally done. But Carter was also anchored in religious and moral values, claiming inner constraints on behavior lacking in some recent presidents. It was not simply that Carter said he would never lie, as American Civil Liberties Union leader Charles Morgan said, "He's the only candidate who's comfortable saying he won't lie."

Carter's opponent in the fall election was President Gerald Ford. Appointed vice president under the Twenty-fifth Amendment to replace Spiro T. Agnew, Ford became president after Nixon's resignation on August 9, 1974. He then appointed Nelson Rockefeller of New York, a man much distrusted by right-wing Republicans, as vice president. At first, Ford brought the country relief from the tawdriness of the Nixon years. It seemed, as he said when taking the oath of office, that "our national nightmare is over." His pardon of Nixon one month later, however, dissipated much of the initial goodwill. A public trial of the ex-president would be excessively punitive, he explained, and the country could not stand such an ordeal. Whatever might be said about the substance of his decision, the way he made it evoked memories of Watergate and concern that he might have made a deal with Nixon. When Ford's press secretary, Jerry ter Horst, heard the news, he resigned. With his credibility undermined, Ford's plain ways and slow speech contributed to a growing perception of him as a well-meaning bumbler. Every time that Ford tripped or fell or misspoke, the press reported it in full. In the White House pressroom, reporters joked that Ford "can't even play President with a helmet." Although no incumbent president had been denied his party's renomination since Chester Arthur in 1884, right-wing Republicans now began looking for a conservative alternative. At a meeting sponsored by the American Conservative Union and the Young Americans for Freedom in February 1975, delegates talked of a third-party effort behind Ronald Reagan and formed a committee under Jesse Helms to look into the matter. Reagan himself urged that conservative efforts be directed to transforming the GOP.

To stave off challenges from the right, Ford announced early, on July 8, 1975, that he would seek another term. He chose Howard H. Callaway of Georgia, a former secretary of the army, to head his campaign, and former deputy defense secretary David Packard to oversee his finance committee. Henry Kissinger, whose détente poli-

cies had infuriated conservatives, was replaced as head of the National Security Council on November 2, 1975, by his deputy, Air Force Lieutenant General Brent Scowcroft. Ford was relieved of the Rockefeller problem when the vice president announced he would not seek his post again. As Callaway had suggested on two occasions the previous summer, opposition to Rockefeller in the South was an extra political burden for the president. This message to the right, however, was blunted because Ford retained Kissinger as secretary of state; moreover, the hawkish secretary of defense, James R. Schlesinger, was replaced by the moderate Donald Rumsfeld; and William E. Colby of the CIA was replaced by the centrist George Bush, the U.S. representative to the Peoples Republic of China.

Ronald Reagan had pretty much decided to make his bid for the presidency in the spring of 1974, while Nixon was still in office. He announced his candidacy on November 20, 1975. "Our nation's capital," he said, "has become the seat of a buddy system that functions for its own benefit—increasingly insensitive to the needs of the American who supports it with his taxes."

Reagan had first captured the hearts of the right with a national television address supporting Barry Goldwater for

This Herblock cartoon shows how the Watergate affair was "dogging" the Republican ticket. (*A Herblock Cartoon, copyright by the Herb Block Foundation*)

president in 1964. His attacks on the welfare "cheats" and student radicals in his successful campaign for the governorship of California in 1966 made him a conservative hero. His pleasant manner and willingness to compromise on tax and welfare programs during his two terms as governor had softened potential opposition from moderates. His campaign for the Republican presidential nomination in 1968, though late and halfhearted, called attention to him as a presidential possibility. Out of office in January 1975, he devoted himself full time to winning a following around the country through his syndicated radio show, news column, and public speeches. In late 1975, he was nearly 65 and facing an appointed, not an elected, president from his own party. His time for another crack at the presidency had come, and it was perhaps a proposition.

Ideologically, Reagan was an implacable opponent of the welfare state, a law-and-order man, a crusading anticommunist who saw the world as a struggle between pure good and pure evil, an opponent of all forms of affirmative action to promote racial equality. On these matters he was considerably to the right of the Republican moderates clustered around Ford.

The ideological battle was joined shortly before the New Hampshire primary. On February 10, Reagan lambasted the Ford–Kissinger detente policies in a speech at Phillips Exeter Academy in New Hampshire. "The balance of forces has been shifting gradually toward the Soviet Union since 1970," he said. "Let us not be satisfied with a foreign policy whose principal accomplishment seems to be our acquisition of the rights to sell Pepsi-Cola in Siberia." Ford, in a press conference on February 17, claimed that Reagan was too far to the right to win the general election—pointing to Reagan's earlier statements that Social Security should be made voluntary and his more recent suggestion that Social Security funds be invested in the stock market and that $90 billion in federal expenditures be cut by transferring federal programs to the states.

Ford had the support of most party leaders. But Callaway had difficulties in setting up a good campaign organization, Packard had trouble raising the big dollars they thought would roll in, and Reagan won over key people in New Hampshire. Yet Ford took New Hampshire on February 24 by a razor-thin margin (50.6 to 49.4 percent), Massachusetts on March 2 (64.4 to 35.6 percent), Vermont on March 2 (84 to 15.2 percent), Florida on March 9 (52.8 to 47.2 percent), and Illinois on March 16 (58.9 to 40 percent). The *Washington Post*'s delegate count now gave Ford 166 delegates to Reagan's 54, with 51 uncommitted. With these losses, the contributions to Reagan began to slow down. The Reagan people—running a net debt of nearly $1 million—trimmed their spending to barely half of what it had been in February. Nine Republican governors suggested that Reagan withdraw to promote party unity. On

March 20, his campaign manager, John Sears, engaged in tentative talks with presidential counselor Rogers C. B. Morton to discuss the possible Ford contributions to the Reagan campaign debt should Reagan withdraw.

The next series of primaries, however, were in states where Barry Goldwater had shown his greatest strength in 1964. In North Carolina on March 23, Reagan beat Ford by 52.4 to 45.9 percent. The small turnout (40 percent) gave weight to Jesse Helms's right-wing followers and to Reagan's television speeches, run in the last four days of the campaign. Twenty-seven percent of those who voted for Reagan, according to an NBC News poll, made up their minds in the last week.

In a national television address on March 31, Reagan elaborated on the foreign policy critique presented in his Exeter speech and raised $1.5 million. The cutoff of the Federal Election Commission payout on March 22—occasioned by conflicts over the makeup of the commission—had seriously crippled an already debt-ridden campaign. These fresh funds put Reagan back on track for the crucial Texas campaign.

Although Ford won Wisconsin (55.2 to 44.3 percent) on April 6, he was completely swamped in Texas on May 1. Reagan swept every congressional district and won all 96 delegates. Texas was the first open primary and, with Wallace out of the Democratic race as a real contender, thousands of Wallace supporters crossed over to vote for Reagan. Charges that the Ford administration was engaged in secret negotiations to "give away" the Panama Canal was an especially important factor in the Texas vote.

Three days later, on May 4, Reagan won in Indiana, Georgia, and Alabama. Reagan surged ahead in the delegate count, taking 357 to Ford's 297. It was a disastrous showing for a sitting president. Ford's run of losses had not been equaled since Theodore Roosevelt challenged President William Howard Taft in 1912. At Ford Committee headquarters that night, Rogers Morton, who replaced Callaway as campaign manager on March 30, said, "I'm not going to rearrange the furniture on the deck of the Titanic." On March 11, Reagan beat Ford in Nebraska (54.6 to 45.4 percent), although Ford took West Virginia (56.6 to 43.4 percent).

On May 18, Ford was back in the running, defeating Reagan nearly two to one in his home state of Michigan. This time independents went heavily for Ford and thousands of Democrats, in a massive turnout, heeded the plea of Republican leaders in the state to cross over to vote for their native son. In Maryland the same day, Ford beat Reagan 57.9 to 42.1 percent.

After this victory, Ford held his own in a tight race down to the June 8 primaries and through five weeks of caucuses. Ford won most of the traditionally moderate states of the Midwest and Northeast. On May 25, he took Kentucky, Oregon, and Tennessee in close races. (Reagan hurt himself in the latter primary when he told reporters in Knoxville that he would consider returning the TVA to the private sector.) On June 1, Ford won in Rhode Island. On June 8, he won New Jersey (where Reagan had entered no delegate candidates) and Ohio (where Ford had the support of the governor and the Republican congressional delegation). On May 24, the Ford campaign also received a big boost when 119 previously uncommitted New York delegates voted to endorse him. The vote was engineered by Nelson Rockefeller, who earlier in 1976 had flirted with the possibility that he might enter as a presidential candidate should the convention be deadlocked between Reagan and Ford.

Reagan took most of the more conservative West and South. He swamped Ford in Arkansas, Nevada, and Idaho on May 25, and in Montana and South Dakota on June 1. Ford then tried to capitalize on Reagan's suggestion in Sacramento that the United States might have to send troops to Rhodesia. Three days before the California primary, the Ford organization ran television ads stating, "When you vote on Tuesday, remember Governor Ronald Reagan couldn't start a war. President Reagan can." Despite that, Reagan won California on June 8, with 65.7 percent of the vote.

After the June 8 primaries, the race was still wide open. Reagan had a total 863 delegates to 958 for Ford, according to the *Washington Post*. Some 260 additional delegates remained to be chosen in the remaining caucus states, and about 164 remained uncommitted from earlier races. For the next five weeks, party leaders and local party activists fought toe to toe for these 424 delegates. Ford secured a majority in Iowa, Delaware, Minnesota, and North Dakota. Reagan took the lion's share in Minnesota, Washington, New Mexico, Montana, and Colorado. In the last two caucuses on July 17, Ford took all of Connecticut's 35 delegates and Reagan all of Utah's 20. On July 6, in the midst of these battles, Reagan appealed to the white ethnic voter in a 60-minute broadcast over the ABC network by characterizing affirmative action as a form of reverse discrimination. "I'd like an opportunity to put an end to this distortion of the principle of equal rights," he said. On July 17, when the final caucus was over, the *New York Times* saw Ford ahead by 1,102 to 1,063 delegates. But the president was still 28 delegates short of the 1,130 needed for nomination. Reagan needed 67.

The next battle was for the approximately 94 delegates who remained uncommitted. As the incumbent, Ford had several advantages. During the spring freeze on federal

President Gerald Ford waves to a crowd from the sunroof of a car in Philadelphia. *(Library of Congress)*

funding, he had been able to draw on White House resources and access to credit, while Reagan had gone without funds. Now he invited whole delegations to dine and drink at the White House, while aides worked on influential politicians in Mississippi (which was holding to the unit rule against party rules) and other uncommitted delegations.

Reagan, on the advice of his strategist, John Sears, countered on July 26 by naming the liberal Republican senator from Pennsylvania, Richard Schweiker, as his prospective running mate. The objective was to broaden Reagan's appeal for the fall campaign and to cut into the Pennsylvania delegation at the convention, where there were still uncommitted votes, and thus start the final bandwagon to Reagan.

Instead, the move enraged conservatives. Clarke Reed, a Reagan supporter and head of the uncommitted Mississippi delegation, announced his "personal" endorsement of Ford after that choice. "This kind of Vice-President," he said, "is too big a price to pay for the nominations." Senator James L. Buckley of New York, supported by Jesse Helms and Illinois representative Dan Crane, stated on August 11 that he would be available as a presidential candidate should there be a deadlock at the convention between Reagan and Ford. His goal was to prevent a first-ballot nomination and to bring pressure on Reagan to drop Schweiker on the second ballot. (Buckley's candidacy was dropped on August 16 after New York State party chairman Richard Rosenbaum warned him that if he persisted in his effort, he would lose the state organization support in his reelection bid that year.) Reagan's move did not even cut into the Pennsylvania delegation as intended. A *New York Times* poll of the Pennsylvania delegation in late July showed only one convert to the Reagan cause. A Gallup Poll on August 12 indicated that the move neither hurt nor helped Reagan with Republican and independent voters at large.

Political strategist John Sears had one last move—a procedural challenge on the floor of the convention at Kansas City to show Reagan's purported second-ballot strength. (The Rules Committee had adopted a rule requiring each delegate to vote on the first ballot as he was pledged to vote under state law and not according to his personal preference.) The Reagan-backed amendment, 16-C, would require Ford to name his vice-presidential choice before the balloting began. If all Reagan supporters voted for 16-C, they might secure a majority that would start a rush to Reagan.

After a debate on August 17, punctuated by boos and scuffles on the floor, Reagan lost the vote on 16-C by 1,069 in favor to 1,180 against, with 10 abstentions. Earlier rumors that the Mississippi delegation would vote against the resolution may have induced some waverers to vote against it. The Mississippi delegation, however, passed on the first roll call and did not deliver its 30 votes against the resolution until after Florida's vote had already given it the coup de grace. A Reagan aide said, "This was the ball game."

Shortly after that vote, the Ford people yielded to another challenge from the Reagan–Helms people and accepted the "morality in foreign policy" plank. A clear rejection of the Ford–Kissinger foreign policies, it commended Soviet dissident Alexander Solzhenitsyn, criticized détente, the Helsinki agreement signed by Ford in 1975, and secret agreements—a slap at the Ford–Kissinger negotiations over the Panama Canal. (Even the platform coming to the floor of the convention reflected earlier concessions to the Reagan–Helms forces on the platform committee—including a call for U.S. military superiority over the USSR, the retention of a mutual defense treaty between the United States and Taiwan, and the endorsement of three constitutional amendments—to "protect unborn children," to bar the assignment of students to schools on the basis of race, and to permit nonsectarian prayers in public schools. A women's task force at the convention had blocked the Reagan–Helms effort to get the Platform Committee to drop the Republican commitment to the Equal Rights Amendment.)

Ford won on the first ballot late at night on August 18 by 1,187 to 1,070. Mississippi, once considered the key to nomination, finally dropped its unit rule before the balloting and gave Ford 16 votes to Reagan's 14.

Reagan came so close to winning the nomination because party rules gave Western and Southwestern states a disproportionate share of the delegates at the expense of the more populous states in the Northeast and Midwest. Ford was more popular with Republican voters as a whole than Reagan (e.g., a Gallup Poll in early July 1976 showed the president leading among Republicans by 61 to 31 percent). Reagan was slightly more popular with conservative voters, as a *New York Times*/CBS poll showed. But his strength was regional, that is, with Southerners and Westerners, and the apportionment provision under which the Republican National Convention operated in 1976 played to his strength.

The fight at the convention also reflected ideological differences. Few Republicans expected to win the election. After a Gallup Poll showed either Ford or Reagan getting only 40 percent of the votes against Carter, delegates responded to the question of whether their man could win with a forlorn "I hope so." The Reagan delegates, considerably more conservative and ideological than the Ford delegates, were mainly interested in inscribing their views in the party platform and in winning control of the party organization. A CBS/*New York Times* poll reported on June 25 that as many as half of the Ronald Reagan supporters were prepared to defect to Carter or boycott the election should Ford win the nomination.

Ford's vice-presidential choice was motivated by the need to heal these divisions. On August 18, shortly after he had won the nomination, Ford consulted Reagan on six vice-presidential possibilities. They were Senator Robert J. Dole of Kansas, Senator Howard H. Baker Jr. of Tennessee, Treasury Secretary William E. Simon, Commerce Secretary Elliot L. Richardson, former deputy attorney general William D. Ruckelshaus, and former Texas governor John B. Connally. Reagan spoke most warmly of Dole, a tough-talking, sarcastic senator with friends in the Reagan camp. At a press conference the next afternoon, Ford announced Dole as his vice-presidential choice. Jesse Helms allowed his name to be placed into nomination by his ultraright supporters, a move that allowed him to ventilate his ideas before announcing his withdrawal.

In his acceptance speech, Ford attacked congressional Democrats, challenged Jimmy Carter to debate, and said that Washington had gotten away from the people. "You at home, listening tonight, you are the people who pay taxes and obey the law," he said. "It is from your ranks that I come and on your side I stand." At the end of the speech, he invited Reagan to the podium to address the delegates. The party platform is a "banner of bold, unmistakable colors," Reagan said. "We have just heard a call to arms based on that platform." Calling on the party to unite against the Democrats, he ended by telling the delegates, "There is no substitute for victory."

There were several third-party candidates in 1976. On the right there was the segregationist ex-governor of Georgia, Lester Maddox, of the American Independent Party, Tom Anderson of the American Party, and Roger L. MacBride of the Libertarian Party. On the left were Peter Camejo of the Socialist Workers Party and Julius Levin of the Socialist Labor Party. Lyndon H. LaRouche of the U.S. Labor Party tried to appeal to extremists on both the left and right.

The only third-force candidate apt to attract a following large enough to have impact on the election was Eugene McCarthy—the former Democratic senator whose strong showing in the New Hampshire primaries in 1968 had paved the way for Robert Kennedy's campaign and the decision of President Lyndon B. Johnson not to seek reelection. Running as an Independent in 1976, McCarthy's hope was to prevent the major-party candidates from winning a majority in the Electoral College. Republicans, he believed, would prefer to negotiate with other electors than throw the decision to the Democratically controlled House. Ideologically, McCarthy appealed to what he considered a neglected center, raising basic questions about the need to reduce a bloated military establishment, to create stronger institutional checks on U.S. intelligence agencies, to protect natural resources, to refashion a foreign policy in accord with traditional American ideas, and to challenge the lock-hold the two major parties have on the political system. With Senator James Buckley he had successfully challenged the Campaign Finance Law of 1974 in the case of *Buckley v. Valeo;* the 1976 Supreme Court decision had led to the reorganization of the commission and the temporary cessation of federal matching funds. McCarthy's subsequent experience showed the problems that third parties still had under the provisions the Supreme Court allowed to stand. Denied federal matching funds unless they received 5 percent of the vote in the last election, they were still subject to a spending limitation of $1,000 per person and $500 per committee.

In September, the Louis Harris Poll showed McCarthy with about 7 percent of the vote in New York, Illinois, Pennsylvania, Ohio, Michigan, and California. As Democratic Party chairman Robert Strauss noted, his threat was primarily to Carter, for he was drawing about 4 to 1 from the Democrats. The campaign finance law, however, severely limited his funds. Moreover, McCarthy had to spend most of his time mounting legal challenges to the

Republican campaign poster *(Library of Congress)*

ways in which state laws were enforced against him and also to the decision of the League of Women Voters and the networks to limit the presidential debates to Carter and Ford. Although he had expected to be on the ballot in at least 40 states, McCarthy finally appeared in only 29.

At the beginning of the fall campaign, Jimmy Carter seemed almost invincible. Although he had dropped in the polls since the Democratic National Convention, he was still leading Ford by about 15 points. Victory seemed within easy reach, as Hamilton Jordan pointed out in memos of June 2 and August 9. The 10 border and Southern states were almost sure bets. By adding all states that usually voted Democratic, Jordan figured that Carter could win by taking a few major swing states in the North. Not a state would be conceded to the Republicans, although Carter would focus his efforts on the swing states. Ford, however, had a plan that might work. According to the strategy memo John Sears gave him in early August, the way he might win was to "act presidential," to undertake a negative campaign against Jimmy Carter, and to hope that Carter would make enough mistakes to close the gap.

"Acting presidential" meant that Ford should rely on presidential announcements set against the backdrop of the Rose Garden or Oval Office and should prove his superior knowledge and experience in debates with Carter. The negative campaign would exploit vulnerabilities in Carter's support that Robert Teeter had discovered in his polls for Ford. Most people had weak perceptions and uncertain feelings about Carter. The Ford campaign would emphasize Carter's liberalism and reinforce public concern that Carter was really an unknown.

To make the Ford organization more efficient, there was a shakeup at the top shortly after the convention. James A. Baker III replaced Morton as head of the campaign organization. Douglas Bailey and John Deardourff were given complete control over the negative campaign commercials, with the proviso that their work be within the bounds of responsible political discourse.

Carter began on an upbeat note on Labor Day at Warm Springs, Georgia, where he called on all the old Democratic names and symbols and some new ones—pledging through efficient management to balance the federal budget. A few days later, however, he fell into a series of petty exchanges with Ford over FBI director Clarence Kelley's use of an FBI carpenter to install window valences in Kelley's private apartment. In the midst of these exchanges, Carter, the anti-boss candidate, fell deep into the embrace of the biggest boss of all, Mayor Daley of Chicago. Participating in a Chicago torchlight parade on September 9, Carter greeted an enthusiastic Democratic state convention with a tribute to Richard Daley, his "very good friend." Then on September 18, he was put on the defensive by White House charges that Carter wanted to raise taxes for half of all American families. An Associ-

Socialist Workers Party campaign poster *(Library of Congress)*

ated Press interview with Carter released the previous day quoted him as saying his goal was to shift the tax burden "toward those who have higher incomes and reduce the income tax on the lower income and middle income taxpayers." The problem was resolved when Carter pointed out that his phrase "middle income" had been inadvertently dropped in the press release.

Two days later, Robert Scheer's interview with Carter, soon to be published in *Playboy,* was released to newspapers around the country. Carter had outlined his political views and compared himself to past presidents. "But I don't think I would ever take on the same frame of mind that Nixon or Johnson did, lying, cheating, and distorting the truth," he said. What attracted the most attention, however, was Carter's statement that he often looked at women with "lust in his heart," and his use of such sexual colloquialism as "screw" and "shack up."

The reaction among Christian conservatives was strong. In Atlanta, 17 independent Baptist preachers denounced Carter as having "brought reproach to the Christian faith." The Reverend Bailey Smith, once a strong

Carter supporter, spoke of an earlier visit with Carter in Oklahoma when "Carter the politician got down on his knees and prayed heaven down. How could his present use of 'shack up' and 'screw' in *Playboy* be reconciled with this memory?" On the press bus, disbelief washed over the reporters. A CBS correspondent declared, "The campaign is dying right under our feet."

On September 23, in the midst of this flurry, Carter met Ford in debate—the first between presidential candidates since the Nixon–Kennedy exchanges in 1960. Carter spoke of a bureaucratic mess and lack of leadership in Washington and emphasized the need to reorganize the government and to reduce unemployment. Ford stressed the need to hold the lid on federal spending to balance the budget and cited the lowering of unemployment as a major goal. Observers noted that, while Carter seemed nervous and did not look presidential, Ford was no better. When the power failed on the microphones, both men froze—standing without speaking to one another, and looking straight ahead into the air for 27 minutes until power was restored. Afterward, a *New York Times*/CBS poll showed Ford the winner in the debate by 37 to 24 percent, with 39 percent undecided.

The morning after the debate, Carter compounded his problems. Passing through Houston, he told a group of Texas journalists at the airport that *Playboy* had misinterpreted his remarks about Johnson. "My reference to Johnson was about the misleading of the American people; the lying and cheating part referred to President Nixon. And the unfortunate juxtaposition of these two names in the *Playboy* article grossly misinterprets the way I feel about him." On the press plane later that day, national reporters got into a shouting match with Jody Powell and accused Carter of trying to "wing one past the provincials" and themselves. Carter further compounded his problems in San Diego that evening by asking a dozen journalists for advice. Several reporters, already uneasy at having been singled out for this special meeting, saw this as an attempt to manipulate them into becoming part of his campaign. Martin Schram of *Newsday* told Carter that the press was not in the business of advising candidates.

Carter was saved from what could have been a precipitous decline when the media shifted attention to Ford. The president formally opened his campaign at his alma mater, the University of Michigan at Ann Arbor, on September 15. Six days later his problems began. First there were stories that Ford had accepted free weekends from U.S. Steel, Gulf Oil, and other lobbies, and that Charles Ruff, the Watergate special prosecutor, had subpoenaed Ford's campaign financial records. Then, for four days, a vulgar, racist joke by Secretary of Agriculture Earl Butz dominated the media. After this issue was closed by Butz's resignation, the House International Affairs Committee issued a Government Accounting Office report critical of Ford's handling of the *Mayaguez* rescue mission in the spring of 1975.

In the second debate on October 6, Carter tried to put Ford on the defensive, echoing earlier Reagan critiques of Kissinger's shuttle diplomacy, the purported decline in U.S. strength, and a fear of competing with the Soviet Union. Carter also accused the Ford administration of participating in the overthrow of the elected government in Chile, and of attempts to start a new "Vietnam" war in Angola. Ford traded blow for blow—citing Carter's various proposals for cuts in defense spending and his purported willingness to accept a Communist government in NATO. But then, in response to questions about the Helsinki pact, Ford stated, "There is no Soviet domination of Eastern Europe, and there never will be under a Ford Administration."

Ford, initially perceived as having won the debate by a margin of 44 to 35 percent, was losing by 61 to 19 percent the following night after newspaper highlighting of his mistake regarding Eastern Europe. On the campaign trail, Ford was pressed for clarification. The president's failure to admit his mistake until October 12, a week later, prolonged the agony. The final blow came on October 13, when John Dean, appearing on NBC's *Today Show,* suggested that Ford had aided the Nixon White House in an attempt to delay or stop an early Watergate investigation by the House Banking Committee. The bad news, however, came to an abrupt end on October 14, when Special Prosecutor Charles F. Ruff refused to go into the matter raised by Dean and cleared Ford of allegations that he had diverted political contributions for his personal use.

During these three weeks, Carter could have formulated the issues of his campaign. Instead, he took after Ford with evident relish, insisting that Ford's failure to fire Butz showed that no one was leading the nation and that Ford had been brainwashed while behind the Iron Curtain.

In the vice-presidential debate on October 15—the first in U.S. history—Mondale and Dole argued over whether the Democratic or Republican programs would serve the nation best. Dole, whose sarcastic wit had been considered one of his assets, went too far, however, when he argued that World War I, World War II, and the Vietnam and Korean wars were all Democratic wars. Afterward, conservative columnist George Will noted that "until Dole took wing in his debate with Walter Mondale, it was unclear when this campaign would hit bottom."

In the final presidential debate on October 22, Carter toned down his sniping at Ford and spoke of a new spirit in America. In the remaining days on the campaign trail Carter accentuated a traditional Democratic line. (Patrick Caddell had warned him on October 16 that he was hurting himself with personal attacks on the president.) At an old-

Dean Salasek, a farmer from rural Marshalltown, Iowa, watches the presidential debate on September 23, 1976, along with his wife, Carolyn, and sons Brian, 15 (left), and Tim, 7. The scene was a common one across the country as millions of families tuned in to watch President Gerald Ford debate his opponent, Jimmy Carter, in the first presidential debate since 1960. *(© Bettmann/CORBIS)*

fashioned Democratic rally in Dallas on October 31, Carter hit his stride, as he went through a medley of campaign themes. "Ford is a decent man," he said, but he could not provide the bold leadership the country needed. "It takes a deep dedication to a cause . . . to a way of life, that has been exemplified in the past by great Presidents who were Democrats." Then a litany of questions about Ford: "Can you think of a single program that he's put forward that's been accepted? Can you think of a single thing?"

Most of Carter's national advertisements at this point emphasized positive themes he had used in his primary campaign. One advertisement, however, showed Mondale and Dole on a split screen and asked, "Who would you like to see a heartbeat away from the Presidency?" In the South, where Caddell's early October polls had shown Carter threatened with the loss of his most important base, the tone was more negative. One set of television spots emphasized Southern pride and resentment of past ridicule. Another focused on Ford's "soft" dealings with

the Soviet Union and piggybacked on Ronald Reagan's critique of the Ford–Kissinger détente policy. "My view of détente is that it has been a one-way street," Carter said. "The Soviet Union knows what they want in detente, and they have been getting it. And we have been out-traded in almost every instance."

In the meantime, the president was deep into a negative campaign. In mid-October Ford traveled around Illinois in a special train, the *Honest Abe,* describing Carter as a man who "will say anything, anywhere to be President." In the last two weeks of the campaign, commercials based on interviews with people in the street were widely used. In one, six Atlantans observed in soft Southern drawls that Jimmy Carter had not been much of a governor. Another commercial featured a map of Georgia, with an announcer proclaiming that under Carter, "Government spending increased 58 percent . . . Government employees up 28 . . . bonded indebtedness up 20." In a more positive television series, former baseball catcher Joe Garagiola, typified as the average American nice guy, asked Ford questions that he answered with assurance and ease.

At this point, the presidency was both an asset and a liability for the Ford campaign. In October he raised farm price supports, which doubtless helped in the farm states. But as president he was also hostage to bad economic news. Just five days before the election, the Commerce Department's index of leading economic indicators fell by 0.7 percent, the second such drop in two months.

Overall, the campaign had not revolved around high issues or responsible discussions. Instead, it had become a whiny affair where serious questions were drowned out by discussions of whether or not each man was as good as he claimed to be. Although the press contributed to this aspect of the campaign, most journalists blamed the candidates. R. W. Apple complained on October 20, "Neither nominee . . . appears able to decide whether he wants to be a good guy or a rabbit puncher." In a *Chicago Sun-Times* editorial called "The Dirty Duo," Morton Kondracke saw an "increasingly petty, nasty, low-blow campaign, and if voters are turned off by it, it's hard to blame them."

Yet newspapers around the nation made the traditional endorsements. By election day, Ford had secured the backing of two-thirds of the dailies, including the *Chicago Tribune*, the *San Francisco Chronicle*, and the *Cincinnati Enquirer*. The *New York Times* and the *Washington Post* endorsed Carter, while the *Wall Street Journal* and the *Los Angeles Times* followed past policies of not endorsing candidates.

The remarkable thing about the campaign was how far Carter had fallen in the course of only three months. From a 33 percent lead over Ford in the Gallup Polls in late July, he dropped to 23 percent just before the Republican convention. After the Republican convention, his margin was down to 10 percent. Outside the South he was running even with Ford. Since the beginning of modern polling in 1935, no candidate had experienced such a rapid decline between conventions.

At the start of the fall campaign, Carter bounced back in the Gallup Poll to a 15 percent lead. From then on, his lead (with minor fluctuations) gradually evaporated. He held most of the party support he had in early September, but independents moved toward Ford. From a 60 percent peak with the independents in July, Carter was down to 33 percent by mid-October. At that time, Daniel Yankelovich, polling for *Time*, reported that 52 percent of the electorate was "soft" or "undecided"—a figure almost four times that at the same point in 1972.

This decline was partly the result of the breadth of the appeals Carter had made. Unlike his Democratic predecessors, Carter had actively wooed groups no longer a part of the Democratic coalition, with emphasis on conservative themes. One consequence was apathy in the home base, where strong Democratic voters were puzzled by the unfamiliar slant of his appeals. When Carter responded late in the campaign by making a more traditional pitch for the core Democratic vote, he alienated conservatives who had been attracted by him during the summer.

The unease about Carter—evident in both Caddell's and Teeter's polls since the summer—was not just based on a concern about where he stood politically. People were also puzzled by his personality. "There was no way on God's earth," Jody Powell explained later, "that we could shake the fuzziness question in the general election, no matter what Carter did or said." As Hamilton Jordan noted: the voters may have described Carter as fuzzy "when they were unable to verbalize what they really meant." Perhaps they called him fuzzy "because he was a Southerner," or because of the "weirdo factor."

In all probability, this "weirdo" factor was the larger-than-life Carter the media had been projecting in the late

President Gerald Ford, First Lady Betty Ford, Senator Bob Dole, and Elizabeth Dole celebrate winning the nomination amidst floating balloons at the Republican National Convention, Kansas City, Missouri. *(Library of Congress)*

Election of 1976   1411

spring and early summer of 1976. No man could possess the extraordinary virtues Carter seemed to have had in the summer of 1976. No politician can survive as an outsider and not make deals with other politicians or use traditional methods to hold his organization together. No campaign organization could function as smoothly as the Carter organization seemed to perform in the early spring of 1976. No people live in the perfect harmony that seemed to characterize Plains, Georgia. When Carter began to run as an ordinary Democrat in the fall of 1976, to make mistakes and to show human flaws, the press highlighted these incongruities. But if he was not what he seemed at the beginning, then what was he?

By election day, it was not at all clear who would win. The previous Friday, the Louis Harris poll noted that the soft and undecided vote was going over to Ford. The last Gallup Poll before the election showed Carter trailing Ford 46 to 47 percent, with 4 percent undecided. With neither candidate looking particularly strong and issues buried under a cascade of near irrelevancies, many voters stayed home. In the electoral college, Carter won by a narrow margin—297 to 240—the smallest since Woodrow Wilson's victory over Charles Evans Hughes in 1916. (One Washington state elector pledged to Ford cast his vote for Ronald Reagan.) Carter's margin in the popular vote was also slim: 40.8 million votes to Ford's 39.1 million, a margin of only 1.7 million votes. Another 1.6 million votes, 2.1 percent, went to all the other minor candidates. Independent candidate Eugene McCarthy received 740,460 votes nationally, and may have cost Carter Iowa, Maine, Oklahoma, and possibly Oregon. After a long legal battle that had gone all the way to the Supreme Court, McCarthy had been kept off the ballot in New York. Had McCarthy remained on the ballot in that state, he might have tipped the election to Ford. Carter won there by 52.2 to 47.8 percent, a margin of only 4.4 percent.

Although more than 81.5 million Americans voted (up 4 million from 1972), the turnout was only 53.5 percent, the lowest since 1948. Regionally Carter won all the South except Virginia and Oklahoma; he took the few Northern industrial states he needed to put him over the top—New York, Ohio, and Pennsylvania—as well as Massachusetts, Delaware, Maryland, Rhode Island, Wisconsin, Minnesota, Hawaii, and the District of Columbia. Ford won all the West, most of the Midwest, and Oklahoma, Virginia, New Hampshire, New Jersey, Connecticut, Maine, and Vermont.

The Democrats retained their dominance in the Congress—winning the House 292 to 143 (a net gain of one seat) and the Senate 62 to 38 (the same as before). Not since Lyndon Johnson's legislative triumphs after the election of 1964 had a president won such large majorities in both houses. There was no evidence, however, that these Democrats came in on Carter's coattails. In the 12 states that went Democratic in the presidential and senatorial races, Carter led the successful Democrats in only 1. Regional and idiosyncratic factors were most important in determining the outcomes. Nine incumbents seeking reelection had been rejected—the greatest number since the Democratic landslide in 1958. Four of the five Democratic incumbents defeated were from the West, and all from states more conservative than they were. The four defeated Republican incumbents were from the East and one border state. Incumbency was the most important factor in the success of House candidates. Of the 385 incumbents seeking reelection, 366 (95 percent) were reelected. Democrats would end up with 37 governorships, one more than they had before the election. Despite long-term trends in the West toward Republican voting in presidential races, the Democrats wound up controlling every statehouse west of the Mississippi except Iowa, Kansas, and Alaska.

Ironically, the outsider Jimmy Carter owed his victory to the traditional party vote. With no compelling personality to attract or repel, no new issues over which to divide, people fell back to traditional cues. As a Gallup Poll showed, Carter had secured 82 percent of the voters who identified themselves as Democrats, 85 percent of the nonwhite, 63 percent of union families, 58 percent of the manual labor vote, and 57 percent of the Catholic vote. The black vote roughly equaled the vote for Johnson in 1964. Union families voted for Carter at a rate equal to or better than that for any other candidate since 1952 except Johnson in 1964. Most important, both groups turned out for Carter in the states where he needed them most. Without the disproportionately large vote for Carter by union families, his success in New York, Pennsylvania, and Ohio would have been impossible. Blacks helped push him over the top in the North (New York), the South (Louisiana and Mississippi), and Southwest (Texas).

Carter's ability to hold component groups in the traditional Democratic coalition was partly the result of the voter-registration and Election Day turnout drives of the Democratic National Committee, a group backed by the Democratic National Committee, called "Wake up Black America," and organized labor. The AFL-CIO, which had endorsed no one in 1972, undertook in 1976 the biggest, the best organized, and most sophisticated campaign in its history to get out the vote. In Pennsylvania, for example, they helped register 500,000 voters, where Carter's margin of victory was 123,073 votes. Overall, 3 million people were registered—mainly blacks, Latinos, and the poor—in 14 targeted states. Of these new voters, approximately 2.4 million voted Democratic. Total black registration was up 750,000 from 1972; and the black turnout rate was about 70 percent as compared to 58 percent in 1972.

This was not quite the old Roosevelt coalition that Patrick Caddell claimed it to be after the election. In the

Democratic candidate Jimmy Carter won the presidential race of 1976. He is shown here with his wife, Rosalynn Carter, and their daughter, Amy (far right). *(Associated Press)*

South, Carter secured 53.7 percent of the vote, larger than any Democrat since Harry Truman in 1948. But Democratic hopes that he had brought the South permanently back into the Democratic fold were premature. Carter's success was nowhere near Truman's (65.6 percent) and Franklin D. Roosevelt's (81.3 percent in 1932, and 74.1 percent in 1944). Moreover, the composition of this vote differed substantially from theirs. Catalyzed by national Democratic efforts to promote the rights of blacks in the South, whites (including the working class) had been moving to the right since the 1960s and voting Republican in presidential elections. Carter did not receive a majority of this white vote. As a consequence of the Voting Rights Act of 1964, the Democratic registration effort in 1976, and Carter's own appeals, considerably more blacks voted in the South than ever before, and they voted overwhelmingly for Carter. Yet Carter's moderation on the issues and his emphasis on traditional values and efficiency in government brought him more Protestant, small-town, over-50, rural, business and professional votes than the Democratic average in recent years. In taking 46 percent of the Protestant vote, for example, he was 10 percentage points higher than the average Democratic candidate for president since 1952.

Despite the importance of party cues for voters at the end, the election did not mark any reversal of the long-term decline in the importance of political parties in the selection of American presidents. Professional campaign managers and their pollsters played key decision-making roles in both political parties, as they had in every presidential campaign since 1952. Their goal was to fashion appeals to capture voters unanchored by party or ideology. Their success depended on their ability to win favorable coverage in a media that had taken over traditional party functions in defining candidates, articulating issues, and interpreting outcomes.

Even before the New Hampshire primary in 1976, press coverage influenced judgments about who the viable candidates would be. The disproportionate publicity that the winner of the New Hampshire primaries received marked out front-runners. In the Democratic primaries, that publicity was so massive that a relative unknown was transformed almost overnight into a household word. After the Pennsylvania primary, only the ninth of 30, Carter was widely proclaimed as almost unbeatable, and the public tended to agree with the media assessment. In the Republican primaries, the process was less important because over 90 percent of the voters knew and had formed strong impressions about each candidate before the campaign. Throughout the entire campaign, the media paid attention to strategic, organizational, and stylistic considerations rather than substantive issues, reversing the pattern found in earlier elections (e.g., in 1940, as reported by Paul Lazarsfeld and others in *The People's Choice*). During the primary campaign, as Thomas Patterson points out in *The Mass Media Election,* only one policy issue received extended coverage, namely, Ronald Reagan's critique of Ford's foreign policy.

During the general election, despite the efforts of both Carter and Ford, no substantive policy issue received extensive coverage—the headlines and evening television news shows featuring instead the mishaps and possible misdeeds of each candidate. Increasingly indifferent to political organizations, voters relied to an extraordinary degree on the mass media for their assessment of candidates during the 1976 primaries, voting only for individuals they recognized and knew something about from media presentations. The issues and events the public remembered were those featured at the top of the news, and policy interpretations, as public reaction to the foreign policy debate particularly showed, were strongly influenced, if not determined, by media commentary.

This account suggests that the media are not equipped to assume the political functions that the parties used to perform. The media's decisions about how to play stories are based mostly on a vague notion of newsworthiness rather than on political importance. Consequently, trivialities often supplant political substance and, at worst, sensationalism gives professional integrity a back seat. In the selection process, better candidates may be eliminated and lesser ones elevated because of chance political events, last-minute headlines, and a few thousand votes in the early primaries. Most important, the mass media cannot and should not aggregate stands on related issues and offer mechanisms for the implementation of policy, as parties can and ought to do. As the 1976 election shows, the link between public policy and what the voters do at the polls can dissolve as the election becomes a series of scattered, uncertain choices made against a media-colored kaleidoscopic political backdrop.

Inevitably, a winner emerged, but what the election meant to the future of national policy was by no means clear.

—Betty Glad

Selected Bibliography

See Herbert E. Alexander, *Financing the 1976 Election* (1979); Patrick Anderson, *Electing Jimmy Carter: The Campaign of 1976* (1994); Peter Carroll, *It Seemed Like Nothing Happened* (1983); Jimmy Carter, *Keeping Faith* (1982); Gerald R. Ford, *A Time to Heal* (1979); Betty Glad, *Jimmy Carter* (1980); John Robert Greene, *The Limits of Power: The Nixon and Ford Administrations* (1992); Robert T. Hartmann, *Palace Politics: An Inside Account of the Ford Years* (1980); Gerald M. Pomper, *The Election of 1976: Reports and Interpretations* (1977); A. James Reichley, *Conservatives in an Age of Change: The Nixon and Ford Administrations* (1981); Martin Schram, *Running for President, 1976: The Carter Campaign* (1977); Kandy Stroud, *How Jimmy Won: The Victory Campaign from Plains to the White House* (1977); Theodore H. White, *America in Search of Itself: The Making of the President, 1956–1980* (1982); and Jules Witcover, *Marathon: The Pursuit of the Presidency* (1977).

1976 Electoral Map and Statistics

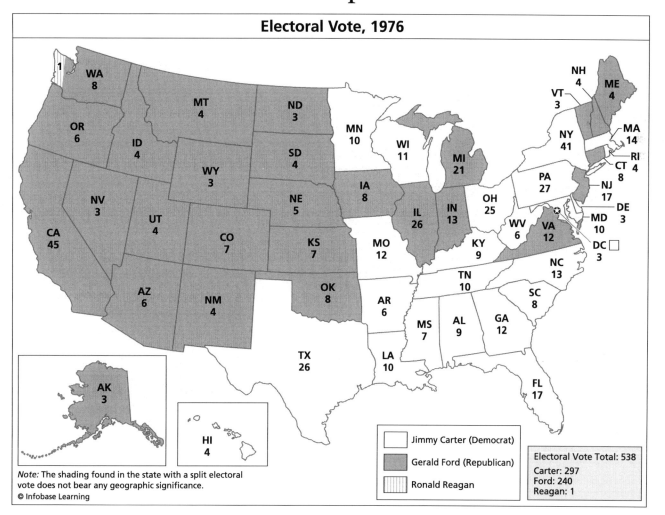

Electoral Vote, 1976

Jimmy Carter (Democrat)
Gerald Ford (Republican)
Ronald Reagan

Electoral Vote Total: 538
Carter: 297
Ford: 240
Reagan: 1

Note: The shading found in the state with a split electoral vote does not bear any geographic significance.
© Infobase Learning

1976 ELECTION STATISTICS

State	Number of Electors	Total Popular Vote	Elec Vote D	Elec Vote R	Elec Vote O*	Pop Vote D	Pop Vote R	Margin of Victory Votes	Margin of Victory % Total Vote
Alabama	9	1,182,850	9			1	2	155,100	13.11%
Alaska	3	123,574		3		2	1	27,497	22.25%
Arizona	6	742,719		6		2	1	123,040	16.57%
Arkansas	6	769,396	6			1	2	230,861	30.01%
California	45	7,867,117		45		2	1	139,960	1.78%
Colorado	7	1,081,135		7		2	1	124,014	11.47%
Connecticut	8	1,381,526		8		2	1	71,366	5.17%
Delaware	3	235,834	3			1	2	12,765	5.41%
District of Columbia	3	168,830	3			1	2	109,945	65.12%
Florida	17	3,150,631	17			1	2	166,469	5.28%
Georgia	12	1,467,458	12			1	2	495,666	33.78%
Hawaii	4	291,301	4			1	2	7,372	2.53%
Idaho	4	340,932		4		2	1	77,602	22.76%
Illinois	26	4,718,833		26		2	1	92,974	1.97%
Indiana	13	2,220,362		13		2	1	169,244	7.62%
Iowa	8	1,279,306		8		2	1	12,932	1.01%
Kansas	7	957,845		7		2	1	72,331	7.55%
Kentucky	9	1,167,142	9			1	2	83,865	7.19%
Louisiana	10	1,278,439	10			1	2	73,919	5.78%
Maine	4	483,208		4		2	1	4,041	0.84%
Maryland	10	1,432,273	10			1	2	86,951	6.07%
Massachusetts	14	2,547,558	14			1	2	399,199	15.67%
Michigan	21	3,653,749		21		2	1	197,028	5.39%
Minnesota	10	1,949,931	10			1	2	251,045	12.87%
Mississippi	7	769,360	7			1	2	14,463	1.88%
Missouri	12	1,953,600	12			1	2	70,944	3.63%
Montana	4	328,734		4		2	1	24,444	7.44%
Nebraska	5	607,668		5		2	1	126,013	20.74%
Nevada	3	201,876		3		2	1	8,794	4.36%
New Hampshire	4	339,618		4		2	1	38,300	11.28%
New Jersey	17	3,014,472		17		2	1	65,035	2.16%
New Mexico	4	416,590		4		2	1	10,271	2.47%
New York	41	6,534,420	41			1	2	288,767	4.42%
North Carolina	13	1,677,906	13			1	2	185,405	11.05%
North Dakota	3	297,094		3		2	1	17,392	5.85%
Ohio	25	4,111,873	25			1	2	11,116	0.27%
Oklahoma	8	1,092,251		8		2	1	13,266	1.21%
Oregon	6	1,029,876		6		2	1	1,713	0.17%
Pennsylvania	27	4,620,787	27			1	2	123,073	2.66%
Rhode Island	4	411,170	4			1	2	46,387	11.28%
South Carolina	8	802,594	8			1	2	104,685	13.04%
South Dakota	4	300,678		4		2	1	4,437	1.48%
Tennessee	10	1,476,346	10			1	2	191,910	13.00%
Texas	26	4,071,884	26			1	2	129,019	3.17%
Utah	4	541,198		4		2	1	155,798	28.79%
Vermont	3	187,855		3		2	1	21,041	11.20%
Virginia	12	1,697,094		12		2	1	22,658	1.34%
Washington	9	1,555,534		8	1	2	1	60,409	3.88%
West Virginia	6	750,674	6			1	2	121,154	16.14%
Wisconsin	11	2,101,336	11			1	2	35,245	1.68%
Wyoming	3	156,343		3		2	1	30,478	19.49%
Total	538	81,540,780	297	240	1	1	2	1,683,247	2.06%

* One elector voted for Ronald Reagan for president.

Carter Democratic		Ford Republican		Others	
659,170	55.73%	504,070	42.61%	19,610	1.66%
44,058	35.65%	71,555	57.90%	7,961	6.44%
295,602	39.80%	418,642	56.37%	28,475	3.83%
499,614	64.94%	268,753	34.93%	1,029	0.13%
3,742,284	47.57%	3,882,244	49.35%	242,589	3.08%
460,353	42.58%	584,367	54.05%	36,415	3.37%
647,895	46.90%	719,261	52.06%	14,370	1.04%
122,596	51.98%	109,831	46.57%	3,407	1.44%
137,818	81.63%	27,873	16.51%	3,139	1.86%
1,636,000	51.93%	1,469,531	46.64%	45,100	1.43%
979,409	66.74%	483,743	32.96%	4,306	0.29%
147,375	50.59%	140,003	48.06%	3,923	1.35%
126,549	37.12%	204,151	59.88%	10,232	3.00%
2,271,295	48.13%	2,364,269	50.10%	83,269	1.76%
1,014,714	45.70%	1,183,958	53.32%	21,690	0.98%
619,931	48.46%	632,863	49.47%	26,512	2.07%
430,421	44.94%	502,752	52.49%	24,672	2.58%
615,717	52.75%	531,852	45.57%	19,573	1.68%
661,365	51.73%	587,446	45.95%	29,628	2.32%
232,279	48.07%	236,320	48.91%	14,609	3.02%
759,612	53.04%	672,661	46.96%	0	0.00%
1,429,475	56.11%	1,030,276	40.44%	87,807	3.45%
1,696,714	46.44%	1,893,742	51.83%	63,293	1.73%
1,070,440	54.90%	819,395	42.02%	60,096	3.08%
381,309	49.56%	366,846	47.68%	21,205	2.76%
998,387	51.10%	927,443	47.47%	27,770	1.42%
149,259	45.40%	173,703	52.84%	5,772	1.76%
233,692	38.46%	359,705	59.19%	14,271	2.35%
92,479	45.81%	101,273	50.17%	8,124	4.02%
147,635	43.47%	185,935	54.75%	6,048	1.78%
1,444,653	47.92%	1,509,688	50.08%	60,131	1.99%
201,148	48.28%	211,419	50.75%	4,023	0.97%
3,389,558	51.87%	3,100,791	47.45%	44,071	0.67%
927,365	55.27%	741,960	44.22%	8,581	0.51%
136,078	45.80%	153,470	51.66%	7,546	2.54%
2,011,621	48.92%	2,000,505	48.65%	99,747	2.43%
532,442	48.75%	545,708	49.96%	14,101	1.29%
490,407	47.62%	492,120	47.78%	47,349	4.60%
2,328,677	50.40%	2,205,604	47.73%	86,506	1.87%
227,636	55.36%	181,249	44.08%	2,285	0.56%
450,825	56.17%	346,140	43.13%	5,629	0.70%
147,068	48.91%	151,505	50.39%	2,105	0.70%
825,879	55.94%	633,969	42.94%	16,498	1.12%
2,082,319	51.14%	1,953,300	47.97%	36,265	0.89%
182,110	33.65%	337,908	62.44%	21,180	3.91%
81,044	43.14%	102,085	54.34%	4,726	2.52%
813,896	47.96%	836,554	49.29%	46,644	2.75%
717,323	46.11%	777,732	50.00%	60,479	3.89%
435,914	58.07%	314,760	41.93%	0	0.00%
1,040,232	49.50%	1,004,987	47.83%	56,117	2.67%
62,239	39.81%	92,717	59.30%	1,387	0.89%
40,831,881	50.08%	39,148,634	48.01%	1,560,265	1.91%

Election of 1980

Election Overview

Election Year 1980

Election Day November 4, 1980

Winning Candidates

- ★ **President:** Ronald Reagan
- ★ **Vice President:** George H. W. Bush

Election Results [ticket, party: popular votes (percentage of popular vote); electoral votes (percentage of electoral vote)]

- Ronald Reagan and George H. W. Bush, Republican: 43,903,230 (50.75%); 489 (90.9%)
- Jimmy Carter and Walter Mondale, Democratic: 35,480,115 (41.01%); 49 (9.1%)
- John Anderson and Patrick Lucey, Independent: 5,719,850 (6.61%); 0 (0.0%)
- Edward Clark and David Koch, Libertarian: 921,128 (1.06%); 0 (0.0%)
- Barry Commoner and LaDonna Harris, Citizens: 233,052 (0.27%); 0 (0.0%)
- Other: 252,303 (0.29%); 0 (0.0%)

Voter Turnout 52.6%

Central Forums/Campaign Methods for Addressing Voters

- Speeches
- Rallies
- Television and print ads
- Debates

Incumbent President and Vice President on Election Day Jimmy Carter and Walter Mondale

Population (1980) 227,726,000

Gross Domestic Product

- $2,788.10 billion (in current dollars: $5,839 billion)
- Per capita: $12,243 (in current dollars: $25,640)

Number of Daily Newspapers (1980) 1,745

Average Daily Circulation (1980) 62,201,840

Households with

- Radio (1980): 79,968,240
- Television (1980): 76,300,000

Method of Choosing Electors: Popular vote (mostly general-ticket system/winner take all)

Method of Choosing Nominees

- Presidential preference primaries
- Caucuses

Key Issues and Events

- Iranian hostage crisis, starting November 1979, and failed rescue attempt in April 1980
- Energy crisis boosts oil prices, which feeds "stagflation," double-digit inflation, sky-high interest rates; low productivity and surprisingly high unemployment
- Carter's "crisis of confidence" and Camp David retreat, summer of 1979
- Even Democrats blame Carter for the country's foreign and domestic problems. Carter's approval ratings hit an all-time low of 29%, November 1, 1979.
- Massachusetts senator Edward Kennedy challenges Carter for the Democratic presidential nomination.
- Favoring less government involvement, Californians vote for Proposition 13 in 1978, which decreases property taxes.

Leading Candidates

REPUBLICANS
- Ronald Reagan, former governor (California)
- George H. W. Bush, former CIA director (Texas)
- John B. Anderson, representative (Illinois)
- Howard Baker, Senate minority leader (Tennessee)
- Philip M. Crane, representative (Illinois)
- John Connally, former governor (Texas)
- Bob Dole, senator (Kansas)
- Ben Fernandez, former special ambassador to Paraguay (California)
- Harold E. Stassen, former governor (Minnesota)
- Lowell Weicker, senator (Connecticut)

DEMOCRATS
- Jimmy Carter, president (Georgia)
- Edward M. Kennedy, senator (Massachusetts)
- Jerry Brown, governor (California)

Trajectory

- On November 4, 1979, Iranian extremists storm the U.S. Embassy in Tehran, ultimately holding 52 Americans hostage for 444 days. The prolonged hostage crisis will overshadow the campaign and doom Jimmy Carter's reelection, making Americans more open to Ronald Reagan's patriotic "Don't tread on me" appeal.
- In a CBS interview broadcast on November 4, 1979, Senator Edward Kennedy fumbles when asked the basic question "Why do you want to be President?" Kennedy's challenge to wrest the nomination from Carter never recovers.
- On January 21, 1980, George H. W. Bush narrowly wins the Iowa caucuses and claims he has the "Big Mo," momentum to catapult him ahead to the Republican nomination.
- At a candidate forum in New Hampshire on February 23, 1980, Ronald Reagan angrily shouts: "I'm paying for this microphone," enhancing his image as a strong leader.
- On February 26, Reagan trounces Bush in the New Hampshire primary and becomes the front-runner.
- At the Republican convention, July 14–17, Reagan considers offering former president Gerald Ford the vice-presidential nomination, with enhanced responsibilities. When CBS newsman Walter Cronkite asks if Ford was thinking of "something like a co-presidency," Ford replies: "That's something Governor Reagan really ought to consider." Furious, Reagan shifts and chooses his leading rival, George H. W. Bush, as his running mate.
- Although the Democratic convention on August 11–14 renominates Carter, Kennedy captures the delegates' hearts—and the nation's attention—with a lyrical concession speech, concluding: "For all those whose cares have been our concern, the work goes on, the cause endures, the hope still lives, and the dream shall never die." After Carter's acceptance speech, Kennedy tarries before joining on the podium and does not raise his hands with the president, depriving Carter of the traditional unity salute and photo op.
- Reagan launches his fall campaign on August 3, 1980, with his first post-convention speech in Philadelphia, Mississippi, the county seat of Neshoba County, where three civil rights workers were murdered in 1964. Pitching to white conservatives, Reagan declares, "I believe in states' rights. . . . I believe we have distorted the balance of our government today by giving powers that were never intended to be given in the Constitution to that federal establishment."
- Reagan's conservatism generates a third-party challenge from moderate Republican John Anderson. The two candidates debate on September 21, 1980. Only willing to debate Reagan, Carter does not attend, and Anderson and Reagan spend much of their debate bashing Carter. Carter's refusal to share a podium with Anderson dooms the other two scheduled presidential debates and a vice-presidential debate. With the election approaching, Reagan ultimately agrees to meet Carter one-on-one.
- Finally meeting for one debate on October 28, Carter foolishly quotes his teenage daughter Amy about the importance of nuclear disarmament. Reagan, acting avuncular, dismisses Carter's criticisms, saying, "There you go again." In his final statement, Reagan asks Americans: "Are you better off than you were four years ago?" The Gallup Poll estimates that Carter drops 10 percentage points after the debate, during the campaign's final two days, one of the most dramatic shifts ever observed, as Reagan ekes out a victory.

Conventions

- Republican National Convention: July 14–17, 1980, Joe Louis Arena, Detroit
- Democratic National Convention: August 11–14, 1980, Madison Square Garden, New York

Ballots/Nominees

REPUBLICANS
Presidential first ballot
- Ronald Reagan 1,939 (97.44%)

- John Anderson 37 (1.86%)
- George H. W. Bush 13 (0.65%)
- Anne L. Armstrong 1 (0.05%)

DEMOCRATS
Presidential first ballot
- Jimmy Carter 2,123 (64.04%)
- Edward Kennedy 1,151 (34.72%)
- William Proxmire 10 (0.30%)
- Koryne Kaneski Horbal 5 (0.15%)
- Scott M. Matheson Sr. 5 (0.15%)
- Ronald V. "Ron" Dellums 3 (0.09%)
- Robert C. Byrd 2 (0.06%)

INDEPENDENT, NATIONAL UNITY
- President: John Anderson, congressman (Illinois)
- Vice President: Patrick Lucey, Democratic former governor (Wisconsin) and ambassador to Mexico (appointed by President Carter)

LIBERTARIAN PARTY
- President: Edward Clark
- Vice President: David H. Koch (1 million votes and on the ballot in all 50 states)

SOCIALIST PARTY USA
- President: David McReynolds (first openly gay man to run for president)
- Vice President: Sister Diane Drufenbrock

CITIZENS PARTY
- President: Barry Commoner
- Vice President: La Donna Harris

COMMUNIST PARTY USA
- President: Gus Hall
- Vice President: Angela Davis. Rock star Joe Walsh runs a mock campaign as a write-in candidate, promising to make his song "Life's Been Good" the new national anthem if he wins, and promising "Free Gas for Everyone."

Primaries

- Republican Party: 35; 76.0% delegates (no Vermont nonbinding primary)
- Democratic Party: 34; 71.8% delegates (no Vermont nonbinding primary)

Primaries Results

REPUBLICANS
- Ronald Reagan 7,709,793; 59.79%
- George H. W. Bush 3,070,033; 23.81%

- John Anderson 1,572,174; 12.19%
- Howard Baker 181,153; 1.40%
- Philip M. Crane 97,793; 0.76%
- John Connally 82,625; 0.64%
- Unpledged 68,155; 0.53%
- Others 33,217; 0.26%

DEMOCRATS
- Jimmy Carter 10,043,016; 51.11%
- Edward Kennedy 7,381,693; 37.57%
- Unpledged 1,288,423; 6.56%
- Jerry Brown 575,296; 2.93%
- Lyndon H. LaRouche Jr. 177,784; 0.90%
- Others 79,352; 0.40%

Party Platform

REPUBLICANS
- "Make America great again"
- Restore the nation's military strength; promote national security; increase defense spending
- Supply-side economic policy
- Balance budget within three years ("the beginning of the end of inflation"); lower taxes; repeal the "Windfall Profit Tax"
- Cut welfare rolls
- Drop endorsement of Equal Rights Amendment after 40 years of support
- Dedication to women's rights, appoint a woman to cabinet, first female justice to the Supreme Court

DEMOCRATS
- No "grand plan"
- Include Kennedy proposals on wage and price controls.
- Support the Equal Rights Amendment.
- Criticize Reagan's economic plan.
- Applaud Carter for stopping Republican push to dismantle the Great Society.

Campaign Tactics

- Negative, sobering campaign: Most Americans polled have negative feelings about both candidates,
- Democratic Party: Carter defensive, more convincing on Reagan's flaws than his own strengths
- Attacks on Reagan as a modern Goldwater who would trigger nuclear apocalypse, or simply as too old.
- Billygate: Embarrassing revelations that Carter's brother accepted $220,000 for lobbying from the Libyan government

- Republican Party: Masterful use of the media, especially radio and television
- Skillful avoidance of difficult questions, emphasis on tone, vision
- "Meanness issue": Carter smiled much in 1976, but many critics see a surprising mean streak as president.
- Reagan mixes attacks on "big government" with upbeat vision of a return to tradition and patriotism.
- Republicans fear Reagan as gaffe-prone, carefully stage-manage his appearances.
- Sometimes the "gaffes" are exactly what he means, such as calling Vietnam a "noble cause."
- Reagan hailed as "the Great Deflector," "the greatest television candidate in history."
- Reagan campaign fears an "October Surprise," a last-minute deal rescuing the hostages, and Carter's presidency.

INDEPENDENT PARTY
- Offers a moderate Republican alternative to Reagan's conservatism.
- Secures support of the Liberal Party in New York State; on the ballot in all 50 states.
- Supports gun control, strategic arms limitation agreement with Russia, Equal Rights Amendment, 50 cents tax on a gallon on oil; revitalizing mass transportation systems.

Debates
- September 21, 1980: Presidential debate in Baltimore (Reagan–Anderson)
- October 28, 1980: Presidential debate in Cleveland (Carter–Reagan)
- The League of Women Voters sponsors the debates for 1980; the original plan called for three presidential, one vice-presidential.
- Anderson is invited to debate with the major party candidates because of his poll standing. Carter is not interested in participating in the debates this time but especially refuses to debate with Anderson. Reagan insists on Anderson's participation.
- First debate, September 21 in Baltimore, with Reagan and Anderson. Moderator is Bill Moyers. Candidates spend most of the debate criticizing Carter.
- Anderson's participation in the remaining planned debates remains controversial. The second presidential debate and the vice-presidential debate are canceled as a result.
- Nearing the end, Reagan agrees to Carter's demands for the debate.

- Second debate, October 28, in Cleveland. Moderator is Howard K. Smith. It is the turning point of the campaign with 100 million viewers.
- No other presidential debates in subsequent elections have changed the course of a campaign as much as the 1980 debate did.

Popular Campaign Slogans
REPUBLICANS
- "Let's Make America Great Again"
- "The Time Is Now"

DEMOCRATS
- "Carter-Mondale: Keep Them Working for You"
- "Re-Elect Carter-Mondale: A Tested and Trustworthy Team"

Campaign Songs
REPUBLICANS
- "California, Here We Come"

DEMOCRATS
- "Don't Let 'Em Take It Away"

Influential Campaign Appeals or Ads
REPUBLICANS
- Effective mocking Carter as helpless.
- Political cartoon, published the day after the election, shows Amy Carter sitting in Jimmy's lap with her shoulders shrugged asking, "The economy? The hostage crisis?"

DEMOCRATS
- Rather than defend his own record, Carter attacks Reagan, portraying him as an extremist, a racist, and a warmonger. Public perceives Carter as "mean."
- Both Carter and the media attack Reagan's "gaffes," including doubts about the theory of evolution, suggesting trees caused more air pollution than cars, and calling Vietnam a "noble cause." One sign hanging on a tree at a campaign stop says, "Chop Me Down Before I Kill Again."

Campaign Finance
- Reagan: $29,188,188 (in current dollars: $72,084,600)
- Carter: $29,352,767 (in current dollars: $72,491,000)

- Anderson's limit of $18.5 million allows private fund-raising.
- Carter and Reagan each spend about $15 million on television ads, Anderson under $2 million.
- Anderson spends $17.6 million (Federal Election Commission funds after election).

- Political action committees (PACs) flood the system, and especially Republicans, with cash. 1976: 450 corporate PACs to 303 pro-labor PACs; 1980: 1,226 corporate and business PACs to 318 labor PACs.

Defining Quotations

- "If Kennedy runs, I'll whip his ass." *President Jimmy Carter to a group of congressmen at a White House dinner, June 11, 1979, regarding rumors that Senator Edward Kennedy intends to run against him for the Democratic nomination*
- "At the height of the Civil War, Abraham Lincoln said, 'I have but one task and that is to save the Union.' Now I must devote my considered efforts to resolving the Iranian crisis." *Jimmy Carter in late 1979*
- "The 1980 election should not be a plebiscite on Ayatollah [Ruhollah Khomeini] or Afghanistan. The real question is whether America can risk four more years of uncertain policy and certain crisis—of an administration that tells us to rally around their failures—of an inconsistent non-policy that may confront us with a stark choice between retreat and war. These issues must be debated in this campaign." *Edward Kennedy, "Sometimes a Party Must Sail Against the Wind," Georgetown University, January 28, 1980*
- "Mush from the wimp." Boston Globe *headline ridiculing Carter that was inserted as a joke but mistakenly published in over 160,000 copies of its March 15, 1980, edition*
- "So what I'm saying is, it just isn't going to work. . . . what I call a Voodoo economic policy." *George H. W. Bush at Carnegie Mellon University, April 10, 1980, condemning Reagan's "supply side" plan to cut taxes but raise government revenue*
- "If I should do anything to lessen the importance paid by us to the hostages' lives and safety and freedom, it would obviously be a reflection on our own Nation's principles." *Jimmy Carter, question-and-answer session in the White House with reporters from Pennsylvania, April 19, 1980*
- "It was a bloodbath. We have had a civil war in the party, and civil wars do not mend nicely. And that's what we had. A civil war between the northern and the southern wings of the Democratic Party." *Carter's pollster, Patrick Caddell, looking back on the Kennedy–Carter fight*
- "We must have the clarity of vision to see the difference between what is essential and what is merely desirable, and then the courage to bring our government back under control and make it acceptable to the people." *Ronald Reagan, presidential nomination acceptance speech, July 17, 1980*
- "I've learned that for a President, experience is the best guide to the right decisions. I'm wiser tonight than I was 4 years ago." *Jimmy Carter, remarks accepting the presidential nomination at the 1980 Democratic National Convention in New York, August 14, 1980*
- "I'm told I can't use the word depression. Well, I'll tell you the definition. A recession is when your neighbor loses his job and a depression is when you lose your job. Recovery is when Jimmy Carter loses his!" *Ronald Reagan, Labor Day speech at Liberty State Park, New Jersey, September 1, 1980*
- "I would rather have a competent extremist than an incompetent moderate." *Former Watergate scandal prosecutor Leon Jaworski after accepting the honorary Democrats for Reagan chairmanship, September 29, 1980*
- "You'll determine whether this America will be unified, or, if I lose this election, whether Americans might be separated black from white, Jew from Christian, North from South, rural from urban." *Jimmy Carter at a Chicago fund-raiser, October 6, 1980*
- "I had a discussion with my daughter Amy the other day, before I came here, to ask her what the most important issue was. She said she thought nuclear weapons and the control of nuclear arms." *Jimmy Carter, presidential debate, October 28, 1980*
- "There you go again." *Ronald Reagan dismissing Jimmy Carter's criticisms during presidential debate, October 28, 1980*
- "Are you better off than you were four years ago? Is it easier for you to go and buy things in the stores than it was four years ago? Is there more or less employment in the country than there was four years ago? Is America as respected throughout the world as it was? Do you feel that our security is safe, that we're as strong as we were four years ago? If you answer all of these questions yes, why then I think your choice is very obvious as to who you'll vote for. If you don't agree, if you don't think that this course that we've been on for the last four years is what you would like to see us follow for the next four, then I could suggest another choice that you have." *Ronald Reagan's conclusion, presidential debate, October 28, 1980*
- "What's to spoil? Spoil the chances of two men at least half the country doesn't want?" *John Anderson on the campaign trail, fall 1980*
- "The fact that by comparison Jerry Ford has been elevated to the rank of elder statesman is sufficient

reason to vote against Carter. . . . [But Reagan's] economics are incomprehensible . . . and Reagan's urgings that we be No. l in arms means only an accelerated arms race. He's shallow, superficial, and frightening in that respect. . . . I guess I'm counting on the fact that the Government will be too paralyzed to be dangerous under Reagan. I think it's horrible that we're put in the position that whatever we do we feel we're making the wrong decision" *Mark Blank, a retired professor living in a Philadelphia suburb, to* Time, *November 3, 1980*

- "The hostage crisis had come to symbolize the collective frustration of the American people. And in that sense, the President's chances for re-election probably died on the desert of Iran with eight brave soldiers who gave their lives trying to free the American hostages." *Hamilton Jordan, Carter's chief strategist looking back*

Lasting Legacy of Campaign

- Largest swing of voters in final 48 hours of campaigning since polling began
- This campaign is an "ABC" election—Anybody but Carter, more a repudiation of Carter than a Reagan or conservative mandate.
- Start of the Reagan Revolution

Election of 1980

After nearly half a century of the Democratic New Deal and successor variations, including three Republican presidencies that paid lip service to many of its basic tenets, the election of 1980 at last brought a clean and dramatic break. Ronald Reagan became the first true embodiment of classic Republican conservatism to reach the White House since Herbert Hoover had left it in defeat in 1933.

Dwight Eisenhower, Richard Nixon, and Gerald Ford all had voiced the required conservative rhetoric but often bowed to the realities (except in Eisenhower's first two years) of mixed party responsibility in Washington and of government as adjuster of economic and social inequities. For Reagan, though, the rhetoric was the reality, and his election ushered in a right-wing revolt that had been promised—or threatened—ever since the disastrous presidential candidacy of Barry Goldwater in 1964. Reagan campaigned throughout 1980 to "get the government off the backs of the people" and then proceeded, in his fashion, to try to do just that.

Though the country had been moving gradually toward the right, the election of 1980 was not so much an unvarnished demand for Ronald Reagan and his conservative views as it was a rejection of the Democratic incumbent, Jimmy Carter, whose four years in the presidency had been indecisive and disappointing. Carter, a one-term governor of Georgia before his surprising rise to power in 1976, was himself essentially an economic conservative who had won election in the aftermath of the Watergate scandal, Nixon's resignation, and Ford's suspicious pardon of Nixon shortly after the presidential resignation. The movement to the right was thus obscured, and Carter was able to ride public disenchantment to his own victory. Carter lost public favor because he was not able to cope with soaring inflation and unemployment, and because he could not bring a satisfactory resolution to the major foreign policy crisis of his administration—the holding of 52 American hostages in Iran for more than a year. For a time, Carter's appeal reached such a low that a member of his own party, Senator Edward M. Kennedy of Massachusetts, youngest brother of the late president, was able to seriously challenge him for the nomination. Although Kennedy failed in that endeavor, his challenge further undermined Carter's strength as the incumbent in the general election. Reagan, after having captured the Republican nomination with relative ease, had only to demonstrate that he was an acceptable alternative to the unpopular man in the White House. In this undertaking, Reagan had the unwitting collaboration of Carter himself in an election that turned more on personality, style, and circumstance than it did on ideology and campaign techniques.

At the outset, the election of 1980 promised to be a model of the refinement of presidential politics as technology. Since Franklin D. Roosevelt's use of radio to persuade voters, presidential campaigns had increasingly become the domain of the professional practitioners—consultants, speechwriters, television advertising men, media manipulators. Now, at last, on the Republican side there appeared to be the perfect marriage: the political technocrats and a candidate, Reagan, who had been a professional actor. They would write the script, he would perform it on the stump, and the whole product would be neatly packaged for the media.

It would be all so tidy and predictable—except that presidential campaigns and elections seldom follow a precise script. They often are too susceptible to events and circumstances beyond the foresight or the control of the technocrats, or of the candidates either, and this fact was particularly true in 1980. And so, in the end, the contest between Jimmy Carter and Ronald Reagan came down to the manner in which the man required by his constitutional obligations to cope with the events and circumstances of the time—President Carter—did so, or failed to do so. Reagan did, to be sure, enunciate most of the conservative dogma in the course of the campaign, and later his overwhelming election would be labeled by many a "revolution" based on ideology. But, in fact, the victory was based more on public revulsion toward Carter personally, and his performance in office.

Carter's beginnings as president did not presage the crisis of confidence that brought him down four years later. His campaign in 1976 as a candidate who put his confidence in the good judgment, and the goodness, of the American people created an aura of optimism and even intimacy that he augmented with an unannounced, unprecedented, dramatic walk down Pennsylvania Avenue after his inauguration. He seemed, in that gesture, to confirm that this president intended to live up to his campaign words about staying close to the people who had elected him, and being guided by their wisdom. In his first weeks and months in office, Carter conspicuously attempted to do so, or at least to nurture that impression. He made spontaneous visits to government offices to talk to the civil servants who now toiled under him; he took voters' calls phoned into the Oval Office on a special line; dressed in a cozy sweater, he delivered a televised fireside chat to the nation; he sent his young daughter, Amy, to public school; and he held town meetings in small communities around the country.

These gestures, however, were not enough to navigate the shoals of a Washington about which, as a former small-state governor with a thinly veiled contempt for the federal bureaucracy, he was inadequately informed. Almost at once, he irritated Congress by drawing up a "hit list" of locally cherished federal water projects and attempting to kill them off without consulting Capitol Hill. In a single stroke, this move unveiled Carter's inexperience in dealing with the federal legislature and his disinclination to govern by compromise rather than by force of his own rigid convictions.

Not only did Carter not know his way around the Washington establishment; worse, he surrounded himself with aides, many from his own Georgia, who were equally uninformed about the ways of the capital city, and in some cases even more insensitive to its power brokers. Those cabinet appointees who did know the Washington ropes, and who were selected amid Carter's pledges that they would be independent and would have ready access to him, soon found that the Georgia guard diminished the worth of those promises. Eager to get things done, Carter overloaded congressional circuits with a flood of legislative proposals and then complained impatiently about lack of action, further irritating even members of his own party on the Hill. On top of all this, Carter demonstrated a self-destructive willingness to tolerate and even excuse the ineptness of some aides and the penchant of others to conduct themselves with an arrogance that only complicated the new president's relationships with Congress.

As a candidate, Carter repeatedly emphasized the need to raise government up to the high standard of ethics from which it had fallen during the Watergate nightmare. This outspoken disdain for dishonesty in government returned to haunt him, however, in the summer of 1977 when it was disclosed that his director of the budget, Georgia banker Bert Lance, had been involved in highly questionable banking practices, including the acceptance of large overdrafts by himself, his wife, and other relatives at his own bank. When the comptroller of the currency issued a damning report, Carter incredibly chose to interpret it as a vindication, even to the point of holding a televised press conference with Lance and telling his man, "Bert, I'm proud of you." Additional revelations several weeks later forced Lance to resign. Carter stood by him to the end, and in a teary statement said he didn't think "there's any way that I could find anyone to replace Bert Lance that would be, in my judgment, as competent, as strong, as decent, and as close to me as a friend and adviser as he has been." That statement may have eased the pain for Lance, but it did nothing to stem the erosion of Carter's standards of ethics in government.

One notable irony of the Carter White House years was that a man whose only governmental experience had been in domestic policies as a governor saw his tenure dominated by foreign affairs. Carter's most pressing domestic problems—rising inflation and joblessness—were exacerbated by soaring world oil prices, but after challenging the American people to take on the energy crisis as "the moral equivalent of war," he backed off, leaving confusion and diminished public confidence in his wake. Frustrated by his inability to cope with a debilitating economic picture, the foreign policy neophyte turned his attentions to problems abroad, where ultimately he found the greatest achievement of this White House term, as well as his greatest heartbreak.

At the core of American concerns in the Middle East, beyond the dependency on the region's oil, was the continuing enmity between Israel and the Arab world. Carter considered the conflict at once the most vexing problem and the area of greatest opportunity for American diplomacy, and after private meetings in his first year in office with President Anwar Sadat of Egypt and Prime Minister Menachem Begin of Israel, he worked single-mindedly to bring about a resolution of their differences.

The task seemed an impossible one. But with patience and determination Carter nursed the effort along, until at last Sadat broke the ice with a dramatic visit in November 1977 to Jerusalem. Sadat's discussions with Begin constituted public recognition by Egypt of Israel's right to exist as a state. Throughout the ebb and flow of the tenuous Sadat–Begin relationship in the months that followed, Carter devoted a remarkable amount of his time and energies to the role of peacemaker, finally astonishing the world by bringing the two leaders together for marathon discussions at Camp David, in the Maryland hills north of Washington. Laboring tirelessly himself as mediator over a 13-day period, shuttling between Sadat and Begin for hours on end of reasoning and cajoling, Carter helped hammer out in September 1978 a peace treaty between the two longtime enemy states that was not only historic for the Middle East but the showcase achievement of the Carter administration.

This triumph raised Carter's stock in the world community, but it did nothing to combat the growing image at home of an administration incapable of dealing with the critical pocketbook issues that so often determine the outcome of national elections. Unemployment and the inflation rate both continued to rise, and as Carter seemed unable to arrest the trend, the Republicans began

to look to the 1980 election with increasing hope. Only five years after the Watergate fiasco that many thought at the time would cripple the GOP for years to come, the party was regrouping to make a serious run at the White House again, with a host of potential candidates in the wings.

Foremost of these was the man who had unsuccessfully challenged incumbent Gerald Ford in 1976, the former governor of California, Ronald Reagan. But because Reagan would be 70 years old in 1981, there were widespread doubts about his electability, and indeed about whether he would even seek the nomination again. A long list of other prospects was forming, including Senate Minority Leader Howard H. Baker of Tennessee; Senator Robert Dole of Kansas, Ford's 1976 running mate; former secretary of the treasury (and former Democrat) John B. Connally; former United Nations ambassador George Bush of Texas; former White House chief of staff General Alexander Haig, now commander of the North Atlantic Treaty Organization; former secretary of the treasury William Simon; and Representatives John B. Anderson and Philip Crane of Illinois and Jack Kemp of
(continues on page 1426)

Republican presidential hopefuls and moderator Howard K. Smith during the presidential forum sponsored by the League of Women Voters in Chicago on March 12, 1980. From left: Philip Crane, George H. W. Bush, Howard K. Smith, Ronald Reagan, and John Anderson. *(Charles Kelly/Associated Press)*

☆ ☆ ☆

1980 ELECTION CHRONOLOGY

1977

September 21, 1977: After weeks of controversy over his questionable banking practices, Bert Lance, President Jimmy Carter's director of the budget, resigns. The scandal has nevertheless undermined Carter's credibility in calling for greater ethics in government.

1978

June 6, 1978: California voters approve Proposition 13, an initiative to impose a ceiling on income taxes. Ronald Reagan, who had pushed the proposal as governor, praises its passage: "It's time to cut the government's allowance."

August 7, 1978: Hoping to replicate Jimmy Carter's grassroots success, Republican representative Philip Crane of Illinois declares his candidacy for the presidency. Others who follow yet fail to get traction, just like Crane, include Howard H. Baker, John Connally, Alexander Haig, Jack Kemp, and William Simon.

September 17, 1978: After 12 days of secret negotiations at Camp David and with Jimmy Carter's encouragement, Israeli prime minister Menachem Begin and Egyptian president Anwar Sadat agree on the framework for a peace treaty between Egypt and Israel.

1979

July 15, 1979: After consulting with legislators and pollsters for eight days, Jimmy Carter gives a major energy policy speech warning of "a crisis of confidence" in America "that strikes at the very heart and soul of our national will." Although he does not use that word, the "malaise" speech makes Carter the butt of jokes for weeks to come.

November 1, 1979: Gallup Polls show Jimmy Carter's public approval ratings at a dismal 29 percent.

November 4, 1979: Iranian extremists storm the U.S. Embassy in Tehran, protesting the American decision allowing the deposed shah of Iran to seek cancer treatment in the United States. The Iranians ultimately will hold 52 Americans hostage for 444 days.

November 4, 1979: While being interviewed by Roger Mudd on a CBS television documentary, Massachusetts Senator Ted Kennedy, planning to challenge President Carter for the Democratic nomination, gives a rambling, uncertain answer to the question "Why do you want to be president?"

December 24, 1979: Soviet forces invade Afghanistan. President Carter announces that he will stay off the campaign trail to deal with the crisis.

1980

January 7, 1980: Sticking to his "Rose Garden Strategy," and now leading in the polls, Carter withdraws from a previously scheduled debate with Kennedy and California Governor Jerry Brown.

January 21, 1980: Former U.S. ambassador to China and former CIA director George H. W. Bush narrowly wins the Iowa caucuses and claims he has the "Big Mo," momentum to catapult him ahead to the Republican nomination. President Carter beats Senator Kennedy by 59 to 31 percent in the caucuses.

January 28, 1980: Speaking at Georgetown University, Kennedy denounces Carter's aloofness, saying: "If the Vietnam War taught us anything, it is precisely that when we do not debate our foreign policy, we may drift into deeper trouble."

February 23, 1980: At a candidate forum in New Hampshire, former California governor Ronald Reagan angrily shouts, "I'm paying for this microphone," enhancing his image as a strong leader.

February 26, 1980: Reagan trounces Bush in the New Hampshire primary and becomes the frontrunner. Carter beats Kennedy by 49 to 38 percent.

March 1, 1980: The United States votes with the U.N. Security Council to rebuke Israel for increasing its settlements in the Arab territories acquired during the 1967 war. The move is condemned by American Jewish groups, as well as by Kennedy. President Carter backpedals, calling the vote "an error."

March 4, 1980: Representative John B. Anderson of Illinois, a long-shot Republican candidate for the nomination, finishes second to Reagan in the Vermont primary and second to Bush in the Massachusetts primary. Anderson's candor excites reporters and college students, especially.

March 18, 1980: Reagan takes the Illinois primary with 48 percent, followed by Anderson with 37 percent and Bush with 11 percent. Carter beats Kennedy.

☆   ☆   ☆

March 25, 1980: Kennedy beats Carter in the New York primary on the strength of his support in the Jewish community.

April 1, 1980: Carter calls a White House press conference at 7:13 a.m. to announce a "positive step" in the Iranian hostage negotiations. It turns out to be false, but he wins the Kansas and Wisconsin primaries.

April 22, 1980: Kennedy wins the Pennsylvania primary.

April 24, 1980: Operation Eagle Claw, a covert military operation to free the hostages in Iran by force, fails, leaving the Iranians with a propaganda victory and further undermining Carter's presidency.

April 25, 1980: Anderson announces he will run as an independent on what he calls a "National Unity Campaign."

June 3, 1980: As the primary season ends, Carter leads the Democrats with 51 percent of pledged delegates, followed by Kennedy with 37 percent. Reagan leads the Republicans with 59 percent of pledged delegates, followed by Bush with 23 percent.

July 1, 1980: Gasoline prices rise to average an unacceptably high $1.24 per gallon.

July 14–17, 1980: The Republican Party holds its national convention at the Joe Louis Arena in Detroit. Ronald Reagan of California wins the nomination on the first ballot, choosing George H. W. Bush of Texas as vice presidential nominee, after briefly considering a "dream ticket" with former president Gerald Ford as a possible running mate.

August 3, 1980: Reagan launches his fall campaign with his first post-convention speech in Philadelphia, Mississippi, the county seat of Neshoba County, where three civil rights workers were murdered in 1964. Pitching to white conservatives, Reagan declares, "I believe in states' rights."

August 11–14, 1980: The Democratic Party holds its national convention at Madison Square Garden in New York City. President Jimmy Carter wins the nomination on the first ballot, again choosing Vice President Walter Mondale as his running mate.

August 12, 1980: Kennedy restores his national reputation with a powerful concession speech embracing liberalism, proclaiming "the work goes on, the cause endures, the hope still lives, the dream shall never die."

August 14, 1980: Carter's acceptance speech lacks the punch of Kennedy's concession.

September 21, 1980: Unwilling to debate the third-party candidate John Anderson, Carter sits out the first candidates' debate in Baltimore. Anderson and Reagan spend much of the debate bashing Carter.

October 6, 1980: President Carter, at a campaign speech in Chicago, warns that a vote for Reagan could mean "Americans might separate black from white, Jew from Christian, North from South, rural from urban." The indictment against his opponent is taken as another example of Carter's "meanness."

October 28, 1980: After much negotiation, Reagan and Carter meet for a final one-on-one debate in Cleveland. While Carter quotes his teenage daughter Amy about the importance of nuclear disarmament, Reagan dismisses Carter's attacks with an avuncular "There you go again. . . ."

October 29, 1980: Gallup polls show Carter has dropped 10 points since the debate, perhaps the most significant last-minute slide in history.

November 2, 1980: Deputy Secretary of State Warren Christopher informs the president of a breakthrough in negotiations with the Iranians. The Reagan camp's constant warnings of an "October surprise" blunt the impact of these developments, as does the Iranians' recalcitrance—the hostages will be released on Inauguration Day.

November 4, 1980: Election Day. Republicans Ronald Reagan and George H. W. Bush eke out a victory with 51 percent of the popular vote, but sweep the Electoral College, carrying 44 states. Democrats Jimmy Carter and Walter Mondale finish with 41 percent of the popular vote, but manage only 49 electoral votes from six states: Minnesota, Rhode Island, West Virginia, Maryland, Hawaii, and Georgia.

December 15, 1980: Presidential electors cast their ballots in their respective state capitals.

1981

January 6, 1981: A joint session of Congress assembles to count the electoral votes.

(continued from page 1423)
New York. Crane, in fact, had already declared his candidacy in August 1978, taking a leaf from the book of early-starting Jimmy Carter in 1975.

Faced with irrefutable signs of political as well as economic trouble, Carter in early July 1979 decided that drastic measures were in order. He retreated to Camp David to prepare a speech to the nation that was first billed as yet another proposal to end the energy crisis, by now manifesting itself in waiting lines and heated tempers at the nation's gasoline pumps. But with nothing essentially new to say, Carter at the last hour decided to postpone the speech and instead summoned his closest White House advisers to consult with him. Among them was Patrick Caddell, his young pollster, who reported a rapidly growing pessimism among the American people about the ability of government to solve national problems.

The hours of consultation at Camp David dragged into days, inevitably creating the impression that some major crisis was at hand. That impression was fed by subsequent decisions to call in other important Democrats—first governors meeting in Louisville, then, in no particular order, mayors and members of the House and Senate, old Washington political hands, economists, religious leaders, labor leaders, businessmen, state legislators, and county officials. Over a period of eight days, nearly 150 individuals of various stripes were called in to tell the president of the United States what was wrong with how he was running the country. It was an incredible spectacle that invited ridicule—and got it in spades.

When the presidential speech finally emerged, it was a curious amalgam of *mea culpa* for Carter's own shortcomings and a warning of, as he put it, "a crisis of confidence" among the American people "that strikes at the very heart and soul of our national will." The talk soon became known as Carter's "malaise speech," although the president never used that word and Caddell vowed he had not either. In the shorthand of reporting, the consensus analysis was that Carter was trying to shift the blame for his failures onto the people, and it did not sit at all well with them.

Carter's vice president, Walter F. Mondale, who had left the Senate to be Carter's running mate in 1976, later insisted that he had opposed the president's handling of the national malaise situation. But Mondale's reported dissent was overruled. Another listener who was particularly distressed at this assessment of the American spirit was Senator Kennedy. Because of fundamental differences he had with the president, Kennedy had for months been considering the idea of challenging Carter for the 1980 Democratic nomination. Kennedy's acknowledged desire to someday regain the White House that tragedy had taken from his brother, John F. Kennedy, was well known.

Others who shared Kennedy's disenchantment with Carter, notably William Winpisinger of the International Association of Machinists, a fiery and profane Carter-hater known to all as "Wimpy," as early as March 1979 had formed a committee to draft Kennedy, but the Massachusetts senator discouraged it, and it went nowhere.

Until Carter's malaise speech, Kennedy had always been able to talk himself out of such a challenge to the incumbent, but now it was not so easy. Kennedy's distress increased sharply a couple of days after the speech, when Carter suddenly announced that he was requesting the resignations of all the members of his cabinet, cabinet-level officials, and senior White House staff—34 individuals in all. The political objective, clearly, was to indicate to the public that Carter meant business and was making a fresh start—while getting rid of some officials who in the view of Carter and the most influential insiders were not playing ball. The targets were Secretary of the Treasury W. Michael Blumenthal, Secretary of Health, Education, and Welfare Joseph Califano, and Secretary of Transportation Brock Adams. Two others who earlier had indicated they wanted to leave, Secretary of Energy James Schlesinger and Attorney General Griffin Bell, were thrown into the pot to augment the appearance of a major housecleaning. Though intended to demonstrate a sure administrative hand on the national tiller, the action was a failure. Instead, the firings were read as more admissions of presidential mistakes and uncertainty, and nowhere were they read more clearly that way than in the mind of Edward Kennedy.

Thus, as the fall of 1979 arrived, first-term president Jimmy Carter, determined to seek and win reelection in 1980, was threatened—both outside and inside his Democratic Party. The Republicans openly rejoiced at the picture of confusion and ineffectiveness that his "malaise summit" and accompanying shakeup had painted, and one by one they declared their intent to challenge him. After Crane there came Connally, Baker, Bush, Dole, Anderson, Senator Larry Pressler of South Dakota, and—the final entrant—Ronald Reagan. At the same time, Ted Kennedy seethed at the mess a president from his own party had wrought with notions, Kennedy said later, that "just ran so contrary to everything I believe in and that I was brought up to believe in."

Nor was that all that jeopardized Carter's reelection chances as the election year approached. On the fourth of November, a mob of young Iranians stormed the American embassy in Tehran, angered by a decision by Carter a week earlier to admit the deposed and ailing Shah of Iran, exiled in Mexico, into the United States for emergency medical treatment. The militants took about 90 hostages and eventually held 52 Americans, demanding the return of the shah under threat that the hostages would be tried, or killed outright.

President Jimmy Carter addresses an audience outside the San Jose City Hall in California as demonstrators raise posters in the background demanding discussion of real issues during the campaign. Carter, seeking a second term, was here to attend a meeting with local energy experts. At left is San Jose mayor Janet Gray Hayes. *(Charles Tasnadi/Associated Press)*

Nearly nine months earlier, armed men had seized the same embassy and had taken 101 persons hostage, but government forces had freed them within four hours. Consequently, the immediate expectation in the Carter White House was that this latest episode, while serious, would be resolved in short order. That expectation, however, proved far off the mark, with disastrous political ramifications at home for Carter.

By this time, Kennedy had already decided to challenge Carter for the Democratic nomination. Although all the early polls indicated that if he ran he would easily defeat the incumbent, once Kennedy began to be perceived as an actual candidate, that prospect plummeted in a startling manner. Ever since the night of July 18, 1969, when Kennedy drove a car off a bridge on the island of Chappaquiddick near Martha's Vineyard in Massachusetts and a young woman passenger drowned, the question of the episode's political impact had hung ominously over Kennedy's career. Now that question was being put to the acid test. Also being tested was the assumption of many Democrats that a national yearning for a return to the Camelot years of John F. Kennedy would make the youngest brother of the slain president their party's strongest candidate.

Kennedy himself, and those closest to him, apparently shared that assumption at the outset. As early as Febru-

ary of 1979, some of them had been meeting, with and without him, to consider the possibility of a challenge. Significantly, however, as one participant noted later, the prime focus of the discussions was always "not on how one would do it if one decided to do it, but whether one should do it."

Carter, too, assumed that Kennedy thought the nomination would be his for the asking, and to disabuse him of that notion—and in the obvious hope of scaring him off—he sent a direct message to Kennedy through a trusted emissary that he intended to seek reelection no matter what happened. In other words, Carter was saying, Kennedy could not count on a repeat of 1968, when Lyndon Johnson had withdrawn in the face of a challenge. Also, in a Democratic Party straw vote in Florida, in which some freelance Kennedy backers sought to pull an upset, the Carter White House committed heavy resources and administered a two-to-one shellacking to the Kennedy forces. So Kennedy had plenty of reason to know by this time that, if he took on the incumbent president, the challenge would be no waltz.

Yet the polls continued to be a glittering lure to Kennedy. As late as November 1, Carter's general approval rating among all voters in the Gallup Poll was at his all-time low—29 percent—and Kennedy led him by two to one as the choice of Democrats for the presidential nomination. Shored up by such data, and stiffened by his dismay at Carter's policies and pessimistic talk, Kennedy set his formal announcement of candidacy for November 7 in Boston.

Three nights before that occasion, however, an event occurred that further crippled Kennedy's candidacy before it had even begun. Kennedy was the subject of a one-hour television documentary written by and featuring one of the day's outstanding television reporters, Roger Mudd, then of CBS News. The documentary traced Kennedy's political and personal career and included segments of two lengthy interviews Mudd had conducted with Kennedy that were nothing short of disastrous for the prospective candidate.

Kennedy's answers were halting, uncertain, and full of vague generalities. One exchange was particularly embarrassing to Kennedy. He was asked by Mudd a question every presidential candidate knows to expect, "Why do you want to be president?" Kennedy responded with a rambling discourse about how the country "has more natural resources than any nation in the world, the greatest technology of any country in the world, the greatest capacity for innovation in the world, and the greatest political system in the world. . . . We're facing complex issues and problems in this nation at this time, but we have faced similar challenges at other times. And the energies and the resourcefulness of this nation, I think, should be focused on these problems in a way that brings a sense of restoration in this country by its people—to—in dealing with the problems that we face—primarily the issues on the economy, the problems of inflation, and the problems of energy. And I would basically feel that—that it's imperative for this country to either move forward, that it can't stand still, or otherwise it moves back."

What made this mushy response especially startling was the fact that it came from a man who for the past 11 years had been confronted almost daily with speculation about an eventual bid for the presidency. Although subsequent surveys indicated the Mudd documentary had been watched by only 15 percent of the American television audience that night (the hit movie *Jaws* was running opposite it on another network), word of it soon set the political community buzzing, to Kennedy's considerable disadvantage. However, another event halfway around the world at roughly the same time as the telecast proved to be even more destructive to the start of his presidential candidacy—the takeover of the American embassy in Tehran.

In times of foreign policy crisis, Americans historically have rallied around their president, and this episode was no exception. The overwhelming impulse was to close ranks behind the national leader, to demonstrate solidarity to the rest of the world, and especially to the Iranian adversaries who were inflicting insult and indignity on United States citizens. As the siege of the embassy continued for days and stretched into weeks, Carter became the beneficiary of the national concern, with tangible political ramifications. By late November, an ABC News/Louis Harris Poll showed for the first time that Carter had moved ahead of Kennedy, 48 to 46 percent, as the choice of Democrats and independents for the Democratic nomination.

Kennedy contributed to his own slide by attacking Carter's decision to admit the shah of Iran to the United States for medical treatment, saying in a television interview that the shah "ran one of the most violent regimes in the history of mankind." Kennedy had ample grounds for making the statement, but in the context of the ongoing crisis, and of his political challenge to Carter, it came off as partisan carping that would only undermine Carter in his efforts to obtain the release of the hostages.

Carter, correctly assessing the political advantage that had come his way, soon went on national television and invoked the Iranian crisis as justification for not campaigning. He and his advisers understood that under the circumstances the most effective campaigning he could do was to perform his duties as president. "At the height of the Civil War," he intoned, "Abraham Lincoln said, 'I have but one task and that is to save the Union.'" Then he added with all due modesty, "Now I must devote my considered efforts to resolving the Iranian crisis." He would leave the burden of campaigning to his vice president, Walter Mondale.

Shortly afterward, Carter's decision to stay off the campaign trail received an added rationale when the Soviet Union invaded Afghanistan. Clearly this was no time for the president of the United States to be out around the country engaging in partisan debate. To the great chagrin of Kennedy and Governor Jerry Brown of California, who had also decided to challenge the incumbent, Carter withdrew from a scheduled debate in Iowa in advance of the precinct caucuses there that would launch the formal contest for 1980 national convention delegates.

In addition, Kennedy's lack of preparation for a serious candidacy was being confirmed now in his own erratic performance on the stump. Less well-known candidates had the luxury of working the kinks out of their speeches and campaign style in relative obscurity; as a Kennedy, the Massachusetts senator burst on the presidential campaign as a major figure expected to perform effectively and appealingly from the first day. He didn't, and he paid a heavy price in news-media criticism and even ridicule, while Carter was enjoying the insulation from public censure that came to an American president conspicuously occupied with a national crisis.

While the intra-party challenge to Carter was stumbling, the Republicans were intensifying their own

Vice President Walter Mondale points to quotes from a speech made by Republican presidential candidate Ronald Reagan as he speaks to labor leaders of the United Food and Commercial Workers Union meeting in Houston. Mondale was hitting at the tax cut proposed by Reagan. *(Ed Kolenovsky/Associated Press)*

competition for the right to run against this seemingly vulnerable first-term president. Ever since Ronald Reagan's impressive challenge to the previous incumbent, Gerald Ford, Reagan's supporters had been organizing and raising money for another try in 1980. California functionaries of his 1976 campaign formed an "independent" group called Citizens for the Republic in 1977 that raised funds to help conservative Republican candidates for lesser offices and to bankroll Reagan's considerable speech-making on the political circuit. The effort kept intact the nucleus of the Reagan campaign operation and bolstered the enthusiasm of his 1976 supporters as well.

In early June of 1978, the voters of Reagan's California, after a long and emotional public debate, pulled off a taxpayers' revolt with overwhelming passage of Proposition 13, an initiative that imposed a ceiling on property taxes. It was an idea that Reagan had pushed without success as governor of California, and he hailed its passage now

as evidence that his goal of "cutting government down to size" was being embraced. Thus encouraged, he continued to tell audiences that the federal government was like a free-spending son. "You can tell him to be less extravagant," Reagan would say, "or you can cut his allowance. Well, it's time to cut the government's allowance." With such appealing if simplistic talk, Reagan remained far ahead of the Republican field in the polls and entered the race in mid-November 1979 as the clear front-runner for his party's nomination.

Of the challengers—Baker, Connally, Bush, Anderson, Dole, and Crane—only the first three were considered to have much chance to stop Reagan, and the first real test was in Iowa. Even before the caucuses there, however, Baker and Connally both showed political weakness in minor state party straw polls, and it was Bush who soon emerged as Reagan's only serious obstacle to the nomination.

George Bush had an impressive string of credentials; in addition to having been United Nations ambassador under Ford, he also had been a member of Congress from Texas, Republican national chairman, director of the Central Intelligence Agency, and special U.S. representative to the Republic of China. He was regarded outside the Republican Party and by its most right-wing elements as a moderate, but he really was as conservative as any of the other candidates except Crane and Reagan. He appealed to many in the party who were unenthusiastic about Reagan because of his age or what was viewed as his ideological rigidity.

Of the three main challengers, Howard Baker was the favorite of the insiders—of the serious observers of the Senate in both the Republican Party and in the news media. He was smart, knowledgeable, agreeable, and effective as the minority leader. But he was also anathema to many conservatives because he had voted, as they put it, to "give away" the Panama Canal. And he was, it turned out, much too cautious politically. He delayed his entry into the race out of an overriding interest in the Senate's business, in particular the matter of ratification of the second strategic arms limitations treaty with the Soviet Union—called SALT II—which he and much of his party opposed. He rationalized that the debate on this critical issue would dominate foreign policy discussion in the country in the year before the presidential election, and he thus would be well positioned to benefit politically from his role as Senate minority leader in the vanguard of the fight against it. SALT II, however, never did become the subject of a great debate in the Senate. In fact, when the Soviet Union invaded Afghanistan, Carter withdrew the treaty from consideration for ratification.

As a late starter in the presidential race, Baker looked for an event at which to demonstrate his strength quickly.

He chose a straw vote at a presidential forum in Maine, where a popular Republican senator, William Cohen, had endorsed him and where a moderate Republican history in the state promised to be very congenial to him. Reagan, aware of that same history, passed up the presidential forum, in keeping with the basic strategy to remain aloof, above the fray. But the other contenders jumped in. Baker's connections in the state, and a vigorous organizational effort, immediately established him as the favorite—an impression to which aides contributed with optimistic talk. Baker flew into Portland with a planeload of reporters primed to give the country a full account of the launching of the Baker campaign. But he delivered a desultory speech on the heels of rousers from Connally and Bush. When the votes were in, Bush had beaten him by 20 votes out of about 900. It was only a straw vote, but Baker had been humbled by losing the expectations game—failing to meet the standard expected of him.

Two weeks later, the same thing happened to Connally in Florida. A strapping and impressive man, Connally, as Nixon's secretary of the treasury, had enhanced his already firm reputation as a strong administrator and forceful personality—as well as a wheeler-dealer in the mold of his old

close friend, Lyndon Johnson. That latter reputation was augmented by his indictment in 1974 on charges that he had taken a dairy lobby bribe in return for his help in obtaining beneficial price-support legislation. After a long trial, Connally was acquitted in 1975, and he remained a favorite of Republican businessmen. But he proved to be a bit too smooth, and subject to suspicion, for most voters.

With Baker wounded as a result of his conspicuous defeat in the Maine straw vote, Connally looked south for an opportunity to move up just behind Reagan in the Republican pecking order. He decided to make a major effort in a similar straw vote at the Florida state convention two weeks later. Reagan was having some organizational problems in Florida, and Connally forces let their hopes get so high that they began to tell reporters their man would run very close to, or even defeat, Reagan. In doing so, they, like the Baker aides in Maine, built expectations too high. Reagan beat Connally handily, and the confident Texan suffered a deflation from which he never recovered.

These early setbacks to two of Reagan's three main rivals for the Republican nomination only cemented the strategy of Reagan's campaign manager, former Nixon political adviser John Sears, to keep his front-running

'IF THIS IS THE ONLY SAFE THING WE CAN DO TO GET BACK ON THE FRONT PAGES, THEN I SAY LET'S DO IT!'

This cartoon by Pat Oliphant shows Ronald Reagan, Jerry Brown, John Connally, and Edward Kennedy, as presidential candidates, running nude in an effort to deflect attention from front-runner Jimmy Carter and to return the presidential campaign, and themselves, to front-page news. *(OLIPHANT © 1979 UNIVERSAL UCLICK. Reprinted with permission. All rights reserved.)*

candidate serenely above the battle. Invited to join all the other Republican candidates in a nationally televised debate in advance of the Iowa precinct caucuses, Reagan declined on grounds that the debate might be "divisive." Thus, the challengers in both major parties were being denied their prime targets in Iowa, Carter having already begged off from the Democratic debate after the Iranian crisis and Afghanistan invasion.

For Carter, not debating was smart politics for an incumbent busy being president at a time of major foreign policy difficulty. Kennedy and Brown could criticize him and his handling of the crises only at their own political peril as the country rallied around him. Each night, as Kennedy and Brown campaigned in Iowa, Carter was seen on the television evening news dealing with the hostage crisis. When caucus night—January 21—arrived, he trounced Kennedy by nearly two to one—59 to 31 percent—with Brown far behind. With that one result, the myth of Kennedy invincibility was shattered.

By this time, the Iowa caucuses had become a major national political story, and Iowans enjoyed the spotlight. They were disappointed, and many were resentful, that Reagan—an adopted son by virtue of having worked as a sports announcer on Iowa radio before going to Hollywood—would snub them by declining their invitation. Convinced by the polls that he was well ahead, and confident that the political organization that had been put in place was adequate to the job, Reagan not only passed up the debate but chose not to campaign in the state, except for an antiseptic final weekend rally outside Des Moines for which loyalists were bused in.

Bush, meanwhile, having weathered the early straw votes and having built an impressive organization of his own in Iowa, campaigned diligently throughout the state. He held his own in the debate that went forward without Reagan, though nothing more than that. He benefited from an organizational effort that was at least the equivalent of Reagan's, and from one other thing—the tremendous interest generated in the caucus process by the invasion of the national news media. On caucus night, more than 110,000 Republicans participated, or more than four times the previous high. The Reagan campaign, confidently basing its grassroots efforts on a much lower figure, calculated that 30,000 votes would be more than enough for Reagan to win. He received 31,348, but with the much higher turnout than anticipated, it was not quite what was needed. Bush won with 33,530, and suddenly the aloof front-runner was in trouble.

Reagan, though, was no flash in the pan. As an ideological candidate, a true believer in the conservative dogma, and the possessor of the talent and professional training necessary to peddle it to voters, all he really needed was to get out among them and start selling. This he did in the first primary, in New Hampshire, with a zest that belied his age and that contrasted sharply with his earlier front-runner's strategy of detachment. Ever since the Eisenhower years, the Republican Party had been moving inexorably, in its heart if not always in its actions, to the right, and in Reagan, Republicans found a candidate who did not temper his views out of any concern that the GOP was the minority party. Indeed, he stoutly believed, and preached, that it could become the majority party only by presenting itself as a clear alternative to the Democrats. The only real question about him among Republican voters was not where he stood, but whether he had the fortitude and stamina at his age to run an effective and winning race against the Democratic nominee. His loss in Iowa forced him to demonstrate that he did, and the New Hampshire primary gave him the opportunity.

One other factor worked to Reagan's advantage in New Hampshire as a result of what had happened in Iowa. Bush, riding the crest of that upset, suddenly was thrust into the national spotlight, and as it shone down on him, questions about his own leadership abilities, his record, and his proposals multiplied and gained greater prominence. Although Bush, like Reagan, was a longtime conservative, he always seemed so acquiescent, so willing to please, that he came off as a rubbery figure. Also, while Bush emphasized the competitive aspects of the nomination fight—the horse race, in the political parlance—Reagan hammered away at all the 10-strike themes of conservatism, from bloated government and welfare cheating to balanced budgets and the Communist threat. The Iowa defeat had dropped him temporarily behind Bush in the polls, but his more vigorous campaigning—including his participation in a debate with all the other candidates—soon erased the Bush lead. Then, one widely publicized event on the final weekend broke the primary wide open, and, in retrospect, removed the last real barrier to Reagan's nomination.

A local newspaper, the *Nashua Telegraph*, proposed a two-man debate between the front-running candidates, Reagan and Bush. Reagan's managers favored the idea because they felt that if Republican voters concluded the choice was between Reagan and the marshmallowy Bush, their man would be the clear winner. Bush's aides, on the other hand, believed that such a debate would confirm Bush's position as the prime, if not only, realistic alternative to Reagan.

The other candidates, however, complained to the Federal Election Commission, which ruled that a two-man debate would be so beneficial to Reagan and Bush that its sponsorship by the newspaper would be an illegal contribution to their campaigns. The Reagan campaign suggested that Reagan and Bush split the costs, and when Bush balked at that idea, Reagan agreed to pay for the whole affair himself. That decision set the stage for one of those dramatic incidents in a campaign that serves to give voters a capsule reading on a candidate, and helps to make him a winner—or a loser.

Reagan campaign manager Sears, still wary about exposing his man in any risk-prone environment and aware that the campaign's internal polls indicated Reagan had already recovered from the Iowa setback, had a brainstorm. Why not diminish the odds of a Reagan mistake in the debate by increasing the number of candidates called on to provide answers in a limited time period from two to seven? And, at the same time, why not be conciliatory to the five who faced being shut out? As Reagan's press secretary at the time, James Lake, put it later, "We didn't need those other candidates out there bad-mouthing us the last three days."

On the morning of the debate, February 23, Sears and Lake called all the other candidates and invited them to participate that night. All of them except Connally, who was pursuing a Southern strategy and was campaigning in South Carolina, agreed to come. The *Nashua Telegraph* still had the role of moderator, and its editors and Bush balked at the idea of expanding the two-man debate, but the Reagan team had made up its mind. A wild scene ensued when Reagan trooped into the high school auditorium debating ground with Dole, Baker, Anderson, and Crane in tow. As they lined up behind the debate table, Bush sat woodenly, staring straight ahead. Reagan took his seat and began making his case for including the others. The moderator, Jon Breen, editor of the paper, looked toward a sound technician and snapped, "Turn Mr. Reagan's microphone off!" It was one of the all-time memorable straight lines in presidential politics, because Reagan, as if on cue, flushed angrily, leaned forward, and shot back, "I'm paying for this microphone, Mr. Green [sic]!"

Bedlam reigned in the auditorium as spectators cheered, applauded, and demanded that chairs be brought out for the four standing candidates. But the newspaper executives and Bush held fast, Bush still staring ahead and looking for all the world like a disapproving teacher's pet in the midst of a blackboard eraser fight. Finally, the rejected four stalked off the platform and the two-man debate went forward, but few remembered afterward what had been said during it. The story was Reagan's heroic attempt to include his four colleagues, and Bush's rigid refusal to let them speak. Not only that; it was a lively, dramatic picture story for television—a great "visual" in the new jargon—with an irate Reagan demanding to be heard in the cause of open debate and a shaken, slightly foolish-looking Bush playing the heavy.

The Nashua scene unfolded on the Saturday night before the primary, and Bush contributed to the dam-

age it inflicted on him by retreating from New Hampshire to spend the final weekend at his home in Texas. On all the Sunday network and local television news shows, and again Monday morning and evening, viewers saw again and again that dramatic segment of "Reagan and the microphone," and then tape of Bush jogging in sunny Houston while Reagan continued to shake hands in snowy New Hampshire. The juxtaposition underscored what was being called a "wimp factor" against Bush in a most emphatic way. Later, after the election, Bush described the whole episode as a "basic sandbag" orchestrated by Sears. But whatever the debate was, George Bush's candidacy was never the same again. On primary day, February 26, Reagan routed him, 50 to 23 percent, with the rest of the field even further behind.

Baker, who received only 13 percent of the New Hampshire vote, finished fourth in both Massachusetts and Vermont the next week and withdrew from the race. Connally bowed out four days later after losing, 54 to 30 percent, to Reagan in South Carolina. Dole and Crane soon followed suit, leaving only Reagan, Bush, and Anderson in the field.

Anderson, the most moderate of the contenders and a man of droll style and humor, had by this time begun to attract a modest following as the common-sense Republican. In the Iowa debate, he had won the crowd over by explaining how Reagan could, as he proposed, cut taxes, increase defense spending and still balance the budget: "It's simple. You do it with mirrors." It was the kind of remark expected from Anderson by those who knew him. He had spent nearly 20 years in the House, and, in his later years, he had been a key figure in the party leadership, admired for his intellectual honesty and political independence. Convinced after nearly two decades in the House that he would rise no higher there, Anderson had decided to make one long-shot bid for the main brass ring before quitting politics altogether.

In the New Hampshire primary, Anderson finished a weak fourth with 10 percent of the vote, but for a brief period thereafter he threatened to replace Bush as Reagan's prime challenger. He ran second to Reagan in Vermont and second to Bush in Massachusetts on March 4, but two weeks later Reagan polished him off in the March 18 Illinois primary. Reagan, with his unerring knack for touching Republican sensitivities, needled Anderson in a televised debate in Chicago for his reluctance to pledge his support for any Republican nominee. "John," Reagan asked in mock sorrow, touching his hand to Anderson's sleeve, "would you really find Ted Kennedy preferable to me?" Reagan beat Anderson in his home state, 48 to 37 percent, and again in neighboring Wisconsin two weeks later. Anderson, persuaded by friends and admirers who took no comfort in the

Independent presidential candidate John Anderson, second from right, addresses a crowd in downtown Minneapolis, Minnesota. *(Jim Mone/Associated Press)*

prospect of a Reagan–Carter race in the fall, announced in late April that he would run as an independent candidate at the head of what he called a "National Unity Campaign."

Bush, meanwhile, hung on, winning the March 25 primary in Connecticut (where he had attended Yale and where his father, Prescott Bush, had been a U.S. senator), but losing in the much more important states of New York (March 25) and Pennsylvania (April 22). On the ropes now, Bush primed for Michigan, where the popular Republican governor, William G. Milliken, had no use for Reagan. Milliken had helped Gerald Ford carry his home state against Reagan in 1976 at a time when Reagan was enjoying a string of primary and caucus successes, and he was determined to deny Reagan Michigan again, and possibly stall his march to the nomination. Milliken and his political organization campaigned diligently for Bush and succeeded in upsetting Reagan in Michigan on May 20, but it was too late.

The very night of Bush's Michigan victory, ABC and CBS News announced in their election telecasts that the delegates Reagan had picked up in a losing cause there, and for his victory in the Oregon primary, were enough to assure his nomination. Bush wanted to press on, but his aides, aware that his campaign lacked the money required to continue what was now a useless venture, closed it down and confronted him with a *fait accompli* he could not reverse. Seven weeks before the Republican National Convention opened in Detroit, Ronald Reagan was certain to win the nomination.

On the Democratic side, the issue was not so conveniently, nor so amicably, resolved. Ted Kennedy had entered the contest against incumbent Jimmy Carter ostensibly because he was profoundly disturbed at where Carter was leading the party and the country, at home and abroad. But the two men had no love for each other, either, and the animosity only multiplied as the campaign progressed.

The drubbing Kennedy took from Carter in the Iowa caucuses on January 21 shook him and his campaign to the core. He had to acknowledge that he had embarked on his presidential bid without adequate preparation and

THE ICEMAN COMETH

This Edmund S. Valtman cartoon shows President Carter watching in dismay as Senator Ted Kennedy approaches carrying two large blocks of ice labeled "Blame for Cold War" and "Wage-Price Freeze." In January 1980, Kennedy, who was opposing Carter for the presidential nomination, gave a major speech at Georgetown University in which he attacked Carter for not being sufficiently firm with the Communists and for not taking steps to control inflation. *The Iceman Cometh* was a play by Eugene O'Neill about a group of homeless misfits who are temporarily beguiled by a flashy salesman who turns out to be mentally deranged. Many people believed in early 1980 that the charismatic Kennedy had a good chance of defeating Carter, who was viewed as incompetent. *(Library of Congress)*

that he had committed some early gaffes, such as his criticism of the shah. But the real problem, he and his chief aides convinced themselves, was the restraint of foreign policy criticism that the hostage crisis and the situation in Afghanistan were imposing on him, and the free ride that Carter the candidate was being given. Kennedy resolved to tackle the problem head-on. In a speech at Georgetown University on January 28, he noted that Hitler's conquest of France and the Low Countries had not stopped public or presidential debate in the 1940s. "If the Vietnam War taught us anything," he said, "it is precisely that when we do not debate our foreign policy, we may drift into deeper trouble."

Kennedy's decision to attack the incumbent's management of foreign affairs in the midst of the Iranian crisis did not adequately gauge the people's inclination to fall in behind their leader under such circumstances. In caucuses in Maine, Kennedy's neighbors rejected him, though narrowly (45 to 39 percent), in favor of Carter. But Kennedy was determined. Attacking Carter in another speech in the same vein at Harvard on February 13, Kennedy chose to interpret the closer Maine result as an indication that "the Presidency can never be above the fray, isolated from the actions and passions of our time. A President cannot afford to posture as the high priest of patriotism."

The next night in a press conference, however, Carter demonstrated the power of the incumbency in political campaigning. "The thrust of what Senator Kennedy has said throughout the last few weeks," the president intoned, "is very damaging to our country and to the establishment of our principles and the maintenance of them, and to the achievement of our goals to keep the peace and get our hostages released."

The force of Carter's indictment was clear in the next primary results in New Hampshire on February 26: Carter 49 percent, Kennedy 38 percent. Kennedy managed to salvage the primary in his home state of Massachusetts, but Carter resumed his winning ways across the South—South Carolina, Georgia, Florida, Alabama—and capped off these victories by trouncing Kennedy in Illinois on March 18, where the support of Chicago's beleaguered first woman mayor, Jane Byrne, only added to the senator's difficulties.

Finally, all Carter had to do to ensure his nomination was defeat Kennedy in New York. If Kennedy lost there, he would have little rationale for continuing his campaign. But there, for the first time, Carter's foreign policy missteps gave the challenger a chance. By confusion or design, the Carter administration several weeks before the New York primary had cast a vote in the U.N. Security Council that had outraged Israel and the American Jewish community. After having twice abstained on similar votes in 1979, the American ambassador voted for a resolution calling on Israel to dismantle civilian settlements in occupied Arab territories, including Jerusalem. When the uproar came, Carter quickly declared the vote a mistake caused by the American U.N. delegation and the White House's "failure to communicate," and he sought to placate irate Jewish voters.

Kennedy adroitly seized on the Carter misstep not only as a question of Carter's support for Israel but also as a measure of his undependability in the conduct of foreign policy. Kennedy's own tremendous support in the Jewish community, combined with growing doubts about Carter's commitment to the Israeli side in the Middle East, gave him the opening he needed. Campaigning strenuously in the closing days, while Carter continued what by now was called his "Rose Garden strategy" of sticking to his presidential duties, Kennedy upset the incumbent in New York on March 25 by a thumping 16 percentage points. White House political strategists began to consider seriously whether the time was not approaching when Carter would have to take to the stump and override a pledge not to campaign until the hostages in Iran were freed.

Before having to confront that possibility, however, Carter still hoped he could extricate the hostages. A United Nations commission had been negotiating with the Iranian government, and on the morning of April 1, hours before voters were to cast ballots in the presidential primaries in Wisconsin and Kansas, Carter called a most unusual early morning televised press conference (7:13 a.m. to be precise) to report a "positive step." Word had come, he said, from Iranian president Abolhassan Bani-Sadr that the hostages would be transferred from the "militants" at the embassy to the government's jurisdiction if the United States ended "all propaganda and agitation" against Iran. Such a step would have been an interim one only, and it never happened, but Carter by his words encouraged the idea that the hostages' outright release might be imminent.

Reporter: "Do you know when they will be actually released and be brought home?"

Carter: "I presume that we will know more about that as the circumstances develop. We do not know the exact time scheduled at this moment."

Carter won the Wisconsin and Kansas primaries handily, but the hostages remained where they were, and pressures on the president to campaign continued. What finally got him out of the Rose Garden and onto the stump, ironically, was not the hostages' release, but a daring military rescue attempt whose abject failure made it more unlikely than ever that they would be set free, but which gave Carter a rationale, however contorted, to start campaigning for renomination.

About three weeks after Carter's false alarm, on his orders six large American transport planes departed on the night of April 24 from a base in southern Egypt and headed for a spot in the Iranian desert, 300 miles southeast of Tehran. There they were to refuel eight American helicopters from the aircraft carrier *Nimitz,* which was stationed in the Gulf of Oman. The helicopters were then to proceed, swooping in over the seized embassy, and land troops who would extricate the hostages. But only six helicopters made it to the refueling point and one developed a mechanical problem when it got there. The plan called for a minimum of six helicopters for the raid, so with Carter's approval it was aborted. As the transports and helicopters prepared to leave the site, one helicopter collided with a transport on the ground, causing a fire that killed eight men. The survivors fled, leaving the Iranians with the wreckage and the American dead with which to reap a propaganda bonanza, which they quickly did.

The disaster became a metaphor for Carter's handling of the hostage crisis, if not for his foreign policy in general. And it came at a most unpropitious time politically, because Kennedy in the wake of his New York primary upset was making notable progress in a strategy aimed at establishing a final rationale for his own nomination. Arguing that the Democratic nominee had to be strong in the industrial heartland of the country, Kennedy campaigned aggressively and won the Pennsylvania primary on April 22 and the caucuses in Michigan (by an eyelash) on April 26, and set his sights on the final big-state primaries in California, Ohio, and New Jersey on June 3.

Five days before those primaries, Carter finally made his first overt campaign appearance of the year, at a rally in Columbus, Ohio. He won that state, but Kennedy captured California and New Jersey. Carter, however, by virtue of the proportional allocation formula used by the party, picked up enough delegates to ensure his nomination—though not without a final row and some embarrassing scenes at the national convention in New York in August.

The Republican convention—or, more accurately, coronation—drew the spotlight first, opening in a rehabilitated downtown Detroit on July 14. With Reagan's nomination certain, the only questions of note were what the platform would say and who would be Reagan's running mate. The Reagan strategists decided at the outset that the platform would not become a battleground, since it meant very little in the scheme of things, anyway. The only issue that generated any fuss was the Equal Rights Amendment, which the platform committee, dominated by Reaganites, threw out of the party's document of principles. This act, which naturally was greeted by loud and emotional protests from the outnumbered Republican feminists, contravened the Republicans' 40-year-old tradition of support for equal rights for women. As for the selection of a running mate, the convention seemed quite content to leave that matter to the presidential nominee—and was astonished when it learned what he had been contemplating.

Well in advance of the convention, Reagan's pollster, Richard Wirthlin, had been surveying voters about a list of prospective running mates. The list included Bush, Baker, William Simon, former secretary of defense Donald Rumsfeld, Senator Richard Lugar of Indiana, Representative Jack Kemp of New York, Representative Guy Vander Jagt of Michigan, Senator Paul Laxalt of Nevada (Reagan's best friend on Capitol Hill), and former president Gerald Ford. Of all these, Ford clearly was the best known and potentially brought more to the ticket than any of the others. But he had flirted earlier with the possibility of running for president again and had turned down the idea. So why would he be interested in running for vice president, a job he had already held?

Reagan was intrigued by the idea, though, especially because he was cool to the most obvious alternative—Bush. Ever since that scene in the high school auditorium in Nashua, Reagan had been put off by Bush's weak performance. "If he can't stand up to that kind of pressure," he told one intimate at the time, "how could he stand up to the pressure of being President?" And he told another, "I have strong reservations about George Bush. I'm concerned about turning the country over to him." Of all the

Balloons spill from the ceiling of Detroit's Joe Louis Arena as presidential candidate Ronald Reagan and members of his family are cheered by delegates at the Republican convention. From right on podium are son Ron, daughter Patti, wife Nancy, Reagan himself, and son Mike holding Reagan grandchild Cameron Michael. *(Associated Press)*

prospects, Reagan plainly preferred Laxalt, but the senator's small-state base, especially with Nevada's extensive gambling interests, worked against his selection.

Prior to Ford's arrival at the convention, he had received feelers about the vice-presidential nomination but had turned them all aside. Nevertheless, Reagan himself broached the subject directly to Ford at private meetings in their Detroit hotel and even arranged to have Ford's secretary of state, Henry Kissinger, discuss with Ford the foreign policy roles he might assume as Reagan's vice president. Soon Ford and Reagan aides were conferring on the possibility. Ford seemed by now to have more than a passing interest, as discussions advanced into what role he might play as vice president in the actual governing process. Inevitably, word of the deliberations soon leaked out, and before long the major television commentators were speculating about the possibility of this incredible "dream ticket."

Ford, interviewed by Walter Cronkite on CBS News, fanned the talk with observations that sounded for all the world as if he were on the verge. "I would not go to Washington . . . and be a figurehead Vice President," he said at one point. "If I go to Washington, and I'm not saying that I am accepting, I have to go there with the belief that I will play a meaningful role across the board in the

basic and the crucial and the important decisions that have to be made in a four-year period." Was he thinking, Cronkite asked, of "something like a co-presidency?" Ford replied, "That's something Governor Reagan really ought to consider."

Reagan, watching the interview in his room, was predictably shocked when the term "co-presidency" was used. Later testimony indicated that the word served as a dash of cold water in the faces of all the principals, showing them with clarity what they all had been toying with—and cooling the interest of the Reagan advisers particularly. Nervously, Reagan pressed Ford for an answer, and was greatly relieved when Ford finally declined. Reagan settled in the end on the obvious choice, Bush, who with customary eagerness accepted.

The Reagan–Ford "dream ticket" had proved illusory, but the two principals' lengthy conversations about it did achieve one thing. They diminished the ill feelings between the two men that had existed since Reagan's challenge to Ford for the 1976 nomination, and Reagan's subsequent failure to campaign very extensively for Ford that year. And it laid down a foundation for Ford's active participation as a campaigner for Reagan in the fall of 1980 in a campaign that would play on the public's dissatisfaction with Carter as Ford's successor.

In his acceptance speech on July 17, Reagan asked, "Can you look at the record of this administration and say, 'Well done'? Can anyone compare the state of our economy when the Carter administration took office with where we are today and say, 'Keep up the good work'? Can you look at our reduced standing in the world today and say, 'Let's have four more years of this'?" The Republican convention roared back: "No!"

The Democratic convention, opening in New York on August 11, produced no similar reconciliation of the party's two main figures, except in the most transparently artificial manner. Although Carter came into the convention with more than a majority of the delegates, the Kennedy forces had one more card to play. They were well aware that Carter, still in the throes of national economic distress and humbled by the seemingly endless Iranian hostage crisis, was running more than 25 percentage points behind Reagan in the public opinion polls. If the delegates, elected to the convention under rules that committed them to vote for the candidate to whom they were pledged, were made free of that firm commitment, might they not be persuaded by the polls to switch to Kennedy, or at least to abandon Carter for some other Democrat? It was worth a try.

Under the euphemism "open convention," a campaign was launched to change the party rules and grant "freedom" to the delegates. But the trouble was that most of the Carter delegates did not want to be free in that sense. They had worked hard to get to the convention, often in bitter primary and caucus fights against Kennedy backers, and they were in no mood to switch, especially to Kennedy. The Carter forces easily turned back the rules challenge by roughly a three-to-two ratio, and Carter's nomination bid had passed its final obstacle.

It remained for Kennedy, however, to provide the two emotional highlights of the convention—one very positive, one extremely negative. The first was a speech he delivered the night before the presidential roll call, in which he had the hall roaring with approval as he touched all the old liberal nerves with cheer lines that in many cases mocked the cautious, middle-of-the-road brand of Democratic policies espoused by Carter. His own candidacy had been criticized for having been a rerun of tired old liberal ideas, and seemingly in defense of it he told the convention:

"The commitment I seek is not to outworn views, but to old values that will never wear out. Programs may sometimes become obsolete, but the ideal of fairness always endures. Circumstances may change, but the work of compassion must continue. It is surely correct that we cannot solve problems by throwing money at them; but it is also correct that we dare not throw national problems onto a scrap heap of inattention and indifference. . . . For those whose cares have been our concern, the work goes on, the cause endures, the hope still lives, the dream shall never die."

The 40-minute demonstration that followed Kennedy's speech was clearly the emotional peak of the convention. Carter's acceptance speech, on August 14 after his nomination for president and that of Walter Mondale for vice president, was an anticlimax. Rather than defending his four years in office, which was an unenviable task, Carter warned of two futures—one of "security, justice and peace" under a second Carter term, one of "despair . . . surrender . . . risk—the risk of international confrontation, the risk of an uncontrollable, unaffordable and unwinnable nuclear arms race" under Reagan.

Kennedy's negative contribution was his late appearance, at the very close of the convention, at a gathering of party stalwarts on the rostrum for pictures with the newly nominated standard-bearer. For days there had been speculation about whether Kennedy would agree to stand with Carter for the traditional victory pose of hands joined over heads. As the convention and the nationwide television audience watched and waited, Carter prowled the Madison Square Garden platform, greeting other senators, governors, mayors, various party officials—but no Kennedy. The senator explained later that his car had been caught in traffic. When he finally arrived, he shook hands perfunctorily with Carter and then strolled around the rostrum with the president of the United States trotting after him like, a Carter intimate said with dismay later, "a puppy dog." It was not an auspicious end for the convention, nor a good beginning for an extremely difficult campaign ahead.

In spite of the very favorable polls, Reagan's political strategists entered the fall campaign with two major concerns. One had to do with their own candidate—whether he had the self-discipline to navigate the course without self-destructing. His aides were well aware that Reagan had a history of making off-the-cuff observations that got him into trouble. That particular penchant was a product more than anything else of his faith in whatever he read or heard, almost without regard to source, that dovetailed with his rather uncomplicated, rigid view of the world. After eight years as a governor and with two presidential nomination campaigns behind him, the Reagan lore abounded with what came to be known, even within his own campaign, as his "horror stories"—accounts of how welfare recipients had ripped off the system for hundreds of thousands of dollars, to give only one example. Also, he did not always appreciate at once the political ramifications of things he said, so it was imperative that the campaign somehow guard against this problem.

The second concern had to do with the opposition. Jimmy Carter as the incumbent president had the power by virtue of his office to affect events—or to appear to affect them—so as to have a decisive impact on the outcome of the election. As early as July, at the Republican convention, Reagan's campaign manager (and later his much beleaguered director of the Central Intelligence Agency), William Casey, had told reporters that one of his major fears was that on the eve of the election Carter might spring an "October surprise"—some foreign policy coup possibly concerning the hostages—that would bring him immediate, short-term voter support.

To guard against such an eventuality, Casey said then, he was establishing "an intelligence operation" to maintain an "incumbency watch" on the administration. No more was said about it, but such an operation was indeed organized under a Casey aide, who, using retired military and CIA personnel, checked on such things as troop and materiel movements via military transport at major American bases in this country and abroad. The effort was, from all later reports, amateurish and of little value. But its very pursuit underscored the concern within the Reagan camp that Carter might indeed try to pull out the election with some "October surprise."

The fear of Reagan's "horror stories" and lack of political sensitivity proved to be a valid one. In a speech to the Veterans of Foreign Wars, he referred to the Vietnam War as "a noble cause"—and triggered a brief rehash of that political nightmare. He stirred up an educational hornets' nest when he told a conference of evangelists that there were "great flaws" in the theory of evolution, and that it might be a good idea if schools taught the creationist theory as well. As Bush prepared to go to Beijing for the Republican ticket, Reagan said he was looking forward to reestablishing official relations with Taiwan. He called Tuscumbia, Alabama, where Carter was kicking off his own campaign, the birthplace of the Ku Klux Klan—it was not. He suggested that volcanic Mount St. Helens in a few months had "probably released more sulfur dioxide into the atmosphere of the world than has been released in the last ten years of auto driving"—a contention immediately rejected by the Environmental Protection Agency, which said manmade sources contributed from 40 to 160 times more pollution each day than did the eruption in Washington State. He said "growing and decaying vegetation" contributed 93 percent of nitrogen oxides that polluted the air, confusing them with nitrous oxides, the natural product of plant respiration. Whereupon he was greeted at one campaign stop by a sign on a tree that said "Chop Me Down Before I Kill Again."

In the midst of these gaffes, which threatened to make Reagan a continuing subject of ridicule and to undermine seriously his credibility, the campaign enlisted the services of one of the Republican Party's most politically sensitive professionals, Stuart Spencer, who had helped run Reagan's gubernatorial campaigns as well as the 1976 Ford campaign against him. Spencer traveled with Rea-

gan as a sort of gaffe preventer and was for the most part successful in curbing the "horror stories" and explaining away those that did pop out of Reagan's mouth.

The fear of an "October surprise" could not be dispelled so easily. It continued to hang over the Reagan campaign until the very end, when reports of eleventh-hour efforts by Carter to extricate the hostages before the election did indeed surface and give the Reagan campaign some last-minute anxiety.

Carter's concern going into the fall campaign, plain and simple, was that voters would base their decision on what they thought about him and his record, and not about Reagan. Although Carter was ready and willing to defend his four years in office, the polls showed conclusively that his administration would require a lot of selling in light of the rising inflation and interest rates at home and the hostage dilemma abroad. No amount of media magic from Carter's campaign technocrats could change the fact that the 1980 election was one in which events, most of them damaging to Carter, were the controlling factors. The best hope for Carter to overtake his challenger was somehow to make the voters think so much less of Reagan or, more specifically, to come to fear his election, that Carter would seem the safer alternative.

Such a strategy was, for obvious reasons, a risky one. Negative campaigning, while demonstrably effective if handled carefully, also can backfire on a candidate, especially if employed against a foe who is well liked by the voters. And asking them to choose the lesser of two evils is in itself a depressant, discouraging voter turnout. The Democrats, as the majority party, usually seek and depend on a large turnout.

This same lesser-of-two-evils approach was dictating the independent candidacy of John Anderson, who was counting on there being enough voters who could not swallow either Carter or Reagan to turn the election his way. This concept seemed to have considerable validity as the fall campaign began, but faded as Reagan demonstrated his acceptability, first in a debate with Anderson in which he held his own, and then with Carter.

Carter's political advisers acknowledged that playing on fears about Reagan was their best bet to divert voters' attention from the Carter record, and they were aware that the ideal way to do so would be to have others, not Carter himself, going after Reagan. One of Carter's remaining strengths was that voters continued to believe that he was a man of great religious conviction and goodwill, and it was essential that this belief not be tarnished. But that rational judgment did not take into consideration Carter's own frustration, and his conviction that Reagan really was a threat to peace.

Thus, early in the campaign, Carter told a Torrance, California, audience on September 22 that the election "will help to decide whether we have war or peace." Reagan, warned by his own advisers in advance that Carter would try to "demonize" him in the campaign, responded with appropriate indignation. "To assume that anyone would deliberately want a war," he lamented, "is beneath decency." In short order, the nation's news media were commenting not only on "the war-and-peace issue" but also on "the meanness issue"—a disturbing penchant by Carter to accuse Reagan of being a heartless wretch and, indeed, a demon. Nevertheless, internal polls did indicate that Carter's negative campaigning was cutting into Reagan's lead.

The president finally went too far in a talk to party workers in Chicago on October 6, warning them that their votes would "literally decide the lives of millions of people in our country and indeed throughout the world. . . . You'll determine whether or not this America will be unified or, if I lose the election, whether Americans might be separated black from white, Jew from Christian, North from South, rural from urban."

The indictment of Reagan as a polarizer proved in time to have considerable validity, but in the context of the campaign it was taken as another example of "meanness" by a desperate incumbent. Reagan, playing the situation for all it was worth, professed sorrow that his opponent could have stooped so low. "I can't be angry," he said. "I'm saddened that anyone, particularly someone who has held that position, could intimate such a thing. I'm not asking for an apology from him. . . . But I think he owes the country an apology."

Such was the political climate when, a week before the election and after much wrangling over arrangements, Carter and Reagan finally met on October 28 in a nationally televised debate in Cleveland. The Reagan strategy earlier had been to avoid any debates, but when, by mid-October, the negative campaigning against Reagan had begun to take its toll, the decision was made to chance it. Also, as the campaign approached its conclusion, Anderson was sinking badly, and the Reagan campaign feared Carter would win over many of Anderson's former supporters unless Reagan did something to woo straying Republicans back into the fold. And, finally, a late debate would give Reagan an opportunity to counter an "October surprise" if Carter were to spring one on him.

As for Carter, the old axiom that incumbents should not debate, endorsed by his advisers, in the end went out the window; he had to get Reagan on the same platform and demonstrate conclusively who was the better risk for the future.

President Jimmy Carter (left) and Republican challenger Ronald Reagan face panelists during their televised debate at the Cleveland Convention Center in Cleveland, Ohio, on October 28, 1980. *(Associated Press)*

As is almost always the case in presidential debates, it was the incumbent who had more to lose and the challenger everything to gain. By this time, Reagan's polls indicated, a negative judgment on Carter already had been made by the voters, but they still had to be convinced that Reagan was up to the job. Merely by holding his own in debate with the incumbent, Reagan would be able to make that point, and he did so. One reason that the challenger did so well, the Democrats argued later, was that the Reagan campaign had managed to get hold of extensive briefing papers prepared for Carter as he readied himself for the debate. Disclosure of this fact after the election led to a lengthy investigation and eventually a court order for the appointment of an independent investigator to determine how the Reagan campaign obtained the papers, and how they were used in preparing Reagan for the debate. A higher court, however, voided that order and effectively shelved the investigation.

In the debate, Carter tried to fan concern about Reagan in handling foreign policy, from the use of military force to nuclear arms control and proliferation of nuclear weapons. He made a strong case that Reagan's policies threatened an acceleration of the arms race, but he undercut his own performance with an inexplicable comment. "I had a discussion with my daughter Amy the other day, before I came here," Carter said at one point, "to ask her what the most important issue was. She said she thought nuclear weaponry and the control of nuclear arms." The notion of relying on the judgment of a 13-year-old in such a matter was, on its face, both baffling and ludicrous, and the ridicule the comment later brought Carter diverted attention from his own reasoned arms-control criticism of Reagan, which later proved quite warranted.

On another occasion, when Carter had Reagan dead to rights in saying that he "began his career campaigning around this nation against Medicare," which was true, Reagan sidestepped by saying simply, "There you go again"—intimating that here was Carter up to his old tricks of unfair allegations. Finally, Reagan scored the forensic coup of the evening with a simple concluding question to the television audience: "Are you better off than you were four years ago?" If so, he said, vote for Carter. If not, vote for him.

President-elect Ronald Reagan, his wife, Nancy, and their family exchange waves with well-wishers during their victory party on November 4, 1980, in Los Angeles. *(Associated Press)*

Although Reagan's pollsters contended later their man had begun to widen his lead even before the debate, there was no doubt that his ability to more than hold his own against the incumbent president finally broke the logjam of concern about him and led to his overwhelming victory a week later.

Arrangements for a debate among the vice-presidential candidates got nowhere. It did not matter. Walter Mondale, George Bush, and former Wisconsin governor Patrick J. Lucey, running with Anderson, all campaigned vigorously but unspectacularly in the shadow of the men who had selected them, and about whom the voters would make their judgment on Election Day.

There remained, however, one final hope for Carter to turn the tables on the last weekend of the campaign. It was the first day of November, but the possibility after all of an October surprise—a few days late—now presented itself. After more months of intrigue and threats in Tehran, the parliament of Iran was meeting to consider the fate of the hostages. There was no telling what their release just three days before the election might do to the emotions of American voters as they faced the choice between Carter and Reagan. For the Reagan campaign, traveling in Michigan and Ohio, the prospect was the only political cloud on the horizon; for the Carter campaign, in Chicago, it was the one event that might yet bail out the desperate incumbent.

Just before four o'clock Sunday morning, November 2, Carter received a phone call from the deputy secretary of state, Warren Christopher, informing him that the Iranian parliament had agreed to release the hostages provided the United States met four demands: pledge noninterference in Iranian affairs, free all frozen Iranian assets in the United States, cancel all American public and private claims against Iran, and return the shah's wealth to Iran. The demands were extreme, but Carter could not afford not to consider them, or at least to use them as a starting point for further negotiations. He decided to return to Washington immediately to be better able, his aides said, to appraise the situation with expert advice and superior communications. But Carter's camp was also thinking about the potential political impact of the president conspicuously rushing back to his desk in the Oval Office to grapple personally with the opportunity. It was just the sort of campaign climax Reagan's strategists had most feared.

That Sunday, as the nation anxiously awaited the outcome of this latest hopeful development—and as its people watched television network reviews of the hostage crisis, now approaching its first anniversary—Carter and his closest aides considered his response. It was determined almost at once that the terms were unacceptable, and to say so was only going to confirm Carter's year-

long failure to obtain the hostages' release. Yet there was no real alternative; indeed, the Reagan campaign had so effectively conditioned the voters by now to be wary of some eleventh-hour gimmick by Carter concerning the hostages that it was difficult even to put the best face on the bad situation.

In the end, Carter went on television and reported that, while the Iranian proposal was "a significant development" that appeared to offer "a positive basis" for further negotiations for the hostages, "I know also that all Americans will want their return to be on a proper basis, which is worthy of the suffering and sacrifices which the hostages have endured." In other words, they were not coming out, and Reagan was home free. Up to the last hour, the campaign of 1980 was the captive not of the new breed of political managers who were said to be taking over the electoral process, but of events outside the control even of the incumbent president.

Carter spent the final day before the election on a mad dash from East Coast to West and back again, but to no avail. On Election Day, November 4, Americans in every section of the country expressed their clear preference for Reagan, if they voted at all. A turnout of just over 52 percent of the eligible voting-age population confirmed that the general apathy of the post–John F. Kennedy years was continuing.

Nationwide, Reagan won 51 percent of the vote to only 41 percent for Carter and 7 percent for Anderson, with the rest split among minor candidates. Reagan won comfortably in the East (5 percentage points), South (8 percent against a Southern candidate), and Midwest (10 percent), and routed Carter in the West (20 percent). He carried 44 states to Carter's 6 and won 489 electoral votes to 49 for Carter.

According to a *New York Times*/CBS News survey of voters leaving their polling places, white males, Catholics, Protestants, independents and defecting Democrats, and voters aged 30 and older with incomes in excess of $15,000 a year and advanced education were Reagan's strongest backers. Whites supported him 55 percent to 36 percent, while blacks backed Carter 82–14, and Hispanics supported the losing incumbent by 54–36. Males preferred Reagan 54–37, women by only 46–45. Catholics went 51–40 for Reagan, Protestants 56–37; even Jews, a traditional anchor in the Democratic constituency, gave him 39 percent, to 45 percent for Carter. Independents favored Reagan 50–34, and 26 percent of Democrats switched to him. Only the 18–21 age group chose Carter, and very narrowly—44–43. Reagan's popularity was demonstrated in direct proportion to voters' increased age, income, and education, with a slight falloff of the Social Security–conscious, 60-plus age group, which also backed him, 54–40. Reagan cracked the normally Democratic blue-collar vote in this survey, 47–46, and trailed Carter only slightly, 44–47, among union-household voters surveyed.

What was more, the Republicans gained control of the Senate for the first time since Eisenhower's first-term election 28 years earlier—strong evidence that a conservative tide was indeed gripping the country. No less than seven liberal Democratic stalwarts were ousted, including the 1972 party standard-bearer, George McGovern of South Dakota.

A major factor in this development was the role played by political action committees (PACs)—groups raising and spending money on behalf of candidates of their choice, or against those to whom they objected. With the direct presidential campaigns financed with federal funds, the PACs either made "independent expenditures" for their presidential choice or for congressional and senatorial campaigns, and in both cases the Republican candidates were by far the major beneficiaries. Whereas in 1976 Federal Election Commission records indicated that corporate PACs, most of them backing Republicans, had outnumbered Democratic-oriented labor PACs, 450 to 303, the ratio had mushroomed by 1980: 1,226 corporate and business PACs to only 318 run by labor unions. Also, 8 of the 10 largest PAC givers to congressional candidates were corporate or conservative political groups.

Yet, so focused had the election year been on Jimmy Carter—his failures and, in the general election, on his personal demeanor as a candidate—that it was debatable whether Reagan's victory meant the country really wanted and expected his undiluted brand of conservatism. He had used the same extravagantly conservative rhetoric in getting elected governor of California, after all, and had turned out to be more moderate and accommodating in his actions than his campaign oratory had suggested he would be.

Polls before and after the election confirmed that voters did, in fact, want to "get the government off our backs," but only in general terms of excessive spending, taxation, and regulation. When it came to government services of nearly every description, they still wanted government to perform them—services from Social Security and hospital care to welfare and unemployment benefits that were the very essence of the New Deal. It would not be until Ronald Reagan took office in January 1981, and he began to convert his rhetoric to sweeping changes in government policy and thought, that the voters who so soundly rejected Jimmy Carter would appreciate what their dislike of the first elected incumbent to be defeated for reelection in nearly three decades had wrought.

In his inaugural address, Reagan repeated a statement that had come to sum up his whole attitude in more than 20 years of political preaching. "In this present crisis," he said, "government is not the solution to our problem; government is the problem. . . . It is my intention to curb the size and influence of the federal establishment. . . . It's not my intention to do away with government. It is rather to make it work—work with us, not over us; to stand by our side, not ride on our back." And, it turned out for good or ill, Ronald Reagan really meant what he said.

—*Jules Witcover*

Selected Bibliography
See Herbert E. Alexander, *Financing the 1980 Election* (1983); Sidney Blumenthal, *The Rise of the Counter-Establishment* (1986); Andrew Busch, *Reagan's Victory: The Presidential Election of 1980 and the Rise of the Right* (2005); Lou Cannon, *Reagan* (1982); Jimmy Carter, *Keeping Faith* (1982); Robert Dallek, *Ronald Reagan* (1984); Elizabeth Drew, *Portrait of an Election* (1981); Rowland Evans and Robert Novak, *The Reagan Revolution* (1981); Thomas Ferguson and Joel Rogers, ed., *The Hidden Election: Politics and Economics in the 1980 Presidential Campaign* (1981); Jack W. Germond and Jules Witcover, *Blue Smoke and Mirrors: How Reagan Won and Why Carter Lost the Election of 1980* (1981); Jeff Greenfield, *The Real Campaign: How the Media Missed the Story of the 1980 Campaign* (1982); Erwin Hargrove, *Jimmy Carter as President* (1988); Steven F. Hayward, *The Age of Reagan: The Fall of the Old Liberal Order 1964–1980* (2001); Hamilton Jordan, *Crisis: The Last Year of the Carter Presidency* (1982); Burton Ira Kaufman, *The Presidency of James Earl Carter, Jr.* (1993); Gil Troy, *Morning in America: How Ronald Reagan Invented the 1980s* (2005); Gerald M. Pomper, *The Election of 1980: Reports and Interpretations* (1981); Austin Ranney, *The American Elections of 1980* (1981); John F. Stacks, *Watershed: The Campaign for the Presidency, 1980* (1981); Peter Steinfels, *The Neo-Conservatives* (1979); John Kenneth White, *The New Politics of Old Values* (1988); and Garry Wills, *Reagan's America: Innocents at Home* (1985). Jonathan Moore, ed., *The Campaign for President: 1980 in Retrospect* (1982), provides excellent firsthand accounts by campaign insiders.

1980 Electoral Map and Statistics

Electoral Vote, 1980

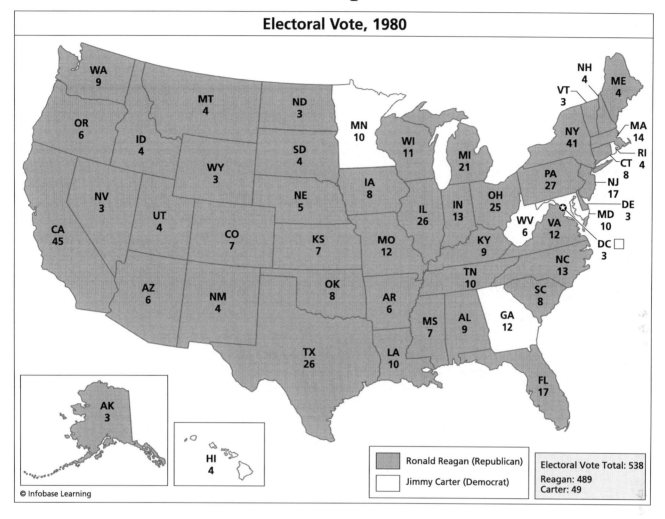

WA 9
OR 6
ID 4
MT 4
ND 3
MN 10
WI 11
MI 21
NH 4
VT 3
ME 4
NY 41
MA 14
RI 4
CT 8
NV 3
UT 4
WY 3
SD 4
IA 8
IL 26
IN 13
OH 25
PA 27
NJ 17
DE 3
MD 10
CA 45
CO 7
NE 5
KS 7
MO 12
KY 9
WV 6
VA 12
DC 3
AZ 6
NM 4
OK 8
AR 6
TN 10
NC 13
SC 8
GA 12
MS 7
AL 9
LA 10
TX 26
FL 17

AK 3
HI 4

Ronald Reagan (Republican)
Jimmy Carter (Democrat)

Electoral Vote Total: 538
Reagan: 489
Carter: 49

© Infobase Learning

1980 ELECTION STATISTICS

State	Number of Electors	Total Popular Vote	Elec Vote R	Elec Vote D	Pop Vote R	Pop Vote D	Margin of Victory Votes	Margin of Victory % Total Vote
Alabama	9	1,341,929	9		1	2	17,462	1.30%
Alaska	3	158,445	3		1	2	44,270	27.94%
Arizona	6	873,945	6		1	2	282,845	32.36%
Arkansas	6	837,582	6		1	2	5,123	0.61%
California	45	8,587,063	45		1	2	1,441,197	16.78%
Colorado	7	1,184,415	7		1	2	284,291	24.00%
Connecticut	8	1,406,285	8		1	2	135,478	9.63%
Delaware	3	235,668	3		1	2	5,498	2.33%
District of Columbia	3	173,889		3	2	1	106,918	61.49%
Florida	17	3,687,026	17		1	2	627,476	17.02%
Georgia	12	1,597,467		12	2	1	236,565	14.81%
Hawaii	4	303,287		4	2	1	5,767	1.90%
Idaho	4	437,431	4		1	2	180,507	41.27%
Illinois	26	4,749,721	26		1	2	376,636	7.93%
Indiana	13	2,242,033	13		1	2	411,459	18.35%
Iowa	8	1,317,661	8		1	2	167,354	12.70%
Kansas	7	979,795	7		1	2	240,662	24.56%
Kentucky	9	1,294,627	9		1	2	18,857	1.46%
Louisiana	10	1,548,591	10		1	2	84,400	5.45%
Maine	4	523,011	4		1	2	17,548	3.36%
Maryland	10	1,540,496		10	2	1	45,555	2.96%
Massachusetts	14	2,524,298	14		1	2	3,829	0.15%
Michigan	21	3,909,725	21		1	2	253,693	6.49%
Minnesota	10	2,051,953		10	2	1	80,933	3.94%
Mississippi	7	892,620	7		1	2	11,808	1.32%
Missouri	12	2,099,824	12		1	2	142,999	6.81%
Montana	4	363,952	4		1	2	88,782	24.39%
Nebraska	5	640,854	5		1	2	253,086	39.49%
Nevada	3	247,885	3		1	2	88,351	35.64%
New Hampshire	4	383,999	4		1	2	112,841	29.39%
New Jersey	17	2,975,684	17		1	2	399,193	13.42%
New Mexico	4	456,237	4		1	2	82,953	18.18%
New York	41	6,201,959	41		1	2	165,459	2.67%
North Carolina	13	1,855,833	13		1	2	39,383	2.12%
North Dakota	3	301,545	3		1	2	114,506	37.97%
Ohio	25	4,283,603	25		1	2	454,131	10.60%
Oklahoma	8	1,149,708	8		1	2	293,544	25.53%
Oregon	6	1,181,516	6		1	2	114,154	9.66%
Pennsylvania	27	4,561,501	27		1	2	324,332	7.11%
Rhode Island	4	416,072		4	2	1	43,549	10.47%
South Carolina	8	890,083	8		1	2	13,647	1.53%
South Dakota	4	327,703	4		1	2	94,488	28.83%
Tennessee	10	1,617,616	10		1	2	4,710	0.29%
Texas	26	4,541,637	26		1	2	629,558	13.86%
Utah	4	604,222	4		1	2	315,421	52.20%
Vermont	3	213,207	3		1	2	12,707	5.96%
Virginia	12	1,866,032	12		1	2	237,435	12.72%
Washington	9	1,742,394	9		1	2	215,051	12.34%
West Virginia	6	737,715		6	2	1	33,256	4.51%
Wisconsin	11	2,273,221	11		1	2	107,261	4.72%
Wyoming	3	176,713	3		1	2	61,273	34.67%
Total	538	86,509,678	489	49	1	2	8,423,115	9.74%

Reagan Republican		Carter Democratic		Anderson Independent		Clark Libertarian		Others	
654,192	48.75%	636,730	47.45%	16,481	1.23%	13,318	0.99%	21,208	1.58%
86,112	54.35%	41,842	26.41%	11,155	7.04%	18,479	11.66%	857	0.54%
529,688	60.61%	246,843	28.24%	76,952	8.81%	18,784	2.15%	1,678	0.19%
403,164	48.13%	398,041	47.52%	22,468	2.68%	8,970	1.07%	4,939	0.59%
4,524,858	52.69%	3,083,661	35.91%	739,833	8.62%	148,434	1.73%	90,277	1.05%
652,264	55.07%	367,973	31.07%	130,633	11.03%	25,744	2.17%	7,801	0.66%
677,210	48.16%	541,732	38.52%	171,807	12.22%	8,570	0.61%	6,966	0.50%
111,252	47.21%	105,754	44.87%	16,288	6.91%	1,974	0.84%	400	0.17%
23,313	13.41%	130,231	74.89%	16,131	9.28%	1,104	0.63%	3,110	1.79%
2,046,951	55.52%	1,419,475	38.50%	189,692	5.14%	30,524	0.83%	384	0.01%
654,168	40.95%	890,733	55.76%	36,055	2.26%	15,627	0.98%	884	0.06%
130,112	42.90%	135,879	44.80%	32,021	10.56%	3,269	1.08%	2,006	0.66%
290,699	66.46%	110,192	25.19%	27,058	6.19%	8,425	1.93%	1,057	0.24%
2,358,049	49.65%	1,981,413	41.72%	346,754	7.30%	38,939	0.82%	24,566	0.52%
1,255,656	56.01%	844,197	37.65%	111,639	4.98%	19,627	0.88%	10,914	0.49%
676,026	51.31%	508,672	38.60%	115,633	8.78%	13,123	1.00%	4,207	0.32%
566,812	57.85%	326,150	33.29%	68,231	6.96%	14,470	1.48%	4,132	0.42%
635,274	49.07%	616,417	47.61%	31,127	2.40%	5,531	0.43%	6,278	0.48%
792,853	51.20%	708,453	45.75%	26,345	1.70%	8,240	0.53%	12,700	0.82%
238,522	45.61%	220,974	42.25%	53,327	10.20%	5,119	0.98%	5,069	0.97%
680,606	44.18%	726,161	47.14%	119,537	7.76%	14,192	0.92%	0	0.00%
1,057,631	41.90%	1,053,802	41.75%	382,539	15.15%	22,038	0.87%	8,288	0.33%
1,915,225	48.99%	1,661,532	42.50%	275,223	7.04%	41,597	1.06%	16,148	0.41%
873,241	42.56%	954,174	46.50%	174,990	8.53%	31,592	1.54%	17,956	0.88%
441,089	49.42%	429,281	48.09%	12,036	1.35%	5,465	0.61%	4,749	0.53%
1,074,181	51.16%	931,182	44.35%	77,920	3.71%	14,422	0.69%	2,119	0.10%
206,814	56.82%	118,032	32.43%	29,281	8.05%	9,825	2.70%	0	0.00%
419,937	65.53%	166,851	26.04%	44,993	7.02%	9,073	1.42%	0	0.00%
155,017	62.54%	66,666	26.89%	17,651	7.12%	4,358	1.76%	4,193	1.69%
221,705	57.74%	108,864	28.35%	49,693	12.94%	2,067	0.54%	1,670	0.43%
1,546,557	51.97%	1,147,364	38.56%	234,632	7.88%	20,652	0.69%	26,479	0.89%
250,779	54.97%	167,826	36.78%	29,459	6.46%	4,365	0.96%	3,808	0.83%
2,893,831	46.66%	2,728,372	43.99%	467,801	7.54%	52,648	0.85%	59,307	0.96%
915,018	49.30%	875,635	47.18%	52,800	2.85%	9,677	0.52%	2,703	0.15%
193,695	64.23%	79,189	26.26%	23,640	7.84%	3,743	1.24%	1,278	0.42%
2,206,545	51.51%	1,752,414	40.91%	254,472	5.94%	49,033	1.14%	21,139	0.49%
695,570	60.50%	402,026	34.97%	38,284	3.33%	13,828	1.20%	0	0.00%
571,044	48.33%	456,890	38.67%	112,389	9.51%	25,838	2.19%	15,355	1.30%
2,261,872	49.59%	1,937,540	42.48%	292,921	6.42%	33,263	0.73%	35,905	0.79%
154,793	37.20%	198,342	47.67%	59,819	14.38%	2,458	0.59%	660	0.16%
441,207	49.57%	427,560	48.04%	14,150	1.59%	4,975	0.56%	2,191	0.25%
198,343	60.53%	103,855	31.69%	21,431	6.54%	3,824	1.17%	250	0.08%
787,761	48.70%	783,051	48.41%	35,991	2.22%	7,116	0.44%	3,697	0.23%
2,510,705	55.28%	1,881,147	41.42%	111,613	2.46%	37,643	0.83%	529	0.01%
439,687	72.77%	124,266	20.57%	30,284	5.01%	7,226	1.20%	2,759	0.46%
94,598	44.37%	81,891	38.41%	31,760	14.90%	1,900	0.89%	3,058	1.43%
989,609	53.03%	752,174	40.31%	95,418	5.11%	12,821	0.69%	16,010	0.86%
865,244	49.66%	650,193	37.32%	185,073	10.62%	29,213	1.68%	12,671	0.73%
334,206	45.30%	367,462	49.81%	31,691	4.30%	4,356	0.59%	0	0.00%
1,088,845	47.90%	981,584	43.18%	160,657	7.07%	29,135	1.28%	13,000	0.57%
110,700	62.64%	49,427	27.97%	12,072	6.83%	4,514	2.55%	0	0.00%
43,903,230	50.75%	35,480,115	41.01%	5,719,850	6.61%	921,128	1.06%	485,355	0.56%

Election of 1984

Election Overview

Election Year 1984

Election Day November 6, 1984

Winning Candidates

- ★ **President:** Ronald Reagan
- ★ **Vice President:** George H. W. Bush

☆　☆　☆

Election Results [ticket, party: popular votes (percentage of popular vote); electoral votes (percentage of electoral vote)]

- Ronald Reagan and George H. W. Bush, Republican: 54,455,472 (58.77%); 525 (97.6%)
- Walter Mondale and Geraldine Ferraro, Democratic: 37,577,352 (40.56%); 13 (2.4%)
- Other: 620,409 (0.67%); 0 (0.0%)

Voter Turnout 53.1%

Central Forums/Campaign Methods for Addressing Voters

- Speeches
- Rallies
- Television/print ads
- Debates

Incumbent President and Vice President on Election Day Ronald Reagan and George H. W. Bush

Population (1984): 236,394,000

Gross Domestic Product

- $3,931 billion (in current dollars: $6,577 billion)
- Per capita: $16,629 (in current dollars: $27,823)

Number of Daily Newspapers (1980) 1,745

Average Daily Circulation (1980) 62,201,840

Households with

- Radio (1980): 79,968,240
- Television (1980): 76,300,000

Method of Choosing Electors: Popular vote (mostly general-ticket system/winner take all)

Method of Choosing Nominees

- Presidential preference primaries
- Caucuses

Key Issues and Events

- Economic recovery
- 1982 midterm elections: Republicans lose 27 seats in the House
- The Reagan Revolution
- Reagan reduces domestic government spending marginally.
- Reagan cuts taxes and increases defense spending significantly.
- Patriotism and optimism stirring
- Fears of nuclear war
- Budget deficit growing

Leading Candidates

REPUBLICANS
- Ronald Reagan, president of the United States (California)
- Harold E. Stassen, former governor (Minnesota)
- Ben Fernandez, Republican National Hispanic Assembly chairman (California)

DEMOCRATS

- Walter Mondale, former vice president and former senator (Minnesota)
- Gary Hart, senator (Colorado)
- Jesse Jackson, reverend and civil rights activist (Illinois)
- John Glenn, senator (Ohio)
- George McGovern, former senator (South Dakota)
- Reubin Askew, former governor (Florida)
- Alan Cranston, senator (California)
- Ernest Hollings, senator (South Carolina)

Trajectory

- Vice President Walter Mondale wins the Democratic Iowa caucuses on February 20, 1984, confirming the polls showing him leading the pack of eight Democratic candidates. In early 1983, Mondale outpolled President Ronald Reagan, who now sweeps the Republican caucuses with minimal opposition.
- Senator Gary Hart upsets Mondale in the New Hampshire primary, February 28, winning 41 percent of the vote. Hart wins by calling Mondale a hostage to the "special interests."
- Mondale wins enough on the first "Super Tuesday," March 13, to stay in the race, carrying Georgia and Alabama, but Hart's "Yuppie Crusade" wins Massachusetts, Rhode Island, and Florida. The field narrows to Hart, Mondale, and the Reverend Jesse Jackson, the first serious African-American candidate, who generates great enthusiasm among minorities but whose calls for a "rainbow coalition" are undermined by a *Washington Post* story that he called New York "Hymietown," and Jews "Hymies."
- Mondale invokes a Wendy's commercial to mock Gary Hart during a debate before the New York primary, asking, "Where's the beef?" in Hart's rhetoric about "New Ideas." Mondale's attack helps derail Hart's campaign, as Mondale receives 45 percent of the vote in New York on April 3, compared to 27 percent for Hart and 25 percent for Jackson.
- Seeking to energize his candidacy, Mondale nominates the first female vice-presidential candidate on a major party ticket. New York representative Geraldine Ferraro is soon hounded by irregularities in her husband's real estate business and Catholic clerics' condemnation of her pro-choice stance.
- President Reagan opens the Los Angeles Olympics on July 28 and presides over an enthusiastic, red-white-and-blue-festooned Republican convention in mid-August. The triumphal shouts of "U.S.A., U.S.A." at both events affirm Reagan's patriotic message that, as his most famous campaign commercial will claim, "It is morning again in America."
- Mondale's lackluster campaign receives a boost on October 7 during the first presidential debate in Louisville, Kentucky. Reagan rambles, especially during his conclusion. Mondale is sharp, aggressive, relentless. The next day the pro-Reagan *Wall Street Journal* asks: "Is Oldest U.S. President Now Showing His Age?" The Reagan camp's claim that the president was "overprepared" makes things worse.
- On October 21, at the second debate, Reagan also stumbles. But he appears more confident, and dismisses the age issue with a knockout blow, saying, "I want you to know that also I will not make age an issue of this campaign. I am not going to exploit for political purposes my opponent's youth and inexperience."

Conventions

- Democratic National Convention: July 16–19, 1984, Moscone Center, San Francisco
- Republican National Convention: August 20–23, 1984, Reunion Arena, Dallas

Ballots/Nominees

REPUBLICANS
Presidential first ballot
- Ronald Reagan 2,233
- Abstaining 2

Vice-presidential ballot
- George H. W. Bush 2,231
- Abstaining 2
- Jack Kemp 1
- Jeane Kirkpatrick 1

DEMOCRATS
Presidential ballot
- Walter Mondale 2,191
- Gary Hart 1,200.5
- Jesse Jackson 465.5
- Thomas Eagleton 18
- George McGovern 4
- John Glenn 2
- Joe Biden 1
- Lane Kirkland 1

Vice-presidential ballot
- Geraldine A. Ferraro 3,920
- Shirley Chisholm 3

Primaries

- Republican Party: 30; 71.0% delegates
- Democratic Party: 30; 62.1% delegates

Primaries Results

REPUBLICANS

- Ronald Reagan 6,484,987; 98.78%
- Unpledged 55,458; 0.84%
- Harold E. Stassen 12,749; 0.19%

DEMOCRATS

- Walter Mondale 6,952,912; 38.32%
- Gary Hart 6,504,842; 35.85%
- Jesse Jackson 3,282,431; 18.09%
- John Glenn 617,909; 3.41%
- George McGovern 334,801; 1.84%
- Unpledged 146,212; 0.81%

Primary Debates

- Eleven Democratic primary debates, with the first one on October 13, 1983, the last one on June 3, 1984.
- The March 11, 1984, debate in Atlanta is the "Where's the Beef?" debate.

Party Platform

REPUBLICANS

- "From freedom comes opportunity; from opportunity comes growth; from growth comes progress"
- Faith in free enterprise
- Call for a balanced budget
- Line-item veto
- Regulatory reform
- "There is a profound moral difference between the actions and ideals of Marxist-Leninist regimes and those of democratic governments."

DEMOCRATS

- Reduce deficit
- Education, training, and retraining
- "Confront . . . the growing problems in our infrastructure."
- "The Reagan Administration has virtually wished away the role of government."
- "Recovery built on debt"
- Fears nuclear arms race will spiral out of control

Campaign Innovations

- The Tuesday Team, an ad-hoc ad agency to reelect Reagan led by Hal Riney

- "It's Morning Again in America": classic gauzy, soft-sell ad campaign
- "Line of the day": Reagan's staff pitched one idea per daily news cycle

Campaign Tactics

REPUBLICANS

- Reagan runs as the candidate of peace, prosperity, and patriotism.
- Masterful use of media, with red-white-and-blue television and radio ads produced by top advertising executives
- Campaign of balloon drops, big rallies, and splashy photo ops
- Reagan balances busy campaign schedule with presidential duties at home and foreign trips to London and "so-called Communist China."
- Emphasizes economic boom after "Carter–Mondale" recession and inflation
- Ignores deficit
- Reagan never mentions Mondale directly—"what's his name"
- Deflects claims of being a hawk by calling for arms controls negotiations with the Soviet Union

DEMOCRATS

- Traditional campaign with big Labor Day opening, reliance on unions—but few people march in Labor Day parades anymore as union influence declines.
- Mondale less comfortable on television, wants a more substantive campaign.
- Tries characterizing Ronald Reagan as a bigoted Scrooge and an ignorant Mr. Magoo but confuses elusive "swing" voters.
- Comes off looking pessimistic, negative.
- Attacks on Reagan's hawkishness, insensitivity to poor, the growing deficit
- Mondale's call to be responsible and raise taxes backfires, tagged as a "tax and spend."
- Gets some traction by questioning Reagan's age after the first debate, but Reagan's comeback in the second debate ends the issue.

Debates

- October 7, 1984: Presidential debate in Louisville, Kentucky
- October 11, 1984: Vice-presidential debate in Philadelphia
- October 21, 1984: Presidential debate in Kansas City, Missouri

Popular Campaign Slogans

REPUBLICANS

- "It's Morning Again in America"
- "Bringing America Back: Prouder, Stronger, Better"
- "America Is Too Great for Small Dreams"
- "Leadership That's Working"

DEMOCRATS

- "America Needs New Leadership"
- "Mondale/Ferraro: For the Family of America"
- "America Needs a Change"

Campaign Songs

- Republican Party: "God Bless the U.S.A."
- Democratic Party: "Gonna Fly Now"

Influential Campaign Appeals or Ads

REPUBLICANS

- "It's morning again in America. Today more men and women will go to work than ever before in our country's history. With interest rates at about half the record highs of 1980, nearly 2,000 families today will buy new homes, more than at any time in the past four years. This afternoon 6,500 young men and women will be married, and with inflation at less than half of what it was just four years ago, they can look forward with confidence to the future. It's morning again in America, and under the leadership of President Reagan, our country is prouder and stronger and better. Why would we ever want to return to where we were less than four short years ago?"
- "Ronald Reagan—Leadership That's Working"
- "Bear in the woods" ad (titled "Bear")—the Soviet Union as a lumbering threat
- Ad commemorating the 40th anniversary of the troops landing at Normandy moves Secret Service agents—and Mondale campaign workers—to tears
- "America's Back"

DEMOCRATS

- One ad plays Crosby, Stills, Nash, and Young singing their 1960s hit "Teach Your Children" in the background, juxtaposes images of children playing with footage of ICBMs launching.
- Mondale's discomfort with media undermines his message.

Campaign Finance

- Reagan: $40,400,000 (in current dollars: $79,127,600)
- Mondale: $40,400,000 (in current dollars: $79,127,600)

Defining Quotations

- "And I know myself: I am ready. I am ready to be President of the United States." *Former vice president Walter Mondale launching his campaign, February 21, 1983*
- "A New Generation of Leadership: Committed to America's traditional values. Gary Hart is impatient with yesterday's politics. He was the first announced presidential candidate to renounce campaign contributions from special interest Political Action Committees. In 1983, Gary Hart published *A New Democracy*, a forward-looking book detailing his plans for governing the nation. Gary Hart is the youngest candidate for President. At 46, he is young enough to bring vitality and energy to the Presidency. Yet he has served almost ten years in the U.S. Senate." *Gary Hart for President 1984 campaign brochure*
- "It's time for a change. Our time has come!" *Jesse Jackson at Democratic National Convention, San Francisco, July 17, 1984*
- "Let's tell the truth. Mr. Reagan will raise taxes, and so will I. He won't tell you. I just did." *Walter Mondale, Democratic nomination acceptance speech, July 19, 1984*
- "Government of the rich, by the rich, and for the rich." *Walter Mondale, Democratic nomination acceptance speech, July 19, 1984*
- "My fellow Americans, I am pleased to tell you I just signed legislation which outlaws Russia forever. The bombing begins in five minutes." *Ronald Reagan ad-libbing during a radio test, August 11, 1984*
- "The choices this year are not just between two different personalities or between two political parties. They're between two different visions of the future, two fundamentally different ways of governing—their government of pessimism, fear, and limits, or ours of hope, confidence, and growth. Their government sees people only as members of groups; ours serves all the people of America as individuals. Theirs lives in the past, seeking to apply the old and failed policies to an era that has passed them by. Ours learns from the past and strives to change by boldly charting a new course for the future. Theirs lives by promises, the bigger, the better. We offer proven, workable answers." *Ronald Reagan, second presidential nomination acceptance speech, August 23, 1984*
- "I would rather lose a campaign about decency than win a campaign about self-interest. I don't think this nation is composed of people who care only for themselves." *Walter Mondale during the first debate against Reagan, October 7, 1984*

- "I was about to say to him very sternly, 'Mr. Mondale, you are taxing my patience.' And then I caught myself. Why should I give him another idea? That's the only tax he hasn't thought about." *Ronald Reagan in Ohio about Mondale's proposed tax increase, October 12, 1984*
- "Four years ago we began to navigate by some certain, fixed principles. Our North Star was freedom, and common sense our constellations. We knew that economic freedom meant paying less of the American family's earnings to the government, and so we cut personal tax rates by 25 percent. We knew that inflation, the quiet thief, was stealing our savings, and the highest interest rates since the Civil War were making it impossible for people to own a home or start an enterprise. And let me interject a news note, in case you've been busy this morning and haven't heard it: Led by Morgan, the bank, two other major banks joined them, and the prime rate came down to 12 percent as of this morning. And I'm sure that the other banks will soon follow. . . . We knew that our national military defense had been weakened, so we decided to rebuild and be strong again. And this we knew would enhance the chances for peace throughout the world. It was a second American revolution, and it's only just begun. But America is back, a giant, powerful in its renewed spirit, its growing economy, powerful in its ability to defend itself and secure the peace, and powerful in its ability to build a new future. And you know something? That's not debatable." *Ronald Reagan, campaign speech in Fairfield, Connecticut, October 26, 1984*
- "America's best days lie ahead, and—you ain't seen nothin' yet!" *Ronald Reagan, victory speech, November 7, 1984*
- "Reagan is the most popular figure in the history of the United States. No candidate we put up would have been able to beat Reagan this year." *Speaker "Tip" O'Neill after the election*

Lasting Legacy of Campaign

- Geraldine A. Ferraro becomes the first woman nominated by a major party.
- Jesse Jackson's "Rainbow Coalition" involves more African Americans and minorities in the political process.
- Reagan's media-savvy, sound bite–laden, patriotic campaign sets a template for electioneering and governing that both Democrats and Republicans follow.

Election of 1984

The 1984 election was a contest between a president and a party. Ronald Reagan, attractive and articulate, relaxed and amiable, was a highly skilled campaigner running for reelection in a time of peace and rising prosperity. His political base was relatively narrow and the Republican Party weak in much of the country, but in an age of media politics, Reagan's strength as a television campaigner was to prove an enormous asset.

Opposing Reagan was the powerful, heterogeneous, and often uneasy coalition known as the Democratic Party. Beginning with their capture of the House of Representatives in the midterm election of 1930 and benefiting from the inspired leadership of Franklin D. Roosevelt during the ordeals of the Great Depression and World War II, the Democrats supplanted the Republicans as the nation's majority party. By 1984, events had eroded the dominance they had once enjoyed. Still, as the year opened, the Democrats controlled the House of Representatives as they had for 50 of the previous 54 years, and seemed likely to retain that control in November, regardless of the outcome in the presidential race. With 45 seats in the Senate, they were favored to make gains that, if not large enough to recapture the majority they had lost in 1980, would probably put them in position to do so in 1986. The Democrats controlled 35 of the 50 governorships, and 34 of the state legislatures completely and one of the two chambers in four other states.

The Democrats in the midterm election of 1982 regained 26 of the 33 House seats they had lost two years earlier. This strong showing had damaged the theory, tentatively advanced by some commentators, that 1980 might be a "critical election," heralding the return of the Republicans as the natural majority party.* In terms of expressed political preference, the Gallup Poll in 1983 reported that 44 percent of voters were Democrats, 25 percent were Republicans, and 31 percent were Independents.

Reagan's political strength was similar to that of Dwight D. Eisenhower. It was a personal, not a party, phenomenon. Without Reagan, the Republicans would be

---

* V. O. Key had described the elections of 1800, 1828, 1860, 1896, and 1932 as "critical" because they registered in each instance a new balance of social forces and set the political pattern for the next several decades.

much weaker. The first major political event of the year, therefore, was Reagan's decision to seek reelection despite his age. At 73, he was already the oldest man ever to serve in the White House. The Democrats dared not make Reagan's advanced age an issue; his evident physical vigor and unbroken record of good health made the fact of his age a matter for public admiration rather than concern. This admiration was bolstered by the president's insouciant response to the shooting attempt on his life in March 1981. "I forgot to duck," he joked to his wife. As he was about to undergo surgery for removal of the bullet, he wisecracked to the surgeons, "I hope you are all Republicans."

If reporters noted that Reagan worked only five or six hours a day, spent long weekends at Camp David, and took frequent vacations, this, too, was not something the Democrats could easily convert into an issue. After President Carter's long hours and studious work, and the earlier crises of the Nixon and Johnson years, Americans seemed relieved to have a president who coped with the job without strain and with unfailing equanimity and good humor. Reagan had hung President Calvin Coolidge's portrait in the Cabinet Room as a symbol of his esteem for that Republican predecessor. Like Coolidge's famous naps, Reagan's relaxed approach to the presidency was not only acceptable to the country but actually reassuring. It was as if the man at the top was signaling the nation that things were not as bad as the news media would have the public believe.

Reagan's administrative style was not an accommodation to his advancing years. It was a continuation of the way he had governed California for eight years from 1967 to 1975. He viewed himself as a chairman of the board, rather than as an active executive. He delegated to senior aides most of his administrative power over appointments, legislation, the budget, and supervision of departments and agencies. He involved himself on a day-to-day basis in only a few issues. He was content to provide broad policy direction and to serve as his administration's most persuasive spokesman. At the middle and upper levels of his administration, there were frequent struggles for power and for control of policy among cabinet officers and factions of the White House staff. Rivals waged ideological and personal feuds through "leaks" to the press. These conflicts did the president no political harm; Reagan stayed above these battles, clearly unconcerned about any inefficiency or loss of morale that infighting might produce, and serenely confident of his ability to impose his will if and when he chose to do so. Since the huge expansion of the activities of the federal government had begun under Franklin Roosevelt a half-century earlier, no president had governed with such a loose rein.

Reagan was unfamiliar with the details or even the main issues in many disputes, both foreign and domestic.

President Reagan did not change his stance on the government, even after he became its head. While president he often attacked "Washington" and "the bureaucracy" in his speeches. This benefited his campaign for reelection in 1984, as he presented himself as allied with his fellow citizens. *(Library of Congress)*

Indeed, the breadth of his ignorance was sometimes startling. In October 1983, for example, at a time when U.S.–Soviet arms control negotiations were breaking down, the *New York Times* reported that Reagan told a group of visitors that he had only recently learned that most of the Soviet nuclear deterrent force was in land-based rather than submarine-based missiles. Surprisingly, this disclosure evoked relatively little public comment.

Like Eisenhower, but to an even greater extent, Reagan stayed politically popular by distancing himself in public from his own administration. Scandals occurred and controversies flared, but the president, not ever having involved himself closely with most of these appointees or the problems confronting them, was untouched.

Having been elected as an opponent of big government, Reagan said in his inaugural address, "Government is not the solution to our problem. Government is the problem." Once in office, he continued in speeches around the country to attack "Washington" and "the bureaucracy." He fostered the belief that he and his fellow citizens were allies against the government rather than that he had been chosen by them to direct the affairs of that government.

Reagan's detached style of governing, his distancing himself from his own appointees and the career bureaucracy, and his blithe cheerfulness and imperturbable optimism were central to the political problem faced by the Democrats in 1984. Reagan was dubbed "the Teflon *(continues on page 1454)*

★ ★ ★
1984 ELECTION CHRONOLOGY

1982
November 2, 1982: Democrats gain 26 seats in the House of Representatives during the midterm elections—along with great confidence that the "Reagan Recession" and concern over President Ronald Reagan's budget cuts will return the Democrats to the White House in 1984.

1983
February 17, 1983: Senator Gary Hart of Colorado declares his candidacy for the 1984 Democratic presidential nomination. Hart is polling at about 1 percent support compared to better known candidates such as Ohio senator (and former astronaut) John Glenn, California senator Alan Cranston, South Carolina senator Fritz Hollings, and the front-runner, former vice president Walter Mondale.

February 21, 1983: Former vice president Mondale launches his campaign with great confidence, saying: "And I know myself: I am ready. I am ready to be President of the United States." Mondale is especially confident because, thanks to the "Hunt Commission," 14 percent of delegates to the Democratic Convention are "superdelegates," officeholders likely to support him as the establishment candidate.

March 8, 1983: President Reagan denounces the Soviet Union as "an evil empire."

December 29, 1983: The Reverend Jesse Jackson, a Democratic presidential candidate, travels to Syria to try to release Navy Lt. Robert O. Goodman Jr., whose plane was shot down over Lebanon. Jackson succeeds, prompting admiration—and admonitions about diplomatic grandstanding.

1984
January 25, 1984: President Reagan delivers the 1984 State of the Union Address, rejoicing: "There is renewed energy and optimism throughout the land. America is back, standing tall, looking to the eighties with courage, confidence, and hope."

January 29, 1984: President Reagan launches his reelection campaign.

February 13, 1984: In the 37th and 38th paragraphs of a 52-paragraph profile of Jesse Jackson, the *Washington Post* reports that Jackson, after saying to an African-American reporter "let's talk black talk," referred to Jews as "Hymie" and New York as "Hymietown."

February 20, 1984: Mondale wins the Democratic Iowa caucuses, confirming the polls showing him leading the pack of eight Democratic candidates. Throughout 1983, Mondale frequently outpolled President Reagan, who now sweeps the Republican caucuses with minimal opposition.

February 26, 1984: Jackson finally apologizes for his "Hymietown" remarks, only to be dogged for the next few weeks by his hesitation to distance himself from the threatening remarks to Jews and the *Washington Post* reporters from the Nation of Islam leader, Louis Farrakhan.

February 28, 1984: Senator Gary Hart upsets Mondale in the New Hampshire primary, winning 41 percent of the vote. Hart wins by calling Mondale a hostage to the "special interests." Hart will follow this up with victories in the Maine caucuses and Vermont primary.

March 13, 1984: Mondale wins enough on the first "Super Tuesday" to stay in the race, carrying Georgia and Alabama, but Hart's "Yuppie Crusade" wins Massachusetts, Rhode Island, and Florida. The field narrows to Hart, Mondale, and Jackson, the first serious African-American candidate, who generates great enthusiasm among minorities but whose calls for a "rainbow coalition" are undermined by his slurs against Jews.

March 20, 1984: Mondale comes from behind to win the Illinois primary, with 40 percent to Hart's 35 percent and Jackson's 20 percent. Hart has been enduring intense scrutiny by reporters wondering why he tried covering his name change from Hartpence to Hart and lied about his age by a year.

April 3, 1984: Mondale receives 45 percent of the vote in New York, compared to 27 percent for Hart and 25 percent for Jackson. During a debate before the primary, Mondale invoked a Wendy's commercial to ask "Where's the beef?" in Gary Hart's rhetoric about "New Ideas."

April 26, 1984: As the Democrats squabble and weaken, Mondale in particular, Reagan acts presidential, arriving for a state visit in China.

June 6, 1984: In Normandy, on his way to the G-7 summit, Reagan speaks at the ceremonies marking the 40th anniversary of D-Day. Snippets of the speeches make extremely effective campaign commercials that bring tears to the eyes of patriots from both parties.

July 12, 1984: Seeking to energize his candidacy, Mondale nominates New York representative Geraldine Ferraro, the first female vice-presidential candidate on a major party ticket. Ferraro is soon hounded by word of irregularities in her husband's real estate business and Catholic clerics' condemnation of her pro-choice stance.

July 16, 1984: The Democratic National Convention meets at the Moscone Center in San Francisco to nominate Walter F. Mondale from Minnesota for president and Geraldine Ferraro from New York for vice president.

July 17, 1984: Jesse Jackson gives a rousing oration at the Democratic convention, declaring: "It's time for a change. Our time has come!"

July 19, 1984: The excitement generated by the Ferraro choice boosts Mondale. Mondale himself is resolute when accepting the nomination, denouncing Reagan's "Government of the rich, by the rich, and for the rich" and saying, "Let's tell the truth. Mr. Reagan will raise taxes, and so will I. He won't tell you. I just did." Right after the convention, Gallup estimates that Mondale is leading Reagan 48 to 46 percent.

July 28, 1984: President Reagan opens the Los Angeles Olympics. The triumphal shouts of "U.S.A., U.S.A." affirm Reagan's patriotic message that, as his most famous campaign commercial will claim, "It is morning again in America."

August 11, 1984: Ad-libbing to test radio equipment, Reagan says: "My fellow Americans, I am pleased to tell you I just signed legislation which outlaws Russia forever. The bombing begins in five minutes."

August 20–23, 1984: The Republican National Convention meets at Reunion Arena in Dallas to renominate President Ronald Reagan as president and Vice President George H. W. Bush as vice president.

August 21, 1984: Geraldine Ferraro mounts a detailed defense of her family finances at a lengthy news conference but is soon targeted by Archbishop John J. O'Connor of New York for being pro-choice.

September 28, 1984: Reagan hosts Soviet foreign minister Andrei Gromyko in the White House, disproving Democratic charges that Reagan's leadership will lead to war.

October 7, 1984: Mondale's lackluster campaign receives a boost during the first presidential debate in Louisville, Kentucky. Reagan rambles, especially during his conclusion. Mondale is sharp, aggressive, relentless.

October 8, 1984: The pro-Reagan *Wall Street Journal* asks: "Is Oldest U.S. President Now Showing His Age?" The Reagan camp's claim that the president was "overprepared" makes things worse.

October 12, 1984: Reagan takes an old-fashioned whistle-stop railroad train campaign tour through Ohio. At one stop he quips: "I was about to say to him very sternly, 'Mr. Mondale, you are taxing my patience.' And then I caught myself. Why should I give him another idea? That's the only tax he hasn't thought about."

October 21, 1984: At the second presidential debate, Reagan also stumbles. But he appears more confident, and dismisses the age issue with a knockout blow, saying, "I want you to know that also I will not make age an issue of this campaign. I am not going to exploit for political purposes my opponent's youth and inexperience."

November 6, 1984: Ronald Reagan wins by a landslide, carrying 49 states, securing 525 electoral votes, two more than Franklin Roosevelt in 1936. His popular vote margin of 59 percent to 41 percent is also impressive, although his failure to campaign more effectively for his party is evident as Republicans lose two Senate seats and only gain 14 House seats.

December 17, 1984: Presidential electors cast their ballots in their respective state capitals.

1985

January 7, 1985: A joint session of Congress assembles to count the electoral votes.

(continued from page 1451)
President: nothing sticks to him." It was significant that in the fourth year of his presidency there were no anti-Reagan jokes of the kind that normally circulate about presidents. There seemed to be no audience for them. Politicians of both parties reported that many constituents disagreed with the president's policies, distrusted his intentions, or questioned his competence, and yet avowed that they liked him personally. Democrats in Congress and at the state level were consequently reluctant to mount against him the kind of sustained attacks that had weakened other recent presidents.

This liking for Reagan did not have the firm foundation of respect for past accomplishments that undergirded the liking for Eisenhower in the 1950s. Nor was there the profound gratitude and loyalty from broad masses of people that Franklin D. Roosevelt's innovative programs had evoked. Still less was Reagan a hero who inspired emulation and enthusiasm, particularly among younger voters, as John F. Kennedy did. The liking for Reagan was a reflection of his sunny disposition, a reciprocation of his positive approach. It also correlated closely with the trend of the economy.

Reagan came to office committed to a counterrevolution in economic and social policy and in foreign affairs. He sought to reverse the growth in big government and to abolish or reduce the size of the government programs in education, health care, job training, housing, legal aid, and environmental protection. Some of the programs had originated in the Roosevelt New Deal of the 1930s and others in the Kennedy–Johnson administrations of the 1960s.

Reagan was a "born-again" conservative. As a Hollywood actor, he had been well known in the Democratic Party and active in liberal causes. He voted four times for Roosevelt and for Harry Truman in 1948. He shifted sharply to the right during the 1950s. By the time he reemerged on the political scene as a television evangelist for Barry Goldwater in the 1964 campaign, Reagan had adopted the free-market economics and minimal-government theory last espoused in the White House by Herbert Hoover. Reagan, first as a paid lecturer and television program host for the General Electric Company and then as a candidate for state and national office, preached his new beliefs in simple terms and with the fresh enthusiasm of a convert. He was that rare figure in any nation's politics: an ideologue with charm. He mixed the economics of Herbert Hoover with the jokes of Bob Hope; he softened and warmed the stark creed of competitive individualism with sentimental stories and happy-ending anecdotes from the *Reader's Digest.*

Interpreting his 1980 mandate broadly, Reagan proposed in 1981 a fundamental reshaping of the relationship between the federal government and the individual citizen in a way that had not been attempted since the New Deal. He pushed through a budget that tightened eligibility standards and cut appropriations for Medicaid, food stamps, student loans, job training, student lunch programs, aid to the handicapped, and aid to the arts and humanities. In subsequent budgets, he continued this downward pressure. In his first three years in office, for example, government spending on job training and public employment programs fell from $9.2 billion to $5.2 billion.

Reagan recommended abolition of the Department of Education, which had been established in 1979, but Congress resisted this change. The first Reagan budget reduced federal spending for elementary, secondary, and vocational education programs from $7 billion to $6.5 billion. In subsequent years, Congress rejected even steeper cuts that he proposed. In the resulting compromises, spending for all education programs stayed approximately level with 1981 figures, which, as critics pointed out, was a concealed cut in real terms since spending did not take account of inflation.

Reagan persuaded Congress to consolidate 30 health programs, previously targeted for specific categories of people and administered under strict federal regulations, into three block grants; states received wide discretion as to their administration. Critics argued that since these grants were not indexed for inflation, the change would mean a decline in the quality of health assistance for low-income individuals, particularly in the poorer states, which would not use state funds to make up the shortfall in federal money.

Reagan in 1981 proposed cutting Social Security benefits and gradually raising the retirement age to 68 by the year 2000. These proposals reflected his longstanding preoccupation with the "actuarial unsoundness" of the Social Security system.* When his recommendations aroused a storm of protest from Congress and the senior-citizens lobby, Reagan backed off. Eventually, a bipartisan commission worked out a compromise that Congress approved in 1983. It raised the system's revenues and at least temporarily defused Social Security as a political issue.

The Reagan counterrevolution in domestic policy was more than offset in its fiscal effect by a dramatic rise in defense spending. Reagan raised the defense budget in his first year by $30 billion—about 14 percent—to a level of $222 billion, and increased it by smaller but still substan-

---

* His provocative remarks about Social Security had alarmed elderly Republican voters in the New Hampshire and Florida primaries in 1976 and probably cost Reagan victory over President Gerald Ford in the contest for the nomination that year.

tial percentages in each subsequent year. By 1984, defense spending had reached $284 billion.

A major feature of Reagan's program was the 1981 tax bill, which cut personal income taxes by 25 percent over a three-year period and provided in dollar terms the largest income tax reduction in history. The bill reduced the surtax on the highest incomes from 70 percent to 50 percent, lowered the capital gains tax, and greatly reduced estate and gift taxes. By liberalizing amortization and depreciation schedules, the bill provided a huge tax reduction to corporations. Reagan professed confidence that, as with the much smaller Kennedy–Johnson tax cut enacted in 1964, lower rates would actually produce higher revenues by stimulating business activity.

When during the 1980 primary campaign Reagan had promised to reduce taxes, increase defense spending, and also balance the budget, his party rivals said these objectives were so self-contradictory that they would be impossible to achieve. George Bush, later to become Reagan's vice president, deprecated the agenda as "voodoo economics." When Congress actually voted this program into effect in the spring and summer of 1981, many from both parties voted for it while suspending their disbelief. Senator Howard Baker, the Senate Republican floor leader, described the Reagan economic program as a "riverboat gamble."

For a lengthy period, it looked as if Reagan had lost this gamble. Coincidentally with his signing of the budget and tax bills, a severe recession began. This deepened in 1982 to become the worst economic decline the nation had experienced in the 40 years since the end of the Great Depression. Twelve million persons, or more than 10 percent of the workforce, were unemployed. Business bankruptcies and farm foreclosures reached 50-year highs. Reagan won his 1980 debate with Carter when he urged viewers to ask themselves, "Am I better off today than I was four years ago?" At the end of Reagan's first year, an opinion poll asking Americans the same question reported that 67 percent said no and only 32 percent said yes. Reagan's own job approval rating as president slipped by December 1982 to 41 percent, well below the levels of his modern predecessors at a comparable point in their first term; it was the most precipitous decline in popularity any president had experienced in his first two years in office.

Reagan had the confidence of a true believer. He stubbornly refused to change course. In the winter of 1982–83, when his political fortunes were at a low ebb and commentators spoke of him as a one-term president and of his need to "revitalize" his failing administration, Reagan cheerily assured the nation that the worst was over and an upturn was sure to begin. That winter the economy began a modest recovery that quickened as the year progressed and turned in 1984 into a roaring boom. Unemployment

fell to the 7 percent it had been when Carter left office. Gross national product spurted ahead at an 8 percent rate. An international glut of oil and a worldwide collapse in commodity prices brought the inflation rate in early 1984 to 3 percent, the lowest rate since 1972, when the Nixon-imposed price controls were in effect. Reagan looked like a prophet. His popularity ratings moved steadily upward in the spring of 1984.

One large, awkward problem remained. As his critics had foreseen and his own supporters had feared, "supply side" economics did not produce a budget miracle. Deficits reached the $200 billion range and seemed likely to stay there for the next several years, even if full employment were achieved. Because of the deficit, interest rates remained at 12 percent, abnormally high for a recovery period by historical standards. For decades, Reagan had preached that huge deficits were dangerous and sinful. As recently as September 25, 1982 in a radio broadcast, he declared, "There's only one major cause of our economic problems: government spending more than it takes in and sending you the bill. There's only one permanent cure: bringing government spending in line with government revenues."

Now Reagan tactically shifted his ideological ground. While taking credit for the brisk economic recovery, he deprecated the importance of deficits. This dispute was to provide a major theme in the subsequent campaign.

In the early years of his administration, Reagan disappointed one section of his supporters by his refusal to allow the so-called "social issues" to compete for congressional attention with his economic program. As 1984 drew near, Reagan gave these issues increasing prominence in his speeches. He supported a constitutional amendment to outlaw abortions and another to restore organized prayer in the public schools. He urged tax credits for parents paying tuition for church-related and other private schools. None of these measures could muster the necessary majorities in Congress.

These social issues were the political fallout from the liberal decisions of the Supreme Court under the leadership of Chief Justice Earl Warren and (on the question of abortion) under Chief Justice Warren Burger. Previous conservative Republican candidates—Goldwater, Nixon, and Ford—had made use of these issues. Reagan, a more skillful public speaker than any of his recent Republican predecessors, was unusual in his ability to dramatize these issues and in the prominence that he chose to give them. These issues enabled him to appeal to two separate constituencies: conservative Roman Catholics in the big cities and suburbs of the North and fundamentalist "Moral Majority" Protestants, largely in the South.

Critics saw a certain irony in Reagan's championship of these fundamentalist causes, pointing out that he was unique among recent presidents in that he attended religious services only once or twice a year. Also, before going to Washington, Reagan had spent years associating with people in Hollywood circles whose sophisticated lifestyles reflected values sharply different from those of conservative Catholics and fundamentalist Protestants.

Reagan's support for government legislation on specific social issues involved him in obvious philosophical paradoxes and inconsistencies. For instance, though he argued for limiting government's responsibilities in the economic sphere, he endorsed government intervention in family life to decide the question of abortion. Likewise, though he had previously taken the view that the legal age for drinking alcoholic beverages should be left to the states to determine, he reversed himself in July 1984 and signed a federal law designed to compel the states to establish 21 as the minimum drinking age, a measure intended to reduce deaths caused by young drunken drivers. Again, though he deplored violent street crime, he opposed further legislation controlling handguns.

In decided contrast to his elaborate domestic agenda, Reagan entered office with only a few simple notions about international problems and rather hazy ideas about the rest of foreign affairs. His fundamental convictions were that the Soviet Union was responsible for creating most international problems and for worsening those that it did not create. He felt that the Communist leaders understood only the language of power and, consequently, that it was necessary for the United States to have a large and rapid buildup of military weapons.

Reagan's most famous statement of his worldview came on March 8, 1983, in an address to a convention in Orlando, Florida, of the National Association of Evangelicals, the largest organization of fundamentalist Protestants, representing approximately 3 million people. Reagan declared that Soviet Communism is "the focus of evil in the modern world." He denounced the proposal for a freeze of nuclear weapons at existing levels without prior Soviet arms reductions as "a very dangerous fraud." He said,

> That is merely the illusion of peace. The reality is that we must find peace through strength . . . In your discussion of the nuclear freeze proposals, I urge you to beware the temptation of pride—the temptation of blithely declaring yourselves above it all and label both sides equally at fault, to ignore the facts of history and the aggressive impulses of an evil empire.

As he usually did in his speeches, Reagan illustrated these remarks with homely stories. He told of hearing a young father discussing Communism with his daughters.

He quoted the father approvingly: "I would rather see my little girls die now, still believing in God, than have them grow up under Communism and one day die no longer believing in God."

Urging his listeners to "pray for the salvation of all those who live in that totalitarian darkness," Reagan said, "There is sin and evil in the world, and we are enjoined by Scripture and the Lord Jesus to oppose it with all our might."

His audience interrupted Reagan frequently with strong applause. At the end, the crowd rose in a standing ovation as the orchestra played "Onward, Christian Soldiers."

Many observers, including some who shared Reagan's perception of the essential character of the Soviet regime and of the importance of American military strength in undergirding American foreign policy, were nonetheless dismayed at the ineptitude and sterility that marked his administration's conduct of foreign affairs. After 18 months in office, Reagan fired his first secretary of state, General Alexander Haig. Having served as deputy national security adviser under Henry Kissinger and then as White House chief of staff in the Nixon administration, Haig was accustomed to serving a president deeply interested in foreign affairs. He could never adapt to the reality that Reagan, preoccupied with domestic issues, had only a modest interest in the subject. In his memoir, *Caveat*, Haig repeatedly complained that Reagan refused to set aside an hour a week for the two men to confer in private, that his daily reports to the president went unanswered, and that his conversations and memoranda on sensitive topics often appeared "leaked" in the next day's *Washington Post* or *New York Times*. Reagan allowed his senior White House staff to treat Haig in the dismissive and manipulative manner that Nixon's senior aides had treated most cabinet officers in charge of domestic departments.

Blaming his difficulties on hostile intrigues by White House aides overly concerned with politics and with the cosmetic effects of foreign policy, Haig wrote in his memoir, "The impulse to view the Presidency as a public relations opportunity and to regard government as a campaign for reelection (which, of course, it is, but within limits) distorts balance, frustrates consistency, and destroys credibility." When Haig protested once too often against these presidential aides and threatened in June 1982 to resign, Reagan accepted a resignation that Haig had not yet actually submitted.

George Shultz, Haig's successor, had earned a high reputation for competence and political finesse in the Nixon administration, in which he served successively as secretary of labor, budget director, and secretary of the treasury. After Haig's stormy tenure, Shultz restored calm and harmony to relations between the State Department and the White House.

As 1984 opened, though, the Reagan administration was still seeking in vain for its first foreign policy success. Reagan, who had mounted strong attacks on many of his predecessor's foreign policy achievements, spent much of his time in office backing away from his earlier statements. Friendly relations between the United States and China were impaired because Reagan's sympathies for the old nationalist regime in Taiwan aroused Chinese suspicions. After three years of negotiations, Reagan was able to visit China in 1984 and lay most of these suspicions to rest. Reagan made no effort to disturb the Panama Canal treaties; in July 1984 he warmly welcomed the president-elect of Panama to the White House. On this occasion, Bernard Gwertzman, longtime diplomatic correspondent of the *New York Times,* wrote:

> As the Reagan Administration struggles with its Central American policy, the solid relations between the United States and Panama, one of the side benefits from the treaties, are a major source of satisfaction to the Administration. Imagine the Administration's problems if in addition to El Salvador and Nicaragua, it also had to worry about protecting the Panama Canal against a hostile Panama.

Despite his harsh rhetoric toward Communism, Reagan paradoxically followed a softer policy toward the Soviet Union than Carter had adopted in his last year in office after the Soviet invasion of Afghanistan. A few weeks after taking office, Reagan lifted the Carter-imposed embargo on grain sales to the Soviet Union. When the Soviet Union used the Polish army as a proxy to crack down on the Solidarity movement in Poland, Reagan shied away from using strong measures, such as declaring Poland in default on its foreign debt. Reagan administration efforts to block the construction of a Soviet natural gas pipeline to Western Europe had to be abandoned when America's European allies refused to cooperate.

Reagan achieved a success of sorts when the European members of the NATO alliance resisted Soviet pressure and went ahead in December 1983 with the installation of intermediate-range ballistic missiles in Britain, Germany, and Italy in response to the prolonged Soviet buildup of similar missiles. This carried through a NATO decision negotiated by Carter in December 1979 that provided for the installation of these missiles unless an agreement to limit them had been reached with the Soviet Union within four years. Whether a different administration from that of Reagan could have achieved such an agreement is a moot question. The Reagan administration had difficulty making up its collective mind as to whether any compromise with the Soviet Union was possible. In January 1983, the president fired Eugene Rostow, director of the Arms Control and Disarmament Agency, on the grounds that he had exceeded his authority in trying to reach an agreement with the Russians. Rostow's ouster confirmed a widely held impression that Reagan was not interested in an arms control agreement unless it involved sweeping Soviet concessions. In the absence of such concessions, he believed a continuation of the American military buildup would put useful pressure on the Soviet Union and eventually produce a more conciliatory Soviet policy. In the autumn of 1983, the Soviet government made good on its longstanding threat to withdraw from arms control talks if the Western powers installed intermediate-range ballistic missiles. All arms control negotiations came to a halt.

Reagan's political strategists had hoped that he would be able in 1984 to emulate Nixon's 1972 strategy, that is, they wanted him to attend a summit meeting with the head of the Soviet government, sign an arms-control agreement, and enter the campaign having effectively deprived the Democrats of the peace issue. As part of this attempt to reach an election-year thaw, Reagan in July 1984 lifted the ban Carter had imposed in 1980 on Soviet trawlers fishing within 200 miles of the U.S. coastline; the old 3-mile limit was restored. The Russians, however, appeared to take the president's strident anticommunist rhetoric more seriously than his own political staff did. Despite repeated Reagan overtures, they refused during the first half of the year to signal any willingness to meet with him before the election.

Reagan encountered his most spectacular setback in the Middle East. His initial hopes to construct an anti-Soviet consensus that would include both Israel and its Arab neighbors soon flickered out. In the spring of 1982, the administration offered only modest warnings when Israel began to move militarily into southern Lebanon to push back the army of the Palestine Liberation Organization. Some critics contended that then Secretary of State Haig actually encouraged this Israeli move, but the evidence now available is inconclusive. What is clear is that, as the Israeli army expanded its operations and eventually reached the Lebanese capital of Beirut, the Reagan administration became alarmed by the number of civilian casualties in Lebanon and the resulting bad publicity the invasion received on American television.

As the fighting around Beirut neared its climax, Haig, because of his difficulties in dealing with the president, finally left office. His successor, Secretary Shultz, and the roving U.S. ambassador in the region, Philip Habib, then put maximum pressure on the fragile Lebanese government and on Israel to reach an agreement providing for Israeli withdrawal from Beirut following the departure of the shattered PLO army into exile. The Reagan administration was unduly confident of its ability to persuade Syria to make a complementary military withdrawal from Lebanon once the Israelis backed off. Instead, the Soviets used this time to reequip its defeated Syrian client. Syria, thus strengthened, proved adamant in resisting American diplomatic pressure and reasserted its presence in Lebanon.

Some 1,400 U.S. Marines had been stationed around the Beirut Airport as part of an international peacekeeping force. They became hostage to a policy the political foundations of which had disintegrated; there was no strong Lebanese government for the peacekeeping force to support. Lebanese Muslim factions backed by Syrian firepower began attacking the marine position. In November 1983, a suicide terrorist drove a bomb-laden truck into the marine encampment and set off an explosion that killed 241 marines and wounded many others. Even after this catastrophe, Reagan continued to defend his placing the marines in this tactically vulnerable and politically pointless position, and to question the courage of those who urged a withdrawal. Then he reversed course. The *Wall Street Journal* reported that "on February 7 [1984], the day the Administration announced the withdrawal of U.S. Marines from Beirut, the President was heading for California to begin a vacation. He delayed the start of his holiday for only about 20 minutes to review a statement disclosing the abrupt policy switch, and he never appeared in public to announce the withdrawal."

Eight Democratic Party figures sought their party's nomination to oppose Reagan. Although they varied in experience and the extent of their familiarity to the public, none was a frivolous candidate and each could stake out some plausible claim to party leadership. As a group, they represented the range of political sentiment among Democrats: radical, liberal, moderate, conservative.

The two best-known candidates were former vice president Walter F. "Fritz" Mondale of Minnesota and Senator John Glenn of Ohio. Mondale carried the heavy burden of being identified with the unpopular, rejected Carter administration. As against that negative, Mondale was personally well known and warmly supported by the leaders of the many different interest groups traditionally identified with the Democratic Party: the AFL-CIO, the teachers associations, the black, Jewish, and Hispanic communities, women's rights activists, environmentalists, the elderly, and peace organizations. Under the changed rules for the 1984 convention that gave members of Congress, governors, and party officials a large bloc of guaranteed seats, Mondale had an added advantage. Insofar as a party establishment could be said to exist, Mondale was its favorite because many governors, big-city mayors, and members of Congress had found him

a sympathetic and knowledgeable ally in Washington during the Carter years. Mondale also had kept together an able political staff regarded by many as the best since John F. Kennedy's group in 1960.

Glenn's assets were the converse of Mondale's. Except in the Deep South, Glenn had little support in the party establishment or the traditional interest groups. His political staff was made up of "hired guns" who had worked in many previous campaigns, but they were not a team and were not used to working with Glenn or with one another. As the first man to orbit the earth, a Marine Corps hero, and a ruggedly handsome man from a small town, Glenn projected an Eisenhoweresque image that would be attractive to conservative Democrats and Republican-leaning independents in the Middle West and South, where national Democratic candidates had been weak. His success in winning reelection to the Senate from Ohio by a margin of more than a million votes in the face of the Reagan victory in 1980 underscored Glenn's broad, almost nonpartisan appeal. If nominated, one supposed he might be a formidable candidate.

Three U.S. senators of widely diversified backgrounds competed with Mondale and Glenn for the party's middle ground. Alan Cranston of California rivaled Glenn as a spectacularly successful vote-getter in his own state. As assistant floor leader, he was an acknowledged master of parliamentary maneuvers and legislative coalition-building in the Senate. At 69, Cranston was three years younger than Reagan, and as a longtime runner he was in superb physical condition. Yet, with his bald head and severely lean face, Cranston looked older than the president, and his personal style was colorless. Making arms control and the nuclear freeze the dominant theme of his campaign, Cranston gambled that he could ride the peace issue to the nomination as George McGovern had done a dozen years earlier.

Senator Gary Hart of Colorado had been McGovern's manager in the 1972 campaign. Since coming to the Senate in 1974, he had positioned himself closer to his party's center. His appeal in 1984 was generational and nonideological. He stressed the need for new ideas, for a party commitment to the overriding importance of economic growth, and for emancipation of the party from old interest-group alignments. He spoke of promoting new technologies and assisting an economy in transition from heavy industry to information and services. Hart made a conscious effort to evoke memories of John F. Kennedy. Indeed, Hart's cool, reserved personality did remind some people of the young JFK; the co-chairman of his national campaign committee was longtime Kennedy associate Theodore C. Sorensen. As the 1984 campaign began, Hart was an unknown factor. Many politicians and media people thought he was conducting a dry run for a more serious campaign in 1988.

Senator Fritz Hollings of South Carolina at 62 was a veteran of 18 years in the Senate. An unclassifiable independent in his thinking, he could be termed a moderate liberal. He was a critic of the oil industry, attacking the depletion allowance as excessive and supporting the Carter administration's windfall-profits tax. He had been a crusader against hunger and malnutrition in the 1960s and had made a name for himself as a supporter of civil rights legislation and as a strong proponent of the federal programs of nutritional assistance for women, infants, and children. Hollings, however, was also a staunch advocate of big military budgets, not a popular position among liberal activists who were influential in Northern and Western presidential primaries. Hollings urged a one-year, across-the-board budget freeze of everything from military spending to Social Security as a way of scaling back the Reagan deficit. He argued that only if the Democrats made themselves credible to the country as the party that could manage the economy and the national defense could they hope to regain power. Tall, handsome, white-haired, and blessed with a rich baritone voice, Hollings looked like Hollywood's vision of a U.S. senator.

Former governor Reubin Askew of Florida was the second Southerner in the race. Highly esteemed in eight years as governor, he had served in the last two years of the Carter administration as U.S. special trade representative. He was the conservative candidate in the Democratic field, the only one opposing abortion and homosexual rights and openly critical of the AFL-CIO. On education, civil rights, and economic issues, however, Askew was not conservative by the standard of Reagan supporters. Askew had declined McGovern's invitation in 1972 to be his vice-presidential running mate. Had he accepted, he would have entered the 1984 campaign better known. As it was, he was unfamiliar to most voters and never overcame his initial invisibility.

At the opposite end of the political spectrum from Askew were former Senator George McGovern and the Reverend Jesse Jackson. Against the advice of most of his former supporters, McGovern entered the race, frankly recognizing that he had almost no chance. Instead of becoming the comic Harold Stassen-type figure that his admirers feared, McGovern made his brief participation in the 1984 campaign a successful blend of idealism and nostalgia. He criticized what he regarded as excessive defense spending, assailed cold war attitudes in foreign policy in Central America and elsewhere, and unequivocally advocated New Deal and New Frontier social programs. His candor and undiminished eloquence won renewed respect from many Democrats. Also, his posture as a peacemaker among his rivals responded to the anxiety of many Democrats who feared that the long and diffi-

cult string of state primaries was breeding party disunity. McGovern was handicapped, however, by a lack of funds and by the media's low expectations for him.

Jackson, a black minister, was the youngest, least predictable, and most controversial of the eight candidates. He was not the first black to seek the Democratic presidential nomination; Representative Shirley Chisholm of New York had been a candidate in 1972 without attracting any significant support. Born and reared in South Carolina, Jackson was a Baptist minister, and black churches were the support network for his primary campaign. Having served on the staff of the Reverend Martin Luther King Jr. until the latter's assassination, Jackson then formed his own Chicago-based organization, PUSH (People United to Save Humanity). He lectured widely in churches and schools, urging young blacks to better themselves through education and hard work. He used threats of black consumer boycotts to persuade some organizations to sign "economic covenants," opening up more jobs to blacks.

Jackson made his debut in national politics at the Miami Beach convention in 1972, where he led the Illinois delegation that was seated in place of one headed by Chicago's Mayor Richard Daley. During the Carter years, Jackson had been an outsider; U.N. Ambassador Andrew Young was the nation's most prestigious black leader. Carter also dealt regularly with Coretta King, the widow of the slain civil rights leader, and with black big-city mayors, led by Coleman Young of Detroit. In 1978, Jackson accepted an invitation from William Brock, then chairman of the Republican National Committee, to address the organization. If the GOP leadership would work with him, Jackson said, he would deliver blacks out of their "bondage" to the Democratic Party. Nothing came of this overture.

In 1983, Jackson began positioning himself to seek the Democratic nomination. By the time he announced his candidacy in the autumn of that year, most of the nation's black mayors and other leaders of the black political establishment had aligned themselves with Mondale. Jackson proved a formidable competitor. The most effective orator in the campaign, he delivered lengthy talks containing applause lines that he had crafted and polished in the course of hundreds of speeches over the previous 15 years. Like William Jennings Bryan's "cross of gold" speech at the 1896 convention, Jackson's principal speech was a work of art that had been years in the making. In a way that no other black leader had succeeded in doing, he mixed the bravado, the knowingness, and the "street smarts" of alienated, working-class, big-city blacks with the more traditional rhetoric of moral uplift and Biblical imagery familiar to churchgoing blacks. His radicalism also

Reverend Jesse Jackson mixes with voters in New York City. *(Mario Cabrera/Associated Press)*

appealed to some left-wing white Democrats. Where his rivals called for slowing down the rate of increase in the Pentagon budget, Jackson urged a sharp reduction in military spending. Where his rivals coupled calls for a peaceful solution in Central America with denunciation of Communism, Jackson (and McGovern) called for restoration of diplomatic relations with Cuba and for cooperation with the Sandinista government in Nicaragua. Of the 3 million votes he polled in the primaries, Jackson received 22 percent of them from whites.

Jackson was a master at manipulating the media: he anticipated its needs, had a flair for creating news, and dressed up his opinions in provocative language. He began his campaign with a publicity coup. He flew to Syria and negotiated the release of Lieutenant Robert Goodman Jr., a black Navy flier who had been shot down and captured while bombing Syrian positions in Lebanon. Though criticized in advance for going outside nor-

mal diplomatic channels, Jackson demonstrated that he could negotiate as skillfully with an Arab head of state as with Chicago politicians or corporate executives.

The political season began in what seemed preordained fashion when Mondale—well organized, well financed, and far ahead in the opinion polls—swept to victory in the Iowa caucuses. Hart was a distant second, McGovern third, and Cranston fourth. Within a few days, however, private polling in New Hampshire showed that Mondale's previously huge lead was rapidly shrinking. The movement was toward Hart. On February 28, the voters confirmed the pollsters' reports. Hart won with 41 percent of the vote. This was followed within a few days by Hart victories in the Maine caucuses and the Vermont primary. The field suddenly narrowed to five as Cranston, Hollings, and Askew withdrew.

March 13 was the first "Super Tuesday" of the campaign; Massachusetts, Rhode Island, Georgia, Florida, and Alabama voted on that day. If Mondale's nominal support in New England had materialized, this was the day on which his managers had hoped he would preempt the nomination. As it was, it became the day on which he had to make a comeback or see his campaign collapse. Increasingly, Mondale looked as if he might go the way of Edmund S. Muskie in 1972, another respected candidate of the party leaders but one who failed to ignite voter enthusiasm.

When a *Boston Globe* poll showed him trailing Hart in Massachusetts by 15 points, Mondale chose to make his stand in the South. This decision underscored the uselessness of endorsements by elected officials. In Massachusetts, Mondale had the endorsement of Governor Michael Dukakis, other state officials, and three influential congressmen. In Maine, he had been backed by Governor Joseph Brennan and Senator George Mitchell. Ignoring endorsements, voters were looking for a "new face."

The South was critical not only for Mondale but also for Glenn and Jackson, neither of whom had scored well in Iowa or New England. Glenn had to demonstrate that in the South, the nation's most conservative region, he had political muscle as a war hero and astronaut. Jackson had to do well among blacks in the South or his campaign would lose its credibility. Hart, Mondale, Glenn, and Jackson spent two weeks crisscrossing the neighboring states of Georgia, Florida, and Alabama in what became a regional primary. With Massachusetts and Rhode Island now conceded to Hart, it became essential for Mondale to win at least two of the three Southern states.

He barely managed to do so. Mondale carried Georgia with 31 percent of the vote to Hart's 27 percent (Jackson 21 percent, Glenn 18). He carried Alabama more decisively with 34 percent, while Glenn edged Hart for second place, each getting 21 percent while Jackson was close behind with 19 percent. Hart carried Florida with a shade under 40 percent of the vote (Mondale 33, Jackson 12, Glenn 11).

Glenn's failure to win any of the three Southern states destroyed his candidacy. McGovern, having made his continuance in the race contingent on carrying Massachusetts, the only state to support him over Nixon in 1972, also withdrew when he polled only 21 percent of the vote, finishing third behind Hart and Mondale. The first Super Tuesday thus narrowed the field to three and, in effect, to two, since no one expected the party to nominate Jackson.

The March 13 primaries came very close to making Hart the nominee. Had Mondale failed to carry Georgia, where he had the support of former president Carter and where he was widely and favorably known, the former vice president might well have withdrawn from the race, making Hart the *de facto* winner four months in advance of the convention. The imponderables could be argued

either way. If Jackson had not entered the race, many black voters would have supported Mondale. If Glenn had withdrawn sooner, his supporters might have gone to Hart and given him a clean sweep in the South.

Although Hart carried more states and polled more votes on March 13, Mondale did well enough to reestablish his candidacy. He told his cheering supporters that evening, "When this race began, it looked like Mondale doing a 100-yard dash. Then it looked like Hart doing a 100-yard dash. But tonight that's all changed. It's going to be a marathon all the way."

It proved an accurate forecast.

Illinois was the next primary state. There, on March 20, Mondale turned the pre-convention contest around. Polls taken for both candidates on March 15 and 16 showed Hart six to eight points ahead. It was his victory to win if he could hold his lead.

Since leaping into national prominence, Hart had been harassed by news stories pointing out that his family name had originally been Hartpence and that he had shortened it to Hart, that various documents and biographical listings had reported him to be a year younger than he actually was, and that he had changed his religion from that of his parents. None of these personal details should have caused Hart any serious difficulty, but he complicated matters by giving confusing, defensive, and sometimes inconsistent explanations. In Illinois, he highlighted these questions by attacking Mondale for running a television advertisement about them. When it turned out that no such Mondale advertisement existed, Hart had to apologize. More serious was his uncertainty as to how to handle Cook County Democratic chairman Edward Vrdolyak. For months, Hart had been assailing Mondale as the candidate of established interests and of party insiders like Vrdolyak. In Illinois, a week before the primary, the Hart campaign ran a television commercial attacking Mondale and Vrdolyak. Then Hart had second thoughts. Vrdolyak was engaged in a bitter feud with Chicago Mayor Harold Washington, a black. Although Washington and Jackson were not personally or politically close, there was little doubt that the city's large black vote would go heavily to Jackson. What black votes Jackson did not get would go mostly to Mondale, who was favorably known in the black community for his civil rights record. If Hart antagonized those white voters sympathetic to Vrdolyak, he would have little support in Chicago. On the Friday before the primary, the Hart organization announced that the television commercial was an error and would be withdrawn, although some stations continued to run it over the weekend.

These mixups over the nonexistent Mondale advertisement and the ill-advised anti-Vrdolyak advertisement could be explained by the fatigue of a candidate who had been campaigning without pause and under intense pressure for several weeks. They could also be explained by the inexperience of his staff, most of whom had never participated in a national campaign. Whatever the explanation, these tactical errors damaged Hart's reputation for competence and leadership among the voters who were his base: the students, the independents, and the young urban professionals frequently referred to as "Yuppies." Hart carried these voters in Illinois by much narrower margins than he had in New England and in Florida. Mondale won the primary with 40 percent to Hart's 35 percent and Jackson's 20 percent.

The New York primary occurred two weeks later. Hart again seriously miscalculated. In other states, he had shown courage and consistency in defending controversial votes he had cast as a senator from Colorado that might not be universally popular. In Michigan, for example, he defended to automobile workers his vote against the government rescue of the Chrysler Corporation and his opposition to "domestic content" legislation that would restrict the importation of Japanese automobiles. In New York, he began with an analogous problem. He was on record against moving the United States Embassy from Tel Aviv to Jerusalem. Israel had proclaimed Jerusalem as its capital, but most nations were reluctant to acknowledge the change because of conflicting Arab claims to the city. In New York, approximately 30 percent of the voters in a Democratic primary are Jewish. Mondale had long cultivated Jewish support and was on record in favor of moving the embassy to Jerusalem. Rather than stand his ground, Hart repudiated an earlier statement as having been written in error by a staff member, and then changed his position to conform with that of Mondale. Many voters felt the "staff mistake" explanation was implausible. Others, including a sizable number of Jews, felt the significance of the embassy issue had been grossly exaggerated and constituted pandering for Jewish votes.

In a debate in New York, Mondale sprang on Hart what became the most famous line of the primary season: "Where's the beef?" Hart had been stressing the need for new ideas and a new politics. By borrowing the punchline from a popular, well-known television commercial for a chain of fast-food restaurants, Mondale epitomized in three words his telling argument that Hart's ideas were not new and had little substance.

For the first time, Mondale benefited directly from the support of a major officeholder. Governor Mario Cuomo of New York not only endorsed him but also lent his son Andrew to manage the Mondale campaign in the state, recruited the principal state campaign aides, and imposed his own television consultant and his own television advertising strategy. The resulting landslide victory (Mondale 621,802, Hart 380,298, Jackson 355,315) enhanced Cuomo's prestige and restored Mondale as the man to beat for the nomination.

The New York disaster for Hart was followed by major defeats in Pennsylvania, Missouri, Tennessee, and Texas. By early May, Mondale had more than 1,500 of the 1,967 delegates needed to win, while Hart had only half as many. Technically, Mondale could still be stopped, but it was now certain that Hart could not go to the convention as the leader on the first ballot. Still, Hart refused to yield. On May 8, while Mondale was winning Maryland and North Carolina, Hart caused a renewed flurry of interest with close, upset victories in Ohio and Indiana.

True to its grueling marathon quality, the primary season came to a hard-fought conclusion on June 5 when Mondale carried New Jersey, while Hart won in California. The steady drift of uncommitted delegates to join the probable winner enabled Mondale to claim the nomination on the following day.

In the interval between his long-delayed proclamation of triumph and the Democratic convention, Mondale faced two delicate political problems. One was a rapprochement with Jesse Jackson and the other was the choice of a running mate.

Although never in serious contention for the nomination, Jackson, by his stylish performance in the debates and on television talk shows and by his convincing display of voting strength in black neighborhoods across the country, had achieved a major objective. He had established himself as the foremost spokesman of the black community, a position of leadership that no one had occupied since the death 16 years earlier of Martin Luther King. He had polled more than 3 million votes, won the primaries in South Carolina, Louisiana, and the District of Columbia, and carried several cities, including Philadelphia.

Jackson claimed to be leading a "rainbow coalition" of minorities and disadvantaged groups. In reality, Mondale was the true leader of a rainbow coalition. He drew some black support in every state (always doing much better in this regard than Hart). When it counted, as in Texas, Hispanic voters preferred him over Jackson by a wide margin. Although Jackson received 22 percent of his votes from whites, the powerful thrust of his candidacy came from blacks. His candidacy was a black show of strength.

In rallying that strength, Jackson had aroused fear and distrust among Jewish voters. Prefacing his remarks to two African-American reporters with the cryptic comment "let's talk black talk," Jackson early in the year used the terms "Hymie" and "Hymietown" to refer to Jews and to New York City. After first denying the comment, Jackson in an appearance at a synagogue in New Hampshire

Walter Mondale speaking at the Democratic National Convention in San Francisco (*Library of Congress*)

in February expressed regret and said of his use of these derogatory terms, "It was wrong."

This controversy had barely subsided when Louis Farrakhan, the Chicago-based leader of the Nation of Islam, leaped from obscurity to notoriety. Farrakhan, a Jackson supporter, made a threat of physical retaliation against the black reporter for the *Washington Post* who was the source of the story about Jackson's earlier remarks. In subsequent speeches and interviews, Farrakhan referred to Judaism as a "gutter religion," described Adolf Hitler as "wickedly great," and termed the establishment of Israel an "outlaw act."

Jackson refused at first to repudiate Farrakhan. He apparently calculated that Jews and others who were offended by these remarks were not going to vote for him anyway, while if he denounced Farrakhan he would lose prestige among those isolated and alienated inner-city blacks to whom the Black Muslim movement appeals. Eventually, under intense pressure from Jewish organizations and from adverse editorial comment in the media, Jackson characterized Farrakhan's statements as "reprehensible and morally indefensible," but he was careful not to reject Farrakhan and his following.

Independent of these controversies, Jackson was a suspect figure in the Jewish community because of his atti-

tude toward Middle East issues. He repeatedly called for the creation of an independent Palestinian Arab state. In 1979, when Andrew Young was forced to resign as U.S. ambassador to the United Nations because of his unauthorized contacts with the Palestine Liberation Organization (PLO) representative in New York, Jackson attributed his removal to "Jewish pressure." Subsequently, Jackson visited the Middle East, met with Yasser Arafat, the head of the PLO, and publicly embraced him.

Mondale, who had always enjoyed strong support from both the black and Jewish communities, was eager to diminish the antagonism swirling around Jackson without offending either group. Timothy F. Hagan, cochairman of the Mondale campaign in Ohio, and Rabbi Marvin Hier of Los Angeles coauthored a proposed plank in the Democratic platform. It read, "The Democratic Party takes this opportunity to reaffirm its adherence to pluralistic principles and to repudiate and completely dissociate itself from people who promote all forms of hatred, bigotry, racism, and anti-Semitism."

Although this proposed language seemed so banal as to be unobjectionable to anyone, some Jackson supporters did object. Representative Mickey Leland of Texas, chairman of the Black Caucus in the Democratic National Committee, saw it as an attack on Farrakhan and therefore an oblique attempt to embarrass Jackson. Leland said, "I think it's very divisive. It's obviously taking a shot at Farrakhan. We give Farrakhan credence by doing that."

Since the resolution had been put forward too late to meet the Platform Committee's deadline, it required a two-thirds majority of the delegates to bring it up for a vote. To avoid even the possibility of an embarrassing black–Jewish clash on television, the Mondale managers persuaded the authors of the resolution to withhold it until the meeting of the Democratic National Committee on the day after the convention. It was then approved unanimously. Meanwhile, in his address to the convention on the third evening, Jackson included conciliatory language toward his Jewish critics.

"If in my low moments, in word, deed or attitude, through some error of temper or tone, I have caused discomfort, created pain or revived someone's fears, that was not my intention," he said.

Recalling many joint efforts of blacks and Jews in behalf of "social justice at home and peace abroad," he declared, "When all is said and done, we must forgive each other, redeem each other and move on."

Jackson's words were warmly received by most Jewish leaders and Jewish delegates and did much to dispel the gathering rancor.

Jackson's speech was a personal triumph, and he left San Francisco with enhanced prestige. He had failed, however, to extract any substantial concessions on the platform from Mondale. The nominee resisted Jackson's proposals for an outright endorsement of affirmative action and racial quotas in employment, for the abolition of two-stage primaries in which the candidate who fails to achieve a majority faces a runoff, and for a substantial federal program of public works and public jobs to relieve unemployment.

As the general campaign proceeded, Jackson faded in importance. Because of their pronounced hostility to Reagan's domestic policies, black voters clearly had no impulse to shift from their traditional Democratic loyalty. Jackson's support for the Democratic ticket and his efforts to register new voters were positive influences, but it soon became clear that the Democrats had serious problems with white voters. Unless Mondale could overcome them, no outpouring of black support could possibly save him.

Fundamental pessimism about the outlook for victory in November dominated Mondale's choice of a running mate. First, he concluded that he could not break Reagan's grip on the South and West. The president would have an unshakable base of more than 200 of the 270 electoral votes needed to win. This assumption meant that it would make little sense to choose a conservative Southerner such as Senator Sam Nunn of Georgia or Senator Lloyd Bentsen of Texas to achieve a conventional North–South regional balance. No Southerner in second place on the ticket could prevent Reagan from winning most of the South. If victory could be achieved for the Democrats, it could probably only come about by doing exceptionally well in traditional Democratic strongholds in the Northeast and the industrial Middle West. A possible pattern for victory envisaged by Mondale and his strategists was modeled approximately on John Kennedy's narrow victory in 1960 and on Hubert Humphrey's near miss in 1968. It presumed Mondale would win four of the six New England states (Maine, Massachusetts, Rhode Island, and Connecticut), all of the Middle Atlantic states (New York, New Jersey, Pennsylvania, Delaware, Maryland, West Virginia, and the District of Columbia), six states in the Middle West (Ohio, Michigan, Illinois, Missouri, Wisconsin, and Minnesota), three in the South (Georgia, Arkansas, and Texas), and one in the Far West (Hawaii). This combination would produce 275 electoral votes.

This minimal strategy argued for choosing a popular figure from the Northeast to complement Mondale's presumed strength as a Middle Westerner. Mondale had been impressed by Governor Cuomo's effectiveness in the New York primary. However, rejecting repeated overtures, Cuomo convinced Mondale that he was not available to run.

A second pessimistic calculation was that Mondale's personality failed to excite and motivate voters. His political skills, notably his alertness and self-discipline as a debater, had enabled him to take advantage of Hart's weaknesses and inconsistencies. Those skills, together with his solid support from interest-group constituencies, had won him the nomination, but they would not suffice in a general election. He needed to do something dramatic to dispel his gray image. Proceeding on this assumption, Mondale decided that if Cuomo was not available he should choose a running mate who would be a "first"—the first woman or the first black or the first Hispanic.

Polling data indicated that only one candidate would add discernible strength to a Mondale ticket. That was Hart, but Hart had no interest in the vice presidency and refused to make any of the tactical and rhetorical concessions needed to ease the way toward an accommodation. Mondale did not want Hart urgently enough to make a firm offer. Polls also suggested that, of the kinds of candidates who would represent an historic "first," a woman would attract additional votes for Mondale. A majority responded that a black or Hispanic vice-presidential candidate would be acceptable, but the number of "don't know" and "undecided" voters was sufficiently large to provide no clear guidance. Mondale was not matched up with particular candidates in trial runs because none of the candidates under consideration was sufficiently well known nationally to make a reliable poll possible.

In late June and early July at his home in North Oaks, Minnesota, Mondale interviewed Tom Bradley, the black mayor of Los Angeles, Henry Cisneros, the Hispanic-American mayor of San Antonio, and Dianne Feinstein, the mayor of San Francisco. Finally, he met with Representative Geraldine Ferraro of New York, the chairperson of the Platform Committee. She was a protégée of House Speaker Thomas P. O'Neill and also came strongly recommended by Cuomo, who argued that she would appeal to Italian-American as well as women voters.

Mondale's aides were closely divided between Feinstein and Ferraro. Two calculations tipped the decision in favor of Ferraro. Mondale did not believe even a Californian on his ticket could deprive Reagan of the electoral votes of his home state, whereas Ferraro would help in New York, a state indispensable to the Democrats. Secondly, Feinstein, once divorced, once widowed, and now married for the third time, was serving as mayor of a city known as the "gay capital of America." She would project traditional family and neighborhood values less successfully than Ferraro, a Roman Catholic, a wife for 24 years, a mother of three children, and a former assistant prosecutor. A final touch in Ferraro's favor was that the racially and ethnically mixed district in Queens that she had represented in Congress for six years was the photographic backdrop used in the "All in the Family" television series.

With Reagan making inroads among normally Democratic blue-collar and lower-middle-class Catholic voters in the big cities and suburbs, Mondale judged Ferraro's religion and ethnic background as important assets.

"This is an exciting choice!" Mondale exclaimed when he revealed his choice of Ferraro one week before the convention opened. His decision achieved its immediate objective of creating a burst of excitement and favorable publicity in the days leading up to the San Francisco convention. Regardless of the outcome of the election, Mondale had lowered a historic barrier against women participating at the highest level of national politics.

The large imponderable was whether Ferraro would widen the "gender gap" between male and female voters to an extent that would help the Democrats significantly. In 1980, 6 million more women voted than did men. Reagan, who won the white male vote decisively, barely edged out Carter among the women, 46 percent to 45 percent. Polls throughout the subsequent four years had consistently shown that a majority of women had less confidence in Reagan than did men because they viewed his foreign policy as bellicose and his domestic policies as lacking in compassion.

Having made his bold move on the vice presidency, Mondale then committed an astonishing lapse of political judgment. On the weekend before the convention opened, he announced that he was dismissing Charles Manatt as Democratic national chairman and naming Bert Lance to direct his campaign. After having to resign as director of the Office of Management and Budget in the Carter administration in 1977, Lance was indicted for alleged violations of federal banking laws. A jury acquitted him on most of the charges but failed to reach a verdict on three. Deciding these were not sufficiently weighty to justify a second trial, the judge dismissed them. Lance resumed his banking career and made a political comeback as chairman of the Georgia Democratic Party. He had been helpful in rallying support to Mondale in the crucial Georgia primary in March and had a wide, friendly acquaintance with other Southern politicians. Having passed over the South in the choice of a running mate, Mondale wanted to make a gesture to that region. Other politicians and political commentators, however, found it hard to understand why Mondale would want to revive memories of the "Bert Lance affair" and underscore his own association with the Carter administration.

Democratic candidates Walter Mondale and Geraldine Ferraro wave to supporters during a rally in New York, July 31, 1984. *(Richard Drew/Associated Press)*

Adverse reaction to the Lance appointment undercut the euphoria over the Ferraro selection. Mondale backed away from his mistake, allowing Manatt to remain as national chairman and Lance to withdraw. This bungling harmed Mondale's prospects in Georgia, one of the few Southern states where he might have been competitive against Reagan. It also for the first time stirred doubts in the political community as to whether Mondale's senior staff, a tightly closed group made up mostly of younger Minnesotans, was as astute as their reputation had suggested.

The platform on which the Mondale–Ferraro ticket campaigned was unequivocally liberal. When contrasted with the program adopted the following month by the Republicans at their Dallas convention, the Democratic platform drew the philosophical line between the two parties more sharply than at any time since the Johnson vs. Goldwater contest 20 years earlier.

On defense spending and military power, the Republican platform praised the Reagan military buildup and pledged "to do everything necessary so that, in case of conflict, the United States would clearly prevail." The Democrats stated, "We will reduce the rate of increase in defense spending. . . . True national security requires urgent measures to freeze and reverse the arms race, not the pursuit of the phantom of nuclear superiority or futile Star Wars' schemes."

On Central America, the Republican platform declared, "The entire region . . . is gravely threatened by Communist expansion, inspired and supported by the Soviet Union and Cuba. . . . We support continued assistance to the democratic freedom fighters in Nicaragua." The Democratic platform said, "We need to develop relations based on mutual respect and mutual benefit. Beyond essential security concerns, these relations must emphasize diplomacy, development and respect for human rights. . . . We must terminate our support for the contras and paramilitary groups in Nicaragua."

With regard to the income tax, the Republicans pledged themselves to "eliminate the incentive-destroying effects of graduated tax rates. . . . We therefore support tax reform that will lead to a . . . modified flat tax." The Democrats countered, "We will enhance the progressivity of our personal income tax code."

Concerning health care, the Republicans stated, "Many health problems arise within the family and should be dealt with there. . . . We will not tolerate the use of federal funds, taxed away from parents, to abrogate their role in family health care." The Democrats said, "We reaffirm our commitment to the long-term goal of comprehensive national health insurance."

On education, the Republican platform stated, "We believe that education is a local function, a state responsibility, and a federal concern. The federal role in education should be limited." The Democratic platform said, "While education is the responsibility of local govern-

ment, local governments already strapped for funds by this administration cannot be expected to bear alone the burden. . . . We call for the immediate restoration of the cuts in funding of education programs by the Reagan Administration."

With regard to nuclear power, the GOP platform stated, "We will work to eliminate unnecessary regulatory procedures so that nuclear plants can be brought on line quickly, efficiently, and safely." The Democratic plank: "The Democratic Party strongly opposes the Reagan Administration's policy of aggressively promoting the further subsidizing of nuclear power." The Democrats also promised to "revitalize" the Environmental Protection Agency, while the Republicans were silent on that scandal-ridden agency.

Several perennial issues reappeared in one or both platforms. The Democrats said that ratification of the Equal Rights Amendment would be "a top priority." The Republican platform was silent on the ERA. With regard to "right to work," the Democrats promised to repeal section 14(b) of the Taft–Hartley Act. The Republicans said, "We reaffirm our longstanding support for the right of states to enact 'right to work' laws under section 14(b) of the Taft–Hartley Act." The Republicans also made a cautious bow toward the restoration of the gold standard, saying that it "may be a useful mechanism . . . to sustain price stability." The Democrats were silent on the gold standard.

These opposing planks contradicted the myth that the two major parties had few serious differences and were becoming indistinguishable. Since Ferraro had chaired the Platform Committee and Mondale's aides had carefully monitored the platform's language, the adoption of the platform and the nomination of Ferraro for vice president expressed the liberal consensus and ideological harmony that, for better or worse, prevailed among the Democrats.

The Democrats were well aware that the images projected at the convention to the television audience would probably influence voters far more than the platform that was adopted. In terms of imagery, the San Francisco convention was an almost unqualified success. Governor Cuomo as keynote speaker demonstrated that he was Reagan's equal in the art of talking both to the live audience in the hall and the vastly larger audience watching on television. He expressed emotional force and evoked enthusiasm from his immediate listeners without losing the conversational tone and psychological intimacy necessary to hold the attention of television viewers. He challenged Reagan directly by taking back for the Democrats the now fashionable themes of family, neighborhood, and community and using them to justify not the individualism and competition of the marketplace but the caring and compassion of government acting with social responsibility. He said:

> The difference between Democrats and Republicans has always been measured in courage and

confidence. The Republicans believe the wagon train will not make it to the frontier unless some of our old, some of our young, and some of our weak are left behind by the side of the trail. The strong will inherit the land!

We Democrats believe that we can make it all the way with the whole family intact. We have. More than once. Ever since Franklin Roosevelt lifted himself from his wheelchair to lift this nation from its knees. Wagon train after wagon train. To new frontiers of education, housing, peace. The whole family aboard. Constantly reaching out to extend and enlarge that family. Lifting them up into the wagon on the way. Blacks and Hispanics, people of every ethnic group, and Native Americans—all those struggling to build their families and claim some small share of America. For nearly 50 years we carried them to new levels of comfort, security, dignity, even affluence.

Some of us are in this convention to remind ourselves where we come from and to claim the future for ourselves and for our children.

The bitter rivals of 1980, former President Carter and Senator Edward M. Kennedy, made supportive appearances. Carter addressed the delegates briefly on opening night; Kennedy introduced Mondale for his acceptance speech. Hart and Jackson both made major speeches before the balloting began. Although their remarks were conciliatory and Mondale's first-ballot victory was assured, neither withdrew. Mondale was nominated with 2,191 votes, while Hart had 1,200.5 and Jackson 465.5.

In accepting, Mondale made a direct appeal to those who had voted for Reagan four years earlier:

I heard you. And our party heard you. After we lost, we didn't tell the American people that they were wrong. Instead, we began asking you what our mistakes had been. . . . Tonight we come to you with a new realism: ready for the future, and recapturing the best in our tradition.

We know that America must have a strong defense, and a sober view of the Soviets. We know that government must be as well-managed as it is well-meaning. We know that a healthy, growing private economy is the key to our future.

Look at our platform. There are no defense cuts that weaken our security; no business taxes that weaken our economy; no laundry lists that raid our treasury. We are wiser, stronger, and focused on the future.

Assailing Reagan's budget deficit and promising to cut it by two-thirds, Mondale promised to raise taxes:

Let's tell the truth. Mr. Reagan will raise taxes, and so will I. He won't tell you. I just did.

This was a move almost as unorthodox as choosing a woman for a running mate. Though known for his caution, Mondale had made two bold moves, knowing that he had to go for broke if he was to have any chance of winning.

The Mondale staff had distributed thousands of small American flags to the delegates and visitors. The television cameras closed out the convention on a living tableau of massed thousands linking arms, waving flags, and singing "God Bless America." If patriotism could be reclaimed from Reagan and the Republicans, the Democrats were making the effort.

A Gallup Poll taken for *Newsweek* immediately after the convention put Mondale ahead of Reagan 48 percent to 46 percent. The Ferraro nomination and the well-managed convention seemed to have paid off.

This Herblock cartoon criticizes President Reagan's attitude toward the homeless. (*A Herblock Cartoon, copyright by the Herb Block Foundation*)

The Republicans gathered for their national convention in Dallas on August 20 under ideal circumstances for the party in power. The nation was at peace. The economy was booming. (The gross national product, which had been rising since the recession ended in late 1982, leaped ahead at an annual rate of 7.6 percent in the second quarter of 1984). The incumbent president was personally popular and politically in command of his party. For observers with long memories, the Reagan "coronation" in Dallas was strongly reminiscent of the San Francisco convention that renominated Dwight D. Eisenhower in 1956.

No serious controversies marred the prevailing mood of optimism and triumph. None of the other speakers competed with Reagan for admiration or attention in the way that Cuomo and Jackson had rivaled Mondale. The keynote speaker was U.S. Treasurer Katherine Ortega, chosen not for her oratorical skills but for her symbolism as a woman and a Hispanic. The stronger speech on the first evening was delivered by Jeane Kirkpatrick, the ambassador to the United Nations and still nominally a Democrat, who berated her party for departing from the stress on military strength and anticommunism that had characterized the Democratic administrations of Truman, Kennedy, and Johnson. Vice President Bush and his prospective rivals in 1988, Senators Howard Baker and Robert Dole and Representative Jack Kemp, made speeches, none of which notably stirred the delegates.

Senator Barry Goldwater took the delegates on a stroll down memory lane. He did not have to remind them that it was with a speech in his campaign 20 years earlier that Reagan had made his national political debut. Reagan's triumph was the delayed justification of the conservative crusade that Goldwater had begun a quarter-century earlier. Goldwater savored the moment and revived half-forgotten rhetoric and campaign themes. He blamed four wars in the 20th century on "the foreign policy and defense weakness of Democratic Administrations." Quoting from his own acceptance speech of 1964, he said, "Let me remind you, extremism in the defense of liberty is no vice."

After his speech, Goldwater in an interview with ABC News disclosed that on some issues the Republican Party had drifted to a more extreme position than his own.

He deplored the platform's rejection of abortion in all circumstances and its demand for a constitutional amendment to restore prayer in the schools.

"I don't think it [abortion] should be in politics at all," Goldwater said. "Then we get into school prayer. The decision of the Supreme Court on school prayer was a proper one. No government should write a prayer, and make my children use it—or anybody's children use it."

It was precisely on these "social issues" that Reagan and the convention managers overreached themselves and lost votes that they might otherwise have won. At an ecumenical prayer breakfast on August 23, the last day of the convention, Reagan said, "The truth is, politics and morality are inseparable, and as morality's foundation is religion, religion and politics are necessarily related. We need religion as a guide."

He asserted that the desire of a majority of Americans to have voluntary prayer in public schools was being frustrated by opponents "in the name of tolerance, freedom, and openmindedness."

"Isn't the real truth that they are intolerant of religion? They refuse to tolerate its importance in our lives."

Fundamentalist evangelical Protestants dominated the prayer breakfast. Their clergymen such as the Reverend Jerry Falwell, the founder of the Moral Majority movement, and the Reverend Wallie Amos Criswell, a leader of the conservative wing of the Southern Baptist Convention, were prominent among the clergymen who opened and closed the convention sessions with prayer.

Although Reagan, at the prayer breakfast and in appearances later in the campaign before Mormon and Jewish groups, was careful to note that he was neutrally benevolent toward all religions, his remarks in Dallas and his association with fundamentalist Protestants set off shock waves among Jewish voters. As a small minority in a nation with a Christian majority, Jews had been sensitized by the tragic history of their people in other countries to react whenever a political leader began to identify the state with ideals of the dominant religion. Elsewhere, it had often been the signal for the onset of anti-Semitic persecution. In the Democratic primaries in the spring, the anti-Semitic overtones of the Jackson campaign had opened up for Republican strategists the prospect that Reagan could further enhance the support he had gained among Jewish voters in 1980. As the campaign developed, however, Jackson faded from the news, and the fear of fundamentalist Protestant influence on Reagan became the dominant concern for many Jewish voters. (On Election Day, Jews by a margin of 66 percent to 32 percent would return to their traditional Democratic allegiance. This contrasted with the 1980 results: Carter 45 percent, Reagan 39 percent, and Anderson 15 percent.)

But at the GOP convention in August, the depth of Reagan's overall popular support was evident. Senator Paul Laxalt of Nevada made the nominating speech for Reagan as he had four years earlier. Reagan in effect was presented to the convention for his acceptance speech by an 18-minute film starring himself. The Columbia Broadcasting System and the American Broadcasting Company declined to show the film on the grounds that it was propaganda, not news, but the National Broadcasting Company put it on the air, as did the Cable News Network. (The three major networks had refused to run a similar film about Mondale shown at the Democratic convention.) The theme of the Reagan film was that his administration represented a new morning, a new beginning for America. In a rapid sequence of images, none of them lasting longer than a few seconds, Americans in different walks of life and from different ethnic backgrounds were shown at sunrise and at flag-raisings. There were numerous pictures featuring the American flag as Reagan's voice spoke of a "reawakening of patriotism in our country." A singer with a husky male voice sang a song, "God Bless the U.S.A." Its lyrics were, in part,

> If tomorrow all the things were gone
> I've worked for all my life,
> And I had to start again
> With just my children and my wife,
> I'd thank my lucky stars to be living here today,
> 'Cause the flag still stands for freedom,
> And they can't take that away.
> And I'm proud to be an American. . . .
> And there ain't no doubt I love this place.
> God bless the U.S.A.

The film included excerpts from dramatic and ceremonial moments in the previous four years. News footage on the attempted assassination of 1981 was shown, and the president's voice was heard saying that Terence Cardinal Cooke of New York had visited him in the hospital and said, "God must have been sitting on your shoulder."

"And I told him," Reagan is heard saying on the film, "he must have been. I told him, 'Whatever time I've got left, it now belongs to someone else.'"

The film had several scenes of Reagan's trip to Normandy battlefields of World War II on the 40th anniversary of D-Day. It moved on to show Reagan surrounded by the U.S. Olympic Team. After a huge close-up of Reagan and a brief silence, there was the sound of "Ruffles and Flourishes." Then an announcer's voice on the soundtrack said, "Ladies and gentlemen, the President of the United States."

Time magazine described the Reagan film as "something of a cross between a Pepsi-Cola commercial (happy young people, catchy music) and [the 1984 film] *The Natural* (mythic baseball heroism inspired by love and personal fidelity backlighted by the sun, awash with violins). That was no surprise: the 18-minute movie was crafted, in large part, by Phil Dusenberry, co-author of the screenplay for *The Natural* and vice chairman and executive creative director of the BBDO, Inc., advertising agency, which handles the Pepsi account."

Reagan, who had made his living as a film actor and then as the host of a television program, was the first president since Kennedy to bring television successfully into the service of his political ends. Television was to Reagan what radio had been to Franklin Roosevelt. In the film about Reagan shown at the Dallas convention, which was also narrated by Reagan, the blending of television and politics, and the use of television as simultaneously a medium for entertainment, for advertising, and for political propaganda, were brought to the highest peak of craftsmanship yet achieved.

Reagan's acceptance speech, although highly effective in evoking applause from his audience, was regarded by most commentators as anticlimactic. It was devoted largely to a point-by-point response to criticisms leveled by Mondale and other speakers at the Democratic convention. Reagan heavily underscored the contrasts as he saw them between America in 1984 and four years earlier. He set forth his central message in this paragraph near the end of his address:

> We promised we'd reduce the growth of the Federal Government, and we have. We said we intended to reduce interest rates and inflation, and we have. We said we would reduce taxes to provide incentives for individuals and business to get our economy moving again, and we have. We said there must be jobs with a future for our people, not government make-work programs. And, in the last 19 months, six and a half million new jobs in the private sector have been created. We said we would once again be respected throughout the world, and we are. We said we would restore our ability to protect our freedom on land, sea and in the air, and we have.
>
> We bring to the American citizens in this election year a record of accomplishment and the promise of continuation.

Polls taken as the Republican convention ended showed that the Reagan–Bush ticket had regained the considerable lead that it had enjoyed in June. Between the two conventions, the Olympic Games had been held in Los Angeles, games that Reagan had opened and that Mondale had not attended. The many gold medals won by American athletes indirectly reinforced Reagan's theme of revitalized American patriotism and self-confidence. Unless Reagan stumbled badly, he appeared to be headed for a decisive victory.

Democratic planning for the fall campaign was not complicated by a third party in the field. John Anderson in the spring had abandoned his effort to keep a third party alive, and he endorsed Mondale after his nomination. Democrats hoped to develop a partisan theme that would reinvigorate the Democratic coalition, hold the 41 percent of the total vote that Carter had won in 1980, and add at least two-thirds of the 6.7 percent of the vote that Anderson had attracted. In addition, they planned a registration drive to maximize their black support. If they could stay in contention in the last two months of the campaign with their support at, say, 46 or 47 percent, they would be in a position to close the gap if they received one or two lucky breaks.

It was soon apparent that the Democrats were unable to present an effective campaign theme and that luck was running against them. From an intellectual standpoint, the lack of a unifying theme was understandable. What theme could tie together such national and world problems as the budget deficits, arms control, the Middle Eastern stalemate, the Nicaraguan revolution, and the Soviet invasion of Afghanistan? But what was intellectually defensible was politically disadvantageous. In an age of television, presidential campaigns had to a large extent become media events, with candidates' speeches written and campaign events planned to play well on the network evening news shows. The news that a candidate generated and the commercials that his campaign paid for were designed to reinforce one another.

Reagan achieved this synergistic effect. His theme was confidence, optimism; America is back and standing tall. His advertising replayed patriotic and upbeat images from the film shown at the Dallas convention. The news programs showed him delivering the same message in highly simplified form: "We think in America every day is the 4th of July. Our opponents think every day is April 15!"

Mondale unveiled his plan to reduce deficits by increasing taxes on corporations and well-to-do individuals, but unless and until voters experienced the effect of the deficit in their own lives, the deficit remained a problem that was difficult to grasp. Having defended Keynesian deficits for two generations, the Democrats were ill at ease in their new role as budget balancers. Few Democratic candidates at the state and local levels associated themselves with Mondale's tax increase and budget deficit proposals.

Polling by the Gallup organization showed that his tax-increase proposal seriously eroded popular support for the national Democratic ticket and that this began to be apparent within a few days of the end of the Democratic convention. The Reagan managers were later astonished to learn that Mondale had made this critically important decision without "market testing" it by advance polling. There was abundant polling evidence of a widespread public uneasiness about the size of the Reagan deficits but no specific information as to how the public would react to a Democratic call for higher taxes.

Data from the polls also indicated that Reagan was perceived as favoring the rich, and Democrats had hoped to exploit the "fairness" issue. In reality, it seemed only to arouse black and Hispanic voters, who were already heavily Democratic and who traditionally did not register or vote in as high proportions as other groups.

This caricature by David Levine shows Democratic candidate Walter Mondale wearing a beanie and juggling many hats. (© *Estate of David Levine, courtesy of Forum Gallery, New York, N.Y.*)

Mondale stressed the importance of arms control, promised to freeze nuclear weapons, and urged annual summit meetings with Soviet leaders. He warned against the danger of becoming embroiled in a Vietnam-style conflict in Central America. In the absence of any immediate crisis in U.S.–Soviet relations or of any situation in which American troops were engaged in combat, these peace issues did not catch on with any voters except convinced liberals.

The Soviet leadership blunted the arms-control issue in September when it sent Foreign Minister Andrei Gromyko to visit President Reagan at the White House. This was interpreted as a signal that the Russians foresaw a Reagan victory and were prepared to do business with him on arms control in his second administration, notwithstanding his harsh anticommunist rhetoric and their own walkout from the Geneva conference in 1983. Many voters may have concluded that Reagan's tough talk and sustained arms buildup would pay more dividends than the Democrats' conciliatory approach.

The Mondale campaign's lack of a cohesive theme was reflected in the fumbling of its television advertising. The choice of a political consultant or an advertising firm to produce the Mondale commercials was one of the fundamental decisions of the campaign. Yet by the beginning of September a selection had not been made. When one campaign manager finally chose to split the advertising budget among five different firms, three of them rejected the offer, insisting that they wanted total control or they would not participate. The upshot was that Mondale advertising limped through the campaign. This failure was a major reason for the magnitude of Mondale's defeat. He and his senior staff, most of them lawyers, had shown themselves in the primaries and conventions to be skillful political organizers on a state-by-state basis, but once a presidential candidate is nominated, the general election campaign is not a state campaign writ large. As he demonstrated in the two debates, Mondale was a competent television performer, but his own and his staff's inability to conceive of the fall campaign in television terms was a critical weakness.

Meanwhile, Lady Luck was riding the Reagan plane. Not only did Gromyko choose to come to Reagan's assistance, but two successive misfortunes hit Geraldine Ferraro. The first involved her family finances. During her six years in Congress, she had sought to separate her political career from her husband's real estate business. She had filed separate income tax returns and had refused to include his earnings on the annual financial disclosure statement required of members of Congress. When challenged on these practices after her nomination, Ferraro impulsively said that she would make public both her own and her husband's tax returns. This went beyond the legal requirement of the federal election laws and beyond normal political practice. When Senator Dole was the Republican vice-presidential candidate in 1976, for example, he had not disclosed the tax returns of his wife, who pursued her own career.

Ferraro's husband, John Zaccaro, balked at fulfilling his wife's promise because, as he claimed, full disclosure might embarrass him in the conduct of his real estate operations. She tried to pass off this refusal with a light remark, telling reporters that anyone married to an Italian husband would know how stubborn such a man could be. Predictably, this remark failed to settle the matter. The press began to investigate Zaccaro's business activities vigorously on the possibility that he was hiding something scandalous. One impropriety did turn up. As court-appointed conservator of the property of a wealthy senile woman, Zaccaro had borrowed (and later repaid with 12 percent interest) $175,000 from the estate to invest in one of his own real estate deals, a practice frowned on by probate courts but not explicitly forbidden by law in New York. When this episode became news, the court removed Zaccaro as conservator. Meanwhile, he had relented and agreed to allow his wife to make his income tax returns public.

The returns of Ferraro and her husband were released to reporters one day in advance of a news conference that she had called. She answered questions from 200 reporters for an hour and 40 minutes. The session was televised live. Her performance was a spectacular personal triumph. *Time* magazine reflected the consensus view when it wrote, "The questions, about her family finances and personal ethics, were complicated and often barbed, yet she managed to seem neither combative nor defensive. Her manner was precise and serious, but relaxed and good-humored too. Her answers were lucid and carefully organized, anecdotal and unpretentious."

Ferraro had no sooner battled back on that front when she was attacked on another. Archbishop John J. O'Connor of New York denounced her for her views on abortion. Ferraro in 1982 had sent a letter to approximately 50 Catholic colleagues in the House of Representatives enclosing a pamphlet from a group, Catholics for a Free Choice, and inviting them to a briefing. In her letter, she wrote, "Catholic lawmakers . . . have experienced moral and political doubt and concern. That is what the briefing and this monograph are all about. They show us that the Catholic position on abortion is not monolithic and that there can be a range of personal and political responses to the issue."

Referring to this letter, Archbishop O'Connor accused her in September 1984 of giving "the world to understand that Catholic teaching is divided on the subject" of abortion. "There is no variance, there is no flexibility, there is no leeway," he declared. He repeated this charge in televised interviews and news conferences over the next week. He climaxed these criticisms with the comment, "Her quarrel is not with me but with the Pope."

During this same period in the first half of September, Archbishop Bernard Law of Boston and 18 other bishops in New England issued a joint statement describing abortion as "the critical issue" of the campaign, and Cardinal John Krol of Philadelphia introduced President Reagan at a Polish festival and extolled his views. Antiabortion demonstrators from the Right to Life movement attended every Ferraro rally, chanting "baby killer."

The effect of this clerical cannonading was to throw Ferraro again on the defensive and distract public attention from the anti-Reagan message she was trying to deliver. Ferraro's position on the abortion issue was no different from that of Governor Cuomo, Senator Kennedy, and many other Catholic political leaders who had refused to join their church's crusade for a constitutional amendment outlawing abortion. She had not ever been publicly criticized by the archbishop of her own diocese of Brooklyn and Queens. That she was attacked so vociferously by Archbishop O'Connor in the neighboring Manhattan diocese and implicitly by Archbishop Law of Boston was an example of the bad luck that shadowed the Democratic campaign. Both these prelates had been appointed only a few months earlier; their predecessors, Cardinal Cooke of New York and Cardinal Humberto Medeiros of Boston, were lower-keyed figures who had generally avoided public battles with political figures.

The abortion controversy was particularly damaging because it undercut much of the rationale for choosing Ferraro. As a wife and mother, a Catholic and an Italian-American, she was expected to appeal particularly to socially conservative Catholic Democrats who in recent presidential elections had begun to stray from the party of their parents. Insofar as such voters were influenced by the opinion of leading bishops, she had been effectively neutralized. Columnist Mary McGrory noted the irony: "Here she is, a lifelong Catholic, a product of Catholic schools and colleges. She goes to Mass every Sunday, and the hierarchy of her church is acting like an arm of the Reagan re-election committee. Ronald Reagan, who never puts a foot inside a church, is acclaimed as the nation's spiritual leader, introduced by cardinals and invited to ring monastery bells."

By early October, the gap between Reagan and Mondale was widening. All Democratic hopes of turning the election around or even making it reasonably close now depended on the two televised debates, scheduled for Sunday, October 7, in Louisville, Kentucky, and October 21 in Kansas City, Missouri. The Democrats had originally pressed for six debates but, realistically, had settled for two between Mondale and Reagan and one between Ferraro and Bush. There was some risk for Reagan in agreeing to any. Since the modern practice of presidential debates had begun, debates had worked in favor of the challenger (Kennedy over Vice President Nixon in 1960, Carter over President Ford in 1976, and Reagan over President Carter in 1980). His agreement to debate was a measure of Reagan's confidence in his communication skills and his conviction that the major issues of peace and prosperity were working in his favor.

The Louisville debate was confined to domestic affairs. The outcome fulfilled Mondale's hopes and interjected a dash of doubt into the rising Republican euphoria. Mondale came across on television as relaxed, self-confident, and occasionally witty. He kept Reagan on the defensive through much of the 90 minutes. The president had been heavily briefed and at times sounded almost like Jimmy Carter in rattling off facts and statistics. Mondale, by contrast, adopted the Reaganesque approach of being personally mellow and putting forward his ideas in broad, philosophical terms. This reversal of roles was striking in the closing statements of the two candidates.

Reagan framed the debate by asking again the question he had asked four years earlier: "Are you better off than you were four years before?" He then gave a fact-laden memorized answer in which he said in part:

Well, let's put it this way, in the first half of 1980 gross national product was down a minus 3.7 percent. The first half of '84 it's up 8.5%. Productivity in the first half of 1980 was down a minus 2 percent. Today it is up plus 4 percent. Personal earnings after taxes per capita have gone up almost $3,000 in these four years. In 1980 or 1979 the person with a fixed income of $8,000 was $500 above the poverty line, and this maybe explains why there are the numbers still in poverty. By 1980 that same person was $500 below the poverty line.

Mondale responded:

The President's favorite question is, "Are you better off?" Well, if you're wealthy, you're better off. If you're middle income, you're about where you were, and if you're of modest income, you're worse off. That's what the economists tell us. But is that really the question that should be asked. Isn't the real question, "Will we be better off? Will our children be better off?" . . .

Are we better off with this arms race? Will we be better off if we start this "Star Wars" escalation into the heavens? Are we better off when we deemphasize our values in human rights? Are we better off when we load our children with this fantastic debt? Would fathers and mothers feel proud of themselves if they loaded their children with debts like this nation is now, over a trillion dollars, on the shoulders of our children? Can we be—say, really say, that we will be better off when we pull away from sort of that basic American instinct of decency and fairness?

I would rather lose a campaign about decency than win a campaign about self-interest. I don't think this nation is composed of people who care only for themselves.

Reagan had earlier used another famous line from his 1980 debate: "There you go again." He used it this time to deny Mondale's charge that he had a secret plan to raise taxes if he were reelected.

Mondale was prepared. Resting an elbow on the lectern and turning to face the president, he asked:

Remember the last time you said that? You said it when President Carter said you were going to cut Medicare, and you said, "Oh, no, there you go again, Mr. President." And what did you do right after the election? You went out and tried to cut $20 billion out of Medicare. And so when you say, "There you go again," people remember this.

THERE HE GOES AGAIN.

This Pat Oliphant cartoon shows President Reagan effortlessly dancing across ice floes labeled "Beirut," "Education," "Deficit," "Nuclear Arms," and "Central America." In the background, Walter Mondale and others are unable to leap across the treacherous floes. *(OLIPH-ANT © 1984 UNIVERSAL UCLICK. Reprinted with permission. All rights reserved.)*

Reagan looked surprised and angry. At other times in the debate, he paused and visibly groped for facts that he needed to complete a sentence but could not quite remember. For the first time, Reagan's age and his often shaky grasp of information seemed to come together and to put in question his fitness to serve as president for another four years. The *Wall Street Journal,* by coincidence, ran a long front-page story on Reagan's age and mental and physical fitness on the day following the debate. This story provided television commentators that evening with an armory of facts and examples on this theme. These stories and commentaries reinforced the impression of telephone polls, taken on Sunday evening and on the next day, that Mondale had won the debate decisively.

"Today we have a brand new race," Mondale said exultantly on October 8 as he marched up Fifth Avenue in the Columbus Day parade, cheered by newly heartened Democrats. But it was not quite as dramatic as that. His good showing enabled him to cut into the president's pre-debate lead of 15 to 20 points in various opinion polls. A second, even more decisive victory in the Kansas City debate would be necessary to bring him genuinely into contention.

It was not to be, despite the fact that, if anything, Mondale outdebated Reagan on foreign policy issues on

October 21 more clearly than he had on domestic issues two weeks earlier. On the very first question, Reagan misspoke about the Central Intelligence Agency's role in Nicaragua and had to correct himself. In the middle of the debate, he gave a long, rambling answer about Biblical prophecies regarding Armageddon. In his closing statement, he ran out of time before he could complete a metaphorical journey down the coastal highway of California.

But these vagaries did not count as much with the public and most commentators as did the fact that, unlike the first debate, Reagan appeared relaxed and confident. When a reporter raised the issue of age, Reagan brought down the house with this reply: "I want you to know that also I will not make age an issue of this campaign. I am not going to exploit for political purposes my opponent's youth and inexperience."

Reagan effectively attacked Mondale's voting record in the Senate on defense issues: "He has a record of weakness with regard to our national defense that is second to none." He also counterattacked skillfully on the human rights issue, asserting that the greatest losses of human rights occur when a country is lost to Communism or extremism and that Afghanistan and Iran had not been "lost on my watch."

Mondale once again was crisp and cogent, making his points firmly and yet not crossing the line into personal attacks on Reagan. On issues such as the failure to protect the marines in Lebanon and the failure to achieve arms control with the Soviet Union, he poked holes in the administration's record. But he did not demolish Reagan's credibility nor did Reagan oblige him by shooting himself in the foot as President Ford had done in the 1976 debate when he asserted that Poland was not under Russian domination.

Opinion polls and press reaction indicated that the debate was regarded as a draw or possibly even a Reagan victory. Gloom settled on Mondale and his entourage. Although his crowds grew to huge size in the last two weeks as loyal partisans turned out to wish him well, Mondale knew that he could not overtake Reagan. In the end, the debates had made no difference. The majority of the people felt comfortable with Reagan and were determined to reelect him, barring some extraordinary event that shook their confidence. Mondale had earned respect by his highly competent performance in the two debates, but he had not shaken the public's loyalty to the incumbent.

On November 6, Ronald Reagan achieved one of the great political triumphs of American history. He carried 49 states, losing only Mondale's home state of Minnesota and the District of Columbia. His total of 525 electoral votes surpassed Roosevelt's modern record of 523 in 1936. His popular vote margin of 59 percent to 41 percent placed him close behind Harding, Roosevelt, Johnson, and Nixon among landslide winners. His immense triumph, however, was, like Nixon's in 1972, a personal rather than a party success. His party lost two seats in the Senate, reducing its margin to 53 to 47, while it gained 14 seats in the House, where Democrats remained in control, 253 to 182.

The indifferent results in Congress suggested to many analysts that 1984 was probably no more a "critical election" than was 1980. But others argued that Reagan's election demonstrated retroactively that Nixon's first victory in 1968 had been a classic "critical election." They held that Nixon's slight margin over Humphrey had masked that election's significance but that his victory did, in fact, mark a definite turn to the right in American politics. If the vote for George C. Wallace, a nonliberal and implicitly racist candidate, was added to that of Nixon, together they represented 57 percent of the electorate. Nixon alone obtained 61 percent in 1972. Reagan's 59 percent of the popular vote in 1984 conformed closely to this pattern.

Kevin Phillips, author of *The Emerging Republican Majority,* pointed out that Nixon and Reagan drew from the same sources of strength. In a *New York Times* article in 1985, he wrote, "The regional, Protestant fundamentalist, ethnic and racial contours of Nixon's 1972 victory all closely foreshadowed those of Reagan's 1984 triumph."

Phillips argued further that major realigning elections seem to occur every 28 to 36 years—in 1800, 1828, 1860, 1896 and 1932. Another was due around 1968, and it came. The five realignment periods all shared a common pattern: in each case, the party newly ascending to power invariably controlled the White House for at least 16 of the first 20 years following the watershed, and such 16- to 20-year party hegemonies have occurred only in these circumstances. "By January 1989, the Republicans will have controlled the Presidency for 16 of the previous 20 years. . . . What we are seeing now is the last great crest of a much older [than 1980] political wave: a 'conservative' (or more appropriately, nonliberal) national era that began some 17 or 18 years ago and is now in late middle age."

Seen in the context of GOP victories in four out of the last five presidential elections, Carter's narrow win in 1976 could be regarded as a fluke event attributable to post-Watergate malaise. But how was one to explain continued Democratic predominance in the House of Representatives and control or near parity in the Senate? Perhaps this could be accounted for by the split-level politics of the South. At the presidential level, white Southerners—and notably, white male voters—had shifted to overwhelming opposition to the national Democratic Party. Even in

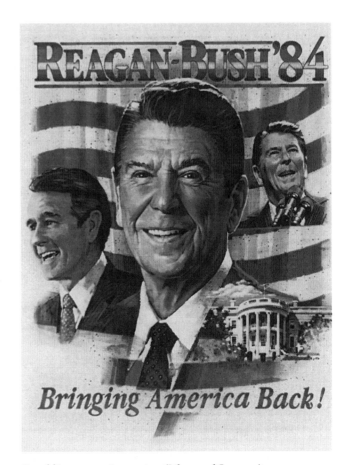

Republican campaign poster *(Library of Congress)*

the two Carter campaigns, a majority of white Southerners had voted for the Republican candidate in preference to a native Georgian. Only Carter's strong support from black voters had enabled him to win 10 of the 11 Southern states in 1976. In 1984, Reagan carried 72 percent of the white vote in the South. But at the local and congressional level, Southerners remained faithful to the Democrats. In a generation, the GOP had managed to make itself competitive in most Southern states in campaigns for the U.S. Senate. In 1962, there was only one Republican senator from the region—John Tower of Texas. After the 1984 election, Republicans held 10 of the South's 22 seats in the Senate. Eventually, white Southerners abandoned their split-level approach to politics and began voting Republican in House elections as well. The result, in 1994, would be an end to the half-century of national Democratic dominance in the House of Representatives.

A radically different and, for the Democrats, a potentially less gloomy interpretation was offered by the young political writer, Sidney Blumenthal. In *The Permanent Campaign,* he debunked the "critical election" theory:

> American politics is not necessarily about to experience a completion and rebirth at once; history is not a drama with a recurring fourth act. The realignment theory is useful today, but mostly as a counter-model. For it is a good guide to what is not happening.
>
> A majority of the electorate, in fact, has not been formed into a new coalition, and the party system has not been revitalized. Instead, there is a dealignment of voters; their partisan loyalties are shallower with each succeeding election. They do not adhere to the faith of their fathers. They are often willing to take a chance with a fresh face who seems to articulate their concerns of the moment. They are less committed to party than to personalities, and their commitment to personalities is ephemeral. . . .
>
> The media have taken over much of the role of the party as the intermediary between politicians and public. . . . Politicians are no longer able to rely on the security of the party machinery. They are obliged to wage individualized campaigns that become permanent in the attempt to govern.

If Blumenthal's analysis was sound, the Democrats did not need to fear that they were victims of an inexorable cyclical trend, whether it began in 1968 or 1980. Rather, they needed only to seek and find a new leader who understood the potential of television as a political tool. A fresh personality with a new style who could proj-

ect appealing media images could capture the drifting voters in the dealigned center of American politics and manufacture his own landslide. In terms of this analysis, Democrats in 1984 made a fundamental error in nominating the "old-politics" Mondale rather than the "new-politics" Hart. In March 1984, after his early primary victories, Hart defeated Reagan in a Gallup Poll matchup, 52 percent to 43 percent. This is tantalizing, if inconclusive, evidence for the theory that Reagan, even with the powers of incumbency and the issues of peace and prosperity working in his favor, was vulnerable to the appeal of a new face capable of attracting the fickle loyalties of millions of restless political consumers.

The "critical-elections" theory and the media-as-master theory would be best seen as complementary interpretations. The political realignment of the South that resulted from the civil rights revolution of the 1960s was a major influence in the Republican presidential victories after 1964. To that extent, it had given the political era since 1968 a distinctive character. During this period, the rise in political importance of television and the decline in power of state and local party organizations created a new volatility in the nation's politics. Television bred the cult of novelty: new faces, new styles, new advertising slogans. Party organizations were forces for stability, stressing loyalty as against the lure of change and retarding rapid swings of opinion. As television surged and the parties ebbed, landslide victories became more frequent. Public opinion polling, which tended to give ephemeral moods an air of authority and nascent trends an air of inevitability, reinforced the destabilizing effects of television.

Reagan's significance could ultimately be more cultural than political, more as a totem than a chief. He became genial host to a vast national audience of balance-the-budget conservatives, "supply-side" radicals, and monetary zealots; of right-to-life moralists and "swinging-single" urban young people; of those comfortable with change as well as of those yearning for a restoration of stability. By its very nature, this union of divergent social tendencies was destined to be temporary. They could not be a permanent coming together of those who seek a restoration of old pieties and a reinvigoration of old inhibitions with those who delight in sexual and social freedoms. Any shift in the balance of forces threatened to bring disillusionment either to fundamentalist or Yuppie and dissolve the fragile equilibrium into incoherence.

If Calvin Coolidge in the 1920s was a puritan in Babylon, Reagan in the 1980s could be seen as a neo-Victorian in an age of liberation. His moralistic rhetoric looked backward to the stern moral code of the past, to an idealization of work, faith, family, and neighborhood. His philosophy of economics and government looked forward to a loosening of public restraints and communal responsibility, to an exaltation of individualism and libertarian self-fulfillment. Like Coolidge, Reagan could perform his symbolic moral role and reconcile irreconcilable forces in the culture only as long as prosperity smothered conflict and sustained a public mood of optimism. The 1984 election was an act of hope that Reagan's luck would hold and swelling affluence validate his optimism.

—*William V. Shannon*

Selected Bibliography

See Paul Abramson, John Aldrich, and David Rhode, *Change and Continuity in the 1984 Elections* (1986); Herbert E. Alexander and Brian A. Haggerty, *Financing the 1984 Election* (1987); Lucius J. Barker. *Our Time Has Come: A Delegate's Diary of Jesse Jackson's 1984 Presidential Campaign* (1988); Lou Cannon, *President Reagan: The Role of a Lifetime* (1991); Elizabeth Drew, *Campaign Journal: The Political Events of 1983–1984* (1985); Morris Fiorina, *Retrospective Voting in American National Elections* (1981); John Forest, *Warriors of the Political Arena: The Presidential Election of 1984* (1986); Jack W. Germond and Jules Witcover, *Wake Us When It's Over: Presidential Politics of 1984* (1985); Peter Goldman and Tony Fuller, *The Quest for the Presidency 1984* (1985); William A. Henry III, *Visions of America: How We Saw the 1984 Election* (1985); Anthony King, ed., *The New American Political System* (2nd ed., 1990); Jane Mayer and Doyle McManus, *Landslide: The Unmaking of the President, 1984–1988* (1988); Michael Nelson, ed., *The Elections of 1984* (1985); Gerald Pomper, ed., *The Election of 1984* (1985); Gerald M. Pomper, *The Election of 1984: Reports and Interpretations* (1985); Larry Speakes, *Speaking Out: The Reagan Presidency from Inside the White House* (1988); Martin Wattenberg, *The Rise of Candidate-Centered Politics* (1991); and Garry Wills, *Reagan's America: Innocents at Home* (1988).

1984 Electoral Map and Statistics

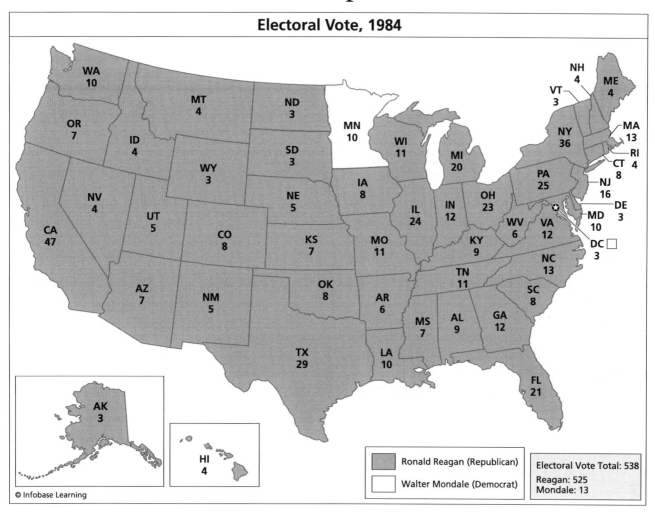

Electoral Vote, 1984

Ronald Reagan (Republican)	
Walter Mondale (Democrat)	

Electoral Vote Total: 538
Reagan: 525
Mondale: 13

© Infobase Learning

1984 ELECTION STATISTICS

State	Number of Electors	Total Popular Vote	Elec Vote R	Elec Vote D	Pop Vote R	Pop Vote D	Margin of Victory Votes	Margin of Victory % Total Vote
Alabama	9	1,441,713	9		1	2	320,950	22.26%
Alaska	3	207,605	3		1	2	76,370	36.79%
Arizona	7	1,025,897	7		1	2	347,562	33.88%
Arkansas	6	884,406	6		1	2	196,128	22.18%
California	47	9,505,423	47		1	2	1,544,490	16.25%
Colorado	8	1,295,381	8		1	2	366,844	28.32%
Connecticut	8	1,466,900	8		1	2	321,280	21.90%
Delaware	3	254,572	3		1	2	50,534	19.85%
District of Columbia	3	211,288		3	2	1	151,399	71.66%
Florida	21	4,180,051	21		1	2	1,281,534	30.66%
Georgia	12	1,776,093	12		1	2	362,094	20.39%
Hawaii	4	335,846	4		1	2	37,896	11.28%
Idaho	4	411,144	4		1	2	189,013	45.97%
Illinois	24	4,819,088	24		1	2	620,604	12.88%
Indiana	12	2,233,069	12		1	2	535,749	23.99%
Iowa	8	1,319,805	8		1	2	97,468	7.39%
Kansas	7	1,021,991	7		1	2	344,147	33.67%
Kentucky	9	1,370,461	9		1	2	283,193	20.66%
Louisiana	10	1,706,822	10		1	2	385,713	22.60%
Maine	4	553,144	4		1	2	121,985	22.05%
Maryland	10	1,675,873	10		1	2	91,983	5.49%
Massachusetts	13	2,559,453	13		1	2	71,330	2.79%
Michigan	20	3,801,658	20		1	2	721,933	18.99%
Minnesota	10	2,084,449		10	2	1	3,761	0.18%
Mississippi	7	940,192	7		1	2	229,285	24.39%
Missouri	11	2,122,771	11		1	2	425,605	20.05%
Montana	4	384,377	4		1	2	85,708	22.30%
Nebraska	5	652,090	5		1	2	272,188	41.74%
Nevada	4	286,667	4		1	2	97,115	33.88%
New Hampshire	4	388,954	4		1	2	146,656	37.71%
New Jersey	16	3,217,862	16		1	2	672,307	20.89%
New Mexico	5	514,370	5		1	2	105,332	20.48%
New York	36	6,806,810	36		1	2	545,154	8.01%
North Carolina	13	2,175,361	13		1	2	522,194	24.00%
North Dakota	3	308,971	3		1	2	95,907	31.04%
Ohio	23	4,547,619	23		1	2	853,120	18.76%
Oklahoma	8	1,255,676	8		1	2	476,450	37.94%
Oregon	7	1,226,527	7		1	2	149,221	12.17%
Pennsylvania	25	4,844,903	25		1	2	356,192	7.35%
Rhode Island	4	410,492	4		1	2	14,974	3.65%
South Carolina	8	968,540	8		1	2	271,069	27.99%
South Dakota	3	317,867	3		1	2	84,154	26.47%
Tennessee	11	1,711,993	11		1	2	278,498	16.27%
Texas	29	5,397,571	29		1	2	1,484,152	27.50%
Utah	5	629,656	5		1	2	313,736	49.83%
Vermont	3	234,561	3		1	2	40,135	17.11%
Virginia	12	2,146,635	12		1	2	540,828	25.19%
Washington	10	1,883,910	10		1	2	244,318	12.97%
West Virginia	6	735,742	6		1	2	77,358	10.51%
Wisconsin	11	2,212,016	11		1	2	202,953	9.18%
Wyoming	3	188,968	3		1	2	79,871	42.27%
Total	538	92,653,233	525	13	1	2	16,878,120	18.22%

Reagan Republican		Mondale Democratic		Others	
872,849	60.54%	551,899	38.28%	16,965	1.18%
138,377	66.65%	62,007	29.87%	7,221	3.48%
681,416	66.42%	333,854	32.54%	10,627	1.04%
534,774	60.47%	338,646	38.29%	10,986	1.24%
5,467,009	57.51%	3,922,519	41.27%	115,895	1.22%
821,818	63.44%	454,974	35.12%	18,589	1.44%
890,877	60.73%	569,597	38.83%	6,426	0.44%
152,190	59.78%	101,656	39.93%	726	0.29%
29,009	13.73%	180,408	85.38%	1,871	0.89%
2,730,350	65.32%	1,448,816	34.66%	885	0.02%
1,068,722	60.17%	706,628	39.79%	743	0.04%
185,050	55.10%	147,154	43.82%	3,642	1.08%
297,523	72.36%	108,510	26.39%	5,111	1.24%
2,707,103	56.17%	2,086,499	43.30%	25,486	0.53%
1,377,230	61.67%	841,481	37.68%	14,358	0.64%
703,088	53.27%	605,620	45.89%	11,097	0.84%
677,296	66.27%	333,149	32.60%	11,546	1.13%
822,782	60.04%	539,589	39.37%	8,090	0.59%
1,037,299	60.77%	651,586	38.18%	17,937	1.05%
336,500	60.83%	214,515	38.78%	2,129	0.38%
879,918	52.51%	787,935	47.02%	8,020	0.48%
1,310,936	51.22%	1,239,606	48.43%	8,911	0.35%
2,251,571	59.23%	1,529,638	40.24%	20,449	0.54%
1,032,603	49.54%	1,036,364	49.72%	15,482	0.74%
581,477	61.85%	352,192	37.46%	6,523	0.69%
1,274,188	60.02%	848,583	39.98%	0	0.00%
232,450	60.47%	146,742	38.18%	5,185	1.35%
460,054	70.55%	187,866	28.81%	4,170	0.64%
188,770	65.85%	91,655	31.97%	6,242	2.18%
267,051	68.66%	120,395	30.95%	1,508	0.39%
1,933,630	60.09%	1,261,323	39.20%	22,909	0.71%
307,101	59.70%	201,769	39.23%	5,500	1.07%
3,664,763	53.84%	3,119,609	45.83%	22,438	0.33%
1,346,481	61.90%	824,287	37.89%	4,593	0.21%
200,336	64.84%	104,429	33.80%	4,206	1.36%
2,678,560	58.90%	1,825,440	40.14%	43,619	0.96%
861,530	68.61%	385,080	30.67%	9,066	0.72%
685,700	55.91%	536,479	43.74%	4,348	0.35%
2,584,323	53.34%	2,228,131	45.99%	32,449	0.67%
212,080	51.66%	197,106	48.02%	1,306	0.32%
615,539	63.55%	344,470	35.57%	8,531	0.88%
200,267	63.00%	116,113	36.53%	1,487	0.47%
990,212	57.84%	711,714	41.57%	10,067	0.59%
3,433,428	63.61%	1,949,276	36.11%	14,867	0.28%
469,105	74.50%	155,369	24.68%	5,182	0.82%
135,865	57.92%	95,730	40.81%	2,966	1.26%
1,337,078	62.29%	796,250	37.09%	13,307	0.62%
1,051,670	55.82%	807,352	42.86%	24,888	1.32%
405,483	55.11%	328,125	44.60%	2,134	0.29%
1,198,800	54.19%	995,847	45.02%	17,369	0.79%
133,241	70.51%	53,370	28.24%	2,357	1.25%
54,455,472	58.77%	37,577,352	40.56%	620,409	0.67%

Election of 1988

Election Overview

Election Year 1988

Election Day November 8, 1988

Winning Candidates

- ★ **President:** George H. W. Bush
- ★ **Vice President:** Dan Quayle

Election Results [ticket, party: popular votes (percentage of popular vote); electoral votes (percentage of electoral vote)]

- George H. W. Bush and Dan Quayle, Republican: 48,886,597 (53.37%); 426 (79.2%)
- Michael Dukakis and Lloyd Bentsen, Democratic: 41,809,476 (45.65%); 111 (20.6%)
- Ron Paul and Andre Marrou, Libertarian: 431,750 (0.47%); 0 (0.0%)
- Other: 466,863 (0.51%); 0 (0.0%)

Voter Turnout 50.2%

Central Forums/Campaign Methods for Addressing Voters

- Stumping
- Speeches
- Rallies
- Print and television ads
- Debates

Incumbent President and Vice President on Election Day Ronald Reagan and George H. W. Bush

Population (1988) 245,061,000

Gross Domestic Product

- $5.1 trillion (in current dollars: $7.614 trillion)
- Per capita: $20,813 (in current dollars: $31,069)

Number of Daily Newspapers (1990) 1,655

Average Daily Circulation (1990) 62,649,218

Households with:

- Radio: 91,100,000
- Television: 92,100,000

Method of Choosing Electors: Popular vote (mostly general-ticket system/winner take all)

Method of Choosing Nominees:

- Presidential preference primaries
- Caucuses

Key Issues and Events

- Fight over Ronald Reagan's legacy—George H. W. Bush as heir
- Iran-Contra scandal tarnishes Reagan and Bush.
- Democrats gain control of the Senate in the 1986 midterm elections.
- Economic crash of 1987 and rejection of Judge Robert H. Bork as Supreme Court nominee further weaken Reagan.
- Republicans call Democrats soft on crime and too willing to raise taxes.
- Culture wars over abortion, liberalism, race.
- Cold war ending becomes triumph for Reagan.

Leading Candidates

REPUBLICANS

- George H. W. Bush, vice president (Texas)
- Bob Dole, senator (Kansas)
- Pat Robertson, televangelist (Virginia)
- Jack Kemp, representative (New York)
- Pierre S. du Pont, governor (Delaware)

- Alexander Haig, former secretary of state (Pennsylvania)
- Ben Fernandez, Republican National Hispanic Assembly chairman (California)
- Paul Laxalt, former senator (Nevada)
- Donald Rumsfeld, former secretary of defense (Illinois)
- Harold E. Stassen, former governor (Minnesota)

DEMOCRATS

- Michael Dukakis, governor (Massachusetts)
- Jesse Jackson, reverend and civil rights leader (Illinois)
- Al Gore, senator (Tennessee)
- Dick Gephardt, representative (Missouri)
- Paul Simon, senator (Illinois)
- Gary Hart, former senator (Colorado)
- Bruce Babbitt, former governor (Arizona)
- Joe Biden, senator (Delaware)

Trajectory

- The Democratic front-runner, Colorado senator Gary Hart, withdraws abruptly from the campaign on May 8, 1987, after being caught by a photographer with his girlfriend, Donna Rice. In December, Hart will return to the race but will be ineffectual.
- Vice President George H. W. Bush comes in a surprising third in the Republican Iowa caucuses on February 8, with only 19% support, behind Senator Bob Dole at 37% and televangelist Pat Robertson at 25%. Missouri congressman Dick Gephardt wins the Iowa caucuses on the Democratic side, but reporters dismiss his victory as mere neighborly solidarity.
- Bush wins a hard-fought comeback contest in the New Hampshire primary on February 16. That night, Dole reinforces his image as a hatchet man by blurting out on TV to Bush: "Stop lying about my record." Governor Michael Dukakis wins the Democratic primary as a technocratic "Atari Democrat" promising to mass-produce the "Massachusetts Miracle."
- Dukakis wins eight states plus American Samoa on "Super Tuesday," March 8. Senator Al Gore wins six Southern states, the Reverend Jesse Jackson wins another five Southern states, and Dick Gephardt wins his native Missouri. When Senator Paul Simon wins his home state of Illinois a week later, the Democrats will have the highest number of candidates winning at least one primary in a campaign since the McGovern reforms of 1971. Bush sweeps all 16 Republican contests.

- On March 26, Jackson wins the Michigan caucuses with 55 percent of the vote, pulling ahead in the Democratic delegate count. Reporters will call 1988 "the Year of Jackson," marveling at his 11 electoral victories and 6.9 million votes.
- Ultimately, Dukakis prevails with a big win in New York and a sweep on June 8 of California, New Jersey, Montana, and New Mexico.
- Speakers pummel Bush at the Democratic National Convention, July 18–21. Senator Edward Kennedy rouses the convention, citing Bush's dithering or dodging as he and the crowd shout: "Where was George?" These attacks give Dukakis a 20-point lead in polls but help a furious Bush rationalize his own slash-and-burn tactics in the fall.
- George H. W. Bush tries prevailing over what in the fall of 1987 Newsweek had harshly called "the Wimp Factor" with a strong campaign launch at the Republican convention, August 15–18. Bush promises to tell Congress "Read my lips: No new taxes." Bush also makes a surprise choice for vice president, turning to a young Indiana senator, Dan Quayle.
- While claiming, "This election is not about ideology, it is about competence," Dukakis runs a surprisingly ham-handed and spiritless campaign. In one of the most embarrassing photo ops ever, Dukakis is photographed riding an M1 Abrams tank at the General Dynamics plant in Sterling Heights, Michigan, on September 13, looking like "Snoopy" ready to take on the Red Baron.
- On October 5, the Bush campaign broadcasts "Revolving Door," an attack ad blaming Dukakis for the vicious kidnapping-rape-and-murder spree of Willie Horton, a black murderer exploiting a Massachusetts prison furlough program. An independent PAC had been broadcasting a less subtle version since September 21. These ads are part of the Republicans' aggressive campaign, mocking Dukakis as a "card-carrying member" of the American Civil Liberties Union, dismissing liberalism as a pejorative, "the L-word," accusing Dukakis of polluting Boston Harbor and preventing Massachusetts students from saying the "Pledge of Allegiance."
- On October 5, Dan Quayle, debating Dukakis's running mate, Senator Lloyd Bentsen, claims to have as much experience as John Kennedy had in 1960. Bentsen chides his younger colleague: "Senator, I served with Jack Kennedy. I knew Jack Kennedy. Jack Kennedy was a friend of mine. Senator, you're no Jack Kennedy."

- During the second presidential debate in Los Angeles, on October 13, Dukakis responds blandly, clinically, when the CNN anchor Bernard Shaw asks whether he would still oppose the death penalty if his wife were raped and murdered. After the debate, the Gallup Poll estimates that Bush is leading 49–43, an astonishing turnaround.

Conventions

- Democratic National Convention: July 18–21, 1988, The Omni, Atlanta
- Republican National Convention: August 15–18, 1988, Louisiana Superdome, New Orleans

Ballots/Nominees

REPUBLICANS
- George H. W. Bush (acclamation)

DEMOCRATS
Presidential ballot
- Michael Dukakis 2,876.25
- Jesse Jackson 1,218.5
- Richard Stallings 3
- Joe Biden 2
- Dick Gephardt 2
- Gary Hart 1
- Lloyd Bentsen 1

Vice-presidential ballot
- Lloyd Bentsen 4,162

Primaries

- Republican Party: 37; 76.9% delegates
- Democratic Party: 37; 66.6% delegates

Primaries Results

REPUBLICANS
- George H. W. Bush 8,258,512; 67.91%
- Bob Dole 2,333,375; 19.19%
- Pat Robertson 1,097,446; 9.02%
- Jack Kemp 331,333; 2.72%
- Unpledged 56,990; 0.47%

DEMOCRATS
- Michael Dukakis 9,898,750; 42.46%
- Jesse Jackson 6,788,991; 29.12%
- Al Gore 3,185,806; 13.67%
- Dick Gephardt 1,399,041; 6.00%
- Paul Simon 1,082,960; 4.65%
- Gary Hart 415,716; 1.78%
- Unpledged 250,307; 1.07%

Party Platform

REPUBLICANS
- "Kinder, gentler" version of Reaganism
- Cut the deficit but "no new taxes"
- Aid democracy and the contras in Central America
- Family values
- Advance the Strategic Defense Initiative
- For school prayer
- For the death penalty
- For a constitutional amendment banning abortion

DEMOCRATS
- End Reagan Revolution
- Reduce the federal budget deficit with cuts, especially the Pentagon
- "Stop the illegal war in Central America"
- Help the elderly
- Serious action on energy and the environment
- Fight AIDS
- Public investment in infrastructure
- Anti–death penalty
- Pro-choice on abortion

Campaign Innovations

- Use of focus groups and other corporate marketing tools to hone message, reach voters
- "Dukakis in a tank" becomes shorthand for a public relations move that backfires.
- "Sound bites" and "photo ops" become part of the regular vocabulary of campaign coverage and spread through American life.
- A "Willie Horton" becomes shorthand for a harsh, unfair, but effective ad or campaign salvo.

Campaign Tactics

REPUBLICANS
- The Republican operative Lee Atwater has his aide James Pinkerton summarize the most effective attacks against Dukakis on a 3 x 5 index card and test them with focus groups.
- The result is the Bush campaign's relentless attack on Dukakis for the Willie Horton prison furlough debacle, polluting Boston Harbor, and limiting the Pledge.
- Balance the harsh, slashing attacks on Dukakis with Reaganesque appeals to patriotism.
- Bush as the heir to Reagan, living the values Reagan salutes
- Bush promises a "kinder, gentler" form of conservatism.
- The uptight Bush tries loosening up, becoming more personal, even indulging in public displays of affection with his wife, Barbara.

DEMOCRATS

- Dukakis wants to win a campaign of substance not style, on issues not attacks.
- Nevertheless, he criticizes the Reagan years but gets little traction with the cold war ending and the economy booming.
- Democrats pillory Quayle as unprepared for higher office.

Debates

- September 25, 1988: Presidential debate in Winston-Salem, North Carolina
- October 5, 1988: Vice-presidential debate in Omaha, Nebraska
- October 13, 1988: Presidential debate in Los Angeles

Popular Campaign Slogans

REPUBLICANS

- "Kinder, Gentler Nation"
- "I want to be remembered as the education president"
- "Building on America's Strength"; "For a Strong America"
- George Bush, "The Leader America Needs for the Future"

DEMOCRATS

- "It's Time to Say YES"
- "This election is not about ideology, it is about competence."
- "Mike Dukakis. A strong leader for a strong America."
- "Mike Dukakis. American know-how is back."

Campaign Songs

REPUBLICANS

- "This Land Is Your Land"

DEMOCRATS

- "America"
- "Fanfare for Michael Dukakis"

Influential Campaign Appeals or Ads

REPUBLICANS

- Willie Horton ad, charging Dukakis with releasing a black prisoner on a Massachusetts prisoners' weekend furlough program who then raped and terrorized a woman in Maryland. Dukakis "allowed murderers to have weekend passes," the narrator intones: "weekend Prison Passes . . . Dukakis on Crime."

- The Americans for Bush arm of an independent PAC, the National Security Political Action Committee, spends $8.5 million broadcasting the ad, which is then broadcast repeatedly for free on news channels.
- "Revolving Door": the more subdued Bush campaign version, warns: "Now Michael Dukakis says he wants to do for America what he's done for Massachusetts."
- "Boston Harbor" depicts environmental pollution in Boston Harbor as America's future.
- "'What is it about the Pledge of Allegiance that upsets him so much?' Bush asks about Dukakis, at a campaign rally. 'It is very hard for me to imagine that the Founding Fathers—Samuel Adams and John Hancock and John Adams—would have objected to teachers leading students in the Pledge of Allegiance to the flag of the United States.'" Governor Dukakis vetoed a 1977 bill that would have compelled teachers to lead their classes in the pledge.

DEMOCRATS

- "Quayle: Just a heartbeat away."
- Counter to Willie Horton ad: "In 1968, George Bush helped an ex-convict fund a halfway house for early released felons in Houston, Texas. In 1982, one of those prisoners raped and murdered a minister's wife."

Campaign Finance

- Bush $46,100,000 (in current dollars: $79,301,000)
- Dukakis $46,100,000 (in current dollars: $79,301,000)

  - General election spending is now $408.3 million.

Defining Quotations

- "Throughout his life, George Bush has shown—time and time again—that he has the ability, integrity and leadership required to meet and overcome tough challenges. His years of experience in private business and at the highest levels of our government have earned him the reputation as a man who gets the job done right. He has the range of experience, the commitment to excellence and the vision of peace and economic opportunity for America that we need in our next President. At the center of George Bush's life is his family. His parents instilled in him strong values that are the basis for his exemplary achievements and it is as a family man that the Vice President speaks out on the important issues America faces and the need to protect our future." *George H. W. Bush for President, 1988 campaign brochures*

- "Democratic values in action: Mike Dukakis and the Massachusetts Miracle. Mike Dukakis doesn't just talk about Democratic values. He puts them into action. Since he's been Governor, the unemployment rate in Massachusetts has gone from more than 11 percent to less than 4 percent. No wonder it's called the Massachusetts Miracle. . . . Mike Dukakis is a modern leader with a classic American success story. He's the son of Greek immigrants who came to this country 75 years ago, searching for better lives. His father became a family doctor, his mother a schoolteacher." *Mike Dukakis for President, 1988 campaign brochures*

- "Poor George, he can't help it, he was born with a silver foot in his mouth." *Texas state treasurer Ann Richards at the Democratic National Convention in Atlanta, keynote address, July 18, 1988*

- "When I look out at this convention, I see the face of America: red, yellow, brown, black, and white. We are all precious in God's sight—the real rainbow coalition." *Jesse Jackson at the Democratic National Convention, July 19, 1988*

- George Bush is a "toothache of a man" who was "born on third base [and] thought he had hit a triple." *Texas agricultural commissioner Jim Hightower at the Democratic National Convention, July 20, 1988*

- "In the Dukakis White House, as in the Dukakis State House, if you accept the privilege of public service, you had better understand the responsibilities of public service. If you violate that trust, you'll be fired; if you violate the law, you'll be prosecuted; and if you sell arms to the Ayatollah, don't expect a pardon from the President of the United States." *Michael Dukakis, "A New Era of Greatness for America," address accepting the presidential nomination at the Democratic National Convention in Atlanta, July 21, 1988*

- "For we're a nation of community; of thousands and tens of thousands of ethnic, religious, social, business, labor union, neighborhood, regional and other organizations, all of them varied, voluntary and unique. This is America: the Knights of Columbus, the Grange, Hadassah, the Disabled American Veterans, the Order of Ahepa, the Business and Professional Women of America, the union hall, the Bible study group, LULAC, 'Holy Name'—a brilliant diversity spread like stars, like a thousand points of light in a broad and peaceful sky. Does government have a place? Yes. Government is part of the nation of communities—not the whole, just a part. And I do not hate government. A government that remembers that the people are its master is a good

and needed thing." *George H. W. Bush, nomination acceptance address, Republican National Convention, New Orleans, August 18, 1988*

- "I'm the one who believes it is a scandal to give a weekend furlough to a hardened first degree killer who hasn't even served enough time to be eligible for parole. I'm the one, I'm the one, who says a drug dealer who is responsible for the death of a policeman should be subject to capital punishment. And I'm the one who will not raise taxes. My opponent, my opponent now says he'll raise them as a last resort, or a third resort. But when a politician talks like that, you know that's one resort he'll be checking into. My opponent, my opponent won't rule out raising taxes. But I will. And the Congress will push me to raise taxes and I'll say no. And they'll push, and I'll say no, and they'll push again, and I'll say, to them, 'Read my lips: No new taxes.'" *George H. W. Bush, acceptance address, Republican National Convention, New Orleans, August 18, 1988*

- Dan Quayle: "I have as much experience in the Congress as Jack Kennedy did when he sought the presidency." Bentsen: "Senator, I served with Jack Kennedy. I knew Jack Kennedy. Jack Kennedy was a friend of mine. Senator, you're no Jack Kennedy." Quayle: "That was really uncalled for, Senator." Bentsen: "You are the one that was making the comparison, Senator, and I'm one who knew him well. And frankly I think you are so far apart in the objectives you choose for your country that I did not think the comparison was well-taken." *Quayle-Bentsen exchange at the vice-presidential debate, October 5, 1988*

- Bernard Shaw (CNN anchor): "By agreement between the candidates, the first question goes to Gov. Dukakis. You have two minutes to respond. Governor, if Kitty Dukakis were raped and murdered, would you favor an irrevocable death penalty for the killer?" *Michael Dukakis:* "No, I don't, Bernard. And I think you know that I've opposed the death penalty during all of my life. I don't see any evidence that it's a deterrent, and I think there are better and more effective ways to deal with violent crime. We've done so in my own state. And it's one of the reasons why we have had the biggest drop in crime of any industrial state in America; why we have the lowest murder rate of any industrial state in America." *Opening exchange, second presidential debate, October 13, 1988*

- "And the American people are wonderful when it comes to understanding when a campaign ends and the world of business begins." *George H. W.*

Bush, president-elect's news conference in Houston, November 9, 1988

- "In 1988, fighting Dukakis, I said that 'I would strip the bark off the little bastard' and 'make Willie Horton his running mate.' I am sorry for both statements: the first for its naked cruelty, the second because it makes me sound racist, which I am not." *Lee Atwater, Bush's campaign manager, before his death in 1991, in the February 1991 issue of* Life

Lasting Legacy of Campaign

- Introduction of regional primaries: 21 Democratic contests on Super Tuesday, March 8, 1988, heavy concentration of Southern primaries with a few other states and American Samoa.

- On Super Tuesday, more convention delegates are picked in both parties than had ever been chosen before in one day.
- Greek community raises millions of dollars for Michael Dukakis in an expression of ethnic solidarity.
- Trivialization of presidential politics; campaign did not focus on the major issues but rather character attacks; mean-spirited, negative campaign
- Power of independent PACs like the National Security PAC, which was so effective in spreading the Willie Horton campaign
- Sense of Democratic anger at Bush's tactics (overlooking how speakers pilloried Bush at the Democratic convention), vowing to win by being tough next time

Election of 1988

Right after his election as 41st president of the United States, George Herbert Walker Bush, tried to get something off his chest. "The American people," he said, "are wonderful when it comes to understanding when a campaign ends and the world of business begins." With the campaign behind him, he added, and presidential politics over, it was time to think about real work.

Bush was obviously the hoped-for political heir to Ronald Reagan. "In 1960 the plate tectonics of American politics favored Nixon," explained former Lyndon Johnson aide John Roche in the *National Review*, "but what a Marxist would call 'subjective' factors—fine organization, a vivid candidate, and Ike's aloofness—tipped it by a whisker. In 1988 the plate movement favors the Republicans even more strongly, and it seems highly unlikely to me that even the strangely diffident George Bush can throw it away." He stood to benefit from a return to economic stability, relaxed cold-war tensions and, in many ways most crucial, revulsion over domestic disorder widely associated with the failures of Democratic liberalism.

At 64, the vice president was 9 years older than the Democratic candidate, Governor Michael Dukakis of Massachusetts. His interest in politics dated back to his early years as a businessman on the West Texas oil fields, when, in Houston, he created Harris County's Republican Party. After failing to defeat incumbent Senator Ralph Yarborough in 1964, Bush was elected to the 90th Congress in 1966. He struck out in a second attempt at the Senate, losing in 1970 to a talented and well-heeled Democrat from South Texas, Lloyd Bentsen, a significant setback for the youthful and energetic Republican.

During the next two decades, Bush compiled an impressive vita. He served in a series of appointive positions, for both the Nixon and Ford administrations: ambassadorships to the United Nations and the People's Republic of China (as head of the American Liaison Office), chairmanship of the Republican National Committee, and director of the Central Intelligence Agency. His great liability as he tried to advance toward the presidency was his reputation as a "wimp," which came out of his 1980 primary campaign against Ronald Reagan. Republican right-wingers were also unhappy that he had referred to their hero's fiscal program as "voodoo economics," and nobody was satisfied that his claim to have been "out of the loop" was sufficient to explain his role in the arms-for-hostages affair, usually known as the Iran–Contra scandal, which embarrassed the Reagan administration. Bush in 1988 had at least a taint of responsibility for the international fiasco that involved trying to free American hostages and funding anticommunist contra fighters in Central America.

Democrats, at the same time, were in decline after having passed the turning point of postwar American liberalism. New Dealers were becoming rare. Pragmatic moderation, if not outright conservatism, was all the rage. The term "big government" became an epithet (a characterization advanced so effectively by Reagan), the embodiment of the power shift. "One is tempted to conclude that the most significant political change in the 1980s is this generational rejection of the Democratic Party," wrote political analyst Patrick Caddell in 1987. Not since John Kennedy's election in 1960 had the party won the White House with a non-Southern candidate. Population shifts became at least as important

George H. W. Bush *(The White House)*

in American presidential politics as questions of money, war, and peace.

But race remained central, the key to understanding American politics and culture. The old New Deal coalition, especially the alliance between what had been the urban North and the rural South, withered under the stress of the new demographics. Divisions along color lines conditioned a realignment in which traditionalists turned to the GOP. Liberalism in Washington (more and more synonymous with hostility toward Jim Crow–era segregation), tolerated and still beneficial in some quarters, repelled Democrats devoted to the politics of anti-communism and local control.

Lyndon Johnson's Great Society programs and the antiwar movement, with its unsettling counterculture, became identified with "permissiveness." Permissiveness, disorder, and race went hand in hand. The increasing pattern of social instability during a period of economic and social dislocation became most visible in rising rates of crime that were easily associated with traditional urban Democratic strongholds, especially those with heavy concentrations of minorities.

Inseparable from all this was the mantra of "law and order," often used as post–civil rights movement code language. Governor George Wallace of Alabama combined with Richard Nixon's "southern strategy" in 1968 to mobilize 57 percent of the votes against the presidential candidacy of Johnson's vice president, Hubert Humphrey.

Nothing, not even the threat of the Soviet Union and crime itself, became as insidiously contentious as the sensitivities of racial justice. A student of poverty and race at Harvard and the Massachusetts Institute of Technology, Daniel Patrick Moynihan, stumbled over the hazards of what came to be called "political incorrectness" when he published a serious analysis of the difficulties of impoverished black families. "Indeed," wrote William Julius Wilson in *The Truly Disadvantaged,* "one of the consequences of the heated controversy over the Moynihan report on the Negro family is that those liberal social scientists, social workers, journalists, policy-makers, and civil rights leaders have been, until very recently, reluctant to make any references to race at all when discussing issues such as the increase of violent crime, teenage pregnancy, and out-of-wedlock births."

Prominent in the atmosphere that was hyperventilated by the political process was the Reverend Jesse Jackson's candidacy in 1984. As the founder of Operation Push in Chicago and the molder of what evolved into the Rainbow Coalition, Jackson appeared to many civil rights activists as the heir of the martyred Martin Luther King Jr. His message combined black self-reliance and the responsibility of white society for lifting the underclass. As Andrew Kopkind put it, "He traversed lines of class and race—African-American, Native Americans, Arab-Americans, field workers, white displaced farm and factory families, the underclass and the working poor—to create a genuine populist force that played serious politics in the highest national arena." In 1984 he managed to draw a fifth of all the votes cast in primaries and caucuses, attracting some three and a half million Americans to his candidacy, and came into the Democratic convention at San Francisco that year behind only Gary Hart and Walter Mondale. His oratory fired the convention and the national television audience. His pulpit, one writer noted, "was the television camera lens."

In 1984, Jackson was the first African-American candidate for a major party nomination, making far greater impact on the campaign than Frederick Douglass had in 1888 or Shirley Chisholm had in 1972. Jack Germond and Jules Witcover, in the most detailed study of the campaign, thought that Jackson saw his candidacy "as a vehicle for attracting attention to a cause and if it skewed the Democrats' process in seeking a presidential nominee, so be it." His followers ranged "from the moderate, older supporters of Dr. King's conciliatory approach to the angry militants" behind the black nationalist fire-eating bigotry of Louis Farrakhan. Some surveys before the 1988 convention in Atlanta showed that about 23 percent of the white electorate persisted in opposition to any black presidential candidate, meaning, as Marshall Frady pointed out, that Jackson, at the age of 46 in 1988, would have to get more than 60 percent of the rest of the white vote to "even stand a chance of gaining a majority in the general election." Projections for the convention indicated that he would not win much more than 700 delegates.

Even before the start of the decade of the 1980s, demographers noted a return flow of blacks to the South. There was clear evidence that efforts toward racial integration were backfiring. Charles Murray was especially effective in his 1984 polemic against government programs to aid the poor, *Losing Ground.* Murray argued that such "reforms" actually undermined the economic plight of the intended beneficiaries. From an increasing number of conservative think-tanks came influential op-ed articles in such journals of opinion as *National Review, Human Events,* and the *American Spectator* taking special aim at liberal programs. There were also gloomy assessments on the editorial pages of the *Wall Street Journal* about the failures, even destructiveness, of policies portrayed as misguided, even self-serving, liberalism. Moynihan's *Maximum Feasible Misunderstanding: Community Action in the War on Poverty* held that the social welfare professionals themselves were often the most likely beneficiaries of government programs.

To whatever extent Moynihan and others attempted to make historical and sociological distinctions, the question often came down to a combination of race and class, as Anthony Lukas's *Common Ground* depicted the school-busing conflicts in Boston. New York City expe-

This Kevin Kallaugher cartoon shows presidential hopeful Jesse Jackson with a bucket of black paint, painting a rainbow. Frustrated at being seen only as a black candidate, Jackson took steps in April 1986 to formally establish his Rainbow Coalition, which he billed as a progressive force within the Democratic Party, based on the needs of a wide variety of constituents. *(Kevin Kallaugher, www.kaltoons.com)*

rienced setbacks that questioned liberal assumptions since the Supreme Court's 1954 desegregation decision in *Brown v. Board of Education.* A strike of teachers against school decentralization in the nation's largest city embittered many blacks toward the heavily Jewish educators union. In urban areas outside the South, residential patterns showed segregation instead of continuing progress toward integration, a turning away from faith in the democratic ideals of racial harmony. Politically, in the South and in much of the country, the face of Republican politics was continuing to get whiter, as it had been doing since Roosevelt's day, and blacks were increasingly identified with the modern Democratic Party. A younger generation of Democrats in the 1970s and 1980s was less attached to New Deal liberalism. Some, especially congressional freshmen, were "Watergate babies" elected in the after-wash of the Nixon scandals; the others were associated in the press with the name of a newly popular computer game and described as "Atari Democrats," nonideological types who subordinated political passions to faith in progress by "high-tech" solutions.

One of them, Michael Dukakis, first elected governor of Massachusetts in 1975, was much less known than Vice President Bush. He was, in fact, so much of a "blank slate in voters' minds," as one reporter wrote, that "Bush had to be the first to write on it." The son of Greek immigrants and the bearer of a "foreign-sounding" name, he had yet to earn a national reputation. He was just another Democratic chief executive from the Northeast, intelligent, competent, honest, "a technocrat, something of a mechanic," neither a 1960s-style liberal nor a flamboyant reformer, more WASPish than ethnic in his ways, and personally so conservative that he "believed in Reason with the faith of the eighteenth-century Enlightenment." Dukakis was more pragmatic than the left-liberalism associated with post–Great Depression Democrats, more Atari than "lefty." In an era after the "can-do" leadership of a JFK and the political cynicism of the Nixon years, managerial types like Dukakis were prized for helping to relieve the distress of the body politic. He was so disdainful of politics as usual that he placed what he thought was the fiscal health of Massachusetts ahead of his pledge not to raise taxes. The result was somewhat of a shock. The nation's most serious, conscientious young governor, Dukakis, was defeated for reelection in his party's primary by an unknown businessman, Ed King. But in 1983 voters returned him to the governorship after a four-year hiatus with an overwhelming majority. He then became the beneficiary of a new generation of electronics and computer industries that prospered along the Route 128 perimeter outside of Boston.

Dukakis was in his glory. The National Governors Association cited him in 1986 as the "most effective gov-

1988 ELECTION CHRONOLOGY

1986

November 4, 1986: In the midterm congressional elections, Democrats regain control of the Senate for the first time in six years.

1987

March 4, 1987: President Ronald Reagan, in a televised address to the nation, finally accepts "full responsibility" for the Iran-Contra scandal that had been plaguing his administration.

May 8, 1987: The front-runner for the 1988 Democratic nomination, Colorado senator Gary Hart, withdraws abruptly from the campaign after being photographed with his girlfriend, Donna Rice. He will later return to the race, but will be ineffectual.

August 23, 1987: Another leading Democrat, Senator Joseph Biden, dooms his campaign by echoing a speech of the British Labor leader, Neil Kinnock. By mid-September rivals will have leaked a videotape of Biden's Iowa State Fair debate summation to reporters, wherein he tells Kinnock's life story as his own, forcing Biden to withdraw.

1988

February 8, 1988: Vice President George H. W. Bush comes in a surprising third with only 19 percent support behind Senator Robert Dole at 37 percent and televangelist Pat Robertson at 25 percent in the Republican Iowa caucuses. In the Democratic caucuses, two Midwestern candidates lead, Missouri representative Richard Gephardt at 31 percent and Illinois Senator Paul Simon at 27 percent, while Governor Michael Dukakis of Massachusetts does quite well, with 22 percent.

February 16, 1988: Bush wins a hard-fought comeback campaign in the New Hampshire primary, defeating Dole 38 percent to 29 percent. Dukakis soundly defeats his closest challenger, Richard Gephardt, 36 to 20 percent.

March 8, 1988: On "Super Tuesday," Bush sweeps all 16 Republican contests. Democrats have a less conclusive day as Dukakis wins eight states and American Samoa, Tennessee Senator Al Gore wins six states, and the Reverend Jesse Jackson wins five. Democrats gird for what most assume will be a lengthy nomination battle ahead.

March 26, 1988: Jackson wins the Michigan caucuses with 55 percent of the vote, putting him ahead in the delegate count. Democrats begin to worry that Jackson, seen as unelectable in a general election, might end up as the nominee instead of Dukakis, who is polling well ahead of Bush.

May 25, 1988: The Republican operative Lee Atwater has his aide James Pinkerton summarize the most effective attacks against Dukakis and test them with a focus group in Paramus, New Jersey. The results convince the Bush team to go negative.

June 8, 1988: After a big win in the New York primary on April 19, Dukakis sweeps California, New Jersey, Montana, and New Mexico to seal the Democratic nomination.

June 22, 1988: Cashing in on public worries about crime and drugs, Bush attacks Dukakis's membership in the American Civil Liberties Union while speaking to the National Sheriffs' Association in Louisville, Kentucky. Echoing an attack first made by Al Gore's playbook and that was effective with the Paramus focus group, Bush highlights the case of Willie Horton, a convicted murderer who kidnapped and raped a woman while on a weekend furlough from a Massachusetts prison.

---

ernor" in the nation. His chief political promoter touted the economic revival as the "Massachusetts miracle." "It's a record that combines progressive values with a sense of fiscal responsibility," he said. It was, nevertheless, also true that he still had not become a "household name." It was New York's governor, Mario Cuomo, rather than

Dukakis, who emerged as the most compelling personality after the fumbled national aspirations of Ted Kennedy. Cuomo continued to hover over the Democratic field. His potential, made even brighter by the national following he attracted as a result of his keynote address at the 1984 convention, made the 1988 situation more intriguing.

July 4, 1988: Michael and Kitty Dukakis host Jesse and Jacqueline Jackson in Brookline, Massachusetts. Dukakis wants peace. Jackson wants the vice presidency. The lunch does not go well.

July 18–21, 1988: At the Democratic National Convention in Atlanta, speakers pillory Vice President Bush. Senator Edward Kennedy rouses the convention, citing Bush's dithering or dodging as he and the crowd shout: "Where was George?" These attacks give Dukakis and his running mate, Lloyd Bentsen, a 20-point lead in polls but help a furious Bush rationalize his own slash-and-burn tactics in the campaign.

August 15–18, 1988: The Republican National Convention meets in New Orleans to nominate George H. W. Bush for president.

August 16, 1988: Bush announces on August 16 that he has chosen the young, conservative Indiana senator J. Danforth Quayle as his running mate. Reporters pounce on Quayle as unqualified and callow.

August 18, 1988: In his acceptance speech, Bush promises to deny congressional requests for tax increases with the memorable phrase, "Read my lips: No new taxes." Bush also promises a "kinder, gentler" approach that celebrates volunteerism, which generates "a thousand points of light."

August 24, 1988: At a rally in Los Angeles, Bush attacks Dukakis over his 1977 veto of a bill mandating that the Pledge of Allegiance be said in Massachusetts schools.

September 13, 1988: Trying to reverse his image as soft on defense, Dukakis climbs into an M1 Abrams tank at the General Dynamics Plant in Sterling Heights, Michigan, and says "rat-tat-tat," emulating the sound of the tank's gun. The image is widely pilloried, and the phrase "Dukakis in a tank" becomes shorthand for a campaign public relations ploy that backfires.

September 25, 1988: At the first presidential debate in Winston-Salem, North Carolina, Bush again attacks Dukakis for supporting the Massachusetts furlough program that freed Willie Horton, echoing anti-Dukakis ads that started airing on September 21. Dukakis also attacks Bush on the crime issue, noting the administration's links with drug trafficking in Central America.

October 5, 1988: At the vice-presidential debate in Omaha, Nebraska, Quayle attempts to allay concerns about his lack of experience by noting that he has as much experience as John F. Kennedy had in 1960. Bentsen replies with the devastating: "Senator, I served with Jack Kennedy. I knew Jack Kennedy. Jack Kennedy was a friend of mine. Senator, you're no Jack Kennedy."

October 13, 1988: During the second presidential debate, CNN anchor Bernard Shaw asks Dukakis whether he would support the death penalty if his wife were raped and murdered. Dukakis delivers a bland, emotionless response about the ineffectiveness of capital punishment. After the debate, the Gallup Poll estimates that Bush is leading 49–43, a shocking turnaround.

November 8, 1988: On Election Day, Bush wins 53.37 percent of the vote and 40 states, to Dukakis's 45.65 percent, 10 states, and the District of Columbia. In his victory speech, Bush reiterates his call for a "kinder, gentler nation."

December 19, 1988: Presidential electors cast their ballots in their respective state capitals. One West Virginia elector reverses her vote for the Democratic ticket, choosing Bentsen as president and Dukakis as vice president.

1989

January 4, 1989: A joint session of Congress assembles to count the electoral votes.

One can speculate about how far Michael Dukakis would have gone without John Sasso. Still in his thirties, Sasso had already become a legendary expert on the ins and outs of Massachusetts politics. A veteran of Ted Kennedy's primary election campaign of 1980 and Dukakis's successful second run for the governorship, he was chief of staff and chief political aide. Without Sasso, dubbed by the *Boston Globe* the "Larry Bird of politics" after the superstar basketball player for the Celtics, Dukakis's career may well have been confined to the state legislature. Without Sasso, there would have been no such packaging as the "The Miracle of

Massachusetts." With Sasso's guidance and caution to mute his liberal instincts, Dukakis joined with a business professor from Harvard, Rosabeth Moss Kanter, to publish a campaign book with the buoyant title of *Creating the Future: The Massachusetts Comeback and Its Promise for America.*

Sasso's value was reemphasized in the flap that took place over the plagiarism charges that forced Senator Joe Biden of Delaware to withdraw his candidacy. It was Sasso who learned that Biden had lifted whole passages from a speech by British Labour Party leader Neil Kinnock and had leaked the story to Maureen Dowd at the *New York Times* and to NBC News. The resulting imbroglio led to his own resignation from the Dukakis staff. When matters got tough during the latter part of the 1988 presidential campaign, Sasso returned to the fight.

"Dukakis' great strength was that he wasn't like Hart, who wasn't like Mondale, who wasn't like Carter, who wasn't like McGovern, who wasn't like Humphrey, who was unfortunately Lyndon Johnson's underling," wrote journalist Sidney Blumenthal. Dukakis's great fortune was that he even became a serious contender. He led the pack, with only Jackson even close.

Jackson was clearly the most articulate, the most passionate, the most programmatic, the most charismatic in the short field of the party's contenders. It was so full of relative lightweights that pundits scoffed at them as "Snow White and the Seven Dwarfs." Jackson's makeup contained more than a whiff of anti-Semitism, especially after an earlier reference to New York City as "Hymietown." Democratic Party leaders, sensitive to their significant Jewish base, were more fearful of an actual Jackson victory than a Dukakis loss. In 1984, when Walter Mondale failed to unseat Reagan, Jackson's candidacy inspired overwhelming support from blacks, but, as one critic of the campaign pointed out in an analysis published afterward, "from almost no other voters."

Michael Dukakis *(Library of Congress)*

Well remembered from four years earlier was the report from liberal journalist Wilson Carey McWilliams that "To white voters, Jackson suggested an inner-city hustler with an aura of financial sleaziness, self-promoting and injudicious, while Jackson's ventures into foreign *policy* were at *least* leftist and arguably unpatriotic." George Bush showed his contempt for Jesse Jackson in the spring of 1988 when he said he refused to be "out-hustled by the hustler from Chicago."

As Mario Cuomo was well aware, by deciding to become a candidate, he could find himself caught in the crossfire between New York's Jewish and black voters. That prospect, at least for the moment, was repugnant to the eloquent Democratic governor. He preferred to remain in the mansion at Albany. Elizabeth Drew, the perceptive Washington correspondent of the *New Yorker*, caught the drift of the Cuomo dilemma in April, when she noted how discouraged he was by the local racial situation. By staying out of the race himself, he left the party bereft of a powerful alternative to Jackson. As the more potent Democrats—Sam Nunn, Kennedy, and Cuomo—dropped out, and as such less-known possibilities as Al Gore Paul Simon, Dick Gephardt, and Bruce Babbitt failed to excite voters, one of the stars of the 1984 campaign, Gary Hart, was caught philandering, and Joe Biden (with an assist from Sasso) followed out the door, Dukakis became the party's "great white hope." Nevertheless, the message received by the nation during much of the spring was more Jackson's than Dukakis's.

The Gallup people appended a special point to their April 7 poll report:

> Despite Jesse Jackson's considerable success in rallying white primary voters to his cause, his candidacy remains plagued by the large number of whites who continue to hold negative opinions about him. Roughly two-fifths of all voters (38%) currently have unfavorable opinions about Jackson, nearly the same as the proportions who expressed similar views last April (41%) and September (45%). As in the earlier polls, negative assessments now are found almost exclusively among whites (43%), compared to only 8% of nonwhites. Solid majorities of voters give Jackson high marks for his honesty and sincerity (72%), as a champion of social justice (60%), and as a strong and forceful leader (56%). However, pluralities doubt that he is capable of dealing with the complex issues that face a president, or that he could manage the federal government, deal effectively with foreign leaders, or improve respondents' economic conditions. Substantial numbers also question Jackson's

ability, if elected, to represent all Americans, and they criticize his stands on the issues as too extreme. These perceptions doubtless contribute to Michael Dukakis' superior showing to Jackson in test elections against George Bush, the probable Republican nominee. In the recent *Newsweek* poll conducted by Gallup, Bush is the choice of 49% of registered voters nationwide to 44% for Dukakis, with 7% undecided. Confronting Jackson, Bush enjoys a commanding 58-to-32% lead, with 10% undecided.

Under such circumstances, Dukakis was not just the party's best hope. He was their only hope. After the Massachusetts governor's impressive showing on what was called "Super Tuesday" on March 8 (the closest thing yet to a national primary, involving 21 states and countless media markets) and even after his victory in Pennsylvania on April 27, which enabled him to clinch the delegate count, Jackson remained the major problem. Jackson's most exacting biographer, Marshall Frady, has, in fact, suggested that the concept of Super Tuesday was pushed by the conservatively inclined Democratic Leadership Council as a barrier against the black candidate by confronting him with a sort of Waterloo in the form of a bloc of hostile voters on a single day. Little did they anticipate how effectively blacks would coalesce behind their candidate to offset the roadblock. Their man ended up with a third of the Southern delegates.

His strong showing in Michigan pumped up his media attention from 3.3 minutes a day the previous week to 21.7 minutes afterward, according to a top aide, Elizabeth Colton. That whole primary season came to an end June 8, when Jackson lost all four primary states: New Mexico, California, Montana, and New Jersey. At that point, Dukakis had essentially won the nomination, helped by enthusiastic Greek-Americans, who enabled his primary campaign to reach its $23 million spending limit. In many ways, however, just as in some professional sports where the "real season" consists of the post-schedule playoffs, the Democratic political focus then homed in on the battle between the two primary front-runners, the African-American progressive and the party stalwart moderate.

And Reverend Jackson did his best to make life hard for the governor. Not only would he continue to use his clout in the manner of other significant contenders to share prominence and power, but, rather than merely fall in line behind the front-runner in the interest of party unity, Jackson pushed hard to say, in effect, that the victory was almost his as much as Dukakis's.

The votes had hardly been counted from the California primary when he made clear that he would not concede. "The notion that we'll just fold up now is as crazy as 'Can

a black run?' We have brought progressive political ideas back as a permanent force in American politics." Later, rhetorically, he asked, "What has Jesse built? I've built a family. I've rebuilt the progressive wing of the Democratic Party. I've expanded our party. We can only talk of winning because of what we built in '84 and did in '85, '86 and '87. What have I built? I've built a movement to shift to humane priorities at home and human rights abroad."

Throughout the primary season, he was the anti-establishment Democrat, the prod from the left. When everybody was worried about Reagan's legacy of budget deficits, Jackson boosted a national health insurance program, increased spending to create jobs, diluting the tax windfall that Reagan had given to the rich, paring the military budget, and, even more than Gephardt, heaping scorn on those who had taken up the banner of globalization. Jackson, anticipating many of organized labor's complaints in the following decade, then charged multinationals with more interest in "green, green, green" than in "red, white, and blue."

Another significant Jackson challenge was to pressure Dukakis to name him as his running mate. He had drawn more votes than had any second-place runner-up in primary history, some 7 million to Dukakis's 10 million. But the Gallup Poll continued to show that only 27 percent of Democrats considered Dukakis obligated to Jackson. Dukakis could neither choose him nor alienate him and his followers. Jackson kept a special caravan of buses rolling, as though the primary season were still in full bloom. His Rainbow Express, as it was called, gave him the additional attention to demand special recognition for the party's presidential campaign. If not the vice presidency, he wanted "shared victory and shared responsibility" with Governor Dukakis, which added up to a vague, unprecedented partnership with the presidential and vice-presidential nominees. On a Sunday *Face the Nation* telecast, he called for working it all out in direct meetings with Dukakis: "We're up against an American original," suggested a Dukakis adviser about Jackson, whose biographer has ventured to write that "Jackson may in fact be the most original figure, all things considered, ever to have reached such importance to the nation's civil life."

Michael and Kitty Dukakis invited the Jacksons for lunch at their Brookline home on July 4. Jackson was not about to make it easy for Dukakis. If he did not give him a place on the ticket, then the governor had to accept his demands for a suitable party platform. That meeting, by every account, was strained and unproductive. Both Jacksons came away from the meeting complaining that they had been "violated" and used only "as part of a charade" by Dukakis.

A few days later, the usually reticent Dukakis said, "Jesse Jackson can do anything he wants to do. I'm going to the convention, and I'm going to win it." At Atlanta, the site of the Democratic National Convention, Dukakis reached out for his running mate by choosing an establishment Texan, Senator Lloyd Bentsen, to shore up the party's national base. It was obviously more important to reconstitute the JFK–LBJ Boston–Austin axis of 1960 than to mollify Jackson. Jackson seethed "with inner rage" when Dukakis made his announcement with not an advance word to the leader of the Rainbow Coalition. Jackson did get a featured role at the Atlanta convention and was showcased on the podium with his wife. The event became a prime-time feature for delirious Democrats, some 12,500 jumping to their feet. Jackson, the preacher, was at his best, his speech interrupted by applause 55 times and drawing 18 standing ovations. "When I look out at this convention," he told them, "I see the face of America: red, yellow, brown, black, and white. We are all precious in God's sight—the real rainbow coalition." It was, reported Dan Rather for CBS, "thunder and lightning from Jesse Jackson. He shook the hall in his own way, just as he has shaken up the Democratic Party." It was the high point of the Jackson thrust.

Less effective in Jackson's behalf was the party's platform. Rather than accede to a Jacksonian demand for the realization of Palestinian aspirations and regional stability, the Dukakis version omitted any references to the "rights" of Palestinians in favor of simple, pro-Israel language calling on the Palestine Liberation Organization to comply with previous United Nations resolutions. Despite momentous developments under Mikhail Gorbachev in the Soviet Union, with individual republics straining to abandon the Kremlin's bloc under the opening made easier by glasnost and perestroika, and Reagan's own acceptance of rapprochement with Moscow, both platforms clung to a conventional cold war mindset. The Democrats, for example, declared abhorrence toward the concept of relaxing "our vigilance on the assumption that long-range Soviet interests have permanently changed." For their part, Republicans held fast to their repugnance toward abortion under all conditions and just about buried the notion of "liberalism" as relevant to American political dialogue.

The Gallup Poll trial heat taken in April 1988 had Vice President Bush and Governor Dukakis only 2 points apart. Gallup's mid-May figures showed Bush 16 points below Dukakis.

In Maine, on the Memorial Day weekend, the atmosphere was that of a "low time" for the Bush team. His inner circle assumed that Bush needed little preparation on international matters, so they emphasized domestic policies as well as the logistics of campaign politics. Dukakis's continuing ability to keep his political distance from Jesse Jackson gave him some aura of strength and

reinforced his reputation as a moderate. A third of the Democrats who had voted Republican in 1984 were seen as ready to resume normal voting habits.

"Movement" conservatism built on the legacy of Barry Goldwater hoped that the vice president would carry on in the Reagan tradition. The Republican Party that Bush fell into, as the son of Prescott Bush, the party moderate first elected to the senate from Greenwich, Connecticut, in 1952, was in 1988 far more heartland and Southern, and decidedly more given to right-wing rhetoric. "When he hears it now," wrote journalist Fred Barnes, "he likes the polarizing language. Eight years of Ronald Reagan has done that, and a lot more, to Bush."

Retaining the Democratic blue-collar vote so attracted to Reagan was the accomplishment of the most intensive and hard-hitting media campaign yet seen in American presidential politics. As Democratic political consultant Robert Squier has written, Republicans excelled at bringing "direct mail fund-raising, television, radio, and computers to the center of their party." As early as May, television advertising expenditures for the Bush campaign were expected to exceed $25 million (which helped make it the most expensive ever up to that time). Better funded than anything the Democrats could mount, with shrewder talent at their command, the Republicans managed to turn the trick of converting the diffident Dukakis into a way-out leftist.

With the help of some deft political strategy, featuring an "air war" managed by media expert Roger Ailes and a "ground war" plotted by the youthful consultant Lee Atwater, who understood better than anyone else the value of winning the bloc of Southern states that was contested on Super Tuesday, Bush turned back all rivals, principally Bob Dole, Pat Robertson, and Jack Kemp. In New Orleans for his party's nominating convention, he reached for the element of surprise by nominating as his running mate Senator Dan Quayle of Indiana, a youthful conservative. The choice of Quayle was popular among the Republican right wing and its religious fundamentalist backers. It also startled Bush's inner circle. Within hours, it was obvious that Quayle was unprepared for a media barrage about allegations concerning his academic background and service in the National Guard during the Vietnam War. His low moment, and one of the campaign's disasters, came when he compared himself to John F. Kennedy in the single vice-presidential debate, provoking his Democratic rival, Lloyd Bentsen of Texas, to say, "Senator, I served with Jack Kennedy. I knew Jack Kennedy. Jack Kennedy was a friend of mine. Senator, you are no Jack Kennedy."

Bush's early regret that he had chosen Quayle was more than overshadowed by the long-term consequences of his reiteration, during his acceptance speech, of a pledge he had made during the campaign. To emphasize

Delegates display opposing candidate choices during the opening session of the Democratic National Convention at the Omni Hotel in Atlanta, July 18, 1988. *(Phil Sandlin/Associated Press)*

that he meant to keep his promise, he said, "The Congress will push me to raise taxes, and I'll say no. And they'll push, and I'll say no. And they'll push again, and I'll say to them, 'Read my lips: No new taxes.'"

His acceptance speech in the Louisiana Superdome that called for a "kinder and gentler nation" sounded to some GOP hardliners uncomfortably critical of the Reagan years. His call for social progress by using "a thousand points of light" heralded a new voluntarism. But the tone of the convention was nevertheless a testimonial to the past eight years. Enough hard-hitting attacks against Democratic liberalism from such sources as Pat Robertson, and even by so moderate a Republican as Governor Thomas H. Kean of New Jersey, reinforced by a conservative platform, kept alive optimism about a Reaganite succession. The Dukakis lead in the polls dropped to just nine points after the Republicans disbanded, leaving the Bush camp to move forward with attack plans that had been developed after the primaries.

Bush always prided himself on being his own man. Unlike Reagan, Bush was neither passive nor indifferent about details. He never assumed that handlers could be trusted to know what was best. Whether, as during the primaries, he had a staff of advisers or a single head, James Addison Baker III, to plot the course to the November election, Bush followed a "hands-on" style. But there were limits to that "hands-on" style. His advisors, citing the early Dukakis advantage, convinced him to accept "red meat." They argued that the governor could be painted as a dangerous liberal. Bush's campaign researchers were able to feed him enough material that carried the potential for doing just that.

They would show that Dukakis was heir to the failed liberalism of the 1960s. He was, in fact, not a moderate but the epitome of "the L-word," a "liberal." He was a "card-carrying" member of the American Civil Liberties Union, an allusion that cleverly re-evoked McCarthy period charges of subversive associations. He vetoed a bill requiring Massachusetts schoolchildren to recite the Pledge of Allegiance. He failed to clean up the polluted mess in Boston Harbor. He even had the misfortune to have the state's economy take a downward turn while the campaign progressed—all that from the Sasso-heralded architect of the "Massachusetts Miracle." One Republican senator from Idaho, Steve Symms, even pushed a rumor that Kitty Dukakis had joined left-wing protesters in burning an American flag. Bush himself so stridently wrapped himself and his campaign in the American flag that his chief public relations man, Roger Ailes, finally concluded that he had gone "a flag too far." R. W. Apple Jr., capturing the newly combative Bush for the *New York Times,* wrote, "Ronald Reagan ran campaigns based on gaining the people's confidence, while Mr. Bush is evidently trying to destroy any confidence that people might have in Governor Dukakis."

Lee Atwater and Roger Ailes quickly understood that the case of Willie Horton, a convict in a Massachusetts state prison, could destroy Dukakis's candidacy. The Democratic governor had granted a furlough to Horton, a murderer serving a life sentence. Horton, a black man, then used his time away from jail to savage a young couple in Maryland, raping the woman. The incident had long been a topic of outrage in Massachusetts. Granting furloughs to lifers without a chance of parole was a legitimate issue. Other states, and the federal prison system itself, used furloughs, but to grant it to lifers was another matter.

At a meeting of Southern Republican leaders in June, Atwater appeared to others as "almost manic" at the prospect of producing Horton ads with pictures linking him to Jackson and Dukakis. At Atlanta, just before the Democrats held their convention in that city and when reporting that Dukakis and his wife had hosted the Jacksons on July 4, Atwater told a group of Southern Republicans that "maybe he'll put this Willie Horton guy on the ticket after all is said and done." The use of Horton as a surrogate for Jackson could not have been handier. Eric Alterman has pointed out that Atwater needed "to force the national Democratic party to shore up its base with black voters, particularly the black Democratic leader Jesse Jackson, and thereby further alienate white conservatives."

Intrinsically explosive, the Horton incident had been picked up and turned against the governor during that year's New York primary by Al Gore. Finally, faced with continuing pressure from the state legislature as well as Gore, Dukakis conceded the point and the furlough program was rescinded. But the reversal came in the spring of 1988, too late for Horton's victims, and too late for the governor himself.

The Willie Horton issue became a classic example of how to exploit racial divisions, even while making plausible-sounding denials of guilt. Republicans used it in their air war, and Bush repeatedly took Dukakis to task

for the furlough. Americans were inundated with the menacing face of Willie Horton. The murderer became a graphic reminder of how social experimentation could backfire. "If ever there has been a distortion of fact or history," Bush complained nearly four years later, "it is making Willie Horton a race issue instead of a prison furlough issue." In reality, it was both, a prison furlough issue, which had sufficient political implications in itself but, making it far more sensitive, a matter that was more upsetting to the public's psyche, the specter of murderous blacks turned loose.

The Willie Horton image that assaulted public sensitivities could have been supplied by "central casting." His angry-looking black face, viewed via prison mug shots, seemed dramatic confirmation of what everybody had heard about poverty and urban ghettos. Focus groups verified the campaign's possession of its own "ultimate weapon," and all the risks that went with it. Having "the bomb" was one thing; using it was another. Horton's race made it both more devastating and dangerous, which Bush's aides readily pointed out, even when conceding that they were worried about creating an ugly backlash. "There was no effort that I know of of anybody trying to exploit race," said Bush political director Ron Kaufman, "particularly the people who understood it best like Lee Atwater." Jim Pinkerton, the staff's intellectual and somewhat maverick conservative, who directed the research into Horton, recalled that "Nobody would tell Bush. He would have been upset" to hear that the man was black.

The findings, when seen by Bush at Kennebunkport, bolstered those who were urging an attack campaign. Atwater, the brashest of the aides, warmed to the prospect. The Jackson–Dukakis get-together at Brookline became a windfall for Republicans throughout the country. The ads that came out of Bush's own campaign, created by public relations man Sig Rogich and Ailes, were politically correct. They prudently left it to others to establish the connection between Willie Horton and his race. One of the more widely used ads, in fact, carefully staged a procession of *white men* going through a revolving door, a not very subtle reminder of what conservatives had been deploring as "revolving-door justice." The menacing picture of Horton himself was the work of independent filmmakers Floyd Brown and Larry McCarthy, former associates of Ailes, but nobody was ever able to prove that they were encouraged by Bush's media man. The campaign's chairman, Jim Baker, later claimed that the official Bush campaign was innocent of such tactics, pointing out that they had sent a letter, belated as it was, calling on the guilty

---

(opposite page) This is a copy of the letter that was distributed by the Maryland Republican Party linking Massachusetts governor Michael Dukakis with murderer Willie Horton. Representative Helen Bentley and Senate candidate Alan Keyes of Maryland held news conferences in Baltimore on November 1, 1988, to denounce the letter. *(Associated Press)*

DUKAKIS

IS THIS YOUR PRO-FAMILY

TEAM FOR 1988 ?

HORTON

Dear Fellow Marylander:

By now, you have heard of the Dukakis/Bentsen team.

But have you heard of the Dukakis/Willie Horton team?

This is the real team which voters, in particular pro-family voters, should be concerned about because it's the Dukakis/Willie Horton team which really tells what you can expect if Mike Dukakis is elected in November.

You see, Willie Horton is the Massachusetts killer Dukakis released as part of his prison furlough program for first degree murderers sentenced to life without parole. Like fifty-eight of his fellow killers, he decided not to return to prison when his weekend of fun was over.

Like many of his fellow escapees, Horton committed further violent crimes while on his "extended" furlough. In Horton's case, he came to Maryland to ply his trade.

The Dukakis/Horton story began on the night of October 26, 1974 when Horton robbed a gas station in Massachusetts. Horton, on parole at the time for assault with intent to murder, wasn't satisfied with merely robbing the 17 year-old station operator. So, he stabbed the boy 19 times, stuffed him into a trash can and left the boy to die.

Horton was captured and convicted of armed robbery and first-degree murder in May of 1975. Unfortunately for honest citizens, Massachusetts' new governor Mike Dukakis had, several weeks earlier, vetoed the death penalty bill in Massachusetts. Horton was sentenced to life imprisonment without parole.

Thus was the Dukakis/Horton team born.

By 1986, Horton was receiving weekend furloughs from Dukakis. After one of his "weekend vacations" Horton, surprisingly enough, failed to return to custody.

Horton was able to run as a direct result of his teammate Mike Dukakis' actions. You see, in 1975 the Massachusetts'

(Over, please)

producers to "cease and desist." Everyone understood that the point had already been firmly established in the mind of American voters. What is additionally obvious is that for all Bush's personal detachment from such tactics, he allowed them to be used to good effect without ever making a statement openly disavowing the relevance of race. A nation already apprehensive about the ambitions of Jesse Jackson was almost uniquely conditioned to respond with irrational fear against any potential leader who would leave them as vulnerable as that Maryland couple. Throughout the country, individual enthusiasts and local Republican committees took up the cry. One such flyer, from a Californian, pegged Jackson as "the century's classic example of black revolutionary failure" and warned that the "Democratic Party platform brings America closer to communism." In North Dakota, voters were urged by local Republican groups to "imagine life with Jesse Jackson as Secretary of State."

Bush could argue that the handling by Dukakis of the Willie Horton case was *not* a race issue. It was a legitimate question about safeguarding society from hardened criminals. The furlough matter had been prominent in Massachusetts for some time. The *Lawrence Eagle-Tribune*'s coverage about how Horton had murdered a youthful gas station attendant and been able to nevertheless gain freedom for a weekend that enabled him to go on a rampage was told in nearly 200 articles that reflected popular concern. Those who argued that it was not a mere manufactured sensation for political advantage also pointed to the Pulitzer Prize awarded to the paper for its reportage. The July issue of the *Reader's Digest* helped to spread national interest with a popular account by Robert James Bidinotto.

In the face of all that, Dukakis proved himself entirely inadequate. How could he have so underestimated the power of the issue? His campaign manager, Susan Estrich, had herself been a rape victim. In what may have been the single most painful moment of all to Democrats, Dukakis's answer to a hypothetical question posed by a black television news anchor, Bernard Shaw, during the second of the two presidential debates about how he would react if his wife were raped, confirmed his reputation as a bloodless technocrat.

Mostly, by then, it had become routine to poke fun at Dukakis's inadequacies. Nothing provoked as much merriment, especially from the Bush camp (even leading them to use the photos in anti-Dukakis commercials), as the sight of the Democratic candidate in an M-1 battle tank, waving from the open turret and looking silly and wearing an ill-fitting helmet. Reporters present on the scene laughed so hard they could be heard on the film soundtrack. And *Bush was supposed to be the wimp!* As the campaign went on, much more was made of Duka-

kis's weaknesses. Foremost, perhaps, was his reluctance to respond quickly and effectively to charges made by the opposition. When Dukakis, discussing the Iran–Contra scandal, said of Reagan, "A fish rots from the head down," the president came back swiftly: "I am not going to pick on an invalid."

The outcome was clear before Election Day. "We saw the floor fall in that weekend after the second debate," said Estrich, as viewers unhesitatingly rated Bush the clear winner by a large margin. The first major survey of opinion following the debates confirmed that Bush had opened up a large lead, 17 percent, according to both the *New York Times* and ABC/*Washington Post* polls. "Too good to be true," wrote Barbara Bush in her diary. Not until the closing days of the campaign did Dukakis do anything but remain on the defensive about liberalism, and, when he did, he argued the point as many Democrats thought he should have done all along. "Yes, I'm a liberal," he said in Bakersfield, California. But it was too late to change course.

So it was too late also to fully mend the tension between Dukakis and Jackson, which continued to revolve around mutual political and personal wariness. The fiery (especially when compared with Dukakis) Jackson's pressures on Dukakis made life uncomfortable for the governor. "Dukakis is in big trouble with the black community," said a black pollster based in the South. "That's all I'm hearing. People say they are uncomfortable with Dukakis because the commitments made to Jackson at the convention are not materializing."

The perceived wisdom was that the party's presidential candidate continued to keep his distance, although he diluted that somewhat in mid-September when he appeared with Jackson at the annual "legislative weekend" of the Congressional Black Caucus Foundation. Donna Brazile, who served as a member of Jackson's senior staff four years earlier but had since gone to work for Dukakis as the campaign's deputy field director, then reported that two months of negotiations with John Sasso had concluded with an agreement. Jackson would campaign in key states, especially in the South. Jackson's anger over Dukakis's fear about alienating Reagan Democrats nevertheless did not keep him from moderating his own tone. The party "needed both a left wing and a right wing to be able to fly," he even said, and had to "recognize that fiscal constraints made it impossible to do many of the things that needed to be done." Still, when he spoke at a rally in New Haven less than a week before Election Day, he boasted that he had covered more ground and addressed more people than Dukakis and Bentsen combined. Concentrating now on law and order, he said, "You can't fight high crime by having easy access to guns and not enough police." The Reagan administra-

President-elect George H. W. Bush waves to the Houston rally honoring him while surrounded by his family on November 9, 1988, a day after his election to the nation's top office. To his right stands his oldest son, future president George W. Bush. *(Associated Press)*

tion, argued Jackson, was responsible for the big budget deficit, negative balance of trade numbers, and thriving drug market. Long before that rally in a chapel on the Yale campus in the presence of a crowd of some 1,400, it was clear that Dukakis's skittishness over Jackson had turned off many black voters and that none of that mattered very much any longer because the Democratic campaign was in disarray.

The 40-state Bush–Quayle 426-electoral-vote sweep came on the strength of 53.4 percent of the popular vote. Bush came out of Election Day, as the *Economist* of London noted, a changed man: confident, in control, and enjoying himself. He was no longer the often strident campaigner who excoriated his opponents with the "L-word." He was once again the gentleman, reverting to what others noted were his East Coast WASPy ways. "George is simply not comfortable when he tries to be tough," noted one of his bosses, Richard Nixon, in 1992. "He comes through as shrill rather than strong. All of us who know him know that George Bush is not a hater." And Bush, for his part, was eager to forget that he had waged a scurrilous campaign, one that left the Demo-

cratic opposition ill disposed to cooperate and ready for vigorous partisanship.

Bush won in 1988 not only by promising "no new taxes" but by demonstrating that, like Charles Atlas of the 95-pound weakling fame, he had become muscular. The American people wanted a strong man in the presidency—not a Dukakis, not another Carter, but more a Harry Truman—at a point when "law and order" was right up there with economics as a defining issue. In the end, though, the great probability is that Jesse Jackson's discomfiting of Michael Dukakis had its impact on the black vote, which it has been estimated fell as much as 10 or 11 percent below the 1984 level. Whether Willie Horton was a surrogate bogeyman for Jesse Jackson, a blatant appeal to racism, or a valid point about crime and punishment, the issue worked. "We never recovered," a top Dukakis adviser later conceded about African Americans turned off from the whole process.

While Dukakis was plainly a loser, the Democrats managed to preserve their congressional control, even broadening it slightly for the 101st Congress, helping to accentuate his failure even more. When casting presidential ballots, voters seemed to be "doing penance for the 1960s," as a *Time* correspondent put it, "when too many voters considered themselves then to be the party of militant blacks, meddlesome social workers, uppity feminists, and draft-card-burning protesters." Conservative Americans knew how to peel away the remnants of the old New Deal coalition. Dukakis helped to simplify their task.

—*Herbert S. Parmet*

Selected Bibliography

See Herbert E. Alexander and Monica Bauer, *Financing the 1988 Election* (1991); Sidney Blumenthal, *Pledging Allegiance: The Last Campaign of the Cold War* (1990); Richard Ben Cramer, *What It Takes: The Way to the White House* (1992); Elizabeth Drew, *Election Journal: Political Events of 1987–1988* (1989); Jack W. Germond and Jules Witcover, *Whose Broad Stripes and Bright Stars? The Trivial Pursuit of the Presidency, 1988* (1989); Michael L. Gillette, interviewer, *Snapshots of the 1988 Presidential Campaign* (3 vols., 1992); Penn Kimball, *Keep Hope Alive! Super Tuesday and Jesse Jackson's 1988 Campaign for the Presidency* (1991); Jane Mayer and Doyle McManus, *Landslide: The Unmaking of the President, 1984–1988* (1988); Herbert S. Parmet, *George Bush: The Life of a Lone Star Yankee* (1997); Gerald M. Pomper, *The Election of 1988: Reports and Interpretations* (1989); David R. Runkel, ed., *Campaign for President: The Managers Look at '88* (1989); Michael Schaller, *Reckoning with Reagan: America and Its President in the 1980s* (1992); Paul Simon, *Winners and Losers: The 1988 Race for the Presidency: One Candidate's Perspective* (1989); Bill Turque, *Inventing Al Gore* (2000); and George Will, *The New Season: A Spectator's Guide to the 1988 Election* (1987).

1988 Electoral Map and Statistics

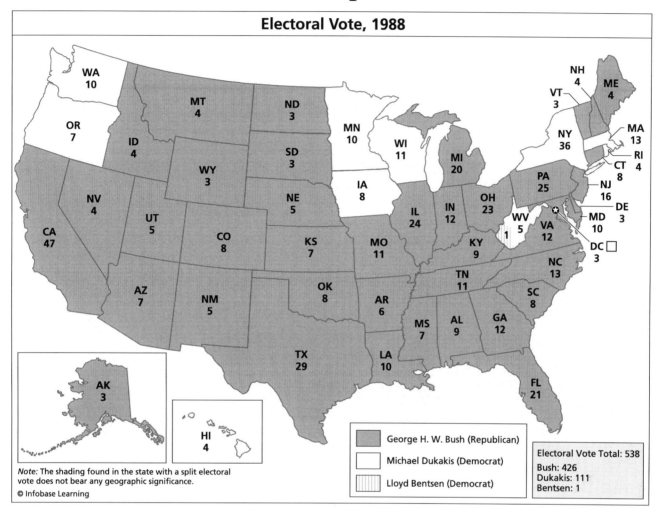

Electoral Vote, 1988

George H. W. Bush (Republican)

Michael Dukakis (Democrat)

Lloyd Bentsen (Democrat)

Note: The shading found in the state with a split electoral vote does not bear any geographic significance.

© Infobase Learning

Electoral Vote Total: 538
Bush: 426
Dukakis: 111
Bentsen: 1

1988 ELECTION STATISTICS

State	Number of Electors	Total Popular Vote	Elec Vote R	Elec Vote D	Elec Vote O*	Pop Vote R	Pop Vote D	Margin of Victory Votes	Margin of Victory % Total Vote
Alabama	9	1,378,476	9			1	2	266,070	19.30%
Alaska	3	200,116	3			1	2	46,667	23.32%
Arizona	7	1,171,873	7			1	2	248,512	21.21%
Arkansas	6	827,738	6			1	2	117,341	14.18%
California	47	9,887,064	47			1	2	352,684	3.57%
Colorado	8	1,372,394	8			1	2	106,724	7.78%
Connecticut	8	1,443,394	8			1	2	73,657	5.10%
Delaware	3	249,891	3			1	2	30,992	12.40%
District of Columbia	3	192,877		3		2	1	131,817	68.34%
Florida	21	4,302,313	21			1	2	962,184	22.36%
Georgia	12	1,809,672	12			1	2	366,539	20.25%
Hawaii	4	354,461		4		2	1	33,739	9.52%
Idaho	4	408,968	4			1	2	106,609	26.07%
Illinois	24	4,559,120	24			1	2	94,999	2.08%
Indiana	12	2,168,621	12			1	2	437,120	20.16%
Iowa	8	1,225,614		8		2	1	125,202	10.22%
Kansas	7	993,044	7			1	2	131,413	13.23%
Kentucky	9	1,322,517	9			1	2	153,913	11.64%
Louisiana	10	1,628,202	10			1	2	166,242	10.21%
Maine	4	555,035	4			1	2	63,562	11.45%
Maryland	10	1,714,358	10			1	2	49,863	2.91%
Massachusetts	13	2,632,805		13		2	1	206,762	7.85%
Michigan	20	3,669,163	20			1	2	289,703	7.90%
Minnesota	10	2,096,790		10		2	1	147,134	7.02%
Mississippi	7	931,527	7			1	2	193,969	20.82%
Missouri	11	2,093,228	11			1	2	83,334	3.98%
Montana	4	365,674	4			1	2	21,476	5.87%
Nebraska	5	662,372	5			1	2	138,801	20.96%
Nevada	4	350,067	4			1	2	73,302	20.94%
New Hampshire	4	450,525	4			1	2	117,841	26.16%
New Jersey	16	3,099,553	16			1	2	422,840	13.64%
New Mexico	5	521,287	5			1	2	25,844	4.96%
New York	36	6,485,683		36		2	1	266,011	4.10%
North Carolina	13	2,134,370	13			1	2	347,091	16.26%
North Dakota	3	297,261	3			1	2	38,820	13.06%
Ohio	23	4,393,699	23			1	2	476,920	10.85%
Oklahoma	8	1,171,036	8			1	2	194,944	16.65%
Oregon	7	1,201,694		7		2	1	56,080	4.67%
Pennsylvania	25	4,536,251	25			1	2	105,143	2.32%
Rhode Island	4	404,620		4		2	1	47,362	11.71%
South Carolina	8	986,009	8			1	2	235,889	23.92%
South Dakota	3	312,991	3			1	2	19,855	6.34%
Tennessee	11	1,636,250	11			1	2	267,439	16.34%
Texas	29	5,427,410	29			1	2	684,081	12.60%
Utah	5	647,008	5			1	2	221,099	34.17%
Vermont	3	243,333	3			1	2	8,556	3.52%
Virginia	12	2,191,609	12			1	2	449,363	20.50%
Washington	10	1,865,253		10		2	1	29,681	1.59%
West Virginia	6	653,311		5	1	2	1	30,951	4.74%
Wisconsin	11	2,191,608		11		2	1	79,295	3.62%
Wyoming	3	176,551	3			1	2	39,754	22.52%
Total	538	91,594,686	426	111	1	1	2	7,077,121	7.73%

* One elector voted for Lloyd Bentsen for president.

Bush Republican		Dukakis Democratic		Others	
815,576	59.17%	549,506	39.86%	13,394	0.97%
119,251	59.59%	72,584	36.27%	8,281	4.14%
702,541	59.95%	454,029	38.74%	15,303	1.31%
466,578	56.37%	349,237	42.19%	11,923	1.44%
5,054,917	51.13%	4,702,233	47.56%	129,914	1.31%
728,177	53.06%	621,453	45.28%	22,764	1.66%
750,241	51.98%	676,584	46.87%	16,569	1.15%
139,639	55.88%	108,647	43.48%	1,605	0.64%
27,590	14.30%	159,407	82.65%	5,880	3.05%
2,618,885	60.87%	1,656,701	38.51%	26,727	0.62%
1,081,331	59.75%	714,792	39.50%	13,549	0.75%
158,625	44.75%	192,364	54.27%	3,472	0.98%
253,881	62.08%	147,272	36.01%	7,815	1.91%
2,310,939	50.69%	2,215,940	48.60%	32,241	0.71%
1,297,763	59.84%	860,643	39.69%	10,215	0.47%
545,355	44.50%	670,557	54.71%	9,702	0.79%
554,049	55.79%	422,636	42.56%	16,359	1.65%
734,281	55.52%	580,368	43.88%	7,868	0.59%
883,702	54.27%	717,460	44.06%	27,040	1.66%
307,131	55.34%	243,569	43.88%	4,335	0.78%
876,167	51.11%	826,304	48.20%	11,887	0.69%
1,194,644	45.38%	1,401,406	53.23%	36,755	1.40%
1,965,486	53.57%	1,675,783	45.67%	27,894	0.76%
962,337	45.90%	1,109,471	52.91%	24,982	1.19%
557,890	59.89%	363,921	39.07%	9,716	1.04%
1,084,953	51.83%	1,001,619	47.85%	6,656	0.32%
190,412	52.07%	168,936	46.20%	6,326	1.73%
398,447	60.15%	259,646	39.20%	4,279	0.65%
206,040	58.86%	132,738	37.92%	11,289	3.22%
281,537	62.49%	163,696	36.33%	5,292	1.17%
1,743,192	56.24%	1,320,352	42.60%	36,009	1.16%
270,341	51.86%	244,497	46.90%	6,449	1.24%
3,081,871	47.52%	3,347,882	51.62%	55,930	0.86%
1,237,258	57.97%	890,167	41.71%	6,945	0.33%
166,559	56.03%	127,739	42.97%	2,963	1.00%
2,416,549	55.00%	1,939,629	44.15%	37,521	0.85%
678,367	57.93%	483,423	41.28%	9,246	0.79%
560,126	46.61%	616,206	51.28%	25,362	2.11%
2,300,087	50.70%	2,194,944	48.39%	41,220	0.91%
177,761	43.93%	225,123	55.64%	1,736	0.43%
606,443	61.50%	370,554	37.58%	9,012	0.91%
165,415	52.85%	145,560	46.51%	2,016	0.64%
947,233	57.89%	679,794	41.55%	9,223	0.56%
3,036,829	55.95%	2,352,748	43.35%	37,833	0.70%
428,442	66.22%	207,343	32.05%	11,223	1.73%
124,331	51.10%	115,775	47.58%	3,227	1.33%
1,309,162	59.74%	859,799	39.23%	22,648	1.03%
903,835	48.46%	933,516	50.05%	27,902	1.50%
310,065	47.46%	341,016	52.20%	2,230	0.34%
1,047,499	47.80%	1,126,794	51.41%	17,315	0.79%
106,867	60.53%	67,113	38.01%	2,571	1.46%
48,886,597	53.37%	41,809,476	45.65%	898,613	0.98%

Election of 1992

Election Overview

Election Year 1992

Election Day November 3, 1992

Winning Candidates

- ★ **President:** Bill Clinton
- ★ **Vice President:** Al Gore

Election Results [ticket, party: popular votes (percentage of popular vote); electoral votes (percentage of electoral vote)]

- Bill Clinton and Al Gore, Democratic: 44,909,806 (43.01%); 370 (68.8%)
- George H. W. Bush and Dan Quayle, Republican: 39,104,550 (37.45%); 168 (31.2%)
- Ross Perot and James Stockdale, Independent: 19,743,821 (18.91%); 0 (0.0%)
- Andre Marrou and Nancy Lord, Libertarian: 290,087 (0.28%); 0 (0.0%)
- Other: 375,729 (0.36%); 0 (0.0%)

Voter Turnout 55.2%

Central Forums/Campaign Methods for Addressing Voters

- Stumping
- Speeches
- Rallies
- Television interviews, talk show appearances
- Print and television ads
- Debates

Incumbent President and Vice President on Election Day George H. W. Bush and Dan Quayle

Population (1992) 256,922,000

Gross Domestic Product

- $6.342 trillion (in current dollars: $8.287 trillion)
- Per capita: $24,686 (in current dollars: $32,255)

Number of Daily Newspapers (1990) 1,655

Average Daily Circulation (1990) 62,649,218

Households with

- Radio (1990): 91,100,000
- Television (1990): 92,100,000

Method of Choosing Electors Popular vote (mostly general-ticket system/winner take all)

Method of Choosing Nominees

- Presidential preference primaries
- Caucuses

Key Issues and Events

- End of cold war: Berlin Wall down, East and West Germany unite, Soviet Communism ends.
- Gulf War: International coalition led by the United States stops Iraq's invasion of Kuwait.
- Bush budget deal in 1990: Democratic Congress raises taxes while imposing spending cuts; Bush breaks his 1988 campaign pledge: "Read my lips: No new taxes."
- March 1991 polls: President Bush has an 88% approval rating after the Gulf War.
- 1991 recession: Gross domestic product down, unemployment rate at over 6%.
- Racially inspired Los Angeles riots begin on April 29, 1992.
- Bush himself seems adrift, disconnected.

Leading Candidates

DEMOCRATS

- Bill Clinton, governor (Arkansas)
- Paul Tsongas, former senator (Massachusetts)
- Jerry Brown, former governor (California)
- Bob Kerrey, senator (Nebraska)
- Tom Harkin, senator (Iowa)
- Douglas Wilder, governor (Virginia)
- Larry Agran, former mayor (Irvine, California)

REPUBLICANS

- George H. W. Bush, president of the United States (Texas)
- Pat Buchanan, conservative columnist (Virginia)
- Harold E. Stassen, former governor (Minnesota)

Trajectory

- In a special *60 Minutes* segment broadcast after the Super Bowl on January 26, 1992, Arkansas governor Bill Clinton and his wife, Hillary Rodham Clinton, appear on CBS acknowledging problems in their marriage. Clinton fights charges he evaded the draft during the Vietnam War along with the adultery allegations. Relentlessly focusing on "the economy, stupid" earns him a second-place finish in New Hampshire on February 18 and bragging rights as the "Comeback Kid."
- Among Republicans, the renegade conservative Pat Buchanan surprises President George H. W. Bush by winning nearly 40 percent of the New Hampshire vote. Bush, whose 88 percent popularity ratings at the end of the Gulf War in January 1991 discouraged most leading Democrats from running against him, sees his popularity plummet as the recession persists.
- On "Super Tuesday," March 10, Clinton sweeps the primaries in the South. Yet even as Clinton racks up enough delegates to win, doubts about him persist. Former California governor Jerry Brown grassroots campaign wins the Connecticut primary on March 24. Building up to the New York primary on April 7, Clinton stumbles again with artful dodges that he tried marijuana but "did not inhale." Nevertheless, he wins New York.
- On June 4, Ross Perot, running as an Independent candidate pledging to cut the budget deficit, leads the national public opinion polls with support from 39% of the voters, versus 31% for Bush and 25% for Clinton, suggesting that his third-party candidacy may make a huge impact.
- Frustrated, Clinton launches a "Manhattan Project" to reengineer his image by playing saxophone on *Arsenio Hall* and denouncing rapper Sister Souljah for her racial demagoguery on June 13 at Jesse Jackson's Rainbow Coalition conference.
- Clinton's choice of a running mate on July 9 generates enthusiasm, as his fellow Southern baby boomer, Al Gore, helps reinforce Clinton's message of dynamic change.
- On July 16, the last day of the Democratic convention, Perot abruptly abandons his self-financed third-party insurgency. Perot's withdrawal reflects confidence in Clinton, who is reintroducing himself as the "Man from Hope," a small-town kid who made good.
- The Republican convention August 17–20 is an exercise in damage control that causes new damage. President Bush apologizes for breaking his "no new taxes" vow. Bush's "kinder, gentler" message is upstaged by Patrick Buchanan's fiery, polarizing call for a "culture war."
- Perot plunges back into the race October 1, just in time to become the first Independent party candidate to participate in the general election debate with both major party candidates.
- After the second of three debates, following a town hall format, on October 15, President Bush is pilloried for having glanced at his watch as an undecided voter in the audience asked, "How has the national debt personally affected each of your lives?" In fact, Bush glanced before the question was asked, but nevertheless answered the question awkwardly. Clinton, in his element, felt the questioner's pain, asking, "Tell me how it's affected you again?"
- Flummoxed by Clinton's near perfect political pitch in the fall, Bush proclaims, "For the rest of the way, we're going 100 percent negative." Clinton, aided by his effective "War Room" back in Little Rock, dodges Republicans' bullets and returns fire aggressively.
- Amid the crossfire, any chance Bush has of winning vanishes on October 30, when the Iran-Contra special prosecutor, Lawrence Walsh, reindicts former defense secretary Caspar Weinberger. Still, Clinton only wins 43 percent of the popular vote.

Conventions

- Democratic National Convention: July 13–16, 1992, Madison Square Garden, New York
- Republican National Convention: August 17–20, 1992, Astrodome, Houston

Ballots/Nominees

REPUBLICANS

Presidential first ballot

- George H. W. Bush 2,166

- Pat Buchanan 18
- Former ambassador Alan Keyes 1

Vice-presidential ballot
- Dan Quayle renominated by voice vote

DEMOCRATS
Presidential first ballot
- Bill Clinton 3,372; 80.27%
- Jerry Brown 596; 14.19%
- Paul Tsongas 209; 4.98%
- Robert Casey 10; 0.24%
- Pat Schroeder 8; 0.19%
- Larry Agran 3; 0.07%
- Ron Daniels 1; 0.02%
- Al Gore 1; 0.02%
- Joe Simonetta 1; 0.02%

THIRD PARTY CANDIDATES AND NOMINATIONS
INDEPENDENT CANDIDATE
- Ross Perot damages his credibility by withdrawing from the race in July, only to reenter it in October. Even worse, he claims he withdrew because Republican dirty tricksters were trying to ruin his daughter's wedding.
- For the vice presidency, Perot nominates a former prisoner of war, James Stockdale, who becomes something of a laughingstock by appearing clueless and meandering during the vice-presidential debate.

INDEPENDENT CANDIDATE
- Ralph Nader urges members of both parties to write in his name in the New Hampshire primaries. He receives 3,054 of the 170,333 Democratic votes and 3,258 of the 177,970 Republican votes cast.

INDEPENDENT CANDIDATE
- Drew Bradford (New Jersey) receives 4,749 votes, 12th overall (.14% of the popular vote in New Jersey, .01% nationwide).

INDEPENDENT CANDIDATE
- Delbert L. Ehlers (Iowa) finishes 6th in home state and receives more votes than Libertarian Andre Marrou in Iowa, finishing 18th nationwide (1,149 votes, .09% of the popular vote in Iowa).

LIBERTARIAN PARTY
- Andre Marrou, former Alaska representative and the party's 1988 vice-presidential candidate for president, and Nancy Lord. Marrou/Lord ticket makes the ballot in all 50 states and Washington, D.C., and receives 291,627 votes (0.28% of the popular vote).

POPULIST PARTY
- Bo Gritz, former U.S. Army Special Forces officer and Vietnam veteran, receives 106,152 votes nationwide (0.10% of the popular vote).

NEW ALLIANCE PARTY
- Lenora Fulani, psychotherapist and political activist and 1988 presidential nominee, and Maria Elizabeth Munoz receive 73,622 votes (0.07% of the popular vote).

U.S. TAXPAYERS PARTY
- Howard Phillips, conservative political activist, and Albion Knight Jr. receive 43,369 votes (0.04% of the popular vote).

NATURAL LAW PARTY
- John Hagelin, scientist and researcher, and Mike Tompkins, on the ballot in 32 states, draw 39,000 votes (0.04% of the popular vote).

Primaries
- Democratic Party: 40; 77.1% delegates
- Republican Party: 39; 67.8% delegates

Primaries Results
DEMOCRATS
- Bill Clinton 10,482,411; 51.99%
- Jerry Brown 4,071,232; 20.19%
- Paul Tsongas 3,656,010; 18.13%
- Unpledged 750,873; 3.72%
- Bob Kerrey 318,457; 1.58%
- Tom Harkin 280,304; 1.39%
- Lyndon LaRouche Jr. 154,599; 0.77%
- Eugene McCarthy 108,678; 0.54%
- Charles Woods 88,948; 0.44%
- Larry Agran 58,611; 0.29%

REPUBLICANS
- George H. W. Bush 9,199,463; 72.84%
- Pat Buchanan 2,899,488; 22.96%
- Unpledged 287,383; 2.28%
- David Duke 119,115; 0.94%

Party Platform
DEMOCRATS
- Champion economic growth
- Promise health care reform

- Deploy military force overseas when necessary
- Impose two-year limit on welfare benefits
- Defer to states to enact death penalty statutes
- Pro-choice on abortion

REPUBLICANS
- Oppose increasing taxes
- Strengthen families
- Promote parental choice in school choice
- Anti-abortion

Campaign Innovations

- "The Larry King era": TV talk shows hosted by Larry King, Phil Donahue, Arsenio Hall, and Oprah Winfrey allow candidates to speak freely in informal settings with friendly hosts and answer questions from the studio audience or from call-ins.
- "Sister Souljah Moment": During the campaign, Bill Clinton publicly denounced rapper Sister Souljah's comments on race. The incident later led to the use of the term "Sister Souljah Moment" to indicate a politician's criticism of apparent allies reputed to be extremists so as to appear brave and independent to reporters and voters.

Campaign Tactics

DEMOCRATS
- Speeches, interviews, and talk show appearances
- "It's the economy, stupid": emphasizing governance, jobs, substance not character
- Run ads with graphs, statistics, and quotations to show seriousness
- "War Room" to respond immediately to every Republican attack
- Bill Clinton appears on Arsenio Hall and plays the saxophone.
- "Sister Souljah Moment"—demonstrates Clinton's independence from the typical "sixties liberal" approach of the Democratic Party by denouncing African-American racial demagoguery at a Rainbow Coalition event
- Immediately following the Democratic convention, the Clintons and Gores maintain momentum by taking a six-day, 1,000-mile bus tour from New York to St. Louis with the slogan, "On the Road . . . to Change America." The tour generates enthusiastic crowds.

REPUBLICANS
- Negative tactics, paralleling the attacks used so effectively in 1988
- Negative advertising, questioning Clinton's character and patriotism

- President Bush, although reluctant at first, goes on the talk-show circuit to campaign for reelection.

INDEPENDENT
- Ross Perot, a Texas billionaire, announces his candidacy on *Larry King Live.*
- Perot says he will run for the presidency if volunteers get his name on the ballot in all 50 states, which they do.
- Perot stars in "infomercials," paid TV advertisements of a half hour or more, addressing the issues, especially the budget deficit: "I'm just going to sit down, and talk to the American people."
- Perot's United We Stand, America organization runs his campaign. Perot only starts appearing at rallies nine days before the campaign ends.

Debates

- Perot and his running mate included in the debates
- October 11, 1992: Presidential debate in St. Louis, Missouri
- October 13, 1992: Vice-presidential debate in Atlanta
- October 15, 1992: Presidential debate at University of Richmond, Virginia. Carole Simpson of ABC News moderates a town hall debate, relaying questions about the issues directly from the audience of undecided voters.
- October 19, 1992: Presidential debate in East Lansing, Michigan

Popular Campaign Slogans

DEMOCRATS
- "It's the economy, stupid"
- "A New Covenant to Make America Work Again!"
- "Don't stop thinking about tomorrow"
- "It's Time to Change America"
- "Putting People First"
- "Change vs. more of the same"
- "Don't forget health care"
- "Putting People First . . . for a Change."

REPUBLICANS
- "Stand by the President 1992"
- "Let's Re-Elect Our Desert Storm Commander in Chief in '92"

INDEPENDENT
- Ross Perot "Ross for Boss"

Campaign Songs

- Democratic Party: "Don't Stop"

- Republican Party: "This Land Is Your Land"
- Independent Party—Perot: "Crazy"

Influential Campaign Appeals or Ads

DEMOCRATS
- Clinton's centrist message as a "New Democrat" stemming from the moderate "Democratic Leadership Council" attracts millions.
- Clinton's centrist appeal: "We can be pro-growth and pro-environment, we can be pro-business and pro-labor . . . we can be pro-family and pro-choice."
- Attacks Bush as an "out of touch" president

REPUBLICANS
- Attacking Clinton as a "pot-smoking, philandering draft-dodger"—focus on character issue
- Mock "Slick Willie's . . . waffling," dismissing Clinton as a "pander bear," in the cutting words of his chief Democratic rival, Paul Tsongas.
- Pushing on the issues of "T&T," trust and taxes, Bush condemns Clinton and Gore as "Governor Taxes and the Ozone Man."
- Bush says at a Michigan campaign rally on October 29: "My dog Millie knows more about foreign policy than these two bozos."

Campaign Finance

- Bush $55,240,000 (in current dollars: $80,123,200)
- Clinton: $55,240,000 (in current dollars: $80,123,200)

  - General election spending is now $528.6 million
  - 4% of the voting population contributes to candidates on some level
  - 80% of all congressional campaign money is donated by PACs or individuals giving at least $200

Defining Quotations

- "Why am I running? Because we Republicans can no longer say it is all the liberals' fault. It was not some liberal Democrat who declared, 'Read my lips! No new taxes!' then broke his word to cut a back room budget deal with the big spenders. It was not Edward Kennedy who railed against a quota bill, then embraced its twin. It was not Congress alone who set off on the greatest social spending spree in 60 years, running up the largest deficits in modern history. No, that was done by men in whom we placed our confidence and our trust, and who turned their backs, and walked away from us. What is the White House answer to the recession caused by its own breach of faith? It is to deny we even have a recession. Well, let them come to New Hampshire." *Pat Buchanan's campaign launch, New Hampshire State Legislative Office Building, December 10, 1991*

- "I think the American people, at least people that have been married for a long time, know what it means and know the whole range of things that it can mean. . . . I have acknowledged wrongdoing, I have acknowledged causing pain in my marriage. I have said things to you tonight and to the American people from the beginning that no American politician ever has. I think most Americans who are watching this tonight, they'll know what we're saying. They'll get it. . . . Wait a minute, wait a minute, wait a minute. You're looking at two people who love each other. This is not an arrangement or understanding; this is a marriage." *Bill Clinton on* 60 Minutes, *January 26, 1992*

- "You know, I'm not sitting here as some little woman standing by my man, like Tammy Wynette. I'm sitting here because I love him and I respect him and I honor what he's been through and what we've been through together. And, you know, if that's not enough for people, then, heck, don't vote for him." *Hillary Clinton on* 60 Minutes, *January 26, 1992*

- "The decision not to be a resister and the related subsequent decisions were the most difficult of my life. I decided to accept the draft in spite of my beliefs for one reason: to maintain my political viability within the system. For years I have worked to prepare myself for a political life characterized by both practical political ability and concern for rapid social progress. It is a life I still feel compelled to try to lead. I do not think our system of government is by definition corrupt, however dangerous and inadequate it has been in recent years (the society may be corrupt, but that is not the same thing, and if that is true we are all finished anyway)." *Letter of Bill Clinton to Col. Eugene Holmes, December 3, 1969, read on* Nightline, *February 12, 1992*

- "For three weeks, of course, I've had some problems in the polls. All I've been asked about by the press are a woman I didn't sleep with and a draft I didn't dodge. Now I'm going to try to give them this election back, and if I can give it back to them and fight for them and fight for their future, I think we've got a chance to do well here and I know we can go beyond here and continue to take this fight to the American people." *Bill Clinton responding to Ted Koppel's persistent questioning on* Nightline, *February 12, 1992*

- "I experimented with marijuana a time or two. And I didn't like it, and didn't inhale, and never tried it again." *When Marcia Kramer asks why Clinton always answered previous questions about drug use by saying, "I never broke the laws of my country," he replies:* "That's not the specific question I've been asked in the past. If anybody had asked the question, I'd have answered it." *Bill Clinton on WCBS-TV in New York, March 29, 1992*

- "Clinton experimented with marijuana but he said he didn't inhale and he didn't enjoy it. That's the trouble with the Democrats. Even when they do something wrong, they don't do it right." *Johnny Carson on the* Tonight Show *a few days later*

- "That's why we need a new approach to government, a government that offers more empowerment and less entitlement.... A government that is leaner, not meaner; a government that expands opportunity, not bureaucracy; a government that understands that jobs must come from growth in a vibrant and vital system of free enterprise. I call this approach a New Covenant, a solemn agreement between the people and their government based not simply on what each of us can take but what all of us must give to our Nation." *Bill Clinton, "A Place Called Hope," acceptance speech to the Democratic National Convention, July 16, 1992*

- "We offer our people a new choice based on old values. We offer opportunity. We demand responsibility. We will build an American community again. The choice we offer is not conservative or liberal. In many ways, it is not even Republican or Democratic. It is different. It is new. And it will work. It will work because it is rooted in the vision and the values of the American people." *Bill Clinton, "A Place Called Hope," acceptance speech to the Democratic National Convention, July 16, 1992*

- "We must take back our cities, and take back our culture, and take back our country." *Pat Buchanan at the Republican National Convention, August 17, 1992*

- "Now let me say this: When it comes to taxes, I've learned the hard way. There's an old saying, 'Good judgment comes from experience, and experience comes from bad judgment.' Two years ago, I made a bad call on the Democrats' tax increase. I underestimated Congress' addiction to taxes. With my back against the wall, I agreed to a hard bargain: One tax increase one time in return for the toughest spending limits ever. Well, it was a mistake to go along with the Democratic tax increase, and I admit it. But here's the question for the American people. Who do you trust in this election? The candidate who's raised taxes one time and regrets it, or the other candidate who raised taxes and fees 128 times and enjoyed it every time?" *President George H. W. Bush, remarks accepting the presidential nomination at the Republican National Convention in Houston, August 20, 1992*

- "Well, they've got a point, I don't have any experience in gridlock government, where nobody takes any responsibility for anything and everybody blames everybody else. I don't have any experience in creating the worst public school system in the industrialized world, the most violent, crime-ridden society in the industrialized world. But I do have a lot of experience in getting things done.... I've got a lot of experience in not taking ten years to solve a ten-minute problem." *Ross Perot, first presidential debate, St. Louis, Missouri, October 11, 1992*

- "I offer a new approach. It's not trickle down economics. It's been tried for 12 years and it's failed. More people are working harder for less, 100,000 people a month losing their health insurance, unemployment going up, our economy slowing down. We can do better. And it's not tax and spend economics. It's invest and grow, put our people first, control health care costs and provide basic health care to all Americans, have an education system second to none and revitalize the private economy. That is my commitment to you. It is the kind of change that can open up a whole new world of opportunities to America as we enter the last decade of this century and move towards the 21st century. I want a country where people who work hard and play by the rules are rewarded, not punished. I want a country where people are coming together across the lines of race and region and income. I know we can do better. It won't take miracles and it won't happen overnight, but we can do much, much better if we have the courage to change. Thank you very much." *Bill Clinton, final statement, third presidential debate, East Lansing, Michigan, October 19, 1992*

Lasting Legacy of Campaign

- All three major candidates are from the South; two are Texans (Bush and Perot).
- Both Clinton and Gore are Southerners, contrary to the conventional strategy of having a geographically balanced ticket.
- Clinton-Gore ticket is the youngest in the 20th century, with Clinton at 45 and Gore age 44.
- The debates are the first to include an Independent candidate along with both major party nominees.

- National debut of Hillary Rodham Clinton during the "year of the woman," with 6 women elected to the Senate and 48 to the House.

- Clinton's centrism reflects the impact of the Reagan years on American ideology, even as his campaign claims to repudiate the Reagan-Bush doctrine.

Election of 1992

The 1992 presidential election took place against the backdrop of a world transformed by the dissolution of the Soviet Union and the end of the cold war. President George Bush, who took the oath of office in the same year that the Berlin Wall came crashing down, hoped to reap the political benefit from the end of the cold war. But the revolutions in Eastern Europe and the Soviet Union also sent shockwaves through American politics. Over the previous half-century the threat of Soviet aggression abroad and Communist subversion at home forged a fragile consensus in favor of an interventionist foreign policy. The end of the cold war not only refocused public attention on pressing domestic needs, it exposed old fissures in the Republican coalition between internationalists and isolationists. "We did not realize how much we had been leaning on the Berlin Wall until we tore it down," said one White House aide.

Bush, who relished the opportunity to play a role on the international stage, earned high marks for his deft handling of the transfer of power in the Soviet Union. His greatest achievement, however, took place in the Persian Gulf. In August 1990, elite Iraqi army troops smashed across the border of Kuwait. President Bush saw the invasion as a direct challenge to U.S. leadership in the post–cold war world. "This must be reversed," he announced after learning of the attack. Over the next few months, in an impressive display of international diplomacy, Bush rallied world opinion and a reluctant Congress to support military intervention to expel Saddam Hussein from Kuwait. In January 1991, a coalition of nations led by the United States launched Operation Desert Storm, a massive military assault that forced Iraqi troops out of Kuwait in less than 100 hours.

The victory in the Gulf War pushed the president's popularity to unprecedented heights—as much as 90 percent in some polls. Republicans were gleeful, especially since many leading Democrats in Congress had voted against the war. "The smart money in Washington says the 1992 campaign ended when the cease-fire began in Kuwait," observed one journalist. Even without the advantage of military victory, Republicans claimed an "electoral lock" on the presidency. Since 1968, 21 states with 191 electoral votes—70 percent of the 270 needed to win—voted Republican in each election. Only the District of Columbia, with 3 electoral votes, had voted consistently for the Democrats.

Confidence in a Bush victory rested on the assumption that the war would be a central issue in the 1992 presidential campaign. Even before most of the troops returned home, there were reasons to question that assumption. With the cold war over, and with no clear foreign threat to distract them, Americans were beginning to focus more attention on problems at home. In 1991, a *Los Angeles Times* poll revealed that by a whopping margin of 83 to 15 percent, voters wanted presidential candidates to concentrate on domestic issues, not foreign affairs. Bush, however, had never established a clear sense of domestic priorities or articulated a clear vision for where he wanted to move the nation. A *Doonesbury* cartoon had him saying on his first morning in office, "So far today, I've said the Pledge [of Allegiance], I haven't joined the ACLU [American Civil Liberties Union] and I haven't furloughed any murderers. I've delivered on my entire mandate, and it isn't even lunch yet."

A slowing economy was the most serious problem facing the nation. After seven booming years, the economy began to sputter. While the gross national product increased at an anemic 2.2 percent, unemployment crept upward, housing starts dropped, and consumer confidence hit new lows. The federal deficit continued its upward spiral to $290 billion in 1992, with forecasters predicting it would rise to $331 billion in 1993. The government was spending $200 billion in interest—15 percent of all spending—to pay interest on the debt. "The United States has never been less threatened by foreign forces than it is today," observed the *New York Times*, "but the unfortunate corollary is that never since the Great Depression has the threat to domestic well-being been greater."

The public clamored for the president to take decisive action to revive the ailing economy, but Bush and his advisers decided to take a hands-off approach. "I don't think it's the end of the world even if we have a recession," said Treasury Secretary Nicholas Brady. "We'll pull out of it again. No big deal." While the president remained largely indifferent to the domestic agenda, repeating the Reagan mantra of smaller government and lower taxes, public opinion had undergone a significant shift since the early 1980s. By 1992, over 65 percent of Americans favored more federal spending to create jobs; 74 percent called for increased spending on education and health care. The anti-tax revolt of the 1970s and '80s receded as many Americans said they would be willing to pay higher taxes if it led to improved medical care and education.

Trapped between a crippling budget deficit and growing demands for more social services, Bush was forced to abandon his "Read my lips: No new taxes" pledge, made in dramatic fashion at the 1988 Republican convention. He justified the switch by claiming that he only learned about the severity of the budget deficit after assuming the presidency. "I've started going into the numbers, finally," Bush said referring to the federal deficit, "and they're enormous." In 1990, the president agreed to a budget compromise with congressional Democrats that included $133 billion in new taxes. Most observers agreed with the decision to raise taxes, but few were convinced that Bush only learned of the problem after the election. The *New York Post*'s front page screamed the reaction: READ MY LIPS: I LIED.

The serious social problems that plagued the nation, and the president's lack of leadership, came into sharp focus when riots tore through Los Angeles in April 1992. The riots commenced after a mostly white jury in a Los Angeles suburb acquitted four white and Hispanic police officers accused of savagely beating an African-American motorist, Rodney King. The jury arrived at the verdict despite the existence of a videotape showing the officers delivering numerous blows to a seemingly defenseless King. Shortly after the verdicts were announced, African Americans in South Central Los Angeles erupted into the most deadly urban riot in over a century. By the time they ended three days later, 58 people lay dead, over eight hundred buildings were destroyed, and thousands more were damaged or looted. The president's initial response was to blame the riots on failed liberal social programs from the 1960s. When that explanation failed to convince people or reassure the nation, Bush traveled to the riot area and promised more federal aid. But for many people, the response was too little, too late. "He can't even fake it," sighed an administration official.

By 1992, many Americans had come to the conclusion that Bush was a decent man but a bad president, out of touch with the concerns of everyday Americans. His overall approval rating sagged to 34 percent, with fewer than 20 percent of the public approving his handling of the economy. During the 1980s, Reagan managed to appeal to the white middle class at the same time that he pursued supply-side economic policies that benefited the wealthy. But Bush lacked Reagan's common touch. The patrician Bush, often photographed riding on a golf cart or vacationing at his summer house in Maine, appeared indifferent to the anxiety of millions of Americans worried about losing their jobs. "He's off fishing and golfing instead of being in the White House, taking care of the country," declared a disgruntled Reagan Democrat.

When asked who had benefited most from the Reagan–Bush policies, 82 percent said the rich. Revealing Bush's vulnerability, nearly 60 percent said a Democratic president would be more likely to care about the needs of the middle class.

Already politically weakened by a struggling economy and low job approval, Bush had to fend off a primary revolt from Patrick Buchanan. The former Reagan speechwriter scored a surprising victory in the Iowa caucuses by attacking Bush as a captive of the Washington establishment who had lost touch with voters. Buchanan's challenge revealed how the end of the cold war had exposed old tensions in the Republican coalition. The slogan for his campaign—America First—was a throwback to the discredited isolationist movement of the 1930s. Rejecting the internationalist assumptions of mainstream Republicans, Buchanan called for an end to all foreign aid, the withdrawal of American troops from Korea and Europe, and an end of U.S. payments to the World Bank. "How other people rule themselves is their own business," he told cheering crowds. "To call it a vital interest of the United States is to contradict history and common sense." Most of all, Buchanan campaigned as a cultural warrior who attacked the president from the right on every "hot button" social issue. One Buchanan commercial showed a clip from a federally funded film showing African-American men dancing together. "Even after good people protested," the narrator states, "Bush continued to fund this kind of art."

While Buchanan sharpened his ideological attacks in the New Hampshire primary, the president fumbled around for a message to justify his candidacy. "Message: I care," he declared in his clumsy shorthand. "Don't cry for me, Argentina," he told a crowd of puzzled businessmen in Dover. Fearful of alienating the party's conservative base, which he was going to need in November, Bush avoided direct attacks on Buchanan. Trying to show that he was in touch with young people, the president quoted a country song by the Nitty Gritty Dirt Band. But he spoiled the attempt by calling them the Nitty Ditty Nitty Gritty Great Bird. At another appearance he startled observers, and rattled the stock market, by saying the economy was "in free fall," but then later retreated, saying it was not really that bad. "His re-election campaign lacks direction because he does," noted the *New Yorker*'s Elizabeth Drew. "He seems to have no clear idea why he should be re-elected."

The president's superior organization, and Republican fear of Buchanan's extremism, allowed Bush to win a narrow 53–37 victory in New Hampshire. But the fiery conservative forced Bush to campaign across the country while enduring a long primary season of punishing ver-

(continues on page 1512)

1992 ELECTION CHRONOLOGY

1988
August 18, 1988: Vice President George H. W. Bush, accepting his party's nomination for president, promises to refuse congressional requests to raise taxes with the memorable phrase, "Read my lips: No new taxes."

1989
November 9, 1989: The Berlin Wall falls, paving the way for the reunification of Germany and the fall of Communism throughout Eastern Europe and the Soviet Union.

1990
August 2, 1990: Saddam Hussein's Iraq invades neighboring Kuwait.

November 5, 1990: In a move deeply unpopular with conservative Republicans, President Bush signs into law a budget deal with the Democratic Congress that raises taxes, breaking his earlier pledge. This move will haunt him throughout the 1992 campaign.

November 6, 1990: In midterm elections, the Republicans lose eight seats in the House, one in the Senate.

1991
March 1991: Shortly after leading allied forces to victory in the Persian Gulf War against Iraq, Bush's approval rating shoots up to 88 percent. Leading Democrats feel increasingly gloomy about their prospects for 1992, but a worsening recession will soon take a toll on Bush's popularity.

October 3, 1991: Arkansas governor Bill Clinton officially enters the crowded Democratic field as he announces his candidacy for president in Little Rock.

December 15, 1991: Tom Brokaw moderates the first nationally televised debate of the primary season among the "Six Pack," the six leading Democratic candidates: Jerry Brown, former governor of California; Governor Bill Clinton of Arkansas; Senator Tom Harkin of Iowa; Senator Bob Kerrey of Nebraska; Paul Tsongas, former senator of Massachusetts; and Governor L. Douglas Wilder of Virginia.

1992
January 17, 1992: Reports begin to surface that Clinton has had numerous extramarital affairs, including a long one with Arkansas state employee Gennifer Flowers. Clinton at first denies the stories.

January 26, 1992: In a special *60 Minutes* broadcast on CBS right after Super Bowl XXVI, Bill and Hillary Clinton submit to a joint interview. Bill Clinton acknowledges "causing pain in my marriage," but gains many Americans' respect by refusing to go into more detail. Hillary Clinton alienates many Southern women by saying, "I'm not some little woman standing by my man like Tammy Wynette"—the beloved country singer.

February 18, 1992: Despite the allegations of marital infidelity and draft manipulation during the Vietnam War that have him nicknamed "Slick Willie," Bill Clinton finishes a strong second in the New Hampshire primary, with 25 percent of the vote to Paul Tsongas's 33 percent. Claiming a moral victory, Clinton calls himself the "Comeback Kid," and the name sticks. On the Republican side, conservative firebrand Pat Buchanan also finishes second, to President Bush, with 37 percent of the vote to Bush's 53 percent, a big blow to the president.

February 20, 1992: Populist Texas businessman H. Ross Perot announces on *Larry King Live* that he will run for president if his supporters manage to put him on the ballot in all 50 states.

March 6, 1992: Taking off the gloves four days before Super Tuesday, Paul Tsongas calls Bill Clinton a "pander bear" who "will say anything, do anything to get votes."

March 10, 1992: Bush sweeps all eight Republican primaries, eliminating Buchanan as a threat. Clinton sweeps the Southern primaries during Super Tuesday, yet doubts about his character and electability persist.

March 19, 1992: Two days after Clinton scores big victories in Illinois and Michigan, Tsongas suspends his candidacy.

April 7, 1992: After a hard-fought campaign in which he admits that he tried marijuana but "did not inhale," Clinton wins the New York primary

☆ ☆ ☆

with 41 percent of the vote. His toughest opponent now, former California governor Jerry Brown, finishes third, behind Tsongas, who remained on the ballot after suspending his campaign.

April 29, 1992: First of several days of rioting in Los Angeles in reaction to the acquittal of four white police officers in the beating of black motorist Rodney King. Poverty and unemployment in the continuing recession are also major factors.

June 3, 1992: Trailing both Perot and Bush in the polls, Clinton plays "Heartbreak Hotel" on the saxophone during an appearance on the *Arsenio Hall* show as part of his "Manhattan Project" to reengineer his image.

June 13, 1992: At a conference sponsored by Jesse Jackson's Rainbow Coalition, Clinton denounces rap artist Sister Souljah for allegedly promoting violence against whites. The phrase "Sister Souljah Moment" comes to mean a deliberate attempt to appear brave and independent by denouncing partisans or extremists on their home turf.

July 9, 1992: Clinton chooses Tennessee senator Al Gore, a fellow Southern baby-boomer, as his running mate to reinforce the Democrats' message of dynamic change.

July 13–16, 1992: At the Democratic National Convention in Madison Square Garden in New York City, Clinton and Gore win on the first ballot. After the convention, Clinton and Gore take a six-day bus ride from New York to St. Louis, campaigning with their wives, "On the Road … to Change America."

July 16, 1992: Faced with declining poll numbers, Perot abruptly withdraws from the race, claiming, "the Democratic Party has revitalized itself."

August 17–20, 1992: With the Republican National Convention meeting at the Astrodome in Houston, Republicans renominate President George H. W. Bush and Vice President Dan Quayle. Buchanan rallies his supporters by denouncing gay unions, the ban on school prayer, and women in combat, calling on Americans to "take back our cities, and take back our culture, and take back our country." Bush apologizes for breaking his promise not to raise taxes.

August 23, 1992: Bush hires his trusted adviser, James A. Baker III, to be White House chief of staff

and revitalize the Republican campaign. Meanwhile, in Little Rock, Clinton's consultant James Carville runs a "War Room" with a handwritten note on the wall summarizing the Democrats' message: "Change vs. More of the Same"; "The economy, stupid"; and "Don't forget health care."

October 1, 1992: Perot plunges back into the race, apologizing for his earlier decision to quit.

October 11, 1992: Perot becomes the first Independent candidate ever to appear alongside both major party candidates at a presidential debate, as he, Bush, and Clinton square off in St. Louis.

October 13, 1992: Gore and Quayle fiercely attack each other's running mates at the vice-presidential debate in Atlanta. Perot's running mate James Stockdale, has difficulty keeping up with the two seasoned politicians.

October 15, 1992: The second presidential debate is held at the University of Richmond in Virginia, using a "town hall" format in which undecided voters ask candidates questions directly. Bush responds awkwardly and appears to glance at his watch when a questioner asks how the national debt has personally affected his life. Clinton, however, seizes the moment and asks the questioner, "Tell me how it's affected you again?"

October 19, 1992: In his final statement at the third presidential debate in East Lansing, Michigan, Clinton distances himself from both "trickle down" and "tax and spend" economics.

October 25, 1992: Perot damages his credibility when he claims that his earlier withdrawal from the race was due to Republican plans to disrupt his daughter's wedding.

October 29, 1992: Trying to stir excitement but risking his dignity, President Bush attacks Clinton and Gore, saying, "My dog Millie knows more about foreign policy than these two bozos." Bush also labels Gore, an environmental activist, "Ozone Man," or just plain "Ozone." "You know why I call him Ozone Man?" Bush cries in Michigan. "This guy is so far out in the environmental extreme, we'll be up to our neck in owls and outta work for every American. He is way out, far out, man."

(continues)

1992 ELECTION CHRONOLOGY *(continued)*

October 30, 1992: While the Bush and Clinton
camps trade attacks late in the campaign, Iran-
Contra special prosecutor Lawrence Walsh
indicts former Republican defense secretary Caspar Weinberger, effectively ending any remaining
chance Bush had to win the
election.

November 3, 1992: Bill Clinton is elected president, with 43.0 percent of the vote. Bush receives

37.5 percent, while Perot wins 18.9 percent, the
best showing for a third-party candidate since
Theodore Roosevelt in 1912.

December 14, 1992: Presidential electors cast their
ballots in their respective state capitals.

1993
January 6, 1993: A joint session of Congress
assembles to count the electoral votes.

(continued from page 1509)
bal assaults. On March 3, the challenger won over 30 percent of the vote in Georgia, Maryland, and Colorado. "We
can win the nomination," he told supporters in Georgia.
Most Republicans who voted for Buchanan, however, said
they would not support him in the general election. They
simply wanted to register their dissatisfaction with Bush's
leadership by casting a protest vote for his opponent.

Backed into a corner and needing a decisive victory
in the March 10 "Super Tuesday" contests, Bush had no
choice but to attack Buchanan, taking to the airways to
highlight his opponent's opposition to the Gulf War.
Buchanan's support withered in the full media glare, and
Bush coasted to victory, sweeping all eight Republican
primaries, winning by large margins, and securing his
hold on the party's nomination. Party leaders pleaded
with Buchanan to drop his challenge. "When it's over, it's
over," said Robert Dole of Kansas. Buchanan promised to
take his challenge to the Republican convention in Houston. "We may be losing the battle for delegates," he told
supporters, "but we're not losing this national debate, and
everyone knows it."

Bush's early formidable lead in the polls following
the Persian Gulf victory had scared off leading Democratic challengers. One after another, the party's leading
contenders—New York governor Mario Cuomo, House
Speaker Richard Gephardt, Tennessee senator Al Gore—
announced they would not run. Instead, a handful of new
faces dominated the Democratic field. Dubbed the "Six
Pack," they included two sitting governors—Arkansas
moderate Bill Clinton, and Virginia's L. Douglas Wilder,
the first African-American elected to govern a state. Jerry
Brown, the eccentric former governor of California, also
threw his hat into the ring. From the Senate came Vietnam War hero and Nebraska senator Robert Kerry and

Iowa liberal Tom Harkin. Former senator Paul Tsongas
of Massachusetts, who had spent the past seven years battling cancer, planned his return to public life by running
for president.

In a clear sign that domestic concerns would dominate the party's agenda, none of the Democratic challengers claimed expertise in foreign policy. "For the first
time in decades," noted an observer, "knowledge of the
rest of the world seems to count for very little." Not only
did the Democrats lack foreign policy experience, they
made Bush's greatest asset a political liability, attacking
him for spending too much time on solving the world's
problems and not enough addressing the nation's needs.
"If you want to continue to spend $160 billion of your
money to defend Europe from the Soviet Union, or whatever it's called now, take your ballot and put it in the Bush
box," Harkin told receptive audiences in Iowa. "But if you
believe that Europe is strong enough and rich enough
and powerful enough to defend itself if it wants, then take
your ballot and put it in the Democrats' box."

In the weeks leading up to the first primary in New
Hampshire, Arkansas governor Bill Clinton emerged as
the Democratic challenger with the most compelling new
message. Even before the primary, Clinton's face graced
the cover of *Time* magazine, and the *Washington Post*
labeled him the "front-runner." Born in 1946 in Hope,
Arkansas, Clinton attended Georgetown University,
received a Rhodes scholarship to Oxford, then returned
to graduate from Yale Law School. In 1978, at the age of
32, he won election as governor of Arkansas, becoming
the youngest governor in the country. Once in office,
Clinton launched an ambitious reform agenda, including
an effort to modernize the highway system by imposing
an unpopular auto-license fee. Two years later he became
the youngest ex-governor when he lost reelection.

The defeat was a turning point in Clinton's life and helped shape his approach to politics. Carefully analyzing his failure, he concluded that he had tried to do too much too soon, and had relied on too many outside advisers. After polls suggested he could win back his job, a chastened Clinton ran again in 1982, traveling around the state apologizing for his past sins. "I made a young man's mistake," he confessed. Running as a consensus-seeking moderate, he promised to focus on attracting jobs and improving education. At the same time, he abandoned the trappings of his liberal past. He cut his long hair, dumped his liberal advisers, and announced his support for the death penalty.

With his ambition clearly focused on the presidency, Clinton worked hard during the 1980s to develop a national network of contacts. He possessed "the world's largest mental Rolodex," said a friend. Clinton impressed veterans with his intellect and charm. "He is a man of the muddy middle, a consensus builder whose most significant attribute is a fierce need, and great ability, to charm most everyone he meets," observed the journalist Joe Klein. Critics also pointed out that he possessed a insatiable need to please, and often tried to be all things to all people. "We can be pro-growth and pro-environment," he told an audience, "we can be pro-business and pro-labor . . . we can be pro-family and pro-choice." His penchant for shading the truth, and blurring ideological lines, led some people to question whether Clinton believed in anything other than ambition.

In 1990, Clinton began his presidential quest by casting himself as a "New Democrat" who understood the concerns of the struggling middle class. A founding member of the centrist Democratic Leadership Council, a group of moderates formed after Walter Mondale's defeat in 1984, Clinton believed that the party had become too closely identified with the concerns of the poor and minorities. The key to winning back the middle class was to emphasize the values of hard work and family. Campaigning as a cultural conservative, he professed his support for capital punishment, and promised to "end welfare as we know it," to make the streets safer and the schools better, and to provide "basic health care to all Americans." For traditional Democrats he offered a message of economic populism, promising to soak the rich and fight to preserve popular social programs. He proposed a "New Covenant" between the "people and their government to provide opportunity . . . inspire responsibility . . . and restore a sense of community to this great nation." He challenged corporate executives and welfare cheaters. "If you can work, you've got to go to work, because you can no longer stay on welfare forever."

It was Clinton's private life, not his public positions, that aroused the greatest controversy. Throughout his

Hillary Rodham Clinton and Bill Clinton (*Library of Congress*)

public career, Clinton had been dogged by questions of womanizing. The issue came to the surface a few weeks before the New Hampshire primary when Gennifer Flowers, a relatively untalented lounge singer who ended up on the Arkansas state payroll, announced that she had been Clinton's mistress for years—and produced taped phone conversations to prove it. "If they ever hit you with it," Clinton is heard advising her on one of the tapes, "just say no and go on. . . . If everybody is on record denying it . . . no problem." The affair dominated the news for days, until Clinton went on national television with his wife, Hillary Rodham Clinton, at his side, to acknowledge problems in their marriage but deny Flowers's charges, claiming that he had a "friendly but limited" relationship with her. (Years later he admitted to having sex with her.) Viewers were reassured by the Clintons' performance, and the press dropped the story.

No sooner had he dodged that bullet than the *Wall Street Journal* fired another one. Less than two weeks before the primary, the *Journal* challenged Clinton's story about how he managed to avoid the draft during the Vietnam War. Clinton claimed that he had voluntarily placed himself in the draft while he was a Rhodes scholar at Oxford University, but that his number was never called. The *Journal* produced a letter a 23-year-old Clinton had written in 1969 thanking an official for "saving me from the draft," saying that it was the only way he could avoid it while still maintaining his "political viability." The letter suggested manipulation, not luck, had allowed Clinton to avoid the draft.

The combination of sex and draft stories took their toll. The candidate's often evasive answers created the impression that he was less than truthful, reinforcing the perception of Clinton as "Slick Willie." With public trust eroding, Clinton's political career appeared over. In the 48 hours following the draft story, Clinton dropped 17 points in the polls. "I fell like a turd in a well," Clinton later joked. When asked to characterize the impact of the stories, pollster Stanley Greenberg responded with one word: "Meltdown." Some senior staff believed the attacks would prove fatal. "That's it. We're done," thought George Stephanopoulos. Sensing blood, Clinton's primary opponents hammered away at the "character issue." Senator Kerry sneered that Republicans would crack Clinton "like a soft peanut" in a general election campaign.

Clinton responded to the crisis by engaging in a burst of campaign activity. Promising to fight "till the last dog dies," the governor campaigned 18 hours a day, appearing on television shows, standing for long hours at shopping malls and street corners, shaking every hand he could reach, and talking into every ear that would listen. "This was all about Clinton," Stephanopoulos reflected, "his pride, ambition, and anger, his need to be loved and his drive to do good." When he finished second to Tsongas by a 33–25 percent margin, he labeled himself the "Comeback Kid," and prepared to battle Tsongas in Clinton's native South. Unable to connect with voters or raise the funds needed to continue, Kerry, Harkin, and Wilder dropped out of the contest.

Although he had justified his candidacy as a challenge to the party's liberal orthodoxy, Clinton attacked Tsongas from the left, attempting to rally the party's traditional constituency groups—minorities, senior citizens, and organized labor—to his candidacy. Abandoning his "New Democrat" theme, he criticized his opponent for suggesting that entitlement programs needed to be cut, for supporting an energy tax to encourage conservation, and for proposing a capital gains tax cut at the same time he advocated cuts in cost-of-living increases for senior citizens. "Isn't it time we closed the book on the 80s?" Clinton asked in a campaign commercial. The Massachusetts senator responded by calling Clinton a "pander bear" who would say anything to please voters.

On March 10, Clinton overwhelmed Tsongas, carrying eight states in the South, while his opponent had to settle for victories in Massachusetts, Rhode Island, and Delaware. On March 17, Clinton racked up victories in two major industrial states: Illinois and Michigan. Two days later Tsongas suspended his candidacy, seeming to remove the last obstacle in Clinton's road to the nomination.

Many Democrats were still not ready to embrace Clinton as their standard-bearer. When Tsongas stumbled, former California governor Jerry Brown jumped in to take his place as the "anti-Clinton" candidate. Running a guerrilla-style campaign, Brown tapped into public doubts about Clinton's character by scoring wins in Maine, Colorado, and Connecticut. Clinton needed an impressive win in the April 7 New York primary to stop Brown and secure the nomination. A few days before the primary, Clinton added to concern about his character and integrity when he admitted to smoking pot. His claim that he "did not inhale" provoked nationwide derision, but it was his evasiveness that angered most reporters. When asked previously whether he had ever used drugs, he had responded, "I never broke the laws of my country." It was only when asked whether he had broken the laws of some other country that he admitted to trying marijuana.

On the defensive on the character issue, Clinton tried to keep the debate focused on policy. Stressing the theme of economic fairness, he attacked Brown's controversial flat tax, contending that it would hurt the poor and working class. In a futile effort to win black votes, Brown announced that Jesse Jackson would be his first choice for vice president, but the move alienated the state's powerful Jewish constituency. Brown's gaffe and Clinton's relentless attacks worked. On primary day, Brown finished third, 15 points behind Clinton and 3 behind Tsongas, who had already dropped out of the race.

By the end of the primary season, the public expressed disenchantment with both the Democratic and Republican nominees. Bush managed to vanquish his primary opponent, but he failed to inspire public confidence in his presidency. As he laid plans for his party's convention in August, Bush faced polls showing that 80 percent of the public thought the country was on the wrong track. Bush's approval ratings had sunk to lows not seen since the days of Jimmy Carter's malaise. At the same time, nearly 25 percent of registered voters said they were unlikely to vote for Clinton "because of questions about his character."

The chief beneficiary of the public disenchantment was Texas billionaire Ross Perot. To many, Perot embodied the American Dream. He grew up poor in Texarkana, Texas, graduated at the top of his class from the U.S. Naval Academy, and eventually started his own company, Electronic Data Systems. Depending heavily on government contracts, the company grew to be the nation's leading provider of information services. In 1984, Perot sold it to General Motors for $2.5 billion.

In February 1992, Perot announced on a popular television talk show that he would run for president if volunteers placed his name on the ballot in all 50 states. A genius at self-promotion, Perot crafted an image as a tough outsider, a "Rambo in a business suit." With a down-to-earth manner, Perot tapped into public discontent with government and Washington by promising to balance the budget and cut the deficit. What would he do if he won the presidency? "In plain Texas talk," he said, "it's time to take out the trash and clean out the barn." By July, the "populist billionaire" was leading both Clinton and Bush in the polls. In electoral vote-rich California,

Supporters of presidential candidate Ross Perot hold up signs during a rally at the Flemington Fairgrounds in Flemington, New Jersey, on October 25, 1992. A crowd of about 10,000 people showed up for Perot's first campaign stop since reentering the presidential race. *(Mike Derer/Associated Press)*

nearly 41 percent of Bush backers, and 31 percent of Clinton supporters, said they would vote for Perot if he were a candidate in the general election.

Bush campaign aides, who viewed Perot as a more serious threat to their candidate in November than Clinton, spent the spring and early summer attempting to undermine his credibility. They chose to ignore Clinton, who was running a distant third in the polls. It turned out to be a critical miscalculation. While Bush and Perot engaged in a nasty name-calling contest, the Clinton campaign reintroduced its candidate to the American people. The primary campaign had blurred Clinton's "New Democrat" message, while the constant charges about character had eroded public support for his candidacy. If he was going to have any chance of winning in November, Clinton would have to refine his message, sharpen his image, and prove that he was a candidate whom people could trust.

For six weeks leading up to the convention in New York, Clinton worked without distraction painting a positive picture of himself. He developed an effective new slogan: "Putting People First." To sharpen his image

and demonstrate that he could stand up to traditional Democratic interest groups, he went to Jesse Jackson's National Rainbow Coalition Convention and attacked the black rap artist Sister Souljah for making racially antagonistic statements. Two days later, Clinton told the United Auto Workers that he supported the North American Free Trade Agreement. Taking advantage of unconventional media outlets, he told young Americans what type of underwear he wore on MTV. Later he went on a late night talk show, put on dark Ray-Ban sunglasses, and played a few verses of "Heartbreak Hotel" on the saxophone.

Perhaps the boldest move was his selection of a running mate. Four days before the opening of the Democratic convention, he abandoned the unwritten law that a vice-presidential candidate should provide geographical and ideological balance, when he chose fellow Southerner Al Gore, a senator from Tennessee. "There's a little Bubba in both of us," he said. Like Clinton, Gore was a party centrist and a fellow baby boomer. Gore offered the ticket other assets as well. As the leading environmentalist in the Senate, he insulated Clinton from attacks on his record in Arkansas. A Vietnam veteran, Gore was a foreign policy hawk who broke ranks and supported the Persian Gulf War.

The press applauded the selection, viewing it as a daring move that highlighted the campaign theme of generational politics. "Young Guns: The Generational Gamble," cried *Newsweek*. "The Democrats' New Generation," shouted *Time*. CBS's Bill Plante said Clinton choose Gore "to send a message of generational change." The *San Francisco Examiner* noted that the nominee "has chosen to make the 1992 election a battle of generations." Just as important, the selection revealed how mass media had altered the calculation for choosing a vice president. As journalist Chris Matthews observed, Gore's selection "salutes a new development in American political life: the emergence of a new, media-oriented politics in which geography is far less dominant, culture and attitude increasingly important."

In July, the Democrats assembled at New York's Madison Square Garden in a hopeful mood. During the first few days, Clinton managed to transform himself in the eyes of many Americans from a pot-smoking adulterer

who dodged the draft into the middle-class son of a single mother who had devoted his life to public service. The party managed to avoid its usual fights over controversial social issues and to adopt a platform that underscored Clinton's "New Democrat" message. Even the conservative *Wall Street Journal* seemed impressed, observing that, instead of dividing the economic pie, the platform "focuses on making the pie grow." The most important step in Clinton's effort to redefine himself came on Thursday evening when he addressed the nation in his acceptance speech.

Hours before ascending the podium to give the most important speech of his life, Clinton received a boost from an unlikely source—Ross Perot. The unpredictable Perot announced that he was withdrawing from the race, claiming that "the Democratic Party has revitalized itself." The timing could not have been better for Clinton. Perot cut loose his army of Independent voters on the same day that Clinton would command the nation's media with his acceptance address. Clinton took full advantage of the opportunity. He told the convention that he accepted the nomination, "in the name of all those who do the work

Governor Bill Clinton, playing with the band, turns out an impressive version of "Heartbreak Hotel" as Arsenio Hall gestures approvingly in the musical opening of *The Arsenio Hall Show* taping at Paramount Studios in Hollywood, June 3, 1992. *(Reed Saxon/Associated Press)*

and pay the taxes, raise the kids and play by the rules, in the name of the hardworking Americans who make up our forgotten middle class." In a direct appeal to Perot voters, Clinton announced a "New Covenant" with the American people. "We offer opportunity," he declared. "We demand responsibility."

Clinton's speech underscored his attempt to portray his candidacy as a fundamental break with the party's past. The press and the public responded favorably. The *San Francisco Chronicle* declared that Clinton's nomination represented "a historic and dramatic shift for the party." Polls revealed a massive shift to Clinton—more than the expected increase from the intense media coverage. Clinton's favorable rating shot up from 41 to 59 percent, and he jumped from 5 points behind into a 23-point lead over Bush. The increase eclipsed the boost Dukakis received from his nomination four years earlier. After the convention, Perot supporters, by a 2-to-1 margin, preferred Clinton to Bush.

Convinced that Dukakis lost the 1988 election in the days between the convention and Labor Day, Gore and Clinton boarded a bus on the day after the convention and headed toward small-town America. For six days the caravan of buses wound its way along I-80 through the battleground states of New Jersey, Pennsylvania, Ohio, and Illinois. Clinton drew strength from the large crowds that turned out to greet him. "October crowds," he bragged, and it was only July. The combination of the convention and the road trip boosted Clinton's numbers. By the end of July, he was leading Bush by 20 points in the polls. But memories of 1988 prevented the Democrats from getting too excited about the prospect for victory. "The dark shadow of President Dukakis hung over the campaign," noted Clinton campaign aide Gary Ginsberg.

While the Democrats barnstormed Middle America, Bush continued to flounder. He told worried party officials that he was waiting for the Republican convention in Houston to shift into "campaign mode." Convention organizers, however, believed that Perot, not Clinton, would be the president's most dangerous opponent in the fall. As a result, they planned to use the Houston convention to consolidate Bush's support among conservatives. On opening night, vanquished primary opponent Patrick Buchanan set the tone for the gathering by claiming that America was in the midst of a "cultural war." Many of the speakers that followed over the next couple days echoed the theme of cultural conflict, attempting to paint Clinton as a symbol of the radical 1960s. "The gap between us and our opponents is a cultural divide," Dan Quayle told the convention. "It is a difference between fighting for what is right and refusing to see what is wrong." Marilyn Quayle told the nation that "Not everyone demonstrated, dropped out, took drugs, joined the sexual revolution or

dodged the draft." At the same time, delegates adopted a rigidly conservative platform that opposed abortions and denounced gay rights.

Bush faced the biggest challenge of his career as he prepared for his Thursday night speech to the nation. Trailing in the polls, widely perceived as a weak president, he needed to seize control of the agenda and set the tone for the fall campaign. The president began by attempting to build a bridge between his foreign policy triumphs and the challenges at home. "The world is in transition, and we are feeling that transition at home," he said. "The defining challenge of the '90s is to win the economic competition—to win the peace." His agenda for the future, however, consisted of little more than rehashed proposals for unspecified tax and spending cuts. Trying to tap into concerns about Clinton's character, Bush claimed that "trust" was the central issue of the campaign. "The question is," he asked, "who do you trust to make change work for you?"

The convention energized conservatives but alienated many moderates. Republicans tried to use the convention to stake a broad claim to family values, but the harsh tone contradicted the "kinder, gentler" message that Bush successfully conveyed in 1988. Bush failed to articulate a clear sense of domestic priorities for a second term that would give undecided voters a reason to vote for him. An ABC News poll taken after the convention showed 72 percent of those interviewed believed the Democrat "had a vision for the country," while only 54 percent described Bush in those terms. For many viewers, the Republicans seemed defensive, trying to cover Bush's weaknesses by launching personal attacks on Clinton. According to one journalist, the old Republican slogans of "Morning in America" and "Stay the Course" were replaced by "We're Sorry, but It's Not All George Bush's Fault." Polls showed that the trust issue cut both ways. For many Americans, the man who broke his "Read my lips: No new taxes" promise of 1988 had little credibility on the issue of trust.

The fall campaign turned into a referendum on George Bush's domestic leadership. The president's greatest asset, his handling of the Persian Gulf War, barely showed up on the public's radar screen. "Foreign policy has never had less salience," said Democratic pollster Mark Mellman. In 1984, the last time an incumbent ran for reelection, Reagan had used the image of a bear wandering in the woods to underscore the need to elect someone who would stand up to the Soviet threat. Eight years later, said Mellman, "The bear has committed suicide." Instead, voters directed their anger at the administration for the sluggish economy. By October, Bush's job approval rating had sunk to 25 percent, and nearly half of all voters said they would not vote for him under any circumstances.

Clinton entered the fall campaign with a double-digit lead in national polls and comfortable margins in the key battleground states of Pennsylvania, New Jersey, Ohio, and Illinois. Clinton aides were determined to avoid the mistake of the Dukakis campaign, which had failed to respond quickly to Bush's relentless attacks. James Carville, the governor's colorful and pugnacious campaign consultant, established a "War Room" on the fourth floor of Clinton headquarters in Little Rock. From here, Carville and his team monitored Bush's every move, tracked news reports, and prepared instant responses to Republican attack ads. The purpose of the War Room, Stephanopoulos recalled, "was to make us appear relentless, to intimidate, to make anyone who was paying attention think of us as aggressive, different, and a little unpredictable—pretty tough for Democrats." The campaign themes were summed up in a handwritten note Carville posted in the middle of the room: "Change vs. More of the Same"; "The economy, stupid"; and "Don't forget health care."

On the campaign trail, Clinton fused two different strains of populism into a potent political message for change. He told independent suburban white voters of his support for law and order, capital punishment, and individual responsibility. Clearly distancing himself from the party's more liberal past, he described welfare as "a second chance, not a way of life." Before the party faithful, Clinton promised to provide "basic health care to all Americans," to protect social security, and to tax the rich. A charismatic personality and compelling speaker, Clinton called for using the power of the federal government to promote economic growth through education and job training. Most important of all, Clinton developed a style of politics that made him credible as a messenger of change. He understood the impact of television, was comfortable performing for the cameras, and understood the new participatory style of campaigning, where issues were discussed on evening talk shows and in town hall forums.

It was a different story in the White House. After the convention, Bush asked Secretary of State James Baker, a close friend and campaign veteran, to take charge of his faltering effort. Initially, Baker sketched a high-minded strategy: having spent his first term addressing world problems, Bush would devote the same energy to addressing domestic needs. When that message failed to resonate, Bush switched gears and decided that the only way to win was to attack his opponent. "For the rest of the way, we're going 100 percent negative," said a Bush campaign official. Bush tried to link Clinton to the legacy of the Carter administration and the economic stagflation of the 1970s. He hammered on Clinton's pattern of evasion and flip-flops on issues. He criticized his record in Arkansas. "In almost every category, [the state is] lagging."

Bush employed many of the "wedge issues" that Republicans had used so effectively against Democrats in the past. Clinton, Bush said, was an "elitist," an "Oxford-educated . . . social engineer" who preferred European-style socialism to the rugged individualism Bush learned from the Texas oilfields. He questioned Clinton's character and Vietnam draft status, and charged that Clinton was a traditional "tax-and-spend" Democrat who was soft on crime. At the same time, Vice President Dan Quayle barnstormed the nation questioning Clinton's patriotism and his trustworthiness. "The American people want their president to be faithful to their country," he told audiences. "They want a president to be faithful to their principles. They want a president who is faithful to their family." Bush picked up the theme, claiming that Clinton's participation in protests against the Vietnam War was unpatriotic. His campaign issued a press release suggesting that the KGB had arranged a Clinton trip to the Soviet Union in 1969.

The end of the cold war made Republican attacks on Clinton's patriotism appear shrill, and the public backlash forced the Bush campaign to retreat. The response underscored a key difference between 1988 and 1992: cultural "wedge issues" had lost their bite. "Wedge issues don't work on Clinton because he's taken positions that inoculate him," observed a centrist Democrat. The Democratic nominee routinely mentioned his work-oriented welfare views, posed with police officers and their widows at law-and-order events, and emphasized his support for the death penalty. Bush persisted in his attacks on values, despite overwhelming poll evidence showing that voters were more interested in economic issues. "Every time Bush used some of these issues," a frustrated Republican observed, "it would reaffirm with some voters that he was out of touch with the most important issue."

Both candidates were forced to rethink their strategy when, on October 1, Ross Perot jumped back into the race, bitterly urging Americans not to waste votes on "politics as usual." Returning as the titular head of "United We Stand, America," Perot made deficit reduction the centerpiece of his message and spent lots of his own money—more than a million a day—to get the attention of voters. He proposed a harsh mix of spending cuts and increased taxes on upper-bracket income, gasoline, and Medicare and Social Security benefits to save a whopping $750 billion over five years. Neither campaign knew what to make of Perot's reentry into the race: Bush feared that he would be a harsh second voice attacking him; Clinton worried that Perot would muddy his appeal as the spokesman for change.

Perot returned to the race just in time to participate in a series of three presidential debates scheduled over a nine-day period beginning on October 11. The debates were the first to include an Independent candidate along with the two major party nominees. Bush probably wished Perot had stayed away from the first debate in St. Louis. The Independent poked fun at Clinton's claim that his experience in Arkansas made him qualified to be president, comparing Arkansas to a "corner grocery store." He reserved his best shots, however, for Bush, accusing him of mismanaging the economy. When Bush touted his experience in the Oval Office, Perot responded, "I don't have any experience in running up a $4 trillion debt."

The informal format of the second debate in Richmond, Virginia, which allowed candidates to take questions from a studio audience with a moderator directing follow-up questions, played to Clinton's strengths. The debate began with the moderator blunting Bush's assault on Clinton by asking the candidates to refrain from personal attacks. The defining moment came when a woman in the audience asked the candidates how the national debt had impacted them. She meant to say recession, but only Clinton was quick enough on his feet to appreciate the confusion. Perot said that the deficit affected him because he was willing to "disrupt my private life" to run for president. Bush's response seemed to confirm doubts about his candidacy. "I'm not sure I get it," he said. Clinton launched into an "I feel your pain response," walking up to the woman, looking her in the eye, and saying that as the governor of a small state he knew people who were out of work and wondering how they would pay their bills.

Bush, who trailed by wide margins in most opinion polls, seemed to come alive in the final debate, finally making pointed jabs at Clinton. He made Clinton the issue, challenging his record in Arkansas, his "waffling" on the issues, and his record as a tax-and-spend liberal. He warned taxpayers they would have to "lock up your wallets" if Clinton and "a spendthrift Democratic Congress" brought back the days of Jimmy Carter. He called on Clinton "to level with the American people" about his draft record, saying he was unfit to be president. "The bottom line is we simply cannot take the risk on Governor Clinton," he told supporters.

Despite his strong final performance, the debates did little to lift Bush's standing in the polls. In the short run, Perot, whose favorable rating doubled from 25 to 50 percent, emerged the big winner. Worried Democratic officials watched the race tighten as Perot rose in the polls, stealing anti-Bush voters from Clinton in key battleground states. Sensing movement in the polls for the first time, Bush sharpened his "T&T" (trust and taxes) attacks. In the frantic final weeks, Bush referred to Clinton and Gore as "two bozos." Calling the governor "Slick Willie," Bush said, "He is bobbing and weaving, and you cannot do that as president." On another occasion in Wisconsin, he referred to the Democratic ticket as "Governor Taxes

Democratic candidate Bill Clinton (left) shakes hands with Independent candidate Ross Perot as Republican candidate President George H. W. Bush looks from behind during introductions before the final presidential debate at Michigan State University in East Lansing, Michigan, on October 19, 1992. *(Susan Ragan/Associated Press)*

and the Ozone Man." The president's closing attack ad of the campaign showed a picture of Arkansas as a barren wasteland while the narrator recited Clinton's tax-and-spend record as governor.

In the Little Rock "War Room," Clinton aides watched as their candidate's lead dropped from double digits to less than 5 points in the final week. "How scared are you?" George Stephanopoulos asked James Carville. "How scared?" Carville repeated. "I'm this scared: if we lose, I won't commit suicide, but I'll seriously contemplate it." It was Perot, however, who committed political suicide during a damaging interview on the popular CBS show *60 Minutes*. When asked why he had quit the race the first time, Perot claimed that he was the victim of Republican "dirty tricks." "The son of a bitch is a psychiatric case," Bush muttered and the White House officially declared him "paranoid." Not only was Perot's explanation different from the one he had offered in July, it raised questions about his temperament and judgment, and knocked him off-message for days.

Any chance Bush had to pull off a Harry Truman–like comeback died on the Friday before the election, when the special counsel investigating the Iran–Contra affair announced a new grand jury indictment of former defense secretary Casper Weinberger. Included in the indictment was a memo indicating that as vice president Bush had favored swapping arms for hostages. The story dominated news coverage in the final weekend and allowed Clinton to turn the trust issue on its head. "There's no such thing as truth when it comes to him," Clinton told audiences. "He just says whatever sounds good and worries about it after the election."

Voters rewarded Clinton on election night, giving him 43 percent of the popular vote, compared to 37 percent for Bush. Clinton's margin in the Electoral College was far more decisive. He won 31 states and 370 electoral votes. Clinton became only the second Democrat in this century to sweep New England, including two states Bush had called home: Connecticut, where the president grew up, and Maine, where he had a vacation home. The Democratic ticket also cracked the Republican grip on the Rocky Mountain West, winning New Mexico and Colorado, then swept the Pacific Coast, including the biggest prize of the night, California. The all-South ticket won eight Southern and border states, and swept the coasts and the industrial heartland. The ticket ran ahead of the Republicans in every age group, but scored especially well with young voters. Clinton also won a larger percentage of white voters than any Democratic nominee since Jimmy Carter in 1976.

The Democrats retained control of both houses of Congress. Observers triumphantly called 1992 "the year of the woman," as voters sent 6 women to the Senate and 48 to the House of Representatives. California became the first state to elect two women senators—Barbara Boxer and Dianne Feinstein—and Illinois elected the first African-American women to the upper chamber, Carol Moseley Braun.

Most pundits hailed the November election as a triumph for a new Democratic Party. The *New York Times* described the Democrats as "a party redefined." *Time* called it a "new coalition of the 1990s." Some Democratic partisans believed Clinton's victory set the groundwork for a realignment similar to the Roosevelt revolution of the 1930s. "Clinton can carry out another Democratic realignment like Roosevelt's, and fashion a new majority," declared the head of the Democratic Leadership Conference.

A closer look, however, suggested that Clinton's victory did not deviate from recent elections. Between 1980 and 1992, four separate Democratic nominees won between 40 and 45 percent of the popular vote. The Republican range was much wider, swinging from 38 percent in 1992 to 59 percent in 1984. Clinton received the same percentage of the electorate as Hubert Humphrey in 1968. His 43 percent was lower than Dukakis's 45.6 percent in a two-way race in 1988. Only 38 percent of Independents voted for Clinton—the same number who voted for Walter Mondale in 1984. Only 10 percent of Republicans crossed over to vote for him.

Voter surveys showed that economic discontent and a desire for change spearheaded the Democratic victory. The election represented a rejection of the Bush presidency, not a new mandate for reform. "The one thing the election demonstrated clearly was that most voters were tired of George Bush," observed one journalist. The president simply failed to give voters a reason to vote for him. The *New York Times* termed Bush "The Half-Way Man," saying that, for all his foreign policy success, in domestic affairs he "created the disquieting and ultimately fatal impression that he didn't know what to do, and worse, didn't much care." Ironically, polls showed that 69 percent of voters were more concerned about Bush's truthfulness about his role in the Iran–Contra scandal than they were over Clinton's efforts to avoid the Vietnam War draft. As a result, Bush became the third one-term president in 20 years, and the first Republican since Herbert Hoover to be rejected for a second term.

Perot won a bigger share of the vote—19 percent—than any third-party candidate since Teddy Roosevelt scored 27.4 percent in 1912. More than 19 million people voted for him. Although he campaigned in only 16 states, the independent received more than 20 percent of the vote in 31 states. Unlike most third-party candidates, he had the benefit of nearly unlimited financial resources, which allowed him to subsidize the effort to get on the ballot and buy media time. His voters were overwhelmingly white and middle class. He scored best in states with the smallest black population. More than half of his supporters expressed a deep distrust of Washington and elected officials. "I'm like the grain of sand in the oyster that irritates the oyster, and out comes a pearl," Perot said in his concession speech.

In a victory speech to a joyous crowd in Little Rock, Clinton described the election as a "clarion call" to deal with a host of ignored domestic problems and to "bring our nation together." His victory was testament not only to his considerable political skill, but also to a political universe that had been transformed by the shattering of the cold war consensus. The question remained, however: did Clinton's victory, and Bush's defeat, foreshadow a new post–cold war politics dominated by domestic issues and rooted in a desire for moderate change? Bill Clinton's challenge was to transform a plurality victory into a meaningful mandate, and to forge a new post–cold war consensus for the next American century.

—*Steven M. Gillon*

Selected Bibliography

James Ceaser and Andrew Busch, *Upside Down and Inside Out: The 1992 Elections and American Politics* (1993) is scholarly and insightful; and Thomas M. Defrank et al., *Quest for the Presidency, 1992* (1994), gives a great overview. See also Herbert

E. Alexander and Anthony Corrado, *Financing the 1992 Election* (1995); Michael Duffy and Dan Goodgame, *Marching in Place: The Status Quo Presidency of George Bush* (1992); Jack W. Germond and Jules Witcover, *Mad as Hell: Revolt at the Ballot Box, 1992* (1993); Robert E. Levin, *Bill Clinton: The Inside Story* (1992); Dwight Morris and Murielle E. Gamache, *Handbook of Campaign Spending: Money in the 1992 Congressional Races* (1994); Kevin Phillips, *Boiling Point: Republicans, Democrats, and the Decline of Middle-Class Prosperity* (1993); Gerald Pomper et al., *The Election of 1992: Reports and Interpretations* (1993); and Charles T. Royer, ed., *Campaign for President: The Managers Look at 1992* (1994). David Maraniss, *First in His Class: A Biography of Bill Clinton* (1995), is the best Clinton biography.

1992 Electoral Map and Statistics

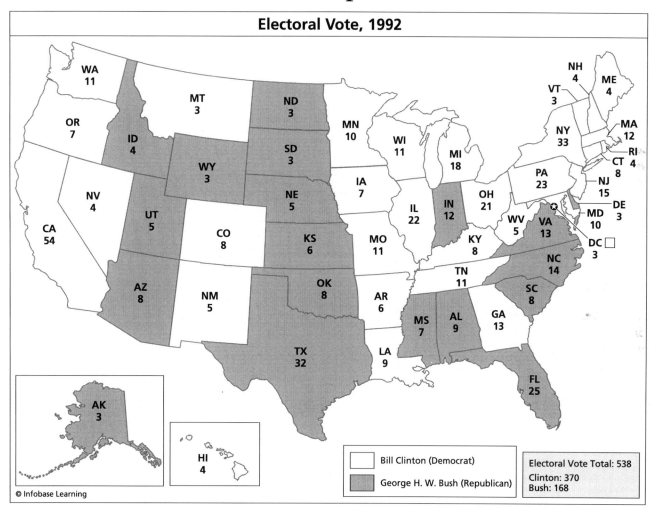

Electoral Vote, 1992

1992 ELECTION STATISTICS

State	Number of Electors	Total Popular Vote	Elec Vote		Pop Vote			Margin of Victory	
			D	R	D	R	I	Votes	% Total Vote
Alabama	9	1,688,060		9	2	1	3	114,203	6.77%
Alaska	3	258,506		3	2	1	3	23,706	9.17%
Arizona	8	1,487,006		8	2	1	3	29,036	1.95%
Arkansas	6	950,653	6		1	2	3	168,499	17.72%
California	54	11,131,721	54		1	2	3	1,490,751	13.39%
Colorado	8	1,569,180	8		1	2	3	66,831	4.26%
Connecticut	8	1,616,332	8		1	2	3	104,005	6.43%
Delaware	3	289,620	3		1	2	3	23,741	8.20%
District of Columbia	3	227,572	3		1	2	3	171,921	75.55%
Florida	25	5,314,392		25	2	1	3	100,612	1.89%
Georgia	13	2,321,133	13		1	2	3	13,714	0.59%
Hawaii	4	372,842	4		1	2	3	42,488	11.40%
Idaho	4	482,114		4	2	1	3	65,632	13.61%
Illinois	22	5,050,157	22		1	2	3	719,254	14.24%
Indiana	12	2,305,871		12	2	1	3	140,955	6.11%
Iowa	7	1,354,607	7		1	2	3	81,462	6.01%
Kansas	6	1,157,256		6	2	1	3	59,517	5.14%
Kentucky	8	1,492,900	8		1	2	3	47,926	3.21%
Louisiana	9	1,790,017	9		1	2	3	82,585	4.61%
Maine	4	679,499	4		1	3	2	56,600	8.33%
Maryland	10	1,985,046	10		1	2	3	281,477	14.18%
Massachusetts	12	2,773,574	12		1	2	3	513,613	18.52%
Michigan	18	4,274,673	18		1	2	3	316,242	7.40%
Minnesota	10	2,347,948	10		1	2	3	273,156	11.63%
Mississippi	7	981,793		7	2	1	3	87,535	8.92%
Missouri	11	2,391,270	11		1	2	3	242,714	10.15%
Montana	3	410,583	3		1	2	3	10,300	2.51%
Nebraska	5	739,283		5	2	1	3	127,002	17.18%
Nevada	4	506,318	4		1	2	3	13,320	2.63%
New Hampshire	4	537,215	4		1	2	3	6,556	1.22%
New Jersey	15	3,343,594	15		1	2	3	79,341	2.37%
New Mexico	5	569,986	5		1	2	3	48,793	8.56%
New York	33	6,926,925	33		1	2	3	1,097,801	15.85%
North Carolina	14	2,611,850		14	2	1	3	20,619	0.79%
North Dakota	3	308,133		3	2	1	3	37,076	12.03%
Ohio	21	4,939,964	21		1	2	3	90,632	1.83%
Oklahoma	8	1,390,359		8	2	1	3	119,863	8.62%
Oregon	7	1,462,643	7		1	2	3	145,557	9.95%
Pennsylvania	23	4,959,810	23		1	2	3	447,323	9.02%
Rhode Island	4	453,477	4		1	2	3	81,698	18.02%
South Carolina	8	1,202,527		8	2	1	3	97,993	8.15%
South Dakota	3	336,254		3	2	1	3	11,830	3.52%
Tennessee	11	1,982,638	11		1	2	3	92,221	4.65%
Texas	32	6,154,018		32	2	1	3	214,256	3.48%
Utah	5	744,068		5	3	1	2	119,232	16.02%
Vermont	3	289,701	3		1	2	3	45,470	15.70%
Virginia	13	2,558,665		13	2	1	3	111,867	4.37%
Washington	11	2,287,565	11		1	2	3	261,803	11.44%
West Virginia	5	683,677	5		1	2	3	89,027	13.02%
Wisconsin	11	2,531,114	11		1	2	3	110,211	4.35%
Wyoming	3	199,884		3	2	1	3	11,187	5.60%
Total	538	104,423,993	370	168	1	2	3	5,805,256	5.56%

Clinton Democratic		Bush Republican		Perot Independent		Others	
690,080	40.88%	804,283	47.65%	183,109	10.85%	10,588	0.63%
78,294	30.29%	102,000	39.46%	73,481	28.43%	4,731	1.83%
543,050	36.52%	572,086	38.47%	353,741	23.79%	18,129	1.22%
505,823	53.21%	337,324	35.48%	99,132	10.43%	8,374	0.88%
5,121,325	46.01%	3,630,574	32.61%	2,296,006	20.63%	83,816	0.75%
629,681	40.13%	562,850	35.87%	366,010	23.32%	10,639	0.68%
682,318	42.21%	578,313	35.78%	348,771	21.58%	6,930	0.43%
126,054	43.52%	102,313	35.33%	59,213	20.45%	2,040	0.70%
192,619	84.64%	20,698	9.10%	9,681	4.25%	4,574	2.01%
2,072,698	39.00%	2,173,310	40.89%	1,053,067	19.82%	15,317	0.29%
1,008,966	43.47%	995,252	42.88%	309,657	13.34%	7,258	0.31%
179,310	48.09%	136,822	36.70%	53,003	14.22%	3,707	0.99%
137,013	28.42%	202,645	42.03%	130,395	27.05%	12,061	2.50%
2,453,350	48.58%	1,734,096	34.34%	840,515	16.64%	22,196	0.44%
848,420	36.79%	989,375	42.91%	455,934	19.77%	12,142	0.53%
586,353	43.29%	504,891	37.27%	253,468	18.71%	9,895	0.73%
390,434	33.74%	449,951	38.88%	312,358	26.99%	4,513	0.39%
665,104	44.55%	617,178	41.34%	203,944	13.66%	6,674	0.45%
815,971	45.58%	733,386	40.97%	211,478	11.81%	29,182	1.63%
263,420	38.77%	206,504	30.39%	206,820	30.44%	2,755	0.41%
988,571	49.80%	707,094	35.62%	281,414	14.18%	7,967	0.40%
1,318,662	47.54%	805,049	29.03%	632,312	22.80%	17,551	0.63%
1,871,182	43.77%	1,554,940	36.38%	824,813	19.30%	23,738	0.56%
1,020,997	43.48%	747,841	31.85%	562,506	23.96%	16,604	0.71%
400,258	40.77%	487,793	49.68%	85,626	8.72%	8,116	0.83%
1,053,873	44.07%	811,159	33.92%	518,741	21.69%	7,497	0.31%
154,507	37.63%	144,207	35.12%	107,225	26.12%	4,644	1.13%
217,344	29.40%	344,346	46.58%	174,687	23.63%	2,906	0.39%
189,148	37.36%	175,828	34.73%	132,580	26.19%	8,762	1.73%
209,040	38.91%	202,484	37.69%	121,337	22.59%	4,354	0.81%
1,436,206	42.95%	1,356,865	40.58%	521,829	15.61%	28,694	0.86%
261,617	45.90%	212,824	37.34%	91,895	16.12%	3,650	0.64%
3,444,450	49.73%	2,346,649	33.88%	1,090,721	15.75%	45,105	0.65%
1,114,042	42.65%	1,134,661	43.44%	357,864	13.70%	5,283	0.20%
99,168	32.18%	136,244	44.22%	71,084	23.07%	1,637	0.53%
1,984,942	40.18%	1,894,310	38.35%	1,036,426	20.98%	24,286	0.49%
473,066	34.02%	592,929	42.65%	319,878	23.01%	4,486	0.32%
621,314	42.48%	475,757	32.53%	354,091	24.21%	11,481	0.78%
2,239,164	45.15%	1,791,841	36.13%	902,667	18.20%	26,138	0.53%
213,299	47.04%	131,601	29.02%	105,045	23.16%	3,532	0.78%
479,514	39.88%	577,507	48.02%	138,872	11.55%	6,634	0.55%
124,888	37.14%	136,718	40.66%	73,295	21.80%	1,353	0.40%
933,521	47.08%	841,300	42.43%	199,968	10.09%	7,849	0.40%
2,281,815	37.08%	2,496,071	40.56%	1,354,781	22.01%	21,351	0.35%
183,429	24.65%	322,632	43.36%	203,400	27.34%	34,607	4.65%
133,592	46.11%	88,122	30.42%	65,991	22.78%	1,996	0.69%
1,038,650	40.59%	1,150,517	44.97%	348,639	13.63%	20,859	0.82%
993,037	43.41%	731,234	31.97%	541,780	23.68%	21,514	0.94%
331,001	48.41%	241,974	35.39%	108,829	15.92%	1,873	0.27%
1,041,066	41.13%	930,855	36.78%	544,479	21.51%	14,714	0.58%
68,160	34.10%	79,347	39.70%	51,263	25.65%	1,114	0.56%
44,909,806	43.01%	39,104,550	37.45%	19,743,821	18.91%	665,816	0.64%

Election of 1996

Election Overview

Election Year 1996

Election Day November 5, 1996

Winning Candidates

- **President:** Bill Clinton
- **Vice President:** Al Gore

Election Results [ticket, party: popular votes (percentage of popular vote); electoral votes (percentage of electoral vote)]

- Bill Clinton and Al Gore, Democratic: 47,400,125 (49.23%); 379 (70.4%)
- Bob Dole and Jack Kemp, Republican: 39,198,755 (40.72%); 159 (29.6%)
- Ross Perot and Pat Choate, Reform: 8,085,402 (8.40%); 0 (0.0%)
- Ralph Nader and Winona LaDuke, Green: 685,435 (0.71%); 0 (0.0%)
- Harry Browne and Jo Jorgensen, Libertarian: 485,798 (0.50%); 0 (0.0%)
- Other: 420,125 (0.44%); 0 (0.0%)

Voter Turnout 49.0%

Central Forums/Campaign Methods for Addressing Voters

- Stumping
- Speeches
- Rallies
- Television interviews, talk show appearances
- Print and television ads
- Debates
- Press, newspapers and magazines, Internet

Incumbent President and Vice President on Election Day Bill Clinton and Al Gore, Democratic

Population (1996) 269,714,000

Gross Domestic Product

- $7.84 trillion (in current dollars: $9.434 trillion)
- Per capita: $29,062 (in current dollars: $34,977)

Number of Daily Newspapers (1995) 1,533

Average Daily Circulation (1995) 58,200,000

Households with

- Radio (1995): 98,000,000
- Television (1995): 98,300,000
- Computer/Internet (1995): 10,857,000

Method of Choosing Electors Popular vote (mostly general-ticket system/winner take all)

Method of Choosing Nominees

- Presidential preference primaries
- Caucuses

Key Issues and Events

- Republicans gain control of both houses of Congress in the 1994 midterm elections, choosing Newt Gingrich as Speaker of the House.
- Republican Congress overreaches. The budget confrontation in late 1995 and 1996 shuts down the federal government. The public blames the Republicans.
- Clinton presidential image improves with his response to Oklahoma City federal building bombing and his "politics of triangulation," pushing V-chips, school uniforms, assault-weapons ban, more police on the streets.

- Clinton still dogged by scandals, by Whitewater special prosecutor
- America at peace, enjoying prosperity, feeling good

Leading Candidates

DEMOCRATS
- Bill Clinton, president of the United States (Arkansas)

REPUBLICANS
- Bob Dole, senator (Kansas)
- Pat Buchanan, columnist (Virginia)
- Steve Forbes, newspaper and magazine publisher (New York)
- Lamar Alexander, former governor (Tennessee)
- Phil Gramm, senator (Texas)
- Alan Keyes, former U.S. ambassador to U.N. Economic and Social Council (Maryland)
- Richard Lugar, senator (Indiana)
- Bob Dornan, representative (California)
- Arlen Specter, senator (Pennsylvania)
- Pete Wilson, governor (California)
- Morry Taylor, businessman (Ohio)
- Harold E. Stassen, former governor (Minnesota)

Trajectory

- During his 1996 State of the Union address, President Bill Clinton declares, "The era of big government is over." Clinton abandons his (and his wife Hillary's) big government health-care reform—which helped the Democrats lose control of Congress in 1994 for the first time in four decades. Following a centrist, poll-driven, "triangulation" strategy, Clinton will govern as "the good father," appealing to "soccer moms," with modest quality-of-life policies, such as V-chips on television sets and school uniforms to restore discipline. With the economy booming and the post–cold war peace intact, Clinton becomes the first Democrat since 1964 to run in primaries essentially unopposed.
- The Republican front-runner, Senator Bob Dole, loses the New Hampshire primary on February 20 by a percentage point to Pat Buchanan, the firebrand conservative commentator. Dole's loss reflects his own difficulties in shifting from legislative insider to charismatic campaigner, as well as the beating that publishing tycoon Steve Forbes's relentless, self-financed, negative ad campaign administered. Ironically, Forbes's splash ultimately helps Dole by scaring off other possible contenders.
- Dole wins in South Carolina on March 2, thanks to his superior organization, thorough fund-raising,

and Republicans' tendency to defer to the anointed front-runner. Dole's momentum builds throughout March but his nomination appears more inherited than earned, his supporters more dutiful than passionate.
- Finance reports filed in April show Clinton has $21 million left to spend until the general campaign starts after the convention, while Dole has only $5 million, having spent his federal funding fighting for the nomination. Dole has little money to counter the Democrats' brilliantly timed ad campaign, which pummels him throughout the spring and is mostly financed by the Democratic National Committee as generic anti-Dole ads, rather than specifically pro-Clinton ads.
- Dole resigns from the Senate on May 15, 1996, to indicate his seriousness, but that move also fails to excite voters.
- At the Republicans' mid-August convention in San Diego, Elizabeth Dole interacts with the crowd, Oprah-style, rather than delivering the usual formal address. Dole's vice presidential choice, the former football star, congressman, and cabinet secretary Jack Kemp, engenders more respect than excitement.
- The Democratic convention starts on August 26 with Bill Clinton's triangulation guru, political consultant Dick Morris, disgraced because he consorted with a prostitute—an uncomfortable reminder of Clinton's indiscretions, the Whitewater scandal, and the new revelations involving sleazy fund-raising techniques in venues ranging from the Lincoln Bedroom in the White House to Buddhist temples. Nevertheless, Clinton gets the coronation he hoped for, with Democrats confident that Dole will not prevent Clinton from building his much vaunted "bridge to the 21st century."
- Many attribute Dole's lackluster campaign to his being, at 72 years old, the oldest candidate running for a first term as president. On September 18 he mentions the "Brooklyn Dodgers," despite their move to Los Angeles 40 years earlier.
- On September 19, through no fault of his own, a railing that Dole is leaning on collapses and he falls off a stage at a rally in Chico, California. Both incidents reinforce the attacks from pro-Clinton ads calling Dole "an aged conservative far from the mainstream," heightening the contrast with Clinton, one of the youngest presidents ever elected.
- The two 90-minute televised debates on October 7 and October 16 do not change the dynamic. Dole

insists: "There's a lot of things wrong with America." Echoing Reagan, Clinton reassures: "We are better off than we were four years ago. Let's keep it going." Only 24 percent of voters say they are following the election "very closely." In 1992, 42 percent followed the campaign closely.

- Bill Clinton wins reelection but fails to get a majority of the popular vote.

Conventions

- Republican National Convention: August 12–15, 1996, San Diego Convention Center, San Diego
- Democratic National Convention: August 26–29, 1996, United Center, Chicago

Ballots/Nominees

DEMOCRATS
Presidential first ballot
- Bill Clinton 4,277; 99.72%
- Abstaining 12; 0.28%

REPUBLICANS
Presidential first ballot
- Bob Dole 1,928; 97.62%
- Pat Buchanan 43; 2.18%
- Phil Gramm 2; 0.10%
- Robert Bork 1; 0.05%
- Alan Keyes 1; 0.05%

Third Party Candidates and Nominations

REFORM PARTY
- President: Ross Perot
- Vice President: Pat Choate
- Ross Perot creates a new party, the Reform Party, financed by a federal subsidy of $30 million, based on his 1992 vote results. Perot can also spend unlimited amounts of his own money as he did in 1992.

UNITED STATES GREEN PARTY
- Ralph Nader (Connecticut) is drafted, not by the Green Party USA but by the individual states' Green parties, who would put his name on the ballot as an Independent.

SOCIALIST PARTY USA
- President: Mary Cal Hollis (Colorado)
- Vice President: Eric Chester (Massachusetts)

LIBERTARIAN PARTY
- President: Harry Browne (Tennessee)
- Vice President: Jo Jorgensen (South Carolina)

CONSTITUTION PARTY (FORMERLY U.S. TAXPAYERS PARTY)
- President: Howard Phillips, chairman of the American Conservative Union

Primaries

- Democratic Party: 37; 81.4% delegates
- Republican Party: 40; 78.8% delegates

Primaries Results

DEMOCRATS
- Bill Clinton 9,706,802; 88.94%
- Lyndon LaRouche 596,422; 5.46%
- Unpledged 411,270; 3.77%

REPUBLICANS
- Bob Dole 9,024,742; 58.82%
- Pat Buchanan 3,184,943; 20.76%
- Steve Forbes 1,751,187; 11.41%
- Lamar Alexander 495,590; 3.23%
- Alan L. Keyes 471,716; 3.07%
- Richard Lugar 127,111; 0.83%
- Unpledged 123,278; 0.80%
- Phil Gramm 71,456; 0.47%
- Robert Dornan 42,140; 0.27%
- Maurice Taylor 21,1800; 14%
- Others 18,261; 0.12%

Party Platform

DEMOCRATS
- End deficit spending
- Balance the federal budget
- Maintain Social Security and Medicare
- Encourage national standards for primary and secondary schools
- Reduce those in need of public funds for welfare
- Protect the National Parks
- Oppose offshore drilling

REPUBLICANS
- Protect the rights of the unborn
- Provide tax relief
- Balance the budget
- Improve education
- Provide affordable health care
- Encourage regulatory reform
- Reject statehood for the District of Columbia
- Affirm English as the nation's language

Campaign Innovations

- First uses of the World Wide Web for campaigning and for keeping track of the candidates

- Clinton's Democratic National Committee–financed advertising blitz in the spring of 1996, traditionally a quiet time for campaigns, and a moment when Senator Bob Dole was out of funds from the primaries, not yet federally funded for the general campaign
- Elizabeth Dole's talk-show style "conversation" with Republican convention-goers
- In *Colorado Republican Federal Campaigning Committee v. Federal Election Commission,* the Court holds that state and local parties cannot be limited in the amount of money spent on behalf of a candidate, as long as that spending is not coordinated with the candidate. This applies to PACs and other independent groups.
- Democrats in California change their primary date from June to March, hoping for more relevance.

Campaign Tactics

DEMOCRATS

- Negative advertising, continuous media spending
- Both campaigns use Internet, but tentatively. Surveys suggest as many as 26 percent of voters use the Internet for some information, but only 7 percent rely on it heavily or exclusively.
- Clinton acts presidential, staying above the fray.
- Clinton as the "good father," a benign centrist presence appealing to soccer moms
- Aggressive fund-raising that opponent charges demeans the White House, with major donors able to stay overnight in the Lincoln Bedroom for a minimum donation of $50,000
- Fund-raising also involved the Clinton people with shady foreign operatives and an embarrassing episode for Al Gore, raising funds at a Buddhist temple where monks can somehow afford to give thousands of dollars in contributions.
- Clinton raises the maximum amount of money allowed for primaries but is unopposed and can save the money to attack the presumptive Republican candidate before the general election begins.
- Democratic National Committee uses "soft money" for "issue advocacy" ads in battleground states.
- Clinton rarely deigns to attack his opponent by name.

REPUBLICANS

- Tries to avoid attacking Clinton directly, fearing enlarging the "gender gap."
- Attempts to return to Reagan playbook, emphasizing patriotism, character, old-fashioned values, but it feels stale.

- Dole resigns from Senate to generate enthusiasm.
- Before the Republican convention Dole promises across-the-board 15% tax cut and an "end to the Internal Revenue Service" as we know it.

Debates

- October 6, 1996: Presidential debate in Hartford, Connecticut
- October 9, 1996: Vice-presidential debate in St. Petersburg, Florida
- October 16, 1996: Presidential debate in San Diego, California

Popular Campaign Slogans

- Democratic Party: "Building a bridge to the 21st century"
- Republican Party: "The Better Man for a Better America"

Campaign Songs

- Democratic: "Don't Stop Thinking About Tomorrow" (reprised from 1992)
- Republican: "Dole Man"

Influential Campaign Appeals or Ads

- Democrats attack "Dole-Gingrich" to link Bob Dole with the less popular, polarizing Speaker of the House, Newt Gingrich.
- Republicans attack Clinton as the "Me Too" president, stealing Republican positions
- Late in the campaign Republicans attack Clinton's lack of character, complaining that his fund-raising turned the White House into "Motel 1600," although the public is more concerned with the Dow Jones, which is riding high.

Campaign Finance

- Clinton: $61,820,000 (in current dollars: $80,180,400)
- Dole: $61,820,000 (in current dollars: $80,180,400)
- Green Party USA: Ralph Nader promises to spend only $5,000. He does not want to be obligated to file a Federal Election Commission financial statement.

Defining Quotations

- "I will seek the presidency with nothing to fall back on but the judgment of the people and nowhere to go but the White House or home . . . and I will then stand before you without office or authority, a private citizen, a Kansan, an American, just a man. For little has come to me except in the hard way, which is good because we have a hard task ahead of us." *Bob Dole, announcing his Senate resignation to jumpstart his flagging bid for the White House as of June 11, 1996*

- "Why? Because some genius in the Clinton administration took the money to fund yet another theory, yet another program and yet another bureaucracy. Are they taking care of you, or are they taking care of themselves? I have asked myself that question. And I say, let the people be free. Free to keep. Let the people be free to keep as much of what they earn as the government can strain with all its might not to take, not the other way around. . . . And it must be said because of misguided priorities there have been massive cuts in funding for our national security. I believe President Clinton has failed to adequately provide for our defense. And for whatever reason the neglect, it is irresponsible." *Bob Dole, address accepting the presidential nomination at the Republican National Convention in San Diego, August 15, 1996*

- "Tonight, my fellow Americans, I ask all of our fellow citizens to join me and to join you in building that bridge to the 21st century. Four years from now, just 4 years from now—think of it—we begin a new century, full of enormous possibilities. We have to give the American people the tools they need to make the most of their God-given potential. We must make the basic bargain of opportunity and responsibility available to all Americans, not just a few. That is the promise of the Democratic Party. That is the promise of America." *Bill Clinton, address accepting the presidential nomination at the Democratic National Convention in Chicago, August 29, 1996*

- "My friends, this election is about two different visions of America's future. As Jack [Kemp] said, our opponents—and they are our opponents; they are not our enemies—offer an old-style liberal vision that puts government first. And Jack Kemp and I offer an optimistic future-oriented vision that puts the American people first. That's the difference! That's the key dividing line in this campaign. They believe in government, and we believe in you. We believe the people. We trust the people of the United States. We trust the people of Missouri! That's the key dividing line in this campaign. They believe in government, and we believe in you," *Bob Dole, at Kemp-Dole rally, St. Louis, Missouri, September 2, 1996*

- "On the most obvious level, the placid waters of the 1996 Presidential campaign suggest a nation at peace with its politics. Many voters may simply choose to stay home. The economy is good, the country is not at war and President Clinton has rebounded from the depths of his unpopularity just two years before." *Adam Nagourney, New York Times, November 3, 1996*

- "When you're an incumbent, and the economy is doing well, boring is good." *George Stephanopoulos, Clinton senior aide and strategist, November 3, 1996*

Lasting Legacy of Campaign

- Lowest voter turnout since 1924
- At 73, Dole is the oldest major party nominee.
- One of the dullest recent campaigns
- Clinton joins Woodrow Wilson and Franklin Roosevelt as the only Democrats reelected in the 20th century.
- Still, Clinton fails to get 50 percent of the popular vote.

Election of 1996

Two issues have dominated American presidential elections for the past 100 years: peace and prosperity. Indeed, some elections have turned on simple economics: which candidate is best for my pocketbook? And so it was in 1996.

By late July, before the campaign had formally begun, before the conventions were gaveled to order, President Bill Clinton seemed to have won the election. His 58 percent job approval rating was the highest since January 1994 just after the State of the Union address in which he had announced a major deficit reduction plan. For the remainder of 1994 and throughout most of 1995, Clinton's approval rating had remained below 50 percent. Increased public support for his performance in office rose during the fall 1995 budget showdown with Congress and remained high from that point on. And, in a July '96 two-way presidential trial heat, Clinton led Bob Dole by 18 percent, about the same lead he held in the Gallup Poll for almost three months. In July, a record 43 percent, up from 30 percent in May, rated national economic conditions as excellent or good compared to 11 percent just prior to the 1992 presidential election. Another record 43 percent, compared to 39 percent in May 1996, thought economic conditions in the country "as a whole are getting better." At approximately this point in the summer of 1992 when George Bush was seeking reelection, the percentage calling the economy

Bob Dole *(Library of Congress)*

"poor" reached 53 percent, and 65 percent of registered voters replied the economy was "getting worse."

The Labor Department reported that the unemployment rate had dropped in June to a six-year low of 5.3 percent—4.6 percent among adults and 15.9 percent among teenagers—with employers adding 348,000 workers to their payrolls. Job losses through layoffs and plant closings reached historic lows. Since Clinton took office in January 1993, about 9 million new jobs had been created (versus 1.7 million under Bush); the president had promised 8 million. Inflation held below a 3 percent annual rate compared to 4.2 percent for Bush. All of which meant that the misery index by July '96, the rate of inflation added to the rate of unemployment, hovered at a three-decade low. During the 1995 budget battle, Bob Dole and his fellow Republicans accused the Clinton administration of using unrealistic rosy assumptions about economic growth to make its deficit reduction program add up. Enactment, Dole predicted, would cause a recession and even higher deficits. The opposite occurred, and the resulting drop in interest rates laid the

foundation for sustained economic expansion. It seems that the White House figures were too conservative.

By July '96, the dollar had gained 10 percent in value over 12 months, as exports zoomed to record levels. Home sales neared a five-year high. Mortgage loan applications soared 20 percent ahead of 1994, the last good year for housing. By mid-July, retail sales had rebounded from the tepid Christmas season, particularly for high-ticket items as consumers went on a buying spree. Auto sales rose sharply, running at an annual rate of 1.5 million new vehicles. Manufacturers added extra shifts to meet the demand. Overall, the economy grew at a robust annual rate of 4.2 percent during the spring. It was the best quarterly performance in two years and a sharp turnaround from the lackluster growth rate of 0.3 percent during the fall of 1995.

Measured by the Dow–Jones Industrial Average, the stock market grew by almost 75 percent since Clinton's inauguration. While, by far, the biggest winners in this unexpected run-up had been the richest Americans, middle-income families also benefited. Forty percent of American families owned shares, usually through mutual funds and retirement accounts. The value of these holdings had increased a whopping $1.6 trillion! The financial markets were initially skeptical of Clinton. They thought he would increase the bloated national deficit. But the president showed surprising deference to Wall Street and the Federal Reserve Board. He now generated criticism from liberals for focusing on deficit reduction.

Less than two years before, in the 1994 midterm elections, enough middle-income voters turned against the Democrats to give the Republicans control of Congress for the first time since 1956. The president, however, brilliantly regained his political footing. He championed Social Security and Medicare, even when confronted with two government shutdowns. He vetoed Republican measures to cut taxes and curb social programs. He supported environmental protection as well as consumer health and safety regulations over business profits. He enhanced his political standing by shaming congressional Republicans to finally accept an increase in the minimum wage that would affect about 10 million of America's lowest paid workers. Shrewdly, Clinton adopted the Republican promise to balance the budget early in the next century, thus inoculating himself against the charge that he was a "tax-and-spend liberal." In fact, he abandoned many liberal themes, such as guaranteed health care, enunciated during the first two years of his presidency and now stressed traditional values—fighting tobacco companies for selling cigarettes to minors, tightening federal drinking water standards, supporting school uniforms, more police on the streets, an assault-weapons ban, the death penalty victims' rights bill, and V-chips—issues designed to bring the wayward back to

1996 ELECTION CHRONOLOGY

1994
November 8, 1994: Campaigning on their "Contract with America" and playing on Americans' growing disgust with President Bill Clinton, Republicans capture both the Senate and, for the first time in four decades, the House of Representatives.

1995
April 19, 1995: Timothy McVeigh bombs the Alfred P. Murrah Federal Building in Oklahoma City, killing 168 people. Clinton's tough response to the bombing improves his presidential image.

November 14, 1995: The first of two brief shutdowns of the federal government begins, due to a budget confrontation between Clinton and Congress. The public blames the Republicans for the impasse.

1996
January 23, 1996: Abandoning earlier big-government proposals such as health-care reform, Clinton declares in his State of the Union address that "the era of big government is over." He will follow this centrist, poll-driven, "triangulation" strategy for the remainder of the campaign, and his presidency.

February 20, 1996: Conservative fireband Pat Buchanan captures 27 percent of the vote in the New Hampshire Republican primary, narrowly defeating front-runner Senator Robert Dole of Kansas, who receives 26 percent.

February 24, 1996: Publishing tycoon Steve Forbes, buoyed by his self-financed negative ad campaign, wins the Delaware Republican primary with 33 percent of the vote, defeating Dole and Buchanan, neither of whom campaigned in the state.

March 2, 1996: Dole wins the South Carolina primary with 45 percent of the vote, to Buchanan's 29 percent. Dole's momentum builds throughout the month of March, but his nomination appears more inherited than earned, his supporters more dutiful than passionate.

April 18, 1996: In reports filed with the Federal Election Commission, the Clinton campaign reveals it has $16 million on hand. Two days later, the Dole campaign admits that after its tough primary battle it has only $2 million left. Clinton takes advantage of this discrepancy by flooding the airwaves with ads attacking Dole throughout the spring, traditionally a quiet time for presidential campaigns.

May 15, 1996: Dole resigns from the Senate to indicate his seriousness about the presidential race, but the move fails to ignite Republicans' passion.

June 5, 1996: Presenting himself as the peace and prosperity president, Clinton reports to Congress: "The economy has created 8.5 million new jobs since January 1993—almost all of them in the private sector. The combined rate of unemployment and inflation is at its lowest level in more than 25 years."

August 5, 1996: Dole unveils his economic plan, featuring a 15 percent across-the-board personal income tax cut. This leaves him vulnerable to Democratic charges that social programs would be at risk in a Dole administration.

August 12–15, 1996: At their national convention in San Diego, Republicans nominate Robert Dole for president and former New York representative Jack Kemp for vice president.

August 18, 1996: Ross Perot wins the nomination for the fledgling Reform Party at the Reform national convention in Valley Forge,

the Democratic fold. The aim—to drive the Republicans to a point where they lost their effective issues. By agreeing in late July, for example, to sign a sweeping GOP welfare bill, the president defied leaders in his own party and ended a 61-year Democratic promise of federal aid

to the nation's poor—but he fulfilled a 1992 campaign pledge to "end welfare as we know it." This was the ultimate example of Clinton's new political strategy of "triangulation"—being the connective balance between the too-liberal Democrats and the too-conservative Repub-

☆   ☆   ☆

Pennsylvania. Based on Perot's 1992 vote results, the new party will benefit from a $30 million federal subsidy.

August 22, 1996: President Clinton signs the Personal Responsibility and Work Opportunity Reconciliation Act, reforming the welfare system. Many liberals are devastated by what they perceive as a sellout; conservatives are pleasantly surprised that Clinton came close to fulfilling his promise of ending "welfare as we know it."

August 25, 1996: Clinton boards a 3-locomotive, 13-car train, to take a four-day, five-state train trip to the Democratic National Convention in Chicago, on a trip combining nostalgia for whistle-stopping with hard-hitting partisanship.

August 26–29, 1996: President Bill Clinton and Vice President Al Gore are renominated by acclamation at the Democratic National Convention in Chicago. Clinton calls on Americans to build a "bridge to the 21st century."

August 29, 1996: Clinton's chief campaign advisor, Dick Morris, architect of the campaign's emphasis on "family values," resigns after reports surface that he had a year-long relationship with a prostitute. Morris's behavior reminds voters of Bill Clinton's ethical problems, which include allegations of adultery, sexual harassment, and, in the longstanding Whitewater case, financial chicanery.

September 19, 1996: Dole falls off the stage when a railing he is leaning on at a rally in California collapses. Along with a mention the previous day of the long-gone "Brooklyn Dodgers," this event seems to confirm the message of Democratic attack ads that paint the 73-year-old Dole as "an aged conservative far from the mainstream."

October 6, 1996: At the first of two presidential debates, in Hartford, Connecticut, Dole insists "there's a lot of things wrong with America." Clinton, already heavily favored to win, pointedly echoes Ronald Reagan and tells Dole "it is not midnight in America."

October 9, 1996: At the vice presidential debate in St. Petersburg, Florida, Gore and Kemp square off over the economy and social issues.

October 16, 1996: The second presidential debate is held in San Diego. Like the two others, it excludes the Perot ticket because this time Perot fails to poll in significant numbers for much of the campaign.

October 18, 1996: The Democratic National Committee suspends John Huang from further fund-raising activities to defuse a growing controversy surrounding a fund-raising event he organized at the Hsi Lai Buddhist temple in California, despite its tax-exempt religious status. This is only one of many fund-raising controversies that dog Democrats, implicating Vice President Gore as well as President Clinton.

November 5, 1996: Clinton is reelected with 49.2 percent of the vote, his second sub-50 percent finish. Dole receives 40.7 percent, and Perot 8.4 percent. Only 49 percent of eligible voters go to the polls, the lowest turnout since 1924.

December 16, 1996: Presidential electors cast their ballots in their respective state capitals.

1997

January 9, 1997: A joint session of Congress assembles to count the electoral votes.

February 26, 1997: In analyzing a list of 800 or so Clinton White House overnight guests, CNN estimates that Clintons' guests in the Lincoln Bedroom donated at least $5.4 million in combined contributions to the Democratic National Committee during 1995 and 1996, as reporters call the White House "Motel 1600," rented out nightly by the Clintons for fund-raising.

---

licans. Between the New Deal and the Great Society eras, the Republican Party seemed a mild unenthusiastic echo of the Democratic programs. It had worked well for Eisenhower and Nixon. Now Clinton had reversed the echo. Would it work for him?

Clinton, the New Democrat, had become the herald of prosperity, the supporter of a litany of government benefits, and the champion of family values—all with a balanced budget! It is this contradictory image that the president had assiduously cultivated with equal intensity since the 1994 congressional defeats. When the Republican convention assembled, Clinton had bonded with the American people—58 percent saying that, as president, he would provide "very strong or somewhat strong" moral leadership, and 64 percent responding that he "cares about the needs of people like you." With masterly political skill, Clinton was well positioned to run for reelection both as a protector of the middle class and as a defender of fiscal responsibility—and to become the first Democrat since Franklin Roosevelt elected to a second term.

By the beginning of March 1996, Bob Dole had regained his position as the runaway leader among Republicans as their choice for the party's presidential nomination. Dole's standing as the presumptive standard-bearer strengthened among Republicans nationwide. In a March 8–10 Gallup Poll, 57 percent of registered Republicans listed him as their favorite, up from 41 percent right after his February 20th narrow New Hampshire primary loss in a multi-candidate race to Pat Buchanan. Steve Forbes now was in second place with a distant 18 percent, and Buchanan, whose standing among Republicans jumped to 27 percent immediately after New Hampshire, fell to third place (13 percent). At that point, though, many Republicans thought nervously, "Have I gone with a loser?" The senator's lack of energy and frustrating inaction in the face of a resurgent Democratic Party became the major talk show subject. While Republican officeholders and party officials dutifully spoke about how close the November election would be, they worried that the Republican Revolution could be an illusion, and that their 1994 congressional victories did not represent a shift in political ideology but was another symptom of the instability of contemporary American politics.

By July '96, their thinking seemed to crystalize: the problem was not the Republican Party—the problem was Bob Dole. But, in reality, party splits that were hidden by the collapse of the Democrats in 1994 had never gone away—splits over abortion, tax cutting, immigration, affirmative action, the assault weapons ban, and economic priorities. Bob Dole now received the blame for this Republican disunity, and it had a dramatic effect. Dole was sinking fast and might reach a depth from which recovery would be impossible. In fact, it didn't seem as if any campaign organization existed but rather a dreary, disorganized gang searching for ideas and a strategy. Conservative writers and commentators suggested that Dole step aside, but for whom? A July 25–28 Gallup Poll showed that 25 percent of Republicans and 33 percent of voters overall thought that Dole "should drop out and let the Republican Party choose someone else at their convention next month."

The senator had won the Republican caucuses and primaries—and the right to be his party's standard-bearer—but he seemed unable to articulate why he wanted to be president and what his party stood for. His disjointed, rambling speeches, badly stringing one platitude after another, turned off voters (54 percent of registered independents supported Clinton in a mid-July Gallup Poll compared to 36 percent for Dole). The senator appeared old, boring, and dull, a man of the 1950s and 1960s without a defining message for 1996. His judgment seemed unfocused, choosing the same weekend as the bomb explosion at the Atlanta Olympic Games to urge the removal of the Pennsylvania Avenue barricades to protect the White House from terrorism. And, on the day he attempted to jump-start his campaign and reshape the political debate to his advantage by promising a much publicized across-the-board tax cut "to eliminate middle-class economic insecurity, and to finally draw a sharp distinction between the parties," his strategists embraced a Republican platform plank that called for a constitutional amendment to outlaw all abortions. In agreeing to this, Dole, under pressure from Christian conservatives, retreated from his June promise of "tolerance language," recognizing that many Republicans, in good conscience, could favor a right to an abortion.

Indeed, a "gender gap" haunted Dole. In every Gallup survey between mid-January and mid-July, registered women voters' support for Clinton over Dole held steady in the high 50s to the low 60s. Among women, Clinton's lead had been at 19 points or greater for six months and since April had fluctuated between 21 and 30 points. Perhaps this was because of Dole's equivocal abortion stand; then there was also the perceived Republican bashing of Hillary Rodham Clinton. Fifty-three percent of women compared with 38 percent of men held a favorable opinion of the First Lady in a mid-June Gallup survey.

Polling data also suggest that for women voters it is not presidential character but rather the bread-and-butter issues. There seemed to be strong dissatisfaction among women with policies pursued by Speaker Newt Gingrich. Many women were bothered by the tone of the Republican "revolutionaries" and by the content of their programs. They took Medicare very seriously. Younger women usually played the larger role in caring for aging parents. Women were also more sympathetic to social spending, especially on education and programs for children. Dole's pro-life stand helped him with certain groups—married churchgoing women—but his difficulty was that the women who were most pro-choice were the well-to-do, historically a Republican group. This "gender gap" was also found on the issue of Whitewater, where men consistently expressed more critical views than women. In a mid-June Gallup Poll, 27 percent of men but just 16 percent of women, said that Clinton had done something illegal in that land deal. Statistically, Dole could have won the election without carrying a majority of women voters. Ronald Reagan did this in 1980. But, as of July, he stood no chance of winning the election if Clinton's margin among women remained so overwhelming. The dilemma Dole continued to encounter was that his centrist moves, on abortion and gun control, for example, infuriated his conservative base.

Dole's age became an issue. If elected, he would be the oldest man to assume the presidency. Many voters worried that he was too old for the job. The age issue damaged him across party lines, especially among otherwise likely supporters—those who approved of the way he handled his position as Senate majority leader. Older people were more likely than younger to be concerned. Those who accurately knew the senator's age (73) responded that he was too old more than those who understated his age. Overall, 32 percent of American adults in early August said Dole was too old to be president. Forty-two percent of Democrats shared this view compared with 32 percent of independents and 21 percent of Republicans. This represented a sharp 14-point jump among independents since March.

Dispirited Republicans, unable to disguise their cultural and ideological divisions, seemed in disarray, facing a sitting president buoyed by a robust economy. The last Gallup Poll taken prior to the Republican convention showed registered voters supporting Clinton 58 to 35 percent. With Ross Perot included, Clinton received 52, Dole 30, and Perot 12 percent. And, 64 percent of registered voters rated Clinton's first term in office "a success," up sharply when compared to a December 1994 survey in which 44 percent so described his first two years in office.

In personal terms, Clinton also was the most popular of the three presidential candidates, with 62 percent saying they had a favorable impression of Clinton, compared to 49 percent for Dole and 40 percent for Perot. Clinton's high approval ratings and impressive lead were historically similar to those of Ronald Reagan, Lyndon Johnson, Richard Nixon, and Dwight Eisenhower at similar points in their presidencies. Each had double-digit leads in Gallup Poll presidential election trial heats in July of their reelection campaigns, and each had a job approval rating of 55 percent or better. All of these incumbents went on to win a second term handily.

Surveys prior to the Republican convention also suggested that President Clinton's wide lead could be explained by Dole's failure to maximize support from Republican voters. While Clinton received the backing of most registered Democrats nationwide, many Republicans on the eve of their convention were not yet set to vote for Dole—77 percent of Republicans favored Dole while 19 percent said they would vote for Clinton; at the same time, 91 percent of Democrats favored Clinton and only 7 percent went for Dole. Were Dole to increase his support among Republicans to 90 percent, taking these votes from Clinton, the President's lead would drop to

4 points. While Gallup Poll trial election heats showed Dole losing by a substantial margin to President Clinton in the November election, they also told us that the Republican Party was quite competitive with the Democratic Party on most key political issues. While voters gave the economy a much higher rating than they did four years ago, the polls also show that they were evenly divided over which party would do a better job of keeping the country prosperous. The July 25–28 Gallup results were a virtual tie: 42 percent saying the Democrats would do better, 41 percent the Republicans. By contrast, when Clinton defeated George Bush in 1992, the Democratic Party led the Republicans on this issue 48 to 39 percent. Stated Dole's chief of communications, "There is nothing wrong with Bob Dole's campaign that a good economic plan, a good Veep choice, a good convention speech and $74 million won't cure."

"Here in San Diego, the real race begins," said Bob Dole as the Republican convention convened on August 12. The nearly 2,000 delegates were overwhelmingly white (91 percent), male (64 percent), 40 years and older (79 percent), and impressively wealthy. Only 23 percent had family incomes under $50,000, while one in five (18 percent) was a millionaire, with another 18 percent worth $500,000 to $1 million according to a *New York Times/CBS News Poll* of delegates. Two-thirds were attending their first convention. They were more conservative than Republicans generally—indeed, more conservative, their responses indicated, than their candidate, Bob Dole. According to the survey, majorities of the delegates opposed affirmative action to protect racial minorities from discrimination (60 percent), the nationwide ban on assault weapons (51 percent), and public education for the children of illegal immigrants (58 percent). Almost all said the federal government "is doing too many things better left to businesses and individuals" (91 percent). But 56 percent favored a more active government in one area—to do more to promote traditional values. The delegates strongly supported outlawing abortion except in very limited instances, with 11 percent responding "abortion should be permitted in all cases" compared with 27 percent among voters as a whole. Sixty-four percent described themselves as "pro-life," compared with 53 percent of all registered Republicans, while 25 percent said they were "pro-choice" compared with 42 percent of all registered Republicans. Thirty-one percent responded they were evangelical or born-again Christian.

These delegates adopted a rigidly conservative party platform. (A platform is a statement of the party's principles, record, and intended programs. Political parties have had formal platforms since the Democratic Party adopted nine policy resolutions, about 500 words, at its 1840 presidential nominating convention.) The 1996

Republican Party platform, some 40,000 words in length, supported the most conservative issues in American politics: a constitutional amendment that would outlaw abortion, making it illegal even when a woman's life was in danger or when the pregnancy resulted from rape or incest, and endorsed legislation "to make clear that the 14th Amendment's protections apply to unborn children." Beyond abortion, the platform opposed affirmative action but promised to enforce laws against "discrimination based on sex, race, age, creed or national origin," and in the next sentence stated, "We reject the distortion of those laws to cover sexual preference." The platform would have denied "public benefits other than emergency aid" to illegal aliens and suggested that assistance to legal immigrants should be limited. It supported "a constitutional amendment or constitutionally valid legislation declaring that children born in the United States of parents who are not legally present in the United States or who are long-term residents are not automatically citizens." Bob Dole said that he had not read the platform and did not feel bound by it. But extreme party planks are indeed innocuous until they become a threat to the status quo, and this is why so much attention was paid to the Republican Party's platform stand on abortion.

While the platform's statements on social issues received the enthusiastic support of Pat Robertson and Pat Buchanan, Bob Dole seemed more concerned about the economic programs that determine most presidential elections. (Pat Robertson, head of the Christian Coalition, which claimed a membership of 1.7 million, almost defeated Dole in the February 1988 Iowa Republican caucus—previous to that and subsequently, Robertson worked ceaselessly to involve his followers in precinct "grassroots"-level politics, and to elect supportive delegates.) Robertson brought to the Christian right political credibility: the power to deliver votes the way union and big-city political machines used to do for Democrats. His efforts were rewarded at the 1996 Republican convention, when 11% of the delegates said they were members of the Christian Coalition, with 55% favoring the group.

The Christian Coalition's Pat Robertson and Ralph Reed, its executive director, had unofficially supported Dole during the primary campaigns. The dilemma for Dole, and the Republican Party, was to hold on to its traditional freewheeling capitalist base while reconciling its economic programs aimed at Middle America with the agenda of the Christian moralists. After adopting a socially conservative platform, the new message suddenly became the party of inclusion—the big tent—a marked contrast to the 1992 convention, where cultural value speeches by Robertson, Buchanan, and Marilyn Quayle seemed divisive. The made-for-television 1996 convention presented itself to those watching it as a united happy

family—sure we have our differences, but let's first elect Bob Dole and Jack Kemp. The anti-abortion plank in the platform was not mentioned during prime-time television as Dole's strategy emerged—win over moderate voters on economic issues, win states, and win the election. "In 1992, we seemed grim and grumpy and were making lists of people we didn't like," former Tennessee Governor Lamar Alexander said as he walked the convention hall. "This convention is optimistic, progressive, conservative."

Robert Joseph Dole was born into a hard-working blue-collar family on July 22, 1923, in Russell, Kansas. His father, Doran, ran an egg and cream distribution station and, later, a local grain elevator; his mother, Bina, sold Singer sewing machines door to door, traveling the county with them in an old Chevrolet. During the Great Depression, the entire family lived in the basement while the house was rented to oilfield workers. The four Dole children shared one bedroom. World War II permanently interrupted Dole's plans to become a medical doctor. In 1943, at age 20, he enlisted in the Army and was eventually assigned to the 10th Mountain Division. In the Po Valley of Italy, on a ridge known as Monte della Madonna, on April 14, 1945, within weeks of the end of the European war, Lt. Dole was badly wounded. An exploding shell destroyed his right shoulder, fractured vertebrae in his neck and spine, and riddled his body with metal slivers. An experimental dose of streptomycin, then a new wonder drug, saved his life, but could not prevent nearly total paralysis. He had been wounded in so many places that, at age 22, Dole had to relearn how to walk, how to eat. It took him 39 agonizing months in army hospitals to recover. Even then, he never regained the use of his shattered right arm. Dole visited the battle site and the nearby tiny Italian hilltop town many times, sometimes alone, twice with his daughter Robin, and twice with his wife Elizabeth. He referred to April 14, 1945, as "the day that changed my life"—not so much the injuries as the struggle to overcome them. Dole returned to civilian life a driven man.

With the help of his first wife, Phyllis, a physiotherapist whom he married in 1948, he earned a bachelor's and a law degree from the University of Kansas. She did all of his papers until he learned to write left-handed. On the Republican ticket, Dole won election to the Kansas State Legislature (1951–53), as prosecuting attorney of Russell County (1953–61), to the House of Representatives (1961–69), and to the Senate in 1968. A fiercely partisan defender of presidents Richard Nixon and Ronald Reagan, Dole also served as chairman of the Republican National Committee (1971–73). He became the Senate's Republican leader in 1984. In 1976, Gerald Ford, with the endorsement of Ronald Reagan, selected Dole as his vice-presidential running mate. Some blamed Dole's harsh campaign style for the narrow Ford–Dole defeat by only 2 percent of the vote. In 1980 and 1988, he unsuccessfully sought the Republican presidential nomination. While his associates said he mellowed over the years, Dole, they agreed, remained a complex man, charming but sometimes aloof and abrasive, always with partisan instincts and a combative sense of humor—and always at the center of the Republican Party's legislative agenda.

Despite his 27 years in the Senate, there are few major bills that are considered genuinely his. His skills were as a deal maker. Observers noted that Dole was not comfortable with sweeping theories of any sort. When Dole discussed legislation, as he did virtually every day—all day—he rarely spoke in ideological terms, said people who worked with him. Rather, he talked in terms of practical politics: which lawmakers and constituencies would support the measure and which ones would not. Announcing his resignation from the Senate on June 11 after 35 years on Capitol Hill to devote himself fully to the presidential campaign, Dole gave one of the most eloquent speeches of his career. He dwelled on the struggles of his life, declaring that "little has come to me except the hard way." He described himself as drawn to the presidency because of the job's enormous burdens. His campaign, he said, was

"about electing a President who's not attracted to the glories of the office, but rather to its difficulties."

Dole rarely thought in ideological terms. Undoubtedly trying to broaden his own constituency and reinvigorate his campaign, Dole chose Jack Kemp, the 61-year-old former nine-term congressman from New York and secretary of housing and urban development in the Bush administration (1989–93)—and sometime Dole rival—as his vice-presidential running mate. Unlike when Bush chose Dan Quayle eight years before, Kemp received excellent ratings from Republicans, 81 percent saying they had a favorable opinion of him. (Sixty-one percent of the general public responded that Kemp "is qualified to serve as president if it becomes necessary" compared with 32 percent for Quayle in mid-July 1992.) Kemp, though popular among Republicans, had long been at odds with many in his party, including Dole. William J. Bennett, the conservative Republican author, noted though, "People have been saying this campaign doesn't talk enough, doesn't have ideas, doesn't have vision, and here comes Kemp. He has all three."

Bob Dole delivered his acceptance speech on August 15. Standing before a frenzy of flag-waving supporters, the senator spoke to the largest television audience he

Dole and Kemp signs at the Republican National Convention in San Diego, 1996 *(© Joe Sohm/ Visions of America, LLC/ Alamy)*

had ever attracted—estimated between 25 and 30 million. "The Republican Party is broad and inclusive," he declared. "It represents many streams of opinion and many points of view." He also seized the prime-time opportunity to present his plan to cut taxes by 15 percent and to balance the federal budget. Dole depicted the Clinton administration as a "corps of elite who never grew up, never did anything real, never sacrificed, never suffered, and never learned." It was that contrast in values and in personal history that the Republican convention had sought to emphasize, almost completely avoiding public discussion of its highly conservative platform.

Third-party or insurgent candidates have contested every 20th-century presidential election. The votes they received ranged from the minuscule to Theodore Roosevelt's 27.4 percent in 1912. In 1992, Ross Perot, running as an independent, won 18.9% of the vote. Almost 20 million Americans showed that either he had a very substantial following or that a large number of voters remained unmoved by President Bush or Bill Clinton.

On August 11th Perot, a 66-year-old billionaire businessman from Texas who had often pictured himself as a reluctant politician, told the newly created Reform Party meeting in Long Beach, California, "I want to be your President." Former Colorado governor Richard D. Lamm challenged Perot for the nomination. In a unique procedure, those who had signed Reform Party petitions in recent months, an estimated 1.1 million, were able to choose between the two by mail vote, through an Internet website or by telephone—the results tallied under the supervision of Ernst & Young, the accounting firm.

The following week, on August 18, at a second Reform convention held in Valley Forge, Pennsylvania, it was announced that Perot had defeated Lamm by receiving about 65.2 percent of the mere 32,145 votes cast. Once again, Perot entered a presidential election using a third party that he created and financed. In mid-September, he chose Pat Choate, an economist, as his running mate.

In 1992, Perot spent more than $64 million of his own money on his third-party candidacy. In 1996, rather than repeating this, Perot decided to accept federal campaign funds to run his campaign. In 1992, he said, "I'm spending my money on this campaign; the two parties are spending your taxpayer money." In 1996, he explained that he wanted to "make sure the American people get involved" in his campaign effort. Perot denounced the two-party system, promising to "kill that little snake this time."

In Perot's brief acceptance speech, rushing through it to appear on CNN's *Larry King Live,* he ridiculed big government, budget deficits, and trade agreements, like NAFTA, which he said exported American jobs. Perot did not have much success in drawing the huge 1992 crowds. Both Representatives Richard Gephardt, the House Dem-

ocratic leader, and Haley Barbour, the Republican Party chairman, agreed in television interviews that the Reform Party would not be an important factor in the fall election. But Bob Dole apparently took Perot seriously enough to admonish a Pittsburgh audience to ignore Perot because the Republican Party "is the real Reform Party."

While the Reform Party languished, the Green Party, an offspring of the antinuclear environmental movements, nominated Ralph Nader as their presidential candidate on August 19. The well-known consumer advocate told some 300 Greens gathered in Los Angeles for their first national nominating convention that both the Republicans and Democrats are "totally beholden to corporate America." Nader said that he did not hold any hope of winning the election—or that he would make it onto the ballot in all 50 states—but "what we're doing is building for the future." In the few election polls that included Nader as a candidate, he did not break into double digits. What support he showed came mainly in California and at Clinton's expense rather than Dole's.

"I come here to say to you, I'm on my way to Chicago and I'm going on a train," said an exuberant President Bill Clinton in Huntington, West Virginia, as he began

Larry King, left, gestures to Texas businessman Ross Perot during a commercial break in the live broadcast of CNN's *Larry King Live* on Friday, July 17, 1992, in New York. Perot took questions from callers and discussed the possibility of forming a third political party. *(Alex Brandon/Associated Press)*

a four-day five-state trip to the 42nd quadrennial Democratic convention, which opened in Chicago on August 26. This nostalgic return to campaigning by train began in the Democratic stronghold of West Virginia, passed into Kentucky, and then Ohio, and on to Michigan and Indiana, all states crucial to a Democratic victory. "I want to see the people like you that I've been working for, and fighting for, for four years," he repeated at every stop as Democratic candidates for congressional and local offices flanked him. "We are on the right track in this country, and we're going forward."

Of the 4,320 delegates to the Democratic convention, 53% were women, 71 percent white, and 17 percent black. (The Democratic National Committee requires each state to divide its delegation approximately evenly between men and women and to "promote racial diversity.") Sixty-six percent were over age 45—29 percent reported a family income of under $50,000, while 46 percent said their income was over $75,000. Eight percent reported a net worth of more than a million dollars, compared with 18 percent of the Republican delegates. Thirteen percent considered themselves evangelical or born-again Christians, compared with 31 percent of the Republicans. Only 2 percent of that year's delegates had attended the 1968 Chicago Democratic Convention, with its strong memories of violence and discord. In marked contrast to the 1968 mayhem, in 1996 the city of Chicago held a lottery to determine who would be able to protest in a cordoned-off area of Grant Park. Above all, though, the political ideology of the Democrats stood in marked contrast with their Republican counterparts. While no Republicans called themselves liberal, 43 percent described themselves as "very liberal" or "somewhat liberal."

The Democratic delegates had some worries about Clinton—26 percent of those polled, using words they chose, said the President's main weakness was a tendency to compromise, ponder, or waffle on the issues. Another 30 percent cited as his chief weakness his character in general or Whitewater and other administration scandals. But an overwhelming 95 percent said they supported Clinton without reservations or did so with but only minor ones—though a majority of delegates said Clinton should be doing more to help the poor and middle class. More than one in four responded that the president was wrong in signing legislation that changed the nation's welfare system.

But who was Bill Clinton, with his goal to "oversee America's transformation into the 21st century"? What did this 50-year-old former Arkansas governor stand for as he asked Americans to place him in the pantheon beside Wilson, Franklin Roosevelt, Eisenhower, and Reagan, the four 20th-century chief executives who served

two full terms? While his reelection was by no means a sure thing as the Democratic convention renominated him and Vice President Al Gore by acclamation, he continued to hold sizable leads in the polls. Politicians from both parties agreed the odds favored him in November.

In a sense, like FDR, Clinton had two distinct terms kaleidoscoped into his four years in the White House—but in contrast to Roosevelt's right/left first term—Clinton's was left/right. First came 1993–94, when he won a partisan victory on a deficit reduction plan that raised taxes on the affluent; his failed one-year struggle for universal health care—during the 1992 campaign, Clinton repeatedly said that health care was "a right, not a privilege"; his muddled attempt to end the military's ban on gay service-people—fudging his 1992 campaign promise to end the ban on gays in the military; the failure to get Congress to enact his 1993 economic stimulus program, which would have provided $50 billion a year for investment in education, job creation, and repairing the nation's infrastructure.

Then came the switch in emphasis and goals after the 1994 Republican congressional sweeps. Now the president changed gears—as did FDR after the overwhelming 1934 liberal Democratic congressional victories. Roosevelt shifted to the left, Clinton veered to the right. He now proposed a balanced budget plan with sharp reductions in projected Medicare spending; he endorsed conservative-sounding ideas such as school uniforms and teen curfews; he signed a welfare reform bill that cut many aid programs for poor people. By signing the welfare bill, Clinton ended the long-standing cash-assistance program known as Aid to Families with Dependent Children, thus abolishing an entitlement that Roosevelt had signed into law in 1935. The *New York Times* summed it up: "He is a moderate who cannot suppress his liberal impulses, a liberal who cannot escape his moderating instincts. He confounds his friends, who think he has agreed with them, only to find he has not. He confuses his enemies, who think they can work with him only to find they cannot." While this was written about Clinton on the day of his renomination, and titled "The Incumbent as a Riddle," it is an apt description of FDR at the same point in his political career.

Overall, in foreign policy, the president's first term saw a nation at peace. His interventions in Haiti and Bosnia had not been the disasters many predicted. His deployment of naval forces apparently ended a Chinese threat to Taiwan. The Middle East remained relatively calm. Boris Yeltsin was reelected president of Russia—Clinton seemed to have been his unofficial campaign manager. While untested in a major crisis, Clinton had kept the peace. Above all, Americans were not fighting in a foreign war.

Unlike his two Democratic predecessors—LBJ and Jimmy Carter—Clinton, as FDR in 1936, faced no primary challengers. The Democratic Party, both in 1936 and 1996, seemed willing to accept a pragmatic politician short on ideology but strong on bonding with voters. But, unlike Roosevelt, Clinton had not become a beloved figure in the Democratic Party.

President Clinton delivered his acceptance speech on August 29 declaring, "Hope is back in America." He promised to protect programs for children, the elderly—and he listed more than a dozen new initiatives his second term would launch in building "that bridge to the 21st century." Alas, just hours before the delegates and a national television audience would hear Clinton on what was billed as the most important speech of his political career, another scandal surfaced. Dick Morris, the president's chief campaign adviser and the central figure behind the emphasis on family-value themes, resigned after a tabloid newspaper reported that he had a relationship with a prostitute and even let her eavesdrop on his conversations with the president. What hurt was the symbolism. The Morris story brought back the image of sleaze, scandal, and character. In Chicago, the Democrats had held a special "family night," with speeches by Hillary Rodham Clinton and Tipper Gore. The Clintons brought their sheltered 16-year-old daughter, Chelsea, into the limelight for the first time in years. No one could estimate how much, if any, this bizarre story about Morris would hurt the Clinton campaign. Had the White House become a haven for people whose standards and behavior were below what the American people had come to expect in that symbol of the nation? Was former president George Bush's evaluation correct when he told the Republican convention in San Diego that, while he had "worked to uphold the dignity and the honor of the presidency. . . . It breaks my heart when the White House is demeaned, the presidency diminished?" Bob Dole had already expressed his concern about White House staff morality in his acceptance address. Would voters continue to focus on political performance, or would White House scandals move to the forefront of the campaign?

On August 29, the Commerce Department reported that the economy sprinted to an even bigger gain in the spring quarter than earlier estimates. Growth in total output of goods and services for the April–June period was calculated at an annual rate of 4.8 percent, the strongest since the spring of 1994. Moreover, less production was going into inventories and more of it to meet demand. In July, the sale of new single-family homes surged 7.8 percent, the most robust showing since February. And, in August, unemployment reached a five-year low of 5.1 percent, with hourly wage earnings increasing. When Clinton took office in January 1993, unemployment stood at 7.1 percent.

In its first survey after the Democratic convention conducted August 30 through September 1, the Gallup Poll found that, in a three-way race, Clinton led among registered voters 55 percent to Dole's 34 percent, with 6 percent for Perot. The President's approval rating soared to 60 percent, the highest of his presidency—a record 54 percent approved of the way he was handling the economy, the highest he ever ranked on this question. A *New York Times*/CBS News Poll concurred, finding the American public feeling better about the economy than at any other time in the last eight years. An accompanying sign of reassurance for the president was that 7 out of 10 people said the economy was very or fairly good, the largest proportion since 1988. By two to one, Americans who rated the economy that way said they would vote for Clinton.

On Labor Day, the traditional opening of the presidential campaign, each candidate defined his strategy. The president had to appeal to moderate voters and Reagan Democrats to edge his electoral support above 50 percent while keeping traditional Democratic constituencies like women, labor, and minorities. "God bless you," the president exclaimed to a woman among the 25,000 people who packed Voyager Park in DePere, Wisconsin, who was holding up a homemade black-and-white placard proclaiming, "Republicans for Clinton." He added, "I wish I could sign that for you. Give her a hand." And at a rally in St. Louis that day, Bob Dole framed the election as a debate over cutting taxes and reducing the size of government. He reminded his audience of President Clinton's failure to implement his 1992 campaign promise to cut taxes and of his own pledge to slash them for business and individuals. "This election is about two visions of America's future," said Dole. "Our opponents offer an old-style liberal vision that puts government first," he continued. "And Jack Kemp and I offer an optimistic vision that puts the American people first. That's the difference. That's the key dividing line in this campaign. They believe in government, and we believe in you."

The historical odds seemed overwhelming in favor of the incumbent Clinton being reelected. A Gallup Poll analysis of the relationship between projected vote surveys taken in September of election years and the actual vote on Election Day suggests that early September surveys have been highly predictive of the electoral winner in past elections. A Dole victory would require a dramatic shift in public opinion, unprecedented since modern polling began.

As of 1996, there had been 12 presidential elections since World War II, with eight including incumbents seeking reelection. For each election, the Gallup analysis examined public opinion in the first survey conducted in September and compared it to the final election outcome. The average change in the Democratic and Republican candidate gap between these two points in time was about 6 points. This suggests that what Americans say they are going to do in September usually has been fairly close to their actual voting behavior in November.

In only four races had the change in the vote approached or exceeded double digits. The maximum change in the gap between candidates across all 12 elections was 13 points—measured in 1948 when incumbent President Harry Truman came from behind to win over Republican challenger Thomas Dewey.

Other than the 1948 election, the biggest September-to-Election Day switches were in 1968 when Hubert Humphrey came back from a 12-point September deficit behind Richard Nixon to within a point of victory, when incumbent President Gerald Ford came back from an 11-point September gap behind challenger Jimmy Carter to within 2 points of winning in 1976, and when Ronald Reagan moved from a dead-even position with Jimmy Carter in September 1980 to his 10-point victory on Election Day. Based on historical precedent, the maximum

reduction in Clinton's lead that Dole could expect would be 13 points, with a much higher probability that the gap would only change by about 6 points. As Frank Newport, editor-in-chief of the Gallup Poll, noted, Gallup's 1996 Labor Day weekend survey showed Clinton with a 21-point lead over Dole (Clinton 55 percent, Dole 34 percent, Perot 6 percent). As the race stood then, a Dole victory would require a most dramatic event—a major Clinton blunder, a personal health issue, or a new revelation of a previously unknown scandal.

Bob Dole seemed unable to communicate his message. In states essential for a Republican victory—Michigan, Ohio, Missouri, and Iowa, for example—a startling number of swing voters described Dole as mean or vindictive, shifty, too old, inept. Dole still came across as a slashing politician remembered for his highly combative appearances over the years on Sunday morning political talk shows. The senator seemed to be out of step, invoking the politics of nostalgia, the yearning for days past.

Dole made his tax cut the centerpiece of his campaign but he could not adequately explain how entitlement programs would not be cut or the deficit increased. President Clinton asked big questions but offered few

President Bill Clinton *(Library of Congress)*

answers, leaving the impression that his second administration would be able to balance the budget painlessly without touching Medicare and other entitlement programs. Clinton repeated his talk about a "bridge to the 21st century," and that vague rhetoric seemed to define the campaign—not a choice between left or right, liberal or conservative, Republican or Democrat, but a choice between Clinton and the future or Dole and the past. The listless campaign plodded along. Common ephemeral items—buttons, ribbons, posters, automobile bumper stickers—were minimal.

In 1992, economic insecurity and the aftermath of the 1991 recession dominated the presidential campaign and helped push George Bush from office. Commentators wrote about the rage of the Perot voter. In 1994, anger at Washington and disappointment with President Clinton's leadership dominated the midterm elections and drove the Democrats from power in Congress. In 1996, with the economy growing, the voters were more upbeat, more optimistic. The mood change was evident in surveys that documented a startling turnabout in the public mood. The percentage who believed the country "is badly off-track" had shrunk dramatically. For President Clinton, the timing of the uptick could hardly have been better. The voters apparently concluded early on that he probably deserved reelection after presiding over a long recovery that reinforced middle-class confidence in the economy. And this was the problem for Bob Dole and his campaign.

"Don't worry about this election. We're going to win," Dole told more than a hundred Republican congressional members on the morning of September 11. This Capitol Hill meeting was aimed at boosting the sagging morale of many within the party who thought that Dole's inability to dent Clinton's substantial lead in public opinion polls could jeopardize majorities in the House and Senate. This meeting with sympathetic lawmakers came after another difficult week for the Dole campaign. The renewed United States conflict with Iraq virtually wiped the Republican nominee out of the headlines, and Dole's criticism of the Family and Medical Leave Act had handed the Democrats a ready-made issue. The Republican campaign began airing two new television commercials: a 30-second spot promoting Dole's tax-cutting plan and a 2-minute ad called "The Better Man" featuring Dole, his wife Elizabeth, and retired General Colin Powell offering testimony that Dole had the character and integrity to lead the nation. The 15 percent across-the-board tax cut, the $500 child credit, a reshaped Internal Revenue Service, and the balanced budget remained the core message. The theme: "The stakes in this Election? Keeping more of what you earn!"

The Democrats countered with an emotional television commercial pointing out Dole's opposition to social programs, implying that he was out of touch with concerns of working families. Clinton ads portrayed Dole as a cold-hearted extremist, a downright scary alternative whose election would threaten the country's basic values. In rapid-fire cadence, Dole was described as against Medicare, for higher taxes, against aid for education, against unemployment benefits, against more police on the streets, against curtailing tobacco advertisements, and against job leaves for parents with dying children. Unflattering footage made Dole look mean and grumpy. By mid-September, as the Dow–Jones Industrial Average continued to soar, polling surveys showed that more than 12 percent of registered Republican voters nationwide were defecting to Bill Clinton compared with less than 5 percent of Democrats who said they planned to vote for Dole.

Dole's campaign also suffered from poor timing. Being tough on crime was traditionally a Republican issue. The senator proposed an anticrime package that would double federal spending for new prisons and require inmates to do full-time work while incarcerated. But, before he could offer details, President Clinton underscored his own determination to avoid being branded a soft-on-crime Democrat by picking up the endorsement of the nation's largest police organization. Both Clinton and Dole surrounded themselves with uniformed police officers to symbolize their concern over the crime issue, which, next to education, was of most concern to voters. Dole used caustic rhetoric and mountains of statistics to paint Clinton as a liberal who winked at drug use and only sounded tough on crime. "He talks like Dirty Harry, but he acts like Barney Fife," said Dole. But the president had a powerful response—the endorsement of the National Fraternal Order of Police, which had supported George Bush in 1992. Clinton positioned himself as a sort of national police chief, boasting that he had put more police officers on the beat, taken guns away from thugs, and had busted record numbers of violent gangs. While Dole blamed Clinton for crime and drug problems, polls suggested the voters did not, evaluating both candidates as equally capable of reducing the use of illegal drugs, and by 46 to 40 percent that Clinton could handle the crime problem better than Dole.

The presidential campaign meandered through dull speeches and news conferences in search of issues that truly separated the candidates. Medicare? Dole would cut the program by $26 billion, Clinton by $19 billion. Violence? Dole wanted it removed from music lyrics; Clinton promised to V-chip it off television. Dole railed against marijuana; Clinton against tobacco. Character? The American people probably knew everything concerning the character of both men, and they decided that this was not a major issue. In 1992, when the character issue loomed much larger because Clinton was the unknown challenger, voters decided then that it didn't matter. Dole insisted that Clinton had a deep commitment to liberalism. Clinton, he said, was "an old-style, dyed-in-the-wool, big-spending liberal." And the president denied he was a liberal, a denial that probably caused many Democrats to flinch. Clinton recalled that he expanded the application of the death penalty and signed welfare cuts into law—how could he be a liberal?

On October 6, Bill Clinton and Bob Dole met in the Bushnell Theater in downtown Hartford, Connecticut, for the first of two 90-minute televised debates. Dole argued, "There's a lot of things wrong with America," while Clinton followed an upbeat appraisal: "We are better off than we were four years ago. Let's keep it going." He defended his first term, which, he said, saw an improvement in the lives of ordinary Americans. The senator tried to chip away at Clinton's record, asserting that average people would really prosper with his tax cut. Perhaps the most noteworthy aspect of the debate was the temperate civilized tone. Neither had anything new to offer. Overall, there was a notable lack of edge to the exchanges as familiar positions were restated. Dole repeatedly intoned his respect for the president, and Clinton said he liked the senator. Public perceptions about who won the debate closely paralleled candidate preference in the election. Probably very few voters were swayed by this debate in an election almost devoid of major differences. Indeed, 92 percent of those surveyed told a *New York Times*/CBS News Poll they had not changed their mind—and 50 percent described the 1996 presidential campaign as being dull.

Two days after the first debate, Dole shifted to a harsher, more negative message, with the candidate, his surrogates, and his commercials all slamming the character and morality of the president. "Bozo's on his way out," said Dole, who had chided Clinton for failing in his 1992 debates with George Bush to address his opponent with respect as "Mr. President." Asked in a CBS interview if Clinton was "ethically and morally deserving to be President," the senator said he had no comment, but added, "I think you would be right to say I am troubled by it." Dole now began stinging attacks, accusing the president of diminishing his office through a pattern of evasion, half-truths, and "endless violations of public trust," which fostered cynicism and eroded faith in the political system.

Voters seemed indifferent. Only 24 percent of those questioned said they were following the election "very closely" compared with 42 percent in 1992, with viewership for the first presidential debate down nearly 20 percent from four years ago. Network news coverage of the campaign dropped 40 percent in September from 1992. The covers of news magazines turned to adultery, diet pills, and plastic surgery. Large news organizations, which field small armies to scour the nation for trends, seemed pre-

pared for every eventuality except that people would turn them off. They had interviewed soccer moms, angry white males, urban blacks, suburban evangelicals, Reagan Democrats, and Clinton Republicans but detected little passion for either candidate. Even talk-show host Oprah Winfrey passed on booking Dole. The vice-presidential debate between Al Gore and Jack Kemp on October 9 accelerated this ennui. It didn't matter what the questions were. Each was programmed to respond to this exercise in civic duty in the allotted number of seconds. In short, some three weeks before the election, more people seemed fascinated by John F. Kennedy Jr.'s wedding than the contest for his father's old office.

Bob Dole used the October 16th final televised presidential debate in San Diego to attack the ethical record of President Clinton as scandal-tainted and undeserving of a second term. "Many American people have lost their faith in government," said Dole, moving in quickly on the ethics attack in the first minutes of the debate. "They see scandals on almost a daily basis. They see ethical problems in the White House. There's a great deal of cynicism out there."

President Bill Clinton (right) and Senator Bob Dole (left) prepare for opening remarks at their first presidential debate at the Bushnell Theater in Hartford, Connecticut, October 6, 1996. *(Charles Krupa/Associated Press)*

Clinton ignored the accusations and instead invoked the nation's economic health and saw this growth increasing in the next four years. "Compared to four years ago," we're clearly better off," the president stated. "That progress is only the beginning." He challenged Dole's contention that the current state of the economy was the worst in this century. "In February he said we had the best economy in 30 years," reminded Clinton. Then, using an old Ronald Reagan line against Dole, he stared into the camera and stated, "If you believe that the California economy was better in 1992 than today, you should vote for Bob Dole." "You haven't seen anything yet," said Dole in describing his sharp-tongued performance in the debate. It's "a warm-up" for the 19 "go after 'em" days left in the campaign. By the end of the evening, though, neither the invited nor the wider audience seemed stirred.

William Kristol's conservative *Weekly Standard* summed up the gloom of Republican pundits: "One Week to Go: Just How Bad Will It Be?" "A motionless engine" is what Kristol, Fred Barnes, and John Podhoretz labeled the GOP campaign for failing to define meaningful differences between a Dole presidency and a second Clinton administration. The *Washington Post* headline of October 19 had to further depress Republicans: "Democrats Have Shot at Regaining Senate: GOP Majority Imperiled by 10 Races Still Too Close to Call." Perhaps Dole got the message! An avalanche of attack ads painted Clinton and the Democrats as "liberal," "ultraliberal," and "unbearably liberal!" Dole now made the big "L" pejorative. While Clinton had flip-flopped on issues, said Dole, he had also jeopardized the nation's defenses and prestige overseas and had broken his pledge to cut taxes for the middle class. Many voters, he continued, seemed prepared to entrust the White House to him for another four years: "Wake up, America! You're about to do yourselves an injustice if you vote for Bill Clinton!" He promised a 96-hour marathon finale that would focus on the president's "public conduct."

Every national public opinion poll showed Clinton stretching his lead. Even in California, where Dole had made a tactical decision to purchase additional, costly television time and to rework his schedule, he trailed Clinton by 20 points—virtually the same margin as in September. The senator had all but ignored his anti-affirmative action stance. Now, in the battle for California, he returned to it with a vengeance, pounding out his theme that affirmative action was discriminatory and no longer needed. "Every time I drive to work in Washington, D.C., or drive down North Capitol Street and I see dozens and dozens of black men without work, I say to myself, 'What has this law done for them?'" Dole thundered during an anti-affirmative action speech in California. The major gamble for the state's crucial 54 electoral votes failed.

Dole personally made another critical decision. He dispatched his campaign manager to ask Ross Perot to withdraw and endorse the Republican ticket. Top advisers inside the Dole campaign seemed bewildered. One who attended the October 23 meeting said, "I don't know that it's the kind of thing a smart campaign does. . . . I'm stunned. You don't negotiate from weakness. Ronald Reagan taught us that." Perot dismissed the overture as "weird" and "goofy," but he widened his criticism of Clinton, now harshly attacking him for the "huge moral, ethical, and criminal problems facing him."

Clinton stayed above the fray. He focused on the economy: "America's awake and moving in the right direction." He ignored the new scandals. A convicted drug smuggler had attended a White House Christmas party; an April "community outreach" at a Buddhist temple near Los Angeles attended by Vice President Al Gore had turned into a bizarre Democratic fund-raiser, leaving the question of how monks earning $40 monthly stipends managed $5,000 contributions; the head of Taiwan's governing Nationalist Party denied he had donated $15 million to the Clinton reelection fund; a former assistant commerce secretary apparently obtained illegal contributions from an Indonesian corporation. The president stuck to his message as he crisscrossed the country—and he connected with the cheering crowds, reaching out and them back for him. In two days alone, he singled out for conversation, attention, and heavy doses of charm a young woman from the Middle East with immigration problems, a girl with a rare blood disease, a woman distraught over late-term abortions, and a young father leaning to Dole. The president seemed to inspire, and energize himself at the same time. A bond with the people finally emerged.

The 1996 elections had very few surprises and very few upsets. The results seemed almost predictable, as public opinion polling samples again were validated. Almost 92 million voters, roughly 50 percent of those eligible, cast a ballot, proportionately the lowest voter turnout since 1924. Bill Clinton, at age 50, became the first Democrat since FDR—and the third since the Civil War—to win a second consecutive term. He came very close to a goal that had obsessed him for four years: winning a majority of the popular vote—Clinton 47,400,125 (49 percent), Dole 39,198,255 (41 percent), Perot 8,085,402 (9 percent). The electoral vote, with a majority of 270 needed to win, stood at Clinton 379 and Dole 159. The president won with 6 percentage points more of the popular vote, and 9 more electoral votes, than in 1992. Dole carried only the broad band of Great Plains and Mountain states stretching from the Canadian border to Texas, most of the old Cotton South, and Indiana, a Republican island in a Democratic sea that covered the whole northeastern quadrant. The fund-raising scandals that had emerged during the final days of the campaign, and Clinton's refusal to answer questions about them, probably cost him support from Republicans and Independents who were otherwise prepared to cross over to the Democratic ticket.

The 1996 presidential election was not really a race. Clinton started ahead and stayed there. He began his second term, however, as he ended his first one, with a Republican-controlled Congress and an electorate reluctant to give him a clear mandate—41 percent thought Clinton would move in a more liberal direction; 43 percent believed he would stay in the political center. The gender gap, a new phrase for the political lexicon, divided voters—more women voted for Clinton, more men for Dole. The president won the votes of one in five self-described conservatives, one in four members of the religious right, one in eight Republicans, half the nation's Catholic voters, and almost 90 percent of black voters. Clinton ran well ahead of Dole among every age group, including senior citizens, but among 18–29-year-old voters the President ran 19 points ahead. Clinton supporters cared most about the economy—more than 6 in 10 polled said the economy was in good shape and most of them voted for Clinton—education, Medicare, and Social Security. Dole voters seemed more concerned about character, taxes, the deficit, and foreign policy. Exit polls showed that Perot voters gave Dole nearly half their support and split the rest between Clinton and Perot. Something, however, may have been lost in this election: the concept of the president as a paragon. Asked in exit polls if they thought Clinton was "honest," 54 percent responded in the negative. For the first time in American history, a Democrat had been elected to the White House with a Congress controlled by the opposition. "We have little faith to let either of you govern unchaperoned," the voters seemed to be saying. "The nation has too many problems to be solved to trust either of you to do it alone." Voters elected a moderate Democratic president to carry out a moderate Republican agenda. Clinton was so sensitive to voters' apprehensions that he avoided campaigning for a Democratic Congress. And, in the closing weeks, Republicans even stopped talking about Bob Dole and reminded voters that, if they planned to vote for Clinton, a Republican Congress would be needed to keep him in line.

In retrospect, Bob Dole never stirred any emotion as a candidate. He seemed wooden, almost detached from the everyday problems faced by Americans. Clinton, on the other hand, came across as the ultimate average American, someone who had tangled personally with virtually every key family issue of the times—a fractured home, an abusive parent, drugs, the morality of Vietnam, infidelity, and dubious business experiences. Bill Clinton emerged as the candidate most in touch with the people, a candidate who felt their pain.

Flooded by "soft money" contributions, the 1996 presidential election was the costliest in American history up until that time. Costly commercials caused the Democrats and the Clinton White House to use dubious fund-raising methods, which raised serious ethical questions during the second Clinton administration.

—*Fred L. Israel*

Selected Bibliography

This article relied heavily on Gallup Poll data, especially the volumes for 1995 and 1996. For the past 70 years, we have been able to measure public opinion. Intellect and technology then combined to perfect the sampling procedure—the public opinion poll. Almost immediately, elected officials became fascinated with polls. And, with one exception, every administration since Franklin D. Roosevelt's has made extensive use of polling data. The exception, of course, was President Harry Truman and his associates.

Polls are but a statistical snapshot of a moment in time. They reflect the process but are not part of it. George Gallup conducted his first public opinion poll in September 1935. He believed that scientific polling overcame an obstacle to democracy: the absence of a way to measure public opinion accurately and continuously. Dr. Gallup considered polls an ongoing referendum on the issues of the day, and certainly not as a spectator sport as to who wins and who loses.

Since 1935, the Gallup Poll has asked more than 50,000 questions of more than 6 million people. Gallup interviewers have polled the American people on virtually every conceivable topic, from political issues to such social problems as health care and AIDS. These records are a superb source for understanding American public opinion since the New Deal. The bulk of the questions, however, have dealt with government—its policies and problems.

See also James W. Ceaser and Andrew Busch, *Losing to Win: The 1996 Elections and American Politics* (1997); Rodolfo O. De la Garza and Louis DeSipio, ed., *Awash in the Mainstream: Latino Politics in the 1996 Elections* (1999); John C. Green, ed., *Financing the 1996 Election* (1999); Bob Woodward, *The Choice: How Clinton Won* (2005); Dick Morris, *Behind the Oval Office: Getting Reelected Against All Odds* (1999); Gerald Pomper et al., *The Election of 1996: Reports and Interpretations* (1997); and Harvey L. Schantz, ed., *Politics in an Era of Divided Government: The Election of 1996 and Its Aftermath* (2000).

1996 ELECTION STATISTICS

State	Number of Electors	Total Popular Vote	Elec Vote D	Elec Vote R	Pop Vote D	Pop Vote R	Pop Vote Ref	Margin of Victory Votes	Margin of Victory % Total Vote
Alabama	9	1,534,349		9	2	1	3	106,879	6.97%
Alaska	3	241,620		3	2	1	3	42,366	17.53%
Arizona	8	1,404,405	8		1	2	3	31,215	2.22%
Arkansas	6	884,262	6		1	2	3	149,755	16.94%
California	54	10,019,484	54		1	2	3	1,291,455	12.89%
Colorado	8	1,510,704		8	2	1	3	20,696	1.37%
Connecticut	8	1,392,614	8		1	2	3	252,631	18.14%
Delaware	3	271,084	3		1	2	3	41,293	15.23%
District of Columbia	3	185,726	3		1	2	4	140,881	75.85%
Florida	25	5,303,794	25		1	2	3	302,334	5.70%
Georgia	13	2,299,071		13	2	1	3	26,994	1.17%
Hawaii	4	360,120	4		1	2	3	91,069	25.29%
Idaho	4	491,719		4	2	1	3	91,152	18.54%
Illinois	22	4,311,391	22		1	2	3	754,723	17.51%
Indiana	12	2,135,842		12	2	1	3	119,269	5.58%
Iowa	7	1,234,075	7		1	2	3	127,614	10.34%
Kansas	6	1,074,300		6	2	1	3	195,586	18.21%
Kentucky	8	1,388,708	8		1	2	3	13,331	0.96%
Louisiana	9	1,783,959	9		1	2	3	215,251	12.07%
Maine	4	605,897	4		1	2	3	126,410	20.86%
Maryland	10	1,780,870	10		1	2	3	284,677	15.99%
Massachusetts	12	2,556,785	12		1	2	3	853,656	33.39%
Michigan	18	3,848,844	18		1	2	3	508,441	13.21%
Minnesota	10	2,192,640	10		1	2	3	353,962	16.14%
Mississippi	7	893,857		7	2	1	3	45,816	5.13%
Missouri	11	2,158,065	11		1	2	3	135,919	6.30%
Montana	3	407,261		3	2	1	3	11,730	2.88%
Nebraska	5	677,415		5	2	1	3	126,706	18.70%
Nevada	4	464,279	4		1	2	3	4,730	1.02%
New Hampshire	4	499,175	4		1	2	3	49,682	9.95%
New Jersey	15	3,075,807	15		1	2	3	549,251	17.86%
New Mexico	5	556,074	5		1	2	3	40,744	7.33%
New York	33	6,316,129	33		1	2	3	1,822,685	28.86%
North Carolina	14	2,515,807		14	2	1	3	118,089	4.69%
North Dakota	3	266,411		3	2	1	3	18,145	6.81%
Ohio	21	4,534,434	21		1	2	3	288,339	6.36%
Oklahoma	8	1,206,713		8	2	1	3	94,210	7.81%
Oregon	7	1,377,760	7		1	2	3	111,489	8.09%
Pennsylvania	23	4,506,118	23		1	2	3	414,650	9.20%
Rhode Island	4	390,284	4		1	2	3	128,367	32.89%
South Carolina	8	1,149,457		8	2	1	3	69,407	6.04%
South Dakota	3	323,826		3	2	1	3	11,210	3.46%
Tennessee	11	1,894,105	11		1	2	3	45,616	2.41%
Texas	32	5,611,644		32	2	1	3	276,484	4.93%
Utah	5	665,629		5	2	1	3	140,278	21.07%
Vermont	3	258,449	3		1	2	3	57,542	22.26%
Virginia	13	2,416,642		13	2	1	3	47,290	1.96%
Washington	11	2,253,837	11		1	2	3	282,611	12.54%
West Virginia	5	636,459	5		1	2	3	93,866	14.75%
Wisconsin	11	2,196,169	11		1	2	3	226,942	10.33%
Wyoming	3	211,571		3	2	1	3	27,454	12.98%
Total	538	96,275,640	379	159	1	2	3	8,201,370	8.52%

Clinton Democratic		Dole Republican		Perot Reform		Nader Green		Others	
662,165	43.16%	769,044	50.12%	92,149	6.01%	0	0.00%	10,991	0.72%
80,380	33.27%	122,746	50.80%	26,333	10.90%	7,597	3.14%	4,564	1.89%
653,288	46.52%	622,073	44.29%	112,072	7.98%	2,062	0.15%	14,910	1.06%
475,171	53.74%	325,416	36.80%	69,884	7.90%	3,649	0.41%	10,142	1.15%
5,119,835	51.10%	3,828,380	38.21%	697,847	6.96%	237,016	2.37%	136,406	1.36%
671,152	44.43%	691,848	45.80%	99,629	6.59%	25,070	1.66%	23,005	1.52%
735,740	52.83%	483,109	34.69%	139,523	10.02%	24,321	1.75%	9,921	0.71%
140,355	51.78%	99,062	36.54%	28,719	10.59%	156	0.06%	2,792	1.03%
158,220	85.19%	17,339	9.34%	3,611	1.94%	4,780	2.57%	1,776	0.96%
2,546,870	48.02%	2,244,536	42.32%	483,870	9.12%	4,101	0.08%	24,417	0.46%
1,053,849	45.84%	1,080,843	47.01%	146,337	6.37%	0	0.00%	18,042	0.78%
205,012	56.93%	113,943	31.64%	27,358	7.60%	10,386	2.88%	3,421	0.95%
165,443	33.65%	256,595	52.18%	62,518	12.71%	0	0.00%	7,163	1.46%
2,341,744	54.32%	1,587,021	36.81%	346,408	8.03%	1,447	0.03%	34,771	0.81%
887,424	41.55%	1,006,693	47.13%	224,299	10.50%	1,121	0.05%	16,305	0.76%
620,258	50.26%	492,644	39.92%	105,159	8.52%	6,550	0.53%	9,464	0.77%
387,659	36.08%	583,245	54.29%	92,639	8.62%	914	0.09%	9,843	0.92%
636,614	45.84%	623,283	44.88%	120,396	8.67%	701	0.05%	7,714	0.56%
927,837	52.01%	712,586	39.94%	123,293	6.91%	4,719	0.26%	15,524	0.87%
312,788	51.62%	186,378	30.76%	85,970	14.19%	15,279	2.52%	5,482	0.90%
966,207	54.25%	681,530	38.27%	115,812	6.50%	2,606	0.15%	14,715	0.83%
1,571,763	61.47%	718,107	28.09%	227,217	8.89%	4,734	0.19%	34,964	1.37%
1,989,653	51.69%	1,481,212	38.48%	336,670	8.75%	2,322	0.06%	38,987	1.01%
1,120,438	51.10%	766,476	34.96%	257,704	11.75%	24,908	1.14%	23,114	1.05%
394,022	44.08%	439,838	49.21%	52,222	5.84%	0	0.00%	7,775	0.87%
1,025,935	47.54%	890,016	41.24%	217,188	10.06%	534	0.02%	24,392	1.13%
167,922	41.23%	179,652	44.11%	55,229	13.56%	0	0.00%	4,458	1.09%
236,761	34.95%	363,467	53.65%	71,278	10.52%	0	0.00%	5,909	0.87%
203,974	43.93%	199,244	42.91%	43,986	9.47%	4,730	1.02%	12,345	2.66%
246,214	49.32%	196,532	39.37%	48,390	9.69%	0	0.00%	8,039	1.61%
1,652,329	53.72%	1,103,078	35.86%	262,134	8.52%	32,465	1.06%	25,801	0.84%
273,495	49.18%	232,751	41.86%	32,257	5.80%	13,218	2.38%	4,353	0.78%
3,756,177	59.47%	1,933,492	30.61%	503,458	7.97%	75,956	1.20%	47,046	0.74%
1,107,849	44.04%	1,225,938	48.73%	168,059	6.68%	2,108	0.08%	11,853	0.47%
106,905	40.13%	125,050	46.94%	32,515	12.20%	0	0.00%	1,941	0.73%
2,148,222	47.38%	1,859,883	41.02%	483,207	10.66%	2,962	0.07%	40,160	0.89%
488,105	40.45%	582,315	48.26%	130,788	10.84%	0	0.00%	5,505	0.46%
649,641	47.15%	538,152	39.06%	121,221	8.80%	49,415	3.59%	19,331	1.40%
2,215,819	49.17%	1,801,169	39.97%	430,984	9.56%	3,086	0.07%	55,060	1.22%
233,050	59.71%	104,683	26.82%	43,723	11.20%	6,040	1.55%	2,788	0.71%
504,051	43.85%	573,458	49.89%	64,386	5.60%	0	0.00%	7,562	0.66%
139,333	43.03%	150,543	46.49%	31,250	9.65%	0	0.00%	2,700	0.83%
909,146	48.00%	863,530	45.59%	105,918	5.59%	6,427	0.34%	9,084	0.48%
2,459,683	43.83%	2,736,167	48.76%	378,537	6.75%	4,810	0.09%	32,447	0.58%
221,633	33.30%	361,911	54.37%	66,461	9.98%	4,615	0.69%	11,009	1.65%
137,894	53.35%	80,352	31.09%	31,024	12.00%	5,585	2.16%	3,594	1.39%
1,091,060	45.15%	1,138,350	47.10%	159,861	6.62%	0	0.00%	27,371	1.13%
1,123,323	49.84%	840,712	37.30%	201,003	8.92%	60,322	2.68%	28,477	1.26%
327,812	51.51%	233,946	36.76%	71,639	11.26%	0	0.00%	3,062	0.48%
1,071,971	48.81%	845,029	38.48%	227,339	10.35%	28,723	1.31%	23,107	1.05%
77,934	36.84%	105,388	49.81%	25,928	12.25%	0	0.00%	2,321	1.10%
47,400,125	49.23%	39,198,755	40.72%	8,085,402	8.40%	685,435	0.71%	905,923	0.94%

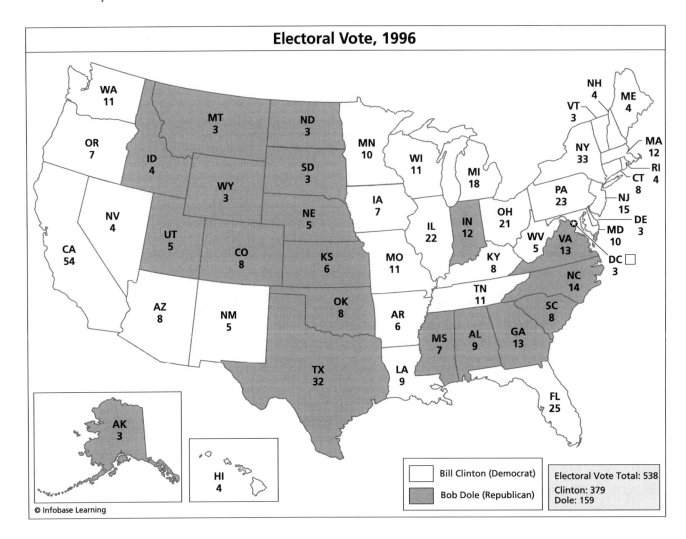

Electoral Vote, 1996

WA 11
OR 7
ID 4
MT 3
ND 3
SD 3
WY 3
NE 5
MN 10
WI 11
IA 7
MI 18
NH 4
ME 4
VT 3
NY 33
MA 12
RI 4
CT 8
PA 23
NJ 15
DE 3
MD 10
NV 4
UT 5
CO 8
KS 6
IL 22
IN 12
OH 21
WV 5
VA 13
KY 8
DC 3
CA 54
AZ 8
NM 5
OK 8
MO 11
AR 6
TN 11
NC 14
SC 8
MS 7
AL 9
GA 13
TX 32
LA 9
FL 25
AK 3
HI 4

Bill Clinton (Democrat)
Bob Dole (Republican)

Electoral Vote Total: 538
Clinton: 379
Dole: 159

© Infobase Learning

Election of 2000

Election Overview

Election Year 2000

Election Day November 7, 2000

Winning Candidates

- ★ **President:** George W. Bush
- ★ **Vice President:** Richard Cheney

Election Results [ticket, party: popular votes (percentage of popular vote); electoral votes (percentage of electoral vote)]

- George W. Bush and Richard Cheney, Republican: 50,460,110 (47.87%); 271 (50.4%)
- Al Gore and Joseph Lieberman, Democratic: 51,003,926 (48.38%); 266 (49.4%)
- Ralph Nader and Winona LaDuke, Green: 2,883,105 (2.73%); 0 (0.0%)
- Patrick Buchanan and Ezola Foster, Reform: 449,225 (0.43%); 0 (0.0%)
- Harry Browne and Art Olivier, Libertarian: 384,516 (0.36%); 0 (0.0%)
- Other: 236,593 (0.22%); 0 (0.0%)

Voter Turnout 50.4%

Central Forums/Campaign Methods for Addressing Voters

- Stumping
- Speeches, rallies
- Television interviews, talk show appearances
- Print and television ads
- Debates
- Press, newspapers and magazines
- Internet

Incumbent President and Vice President on Election Day Bill Clinton and Al Gore

Population (2000) 282,413,000

Gross Domestic Product

- $9.952 trillion (in current dollars: $11.226 trillion)
- Per capita: $35,237 (in current dollars: $39,750)

Number of Daily Newspapers (2000) 1,480

Average Daily Circulation (2000) 55,800,000

Households with

- Radio (2000): 100,500,000
- Television (2000): 101,000,000
- Computer/Internet (2000): 43,639,000

Method of Choosing Electors Popular vote (mostly general-ticket system/winner take all)

- Had the ballot recount continued, the Florida legislature was prepared to appoint the Republican slate of electors to avoid missing the federal deadline for choosing electors.

Method of Choosing Nominees

- Presidential preference primaries
- Caucuses

Key Issues and Events

- Democrats boosted by peace and prosperity under Clinton
- Republicans are encouraged by backlash against Clinton sex scandals and Gore fund-raising she-

nanigans in 1996. George W. Bush benefits from great name recognition, thanks to his father, George H. W. Bush. Bush promises "Compassionate Conservatism" and tax cuts. Gore is ambivalent about Clinton's legacy.

Leading Candidates

REPUBLICANS
- George W. Bush, governor (Texas)
- John McCain, senator (Arizona)
- Alan Keyes, former ambassador to United Nations Economic and Social Council (Maryland)
- Steve Forbes, businessman (New York)
- Gary Bauer, former president of Family Research Council (Virginia)
- Orrin Hatch, senator (Utah)
- Elizabeth Dole, former U.S. secretary of transportation, secretary of labor, and senator (North Carolina)

DEMOCRATS
- Al Gore, vice president of the United States (Tennessee)
- Bill Bradley, former senator (New Jersey)

REFORM PARTY
- John B. Anderson, former representative from Illinois, former Independent presidential candidate (Florida)
- David L. Boren, former senator (Oklahoma)
- Pat Buchanan, former speechwriter and senior adviser to President Richard Nixon (Virginia)
- Charles E. Collins, former school board chairman for a rural Florida county (Georgia)
- John Hagelin, past and then-current Natural Law Party candidate (Iowa)
- Ross Perot, 1996 presidential nominee (Texas)
- Donald Trump, real estate developer (New York)

Trajectory

- George W. Bush, advocating a "compassionate conservatism," wins the Republican Iowa caucuses on January 24, 2000, with 41 percent of the vote, having dominated the "invisible primary" of 1999 with the most name recognition and the best fund-raising, amassing $67 million by winter 2000. Vice President Al Gore has an even more impressive win in Iowa, beating former senator Bill Bradley handily 63 percent to 35 percent.
- In New Hampshire, on February 1, Gore triumphs again, although Bradley surges, getting 46.3 percent to Gore's 50.4 percent. Bradley's strong showing stirs media interest, albeit temporarily. Meanwhile, Senator John McCain with his charming, media-friendly "Straight Talk Express" turns the race upside down by humiliating Bush with a 49 percent to 30.2 percent win.
- After a vicious campaign marked by "push polls" spreading rumors and racial demagoguery, Bush wins South Carolina's "First in the South" primary on February 19, with 53 percent to McCain's 42 percent. The harsh tactics enrage McCain.
- With Bradley enjoying adoring press coverage, he and Gore debate very aggressively against one another at Harlem's Apollo Theatre on February 22.
- On "Titanic Tuesday," March 7, 11 primaries and 6 caucuses essentially decide both nominations. Gore earns nearly three-quarters of the votes cast that day and wins all 11 Democratic primaries. Bush wins 56.9 percent of the votes and seven of the 11 Republican primaries.
- On the eve of the Republican National Convention, which begins on July 31 in Philadelphia, the head of Bush's vice-presidential search committee, Richard Cheney, becomes Bush's nominee for vice president. Bush delivers a surprisingly effective acceptance address on August 3, mocking Democrats with the chant: "This administration had its chance. They have not led. We will."
- With Cheney having resided in Texas for 10 years, and Bush the governor of Texas, his home state, Cheney has to change back his voter registration to his home state of Wyoming to accept nomination as vice president. The Constitution prohibits electors from voting for two candidates from the same state.
- At the Democratic Convention, August 14 to 17, President Clinton almost steals the show with "The Walk," as a hand-held camera follows him through the Staples Center's backstage before he saunters onstage to wild applause. Gore asserts himself with his own surprising choice for vice president, Senator Joseph Lieberman, who denounced Clinton's dalliance with Monica Lewinsky. "I stand here tonight as my own man and I want you to know me for who I truly am," Gore proclaims. Most dramatically, before the speech, Gore gives his wife Tipper a passionate, three-second kiss to disprove caricatures of him as robotic. The convention sends Gore into the general campaign with a lead over Bush.
- At a Labor Day event in Naperville, Illinois, on September 4, an open microphone captures Bush muttering to Cheney: "There's Adam Clymer—

major league asshole—from the *New York Times*." Cheney's response, "Oh yeah, big time," earns him the nickname "Big Time," while Bush's frank admission, "I regret people heard the comments," contains the damage.

- Election relatively boring until Election Day: "Gush and Bore"
- At the first debate on October 3, Bush holds his own, defying expectations that Gore will crush him. Gore's exasperated sighs and winces as Bush speaks make Gore look aggressive and unpresidential.
- The third debate, October 17, involves the sharpest exchanges between the two candidates. The debates, which attract huge audiences because the race is so tight, deliver no knockout blows with few defining moments. Still, Bush inches ahead of Gore in most polls during October.
- On November 2, just days before the election, leaked police documents reveal that Bush had been arrested for drunk driving in Kennebunkport, Maine, in 1976. Bush acknowledges he was arrested and paid the fine—a decade before swearing off alcohol. Still, Karl Rove, Bush's chief political adviser, later concludes that the news disillusioned millions of evangelical voters from voting for Bush on Election Day, and the race narrowed in the last week.
- Bush and Gore deadlock on Election Day, November 7, 2000, with Florida's electoral votes in dispute. Thousands of Jewish senior citizens mistakenly vote for Pat Buchanan rather than Al Gore due to the confusing "Butterfly Ballot," while most of the 97,421 votes Ralph Nader of the Green Party receives in Florida probably would have shifted the election to Gore had Nader not run.
- On election night Gore leads in the popular vote by half a million; however, neither candidate receives a majority of 270 in the Electoral College. The election hinges on Florida's 25 electoral votes, which would take either candidate beyond the 270 mark.
- The numbers fluctuate all evening and into the early night. Voter exit polls indicate a lead for Gore, and many TV news sources call the election for Gore based on early returns. However, the count shifts in Bush's favor, prompting Gore to concede by phone to Bush. When Bush's lead narrows, Gore withdraws his concession.
- The Florida vote is so close it triggers the law mandating an automatic statewide machine recount, which gives Bush the state by under 400 votes.
- Dispute over Florida's electoral votes lasts 36 days.

- "Butterfly ballots": The Gore campaign discovers balloting errors in the three critical counties in the state and demands a hand recount. The Bush campaign opposes the recount.
- The Battle of the Ballots: Continuing disagreements about recounting the votes, with press conferences, lawsuits, court hearings, and demonstrations.
- Gore argues that in four counties, Broward, Miami-Dade, Palm Beach, and Volusia, faulty voting machines discarded legitimate votes that would have swayed the election to Gore.
- The controversial votes are in counties where Gore was leading. Katherine Harris, a Bush supporter and Florida's secretary of state, refuses to authorize the recount or extend the deadline to report the vote count beyond November 14. Gore appeals to the Florida Supreme Court.
- After weeks of hand recounts and legal squabbles, the Florida Supreme Court on November 21 unanimously sides with Gore, requiring the recounts to continue and saying state election officials must accept recounts as late as November 26.
- Two of the counties commence their recounts on November 22. Miami-Dade halts the recounts after Republicans mob the county offices. Miami-Dade officials resubmit their original counts, claiming otherwise they would miss the deadline. Palm Beach County misses the recount deadline.
- On November 26, Florida secretary of state Katherine Harris and the state canvassing board certify Bush the winner of Florida's electoral votes, by 537 votes over Gore.
- Gore and the Democrats contest the results in Florida's Supreme Court. The justices vote four to three in Gore's favor on December 8, ordering that the more than 45,000 uncounted ballots in the 67 counties be reviewed in a hand count.
- Republicans immediately appeal to the U.S. Supreme Court, claiming the recount violates Bush's Fourteenth Amendment right to equal protection and requesting some "legal finality."
- On December 9, the Supreme Court votes 5–4 to halt the recount and hears arguments from both sides on December 11.
- Late Tuesday night, December 12, a divided Supreme Court, issuing six separate written opinions in *Bush v. Gore,* halts any recounts, finding there is no time to conduct a new recount that would be constitutional under the equal protection clause. A 5–4 ruling decides that no uniform standards exist to determine voters' intentions. Recounts also could not be completed by the December 12 "safe harbor"

deadline and before the December 18 Electoral College vote. Therefore the certified vote is upheld. This ruling gives Florida's 25 electoral votes to George W. Bush, and Al Gore graciously concedes the election on Wednesday.

Conventions

- Green Party National Nominating Convention: June 24–25, 2000, Denver, Colorado
- Republican National Convention: July 31–August 3, 2000, First Union Center, Philadelphia
- Democratic National Convention: August 14–17, 2000, Staples Center, Los Angeles
- Natural Law Party, August 31–September 2, 2000, Arlington, Virginia

Ballots/Nominees

REPUBLICANS
Presidential first ballot
- George W. Bush 2,058; 99.66%
- Alan Keyes 6; 0.29%
- John McCain 1; 0.05%

DEMOCRATS
Presidential first ballot
- Al Gore 4,328; 99.79%
- Abstaining 9; 0.21%

Vice-presidential ballot
- Joseph Lieberman, unanimously

THIRD PARTY CANDIDATES & NOMINATIONS
GREEN PARTY
Presidential ballot
- Ralph Nader (District of Columbia) 295
- Jello Biafra (California) 10
- Stephen Gaskin (Tennessee) 10
- Joel Kovel (New York) 3
- Abstain 1
- The Green Party appears on 44 of the 51 ballots nationally (43 states and D.C.)

LIBERTARIAN PARTY
Presidential ballot
- Harry Browne (Tennessee) 493
- Don Gorman (New Hampshire) 166
- Jacob Hornberger (Virginia) 120
- Barry Hess (Arizona) 53
- Others 23
- Write-ins 15
- David Hollist (California) 8

- The Libertarian Party's National Nominating Convention: Harry Browne of Tennessee for president; Art Olivier of California for vice president.
- Browne is nominated on the first ballot and Olivier receives the vice-presidential nomination on the second ballot.
- The Libertarian Party appears on 50 of 51 ballots.

CONSTITUTION PARTY
- The Constitution Party is on the ballot in 41 states.

President
- Howard Phillips (3rd nomination)
- Herb Titus
- Mathew Zupan

Vice-presidential ballot
- Curtis Frazier (Missouri)

NATURAL LAW PARTY
- John Hagelin (Iowa)
- Nat Goldhaber (California)
- Unanimous decision without a roll-call vote; party on 38 of the 51 ballots nationally

Primary Debates

REPUBLICANS
- October 22, 1999: Republican candidates debate in Durham, New Hampshire
- October 29, 1999: Republican candidates debate in Hanover, New Hampshire
- December 2, 1999: Republican candidates debate in Manchester, New Hampshire
- December 6, 1999: Republican candidates debate in Phoenix, Arizona
- December 13, 1999: Republican candidates debate in Des Moines, Iowa
- January 6, 2000: Republican candidates debate in Durham, New Hampshire
- January 7, 2000: Republican candidates debate in Columbia, South Carolina
- January 10, 2000: Republican candidates debate in Grand Rapids, Michigan
- January 15, 2000: Republican candidates debate in Johnson, Iowa
- January 26, 2000: Republican candidates debate in Manchester, New Hampshire
- February 15, 2000: Republican candidates debate in Columbia, South Carolina

DEMOCRATS
- October 28, 1999: Democratic candidates debate in Hanover, New Hampshire

- December 17, 1999: Democratic candidates debate in Nashua, New Hampshire
- December 19, 1999: Democratic candidates debate in Washington, D.C.
- January 5, 2000: Democratic candidates debate in Durham, New Hampshire
- January 8, 2000: Democratic candidates debate in Johnson, Iowa
- January 17, 2000: Democratic candidates debate in Des Moines, Iowa

Primaries/Caucus Results

REPUBLICANS
Iowa caucus
- Bush 41%
- Forbes 30%
- Keyes 14%
- Bauer 9%
- McCain 5%
- Hatch 1%

New Hampshire primary
- McCain 49%
- Bush 30% (Gary Bauer dropped out)

South Carolina primary
- George W. Bush 53%
- John McCain 42%
- Alan Keyes 5%

Super Tuesday
- Bush wins New York, Ohio, Georgia, Missouri, California, Maryland, and Maine
- McCain wins Rhode Island, Vermont, Connecticut, and Massachusetts (drops out)

DEMOCRATS
Iowa caucus
- Al Gore 63%
- Bill Bradley 35%

New Hampshire primary
- Al Gore 50%
- Bill Bradley 46%

Primaries Results (delegate totals)

REPUBLICANS
- George W. Bush 12,034,676; 62.00% (1526)
- John McCain 6,061,332; 31.23% (275)
- Alan L. Keyes 985,819; 5.08% (23)
- Steve Forbes 171,860; 0.89% (10)
- Unpledged 61,246; 0.32% (2)

- Gary L. Bauer 60,709; 0.31%
- Others 16,103; 0.08% (1)
- Orrin G. Hatch 15,958; 0.08% (0)

DEMOCRATS
- Al Gore 10,885,814; 75.37% (3,007)
- Bill Bradley 3,027,912; 20.96% (522)
- Lyndon H. LaRouche Jr. 276,075; 1.91%
- Uncommitted 207,285; 1.4%
- Other 46,102; 0.32%
- Abstentions 9

Party Platform

REPUBLICANS
- Call for "compassionate conservatism"
- Cut taxes
- Oppose gays in the military
- Pro-life on abortion
- Reform Social Security

DEMOCRATS
- Maintain fiscal discipline
- Boost education
- Reform health care
- Need campaign finance reform
- Pro-choice on abortion

Campaign Innovations

- "Push polling" by Bush forces in South Carolina before the state's primary, advancing smears in the guise of survey questions, spreads rumors that McCain's adopted Bangladeshi-born daughter was an African-American child he fathered out of wedlock.
- Out-of-state advocacy groups have big impact in Republicans' South Carolina primary.
- "Infotainment": both candidates work the talk-show and comedy-show circuit aggressively, being hosted by Oprah Winfrey, David Letterman, Regis Philbin, Rosie O'Donnell, and Jay Leno, and appearing on *Saturday Night Live*.

Campaign Tactics

REPUBLICANS
- Bush aides organize an impressive fund-raising apparatus, with experts at "bundling," grouping donations together, so he can be flush with cash.
- Try to tag Gore as part of the "Clinton-Gore" administration and tarred by scandal
- Karl Rove's careful, focused strategy is tailored to the specific needs of groups, especially Christian Evangelicals.

- Republican Leadership Council runs pro-Nader ads to split the "liberal" vote.
- Vice-presidential candidate Dick Cheney stumps nationwide.

DEMOCRATS
- Gore distances himself from President Clinton because of the Monica Lewinsky scandal and subsequent impeachment, but Gore still wants to benefit from Clinton's campaigning and fund-raising skills.
- Clinton is willing to stump for Gore, but Gore does not want the campaign and press to focus on Clinton, which may have cost Gore votes in the long run.
- Focus on Bush's gaffes and inexperience
- Gore and Lieberman take an old-fashioned trip down the Mississippi River on the evocative *Mark Twain* riverboat.
- Publicity pitch in final weeks to convince Nader supporters that Gore supports many of the same issues and has a higher likelihood of winning the election
- Vice-presidential candidate Joe Lieberman campaigns in a nationwide tour.

GREEN PARTY
- "Super-rallies": large rallies in sports arenas with a celebrity master of ceremonies

Debates
- October 3, 2000: Presidential debate in Boston, Massachusetts
- October 5, 2000: Vice-presidential debate in Danville, Kentucky
- October 11, 2000: Presidential debate in Winston-Salem, North Carolina
- October 17, 2000: Presidential debate in St. Louis, Missouri

Popular Campaign Slogans

REPUBLICANS
- "Compassionate conservatism"
- "Reformer with results"
- "Prosperity with a Purpose"
- "Reasonable Change"
- "Renewing America's Purpose Together"
- "New Kind of Republican"
- "Leave no child behind"
- "Real plans for real people"

DEMOCRATS
- "Prosperity and Progress"
- "Prosperity for America's Families"

GREEN PARTY
- "Government of, by, and for the people . . . not the monied interests"

Campaign Songs

REPUBLICANS
- "I Won't Back Down" (Tom Petty threatens to sue Bush if he does not stop using the song. Petty performs the song at Al Gore's home minutes after he concedes the election.)
- "We the People"
- "Right Now"

DEMOCRATS
- "You Ain't Seen Nothin' Yet"
- "Let the Day Begin"

Influential Campaign Appeals or Ads

- Bush promises to restore "honor and dignity" to the presidency and White House
- Bush promotes bipartisanship
- Gore treats Bush as gaffe-prone, dumb, inexperienced, and incompetent

Campaign Finance

- Bush: $67,560,000 (in current dollars: $79,839,700)
- Gore: $67,560,000 (in current dollars: $79,839,700)

Defining Quotations

- "This boy, this son of ours, is not going to let you down." *George H. W. Bush campaigning for his son in New Hampshire, January 29, 2000*
- "He's going to walk right into our punch in South Carolina." *Bush campaign aide after New Hampshire, speaking about John McCain, February 1, 2000*
- "If he's a reformer, I'm an astronaut." *John McCain talking about George W. Bush on the campaign trail in Michigan, February 20, 2000*
- "People just don't pay attention." *Representative Patrick Kennedy complaining of public apathy, quoted in the* Boston Globe, *July 23, 2000*
- "Our current president embodied the potential of a generation—so many talents, so much charm, such great skill. But in the end, to what end? So much promise to no great purpose." *George W. Bush, address accepting the presidential nomination at the Republican National Convention in Philadelphia, August 3, 2000*
- "If Al Gore has differences with the president, he ought to say loud and clear what they are. I don't

think President Clinton is an issue as we go forward. There's no question the president embarrassed the nation. Everybody knows that. . . . Americans want to be assured that the next administration will bring honor and dignity to the White House. Are they going to hold Al Gore responsible for missed opportunities? I mean, either you're part of an administration or you're not part of an administration is how I view it. I think he needs to stand up and say if he thought the president were wrong on policy and issues, he ought to say where." *George W. Bush, Associated Press interview, August 11, 2000*

- "Not so long ago, a balanced budget seemed impossible. Now our budget surpluses make it possible to give a full range of targeted tax cuts to working families. . . . But let me say it plainly: I will not go along with a huge tax cut for the wealthy at the expense of everyone else and wreck our good economy in the process." *Al Gore, address accepting the presidential nomination at the Democratic National Convention in Los Angeles, August 17, 2000*
- "A lot of folks don't think I can string a sentence together. Expectations were so low all I had to do was say, 'Hi, I'm George W. Bush.'" *Bush talking about the first debate, October 3, 2000*
- "The sigh kept Gore from winning the debate." *Margaret Carlson of CNN and* Time *after the first debate, October 3, 2000*
- "I don't think our troops ought to be used for what's called nation-building." *George W. Bush, second presidential debate, October 11, 2000*
- "If we say somebody's carried the state, you can take that to the bank. Book it." *Dan Rather of CBS on election night, November 2, 2000*
- "Sip it, savor it, cup it, Photostat it, underline it in red, press it in a book, put it in an album, hang it on the wall: George W. Bush is the next President of the United States." *Dan Rather of CBS on election night, November 2, 2000, hours before the 36-day deadlock begins*
- "Circumstances have changed." *Al Gore to George W. Bush, retracting his concession on election night*
- "One thing, however, is certain. Although we may never know with complete certainty the identity of the winner of this year's Presidential election, the identity of the loser is perfectly clear. It is the Nation's confidence in the judge as an impartial guardian of the rule of law." *Justice John Paul Stevens' stinging dissent in* Bush v. Gore, *December 12, 2000*
- "I know America wants reconciliation and unity. I know Americans want progress. And we must seize this moment and deliver. Together, guided by a spirit of common sense, common courtesy and common goals, we can unite and inspire the American citizens." *George W. Bush, victory speech, December 13, 2000*

Lasting Legacy of Campaign

- First time the Supreme Court decides an election
- Closest election since 1876
- Third time since 1824, along with 1876 and 1888, that the losing candidate won the popular vote and the new president won only by virtue of the electoral vote
- Lingering bad feelings among Democrats, who claim that Bush and the Republicans "stole" the election
- Fears that the American system itself is flawed—even as most Americans accept the decision in a mark of constitutional conservatism

Election of 2000

No president was elected on Election Day 2000. The day appointed, Tuesday, November 7, turned out to be the beginning of a very different kind of affirmation of American democracy. For 36 days a political struggle between the campaigns of Vice President Al Gore and Texas governor George W. Bush gripped national attention, the outcome swaying in dramatic rhythm, one way, then the other. Through it all, the citizenry remained calm, even developing something of a studious interest in the exotic civics lesson that played out in the struggle for that priceless reward of American political life, the White House.

That the popular vote did not determine the victor came as a general shock, because almost always it had in American history. In the days after the election, Americans would be instructed in the rules of the Electoral College, an arcane eighteenth-century device that apportioned electoral votes on the basis of the size of a state's population. For most states, including Florida, a candidate won all electoral votes no matter how tiny his successful margin in the popular vote. With Florida's 25 electoral votes temporarily in suspension because of raging arguments over the proper counting of the popular vote, neither George W. Bush nor Al Gore had won the

270 electoral votes required for election. Simply put, who-ever won Florida's electoral votes won the presidency.

On December 12, 2000, for the first time in American history, the U.S. Supreme Court, in a 5–4 decision, chose the president of the United States. While the ascent of George W. Bush provoked as much opposition as appro-bation, it did reflect the election results. Statistically, the American electorate had produced a tie.

Immediately after the Supreme Court ruled, the Republicans established a beachhead in Washing-ton, commanded by Vice President-elect Dick Cheney. Already dubbed the *consigliere* of the fledgling admin-istration, Cheney conveyed a slow ease and remarkable familiarity with issues and the politicians attached to them. His longevity in Washington power circles went back to the Ford administration and continued through

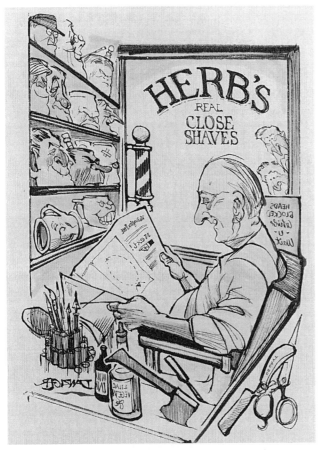

This Jeff Danziger caricature shows the legendary political car-toonist Herbert Block, known as "Herblock," sitting in a chair in his barbershop, looking at a spread for the *Washington Post* edito-rial page with space designated for his next cartoon. He appears to be chuckling to himself as he plans how to fill the space. Al Gore and George W. Bush anxiously peer in through the shop window. On the shelves before Herblock are heads of previous presidential "customers" from past campaigns, including FDR, Reagan, Nixon, and Carter. *(Jeff Danziger, New York Times Syndicate)*

a well-received stint as the first President Bush's secre-tary of defense, particularly during the Gulf War. Subse-quently, as a Texas oil and gas executive, he had cemented a relationship with the semi-obscured power of major corporate interests, for whom recapture of the White House promised so much. Gray, balding and rotund, Cheney always seemed significantly "older," particularly when compared to George W. Bush, even though they were separated by just five years. Cheney captured the media's attention through December as the unusual inau-guration approached.

Inauguration Day has often presented Americans with a stirring exhibition of symbolic pomp. The events in Washington on January 20, 2001, particularly inter-esting for the cast of characters assembled on the west face of the Capitol, also achieved historical distinction. Certainly the scene defied probability. Bush the elder defeated by Clinton succeeded by Bush the younger. John Adams, the only other president whose son served in the White House, had to wait a quarter-century after losing his reelection bid before John Quincy Adams became president in 1825. The Bushes had the exquisite pleasure of witnessing the dismissal from the national stage of the man whom they had fervently despised for years.

There stood the new president, taking his oath from Chief Justice William Rehnquist, architect of the Court's conservative majority. Bush spoke briefly and well, the new presidency began, and the new president finally required some definition. The questions about his qualifications for office accurately reflected a man long underestimated.

Elected Texas governor in a stunning upset over incumbent Democrat Ann Richards in November 1994, Bush claimed national potential through pedigree as well as by electoral success. In the Texas State House, he concentrated on a limited number of issues. Faced with a weak gubernatorial system that invests authority in the legislature, Bush gained stature through his charm and by willingness to compromise with the agenda of the entrenched bipartisan coalition that permanently runs the Lone Star State. He did push forward major reforms in education while broadening the traditional Republi-can base through particular attention to Hispanic con-cerns. Casually using serviceable Spanish, Bush conveyed empathy toward the aspirations of Texas Latinos, picking up support as he developed a political identification dis-tinct from his roots in the Eastern establishment.

By the summer of 1997, Governor Bush had become an occasional face at the incessant "cattle calls" of presiden-tial hopefuls. At the Midwest GOP Leadership Confer-ence in Indianapolis in July, he appeared in a crowd that included Speaker of the House Newt Gingrich, former vice president Dan Quayle, Oklahoma representative J.

C. Watts, Lamar Alexander, Alan Keyes, and Tennessee senator Fred Thompson.

Shunning flamboyance, Bush seemed to content himself with pious generalities in public and informal socializing with political professionals at a limited and carefully selected number of appearances outside Texas. At the same time, and almost imperceptibly, he ingratiated himself with a rising generation of substantial national figures. Meanwhile, in Washington, the existing GOP power base set about to destroy itself.

Into the mid-1990s, Republican power rested with Gingrich. Architect of the party's historic seizure of Congress in 1994, the magnetic and cocky Gingrich made himself into a media celebrity as well as the undisputed repository of congressional authority. After four decades in the minority, the Republicans had returned to power promising to alter the very nature of American politics. Gingrich, charismatic and willful, led this "revolution" to victory in the 1994 midterm election, picking up an astonishing 52 seats in the House.

Newt Gingrich arrived at the pinnacle of political celebrity armed with audacity. In the 1980s, he delighted in uncompromising attacks on both parties from the back benches of the House, where he represented a suburban Atlanta district. Gingrich regularly attacked the moderation of President George H. W. Bush's policies, including criticizing the 1992 election campaign. The pugnacious Georgian swept into power in the historic 1994 by-elections at the head of a small army of right-wing Republican representatives for whom Gingrich was both leader and guru. Named "Man of the Year" in 1995 by *Time*, Gingrich stood astride American politics. It was during this period that President Clinton told a national press conference that he, the president of the United States, still remained relevant. Pundits began referring to Gingrich as the American Prime Minister.

Gingrich's undoing came at the hands of Clinton, the despised foe of virtually all Republicans. In the protracted struggle over spending, balancing the budget, paying the national debt, and protecting the sacred entitlements of Social Security and Medicare, the Republicans seemed to hold the popular advantage in the scuffles preceding the 1996 presidential election. In November 1995, the GOP engaged in high-stakes budget negotiations that produced a deadlock so serious that the U.S. government for all intents and purposes shut down for six days. Clinton blamed Republican congressional leaders Gingrich and Dole. It stuck.

In the midst of the great showdown, Gingrich told reporters that his decision to fight so strongly against the president arose through an entirely unrelated event. A large official delegation of prominent Americans had flown to the funeral of assassinated Israeli prime minis-

ter Yitzhak Rabin, stopping over in Israel for a matter of hours before heading back home. On the trip, the president had ignored him, the speaker reported. He had been remanded to a back seat and upon return to Washington forced to deplane from a rear door. "This is petty. I'm going to say up front: It's petty . . . but I think it's human," Gingrich said while what some reporters described as "pouting." The New York *Daily News* ran a front-page cartoon of "Baby Newt" in a diaper throwing a tantrum. He never fully recovered. The party would need new leadership.

Early in 1998, syndicated conservative columnist Robert Novak cited a "secret 2000 presidential 'straw vote' of Republican state chairmen" that showed overwhelming support for Governor Bush, "with nobody else a close second." Republican media pundit Mary Matalin, veteran of the 1988 and 1992 campaigns of the elder Bush, told the Houston *Chronicle* simply that "He's going to be the nominee. . . . He's going to be the next President of these United States."

Month after month, Bush held off his suitors and steadily reprised standard themes, always emphasizing his preoccupation with his own reelection in November. Not always adroitly but usually effectively, he withstood periodic negative groundswells, particularly against the death penalty, the use of which propelled Texas into the undesired status of world leader in state-sanctioned capital punishment. Early in 1998, Bush came under great pressure to reprieve a killer-turned-jailhouse-preacher named Karla Faye Tucker. Even fundamentalist Christian conservatives admired her prison rehabilitation—she actually married a prison chaplain after becoming born again. With apparently little reflection, Bush ordered the execution, explaining blandly that he had to enforce all state laws.

In November 1998, Bush achieved reelection as governor in an impressive landslide. On the same day, competing forces in national Republican politics destroyed themselves. The 1998 congressional elections proved to be a disaster for Gingrich and House Republican authority. Against prevailing odds, and in dizzying order, the Democrats actually gained seats, and the once-mighty Gingrich resigned as Speaker and left Congress altogether. Instantly, the leverage of Republican authority moved out of Washington. Into the void advanced a dozen prospective presidential nominees, none as well situated as the governor of Texas. Perhaps more than the public understood, the national command of the GOP passed in one shocking election from Newt Gingrich to George W. Bush.

Even after the Speaker's noisy exit from the national political stage, he left behind as his most ardent follow-

(continues on page 1558)

☆   ☆   ☆

2000 ELECTION CHRONOLOGY

1996
April 29, 1996: Vice President Al Gore makes a fund-raising visit to the Hsi Lai Buddhist temple in California, despite its tax-exempt religious status. The normally penurious nuns show a remarkable ability to write thousand-dollar checks.

1997
March 3, 1997: In a press conference defending his phone calls from the White House soliciting Democratic campaign contributions during the 1996 campaign, Vice President Gore—long known as a model of rectitude, now tagged as Clinton's "solicitor-in-chief"—repeats the phrase "There is no controlling legal authority that says this was in violation of law" seven times one way or another.

1998
November 3, 1998: Republicans are shocked that the Democrats gain five seats in the House of Representatives during the midterm elections—widely interpreted as a message from voters to stop scandal-mongering and returning to governing. Speaker of the House Newt Gingrich resigns in response. A rare bright spot for the Republicans that day is Texas governor George W. Bush's reelection landslide.

December 19, 1998: The House of Representatives impeaches President Bill Clinton on perjury and obstruction of justice charges related to his relationship with former White House intern Monica Lewinsky. Clinton vows to fight the charges and remain in office.

1999
February 12, 1999: The Senate acquits Clinton.

June 12, 1999: On his first campaign trip to Iowa, Governor Bush proclaims: "I am running for president; there's no turning back." At the time he faces an extremely crowded field that includes former cabinet secretaries Lamar Alexander and Elizabeth Dole, along with senators John Ashcroft and Bob Smith, all of whom will soon drop out.

September 27, 1999: Former Vice President Dan Quayle drops out of the Republican race, saying he cannot compete with George W. Bush's name recognition and fund-raising ability.

December 13, 1999: The Republican candidates gather in Des Moines, Iowa, for the first debate with all of them present. The six are former Reagan administration official Gary Bauer, Texas governor George W. Bush, publisher Steve Forbes, Utah senator Orrin Hatch, former ambassador Alan Keyes, and Arizona senator John McCain,

December 30, 1999: The Bush campaign announces it raised a record $67 million, proof of how George W. Bush, advocating a "compassionate conservatism," has dominated the "invisible primary," the fund-raising and networking with supporters, politicians, and reporters, before any voting in primaries or caucuses.

2000
January 24, 2000: Bush defeats Forbes 41 percent to 30 percent in the Republican Iowa caucus. On the Democratic side, Vice President Al Gore wins decisively over former New Jersey senator Bill Bradley, 63 percent to 35 percent.

February 1, 2000: Despite losing to Gore 50.4 percent to 46.3 percent in the Democratic New Hampshire primary, Bradley stirs media interest with his strong second-place showing. McCain's charming, media-friendly "Straight Talk Express" powers him to a resounding 49-to-30.2-percent victory over Bush.

February 19, 2000: After a vicious campaign marked by "push polls" spreading racial smears against McCain in the guise of survey questions, Bush wins South Carolina's "First in the South" primary over McCain by a margin of 53 percent to 42 percent.

February 22, 2000: With Bradley enjoying adoring press coverage, he and Gore debate each other aggressively at Harlem's Apollo Theatre.

March 7, 2000: "Titanic Tuesday" (not just "Super Tuesday") essentially decides both races, with Gore winning all 11 Democratic primaries and

Bush winning 7 out of 11 Republican primaries. Gore earns nearly three-quarters of the votes cast that day, and Bush wins 56.9 percent of the votes.

April 11, 2000: Bush seeks to bolster his image as a centrist "compassionate conservative" by unveiling a package of tax credits designed to help lower-income Americans purchase health insurance and homes.

July 25, 2000: Bush announces that former defense secretary Richard Cheney, head of his vice presidential search committee, will be his candidate for vice president. Bush praises Cheney's "great integrity, sound judgment and experience."

July 31–August 3, 2000: Philadelphia hosts the Republican National Convention, which nominates George W. Bush of Texas for president and Richard Cheney of Wyoming, although quite recently of Texas, for vice president on the first ballot.

August 3, 2000: Bush delivers a surprisingly effective acceptance address, mocking Democrats with the chant: "This administration had its chance. They have not led. We will."

August 7, 2000: Seeking to distance himself from the Clinton scandals, Gore selects as a running mate Connecticut senator Joseph Lieberman, who criticized Clinton's affair with Lewinsky. Lieberman will become the first Jew on a major party ticket.

August 14, 2000: The Democratic National Convention begins in Los Angeles. The Democrats will nominate Al Gore of Tennessee for president and Connecticut senator Joseph Lieberman for vice president. The first night of the convention Clinton steals the show with "The Walk," as a hand-held camera follows him through the Staples Center's backstage before he saunters onstage to wild applause.

August 17, 2000: In his acceptance speech, Gore seeks to distance himself from Clinton, proclaiming: "I stand here tonight as my own man and I want you to know me for who I truly am." Most dramatically, before the speech, Gore gives his wife Tipper a passionate, three-second kiss to disprove caricatures of him as robotic. The conven-

tion sends Gore into the general campaign with a lead over Bush.

September 4, 2000: At a Labor Day event in Naperville, Illinois, an open microphone captures Bush muttering to Cheney: "There's Adam Clymer—major league asshole—from the *New York Times*." Cheney's response, "Oh, yeah, big time," earns him the nickname "Big Time," while Bush's frank admission, "I regret people heard the comments," contains the damage.

September 11, 2000: Seeking a warmer image, Gore appears on Oprah Winfrey's talk show— a stretch for Oprah herself, who usually has avoided politicians thus far. Addressing an audience that averages 22 million viewers a week, three-fourths of them women, Gore comes across, the *New York Times* noted, "as a sensitive and devoted family man." Bush soon appears on Oprah, and both candidates also appear on David Letterman's talk show as well as many others.

October 3, 2000: At the first presidential debate in Boston, Bush holds his own, defying expectations that Gore will crush him. In fact, Gore's exasperated sighs and winces as Bush speaks make Gore look aggressive and unpresidential.

October 5, 2000: Cheney and Lieberman stage a low-key and civil vice-presidential debate in Danville, Kentucky.

October 11, 2000: At the second presidential debate in Winston-Salem, North Carolina, Bush criticizes Clinton-era military campaigns such as those in Somalia and the Balkans, saying, "I don't think our troops ought to be used for what's called nation-building."

October 17, 2000: In the third and final presidential debate, Gore, trailing slightly in the polls, continues in his recent left-of-center, populist bent, pledging to "fight for the middle-class families and working men and women who are sick and tired of having their parents and grandparents pay higher prices for prescription drugs than anybody else." The debates continue to attract huge audiences because the race is so tight, but deliver no knockout blows. Still, Bush inches ahead of Gore in most polls during October.

(continues)

2000 ELECTION CHRONOLOGY (continued)

November 2, 2000: Leaked documents reveal that Bush had been arrested for drunk driving in 1976 in Kennebunkport, Maine. Bush acknowledges he was arrested and paid the fine—a decade before swearing off alcohol. Bush's chief political adviser, Karl Rove, later concludes that the news disillusioned millions of evangelical voters from voting for Bush on Election Day.

November 5, 2000: Both candidates appear with taped segments on *Saturday Night Live*'s "Presidential Bash 2000," acknowledging just how many Americans, especially younger citizens, are relying on comedy shows for news. In Bush's skit, he says he is "amvibalent" toward an "offensible" program. Gore mocks his own behavior during the first debate, rolling his eyes and sighing melodramatically.

November 7, 2000: On election night, Gore leads in the popular vote by half a million, but the election hinges on the close result in Florida, with its 25 electoral votes. The only certainty about Florida is that the result is close enough to trigger an automatic statewide machine recount, which will show Bush 327 votes ahead of Gore. The left-wing Green Party candidate Ralph Nader receives nearly 100,000 votes in Florida.

November 8, 2000: As the Florida count shifts in Bush's favor, Gore concedes by phone. When the vote narrows again, Gore retracts his concession at 4:05 a.m., noting that "circumstances have changed."

November 8, 2000: Democratic officials charge that the "butterfly" ballot design in use in Palm Beach County caused many Jewish senior citizens who wanted to vote for Gore to vote mistakenly for Reform Party candidate Pat Buchanan instead. Democrats begin to demand hand

recounts in this and other counties in which they identified voting irregularities.

November 13, 2000: As some Democratically controlled counties continue the lengthy process of hand recounts, Florida secretary of state Katherine Harris, a Bush supporter, refuses to extend the deadline for vote certification beyond November 14. The Florida Supreme Court later orders the deadline extended to November 26.

November 26, 2000: Amid continued recounts and demonstrations, Katherine Harris and the state canvassing board certify Bush the winner of Florida's electoral votes, by 537 votes over Gore.

December 8, 2000: The Florida Supreme Court reverses Harris's decision, ordering that the more than 70,000 uncounted ballots in Florida's 67 counties be reviewed in a hand count.

December 9, 2000: The U.S. Supreme Court stays the Florida recount ruling while it considers an appeal by Republicans.

December 12, 2000: By a 5-to-4 margin, the Supreme Court halts the recount, on grounds that no uniform standards exist to determine voters' intentions. The earlier certified results are therefore upheld, effectively making Bush the president-elect.

December 18, 2000: Florida electors meet in Tallahassee to cast their 25 electoral votes for Bush, as electors across the country meet in their respective state capitals. Bush wins the election, 271 electoral votes to 266. This marks only the second time since 1824 that the candidate with the highest number of popular votes on Election Day does not win the election.

2001
January 6, 2001: A joint session of Congress assembles to count the electoral votes.

(continued from page 1555)

ers in the House a strong-willed band of partisans who were determined to impeach President Clinton, even against the clear preferences of the large majority of the American electorate. Shortly before the November elec-

tions, Special Prosecutor Kenneth Starr released his long-anticipated report, which would become the basis for the Republican House to issue articles of impeachment against the president. The Starr document, quickly reproduced in book form, widely excerpted in newspapers and available on the Internet, emphasized lurid descriptions of Clinton's sexual liaison with Monica Lewinsky. After an initial media frenzy that threatened to destroy the president, a backlash soon suggested the popular aversion to political overkill.

Yet through the holiday season and into January 1999, the House Republican leadership pushed on, even after lack of sufficient support in the Senate foreshadowed defeat. Republican pollster Frank Luntz termed the campaign against the president "the stupidest single political decision I know of." As a consequence, as Clinton held onto the White House through all the political assaults, the once-mighty Republican House majority lost its grip on national power. The battle to succeed Bill Clinton would feature a Republican attitude that all Washington insiders were a problem to be confronted. No candidate reiterated this theme more frequently than the triumphantly reelected governor of Texas.

The size of Bush's reelection added to his political resume in a number of useful ways. In capturing nearly 7 of every 10 votes, he won two-thirds of the women's vote, almost 50 percent of Hispanics, and about a third of Democrats. He carried the rest of the statewide GOP ticket into office with him. Assessments of the victory emphasized Bush's successful commitment to education as measured by the establishment of statewide standards, marked increases in test scores, and funding of bilingual education. By contrast, his own party in Washington had until recently called for the abolition of the Department of Education and blocked President Clinton's national public school construction fund. Shortly after Election Day, the prominent educational scholar Diane Ravitch noted, "Bush is so far ahead of the national party that the people in Washington can't even see how behind they are."

By the time that Bush formally announced his candidacy for the presidency in June 1999, a gaggle of alternative Republican candidates still filled the political stage. Lamar Alexander, former governor of Tennessee and secretary of education under President George H. W. Bush, had good name recognition from earlier runs, sufficient financial backing, and organizational support in early primary states, particularly Iowa. Next in line came the multimillionaire Steve Forbes, an indefatigable campaigner who by 1998 had moved himself distinctly to the right wing of the party. Press accounts usually mentioned former vice president Dan Quayle, and such other supplicants of the religious right as Gary Bauer, a well-known religious conservative, senators John Ashcroft of Missouri, and Bob Smith of New Hampshire, as well as Alan Keyes, a flamboyant African-American conservative whose riveting oratory always attracted attention. Occasionally, veteran Republican fixture Jack Kemp

appeared, and political mention included Representative John Kasich of Ohio, Elizabeth Dole, governors John Engler of Michigan, Tommy Thompson of Wisconsin, and Pete Wilson of California. Most of them refused to leave without a fight.

Lamar Alexander derided Bush's notion of "compassionate conservatism" as "weasel words . . . cleverly and deliberately put together to confuse people by meaning nothing." Quayle called the term "silly and insulting." Forbes declared that "sneakymouthed rhetoric and poll-tested clichés are no substitute for a muscular, substantive agenda." Bauer contented himself by ridiculing former President Bush's "kinder and gentler" approach as political disaster. The negative verbiage notwithstanding, all references were aimed at an obvious front-runner sated with cash. By June 1999 he had $39 million, by September $50 million. Republican power brokers had clearly made their choice: the self-styled "compassionate conservative."

Bush continued raising funds at a record pace. He would raise $96.3 million for the primary campaign alone from more 300,000 individual donors representing all 50 states. Crucial help came from more than 246 "pioneers," who raised $100,000 for Bush by "bundling," collecting the federally mandated limit of $1,000 from at least 100 friends. Eventually, at least 104 "pioneers" would receive Bush administration appointments, including 23 ambassadorships and 3 cabinet posts.

By contrast, Bush's general election rival, Al Gore, would accept federal funds and restrictions, carefully husbanding the $40.5 million allocated to him for the primaries. For the general election, each would accept $67.6 million from the taxpayers, although the national party committees, the local party committees, independent advocacy groups, and particular interest groups would spend millions more. Ultimately, the system was flooded with so much "soft money"—contributions to the political parties or other organizations and not to the more closely regulated campaigns—that the Bipartisan Campaign Reform Act, also known as the McCain-Feingold Act, would prohibit unregulated contributions to national party committees beginning in 2002.

Convinced of the inevitability of Bush's candidacy even before he formally announced, the GOP establishment in Washington capitulated. In May on Capitol Hill, House Speaker J. Dennis Hastert, Majority Leader Dick Armey, Conference Chairman J. C. Watts, and Tom DeLay, the redoubtable House Republican whip, met with Karl Rove and Karen Hughes, who ran the Texas governor's campaign. "These discussions," Ms. Hughes remarked, "are about the agenda that would emerge from the 2000 presidential campaign should Governor Bush be elected President."

"I am running for President of the United States; there's no turning back and I intend to be the next President of the United States," Bush proclaimed on June 12, 1999, as he swept across the country from Texas through Iowa and on to Massachusetts and New Hampshire. Along the way, he unveiled a stock campaign speech that would serve him for the next 17 months. He pledged to cut taxes, reduce welfare, fight crime, improve schools, and promote personal responsibility—everything to be done compassionately and conservatively. When the energetic new candidate also spent a day with his famous parents at the ancestral Bush home in Kennebunkport on the Maine coast, the occasion produced saturation media coverage of an array of comfortable images with George and Barbara Bush. Comparisons between father and son were inevitable.

The younger man routinely referred to himself as George W., or simply "W," or "Dubya," in Texas patois. Friendly observers were impressed with his energy and persistence, as well as a quick if acerbic wit that seemed designed to deflate complexity. More significantly, his life had been largely determined by the advantages accruing to a child of wealth and power. Like the Kennedys, a comparison that the Bushes detested, the children had access to elite educational institutions, business opportunities, and political feasibility. Uniquely, though, his degrees from Yale and Harvard appeared to make George W. uncomfortable, as somehow diminishing Texas authenticity.

The essence of the family's story over the past half-century was the move from the New England patrician class to the hard-knuckle cultural bramble of Texas. The former president was the family pioneer in the move into the havoc of the west Texas oil patch, and ever more he would insist on asserting Texan accreditation, even claiming a Houston hotel as official "home address" during his presidency. Yet the cultural transfusion was never complete with the father, who remained more comfortably associated with the style of Yale and elite clubs, old money, and the ancestral home on the Maine seacoast.

On the other hand, there was no ambiguity in George W. Bush's Texas identity. Around the time of his inauguration, lavish stories on the subject of the Bush ranch appeared in newspapers across the country. Vaguely near Waco but isolated even from Crawford, the nearest village, the ranch sat on pristine if raw countryside. The house had neither cable television nor satellite dish. The new president delighted in escorting visitors across the vast expanse of 1,600 acres, describing flora and fauna with impressive detail. The ranch was strictly blue jeans and Stetson, pickup trucks and barbecues. "This is home," he often declared.

By the summer of 1999, the younger George Bush, despite his light resume and scant national standing, commanded the Republican battle for the White House. Although the GOP field remained large, the nomination was his to lose. On the Democratic side, Governor Bush's likely opponent had also outdistanced his competition. Yet the contrast in the two men could hardly have been greater. The political force represented by Albert Gore Jr. seemed to make the campaign and election routine precursors to the inauguration of President Gore: literally born into political power, mentored by his father and namesake, a senator from Tennessee, early civil rights advocate, populist, Vietnam War objector, and an imperious man, ambitious for himself and his boy.

Al Gore's birth on March 31, 1948, was noted on page one of the Nashville *Tennessean* at the senator's insistence. The Gores kept a suite in the Fairfax Hotel along Washington's elegant Embassy Row. For as long as Congress stayed in session each year, young Al Gore lived in the odd confines of a big city hotel. In Washington he attended the exclusive St. Albans School. For the rest of the year, he lived an opposite life as a country boy on the family farm near Carthage, Tennessee. Accounts of the young Al Gore's socializing reveal a careful, highly disciplined boy and young man in thrall to the giant shadow cast by his father.

Ivy League colleges in the mid-1960s forced many young men to confront unusual issues in the seminar room, to make difficult moral choices, to dispute the dark side of capitalism and the obvious anomalies of "the system," and to face conflict between legitimate self-interest and idealism. The campus-based antiwar movement burgeoned, ranging from serious radicals of all ages to an accompanying army of young people whose cultural movement embraced untraditional forms of music, dress and behavior.

At Yale, George W. Bush managed to remain oblivious to this famous historical moment, and stayed within the venerable cocoon of Skull and Bones, the elite secret society. Al Gore's days at Harvard were not completely dissimilar, although Bush took pride in anti-intellectualism and Gore remained a serious student.

As a political traditionalist, Gore eschewed the radicalism that attracted some of his friends. With his election as chairman of the Freshman Council in the fall of 1965, he dutifully dealt with issues of football tickets and the quality of cafeteria meatloaf, derided at every turn by his more hip suite mates. A football player from Texas then known as Tom Jones rode Gore hard for his "high school" preoccupations. Gore soon dropped campus politics entirely, and would always remain close to Tommy Lee Jones.

Gore's Harvard years are temptingly simple to summarize. Thrown into a competitive zoo of putatively

George W. Bush *(Eric Draper/U.S. Defense Department)*

brilliant scholars and athletes, he competed. He landed in an end-of-the-bench seat on the freshman basketball team. But he played some. In select seminars, he sought to balance the disturbing formulae of Marx and Freud with the practical politics and institutions of his famous father. The senator and his son headed for the Democratic National Convention in Chicago in the late summer of 1968, seeking to represent principled dissent against the mushrooming debacle in Vietnam.

Father and son remained inside the cavernous meeting hall as outside American radicalism sought to take the streets. Al helped the senator prepare a rousing antiwar speech, a stance the elder Gore had championed since the first major American troop buildup in 1965. The American political process would fail to come to terms with the debacle of Vietnam, leaving a poisonous legacy. Al Gore, son of an antiwar dove whose position would soon cost him his Senate seat, decided to enlist.

In the summer of 1969, Gore left Harvard with an honors degree and a determination to join the U.S. Army. Many others of his celebrated generation proceeded in exactly opposite directions, wrangling graduate student exemptions or whatever expedient meant avoiding a military tour in Vietnam. The actual nature of his military service during the few months Gore spent in Vietnam is less interesting than the mere act of his being there. Assigned to a public affairs post, he either remained office-bound or, from time to time, moved circumspectly around the country. His encounters with broken and angry front-line troops were nonetheless quite real.

Returning home, now 23 and married, Gore eschewed politics, studying religion and law and working as a reporter for the *Tennessean*. He returned to Washington as a congressman from Tennessee in 1977, moved to the Senate in 1985, mounted a tepid bid for the presidency in 1988, and watched for his main chance.

The 1991 Cleveland national convention of the centrist Democratic Leadership Council provided a casting call for "moderate" Democratic hopefuls for the wide-open 1992 nomination. Both Gore and Clinton addressed this arena full of political pros. The Arkansas governor set aside prepared remarks and spoke extemporaneously, in full passion policy-wonk-with-charm mode. He galvanized the crowd. Gore, later, put them to sleep.

The ultimate production of the unlikely Clinton–Gore ticket of 1992 depended on a series of events and careful calculation by both parties. The men had no personal relationship. Oddly, even after 15 years as prominent politicians, Gore and Clinton scarcely knew each other. Similarities in age and regional political culture—even their common centrist policies—seemed diminished by differences in character and experience. During the run-up to the 1992 race, in a story recorded by *Washington Post* journalists, Gore, asked about Clinton by a fellow Tennessee Vietnam vet, replied, "He's the kind of guy we would have beat the [expletive] out of."

Gore's foreign policy credentials, including Vietnam service and support for the Gulf War, would supposedly counterbalance deficiencies in the biography of Clinton's background, which featured antiwar activism, graduate school deferment to study in England, and duplicitous relations with his draft board.

Governor Clinton's advisers considered Gore's liabilities as well. A ticket of two middle-aged representatives of adjoining small Southern states seemed bizarre to traditional political thinkers. The Tennessean also bore the image of dullness and often seemed perfectly wooden on the stump. At the same time, Gore was regarded in Washington as exceedingly ambitious, which the exceedingly ambitious Clintonites carefully noted. Ultimately, the harsh political wisdom of Machiavelli would prevail, and the men would find each other.

Gore's political presence benefited from a portfolio of responsibilities that exceeded any of his vice-presidential predecessors. His initial deal with Clinton included effective control of all aspects relating to the environment, but also policy formulation associated with the burgeoning Internet, bureaucratic efficiency through "reinventing government," and space and disarmament issues. Gore mastered the prolix detail on all issues as the means to serving a president whose enthusiasms and scattershot pragmatism constituted simply a different life force than that of the precise Gore. Clinton the impressionist, Gore the programmer. Deferential in the public eye, the vice president sought in private to be useful. Clinton looked boldly at daunting crises, including those of his own making. Gore fought self-doubt. At the same time, observers noted, Gore, having made a decision, showed resilience if not stubbornness in holding to carefully calculated positions. Clinton remained at the ready for maneuver and deal.

Two celebrated episodes of the Clinton years shadowed Gore's campaign for the presidency. One involved fundraising, that is, the thinly disguised habit of both political parties of soliciting huge and largely unregulated "contributions" from the wealthiest sectors of America, individuals and corporate titans most of whom pursued self-interest through the vast brokerage of government power.

Through the White House years, on regular occasions a "call list" appeared on Gore's desk, identifying people prominent in business and the arts. Within limits provided by his lawyers, Gore made the calls, regardless of the seemingly obvious implications of unseemliness. By so doing, of course, he followed an established pattern followed by virtually all Washington politicians. As the presumptive rising president, however, Gore had higher visibility.

In March 1997, the legendary Bob Woodward of the *Washington Post* reported on Gore's role as the Democrats' "solicitor-in-chief." Stung, Gore defended himself in a press conference he called to protest his innocence. Throughout this degrading money-grubbing process, Gore had attempted to insulate himself through legal opinion. He took one of his lawyer's phrases into the White House briefing room. Seven times during reporters' questioning, the vice president robotically intoned that "there is no controlling legal authority" on the subject at hand. The phrase would stick.

Much more difficult for Gore was the insoluble dilemma produced by the Lewinsky sex scandal. The president lied to the vice president, just as he did to his own family and the country at large. Yet Gore's linkage with Clinton compelled him to endure the relentless scandal that consumed America throughout 1998, culminating in the tawdry impeachment proceedings. Clinton, impeached and disgraced, survived with Gore at his side, most notably at a publicly televised "victory" rally at which Gore called Clinton a "great president." This association would also come into play in 2000, however obviously Gore sought to create space from the ubiqui-

tous Clinton. Most tellingly, on December 5, 1998, his ascendant forebear, "Senator Senior," died. Gore returned to Tennessee for the mournful occasion as Washington broiled in impeachment fury.

Gore survived all, of course, and moved to the head of the pack chasing the Democratic nomination. By the middle of 1999, as Bush seemed to overwhelm his Republican competitors with campaign funds, Gore jousted with the formidable former New Jersey senator Bill Bradley. This configuration defied political punditry. Gore, seven years the vice president in an administration presiding over an unprecedented bull market, should have benefited richly from peace and prosperity. Instead, going into the primary season, Bradley had raised enough money to stay in the game and even led polls in New York and California, significant Democratic redoubts.

The Republican race should have been a free-for-all. Yet even before New Hampshire, Bush's superbly oiled machine had chased away Kasich, Alexander, and Bob Smith. In October, Elizabeth Dole, running second in GOP polls—albeit at great distance—left the race. She had raised a mere $5 million at a time when Governor Bush's war chest contained $57 million. As Mrs. Dole left the race, Arizona Senator John McCain announced his candidacy. Most observers downplayed the significance of the arrival of the combative former POW, so unpopular with the GOP establishment because of unsparing opposition to unrestricted political soft money. He seemed just another recruit in the lost legion of Republicans in New Hampshire. None of them—McCain, Steve Forbes, Gary Bauer, Sen. Orrin Hatch, and Alan Keyes—had yet hit double digits in national polls, while Bush's numbers reached 53 percent, and rising.

In a dramatic assertion of confidence, Bush blindsided the Republican House leadership and its announced intention to defer tax relief for moderate wage earners. To the stupefaction of Speaker Hastert and two Texas powerhouses, Majority Leader Armey and Whip DeLay, Bush decried Republican efforts to "balance their budget on the backs of the poor."

A clamor arose in the media, Bush held his ground, and his campaign sailed on. Republican members of Congress were also out of political options. The only other tenable candidate, Senator McCain, absolutely terrified powerful GOP interests.

Over the early months of 2000, McCain became an authentic American hero, almost despite himself. With a record rife with rascality sufficient to sink a normal presidential candidate, the silver-haired McCain delighted in acknowledging his transgressions. As an aura of authenticity descended, John McCain threatened the Bush machine in the New Hampshire and South Carolina primaries.

The measure of the man drew heavily on a daunting family legacy. Both his father and grandfather, indifferent students at Annapolis, became four-star admirals, his father rising to command all U.S. forces in the Pacific during the Vietnam War. Next in line, the senator, John Sidney McCain III, more than observed family legacy as a midshipman, graduating fifth from the bottom of his Naval Academy class.

Well into the process of achieving his own four-star naval career, McCain took his jet off the deck of the U.S.S. *Oriskany* on October 26, 1967, headed for Vietnam, and ended the day shot down, nearly killed, captured, and imprisoned. His tortured saga over the following five and a half years became familiar to the American people during the 2000 campaign, amplified by McCain's simultaneous publication of *Faith of My Fathers,* a celebration of his father and grandfather and the military ethos that produced the three men. Refusing release offered to embarrass his father the admiral, McCain remained holed up in deplorable conditions with his military peers.

Upon release he tried mightily to repair a shattered body, succeeded in getting back into the air, but realized that physical deterioration would inexorably disqualify him, meaning no command assignment, no flag rank. Consequently, in 1977 he became the navy's liaison to the U.S. Senate, a job combining tending to naval interests and weaving a social network in the nation's premiere old boys' club. He proved very good at the job, senators generally liking the war hero bad boy. Despite normal danger signs—his marriage fell apart, there were rumors of womanizing—McCain's penchant for politics drew attention. Major political lords—Ross Perot, Ronald Reagan—sought his public company. He resigned from the navy and set his sights on Capitol Hill.

Divorced in 1979, he soon married the daughter of a wealthy Phoenix businessman. At the wedding, Senator William Cohen (R-ME) stood as best man, Sen. Gary Hart as an usher. Settling in Phoenix, McCain ingratiated himself with wealthy conservative power brokers. He stood for a House seat in 1982, depicted as a "carpetbagger" by local rivals in the race. Where was his real home, he was asked. "As a matter of fact, the place I lived the longest in my life was Hanoi." Case closed, election secured. A seat in the Senate waited on the retirement of Republican icon Barry Goldwater in 1986. From the beginning, McCain never met serious political opposition in Arizona, despite enduring the most embarrassing moment of his public life.

Arizona's premiere influence peddler, a man named Charles H. Keating Jr., led a fabled existence, courtesy of the land development and banking deals that provided excess millions and the attention of politicians. McCain accepted the largesse, political contributions, private jet transportation, and vacations in the Bahamas. Other public men did the same, four Democratic senators joining McCain in deferring to Keating's request to meet with federal regulators interested in the farcically named Lincoln Savings and Loan. There followed a televised investigation into the "Keating Five," a harrowing experience that nonetheless changed McCain's life. The Lincoln thrift went bankrupt, eventually costing the public treasury $3.4 billion for the bailout. Keating went to jail. McCain, cited for "poor judgment," moved on to become the champion of a radical reform effort to abolish "soft money," that is, the unregulated flood of cash that sustains modern American politics.

With apparent ease and certainly with effect, McCain would henceforth describe himself and other politicians as tainted by special-interest riches. As he gleefully advanced his politically outrageous crusade, the Arizona senator's popularity with his peers nearly disappeared. Off-the-record comments from the Republican side of the Senate produced an interesting composite picture of their colleague: simply annoying, sanctimonious, unnecessarily personal and emotional, a bad party man. As Governor Bush rang up endorsements from the party's leaders, just four senators supported McCain. Thirty-five chose Bush.

Despite his suspect standing in his own party, McCain lit a bright fire on the campaign trail. His perpetual bus tour, the "Straight Talk Express," captivated the public. A flowing stream of journalists and politicians climbed aboard to crowd around the senator, who provided a continuous press conference as the vehicle sped over the snowy New Hampshire landscape. Cameras rolled as media heavyweights vied with local correspondents to joust and laugh with the indefatigable McCain. It seemed obvious, on the round-the-clock political shows, that McCain was having the time of his life. He visibly gained confidence as the cheering crowds responded, using simple but plausible political attacks on his well-heeled adversary, the Texas governor. Raspy voiced, his face alternately wreathed in a smile or frown, he spoke with passion but also made fun of himself—a wondrous formula in the age of television. McCain instantly emerged a real threat to the Bush ascendancy.

The first real combat in New Hampshire occurred in Durham on January 6, 2000, six Republicans providing the action. The previous evening, Gore and Bradley had stood on the same stage at the University of New Hampshire and politely jabbed at each other. The Republicans provided theater. Governor Bush moved quickly to control the damaging memory of his father's pledge on taxes. "This is not only no new taxes," he said referring to his promise, "this is tax cuts, so help me God." Senator McCain changed the subject. With a broad grin he "confessed" that all politicians, himself specifically included, should be suspected of taint from the wash of available and unaccountable cash that filled Washington. Bush scolded him for supporting a campaign money reform policy that "Al Gore is applauding." McCain counterattacked, charging that new national commercials depicting Bill Clinton morphing into McCain were the product of a hidden Bush surrogate group. At least, McCain beamed, "get a better picture."

The four other men on the stage stood alongside seeking attention. Keyes denounced homosexuality. Hatch blasted Fidel Castro. Forbes found Bush defective on tax reform. Bauer hit at Bush's father. National television ratings indicated that the American public had warmed to the contest, and more debates quickly followed.

A week before the February 1 New Hampshire contest, the Iowa caucus results came in. Although its rules exceeded ready grasp by all but the most confirmed political devotees, the numbers resounded: Gore trounced Bradley by 63 to 35 percent. On the Republican side, Bush captured 41 percent in a six-man field. McCain, husbanding resources for New Hampshire, did not campaign, and tallied a token 5 percent. Forbes won a strong 30 percent for second place, raising his hopes in New Hampshire. However earnestly the wealthy publisher repeated his flat-tax proposal, the days before the vote belonged to Bush and McCain.

Imagining the coming presidential debates, McCain pledged "to beat Al Gore like a drum." Governor Bush, he claimed, would have nothing to say, since he "is defending the system that has corrupted and debased the system of government."

For his own part, in the final hours Bush produced two more prominent supporters, his mother and father, who told a cheering crowd that "this boy, this son of ours, is not going to let you down."

On the Democratic side, Vice President Gore also took off the gloves, since Senator Bradley's poll numbers had crept upward close to primary day. Gore decried the "personal vilification" he had ostensibly suffered through Bradley's "manipulative attack." Gore supporters in Washington echoed the denunciation, a sure sign of concern. Final polls confirmed the closeness of both party races. Bradley's candidacy seemed imaginable.

Bradley's hold on the political imagination rested on his apparent mastery of the basic elements of American heroism. Self-effacing, stoic, and intensely private, he appeared solemn even in the midst of the chaotic life he chose in professional basketball and politics. Darkly handsome, athletic and intellectual, the young man from the Mississippi River town of Crystal City, Missouri, often heard elders proclaim that "he will someday be President." As a Princeton undergraduate in the early 1960s, he carried an Ivy League team to heights normally

reserved for collegiate basketball factories. As a New York Knick, he melded invaluable skills into a team concept nonpareil—"finding the open man" became a convention for teamwork. Playing beside men of obviously superior athletic skills, Bradley, silent and dependable, cool amidst howling crowds and flying elbows, prevailed. Sports scribes unanimously agreed that he "couldn't run, couldn't jump," through a career that led to induction in the Naismith Memorial Basketball Hall of Fame.

In the New Hampshire primary on February 1, Gore bested Bradley by 5 points, as McCain swamped Bush by 18. Despite the Republican shocker, one senior Bush adviser confidently knew what came next, stating, "He's going to walk right into our punch in South Carolina." In the meantime, McCain's unlikely triumph excited newspaper headlines and political pundits everywhere.

Bush immediately raced to the right in South Carolina, running on religious rectitude, a clearer opposition to abortion than he had shown elsewhere, and a much featured appearance at Bob Jones University in Greenville. There, under the gaze of Dr. Bob Jones III, grandson of

With a backdrop of the Kingdome and the Seattle Mariners ballpark, Democratic presidential candidate Bill Bradley addresses a rally at Victor Steinbrueck Park, February 11, 2000, in Seattle. Bradley made appeals to women voters and to striking Boeing workers. At right is Washington auditor Brian Sonntage. *(Elaine Thompson/Associated Press)*

the original evangelist whose literal comprehension of the Bible had been observed for 75 years, Bush waxed in the company of friendly students, whose attendance, like so much of their lives, was obligatory. This erstwhile redoubt of the segregationist South remained a secure right-wing enclave. From it, Bush mounted an offensive that overwhelmed McCain with cash. Bush's treasury touched $69 million, McCain's $14 million. The champion opponent of soft money badly needed more of it himself.

In the end, Bush would prevail in South Carolina easily, by 11 points. Yet the three weeks of campaigning produced such hot-button turmoil that 600,000 South Carolinians voted, twice the primary number of 1996. Campaign funds rained down all over the state, Bush spending $3 million each week. The money bought saturation advertising on television and radio, Bush's resources dominating, hammering McCain high and low. Out-of-state advocacy groups like "Right to Life" and "Americans for Tax Reform" swooped in on McCain. While coordination between a presidential candidate and a national advocacy group is illegal, the conspiracy is nearly impossible to prove, particularly in a quick moving, snap election.

"Push polls" are in fact scripted telephone calls designed to smear an opponent, often through the unsupported interrogatory, "Did you know that he [fill in the allegation]" "Did you know that McCain left his crippled first wife?" "Did you know that Cindy McCain is/was a drug addict who stole money from a kids' fund?" So-called "Christian talk radio" chimed in. According to Representative Lindsay Graham, a broadcaster stated that at home in Arizona McCain kept a backyard pentagram, a five-pointed star widely identified with witchery and the occult. A fringe veterans group denounced McCain for "abandoning" veterans. The booming national radio voices of Rush Limbaugh and Pat Robertson contributed, the former calling McCain "a liberal," and the fundamentalist television reverend declaring that McCain would destroy the GOP. Bush himself made reference, incorrectly as it turned out, to a group of gay Republicans who had endorsed his opponent.

On primary day, Bush received 53 percent and McCain 42 percent. The South Carolina Republican primary campaign proved one simple Republican reality that, however keenly felt, could not be admitted: the party establishment regarded McCain as a Manchurian Candidate, perhaps even a liberal.

The first days of March would determine the primary war. Intense national campaigning featured 18 different contests leading up to "Titanic Tuesday," March 7, when the determining votes were to be cast.

The Republican joust continued to attract the most attention primarily because of the Arizona maverick. "If

he's a reformer," McCain proclaimed of Bush after South Carolina, "I'm an astronaut." The Arizona senator had captured Michigan's 58 delegates on February 22, also winning his home state, where the GOP governor of Arizona led his opposition. At this point, he made a major strategic mistake, however much he enjoyed doing it. McCain went into the heart of the Christian Coalition to denounce its leading practitioners.

Christian political chieftains Pat Robertson and Jerry Falwell, each for years presumed to be able to influence masses of voters, were "agents of intolerance who shame our faith, our party and our country," McCain told a rapt crowd in Virginia Beach on the eve of the Virginia primary. He even drew a parallel between Robertson and Falwell on the one side and Muslim extremist Louis Farrakhan and the Reverend Al Sharpton on the other.

So compelling was the political theater provided by McCain's crusade that, as Mary McGrory of the *Washington Post* noted, "We had almost forgotten that Al Gore and Bill Bradley were still around." On February 22, at Harlem's famed Apollo Theater, Bradley and Gore engaged in such a fierce "debate" that, as the *New York Times* reported, it "repeatedly seemed on the verge of getting out of control." The two men, each with an essentially centrist voting record, leveled extreme charges against each other. The raft of issues included guns, racial profiling, equal opportunity, health care, and reparations for slavery. However observers scored the contest, Gore won, if only because of superior organizational muscle. With money and good prospects, the vice president had attracted the public support of the African-American political elite, including Representative Charles Rangel, state controller and gubernatorial hopeful H. Carl McCall, former mayor David Dinkins, and the influential former congressman, the Rev. Floyd Flake. Bradley's principal African-American supporter was film director Spike Lee. Throughout New York State as elsewhere, the power of incumbency and vision of electoral continuity clearly asserted itself among the Democrats.

Senator Bradley decided to spend most of his remaining time and resources in Washington State, where a political culture featuring tolerance and environmental concern represented an opportunity to score a noteworthy victory. Bradley desperately needed the win. His very survival depended on it. Immediately—and stunningly—the next flurry of primaries restored the regular order of political power. Between March 1 and 8, both Bradley and McCain were knocked out. Bradley, humbled by Gore in Washington State by 68–21 percent, limped on to New York and California, where a similar fate awaited.

McCain would also lose big battles and disappear from the campaign trail in March, eight months before the election. At the same time, the nature of his defeat presaged a larger struggle for the future of the GOP. Bush defeated him in the Virginia primary by 53–44 percent, after which voter analysis disclosed a clear fissure in party preference. The Texas governor won the Christian conservative vote by 8 to 1. Overall, registered Republicans voted for the Texas governor 63–33 percent, and he also won the gender vote by a similar proportion. Among "independent" voters, however, the Arizona insurgent triumphed by a two-to-one margin, an appeal to an electorate that he matched across the nation. McCain, in defeat, created a legacy that would remain well beyond Bush's election.

When he became the only contender for the Republican presidential nomination, Bush moved promptly to the center. In Super Tuesday victory remarks before a joyous following in Austin, he proclaimed that "Republicans must expand on prosperity and extend it to those who still struggle," adding, "We must also be a strong nation that cares for the weak and the forgotten. . . . We must be a party of inclusion, the party of a generous heart and an open door."

In Nashville on the same evening, Gore struck a similar note: "This year in this election we are the party of the mainstream." At the end of the day, finally, the two men faced each other, one destined for the White House, the other for an uncertain future. The high-stakes game, scheduled to play out over the next eight months, would present a maladroit drama of an overlong and tedious first act, a second act mixing drama and melodrama, and then a swift and astonishing denouement.

America's election cycles, unique among democratic nations primarily because of their marathon character, include long weeks of torpor. Over nearly five months between Super Tuesday in March and the national conventions in August, Vice President Gore and Governor Bush regularly but unsuccessfully attempted to command public attention. The national committees of the two parties churned out press releases without discernible effect. Prominent political figures appeared on the Sunday morning talk shows, one appearance melding inconclusively into the next. "People just don't pay attention," confessed Rhode Island representative Patrick Kennedy, head of the Democratic House campaign effort.

In the last days of July, Bush shocked the nation by selecting Dick Cheney as his vice-presidential running mate. Choosing the former secretary of defense, 59, produced a range of lively editorial opinion. His extensive resume also included several heart incidents, some requiring surgery. Cheney represented the political symbiosis between Governor Bush and former president Bush, who himself lobbied for Cheney's appointment. Much of the national commentary on the new Republican ticket invidiously contrasted Cheney's political heft with that of Governor Bush. They were, their partisan foes chortled, two Texas oil men.

The four-day GOP convention in Philadelphia fit perfectly into the modern American version of political marketing. Conventions had long since ceased to perform their original function of on-the-spot combat for nomination, a hoary tradition that contributed some of the most colorful pages in American history. In modern conclaves, all decisions have been made beforehand, and the public proceedings are deftly designed as "infomercials" intended to sell the party and its candidates. In this spirit, the Republicans presented to the media a unique perception of themselves.

The succession of speakers who came to the podium represented the most fulsome recipe of American diversity: people of color and ethnic variety, women, campfire girls, professional athletes, single mothers, a rabbi, an imam, and a Greek Orthodox archbishop scattered among the politicians, including a gay member of Congress. ShowTime featured the rocker Chaka Khan, a Hispanic choral group, and a small army of African-American singers and dancers. The stage cast, the focus of the cameras, was a contrast to the audience of delegates, who well represented the white suburban base of the GOP.

The normally phlegmatic Cheney served red-meat rhetoric, to the crowd's delight, tearing into "Clinton–Gore." In rhythm he intoned, "The wheel has turned . . . and it is time . . . It is time for them to go," the throng responding, "Go! Go! Go!" The next night, presidential candidate Bush proved an even better performer. His speech, nearly 4,000 words, had evolved from multiple drafts and careful preparation by Bush, whose public speaking still sometimes attracted ridicule. On this evening, before a national audience and his own party faithful, both the substance and delivery by the candidate drew praise. Usual skeptics, like the *New York Times* and *Washington Post,* were positive.

In the two-week interim between conventions Gore, too, had upset political convention by choosing Senator Joseph I. Lieberman as his running mate. The Connecticut senator's national reputation rested on his moral edge, most prominently displayed when from the Senate floor he flayed Clinton's dalliance. Lieberman also associated himself with conspicuous, if ineffectual, efforts to decrease the degrading content of television and films. The loquacious Lieberman occupied the moderate center of the party, had excellent connections in the Senate, and was a remarkably adept retail politician in Connecticut. As the first Jew to occupy a place on a major national ticket, he carried with him a visible ethnic *frisson* balanced on the novel phenomenon of proclaiming his religious beliefs, thus inviting either tolerance or bigotry.

In Los Angeles on Monday evening, August 14, thousands of politically charged Democrats from across the nation settled into the Staples Center, home of the Los Angeles Lakers of the National Basketball Association. Outside, largely ignored by delegates and media alike, phalanxes of youngish protesters surged toward the futuristic arena, contained by riot-gear-clad police who soundly executed instructions to preserve order. Many demonstrators had made the cross-country trek after performing their noisy rituals in tandem with Philadelphia cops.

The four-day party festival continued without interruption. It bore much resemblance to the other convention. All significant business had been prearranged. The medley of speakers coming on camera reflected party diversity, all major constituencies dutifully represented. Once again, the major television networks dedicated a simple two-hour "window" for the national audience. One dramatic element did distinguish the Democrats' opening night: President Clinton opened for Vice President Gore.

Their edgy relationship, however transparent, had ended with the Lewinsky scandal. Estrangement accompanied by animosity would increase over time. First, however, they were compelled to share a convention that

for each assumed the highest importance. For Clinton, legacy. For Gore, the ultimate political prize.

Clinton's staged entrance to the arena suggested all the flamboyant elements that enchanted his supporters and maddened his enemies. Suddenly, he loomed up on the giant screens around the arena and simultaneously on prime-time television. Alone, somewhere deep behind the podium, he walked down a corridor, turned into its continuation, smiling, confident, striding, turning at right angles inside a designer maze. For nearly two minutes he strolled on, seemingly happy to be trapped behind stage. "The Walk," said Hollywood producer and longtime Clinton pal Harry Thomason, its creator, sought to mirror "High Noon," the classic film homage to a righteous lone gunslinger. Comfortable with the panache, the outgoing president finally came on stage and spoke about himself, and Al Gore.

The 40-minute speech met Clinton's high oratorical standards. In ringing endorsement of the Gore–Lieberman ticket, Clinton reprised the record of his own administration. Thus, the president proclaimed, "we built our bridge to the twenty-first century. We crossed it together.

Democratic presidential nominee Al Gore and his running mate, Senator Joe Lieberman, wave to the crowd at the Democratic National Convention in Los Angeles, August 17, 2000. (© Joe Sohm Visions of America LLC/Alamy)

And we're not going back." He then referred to his vice president's social values, political effectiveness, and family loyalty in the loftiest terms. He concluded, "More than anybody else I've known in public life, Al Gore understands the future and how sweeping changes can affect Americans' daily lives." Political strategy having insisted that Gore be anywhere but Los Angeles for the Clinton performance, Gore commented from half a continent away, in St. Louis. Asked about the president's oration, Gore coolly told a reporter, "I thought he made a very strong case for the policies that have helped to produce this progress and prosperity."

Other featured Democrats occupied the delicate space over the next two days prior to Gore's acceptance of the nomination. First Lady Hillary Rodham Clinton, candidate for a Senate seat in New York, spoke during prime time before her husband. Subsequently, familiar luminaries took the spotlight. Massachusetts senator Edward M. Kennedy and many members of his family engaged in their special rendering of tradition and nostalgia. Jimmy Carter, ignored by the 1996 convention, received a moving tribute. Meanwhile, Clinton left the city to meet Gore in an elaborately staged "passing the torch" event.

What then unfolded reflected the Gore camp's strong belief that close public association with Clinton represented a political liability. The symbolic meeting took place in an odd setting, a remote small town, Monroe, Michigan. Before 15,000 people in 95-degree heat, the two men embraced, each spoke, and then Bill, Hillary, and Chelsea Clinton left the stage, literally and symbolically, to Al and Tipper Gore. Back at the Staples Center, attention had turned to vice-presidential nominee Joe Lieberman's riveting charge to the delegates.

The Connecticut senator reveled in his own life as a paean to America's virtue and promise. Introduced by his wife Hadassah, child of Holocaust survivors, an energized Lieberman stressed tolerance, equal rights, and opportunity, citing his immigrant forebears of modest means. He embraced Jewish identity, and found a parallel with the politically sacred name of John F. Kennedy, Democrat and only Roman Catholic president in American history. The other theme of the speech was a predictable, if lively and often sardonic, offensive against "my friends" the Republicans. Lieberman, well received in the convention hall and by the nation's press, nearly equaled the performance of Clinton. Both raised the bar for Gore's appearance the following night.

With uncharacteristic brio, Gore immediately sought to counter his wooden image. Bounding onto the stage, he threw his arm around Tipper and bent into a languorous kiss, producing a red-faced wife and several days' discussion around the nation. To answer the Clinton Question,

he announced, "We're entering a new time. We're electing a new president. And I stand here tonight as my own man, and I want you to know me for who I truly am."

Gore finished to a standing ovation as the stage filled with the candidates and their wives and families in the familiar American political scene of martial music, the red-white-and-blue, candidate signs and balloons and confetti. The finalists in place, the citizens of the United States, without noticeable general interest, faced seven weeks of the 2000 presidential campaign. At least.

A basic rule of American politics grants presidential candidates a "bounce" in poll numbers immediately after their respective conventions, and so it was in August 2000. Governor Bush left the Philadelphia meeting with a 49–38 percent bulge, but Vice President Gore came to prevail after Los Angeles by 52–48 percent. In fact, the early stages of the fall campaign made clear the nearly even split between the men that would prevail until the bitter end.

Neither Gore nor Bush possessed the natural political magic on the campaign trail of a Reagan or Clinton. Both thus spent the several weeks prior to the first debate in early October perfecting modes of attack, defense, and image projection. After Los Angeles, Gore and Lieberman took a Mississippi River trip aboard the *Mark Twain,* a paddle-wheeled river steamboat replica actually powered by diesels. The men dressed in denim and cowboy boots for stops at river ports, where they were well received by residents of Iowa, Illinois, and Missouri, and also enjoyed ample media exposure. Meanwhile, Gore's advertising task force had prepared attacks on Bush, reprising the sensitivities of the South Carolina primary, particularly Bob Jones University and the Confederate symbol on that state's flag.

The Bush forces were ready with a commercial showing Gore at the infamous Buddhist Temple fund-raiser coupled with the vice president's presenting himself as a champion of campaign finance reform. The Texas governor had just embarked on a concentrated Labor Day schedule when he committed the first major gaffe of the race. In an open-microphone whisper to Cheney on a stage in Naperville, Illinois, Bush indicated the nearby presence of a veteran reporter assigned to the Republican canvass. "There's Adam Clymer—major league asshole—from the *New York Times.*" Cheney's response would earn him a permanent nickname: "Oh, yeah, big time." For the next several days, the Bush camp responded well to the small crisis. Clymer's reports had been unfair, communications director Karen Hughes maintained. From New York, the *Times* steadfastly insisted on their man's objectivity. Gore forces piled on Bush. The candidate himself uttered a plaintive truth: "I regret people heard the comments."

Consumer advocate and Green Party presidential candidate Ralph Nader (left) shares a moment with Jay Leno during Nader's visit to *The Tonight Show* on September 12, 2000. *(Reed Saxon/Associated Press)*

Just after Labor Day, Gore appeared on the nationally syndicated *Oprah,* a permanent item in the daily schedule of about 22 million Americans, overwhelmingly women. Following a formula honored by all politicians appearing in an uncertain situation, the vice president teased himself, acknowledging his woodenness even as he discussed the passionate convention kiss with Tipper. Gore tailored the message to the audience, honoring family and promising a tax cut to a working parent opting to spend more time at home.

Shortly thereafter, the vice president faced a tougher media challenge by appearing on the *Late Show with David Letterman.* He jousted ably with the sardonic comedian, at one point reflecting on the famous kiss. "I have been surprised at the amount of commentary and reaction to it. I really have," Gore said, "because to me, that was just a little peck." Letterman replied, "Al, how long have you been on the road?" Soon, Governor Bush booked a date with Letterman.

Bush also turned up on *Oprah,* spending a relaxed hour combining self-deprecating admission with glimpses of policy. He discussed the importance of family and admitted to a "problem with alcohol," solved when he went on the wagon at age 40. He pumped for significant tax cuts,

telling an audience member, "I think you should be putting money back in your pocket." The crowd responded enthusiastically.

One or both candidates would eventually appear with Regis Philbin, Rosie O'Donnell, and Jay Leno, and on *Saturday Night Live,* whose caustic satires portrayed Bush as stupid and Gore as robotic. Lowlights included Gore attempting to hypnotize Philbin and Bush promising to place a mechanical bull in the White House. That even Green Party presidential candidate Ralph Nader, a notoriously unfunny man, appeared on Letterman best proves the point of permanently altered campaign requirements.

At the same time, most days followed the normal cadences of attack and defend, always with an eye to the local and national television cameras. Standard themes became fixed. Republican candidates persistently emphasized "Clinton–Gore" ethical shortcomings. Bush, clearly gaining confidence in public, told a CNN political show audience on September that while "the vice president is a good family man, no question about that . . . he has been a part of an administration that violated financing laws." Evidence? The Buddhist Temple, fund-raising phone calls from the White House, and "no controlling legal authority."

The positive side of GOP campaigning emphasized tax cuts and reduction of the role of the federal government. Bush told CNN's *Money Line* of a 10-year $1.3 billion tax relief plan, to be taken from the federal surplus after ensuring Social Security, prescription drug coverage, education reform, military reconstruction, and the needs of the environment. All this, he insisted, would be accomplished by shrinking the government. Gore, he charged, mistrusted the people and favored multiplying federal programs. The vice president returned the fire, of course. Over and over, he repeated themes first struck months ago.

The major contenders went into their first debate on October 3 deadlocked at about 45 percent each. Nader stood at 4 percent, while Pat Buchanan hovered at an unsteady 1 percent. For two decades, Buchanan, powerful orator and infighter, championed right-wing causes from within the GOP, including isolation in foreign policy, an effective end to immigration, skepticism about the Holocaust and Israel, and opposition to economic globalization. Once a potent force, Buchanan in 2000

relied on the $12.6 million allocated by the Federal Election Commission on September 14. Four days later, his campaign began with a speech at Bob Jones University. The crowd roared approval when he pledged to kick the United Nations out of the United States, with the message, "If you have trouble leaving, we'll send up 10,000 Marines to help you pack." Three weeks later, he appeared in Boston to demand entry into the presidential debate. For the day, he joined forces with ideological opposite Nader. Eventually, Buchanan's $12.6 million in federal funds only yielded him just under a half-million votes, 0.4 percent of the popular vote. Nader, who did not take federal funds and raised under $10 million, won 2.9 million votes, almost 3 percent of the total.

The Commission on Presidential Debates held to a ruling excluding candidates who failed to achieve at least a 15 percent rating in several polls, thus denying Buchanan and Nader. Both protested mightily, Nader actually being carted away by police and threatened with arrest. "Pitch-

Democratic candidate Al Gore (left) and Republican candidate George W. Bush present their views during the first presidential debate, October 3, 2000, at the Clark Athletic Center on the campus of the University of Massachusetts in Boston. *(Ron Edmonds/Associated Press)*

fork Pat" was a spent force, however, and never became a factor in the race. Nader persisted, significantly so.

Bush v. Gore, round one. Regarding the oratorical context, Bush had recently told a reporter, "Now I understand that he's a great debater, but I've got something to say." He had surely done well enough in a number of matches with the formidable McCain, yet the aura of intellectual inferiority clung to the Texas governor. Later, he would observe, with a twinkle, "A lot of folks don't think I can string a sentence together. Expectations were so low all I had to do was say, 'Hi, I'm George W. Bush.'" Actually, Bush did well enough.

As predicted, Gore hammered at issues, taking as holy causes prescription drugs, Medicare, and Social Security, warning that Bush's mania for tax cuts endangered their integrity. Facts came as drumbeats sounding across the territory of foreign and domestic accomplishments and prospects. Bush popped in with vague general responses, emphasizing that he supported individuals while Gore favored government. At another point, the Texan reminded everyone that "Clinton–Gore" had been around for eight years but had not found time to accomplish what the vice president only now indicated were urgent priorities. Gore, indefatigable, revealed his own deep knowledge and, in several cases, caused Bush to respond weakly, for instance, not knowing that Russia supported the Yugoslav tyrant Milosevic. While Bush spoke, Gore's facial gestures suggested disgust, which he underscored with audible heavy sighs.

Meanwhile, the vice-presidential candidates squared off in their only joint appearance, on October 5, in Danville, Kentucky. The civilized exchange between the two veteran politicians probably pleased observers interested in "just the issues." Lacking drama, the debate did provide moments of levity. "Did Al Gore make promises in 1992?" Lieberman asked. "Absolutely. Did he deliver? Big time, if I may put it that way. And I'm pleased to see, Dick, from the newspapers, that you're better off than you were eight years ago, too."

These references were to Cheney's support of Bush's obscenity about the reporter, and to the extraordinary income Cheney had amassed from the oil and gas industry. He replied without missing a beat: "I can tell you, Joe, that the government had absolutely nothing to do with it." Lieberman then went one joke too far when he quoted his wife as wishing that the Liebermans could "go out into the private sector." Cheney flashed back, "Well, I'm going to try to help you do that, Joe."

In the second presidential debate, in Winston-Salem, North Carolina, the candidates interacted only with PBS anchor Jim Lehrer, in what was billed as "a more informal exchange." The three men sat around a table and proceeded through the familiar litany of domestic and international items. Occasionally the dialogue took on a sharp edge, as when they repeated positions on gun control. Analysts noted two principal differences in this second contest. Bush, well-briefed and sharp on foreign policy matters, seemed confident and "presidential." Gore, reacting to earlier criticism, softened his posture markedly. "I agree with the governor," he responded repeatedly. Tracking polls continued to predict a dead heat.

A few days later, in St. Louis, the last debate unfolded in a "town hall" format thought to favor the more experienced Gore. Both men were able to move around the stage, back and forth toward the audience and toward each other while exchanging barbs. Gore seemed much more aggressive in affirming and parrying points on health care, size of government and taxes. Bush held his own, at one dramatic point effectively muting an accusatory question from the audience on capital punishment in Texas.

The Texas governor also demonstrated resilience in the face of Gore's attempts at visual drama, as when the vice president stepped toward him as Bush spoke. Bush responded through body language, smiling, relaxing his frame, appearing to snort, showing his trademark smirk. "He tried to psyche the governor out," strategist Karl Rove told the press, "and it did not work." The Gore campaign chairman disagreed. "They weren't tactics," he insisted, "what it was, was somebody showing they could be in command of an evening, and therefore be commander-in-chief."

Through the exhausting final days, both men stuck to established routines. Bush appeared on *Saturday Night Live* spouting malapropisms, claiming to be "amvibalent" toward an "offensible" program. In his turn, Gore rolled his eyes and sighed.

Mighty exertions into popular culture as well as daily policy proclamations failed to resolve the deadlock forecast by the polls. As Election Day neared and Gore still failed to seize his predicted advantage, pressure increased to enlist, finally, the missing thrust of Bill Clinton.

By design, Gore would remain, whatever the consequences, "my own man." He even broke with Clinton during the furious squabble over Cuban refugee child Elian Gonzalez, the vice president calling for permanent residence status for the boy in a transparent overture to anti-Castro forces in Miami. The gamble of shunning the president translated into rejecting the full visible support of one of the greatest natural politicians in American history. Clinton remained extraordinarily popular (and ferociously unpopular), but on the margins emphatically sustained by an approval rating historically high for an eight-year incumbent of the White House. The popular propensity to forgive Clinton's transgressions indicated his political value to his successor. Gore and his advisers disagreed.

This Ann Telnaes cartoon shows a sleepy-eyed man with a bowl in his hand standing before an open pantry with two large boxes of breakfast cereals on the shelf, "Gore Bran" with Al Gore on the box, and "Frosted Flake" on which George W. Bush appears wearing a propeller beanie, plus a "variety pak" lampooning the minor-party candidates. *(Ann Telnaes Editorial Cartoon © 2000 Ann Telnaes. Used with permission of Ann Telnaes and the Cartoonist Group. All rights reserved.)*

The economy continued to roar, prosperity washed the nation, the federal budget surplus for fiscal year 2000 reached an unprecedented level of $230 billion, the nation remained at peace, and the sitting vice president could not take advantage. Clinton remained tied to the White House.

On the edge of Election Day, mysterious sources uncovered a 25-year-old driving-while-intoxicated charge against Bush. Media scrutiny intensified as each campaign responded cautiously, on eggshells awaiting public response. In fact, nothing materialized, general common sense prevailing that a young man had made a mistake a long time ago. In this non-tempest lay the concealed message that George W. Bush enjoyed a solid enough public standing. Trivial error would not sink him, as had once been suspected. The polls reflected a tie as Election Day arrived.

The quadrennial main event of American politics is now a media circus of elaborate dimension. The networks and burgeoning cable operations have agreed to a muscular competitiveness, seeking victory in popular ratings, each calling attention to themselves like brash hucksters. As Election Day 2000 passed westward from the Atlantic coast toward remote Alaska and distant Hawaii, early returns, exit polls, and trend analysis continued. Despite the well-cultivated illusion that one or another group of familiar faces possessed special insight or information, all information came from the same source, produced by Voter News Service, a consortium created for the occasion by ABC, CBS, NBC, CNN, Fox, and the Associated Press.

By mid-evening, every national television outlet had embarrassed itself. NBC gave Florida to Gore at 7:49 EST, and 10 minutes later the others all agreed. CBS's Dan Rather assured his viewers, "If we say somebody's carried the state, you can take that to the bank. Book it." In the control rooms, however, reality remained elusive due to incorrect information generated by Voter News Service.

By 10 p.m. the networks reversed the Florida decision, declaring the state "too close to call." Just after 2 a.m., Fox presented Florida to Bush and proclaimed him the president-elect; the other networks quickly following. Rather even outdid himself: "Before the trail goes completely cold, let's give a tip of the Stetson to the loser, Vice President Al Gore, and at the same time a big tip and a hip-hip-hooray and a big Texas howdy to the new President of the United States." This time, and once again, the veteran anchorman had no doubts: "Sip it, savor it, cup it, Photostat it, underline it in red, press it in a book, put it in an album, hang it on the wall: George W. Bush is the next President of the United States." Two hours later, he took it back. All his colleagues again agreed. No one had been elected.

By this time, those millions of Americans still fighting sleep to learn of the next president had been misinformed twice by all of its principal sources of information. When they all re-reversed themselves, CNN pundit Jeff Greenfield cracked, "Oh waiter, one order of crow."

Dawn approached Nashville as Al Gore's motorcade sped toward the rambling War Memorial Plaza, where he would tell his supporters that he had telephoned George Bush in Austin to concede. Thousands awaited the chagrined vice president as steady rain added poignancy. At Gore headquarters, amidst the detritus of the long heartbreaking evening, a veteran Democratic operative from Massachusetts named Michael Whouley stared at continuing television accounting of the Florida vote, which had Gore closing to within a few thousand. Whouley thought that the thin margin should prevent concession, whatever the networks said, and urgently tried to contact the Gore motorcade. Beeper communication established as the vice president neared the plaza, the frantic aide yelled, "This thing in Florida has changed." Now the difference looked like but 600 votes. Campaign chief William Daley, convinced, convinced Gore. There would be no public concession. Gore phoned Bush just an hour after he had conceded.

Gore: Circumstances have changed.
Bush: Let me make sure I understand. You're taking back your concession?
Gore: Well, you don't have to be snippety with me.
Bush: Well, Mr. Vice President, you got to do what you got to do.

Gore: Let me explain something. Your younger brother is not the ultimate authority on this. . . . It's not in any way clear I have lost, and until it is clear, I can't concede.

Florida law requires a recount when the difference between contenders is less than 0.005 percent. With fate in the balance, election officials across the state immediately began to recount nearly 6,000,000 votes, and await overseas ballots. The Republican secretary of state, Katherine Harris, would certify the results. Governor Jeb Bush recused himself from official participation in his brother's struggle.

"Recount," of course, immediately became a misnomer. Cries of deception and intimidation had arisen in South Florida even before the polls closed, first with the suddenly infamous "butterfly ballot." In one Palm Beach County district studded with condos heavily populated with Jewish senior citizens, 3,407 "butterfly ballot" votes for Pat Buchanan constituted about 20 percent of his entire total statewide. A later survey failed to find one voter who favored Buchanan. As the days passed, powerful teams representing both candidates arrived in Florida to haggle. Within a next few hours, tens of thousands of "butterfly ballots" would be deemed invalid, punched twice, arguably out of frustration after a "mistake." Republicans reveled in the news that a Palm Beach election supervisor, a Democrat, had designed the ballot.

Lawyers, public relations staffers, and political operatives skilled in the covert machinations common to political crises loomed up around the state. Former secretary of state Warren Christopher, a veteran of emergencies foreign and domestic, headed the Gore forces. Former secretary of state James A. Baker III, Bush family loyalist thought to have absorbed some blame for President Bush's failure in 1992, marshaled the team of George Bush the younger.

Immediately, both sides went to court. Thus began an often-obscure war of injunctions, stays, and appeals that would rage for a month and stop only at the U.S. Supreme Court. On Saturday, November 11, Bush's forces went into Federal District Court in Miami to protest the "arbitrary and unconstrained decision-making authority" ostensibly practiced by local election officials presiding over recounts. Shortly thereafter, as if to focus the issue, officials in heavily Democratic Palm Beach County ordered the review of 425,000 votes, including those where the "chad" had not fully cleared the hole in the ballot. Page one of the New York Times on Sunday, November 12, featured a photograph of a Florida judge holding a "dangling chad" up to the light, flanked by a Republican observer on one shoulder and a Democrat on the other.

The Miami federal judge rejected the Republican bid to halt recounts. As they continued, Florida secretary of state Harris, a member of Governor Jeb Bush's cabinet, told reporters that within hours she would enforce a deadline for the reporting of all official vote tallies from across the state. The Democrats prevailed against Harris in state court. The recounting continued, Bush's lead bobbing slightly at just a few hundred votes. The political warfare escalated.

In the end, the Republicans, better organized, with more money, in control of vital state patronage positions and, perhaps, hungrier and tougher, would prevail.

Over these days, as the media blared, for public consumption the two candidates sought to offer attractive images for the ubiquitous cameras. Both overstepped. In Bush's case, the scene offered to the public came from his remote Texas ranch, where the living room had been transformed into a plausible stage set of the Oval Office. The Texas governor, surrounded by advisers, backed by a crackling fireplace, seemed deep in serious discussion with serious people, acting "presidential." Gore, for his part, remained in the nation's capital, most prominently engaged in a backyard family football game with his children and a gaggle of attractive young people. This Kennedyesque scene, according to reports, represented the only known Gore family football outing over his many years in Washington.

On November 15, a Wednesday evening, the vice president unexpectedly went on national television. In his deliberate fashion, he spoke of the reasonableness of supplementing voting machine counts ("Machines can sometimes misread or fail to detect the way ballots are cast") with "complete hand counts," specifically in Palm Beach County, Miami-Dade County, and Broward County. If Bush wished, he continued, the entire state could be recounted. Whatever the method chosen, Gore stressed, "I will abide by the result, I will take no legal action to challenge the result, and I will not support any legal action to challenge the result." Arrestingly, Gore concluded by calling for a personal meeting with Bush "to reaffirm our national unity."

The Republican forces responded with a two-pronged counterattack. Shortly after Gore's television appearance, Katherine Harris announced that it was "my duty under Florida law" to reject any county's requests to update totals. Meanwhile, the Bush forces, shocked by Gore's unexpected prime-time broadcast, sprang into action. The governor hurriedly left his ranch and raced 100 miles to the mansion in Austin. Just over three hours after Gore's appearance, and belying the emergency nature of the situation, Bush effectively responded. He opposed recounts because the standards varied from county to county, appearing subjective and arbitrary. The votes have

already been counted and recounted, he argued, and "the way to conclude this election in a fair and accurate and final way is for the State of Florida to count the remaining overseas ballots, add them to the certified vote and announce the results, as required by Florida law." There would be no meeting between the two men.

As the ides of November passed, the nation remained manifestly calm, yet the nonstop political talk shows inherited dramatic new material every day. The Florida Supreme Court made its first appearance on the national stage with a ruling that Palm Beach and Broward Counties, putatively Democratic, could continue recounts. Gore forces also went to court to stop Secretary Harris from refusing to accept fresh tallies. Bush lawyers traveled to Atlanta with an appeal to the U.S. Court of Appeals for the 11th Circuit, arguing that the absence of clear state criteria for counting votes amounted to an unconstitutional violation of voting rights. The Bush lead held at 300 votes.

Back in Tallahassee, the Florida Supreme Court ruled that the state could not certify the result. First, the court must rule on the disputed votes still being examined in the three heavily Democratic counties, as well as add in the overseas tallies that continued to arrive.

Ten days after Election Day, Bush's lead in the Florida popular vote stood at 750. Beside that modest number towered the figure of 1.5 million votes to be recounted in areas with a strong Gore predisposition. A further blow to Bush came from Atlanta, where the Circuit Court refused to halt recounts. Some good news accompanied the completion of overseas ballots, decidedly for Bush, raising his lead to 930. Yet even this ordinary procedure of counting the votes of overseas American citizens, many of them service people, produced extraordinary political diatribe.

Bush lawyers acquired a five-page Gore strategy letter, the subject of which detailed ways to dispute military absentee ballots, which were thought to favor Bush heavily. A prominent Bush surrogate in Florida, Montana governor Marc Racicot, launched the withering counterattack: "The Vice President's lawyers have gone to war . . . against the men and women who serve in our armed forces," he charged. Heavy Republican artillery followed on local and national political talk shows. This piece of political theater's mastermind, a veteran GOP operative named Warren Tompkins, had last achieved national press attention nine months earlier in the now-memorable South Carolina primary that smeared Senator McCain. Tompkins pursued the antimilitary theme through powerful figures like Florida resident and Gulf War hero General Norman Schwarzkopf. Just returned from a Texas hunting trip with former President Bush, Schwarzkopf appeared before television cameras to note that "it is a very sad day" when soldiers in "danger on a daily basis" were excluded from the vote on a "technicality." Behind the public relations onslaught, Bush lawyers insinuated themselves into the local political infrastructure. They sought to maximize the counting of overseas absentee votes from safely Republican areas, and to impose stringent regulations in those areas that leaned toward Gore.

After a six-month inquiry into possible manipulation of these votes, the *New York Times* on July 15, 2001, concluded, "Under intense pressure from the Republicans, Florida officials accepted hundreds of overseas absentee ballots that failed to comply with state laws." The *Times*'s statistical analysis concluded that discarding these flawed ballots would not have changed the outcome. In essence, the vote produced a statistical dead heat. The *Times* found no evidence of fraud.

The spotlight shifted to the seven justices of the Florida Supreme Court, six of them more or less identified with the Democrats. During oral arguments, Chief Justice Charles T. Wells discussed the significance of the date December 12 with Gore attorney David Boies. He asked Boies if all aspects of Florida voting "have to be finally determined by that date. . . . Do you agree with that?" Boies admitted that he did. The date in question, sometimes referred to as a "safe harbor," would allow for the designation of Florida electors in time for the December 18 meeting of the Electoral College. Boies's admission would later be used against him in the strongest measure.

On November 22, the court unanimously held that the South Florida recounts should proceed to completion within the following five days. The justices provided no definitive formula for evaluating the variety of chads. Republicans sprang to the cameras. Utah senator Orrin G. Hatch, chairman of the Judiciary Committee, found "constitutional errors of great proportions . . . [designed] to give the election to Gore." In Tallahassee, James Baker, flushed and agitated, derided the court, which "decided to change the rules in the middle of the game." Hammer blows continued, testing even the voracious appetite of 24-hour political channels. In Washington, Dick Cheney suffered another heart attack and went into the hospital. In Miami, the largest reservoir of potential votes for Gore simply disappeared.

Miami-Dade County, largest enclave of Democratic votes in the state, abruptly decided not to continue with recounts. The official reason cited an inability to meet the deadline four days hence. This immediately followed a threatening series of events at the office of the election supervisor. As the canvassing board had settled to begin recounts, protesters, waving Bush/Cheney signs, listened to partisan rhetoric, including the claim by New York rep-

resentative John Sweeney that "thugs in that building are trying to hijack the election." Unruliness fueled the horde, which advanced into the building to the room where the canvassing board sat, banging on the door, shouting "voter fraud," and "let us in." Sheriff's deputies arrived to protect a surrounded local Democratic official. Two cameramen went to the ground in the melee. Shortly thereafter, the board abandoned the recount. A Republican lawyer wryly commented, "I think the Board must have searched their hearts deeply and changed their position when they realized that the results of the recount would not be deemed legitimate."

This tortured political mess included, ironically, the Democrats' own intrigues. Cuban-Americans were still angry over President Clinton's decision to return Elian Gonzalez to his father in Cuba. "The Cubans in Miami remember Elian," one commentator noted, adding "the Democrats have never been tough enough on Cuba." According to another observer, "If you're a judge or a mayor in this town, you have no choice but to think how this issue will play out in the Cuban community." As the county canvassing board shut down without a whimper, the powerful and popular Democratic mayor of Miami-Dade, Alexander Penelas, failed to lift a finger for Gore. On November 24, the Florida High Court, conferring on Thanksgiving Day, unanimously rejected the Gore appeal on the Miami-Dade recount.

As the Gore forces recoiled, wire services announced that Bush had requested the intervention of the U.S. Supreme Court. The language addressed to the Court reflected the increasing panic of the situation. The recount process was "selective, capricious and standardless [sic] . . . riddled with severe and pervasive irregularities . . . manifest inconsistencies in counting methods and a politically charged, partisan atmosphere, all of which have combined to spawn a process that now borders on anarchy." To general amazement, the Supreme Court ordered arguments on *Bush v. Gore*.

Regardless, within 48 hours of the Supreme Court bombshell, Florida secretary of state Harris announced Bush's "official" capture of the Florida popular vote, his margin put at 537, and thus Florida's 25 electoral votes, which would produce the 271 minimum needed for victory. Bush went before cameras in Austin and claimed the presidency. Gore refused to concede and announced another round of court proceedings. In fact, all over Florida, over 100 attorneys pursued lawsuits on both sides. Bush forces had suits against several counties over the question of counting overseas ballots. "Private citizens" sued Seminole County over thousands of absentee ballots. Two "citizens' suits" contested the legality of the "butterfly ballot." In Washington, the Supreme Court had taken under advisement

Bush v. Gore. Meanwhile, the state legislature added to the political tension.

The Republican-dominated legislature, also with an eye on time, declared its interest in a special session for the purposes of designating the state's 25 electors, who would be pledged to Bush. A constitutional nightmare appeared. Should Gore prevail in the courts, and in ensuing recounts, eventually winning the state, a slate of electors would emerge pledged to him. Two slates of electors? Only in the corrupted 1876 election had the political system frozen so solid.

That election, like the 2000 contest, had produced a statistical tie and sent the outcome into the uncertain precincts of the Electoral College. Three Southern states—South Carolina, Florida, and Louisiana—had sent in double returns to Congress. Republican election boards, buttressed by federal troops protecting the vote and livelihood of former slaves, refused to accept evident Democratic majorities. The Democrats, representing resurgent traditional interests intent on removing federal power and ending Reconstruction, sent in their own returns. Passions transcended compromise, and for weeks Congress debated. The Republican Senate stood behind Rutherford B. Hayes. The Democratic House held for Samuel J. Tilden. With no clear way out, Congress appointed a 15-member Electoral Commission to resolve the dispute. As the inaugural date of March 4, 1877, approached, Democrats offered a deal: They would accept Hayes if all federal troops left the South, thus restoring white rule to the old Confederacy and permitting the racial accommodations and advances of the Reconstruction period to be reversed. The Republicans agreed to the deal. On March 2, 1877, the commission voted eight to seven that Hayes had 185 electoral votes and Tilden 184, thus giving Hayes the presidency. Hayes, on his way from Ohio to Washington before this final decision, arrived in time for his own inauguration. The deal signaled the end of Reconstruction, and within a generation the American South became widely segregated.

All the legal warfare, costing millions in fees, would soon be mooted merely by the passage of time. The inexorable turn of the calendar posed the greatest danger for Gore. Florida's electors would have to be designated before the "safe harbor" of December 12, a date six days prior to the meeting of the Electoral College itself. Gore's case before Leon County Circuit Judge N. Saunders Sauls began in Tallahassee on December 3. The judge had refused to permit ongoing recounts before or during the case, although he did allow disputed ballots to be transported from South Florida to the capital city in the north.

With a national television audience watching, Judge Sauls listened carefully to minute descriptions of chad varieties and their putative legitimacy, or lack thereof.

Boies, a celebrated New York litigator and head of the Gore law assemblage, maintained regarding the disputed ballots that, "There is sufficient evidence that those votes could change or at least place in doubt the results of the election." His counterpart, Barry Richard, perhaps the most powerful local presence in any Florida courtroom, retorted that such consideration required "that this court should disregard all of the actions of the various canvassing boards that are under challenge here and should begin anew an assessment and a count of all of the votes that the plaintiffs challenge."

Thus began the nine-hour Saturday session. Convoluted questions and extended answers, objections, and responses dragged out the hours, to the consternation of the Gore people. The Sunday session would be even worse for them. On that long day, in Judge Sauls's slightly shabby courtroom, its inelegant facilities exposed by fluorescent lighting, the crowd of politicos and expensive lawyers spent 14 hours. At the end, Sauls provided a grace note for both sides, saying, "I suppose at this time, counsel, I must tell you it was a case well tried and argued." Outside both Boies and Richard proclaimed their optimism. Judgment came swiftly.

The very next day, December 4, Judge Sauls rejected every argument advanced by Gore's lawyers. They failed, he said, to prove a "reasonable probability" that the election results would be different had disputed ballots been counted. Sauls told a hushed courtroom that "the evidence does not establish any illegality, dishonesty, gross negligence, improper influence, coercion or fraud in the balloting and counting processes." One Bush lawyer exulted, "This was as complete a victory as I've ever gotten in a trial."

On Friday and Saturday, December 8 and 9, as never before, the American political system disappeared into courthouses. On Friday, an angry and divided Florida Supreme Court, voting 4 to 3, ordered a recount "in all Florida counties where there was an undervote," that is, a review of approximately 45,000 cases where a ballot recorded no vote for president. Canvassing officials were to begin the next day, Saturday, and conclude by 2 p.m. on Sunday. The majority opinion took the approach that Judge Sauls had erred by misinterpreting the law at several key points. It alluded to widely aired complaints of irregularities from African-American districts in Miami-Dade County, concluding that "although the time constraints are limited, we must do everything required by law to ensure that legal votes that have not been counted are included in the final election results." Governor Bush's legal team immediately appealed the ruling to the U.S. Supreme Court.

The next day, as the recounting continued, a veritable scoreboard reflected the tally. Bush led by 154 votes (or

Gore and Lieberman supporters protest in front of the Supreme Court building during the oral argument of *Bush v. Gore*, December 11, 2000. (© *Danita Delimont/Alamy*)

191). At 2:45 p.m. EST on this Saturday, as a significant national audience watched officials in several Florida districts try to "recount the undercount," a bulletin staggered the country. From Washington, suddenly and against all odds, the Supreme Court of the United States, split 5 to 4, ordered the immediate halt of all electoral board activities in Florida. The Court's majority consisted of Chief Justice William H. Rehnquist and Justices Sandra Day O'Connor, Antonin Scalia, Anthony M. Kennedy, and Clarence Thomas. Dissenting were Justices John Paul Stevens, David H. Souter, Ruth Bader Ginsburg, and Steven G. Breyer. The deep and complex divide among the nine men and women could not have been more fundamental.

On the simple question of appropriate jurisdiction, "liberals" and "conservatives" had reversed positions. The conservative majority faced the paradox of overruling the authority of a state supreme court, a familiar fault line in the American federal system in which the conservative legacy had resolutely opposed centralization of power. The Court's "liberals" would support the authority and decision of the state court, reversing the tradition

of such jurists to champion federal judicial supremacy. More immediately, accepting and deciding *Bush v. Gore* would mock the Court's historic attempt to preserve its majesty through insulation from party politics.

The justices advertised their differences. Stevens, the Court's longest-sitting member and most consistent liberal, wrote that in accepting the case "the majority has acted unwisely." Both the election and history were in the balance, he believed: "Preventing the recount from being completed will inevitably cast a cloud on the legitimacy of the election." Responding in a separate opinion for the majority, Scalia virtually claimed victory: "It suffices to say that the issuance of the stay suggests that a majority of the court, while not deciding the issues presented, believe that the petitioner [Bush] has a substantial probability of success."

Both sides would have 24 hours to deliver briefs—on a Sunday—on Bush's motion to quash the Florida court's approval of recounts. The justices would hear arguments on the following day and then decide. This action took place two days before the December 12 deadline for state certification of electors.

On Monday morning, December 11, the justices assembled to hear once more the now-familiar arguments. From the Bush side, led by Theodore B. Olsen, longtime Republican legal luminary in Washington, the theme would be that recounting in Florida was both illegal and unconstitutional. The Gore forces, again directed by David Boies, would maintain "the right of voters to have their ballots counted." For 90 minutes, the most intense legal seminar in American history took place before a select audience, with millions following a near-simultaneous audio transcription.

The justices set the tone immediately. A minute or so after launching into his opening, Olsen heard Justice Kennedy demand, "Can you begin by telling us our federal jurisdiction? Where's the federal question here?" Olsen responded, and the colloquies soon involved all other justices except Clarence Thomas, who, as was his practice, remained silent. Souter and Breyer angled for a position that would establish a single criterion for recounting, with an eye to sending the case back to Florida. Scalia, on the opposite approach, inquired regarding chads and stated the view that imperfect perforations were the result of mistakes made by voters, a situation that did not produce a wrong. Rehnquist sought clarification on some facts. O'Connor probed the murky area between legislative and judicial authority; Stevens picked up O'Connor's point, questioning Olsen's contention that the Florida Supreme Court did not possess sufficient authority to review the legislature's electoral design. Ginsburg further developed the Souter–Breyer theme of finding a universally acceptable standard for recounting.

At one point, when Olsen seemed to approach an accommodation with the "single criterion" idea of Souter, Breyer, and Ginsburg, Scalia interjected a sharp corrective: "It's part of your submission, I think," he posed rhetorically for Olsen, "that there is no wrong when a machine does not count those ballots that it's not supposed to count." "That's absolutely correct, Justice Scalia," replied Olsen.

The Gore team's strategy depended on attracting as swing votes O'Connor and Kennedy. To that end, Boies advanced the proposition of the appropriateness of the Florida court's 4–3 ruling ordering the resumption of recounts. Here the case hung for the continuation of Gore hopes. Neither swing vote appeared to move, both justices taking Boies to task on the implications of his argument. "We can't send this back for more fact-finding," a laconic Souter admitted.

Office lights in the Court building burned through the night on Monday. The next day a large part of the nation hovered near television. Public opinion remained remarkably calm even as commentators pointed to an eventual loss of patience, with all that implied. On the Court grounds the media poised, on call, surrounding the press entrance with the twisted gaggle of electronic gear now common to all public events. Correspondents gossiped in small groups. Just after 10 p.m. ET, the undercurrent rose. "Something is happening," television viewers were told. A bizarre tableau immediately materialized.

Television "runners" were seen grabbing at the sheaves of paper coming from the Court's press office. They ran, literally, to the waiting reporters, who tried to make sense of what they held in their hands, turning pages, scanning, producing instant interpretation, all the while live on the networks and cable channels.

As viewers flipped channels over the next hour, they received wildly different accounts of the meaning of the 67-page decision. Several journalists and their legal pundits believed the Court would allow the Florida recounts to proceed. Dan Rather of CBS thought that the opinion did not make Bush president. Pete Williams and Dan Abrams of MSNBC surmised the opposite. CNN's Bernard Shaw, Judy Woodruff, and Roger Cossack clung to the determination that Florida would recount.

Clarity formed overnight. For the first time in American history, the U.S. Supreme Court effectively chose the president of the United States. The Court divided 5–4, the same majority that had accepted jurisdiction in *Bush v. Gore*. Their opinion stressed the approach of midnight, the "safe harbor" date of December 12. Time had run out, they held, making it impossible to recount votes while at the same time respecting "minimal constitutional standards." Boies's admission of the "safe harbor" deadline returned in the hands of those who used it against him with great effect. The Court acted with dispatch, conflating the December 12 "deadline" with the equal protection clause:

> Upon due consideration of the difficulties identified to this point, it is obvious that the recount cannot be conducted in compliance with the requirements of equal protection and due process without substantial additional work. . . . Because it is evident that any recount seeking to meet the December 12 date will be unconstitutional for the reasons we have discussed, we reverse the judgment of the Supreme Court of Florida ordering a recount to proceed.

Justices Souter, Breyer, and Ginsburg had agreed that the lack of a standard threatened equal protection (which contributed to the second court decision that would be announced simultaneously by a misleading 7–2 count). With vehemence, the dissenters argued the necessity of creating that standard and proceeding with the recount.

They lost. Justice Stevens's biting protest received wide coverage:

> What must underlie petitioners' entire federal assault on the Florida election procedures is an unstated lack of confidence in the impartiality and capacity of the state judges who would make the critical decisions if the vote count were to proceed. Otherwise, their position is wholly without merit. The endorsement of that position by the majority of this Court can only lend credence to the most cynical appraisal of the work of judges throughout the land. It is confidence in the men and women who administer the judicial system that is the true backbone of the rule of law. Time will one day heal the wound to that confidence that will be inflicted by today's decision. One thing, however, is certain. Although we may never know with complete certainty the identity of the winner of this year's Presidential election, the identity of the loser is perfectly clear. It is the Nation's confidence in the judge as an impartial guardian of the rule of law.
>
> I respectfully dissent.

The media, with its insatiable appetite, filled the airwaves with law professors, most of them hostile to the decision. "Partisan politics," said Richard Briffault of Columbia Law School; "very contrived," added Susan Low Bloch of Georgetown Law School; "outrageous," declared Larry Kramer of New York University Law

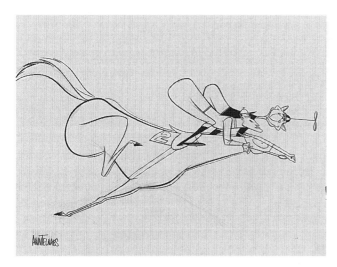

This Ann Telnaes cartoon shows Gore and Bush as jockeys on race horses in an apparent dead heat. While Gore looks determined, Bush, wearing a propeller beanie, claims the lead and the victory. *(Ann Telnaes Editorial Cartoon © 2000 Ann Telnaes. Used with permission of Ann Telnaes and the Cartoonist Group. All rights reserved.)*

School. Several legal scholars suggested a parallel with two of the most repugnant decisions in Court history—*Dred Scott* and *Plessy v. Ferguson*—each a justification of racism. Other students of the Court suggested the decision might offer precedents, in federal–state judicial relations or in the interpretation of equal protection. All of the justices in the majority had lengthy records in opposition to an elastic (or "liberal") interpretation of the equal protection clause, until they embraced it in *Bush v. Gore*. Or, perhaps, was the majority opinion so crafted that it amounted to a unique ad hoc solution to a specific problem? Conservative scholars, supporting the decision, stressed the burgeoning national crisis if the public rose in frustration, or, more likely, if a bitterly partisan Congress staged a reenactment of 1876.

In the frenzied hours after the decision, Gore's strategists in Washington and Florida, encouraged by the vice president, scrutinized the majority opinion seeking mechanisms that would allow his campaign to continue. They continued through the night and into the new day before bowing to a rising consensus, even among partisan supporters, that Gore concede.

On December 13, 36 days after "election day," the president-elect of the United States addressed the nation in evening prime time, from the precisely chosen chamber of the Texas House of Representatives in the capitol building in Austin. The Speaker of the House, Democrat Pete Laney, introduced Bush to a jubilant throng, with the theme of bipartisanship strung through the packed hall together with the Christmas ornaments. "I was elected not to serve one party, but to serve one nation," Bush insisted. "Whether you voted for me or not, I will do my best to serve your interests, and I will work to earn your respect."

An hour earlier, Al Gore had placed a brief call to concede personally to "the president-elect," the first time he had used the term, and to offer formal congratulations. The vice president reminded Governor Bush of the adventure that the two men had had when last they spoke—"and I promised not to call him back this time." Gore had then gone on national television for an eight-minute speech widely characterized as eloquent and gracious. He emphasized his disagreement with the Court's decision, but "I offer my concession."

As Washington welcomed the holidays, a normal atmosphere generally reasserted itself. To be sure, grumbling about the Court would continue, probably well into the future. Correspondingly, assessment of the two campaigns remained firmly in vogue, particularly when the final certified tallies underscored the dimensions of the electoral split. Gore won the popular vote by about 500,000, winning 20 states and the District of Columbia, with 266 electoral votes. One Gore elector in the District

1580 History of American Presidential Elections

of Columbia cast a blank ballot in protest. Bush won 30 states and 271 electoral votes, one more than the needed majority in the Electoral College. Florida's deciding tally of 537 votes out of 5,963,110 officially counted captured the conclusive 25 electoral votes. Who "won" Florida? "No one is ever going to know," said Illinois representative John Shimkus (R-IL). "There will be a burden to acknowledge that."

In spite of the precarious outcome, Gore met sharp negative criticism. He failed to translate eight years of popular incumbency against a candidate with scant political experience and questionable campaign skills. He lost his ancestral home state, Tennessee, and even Democratic redoubt West Virginia, when a victory in either would have won the White House. Critics feasted on his ineffective public demeanor. Early in the campaign, dubious advice transformed Gore's image from pinstriped power suit to earth-toned casual wear, a metaphor for plasticity. His subpar performances in the three debates disappointed the vice president's campaign as much as they braced the supposedly overmatched Bush. Obviously, on the other hand, Gore bore unasked-for liabilities. The Nader campaign, tiny but resilient, drew off a crucial slice of progressive votes. The largest problem of all, his erstwhile partner President Clinton, was judged to be more burden than benefit. Yet on the stark and incomplete ground of pure political ability, the distinction between Clinton and Gore seems as clear as between winner and loser.

Bush's minimalist campaign always identified him as the "outsider" pledged to fight the intrigues, excesses, gridlock, and bitter partisanship found in, as he invariably identified it, "Washington, D.C." What he favored, as his simple messages about decency and civility implied, was limited government, a major tax cut, education reform, and monogamy in the White House.

And so the Bush Restoration came to Washington to take power and as decorously as possible to exact revenge on Clinton for the family humiliation of 1992. For his part, Clinton's long good-bye embarrassed supporters and restoked the bile of enemies. On Inauguration Day, a uniquely American tragicomedy unfolded with all the characters present: Presidents Bush, Clinton, and Bush, rejected former vice president Gore, Chief Justice Rehnquist, who presided over Clinton's impeachment and the younger Bush's ascension, and the eight other justices who milled about each other now away from the center of the stage.

—*J. F. Watts*

Selected Bibliography

See William J. Crotty, *America's Choice 2000: Entering a New Millennium* (2001); E. D. Dover, *Missed Opportunity: Gore, Incumbency, and Television in Election 2000* (2000); Kathleen Hall Jamieson and Paul Waldman, eds., *Electing the President, 2000: The Insider's View* (2001); Daron R. Shaw, *The Race to 270: The Electoral College and the Campaign Strategies of 2000 and 2004* (2006); Washington Post Staff, *Deadlock: The Inside Story of America's Closest Election* (2000), which offers a very useful starting point for understanding the whole election; and Stephen J. Wayne, *The Road to the White House, 2000* (2000).

On the Bush-Gore deadlock, see Bruce A. Ackerman, *Bush v. Gore: The Question of Legitimacy* (2002); Vincent Bugliosi, *The Betrayal of America: How the Supreme Court Undermined the Constitution and Chose Our President* (2001); James W. Ceaser and Andrew E. Busch, *The Perfect Tie: The True Story of the 2000 Presidential Election* (2001); Alan M. Dershowitz, *Supreme Injustice: How the High Court Hijacked Election 2000* (2001); Richard A. Posner, *Breaking the Deadlock: The 2000 Election, the Constitution, and the Courts* (2001); Jack Rakove ed., *The Unfinished Election of 2000* (2001); Bill Shannon, *At Any Cost: How Al Gore Tried to Steal the Election* (2001); Jeffrey Toobin, *Too Close To Call: The Thirty-Six-Day Battle to Decide the 2000 Election* (2001); Mark Whitman, *Florida 2000: A Sourcebook on the Contested Presidential Election* (2003); and Charles L. Zelden, *Bush v. Gore: Exposing the Hidden Crisis in American Democracy* (2008).

2000 Electoral Map and Statistics

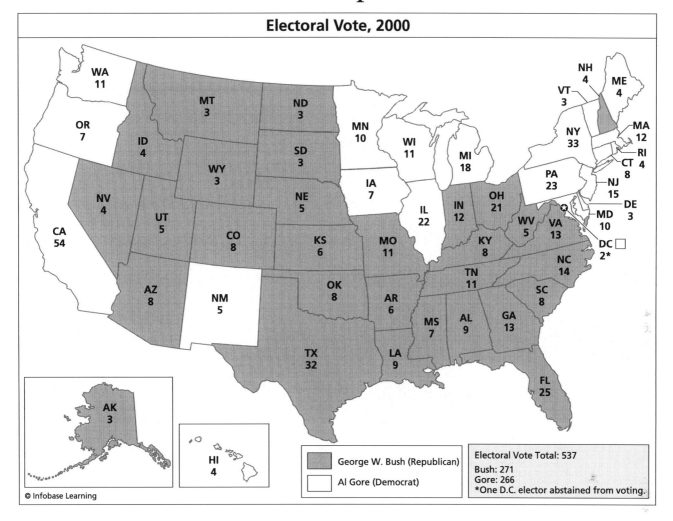

Electoral Vote, 2000

George W. Bush (Republican)

Al Gore (Democrat)

Electoral Vote Total: 537
Bush: 271
Gore: 266
*One D.C. elector abstained from voting.

© Infobase Learning

2000 ELECTION STATISTICS

State	Number of Electors	Total Popular Vote	Elec Vote R	Elec Vote D	Elec Vote A*	Pop Vote R	Pop Vote D	Pop Vote G	Margin of Victory Votes	Margin of Victory % Total Vote
Alabama	9	1,672,551	9			1	2	3	248,807	14.88%
Alaska	3	285,560	3			1	2	3	88,394	30.95%
Arizona	8	1,534,113	8			1	2	3	96,311	6.28%
Arkansas	6	921,781	6			1	2	3	50,172	5.44%
California	54	10,965,856		54		2	1	3	1,293,774	11.80%
Colorado	8	1,741,365	8			1	2	3	145,518	8.36%
Connecticut	8	1,459,525		8		2	1	3	254,921	17.47%
Delaware	3	327,622		3		2	1	3	42,780	13.06%
District of Columbia	3	201,894		2	1	2	1	3	153,850	76.20%
Florida	25	5,963,110	25			1	2	3	537	0.01%
Georgia	13	2,596,804	13			1	2	4	303,490	11.69%
Hawaii	4	367,951		4		2	1	3	67,441	18.33%
Idaho	4	501,621	4			1	2	3	198,300	39.53%
Illinois	22	4,742,123		22		2	1	3	569,605	12.01%
Indiana	12	2,199,302	12			1	2	3	343,856	15.63%
Iowa	7	1,315,563		7		2	1	3	4,144	0.31%
Kansas	6	1,072,216	6			1	2	3	223,056	20.80%
Kentucky	8	1,544,187	8			1	2	3	233,594	15.13%
Louisiana	9	1,765,656	9			1	2	3	135,527	7.68%
Maine	4	651,817		4		2	1	3	33,335	5.11%
Maryland	10	2,025,480		10		2	1	3	331,985	16.39%
Massachusetts	12	2,702,984		12		2	1	3	737,985	27.30%
Michigan	18	4,232,711		18		2	1	3	217,279	5.13%
Minnesota	10	2,438,685		10		2	1	3	58,607	2.40%
Mississippi	7	994,926	7			1	2	3	168,266	16.91%
Missouri	11	2,359,892	11			1	2	3	78,786	3.34%
Montana	3	410,997	3			1	2	3	103,052	25.07%
Nebraska	5	697,019	5			1	2	3	202,082	28.99%
Nevada	4	608,970	4			1	2	3	21,597	3.55%
New Hampshire	4	569,081	4			1	2	3	7,211	1.27%
New Jersey	15	3,187,226		15		2	1	3	504,677	15.83%
New Mexico	5	598,605		5		2	1	3	366	0.06%
New York	33	6,822,668		33		2	1	3	1,704,533	24.98%
North Carolina	14	2,911,262	14			1	2	-	373,471	12.83%
North Dakota	3	288,267	3			1	2	3	79,568	27.60%
Ohio	21	4,705,457	21			1	2	3	165,019	3.51%
Oklahoma	8	1,234,229	8			1	2	-	270,061	21.88%
Oregon	7	1,533,968		7		2	1	3	6,765	0.44%
Pennsylvania	23	4,913,119		23		2	1	3	204,840	4.17%
Rhode Island	4	409,112		4		2	1	3	118,953	29.08%
South Carolina	8	1,383,777	8			1	2	3	220,387	15.93%
South Dakota	3	316,269	3			1	2	-	71,896	22.73%
Tennessee	11	2,076,181	11			1	2	3	80,229	3.86%
Texas	32	6,407,637	32			1	2	3	1,365,893	21.32%
Utah	5	770,754	5			1	2	3	312,043	40.49%
Vermont	3	294,308		3		2	1	3	29,247	9.94%
Virginia	13	2,739,447	13			1	2	3	220,200	8.04%
Washington	11	2,488,745		11		2	1	3	138,788	5.58%
West Virginia	5	648,124	5			1	2	3	40,978	6.32%
Wisconsin	11	2,598,607		11		2	1	3	5,708	0.22%
Wyoming	3	218,351	3			1	2	3	87,466	40.06%
Total	538	105,417,475	271	266	1	2	1	3	543,816	0.52%

* One elector abstained from voting.

Bush Republican		Gore Democratic		Nader Green		Buchanan Reform		Others	
944,409	56.47%	695,602	41.59%	18,349	1.10%	6,364	0.38%	7,827	0.47%
167,398	58.62%	79,004	27.67%	28,747	10.07%	5,192	1.82%	5,219	1.83%
781,652	50.95%	685,341	44.67%	45,645	2.98%	12,373	0.81%	9,102	0.59%
472,940	51.31%	422,768	45.86%	13,421	1.46%	7,358	0.80%	5,294	0.57%
4,567,429	41.65%	5,861,203	53.45%	418,707	3.82%	44,987	0.41%	73,530	0.67%
883,745	50.75%	738,227	42.39%	91,434	5.25%	10,465	0.60%	17,494	1.00%
561,094	38.44%	816,015	55.91%	64,452	4.42%	4,731	0.32%	13,233	0.91%
137,288	41.90%	180,068	54.96%	8,307	2.54%	777	0.24%	1,182	0.36%
18,073	8.95%	171,923	85.16%	10,576	5.24%	0	0.00%	1,322	0.65%
2,912,790	48.85%	2,912,253	48.84%	97,488	1.63%	17,484	0.29%	23,095	0.39%
1,419,720	54.67%	1,116,230	42.98%	13,432	0.52%	10,926	0.42%	36,496	1.41%
137,845	37.46%	205,286	55.79%	21,623	5.88%	1,071	0.29%	2,126	0.58%
336,937	67.17%	138,637	27.64%	12,292	2.45%	7,615	1.52%	6,140	1.22%
2,019,421	42.58%	2,589,026	54.60%	103,759	2.19%	16,106	0.34%	13,811	0.29%
1,245,836	56.65%	901,980	41.01%	18,531	0.84%	16,959	0.77%	15,996	0.73%
634,373	48.22%	638,517	48.54%	29,374	2.23%	5,731	0.44%	7,568	0.58%
622,332	58.04%	399,276	37.24%	36,086	3.37%	7,370	0.69%	7,152	0.67%
872,492	56.50%	638,898	41.37%	23,192	1.50%	4,173	0.27%	5,432	0.35%
927,871	52.55%	792,344	44.88%	20,473	1.16%	14,356	0.81%	10,612	0.60%
286,616	43.97%	319,951	49.09%	37,127	5.70%	4,443	0.68%	3,680	0.56%
813,797	40.18%	1,145,782	56.57%	53,768	2.65%	4,248	0.21%	7,885	0.39%
878,502	32.50%	1,616,487	59.80%	173,564	6.42%	11,149	0.41%	23,282	0.86%
1,953,139	46.14%	2,170,418	51.28%	84,165	1.99%	2,061	0.05%	22,928	0.54%
1,109,659	45.50%	1,168,266	47.91%	126,696	5.20%	22,166	0.91%	11,898	0.49%
573,230	57.62%	404,964	40.70%	8,126	0.82%	2,267	0.23%	6,339	0.64%
1,189,924	50.42%	1,111,138	47.08%	38,515	1.63%	9,818	0.42%	10,497	0.44%
240,178	58.44%	137,126	33.36%	24,437	5.95%	5,697	1.39%	3,559	0.87%
433,862	62.25%	231,780	33.25%	24,540	3.52%	3,646	0.52%	3,191	0.46%
301,575	49.52%	279,978	45.98%	15,008	2.46%	4,747	0.78%	7,662	1.26%
273,559	48.07%	266,348	46.80%	22,198	3.90%	2,615	0.46%	4,361	0.77%
1,284,173	40.29%	1,788,850	56.13%	94,554	2.97%	6,989	0.22%	12,660	0.40%
286,417	47.85%	286,783	47.91%	21,251	3.55%	1,392	0.23%	2,762	0.46%
2,403,374	35.23%	4,107,907	60.21%	244,060	3.58%	31,703	0.46%	35,624	0.52%
1,631,163	56.03%	1,257,692	43.20%	0	0.00%	8,874	0.30%	13,533	0.46%
174,852	60.66%	95,284	33.05%	9,497	3.29%	7,288	2.53%	1,346	0.47%
2,351,209	49.97%	2,186,190	46.46%	117,857	2.50%	26,724	0.57%	23,477	0.50%
744,337	60.31%	474,276	38.43%	0	0.00%	9,014	0.73%	6,602	0.53%
713,577	46.52%	720,342	46.96%	77,357	5.04%	7,063	0.46%	15,629	1.02%
2,281,127	46.43%	2,485,967	50.60%	103,392	2.10%	16,023	0.33%	26,610	0.54%
130,555	31.91%	249,508	60.99%	25,052	6.12%	2,273	0.56%	1,724	0.42%
786,426	56.83%	566,039	40.91%	20,279	1.47%	3,520	0.25%	7,513	0.54%
190,700	60.30%	118,804	37.56%	0	0.00%	3,322	1.05%	3,443	1.09%
1,061,949	51.15%	981,720	47.28%	19,781	0.95%	4,250	0.20%	8,481	0.41%
3,799,639	59.30%	2,433,746	37.98%	137,994	2.15%	12,394	0.19%	23,864	0.37%
515,096	66.83%	203,053	26.34%	35,850	4.65%	9,319	1.21%	7,436	0.96%
119,775	40.70%	149,022	50.63%	20,374	6.92%	2,192	0.74%	2,945	1.00%
1,437,490	52.47%	1,217,290	44.44%	59,398	2.17%	5,455	0.20%	19,814	0.72%
1,108,864	44.56%	1,247,652	50.13%	103,002	4.14%	7,171	0.29%	22,056	0.89%
336,475	51.92%	295,497	45.59%	10,680	1.65%	3,169	0.49%	2,303	0.36%
1,237,279	47.61%	1,242,987	47.83%	94,070	3.62%	11,471	0.44%	12,800	0.49%
147,947	67.76%	60,481	27.70%	4,625	2.12%	2,724	1.25%	2,574	1.18%
50,460,110	47.87%	51,003,926	48.38%	2,883,105	2.73%	449,225	0.43%	621,109	0.59%

Election of 2004

Election Overview

Election Year 2004

Election Day November 2, 2004

Winning Candidates

* **President:** George W. Bush
* **Vice President:** Richard Cheney

Election Results [ticket, party: popular votes (percentage of popular vote); electoral votes (percentage of electoral votes)]

* George W. Bush and Richard Cheney, Republican: 62,040,611 (50.73%); 286 (53.2%)
* John Kerry and John Edwards, Democratic: 59,028,432 (48.26%); 251 (46.7%)
* Ralph Nader and Peter Camejo, Independent: 465,650 (0.38%); 0 (0.0%)
* Michael Badnarik and Richard Campagna, Libertarian: 397,265 (0.32%); 0 (0.0%)
* Other: 363,579 (0.30%); 0 (0.0%)

Voter Turnout 56.2%

Central Forums/Campaign Methods for Addressing Voters

* Speeches
* Rallies
* Television ads
* Debates
* Web sites, e-mail, blogs, XML/RSS feeds

Incumbent President and Vice President on Election Day George W. Bush and Richard Cheney

Population (2004) 293,348,000

Gross Domestic Product

* $11.868 trillion (in current dollars: $12.264 trillion)
* Per capita: $40,456 (in current dollars: $41,806)

Number of Daily Newspapers (2004) 1,457

Average Daily Circulation 54,600,000

Households with

* Radio: 108,300,000
* Television: 109,000,000
* Computer/Internet (2003): 62,000,000; 70% of total households online by July 2005

Method of Choosing Electors Popular vote (mostly general-ticket system/winner take all)

Method of Choosing Nominees

* Presidential preference primaries
* Caucuses

Key Issues and Events

* "Bushophobia"—irrational liberal hatred of Bush
* Charges that Bush stole the 2000 election and lied his way into the Iraq war
* September 11, 2001, terrorist attacks in New York, Washington, and Pennsylvania and the ensuing "War on Terror"
* Wars in Afghanistan and Iraq
* Polarized nation: red states v. blue states; conservatives vs. liberals
* In the 2002 midterm elections Republicans maintain control of House of Representatives, gain four

seats, and recapture the Senate by winning two additional seats.

- Health Care—tens of millions of Americans uninsured.
- Education: No Child Left Behind Act
- Bush proposes Social Security reform.
- Continuing struggle over taxes, budget deficit
- May 2003, Bush prematurely declares "Mission Accomplished" in Iraq.
- December 2003, Saddam Hussein's capture boosts American morale after months of terrorism and chaos in Iraq, but the violence continues.

Leading Candidates

REPUBLICANS
- George W. Bush, president of the United States (Texas)

DEMOCRATS
- John Kerry, senator (Massachusetts)
- John Edwards, senator (North Carolina)
- Howard Dean, former governor (Vermont)
- Wesley Clark, retired general (Arkansas)
- Dennis Kucinich, representative (Ohio)
- Al Sharpton, reverend and civil rights activist (New York)
- Joseph Lieberman, senator (Connecticut)
- Richard Gephardt, representative (Missouri)
- Carol Moseley Braun, former senator (Illinois)
- Bob Graham, senator (Florida)

Trajectory

- The worst terrorist attack in American history, on September 11, 2001, defines George W. Bush's presidency and will shape the 2004 campaign.
- President Bush, facing minimal opposition, wins the Republican caucuses in Iowa, while Senator John Kerry wins the Democratic caucuses, with nearly 38 percent of the vote on January 19, 2004. For Kerry this marks a comeback after months of watching Howard Dean surge with his Internet-fueled campaign.
- Dean's campaign never recovers from Dean's "scream" during his Iowa concession speech the night of January 19.
- On February 3, Kerry wins five of seven contests and is well on his way to clinching the nomination. Senator John Edwards will continue fighting for another month, without posing much of a threat.
- During a Kerry campaign swing through West Virginia on March 16, a heckler derides the senator for failing to support an $87 billion appropriation for the troops. Exasperated by the persistent

questioner, trying to explain his legislative strategy, Kerry exclaims: "I actually did vote for the $87 billion before I voted against it." Within 24 hours the sentence is immortalized in a Republican campaign commercial branding Kerry a "Flip-Flopper."

- On April 28, CBS reports acts of torture and sexual humiliation perpetrated by American soldiers at Iraq's massive Abu Ghraib prison. The news intensifies the Democratic fury against Bush.
- Kerry caps a successful Democratic convention in his hometown, Boston—featuring, among other highlights, the extraordinary, eloquent national debut of Senate candidate Barack Obama—with an effective acceptance address on July 29. "I'm John Kerry and I'm reporting for duty," he says to great applause, while warning ominously, "This is the most important election of our lifetime."
- As Kerry enjoys his modest post-convention "bounce," leading Bush 50 to 44 percent, Swift Boat Veterans for Truth launch ads against his Vietnam record in three swing states on August 5. These and other commercials, along with a best-selling book, will constitute one of the most effective advertising attacks in campaign history. Kerry, saving his money for September and seeking to preserve his dignity, foolishly fails to respond.
- Speakers at the Republican National Convention pummel Kerry, led by the renegade Democrat Zell Miller. Bush's acceptance address on September 2 is more upbeat, following the convention theme: "Fulfilling America's Promise by Building a Safer World and a More Hopeful America." Meanwhile, outside, hundreds of thousands of anti-Bush protesters constitute the largest demonstration against a party convention in history.
- CBS's veteran news anchor Dan Rather broadcasts a report on *60 Minutes II* on September 8, claiming Bush shirked his duty while serving in the Air National Guard from 1972 to 1973. In a major victory, bloggers quickly prove the documents, supposedly written by Bush's commander, the late Lieutenant Colonel Jerry B. Killian, to be forgeries. Rather soon resigns.
- At the first of three presidential debates on September 30, at the University of Miami, President Bush scowls too much and appears far too impatient with Kerry, whose smooth performance boosts his standing.
- By the third debate, October 13, Bush is calmer and more in command, but the debates allow Kerry to appear presidential and authoritative, while Bush appears testy and diminished.

- On the eve of the election, October 29, 2004, the al-Jazeera network broadcasts a tape from Osama bin Laden, the head of al-Qaeda. Bin Laden takes responsibility for 9/11—and helps reinforce Bush's message that the terror threat continues.
- Ohio electoral votes contested for data irregularities. Robert F. Kennedy Jr.: "the widespread irregularities make it impossible to know for certain that the [Ohio] outcome reflected the will of the voters."
- Representative Stephanie Tubbs Jones of Ohio and Senator Barbara Boxer of California, both Democrats, raise objections to the Ohio Certificate of Vote. Both houses voted to override the objection, 74 to 1 in the Senate and 267 to 31 in the House of Representatives.
- *Moss v. Bush:* Charging fraud and seeking to challenge Bush's electoral votes in Ohio. The case is dismissed.
- One Minnesota elector voted for John Edwards for both president and vice president.

Conventions

- Democratic National Convention: July 26–29, 2004, FleetCenter, Boston
- Republican National Convention: August 30–September 2, 2004, Madison Square Garden, New York

Ballots/Nominees

REPUBLICANS
President
- George W. Bush 2,508; 99.96%

Vice President
- Richard Cheney nominated by voice vote

DEMOCRATS
President
- John Kerry 4,253; 98.40%
- Dennis Kucinich 43; 0.99%
- Abstention 26; 0.60%
- Total 4,322; 100.00%

Vice President
- John Edwards chosen by acclamation

Primary Debates

- Sixteen Democratic primary debates, starting on April 9, 2003, with the last one on Feb. 29, 2004. The organizers usually are interest groups representing, among others, the pro-choice community, the elderly, labor unions, African-Americans, Hispanics, and women.

NOTABLE DEBATES

- May 3, 2003, University of South Carolina campus in Columbia during South Carolina's Democratic Weekend. George Stephanopoulos of ABC News moderates: Braun, Dean, Edwards, Gephardt, Graham, Kerry, Kucinich, Lieberman, and Sharpton
- January 22, 2004: Democratic debate in Manchester, New Hampshire
- January 29, 2004: Democratic debate in Greenville, South Carolina

Primaries/Caucuses Results

REPUBLICANS
- George W. Bush 7,853,893; 98.06%
- Uncommitted 91,926; 1.15%
- Unidentified scattering 37,104; 0.46%
- Bill Wyatt 10,937; 0.14%

DEMOCRATS
- John Kerry 9,930,497; 60.98%
- John Edwards 3,162,337; 19.42%
- Howard Dean 903,460; 5.55%
- Dennis J. Kucinich 620,242; 3.81%
- Wesley Clark 547,369; 3.36%
- Al Sharpton 380,865; 2.34%
- Joe Lieberman 280,940; 1.73%
- Uncommitted 157,953; 0.97%
- Lyndon LaRouche 103,731; 0.64%
- Carol Moseley Braun 98,469; 0.60%
- Richard Gephardt 63,902; 0.39%
- Unidentified scattering 12,525; 0.08%
- Randy Crow 6,398; 0.04%
- Mildred Glover 4,050; 0.02%
- Bill McGaughey 3,161; 0.02%
- George Ballard 2,826; 0.02%
- Others 3,527; 0.02%

Party Platform

REPUBLICANS
- Maintain war on terror
- Keep vigilant on national security
- Create an "ownership society"
- Support a constitutional amendment guaranteeing that an "unborn child has a fundamental individual right to life"
- Define marriage as being between a man and a woman

DEMOCRATS
- Need energy independence
- More environmental protection
- Strengthen military
- Enhance homeland security

Campaign Innovations

- Internet as an organizing tool; first generation of social networking tools like "Meetup"
- Fund-raising over the Internet brings in many small contributions
- Web sites; e-mail; blogs; e-advertising; online organization; XML/RSS feeds
- The use of electronic voting systems spreads.
- Colorado Amendment 36 proposes distributing Colorado's electoral votes proportionally rather than winner take all—it fails to pass on Election Day.

Campaign Tactics

REPUBLICANS
- Bush shifts from big-tent, compassionate conservatism in 2000 to a red-meat, red-state–oriented approach.
- Both campaigns focus on "wedge issues" to mobilize their core supporters, with Bush's "Brain," Karl Rove, estimating that the 3–5 million Christian evangelicals he is targeting constitute approximately 40 percent of the Republican Party.
- Rally around the flag during a time of national crisis.
- "527s" help pummel Kerry as a traitor to his fellow Vietnam veterans by opposing the Vietnam War so publicly and self-servingly.

DEMOCRATS
- Kerry refuses to renounce his initial support for the Iraq War. Instead, he attacks Bush's execution of the war.
- The Democrats mock Bush's campaign promise to be a "uniter not a divider," listing it as the first of "Bush's Broken Promises."
- The "Anybody But Bush" disgust for the president as stupid, as a liar, as incompetent feeds an intensity in the campaign.

Debates

- September 30, 2004: Presidential debate at University of Miami, moderated by Jim Lehrer of PBS. Kerry performs well; Bush is criticized for his harsh demeanor.
- October 5, 2004: Vice-presidential debate at Case Western Reserve University in Cleveland, Ohio, moderated by Gwen Ifill of PBS.
- October 8, 2004: Presidential debate at Washington University in St. Louis, Missouri, moderated by Charles Gibson of ABC. Bush performs better but still appears angry and flustered, unlike the cool Kerry.
- October 13, 2004: Presidential debate at Arizona State University, moderated by Bob Schieffer of CBS News. Bush does not triumph in the third debate, which emphasizes the economy. The debates boost Kerry's poll numbers because he appears more presidential.

Popular Campaign Slogans

REPUBLICANS
- "Yes, America Can!"
- "Heart and Soul"
- "Moving America Forward"
- "A Safer World and More Hopeful America"
- "Steady leadership in times of change"

DEMOCRATS
- "Comeback Kerry"
- "Let America Be America Again"
- "A stronger America begins at home"
- "A safer, stronger, more secure America"
- "The real deal"
- "The courage to do what's right for America"
- "Together, we can build a stronger America"
- "A lifetime of service and strength"
- "A new team, for a new America"
- "Stronger at home, respected in the world"
- "America deserves better"
- "Help is on the way!"
- "Don't change horsemen in mid-apocalypse"

Campaign Songs

REPUBLICANS
- "Only in America"
- "Wave on Wave"

DEMOCRATIC
- "No Surrender"
- "Fortunate Son"

Influential Campaign Appeals or Ads

REPUBLICANS
- "Safer, Stronger"
- Ad ridiculing Kerry's "fog" about supporting the troops
- Image of Kerry windsurfing in Nantucket target of a Bush advertisement: "In which direction would John Kerry lead? Kerry voted for the Iraq war, opposed it, supported it, and now opposes it again. He bragged about voting for the $87 billion to

support our troops before he voted against it. John Kerry. Whichever way the wind blows."
- John Kerry as a flip-flopper
- Jerome R. Corsi and John O'Neill's *Unfit for Command: Swift Boat Veterans Speak Out Against John Kerry* becomes a huge best seller pillorying Kerry.

DEMOCRATS
- "One thousand U.S. casualties. Two Americans beheaded just this week. The Pentagon admits terrorists are pouring into Iraq." Yet, "in the face of the Iraq quagmire, George Bush's answer is to run a juvenile and tasteless attack ad."
- Questions the reliability of President Bush's information about Iraq and Bush's brainpower
- Promises to restore "trust and credibility" to the White House

Campaign Finance

Amounts for each candidate for the general campaign (federal financing in return for spending limits):
- Bush: $74,260,000 (in current dollars: $80,387,000)
- Kerry: $74,260,000 (in current dollars: $80,387,000)

Estimated total spent on each campaign, start to finish:
- George W. Bush $367,227,801 = $5.92 per vote
- John Kerry $326,236,288 = $5.52 per vote
- Ralph Nader $4,566,037 = $9.85 per vote
- The Bipartisan Campaign Reform Act of 2002 (the McCain-Feingold Bill) prohibits "soft money," meaning unregulated contributions to national political parties when a candidate accepts public financing and spending limits.
- McCain-Feingold Bill helps 527s proliferate. Named after Section 527 of the Internal Revenue Code, these groups can raise almost unlimited funds as long as they do not coordinate their plans with a candidate.

Defining Quotations

- "In the wake of September 11, who among us can say with any certainty to anybody that the weapons might not be used against our troops or against allies in the region?" *Senator John Kerry, October 9, 2002, in his Senate speech explaining why he voted for the "pro-war" resolution authorizing force in Iraq*
- "What I want to know is what in the world so many Democrats are doing supporting the President's unilateral intervention in Iraq." *Howard Dean addressing the California State Democratic Convention, March 15, 2003*

- "Not only are we going to New Hampshire, Tom Harkin, we're going to South Carolina and Oklahoma and Arizona and North Dakota and New Mexico, and we're going to California and Texas and New York. . . . And we're going to South Dakota and Oregon and Washington and Michigan, and then we're going to Washington, D.C., to take back the White House! Yeah!!!" *Howard Dean's "scream" at the Iowa caucus concession speech, January 19, 2004*
- "An amazing thing happened in the presidential contest of 2004. For the first time in my life, maybe the first time in history, a candidate lost but his campaign won. . . . Nothing less than the first shot in America's second revolution, nothing less than the people taking the first step to reclaiming a system that had long ago forgotten they existed. This was democracy bubbling to the surface." *Joe Trippi, architect of Dean's net-roots campaigning techniques*
- "I actually did vote for the $87 billion before I voted against it." *John Kerry responding to a persistent questioner while stumping in West Virginia, March 16, 2004*
- "I wish you'd have given me this written question ahead of time so I could plan for it. I'm sure something will pop into my head here in the midst of this press conference, with all the pressure of trying to come up with answer, but it hasn't yet." *George W. Bush, prime-time press conference, response to a reporter's question about what mistakes he has made since 9/11, April 13, 2004*
- "Nobody wants to be the war president. I want to be the peace president." *George W. Bush at a reelection rally, Cedar Rapids, Iowa, July 20, 2004*
- "There's not a liberal America and a conservative America; there's the United States of America. There's not a black America and white America and Latino America and Asian America; there's the United States of America. The pundits, the pundits like to slice and dice our country into red states and blue states: red states for Republicans, blue states for Democrats. But I've got news for them, too. We worship an awesome God in the blue states, and we don't like federal agents poking around our libraries in the red states. We coach Little League in the blue states and, yes, we've got some gay friends in the red states. There are patriots who opposed the war in Iraq, and there are patriots who supported the war in Iraq. We are one people, all of us pledging allegiance to the stars and stripes, all of us defending the United States of America." *Barack Obama, Democratic National Convention keynote address, July 27, 2004*

- "I'm John Kerry and I'm reporting for duty . . . This is the most important election of our lifetime. My first pledge to you tonight: As president, I will restore trust and credibility to the White House. . . . Now, I know there that are those who criticize me for seeing complexities—and I do—because some issues just aren't all that simple. Saying there are weapons of mass destruction in Iraq doesn't make it so. Saying we can fight a war on the cheap doesn't make it so. And proclaiming 'Mission accomplished' certainly doesn't make it so. The future doesn't belong to fear; it belongs to freedom." *John F. Kerry, address accepting the presidential nomination at the Democratic National Convention in Boston, July 29, 2004*

- "For more than thirty years, most Vietnam veterans kept silent as we were maligned as misfits, drug addicts, and baby killers. Now that a key creator of that poisonous image is seeking the Presidency we have resolved to end our silence." *Swift Boat Veteran and POWS for Truth, home page, part of a campaign launched in August 2004*

- "Senator Kerry has made it clear that he would use military force only if approved by the United Nations. Kerry would let Paris decide when America needs defending. I want Bush to decide. . . . John Kerry, who says he doesn't like outsourcing, wants to outsource our national security. . . . This politician wants to be leader of the free world. Free for how long?" *Senator Zell Miller, Georgia Democrat, Republican National Convention keynote address, September 1, 2004*

- "You may have noticed I have a few flaws, too. People sometimes have to correct my English. I knew I had a problem when Arnold Schwarzenegger started doing it. Some folks look at me and see a certain swagger, which in Texas is called 'walking.' Now and then I come across as a little too blunt, and for that we can all thank the white-haired lady sitting right up there." *George W. Bush, address accepting the presidential nomination at the Republican National Convention in New York City, September 2, 2004 (and pointing to his mother, Barbara Bush)*

- "Again, my opponent and I have different approaches. I proposed and the Congress overwhelmingly passed $87 billion in funding needed by our troops doing battle in Afghanistan and Iraq. My opponent and his running mate voted against this money for bullets and fuel and vehicles and body armor. . . . This moment in the life of our country will be remembered. Generations will know if we kept our faith and kept our word. Generations will know if we seized this moment, and used it to build a future of safety and peace. The freedom of many, and the future security of our Nation, now depend on us. And tonight, my fellow Americans, I ask you to stand with me." *George W. Bush, address accepting the presidential nomination at the Republican National Convention in New York City, September 2, 2004*

- "I would not have done just one thing differently than the president on Iraq, I would have done everything differently than the president on Iraq. . . . You've about 500 troops here, 500 troops there and it's American troops that are 90 percent of the combat casualties and it's American taxpayers that are paying 90 percent of the cost of the war. It's the wrong war, in the wrong place at the wrong time." *John Kerry, at Racine, West Virginia, September 6, 2004*

- "The advance of liberty is the path to both a safer and better world." *George W. Bush in speech to U.N. General Assembly, September 21, 2004*

- "When our country's in danger the president's job is not to take an international poll. The President's job is to defend America." *George W. Bush, barnstorming Ohio, October 2, 2004*

Lasting Legacy of Campaign

- 2004 is America's first billion-dollar election campaign.
- Bush wins, but the enmity generated makes governing difficult.

Election of 2004

The one-line historical verdict regarding the 2004 election is simple: not for the first time in American history, and probably not for the last time, a war president won reelection during wartime. Republican president George W. Bush beat Democratic senator John F. Kerry by echoing Abraham Lincoln's 1864 reelection appeal: "Don't swap horses while crossing the river." This tale's fascinating twist is just how close Kerry came to winning, nevertheless. Even with the historical deck stacked in President Bush's favor, despite a campaign bookended by Iraqi leader Saddam Hussein's capture toward the beginning and a threatening Osama bin Laden tape at the end, Republicans needed excellent organization, aggressive messaging, millions of dollars, an assist from the culture wars, and major Democratic missteps to win.

The deadly terrorist attacks of September 11, 2001, defined the Bush presidency and the 2004 campaign. On a bright September morning, 19 Jihadists hijacked four transcontinental flights, turning these civilian airplanes filled with innocents and loaded with fuel into massive suicide bombs. One jet hit the North Tower of New York's World Trade Center, one jet hit the South Tower, one jet hit the Pentagon, and one jet crashed into a field near Shanksville, Pennsylvania, after passengers and surviving crew members stormed the commandeered cockpit. Osama bin Laden's al-Qaeda terrorists murdered nearly 3,000 people that day.

Having witnessed on television planes exploding, towers collapsing, mass murder in familiar settings, a new terror seized Americans. After those ugly September days, many feared a wave of similar attacks. Many feared a new reality of constricted choices, as "the world would never be the same."

Amid the terror, some hope flourished too. The rescuers' nobility, the victims' biographies, etched into the country's collective soul, reaffirmed America's national identity. Many reevaluated the 1990s' boom times as superficial. They vowed to love life more, to hug loved ones harder, to search for meaning more intensely, to spend more time doing great, selfless things. Initially, proposals to commemorate 9/11 as a day for national volunteer service proved popular.

Shocked by the attacks, President Bush stumbled initially but soon found his stride. After nearly nine months in office, perhaps this rookie president's greatest accom-

This aerial view shows what remained of one of the 110-story World Trade Center towers after the terrorist attacks on September 11, 2001. *(Eric J. Tilford/U.S. Navy)*

plishment had been asserting his legitimacy despite his electoral deadlock in 2000 with Vice President Al Gore. The Supreme Court eventually ended the 36-day standoff in December 2000, giving Bush the presidency. Partisan Democrats remained embittered, though, noting Bush lost the popular vote by half a million ballots. In a mark of the Constitution's enduring power, most Americans accepted Bush as president.

President Bush refused to govern as an accidental president. In early February 2001, Bush proposed a ten-year $1.6 trillion tax cut. Democrats' $1.2 trillion counter-proposal made the question "how large," not "whether," ceding victory to Bush.

The president farmed out his political dirty work to his political consultant, Karl Rove. Often touted as Bush's "brain," possessing an arithmetical strategic mind hardened by partisan warfare, Rove sought the winning margin, even if narrow. Rove's governing strategy in looking toward the 2004 election focused on recapturing the 3–5 million evangelical Christian conservatives who had not voted for Bush in 2000.

Bush critics portrayed Bush as a dummy, needing a ventriloquist like Rove. James Moore and Wayne Slater wrote best-selling books labeling Rove "likely the most powerful unelected official of our time." Moore and Slater treated Rove's aggressive fund-raising and "politics of deception" as revolutionary, rather than the latest chapter in a long history of political gamesmanship. This caricature absolved noble, outfoxed Democrats of responsibility for losing elections. It assumed that Republicans governed only by manipulating gullible Americans.

Like former president Ronald Reagan, Bush did not mind being "misunderestimated," as he, a Yale College and Harvard Business school graduate, once said. Born to George Herbert Walker and Barbara Pierce Bush on July 6, 1946, the grandson of Senator Prescott Bush, George W. Bush was known to be affable and fun-loving. He also was a big drinker when young but stopped drinking when he turned 40 in 1986. "When I was young and irresponsible," he said, "I was young and irresponsible."

After that, Bush began to blossom professionally. He advised his father informally but effectively during George H. W. Bush's 1988 presidential campaign and one-term presidency. In 1989, Bush became a co-owner of major league baseball team, the Texas Rangers. He cashed out in 1998 with $14.9 million, having earned nearly a 25-fold return on his investment and a golden reputation for leading the club with brio. In 1994, he unseated popular Texas governor Ann Richards and easily won re-election in 1998.

In building his political career, Bush disarmed critics. Tempering genuine charm with brutish cunning, backed by go-for-broke loyalists like Karl Rove, he knocked out his top rival for the 2000 Republican nomination, Senator John McCain. These skills kept Republicans focused during the drawn-out electoral deadlock.

Nevertheless, shortly after the inauguration, the vaunted Rove-Bush team overstepped. The Republicans controlled the evenly split Senate only through Vice President Richard Cheney's tie-breaking vote. In May 2001, when the Senate's Republican caucus endorsed massive education cuts, Vermont senator James Jeffords deserted his party and became an Independent. His defection made the Democrats the majority party in the Senate by a 50–49 vote.

The president persevered. Unlike Ronald Reagan, who frustrated conservatives by compromising frequently, and George H. W. Bush, whose moderation alienated conservatives, George W. Bush advanced the conservative social agenda and economic vision. Bush's "faith-based initiative" mobilized churches to tackle social problems, worrying liberals who feared the intrusion of church on state matters. He rejected the Kyoto protocols to reduce greenhouse gas emissions, infuriating environmentalists. He hailed the "sanctity of life," dismaying pro-choice feminists.

Bush's tone also alienated liberals. Bush brought a crisp, corporate feel back to the White House. He expected discipline, punctuality, clean living, and clean language from his staff. But if the West Wing felt like a Boy Scout convention, filled with earnest, well-dressed, white-bread types, the president himself remained too much the frat boy. Bush's mischievous streak, his promiscuous knighting of friends with nicknames, his lopsided and often misfiring grin, and his loping walk telegraphed a mix of aristocratic entitlement and devil-may-care insouciance that drove journalists, academics, and Democrats crazy.

After the president consolidated power in his first spring and signed the tax-cut package in the summer, his domestic initiatives stalled. The president's month-long vacation in August 2001 at his Crawford, Texas, ranch reminded reporters of Ronald Reagan's lazy days at his California ranch. Little did anyone realize just how negligent this lassitude would appear shortly after Bush returned to Washington in September.

As the Twin Towers collapsed, the Pentagon smouldered, and America's post–cold war sense of security crumbled on 9/11, Bush steadied himself quickly. Visiting the World Trade Center ruins, hugging a rescue worker while addressing others through a megaphone, he telegraphed a humanity, a physicality, that reassured Americans. "Great harm has been done to us," Bush told Congress. "And in our grief and anger we have found our mission and our moment."

Bush's headstrong, can-do cowboy patriotism made him seem the right man for the job. His Texas swagger inspired most Americans when dithering would have demoralized. His restrained statesmanship and condemnation of vigilante violence as "not the America I know" saved Arab Americans from acts of mass revenge. On September 17, while visiting a Washington-area mosque, the Islamic Center, Bush declared: "Americans who mistreat Muslims should be ashamed. . . . In our anger and emotion, our fellow Americans must treat each other with respect." As Americans rallied around their leader, Bush's popularity rating soared to 90 percent.

Unwisely echoing recent predecessors' sweeping, unsuccessful wars on poverty and on drugs, President Bush declared a "war on terror." His Treasury Department choked the terrorist cash flow—one of many initiatives developed before September 11 but shelved as part of what was now called the "September 10" mindset. The USAPatriot Act, an acronym for the Uniting and Strengthening America by Providing Appropriate Tools Required to Intercept and Obstruct Terrorism Act of 2001, empowered federal law enforcement agencies in the fight. Addressing "every nation" via a special joint session of Congress on September 20, Bush said: "Either you are with us or you are with the terrorists." Bush applied American might to disrupt al-Qaeda, the terrorist group behind the 9/11 attacks, and depose Afghanistan's Taliban leaders, who sheltered Osama bin Laden, the group's leader. America's invasion of Afghanistan in October initially worked. The Taliban fled, giving Americans a quick sense of victory.

Momentarily, Bush became a bipartisan hero. Even former Clinton aides praised Bush and his "dream team" of Secretary of State Colin Powell, Secretary of Defense Donald Rumsfeld, National Security Adviser Condoleezza Rice, and Vice President Dick Cheney. As 2002 began, President Bush earned praise for his "realism," the foreign policy establishment's highest compliment. He pulled off the paradox epitomized by his 2002 State of the Union introduction: "As we gather tonight, our nation is at war, our economy is in recession and the civilized world faces unprecedented dangers. Yet the state of our union has never been stronger."

Domestically, the president's State of the Union address celebrated a major bipartisan achievement, the No Child Left Behind Act, co-sponsored by the leading liberal senator, Ted Kennedy. This legislation created national benchmarks for student progress and helped fulfill Bush's campaign vow to govern as a "compassionate conservative." For all the talk of America the polarized, Democrats and Republicans still shared many common assumptions, goals, and policies. Bush governed within the same post–Great Society "Third Way" consensus that forced Ronald Reagan, a conservative, to maintain the welfare state and stopped Bill Clinton, a liberal, from

2004 ELECTION CHRONOLOGY

2001

September 11, 2001: Islamist terrorists hijack four commercial airplanes, crashing two into the Twin Towers of the World Trade Center in New York City, one into the Pentagon, and one in rural Pennsylvania. There were no survivors from the flights, and nearly 3,000 Americans were killed in the attacks. The ensuing American "War on Terror" becomes controversial and bloody, with America enmeshed in long, complicated wars in Afghanistan and Iraq.

2003

June 24, 2003: Campaigning intensively since May 2002, Howard Dean, the former governor of Vermont, formally announces his intention to seek the presidency, buoyed by his effective use of social networking tools such as Meetup.com to raise money and mobilize supporters.

September 2, 2003: Massachusetts senator John Kerry announces his candidacy in South Carolina, worrying now that Dean may overwhelm him in New Hampshire and Iowa.

December 9, 2003: Former vice president Al Gore endorses Howard Dean, disappointing Gore's former running mate, Joe Lieberman. Dean appears to be the Democratic frontrunner.

December 13, 2003: U.S. soldiers in Iraq capture Saddam Hussein nearly nine months after the American invasion in March 2003.

2004

January 19, 2004: Kerry wins the Iowa caucuses with 38 percent of the vote; North Carolina senator John Edwards finishes close behind with 32 percent. Dean finishes third with just 18 percent.

That night, trying to reassure supporters, Dean screams into his microphone on national television, a move that is widely lampooned.

January 23, 2004: Dr. David Kay of the Iraq Survey group resigns, saying he has found no weapons of mass destruction in Iraq.

January 27, 2004: Kerry wins the New Hampshire primary, solidifying his position as the Democratic front-runner with 39 percent of the vote. Dean comes in second with 26 percent. General Wesley Clark, who skipped Iowa's caucuses in favor of New Hampshire, comes in just ahead of Edwards, both garnering approximately 12 percent of the vote. Lieberman, also relying on the New Hampshire primary to launch his candidacy, comes in fifth with 9 percent.

February 3, 2004: On "Mini-Tuesday," the first multi-state day of primary elections, Kerry takes five of the seven states up for grabs (Arizona, Delaware, Missouri, New Mexico, and North Dakota). Clark gains a badly needed victory in Oklahoma while Edwards carries South Carolina in primaries near their respective home states. Lieberman drops out.

February 17, 2004: Kerry wins the Wisconsin primary with 40 percent of the vote, while Edwards finishes close behind with 34 percent. Dean gets only 18 percent.

February 19, 2004: Dean suspends his campaign.

March 2, 2004: Now campaigning only against Edwards, Kerry racks up victories on Super Tuesday, winning California, Connecticut, Georgia, Maryland, Massachusetts, Minnesota, New York, Ohio, and Rhode Island. Dean wins Vermont, though this no longer makes any difference.

---

expanding it. In November 2003, a similar bipartisan spirit would pass the Medicare Modernization Bill as Democrats and Republicans united to address healthcare concerns without undertaking sweeping reforms.

The debate over whether the United States should invade Saddam Hussein's Iraq in response to the terrorism polarized the country. Following 9/11, Bush administration officials asserted a new "right of preventive, or peremptory, self-defense." In his January 2002 State of the Union address, Bush identified "an axis of evil," consisting of Iraq, Iran, North Korea, "and their terrorist allies . . . arming to threaten the peace of the world." Bush and his team targeted Iraq first because Americans already viewed Saddam Hussein as evil, unpredictable, and dangerous. Under Hussein,

☆   ☆   ☆

March 3, 2004: Edwards drops out of the race while praising Kerry, who responds warmly, fueling speculation that Kerry will tap Edwards as his running mate.

March 16, 2004: At Marshall University in Huntington, West Virginia, a heckler asking repeatedly about Kerry's vote against an additional $87 billion for the wars in Iraq and Afghanistan prompts Kerry's exasperated response: "I actually did vote for the $87 billion before I voted against it." The Bush camp pounces on this as a typical Kerry "flip-flop."

April 13, 2004: During the first prime-time presidential press conference in more than a year, a reporter asks President Bush what mistakes he has made since 9/11. Bush answers: "I'm sure something will pop into my head here in the midst of this press conference, with all the pressure of trying to come up with an answer, but it hadn't yet."

April 28, 2004: CBS reports acts of torture and sexual humiliation by U.S. soldiers at Iraq's massive Abu Ghraib prison. President Bush condemns the brutality.

June 11, 2004: Six days after Ronald Reagan dies at age 93, Bush eulogizes the former president before a nationwide TV audience.

July 6, 2004: Kerry selects Edwards as his running mate.

July 26–29, 2004: The Democratic National Convention meets in Boston, to nominate John Kerry for president and John Edwards for vice president. The convention's highlight is the keynote address delivered by Senate candidate Barack Obama of Illinois on July 27.

August 5, 2004: Swift Boat Veterans for Truth broadcasts its first TV ad attacking Kerry's military service record.

August 30–September 2, 2004: The Republican National Convention meets in New York City to renominate President George W. Bush and Vice President Richard Cheney. Members of more than 800 anti-Bush groups protest.

September 8, 2004: *Sixty Minutes II* uses a memo from Lieutenant Jerry B. Killian to accuse Bush of shirking his duty while serving in the Air National Guard. Bloggers quickly prove the documents are forged.

September 30, 2004: Bush and Kerry square off in their first debate, held at the University of Miami. Many criticize Bush for scowling.

October 5, 2004: In the vice presidential debate at Case Western Reserve University in Cleveland, Edwards more than holds his own against Cheney.

October 8, 2004: Bush and Kerry engage in a second debate at Washington University in St. Louis, this time in a town hall format. Bush improves but still appears angry and flustered.

October 13, 2004: The third presidential debate at Arizona State University is also not decisive but marginally better for Kerry.

October 29, 2004: Terrorist Osama bin Laden releases another threatening videotape, which boosts Bush's poll ratings.

November 2, 2004: Thanks to strong Republican turnout, President Bush wins the popular vote by 3.5 million votes and takes the Electoral College, thanks to a slim margin of victory in Ohio.

December 13, 2004: The presidential electors cast their votes in their state capitals.

2005

January 6, 2005: Congress meets in a joint session to count the electoral votes.

Iraq had attacked both Iran and Kuwait. Hussein struggled against the United States following the end of the Gulf War in 1991. Knowing that Iraq's dictator had spent two decades seeking nuclear, chemical, and biological weapons, Bush believed Iraq posed an imminent threat with WMDs—Weapons of Mass Destruction—and also believed, despite little evidence, that Hussein assisted al-Qaeda.

By the spring of 2002, the emerging War on Terror was more subtle and intermittent than many anticipated. While an apocalyptic, nihilistic Islamist ideology united those who bombed nightclubs in Bali, trains in Madrid, housing complexes in Riyadh, and buses in Jerusalem, no world war developed. In the United States, the terrorists failed to attack again throughout the Bush years. The president, while prosecuting the war aggressively, urged Americans to return to the shopping malls, to keep living their lives rather than sacrificing for some broader goal.

President Bush plunged into the 2002 congressional midterm race enthusiastically, evoking former president Andrew Johnson's "Swing around the circle" in 1866 and Franklin Roosevelt's electoral assault against conservative Southern Democrats in 1938. Bush delivered 87 speeches and visited 13 states in one two-week stretch alone, while raising millions of dollars for Republican candidates. "Is the presidency of the United States a part-time job?" the *Washington Post* columnist Mary McGrory wondered.

Bush's "Pit-Stop Presidency" made policy sense. Bush—and Rove—feared the historical "curse" whereby most presidents saw their parties lose congressional seats during midterm elections. In the fall of 2002 Bush was pitching the war against Iraq to the public, while improving his chances of selling it to Congress. "There is a threat to the U.S. and our close friends and allies in Iraq," the president thundered. "The leader of Iraq is a man who for 11 years has deceived the world. He said he wouldn't have weapons of mass destruction."

The hysteria driving the Iraqi war debate made "September 11" the preserve of the supposed warmongers as many war sceptics deemed the mass murders the predictable response to American "aggression." Antiwar protesters treated "Bushitler" as the villain and Saddam Hussein as the victim, waving anti-American and anti-Semitic placards at rallies the world over. The "peaceniks" mocked Bush's IQ; a Canadian official called Bush a "moron." In a case of Freudianism run amok, some speculated about Bush's desire to finish his father's work in Iraq. Others blamed America's oil addiction.

The pro-war side was equally strident. The administration called murky evidence suggesting possible WMDs or al-Qaeda ties clear proof that Hussein was going nuclear and conspiring with bin Laden. Bureaucratic trench warfare distorted intelligence assessments into briefs selling the war. Pro-war advocates overestimated Iraqis' willingness to embrace democracy. By being so definitive, Bush and his allies all but invited charges of lies and conspiracies if the mission soured.

Weeks before the midterm elections, Bush shrewdly asked Congress to authorize the use of force in Iraq, if necessary. Bush's father, President George H. W. Bush, had made a similar request before the first Gulf War in 1990–91. "In the wake of September 11," asked Senator John Kerry, who supported the resolution, "who among us can say with any certainty to anybody that the weapons might not be used against our troops or against allies in the region?" Even some war sceptics assumed Hussein had lethal weapons and warned he would use them if attacked. On October 10, 2002, the House of Representatives voted 296 to 133 to authorize using force in Iraq. The next day the Senate passed the resolution 77 to 23.

Bush's efforts paid off on Election Day that November. Republicans gained eight seats, kept control of the House of Representatives, and recaptured the Senate by winning two additional seats. "What this victory confers on the President, above all, is legitimacy," ABC news reported.

Nevertheless, Bush's victory was costly. Many Republicans, riled by his rhetoric, campaigned aggressively. They treated patriotism, the War on Terror, and a new, post-9/11 phrase—"Homeland Security"—as their issues and all doubters as traitors. The attack that unseated Democratic Georgia senator Max Cleland was particularly harsh, questioning the patriotism of this decorated

This Ann Telnaes cartoon shows President Bush as the Pied Piper gleefully leading eager Americans into war against Saddam Hussein and Iraq. *(Ann Telnaes Editorial Cartoon ©2003 Ann Telnaes. Used with permission of Ann Telnaes and the Cartoonist Group. All rights reserved.)*

Vietnam War veteran, who lost two legs and his forearm in the war.

Resenting the Republican tactics, Democrats became increasingly strident. Their "Bushophobia" led them to charge that Bush stole the 2000 election and was lying his way into the Iraq War. Some even suggested that Bush did not prevent the 9/11 tragedy to advance his "neoconservative agenda."

As the Iraqi War debate intensified, the United States looked increasingly polarized. The Bush-Gore deadlock of 2000 was only one of many indicators of an electorate that rivaled the one from the 1880s and 1890s in being so closely divided on many defining issues. Bill Clinton had served two terms in the 1990s without ever winning a popular majority, and ended his term impeached but not convicted after a poisonous partisan battle. The seesawing in Congress reflected similar divisions.

Many of the ties that had long bound Americans were unraveling. The rise of cable television ended the domination of the "Big Three" television networks—CBS, NBC, and ABC—that had once forged common cultural and political touchstones. Nearly four decades of Nixon and Reagan conservatives bashing the "liberal media" encouraged the rise of Fox News as a conservative alternative, and the growing perception of the "mainstream media" as left-leaning. The Internet, rather than fostering a national or even global community as some foresaw, often produced a shrill, fragmented blogosphere.

In Washington, both parties had constructed competing institutional, ideological, and social universes. Republicans assumed congressional power in 1994, vowing revenge after decades of Democratic high-handedness. The parties were more united internally but less committed to compromising with each other. Reaganism killed liberal Republicanism, just as the civil rights revolution made the race-baiting conservative Southern Democrat an increasingly endangered species. A take-no-prisoners headline-driven emphasis on positioning the party to score points undermined the tradition of congressional coalition building and consensus. An odd alliance of African-American Democrats and white Republicans redistricting congressional seats after the 1990 and 2000 census created more districts that were either overwhelmingly Democratic or overwhelmingly Republican. These districts more frequently elected firebrands to Congress, whereas mixed districts produced more moderate members. The high cost of politics gave incumbents the inside track on fund-raising, further insulating ensconced extremists from moderating electoral pressures.

The culture wars of the 1960s, 1970s, and 1980s, battling about affirmative action, abortion, gun control, crime prevention, taxation, and defense spending, often reinforced one political identity or another. In the 1990s,

network television electoral maps began charting states that voted Republican in red and states going Democratic in blue. The paradigm became familiar during the Bush-Gore post-election purgatory in 2000. The red-blue dichotomy summarized a growing political polarization, which, the Republican strategists believed, involved geography, religion, consumer preferences, lifestyles, and core values along with political attitudes and party affiliations. This red state–blue state paradigm caricatured the nation as hopelessly divided between provincial, heavily rural, traditional, pro-life, gun-toting, tax-cutting, beer-swilling, God-fearing red staters and cosmopolitan, overwhelmingly urban, progressive, pro-choice, gun-controlling, big government–loving, Chardonnay-sipping, secular blue staters.

As the 2004 presidential election approached, the logical Democratic candidate was Al Gore. The former vice president—who won a half-million more votes than Bush in 2000—could have made the 2004 contest a redo of 2000. But Gore seemed disinclined to run. Rather than leading the opposition to Bush, he faded away initially. After September 11, Bush's poll ratings soared, and even Gore's closest allies doubted he would have been as decisive in the crisis as Bush had been.

Nevertheless, speculation about Gore's plans clouded the "invisible primary," the period before any caucuses or primaries when candidates round up endorsements, establish organizations, woo reporters, and raise money. Gore's 2000 running mate, Senator Joseph Lieberman of Connecticut, loyally deferred to Gore and thus watched his own prospects and his reputation for decisive leadership dim as Gore dithered. Vermont governor Howard Dean formed a presidential exploratory committee in May 2002, modeling his campaign on Jimmy Carter's successful grassroots venture of 1976. A Yale undergrad who became a doctor, and the son of a Park Avenue stockbroker, Howard Brush Dean III built his practice in rural Vermont, gradually plunging into politics. He served as lieutenant governor while still practicing medicine from 1987 until 1991, when the governor died suddenly. Dean became governor, then was elected to two five-year terms. Serving until 2003, Dean governed as a calm, bridge-building centrist. Campaigning for president, Dean sounded like the pugnacious New Yorker he had been rather than the mellow country physician he had become. Dean tapped into Democrats' anger. Echoing the late liberal senator Paul Wellstone, Dean insisted he represented the "Democratic wing of the Democratic Party."

Massachusetts senator John Kerry announced his intentions to run in December 2002, campaigning more conventionally as a war veteran turned senator. John Forbes Kerry—another JFK—was a Golden Boy from yes-

John Kerry *(U.S. Congress)*

teryear, born in 1943, the well-bred son of a Foreign Service officer. A St. Paul's School preppie, a Skull-and-Bones Yalie, Kerry spent his youth hobnobbing and high-flying. Feeling financially inadequate among the mega-wealthy, torn between his social set's frivolity and his public-service–oriented seriousness, Kerry demonstrated an ambition that distinguished him from his world of cotillions and trust funds. Kerry served in the Navy for four years, from 1966 to 1970, spending parts of the last two years in Vietnam. He commanded a Fast Patrol Craft (PCF), also called a Swift Boat—heavily armed, lightly armoured, for maximum speed. Kerry earned three Purple Hearts for minor injuries received in battle, and a Silver Star for leading his men out of an ambush, charging and killing an enemy soldier.

Honorably discharged as a lieutenant, on returning home Kerry grew his hair long, had nightmares, and vented rage. He was the first Vietnam veteran to testify before Congress, detailing the recollections of veterans alleging war crimes: "They told the stories at times they had personally raped, cut off ears, cut off heads . . . ran-

domly shot at civilians, razed villages in fashion reminiscent of Genghis Khan . . . and generally ravaged the countryside of South Vietnam. . . ." Still, while serving on the Executive Committee of Vietnam Veterans against the War he also tried moderating antiwar radicals. Kerry joined hundreds of others in throwing away their ribbons and medals in front of the U.S. Capitol. "I'm not doing this for any violent reasons," Kerry said as he seemingly disposed of his medals, "but for peace and justice, and to try and make this country wake up once and for all." Trying to present the movement's best public face, Kerry demonstrated his great skill: his ability to speak American to Americans.

Nevertheless, a reputation as an unprincipled glory hound had dogged him since his youth. On the campaign trail, Democrats dismissed him as JFK, not John Forbes Kerry but "Just For Kerry," a grandstanding political will o' the wisp who would say whatever was necessary to get elected. During Christmas 2003, "Iowans for Dean" would try giving Kerry a present: flip-flops, reinforcing the impression that would help doom Kerry's candidacy.

In December 2002, Gore finally announced he would not run. Senator Lieberman launched his campaign the next month. Other Democratic candidates quickly jumped in: former Illinois senator Carol Moseley Braun, North Carolina senator John Edwards, Missouri congressman Richard "Dick" Gephardt, Florida senator Bob Graham, Ohio congressman Dennis Kucinich, and the Reverend Al Sharpton of New York. These candidates' views ranged widely. Lieberman supported Bush's War on Terror and was increasingly to most Democrats' right, especially on foreign policy, while Braun, Kucinich, and Sharpton veered sharply left overall.

Amid the latest crop of candidates, John Edwards stood out by auditioning to be the Bill Clinton of 2004, the centrist Southern Democrat who wins the White House by wooing the nation. A former trial lawyer, Edwards had the choirboy looks, silky smooth manner, and silver tongue of a striving Southerner who had talked his way from modest beginnings as a millworker's son to multimillionaire status and a U.S. Senate seat. Edwards had voted for the Iraq War but was an economic populist. Yet he lacked a presidential gravitas, reminding too many of the fey former vice president Dan Quayle.

Meanwhile, as the Democrats jockeyed for position, President Bush, empowered by the 2002 midterm elections, led the nation to war against Iraq. While Democrats agonized over what stand to take—and many ultimately supported the president—Republicans continued alienating Democrats by questioning critics' patriotism. Representative Tom Delay, the Texas Republican and powerful House leader, blasted "the timid counsel of those who would mortgage our security to the false promises of wishful thinking and appeasement."

Amid the Iraq debate in 2002, many marveled at the changes in America and its president that September 11 had wrought. Back in pre–9/11 2001, a seemingly callow, untested, grammatically challenged president had been inaugurated, having lost the popular vote and having survived a bitter fight over ballot counting in Florida. At the time, President Bush frequently broadcast a deer-in-the-headlights look on camera. Words would float around, unmoored to conventional rules of diction and sometimes flying in the face of facts or logic. The George Bush now leading his nation into war found a voice and a vision. While no Winston Churchill, he looked squarely into the camera, speaking in crisp, clear sentences, and led.

Rarely in this age of poll-driven politics had an American leader defied the conventional wisdom, dismissed so many domestic and international experts so boldly and calmly. Bush did not falter during the tense buildup to this "trust me" war, an invasion whose legitimacy rested on Americans' faith in their president. He also did not adjust, learn, mollify, or compromise. The only time Clinton had shown such determination was in his efforts to save himself during the Monica Lewinsky scandal. Even Franklin Roosevelt laid the groundwork for America's entry into World War II more subtly, through half-steps such as the Lend-Lease program.

On March 19, 2003, President Bush delivered a nationally televised prime time address launching a "broad and concerted campaign" to disarm Iraq. "Operation Iraqi Freedom" sought to "shock and awe" Iraq's leaders into submission. By April 9, the American-led coalition forces had taken Baghdad, toppling Saddam Hussein's huge statue in central Baghdad. On May 1, 2003, the president landed a Navy S-3B Viking on the aircraft carrier USS *Abraham Lincoln* in the Pacific Ocean. He delivered a victory speech behind a huge banner proclaiming "MISSION ACCOMPLISHED."

From one perspective, Bush's move into Iraq was heroic and historic. Had stability followed Hussein's fall in Iraq, historians might have hailed Bush as courageous, even visionary. And while it is circular to say that had he succeeded in Iraq he would have been a success, in a democracy, the riskier the step, the faster and clearer the success must be.

The mission in Iraq, however, was anything but accomplished. American prestige plummeted in mid-April when Iraqis looted buildings throughout Baghdad, notably the National Museum of Antiquities. More than 170,000 priceless archaeological treasures were lost or destroyed. Then, acts of terrorism erupted. On August 19, a truck bomb decimated the United Nations headquar-

ters in Baghdad, killing 22 people, including the top U.N. envoy in Iraq, Sergio Vieira de Mello. Ten days later, a car bomb outside the Imam Ali Mosque in Najaf killed 125, including a top Shiite cleric.

Iraq's slide into bloody, sectarian chaos, with Americans caught in multiple crossfires, derailed the Bush presidency. The weapons of mass destruction that Bush targeted were never found, and may never have existed—which kept Americans debating the war's premise. Secretary of Defense Donald Rumsfeld's confidence in a lean, agile army rather than a large, overwhelming force further strained the country's patience. The many international protests emboldened the war's critics at home.

Considering how messy the mission proved to be, Americans demonstrated remarkable patience. The 9/11 trauma kept many Americans loyal to the president and the war effort. Throughout the 2004 campaign, many antiwar critics were frustrated by their failure to convince millions to abandon the president. Democrats were cautious. "I don't think any United States senator is going to abandon our troops and recklessly leave Iraq to whatever follows as a result of simply cutting and running," Senator Kerry said in September 2003. A year later, as the Democratic presidential nominee, Kerry honorably refused to renounce his initial support for the war. Instead, Kerry attacked Bush's execution of the war.

Other Democrats were more vehement. The financier George Soros pumped over $15 million into Moveon.org and other groups to oppose Bush's reelection. Accusing Bush of embracing a "supremacist ideology," Soros—who survived Nazi-dominated Hungary during World War II—told reporters: "When I hear Bush say, 'You're either with us or against us,' it reminds me of the Germans. My experiences under Nazi and Soviet rule have sensitized me." Backed by Soros and others, Moveon.org and similar groups attacked the president in equally inflammatory terms, tapping into the blogosphere's growing power and vitriol.

The more elusive success in Iraq appeared, the more doubts about Bush's original intentions grew. In October 2003, David Kay, the head of the Iraq Survey Group seeking to catalogue Saddam Hussein's arsenal of weapons of mass destruction, released his interim report. In that report and in his final conclusion in January 2004, Kay said he found no WMDs. Kay acknowledged that while Hussein had sought many different weapons, he believed the intelligence community had failed both presidents Clinton and Bush by incorrectly assuming that Hussein was developing nuclear weapons. Still, the headlines emphasized the phantom WMDs. Most Democrats assumed Bush and his aides had lied their way into the war they wanted. Kerry, sharpening his message, called

Iraq "the wrong war, in the wrong place, at the wrong time."

In mid-December 2003, American soldiers in Iraq captured a bearded, wild-looking Saddam Hussein hiding in what soldiers called a "spider hole," a cramped, one-person foxhole. The Iraqi strongman's humiliating end boosted Bush's standing and somewhat blunted the war issue as the Democratic race intensified.

Since the 1970s, as presidential primaries proliferated, so did the number of forums and televised debates. The nine 2004 Democratic candidates first debated each other on May 3, 2003, at the University of South Carolina campus in Columbia during South Carolina's Democratic Weekend. George Stephanopoulos, the Clinton aide turned ABC News anchor, moderated the discussion between Braun, Dean, Edwards, Gephardt, Graham, Kerry, Kucinich, Lieberman, and Sharpton. During the next nine months, a gradually dwindling group would meet in over a dozen more televised debates and many more forums. Often media organizations and political organizations cosponsored. CNN and "Rock the Vote" hosted at historic Faneuil Hall in Boston. The Congressional Black Caucus Political Education Leadership Institute and Fox News Channel sponsored a debate at Morgan State University in Baltimore. Governor Bill Richardson and the Congressional Hispanic Caucus hosted a Democratic National Committee–sanctioned debate at the University of New Mexico in Albuquerque, broadcast on Univision and PBS stations. The organizers usually were interest groups, representing, among others, the pro-choice community, the elderly, labor unions, African-Americans, Hispanics, and women.

The televised debates proved irresistible to minor candidates like Al Sharpton and Dennis Kucinich. Neither had a serious chance of winning, but the race's volatility prevented debate organizers from establishing popularity thresholds at first. Sharpton used the debates to rehabilitate his reputation and challenge the Reverend Jesse Jackson to become the media's go-to guy on African-American issues. Kucinich, in 2004, and again in 2008, used the exposure to articulate a more populist, radical, antiwar, big government vision that made the leading Democratic candidates look cautious and conservative.

The big winner of the televised debates, at least initially, was Howard Dean. Dean's message fit the politics of the moment and the politics of most primaries, which play to partisans. Dean's movement grew thanks to Joe Trippi, a consultant who trusted the Internet as an organizing tool—and a pathway to progress. The Dean campaign began in May 2002 with seven staffers, 432 known supporters, and $100,000. By early 2004 Dean was leading the polls and had raised $50 million, with a record-breaking $15.8 million in one quarter alone, most of it in $100 donations or less.

Deploying the first generation of social networking tools like "Meetup," the Dean campaign embraced the Internet age's key tenets, developing a grassroots campaign with decentralized authority. Dean recruited nearly 600,000 "Deaniacs," many of them political novices committed to reviving American democracy. "The Internet community is wondering what its place in the world of politics is," Dean preached. "Along comes this campaign to take back the country for ordinary human beings, and the best way you can do that is through the Net. We listen. We pay attention. If I give a speech and the blog people don't like it, next time I change the speech."

Trippi took credit for this approach, but Dean disagreed. "We fell into this by accident," Dean told *Wired* magazine. The "community taught us. They seized the initiative through Meetup. They built our organization for us before we had an organization."

In the modern, highly scrutinized campaign, Dean's passion attracted partisans but worried staffers. In November 2003, Dean had to backtrack after saying, "I still want to be the candidate for guys with Confederate flags in their pickup trucks." The quick-to-condemn chorus tut-tutted about Dean's stereotyping—as if good ol' Southern boys needed their own anti-defamation league. But Dean was speaking shorthand, hoping to court conservative Southern Democrats, not just Northeastern liberals. Nevertheless modern campaigning left little margin for error—or room for creative expression—and reporters waited for Dean to overstep.

Still, as 2003 came to a close, the media decided Dean had become the campaign's hottest phenomenon. The former Vermont governor graced the cover of both *Time* and *Newsweek* within a matter of months. On December 9, 2003, Gore endorsed him, crushing Lieberman's presidential prospects while confirming Dean's front-runner status.

Dean's ascent galvanized the listless Kerry campaign. In November, Kerry had fired his campaign manager and replaced him with Ted Kennedy's disciplinarian chief of staff, Mary Cahill. Emboldened, Kerry challenged the president: "Bring it on." This rhetorical hijacking took Bush's controversial challenge in July to Iraqi insurgents—"Bring 'em on"—to suggest that this war-tested Democrat could debate national security with the Republican president.

Most important, Kerry finally agreed to "bust the caps," breaking out of the financial straitjacket candidates accepted in return for federal funding. Kerry, Dean, and most Democrats believed in campaign finance limits and public financing—except when politically inconvenient. Campaign finance legislation made fund-raising more difficult and limited amounts to spend state by state while providing public funding. Dean first "busted the caps," to exceed state-by-state spending limits and the overall $45 million ceiling for those receiving federal matching funds. Dean's Internet fundraising was too successful to abandon. Dean held a farcical Internet "plebiscite" to get Deaniacs' "permission" to abandon the financial limits. Following the season's operative Democratic logic— "Anybody But Bush"—they approved, especially because Bush raised so much money he did not even pretend to accept the financial limits.

Kerry was more conscience-stricken, especially because he had helped pass the campaign finance legislation. But with his campaign sinking and Dean soaring, Kerry adapted. He mortgaged his Beacon Hill townhouse and began the humiliating hunt for campaign cash, the bane of most politicians' existence.

Since George McGovern lost in 1972 and Michael Dukakis lost in 1988, many moderate Democrats distrusted the primary process. They feared that party activists chose partisan nominees who could not capture swing votes in November. Dean's growing momentum, centrists' growing fears, and Americans' perennial yearning for a king-like figure floating above the fray boosted General Wesley Clark's campaign. As supreme allied commander–Europe of NATO from 1997 to 2000, Clark led allied forces during the Kosovo War. After a "Draft Clark" effort modeled on the 1952 "Draft Eisenhower" campaign took off in April 2003, Clark became the last Democratic candidate to enter the race that September.

Clark was apolitical, noncontroversial, and inexperienced. He supported abortion rights and affirmative action but most Democrats could not forgive his votes for Ronald Reagan. Running as the general tough enough to oppose the Iraq War, he nevertheless admitted he might have supported the initial congressional resolution. His biggest error, however, was foregoing the Iowa caucuses.

Back in 1972, a mercurial offset printing press forced Iowa Democrats to hold their precinct caucuses in January. The early date allowed enough time to duplicate and distribute the results during the caucus's many voting rounds. This arrangement made their vote the first in the nation. Iowans loved the attention. Four years later, Iowans promoted their caucus to candidates and reporters. "I knew each wanted to be where the other was," the Democratic state chairman, Tom Whitney, later recalled, identifying the symbiotic relationship between politicians and the press. Jimmy Carter's surprise win in Iowa catapulted him to the presidency.

The Iowa caucuses joined the New Hampshire primary as the campaign's opening one-two punch. Since 1920 New Hampshire has held the nation's first primary in every presidential election. In 1977, New Hampshire

law mandated that it always be first. But Iowa holds its caucuses, and as a result, citizens in these two states have maintained a disproportional impact on choosing each party's nominee.

By sitting out Iowa, Clark allowed Kerry to emerge as the tough Democrat and the safe alternative to Dean. Kerry hovered above the fray as Howard Dean and Richard Gephardt of neighboring Missouri, both going for broke in Iowa, trained their firepower on each other. Just before the Iowa caucuses, targeting the candidate he perceived as his greatest threat, Kerry dismissed Edwards as a novice. The 60-year-old Kerry then said of the 50-year-old Edwards, "When I came back from Vietnam in 1969 I don't know if John Edwards was out of diapers then. Well, I'm sure he was out of diapers." Edwards, who was 16 at the time, later responded: "In 1969, I was sitting around a kitchen table with my parents trying to figure out how we would pay for college like so many Iowans do every single day. And that is a difference between me and Senator Kerry." Kerry questioned the baby-faced Edwards's gravitas; Edwards replied with a populist jab against Kerry, the kept man who financed his campaign by mortgaging his mansion.

Kerry was dancing on the head of a pin. While President Bush could seem maddeningly simplistic in a complex world, candidate Kerry reveled in nuances and

This Ann Telnaes cartoon shows the Democratic donkey standing on a scale while attempting to support all the party's presidential candidates: (clockwise from center) Howard Dean, Dennis Kucinich, Carol Moseley Braun, Wesley Clark, John Kerry, Dick Gephardt, John Edwards, Al Sharpton, and Joseph I. Lieberman. (*Ann Telnaes Editorial Cartoon © 2004 Ann Telnaes. Used with permission of Ann Telnaes and the Cartoonist Group. All rights reserved.*)

contradictions. An antiwar candidate who voted for the war in Iraq but against the latest reconstruction appropriation for the war-torn nation, Kerry also ran as the populist foe of privilege, despite being a multimillionaire Boston Brahmin Yalie who never married a woman worth less than $300 million. *Tour of Duty: John Kerry and the Vietnam War,* historian Douglas Brinkley's contribution to the two-century-old genre of campaign biographies, perpetuated another great paradox defining Kerry's campaign: glorifying military exploits in a war he hated.

The book excited Republicans with the prospect of casting Kerry as a Jane Fonda–loving, pot-smoking traitor-dilettante who ran antiwar protests from the comfortable perch of swanky Georgetown friends. Yet Democrats rejoiced that this JFK was no Michael Dukakis. Ramrod straight, with a chestful of medals and a massive Dudley

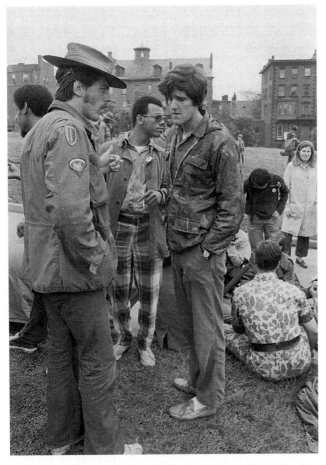

John Kerry (right) of Waltham, Massachusetts, talks with other Vietnam veterans against the war at the foot of Bunker Hill monument prior to a march to Boston Common in Boston, May 31, 1971. The demonstration against the Vietnam War with a trek from Concord to Boston traced in reverse Paul Revere's 1775 midnight ride. Most of the demonstrators spent a night in a makeshift jail in Lexington after defying a ban on overnight use of Battle Green, site of the first battle of the American Revolution. *(Associated Press)*

Do-Right chin only a mother, the *Doonesbury* cartoonist Garry Trudeau, or a Mount Rushmore sculptor could love, Kerry was not easily caricatured as a subversive. Moreover, he was not afraid to fight. Many veterans demonstrated deep loyalty to Kerry, reflecting volatile "Band of Brothers" emotions Republican character assassins had to avoid unleashing when attacking him.

On Martin Luther King Day, January 19, 2004, Iowa's Democrats spoke through their caucuses. Approximately 120,000 mostly white, heavily rural, disproportionately liberal participants representing perhaps .0004 of the nation's 290 million people enjoyed their moment in the sun—and the campaigns' estimated expenditure of $90 per caucus goer. An estimated 950 reporters from 27 states and 13 countries swooped down on the happy Iowans.

Iowa produced some surprises. Doing poorly in the polls, Carol Moseley Braun, the former senator from neighboring Illinois, dropped out days before the caucuses and endorsed Dean. Similarly, Gephardt sputtered, getting just 10.6 percent of the vote, dooming his campaign. The biggest surprise, despite all the hype in a state similar to Vermont and seemingly open to his outsider's message and grassroots approach, was that Howard Dean came in third, winning 18.6 percent of votes.

Even worse for Dean, his concession speech made him a laughingstock. Trying to pump up 3,500 disappointed supporters, Dean played to the crowd rather than to the unforgiving television cameras. "Not only are we going to New Hampshire, Tom Harkin," Dean bellowed, acknowledging Iowa's senator who endorsed him, "we're going to South Carolina and Oklahoma and Arizona and North Dakota and New Mexico, and we're going to California and Texas and New York. . . . And we're going to South Dakota and Oregon and Washington and Michigan, and then we're going to Washington, D.C., to take back the White House! Yeah!!!"

The louder Dean shouted, the more angrily he barked, the less ready-for-prime-time he seemed. His climactic "Yeah" was a long, guttural growl. Dean's "primal scream" went viral on the Internet as Americans mocked Dean's "I have a scream speech" on King's birthday.

Eventually, reporters admitted that thousands of supporters screaming at Dean made the noise in the room deafening. All this was lost on television, because Dean's unidirectional microphone and the camera focused on Dean, not the scene. The 663 times that news channels replayed the scream over the next four days prompted retrospective journalistic apologies when it was too late.

Howard Dean's campaign never recovered from "the scream." His Iowa failure raised doubts he could translate his Internet insurgency into ballot box success. Dean became another Paul Tsongas or Bill Bradley—independent liberal voices from the 1992 and 2000 campaigns whom reporters enjoyed building up, then taking down.

Nevertheless, Dean's techniques revolutionized presidential campaigning. "An amazing thing happened in the presidential contest of 2004," Joe Trippi gushed. "For the first time in my life, maybe the first time in history, a candidate lost but his campaign won." Trippi labeled Dean's failed campaign "the first shot in America's second revolution, nothing less than the people taking the first step to reclaiming a system that had long ago forgotten they existed. This was democracy bubbling to the surface." In spring 2003, John Kerry's campaign manager at the time, Jim Jordan, could still insist "there are no votes on the Internet"—but not for much longer. The Dean campaign's pioneering legacy would become clear in 2008, when Barack Obama's campaign perfected Dean's net-roots campaigning techniques.

Iowa's surprise winner, with nearly 38 percent of the vote, was John Kerry, a statistically insignificant 6 points ahead of John Edwards. Kerry's comeback strategy had worked. Kerry surged ahead by emphasizing his wartime heroics, his governmental experience, and his disdain for George W. Bush.

Unlike Dean, Kerry needed to appear more emotional, more authentic, less slick, and less senatorial. At his victory party, after the aging liberal lion, Ted Kennedy, shouted by way of introducing Kerry, Kerry instinctively lowered the emotional temperature. His victory speech contained just enough populist anger against Bush and "the special interests" to rile the crowd, but not so much that he lost his cool, his viewers back home—or his voice.

With Kennedy at his side and Iowans shouting "JK all the way," Kerry posed as the Kennedy legatee. John F. Kennedy had PT-109, Kerry had his Vietnam Swift Boat; both Kennedy and Kerry combined an aristocrat's panache with the liberal's social conscience. Rivals targeted Kerry as another Michael Dukakis, an effete, Ivy League liberal out of touch with real Americans—and coddled by his billionaire wife, Teresa Heinz, mistress of the ketchup fortune.

Eight days after the Iowa caucuses, the nation turned its attention to New Hampshire, where the first primary was held on January 27, 2004. The Democrats mostly agreed that health care needed reforming, education needed improving, the middle class needed protecting, and George W. Bush needed retiring. Polls suggested Kerry's "electability" swayed many of the 220,000 Democrats voting that day. Kerry won just over 84,000 votes, 39 percent of the total, securing 13 of the total 4,322 Democratic delegates. Dean, from neighboring Vermont, came in second with 26 percent. Clark, who skipped Iowa to concentrate on New Hampshire, nosed ahead of Edwards, with both garnering approximately 12 percent

of the vote. Lieberman, also relying on the New Hampshire primary to launch his candidacy, came in a poor fifth with 9 percent.

Since the 1960s, Americans had improvised a democratic but chaotic nominating process. Each state party could decide when to hold its primary or caucus, but the national parties tried micromanaging the timing—as did some state legislatures, like New Hampshire, which insisted on holding the first primary. States worried about losing influence if they were too early or too late in the season, if they were clumped with other states or alone. Some party leaders advocated regional primaries; others wanted geographic diversity. Since 1984, the primary schedule pivoted around "Super Tuesday," the day in February or March featuring the most primaries and caucuses. In 2004, February 3 was "Mini-Tuesday" or Super Tuesday I, with seven states in play, followed by March 2, Super Tuesday, or Super Tuesday II, with nine states holding primaries and Minnesota caucusing.

The momentum from Iowa and New Hampshire propelled Kerry to victory on Mini-Tuesday, when he won five states stretching from the Northeast to the Southwest. Clark won Oklahoma while Edwards carried South Carolina, each benefiting from the proximity to their respective home states. After campaigning intensely in Delaware and losing, Lieberman dropped out.

The Kerry juggernaut continued. He won the Wisconsin primary on February 17 with 40 percent of the vote. Edwards finished a strong second, with 34 percent, emerging as an appealing young voice trying to spark a pro-middle-class populism, even as Kerry's experience reassured more voters. Dean received only 18 percent of the vote and faded from the race.

On Super Tuesday, March 2, Kerry won nine states, including California and New York. The next day, Edwards quit the race with gracious words for Kerry, the front-runner. In return, Kerry called Edwards a "valiant champion of the values for which our party stands." The warm exchange fueled speculation that Kerry, now the presumptive nominee, would tap Edwards as his running mate.

As the Democrats slugged it out over the winter, the Republicans enjoyed their rare respite from a nomination fight. President Bush—or "43," as he liked to be called, meaning the 43rd president—worked hard to unify his party and placate the right, remembering that Pat Buchanan's run to George II. W. Bush's right in 1992 helped doom "41's" efforts. Despite Bush's easy renomination, he was having a hard time governing. The Iraq debacle undermined his claims to competence.

Bush, however, relished taking on John Kerry. Bush was among the select few who could look down at his fellow Yalie John Forbes Kerry as a social climber with

Presidential candidate John Kerry campaigns in Albuquerque, New Mexico, September 16, 2004. (© *Jonathan A. Meyers/Stock Connection Distribution/Alamy*)

a pedigree but no real family wealth. In turn Kerry, an intellectual politician, bristled at the once hard-partying frat boy who reduced everything to a punchline. At one point Kerry would exclaim, "I can't believe I'm losing to this idiot." Aware of the tension, and Kerry's tendency to sound hi-falutin', Bush's people tried annoying the senator. Riffing off the famous Clinton War Room sign "It's the economy, stupid," the Bushies' sign read: "It's the hypocrisy, stupid."

In mid-March 2004, the Bush strategy succeeded. As Senator Kerry stumped around West Virginia, a critical swing state, Republicans ran an ad mocking Kerry. A deep voice demanded that "Mr. Kerry" vote for or against funding the troops in Iraq and Afghanistan. The ad suggested Kerry had voted "no" repeatedly. That afternoon, a heckler at a veterans' meeting derided the senator for failing to support the troops. Kerry explained he wanted to support the troops while supporting an amendment rolling back President Bush's tax cut for the rich. Kerry voted

for the funding legislation with the anti-tax-cut amendment, then opposed the resolution when the amendment failed. Exasperated by the persistent questioner, Kerry exclaimed: "I actually did vote for the $87 billion before I voted against it."

Bush's advisers, who had watched Dean and other Democrats deride Kerry's flip-flopping, pounced. The Bush campaign quickly produced an ad ridiculing Kerry's "fog" about supporting the troops. As with the 1988 Willie Horton ad caricaturing Michael Dukakis as soft on crime, the commercial was broadcast many more times for free on news shows than as a paid political message. Eight months later, on Election Day, Senator Kerry would still be defined by his logical, yet politically foolish, declaration.

While the flip-flopping charge dogged Kerry, the Iraq War became Bush's albatross. On April 28, CBS reported acts of torture and sexual humiliation by U.S. soldiers at Iraq's massive Abu Ghraib prison. President Bush condemned the brutality. But he and Secretary of Defense Donald Rumsfeld fostered the cowboy culture that condoned such abuses. Increasingly, Democrats scorned the Republicans for invoking Abraham Lincoln's remarks when running for reelection in 1864 that Americans "have concluded it is not best to 'swap horses while crossing the river,'" by saying "Don't change horsemen in mid-apocalypse."

Bush's allergy to self-criticism frustrated his opponents. The blue-chip, bipartisan National Commission on Terrorist Attacks upon the United States, had been meeting since 2003. The 9/11 Commission, as it was popularly called, analyzed what went wrong on that awful day to avoid future catastrophes. Many awaited the final report, released on July 22, 2004, although Bush seemed dismissive. On April 13, 2004, during the first prime-time presidential press conference in more than a year, a reporter asked the president what mistakes he had made since 9/11. "I wish you'd have given me this written question ahead of time so I could plan for it," Bush joked, then paused. "I'm sure something will pop into my head here in the midst of this press conference, with all the pressure of trying to come up with answer, but it hadn't yet." He never answered the question adequately.

The troubles in Iraq and Bush's own personality fed a vicious backlash against the president. The serious charge that the president lied to the American people became widespread. Moveon.org sponsored an Internet ad contest, "Bush in Thirty Seconds," resulting in two ads comparing the president to Adolf Hitler, claiming, "What were war crimes in 1945 is foreign policy in 2003." When Republicans objected, Moveon.org quickly pulled the ads.

In late June, Michael Moore's film *Fahrenheit 9/11* eviscerated the president as clueless and corrupt. It earned

$23.9 million its first weekend, unprecedented for a documentary, and quickly broke the $100 million mark. Moore made valid points about Bush's politicization of the war. But Moore misleadingly treated September 11 as a Republican coup to terrify Americans and fight the Iraqis, rather than as a story of Islamist terrorist evil exploiting American—and Western—complacency.

Bush had received a surprising boost in early June in his eulogy to Ronald Reagan, who died on June 5. The American tendency to remember presidents graciously fosters American nationalism. Still, the eulogizing that culminated in Reagan's funeral on June 11, 2004, exceeded the usual mourning rituals for American statesmen. Democrats who built their careers opposing the man now praised this optimistic patriot who helped win the cold war. President Bush wrapped himself in Reagan's mantle, as commentators spent a week celebrating the "Reagan Revolution" and touting Bush as his successor.

While the Reagan funeral made Bush look presidential, Kerry was consistently cast as the challenger. Kerry did not marshal resources or manage expectations well.

He worried that accepting the Democratic nomination in late July, with Bush being nominated over a month later, would handicap his campaign. The federal spending limits for the general campaign began upon nomination. When the Democrats originally scheduled their convention, they desired the extra month of federal funding. But in the spring, with Kerry fund-raising effectively, he considered postponing his nomination to spread the $75 million in public financing for the general election over two months rather than three. "Mr. Kerry embraced the rules when they helped him but now wants to ignore them when they don't," the *Wall Street Journal* sniped.

Kerry tried to keep reporters interested and supporters motivated during the long stretch from March, when he clinched the nomination, to July, when he would accept the nomination. Craving front-page stories, journalists get surly when the story lags. In the vacuum, reporters began picking at the Kerry campaign, while speculating wildly about who his running mate might be.

Kerry ultimately chose John Edwards. The North Carolina senator had impressed many with his charisma,

President Bush speaks during funeral services for former president Ronald Reagan at the National Cathedral in Washington, June 11, 2004. *(Charles Dharapak/Associated Press)*

smarts, and populist passion. Democrats hoped Edwards's smile would trump Vice President Richard Cheney's snarl; Edwards's indignation could blunt Cheney's self-righteousness. Yet there was little chemistry between the two senators. Post-election rumors would claim Kerry preferred Dick Gephardt. Edwards barely affected the race. He did not even deliver his home state of North Carolina.

The Democratic National Convention took place as scheduled, in Boston, Kerry's hometown. Opening night, July 26, featured the Democrats' headliners: Jimmy Carter, Bill Clinton, Al Gore, and Hillary Rodham Clinton. On Tuesday, Kerry's wife Teresa spoke, along with the young politician Kerry chose to deliver the keynote address, Illinois state senator Barack Obama, who was running for the U.S. Senate. Obama was so obscure that the "big three" networks—ABC, CBS, and NBC—did not broadcast his speech. Of course, in the age of Internet, network television was no longer the great American agenda-setter.

Preaching a nationalist gospel for a multicultural America and resurrecting a national sense of community amid the boom years' selfishness, Obama proclaimed, "If there's a child on the south side of Chicago who can't read, that matters to me, even if it's not my child." Most dramatically, he repudiated "the pundits" who "like to slice and dice our country," pitting a provincial, rural, conservative "red" America against a cosmopolitan, urban, liberal "blue" America. Instead, Obama celebrated a red, white, and blue "*United* States of America." With this electrifying speech, Obama made the most impressive national convention debut since William Jennings Bryan's Cross of Gold speech in 1896.

Although it would never make the oratorical hall of fame, Kerry's acceptance speech worked. Surrounding himself with old battle-scarred comrades, determined to show that Democrats were fighting patriots, too, he declared: "I'm John Kerry and I'm reporting for duty," triggering frenzied applause. Kerry insisted, "This is the most important election of our lifetime." Emphasizing a central Democratic theme, he made "my first pledge to you tonight: As president, I will restore trust and credibility to the White House." Trying to neutralize the flip-flop issue while questioning Bush's smarts and integrity, Kerry said: "Now, I know there that are those who criticize me for seeing complexities—and I do—because some issues just aren't all that simple. Saying there are weapons of mass destruction in Iraq doesn't make it so. Saying we can fight a war on the cheap doesn't make it so. And proclaiming 'Mission accomplished' certainly doesn't make it so." More broadly he insisted: "The future doesn't belong to fear; it belongs to freedom."

Reflecting Reagan's influence, Kerry mentioned the late president, spoke about breaking with his own party to vote for a balanced budget, and remembered fighting to deploy 100,000 additional police officers. Showing he was a tough national security Democrat with a heart, he had harsh words for terrorists, soothing words for the 9/11 victims, and warm words for those struggling "here at home," where "wages are falling, health-care costs are rising, and our great middle class is shrinking."

Kerry's speech confirmed that the Democrats were pitching much of the 2004 campaign on two intelligence failures: doubting the reliability of President George W. Bush's information about Iraq and, more broadly, doubting Bush's brainpower. In this age of Jon Stewart and Jay Leno, television comedians who supplied young Americans with more news than any other source, the president as village idiot was a staple of late night comedy. A Google Search mid-campaign for "Bush and Stupid" yielded 1,760,000 hits; by contrast, "Kerry and Flip Flop" yielded 163,000. This disparity demonstrated that the election remained a referendum on the incumbent.

Bush himself mocked this perception of him as a dummy, playing the happy-go-lucky all-American who stumbled upward, rather than the overachiever clawing his way to the top. "You may have noticed I have a few flaws, too. People sometimes have to correct my English," Bush joked at the Republican National Convention. "I knew I had a problem when Arnold Schwarzenegger started doing it."

Some supporters made the presidential intelligence question another wedge issue in the culture wars. In the *New York Times Magazine*, reporter Ron Suskind recalled Bush adviser Mark McKinnon's challenge in late 2002. "You think he's an idiot, don't you?" McKinnon said. Rejecting Suskind's denial, McKinnon continued: "No, you do, all of you do, up and down the West Coast, the East Coast, a few blocks in southern Manhattan called Wall Street. Let me clue you in. We don't care. You see, you're outnumbered 2 to 1 by folks in the big, wide middle of America, busy working people who don't read the *New York Times* or *Washington Post* or the *L.A. Times.* . . . They like the way he walks and the way he points, the way he exudes confidence. They have faith in him. And when you attack him for his malaprops, his jumbled syntax, it's good for us. Because you know what those folks don't like? They don't like you!"

The stupidity slur undercut Democrats' simultaneous indictment of Bush as a callous ideologue. In 1984 Walter Mondale and his allies had tried characterizing President Reagan as a bigoted Scrooge and an ignorant Mr. Magoo but confused elusive "swing" voters. Americans doubted someone was both clueless and malevolent.

Bush, like Reagan, tapped into long-standing American suspicions about smart politicians being too smooth, too clever. Long before Dwight Eisenhower the man of action beat Adlai Stevenson the "egghead," American voters prized the rough-hewn plain-speakin' frontiersman above the hypereducated silver-tongued urbanite. In 1980, Reagan contrasted his bold, simple vision with Jimmy Carter's intellectually oriented temporizing and micromanagement. Bush positioned himself as a man of clarity, if not eloquence, as opposed to his "slick" predecessor—and opponent. "Even when we don't agree, at least you know what I believe and where I stand," Bush said in his acceptance speech.

This populist critique of the too-intellectual president played to ideas increasingly popular among scholars. Harvard University psychologist Howard Gardner's theory of multiple intelligences suggested that Justice Oliver Wendell Holmes's claim that Franklin D. Roosevelt possessed a second-rate intellect but a first-class temperament could have been a compliment. "Smart comes in all kinds of different ways," President Bush averred.

While the Democrats' two lines of attack contradicted each other, the Republicans' main lines of attack reinforced each other. Republicans added the claim that Kerry was no hero to the charge that he flip-flopped. The overlapping message suggested Kerry was too callow and craven to be president.

In August, just as Kerry enjoyed a modest post-convention "bounce" giving him a small lead over President Bush of 50 percent to 44 percent among likely voters, a new group called Swift Boat Veterans for Truth launched one of the most effective advertising attacks in campaigning history. In widely publicized commercials, a best-selling book, and numerous other media initiatives, approximately 250 of the 3500 veterans who served on Swift Boats during Vietnam attacked Kerry's character and defining political narrative as a war hero. "For more than thirty years, most Vietnam veterans kept silent as we were maligned as misfits, drug addicts, and baby killers," the group charged. "Now that a key creator of that poisonous image is seeking the presidency we have resolved to end our silence."

Kerry's critics were refighting the political battles of Vietnam nearly three decades after Saigon's fall. The Swift Boat Veterans could not forgive Kerry—and so many other baby boomers—for opposing the war so vehemently. They believed that Kerry's high-profile role as a veteran denouncing the war, charging American soldiers with "crimes committed on a day-to-day basis with the full awareness of officers at all levels of command," when other American soldiers were in enemy's hands, was treasonous. "In a time of war, can America trust a man who betrayed his country?" one commercial asked.

Swift Boat Veterans for Truth, which eventually evolved into Swift Vets and POWs for Truth, was a 527 group, the result of the latest attempt to limit money's influence in politics. President Bush had reluctantly signed the Bipartisan Campaign Reform Act of 2002, also known as the McCain–Feingold Act, seeking to limit the "soft money" political parties' national committees pumped into campaigns when the candidates accepted public financing and spending limits. Following the law of unintended consequences that always haunted campaign finance reform, McCain-Feingold helped 527s proliferate. Named after Section 527 of the Internal Revenue Code, these groups could raise almost unlimited funds as long as they did not coordinate their plans directly with a candidate.

Democrats first exploited the loophole with the most prominent anti-Bush group, Moveon.org, producing many commercials. Overall, 527s spent about $300 million during the election, helping to make 2004 America's first billion-dollar presidential campaign. The Swift Boat Veterans had the biggest impact, even bequeathing a new verb to American politics. After Kerry, politicians vowed not to be "swiftboated."

Kerry miscalculated by not fighting back. The Swiftboat attacks began in August, when Kerry was conserving cash for the fall campaign. Americans wanted to see fireworks. Without the candidate's rejoinder, many swing voters began believing the charges.

From August 30 to September 2, the Republican National Convention continued harping on Kerry's weakness. Convening in New York City to emphasize the 9/11 connection, the Republicans politicized the terrorism issue. Georgia senator Zell Miller, a Democrat, crossed party lines to pummel Kerry in a keynote address. "Senator Kerry has made it clear that he would use military force only if approved by the United Nations," Miller sneered. "Kerry would let Paris decide when America needs defending. I want Bush to decide. . . . John Kerry, who says he doesn't like outsourcing, wants to outsource our national security." Delivering the knockout blow, Miller snapped: "This politician wants to be leader of the free world. Free for how long?"

In his acceptance speech, George W. Bush was more statesmanlike but equally muscular. He targeted Kerry's flip-flop on the $87 billion "for bullets and fuel and vehicles and body armor." Bush observed that "when pressed," Kerry "said it was a 'complicated' matter." Bush proclaimed: "There's nothing complicated about supporting our troops in combat."

"This election will also determine how America responds to the continuing danger of terrorism," Bush stated, "and you know where I stand." He recalled visiting the World Trade Center rubble three days after the

Safeguarding Our Freedoms

Titled "Safeguarding Our Freedoms," this Jeff Danziger cartoon shows the Statue of Liberty sitting in a corner of a jail cell, while Vice President Richard Cheney, holding the keys in one hand, tells her, "You'll be completely safe in here," and President George Bush tells her, "Remember, we love freedom." Danziger reflects concern for civil liberties during the War on Terror and increased homeland security. *(Jeff Danziger, New York Times Syndicate)*

attacks. "Workers in hard hats were shouting to me, 'Whatever it takes.' A fellow grabbed me by the arm, and he said, 'Do not let me down.' Since that day, I wake up every morning thinking about how to better protect our country. I will never relent in defending America—whatever it takes."

As Republicans celebrated inside Madison Square Garden, protestors belonging to more than 800 anti-Bush groups gathered outside. The day before the convention began, on Sunday, August 29, United for Peace and Justice organized a huge march past the convention site. Crowd estimates varied from 250,000 to 800,000, making it the largest protest against a political convention and one of the largest protests in American history. Protestors chanted "No More Bush," denouncing the Iraq War, environmental degradation, the lack of AIDS research funding, and the spread of poverty. Most of the protests were peaceful but 1,800 protestors were arrested—another convention record. Most charges were dropped, prompting charges of police overreaction. The protests, while color-

ful, reflected the ominous undertone of national division and despair in Bush's America.

During the Republican convention, photographers captured Kerry windsurfing off the Nantucket Coast, where he and Teresa owned one of their five homes. To many, the image of Kerry windsurfing conveyed his haughtiness and fickleness—and Republicans raced to exploit it. Soon a new Bush advertisement asked, "In which direction would John Kerry lead?" as the Democratic candidate tacked left and right. "Kerry voted for the Iraq war, opposed it, supported it, and now opposes it again," the narrator said. "He bragged about voting for the $87 billion to support our troops before he voted against it." The ad concluded: "John Kerry. Whichever way the wind blows."

If Kerry was culturally tone deaf, Bush was intellectually tone deaf. Democrats responded to the mocking of Kerry's leisure time pursuits with hard-hitting attacks against Bush's governance. In late September, when the windsurfing ad ran against Kerry, the Democrats quickly aired a commercial called "Juvenile." The narrator proclaimed: "One thousand U.S. casualties. Two Americans beheaded just this week. The Pentagon admits terrorists are pouring into Iraq." Yet, "in the face of the Iraq quagmire, George Bush's answer is to run a juvenile and tasteless attack ad."

Barely a week after the convention, CBS's veteran news anchor Dan Rather broadcast a report on *"60 Minutes II"* claiming Bush shirked his duty while serving in the Air National Guard from 1972 to 1973. Memoranda supposedly written by Bush's commander, the late Lieutenant Colonel Jerry B. Killian, corroborated the rumors, which had dogged Bush for years. Bloggers quickly proved the documents to be forgeries, noting that the centering of the type on the page was standard in the computer era yet rare in the early 1970s.

In a defining moment for the blogosphere in its revolution against mainstream media dominance, a former CBS News executive vice president, Jonathan Klein, dismissed the skeptical bloggers as lacking the CBS News team's authority: "You couldn't have a starker contrast between the multiple layers of check and balances [at *60 Minutes*] and a guy sitting in his living room in his pajamas writing," Klein quipped on television, while debating the issue. The fact that the segment's producer was fired and Dan Rather resigned in disgrace shook the media's credibility and made the "guys in pajamas" folk heroes.

The big three networks were under attack from the blogosphere and from cable channels. During the Democratic convention, for the first time, a cable news channel, CNN, boasted higher ratings than the big three networks' news shows. Meanwhile, promising to be "fair and balanced," Fox News offered a gung-ho, patriotic, pro-Bush perspective that cemented Bush supporters' loyalty.

Increasingly, Republicans and Democrats played to their respective bases. Bush's pollster, Matthew Dowd, concluded that "independents or persuadable voters in the last 20 years had gone from 22 percent of the electorate to 7 percent of the electorate in 2000." Traditionally, Dowd argued, everyone yelled, "Swing voters, swing voters, swing voters, swing voters, swing voters." To win in 2002, then 2004, Republicans mobilized their core supporters, seeking the 3–5 million conservatives and evangelicals Karl Rove estimated had stayed home on Election Day 2000.

The campaign focused on "wedge issues" to motivate the Christian evangelicals constituting approximately 40 percent of the Republican Party. "Elections are always about values," Dowd preached. "They're not about issues." Republicans charged that Democrats would encourage gay marriage, high taxes, mass abortions, and retreats from Iraq and Afghanistan. They painted Kerry as a decadent, flip-flopping, France-loving, big government, out-of-touch, '60s-addled, libertine, elitist city-slicker, more *Mother Jones* than *Field and Stream*, more NASDAQ than NASCAR, more Porsche than pick-up truck, more windsurfer than churchgoer, a dissident, not a patriot.

Bush happily shifted from his big-tent compassionate conservatism in 2000 to a red-meat, red-state–oriented approach. Unlike Ronald Reagan in 1984, Bush did not want a "lonely victory." He wanted to solidify Republican congressional strength and leave the Republican Party "stronger, broader and better."

Bush's unapologetic, surprisingly passionate campaign earned grudging admiration. Even the *New York Times* described him as a "street-smart, intuitive politician" and "a president of consequence." The *Times* also noted the criticism that "a president who always knows what he thinks never has to ponder the details; dogmatism saves time, and everything becomes strategy."

Bush's swagger became a campaign issue. The Democrats mocked Bush's 2000 campaign promise to be a "uniter not a divider," listing it as the first of "Bush's Broken Promises." Republican senator Chuck Hagel of Nebraska feared the lack of bipartisan cooperation posed a greater threat than terrorism. He recalled warning the president early on: "You're going to need the trust and relationships that you build on Capitol Hill." Hagel sighed, "They didn't do that."

As the 2004 presidential campaign entered debating season—with three 90-minute Kerry-Bush appearances and a fourth vice-presidential debate—campaign aides, journalists, and viewers searched for that defining gaffe, the dramatic sound bite or image that transforms the campaign. Reporters recalled Ronald Reagan's "There you go again" quip to Jimmy Carter in 1980; an aging President Reagan's rebound rejoinder to his younger challenger in 1984, "I'm not going to make an issue about Mr. Mondale's age and experience"; and Senator Lloyd Bentsen's body blow in 1988 to his greener colleague and vice presidential rival, Dan Quayle: "Senator, you're no Jack Kennedy." But such moments were rare.

More frequently, debates were dull. Journalists placed themselves on banana peel patrol, inhibiting candidates who feared minor slips' becoming major embarrassments. Media reports invariably influenced the outcome. Republicans' initial polling in 1976 estimated that Gerald Ford beat Jimmy Carter during the second debate. Most viewers ignored the president's gaffe suggesting Eastern Europe was free. Yet with each round of the ensuing news cycles emphasizing Ford's gaffe, Ford lost ground. Later, "spin alleys" developed outside the debating halls, with both parties unleashing their respective attack dogs to feed the media beast and shape the "postgame" show.

Voters also deserved blame. Citizens demanded issue-oriented exchanges. But when candidates focused on "just the facts," most voters stopped paying attention.

In Ohio, one undecided voter gripped Senator Kerry's hand and asked: "What are you going to tell somebody like me, who is on the fence?" Denouncing President Bush's handling of Iraq, Kerry stared straight into her eyes and said, "I know how to get it done." The voter swooned: "I'm voting for him. He was not so uppity as to overlook me."

Here was the key to the campaign, which rationalists and reporters overlooked at their peril. Americans wanted to be heard and seen; they wanted to sense that the candidate cared. A shrewd candidate addressed important issues while also talking about issues to demonstrate empathy. The challenge in the debates—as in most democratic politics—was not just to get the right answer but to answer in the right way.

It was easy to ridicule the presidential campaign. It was easy to snicker that the candidates squabbled about the wrong war (Vietnam) while ignoring the relevant conflict (Iraq). It was easy to caricature the two candidates: Senator Kerry's poofy hairdo and monumentally long chin and President Bush's beady-eyes and schoolboy grin. It was easy to dismiss the debates as carefully scripted, artificially choreographed joint appearances.

The first presidential debate, held at the University of Miami on September 30, however, silenced the naysayers and sobered the critics. There was no defining exchange. Inevitably, after the debate, which emphasized foreign affairs and homeland security, Democrats waxed eloquent about Kerry's eloquence; Republicans consistently emphasized the president's consistency. What was extraordinary was the debate's sheer ordinariness—in the American context. In a world of dictators and terrorists, these two rivals dueled verbally but remained gracious. When the moderator Jim Lehrer invited discussion of "underlying character issues," Bush saluted Kerry's "service" to the nation. Kerry replied: "I'm not going to talk about a difference of character. I don't think that's my job or my business." The gentlemanly tone was shrewd; Americans respond to mudslinging while demanding that their politicians act statesmanlike.

All this made the first debate healing, reassuring. With America-bashing becoming a popular worldwide sport, with Bushophobia rampant in Europe and Canada, it was illuminating to see the principles that united Senator Kerry and President Bush—including zero tolerance for terror at home and abroad. With ideologues rationalizing terrorism and excoriating free countries fighting terror, with pessimists doubting democracy's resilience during trying times, this peaceful conversation conducted before 62.5 million viewers was inspiring.

During the debate, Kerry scribbled notes as Bush spoke; he kept calm and delivered his words effectively. Most observers believed Kerry won. Commentators,

including the *Washington Post*'s Dana Milbank, criticized Bush's scowling demeanor, comparing it to Al Gore's sighing in 2000 and George H. W. Bush's glance at his wristwatch in 1992. When Kerry criticized Bush for only convincing the United Kingdom and Australia to join the invasion of Iraq, stating, "We can do better," Bush weakly replied, "Well, actually, he forgot Poland."

Even as the president's aides spun desperately, hailing their chief, key insiders confronted Bush. "I was not irritated," Bush insisted. "Sir, you were," his communications adviser Karen Hughes insisted. "I don't know what happened," First Lady Laura Bush said to her husband. "You've got to be yourself, and you weren't."

A week later, in the October 5 vice-presidential debate at Case Western Reserve University in Cleveland, John Edwards confronted Vice President Dick Cheney more effectively than Joe Lieberman had four years before. Edwards questioned Cheney's record at Halliburton, the energy conglomerate Cheney once led. Cheney retorted: "If you go, for example, to FactCheck.com, an independent Web site sponsored by the University of Pennsylvania, you can get the specific details with respect to Halliburton." The university actually ran FactCheck.*org*, while FactCheck.*com* sold dictionaries and encyclopedias. Cheney's mistake led many viewers to the wrong Web site and, resenting the extra traffic, Democrats at FactCheck.com redirected them to George Soros's anti-Bush website.

When Bush and Kerry met again on October 8 at Washington University in St. Louis, they followed a town hall format, answering questions citizens posed. Bush performed better but still appeared angry and flustered, unlike the cool Kerry. Bush's attempts at humor largely fell flat. The president cut off moderator Charlie Gibson after Kerry accused him of invading Iraq unilaterally. "Let me just answer what he just said about going alone," Bush said. "You tell [British prime minister] Tony Blair we're going alone! Tell Tony Blair we're going alone!"

Given two minutes to conclude, each candidate articulated a different domestic vision—after spending much of the debate and the campaign dueling about Iraq and America's reputation in the world. Focusing on the "crisis here at home," Kerry announced: "I have a plan to provide health care to all Americans. I have a plan to provide for our schools so we keep the standards, that we help our teachers teach and elevate our schools by funding No Child Left Behind. I have a plan to protect the environment so that we leave this place in better shape. . . ." Responding, Bush offered a Reaganesque formula "to keep this economy going: keep the taxes low, don't increase the scope of the federal government, keep regulations down, legal reform, a health care policy that does not empower the federal government but empow-

John Edwards (right) responds to Dick Cheney (left) during the vice-presidential debate in Cleveland, October 5, 2004. *(Ron Edmonds/ Associated Press)*

ers individuals, and an energy plan that'll help us become less dependent on foreign sources of energy."

Finally, on October 13, Bush shed the anger and impatience. Still, he did not win the third encounter decisively at Arizona State University, which emphasized the economy. Commentators said these presidential debates mattered—for a change—boosting Kerry's poll numbers because he appeared more presidential.

As Kerry and Bush clashed, two competing stereotypes of America clashed too. Americans heard that their nation was cranky, divided between "red" and "blue." Yet they also heard about the pathetic voter-turnout rate of barely 50 percent, and a soporific culture preferring leisure to politics, shopping to voting, consumerism to idealism.

At worst, both stereotypes were true. Americans were enduring ugly, polarized partisanship without the positive benefits of civil, constructive, mass political engagement. If, despite experiencing 9/11, Americans simply recreated 2000's partisan divide, partisanship was preventing Democrats and Republicans from adjusting their worldviews to fit new world realities.

That failure loomed large in America's bookstores, usually oases of reason. Readers were overwhelmed by the crossfire of complaints. Seymour Hersh's *Chain of Command* claimed Bush "made the world a more dangerous place for America," while Richard Miniter's *Shadow War* detailed "how Bush is winning the war

on terror." Historian Douglas Brinkley praised John Kerry's noble *Tour of Duty* while a Swift Boat veteran, John E. O'Neill, and Jerome Corsi branded Kerry *Unfit for Command*. Yet, amid the hysteria, despite polls suggesting 70 percent of Americans felt particularly deeply about this campaign, on Election Day, hundreds of thousands of partisans had to spend all day cajoling millions to vote. It was hard to believe the country was so polarized yet so blasé.

Maybe there was more to America than fire-breathing evangelicals, apocalyptic liberals, and robotic couch potatoes. This campaign, like all campaigns, struggled with the candidate's conundrum—how to mobilize millions to debate their futures without succumbing to demagoguery or superficiality? But given the long, colorful history of American invective, Americans did well in 2004. The red, white, and blue trumped the red versus the blue. The three debates attracted 160.4 million viewers, while the first debate's viewership was 35 percent larger than the one in 2000.

Kerry and Bush demonstrated their conflicting worldviews, temperaments, issue prescriptions—and their common patriotism. Bush opposed abortion, Kerry supported choice. Bush spoke about shrinking government, Kerry talked about improving America's infrastructure. Bush wanted to privatize Social Security, Kerry wanted to preserve it. At the same time, both affirmed the prevailing center-right consensus forged by Ronald Reagan, then Bill Clinton. Tacking right, Kerry supported the war and vowed not to raise taxes. Tacking left, Bush touted his No Child Left Behind education reform and emphasized how much stem cell research he allowed.

Note the bells that did not ring in 2004—no violence, no mass arrests. The economy worked; it was business as usual. Osama bin Laden released a videotape just before the election that triggered no panic. Headlines highlighted the dysfunctional, overlooking the functional. Yet Jon Stewart, a comedian claiming the ear of young America, chided the Democrats and Republicans dueling daily on CNN's *Crossfire* for being so shrill and polarizing, resulting in the program's cancellation. And the Democrats' rising star, Barack Obama, repudiated the red-versus-blue paradigm. Every four years Americans exhaust their vocabularies demonizing each other, then revert to their naturally nicer state. Perhaps this election demonstrated the best of both worlds, a democratic society where passionate opinions are expressed without resorting to violence, without getting too nasty.

The focus on red-versus-blue America should not have obscured another important headline: the United States of America was becoming increasingly conservative. Unlike Gerald Ford in 1976, Jimmy Carter in 1980, and George H. W. Bush in 1992, George W. Bush won re-election, capturing 62,040,611 votes to Kerry's 59,028,432 and winning the electoral college 286 to 251. Bush's victory margin of 3 million votes crossed the 50 percent popularity threshold that had eluded Bill Clinton in 1996. Bush became the first president with a popular vote majority since 1988, even as Democrats played out scenarios whereby a shift of less than 60,000 votes in Ohio from Bush to Kerry, out of more than 5.5 million cast, would have given Kerry 20 more electoral votes and the White House. The House of Representatives remained Republican and quite partisan, after a net gain of three seats. The Senate remained Republican, with a net gain of four seats and Democrats reeling from the loss of their leader, Senator Tom Daschle of South Dakota. For the first time since 1952 the Republicans clearly dominated the House, the Senate, and the White House. Nearly two-thirds of the state governors also were Republican. Referenda in eleven states outlawed gay marriage.

America's center of political gravity had shifted. John Kerry had to lean right. He supported the war in Iraq and repudiated Howard Dean. He vowed not to raise taxes for the middle class. Although he endorsed a more compassionate social agenda, Kerry avoided the "L word," liberal, a label with a proud American pedigree, which Republicans cleverly reduced to an epithet. Kerry understood that even in 2004, Americans still lived in a Reaganized

America. Reagan's conservative counterrevolution mobilized evangelicals, united Republicans, taught conservative politicians how to exploit cultural wedge issues. There were still millions of American liberals, many progressive policies remained deeply entrenched, and American tradition values consensus and compromise. Yet a politically conservative status quo explained Bush's victory along with a growing baseline of social liberalism that Republicans had to respect.

The 2004 election was close—but not as close as 2000. The voting patterns were similar, although New Hampshire went Democratic, Iowa and New Mexico went Republican. The electoral map confirmed impressions of blue Democratic cosmopolitans opposing red Republican traditionalists. When 22 percent in Election Day exit polls said "values" swayed their votes, reporters proclaimed an unbridgeable chasm and a stable electoral deadlock. This conclusion was misleading. In the exit polls, 34 percent identified national security as important, but those answers were divided between Iraq and terrorism. "Security Moms" helped Bush win, with his percentage of the women's vote growing from 2000. Similarly, when the answers were grouped by category, 25 percent most worried about economic issues.

The Rove-Dowd mobilization strategy worked. Republicans voted in equal numbers to Democrats, a historic first made more impressive by the fact that the Democrats were more numerous than their rivals. Seventeen million more people voted in 2004 than 2000, a 14 percent increase. The 60 percent turnout of eligible voters approached 1992's total of 61.5 percent. Bush's voting percentage increased almost everywhere except Vermont and South Dakota.

Commentators attributed Bush's victory to Karl Rove's skills, Kerry's lack of personal charisma, the public's fear of terrorism, and Bush's caricature of Kerry. "For eight months, the Bush campaign kept up a relentless attack on Kerry as a flip-flopper," wrote William Schneider in the *National Journal*. "It started on March 3, when Bush said, 'Senator Kerry has been in Washington long enough to take both sides on just about every issue.' It ended at midnight the night before the election. At his final campaign rally in Dallas, Bush recounted Kerry's vote against funding for the troops in Iraq. 'And then he entered the flip-flop hall of fame,' Bush said. 'And as he entered that hall of fame,' he said, 'I actually did vote for the $87 billion before I voted against it.'"

Still Kerry had come close to winning—or actually Bush had come close to losing. Oil prices were up and the economy was down. More people were pessimistic about the future than optimistic. It was the narrowest incumbent victory ever, merely 2.5 percent, even slimmer than

Woodrow Wilson's 3.2 percent victory margin in 1916. Clinton had 8.5 percent in 1996 and Richard Nixon had 23.2 percent in 1972.

Most troubling, the Bushophobia lingered. Traditionally, the end of a campaign begins a time of healing. In November 2004, however, many dumbfounded Democrats concluded that anyone who chose George W. Bush had to be as "ignorant" or "repellent" as he was.

The *New York Times* led the howl of the blue states. The *Times* published historian Garry Wills's lament calling Election Day "The Day the Enlightenment Went Out." America's "fundamentalist zeal, . . . religious intolerance, fear of and hatred for modernity," Wills claimed, now resembled "the Muslim world, . . . Al Qaeda, . . . Saddam Hussein's Sunni loyalists." *New York Times* columnist Maureen Dowd sneered: "W. ran a jihad in America so he can fight one in Iraq." A map darting around the Internet showed North America divided into two countries: cosmopolitan "blue" America, constituting the Northeast, the West Coast, and Canada, renamed "the United States of Canada," and the benighted American Midwest and Sunbelt, renamed "Jesusland."

The 2004 campaign produced an anomalous result. George W. Bush had tremendous power and political capital, which he was ready to use. But Democrats harbored tremendous resentment. Bush's second term would reflect the need to have public opinion behind you, not just power. The reelected president would not succeed in advancing his agenda, hobbled as he would be by a natural disaster in New Orleans, continuing wars in Iraq and Afghanistan, and, then, in the fall of 2008, an earth-shattering financial crisis.

—*Gil Troy*

Selected Bibliography

Douglas Brinkley, *Tour of Duty: John Kerry and the Vietnam War* (2003), is Kerry's authorized campaign biography. John E. O'Neill and Jerome R. Corsi, *Unfit for Command: Swift Boat Veterans Speak Out Against John Kerry* (2004), is the book version of the famous (or infamous) attack on Kerry that helped derail his campaign. James W. Ceaser and Andrew E. Busch, *Red Over Blue: The 2004 Elections and American Politics* (2005), is an excellent, thought-provoking academic study. Evan Thomas and the Staff of *Newsweek, Election 2004: How Bush/Cheney '04 Won and What You Can Expect in the Future* (2004) is a great play-by-play. See also William J. Crotty, *A Defining Moment: The Presidential Election of 2004* (2004); John C. Green, Mark J. Rozell, and Clyde Wilcox, eds., *The Values Campaign? The Christian Right and the 2004 Elections* (2004); John F. Kennedy School of Government Institute of Politics, *Campaign for President: The Managers Look at 2004* (2006); Bill Kristol, *What's at Stake: The War on Terror and the 2004 Election* (2004); Charles Lewis, *The Buying of the President, 2004: Who's Really Bankrolling Bush and His Democratic Challengers: And What They Expect in Return* (2004); David B. Magleby, Anthony Corrado, and Kelly D. Patterson, eds., *Financing the 2004 Election* (2006); William G. Mayer, *The Making of the Presidential Candidates 2004* (2004); Mark Crispin Miller, *Fooled Again: How the Right Stole the 2004 Election & Why They'll Steal the Next One Too (Unless We Stop Them)* (2005); Larry Sabato, *Divided States of America: The Slash and Burn Politics of the 2004 Presidential Election* (2005); Walter Shapiro, *One-Car Caravan: On the Road with the 2004 Democrats Before America Tunes In* (2003); Daron R. Shaw, *The Race to 270: The Electoral College and the Campaign Strategies of 2000 and 2004* (2006); Andrew Paul Williams and John C. Tedesco, eds., *The Internet Election: Perspectives on the Web in Campaign 2004* (2006).

2004 ELECTION STATISTICS

State	Number of Electors	Total Popular Vote	Elec Vote R	Elec Vote D	Elec Vote *	Pop Vote R	Pop Vote D	Margin of Victory Votes	Margin of Victory % Total Vote
Alabama	9	1,883,449	9			1	2	482,461	25.62%
Alaska	3	312,598	3			1	2	79,864	25.55%
Arizona	10	2,013,893	10			1	2	210,770	10.47%
Arkansas	6	1,054,945	6			1	2	102,945	9.76%
California	55	12,421,857		55		2	1	1,235,659	9.95%
Colorado	9	2,130,325	9			1	2	99,531	4.67%
Connecticut	7	1,578,769		7		2	1	163,662	10.37%
Delaware	3	375,270		3		2	1	28,492	7.59%
District of Columbia	3	227,586		3		2	1	181,714	79.84%
Florida	27	7,609,810	27			1	2	380,978	5.01%
Georgia	15	3,304,481	15			1	2	548,105	16.59%
Hawaii	4	429,013		4		2	1	37,517	8.74%
Idaho	4	598,447	4			1	2	228,137	38.12%
Illinois	21	5,274,322		21		2	1	545,604	10.34%
Indiana	11	2,468,002	11			1	2	510,427	20.68%
Iowa	7	1,506,908	7			1	2	10,059	0.67%
Kansas	6	1,187,756	6			1	2	301,463	25.38%
Kentucky	8	1,796,079	8			1	2	356,706	19.86%
Louisiana	9	1,943,106	9			1	2	281,870	14.51%
Maine	4	740,752		4		2	1	66,641	9.00%
Maryland	10	2,386,678		10		2	1	309,790	12.98%
Massachusetts	12	2,912,388		12		2	1	732,691	25.16%
Michigan	17	4,839,252		17		2	1	165,437	3.42%
Minnesota	10	2,828,387		9	1	2	1	98,319	3.48%
Mississippi	6	1,152,365	6			1	2	226,887	19.69%
Missouri	11	2,731,364	11			1	2	196,542	7.20%
Montana	3	450,445	3			1	2	92,353	20.50%
Nebraska	5	778,186	5			1	2	258,486	33.22%
Nevada	5	829,587	5			1	2	21,500	2.59%
New Hampshire	4	677,738		4		2	1	9,274	1.37%
New Jersey	15	3,612,137		15		2	1	241,427	6.68%
New Mexico	5	756,304	5			1	2	5,988	0.79%
New York	31	7,391,741		31		2	1	1,351,713	18.29%
North Carolina	15	3,501,007	15			1	2	435,317	12.43%
North Dakota	3	312,833	3			1	2	85,599	27.36%
Ohio	20	5,627,908	20			1	2	118,601	2.11%
Oklahoma	7	1,463,758	7			1	2	455,826	31.14%
Oregon	7	1,836,782		7		2	1	76,332	4.16%
Pennsylvania	21	5,769,590		21		2	1	144,248	2.50%
Rhode Island	4	437,134		4		2	1	90,714	20.75%
South Carolina	8	1,617,730	8			1	2	276,275	17.08%
South Dakota	3	388,215	3			1	2	83,340	21.47%
Tennessee	11	2,437,319	11			1	2	347,898	14.27%
Texas	34	7,410,765	34			1	2	1,694,213	22.86%
Utah	5	927,844	5			1	2	422,543	45.54%
Vermont	3	312,309		3		2	1	62,887	20.14%
Virginia	13	3,198,367	13			1	2	262,217	8.20%
Washington	11	2,861,713		11		2	1	205,307	7.17%
West Virginia	5	755,887	5			1	2	97,237	12.86%
Wisconsin	10	2,997,007		10		2	1	11,384	0.38%
Wyoming	3	243,428	3			1	2	96,853	39.79%
Total	538	122,303,536	286	251	1	1	2	3,012,179	2.46%

* One elector voted for John Edwards.

Bush Republican		Kerry Democratic		Nader Independent		Others	
1,176,394	62.46%	693,933	36.84%	6,701	0.36%	6,421	0.34%
190,889	61.07%	111,025	35.52%	5,069	1.62%	5,615	1.80%
1,104,294	54.83%	893,524	44.37%	2,773	0.14%	13,302	0.66%
572,898	54.31%	469,953	44.55%	6,171	0.58%	5,923	0.56%
5,509,826	44.36%	6,745,485	54.30%	21,213	0.17%	145,333	1.17%
1,101,256	51.69%	1,001,725	47.02%	12,718	0.60%	14,626	0.69%
693,826	43.95%	857,488	54.31%	12,969	0.82%	14,486	0.92%
171,660	45.74%	200,152	53.34%	2,153	0.57%	1,305	0.35%
21,256	9.34%	202,970	89.18%	1,485	0.65%	1,875	0.82%
3,964,522	52.10%	3,583,544	47.09%	32,971	0.43%	28,773	0.38%
1,914,254	57.93%	1,366,149	41.34%	2,231	0.07%	21,847	0.66%
194,191	45.26%	231,708	54.01%	0	0.00%	3,114	0.73%
409,235	68.38%	181,098	30.26%	1,115	0.19%	6,999	1.17%
2,345,946	44.48%	2,891,550	54.82%	3,571	0.07%	33,255	0.63%
1,479,438	59.94%	969,011	39.26%	1,328	0.05%	18,225	0.74%
751,957	49.90%	741,898	49.23%	5,973	0.40%	7,080	0.47%
736,456	62.00%	434,993	36.62%	9,348	0.79%	6,959	0.59%
1,069,439	59.54%	712,733	39.68%	8,856	0.49%	5,051	0.28%
1,102,169	56.72%	820,299	42.22%	7,032	0.36%	13,606	0.70%
330,201	44.58%	396,842	53.57%	8,069	1.09%	5,640	0.76%
1,024,703	42.93%	1,334,493	55.91%	11,854	0.50%	15,628	0.65%
1,071,109	36.78%	1,803,800	61.94%	4,806	0.17%	32,673	1.12%
2,313,746	47.81%	2,479,183	51.23%	24,035	0.50%	22,288	0.46%
1,346,695	47.61%	1,445,014	51.09%	18,683	0.66%	17,995	0.64%
684,981	59.44%	458,094	39.75%	3,177	0.28%	6,113	0.53%
1,455,713	53.30%	1,259,171	46.10%	1,294	0.05%	15,186	0.56%
266,063	59.07%	173,710	38.56%	6,168	1.37%	4,504	1.00%
512,814	65.90%	254,328	32.68%	5,698	0.73%	5,346	0.69%
418,690	50.47%	397,190	47.88%	4,838	0.58%	8,869	1.07%
331,237	48.87%	340,511	50.24%	4,479	0.66%	1,511	0.22%
1,670,003	46.23%	1,911,430	52.92%	19,418	0.54%	11,286	0.31%
376,930	49.84%	370,942	49.05%	4,053	0.54%	4,379	0.58%
2,962,567	40.08%	4,314,280	58.37%	99,873	1.35%	15,021	0.20%
1,961,166	56.02%	1,525,849	43.58%	1,805	0.05%	12,187	0.35%
196,651	62.86%	111,052	35.50%	3,756	1.20%	1,374	0.44%
2,859,768	50.81%	2,741,167	48.71%	0	0.00%	26,973	0.48%
959,792	65.57%	503,966	34.43%	0	0.00%	0	0.00%
866,831	47.19%	943,163	51.35%	0	0.00%	26,788	1.46%
2,793,847	48.42%	2,938,095	50.92%	2,656	0.05%	34,992	0.61%
169,046	38.67%	259,760	59.42%	4,651	1.06%	3,677	0.84%
937,974	57.98%	661,699	40.90%	5,520	0.34%	12,537	0.77%
232,584	59.91%	149,244	38.44%	4,320	1.11%	2,067	0.53%
1,384,375	56.80%	1,036,477	42.53%	8,992	0.37%	7,475	0.31%
4,526,917	61.09%	2,832,704	38.22%	9,159	0.12%	41,985	0.57%
663,742	71.54%	241,199	26.00%	11,305	1.22%	11,598	1.25%
121,180	38.80%	184,067	58.94%	4,494	1.44%	2,568	0.82%
1,716,959	53.68%	1,454,742	45.48%	2,393	0.07%	24,273	0.76%
1,304,894	45.60%	1,510,201	52.77%	23,283	0.81%	23,335	0.82%
423,778	56.06%	326,541	43.20%	4,063	0.54%	1,505	0.20%
1,478,120	49.32%	1,489,504	49.70%	16,390	0.55%	12,993	0.43%
167,629	68.86%	70,776	29.07%	2,741	1.13%	2,282	0.94%
62,040,611	50.73%	59,028,432	48.26%	465,650	0.38%	768,843	0.63%

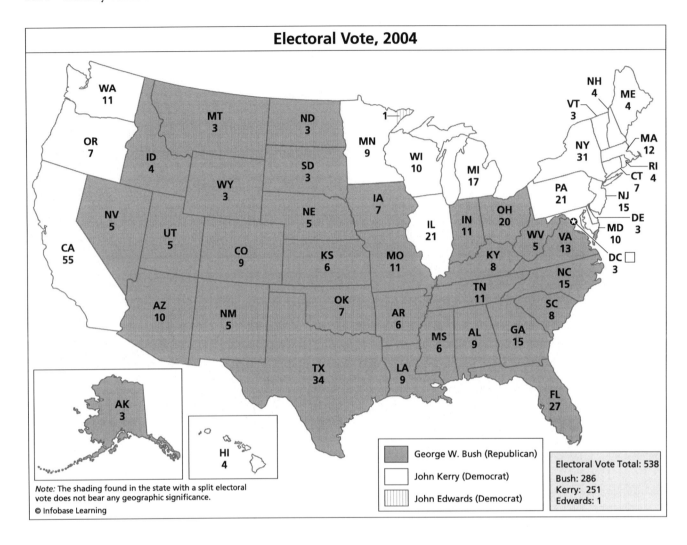

Electoral Vote, 2004

WA	11
OR	7
MT	3
ND	3
MN	9
1	
NH	4
ME	4
VT	3
ID	4
SD	3
WI	10
MI	17
NY	31
MA	12
WY	3
IA	7
IN	11
OH	20
PA	21
RI	4
CT	7
NV	5
NE	5
IL	21
WV	5
NJ	15
CA	55
UT	5
CO	9
KS	6
MO	11
KY	8
VA	13
DE	3
MD	10
DC	3
NC	15
AZ	10
NM	5
OK	7
AR	6
TN	11
SC	8
MS	6
AL	9
GA	15
TX	34
LA	9
FL	27
AK	3
HI	4

Note: The shading found in the state with a split electoral vote does not bear any geographic significance.

© Infobase Learning

■ George W. Bush (Republican)
□ John Kerry (Democrat)
▥ John Edwards (Democrat)

Electoral Vote Total: 538
Bush: 286
Kerry: 251
Edwards: 1

Election of 2008

Election Overview

Election Year 2008

Election Day November 4, 2008

Winning Candidates

- ★ Barack Obama
- ★ Joseph Biden

Election Results [ticket, party: popular votes (percentage of popular vote); electoral votes (percentage of electoral vote)]

- Barack Obama and Joseph Biden, Democratic: 69,499,428 (52.89%); 365 (67.8%)
- John McCain and Sarah Palin, Republican: 59,950,323 (45.62%); 173 (32.2%)
- Ralph Nader and Matt Gonzalez, Independent: 739,278 (0.56%); 0 (0.0%)
- Bob Barr and Wayne Allyn Root, Libertarian: 523,433 (0.40%); 0 (0.0%)
- Other: 694,561 (0.53%); 0 (0.0%)

Voter Turnout 58.2%

Central Forums/Campaign Methods for Addressing Voters

- Speeches
- Rallies
- Internet, Web sites, blogs, social networking

Incumbent President and Vice President on Election Day George W. Bush and Richard Cheney

Population (2008) 304,530,000

Gross Domestic Product

- $14.4 trillion (in current dollars: $13.3 trillion)
- Per capita: $47,422 (in current dollars: $43,714)

Number of Daily Newspapers (2007) 1,422

Average Daily Circulation (2007) 50,700,000

- *USA Today,* 2,524,965
- *Wall Street Journal,* 2,068,439
- *New York Times,* 1,627,062

Newspapers on the Web

- 80 of the nation's top 100 newspapers offer reporter blogs. On 63 of these blogs, readers could comment on posts written by reporters.
- 76 of the nation's top 100 newspapers offer RSS (Really Simple Syndication) web feeds on their websites. All of these feeds are partial feeds, and none include ads.

Households with

- Radio (2006): 110,500,000
- Television (2006): 110,000
- Computer/Internet (2007): 72,721,000

Method of Choosing Electors

- Popular vote (mostly general ticket system/winner take all)

Method of Choosing Nominees:

- Presidential preference primaries
- Caucuses

Key Issues and Events

- George W. Bush's historically low popularity
- Iraq/Afghanistan wars

- Democrats gained majorities in both houses of Congress in 2006
- Economic crash in September 2008
- Energy crisis
- Democrats worry about the early front-runner, New York senator Hillary Rodham Clinton, and her ability to attract voters, Independents
- Strong chance of first woman president or first African-American president

Leading Candidates

DEMOCRATS

- Barack Obama, senator (Illinois)
- Hillary Rodham Clinton, senator (New York)
- John Edwards, former senator (North Carolina)
- Bill Richardson, governor (New Mexico)
- Joe Biden, senator (Delaware)
- Christopher Dodd, senator (Connecticut)
- Dennis Kucinich, representative (Ohio)
- Mike Gravel, former senator (Alaska)
- Tom Vilsack, former governor (Iowa)

REPUBLICANS

- John McCain, senator (Arizona)
- Mike Huckabee, former governor (Arkansas)
- Mitt Romney, former governor (Massachusetts)
- Rudy Giuliani, former mayor (New York City)
- Ron Paul, representative (Texas)
- Fred Thompson, former senator (Tennessee)
- Duncan Hunter, representative (California)
- Sam Brownback, senator (Kansas)
- Tom Tancredo, former representative (Colorado)
- Tommy Thompson, former governor (Wisconsin)
- Alan Keyes, former ambassador (Maryland)
- Jim Gilmore, former governor (Virginia)

Trajectory

- July 27, 2004, an obscure politician with the unlikely name of Barack Obama electrifies the nation with a lyrical, visionary Democratic convention keynote address.
- Obama wins the Iowa caucus on January 3, 2008, seizing front-runner status from Hillary Rodham Clinton, who had held it for the past year.
- Clinton and John McCain win New Hampshire primary on January 8; however, Obama's "Yes, We Can" concession speech rocks the nation, effectively making the Democratic nomination a two-person race.
- McCain beats Rudy Giuliani in Florida; Giuliani drops out, January 29, 2008.

- Super Tuesday, February 5: McCain triumphs, Clinton and Obama split
- On March 13, ABC reports finding of incendiary anti-American videotapes of the Reverend Jeremiah Wright, Barack Obama's preacher.
- Obama delivers a speech on race and reconciliation at the Constitution Center in Philadelphia, March 18, 2008.
- On June 19, Obama becomes the first presidential nominee to reject public financing—and the attendant spending limits—since the system was established in 1976.
- Obama accepts the Democratic nomination on August 28, the 45th anniversary of Martin Luther King Jr.'s "I Have a Dream" speech.
- McCain's surprise choice as running mate, Sarah Palin, delivers a rousing campaign speech at the Republican convention, September 3, as a "hockey mom" who can take on Obama.
- September 15: The economy crashes.
- September 24: Palin stumbles through an interview with Katie Couric, appearing glib and ignorant.
- After stating, "The fundamentals of our economy are strong," McCain suspends his campaign on September 24, then restarts it on September 26. In contrast to Obama's calm, steady, and disciplined demeanor, McCain's actions appear erratic, and his campaign never recovers.

Conventions

- Constitution Party National Convention, April 23–26, 2008, Kansas City, Missouri
- Libertarian National Convention, May 23–26, 2008, Denver, Colorado
- Green Party National Convention, July 10–13, 2008, Chicago, Illinois
- Reform Party National Convention, July 18–20, 2008, Dallas, Texas
- Democratic National Convention, August 25–28, 2008, Pepsi Center and Invesco Field, Denver, Colorado
- Republican National Convention, September 1–4, 2008, Xcel Energy Center, St. Paul, Minnesota

Ballots/Nominees

DEMOCRATS

Presidential first ballot

- Barack Obama 3,188.5; 72.15%
- Hillary Rodham Clinton 1,010.5; 2.87%
- Abstentions 1.0; 0.00%
- Delegates who did not vote 219.0; 4.96%
- Totals 4,419.0; 100.00%

Vice-presidential ballot
- Joseph Biden, acclamation

REPUBLICANS
Presidential first ballot
- John McCain 2,343; 98.45%
- Ron Paul 15; 0.63%
- Mitt Romney 2; 0.08%
- Delegates that did not vote 20; 0.84%
- Totals 2,380; 100.00%

Vice-presidential ballot
- Sarah Palin, unanimous

Primary Debates

- 19 Democratic debates from April 26, 2007, to April 16, 2008
- 16 Republican debates from May 3, 2007, to January 30, 2008

Primaries Results

DEMOCRATS
- Hillary Rodham Clinton 18,155,676; 47.95%
- Barack Obama 17,952,233; 47.41%
- John Edwards 1,007,069; 2.66%
- Uncommitted 326,775; 0.86%
- Bill Richardson 105,017; 0.28%
- Dennis J. Kucinich 103,267; 0.27%
- Joe Biden 81,623; 0.22%
- Scattering 46,058; 0.12%
- Mike Gravel 40,260; 0.11%
- Chris Dodd 35,203; 0.09%
- Jim Rogers 3,905; 0.01%

REPUBLICANS
- John McCain 9,838,910; 46.49%
- Mitt Romney 4,681,436; 22.12%
- Mike Huckabee 4,281,900; 20.23%
- Ron Paul 1,214,563; 5.74%
- Rudy Giuliani 597,499; 2.82%
- Fred Thompson 303,845; 1.44%
- Uncommitted 70,873; 0.33%
- Alan L. Keyes 59,636; 0.28%
- Scattering 48,004; 0.23%

Party Platform

DEMOCRATS
- Redeploy American troops serving in Iraq
- Pro-choice on abortion
- "Tough and practical" immigration reform
- Health-care reform and access
- Alternative energy technologies
- Fight global warming.
- Amend NAFTA (North American Free Trade Agreement).
- Expand AmeriCorps and Peace Corps programs.

REPUBLICANS
- Increase intelligence-gathering capabilities to combat terrorism and for national security.
- More armed forces support (economic opportunities and health and disability care for veterans)
- Pro-life on abortion
- Oppose amnesty for illegal immigrants.
- English as the official language
- United Nations reform
- Tax relief (economic growth, promote small business)
- Government reform (balanced budget act, ending earmarks in legislation)
- Develop nuclear energy as an alternative to oil.

Campaign Innovations

- In late 2007 both parties mandate that Iowa will always hold the first caucus, and New Hampshire the first primary. Republican state parties failing to comply will lose half their delegate vote, while any renegade Democratic state parties risk having their entire delegation excluded. The Democratic Party also rules that only four states can hold primaries prior to February 5.
- Courting and mobilizing activists, donations, and voters through the Internet.
- Effective usage of campaign websites and social media sites, especially YouTube, MySpace, and Facebook.
- More than 1 million people receive campaign text messages via cell phone.
- Two million people join MyBO, a pro-Obama website fusing social networking with volunteer work.
- More than 5 million people support Obama's profile on social sites like Facebook.
- Thirteen million voters sign up with Obama for America (one-quarter of Obama voters).

Campaign Tactics

DEMOCRATS
- Shrewd tactics and soaring rhetoric fuel Obama's campaign.
- Obama organizes from the bottom up.
- "No drama Obama" recruits disciplined aides who cooperate with one another.
- Obama's early opposition in 2002 to the war in Iraq certifies his independence.

- Obama rejects $84 million in public financing for the general campaign and raises a record-breaking $150 million in September alone, as part of an overall total of $600 million for the general election.
- To shore up his foreign credentials, in late July Obama visits Kuwait, Afghanistan, Iraq, Jordan, Israel, Germany, France, and the United Kingdom. This trip is the most extensive mid-campaign foreign tour a presidential nominee ever undertook.
- Obama maintains a steely, steady, professional calm demeanor that proves reassuring.
- Final Obama surge: Obama addresses crowds of as many as 100,000 voters. His campaign spends $4 million purchasing 30 minutes on CBS, NBC, and Fox.

REPUBLICANS

- McCain appeals to Republican voters as experienced but not tainted by an identification with Bush, vindicated by the Iraq surge, a genuine war hero, and a national leader.
- Negative rhetoric and ads, with McCain spending much of the summer deriding Obama's inexperience, especially in foreign affairs.
- After the third presidential debate, McCain begins campaigning with "Joe the Plumber" (Joe Wurzelbacher), who supposedly represents the average Americans worried that Obama's policies will burden them economically.

Debates

- September 26, 2008: Presidential debate at University of Mississippi (foreign policy/national security), moderated by Jim Lehrer, PBS. Polls show that by 52 percent to 35 percent most Americans deem Obama the winner. McCain appears too prickly.
- October 2, 2008: Vice-presidential debate at Washington University, St. Louis, moderated by Gwen Ifill, PBS.
- October 7, 2008: Presidential debate at Belmont University (town meeting, economy), moderated by Tom Brokaw, NBC News.
- October 15, 2008: Presidential debate at Hofstra University (domestic/economic policy), moderated by Bob Schieffer, CBS News.

Popular Campaign Slogans

DEMOCRATS

- "Change We Can Believe In"
- "Change We Need"
- "Hope"
- "Yes, We Can!"

REPUBLICANS

- "Country First"
- "Drill, Baby, Drill"
- "A Leader We Can Believe In"
- "A Cause Greater Than Self"
- "Reform, Prosperity, Peace"

Campaign Songs

DEMOCRATS

- "Yes, We Can"
- "Better Way"
- "Signed, Sealed, Delivered, I'm Yours"
- "City of Blinding Lights"
- "Higher and Higher"
- "Think"
- "The Rising"
- "Only in America"

REPUBLICANS

- "Take a Chance on Me"
- "Our Country"
- "Raisin' McCain"

Influential Campaign Appeals or Ads

DEMOCRATS

- Obama's call for idealism and a modern multicultural nationalism resonates, especially among young voters, intellectuals, and African Americans.
- will.i.am of the Black Eyed Peas and some other celebrity friends make a music video out of Barack Obama's New Hampshire primary concession speech, making "Yes, We Can" a pop culture as well as political phenomenon.
- The Clinton campaign's most memorable commercial: "It's 3 a.m. and your children are safely asleep. . . . Who do you want answering the phone [at the White House]?"
- "Seven": Depicting McCain as out of touch when he could not respond to the question about how many houses he owned.
- Civil liberties groups and the netroots denounce the updated Foreign Intelligence Surveillance Act (FISA), which McCain pronounces a "vital national security matter." In late June, Obama announces he will vote for the latest version, having opposed an earlier version, because the compromise bill reaffirms the primacy of the FISA courts.
- Comedian Tina Fey on *Saturday Night Live* imitates Sarah Palin's gaffes and missteps on the campaign trail.

REPUBLICANS

- Popular advertisement juxtaposing images of pop stars Britney Spears and Paris Hilton as Germans shout, "Obama, Obama," asks tartly: "He's the biggest celebrity in the world—but is he ready to lead?"
- John McCain emphasizes his patriotism, sense of duty, commitment to old-fashioned values, and heroic biography, saying: "I fell in love with my county when I was a prisoner in someone else's."
- Rumors that Obama is Muslim, attended a radical madrasa in Indonesia, and is, as Palin puts it, an unpatriotic radical "palling around with terrorists."

Campaign Finance

- Obama raises $744,985,624 to John McCain's $368,093,764 for the general campaign for a total of $1,113,079,388.
- The Republican and Democratic National Committees and advocacy groups spend millions more.
- Obama's campaign spends $310 million on airing 570,963 commercials.
- McCain spends $135 million for 274,737 airings.

Defining Quotations

- "You . . . came here because you believe in what this country can be. In the face of war, you believe there can be peace. In the face of despair, you believe there can be hope. In the face of a politics that shut you out, that's told you to settle, that's divided us for too long, you believe that we can be one people, reaching for what's possible, building that more perfect union." *Barack Obama, Springfield, Illinois, campaign launch, February 10, 2007*
- "I am an American running for president. I do not define my candidacy by my religion. A person should not be elected because of his faith nor should he be rejected because of his faith." *Mitt Romney, Texas A&M University, December 6, 2007*
- "I just don't want to see us fall backward as a nation. I mean, this is very personal for me. Not just political. I see what's happening. We have to reverse it. . . . Some people think elections are a game: who's up or who's down. It's about our country. It's about our kids' future. It's about all of us together. Some of us put ourselves out there and do this against some difficult odds." *Hillary Clinton, Portsmouth, New Hampshire, on the eve of the primary, January 7, 2008.*
- "My friends, you know I'm past the age when I can claim the noun 'kid,' no matter what adjective precedes it. But tonight, we sure showed them what a comeback looks like." *John McCain, after his victory in the New Hampshire primary, January 8, 2008*
- "Yes, we can. It was a creed written into the founding documents that declared the destiny of a nation: Yes, we can. . . . It was whispered by slaves and abolitionists as they blazed a trail towards freedom through the darkest of nights: Yes, we can. . . . It was sung by immigrants as they struck out from distant shores and pioneers who pushed westward against an unforgiving wilderness: Yes, we can. . . . Yes, we can, to opportunity and prosperity. Yes, we can heal this nation. Yes, we can repair this world. Yes, we can." *Barack Obama, New Hampshire concession speech, January 8, 2008*
- "For the first time in my adult lifetime, I'm really proud of my country. . . ." *Michelle Obama, in Madison, Wisconsin, February 18, 2008*
- "[It is not] God Bless America . . . No, no, no, God *damn* America." *The Reverend Jeremiah Wright in a 2003 sermon first publicized on March 13, 2009*
- "When we started this race, Barack told us that he wanted the campaign to be a vehicle for involving people and giving them a stake in the kind of organizing he believed in. He is still the same guy who came to Chicago as a community organizer twenty-three years ago. The idea that we can organize together and improve our country—I mean, he really *believes* that." *Obama's political consultant, David Axelrod, tells* Rolling Stone, *published in the March 20, 2008, issue*
- Bitterness over economic troubles made rural voters in Pennsylvania and elsewhere, "cling to guns or religion or antipathy to people who aren't like them." *Barack Obama, April 6, 2008, at a private fund-raising dinner*
- "Our party and our country are better off because of her, and I am a better candidate for having had the honor to compete with Hillary Rodham Clinton." *Barack Obama claiming the Democratic nomination in St. Paul, Minnesota, June 3, 2008*
- "Although we weren't able to shatter that highest, hardest glass ceiling this time, thanks to you, it's got about eighteen million cracks in it. And the light is shining through like never before, filling us all with the hope and the sure knowledge that the path will be a little easier next time." *Hillary Clinton, concession speech, Washington, June 3, 2008*
- "I know how to win wars. And if I'm elected President, I will turn around the war in Afghanistan, just as we have turned around the war in Iraq, with a comprehensive strategy for victory. I know how to do that. . . . In wartime, judgment and experience

matter. In a time of war, the commander in chief doesn't get a learning curve. . . . My friends, flip-floppers all over the world are enraged." *John McCain, Albuquerque, New Mexico, July 15, 2008*

- "With an eye toward the future, with resolve in our hearts, let us remember this history, and answer our destiny, and remake the world once again." *Barack Obama, Berlin, Germany, July 24, 2008*

- "This November, the torch will be passed again to a new generation of Americans, so with Barack Obama and for you and me, our country will be committed to his cause. The work begins anew. The hope rises again. And the dream lives on." *Edward M. Kennedy, speech at the Democratic National Convention, August 25, 2008*

- "America, we are better than these last eight years. We are a better country than this. . . . This moment, this election is our chance to keep, in the 21st century, the American promise alive. . . . We love this country too much to let the next four years look just like the last eight. . . . In Washington, they call this the 'Ownership Society,' but what it really means is that you're on your own. Out of work? Tough luck, you're on your own. No health care? The market will fix it. You're on your own. Born into poverty? Pull yourself up by your own bootstraps, even if you don't have boots. You are on your own. Change happens because the American people demand it, because they rise up and insist on new ideas and new leadership, a new politics for a new time. America, this is one of those moments." *Barack Obama, "The American Promise," address accepting the presidential nomination at the Democratic National Convention in Denver, August 28, 2008*

- "I guess a small-town mayor is sort of like a community organizer, except that you have actual responsibilities. I might add that, in small towns, we don't quite know what to make of a candidate who lavishes praise on working people when they're listening and then talks about how bitterly they cling to their religion and guns when those people aren't listening. No, we tend to prefer candidates who don't talk about us one way in Scranton and another way in San Francisco. . . . I had the privilege of living most of my life in a small town. I was just your average hockey mom and signed up for the PTA. I love those hockey moms. You know, they say the difference between a hockey mom and a pit bull? Lipstick." *Sarah Palin, address accepting the vice-presidential nomination at the Republican National Convention in St. Paul, Minnesota, September 3, 2008*

- "Fight with me. Fight with me. Fight for what's right for our country. Fight for the ideals and character of a free people. . . . We're Americans, and we never give up. We never quit. We never hide from history. We make history." *John McCain, address accepting the presidential nomination at the Republican National Convention in St. Paul, Minnesota, September 4, 2008*

- "Raising taxes on small businesses will kill jobs. Joe the plumber said, 'Look, I've been working all my life, I want to buy the business I'm in, but you're going to raise my taxes.' You know what Senator Obama said? He wants to spread the wealth around." *John McCain, third presidential debate, October 16, 2008*

- "It isn't easy for me to disappoint Senator McCain in the way that I have this morning, and I regret that. I think we need a transformational figure. I think we need a president who is a generational change and that's why I'm supporting Barack Obama, not out of any lack of respect or admiration for Senator John McCain. I found that (John McCain) was a little unsure as to how to deal with the economic problems that we were having. Almost every day there was a different approach to the problem and that concerned me, sensing that he doesn't have a complete grasp of the economic problems that we had." *Colin Powell endorsing Barack Obama on NBC's* Meet the Press, *October 19, 2008*

Lasting Legacy of Campaign

- First African-American nominee and winner
- First Roman Catholic elected vice president
- First female nominated on the Republican Party ticket
- First female major party runner-up for the presidential nomination
- Largest economic cataclysm ever to occur during a general election
- Largest grassroots and netroots campaign ever
- First major party nominee to reject public financing and limits since the system began in 1976
- An unprecedented $5.3 billion spent by all candidates in all presidential and congressional races in 2008 combined, with $1.8 billion spent on the presidential campaign

Election of 2008

The legendary reporter Theodore White described presidential campaigns as moments when Americans weigh the past and assess the present to shape the future. During the 2008 campaign, Americans keenly felt the burdens of their racist and sexist past along with the blessings of their democratic heritage, were shocked by the challenges facing them in the present, and were troubled about the future. This was a record-breaking campaign of firsts—with the first African-American nominee and winner, the first female major party runner-up, the largest economic cataclysm ever to occur during a general election, the largest grassroots and netroots campaign ever, an unprecedented $4.3 billion spent by all candidates combined, and the first time since 1920 that neither a president nor a vice president considered running for the presidency. The campaign ended with Americans reaffirming their faith in their country and themselves by choosing an unlikely savior, a 47-year-old first-term senator used to describing himself as "a skinny guy with a funny name," who had only been in the Senate for two years when he launched his presidential campaign.

George W. Bush's perfect storm of overlapping disasters made Barack Obama president. When President Bush won reelection in 2004, he announced that having amassed political capital, he was ready to use it. Bush looked formidable. He was the first president with a popular vote majority since his father George H. W. Bush won in 1988, the first Republican president reelected since Ronald Reagan in 1984, and the first Republican president elected with control of both houses of Congress since Dwight Eisenhower in 1952. Republicans and pundits predicted a new Republican realignment building on the 1980s' conservative Reagan Revolution.

And yet, Bush's presidency rested on a spongy foundation. Bush only won by 3 million popular votes out of 120 million cast. The electoral vote margin was a narrow 35 votes. Had Democratic Senator John Kerry won

(continues on page 1624)

President Bush's approval ratings dropped dramatically after Hurricane Katrina hit New Orleans in 2005 and Washington failed to effectively respond to its victims. Here a U.S. Coast Guard officer looks for survivors. *(Petty Officer 2nd Class NyloxLyno Cangemi/U.S. Coast Guard)*

☆ ☆ ☆

2008 ELECTION CHRONOLOGY

2007

January 20, 2007: The clear Democratic front-runner, New York senator Hillary Clinton, announces the formation of a presidential exploratory committee.

February 5, 2007: The Republican front-runner in the polls, former New York City mayor Rudolph Giuliani, files a "statement of candidacy."

February 10, 2007: Senator Barack Obama, Democrat of Illinois, announces his candidacy for the Democratic nomination in Springfield, Illinois.

April 25, 2007: Senator John McCain, Republican of Arizona, kicks off his campaign to little acclaim in Portsmouth, New Hampshire.

April 26, 2007: Eight candidates for the Democratic nomination hold their first debate in Orangeburg, South Carolina. They largely avoid criticizing each other in favor of attacking President George W. Bush.

October 30, 2007: During another Democratic debate in Philadelphia, after explaining why New York governor Eliot Spitzer might grant illegal immigrants driver's licenses, Clinton backtracks when attacked. This kind of Clintonesque inconstancy undermines people's faith in her.

November 10, 2007: Obama gives a rousing Jefferson-Jackson Day dinner speech in Iowa.

December 6, 2007: Speaking at Texas A&M University, former Massachusetts governor Mitt Romney confronts the anti-Mormon bigotry he is experiencing.

2008

January 3, 2008: Barack Obama wins the Democratic Iowa caucuses with 37.6 percent of delegate support, while former North Carolina senator John Edwards and Senator Hillary Rodham Clinton virtually tie for second with 29.8 and 29.5 percent, respectively. Former Arkansas governor Mike Huckabee wins the Republican contest with 34.4 percent support, beating the better-funded Mitt Romney, who comes in second with 25.4 percent. Former Tennessee senator Fred Thompson garners 13.4 percent, while McCain comes in fourth with 13.2.

January 5, 2008: In a debate between New Mexico governor Bill Richardson, Edwards, Clinton, and Obama, Clinton is asked why some voters do not consider her likable. Obama interjects, condescendingly: "You're likable enough, Hillary."

January 7, 2008: In a Portsmouth coffee shop with 16 undecided voters covered by about 100 journalists, a woman asks Clinton: "How did you get out the door every day?" Clinton is moved—possibly to tears—as she says: "I mean, this is very personal for me. Not just political. I see what's happening. We have to reverse it."

January 8, 2008: Clinton surprises both pollsters and Obama supporters by winning the New Hampshire Democratic primary, capturing 39 percent of the vote to Obama's 36 percent. The results disappoint John Edwards, who captures just 17 percent. Among Republicans, McCain wins 37 percent, Romney takes 32 percent, Huckabee wins 11 percent.

January 15, 2008: Michigan holds its primary, defying the rules of both parties limiting the number of early primaries and caucuses.

January 26, 2008: After Obama wins the hard-fought South Carolina primary, former president Bill Clinton angers African Americans by comparing Obama's victory to those of Jesse Jackson in 1984 and 1988.

January 28, 2008: Caroline Kennedy and her uncle, Senator Edward Kennedy, endorse Obama.

January 29, 2008: Giuliani comes in a distant third in the Florida primary, despite building his entire strategy on the state.

January 30, 2008: Edwards and Giuliani both drop their presidential bids.

February 5, 2008: In one of the most inconclusive Super Tuesdays for Democrats, Clinton and Obama each pick up enough states to keep their campaigns going strong. Clinton wins California, New York, Massachusetts, and New Jersey. Obama wins Illinois, Georgia, Connecticut, Colorado, and Missouri, along with several smaller states. In the Republican contests, McCain solidifies his status as the front-runner by winning the

most states, including California, New York, and Illinois. Romney takes seven states.

February 7, 2008: Romney drops out of the Republican race.

February 18, 2008: Michelle Obama stirs controversy by saying, "For the first time in my adult lifetime, I'm really proud of my country, and not just because Barack has done well, but because I think people are hungry for change."

February 19, 2008: Obama wins his eighth and ninth straight victories since Super Tuesday by taking Hawaii and Wisconsin, giving him a narrow lead in delegates over Clinton.

February 28, 2008: The Clinton campaign releases its very effective "3:00 a.m." television commercial, saying Hillary Clinton is the one to trust when international crises break out in the middle of the night.

March 4, 2008: As McCain captures the 1,191 delegates necessary to clinch the Republican nomination on "Junior Tuesday," with victories in Ohio, Rhode Island, Texas, and Vermont, Mike Huckabee bows out of the race. Among Democrats, Clinton's victory in Ohio keeps her campaign alive, although Obama is leading in delegates.

March 13, 2008: ABC uncovers videotapes of Obama's pastor and spiritual mentor, the Reverend Jeremiah Wright, denouncing America harshly.

March 18, 2008: In Philadelphia, Obama delves into the difficult question of race in America, defusing the Wright controversy.

April 6, 2008: At a private fund-raiser in San Francisco, Obama speculates that bitterness over economic troubles makes rural voters in Pennsylvania and elsewhere "cling to guns or religion or antipathy to people who aren't like them."

April 22, 2008: Clinton wins Pennsylvania decisively, keeping her candidacy alive.

June 3, 2008: While in St. Paul, Minnesota, assessing the final primary results in Montana and South Dakota as well as a rush of support from superdelegates, Obama claims the Democratic nomination.

June 19, 2008: For the first time since 1976, a nominee rejects public financing, when Obama turns down $84 million in public funding and the attendant limits for the general campaign.

July 14, 2008: The *New Yorker* publishes its July 21 issue with a satirical cartoon cover depicting Obama and his wife, Michelle, as terrorists, complete with an American flag burning in the fireplace and a portrait of Osama bin Laden on the wall.

July 24, 2008: Obama speaks to nearly a quarter-million people in Berlin, Germany, the highlight of his eight-country tour of the Middle East and Europe.

July 30, 2008: The McCain campaign releases a commercial mocking Obama as the "biggest celebrity in the world. But is he ready to lead?"

August 22, 2008: Obama selects Delaware senator Joe Biden as his running mate.

August 25–28, 2008: At the Democratic National Convention in Denver, Colorado, Democrats nominate Barack Obama for president and Joe Biden for vice president.

August 28, 2008: Obama accepts the nomination at Invesco Field before 80,000 people, on the 45th anniversary of Martin Luther King's "I Have a Dream" speech.

August 29, 2008: At a rally in Dayton, Ohio, McCain announces he has picked Alaska's young governor, Sarah Palin, as his running mate.

September 1–4, 2008: The Republican National Convention in St. Paul, Minnesota, nominates John McCain for president and Sarah Palin for vice president.

September 3, 2008: Sarah Palin's acceptance speech triggers great excitement, inspiring McCain to deliver a more effective address the next night.

September 15, 2008: Lehman Brothers goes bankrupt and the Dow Jones Industrial Average plummets 4.4 percent, by 504 points, as the stock market drops sharply.

September 24, 2008: McCain says he is temporarily suspending his campaign to deal with the financial crisis, putting the first presidential debate in doubt.

(continues)

★ ★ ★

2008 ELECTION CHRONOLOGY (continued)

September 25, 2008: McCain, Obama, and other congressional leaders meet with President Bush at the White House.

September 26, 2008: McCain eventually agrees to participate in the first debate, held at the University of Mississippi. Neither candidate makes any real gaffes in the relatively mild debate.

September 29, 2008: House Republicans block passage of a $700 billion economic rescue package, sending the markets even lower.

October 2, 2008: In the most anticipated vice-presidential debate in recent memory, Sarah Palin and Joe Biden duel more or less to a draw.

October 7, 2008: In their second debate, with a town hall format at Belmont University in Nashville, the presidential candidates address the rapidly plummeting economy.

October 15, 2008: In the final presidential debate, McCain keeps invoking "Joe the Plumber," and Obama keeps cool in the face of repeated McCain attacks.

October 19, 2008: Former secretary of state Colin Powell endorses Obama and denounces the anti-Muslim smears circulating on the Internet.

November 4, 2008: Barack Obama is elected the 44th president by a much wider margin than that of the previous two presidential elections.

December 15, 2008: The electors meet in their respective states and choose Barack Obama as president.

2009
January 8, 2009: Congress meets in a joint session to count the electoral votes.

(continued from page 1621)
60,000 more votes in Ohio and captured that state's 20 electoral votes, he would have become president. Republicans' margins in Congress were also narrow, with 231 Republicans to 200 Democrats and one Independent in the House, and 55 Republicans to 44 Democrats with one Independent in the Senate. With this shaky base, Bush presided over a bloody, unpopular, chaotic war in Iraq, a teetering economy, and a divided country with millions who despised him.

Bush's postelection euphoria faded quickly. By July 2007, the president's disapproval rating hit 65 percent, a level of hostility only endured by Harry Truman in 1952 during the Korean War and Richard Nixon in 1974 shortly before he resigned. Perhaps even more worrisome for Republicans, 52 percent of Americans surveyed "strongly" disapproved, with 28 percent calling themselves "angry." In May 2008, a record 71 percent disapproved of Bush, with 68 percent disapproving of the Iraq war. The more unpopular the Iraq war became, the less popular Bush was.

The New Orleans disaster undermined Americans' confidence in Bush's big gamble, the Iraq war. CNN journalist Anderson Cooper remarked that after Katrina "everything changed." After August 2005, Bush never again enjoyed a majority of Americans polled approving his presidency.

Bush's Katrina fumbles replicated his mistakes in Iraq. He seemed unprepared for the scale of resistance there, destructively loyal to Secretary of Defense Donald Rumsfeld, numb to soldiers' suffering, resistant to the bad news, and too rigid in responding to the crisis. Bush failed to convince Americans why the nation should bother remaining in Iraq. The never-found weapons of mass destruction—essential to Bush's justification for going to war—undermined his credibility, while his assertion that a free Iraq would democratize the Middle East seemed far-fetched.

The images of flood-ravaged New Orleans and Iraqi suicide bomber carnage defined Bush's failed presidency. The president's rigidity and seeming imperviousness to criticism made matters worse. His take-no-prisoners stance on social and cultural issues enraged Democrats. The nation's mood soured. Bush's push to privatize Social Security failed. In an unhappy portent of the economic cataclysm that would shake up the 2008 presidential campaign, oil prices skyrocketed.

Eulogies about the end of conservatism and the Republican Party replaced the post-2004 speculation about a renewed Reagan Revolution. In the 2006 midterm elections, Democrats gained 6 Senate seats and 30 seats in the House of Representatives. For the first time since the 1994 "Republican Revolution," Democrats controlled both houses of Congress. Nancy Pelosi, the first female Speaker of the House, was a San Francisco liberal who epitomized the ascendant, assertive, angry, Bushophobic Democratic Party.

Democrats began the 2008 campaign confident as worried Republican candidates invoked the late Ronald Reagan's name frequently while ignoring George W. Bush. None of the five major contenders came from the Bush administration: former New York City mayor Rudolph Giuliani, former Massachusetts governor Mitt Romney, Arizona senator John McCain, former Tennessee senator Fred Thompson, and former Arkansas governor Mike Huckabee. Giuliani's positions on abortion and gay rights were to the party's left, but he hoped his leadership following the terrorist attacks of September 11, 2001, and his reputation as tough on terror would attract voters. Romney's Mormonism made him suspect in the eyes of many evangelical Christians. As governor of Massachusetts, Romney had taken centrist stands, supporting statewide health care, raising taxes, and soft-pedaling his abortion stand. Senator John McCain of Arizona built a national reputation as a maverick and still resented Bush's bullying tactics in the 2000 presidential primaries. Former Tennessee senator Fred Thompson's avuncular manner and fame from television's *Law and Order* made him most suitable to audition as Ronald Reagan's heir, but his reticence to address issues unnerved Republicans. Former Arkansas governor Michael Huckabee's sharp wit during debates contrasted with the president's reputation for being tongue-tied. Several other Republicans jumped into the race, including Texas representative Ron Paul, California representative Duncan Hunter, former ambassador Alan Keyes, Kansas senator Sam Brownback, former Virginia governor Jim Gilmore, former Colorado representative Tom Tancredo, and former Wisconsin governor Tommy Thompson.

Rudy Giuliani dominated the "invisible primary," the lengthy buildup to the campaign when candidates line up supporters and raise money. "America's Mayor" ran on his self-promoting legend as the man who saved New York, fought crime, made it clean, and helped it heal after terrorists hit. Giuliani raised millions, received more news coverage than any other Republican, and watched his leading rival, John McCain, stumble, unable to recapture the magic of his 2000 run. For much of 2007 Giuliani outpolled his fellow Republicans, but gradually, over 16 "debates" beginning with a forum at the Ronald Reagan Presidential Library on May 3, 2007, he began to lose traction. Romney's financial sophistication impressed many. Huckabee's debate zingers drew attention, such as accusing Congress of spending money "like John Edwards at a beauty shop," mocking the populist Democratic candidate whose campaign spent $800 for two haircuts. And, eventually, McCain found his footing. Meanwhile, Giuliani's extramarital affair with the woman who became

his third wife, pro-choice position, shady business associates, and preoccupation with terrorism when Americans were less fearful than in 2001 derailed his candidacy. Watching Giuliani in action, Democratic senator Joe Biden teased: "There's only three things he mentions in a sentence—a noun, a verb, and 9/11."

In the debates, the Republican candidates wanted to appeal to party pride without being burdened by Bush. Americans vacillated between prizing politicians' independence or their party loyalty. Before the Civil War, a "doughface" twisted his words on the slavery issue depending on whether he faced north or south. In 1896, the New York Democratic Party boss David Hill reluctantly supported his party's nominee, William Jennings Bryan, saying, "I am a Democrat still, very still."

Leading up to 2008, the Democrats were not still at all. The Democratic base was energized, furious, and frustrated after two terms of Bush. While boasting they could find a suitable candidate, Democrats feared their party would blow it somehow.

Democrats' anxiety centered on the leading candidate, New York senator Hillary Rodham Clinton. The woman nicknamed "Sister Frigidaire" in high school initially proved inept at the arts of mass seduction that her husband Bill Clinton mastered. As Arkansas's First Lady from 1979 to 1981 and 1983 to 1992, and then as America's polarizing First Lady from 1993 to 2001, she wowed people with her smarts but alienated many with her edge, while her husband Bill Clinton won over people with his charms. Many people still hated her a decade and a half later, even loyal Democrats.

To her credit, Hillary Clinton learned—and matured. Turning 60 in August 2006, she was softer than she had been as an anxious 45-year-old. Fifteen years in the national political maelstrom and amid the celebrity culture's glare taught her how to project that ease publicly. Happy to be running her own political career rather than serving her husband's since she ran for the Senate in 2000, Hillary Clinton was more self-assured, resolved, and charming as New York's senator than she was as First Lady. She laughed more frequently and freely—but still occasionally emitted the forced cackle the comedian Jon Stewart ridiculed. An effective senator who worked with both parties and deferred to Senate veterans, Clinton was surprisingly centrist and hawkish, most notably in initially supporting the Iraq War.

As Edmund Muskie tried (and failed) to do in 1972, as Walter Mondale succeeded in doing in 1984, Hillary Clinton built her campaign assuming her nomination was inevitable. Clinton dominated the "invisible primary" of 2006–2007. After the first of what would be 19 Democratic debates on April 26, 2007, at South Carolina State University, MSNBC's Chris Matthews said of Clinton: "I thought

Republican presidential hopefuls, from left, former Tennessee senator Fred Thompson, former Massachusetts governor Mitt Romney, Arizona senator John McCain, former Arkansas governor Mike Huckabee, former New York City mayor Rudolph Giuliani, and Texas representative Ron Paul pose prior to a Republican debate in Myrtle Beach, South Carolina. *(Mary Ann Chastain/Associated Press)*

she handled herself well as the front runner and kept her status." Matthews's compliment was hard-earned, considering the impressive rivals Clinton faced: Senator Christopher J. Dodd of Connecticut, former senator John Edwards of North Carolina, Governor Bill Richardson of New Mexico, Senator Joseph R. Biden Jr. of Delaware, Representative Dennis J. Kucinich of Ohio, former senator Mike Gravel of Alaska, and Senator Barack Obama of Illinois.

Still, that first debate's first question, about Iraq, which went to Clinton, highlighted one of her vulnerabilities. Clinton's 2002 vote to authorize the use of force in Iraq haunted her campaign. Even as the troop "surge" that President Bush announced in 2007 succeeded, even as the economy replaced Iraq as Americans' top worry, Clinton's pro-war vote made her appear too conventional, too Washington, for millions of restive Democrats. Iowa's antiwar Democrats were particularly unforgiving.

Clinton was also too cautious, too nuanced, too responsible when campaigning. In a defining stum-

ble during the October 30 debate in Philadelphia, she explained why New York governor Eliot Spitzer might grant illegal immigrants driver's licenses. When Senator Dodd objected, Clinton backtracked, saying, "I just want to add, I did not say that it should be done, but I certainly recognize why Governor Spitzer is trying to do it." The candidates—and reporters—pounced. Remembering "Ted Kennedy's inability to explain to Roger Mudd why he was running for president in 1980," the Clintons' former political consultant—and now frequent critic—Dick Morris crowed: "It was one of those few moments when the real candidate is on display and visible to all."

Clinton and her overpaid, disorganized, and disputatious strategists dithered, unsure whether to emphasize her experience or her personality. Eventually, Clinton realized she needed to prove her "likability" to voters, not just her electability or governing ability. But she was better at appearing formidable than likable, especially when her husband was around. At Coretta Scott King's funeral on February 7, 2006, as the campaign began, Bill Clinton wowed the crowd while Hillary stood by looking like a forbidding if flummoxed schoolmarm. Hillary Clinton was handcuffed by sexist stereotypes making it hard for public women to appear charming yet serious. Nancy Reagan was similarly perceived as a brittle "ice queen" married to an affable glad-hander.

The two politicians who emerged as Clinton's main rivals for the nomination in 2007 were maestros of mass magnetism. John Edwards, a former one-term senator from North Carolina and John Kerry's 2004 running mate, balanced his chipper personality and boyish good looks with a tough antiwar stance and pro–little guy populism. Illinois senator Barack Obama was a natural charmer, appearing to be every Democrat's cute, compelling, always successful younger brother, while Hillary Clinton seemed to be the stiff older sister.

Obama's meteoric rise illustrated African-Americans' remarkable progress in America since his birth in 1961 to a black father from Kenya and a white mother from Kansas. Although raised mostly in Hawaii, Obama lived in Indonesia from the ages of six to ten. After graduating from Columbia University in 1983, he became a community organizer in Chicago, and after graduating from Harvard Law School in 1991, he became a civil rights lawyer and law school lecturer. At Harvard, he became the first African-American elected president of the *Harvard Law Review*. This breakthrough led to a book contract for what became his best-selling memoir, published in 1995: *Dreams from My Father: A Story of Race and Inheritance*. In 1996 he won a seat in the Illinois State Senate, and in 2004 he became the Democratic candidate for the U.S. Senate from Illinois.

John Kerry made a surprise selection of Obama to deliver the Democratic National Convention keynote speech in 2004. Obama's spellbinding address articulating a new, multicultural, centrist nationalism made him an overnight sensation. He repudiated the red-state–blue-state analysis—and polarizing demagoguery—of the Clinton-Bush era, insisting: "There's not a liberal America and a conservative America; there's the United States of America." The hall rocked with applause. "There's not a black America and white America and Latino America and Asian America; there's the United States of America. . . ." The applause intensified. "We worship an awesome God in the blue states, and we don't like federal agents poking around our libraries in the red states. We coach Little League in the blue states and, yes, we've got some gay friends in the red states."

At that moment, a star was born. Obama easily won election in Illinois in November—becoming the Senate's only black member. He entered the Senate as a national celebrity and a presidential contender, especially after the release in 2006 of his second best-seller, *The Audacity of Hope: Thoughts on Reclaiming the American Dream*.

Silky smooth, over six feet tall, slim and fit thanks to regular basketball workouts, Obama had that magical ingredient called charisma. He rocketed to the top with celebrity power, boosted by talk show giant Oprah Winfrey's embrace. A cool character, he stirred great passions. As a Harvard-educated lawyer who matured after the 1960s' turmoil, he lacked the edge of Jesse Jackson and the older generation of African-American politicians. Obama ran as a constructive centrist promising to end the Clinton–Bush baby-boom generational squabbling. Senator Joe Biden (who later became Obama's choice for vice president) called Obama "the first mainstream African-American who is articulate and bright and clean and a nice-looking guy." Biden's inarticulate gaffe—for which he immediately apologized—was a rare early stumble into the race issue. Actually, Americans seemed more worried that Obama was too green—inexperienced—than too black.

Like the three leading candidates, the Democratic also-rans were fiercely anti-Bush partisans. Senator Dodd, Senator Biden, Governor Richardson, Representative Kucinich, and former Alaska senator Gravel all had more governing experience than Clinton, Edwards, or Obama. Richardson ran clever, plaintive advertisements, mostly spread via the Internet, lamenting his irrelevance. In one, an actor playing the role of a bored job interviewer ran through Richardson's impressive congressional, diplomatic, and gubernatorial resume and then asked, while chomping on a sandwich: "So what makes you think you can be president?" Every candidate secured equal time at the microphone in the various debates and forums, but these veterans fizzled as candidates.

The campaign quickly became a three-person race. In the first three months of 2007, Clinton and Obama each raised more than $20 million, and Edwards raised more than $12 million. In the summer of 2007, Clinton even outpolled Obama among blacks. By the end of 2007, Clinton had amassed the most superdelegates, the 795 Democratic Party leaders and office-holders with automatic delegate status to serve as ballast in decision-making at the Democratic convention. She also led nationally with 42 percent of likely voters. Obama enjoyed the support of 23 percent of likely voters. Edwards had 16 percent. The others barely registered.

As the candidates prospected for votes and—even more important during the "invisible primary"—money, turf warfare among various states erupted in both parties. The Iowa caucuses and the New Hampshire primary had emerged accidentally as the first in the nation, with the Iowa caucuses slated for January 3, 2008, and New Hampshire's primary on January 8. For more than three decades, the voters in these two particular states enjoyed a dispro-

Presidential candidate Barack Obama campaigning at a rally in Delaware *(mistydawnphoto/Shutterstock)*

portional impact on choosing the nominee. Benefiting financially as well as politically, the states' leaders shrieked any time another state threatened their prime position.

These arbitrary scheduling quirks rendered far larger and more diverse states like Michigan, Florida, and California irrelevant in the nominating process. Kowtowing to Iowa and New Hampshire, the Democratic National Committee's Rules and Bylaws Committee decreed that the season for primaries and caucuses would run from the first Tuesday in February until the second Tuesday in June, except that the Iowa precinct caucuses could be 22 days before that first Tuesday in February, Nevada first-tier caucuses could be 17 days before, the New Hampshire primary could be 14 days before, and the South Carolina primary could be 7 days before. When the Michigan and Florida legislatures nevertheless scheduled their primaries on January 15 and January 29, respectively, the Democratic National Committee initially stripped Michigan of its 128 delegates and 28 superdelegates. Both parties also penalized Florida.

The Iowa caucuses on January 3 upended both races. "OBAMA AND HUCKABEE TRIUMPH," the headlines blared. Obama received 37.6 percent of the vote, Edwards received 29.7 percent, and Clinton received 29.5 percent. On the Republican side, Huckabee had 34.4 percent, Romney 25.2 percent, Thompson 13.4 percent, and McCain 13.1 percent. Forgetting that the Iowa caucus is more like the snap of a starter's pistol than the roar of a rocket launcher, reporters magnified these minor Iowa victories into major national trends. Obama and Huckabee enjoyed a boost in momentum and fund-raising, especially because the 2008 race was already attracting so much attention. Both parties experienced record turnout, fueled by approximately $70 million spent overall. The 239,000 Democratic voters nearly doubled the Republican turnout—and nearly doubled the 2004 Democratic turnout. Many first-timers, especially those younger than 30, flocked to the polls and supported Obama.

The emergence of Obama and Huckabee showed how wide open both party fields were. Before his stirring debut at the 2004 Democratic convention, Barack Obama was so obscure that the "Big Three" networks did not even cover his keynote address. Even though Mike Huckabee had governed Arkansas from 1996 to 2007, he was not known nationally until autumn 2007, when his wisecracks attracted attention in the televised candidate debates.

Shrewd tactics and soaring rhetoric fueled Obama's campaign. His staff ran a ground game that outsmarted and outorganized the supposedly formidable Clinton operation as his politics of hope inspired millions. "No drama Obama" recruited aides who harmonized with one another to make their boss look good as Clinton's squabbling prima donnas backstabbed one another.

"You . . . came here because you believe in what this country can be," Obama had told supporters who, despite the chill of Springfield, Illinois, massed outside to help him launch his presidential quest on February 10, 2007. "In the face of war, you believe there can be peace. In the face of despair, you believe there can be hope. In the face of a politics that shut you out, that's told you to settle, that's divided us for too long, you believe that we can be one people, reaching for what's possible, building that more perfect union." This was vintage Obama, with calls for unity that could have been caricatured as mushy, anchored in his repudiation of the Iraq War. He peddled his centrist message with rhythms that rocked to the beat of the American gospel and rhetoric rooted in the holiest text of America's civic canon, all laced with a redemptive vision.

The youthful Obama articulated a post–baby-boomer sensibility repudiating the Clintons as well as George W. Bush. In his 2004 convention speech, and in *The Audacity of Hope,* Obama championed the "pragmatic, nonideological attitude of the majority of Americans." Obama told of a Washington insider who described the 1950s' civility as "generational." World War II produced politicians united by shared patriotic experiences that trumped partisanship. The 1960s produced politicians still nursing grudges from those times. Obama shaped his identity as the next generation's standard-bearer by rejecting "the smallness of our politics," especially the baby boomers' polarizing politics.

Speaking in Springfield, on that wintry day in February, just days before the Great Emancipator's birthday, Obama blurred his identity with Lincoln's. The "life of a tall, gangly, self-made Springfield lawyer tells us ... that there is power in words," Obama preached. "He tells us that there is power in conviction. . . . He tells us that there is power in hope."

Obama applied the skills he honed as a community organizer in Chicago to presidential campaigning. Knowing Hillary Clinton could beat him in a top-down contest, Obama organized from the bottom up. "When we started this race, Barack told us that he wanted the campaign to be a vehicle for involving people and giving them a stake in the kind of organizing he believed in," Obama's political consultant, David Axelrod, told *Rolling Stone* in March 2008. "He is still the same guy who came to Chicago as a community organizer twenty-three years ago. The idea that we can organize together and improve our country—I mean, he really *believes* that."

Obama's team deployed 159 field organizers throughout Iowa, who in turn mobilized 10,000 volunteers. As journalist Richard Wolffe would report, on one day in mid-June 2007, the Obama organization made 8,279

phone calls. By December, the campaign was calling nearly 25,000 voters daily—and hoping to reach 363,000 voters door to door, nearly three times the total number of Democrats who had caucused in 2004. The field staff trained the volunteers in the strange art of caucusing. Prodded by David Plouffe, Obama's campaign manager, the campaign enlisted Independents and first-time voters. Iowa became the pilot project for a grassroots campaign that revolutionized American politics.

Still, Obama faced a steep learning curve on the campaign trail. When the campaign started, Plouffe later recalled: "We didn't have bank accounts, we didn't have credit card accounts, we didn't have any staff, we didn't have a list of people who were going to do our first serious fundraisers." Obama was unprepared for the relentless pace, the scrutiny, the intensity. He also preferred speeches, which were rarely televised, to the debates. "There's no doubt that the sixty-second format debates, or even ninety seconds, are tough for me. I tend to be a storyteller," Obama confessed to Dan Balz and Haynes Johnson of the *Washington Post*.

Obama believed he was the man for the moment. His exposure to the other candidates, especially Hillary Clinton, confirmed his impression. His early opposition in 2002 to the war in Iraq certified his independence from Washington group think.

Still, as someone who believed in the "power" of *his* words, Obama only really became energized in Iowa after his Jefferson-Jackson Day dinner speech in November 2007. Targeting Clinton without mentioning her, Obama rejected "triangulating and poll-driven positions." He said Democrats always did best "when we led, not by polls, but

The Democratic primary quickly became a three-person race between Barack Obama, Hillary Rodham Clinton, and John Edwards. *(U.S. Federal Government)*

Former Massachusetts governor Mitt Romney speaks to supporters at a rally at the state fairgrounds in Des Moines, Iowa. *(Jonathan Schilling/IowaPolitics.com)*

by principle; not by calculation, but by conviction; when we summoned the entire nation to a common purpose—a higher purpose." Hillary Clinton never spoke that crisply.

Mike Huckabee's rise reflected another modern American political story, the rise of the religious right. Huckabee played to Iowa's evangelicals, calling himself a "Proven Christian Leader" in some ads—until criticism forced him to change the line to "a Proven Leader." Huckabee's appeal implicitly contrasted himself as a true Christian, and thus a true American, with his runner-up in Iowa, Mitt Romney, a Mormon, whose candidacy stirred some bigoted anti-Mormonism. Huckabee's crass appeal, acting as if he was running for America's pastor in chief, violated the delicate unspoken rules in the gray area where religion and politics overlap.

For his part, Romney eloquently rejected "religious tests" for presidents. Speaking on December 6, 2007, at Texas A&M University, Romney said: "I am an American running for president. I do not define my candidacy by

my religion. A person should not be elected because of his faith nor should he be rejected because of his faith." In confronting the anti-Mormon prejudice, Romney recalled John Kennedy's historic plea for religious tolerance in 1960 amid anti-Catholic prejudice. "In this election, the only candidate with three wives is Rudy Giuliani, not Mormon Mitt," Thomas M. DeFrank of the New York *Daily News* snapped, mocking Giuliani's personal entanglements. America had progressed. That Giuliani, Biden, Dodd, and Richardson were Catholic barely merited notice.

Meanwhile, following Iowa, the Clinton juggernaut sputtered. What had once seemed inevitable now seemed improbable. Reporters began eulogizing Clinton's campaign. For a perfectionist like Hillary Clinton, the quick dismissal was torturous. She had worked so hard for so long, so many strategists and pundits had reinforced her presumption that the nomination was hers, she could not comprehend what was happening.

Five days separated Iowa and New Hampshire. Ironically, Clinton's distress helped her in the Granite State. Shortly before the primary, in a typically absurd event in a Portsmouth coffee shop with 16 undecided voters covered by about 100 journalists, a woman asked, "How did you get out the door every day? I mean, as a woman, I know how hard it is to get out of the house and get ready. Who does your hair?" Clinton laughed at first, and joked. Then, she paused and her eyes welled with tears. "I just don't want to see us fall backward as a nation," Clinton began, her voice strained. "I mean, this is very personal for me. Not just political. I see what's happening. We have to reverse it. . . . Some people think elections are a game: who's up or who's down," Clinton said as her voice broke: "It's about our country. It's about our kids' future. It's about all of us together. Some of us put ourselves out there and do this against some difficult odds."

Hillary Clinton's tears reminded observers of how Edmund Muskie's support in 1972 melted away after he cried—or wiped ice and snow from his eyes (it was never clear)—as he defended his wife's honor, and Representative Patricia Schroeder's tearful announcement on September 21, 1987, that she would not run for president. Yet while Muskie was mocked and Schroeder dismissed, Clinton's stock rose. New Hampshire Democrats, especially women, enjoyed seeing the formidable Hillary Clinton's vulnerable side. "It got me," said Jane Harrington, an undecided New Hampshire voter. "I wanted to see who the real Hillary was. That was real."

Clinton also benefited from Obama's arrogance. Jazzed by Iowa, Obama treated New Hampshire as a victory lap, playing to the adoring crowds, not the crusty New England voters. In a four-person debate between Richardson, Edwards, Clinton, and Obama on January 5, Clinton was asked why some voters did not consider her likable. Obama interjected, condescendingly: "You're likable enough, Hillary." As Obama and Edwards attacked Clinton as the status quo candidate, Clinton dismissed Obama as a showboat: "Making change is not about . . . a speech you make," she said. "It is about working hard."

Voters shifted back toward Clinton in the contest's final days. Ultimately, she won 39 percent of the vote in New Hampshire, to Obama's 36 percent. John Edwards received only 17 percent. Democrats now faced a long, drawn-out duel between two larger-than-life candidates.

Senator John McCain, whom reporters had eulogized prematurely with his fourth-place finish in Iowa, won on the Republican side. With the Clinton and McCain New Hampshire "comebacks" after the Obama and Huckabee Iowa "surprises," 350,000 caucusing Iowans and a half million or so New Hampshire voters reminded the pundits that even in modern America's "mediaocracy," the power remains with the people.

Senator John McCain started his campaign paralleling Hillary Clinton's "inevitability" strategy. This grizzled former Navy pilot, the son and grandson of four-star admirals, had been a prisoner of war in Vietnam for over five years, was a two-term congressman, and had served as Arizona's senator since 1987, winning reelection three times. Most reporters loved McCain, especially in 2000, when he spoke candidly on his campaign bus, "The Straight Talk Express." In that spirit, he formally launched his campaign in New Hampshire on April 25, 2007, saying, "I'm not the youngest candidate, but I am the most experienced."

McCain's 2008 campaign, however, started off top-heavy, mismanaged, overhyped, and underfunded. He enraged conservatives, who always doubted him, by advocating a pathway to citizenship for illegal immigrants. He was identified with the Iraq War when the mission was stymied and unpopular. His campaign developed an elaborate $154 million plan to win the Republican nomination that imploded before being implemented due to lack of funds.

By summer 2007, reporters declared McCain's candidacy dead. McCain decided to return to the frank, one-on-one retail campaigning that helped him win New Hampshire in 2000. "I've had tough times in my life—this is a day at the beach compared to some others," McCain said, banking on his heroic status to help him rebound.

The shift worked. McCain won 37 percent of the vote. Romney, despite living in neighboring Massachusetts, only received 32 percent. In a state with fewer evangelicals than Iowa, Huckabee came in third with 11 percent. As supporters cheered "Mac is back" at his victory party, the 71-year-old McCain quipped: "My friends, you know I'm past the age when I can claim the noun 'kid,' no matter what adjective precedes it. But tonight, we sure showed them what a comeback looks like."

In these early, critical contests, Giuliani remained missing in action—by his own choice. Giuliani's fall from front-runner in the polls throughout most of 2007 to primary failure in 2008 was stunning. The decision to skip Iowa and New Hampshire to focus on Florida was foolhardy. But even in Florida, the more voters saw Giuliani, the less they liked him. In a campaign season when voters were tired of a testy, embattled incumbent, they had no patience for a testy, embattled candidate with personal baggage in addition.

A week after the January 8 New Hampshire primary, Romney won the primary in Michigan, where his father had been a popular governor in the 1960s, earning 39 percent of the vote. McCain had 30 percent. Romney also won the Wyoming caucuses just after Iowa, and the Nevada caucuses on January 19, even as he came in fourth in South Carolina on January 26. Going into

Super Tuesday, February 5, each of the three leading Republican contenders represented a different dimension of the Reagan coalition that had shaped American politics for more than a quarter century: Huckabee represented the evangelicals and conservatives; McCain represented the national security types and the neoconservatives; and Romney represented the corporate and technocratic elites.

Thanks to the citizens of Iowa and New Hampshire, the Democratic race became a clash of the titans. Clintonites knew how to win and knew how to lose, nimbly turning setbacks into opportunities for comebacks. Obama remained a dazzling political talent, a silver-tongued, honey-smooth, hope-generating political thoroughbred. Both Obama's Iowa victory speech and his New Hampshire concession were rhetorical gems, while Clinton's New Hampshire victory speech had a lumpy quality that suggested she had not yet learned from her husband or her rival how to sweet-talk the American people.

Obama's New Hampshire concession was particularly impressive. The young senator encouraged his supporters with a fresh burst of political poetry. Obama adapted the United Farm Workers' Spanish slogan *"Sí, se puede"*

(Yes, it can be done), treating it as a historic American slogan. Casting himself as the avatar of hope emerging from a sea of cynics, Obama articulated the "simple" can-do "creed that sums up the spirit of a people: Yes, we can." Creating his own call and response, Obama offered a triptych through American history punctuated by his newfound slogan: "It was a creed written into the founding documents that declared the destiny of a nation: Yes, we can. . . . It was whispered by slaves and abolitionists as they blazed a trail towards freedom through the darkest of nights: Yes, we can. . . . It was sung by immigrants as they struck out from distant shores and pioneers who pushed westward against an unforgiving wilderness: Yes, we can. . . . Yes, we can, to opportunity and prosperity. Yes, we can heal this nation. Yes, we can repair this world. Yes, we can."

The speech became legendary thanks to will.i.am of the group Black-Eyed Peas. The hip-hop star recruited his friend, Jesse Dylan, Bob Dylan's son, to direct a music video with about 30 of their celebrity friends, ranging from the basketball great Kareem Abdul Jabbar to the actress Scarlett Johansson. The video offered a simple musical accompaniment to Obama's "yes, we can" riff,

Presidential candidate John Edwards speaks at a Small Change for Big Change event in California. *(Jose Gil/Shutterstock)*

and spliced in different celebrities echoing Obama's words as a tape of Obama's speech played. Obama's already lyrical speech became infectious, addictive.

Reflecting the Web's centrality in this election, Obama aides played the independently produced video at rallies, promoted it on the campaign website, and spread it through Facebook and other social networking tools. As this video—which ultimately won an Emmy—went viral, a Silicon Valley entrepreneur supporting Hillary Clinton produced a cheesy, kitschy, Disneyfied ditty singing "Hillary for you and me—bring back our de-mo-cra-cy." The contrast between the two videos reflected the growing sex-appeal gap separating the two campaigns.

Even with Clinton's New Hampshire win, Obama's Iowa caucus victory changed the campaign's dynamics irreversibly. Whereas throughout the "invisible primary" Clinton was the front-runner with Obama the upstart, Clinton pursued Obama for six months, until she conceded. Obama had adoring news coverage, an exciting campaign, and a creative organization. In fact, he was *the* story of 2008, reducing everyone around him to a prop.

Bill Clinton was particularly flummoxed by Obama's rise. Clinton assumed his wife would win the Democratic nomination easily, as if it were theirs for the asking. Now, this upstart was excelling in what had been considered Bill Clinton's areas of strength. Now Obama, not Clinton, was the wunderkind, John Kennedy's heir, the natural, the one. Now, Obama, not Clinton, seemed to be the most popular man in the world—and African-Americans' favorite Democrat.

Obama's relationship with the African-American political establishment developed fitfully. Obama was younger, smoother, and seemingly less angry than Jesse Jackson and Al Sharpton. Obama literally was African-American, the son of a Kenyan father and a Kansan mother. Nevertheless, some black activists distrusted him as too white, too cool, too Harvard. Obama's story, from Hawaii to Harvard by way of Indonesia and prep schools—told so famously in his first book, *Dreams from My Father*—was not the typical African-American tale. And Obama viewed his racial identity as a choice—he decided how much of his black heritage to embrace.

Jesse Jackson particularly resented Obama's crossover appeal. In July 2008, while prepping for a Fox News TV appearance, Jackson criticized "Barack" for "talking down to black people"—with the microphone on. Further, as the Fox News anchor Brit Hume delicately put it, Jackson "threatened to cut off a certain part of Obama's anatomy."

For most, the turning point in Obama's relationship with the African-American community came in South Carolina, when Bill Clinton alienated black voters by playing crass racial politics. After Obama won the hard-fought contest on January 26, the former president ever so innocently remembered that Jesse Jackson won South Carolina in 1984 and 1988. The remarks dismissed Obama as a racial fringe candidate, even though Obama more than doubled Hillary Clinton's votes, 55 percent to 27 percent, with John Edwards third at 18 percent. In fairness, Obama won an estimated 78 percent of the black vote, while Hillary Clinton and John Edwards split 75 percent of the white vote. Nevertheless, offended African-American politicos, including the civil rights pioneer congressman John L. Lewis, abandoned Hillary Clinton.

Democrats were being doubly disingenuous. Many pro-Obama black politicians were appealing to black voters to elect the first African-American president. And anyone who doubted that Bill Clinton played politics aggressively had not paid attention during the 1990s.

The backlash against Clinton's demagoguery helped Obama secure the Kennedy imprimatur. On January 27, Caroline Kennedy published an op-ed in the *New York Times* recognizing Obama's potential to be an inspirational "President Like My Father." The next day she joined her uncle, Senator Edward Kennedy, in endorsing Obama.

Four days after coming in third in South Carolina, John Edwards withdrew from the race. Trying to stay relevant, Edwards declined to endorse either Obama or Clinton. On the Republican side, Rudy Giuliani dropped out the same day. Giuliani left with class, endorsing McCain, making McCain's nomination all but inevitable.

Super Tuesday, February 5, 2008, was the keystone to Hillary Clinton's "inevitability" strategy. She and her advisers banked on sweeping the 24 primaries and caucuses that day, conserving few resources in case she failed to clinch the nomination. With 52 percent of the Democratic delegates at stake, the results were inconclusive. Clinton won 834 delegates and 10 states to Obama's 847 delegates and 13 states. Cumulatively, Clinton garnered 8,081,748 votes, 46 percent of those cast that day, while Obama's 7,987,274 votes represented 45 percent cast. Clinton won the crucial big states of California, New York, Massachusetts and New Jersey, while Obama picked up Illinois, Georgia, Connecticut, Colorado and Missouri, among others.

On the Republican side, McCain enjoyed the kind of day Clinton expected. In addition to winning California, New York, and seven other states, McCain sewed up 602 delegates. The closest runner-up, Mitt Romney, won seven states but only 201 delegates, while Huckabee, sputtering, only won four small Southern states and West Virginia.

Despite its inconclusive result, Super Tuesday may have been the Democratic campaign's turning point. Not only did Clinton fail to win big that day, but also her expensive advisers failed to plan for the day after. With his community-organizer instincts, Obama orchestrated intense efforts in small states and caucus states, venues the arrogant Clintonites considered beneath them.

Even on Super Tuesday, Clinton's strategy backfired. Clinton won 54 percent of votes in the New Jersey primary, with 107 delegates at stake. It was not winner take all, however, yielding her just 11 more delegates than Obama. In the caucuses in the small state of Idaho, Obama overwhelmed Clinton and secured 12 more delegates than she did, negating her more dramatic New Jersey victory.

Obama began a winning streak after Super Tuesday, racking up 10 straight victories. Wins on February 19 in Hawaii and Wisconsin gave him a narrow lead in delegates over Clinton. Obama's strategy of seeking delegates wherever possible—and fighting every battle, no matter how small—trumped Clinton's strategy of going for big wins. Reporters Haynes Johnson and Dan Balz note that by February 19, "80 percent of his lead came from caucuses, though they accounted for barely a fifth of the total delegates."

Desperate—and most effective when backed in a corner—the Clinton campaign concentrated on the Ohio and Texas contests on March 4, nicknamed "Junior Tuesday," to establish a firewall against the Obama insurgency. The result was the campaign's most memorable commercial. Clinton broadcast a 30-second spot in Texas that began with the phone ringing as children slept peacefully. "It's 3 a.m. and your children are safely asleep," the narrator asked in a too-calm voice, with patriotic music purring in the background. "Who do you want answering the phone?" Six rings later, Hillary Clinton, the supposedly experienced leader, answered. Color streamed into the picture, as America slept safely and soundly, with the right person in charge.

The contest was getting personal. Defending Obama against Clinton's charge that he was inexperienced, the Clinton anti-impeachment flack and now Obama supporter Greg Craig wrote a devastating memo assessing each foreign policy hot spot where Hillary Clinton claimed she helped as First Lady and demonstrating how marginal a player she was. Some African-American supporters claimed Hillary's ad stirred traditional fears of the black man as a threat to white women and children, while former Democratic vice presidential candidate Geraldine Ferraro foolishly attributed Obama's rise to his race. Ferraro's comments echoed Gloria Steinem's complaints that white men feared a woman candidate more than they feared a black candidate. Despite Obama's desire for a post-racial campaign, racial issues often lurked.

Clinton's counterattack worked. On "Junior Tuesday," she won the primaries in Ohio 53 percent to 45 percent, Texas 51 percent to 48 percent, and Rhode Island 58 per-

cent to 40 percent (Texas had a hybrid system with precinct conventions as well, which Obama eventually won). She became the Comeback Queen by taking some aggressive moves from the Bill Clinton political playbook. She jumped on a *Saturday Night Live* skit that accused the press of coddling Obama by sarcastically suggesting that reporters should offer her rival a pillow to make him comfy during their debate. She was so pleased with *Saturday Night Live*'s portrayal that she guest-hosted March 1, three days before "Junior Tuesday." At the same time, Clinton and her surrogates roughed Obama up over his friendship with a corrupt Chicago operator, Tony Rezko, and over his NAFTA two-step, wherein one Obama adviser assured the Canadian embassy not to worry about his attacks on free trade.

Exit polls on Junior Tuesday showed that most of the voters who decided in the final two weeks chose Clinton. In Ohio, exit polls showed that voters thought she would make a better commander in chief than Obama by 57 percent to 40 percent. Such numbers suggested Americans did not mind having a woman in charge.

Hillary Clinton shrewdly kept her husband under wraps in Ohio and Texas. Senator Clinton relearned the lesson that guided her senatorial career: Bill Clinton commandeered too much attention, undermining her claim to autonomy. Senator Clinton also relearned the lessons of the White House years. Hillary Clinton was more popular as First Lady when she kept to more traditional First Lady–like roles. Americans do not want a husband-wife co-presidency.

Republicans delighted in the Democrats' predicament. After McCain captured the 1,191 delegates necessary to clinch the Republican nomination, with victories in Ohio, Rhode Island, Texas, and Vermont on March 4, Huckabee withdrew. McCain appealed to Republican voters as experienced but not tainted by an identification with Bush, vindicated by the Iraq surge, a genuine war hero, and national leader.

Meanwhile, the Democrats suffered as two strong candidates with legitimate claims clashed. Obama retained a slight yet possibly insurmountable lead in the number of delegates. But having won New York, California, Texas, Ohio, Florida, Michigan, New Jersey, and leading in Pennsylvania, Clinton claimed she would win the states with the biggest electoral votes, and the most critical swing states in November. Clinton also desperately wooed the superdelegates.

As Clinton enjoyed some much-needed momentum from Junior Tuesday, Obama endured his biggest controversy. On March 13, ABC uncovered incendiary videotapes of the Reverend Jeremiah Wright, Obama's preacher and spiritual mentor, denouncing America. "We bombed Hiroshima, we bombed Nagasaki, and we nuked far more than the thousands in New York, and we never batted an eye," Wright said in a sermon after September 11, suggesting "America's chickens" came "home to roost" that day. In a 2003 sermon, Wright mocked the phrase "God Bless America," proclaiming: "No, no, no, God *damn* America. . . ."

Had Clinton's opposition-research team uncovered these tapes before Obama won Iowa in January 2008, she probably would have won the nomination. But by March, Obama had cemented the loyalty of millions of Democrats. Still, the Wright controversy undermined Obama's message of patriotic centrism, especially because just weeks before, Obama's wife, Michelle, had said, "For the first time in my adult lifetime, I'm really proud of my country, and not just because Barack has done well, but because I think people are hungry for change." This line was used to caricature Mrs. Obama as a so-called angry black woman. Implying she had never been proud of her country offended many. Her remarks, together with the Reverend Wright's vitriol, fed fears that Obama was a radical masquerading as a moderate.

After initially hesitating, Obama confronted the challenge. On March 18, he delivered a speech at the Constitution Center in Philadelphia. Obama denounced Wright's words while placing them in the context of America's tortured racial past. Obama rejected Wright's "profoundly distorted view of this country." He warned of the tendency to elevate "what is wrong with America above all that we know is right with America." Obama rooted these statements in African-Americans' historic anguish and affirmed his loyalty to his pastor and his community. By explaining the anger, Obama did what modern politicians rarely do: he acknowledged complexity. By refusing to disown Reverend Wright while disavowing Wright's ideology, Obama avoided charges that he lacked steadfastness by showing his independence of mind.

Using the controversy to restate his life story, Obama described himself as a glorious hybrid, carrying America's past and future in his mixed blood: "I will never forget that in no other country on Earth is my story even possible." He acknowledged that his past "hasn't made me the most conventional candidate. But it is a story that has seared into my genetic makeup the idea that this nation is more than the sum of its parts—that out of many, we are truly one."

Saying "Not this time," Obama challenged Americans to move beyond racism, recriminations, and the campaign's petty distractions. Characteristically, he refused to dwell in the land of wrongs and regrets, pushing toward healing and hope. "This union may never be perfect, but generation after generation has shown that it can always be perfected," he proclaimed, inviting his fellow Americans to transcend the divisions and fix their country.

Obama overstepped occasionally. He unfairly compared the Reverend Jeremiah Wright's years of invective with former vice presidential candidate Geraldine Ferraro's one foolish comment attributing Obama's success to his race. And Obama was too forgiving of his own passivity and Wright's hate-mongering. But the speech succeeded. Americans sought redemption, and Obama played the redeemer brilliantly.

The controversy highlighted the Obama campaign's great mystery. Many Americans wanted to believe he was what he purported to be, that his gift for words would translate into a genius for governance. Yet the questions cropping up were not simply about his inexperience but also his inaction. He never confronted Jeremiah Wright. He sat silently as the United Church of Christ to which he belonged passed a resolution singling out Israel, among all countries, for possible divestment. Still, in a media-besotted world, words mattered—presidential rhetoric could shape an era. Americans of all parties and races liked this candidate's willingness to tackle difficult topics, build rhetorical bridges, and attempt to heal some national wounds.

As the arduous Democratic nomination battle inspired comparisons with the First World War's trench warfare, both candidates struggled to stay positive and "on message." Despite enjoying her opponent's tumultuous March, Clinton was soon struggling with her own blunder, trying to explain how she recalled and described a warm, First-Lady–like welcome in Bosnia in March 1996 as a difficult landing under a hail of gunfire. The controversies must have made both candidates pine for the days of early-20th-century campaigning, when crowds wanted to hear a William Jennings Bryan or a Theodore Roosevelt deliver his standard speech. In the 1920s, radio broadcasts required the new, the fresh, the unrehearsed. The 1928 Republican nominee, Herbert Hoover, missed those "happier speaking times" when candidates "could repeat the same speech with small variations . . . and eloquence [could be] invented by repeated tryouts."

But the candidates were not just stumbling because of, as Hillary Clinton claimed, "the millions of words" they were emitting. The Reverend Wright and Bosnia-under-fire controversies struck at the heart of the respective candidate's identities, zeroing in on vulnerabilities. The disconnect between Obama's words and his preacher's teachings emphasized how little was known about Obama, how he was more defined by his rhetoric than his record. By contrast, Clinton was, perhaps, too well defined. Her unduly heroic description of her Bosnia adventure raised questions about how serious her record was as First Lady. But, even worse, it resurrected all those worries about both Clintons' integrity.

If Otto von Bismarck's long-standing bon mot still held, that law-making is as messy as sausage-making, a carnivore's codicil suggests tough campaigns frequently make mincemeat out of candidates' reputations. As the April 22 Pennsylvania primary loomed, Democrats feared the process would diminish both front-runners. Both Clinton and Obama unintentionally highlighted fundamental paradoxes defining their respective campaigns—and political identities. Clinton continued twisting and turning her First Lady legacy every which way. She exaggerated her influence within the Clinton administration and the greatness of the Clinton record—except when she had to retreat from the record, especially regarding Bill Clinton's welfare reform, which she opposed and now many Democrats criticized.

Voters were equally vexed when Obama in a private fund-raiser on April 6 displayed an Ivy League elitism lurking behind his "Yes We Can" populism. Obama speculated that bitterness over economic troubles made rural voters in Pennsylvania and elsewhere "cling to guns or religion or antipathy to people who aren't like them." Obama—who seldom misspoke—simultaneously insulted gun owners, churchgoers, and opponents of ille-gal immigration, while suggesting that money trouble clouded the little people's good judgment. Demonstrating that the Internet could hurt as well as help, Obama's remarks were reported by Mayhill Fowler, an Obama donor and "citizen journalist," voluntarily feeding campaign-related "content" to the popular *Huffington Post* website. Ironically, the first serious African-American presidential contender was accused of being elitist.

Remarkably, Clinton won the Pennsylvania primary 55 percent to 45 percent, thanks to blue-collar males. This constituency was hostile to her as First Lady and considered to be the group most resistant to her presidential candidacy. Some attributed her success to nostalgia for her husband. Others pointed to how much Clinton had grown as a candidate. Still others feared it took a black candidate to make blue-collar white men finally accept Hillary Clinton.

Clinton's continued crass appeals to "hard-working" white voters, along with her big victories in mostly white states like West Virginia on May 13, risked making the race about race. Obama's North Carolina victory on May 6, based on the large African-American vote, reinforced the impression of growing racial polarization. Despite Amer-

Presidential candidate Hillary Clinton speaking at a campaign rally *(Solaria/Shutterstock)*

ica's tremendous racial progress, both political parties frequently made racial appeals. The elusive white, male, working-class voter, sometimes called Joe Six Pack, sometimes called the Reagan (formerly Roosevelt) Democrat, was subjected to steady if subtle racially based appeals just as in Richard Nixon's "law and order" campaign in 1968.

The Democratic commitment to identity politics also kept race and gender in play. Obama used his base in the African-American community, and the exciting prospects of becoming the first black president, just as Clinton exploited her shot to become the first woman president. Identity politics demanded a one-way street. Blacks could appeal to blacks yet perceive racism in opponents' attacks. Women were praised for reaching out to their sisters and crying "sexism" if criticized.

The 2008 campaign demonstrated how racial and gender-based appeals stressed the body politic. But in a polyglot democracy, subgroup appeals were inevitable. In 1988, Massachusetts governor Michael Dukakis tapped Greek-American pride to finance his campaign. Twelve years later, Senator Joe Lieberman tapped American Jewish pride to raise American Jewish money in trying to become the first American Jewish vice president. These actions were less controversial because the white ethnic immigrants who seemed so foreign when Al Smith ran for president in 1928 were by the late 20th century so much better integrated.

Obama flummoxed the Clintons. These baby boomers ran a surprisingly flat, outdated campaign more television-based than Internet-savvy, more rooted in yesterday's techniques and agendas than today's technologies and trends. In one nostalgic ad in Pennsylvania, Clinton reminisced about playing pinochle, of all things. Once again, Clinton voters skewed older and traditional while Obama's voters were younger and hipper.

With her Pennsylvania primary victory, Clinton again proved to be the Timex candidate. Like the occasionally unfashionable but always durable watch, she showed she "takes a licking but keeps on ticking." The race was so close that Clinton could at least make a moral claim to the nomination because of her big-state wins, her strength in the swing states, and her support in Florida and Michigan, whose votes the Democratic Party negated.

Clinton's opposition toughened Obama for the general election. The primary campaign focused Obama on the need to reach working-class whites. The public's exposure to the Reverend Wright controversy inoculated Obama against further outbreaks. Obama was lucky. By the fall, Americans were more concerned with the economy than with Obama's years of passive acceptance of Wright's repeated assaults on America.

After Obama won the final primaries on June 3 in Montana and South Dakota, he had amassed an estimated 17,822,145 votes to Clinton's 17,717,698. More significantly, he had passed the threshold of 2,117 delegates he needed, 50 percent of the party's 4,233 delegates, ultimately ending with an estimated 2,306.5 delegates to Clinton's 1,973 and Edwards's 4.5. In one of the many turnarounds of 2008, a wave of super-delegates swept toward Obama in the last weeks, delivering him the party establishment along with the nomination. Both camps emphasized the unprecedented nature of the fight, how many people voted, how intense the contest was. For Clintonites, this preserved dignity, bragging rights—and a shot at 2012 if Obama faltered. For Obamaniacs, this made the final few weeks a triumph over a superstar, rather than a stagger toward the finish.

Clinton's impressive swing-state victories and her historic vote total vindicated her decision to hang on, refusing to concede. Grumbling from Edwards's camp that he should not have quit so soon emphasized one of the probable legacies from Clinton's never-say-die campaign: in the future it would be harder to get candidates to withdraw and thus harder for parties to rally around one winner early in the process. Had Clinton quit in February or early March, she would have been remembered as the Ed Muskie of 2008, an overconfident frontrunner whose aides spent too much time quibbling over who would get which West Wing office but produced as little as Muskie did in 1972. Instead, Clinton and her husband angered many Democrats but mobilized millions.

On June 3, Obama claimed the Democratic nomination in St. Paul, Minnesota. "Our party and our country are better off because of her," Obama said in his victory speech, "and I am a better candidate for having had the honor to compete with Hillary Rodham Clinton." Four days later, in Washington, Clinton finally conceded, telling supporters: "Although we weren't able to shatter that highest, hardest glass ceiling this time, thanks to you, it's got about eighteen million cracks in it. And the light is shining through like never before, filling us all with the hope and the sure knowledge that the path will be a little easier next time."

Obama now had to unify the party, prepare for the Democratic National Convention, and rest up for the general campaign. He rejected $84 million in public financing for the general campaign, calculating that the massive sums he could raise would compensate for the damage to his reputation as a reformer. The system is broken, Obama said, justifying his move.

Obama also banked on the adoring press he enjoyed throughout his campaign. After he raised a record $150 million in September alone, on his way to $600 million overall for the general election, a *Washington Post* editorial rhapsodized: "Much of Mr. Obama's money has arrived in small donations. . . . Mr. Obama's haul reflects the enormous enthusiasm his campaign has generated." Yet, the front page of the same edition of the same newspaper said disclosure forms showed Obama bankrolled by the usual "ultra-rich Democratic donors." By contrast, the reporting four years earlier about President George W. Bush's prodigious fund-raising efforts was harsh. "Pioneers Fill War Chest, Then Capitalize," a typical headline claimed. Apparently, Obama's fund-raising was a romantic effort empowering the people; Bush's fund-raising subverted democracy.

These caricatures resonated, reinforcing other popular story lines. For months reporters celebrated Obama's "Yes, We Can" campaign as a people's crusade. And for decades reporters had been lambasting the Republicans as plutocrats. Moreover, these narratives were rooted in truth. Even if mega-donors bankrolled much of the fund-raising, Obama attracted a record number of smaller donors, on-line and off, many of them first-time givers. And claiming that the Republican Party was pro-business was no more controversial than calling Hollywood liberal.

Obama calculated correctly. One of history's most prodigious fund raisers, he raised $639,174,281 to John McCain's $360,167,823 for the general campaign. The total of $999,342,104 did not include the millions spent on the campaign by the Republican and Democratic National Committees, advocacy groups like Moveon .org, interest groups like the AARP, America's largest membership organization for people 50 and over. With this money, Obama's campaign could spend $310 million on airing 570,963 commercials. McCain spent $135 million for 274,737 airings.

Obama's haul—and his renunciation of federal financing—highlighted the campaign finance system's problems. Politicians spent too much time and made too many promises fund-raising. But it was unrealistic to banish money from the system. Money represented power in America. Limits never worked; like water seeping into a cellar, money inevitably seeped into American campaigns.

On a more sobering note, Obama knew his foreign policy and national security credentials were thin and he might end up becoming commander in chief of the world's sole superpower. Voters shared that concern. One *Washington Post*-ABC News poll found that 72 percent of those surveyed believed McCain knew enough about world affairs, but only 54 percent expressed similar faith in Obama.

Celebrating centrism while appealing to progressives, Obama walked a treacherous high-wire act, especially regarding the warrantless wiretapping immunity granted telecommunications companies in the updated Foreign Intelligence Surveillance Act (FISA). Civil liber-ties groups denounced FISA, which McCain pronounced a "vital national security matter." In late June, Obama announced he would vote for the latest version, having opposed an earlier version, because the compromise bill reaffirmed the primacy of the FISA courts.

Obama's most passionate, grassroots supporters were furious. On July 3, Obama posted an explanation on the blog of Joe Rospars, new media director of "Obama for America." Obama said, "Given the choice between voting for an improved yet imperfect bill, and losing important surveillance tools, I've chosen to support the current compromise". Acknowledging his supporters' anger, Obama said, "I cannot promise to agree with you on every issue. But I do promise to listen to your concerns, take them seriously, and seek to earn your ongoing support to change the country. That is why we have built the largest grassroots campaign in the history of presidential politics." Three key Obama policy aides then "chatted" for the next 30 minutes on the "Obama for America" website. Many supporters, even if unconvinced, applauded Obama's responsiveness.

To shore up his foreign credentials, in late July Obama visited Kuwait, Afghanistan, Iraq, Jordan, Israel, Germany, France, and the United Kingdom. While tiptoeing around the Palestinian-Israeli divide, Obama spoke personally when he visited the frequently bombed Israeli town of Sderot. "The first job of any nation-state is to protect its citizens," Obama said. "If somebody was sending rockets into my house, where my two daughters sleep at night, I'm going to do everything in my power to stop that. And I would expect Israelis to do the same thing."

The high point of this foreign tour, the most extensive mid-campaign tour a presidential nominee ever undertook, occurred on July 24, with Obama's address in Berlin, the German capital. In a characteristic overreach, Obama wanted to speak at Brandenburg Gate, the site of President Kennedy's "Ich Bin Ein Berliner" speech in 1963 and Ronald Reagan's "Mr. Gorbachev, tear down this wall" address in 1987. German leaders bristled, and the location was changed to the Victory Column. Masses—as many as 240,000—nevertheless thronged the streets of Berlin to hear Obama identify himself as a "fellow citizen of the world" and proclaim: "With an eye toward the future, with resolve in our hearts, let us remember this history, and answer our destiny, and remake the world once again."

On his trip, Obama avoided any major gaffes and basked in the fawning coverage. The three-network-news-anchor honor guard accompanying Obama guaranteed pope-level coverage. This trip proved once again that Obama's candidacy was the most exciting political story of the decade, and that the election remained all-Obama-all-the-time. This election was Obama's to win or lose.

With this trip, Obama overstepped. Americans "don't want to elect the president of Europe," former Republican representative Vin Weber snapped. McCain's people broadcast a popular advertisement that juxtaposed images of the celebrities Britney Spears and Paris Hilton as Germans shouted, "Obama, Obama," then asked tartly: "He's the biggest celebrity in the world—but is he ready to lead?"

Just over two weeks after Obama returned home, Republicans asked the question again when Russia invaded Georgia on August 8. Senator McCain denounced Russia's actions authoritatively: "In the 21st century nations don't invade other nations."

McCain spent much of the summer deriding Obama's inexperience. Republicans rejected Obama's "September 10" mentality, treating terrorism as a domestic law enforcement issue, not a military threat. "I know how to win wars," McCain said in Albuquerque, New Mexico, in mid-July. "And if I'm elected president, I will turn around the war in Afghanistan, just as we have turned around the war in Iraq, with a comprehensive strategy for victory." Sharpening his elbows, McCain said: "In a time of war, the commander in chief doesn't get a learning curve."

McCain mocked Obama for first opposing the surge in Iraq in January 2007, then acknowledging that more troops in Iraq reduced violence. "My friends, flip-floppers all over the world are enraged," McCain chuckled.

Actually, both candidates' positions were converging, not only about Afghanistan. Obama realized his rhetoric and postures soon could have serious life-and-death implications. Even on his signature issue of opposing the Iraq War, he started talking about procedures, 16-month timetables, and "residual" forces remaining.

McCain unsettled conservatives by also playing to the center. "I count myself as a conservative Republican, yet I view it to a large degree in the Theodore Roosevelt mold," McCain said in July. McCain saw a governmental role in coping with climate change and other environmental challenges as well as regulating campaign finance. "I believe less governance is the best governance, and that government should not do what the free enterprise and private enterprise and individual entrepreneurship and the states can do, but I also believe there is a role for government...," McCain said. "Government should take care of those in America who cannot take care of themselves."

Presidential candidate John McCain campaigning in New Hampshire (*Marc Nozell, Merrimack, New Hampshire*)

This convergence in the campaign was constructive. It was not just the gravitational pull to the center that often occurred after primaries. It was not just the "Oh, boy, I might be president" flight from irresponsible rhetoric. It was what the American people desired, mature leadership expressed in commonsense policies.

The pre-convention period became Obama's lost summer of missed opportunities. Rather than breaking away from McCain, Obama entered convention season looking like just another political mortal. With the modern presidential campaign a struggle over competing story lines, the Republicans shifted the plotline away from talk about 2008 being the Democrats' year, to talk about how the Democrats could appear vulnerable in what should be a Democratic year. Polls through August showed Obama maintaining a slim three- to four-point lead.

By selecting Delaware senator Joe Biden as his running mate, Obama sought to regain control of the campaign narrative with the crucial vice-presidential prop. Spurning Hillary Clinton—partially because of fears her husband would be a loose cannon—Obama chose a tough campaigner, a smart Washington insider, a bridge to working-class whites and, most important, an experienced foreign policy hand. The three others on the short list for vice president, Indiana senator Evan Bayh, Virginia governor Tim Kaine, and Kansas governor Kathleen Sebelius, were less experienced.

Biden was an embarrassment on the 2008 campaign trail, winning only 9,000 votes and finishing fifth in Iowa. Still, he chaired the Senate Foreign Relations Committee, drafted historic legislation such as the Violence Against Women Act of 1994, had held 50-plus Senate hearings, and appeared frequently on Sunday television talk shows. The tragic loss of his first wife and daughter in an automobile accident shortly before he entered the Senate in 1973, his ability to raise his two boys alone and eventually start a new family, his comeback from two brain aneurysms, and his record of 30 years in Washington without a major scandal were all admirable.

On the eve of the Democratic National Convention in Denver, as the early-21st century's Cinderella candidate, Obama found himself competing with himself, with outsized expectations of what he could do. Obama upped the ante historically, choosing to accept his nomination on August 28—the 45th anniversary of Martin Luther King's "I Have a Dream" speech. Obama also upped the ante dramatically, shifting the venue to an 80,000-seat stadium, the Denver Broncos' Invesco Field. Polls showed Obama and McCain in a statistical dead heat.

On opening night in Denver, August 25, Ted Kennedy, the crown prince of the Democratic Party, suffering from a brain tumor that would kill him a year later, anointed the young Illinois senator as Camelot's heir. Channeling his own fiery, heartbreaking "the dream will never die" consolation speech at the 1980 convention after losing the Democratic nomination to President Jimmy Carter, Kennedy proclaimed: "The work begins anew. The hope rises again. And the dream lives on."

Michelle Obama also spoke that night. She uncorked that traditional, magical, American elixir, the American Dream, to prove that she and her husband were neither elitist nor unpatriotic. Mrs. Obama offered her more conventional biography of South-Side-Chicago-girl-made-good to Americanize her husband's famously unconventional biography. Michelle Obama emphasized her humble origins, her parents' values, her up-by-the-bootstraps life story. Blurring her story with his, she proclaimed: "What struck me when I first met Barack was that even though he had this funny name, even though he'd grown up all the way across the continent in Hawaii, his family was so much like mine. . . . Like my family, they scrimped and saved so that he could have opportunities they never had themselves."

The next night, Hillary Rodham Clinton's supporters insisted on placing her name in nomination at the convention. The Obama-Clinton melodrama threatened to begin again. Both Bill and Hillary Clinton were back where they loved to be, front and center, even if this convention was supposed to be Obama's star turn. The roll call—when state delegations cast their ballots for the nominees—evoked a time when these quadrennial gatherings actually made a difference and frequently yielded surprising nominees. But the modern message underlying this traditional ritual was clear. Senator Clinton—and her ex-president husband—wanted to remind the American people that she won more than 17 million votes, including many votes from enthusiastic women devastated by her loss. Whatever Clinton lost by appearing too brazen, she gained more with this power play. Her demand to star in this convention psychodrama underscored her and her husband's relevance.

Obama could not be cowed by the Clintons. He had to be magnanimous without succumbing to the Clinton cyclone. Obama could not play the stolid William Howard Taft of 1908 to the charismatic Theodore Roosevelt. He could not allow former president Bill Clinton to undercut him as Dwight Eisenhower had undermined Richard Nixon in 1960, by asking for a week to remember any of Nixon's vice-presidential accomplishments. Obama also could not allow Hillary Clinton to give the kind of soaring consolation speech, which steals delegates' hearts, as Ronald Reagan did in 1976 or Ted Kennedy did in 1980.

Hillary Clinton's Denver speech fell flat, lacking what George H. W. Bush dismissed as "that vision thing." Clin-

Michelle Obama, wife of Democratic candidate Barack Obama, addresses the audience at the Pepsi Center in Denver, Colorado, on August 25, 2008. *(QQQQQQ Photos)*

ton ticked off various programs she advocated, particular policies she liked, and specific individuals she met while campaigning. She was more gracious—and less destructive—than Reagan was in 1976 or Kennedy was in 1980. Still, she was following the party script, not speaking from her heart, and was quite vague about Obama himself.

The speech illustrated one reason her campaign failed. No overriding idea propelled her candidacy forward, nothing deeper than "it's MY turn." Her speech reflected the diligent grade grubber, not the romantic poet. It was in keeping with her history as Bill Clinton's dutiful behind-the-scenes supporter rather than a Clintonesque riffer who could charm and inspire. In fairness, she was also commanding and moving when she linked her campaign to women's historic aspirations for equality. But even when discussing women's rights, she offered no vision of what women could do for America as women; she triggered no thoughts deeper than "It's our turn."

Bill Clinton, typically, upstaged his wife the next night. He helped rehabilitate his own reputation with his colorful, enthusiastic endorsement. "Everything I learned in my eight years as president, and in the work I have done

since in America and across the globe, has convinced me that Barack Obama is the man for the job," he declared.

Nevertheless, when Hillary Clinton suspended the state-by-state roll-call vote she had demanded, moving for the 2008 Democratic convention to nominate Senator Barack Obama by acclamation, she helped to make history. Network cameras zeroed in on African-Americans, young and old, beaming, as tears poured down their cheeks. For the first time in American history, a major political party had nominated a black man to be president.

The drama of the moment proved more memorable than Obama's actual acceptance speech at Invesco Field. Republicans mocked the Democrats for the Greek columns flanking the stage, saying the "Temple of Obama"—the "Barackopolis"—proved the candidate's grandiosity. Like William Jennings Bryan's acceptance speech in 1896, Obama's acceptance speech was adequate but not up to the high standards he set. The address was more partisan than transcendent, more a predictable call to change than a transformational vision for the 21st century. Declaring that all had gathered "because we love this country too much to let the next four years look just like the last eight," Obama bashed the Republicans' trickle-down philosophy, failing war effort, Katrina mismanagement, and society of selfishness. "In Washington, they call this the 'Ownership Society,' but what it really means is that you're on your own. Out of work? Tough luck, you're on your own. No health care? The market will fix it. You're on your own. . . ." Obama said: "Change happens because the American people demand it, because they rise up and insist on new ideas and new leadership, a new politics for a new time."

Republicans had many reasons to dread their national convention, which began three days later. They were struggling with an unpopular president, polls predicting 2008 would be a Democratic year, a presidential nominee who often seemed listless, and a restive party. To make matters worse, Hurricane Gustav forced the evacuation of New Orleans on the convention's opening day, reviving memories of George W. Bush's massive failure following

Hurricane Katrina. Surprisingly, the Republicans also pulled off a great convention.

The Republicans' best week of the general campaign began even before the convention. To minimize the usual post-convention bounce, John McCain selected his running mate the day after the Democrats dispersed. McCain preferred Senator Joseph Lieberman, a Democratic turned Independent, to run on a national security unity ticket. But evangelicals threatened to disrupt the convention because Lieberman was pro-choice. Others considered included Louisiana governor Bobby Jindall, Minnesota governor Tim Pawlenty, former secretary of homeland security Tom Ridge, and McCain's runner-up, Mitt Romney. Instead, McCain selected Alaska's 45-year-old first-term governor, the former mayor of Wasilla, Sarah Palin, to be the first woman Republicans would nominate for the vice presidency.

Not knowing Palin and disliking surprises, Washington reporters attacked her as inexperienced, untested,

Republican candidates John McCain and Sarah Palin in Albuquerque, New Mexico, on September 6, 2008. Sarah Palin's husband, Todd Palin, is behind the teleprompter, and John McCain's wife, Cindy McCain, is behind Sarah Palin. *(Matthew Reichbach)*

unfamiliar—all of which was true. But she was also a charismatic conservative who could attract evangelicals and cultural traditionalists, many of whom distrusted McCain. Despite trying to represent all-American values, Governor Palin was forced to admit that her 17-year-old daughter Bristol was five months pregnant and would soon marry the father.

The firestorm stoked interest in Palin's acceptance address on September 3, which attracted approximately 37 million viewers. Obama's speech attracted 38.4 million, and Biden's attracted 24 million. Palin's speech made it clear that McCain chose her not just to woo women, not just to shore up the Republican right, but to revive the culture wars. Palin's performance was especially impressive considering the humiliating pounding she and her family had been enduring. Pushing back, Palin claimed to be a martyr targeted by the insular Washington elite.

Palin drew a line between those who serve in the army—and those who do not, between those who live in the bicoastal bubble—and those who live in what she clearly considered the real America. Palin's speech was as sharp as Marilyn Quayle's and Pat Buchanan's 1992 Republican convention speeches but less shrill. She mocked Obama as "a man who has authored two memoirs but not a single major law or reform" and "a man who can give an entire speech about the wars America is fighting, and never use the word 'victory' except when he's talking about his own campaign." In her sharpest zinger, delivered with a smile, she said: "I guess a small-town mayor is sort of like a 'community organizer,' except that you have actual responsibilities." She elicited the biggest laugh after introducing herself as a "hockey mom," explaining that "the difference between a hockey mom and a pit bull" is "lipstick." In plunging the stiletto so deftly, Sarah Palin channeled the depressed Republicans' great hero, Ronald Reagan. Palin punctured the bubble of invincibility encasing Obama after the historic Democratic proceedings in Denver.

Sarah Palin's star turn energized the once listless Republican convention—and spurred John McCain to give one of his best performances. Before a record national viewing audience of 38.9 million on September 4, McCain had a chance to redefine his campaign and his image. Unlike his Democratic rival, McCain was far better volleying with voters than grandly addressing them. But McCain felt vindicated by Palin's success—after a week of naysaying questioning her suitability and his judgment. McCain also felt vindicated by advocating the surge in Iraq, which finally was succeeding.

While much of his acceptance speech was unexceptional, neither as soaring as Obama's nor as mischievous as Palin's, McCain ended with a rousing call to Americans to fight for what was right. Recounting his experiences as a

Illustration of candidates Barack Obama and John McCain *(Kevin Renes/Shutterstock)*

prisoner of war in Vietnam, McCain said he learned from the traumas he endured to live for his country, not just for himself. Culminating with a patriotic haiku shouted above the cheering Republican masses, McCain cried: "Fight with me. Fight with me. Fight for what's right for our country. Fight for the ideals and character of a free people." Using the kind of rhetoric that usually set foreign teeth on edge but Americans loved, McCain concluded: "We're Americans, and we never give up. We never quit. We never hide from history. We make history." McCain's speech reinforced the message that Republicans are patriots who serve, especially in the military, and Democrats are doubters who dodge. But McCain also elegantly saluted Barack Obama and the Democrats as "fellow Americans," endorsing an end to "partisan rancor."

The candidates of 2008 seemed to agree about one thing—America needed a change. Both noticed how sour the national mood was, even before the economic collapse. Barack Obama campaigned for "Change We Can Believe In," having defeated Hillary Clinton, who insisted that she was "Ready for Change." John McCain warned "the old, big-spending, do-nothing, me-first, country-second crowd: Change is coming." A promise to bring about "change" seems the most obvious campaign pledge: After all, most presidential campaigns are romantic quests promising salvation. And post-1960s Democrats spoke of comprehensive change with particular zeal.

As it had in the past, the campaign for change energized the electorate in 2008. The campaign took place on television and on the stump, in sweaty, overcrowded auditoriums rocking with the cheers of thousands and in quiet, lonely workstations, as millions experienced the campaign through the Internet.

In this campaign, the Internet was not just a source of news but one of many platforms for building and expressing support, especially for Obama. As the *Nation* would note: "More than a million people asked for campaign text messages on their cellphones. Two million joined MyBO, a website fusing social networking with volunteer work,

Impersonating Sarah Palin on NBC's *Saturday Night Live* on September 27, 2008, Tina Fey (left) stumbles in answering a question posed by Amy Poehler, who is impersonating CBS news anchor Katie Couric. Fey's impersonations were a huge hit, prompting Palin herself to appear on the show in October. *(Dana Edelson/NBC Universal, Inc.)*

while more than 5 million supported Obama's profile on social sites like Facebook. Most famously, 13 million voters signed up for regular e-mails, fundraising pitches and other communications." By November, a quarter of Obama voters interacted with the Obama network, a vital virtual community.

Following the Republican convention, as polls showed the Republicans pulling ahead, Obama seemed stymied by Palin's stinging critique. Then, the biggest financial cataclysm ever to occur so close to a presidential Election Day mushroomed. Through America's banks, America's entire financial system had gorged on arcane subprime mortgages, which emerged as "toxic assets," destroying venerable firms and rocking the economy. On September 7, three days after the Republican convention ended, the federal government took over Fannie Mae and Freddie Mac, the mortgage giants owning or guaranteeing $5 trillion of the country's $12 trillion mortgage market. On September 14, Bank of America swallowed up the Wall Street firm Merrill Lynch, whose liquidity was evaporating. On September

15, Lehman Brothers, an iconic firm founded in 1850, which was managing $275 billion in assets, went bankrupt. In response, the Dow Jones Industrial Average plummeted 4.4 percent, by 504 points. Within a week, the Dow Jones had dropped by 800 points. On September 17, the insurance leviathan American International Group (AIG) teetered, saved by an emergency federal loan of $85 billion. By Thursday, September 18, U.S. Treasury secretary Henry Paulson and the chairman of the Federal Reserve Bank, Ben Bernanke, were lobbying Congress to authorize a $700 billion bailout. Bernanke, an expert on the Great Depression of the 1930s, warned: "If we don't do this, we may not have an economy on Monday."

The financial meltdown doomed the McCain campaign. Whatever momentum McCain enjoyed after his energized convention vanished amid the fourth major disaster under George W. Bush's watch: following 9/11, Iraq, and Katrina, the financial crisis. The crash seemed to repudiate the entire Reagan Revolution. Watching the collapse on September 15, McCain offered the Hooveresque declaration, "The fundamentals of our economy are strong."

In fairness, Obama did not offer any brilliant solutions either. The financial collapse, combined with the deep hopes Obama generated, raised the stakes in what had already become a historic presidential race. Surprisingly, the Iraq War issue, which originally propelled Obama's campaign, proved less relevant in the general election. Democrats did not like to admit it, and 61 percent of Americans opposed the Iraq surge when Bush—and McCain—pushed it in January 2007, but the troop increase stabilized Iraq. The Iraq question slipped from burning issue to political common denominator, a stand Democrats shared to affirm their collective identity but that swayed few Independents.

McCain undercut his strongest argument for election by appearing unsure and erratic, while Obama emerged as the calm, cool, collected candidate. On September 24 McCain announced he would suspend his campaign and probably skip the first debate on September 26 to fly back to Washington to help solve the crisis. With the debate scheduled for a Friday night when little business would be transacted, his statement seemed absurd, as did his ultimate appearance at the debate, with the crisis unresolved.

At McCain's insistence, President Bush had invited both candidates to a White House meeting with administration officials and congressional leaders the day before, on September 25. Rather than creating a chorus of national unity, it degenerated into a cacophony of partisan posturing. Insiders reported that Obama asked some probing questions while McCain sat silently, impotently. McCain's brief suspension began a downward spiral from which his campaign never recovered.

Fifty-three million viewers watched the first debate, held at the University of Mississippi in Oxford. Neither candidate made a defining gaffe. Both appeared to be competent and idealistic men of character. Still, McCain appeared too prickly, condescendingly dismissing Obama as inexperienced or uncomprehending at least seven times, proclaiming: "I honestly don't believe that Senator Obama has the knowledge or experience" to be president. By contrast, like John Kennedy facing Richard Nixon in 1960, Obama kept his cool. Somehow the 47-year-old upstart Democratic senator appeared the more mature leader than the 71-year-old grizzled Republican senator. Polls showed that by 52 percent to 35 percent most Americans deemed Obama the winner.

The one vice-presidential debate on October 2 also attracted inordinate interest. Palin became the fall's media comet, streaking across the sky and flaming out. Voter interest soared partially because she was a fresh personality and partially because she had stumbled in recent interviews. After a bad interview on ABC, sup-

porters claimed Charles Gibson had been condescending. But CBS's Katie Couric gently lobbed softball questions, which Palin whiffed repeatedly. In one excruciating exchange Couric asked the Alaska governor what newspapers and magazines she read regularly. Palin responded like an undergraduate covering up ignorance with a civics speech: "I've read most of them, again with a great appreciation for the press, for the media." Couric, politely, followed up: "What, specifically?" Palin skated again: "Um, all of them, any of them that have been in front of me all these years." Couric asked again, sweetly: "Can you name a few?" Palin responded with another generalization, "I have a vast variety of sources where we get our news, too," then shifted by defending Alaska as part of America, not a backwater. These goofs fed the Jon Stewart effect that further boosted debate ratings—many people wanted to watch the event live so they could get the jokes about it later, in this case the inevitable Tina Fey imitation of Palin on Saturday Night Live.

As Washington's gaffe-master general, Biden also seemed to be one ill-chosen phrase away from becoming a laughingstock. When Obama introduced him, Biden called his running mate "Barack America." At a Missouri rally Biden introduced State Senator Chuck Graham, saying, "Chuck, stand up," before noticing Graham was a wheelchair-using paraplegic. Biden practiced debating with women to avoid appearing condescending.

With the bar set so low, both candidates performed admirably. Palin appealed directly to voters, with a common touch and a warm smile. She surprised many with a nuanced answer about gay marriage, welcoming diversity of lifestyles in her own family and among her fellow citizens, but still defining marriage as between a man and woman.

Biden was disciplined throughout, aggressive but not bullying. Palin was probably stronger the first half, with Biden's occasional forced, haughty smile making him look too much the senatorial peacock. While Biden did not break new ground intellectually, tagging McCain as George W. Bush redux and wrong on the war, the economy, the environment, and energy, Palin demonstrated the exhaustion of Republican ideology. Echoing Reagan, she insisted that government cannot be the solution to every problem and saluted the United States as a shining city upon the hill. But 28 years after Reagan won the presidency, Republicans needed to move beyond viewing tax cuts and defense buildups as the only recipe for policy success.

As the Republican campaign derailed, Palin became more of a liability. Reports that the Republican National Committee spent $150,000 outfitting Palin and her family undercut her "just folks" image. Leaks from the McCain camp accused her of being uncooperative and uncoachable, undermining the campaign. Rather than attracting

President-elect Barack Obama and his wife, Michelle, with Vice President–elect Joe Biden and his wife, Jill, at their election night rally at Grant Park in Chicago, November 4, 2008. *(Alex Brandon/Associated Press)*

Hillary Clinton supporters, Palin infuriated them with her affect and her policy stands. Ultimately, Palin polarized. In exit polls in November two-thirds of voters considered Biden qualified and 60 percent deemed Palin not qualified, although 74 percent of Republicans considered her qualified, indicating that partisanship shaped the perceptions.

The second debate between Obama and McCain, held on October 7 at Belmont University in Nashville, was supposed to be a slugfest. McCain was in freefall, especially after House Republicans rejected the $700 billion Wall Street bailout on September 29, causing the Dow Jones to drop by 778 points, wiping out an estimated $1.2 trillion. The Town Hall format emphasized give and take between candidate and voter. Six million people submitted questions for the two candidates over the Internet, reflecting Americans' intense engagement in the final month of the campaign.

Despite reporters' gleeful warnings that this was McCain's last chance to ruffle Obama, the gravitational forces that usually polarize American politics were checked that October night. Unwilling to ignore the undecided voters' earnest questions as the stock market imploded, both Obama and McCain answered the questions thoughtfully, even ploddingly. Once again, both candidates offered ritualistic denunciations of the meltdown's economic bogeymen, including Bush's deregulators, greedy Wall Streeters, and corrupt lobbyists.

As Obama's lead stabilized in October, rumors ricocheted around the Internet that he was Muslim, that as a boy he attended a radical madrasa in Indonesia, that he was an unpatriotic radical "palling around with terrorists"—a reference to a slight connection to former radical Bill Ayers. Bush's former secretary of state, Colin Powell, stood out by standing up against the ugliness. Endorsing Obama, Powell blamed McCain and Palin for stirring up the nastiness. Powell denounced those who responded to claims that Obama was Muslim by denying it, as if it were a slur. True, Obama is a Christian, he said. "But the really right answer is, 'What if he is?' Is there something wrong with being a Muslim in this country? The answer's no, that's not America. Is there something wrong with some seven-year-old Muslim-American kid believing that he or she could be president?" Powell told of a New Jersey kid who enlisted after 9/11 and died in Iraq. His headstone had a "crescent and a star of the Islamic faith. And his name was Kareem Rashad Sultan Khan, and he was an American."

The final presidential debate, at Hofstra University in Hempstead, Long Island, on October 15, was as subdued as the first two. McCain remained more of a worried, defensive candidate in search of a strategy than a centered demigod. McCain repeatedly mentioned Joe Wurzelbacher, a plumbing contractor in Holland, Ohio, whose confrontation with Obama days earlier while Obama was campaigning door-to-door was spread via You Tube. McCain made "Joe the Plumber" into an American Everyman, the voice of the people. "Raising taxes on small businesses will kill jobs," McCain charged, noting that small businesses provided 16 million jobs. "Joe the plumber said, 'Look, I've been working all my life, I want to buy the business I'm in, but you're going to raise my taxes,'" McCain recalled. "You know what Senator Obama said? He wants to spread the wealth around."

Wurzelbacher became famous overnight, with a Wikipedia entry, a manager, and a career as an online pundit. This Joe-the-Plumberization of American campaigning harked back to Reagan's ritual of singling out a few representative Americans during his State of the Union addresses. Many candidates in 2008 inserted moments of faux intimacy into their riffs, telling of one voter with whom they bonded on the campaign trail. McCain took it to an extreme.

Obama kept cool despite McCain's attacks. Obama kept his more inspirational self carefully bottled, preferring to let McCain—and the Republicans—stumble. While his calm made him look buoyant, professional, presidential, Obama risked appearing to win by default with no clear mandate.

Obama and McCain agreed on some important issues, such as immigration reform, with both approving the legislation Bush supported, demanding tougher enforcement while also proposing a path to citizenship for some illegal immigrants. Still, the two candidates continued the decades-old defining Republican-Democratic split over faith in government. Despite his post-baby-boomer caution, Obama had more faith in big government than McCain did. He vowed to enact health-care reform, providing coverage to all uninsured Americans. He wanted more investment in infrastructure, a huge play for energy independence, and greater sensitivity to the environment. Obama criticized Bush's my-way-or-the-highway approach to foreign leaders and proposed engaging America's rivals, especially dictatorships seeking nuclear power such as Iran and North Korea. McCain was more skeptical in theory about big government, even though he approved the $700 billion Wall Street bailout package. He promised to improve the health-care system but feared too big and intrusive a plan. He preferred a Reagan-style approach of growing the economy and improving quality of life through private dynamism to Obama's faith in using government programs to manage the economy, energy, and the environment. And McCain considered Obama dangerously naïve in trusting dialogue with the world's dictators.

As always, candidates were forced to address dozens of issues, but the public opinion polls boiled the election down to just a handful of major concerns. One CNN poll on the eve of the election found 57 percent of Americans most concerned with the economy. Beyond that, 13 percent were most concerned about the war in Iraq, another 13 percent mentioned health care first, 10 percent mentioned terrorism, and 5 percent were most concerned with illegal immigration.

In the campaign's final week, Obama and his advisers understood the need for his own concluding surge—to shape an Obama mandate. Addressing adoring crowds of as many as 100,000 voters, he resurrected his "Yes, We Can" spirit. His campaign spent $4 million purchasing 30 minutes on CBS, NBC, and Fox on October 29, for the first extended prime-time candidate infomercial since Ross Perot's 1992 campaign. Obama returned to the healing unity rhetoric that first catapulted him into the political stratosphere with his 2004 convention keynote. "In one week, you can put an end to the politics that would divide a nation just to win an election, that tries to pit region against region, city against town and Republican against Democrat, that asks us to fear at a time when we need hope," Obama proclaimed. "In one week's time, at this defining moment in history, you can give this country the change we need."

In his campaign of nearly perfect pitch, Obama turned in another virtuoso performance. Viewers saw snippets of Obama's 2004 keynote, photos of Obama's parents, and footage of World War II workers affirming Obama's maternal grandparents' all-American pedigree. Viewers heard testimonies from Michelle Obama, Governor Bill Richardson, Illinois senator Dick Durbin, and a retired brigadier general. Viewers saw the candidate at rallies and heard him giving the voters a more direct—and uncharacteristically subdued—pitch.

The campaign responded to criticism that his earlier speeches were too lyrical and vague by setting Obama in a mock Oval Office, speaking substantively. It was refreshing to hear him without his trademark singsong. Obama emphasized the nation was in crisis. This unnerving message upstaged his usual uplifting call for Americans to solve the world's problems by working together.

The roller-coaster campaign culminated in a momentous, magical, redemptive night. Obama defeated McCain 69.50 million to 59.95 million in the popular vote and 365 to 173 in the electoral vote. Both margins of victory dwarfed those of Bush in 2000 and 2004. After 232 years—more than a third of which were marked by slavery—the United States had elected an African-American president. Over 100,000 people gathered in Grant Park in Chicago, emitting a deafening, inspiring, historic roar when Obama clinched the presidency.

Late Tuesday night November 4, and early Wednesday morning, Senators Barack Obama and John McCain

ended the drawn-out, often bitter 2008 campaign magnificently, patriotically. McCain conceded with the grace and nonpartisanship for which he had been famous—and which seemed missing during his campaign. Obama's speech was masterful. Although it started a tad grandiose, as he associated his personal triumph with America's redemption, the rest sparkled. Understanding the daunting challenges ahead, he called, Franklin Roosevelt–style, for a spirit of community and self-sacrifice. He reached out to the more than 59 million Americans who voted against him and to the millions around the world listening in—while warning America's foes not to underestimate him. Telling the story of Ann Nixon Cooper, a 106-year-old African-American woman who voted for him, offered a wonderful triptych of twentieth-century history, punctuated by the supposedly "timeless" but quite contemporary and Obamian credo, "Yes, We Can."

Americans love charismatic leaders singing a compelling, optimistic song. The presidency's unique mix of king and prime minister makes generating hope part of the presidential skill set. The optimism a Franklin Roosevelt or a Ronald Reagan generated boosted the country's mood along with each leader's popular and historical standing. The United States needs an arm-twister-in-chief to get things done and a cheerleader-in-chief to make Americans feel good.

The outpouring of emotion when Obama clinched his victory was thrilling. Little more than a decade earlier, when an overwhelmingly black jury found the football great O.J. Simpson innocent of two murders, cameras recorded cheering blacks and morose whites, emphasizing a split-screen America. On this magical night of overcoming, the cameras showed blacks and whites crying together, laughing together, celebrating together, hoping together, in a tableau of healing.

You needed a heart of stone not to be moved by watching the joy that swept America—but you needed a head of straw not to worry about how Obama would succeed. His calls for unity could last only if he could govern in the same expansive and moderate spirit that his speech that night evoked. Hope is like a balloon, able to entrance and elevate, but easily overinflated or destroyed by just the right pinprick. Politics itself is an odd mix of noble aspirations with ruthless ambition, high-minded ideals with thuggish tactics. Sixteen years earlier, a young, charismatic candidate had come, literally, from a place called Hope. Within weeks of his election, Bill Clinton had frittered away much of the positive emotion surrounding his candidacy. Amid the many challenges Barack Obama faced was the danger of disappointing the millions who placed so much faith in him.

American presidential campaigns are social stress tests, regularly scheduled exercises that highlight the country's social, cultural, and political strengths and weaknesses. The 2008 campaign also demonstrated the country's devastating economic weaknesses. But campaigns also breed optimism, as candidates invite their fellow citizens to remember the past and assess the present, then invest one mortal with the future dreams of 300 million people.

For all the foolishness and frustrations of the two-year, $1.8-billion presidential quest, Americans could enter the two-and-a-half-month transition to Inauguration Day proud of the peaceful, thorough, and open process that selected their next president. Tens of millions of citizens shaped the historic outcome. The scope of Obama's victory—and the victory itself—proved that campaigns mattered, that the fates of individuals and forces could shift dramatically thanks to the democratic process.

Obama made everything look easy, the adoring media made his election look obvious. Neither Obama nor McCain coasted to their respective party's nomination. In 2006 and 2007, Senator Clinton seemed like the Democrats' inevitable choice. Simultaneously, McCain's quest for the Republican nomination almost died. Only once the voting started did McCain revive. Only after Obama won the Iowa caucuses did most people start believing this young, first-term senator just might win it all.

In the general campaign, the lead switched at least three times. The two were tied when the Democratic convention began. Obama surged after his convention, McCain surged after his. Obama started running away with it after the financial meltdown.

In this rollicking, grueling, unpredictable 2008 campaign marathon, America's voters—and politicians— found themselves particularly shaped by the 1960s revolution as they judged, but also partially tried to replicate, the 1980s revolution. McCain represented the sea change in attitudes toward Vietnam veterans that he helped nurture. During the war, many returning soldiers felt rejected by the country they had served. McCain's iconic role, symbolizing patriotism, selflessness, and sacrifice, helped heal many of that war's national wounds. During the October 21, 2007, debate in Orlando, Florida, McCain—the former prisoner of war—highlighted the contrast between his experiences in the 1960s and those of his opponents by mocking Clinton's proposal "to spend one million dollars on the Woodstock Concert Museum. Now, my friends, I wasn't there," McCain smiled. "I'm sure it was a cultural and pharmaceutical event. I was tied up at the time."

Obama, who repeatedly emphasized how young he was during the 1960s, was a child of that decade, born in 1961. The civil rights movement made his candidacy possible. And despite Hillary Clinton's loss, her campaign—along with Sarah Palin's—advanced the women's revolution of the 1960s to the upper reaches of national politics.

As the 1960s cast its shadow, the 1980s Reagan Revolution loomed large, too. When McCain was not channeling Theodore Roosevelt, he invoked Ronald Reagan. Both Roosevelt and Reagan offered the muscular, nationalist, patriotic leadership that McCain admired. Obama admired that leadership style, too. Interviewed in Nevada in January 2008, Obama said Reagan had "changed the trajectory of America in a way that . . . Richard Nixon did not and in a way that Bill Clinton did not." Responding to Hillary Clinton's inevitable derision, Obama explained he was not embracing Reagan's policies, just admiring Reagan as a "transformative leader."

Obama demonstrated a similar ambition and potential. He did not run to be a caretaker. Having matured during the Reagan Revolution, Obama wanted to redefine liberalism as more community-oriented and more sensitive to tradition than 1960s liberalism by balancing rights and responsibilities, government power and individual prerogative.

Of course, the nation's financial meltdown during the campaign directly challenged the 1980s legacy. During the summer, the Russian invasion of Georgia along with continuing worries about Iran and Iraq made pundits predict 2008 would be a foreign policy–oriented election. That assumption prompted Obama to select Biden as a running mate. That hedge—and so many others—diminished in value with the stock market's collapse.

Barack Obama won big on Election Day. He received nearly 10 million more popular votes than McCain and more than twice as many electoral votes. The election came down to five battleground states with 84 electoral votes combined. Obama won four of the five: Florida, Indiana, North Carolina, and Ohio, while virtually tying McCain in Missouri, with each winning 49 percent of the popular vote, but McCain nosing ahead to get Missouri's 11 electors. In winning Indiana as well as Virginia, Obama became the first Democrat to capture those states since 1964.

Exit polls of 16,000 people leaving the voting booths suggested Obama's big win was among youth and minorities. Voters in the 18-to-24 age group voted 68 percent for Obama to 30 percent for McCain, while 69 percent of those 25 to 29 went for Obama. First-time voters also voted for Obama overwhelmingly, by 72 percent to 27 percent. Blacks voted for Obama 96 percent to 3 percent for McCain. Twice as many of those polled attributed their votes to age as a factor rather than race.

The country Obama would lead was a more multicultural and multiracial America. Nearly a third of the 300 million American citizens were "minorities," with 42.7 million Hispanics, 39.7 million blacks, and 14.4 million Asian-Americans. When the campaign began, polls suggested Clinton would win the Hispanic vote. When

McCain emerged as the Republican nominee, the conventional wisdom said he would make inroads among Hispanics because of his sensitivity to the plight of undocumented workers. Ultimately, Obama won two-thirds of the Hispanic vote and nearly two-thirds of Asian-Americans.

Voters also gave Obama strong majorities in both houses of Congress. Democrats gained eight seats in the Senate, dominating Republicans 59 to 41. Democrats gained 21 seats in the House of Representations for a comfortable majority of 257 to 178.

And yet, despite the economic crash, despite Obama's victory, only 51 percent believed government should do more to solve problems. Forty-three percent believed government was doing too much, and 56 percent opposed the government's $700 billion bailout of financial companies. In California, progressives did not know whether to laugh or cry. Obama received an impressive 61 percent of the vote, but 52 percent of that state's electorate approved an amendment to the state constitution banning same-sex marriage. Ironically, the surge in black churchgoing voters for Obama helped pass the gay marriage ban, a reminder that America was more conservative and the electorate more multidimensional than the Democrats' narrative suggested.

All these results, and Obama's cautious, passive approach during the fall campaign, suggested that Obama did not have much of a mandate for change. Americans remained divided about basic issues such as the size of government. But, in November 2008, Americans united to repudiate George W. Bush and the Republicans. Just as Reagan won in 1980 in an ABC election (Anybody But Carter), Barack Obama won a GO George election (Get Out George W. Bush). The financial crash made the election practically unwinnable for the Republicans; Obama's performance in the debate and his don't-rock-the-boat ability to reassure wavering voters closed the sale.

Still, the 2008 campaign—and the redemptive spirit of both Election Night as well as Inauguration Day 2009—showed that Americans hungered for change and inspiration. Inspiring while making hard decisions that might entail sacrifice is a Herculean task. In the inevitably rough days that followed the start of his term, the new president might even have caught himself yearning for the clarity and simplicity of the campaign trail, where oratory could substitute for policy and soundbites could trump substance, even if the accommodations were less plush than those the White House offered.

—*Gil Troy*

Selected Bibliography

Barack Obama, *Dreams from My Father: A Story of Race and Inheritance* (1995, 2004) is Obama's now-legendary autobiography. Barack Obama, *The Audacity of Hope: Thoughts on Reclaiming the American Dream* (2006), demonstrates Obama at his centrist best. John McCain with Mark Salter, *Faith of My Fathers* (1999, 2000) is an eloquent memoir of a genuine American hero and patriot; Dan Balz and Haynes Johnson, *The Battle for America 2008: The Story of an Extraordinary Election* (2009), gives a great overview of the campaign. Richard Wolffe, *Renegade: The Making of a Presidency* (2009), provides great glimpses into Obama himself as he evolved from long-shot celebrity candidate to president. Chuck Todd and Sheldon Gawiser, *How Barack Obama Won: A State-by-State Guide to the History 2008 Presidential Election* (2009), has an excellent introduction to the whole campaign. See also Eric Boehlert, *Bloggers on the Bus: How the Internet Changed Politics and the Press* (2009); Franklin Foer, *Election 2008: A Voter's Guide* (2008); Garrett M. Graff, *The First Campaign: Globalization, the Web, and the Race for the White House* (2007); Mark Halperin and John F. Harris, *The Way to Win: Taking the White House in 2008* (2006); John Heilemann and Mark Halperin, *Game Change: Obama and the Clintons, McCain and Palin, and the Race of a Lifetime* (2010); Gwen Ifill, *The Breakthrough: Politics and Race in the Age of Obama* (2009); William G. Mayer, *The Making of the Presidential Candidates 2008* (2008); David Mendell, *Obama: From Promise to Power* (2007); and Frank Newport et al., *Winning the White House 2008: The Gallup Poll, Public Opinion, and the Presidency* (2009).

2008 Electoral Map and Statistics

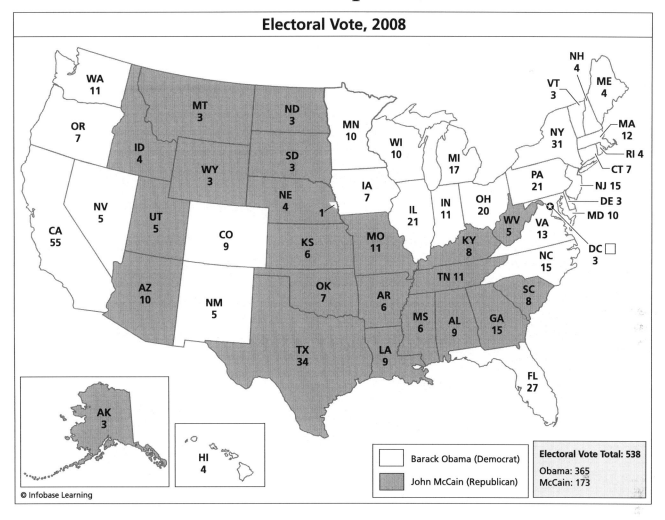

Electoral Vote, 2008

WA 11
OR 7
MT 3
ND 3
MN 10
WI 10
NH 4
VT 3
ME 4
NY 31
MA 12
RI 4
CT 7
ID 4
WY 3
SD 3
MI 17
PA 21
NJ 15
DE 3
MD 10
NV 5
UT 5
NE 4
IA 7
IL 21
IN 11
OH 20
WV 5
VA 13
DC 3
CA 55
CO 9
KS 6
MO 11
KY 8
NC 15
AZ 10
NM 5
OK 7
AR 6
TN 11
SC 8
MS 6
AL 9
GA 15
TX 34
LA 9
FL 27
AK 3
HI 4

Barack Obama (Democrat)
John McCain (Republican)

Electoral Vote Total: 538
Obama: 365
McCain: 173

© Infobase Learning

2008 ELECTION STATISTICS

State	Number of Electors	Total Popular Vote	Elec Vote		Pop Vote		Margin of Victory	
			D	R	D	R	Votes	% Total Vote
Alabama	9	2,099,677		9	2	1	453,067	21.58%
Alaska	3	326,197		3	2	1	70,247	21.54%
Arizona	10	2,303,838		10	2	1	195,404	8.48%
Arkansas	6	1,086,617		6	2	1	215,707	19.85%
California	55	13,560,259	55		1	2	3,262,692	24.06%
Colorado	9	2,401,126	9		1	2	215,004	8.95%
Connecticut	7	1,646,793	7		1	2	368,345	22.37%
Delaware	3	412,616	3		1	2	103,085	24.98%
District of Columbia	3	265,853	3		1	2	228,433	85.92%
Florida	27	8,411,268	27		1	2	236,148	2.81%
Georgia	15	3,931,463		15	2	1	204,636	5.21%
Hawaii	4	453,568	4		1	2	205,305	45.26%
Idaho	4	658,454		4	2	1	166,572	25.30%
Illinois	21	5,528,354	21		1	2	1,388,169	25.11%
Indiana	11	2,755,590	11		1	2	28,391	1.03%
Iowa	7	1,537,123	7		1	2	146,561	9.53%
Kansas	6	1,238,873		6	2	1	184,890	14.92%
Kentucky	8	1,827,587		8	2	1	296,477	16.22%
Louisiana	9	1,951,393		9	2	1	365,286	18.72%
Maine	4	731,163	4		1	2	126,650	17.32%
Maryland	10	2,631,596	10		1	2	669,605	25.44%
Massachusetts	12	3,081,069	12		1	2	795,244	25.81%
Michigan	17	5,010,194	17		1	2	823,940	16.45%
Minnesota	10	2,910,369	10		1	2	297,945	10.24%
Mississippi	6	1,289,384		6	2	1	169,935	13.18%
Missouri	11	2,928,949		11	2	1	3,903	0.13%
Montana	3	482,081		3	2	1	11,723	2.43%
Nebraska	5	801,281	1	4	2	1	119,660	14.93%
Nevada	5	967,848	5		1	2	120,909	12.49%
New Hampshire	4	709,347	4		1	2	68,292	9.63%
New Jersey	15	3,875,393	15		1	2	602,215	15.54%
New Mexico	5	830,158	5		1	2	125,590	15.13%
New York	31	7,640,607	31		1	2	2,052,174	26.86%
North Carolina	15	4,310,789	15		1	2	14,177	0.33%
North Dakota	3	317,738		3	2	1	27,484	8.65%
Ohio	20	5,717,780	20		1	2	262,224	4.59%
Oklahoma	7	1,462,661		7	2	1	457,669	31.29%
Oregon	7	1,827,760	7		1	2	298,816	16.35%
Pennsylvania	21	6,010,967	21		1	2	620,478	10.32%
Rhode Island	4	471,294	4		1	2	131,180	27.83%
South Carolina	8	1,920,969		8	2	1	172,447	8.98%
South Dakota	3	381,975		3	2	1	32,130	8.41%
Tennessee	11	2,601,982		11	2	1	391,741	15.06%
Texas	34	8,087,208		34	2	1	950,695	11.76%
Utah	5	957,481		5	2	1	268,360	28.03%
Vermont	3	325,046	3		1	2	120,288	37.01%
Virginia	13	3,723,260	13		1	2	234,527	6.30%
Washington	11	3,051,846	11		1	2	521,632	17.09%
West Virginia	5	714,868		5	2	1	93,609	13.09%
Wisconsin	10	2,982,653	10		1	2	414,818	13.91%
Wyoming	3	254,658		3	2	1	82,090	32.24%
Total	538	131,407,023	365	173	1	2	9,549,105	7.27%

Obama Democratic		McCain Republican		Nader Independent		Others	
813,479	38.74%	1,266,546	60.32%	6,788	0.32%	12,864	0.61%
123,594	37.89%	193,841	59.42%	3,783	1.16%	4,979	1.53%
1,034,707	44.91%	1,230,111	53.39%	11,301	0.49%	27,719	1.20%
422,310	38.86%	638,017	58.72%	12,882	1.19%	13,408	1.23%
8,274,473	61.02%	5,011,781	36.96%	108,381	0.80%	165,624	1.22%
1,288,633	53.67%	1,073,629	44.71%	13,352	0.56%	25,512	1.06%
997,773	60.59%	629,428	38.22%	19,162	1.16%	430	0.03%
255,459	61.91%	152,374	36.93%	2,401	0.58%	2,382	0.58%
245,800	92.46%	17,367	6.53%	958	0.36%	1,728	0.65%
4,282,367	50.91%	4,046,219	48.10%	28,128	0.33%	54,554	0.65%
1,844,123	46.91%	2,048,759	52.11%	1,165	0.03%	37,416	0.95%
325,871	71.85%	120,566	26.58%	3,825	0.84%	3,306	0.73%
236,440	35.91%	403,012	61.21%	7,175	1.09%	11,827	1.80%
3,419,348	61.85%	2,031,179	36.74%	31,152	0.56%	46,675	0.84%
1,374,039	49.86%	1,345,648	48.83%	909	0.03%	34,994	1.27%
828,940	53.93%	682,379	44.39%	8,014	0.52%	17,790	1.16%
514,765	41.55%	699,655	56.48%	10,527	0.85%	13,926	1.12%
751,985	41.15%	1,048,462	57.37%	15,378	0.84%	11,762	0.64%
782,989	40.12%	1,148,275	58.84%	6,997	0.36%	13,132	0.67%
421,923	57.71%	295,273	40.38%	10,636	1.45%	3,331	0.46%
1,629,467	61.92%	959,862	36.47%	14,713	0.56%	27,554	1.05%
1,904,098	61.80%	1,108,854	35.99%	28,841	0.94%	39,276	1.27%
2,872,579	57.33%	2,048,639	40.89%	33,085	0.66%	55,891	1.12%
1,573,354	54.06%	1,275,409	43.82%	30,152	1.04%	31,454	1.08%
554,662	43.02%	724,597	56.20%	4,011	0.31%	6,114	0.47%
1,441,911	49.23%	1,445,814	49.36%	17,813	0.61%	23,411	0.80%
232,159	48.16%	243,882	50.59%	3,699	0.77%	2,341	0.49%
333,319	41.60%	452,979	56.53%	5,406	0.67%	9,577	1.20%
533,736	55.15%	412,827	42.65%	6,150	0.64%	15,135	1.56%
384,826	54.25%	316,534	44.62%	3,503	0.49%	4,484	0.63%
2,215,422	57.17%	1,613,207	41.63%	21,298	0.55%	25,466	0.66%
472,422	56.91%	346,832	41.78%	5,327	0.64%	5,577	0.67%
4,804,945	62.89%	2,752,771	36.03%	41,249	0.54%	41,642	0.55%
2,142,651	49.70%	2,128,474	49.38%	1,454	0.03%	38,210	0.89%
141,403	44.50%	168,887	53.15%	4,199	1.32%	3,249	1.02%
2,940,044	51.42%	2,677,820	46.83%	42,337	0.74%	57,579	1.01%
502,496	34.35%	960,165	65.65%	0	0.00%	0	0.00%
1,037,291	56.75%	738,475	40.40%	18,614	1.02%	33,380	1.83%
3,276,363	54.51%	2,655,885	44.18%	42,977	0.71%	35,742	0.59%
296,571	62.93%	165,391	35.09%	4,829	1.02%	4,503	0.96%
862,449	44.90%	1,034,896	53.87%	5,053	0.26%	18,571	0.97%
170,924	44.75%	203,054	53.16%	4,267	1.12%	3,730	0.98%
1,087,437	41.79%	1,479,178	56.85%	11,560	0.44%	23,807	0.91%
3,528,633	43.63%	4,479,328	55.39%	5,751	0.07%	73,496	0.91%
327,670	34.22%	596,030	62.25%	8,416	0.88%	25,365	2.65%
219,262	67.46%	98,974	30.45%	3,339	1.03%	3,471	1.07%
1,959,532	52.63%	1,725,005	46.33%	11,483	0.31%	27,240	0.73%
1,750,848	57.37%	1,229,216	40.28%	29,489	0.97%	42,293	1.39%
303,857	42.51%	397,466	55.60%	7,219	1.01%	6,326	0.88%
1,677,211	56.23%	1,262,393	42.32%	17,605	0.59%	25,444	0.85%
82,868	32.54%	164,958	64.78%	2,525	0.99%	4,307	1.69%
69,499,428	52.89%	59,950,323	45.62%	739,278	0.56%	1,217,994	0.93%

Appendix

PRESIDENTIAL ELECTION CAMPAIGN COSTS, 1860–2008 (GENERAL ELECTION ONLY)

Election Year	Campaign	$	In Current $
1860	Lincoln	$100,000	$2,339,068.97
	Douglas	$50,000	$1,169,534.48
1864	Lincoln	$125,000	$1,551,059.45
	McClellan	$50,000	$620,423.78
1868	Grant	$150,000	$2,062,489.86
	Seymour	$75,000	$1,031,244.93
1872	Grant	$250,000	$4,005,885.83
	Greeley	$50,000	$801,177.17
1876	Hayes	$950,000	$17,261,075.89
	Tilden	$900,000	$16,352,598.21
1880	Garfield	$1,100,000	$20,920,457.94
	Hancock	$335,000	$6,371,230.37
1884	Blaine	$1,300,000	$25,936,147.06
	Cleveland	$1,400,000	$27,931,235.29
1888	Harrison	$1,350,000	$27,749,863.64
	Cleveland	$855,000	$17,574,913.64
1892	Harrison	$1,700,000	$36,803,010.64
	Cleveland	$2,350,000	$50,874,750.00
1896	McKinley	$3,350,000	$77,468,369.32
	Bryan	$675,000	$15,609,298.30
1900	McKinley	$3,000,000	$69,374,659.09
	Bryan	$425,000	$9,828,076.70
1904	T. Roosevelt	$2,096,000	$45,863,860.65
	Parker	$700,000	$15,317,129.03
1908	Taft	$1,655,518	$35,093,360.15
	Bryan	$629,341	$13,340,652.52
1912	Taft	$1,071,549	$21,590,014.85
	Wilson	$1,134,848	$22,865,389.42
1916	Hughes	$2,441,565	$45,583,122.56
	Wilson	$1,134,848	$21,187,195.70
1920	Harding	$5,417,501	$55,122,801.80
	Cox	$1,470,371	$14,960,951.41
1924	Coolidge	$4,020,478	$47,845,804.24
	Davis	$1,108,836	$13,195,732.00

Election Year	Campaign	$	In Current $
1928	Hoover	$6,256,111	$74,451,013.59
	Smith	$5,342,350	$63,576,776.76
1932	Hoover	$2,900,052	$43,077,203.06
	F. Roosevelt	$2,245,975	$33,361,581.50
1936	Landon	$8,892,972	$130,195,029.43
	F. Roosevelt	$5,194,741	$76,052,129.41
1940	Willkie	$3,451,310	$50,167,009.55
	F. Roosevelt	$2,783,654	$40,462,200.38
1944	Dewey	$2,828,652	$32,706,128.03
	F. Roosevelt	$2,169,077	$25,079,829.57
1948	Dewey	$2,127,296	$17,962,763.85
	Truman	$2,736,334	$23,105,445.34
1952	Eisenhower	$6,608,623	$50,748,987.62
	Stevenson	$5,032,926	$38,648,883.32
1956	Eisenhower	$7,778,702	$58,196,988.17
	Stevenson	$5,106,651	$38,205,822.49
1960	Nixon	$10,128,000	$69,629,657.84
	Kennedy	$9,797,000	$67,354,044.02
1964	Goldwater	$16,026,000	$105,202,418.52
	Johnson	$8,757,000	$57,485,185.26
1968	Nixon	$25,402,000	$148,542,574.66
	Humphrey	$11,594,000	$67,797,913.97
1972	Nixon	$61,400,000	$298,919,583.73
	McGovern	$30,000,000	$146,051,913.88
1976	Ford	$21,786,641	$77,918,447.40
	Carter	$21,800,000	$77,966,224.96
1980	Reagan	$29,188,188	$72,084,551.82
	Carter	$29,352,767	$72,491,004.03
1984	Reagan	$40,400,000	$79,127,618.86
	Mondale	$40,400,000	$79,127,618.86
1988	Bush	$46,100,000	$79,300,962.81
	Dukakis	$46,100,000	$79,300,962.81
1992	Bush	$55,240,000	$80,123,198.57
	Clinton	$55,240,000	$80,123,198.57
1996	Dole	$61,820,000	$80,180,421.80
	Clinton	$61,820,000	$80,180,421.80
2000	Bush	$67,560,000	$79,839,677.35
	Gore	$67,560,000	$79,839,677.35
2004	Bush	$74,620,000	$80,386,952.78
	Kerry	$74,620,000	$80,386,952.78
2008	Obama	$744,985,624	$744,985,624.00
	McCain	$368,093,764	$368,093,764.00

SOURCE: 1860–1980 (nominal dollars) are from Herbert E. Alexander, *Financing Politics: Money, Elections and Political Reform*, 3rd. ed. (Washington D.C.: CQ Press, 1984), p. 7. Subsequent years are from the Federal Election Commission. CPI updated using the annual CPI of 2006, as well as the CPI for February 2007. CPI drawn from ftp://ftp.bls.gov/pub/special.requests/cpi/cpiai.txt.

Index

Page numbers in *italics* indicate illustrations, photographs, or political cartoons. **Bold** page numbers indicate a major treatment of an election. Page numbers followed by *t* indicate tables. Page numbers followed by *c* indicate chronologies.

C

Cable News Network. *See* CNN
Cabot, George 64, 85
Caddell, Partick
    election of 1972 1363
    election of 1976 1391,
      1394, 1408–1411
    election of 1980 1420,
      1426
    election of 1988 1485
Cahan, Abe 1080
Cahill, Mary 1598
Cain, Harry 1212, 1215
Caldwell, Josiah 592, 593
Caldwell, Willie W. 1014
Calhoun, John C. *232, 287,*
    331, 333, 356, 358, 419, 560
    elections of 1816 and
      1820 151, 152, 161
    election of 1824 170, 171,
      173, 174, 174*c*, 175*c*,
      177–178, 180, 182–187,
      193, 194
    election of 1828 202, 206,
      207*c*, 209, 215, 220, 221
    election of 1832 226,
      227, 229, 230, 232, 233,
      236*c*, 243
    election of 1836 252,
      254, 255, 256*c*, 257,
      264, 273–274
    election of 1840 289,
      292, 294, 305
    election of 1844 324, 325,
      330*c*, 332–336, 338–
      342, 344, 345, 347, 350,
      351, 353, 355, 357
    election of 1848 374, 384
    election of 1852 413, 419
    election of 1856 461
Califano, Joseph 1426
California
    election of 1880 627,
      633*c*, 648
    election of 1944 1142
    election of 1948 1183
    election of 1964 1292*c*
    election of 1968 1328
    election of 1972 1374
    election of 1980 1416,
      1424*c*, 1429
    election of 1996 1542
    election of 2004 1650
California primary
    election of 1964 1302
    election of 1968 1337–
      1338
    election of 1976 1398

Callaway, Howard H. 1402,
    1403
Callender, James Thomson 63
Camejo, Peter 1406, 1584
Cameron, J. Donald 630
Cameron, Simon 454, 465,
    466, 480, 482
Campagna, Richard 1584
The Campaign 383, 397
campaign finance. *See also*
    fund-raising; fund-raising
    scandals
      campaign costs, 1860-
        2008 1654*t*–1655*t*
      election of 1908 846*c*,
        866, 867
      election of 1972 1371
      election of 1976 1386,
        1387, 1390, 1396, 1397,
        1403, 1406
      election of 1980 1419–
        1420
      clection of 1988 1483
      election of 1992 1506
      election of 1996 1527,
        1530*c*, 1531*c*, 1542,
        1543
      election of 2000 1551,
        1552, 1556*c*, 1559,
        1562, 1565
      election of 2004 1587,
        1588, 1598–1599,
        1603
      election of 2008 1618–
        1620, 1623*c*, 1627,
        1637–1638
campaign finance reform
    1392*c*. *See also* McCain–
    Feingold Act
campaign finance scandals
    1542, 1543
Campbell, Angus 1234
Campbell, George W. 209
Campbell, James E. 713, 909
Campbell, Lewis D. 386, 438,
    439
Camp David 1426
Camp David Accords 1423,
    1424*c*
campus unrest. *See* college
    demonstrations
Canada 701, 702
Canfield, Cass 1254
Cannon, Frank
    election of 1896 756
    election of 1904 818
    election of 1908 857
Cannon, James, Jr. 1013

Cannon, Joseph G. *816*
    election of 1904 815,
      817, 821
    election of 1908 841,
      842, 846*c*, 855
    election of 1912 883, 884
Canter, David 420
Capehart, Homer 1206, 1231
Capper, Arthur 1061, 1081
Carey, Henry Charles 439
Carey, Hugh 1396
Cargo, David F. 1318
Carlisle, John G.
    election of 1884 662–664
    election of 1892 713, 724
    election of 1896 741, 748
Carlson, Frank 1210, 1318
Carlson, Margaret 1553
Carman, Harry 1253
Carnegie, Andrew
    election of 1888 694
    election of 1892 732, 733
    election of 1900 782,
      783, 788, 797, 800, 801
    election of 1908 868
Carpenter, Terry 1254
Carr, Julian S. 776
Carroll, Charles 18, 235, 236,
    240
Carroll, George W. 812, 818*c*
Carroll, William 304
Carson, Johnny 1507
Carter, Alton 1391
Carter, Amy 1386, *1412*, 1417,
    1419, 1422, 1440
Carter, Billy 1386, 1391, 1418
Carter, Hugh 1391
Carter, Jimmy *1389, 1391,*
    1397, 1399, 1409, 1412, 1427,
    1434, 1439
    election of 1976 1384–
      1388, 1390–1391,
      1392*c*–1394*c*, 1396,
      1397, 1399–1402,
      1405–1412
    election of 1980 1416–
      1422, 1424*c*, 1425*c*,
      1426–1428, 1431,
      1433–1442
    election of 1984 1457,
      1459, 1467, 1475
    election of 1992 1519
    election of 1996 1539
    election of 2000 1568
    election of 2004 1595,
      1599, 1604, 1605
Carter, Lillian 1386, 1391
Carter, Rosalynn 1386, *1412*

Carter, Thomas H. 731
Carville, James 1511*c*, 1518,
    1519
Cary, Samuel 574, 575, 578*c*,
    592
Casablanca Conference
    1132*c*, 1135
Case, Clifford P. 1318, 1340
Casey, Robert 1504
Casey, William 1438
Cass, George W. 493
Cass, Lewis *380, 381, 389,*
    393, 396, 397, 399
    election of 1844 323,
      325, 332, 336, 338, 342,
      344–347, 350
    election of 1848 373–377,
      378*c*, 379*c*, 380–386,
      388, 390, 392–395,
      397–400
    election of 1852 406,
      411*c*, 413, 414, 418–
      421, 423–425, 430
    election of 1856 439, 452
Castleton, Samuel M. *954*
Castro, Fidel 1279, 1292*c*,
    1296
Catholicism
    election of 1836 268
    election of 1852 430, 432
    election of 1856 446, 458
    election of 1868 533
    election of 1880 646, 647
    election of 1884 670
    election of 1904 832
    election of 1908 870, 872
    election of 1916 930
    election of 1924 981,
      982, 984
    election of 1928 999,
      1000, 1002, 1005*c*,
      1007, 1008, 1010, 1011,
      1013, 1014, 1020
    election of 1932 1029
    election of 1936 1060,
      1078
    election of 1944 1144
    election of 1948 1190
    election of 1960 1262,
      1264–1265, 1267*c*,
      1269, 1270, 1274,
      1280–1282
    election of 1972 1380
    election of 1984 1455,
      1471–1472
Catholic voters
    election of 1936 1089
    election of 1952 1236

election of 1876 586,
597, 620
election of 1884 653
liberals/liberalism
election of 1920 943
election of 1948 1162,
1166, 1176, 1180–1183,
1185, 1188
election of 1952 1218
election of 1960 1262,
1269, 1270
election of 1964 1291
election of 1968 1318,
1331–1332, 1340
election of 1972 1370
election of 1976 1389,
1394
election of 1980 1425c,
1437, 1442
election of 1988 1481,
1486, 1487, 1493
election of 1996 1541,
1542
election of 2004 1591,
1595, 1601, 1610
Libertarian Party
election of 1972 1360,
1361, 1368c, 1369c
election of 1976 1392c,
1406
election of 1980 1416,
1418
election of 1988 1480
election of 1992 1502,
1504
election of 1996 1524,
1526
election of 2000 1547,
1550
election of 2004 1584
election of 2008 1615,
1616
Liberty Party 397, 399
election of 1840 278,
279, 285c, 306
election of 1844 323–
325, 329c, 361–364
election of 1848 374,
382, 399
election of 1852 406, 407,
410c, 411c
election of 1856 448
election of 1932 1046
Lieberman, Hadassah 1568
Lieberman, Joseph 1567, 1599
election of 2000 1547,
1548, 1550, 1552,
1557c, 1566, 1568, 1571

election of 2004 1585,
1586, 1592c, 1595,
1596, 1598, 1601
election of 2008 1637,
1642
Life magazine 1099, 1109
Lilienthal, David 1167, 1207
Limbaugh, Rush 1565
Lincoln, Abraham 472, 479,
481, 485, 560, 705, 959
election of 1836 264, 273
election of 1840 298, 310
election of 1848 376,
379c, 380, 389, 394, 401
election of 1856 438,
439, 459
election of 1860 465–
468, 470, 470c, 471c,
472, 479, 482–485, 487
election of 1864 492–
495, 496c, 497, 497c,
498, 500, 501, 503–
508, 511–514
election of 1868 521, 524
election of 1872 557
election of 2008 1629
Lincoln, Abraham,
assassination of
election of 1864 514
election of 1868 518, 521,
522c
election of 1880 637
Lincoln, Benjamin 2
Lincoln, Levi 80, 82, 105
Lincoln, Robert Todd 654,
661, 677
Lincoln Bedroom campaign
finance scandal 1527, 1531c
Lincoln Savings and Loan
1563
Lindbergh, Charles
election of 1928 1005c
election of 1932 1034
election of 1936 1072
election of 1944 1147
Linderman, Henry Richard
584
Lindsay, John V. 1318, 1319,
1327, 1340, 1341, 1361–
1363, 1368c, 1371–1373
Lindsey, Ben B. 926
Linger, Claude R. 1128
Link, Arthur S. 964
Lippard, George 391, 391
Lippitt, Charles 741
Lippmann, Walter
election of 1924 980,
988, 989, 993

election of 1928 1013
election of 1932 1028,
1038
Literary Digest
election of 1900 800
election of 1920 938
election of 1924 992
election of 1936 1059,
1062, 1065c, 1085,
1088
Littauer, Lucius N. 828
Littleton, Martin 827–828
Livingston, Edward 61
Livingston, Peter 228, 240
Livingston, Robert 83c, 129
Lloyd, David D. 1181
Lloyd, Henry Demarest 784
Lloyd, James M. 1263
Lockwood, Belva Ann 654,
655, 659c, 665, 680c
Lockwood, Daniel S. 663
Locofoco Party 254, 256c,
269, 293–295, 294, 310, 314,
316, 319
Lodge, Henry Cabot 942, 963
election of 1880 626
election of 1884 652
election of 1904 817, 820
election of 1908 852, 861
election of 1916 910, 915,
917
election of 1920 942,
945
election of 1924 972
Lodge, Henry Cabot, Jr.
election of 1936 1086
election of 1952 1202c,
1206, 1210, 1211, 1213,
1222
election of 1956 1247
election of 1960 1261,
1267c, 1273, 1280
election of 1964 1287,
1288, 1292c, 1301–
1305
election of 1968 1340
Loeb, James 1179
Loeb, William 861
Logan, John 661
election of 1868 527
election of 1880 630
election of 1884 652–
654, 656, 658c, 661,
662, 666, 668
Log Cabin 308, 312, 316
Long, Alexander 533
Long, Breckinridge 1084
Long, Chester 861

Long, Huey 1044, 1058, 1061,
1064c, 1071
Long, John D. 787
Longworth, Nicholas 861,
1015
Loomis, Francis 743
Lord, Nancy 1502, 1504
Lorimer, William 806
Los Angeles riots (1992) 1502,
1509, 1511c
Los Angeles Times 702, 904
Louisiana Purchase
election of 1804 80, 83c,
85, 88
election of 1808 95
election of 1848 389
election of 1860 476,
477
Louisville Courier-Journal
election of 1892 724
election of 1896 768
election of 1900 802
election of 1904 822
election of 1932 1043
Love, Alfred H. 680c
Love, John A. 1318
Love, Thomas B. 980, 987
Loveless, Herschel 1263
Lowden, Frank Orren 943,
1014, 1017
election of 1920 935–
937, 940c, 943, 944,
946–948
election of 1924 970,
976, 978, 979
election of 1928 999,
1000, 1016, 1017
election of 1936 1063
Lowenstein, Allard K. 1332,
1337
Lowndes, William 151, 174,
182–183
Lubell, Samuel 1086, 1233–
1235
Lucas, Robert 241
Lucas, Scott W.
election of 1940 1097
election of 1944 1128
election of 1952 1217
Luce, Clare Booth 1213
Luce, Henry 1105, 1108
Lucey, Patrick 1416, 1418,
1441
Luciano, Charlie "Lucky"
1140
Lugar, Richard 1436, 1525
Lukas, Anthony 1487
Lund, Frank 1017